HEALTH IN ANTIQUITY

HEALTH IN ANTIQUITY

Edited by
Helen King

Routledge
Taylor & Francis Group

LONDON AND NEW YORK

First published 2005
by Routledge
2 Park Square, Milton Park, Abingdon, Oxon OX14 4RN

Simultaneously published in the USA and Canada
by Routledge
270 Madison Ave, New York, NY 10016

Routledge is an imprint of the Taylor & Francis Group

Typeset in Garamond by
Newgen Imaging Systems (P) Ltd, Chennai, India
Printed and bound in Great Britain by
TJ International Ltd, Padstow, Cornwall

British Library Cataloguing in Publication Data
A catalogue record for this book is available from the British Library

Library of Congress Cataloging in Publication Data
A catalog record for this book has been requested

ISBN 0–415–22065–3

CONTENTS

CONTENTS

FIGURES

TABLES

CONTRIBUTORS

Robert Arnott is Sub-Dean and Director of the Centre for the History of Medicine of the University of Birmingham Medical School and has recently been appointed the University's Public Orator. A practising archaeologist, he specialises in palaeodisease, health and medicine in the Neolithic and Bronze Age cultures of the Aegean and Anatolia, especially the Minoans, Mycenaeans and the Hittites. His publications include *The Archaeology of Medicine* (Oxford: Archaepress, 2002), which included a major study of Hittite Medicine, *Trepanation* (Lisse: Swets and Zeitlinger, 2003) and numerous articles and chapters in learned journals: *Disease, Healing and Medicine in the Aegean Bronze Age* (Leiden: E.J. Brill) will appear in 2005. He is Vice-President of the Society for Ancient Medicine.

Peter Barefoot is a Fellow of the Royal Institute of British Architects and qualified at the Architectural Association. He has been involved with the design of contemporary hospital buildings and housing for the elderly since 1958, as well as New Town housing in Lancashire. His most recent buildings include ward and outpatient design at St Bartholomew's Hospital, London, and while working on these later projects, he carried out research on the therapeutic quality of design in hospital buildings, which he called 'locotherapy'. Some of his conclusions were published in 1992 in *Technologie per la Sanità* (Bologna: Progetto LM). He is currently completing a study of the ergonomics of staircase design in Minoan palaces and a comparison of the ancient and contemporary libraries at Alexandria.

Chryssi Bourbou is a Research Associate at the Archaeological Services of the Ministry of Culture in Greece. Her main research interests focus on the effects of environmental and cultural stress in ancient Greek populations and sub-adult mortality patterns. She has participated in many excavations and research projects in Greece, Spain and France, and organises workshops on skeletal analysis and palaeopathology at various institutions and universities worldwide. She is currently working on two projects on the bioarchaeology of Crete during the middle-Byzantine centuries (eleventh–twelfth centuries AD) and the effects of Turkish conquest in Crete as evidenced through the bioarchaeological analysis of two sites.

Gillian Clark is Professor of Ancient History in the Department of Classics and Ancient History, University of Bristol. Her main research interest is the intellectual and social history of late antiquity/patristics, and her current project, with Todd Breyfogle and Karla Pollmann, is a collaborative commentary on Augustine, *City of God* (Oxford University Press). Relevant publications include *Women in Late Antiquity: Pagan and Christian Lifestyles* (Oxford: Oxford University Press, 1993); *Augustine: Confessions 1–4* (Cambridge: Cambridge University Press, 1995); *Porphyry: On Abstinence from Killing Animals* (Duckworth/Cornell, 2000) and *Christianity and Roman Society* (Cambridge: Cambridge University Press, 2004).

Sherry C. Fox is Director of the Wiener Laboratory, American School of Classical Studies at Athens, Greece. She is also currently an Adjunct Research Scientist at the Museum of Anthropology, University of Michigan. Her primary research interest is palaeopathology, but she is also trained as a forensic anthropologist. Her archaeological work focuses upon human skeletal analyses from the eastern Mediterranean, with an emphasis on sites in Cyprus dating from the Hellenistic to Byzantine periods.

Karelisa Hartigan is a Professor of Classics at the University of Florida. Her publications focus primarily upon Greek drama and myth and their relationship to the modern world. They include *Muse on Madison Avenue: Classical Mythology in Contemporary Advertising* (Frankfurt am Main: Peter Lang, 2002); *Greek Tragedy on the American Stage* (Westport, CT: Greenwood, 1995); *Ambiguity and Self-Deception. The Apollo and Artemis Plays of Euripides* (Frankfurt am Main: Peter Lang, 1991); *The Poets and the Cities* (Meisenheim am Glan: Anton Hain, 1979) and *The Myths Behind Our Words* (New York: Forbes Custom, 1998). As part of her research on arts and healing in the ancient world and the modern hospital, she has become an improvisational actress with the Arts-in-Medicine programme at the University's hospital.

Ralph Jackson is Curator of the Romano-British Collections at the British Museum. He specialises in Roman metalwork and the archaeology of ancient medicine. His publications on ancient medicine include *Doctors and Diseases in the Roman Empire* (London: British Museum Press, 1988), and current projects include a book on Greek and Roman surgery, a catalogue of the British Museum's medical collections, and, with Dr Jacopo Ortalli, the publication of the remarkable medical assemblage from the 'House of the Surgeon' at Rimini.

Helen King is Professor of the History of Classical Medicine at the University of Reading. Trained in Ancient History and Social Anthropology at University College, London, she has published widely on aspects of ancient medicine and its reception. Her books include *Hippocrates' Woman: Reading the Female Body in Ancient Greece* (London and New York: Routledge, 1998); *Greek and Roman Medicine* (Bristol Classical Press/Duckworth, 2001) and *The Disease of Virgins: Chlorosis, Green Sickness and the Problems of Puberty* (London and New York: Routledge, 2003).

Anna Lagia received her PhD in anthropology at the University of Chicago. Her principal research interest is in bioarchaeology of the Classical, Hellenistic and Roman periods in Athens and the regions of Attica, Beotia and Euboea, but she also works on reconstructing health and dietary patterns in prehistoric populations from the Peloponnese. She has published in journals including *Archäologische Anzeiger*, *Athenische Mitteilungen* and *Eulimene*. She is also interested in developing skeletal standards for Greek populations, and in understanding the presentation of skeletal lesions in terms of disease, and has founded a modern reference human skeletal collection for Greek populations at the University of Athens.

Ray Laurence is a Senior Lecturer at the University of Reading. He has worked extensively on Pompeii and other Roman cities. His publications on this subject include *Roman Pompeii: Space and Society* (London and New York: Routledge, 1994) and *Domestic Space in the Roman World: Pompeii and Beyond* with Andrew Wallace-Hadrill (London and New York: Routledge, 1997). He has also investigated the topic of human ageing in antiquity and published these findings with Mary Harlow in *Growing Up and Growing Old in Ancient Rome: A Life Course Approach* (London and New York: Routledge, 2002). His interest in health in antiquity arose from these two themes of his research.

Dominic Montserrat who died in October 2004 after a long illness worked on aspects of the body in Egypt and in late antiquity. His publications include *Sex and Society in Graeco-Roman Egypt* (Kegan Paul, 1996); *Akhenaten: History, Fantasy and Ancient Egypt* (London and New York: Routledge, 2000); *Changing Bodies, Changing Meanings: Studies on the Human Body in Antiquity* (London and New York: Routledge,

2004); with S.N.C. Lieu, *From Constantine to Julian: Pagan and Byzantine Views, a Source History* (London and New York: Routledge, 1996) and the edited collection *Constantine: History, Historiography and Legend* (London and New York: Routledge, 1998).

Neville Morley is Senior Lecturer in Ancient History at the University of Bristol. His main research interests are ancient economic history, especially the city of Rome, the theory and philosophy of history, and the place of antiquity in nineteenth- and twentieth-century critiques of modernity. His publications include *Metropolis and Hinterland: The City of Rome and the Italian Economy* (Cambridge: Cambridge University Press, 1996); *Writing Ancient History* (London and Ithaca, NY: Duckworth and Cornell University Press, 1999) and *Theories, Models and Concepts in Ancient History* (London and New York: Routledge, 2004), as well as articles on counterfactual history, demography, Marx and Nietzsche. He has just completed a book on trade in antiquity to be published by Cambridge University Press.

Charlotte Roberts is a biological anthropologist in the Department of Archaeology, University of Durham, England (website: www.dur.ac.uk/c.a.roberts/). Her principal research interests focus on the history of disease (palaeopathology), and more specifically the evolution and history of the infectious diseases. She has published over 100 papers in anthropological and archaeological literature. Her books include *The Archaeology of Disease* (second edition, Stroud: Sutton, 1995) with Margaret Cox, *Health and Disease in Britain. Prehistory to the Present Day* (Stroud: Sutton, 2003) and *The Bioarchaeology of Tuberculosis: A Global Perspective on a Reemerging Disease* (Gainesville, FL: University Press of Florida, 2003). She is currently working on the third edition of *The Archaeology of Disease*, a book for the Council for British Archaeology on the study of human remains in archaeology, and is the UK representative for the National Science Foundation supported project – 'History of health in Europe from the Late Palaeolithic to the present.'

Emma Stafford is Lecturer in Classics at the University of Leeds. Her research interests lie in Greek cultural history, especially religion, approached via a combination of literary and material evidence. In addition to articles on various aspects of Greek religion and iconography, her publications include *Worshipping Virtues: Personification and the Divine in Ancient Greece* (Swansea/London: Classical Press of Wales/Duckworth, 2000) edited with Judith Herrin, KCL; *Personification in the Greek World: From Antiquity to Byzantium* (London: Ashgate, 2004) and *Ancient Greece: Life, Myth and Art* (London: Duncan Baird, 2004). She is currently working on *Herakles* for a new series on *Gods and Heroes in the Ancient World* (edited by Susan Deacy, London and New York: Routledge) and on a Greek religion sourcebook.

Sevi Triantaphyllou obtained her first degree in Archaeology (1990) and MPhil in Prehistoric Archaeology (1992) at the University of Thessaloniki. She then completed her MSc in Osteology, Palaeopathology and Funerary Archaeology (1993) and PhD (2000) at the University of Sheffield. Her doctoral thesis on prehistoric skeletal populations from Central and Western Greek Macedonia was published in 2001 by the British Archaeological Reports. She is currently working as an osteo-archaeologist for the Greek Archaeological Service and as a freelance researcher in various projects in the prehistoric Aegean. She held the 1994–95 J.L. Angel Fellowship at the Wiener Laboratory, ASCSA, and was recently awarded a post-doctoral fellowship by the Institute of Prehistoric Aegean (INSTAP) in order to examine the dental micro-wear of prehistoric skeletal populations from Northern Greece, Peloponnese and Crete.

Anastasia Tsaliki is finishing her doctoral research in Biological and Funerary Archaeology at the University of Durham, UK, investigating the phenomena of necrophobia and the anomalous disposal of the dead. Her first degree was in History, Archaeology and History of Art from the University of Athens, Greece, and she holds the MSc in Palaeopathology, Funerary Archaeology and Bone Chemistry. Research interests also involve studies on marginality, ritual crime and the mythology and folklore of the occult. Her publications include 'Vampires beyond legend: A Bioarchaeological Approach' (Proceedings of the XIII European Meeting of the Paleopathology Association, Chieti, Italy, 18–23 September 2000, Edigrafital S.p.A.: Teramo-Italy, 295–300); 'The Capestrano Warrior: artistic caprice or disease?' (*Paleopathology Newsletter*, 119, 2002, 3–11) and 'Spine pathology and disability at Lesbos, Greece' (Paleopathology Newsletter 125, 2004, 13–17).

Nicholas Vlahogiannis is a Senior Fellow in the Department of History, University of Melbourne. His principal research interest is Ancient History, but he has also published articles and chapters on Australian educational and urban history, and modern Balkan history. His publications include *Prinny Hill: The Princes Hill Schools 1889–1989* (Melbourne: Princes Hill Schools, 1988); *More than a School: Glendonald School for Deaf Children, 1951–1991* (with Paul Duerdoth; Melbourne: Deakin University, 1992) and *The Heritage of Hellenism: A Handbook* (Melbourne: ASA Publications, 1997). He is currently working on two projects – *Diplomacy and War: The Foreign Politics of Mithridates Eupator VI, King of Pontus* (Melbourne: Department of History Monograph Series, University of Melbourne) and *Representations of Disability in the Ancient World* (London and New York: Routledge).

John Wilkins is Professor of Greek Culture at the University of Exeter. He has written books on Greek drama including *Euripides: Heraclidae* (Oxford: Oxford University Press, 1993), *The Boastful Chef* (Oxford: Oxford University Press, 2000) and *The Rivals of Aristophanes* (edited with David Harvey; London: Duckworth, 2000). He has also published widely on the history of food and culture including *Food in Antiquity* (edited with David Harvey; Exeter: University of Exeter Press, 1995) and *Athenaeus and his World* (edited with David Braund; Exeter: University of Exeter Press, 2000). He is currently writing books on Galen's nutrition and pharmacology.

ACKNOWLEDGEMENTS

In Chapter 2, Figure 2.1 appears courtesy of Don Ortner and Agnes Stix of the Smithsonian Institution, Washington, DC, USA; Figures 2.2 and 2.3 appear courtesy of University of Athens modern reference collection. In Chapter 5, Figure 5.2, Photo 1 appears courtesy of the Römisch-germanisches Zentralmuseum, Mainz; Photo 2 courtesy of the British Museum and Photo 3, Antikenmuseum Berlin, Staatliche Museen Preussischer Kulturbesitz. Figure 5.7 is from the British Museum, Neg. no. XXII, D (42) and Figure 5.3 is copyright to the author. Figure 5.6 is by Karen Hughes, after Majno. In Chapter 6, Figure 6.1 appears with the permission of Los Angeles County Museum of Art (The William Randolph Hearst Collection) and Figure 6.2 (private collection) with permission of the owner. Figures 6.3 and 6.4 appear courtesy of the Archaeological Receipts Fund. In Chapter 9, Figure 9.1 is copyright to the author. In Chapter 12, Figure 12.1 appears with the permission of The International Hippocratic Foundation; Figures 12.3 and 12.5 are copyright to the author.

ABBREVIATIONS

Abst.	Porphyry, *On Abstinence*
Alex.	Plutarch, *Life of Alexander*
Amm. Marc.	Ammianus Marcellinus
Anth. Pal.	*Palatine Anthology*
Apoll.	Apollodoros
Aq.	Frontinus, *De aquaeductis urbis Romae* (*The Aqueducts of Rome*)
Ath.	Athenaios
Att.	Cicero, *Letters to Atticus*
Aug.	Suetonius, *Life of Augustus*
Bibl.	*Bibliotheca*
CMG	Corpus Medicorum Graecorum
Conf.	Augustine, *Confessions*
De Off.	Cicero, *De Officiis* (*On Duties*)
Div. Iul.	Suetonius, *Life of Caesar*
DK	H. Diels and W. Krantz (1967) *Die Fragmente der Vorsokratiker*, Zurich
DL	Diogenes Laertius
DS	Diodorus Siculus
DW	*Diseases of Women*
Ep.	*Epistles*
GA	Aristotle, *De generatione animalium* (*On the Generation of Animals*)
Geog.	Strabo, *Geography*
HA	Aristotle, *Historia animalium* (*On the History of Animals*)
Hdt.	Herodotos, *The Histories*
IG	*Inscriptiones Graecae* (1873–)
Il.	Homer, *Iliad*
Isthm.	Pindar, *Isthmian Odes*

K	C.G. Kühn (1821–33), *Claudii Galeni opera omnia*, 20 vols, Leipzig
KA	R. Kassel and C. Austin (eds) (1989) *Poetae Comici Graeci*, Berlin and New York: de Gruyter, vol. 7
L	E. Littré (1839–61), *Oeuvres complètes d'Hippocrate*, 10 vols, Paris
Lyc.	Plutarch, *Life of Lycurgus*
Mor.	Plutarch, *Moralia*
NH	Pliny, *Natural History*
Od.	Homer, *Odyssey*
PA	Aristotle, *De partibus animalium* (*On the Parts of Animals*)
Paus.	Pausanias
Per.	Plutarch, *Life of Pericles*
PG	J.-P. Migne (1857–) *Patrologiae cursus completes. Series graeca. Patrologiae Graecae*
Pind.	Pindar
Plut.	Plutarch
PMG	D.L. Page (ed.) (1962) *Poetae Melici Graecae*, Oxford: Clarendon Press
PNI	psychoneuroimmunology
Pol.	Aristotle, *Politics*
ppm	parts per million
Pyth.	*Pythian Odes*
RA	Dionysius of Halicarnassus, *Roman Antiquities*
Rep.	*Republic*
RIBA	Royal Institute of British Architects
RR	Varro, *Res rusticae*
SEG	*Supplementum Epigraphicum Graecum*
Silv.	Statius, *Silvae*
Soph.	Sophocles
Suet.	Suetonius
VA	Philostratus, *Vita Apollonii* (*Life of Apollonius*)
WD	Hesiod, *Works and Days*
WHO	World Health Organisation

INTRODUCTION

What is health?

Helen King

In Plato's *Gorgias*, Socrates refers to a traditional *skolion*, or drinking-song, in which health is described as the greatest blessing for humankind (451e). This much-quoted song, attributed to Simonides or Epicharmos and thus going back to the fifth or even sixth century BC, says:

> To be healthy is best for mortal man,
> second is to be of beautiful appearance,
> third is to be wealthy without trickery,
> and fourth to be young with one's friends.
> (Simonides fr. 651 PMG)

Hygieia, the female personification of Good Health, was often shown standing beside her seated father, the healing god Asklepios. In the well-known hymn to Hygieia – from which the title of Emma Stafford's chapter (Ch. 6) for this volume is taken, and which is also discussed by John Wilkins (in Ch. 7) – the fourth-century BC poet Ariphron claims that without health 'no one is happy' (Athenaios 15.701f–702b) or, in a different translation, 'no one prospers'. Michael Compton (2002: 324–6) has argued that, in the cult of Asklepios, Hygieia provided a focus for healthy worshippers; in the words of the Orphic hymn to her, the goddess is 'sole mistress and queen of all' who is called upon to 'keep away the accursed distress of harsh disease' (Athanassakis 1977: 90; Compton 2002: 319). Stafford's chapter here explores the changing position of Hygieia in ancient Greek cult, and argues that her worship tells us much about attitudes to health in Greece and also in Rome.

Another fragment of Simonides also suggests that health should be placed before other blessings: 'there is no pleasure in beautiful wisdom if a man does not have holy health' (fr. 604 PMG).[1] The relative importance of the 'good things' was something that was discussed in antiquity; in *Against the Ethicists*, 48–66, the second-century AD writer Sextus Empiricus

1

summarised the different viewpoints taken. For philosophers of the Academic or Peripatetic persuasion, health did not hold the top position (*Against the Ethicists*, 59); he cited the Academic Krantor, a philosopher of around 300 BC, for whom it was beaten into second place by virtue or courage (*andreia*). But for Ariphron, Likymnios and Simonides, as well as for 'ordinary folk', health was seen as the prime good. Also writing in the second century AD, Lucian described how he accidentally wished his patron 'Health to you', when correct protocol for the morning salutation required 'Joy to you' (*De lapsu* 1). In the course of a discussion of the different greetings possible, he gives what he claims are historical examples of each. Thus, for example, the Pythagoreans preferred 'Health to you' (*De lapsu* 5), and it was with this greeting that Epicurus often began letters to his dearest friends; it is also very common in tragedy and Old Comedy (*De lapsu* 5–6). Lucian cites the *skolion* and also the Ariphron hymn, the latter being described as 'that most familiar piece of all which everybody quotes' (*De lapsu* 6); all the blessings of the world are worth nothing without health (*De lapsu* 11).

So what is health? For the social sciences, it has been argued that the rise of health to the top of the research agenda is a direct result of its increased importance as a value for us (Pierret 1993) and that this in turn only became possible because of improvements in medical knowledge from the 1940s onwards (Breslow 2000: 40). Within Classics, medicine in the ancient world is now an established field of study; however, the essays in this volume, many based on papers given at a conference organised by Karen Stears at the University of Exeter in September 1994, try to shift the focus of study on to health, looking not only at ancient beliefs about health but also at the health status of the peoples of Graeco-Roman antiquity. The project combines archaeological studies of material remains with work based on literary evidence and includes two very individual accounts of the impact of the ancient world on the health of people today through hospital architecture and through drama therapy.

Our society operates with two competing definitions of health. According to the biomedical definition, health is the absence of disease. This idea of a simple polarity between *hygieia* (health) and *nosos* (disease) was one familiar in the early Roman Empire. Plutarch wrote one of several works on good health surviving from the ancient world (*Advice on Keeping Well*; cf. Corvisier 2001), a treatise in which he argues for moderation in regimen, and particularly in diet, in order to preserve health, and suggests that knowledge of one's healthy self is essential so that the warning signs of imminent disease can be recognised (*Mor.* 127d, 129a, 136e–f). Elsewhere, when explaining the nature of *boulimos* (ox-hunger), Plutarch notes that

> Since any kind of starvation, and particularly *boulimos*, resembles a disease, inasmuch as it occurs when the body has been affected

unnaturally, people quite reasonably contrast it (with the normal
state), as they do want with wealth, and disease with health.

(Table Talk 6.8, *Mor.* 694b)

The construction of disease/health as an opposition akin to want/wealth is,
however, not entirely straightforward. It is much easier to talk about disease
than health; readers of this volume may at times feel that they are learning
more about 'disease in antiquity' than about 'health in antiquity'. Disease
comes in many forms, which can be classified: one part of medicine is to
create this classification. Disease is an addition; it is something one 'has'. In
this sense, it is more like wealth than want; it is possession rather than lack.
To bring in yet another opposition, male/female is often presented as
possession (of the phallus) against absence. 'Female' then becomes the
unmarked term, which lives in the shadow of the marked term. In many
ways, health lives in the shadow of disease, something that many of us have
experienced; it is sometimes only when you are ill that you realise what
'feeling well' was like. It is relevant here that, when the sociologist Janine
Pierret conducted interviews in France and asked people to tell her what
health meant to them, 'it induced talk about illness' (Pierret 1993: 14).

The other understanding of health is a social one (Ruzek *et al.* 1997: 4),
seeing it as positive, rather than negative, and is based on the World Health
Organisation definition offered in 1946: 'a state of complete physical, mental and social well-being and not merely the absence of disease or infirmity'
(cited Gordon 1976: 42; Polunin 1977: 87–8).[2] This has been widely discussed, and is mentioned by several of the contributors to this book;
Roberts *et al.* cite a variation on it which asserts that health is 'more than
mere survival – it is living usefully despite the various diseases and stresses
which challenge all of us'. Praised for its attempt 'to place health in the
broadest human context' (Callahan 1982: 83), the WHO definition has also
been rejected as 'so comprehensive that it equates health with happiness and
thus spoils its good intents' (Nordenfelt 1993: 282); although, of course,
the equation of health and happiness would not have been seen as a problem by Ariphron. When discussing Krantor's views, Sextus Empiricus suggests that most Greeks think 'It is not possible for happiness to exist when
bedridden and sick' (*Against the Ethicists*, 57, trans. Bett 1997: 12), although
Plutarch considered that it was perfectly possible to be a philosopher, general
or king while being weak or sickly (*Mor.* 126c). Unease has been expressed
by modern commentators at the inclusion of 'well-being' in the WHO
definition, as this is seen as something going beyond the state of the body,
and into areas over which doctors have no control. The inclusion of social
factors underlined that 'health' was being extended beyond the domain of
medicine and into politics (Callahan 1982: 81), with the roles of housing,

education and environment being recognised. Those resisting this move protested that 'Medicine can save some lives; it cannot save the life of society' (Callahan 1982: 84). The recent move from health to 'wellness', championed by institutions such as the California Wellness Foundation (Jamner and Stokols 2000), has led to the much-derided WHO definition coming back to prominence (Breslow 2000: 39). In some circles, health has been redefined according to the number of ADLs – activities of daily living, such as the ability to eat, or to go to the toilet unaided – which an individual can manage. In traditional societies, however, well-being has been defined not in terms of the individual but rather according to the relationships which that individual maintains with other people, deities or spirits; as Dominic Montserrat puts it in Chapter 14 on the healing cult of SS Cyrus and John in late antiquity, health is an issue 'of religious, cultural and political significance, going far beyond the concerns of the individual afflicted body'. This does not seem very distant from the WHO definition; nor does John Wilkins's point that the goddess Hygieia 'is associated with wealth, children and power' (p. 138, this volume). Indeed, women's health care activists today also stress that health is 'embedded in communities, not just in women's individual bodies' (Ruzek *et al.* 1997: 13).

While not going as far as ADLs, Galen comments on the use of 'health' in his own day:

> I see all men using the nouns *hygieia* and *nosos* thus . . . For they consider the person in whom no activity of any part is impaired 'to be healthy', but someone in whom one of them is impaired 'to be sick'.
>
> (*On the Therapeutic Method* 1.5.4; trans. Hankinson 1991: 22)

How far is this true? Are there specific activities which one needs to be able to perform in order to consider oneself 'healthy'? Sight is an obvious case in point. In Greek myth, blindness is associated with poetry and the gift of prophecy, but may also be seen as the result of transgression; for example, seeing a goddess bathing. It could be taken to physicians, or treated with amulets (Libanius, *Oration* 1), but it is also the most common condition at the temple of Asklepios at Epidauros.[3] At another temple of Asklepios, Phalysios of Naupaktos presented 2000 gold staters after his sight was restored (Pausanias 10.38), and in Aristophanes (*Ploutos* 634ff.) both the god Ploutos and a blind thief seek the help of Asklepios. In Chapter 10, Nick Vlahogiannis raises the issue of the visibility of health on the body; if disability is 'neither an illness nor a disease', then is a disabled person 'healthy'? What happens when a person is cured of a long-standing disability? King (2001b) examined the blindness visited upon Epizelos at the battle of

Marathon (Herodotos, *Histories* 6.117) and argued that his recovery was not possible, because of the status he received by having been blinded in a great victory by a divine event; precisely because the story Epizelos told was one which made him a hero, his illness narrative could never end in cure. But could he nevertheless be seen as 'healthy'? Where some disability is a public statement written on the body, other forms can be internal, private and personal; King's chapter (Ch. 8) in this volume examines Hippocratic gynaecology, and asks whether, for a woman living within the constraints of these heavily pro-natalist texts, it was possible to be 'healthy' if the reproductive function was impaired.

A further question concerns the power relationships of health: who defines it? In medical sociology and anthropology, the standard use of the terms 'disease' and 'illness' suggests the possibility of a mismatch between patients' sensations of health or its absence, and the medical categories applied by the doctor. As Eisenberg's now-classic definition put it, 'To state it flatly, patients suffer "illnesses"; physicians diagnose and treat "diseases"' (1977: 11). Health can be the absence of disease, or a greater sense of wellness; in the latter case, it becomes the absence of 'illness' rather than of 'disease'. 'Disease', then, tends to be used for the (natural/Western biomedical) doctor's definition, based on structural or functional abnormalities, while 'illness' is the (cultural/traditional, third-world) patient's experience. Although the opposition is used most frequently for anthropological encounters between different medical systems, it is also applicable within any single medical system. Within Western biomedicine, for example, 'disease' conventionally refers to symptoms that can be objectively measured or seen, while 'illness' represents the patient's feelings about the significance of the symptoms extending to their moral and social implications (Helman 1985: 293). Moving on to medical systems in general, we could say that the 'disease' label applied to a patient by a doctor grows out of the system within which he or she is trained and the culture within which the medical encounter takes place whereas the experience of 'illness' is equally culturally specific.

A similar division could be applied to health. Health can be used as the opposite of 'disease', and seen from the doctor's point of view, as something which can be judged by particular signs taught to doctors; in our own culture, it is increasingly seen as something that can be effectively measured by medical technology – x-rays, ultrasound scans and microscopic analysis – with the results being expressed in an apparently neutral, numeric form, in body temperature, white cell count, blood pressure and so on. But the self-proclaimed objectivity of measurement in Western biomedicine has been challenged by work such as that of Annemarie Mol and Marc Berg (1994) on anaemia, which has shown that the symptoms listed as indicating this diagnosis vary considerably between textbooks. The haemoglobin levels, relied upon to diagnose the disease, may in practice vary according to patient's posture, the site from which blood is taken, the time of day, the weather, the amount of fluid drunk by the patient and the method of measurement used.

Health can, however, be seen from the patient's point of view not as the opposite of 'disease' but as opposed to the experience of 'illness'. Some modern works use a model of Asklepios as medical intervention in illness versus Hygieia as the self in search of ways to remain in harmony with nature (Compton 2002: 329; Sassatelli 2003: 82). Being a body, living a body, is a process of interpretation in which we are all engaged. Deciding whether one is 'healthy' or 'ill' can be seen as a social and personal act. My decision to regard myself as 'ill' can depend on a wide range of factors: whether I am able to do all that I have to, or want to do; my knowledge of the severity of my symptoms; and whether the monetary and social costs of taking action outweigh any discomfort I may feel. As Nick Vlahogiannis (Ch. 10, this volume) points out, disease and illness can go with a devaluation of the self; health concerns inclusion, illness exclusion, from parts of social life. In western industrialised society, the decision to be 'ill' relates to the role of worker (Pierret 1993: 17); in order to receive money in lieu of wages, it is necessary to convert illness into a recognised category of disease. John Murray's study of late-nineteenth and early-twentieth century evidence on sick funds usefully summarises 'the cultural inflation of morbidity'; the idea of variation in the 'cultural standards of what constituted sufficient sickness to absent oneself from work' (2003: 237–41). Most scholars believe that the availability of funds to support sick workers led to a fall in the level of illness needed to be defined as 'sick'; however, Murray argued that social, as well as economic, factors affected such self-definition. James Riley's work (1997) suggests that workers did not take time off more frequently, but remained off work for longer at each sickness incident.

Deciding that I am 'ill' may not involve consulting another person, whether family member, friend or health care professional; in the 1970s, it was estimated that 75 per cent of symptoms were treated by the patient only (Levitt 1976). The social valuation of different diseases will affect the patient's response. For example, do those who think they may have AIDS seek help, or do they avoid seeking help because they are afraid of stigma? If the rate of venereal disease is found to be very high in a particular geographic area, does this mean simply that such disease is particularly common there, or is the figure due to less stigma in reporting the symptoms?

So patients may decide they are 'ill', and seek treatment, for a variety of reasons. However, because the medical encounter is about power, the patient's sensation of having crossed from health to illness may not coincide with the doctor's definition of the point at which health becomes disease. Philip Moore's work, *The Hope of Health*, published in 1565, hints at the possibility of a mismatch between doctors' and patients' definitions of health in the sixteenth century: 'it be needful to declare, what health is, and wherein it consisteth, that thereby the ignorant may learn to know when they are in perfect health, and when they be inclined to sickness' (1565: 45). Here, for patient, we read 'the ignorant'. Patients fail to realise when they are sick – they waste the doctor's time by turning up when healthy or staying away when sick and then only presenting when it is too late. This is a theme in Hippocratic medicine too, for a very good reason; blaming the patient for delay in seeking help is a highly convenient way of explaining why the patient died despite having been treated by the doctor. It was not the treatment that killed the patient: no, it was just left too late (e.g. *Prognostics* 1).

It is clear that discrepancy between medical definitions of health and our experiences of it as patients persists in our own culture. Stephen Kellert cites a number of studies of both mental and physical illness that suggest the possible scale of such discrepancies (1976: 224–5). For example, in the 1960s a study of over 10,000 apparently healthy people concluded that a staggering 92 per cent of them had 'some disease or clinical disorder'. A study in 1934 of 1,000 children found 611 had already had their tonsils removed. The remaining 389 were then medically examined, and 174 were considered to need tonsillectomy. This left 215, who were sent to another group of doctors; 99 of them were found to need a tonsillectomy, leaving 116. They were sent to yet more doctors, who recommended tonsillectomy for nearly half of these. Private medical screening feeds on the fear that you can feel absolutely healthy, but in reality you are very sick indeed. In Western biomedicine, although there may be a 'textbook picture' of disease, it is nevertheless accepted that different patients with the same diagnosis will have different symptoms (Helman 1985: 314); it is also possible to have either disease-without-illness, where the patient feels well but laboratory tests show evidence of a disease (Mol and Berg 1994: 256), or illness-without-disease, where the patient feels unwell but laboratory tests show no clinical abnormality. It is even possible for illness to mimic disease, as in Cecil Helman's classic 1985 study of pseudo-angina, in which a patient learns the symptoms of angina by being on the relevant hospital ward.

In ancient Greece, two opposed views of health and disease coexisted. On the one hand, it was believed that the original state of humanity was health; myth described how diseases were released from Pandora's jar along with hunger and hard work (Hesiod, *WD* 102–4), while some medical writers, such as Dicaearchus, believed that the original diet of human beings was free from any of the harmful residues which they thought caused ill health (fr. 49 Wehrli). On the other hand, the writer of the Hippocratic text *On Ancient Medicine* argued that the original state was disease, seen as the result of eating raw and uncooked foods like those consumed by wild beasts; this was gradually overcome by doctors working to create a diet appropriate for people (see further Wilkins, Ch. 7, this volume). In both cases, health is only a pawn in a bigger game, whether that game is myth explaining how all the perceived evils of the world derive from the same point, or medicine claiming the credit for all that is good (King 1999).

The chapters in this collection warn us against making broad generalisations about 'health in antiquity'. Such generalisations often rely on our attempts to construct ourselves in opposition to the past; for example, to romanticise the ancient diet as good and simple and healthy, because we live with preservatives and pollution, a position which is just as insecure as an earlier generation's assumptions that the health of people in antiquity must have been inferior to our own because we are a model of progress. Similarly, Neville Morley (Ch. 11) points out that the literature on the Roman city represents it either as a paragon of health, or as a place of darkness and disease; these two extremes depend in turn on whether architecture or literary evidence is privileged.

Reality, so far as we are able to judge it, was far more complicated. Bob Arnott's chapter (Ch. 1) describes how increased food production could – paradoxically – have led to a poorer diet, as the foods produced were those that could be most easily preserved, which tend to be foods with a high carbohydrate content, low in iron, vitamin C and calcium; it is even possible that increased food production led to sub-clinical malnutrition. Domestication of animals, which we may regard as further progress for human health, may instead have led to a rise in disease, if we take account of the zoonoses, those diseases which can spread to humans from animals; these include tuberculosis, discussed by Charlotte Roberts and her fellow contributors (in Ch. 2). Sherry C. Fox (in Ch. 3) cites evidence that animals lived within the domestic space of the home as early as the mid-fourth century AD: Neville Morley (in Ch. 11) notes that this also increases the incidence of malaria. The move to settled communities meant a greater risk of those diseases spread by proximity, such as respiratory infections (Roberts *et al.* in Ch. 2), while irrigation created an environment in which parasites thrive. The baths associated with the Romans appear 'healthy' but, as Sherry C. Fox reminds us, their practice of sharing toilet sponges would have spread disease.

There is thus no linear progress in human health. While the palaeopathology of the ancient world can tell us what was in fact eaten, John Wilkins looks at dietary theory in the Greek and Roman worlds, raising the issue of when careful control of diet shades into medical use of plants as drugs. He notes the resistance of many ancient writers in the dietetic tradition to the fruit and vegetables which we now consider essential to health; however, dietary advice does seem to have incorporated foods which were available to the poor, rather than claiming that good health could only be achieved with an expensive diet. Here we are reminded of Plutarch's claim that the least expensive foods are the best for health (*Mor.* 123d). Although Sherry C. Fox charts dental caries in the populations of Hellenistic and Roman Paphos and Corinth, Ray Laurence's chapter (Ch. 4) reminds us that the teeth of the Romans could be better than our own, while their height was not as far short of ours as we may expect.

The work collected here also draws attention to the variation that existed between cities of a similar nature and of a similar size. Sherry C. Fox's study of Paphos and Corinth finds a broadly comparable picture, but with some differences. Neville Morley paints a picture of Rome as dominated by hyperendemic malaria, with periodic epidemics of other diseases whereas Alexandria was plagued with leprosy. What of the city and the countryside? Rural men and women were taller than their urban counterparts in Rome, and Morley points out that 'we cannot assume that, because most Roman cities were significantly healthier places to live than the capital, they were necessarily as healthy as the countryside' (p. 197, this volume). Yet the water supply was better in Rome than outside it, and most ancient cities other than Rome itself were healthier than the medieval, early-modern or contemporary Third World city.

The contributors to this volume also address the effects of a constant level of low health, or sudden outbreaks of acute disease, on society. Fox notes those conditions that would have prevented people from reproducing, or even from surviving to the age at which they would be able to reproduce. Vlahogiannis observes the many situations that could lead to disability in the ancient world, including congenital conditions, accidents, occupational injury and battle wounds. Laurence, however, points out the dangers of drawing conclusions from the evidence of bones; for example, palaeopathological evidence of strained joints could be due to hard work, but it could be the result of deliberate body-building. More broadly, Roberts *et al.* note the limits of palaeopathology. What it can tell us depends on the bones which survive, and our samples can be biased in a number of ways; the skeletal remains from the Vesuvian sites studied by Laurence are unusual in that, unlike a sample from a cemetery, 'they represent a living population' (p. 83, this volume). It is also possible that the virulence of disease organisms has changed, while many diseases leave similar 'marks' on the skeleton, and some – such as viruses, as Fox reminds us – no trace at all. Ralph Jackson's chapter (Ch. 5) examines bones from a different perspective, that of bone surgery in the Roman Empire, and concludes that the tools used were 'finely-designed and exquisitely-crafted', and the techniques used 'generally excellent' (p. 118, this volume).

Considerable continuity can be seen in some aspects of ancient health and health care practices. The theme of religion and healing runs through many of the chapters in this collection. Gillian Clark (in Ch. 13) shows how Christians could understand illness as an opportunity to repent, or as an opportunity to share Christ's suffering, but this did not mean that illness in itself became desirable; health remained the goal, and illness was to be healed by doctors or by prayer. Dominic Montserrat shows how, from the fifth century AD onwards, healing was sought at Menouthis by Christians of all persuasions, as well as by Jews and pagans. He extends the discussion of the relationship between classical temple medicine and Hippocratic medicine, showing that humoral theory lay behind many of the treatments offered at the shrine, and that the accounts of miracles given by Sophronius directly engage with Hippocratic and Galenic methods. Before his conversion to Christianity, Cyrus was a doctor, trained in Alexandria, and Sophronius presents him as a holistic healer, capable of leading his patients 'on to good health and life'. As for Aelius Aristides in the second century AD, in a religious context, ill health could be a source of spiritual power (King 1998: 126–30). Miraculous cures are also discussed by Vlahogiannis (Ch. 10) and Hartigan (Ch. 9); Hartigan sets them in the context of modern understandings of the 'placebo effect'.

The humoral tradition led to an interest in adjusting diet according to the season and the climate, which also extended over many centuries. The geography or place of healing was also significant. The influence of SS Cyrus and John is generally localised, becoming more effective the closer it is to the tomb of the martyrs themselves. While Morley looks at how architectural movements such as the 'New Urbanism' have interpreted ancient Rome for their own purposes, Peter Barefoot provides another slant on the reception of ancient architecture and town planning, arguing for 'locotherapy' as a practice as valid now as it was in the ancient world. Karelisa Hartigan's chapter (Ch. 9) similarly uses contemporary approaches to the value of drama in healing in order to raise questions about what may have taken place at the healing shrines of antiquity. Here, she argues, what demonstrates continuity is an aspect of the human mind/body relationship that is constant across the centuries; forms of drama used in therapy can draw on Aristotle's theory of *katharsis*, but modern practice can then be used to raise new questions about what happened within the healing shrines of the ancient world.

Those whose work is represented here would like to contribute to this dialogue between ancient and modern discussions of health. This book has been in gestation for a very long time; some contributors have been waiting for it to appear for a decade whereas others have left the project to publish elsewhere, and new ones have been recruited to take their places. I would like to thank them all for their perseverance and patience with the change of editor, and also to thank Richard Stoneman for his belief that this book would one day appear.

NOTES

1 I owe these and many other references here to Emma Stafford. I would like to thank her, and also Chris Newdick for his valuable comments on contemporary issues of health policy.
2 Preamble to the Constitution of the World Health Organisation as adopted by the International Health Conference, New York, 19–22 June 1946; signed on 22 July 1946 by the representatives of 61 States (Official Records of the World Health Organisation, no. 2, p. 100) and entered into force on 7 April 1948.
3 Iamata A4; A9; A18; A20; B22; B32; C65; possibly D69. On sight, see further Vlahogiannis (Ch. 10, this volume).

1

DISEASE AND THE PREHISTORY
OF THE AEGEAN

Robert Arnott

Historians find war exciting and pestilence dull; they exaggerate
the effects of the former and play down the latter.

(Grove and Rackham 2001)

INTRODUCTION

From the very beginning of human history, infectious diseases have been life
threatening, and have often been instrumental in major social change. For
those engaged in research into the history of human disease, an understanding
of how they work is vitally important to our reconstruction of how people
lived their lives, as their spread is strongly related to social and economic
factors, such as nutrition, demography, community hygiene, ranking and
status. The evidence, most of it skeletal, whether studied by conventional
osteology or by biomolecular science, enables us to create models explaining
the evolution of diseases and their vectors and can help establish a better
overall understanding of these societies and human adaptation to disease.

A brief glance at the indices of many major works in the field shows that
many scholars who have studied the prehistory of Greece and the Aegean,
in the third and second millennia BC (and earlier), have ignored the history
of disease as an important aspect in social reconstruction of Aegean palace
societies and their predecessors. Governed by their own experience of living
amid disease-experienced populations of the West, where almost complete
immunity exists to the many infections that would have killed a great
number of the inhabitants of Knossos or Mycenae, many such scholars are
completely unaware of the social effects of disease and the major consequences that ensued whenever contacts across disease boundaries allowed
a new infection to invade a population that lacked any acquired immunity.

Another mistake often repeated is the belief that the demographic and cultural consequences of improvements in food production must have led to improved nutrition and health. There is now growing evidence to suggest that improved health is not necessarily linked to food production; indeed, the opposite is often likely to be true. The tendency to concentrate on too few crops, possibly leading to environmental changes will, in turn, have increased the potential for nutritional and infectious disease (F.R. Riley 1999: 133).

DISEASES AND PARASITES

Diseases and parasites play an all-pervasive role in every aspect of society. Throughout human history, individuals or even entire communities, large and small, have exhibited varying levels of susceptibility or immunity to infections. These levels of infection can often be hereditary, but are more likely to be the consequence of previous exposure to particular micro-organisms (Haldane 1957; Motulsky 1960). Disease in humans is also a reflection of a mixture of genetic inheritance, ecology and a relationship with those plants and animals with which they share their environment. It is influenced by occupation, diet, settlement location, social structure and religious beliefs. Adjustment of human defences against disease and levels of resistance and immunity are constantly changing and, similarly, as micro-organisms themselves undergo continual adaptation to their environments, prolonged interaction will eventually allow both to survive (Black 1974; McKeown 1988: 4).

It has been suggested that many disease partnerships have failed to survive from antiquity because of the breakdown in the symbiotic relationship between a micro-organism and its host and, thankfully, many of the most lethal pathogenic micro-organisms are poorly adjusted to being parasitical. Some, familiar to us today as the parasites carrying known diseases, are still in the early stages of development and adaptation to their human hosts; although, of course, as we also know, co-existence over time does not produce mutual harmlessness (Smith 1934).

The very earliest settlements in the Aegean, between approximately the eighth and third millennia BC, other than in Thessaly, were scattered rather thinly, the population living in relatively small hamlets (Perlès 2001: 171–2), and most of them would have acquired the same spectrum of parasites in childhood. These infections of a small rural society would not have been a particularly heavy burden, and they clearly failed to inhibit the expansion of population in the period. Within 500 years of the domestication of the first food crops human population would have grown dramatically compared to the previous hunter-gatherer communities living within the same region (Cockburn 1963: 150).

The early development of pastoralism brought with it significant dangers to the human population. Most, if not all, infectious diseases of civilisation have spread to humans from the animal population. In prehistory, contacts were closest with domesticated animals, and it is therefore not surprising that many of the infectious diseases common to humans are also recognisable in animals. For example, of what we call the sporadic zoonotic diseases, smallpox is almost certainly connected with cowpox, and influenza is shared with pigs; other diseases in this category were measles and mumps. Pastoralism brought to humans many different new pathogens, but they did not appear to spread at once. Some of these sporadic zoonoses transmitted from domesticated animals remained occasional and dormant until proto-urbanisation created the conditions for them to spread and sustain crowd transmission.

The change from hunting and gathering to primitive farming was not entirely detrimental to health, as a number of factors become firmly balanced. With the beginning of farming, some stabilisation of general health would have occurred, with the return of female longevity back to the norm that existed during the earlier hunter-gatherer period. This eventually created an excess of survivals over deaths in the very young, and a population increase ensued. The ending of a nomadic existence meant less stress on women during pregnancy, and postnatal adjustment and genetic adaptation of each population to endemic infections will have occurred, especially in malaria, through the balanced polymorphic increase in genetically determined abnormal haemoglobins, allowing for antibody formation with just enough iron and zinc in the diet (Angel 1984). Most of the pathological conditions that existed in these periods will have related to the creation of more stable communities and the formation of permanent villages. Their establishment meant that people began to live in poor conditions and in very close proximity, so that hygiene suffered and individuals were exposed to an increasing number of disease organisms.

Early forms of social organisation may have created dietary and sanitary codes (many of which have survived until the present day) that would have reduced the risk of infection, but it was not just worms and other parasites that flourished in the favourable conditions created by agriculture for their spread amongst the human population. Protozoan, bacterial and viral infections also had an expanded field as the human population, together with their flocks and herds, grew. However, it is only when communities become large enough, where encounters with other individuals become frequent enough, and when people lived in close proximity in poor, unhygienic conditions, that the infections brought about by these micro-organisms spread.

Unfortunately, no soft-tissue remains have been found in the Aegean, so it is therefore only possible to indicate the presence of specific diseases that leave diagnostic lesions on bones of such as poliomyelitis, tuberculosis, brucellosis and pyrogenic infections, which include staphylococcus and salmonellosis. Similarly, it is not possible to confirm the existence of other acute diseases such as cholera, typhoid and smallpox, although they must have been present in a growing population. It is, however, possible to iden- tify from the osteological pathology other specific metabolic diseases and conditions, including avitaminosis, rickets, scurvy, metastatic bone cancer, dental disease and a whole range of instances of osteoarthritis, inflammation and other degenerative diseases of the bone, including gout, and congenital disease and deformities, such as Paget's disease (Arnott 1996: 265, 2004).

Many diseases need relatively high population densities in order to thrive and were quite insignificant to hunter-gatherer bands in early prehistory, becoming significant only with the development of permanent settlement, farming and subsequent population nucleation. In fact, the earliest forms of settlement in small agricultural communities involved new risks of parasitic invasion. Increased contact with human excrement that accumulated in prox- imity to living quarters allowed for a variety of intestinal parasites to thrive. In later urban centres, with the absence of arrangements for sanitation for the population outside the palaces and other elite dwellings, the inhabitants would, as a rule, have used the streets and open squares and areas alongside walls for urination and defaecation. The consequences of this would have been not only an increase in contagious ova, worms and other pernicious parasites, carriers of any number of diseases, but also the contamination of supplies of public drinking water, such as streams, wells and cisterns, thus putting pub- lic health in jeopardy. Other micro-organisms would also have contaminated water supplies, particularly where a community had to rely permanently on one source. For the Aegean, as elsewhere, the existence of closed rural endo- gamous societies will have had a profound epidemiological effect, with various inherited diseases and disabilities that such in-breeding often produces.

In some parts of the Eastern Mediterranean and the Near East, irrigation farming recreated the favourable conditions for the transmission of disease parasites that prevailed in the tropical rain forests from where many of the diseases originally emerged, particularly warm shallow water, in which potential human hosts would provide a more than suitable medium for dis- ease (Kent 1986). Amongst them was infection by the parasitical blood fluke *Schistoma sp.* (which produces schistomiasis), not believed to have been a serious problem in the Aegean, and the *Anopheles* mosquito that spreads malaria, one of the most virulent and prevalent diseases of the Aegean, particularly in the Greek mainland.

Compared to the hinterlands of the large urban centres of the Ancient Near East, such as Ras Shamra (Ugarit) and Troy, the Aegean, with its rain-watered rather than irrigation-watered lands, would have offered a slightly healthier and more disease-free environment into which the population could expand, as patterns of cultivation and land-use did not always invite new forms of parasites. For example, the olive formed part of the wild flora of Greece and, after cultivation, involved little disruption to the existing ecology. The vine was introduced into Greece from the better-watered regions of the North, but similarly caused little alteration to the ecology. This was also the case with wheat and barley, which in their earliest forms are indigenous and so involved few alterations to the older biological balances. As the population density gradually increased, various infections became more common, and during the Late Bronze Age, the population must have increased enough to maintain a large spectrum of diseases. With trade patterns as they existed in the Middle and Late Bronze Ages, many of the coastal regions of the Eastern Mediterranean would have begun to constitute a single disease pool, with diseases communicated through ship-borne trade, over hundreds of miles of sea (Cockburn 1963: 87).

MALARIA

It was Lawrence Angel who first suggested that one of the most virulent, prevalent and handicapping diseases that affected the prehistoric Aegean, and that would have succeeded in having a major influence on the social history of the region, was malaria, in particular *falciparum* malaria, caused by the parasite *Plasmodium falciparum* (Angel 1971: 77–84; Roberts *et al.*, Ch. 2, this volume). He was the first to suggest that porotic hyperostosis, a form of osteoporosis expressed in lesions on the cranial vault and long bones found on a number of skeletal remains (Caffey 1937; Moseley 1965), is a reliable indicator of a genetic form of anaemia, in this case β-thalassaemia, and thus can be used as an index for the frequency of malaria, with which it lives in a symbiotic relationship. *Falciparum* malaria allows selective survival for those children heterozygous for one of several abnormal haemoglobins, β-thalassaemia, sickle-cell anaemia and G6PD deficiency, which prevents amoeboid entrance of the *P. falciparum* sporozoites and thus protects young children until their metabolic systems have had time to develop antibodies. In a particularly malarial environment, many of which existed in the Aegean at the time, the normal children would often die of *falciparum* malaria and those homozygous for an abnormal haemoglobin will often die of the resulting genetic haemolytic disease (Angel 1975: 179). The view that porotic hyperostosis is an indicator of thalassaemia has been challenged, and some believe that it is caused by iron-deficiency anaemia (Stuart-Macadam 1992); however, more recent work tends to support Angel's view (Capasso 1995; Tayles 1996; Lovell 1997).

Malaria is spread by the microscopic *Plasmodium* parasite, which lives in the body of the *Anopheles* mosquito and which transmits the disease to humans through the bite of the female. The parasites move speedily through the bloodstream to the liver, where they breed during an incubation period of approximately fourteen days. Returning to the blood, they then attach themselves to red blood cells, which break down and lead to waves of fever, attacking the patient, dependent upon the type of malaria that they have contracted. Malignant tertian malaria, caused by the *P. falciparum*, is the most lethal, which in modern times produces something like 95 per cent of all deaths from the disease. It spreads within the circulatory system very quickly, causing massive destruction of red cells and hence dangerous levels of anaemia, enlargement of the liver and spleen and then stupor, fits, coma and finally death (Knell 1991: 3).

Malaria became a disease of habitation and farming and, overcoming ecological barriers, shadowed their origins and development, after it emerged from the tropical rain forests south of Sub-Saharan Africa, eventually spreading to the Near East and the northern shore of the Mediterranean by at least the eighth millennium BC (Groube 1996: 123–5). The *Plasmodia* causing malaria are thought to be the descendants of ancient parasites of the intestinal tract of a common ancestor to reptiles, amphibians and birds, all currently infected by different species of *Plasmodia*. In prehistoric Greece, the conversion of a proportion of forestland into farmland and the establishment of the first Early Neolithic settlements created an environment ideally suited to the breeding of mosquitoes. These settlements were often situated by natural freshwater or artificially created habitats such as water storage vessels and stagnant ponds. In fact, coastal settlement sites, with their rich silt soils, and providing excellent land for the grazing of cattle and the growing of wheat and barley, were ideal for the spread of malaria.

Leonard Bruce-Chwatt and Julian de Zuluetta rejected earlier speculation that *P. falciparum* was already active on the Greek mainland by the fifth century BC. They are of the view that it spread on the northern shores of the Mediterranean and southern Europe during the time of the Roman Empire, and attributed all textual references to 'intermittent tertian fever' to the effects of infection by *P. vivax* (Bruce-Chwatt and de Zuluetta 1980: 18–25). Others have argued that *P. falciparum* is very old and that this type of malaria arrived in Greece between the end of the last Ice Age and mid-first millennium BC (Coluzzi *et al.* 2002). One of the most decisive pieces of evidence to support the notion of an early transmission of malaria to the Aegean is connected with a mutation of β-thalassaemia. One of the two most frequent mutations in the Mediterranean today is the B+IVS nt 100 mutation (G→A), which occurs in areas of former Greek colonisation of the Italian peninsular, and attains its highest frequencies today in the Eastern

Mediterranean, being particularly common in Greece. It has been suggested that this particular mutation originated in Greece (and possibly Asia Minor) and was spread westwards to Italy by Greek colonisation from the eighth century BC onwards, implying that *falciparum* malaria must have already become endemic at least in Greece beforehand, pointing to its implied existence during at least the second millennium BC and earlier (Robert Sallares, personal communication 2000).

From the skeletal evidence, Angel was able to conclude that the incidence of malaria reduced during the course of Aegean prehistory, based on a reduction in the number of skeletons positive for porotic hyperostosis which he had identified at a number of sites. For example, 60 per cent of all skeletons studied in the case of Early Neolithic Nea Nikomedia (mid-fifth millennium BC) were positive, as against 20.4 per cent in the case of Middle Helladic Lerna (*c*.1700–1600 BC), a pattern that repeats itself in the whole region (Angel 1971: 77–84). However, this reduction would not have been naturally progressive, creating temporary variations in the pattern of reduction, and it is likely that the establishment of larger settlements by the beginning of the third millennium BC had a temporary determining effect on the course of malaria, as these larger population densities would have produced artificial breeding grounds for the *Anopheles* mosquito. The distribution of malaria in the Aegean was likely to be linked to local environmental conditions, such as in coastal lowland with close proximity to water, for example as at Lerna, thus increasing prevalence for a period. Whilst in earlier prehistory the selection of a habitation site would have been related to a number of factors, experience may have shown that some particular sites may have been unsuitable because of the proximity to mosquito breeding grounds and a prevalence of malaria.

In the Argolid at the beginning of the Middle Helladic period (*c*.1900 BC), coastal sites such as Lerna and Asine (and possibly Argos), with their high frequency of implied malaria, may have been important centres as they would have had access to imported goods, for example from Crete. At this time, Mycenae was relatively obscure, but by the end of the Middle Helladic period, it had become pre-eminent in the Argolid; Lerna and Asine had by now been reduced to being of subsidiary importance. Mycenae's spectacular rise may be attributable in part to it being located a distance away from mosquito breeding grounds and, from the evidence of porotic hyperostosis from the Shaft Graves, experiencing low incidence of the disease.

The existence of widespread *falciparum* malaria on the Greek mainland, up to the end of the Middle Helladic period, mostly in lowland marshy areas, such as the Argolid and Boeotia, would have had a considerable social effect upon both fecundity and the energy and survival potential of small children, which could possibly have led to the creation of a selective microevolutionary process. Malaria, particularly *falciparum* malaria, is a major debilitating disease, prone to relapsing, and is apt to disrupt the whole structure of society. Extensive incidence of malaria in any society can act as a social depressant, often inhibiting creativity and invention, and undermining the whole of its social fabric.

The eventual reduction in the incidence of malaria during the Middle Helladic period on the Greek mainland was largely a result of improvements in farming methods and changes in sea level, which may have destroyed many of the mosquito breeding grounds. The consequence of this was better overall health of the population, with increased fertility and energy, and the population generally rebounding substantially from earlier poorer levels of overall health and nutrition. This would also have meant that existing food supplies would have come closer to meeting the nutritional needs of the population in terms of protein, calories and iron (Bisel and Angel 1985). As a consequence, all these changes would have been a contributory factor towards the great surge of energy and creativity that occurred on the Greek mainland at that time, from which emerged the beginnings of Mycenaean civilisation in around 1600 BC.

Of course, during the Late Bronze Age malaria did not simply disappear. Although the Mycenaeans began the draining of marshy lakes, such as Lake Copais in Boeotia (Kalcyk *et al.* 1986), which would have continued the process of the shrinking of mosquito breeding grounds, large pockets of malaria would have continued to exist, and were even created. For example, coastal infilling caused by sedimentary deposits from rivers would have reversed many of these trends, as happened at the site of Ayios Stephanos, occupied in the Late Helladic IIIA/B period (*c.*1400–1200 BC), and situated on the now marshy Helos Plain in southern Laconia. This population, lacking the gene for thalassaemia, because they were formerly unexposed to malaria, now became exposed and unprotected against the disease. The extraordinarily high percentage of infant burials at the site has malaria as the prime suspect (Janko 1996).

MIGRATION

Migration of peoples during the Aegean Bronze Age and in earlier prehistory would not only have had significant cultural and demographic effects, but also epidemiological consequences. In earlier prehistory, the movement of people would have brought with them their domesticated animals and a host of new pathogens, whether they were the wholesale movement of peoples that some believe introduced agriculture into Europe from the Near East or just a few who quickly mingled with the existing hunter-gatherer population.

Later on, the start of the migration of the proto-Greek speaking Indo-Europeans into the Greek mainland from the north at the end of the Early Helladic period (*c*.2100 BC) may have introduced new diseases, which may have had a devastating effect, when let loose on the existing population in their small and often isolated communities. This may be one of the reasons behind the reduction in population at this time and the nucleation of small communities into larger ones. There is even evidence during the Early Helladic III period (*c*.2100 BC) for a mass burial at Corinth, which might add support to this hypothesis (Waage 1949: 421–2).

The disruptive effect of such epidemics on society is likely to be greater than the mere loss of life. As we know from historical analogies, survivors of such epidemics are often demoralised, and lose all faith in inherited custom and belief, which had not prepared them for such horror. In these circumstances, new infections often manifest their greatest virulence amongst young adults, owing to the excessive vigour of this group's antibody reactions to the invading organism (McNeill 1977: 71). Losses to the population in the 20-year-old plus age bracket are, of course, more lethal to the economy of a society than the deaths of, say, the very old or the very young. Any society that loses a large percentage of its young adults, will find it difficult to maintain itself spiritually, never mind economically (McNeill 1977: 71). The arrival of the Mycenaeans on Crete (*c*.1450 BC), with its associated population influx, may also have had important epidemiological and demographic consequences. The population of newcomers often increases disproportionate to their original size, and when combined with the introduction of new pathogens, which sometimes can cause very serious 'virgin-soil' epidemics, the native population is often decimated and replaced by the newcomers within two or three generations (McNeill 1977: 71–2).

One other problem would have been refugees. A number of events in the Aegean have led scholars to believe that there have been both large and small movements of refugees. Perhaps the best known is the period following the evacuation of Thera before the final eruption in the mid-seventeenth century BC. Involving much greater numbers was the likely concentration into the surviving urban centres on Crete, such as Knossos, following the widespread destructions on the island in the Late Minoan IB period (*c*.1500–1450 BC) (Driessen and Macdonald 1997). As in any society, ancient or modern, refugees need to be fed and, in some manner, housed. This would have created what may have been 'shanty towns' on the periphery of population centres such as Knossos. In these circumstances, one of the greater dangers would have been the outbreak of epidemic diseases which, when combined with a shortage of food, may have led to large-scale mortality.

The end of the Bronze Age came in the twelfth century BC, the time of the legendary siege of Troy, with the destruction of the Mycenaean palaces, many now heavily fortified. The causes suggested include a series of earthquakes, economic recession and social stress, and the wholesale disruption of trade with the Near East caused by invasion and the movement of the 'Sea Peoples'. If widespread climatic change and drought were mainly responsible for the decline and collapse of the Mycenaean world in the twelfth century BC, as has been suggested by Rhys Carpenter and others (Carpenter 1966; Bryson *et al.* 1974), and discussed by Philip Betancourt and Robert Drews (Betancourt 1976; Drews 1993: 77–84), then a natural consequence would have been widespread epidemic disease (e.g. cholera and typhoid) brought about by the shortage of clean drinking water. However, other than the evidence for a possible small-scale localised epidemic at Argos around 1150 BC (Kritzas 1972: 198–201), there appears to be no archaeological or palaeopathological evidence to support such a concept (Dickinson 1974). In any case, scientific studies have shown that there was no apparent change to the flora of the region at this time (Grove and Rackham 2001: 151–66). Whatever the cause, the turmoil of the end of the Bronze Age led many to abandon their homes and emigrate to Asia Minor and Cyprus, after the collapse of the Mycenaean economy and overseas export markets and the desertion of the palaces and towns.

URBANISATION

By the third millennium BC, the larger urban communities in the Near East began to become more densely populated, taking them beyond the critical threshold for the spread of density-dependent diseases. Infectious bacterial and viral diseases will no longer have had any need for an intermediate zoonotic host and therefore could spread more effectively. These diseases – measles, mumps, whooping cough, smallpox, tuberculosis and the rest – remain all too familiar to us (Black 1975: 515). The epidemiological distinction between town and countryside now became much more apparent. Population pressures, causing the overuse of soils, grasslands and woodlands, with farming practices improving slowly in comparison, allowed for endemic diseases also associated with habitation, such as malaria, hookworm, amoebiasis and other forms of dysentery to spread.

In the Aegean during the Bronze Age, similar urban health hazards to those in the Near East could only have emerged in centres with sufficiently large populations; Late Minoan Knossos and various other centres on Crete, such as Gournia and Palaikastro, meet this criterion. In such centres the circulation of diseases would have been intensified through poor hygiene, and contaminated water supplies plus a full array of insect-borne pathogens. The very existence of these urban centres would have created its own intrinsic problems; for example, a breakdown of the transportation of food from the countryside, or even localised war would have created famine conditions, and local crop failures would have been difficult to overcome. This will have been particularly true of the social disruptions that occurred in the Late Minoan IB period (c.1500–1450 BC). Accordingly, these urban centres would have depended upon each other and the countryside to replenish losses from famine, epidemic and endemic diseases. The countryside would often have been healthier, as many of the diseases of the towns were less likely to reach these outlying farming districts. However, once these diseases penetrated the countryside, they would have had a greater epidemiological effect than they had on the urban populations, who were already exposed to them and therefore partially immune.

As Photini McGeorge (1988: 47) has reminded us, the remains of the material culture and architecture of the period have for generations influenced our image of the Aegean Late Bronze Age, particularly Crete. The great art, luxury and wealth of the palace elites have often mistakenly created the false impression of a largely privileged society. From the archaeological and skeletal evidence that has emerged from excavations in recent years, we are now beginning to know something of the reality for those living outside the palaces, often concentrated into small urban centres. Such evidence indicates a picture vastly different from the well-dressed and nourished figures depicted in the iconography of the period. As the result of more recent palaeopathological work on Crete, it is now therefore possible to begin to develop an understanding of the overall effect of what has come to be seen as the process of urbanisation on the individual health of the Late Minoan population. This is vital to our understanding of epidemiology and social conditions in the period (McGeorge 1988: 47, 1992: 43–4).

In the fourteenth century BC and later, following the destruction on Crete of most of the major palaces, and the arrival of the Mycenaeans, the growing population density of Late Minoan Khania, for example, would have been quite conducive to the rapid spread of disease and would have taken its toll on the population, weakening resistance to many diseases such as dysentery, tetanus and hookworm (McGeorge 1992: 46–7). This would have been exacerbated by little or no understanding of the cause of most illnesses, overcrowding, possible ignorance of rudimentary hygiene, poor sanitation, poor food preservation, shared cooking utensils, exposure to human excrement, the lack of physical isolation of the sick, and the probable periodic contamination of drinking water supplies, combined with a meagre, unbalanced and often seasonal diet. Immunity to infection would gradually have begun to disappear, making even childhood diseases often fatal, and the incidence of epidemic disease is likely to have been high. Like many other towns of the period, Khania was also an important overseas trade centre and busy sea-port, trading with the whole of the Eastern Mediterranean, and extended overseas contacts through interactive trade and exchange networks may well have led to the introduction of infectious organisms from overseas (McGeorge 1992: 46–7). McGeorge also interprets the premature incidence of degenerative joint disease, which she associates with excessive strain, as suggesting a life-time of intense physical labour (1992: 43–4).

On the Greek mainland, it is doubtful whether there were ever any Mycenaean population centres of the size of Knossos. However, many of these smaller mainland settlements may well have reached the criteria required for maintaining some density-dependent diseases, with the larger settlements in the Argolid, Messenia and Boeotia possibly even large enough to sustain epidemics on the same scale as on Crete.

HEALTH STATUS, STATURE AND LIFE EXPECTANCY

Our knowledge of health status, stature and life expectancy and its relationship to disease naturally depends upon a critical understanding of the skeletal evidence that is available for the period. Although Halstead (1977: 107) did express the more conventional view for his time that the average age of death was low (not much over 30 for those who reached adulthood) and that most females died during their childbearing years, he did so before the more recent work on the skeletal aging of adults was rethought. Although it is usually speculated that life expectancy would have risen between earlier prehistory and the end of the Bronze Age on the Greek mainland, McGeorge has suggested that, for men in parts of Minoan Crete, despite the so-called 'improved' living conditions, it actually reduced during the course of the Bronze Age, varying on average from 35.24 years[1] in the Early Minoan III period (c.2100 BC) to 30.84 years in the Late Minoan IIIA/B periods (c.1375–1300 BC). This downward trend can be explained by the increase in the number of various infectious diseases and the overall effect of a process of urbanisation on a considerable number of the population. However, for women, their average life expectancy remained roughly constant, between 28.06 years in the Early Minoan III period and 27.32 years in the Late Minoan IIIA/B periods, with the same nutritional and obstetric factors applying throughout the whole of the Bronze Age (McGeorge 1990: 420–3). Although this is based on the well-preserved sample from Armenoi, and may not be representative of the period at more important sites such as Knossos, it does make a statement about the deterioration of living standards at the time (F.R. Riley 1999: 137).

Late Minoan town life was particularly hard for the more vulnerable members of society, such as children. At Khania, located in Western Crete, there was higher child mortality than in the rural population; children aged up to 5 years formed 45 per cent of the total sample studied from the graves. At Armenoi, children and sub-adults up to the age of 16 years formed 31 per cent of the sample, the mortality rate amongst children aged 5–15 years being 15.4 per cent. Of that sample, 22 per cent were under 1 year, 34 per cent were under 2 years and 54.7 per cent were under 5 years (McGeorge 1990: 425–6).

Diseases such as tuberculosis, trauma, infections, acquired haemolytic disease, malaria and enteropathies must have taken their toll, and many childhood diseases such as measles, chickenpox and viral infections would have been fatal, particularly if there were complications such as pneumonia (McGeorge 1990: 427). However, the figure of 56 per cent juvenile mortality in the well-preserved sample from rural Middle Helladic Lerna (Angel 1971: 70) may be exaggerated by malaria. Against a background of inadequate nutrition, poor habitation standards and limited medical care, a high infant mortality was often a feature of the ancient world, where disease was a severe restraint on child survival.

Children suffered particularly from nutritional or disease stress; this is shown on lines of arrested growth, such as those seen on the femora of a child aged approximately 8 years from Tomb 11 at Khania. At some sites on Crete, McGeorge has produced evidence of rickets and probably infantile scurvy or Barlow's disease (McGeorge 1992: 44); this may indicate either a poor and insufficient diet lacking vitamins C and D or, in the case of rickets, the possibility of young children working long hours in sweatshops devoid of sunlight. Failure of lactation by nursing mothers, owing to malnutrition, may have been the cause of death of a number of small children.

Teeth can also tell us something about the stature and health of the population as a whole. The work of Becker (1975: 271–6) at Pezoules Kephala, Karo Zakro and that of McGeorge at Armenoi, for example, show that 28.6 per cent of teeth were lost before death and 17.7 per cent had caries. This is almost double the figures for Middle Minoan Knossos and supports McGeorge's assertion that it was caused by dietary change that emphasised dependence on foods with high carbohydrate content (McGeorge 1990: 423–4). Dental diseases remained much the same at all these sites.

Nutritional stress also has another effect, in that it seriously affects susceptibility to disease. The need to store food surpluses, as the result of improvements in production, can create a bias towards the kind of foodstuffs which can be preserved without deterioration. Cereals, pulses, dried fruits (e.g. figs, prunes, raisins and dates), honey, olive oil and pickled olives can be stored in clay storage jars for up to two years. However, all are high in carbohydrates and, with the exception of beans and lentils, they are deficient in iron, vitamin C and calcium (McGeorge 1990: 424).

Thus, inspite of the improvements, diet may have become poorer for the non-elites, due to a greater dependence on these forms of stored food, with a consequential increase in both infectious diseases and other conditions brought about by a diet deficient in these requirements. Thus, for example, if most of them ate bread made from barley, gruel and vegetables with a little cheese and even less meat protein, then dietary deficiency states would have existed, if only sub-clinically. Clinical manifestation would occur only where there were other reasons for generalised ill health and in increased physiological need, for example, during pregnancy. Equally, sub-clinical malnutrition impairs healing and the body's resistance to infection (McGeorge 1990: 427).

A further consequence of the dietary deficiencies that existed amongst the poor who lived in urban centres might have been protein–calorie malnutrition. It occurs when both calories and protein are insufficient. As a result, during childhood and adolescence, growth is suppressed to conserve calories needed to maintain basic body processes. A child may well have been at risk from nutritional deficiency, possibly by a generally reduced natural defence system caused by the mother, if she was also suffering from the condition. Her milk would be of poor quality and in short supply, and putting the child at further risk, as it is unable to acquire the nutrients or other substances lacking. The most dangerous period for the child would have been the weaning stage. If the new foods were of poor quality or in short supply, this would have led to nutritional stress, especially if the milk was also inadequate.

WOMEN AND CHILDREN

Women, especially in the towns, were also very vulnerable. The greatest threat to women's health may have been the sheer physical exhaustion of frequent, possibly annual pregnancies, with the associated dangers. McGeorge, for example, believes that prolonged lactation may also have caused nutritional draining of body resources of vitamins and other minerals, not easily replaced by the poor diet of the period. Consequently, many women will have died at the time of peak reproductive activity, and the higher frequency of deficiency disease, premature osteoporosis and the increased incidence of tooth loss before death were observed amongst females. These disturbances made women less resistant to other diseases and consequently diminished their overall life expectation compared with that of men (McGeorge 1987: 408).

These ideas that nutritional and other physical stress were primarily due to pregnancy, parturition and lactation have been challenged by

Kimberly Calnan Gray (Gray 1992, 1994) who argues that the primary cause of the earlier mortality of females in the Aegean Bronze Age is rooted in a number of factors relating to malnutrition, commencing at an early age, thus creating a much lower resistance to disease. Behavioural factors, such as occupationally related physical alterations – for example, squatting and femoral neck erosion – will have also been important factor, as may also have been physical abuse. Calnan Gray also believes that additional cultural strictures, such as food rationing during lean periods, may have also perpetuated a cycle of malnutrition stresses into a succeeding generation. Women, she believes, were well adapted to stresses in pregnancy, parturition and lactation. She also points out that parturition in adolescence was not a likely cause, due to delayed age at menarche, itself influenced by malnutrition. Not all women become pregnant and not all women reach term and give birth; not all women experience difficulties during their confinement. Therefore, not all health hazards for women should be ascribed to pregnancy and parturition.

From her work studying the much neglected human skeletal remains of children, from the Middle Helladic graves in the Lower Town at Asine excavated in 1926, Anne Ingvarsson-Sundström (2003) has also studied the complications between the mother's and child's health status. She has noted a number of important factors; for example, that poor maternal malnutrition can be a serious threat to the foetus as it can reduce placental size and reduce foetal nutrition itself, not to mention the possibilities of malnutrition impairing obstetric performance. She suggests that malnutrition would threaten the mother as well, supporting Calnan Gray's views, which include malnutrition being the main killer of women, rather than childbirth hazards or continuous pregnancies. Her other conclusions are that (a) women with a short stature have the highest rate of perinatal deaths; (b) factors like the mother's age (high or low) and number of pregnancies also affect the outcome of birth; (c) if the mother dies, there is little chance of the child's survival; (d) food was probably not distributed fairly amongst the sexes and (e) the introduction of food other than breast milk at about four months would have been a crucial cause of infant mortality. She believes that the combination of the nutritional status of women with their cultural and economic circumstances would have had a huge impact on the fate of neonates.

In contrast, the life expectancy of rural men seems to have been better than for those living in towns. Town-dwelling males, as well as females, were approximately three centimetres shorter than their rural counterparts. This difference in stature points to the urban population being comparatively undernourished, leading to skeletal retardation and reduction in growth. This was likely to be due to the deficiencies in specific components of the diet, perhaps exacerbated by seasonal food shortages. This is supported by the existence of both anaemia and nutritional deficiency reflected by the reduction in stature and bone/enamel hypoplasias, the instance of which increased markedly in the Bronze Age, by the high incidence of deficiency diseases, frequency of ante-mortem tooth loss and by the appearance of density-dependent epidemic disease (McGeorge 1992: 46–7).

MINOAN CRETE

The health status of the Minoan population of Crete would largely have applied to the mainland Mycenaeans. Crete does not appear to have suffered from malaria to the same extent as the mainland did, because if it had, it would have inhibited the growth of the first palace society on the island. As a comparison, at Middle Helladic Lerna, Angel estimated that the average age of death for adult men was 37 years and for adult women 31 years, with an infant mortality rate of 36 per cent (Angel 1971); however, this estimate for males may be too high. By the fifteenth century BC, there were some improvements in physical stature, pelvic depth and dental health, and there was an apparent increase in the life span of men and women and increased fertility and parity. Even a slight decrease in childhood diseases would have led to a decrease in infant mortality. These factors would have led to a rise in population, the greater density putting increased pressure on agriculture and the food supply (Angel 1968: 263–70, 1975: 181–2). This probably created social and medical conditions perhaps not dissimilar to those at Khania, but based, unlike Crete as a whole, on a lower concentration of the population in one place. This may also have resulted in some reaction against overcrowding on the island, perhaps finding expression in an expansion of territory, overseas colonisation – possibly in Western Anatolia and Cyprus – and maybe even localised war (Angel 1975: 181–2).

THE MYCENAEANS

On the mainland, there are also stark regional variations. In contrast to the later towns, for earlier rural centres such as Nichoria in the south-west Peloponnese in the Late Helladic IIA period (c.1500 BC), Sara Bisel estimated the average age at death was again unusually low – females 30 years and males 31.4 years. This might be associated with a severe epidemic that is reflected in a mass unceremonial burial, but Bisel has also calculated that the local population was on the whole healthier than contemporary town-dwelling population groups (Bisel 1992: 355–6), and displays none of the major effects of urbanisation. Taller than average, they had fairly good nutrition, with a greater reliance on protein from eating meat, a little fish and the use of unrefined cereals as well as much softer foods (Bisel 1992: 357). The high incidence of hypoplastic lines in dental enamel, indicating arrested growth in childhood, shows that many suffered frequent episodes of illness or starvation as children, perhaps the result of a crop failure or over-reliance on coarsely ground flour and porridge, which must have been serious enough to interfere with calcium, iron and zinc absorption, but not sufficient to cause death (Bisel 1992: 355–7).

The human skeletal remains found in the Deiras cemetery and the south quarter at Argos gives us the opportunity to examine health and nutrition from a small urban site dated towards the end of the Bronze Age (Charles 1963: 74–5). In the Late Helladic IIIA2 period (c.1350 BC), the average age at death at Argos, according to Robert Charles, is as high as 40 years, and something like 50–100 later, in the Late Helladic IIIB period (c.1300–1200 BC), the average only increased slightly to 41.4 years. Of more significance is the dentition of the occupants of the Deiras cemetery, where 7 out of 43 show evidence of caries, normally associated with a flour-based diet of town dwellers; this was probably due to the introduction in the Late Bronze Age of the Mycenaean crop combination of olives and cereals. Many also have stunted or impacted wisdom teeth, and some even none at all, while in one a canine tooth has not emerged from its socket; these are attributes of town dwellers (Charles 1963: 65, 71). Robert Sallares believes that the diet of the Mycenaeans rested on a small range of rather primitive crops. The primitive husk wheats, emmer and einkorn, were still important and had not yet been replaced by the cereals we know today. Similarly, he believes that the Mycenaeans were not making extensive use of domesticated olive trees and would have relied on obtaining oil from wild olive trees for domestic use and their perfume industry (Sallares 1991: 15–16).

The hypothesis of Sallares supports the work of Bisel and Angel, who have concluded that there were some beneficial aspects of Mycenaean society that affected overall health. Although the non-elite diet would often have been deficient in protein, calories and iron, it was high in roughage from the unrefined cereal, thus assisting in the avoidance of gastrointestinal disorders. There was also no unrefined sugar, and honey was only available for special occasions, therefore contributing to dental health. The reliance on olive oil, an unsaturated fat, rather than quantities of saturated animal fat, means that the overall diet was generally low in cholesterol, but this would not be significant if the adult population did not live long enough to develop heart disease (Bisel and Angel 1985: 205–6). However, owing to protein deprivation or an imbalance of amino acids, one result of this diet would have been a lowered resistance to disease and infection. This would have affected children in particular by the depletion of antibodies, and by interference with macrophage metabolism (Angel and Bisel 1985: 206). Low iron intake is also known to increase susceptibility to infectious disease (Winberg 1974: 952–6). Of course, instances of malaria gradually decreased from earlier periods, and this would have been a major contributory factor to better overall health, increased fertility and energy.

THE ELITES

What, however, of the inhabitants of the palaces at Knossos, Mycenae, Pylos and elsewhere? Of course, they suffered illness and trauma, but their diet, living conditions and medical treatment would have been quite different from the rural and urban non-elite population. From the evidence of Grave Circle B at Mycenae, Angel was able to suggest the stature and overall health of a few of the early male members of a ruling family, interred there during the transition from the Middle to the Late Helladic periods (c.1650–1500 BC) (Angel 1972b: 393–4). They were generally thick-set, sturdy and with relatively short lower limbs, and ranged in height from 1.71 to 1.80 m tall, making them on average 5 cm taller than their subjects; this difference is also reflected in a five-fold improvement in dental health. However, disease is no respecter of class divisions, and in addition to dietary factors, including its seasonality, diseases would have had an equal impact on life expectancy. Other than epidemics, which must have occurred, genetic conditions, such as thalassaemia, malaria, tuberculosis and brucellosis, will have been significant, although vulnerability to disease would have been conditioned by the better quality of their diet and its overall protein content. This confirms the evidence that this is a more prosperous community, with a much higher standard of living. There is one case (131 Myc.) of gallstones, caused by eating too many fatty foods such as meat and by drinking more wine (Angel 1972b: 383).

In the Middle Helladic period it has been estimated that the average person had 6.5 diseased teeth and, by the Late Bronze Age, 6.6. In contrast, those elites buried in the Grave Circle B had only on average 1.3 diseased teeth. This immunity to dental disease, although it may have had a genetic component, is more likely part of a picture of general good health. The lack of lines of enamel growth arrest, and the rarity of porotic hyperostosis, suggests they enjoyed much better health than the common people, despite the same postural and muscular adaption to rough terrain, and instances of arthritis. However, Angel's estimate of the male life expectancy of approximately 36 years, being no greater than the general male population, is explained by the stresses of leadership and physical activities. One skeleton, for example (59 Myc.), shows possible occupational stress from carrying a large shield (Angel 1972b: 381–2). Many of the males have enough head wounds, arthritis and vertebral fractures to indicate they were active and vigorous warriors. There is evidence that the children of these elites escaped partial starvation and illness, and that their growth was prompted by a relatively good diet, as reflected in the state of their teeth (Angel 1972b: 393–4). For the Late Bronze Age, there is as yet insufficient pathological evidence from the major palatial sites to illustrate their precise circumstances, but it is clear from the archaeological evidence that sewage systems, fresh water supply and preferential food supplies were available only to these elites and their households. By the end of the Late Bronze Age, their circumstances can only have improved, not lessened, by the development of forms of medical treatment (Arnott 1996, 2004).

CONCLUSION

It is a tribute to the resilience of the population of the prehistoric Aegean that, in the absence of modern-day therapeutics and the advances of biomedicine, they could, although often handicapped by disease and trauma, survive at all, never mind create advanced cultures. Absurdly romantic notions of gods and heroes and the Trojan War must now be replaced in our minds by an understanding of the harsh reality of a society where life was hard, death and disease were everyday occurrences and the day-to-day ambition of those who lived outside the palaces was simply survival.

ACKNOWLEDGEMENTS

This chapter was first read as a paper to the University of Birmingham History of Medicine and Health Research Seminar held on 23 April 1998 and in part to the Ninth International Congress of Cretan Studies, Elounda, Crete, on 3 October 2001 and I am grateful to all those who stimulated me with ideas during the discussion. I also wish to thank Dr Kimberley Calnan Gray and Dr Anne Ingvarsson-Sundström for permission to make use of their unpublished PhD theses and to the following for their advice or assistance: Keri Brown, Professor Don Brothwell, Dr Photini McGeorge, Dr Ken Wardle and Dr Robert Sallares. This work would not have been possible without the financial support of The Wellcome Trust, to which I remain continually indebted. Much of this manuscript was written whilst working at the INSTAP Study Centre for East Crete and I am indebted to Dr Thomas Brogan and his staff for their hospitality. Finally, I should like to thank the editor, Professor Helen King, for rescuing this book.

NOTE

1 In their work, Angel, McGeorge and others sometimes offer very precise adult skeletal ages, which have now been challenged on osteological grounds. Even with this caution, however, the overall trends that they point to in their results would stand up to scrutiny, even if re-calculated on broader age bands than the precise ages that many now use. It must be understood that the data on demography are still limited and that only a few tentative conclusions are possible.

2

HEALTH AND DISEASE IN GREECE

Past, present and future

Charlotte Roberts, Chryssi Bourbou, Anna Lagia,
Sevi Triantaphyllou and Anastasia Tsaliki

INTRODUCTION

Health is crucial to the well-being of society today, its efficient function and survival; as Angel and Bisel state: '... health is more than mere survival – it is living usefully despite the various diseases and stresses which challenge all of us' (1986a: 12). Disease affects everybody at some point in their lives and many factors predispose populations to acquiring deviations from normal health. The occurrence of disease, its transmission and maintenance in a population, its geographic, prehistoric and historic variation captures the fascination of all. Disease can curtail, or even cease forever, a person's 'normal' function, contribution to and enjoyment of life; it is the one factor in our lives that is more often than not unpredictable. P.J. Brown *et al.* (1996: 183) succinctly state that '... particular diseases ... vary by culture ... (and) ... the nature of interactions between disease and culture can be a productive way of understanding humanity'. Whilst the authors support this viewpoint wholeheartedly, they recognise that not all scholars in archaeology, anthropology, the classics and history study health and disease, but the message forwarded is that looking at health may help other disciplines studying the history and archaeology of Greece to answer questions and test the hypotheses that they may have.

This chapter aims, first, to demonstrate the importance of considering past disease patterns and how they affected populations, how they are studied and what limitations there might be. Second, the study of health in past Greek societies is discussed with reference to the late J. Lawrence Angel, the most prominent person to have made detailed studies of human skeletal material in Greece. Finally, current research on health in Greece in the past is considered, with suggestions as to how its study may progress in the future.

Background

Greece has an incredible history and is a region which has attracted a great deal of attention from both archaeologists and historians. The wealth of material of all types, ranging from magnificent buildings to a range of delicately manufactured artefacts, has survived for study by many people from a range of academic disciplines. In addition to this wealth of material culture, there is also a significant body of literary sources. Together these provide a wide range of data sources for the reconstruction of past human behaviour, change and adaptation. However, whilst pottery and other artefacts, buildings and written records have been studied time and again to answer specific questions about people living hundreds or even thousands of years ago, the remains of the people who provided all these data are often ignored, for a number of reasons. Studies of cemeteries have been focused mostly on aspects of material culture such as pottery and luxury items accompanying the deceased as grave goods, rather than on the remains of the people themselves. The study of funerary archaeology in Greece, where burial practices are being approached in terms of socio-political, economic or other cultural variables, has only recently been developed and has been mostly applied to the southern Greek mainland and Crete (Pullen 1985, 1990; Laffineur 1987; Morris 1987, 1992; Hagg and Nordquist 1990; Tzedakis and Martlew 2002). In this context the physical (or biological) anthropological data of the cemetery usually forms a separate appendix at the end of each cemetery report (e.g. Duckworth 1902–03, 1904, 1913; Hawes 1911; Furst 1932; Breitinger 1939; Musgrave 1976a, 1980a; Bisel 1980a; Coldstream *et al.* 1981; Xirotiris 1982, 1992; Wade 1983; Herrmann 1992) or in monographs or papers written in a rather technical style, often dealing with issues far away from the original questions posed (Boyd 1900–01; Hawes 1909–10; Hasluck and Morant 1929; Furst 1930, 1932; Koumaris 1930; Charles 1958, 1963, 1965; Carr 1960; Poulianos 1967; Gejvall and Henschen 1968; Krukof 1971; Paidoussis and Sbarounis 1975, 1979; Musgrave 1976b, 1985, 1990; Prag *et al.* 1984; Wall *et al.* 1986; Preka-Alexandri 1988; Musgrave and Popham 1991; Triantaphyllou and Chamberlain 1996; Triantaphyllou 1997). These analytical approaches are often closely determined by the biological, medical and anatomical backgrounds of the authors and do not necessarily suggest a lack of interest in archaeological questions. On the contrary, many of them are excellent methodological and systematic works but, although they refer to archaeological material, with the exception of a few cases (Patrick 1967; Halstead 1977; Bisel 1980b; Musgrave 1980b; Xirotiris 1980, 1981, 1986; Bisel and Angel 1985; McGeorge 1988; J.E. Powell 1989; Pappa *et al.* 1998; Triantaphyllou 1998a) they do not contribute significantly to reconstructing the lives of past populations in Greece. There is, thus, a need in Greek biological anthropology for systematic study and co-operation between biological anthropologists, field archaeologists and historians. This is not to say that Greece is the only country in the world where this problem occurs, but it does highlight the point that, without humans, we could say little about the past. Today our world is shaped by us and we are also shaped by it; we adapt to, and change, our environment when conditions demand. This has the potential to be reflected in our bodies, and more precisely in our skeletal remains; to be blunt, we need to see what is happening with humans themselves before we can interpret other evidence in the past. This chapter therefore aims to convey why and how we can study and use the evidence for health and disease to understand the past.

The study of past health and disease: palaeopathology

Health can be defined as 'the state of being bodily and mentally vigorous and free from disease', and disease as 'any impairment of normal physiological function affecting all or part of an organism especially a specific pathological change caused by infection, stress, etc., producing characteristic symptoms; illness or sickness in general' (Hanks 1979). As Bhasin *et al.* (1994: 65) state, 'Health is not a component but is an expression of development; so that the health of a community at a given moment is the very situation of the whole social system seen from a health point of view.' Palaeopathology was described earlier last century by Sir Marc Armand Ruffer, an Anglo-French doctor, as the science of diseases whose existence can be demonstrated on the basis of human and animal remains from ancient times. It is a multidisciplinary and holistic sub-discipline of physical or biological anthropology (the study of the biological evidence for humans from prehistory to the present) which considers many types of evidence ranging from written records to skeletal and mummified remains (e.g. İşcan and Kennedy 1989; Roberts and Manchester 1995; Bourbou 1999a). Not only does it look at the evidence for ill health *per se*, but it also attempts, by considering the cultural context from which the material comes, to understand why certain diseases appear and affect populations at specific time periods (the 'biocultural approach', or also termed 'bioarchaeology'); Roberts and Cox (2003) provide a recent study of British health from prehistory to the present. For example, if we were to imagine a population that starts to settle and practise agriculture rather than hunting and gathering, what changes in their lives would affect the diseases from which they would suffer (Cohen and Armelagos 1984)? They would be living in permanent housing, relying on a more limited range of food sources which may be deficient in important nutrients, domesticating animals and accumulating refuse. Consequently, they may be at risk from developing respiratory and other infections from living in close contact with other members of the community (rather than living in temporary structures in smaller groups). In addition, nutritional deficiency diseases may increase, and diseases such as tuberculosis, affecting animals, may be transmitted to humans. As a modern comparison, today we see a rise in cases of tuberculosis, an infectious disease (Raviglione *et al*. 1995). Why? There are many factors responsible, including more people living in poverty and in crowded and poor housing, deficient diets due to poverty, resistance to the drugs used to treat the disease and deficient immune systems, as in people with HIV (human immunodeficiency virus infection); in the developing world, we could add transmission of the disease from cattle suffering from bovine tuberculosis. Many of these factors are also relevant to the appearance of the infection in the past.

The evidence used to reconstruct health and disease in the past consists of skeletal and mummified remains (considered as primary evidence), contemporary artistic depictions and written records, with reference to disease patterns and their predisposing factors in traditional living societies (e.g. leprosy in India today). All this evidence is interpreted using a clinical base; that is to say, one has to consider how a disease affects the body in a living individual before this can be recognised and interpreted for the past. For example, what is the bony damage in rheumatoid arthritis and what signs and symptoms does the person experience; how common is it today and what causes it? From the information on diseases today one can begin to consider disease in the past. That is not to say that there are no limitations to the study of palaeopathology. It has to be assumed that disease affected the skeleton in the same way in the past as it does today, and that people illustrated and wrote accurately about disease; we have to pay close attention to these particular problems. The appearance of a disease in a skeleton may have altered, for many reasons, over long periods of time. The virulence of the organism could have changed and, hence, its effect on bone, and it is highly probable that many writers and artists recorded the most dramatic and unusual diseases in the past, whilst ignoring those conditions which may not produce visually disturbing features.

Reconstructing the diseases that were present in a population, and their frequency, is not an easy task and is undertaken by a variety of people from a range of backgrounds; these include biological anthropologists specialising in palaeopathology, interested doctors and dentists, anatomists, historians

ROBERTS *ET AL.*

and archaeologists. In the United States the discipline has grown rapidly, whilst in Europe and the rest of the world it has lagged behind in making training in palaeopathology available. In the United Kingdom, for example, postgraduate courses in the study of human remains in archaeology did not begin until the late 1980s and the majority of archaeology departments do not teach undergraduates in this area. Whilst Europe is still catching up, the United States has made significant advances in the biocultural interpretation of disease patterning in past societies and has paved the way for how future studies should be undertaken. For example, standards for data collection in human skeletal remains have been developed (precipitated by the repatriation and reburial issue in North America), and provide a baseline for recording of data, making it potentially possible to compare populations from different geographic regions and time periods (Buikstra and Ubelaker 1994). This is the only way in which information can be generated on how and why, worldwide, diseases have appeared at different points in time, and how different that information is to today's health and disease problems.

In Europe, in recent years, there has been an increase in the population approach to past health and disease (e.g. Lewis *et al.* 1995) rather than a concentration on isolated cases of certain diseases (e.g. Wells 1965). Whilst interesting in itself, and contributing to the evidence for disease in the past, study of one individual suffering from, for example, osteoarthritis in Anglo-Saxon England is hardly very illuminating with respect to osteoarthritis in Anglo-Saxon populations generally. Despite this, however, the discipline has developed from the nineteenth century, where non-human cases of disease were initially recorded, into the twentieth century where more population-based approaches answering specific questions began to emerge, mainly from North American scholars. For example, when did syphilis first appear? Did tuberculosis first occur in the New or Old World? What precipitated the plague to appear and devastate so many populations around the world? We see this trend continuing with the emphasis on the biocultural approach in answering questions, and testing hypotheses about disease in the past, by studying skeletons from large cemetery sites.

Problems in the study of skeletal evidence

First, the skeletal material that palaeopathologists study is highly dependent on what survives in the ground to be excavated, and how carefully it is recovered. Many factors affect survival of bones and teeth (the latter tend to survive better) and these range from how the dead person is disposed of (e.g. cremation versus inhumation), what happens to the body whilst it is in the ground (e.g. grave water content, soil acidity, temperature and humidity, the presence of plants and animals in the grave, a coffin and/or clothing, depth of burial and later disturbance, for example by another grave; Boddington *et al.* 1987), and what methods are used to excavate the skeleton (McKinley and Roberts 1993). For example, the small bones of the hands and feet may not survive or could be missed during excavation, and these preserve vital evidence for some of the joint diseases and conditions like leprosy. Once the skeletons are recovered, the question of how representative of the original population they are needs to be asked. A rural cemetery, for example, may have been totally recovered and could provide a better picture of the community at a single point in time, and yet an urban cemetery is more likely to be incompletely excavated because of constraints on the excavated area caused by standing modern buildings in the vicinity. In effect, a cemetery population is only a sample of the original contributing population and it may be that it is biased in some way (Waldron 1994).

The methods used to examine the evidence for disease are many, but mainly rely on macroscopic and radiographic techniques – most researchers use the former. Microscopic study may be used for confirming diagnosis in problematic cases, and stable isotope and trace element analysis may be used to reconstruct past diet and migration, both relevant to disease (Katzenberg 2000). Of late, ancient DNA (aDNA) and other biomolecules specific to micro-organisms causing disease have been used for diagnosis (see T. Brown and K. Brown 1992 for problems and potential, and Salo *et al.* 1994 for an example). Disease can affect bone in a limited number of ways; namely, by forming bone, destroying bone, or both. These changes on the bone are recorded in detail, noting which bones are affected (their distribution pattern), where on the bone they occur and whether or not the lesions are healed. This latter information is important in determining whether a person was actively suffering from a disease when they died (perhaps a contributory cause of death) or whether they had survived the problem which had then led to resolution and healing of the lesion. Once abnormal changes have been recorded, a number of potential diseases may be forwarded for consideration (differential diagnosis) because many diseases leave similar 'marks' on the skeleton. It is usually their distribution pattern and the characteristics of the lesions that indicate what specific disease was present. The characteristics and patterning of lesions are interpreted with reference to descriptions in the clinical literature of diseases affecting bones and joints (e.g. Resnick 1995). More often than not, it is only possible to categorise disease into broad groups, such as infectious or metabolic disease, but in some circumstances a specific condition may be identified. What is important is that a detailed description of the abnormalities is given (preferably including photographs) so that future workers have access to as much data as possible for potential re-interpretation. Another complication is that not all diseases affect the skeleton so that, for example, the plague, smallpox, cholera, diphtheria, measles, malaria and many tumours will not be seen in the skeleton; this invisible data may only be recognised in visual or written historical records. This makes documentary and iconographic evidence particularly useful in these cases, although the development of aDNA as a tool for diagnosis of disease may help to identify some of these diseases; as in the case of Drancourt *et al.* (1998) on the diagnosis of plague in post-medieval France. Two other major points need to be made. First, just because a skeleton has no abnormal lesions – that is, the bones look normal – does not necessarily mean they did not suffer disease; after all, something killed them! They could have died in the acute stages of the disease before the bones were affected. Second, skeletons with chronic healed lesions may be regarded as the healthy part of a population because they have survived the acute stages of a disease (due to their strong immune system, perhaps), and developed skeletal lesions which have healed; many of these limitations are discussed in the excellent paper by Wood *et al.* (1992).

HEALTH AND DISEASE IN PAST
GREEK POPULATIONS

Early studies of biological anthropology in Greece

The study of health and disease in past Greek skeletal remains has a long history and is documented in Agelerakis's (1995, 1997) description of the development of biological anthropology in Greece. The first studies of skeletal remains in Greece were conducted in the first quarter of the nineteenth century by Rudolf Virchow, the German physical anthropologist (Virchow 1872, 1873, 1891, 1893), but the creation of the Museum of Anthropology in 1886 inaugurates the history of the study of biological anthropology in Greece, it being one of the oldest museums of humankind in Europe (Pitsios 1994: 7). Initially it was housed at the Academy of Athens but, in 1930, it was transferred to the newly built School of Medicine at the University of Athens, of which it has been an integral part ever since. Two researchers were seminal in the creation of the Museum and in the establishment of biological anthropology as a separate discipline in the Greek Academia. Klon Stephanos was the founder and director of the Museum from 1886 to 1915 and was also responsible for the establishment of Anthropology in 1915 as a separate Chair at the University of Athens. Yiannis Koumaris took over the direction of the Museum for another 35 years (1915–50), also being the first Professor of Anthropology at the University of Athens and the founder of the Greek Anthropological Society in 1924 (Pitsios 1993: 36, 1994: 8).

The educational background of both directors of the Museum, as of most of their successors and colleagues, originated from the fields of medicine and biology, and impacted upon the kind of research they pursued. Skeletal analyses concentrated on the analyses of extensive series of human crania (Furst 1930; Koumaris 1930, 1931) within a framework that emphasised morphological similarities explained by genetic diffusion, and aimed to assess 'racial' histories. During the 1960s and 1970s the discovery of significant palaeoanthropological findings in Petralona (Bostanci 1964; Breitinger 1964; Charles 1965; Poulianos 1971a, 1976, 1983) and in Mani (Pitsios 1979, 1985) directed Greek anthropological research interests toward the study of phylogenetic relationships and the exploration of the role that the Greek peninsula played in human evolution.

The same period witnessed an increased interest in studies of living populations that aimed to assess population affiliations through the acquisition of a number of anthropometric and anthropomorphic data (Poulianos 1968, 1971b; Pitsios 1978). Whereas most of these studies offer unique datasets that can prove useful for further analyses, they seldom contain information concerning the biological significance of the observed variations and are, sometimes, driven by an ideological rather than a scientific impetus (e.g. Poulianos 1976, 1977). A dominant trend in skeletal studies in Greece was, and is, highly detailed osteological descriptions, typically appendices to many site reports with long lists of measurements and other observations which, whilst not very useful in isolation, provide raw data for further inferences about ancient lives (Buikstra 1998).

Apart from Angel's work, and until the last few years, most skeletal study in Greece appears to have been focused on anthropometry (looking at variation between and within populations using measurements). Greece, being the crossroads of various cultures throughout its history, offers a flourishing area for the study of movement and intermixing of people. The latter can be seen in the tendency throughout the twentieth century to explore and prove that modern Greeks come originally from their ancient ancestors, mostly ignoring issues of health and adaptation. Biological anthropology, along with other branches of the social and applied sciences such as ethnography, cultural anthropology and the medical sciences, was targeted to support certain political decisions and ideologies, but this is not to say that all of the anthropometric work done had that aim. Even despite this apparent activity in Greece in biological anthropology, in the early 1980s Grmek (1983: 52) claimed that the 'results obtained (in palaeopathology) up to now are incomplete, especially for the classical period', and even as early as the late 1800s there were comments about the incorrect ways archaeologists were excavating skeletons (Grmek 1983: 53), obviously to the detriment of further analysis. Grmek's (1983) work, in fact, is an incredibly useful text on disease in ancient Greece, collating documentary and skeletal evidence for health and disease, a publication which Angel would have found useful for his work.

The contribution of J.L. Angel

J. Lawrence Angel (Figure 2.1) had also always been very interested in human skeletal variation, especially with respect to migration and immigration in the Mediterranean area, but later in his work he tended to focus much more on health and disease. As Buikstra and Hershover (1990) point out (and other authors reiterate), Angel was significantly ahead of his time in the study of skeletal remains, and more specifically health problems.

Figure 2.1 J.L. Angel (courtesy of Don Ortner and Agnes Stix of the Smithsonian Institution, Washington, DC, USA).

He advocated interdisciplinary studies, a regional approach to answering questions, and the application of the study of skeletons to prehistory and history. In addition to the study of Eastern Mediterranean skeletal material (which included modern Greece, Anatolia and Cyprus), he also worked on New World populations (Angel *et al.* 1987) and modern problems (Angel 1949), including forensic anthropological investigations (Angel and Caldwell 1984; Ubelaker 1990), and all this work covered a wide range of subject areas (e.g. microevolution, occupation, obesity, ecology, dental anthropology, palaeodemography, social biology and palaeopathology).

Angel was born in London in 1915 and died in 1986. His father was a sculptor, and mother, a classics scholar (Ortner and Kelley 1988). He studied classics but moved rapidly into physical anthropology, visiting Greece for the first time in 1937 and completing his PhD in 1942. He excavated archaeological sites in Greece, knew much about Greek history and had an interest in contemporary Greece (Jacobsen and Cullen 1990). He also pioneered the study of skeletal material in Greece painstakingly searching for excavated skeletons, fighting bureaucracy, educating archaeologists on the best excavation methods for skeletal material and analysing skeletal material for his research. Angel combined a unique background in classics with studies in human anatomy and biological anthropology (St Hoyme 1988) and was able to bring together diverse disciplines in his analyses, his research being ahead of his time perhaps by as much as two decades (Buikstra 1998). The extent of the impact of Angel's research upon the study of biological anthropology worldwide has been assessed by several authors (Ubelaker 1982; St Hoyme 1988; Buikstra 1990, 1998; Buikstra and Hershover 1990; Jacobsen and Cullen 1990; Kennedy 1990).

Angel's initial interest was in 'racial' history and its relation to culture (1942, 1944a) but he shifted later to a focus on palaeoecology, health and human adaptation (Jacobsen and Cullen 1990) and, although he rejected racism, he admitted that human biological variation existed (Kennedy 1990: 204). From his very early studies Angel was concerned with the issue of 'race' but the notion of 'race' that he used differed drastically from that of his contemporaries. Angel 'interpreted his racial categories not as rigid, genetically determined entities, but as abstract concepts which were useful in defining genetic change and physical characteristics appearing in different frequencies in human populations. In short, his biological types were tools, not biological realities... However, a rejection of racism was never confused with the necessity to admit the existence of human biological diversity' (Kennedy 1990: 205). From the beginning, Angel conceded that 'types' only loosely represent genetic realities; in effect 'they are inflexible and artificial' (Angel 1945: 282). This is a point that Jacobsen and Cullen (1990: 40) note: 'types make vivid the biodynamics of population change, but are too inflexible and artificial in representing genetic reality'. Attitudes to the study of 'race' (now more properly termed as ancestry or ethnicity) in the past have changed since Angel's work and there is much controversy in biological anthropology about whether 'race' can and should be identified, or even discussed, in skeletal remains. This has stemmed from the religious, political and social dimension attached to racial issues today, and the heterogeneity of populations all over the world. People have moved around, migrated and immigrated, and there have been intermarriages between people of different ancestral groups, so that identifying the origin of people based on their skeletons becomes problematic, with traits from many different groups present in the same skeleton. The main point to emphasise is that people may be different, and this 'difference' may be identified in the skeleton, although not always that easily, while that these 'differences' do not reflect any hierarchy among people.

In the 1940s Angel was studying something that became a controversial area in the later part of last century. He used data on cranial measurements he collected to answer questions about population movement. Today we still see the study of 'race' in forensic situations when identification of a skeleton utilises ancestral characteristics visible in the bony structure. This is particularly important because on a missing person list the ancestral origin of each person is stated, so recording this feature is essential in identification. It is important to stress the theoretical framework of Angel's work, which was not shared by many of his contemporaries. Although his classificatory system was based on the type system employed by his mentor (Hooton 1930: 185–6, as noted by Angel 1944a: 336), Angel moved beyond a static typological approach to one that employed a biocultural perspective and focused on the exploration of the nature of human biological variation through the consideration of ecological, social and cultural variables (Angel 1944a, 1946a, 1965, 1966, 1969a). This emphasis of Angel on the process, rather than on the history, of diverse biological conditions also had a great impact on the shaping of the modern palaeopathological approach. Angel belongs to the group of people who were responsible for shifting the research interests of palaeopathology from a static concern with the history of disease to questions concerning the epidemiology of diseases and their relation to other biocultural factors (Ubelaker 1982: 345).

Angel's publications (from 1939 to 1991) number 145 (see Appendix) and include, on the basis of the title, around 60 papers (40 per cent) on aspects of past Mediterranean populations. The total number, however, also includes 17 conference abstracts (some of which eventually became publications); 6 related to forensic anthropology, 8 on New World skeletal material/issues (publications seen later in his life), and 3 book reviews.

Buikstra and Hershover (1990) critique 107 of his publications and show that, throughout his life, his major interest remained in Greece. He published in many areas of physical anthropology, but it was his cemetery reports of skeletal material that figure prominently; it is probably in this area that many physical anthropologists worldwide today produce most publications. In effect, the basic skeletal report is the first piece of work produced for a site, which may then be followed by more specific research as questions and hypotheses develop about the skeletal material as it is being analysed. Apart from his many reports on skeletal material from a variety of archaeological sites in Greece, he had a keen interest in a number of areas of physical anthropology still attracting attention today. These include the biocultural approach to studying past populations (or 'social biology' – this is the approach advocated currently), palaeodemography (many of his papers are still cited today), palaeopathology (notable work was his study of thalassaemia and its relationship to malaria in the Mediterranean which is still a hot topic of debate by historians and biological anthropologists alike, now being tackled using ancient DNA analysis, e.g. Taylor et al. 1997), and occupationally related pathology (which is seeing a major increase in interest today, despite the problems of studying it; Jurmain 1999). He was also keen to state why studying the past was important, almost justifying it as he documented his analyses: he advocated cross-discipline fertilisation at all times for the interpretation of archaeological materials.

A survey of some of his publications shows that, from the start, Angel was not only interested in the biological remains of Greek populations but also in their cultural context, ranging from the funerary customs associated with them to the diseases from which they suffered. His initial publications did focus on the subject of movement of people in the Mediterranean, concentrating on measurements of skulls to define head shapes (e.g. 1945, 1946b), but his attention to detail in recording is laudable at this very early stage of biological anthropological study. Even in 1944 (1944b), however, he was already studying health and disease, and his paper on teeth took a comparative look at both ancient and modern populations, even delving into differences between urban and rural groups, something which is only seriously being considered of late in palaeobiological anthropology (Roberts et al. 1998). In 1947 Angel published his first paper specifically tackling palaeodemography, something he developed in later years, in publications which are still cited today (1968, 1969a,b). He was particularly keen to show the relationship between ecological factors and the structure of past populations, including their health patterns (1972a, 1975). Perhaps one of his most important works was that on the proto-urban population from Middle Bronze Age Lerna in 1971, a time when this population was experiencing a critical time in its history; in fact, Grmek (1983: 56) considers that the monograph was a 'model of the genre'. In this monograph, Angel emphasised that he could only consider these people bioculturally by studying all their physical remains, '... plus from archaeologists and other experts, a knowledge of their environment, their diet and the material objects in their culture, as well as a more or less firm structure of knowledge of hundreds of other sites made into a chronological sequence by a host of scholars and scientists' (1971: 112). This point comes across time and again; namely, that a multidisciplinary approach to reconstruct past human population adaptation and change was the way to proceed. His publications in 1972 and 1975 on the relationship between ecology and population in the Eastern Mediterranean certainly proved that collating all these types of data together made possible a reconstruction of why populations changed, in terms of male/female length of life, and why disease rates altered from 9000 BC to AD 1800. He continued this sort of work well into those publications that appeared in the 1980s.

In the 1960s he began to tackle another question in health and disease, that of the effect of the transition to agriculture on the health of populations, using Neolithic skulls from Sotira. This area of study was given more prominence in 1984 with the publication of a book on palaeopathology at the origins of agriculture, for which Angel produced a paper on Greek populations, leading to many more studies in the same vein (Hill and Armelagos 1990). Later (1964a), he first published on an area of palaeopathology, the thalassaemias, which has prompted much work since then. He showed an association between high sea levels, marshy areas of Greece, malaria and skeletal changes of the genetic anaemia, thalassaemia, well before 2000 BC in Greece. A flurry of papers on this subject were published (1966, 1967, 1977, 1978) and all his skeletal reports noted the presence or absence of this condition. The key to this argument was that the organism causing malaria was a factor for the maintenance of relatively high frequencies of genes for abnormal haemoglobin (Angel 1964a). Since his work, no papers have been published on this subject in Greek populations, although other Greek researchers have considered it (e.g. Lagia 1993). In 1974 he also presented the first real population-based approach to the study of trauma from the seventh millennium BC to the twentieth century in Greece, finding a negative association of fractures with levels of 'civilisation'. Although this was his only paper specifically on this subject, it was influential in the field of biological anthropology, and still stands as one of the few population-based approaches to trauma in the past, others including Jurmain (1991), Lovejoy and Heiple (1981) and Grauer and Roberts (1996). He also considered the association of occupation and skeletal change (1964b, 1982), which has seen a major interest over the last fifteen years (Merbs 1983; Kennedy 1989; Bridges 1990, 1991; Jurmain 1999).

Angel's painstaking work on reconstruction of skulls from fragments of mainly cranial vaults and faces is worth mentioning, although he was limited by the tools available at the time. The extensive use of wire and benzine-based transparent glue often deformed skulls and made the sutures unobservable, and the bones were prone to break at the same or different areas. Without doubting Angel's genius and passion for his work, it is wise for the modern researcher to take these problems into account.

In short, Angel had a wide range of publications on many aspects of biological anthropology and pioneered studies of skeletal material in Greece. He paved the way for the future and highlighted many questions which still need to be asked of extant material and of that which may be excavated in the future. He worked towards successfully bridging the gap between biological anthropology and archaeology, and helped educate the latter in the importance of the efficient and careful retrieval of skeletal remains from the ground. What then of the present and future?

Current work in health and disease in Greek skeletal material

Several developments in a number of institutions in Greece that support the study of human skeletal remains, such as University Departments, the Eforeia/Ephorate of Palaeoanthropology and Speleology, and the Wiener Laboratory of the American School of Classical Studies at Athens (ASCSA) appear very promising for the field of biological anthropology in the region today. The Wiener Laboratory, in particular, honouring the contribution of J.L. Angel to the study of human skeletal remains in the Eastern Mediterranean, offers annually one or two Fellowships for the study of human skeletal remains in Greece. In the Eforeia/Ephorate of Palaeoanthropology and Speleology, a rich environment is offered for interdisciplinary research that functions towards the development of a better understanding of archaeological investigation (Stravopodi 1993a,b; Stravopodi et al. 1999).

The long-standing relationship of anthropology with the departments of biology and medicine at the University of Athens and Thrace has centred research on the fields of evolutionary anthropology (Pitsios 1979, 1985; Papagregorakis and Syropoulos 1988; Pitsios and Liebhaber 1995; Manolis 1996; Manolis and Mallegni 1996) and in the investigation of biological affinities of Greek populations, correlating biological, ethnographic and historical data (Pitsios 1978; Xirotiris 1980, 1986; Karali 1987; Manolis 1991a; Manolis et al. 1995; Panagiaris et al. 1997). Furthermore, research in university departments includes the analysis of historic and prehistoric skeletal remains (Xirotiris 1981, 1982, 1992; Manolis 1991a,b; Manolis et al. 1994; Manolis and Neroutsos 1997; Karali and Tsaliki 2000, 2001a).

Current projects undertaken within the University of Athens include the development of a modern reference collection, initially founded at the

Wiener Laboratory (Pike 1997), and currently curated at the University of Athens, in the Department of Biology (Figures 2.2 and 2.3). The collection aims to contribute to the development of standards for sex and age estimation for Greek populations (Lagia *et al.* 2000), as well as to the identification of diseases from the human skeleton (Lagia 1997; Lagia and Kontanis 1997). Moreover, the creation of the field of Forensic Anthropology at the University of Athens, in the Department of Forensic Medicine and Toxicology (Moraitis *et al.* 2000), is one of the most recent establishments.

A large number of biological anthropological analyses apply current methods of skeletal biology to investigate health and disease patterns in populations from diverse regional and chronological contexts (Agelarakis 1987, 2000; McGeorge 1992; Fox Leonard 1997; Lagia 1999; Triantaphyllou 2001; Bourbou 2003a, 2004a; Bourbou and Rodríguez-Martín 2003; Bourbou in press; Malama and Triantaphyllou 2003; Tsaliki 2003b). There is also an ongoing interest in the identification of specific diseases in the past which is expressed through a series of studies addressing methodological considerations in palaeopathology (Lagia 1993; Eliopoulos 1998; Tsaliki 2002a) and presenting specific pathological conditions (Manolis *et al.* 1994; Arnott 1996; Barnes and Ortner 1997; Bourbou 1998, 2000, 2001a, 2003b, 2004b, in press; Little and Papadopoulos 1998; Lagia and Ruppenstein 1999; Tsaliki 2003a, 2004a).

Recent years have also witnessed a blossoming of analyses that attempt to combine biological anthropological with contextual and other multidisciplinary based data in order to reconstruct aspects of life history and the treatment of the deceased as revealed by human skeletal remains (e.g. Tsaliki 1996, 1997, 2000, 2001, 2002b; Karali and Tsaliki 2001b; Vavouranakis *et al.* 2002). These studies employ current analytical techniques to a theoretical framework and have a population-based approach working at a regional and temporal level with cross-cultural comparisons in some cases (Papathanasiou *et al.* 1995, 2000; Manginis *et al.* 2001; Papathanasiou 2001a,b; Triantaphyllou 2001; Bourbou 2003a, 2004a). The contribution of the field of taphonomy to bioarchaeological analyses has enhanced our understanding of the interaction of human and environmental factors (Moraitis 1998; Moraitis and Koutselinis 2000; Lagia 2002). Special emphasis is also given to sub-groups within a population, such as the sub-adults. The study of infant mortality, until recently a neglected subject in the bioarchaeological literature, has brought to centre stage aspects of the preservation of immature remains or neonatal versus post neonatal mortality, the latter highly associated with poor environmental conditions (Triantaphyllou and Chamberlain 1996; Papadopoulos 2000; Bourbou 2001b).

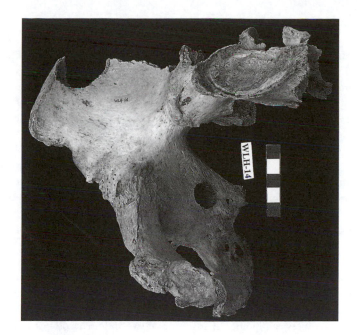

Figure 2.2 Modern example of cancer affecting the pelvic bone in a 65 year old male
who died of metastases ('secondaries') of cancer of the brain (primary site
was the lungs); University of Athens modern reference collection.

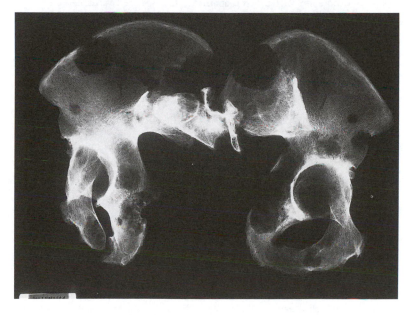

Figure 2.3 Radiograph of Figure 2.2 and the opposite side, also showing destructive
lesions.

Furthermore, researchers have focused attention on regions and chronological periods that were previously ignored (e.g. Tsaliki in press). For example, in Northern Greece the analysis of a large series of skeletal remains from Greek Macedonia has revealed intriguing data about aspects of health and dietary status, demography and mortuary behaviour from the Neolithic to the Early Iron Age (Triantaphyllou 1997, 1998a,b,c, 2000, 2001). These studies indicate an overall tendency towards declining levels of health and oral status in Late Bronze and Early Iron Age populations, and an overall shift from a high reliance on meat consumption to a diet based on carbohydrate foods from the Neolithic and Early Bronze Ages to the Late Bronze and Early Iron Ages. Changes in the treatment of the dead from the Neolithic to the Early Iron Age also suggest a shift in emphasis from individual to lineage-group identity. Meanwhile, there is an ongoing project that attempts to explore similar questions from the same area in historical cemetery populations (e.g. ancient Pydna and Amphipolis; Bessios and Triantaphyllou 2002; Malama and Triantaphyllou 2003; Grammenos and Triantaphyllou 2004). Integrated analyses have inspired an increasing collaboration between biological anthropologists and archaeologists and have resulted in important research findings (Liston 1993; Lagia 2000; Bessios and Triantaphyllou 2002; Malama and Triantaphyllou 2003).

Within the analytical techniques employed in bioarchaeology, bone chemical analyses (e.g. Magou *et al.* 1997; Papathanasiou 2001b; Triantaphyllou 2001; Bourbou and Richards forthcoming) have offered valuable knowledge on the reconstruction of past diets and economic strategies. Triantaphyllou (2001) and Papathanasiou (2001b) have conducted isotopic analysis on prehistoric Greek populations from diverse regions and have reached similar conclusions concerning diet (Van Klinken and Triantaphyllou 1997). In both studies the absence of any signal indicating marine consumption even at coastal sites, and the presence of a primarily terrestrial-based diet are striking (also see Karali 1999 for comment about fluctuations in the consumption of shellfish in Greek prehistory). Garvie-Lok (2001) has taken a further step in bone chemical analysis attempting to reconstruct patterns of diet and mobility in Medieval Greece (twelfth to fifteenth centuries AD).

Future work

It is accepted that for the application of theoretical and methodological advances to take place in the reconstruction of past lifeways it is necessary to have large representative samples of well-documented skeletons. As Buikstra (1991: 174) said, 'The major factors limiting advancement in bioarchaeological research centre are on the quantity and quality of skeletal remains and contextual data. The need for representative samples of sufficiently large size continues to be crucial.' Ubelaker (1982: 346) also notes that 'Ancient disease in a biocultural and epidemiological perspective represents an exciting area of research, but one with many methodological problems. The problems centre on the incomplete evidence for disease and the need for more accurate chronological controls and more exact indicators of subsistence and other cultural variables.' These statements, although intended to describe the situation in a different cultural context, are as urgent as ever in the modern arena of anthropological research in Greece. Despite Angel's monumental efforts, Jacobsen and Cullen (1990) note that a close collaboration of the archaeologist with the biological anthropologist has not yet been achieved. It is also obvious to the researcher that Greek Eforeias (i.e. local archaeological councils), museums and other institutions can lack well-organised, properly curated, and easily accessible skeletal collections.

Education has played an important role in the perpetuation of this phenomenon. For instance, the University of Athens is the largest and oldest University in Greece, established in 1837. Archaeology is being taught in the Department of History, Archaeology and History of Art but the approach to archaeology is traditional and classicistic. Undergraduate students must follow compulsory courses on all three major subjects, with the addition of ancient and modern literature, psychology, philosophy and similar subjects, whereas courses in environmental archaeology, human osteoarchaeology, archaeobotany, archaeozoology and burial archaeology are either optional or non-existent. In addition, the lack of a unified University library is an important drawback. Every discipline has its own small specialised library, housed separately, which prohibits interdisciplinary research. The modules taught in other more recently developed archaeology departments across the country seem more promising and modern in approach.

Within the framework for improving the current status of biological anthropology in Greece, the Department of Biological Sciences, University of Athens has initiated an annual bioarchaeological seminar addressed to the archaeological community. This seminar aims to increase the communication between the disciplines of anthropology and archaeology, providing information about theoretical, technical and methodological advances that take place in the field and about the mutual interest that exists in such collaboration. The seminar emphasises the need for collaboration taking place at all levels of a project, starting from the planning of the research design, moving to sampling strategies, the recovery and conservation of the material and finally to the analysis and interpretation of the results. The Research Team for Environmental

Archaeology of the University of Athens, in collaboration with the Hellenic Society for the Protection of the Environment and the Cultural Heritage, the Department of Chemistry of the University of Athens, the National Research Centre Democritos, and lately the Laboratory of Sea Geology and Oceanography of the Department of Geology, University of Patra, and the Netherlands Institute in Athens (NIA), have organised several seminars which aim to bring together scholars in archaeology, archaeometry, geosciences, environmental studies and biology. It is only within such a collaborative framework that it will be possible to escape from descriptive appendices and integrate analyses and interpretation of cemeteries with problem-oriented research designs.

The accelerated participation of biological anthropology in understanding the past highlights the importance of the participation of a person who understands the analysis of human skeletal remains at cemetery excavations for the most efficient retrieval of skeletal material, together with soil and other samples (Tsaliki 2004b). For example, where an excavator lacks the appropriate training, small foetal bones may be missed and this may result in misinterpretation of the data retrieved from the skeletal material. The limited potential of one single Archaeological Service, namely the Eforeias/ Ephorates of Palaeoanthropology and Speleology, to accommodate for the needs of numerous cemetery excavations that take place throughout Greece, emphasises the need to establish affiliations of biological anthropologists, as well as of organised Laboratories fostering interdisciplinary analysis. Continuous active participation in cemetery excavations will eventually lead to large skeletal collections being properly recorded, maintained and curated. According to a recent public announcement on the website of the Ministry of Culture in June 2003, the President of the Hellenic Democracy signed a decree on the 'New Organisation of the Ministry of Culture'. Among the major changes, it has been announced that the Eforeias/ Ephorates of Antiquities will be increased by 28 units. As a result, every prefecture will house at least one service of the Ministry of Culture. In addition, two Eforeias/Ephorates of Palaeoanthropology and Speleology will be organised, one in Athens and one in Thessaloniki. The number of Archaeological Institutes will also be increased to six. The study of human remains from archaeological sites therefore has much greater potential.

Archaeologically-derived Greek skeletal material provides the opportunity of studying the lives of past populations diachronically with the added benefit of integrating the biological evidence with, for example, contemporary literature, epigraphy, artefacts and architectural remains. Furthermore, the availability of easily accessible data on standards for recording for human skeletal remains (Buikstra and Ubelaker 1994), means that the stage seems set for this to be achieved.

ACKNOWLEDGEMENTS

The authors would like to thank Jane Buikstra for providing a copy of her unpublished paper (1998), which covers much valuable information. Special thanks to Marie-Catherine Bernard for attending to the bibliography, to Don Ortner and Agnes Stix (Department of Anthropology, Smithsonian Institution) for the photograph of J.L. Angel and to Helen King for being patient and waiting for the revision of this chapter, first written in 1998.

APPENDIX: J.L. ANGEL'S BIBLIOGRAPHY

Angel, J.L. (no date) 'Early colonial settlers in Virginia at Carters Grove', manuscript on file: National Anthropological Archives, National Museum of Natural History, Smithsonian Institution, Washington, DC.

—— (1939a) 'Appendix II. Geometric Athenians', in R.S. Young (ed.) *Late Geometric Graves and a Seventh-century Well in the Agora*, Athens: American School of Classical Studies Hesperia, Supplement II, 236–46.

—— (1939b) 'The Babakoy skeleton', *Archiv für Orientforschung*, 13: 28–31.

—— (1940–48) 'Appendix 3. Roman tombs at Vasa: the skulls', *Report of the Department of Antiquities*, Cyprus, 68–76.

—— (1942a) 'A preliminary study of the relations of race to culture, based on ancient Greek skeletal material', unpublished PhD thesis, Harvard University.

—— (1942b) 'Classical Olynthians', in D.M. Robinson (ed.) *Excavations at Olynthus Pt. XI: Necrolynthia*, Baltimore, MD: Johns Hopkins University Press, 211–40.

—— (1943a) 'Treatment of archaeological skulls', in H.L. Shapiro (ed.) *Archaeological Briefs*, 3: 3–8.

—— (1943b) 'Ancient Cephallenians: the population of a Mediterranean island', *American Journal of Physical Anthropology*, 1: 229–60.

—— (1944a) 'A racial analysis of the ancient Greeks: an essay on the use of morphological types', *American Journal of Physical Anthropology*, 2: 329–76.

—— (1944b) 'Greek teeth: ancient and modern', *Human Biology*, 16: 283–97.

—— (1945a) 'Skeletal material from Attica', *Hesperia*, 14: 263–80.

—— (1945b) 'Neolithic ancestors of the Greeks', *American Journal of Physical Anthropology*, 49: 252–60.

—— (1946a) 'Race, type and ethnic group in ancient Greece', *Human Biology*, 18: 1–32.

—— (1946b) 'Social biology of Greek culture growth', *American Anthropologist*, 48: 493–533.

—— (1946c) 'Some interrelationships of classical archaeology with anthropology' (abstract), *American Journal of Physical Anthropology*, 50: 401.

——, Paschkis, K., Matthews, R.A., Schopbach, R. and Swenson, P.C. (1946d) 'Constitutional obesity' (abstract), *American Journal of Physical Anthropology*, 4: 257.

Angel, J.L. (1946e) 'Skeletal change in ancient Greece', *American Journal of Physical Anthropology*, 4: 69–97.

—— (1947a) 'The length of life in ancient Greece', *Journal of Gerontology*, 2: 18–24.

—— (1947b) 'Increase in length of life in ancient Greece' (abstract), *American Journal of Physical Anthropology*, 5: 231.

—— (1948a) 'Health and the course of civilisation', in*tern*, 14: 15–17, 45–8.

—— (1948b) 'Anatomical aspects of obesity' (abstract), *Anatomical Record*, 100: 635–6.

—— (1948c) 'Factors in temporomandibular joint form', *American Journal of Physical Anthropology*, 83: 223–46.

—— (1949) 'Constitution in female obesity', *American Journal of Physical Anthropology*, 7: 433–72.

—— (1950) 'Skeletons', *Archaeology*, 3: 233–41.

—— (1951a) 'Population size and microevolution in Greece', *Cold Spring Harbor Symposia in Quantitative Biology*, 15: 343–51.

—— (1951b) 'Troy: the human remains. Supplemental Monograph 1', in C. Blegen (ed.) *Troy: Excavations Conducted by the University of Cincinnati, 1932–1938*, Princeton, NJ: Princeton University Press.

—— (1951c) 'Table 17. Belt cave, Skull 2, measurements, indices and observations', in C.S. Coon (ed.) *Cave Explorations in Iran*, Philadelphia, PA: University Museum Monographs, 86–8.

—— and Coon, C.S. (1952a) 'Axial skeleton of an Upper Paleolithic woman from Hotu' (abstract), *American Journal of Physical Anthropology*, 10: 252.

—— (1952b) 'The human skeletal remains from Hotu Cave, Iran', *Proceedings of the American Philosophical Society*, 96: 258–69.

—— (1953a) 'Classical archaeology and the anthropological approach', in G.E. Mylonas and D. Raymond (eds) *Studies Presented to David Moore Robinson. Volume II*, St. Louis, WA: Washington University Press, 1224–31.

—— (1953b) 'Appendix II. The human remains from Khirokitia', in P. Dikaios (ed.) *Khirokitia*, London: Oxford University Press, 416–30.

—— (1954a) 'Human biology, health and history in Greece from first settlement until now', *Yearbook of the American Philosophical Society*, 168–72.

—— and Coon, C.S. (1954b) 'La Cotte de St Brelade II: present status', *Man*, 54: 53–5.

—— (1954c) 'Some problems in interpretation of Greek skeletal material: disease, posture and microevolution' (abstract), *American Journal of Physical Anthropology*, 12: 284.

—— (1954d) 'The human skeletal material from the well', in E.B. Wace (ed.) *The Cyclopean Terrace Building and the Deposit of Pottery Beneath It (Part IV of Mycenae 1939–1953)*, Annual of the British School at Athens, 49: 267–91, 288–9.

—— (1955a) 'Roman tombs at Vasa: the skulls', in J.D. Taylor (ed.) *Report of the Department of Antiquities, 1945–1948*, Nicosia, Cyprus, 68–76.

—— (1955b) 'Newly excavated human bones from Greece (1954)', *American Journal of Archeology*, 59: 169.

—— (1956) 'Age change in obesity' (abstract), *American Journal of Physical Anthropology*, 14: 373–4.

—— (1957a) 'Age changes in obesity' (unsigned), *Medical Science*, 1: 33–7.

—— (1957b) 'Genetic factors in obesity' (abstract), *American Journal of Physical Anthropology*, 15: 444–5.

—— (1958) 'Human biological changes in ancient Greece. With special reference to Lerna', *Yearbook of the American Philosophical Society*, 266–70.

—— (1959a) 'Early Helladic skulls from Aghios Kosmas', in G.E. Mylonas (ed.) *Aghios Kosmas: An Early Bronze Age Settlement and Cemetery in Attica*, Princeton, NJ: Princeton University Press, 167–79.

—— (1959b) 'Femoral neck markings and human gait', *Anatomical Record*, 133: 244.

—— (1960a) 'Age change in obesity', *Human Biology*, 32: 342–65.

—— (1960b) 'Human gait, hip joint and evolution' (abstract), *American Journal of Physical Anthropology*, 18: 361.

—— (1960c) 'Physical and psychological factors in human growth', in A.F.C. Wallace (ed.) *Selected Papers of the 5th International Congress of Anthropological and Ethnological Sciences, 1956*, Philadelphia, PA: University of Pennsylvania, 665–70.

—— (1961) 'Appendix 1. Neolithic crania from Sotira', in P. Dikaios (ed.) *Sotira*, Philadelphia, PA: University Museum Monographs, 223–9.

—— (1963) 'Physical anthropology and medicine', *Journal of the National Medical Association*, 55: 107–16.

—— (1964a) 'Osteoporosis: thalassemia?', *American Journal of Physical Anthropology*, 22: 369–74.

—— (1964b) 'The reaction area of the femoral neck', *Clinical Orthopedics*, 32: 130–42.

—— (1964c) 'Prehistoric man', in S.H. Engle (ed.) *New Perspectives on World History*, Washington, DC: National Council for Social Studies.

—— (1965) 'Old age changes in bone density: sex and race factors in the United States', *Human Biology*, 37: 104–21.

—— (1966a) 'Porotic hyperostosis, anemias, malarias and marshes in the prehistoric Mediterranean', *Science*, 153: 760–3.

—— (1966b) 'Appendix. Human skeletal remains from Karatas', in M.J. Mellink (ed.) 'Excavations at Karataş–Semayük in Lycia', *American Journal of Archeology*, 70: 245–57 (with subsequent reports in same journal in 1968, 1970, 1973 and 1976).

—— (1966c) 'Effects of human biological factors in the development of civilisation', *Yearbook of the American Philosophical Society*, 1965: 315–17.

—— (1966d) 'Early skeletons from Tranquillity, California', *Smithsonian Contributions to Anthropology*, 2: 1–19.

—— (1967) 'Porotic hyperostosis or osteoporosis symmetrica', in D.R. Brothwell and A.T. Sandison (eds) *Diseases in Antiquity: A Survey of the Diseases, Injuries and Surgery of Earlier Human Populations*, Springfield, IL: Charles Thomas, 378–89.

—— (1968a) 'Ecological aspects of paleodemography', in D.R. Brothwell (ed.) *The Skeletal Biology of Earlier Human Populations*, Symposia of the Society for the Study of Human Biology, Vol. 8, London: Pergamon Press, 263–70.

—— (1968b) 'Human skeletal material from Slovenia', *Bulletin of the American School of Prehistoric Research*, 25: 75–108.

—— (1968c) 'The bases of paleodemography' (abstract), *American Journal of Physical Anthropology*, 29: 137.

Angel, J.L. (1968d) 'Appendix. Human remains at Karataş', *American Journal of Archeology*, 72: 260–3.

——, Stutts, M. and Mayer, J. (1968e) Obesity article (title unknown), in J. Mayer (ed.) *Overweight: Causes, Cost and Control*, New Jersey: Englewood Cliffs.

—— (1969a) 'The bases of paleodemography', *American Journal of Physical Anthropology*, 30: 427–37.

—— (1969b) 'Paleodemography and evolution', *American Journal of Physical Anthropology*, 31: 343–53.

—— (1969c) 'Appendix II. Human skeletal material from Franchthi Cave', *Hesperia*, 38: 380–1.

—— (1970) 'Appendix. Human skeletal remains at Karataş', in M.J. Mellink (ed.) 'Excavations at Karataş–Semayük and Elmali, Lycia, 1969', *American Journal of Archeology*, 74: 253–9.

—— (1971a) *The People of Lerna: Analysis of a Prehistoric Aegean Population*, Princeton, NJ: American School of Classical Studies at Athens.

—— (1971b) 'Early Neolithic skeletons from Çatal Hüyük: demography and pathology', *Anatolian Studies*, 21: 77–98.

—— (1971c) 'Genetic and social factors in a Cypriote village', *Human Biology*, 44: 53–79.

—— (1971d) 'Diseases and culture in the ancient Eastern Mediterranean', in V.V. Novotny (ed.) *Proceedings of an Anthropological Congress Dedicated to Ales Hrdlicka*, 30 August–5 September, 1969, Praha, Humpolec: Praha Academeia, 503–8.

—— (1971e) 'Human skeletal material from the Church of Holy Apostles', in A. Frantz (ed.) *The Church of the Holy Apostles. The Athenian Agora, Volume 20*, Princeton, NJ: American School of Classical Studies at Athens, 30–1.

—— (1971f) Review of S. Jarcho (ed.) 'Proceedings of a Symposium on Human Paleopathology, 1966', *Journal of the History of Medicine and Allied Sciences*, 26: 220–1.

—— (1972a) 'Ecology and population in the Eastern Mediterranean', *World Archaeology*, 4: 88–105.

—— (1972b) 'A Middle Palaeolithic temporal bone from Darra–i–Kur, Afghanistan', *Transactions of the American Philosophical Society*, 62: 54–6.

—— (1972c) 'Teeth, health and ecology: pitfalls of natural experiments' (abstract), *American Journal of Physical Anthropology*, 37: 428.

—— (1972d) Review of Gy. Ascadi and J. Nemeskeri, 'History of human life span and mortality', *American Journal of Physical Anthropology*, 36: 300–2.

—— (1972e) 'Biological relations of Egyptian and Eastern Mediterranean populations during pre–Dynastic and Dynastic times', *Journal of Human Evolution*, 1: 307–13.

—— (1972f) 'Late Bronze Age Cypriotes from Bamboula: the skeletal remains', in J.L. Benson (ed.) *Bamboula at Kourion: The Necropolis and the Finds Excavated by J.F. Daniel*, Philadelphia, PA: University of Pennsylvania Press, 148–55.

—— (1973a) 'Biological relations of Egyptians and Eastern Mediterranean populations during pre–Dynastic and Dynastic times', in D.R. Brothwell and B.A. Chiarelli (eds) *Population Biology of the Ancient Egyptians*, London: Academic Press, 307–13.

—— (1973b) 'Early Neolithic people of Nea Nikomedia', in I. Schwidetzky (ed.) *Fundamenta. Monographien zur Urgeschichte Series B. Die Anfänge des Neolithikums vom Orient bis Nordeuropa*, Cologne: Bohlau Verlag, 103–12.

—— (1973c) 'Skeletal fragments of Classical Lycians', in M.J. Mellink (ed.) 'Excavations at Karataş–Semayük and Elmali, Lycia, 1972', *American Journal of Archeology*, 77: 303–7.

—— (1973d) 'Human skeletons from grave circles at Mycenae', in G.E. Mylonas (ed.) *Taphikos Kyklos B ton Mykenon*, Athens: Library of the Archaeological Society in Athens, 73, 379–97.

—— (1973e) 'Neolithic human remains (Franchthi Cave)', *Hesperia*, 42: 277–82.

—— (1973f) 'Late Bronze Age Cypriotes from Bamboula', in J.L. Benson (ed.) *Bamboula at Kourion: The Necropolis and the Finds Excavated by J.F. Daniel*, Philadelphia, PA: University of Pennsylvania Press, 148–65.

—— (1973g) 'Prehistoric malaria in the Near East' (abstract), *Paleopathology Association Newsletter*, 1: 2–3.

—— (1974a) 'Patterns of fractures from Neolithic to modern times', *Anthropologiai Kozlmenyek*, 18: 9–18.

—— (1974b) 'Occurrence of some pathologies, ancient and modern' (abstract), *American Journal of Physical Anthropology*, 40: 129–30.

—— (1974c) 'Bones can fool people', *FBI Law Enforcement Bulletin*, 43: 16–20, 30.

—— (1974d) 'The cultural ecology of general versus dental health', in W. Bernhard and A. Kandler (eds) *Bevölkerungsbiologie*, Stuttgart: G. Fisher Verlag, 382–91.

—— (1975a) 'Paleoecology, paleodemography and health', in S. Polgar (ed.) *Population, Ecology and Social Evolution*, The Hague: Mouton, 167–90.

—— (1975b) Comment on 'New evidence for a late introduction of malaria into the New World', *Current Anthropology*, 16: 96.

—— (1975c) 'Middle class skeletal differences', *American Journal of Physical Anthropology*, 42: 288.

—— (1975d) 'Porotic hyperostosis, anemias, malarias and marshes in the prehistoric Eastern Mediterranean (with tables revised for printing)', in P. Reining and I. Tinker (eds) *Population Dynamics, Ethics and Policy*, Washington, DC: American Association for the Advancement of Science, 96–8.

—— (1975e) 'Human skeletons from Eleusis', in G.E. Mylonas (ed.) *Ditikon Nekrotapheion tes Eleusinos (The South Cemetery of Eleusis)*, Athens: Library of the Archaeological Society of Athens, 81, 435–8.

—— (1976a) 'Appendix. Early Bronze Age Karatas people and their cemeteries', *American Journal of Archeology*, 80: 385–91.

—— (1976b) 'Colonial to modern skeletal change in the U.S.A.' (abstract), *American Journal of Physical Anthropology*, 44: 164.

—— (1976c) 'Introduction to symposium in honor of T. Dale Stewart', *American Journal of Physical Anthropology*, 45 (3, part 2): 521–30.

—— (1976d) 'Colonial to modern skeletal change in the U.S.A.', *American Journal of Physical Anthropology*, 45: 723–36.

—— (1977a) 'Anemias of antiquity: Eastern Mediterranean', in E. Cockburn and A. Cockburn (eds) *Porotic Hyperostosis: An Enquiry*, Paleopathology Association Monograph No. 2, 1–5.

Angel, J.L. (1977b) Review of R.T. Steinbock, 'Paleopathological Diagnosis and Interpretation', *Paleopathology Association Newsletter*, 17: 18–19.

—— (1977c) 'Porotic hyperostosis in the Eastern Mediterranean' (abstract), *American Journal of Physical Anthropology*, 47: 115.

—— and Cherry, D.G. (1977d) 'Personality reconstruction from unidentified remains', *FBI Law Enforcement Bulletin*, 46: 12–15.

—— (1977e) 'Appendix 5. Human skeletons', in J.E. Coleman (ed.) *Kephala. A Late Neolithic Settlement and Cemetery*, Princeton, NJ: American School of Classical Studies at Athens, 133–56.

—— (1978a) 'Porotic hyperostosis in the Eastern Mediterranean', *Medical College of Virginia Quarterly*, 14: 10–16.

—— (1978b) 'Pelvic inlet form. A neglected index of nutritional status' (abstract), *American Journal of Physical Anthropology*, 48: 378.

—— (1979a) 'Osteoarthritis in Prehistoric Turkey and Medieval Byzantium', *Henry Ford Hospital Medical Journal*, 27: 38–43.

——, Phenice, T.W., Robbins, L.H. and Lynch, B.M. (1980a) *Lopoy and Lothagam. No. 2 Late Stone Age Fishermen of Lothagam, Kenya*, East Lansing, MI: Michigan State University Museum Anthropological Series 3(2).

—— (1980b) 'The Lothagam site skeletons (1965–1966 collection)', in J.L. Angel, T.W. Phenice, L.H. Robbins and B.M. Lynch (eds) *Lopoy and Lothagam. No. 2 Late Stone Age Fishermen of Lothagam, Kenya*, East Lansing, MI: Michigan State University Museum Anthropological Series 3 (2), 151–65.

—— (1980c) 'Early Bronze Age Anatolians' (abstract), *American Journal of Physical Anthropology*, 52: 201.

—— (1980d) 'Physical anthropology: determining sex, age and individual features', in A. Cockburn and E. Cockburn (eds) *Mummies, Disease and Ancient Cultures*. Cambridge: Cambridge University Press, 241–57.

—— (1981a) 'History and development of paleopathology', *American Journal of Physical Anthropology*, 56: 509–15.

—— (1981b) 'Aidan Cockburn (1912–1981). A memorial', *Paleopathology Association Newsletter*, 36: 2–3.

—— (1981c) 'Physical anthropological analysis', Appendix 2 in S.A. Burston and R.A. Thomas (eds) *Archaeological Data Recovery at Catocin Furnace Cemetery, Frederick County, Maryland*, Baltimore, MD: Department of Transportation.

—— and Olney, L.M. (1981d) 'Skull base height and pelvic inlet depth from prehistoric to modern times' (abstract), *American Journal of Physical Anthropology*, 54: 197.

—— (1981e) 'Skull base and pelvic changes from Paleolithic to modern times', in E. Cockburn (ed.) *Papers on Paleopathology Presented at the Annual Meeting of the Paleopathology Association,* Detroit, MI: Paleopathology Association, p. 1.

—— (1981f) 'The armor and Drummond–Harris sites, Governor's Landing, Virginia', manuscript on file: National Anthropological Archives, National Museum of Natural History, Smithsonian Institution, Washington, DC.

—— (1981g) 'Skull base height and pelvic inlet depth from prehistoric times', *American Journal of Physical Anthropology*, 54: 197.

—— (1982a) 'Osteoarthritis and occupation (ancient and modern)', in V.V. Novotny (ed.) *Second Anthropological Congress of Ales Hrdlicka*, Pragensis: Universitas Carolina, 443–6.

—— and Zimmerman, M. (1982b) 'T. Aidan Cockburn, 1912–1981: a memorial', *American Journal of Physical Anthropology*, 58: 121–2.

—— (1982c) 'Adult dental conditions as an indicator of childhood health and nutrition' (abstract), *American Journal of Physical Anthropology*, 57: 167.

—— (1982d) 'Identification from burnt bones' (abstract), paper presented at the 34th Annual Meeting of the American Academy of Forensic Sciences, Orlando, Florida, program abstracts, H24: 101.

—— and Olney, L.M. (1982e) 'A new measure of growth efficiency: skull base height', *American Journal of Physical Anthropology*, 58: 297–305.

—— (1982f) 'Ancient skeletons from Asine', in S. Diets (ed.) *Asine II. Results of the Excavations East of the Acropolis 1970–1974*, Stockholm: Paul Astroms Forlag, 105–38.

—— (1983a) 'Health status of colonial iron–worker slaves' (abstract), *American Journal of Physical Anthropology*, 60: 170–1.

—— and Kelley, J.O. (1983b) 'The workers of Catoctin Furnace, Maryland', *Maryland Archeology*, 19: 2–17.

—— (1984a) 'Experiment in human growth response to improving diet and disease control', *American Journal of Physical Anthropology*, 63: 134.

—— (1984b) 'Variation in estimating age at death of skeletons', *Collegium Antropologicum*, 8: 163–8.

—— (1984c) 'Health as a crucial factor in the changes from hunting to developed farming in the Eastern Mediterranean', in M.N. Cohen and G.J. Armelagos (eds) *Paleopathology at the Origins of Agriculture*, Orlando, FL: Academic Press, 51–70.

—— and Caldwell, P. (1984d) 'Death by strangulation: a forensic anthropological case from Wilmington, Delaware', in J. Buikstra and T. Rathburn (eds) *Human Identification. Case studies in Forensic Anthropology*, Springfield, IL: Charles Thomas, 168–75.

—— (1985a) 'Bony effects of vanity on spinal pain: 18th century stays versus later corsets', paper presented at the Physical Anthropology Section of the 37th Annual Meeting of the American Anthropological Association, Washington, DC.

——, Kelley, J.O., Parrington, M. and Pinter, S. (1985b) 'Stresses of first freedom: 19th century Philadelphia', *American Journal of Physical Anthropology*, 66: 140.

—— (1985c) 'The forensic anthropologist's examination', *Pathologist*, 39: 48–57.

—— (1985d) 'Performance evaluations. Unpublished memorandum to W.G. Melson, 6th September 1985', manuscript on file in the National Anthropological Archives, Smithsonian Institution, Washington, DC.

—— and Bisel, S.C. (1985e) 'Health and nutrition in Mycenean Greece. A study in human skeletal remains', in N.C. Wilkie and W.P.D. Coulson (eds) *Contributions to Aegean Archaeology*, Minneapolis, MN: Centre for Ancient Studies, University of Minnesota, 197–209.

—— and Bisel, S.C. (1986a) 'Health and stress in an early Bronze Age population', in J.V. Canby, E. Porada, B.S. Ridgeway and T. Stech (eds) *Ancient*

Anatolia: Aspects of Change and Cultural Development. Essays in Honor of Machteld J. Mellink, Madison, WI: University of Wisconsin Press, 12–30.

—— and Kelley, J.O. (1986b) 'Description and comparison of the skeleton', in A.E. Close (ed.) *The Wadi Kubbaniyan Skeleton: A Late Paleolithic Burial from Southern Egypt*, Dallas, TX: Southern Methodist University Press, 53–70.

—— and Zimmerman, M. (1986c) *Dating and Age Determination of Biological Materials*, London: Croom Helm.

——, Suchey, J.M., İşcan, M.Y. and Zimmerman, M.R. (1986d) 'Age at death estimated from skeletons and viscera', in M. Zimmerman and J.L. Angel (eds) *Dating and Age Determination of Biological Materials*, London: Croom Helm, 179–220.

—— (1986e) 'The physical identity of the Trojans', in M.J. Mellink (ed.) *Troy and the Trojan War. A Symposium Held at Bryn Mawr College, October 1984* (Department of Classical and Near Eastern Archeology), Bryn Mawr, PA: Bryn Mawr College Press, 63–76.

—— and Kelley, J.O. (1986f) 'The human skeletal material from Franchthi Cave', unpublished manuscript.

—— and Bioel, S.C. (1986g) 'The human skeletal material from Franchthi Cave', manuscript on file: Program in Classical Archeology, Indiana University, Bloomington, IN.

—— (1986h) 'Ecological aspects of paleodemography', in D. Brothwell (ed.) *The Skeletal Biology of Earlier Human Populations*, Oxford: Pergamon Press, 263–70.

——, Kelley, J.O., Parrington, M. and Pinter, S. (1987) 'Life stresses of the free black community as represented by the First African Baptist Church, Philadelphia, 1823–1841', *American Journal of Physical Anthropology*, 74: 213–29.

—— (1988) 'Graphic reproduction of the head and face from skull', in C. Feller (ed.) *Selected Papers from the Proceedings of the 7th Annual Conference of the Guild of Natural Science Illustrators*, Washington, DC: Guild of Natural Science Illustrators, 6–8.

—— and Kelley, J.O. (1991) 'Inversion of the posterior edge of the jaw ramus. A new race trait', in G.W. Gill and J. Rhine (eds) *Skeletal Race Identification: New Approaches in Forensic Anthropology*, Albuquerque, NM: University of New Mexico Press.

3

HEALTH IN HELLENISTIC
AND ROMAN TIMES

The case studies of Paphos, Cyprus
and Corinth, Greece

Sherry C. Fox

INTRODUCTION

The study of ancient health draws upon a variety of evidence including ancient literary sources, coprolites and other latrine contents and, perhaps most importantly, human remains themselves. Sometimes these distinct strands of evidence support each other, but in other instances they do not. Epidemics recorded by writers during the Roman Empire, for example (Patrick 1967), with the exceptions of smallpox and rubella (Ortner and Putschar 1981), do not appear to have produced bony responses detectable in preserved human remains. Many ancient societies, however, were not literate, and even those that were have left behind written records often few in number, incomplete, or unclear. Nevertheless, historical sources are important for illuminating aspects of ancient health such as medical treatments (Jackson 1988). Commentaries on ancient medicines in Cyprus, for example, can be found in the works of Aristotle, Pliny and Galen (Wallace and Orphanides 1990).

Archaeological discoveries also attest to ancient medical practices. The excavation of a surgeon's tomb in the eastern necropolis of Paphos, Cyprus, revealed different types of medical implements in use during the Roman period (Michaelides 1984), as well as evidence of medications, some of which were copper-based (Foster *et al.* 1988). Analysis of latrine contents often provides useful information about intestinal worms and diarrhoea suffered by the inhabitants of a particular site, but cannot connect the health problems identified with specific individuals. Conditions of hygiene, water supply and sewage disposal are also concerns in reconstructing ancient human health. For example, the practice of reusing common toilet sponges during Graeco-Roman times probably contributed to the spread of disease (Scobie 1986). Even in the most hygienic of Roman public baths, bacteria would undoubtedly have been found. Furthermore, at least during the Roman period, lead was often used in water pipes and the wine-making process, which must have resulted in instances of lead poisoning (Steinbock 1979). Cultural practices associated with personal hygiene, bathing and drinking clearly had a potential effect upon health.

Palaeopathological analysis of human remains themselves provides specific health data for individuals that can then be combined to reconstruct the overall health of a population. Such individual health data generally consist of skeletal evidence for palaeopathology (ancient disease and trauma), except in those rare instances where soft tissue has also been preserved through mummification or other processes. Palaeopathological data nevertheless have their limitations, since, for example, most viruses leave no trace upon the human skeleton. What can show up in bone are bacterial and other infections, diseases and bone-related traumata.

The analysis of human remains, particularly of material constituting a skeletal series, can also provide general demographic information including distributions of sex, age and stature. With such data in hand, researchers can begin to estimate the rate of infant mortality, male and female longevity and average life span for an ancient population. In addition, patterns of disease and trauma may be discerned, revealing, for example, the most common health problems that a population may have experienced. The question then arises whether the population was affected by diseases and traumata with evolutionary implications, which may have prevented people from reproducing or even living to reproductive age.

Although we have learned a great deal from human skeletal remains about Eastern Mediterranean prehistoric peoples, relatively few skeletal studies within this region have been conducted on human material from later periods of antiquity. Consequently, our knowledge of health in the Eastern Mediterranean during Hellenistic and Roman times, based upon palaeopathological analysis, is limited. One explanation for the dearth of human skeletal analyses on Hellenistic–Roman material is that cremation was the preferred burial custom throughout much of the Graeco-Roman world (Kurtz and Boardman 1971).[1] Furthermore, the palaeopathological study of health in post-Bronze Age antiquity has been affected by the failure of archaeologists to retain human skeletal material during their excavations. In cases where human bones were collected, occasionally only crania or skulls were kept for analysis.

The study summarised here is a comparative analysis of human skeletal remains, dating to the Hellenistic and Roman periods, from the sites of Paphos, Cyprus and Corinth, Greece (Figure 3.1) (Fox Leonard 1997).[2] At both sites, inhumation was predominant, and all human remains encountered

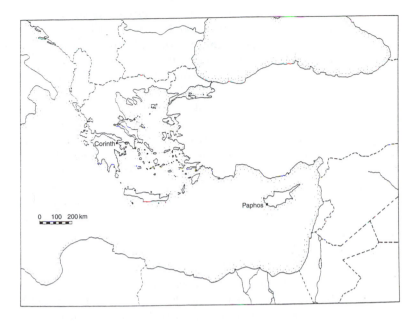

Figure 3.1 Paphos, Cyprus and Corinth, Greece in the Eastern Mediterranean.

during excavation were retained for eventual analysis. The samples minimally comprise 275 individuals from Paphos and 94 individuals from Corinth. These two case studies illustrate the palaeopathological approach to reconstructing ancient health which I have described, and add two more pieces to the puzzle of human health in the Eastern Mediterranean during Hellenistic and Roman times.

MATERIALS AND METHODS

Human skeletal remains were analysed from two sites dating to the Hellenistic and Roman periods: Paphos, Cyprus and Corinth, Greece. The purpose of the research is to compare health from samples of these two skeletal series by identification of palaeopathological lesions. Dental and osseous palaeopathological lesions afflicting individuals within each site are identified and recorded along with demographic data on individual sex and age. The prevalence of identified diseases and traumata are calculated and disease patterns elucidated. Diseases with evolutionary implications are identified, such as ailments that may have prevented individuals from surviving to reproductive age or from reproducing.

The human skeletal series from Paphos comprises the largest known collection of human remains from the Cypriot Hellenistic and Roman periods. Included in this study are skeletal remains recovered from 31 tombs during the period 1980–83 and now housed in the Paphos District Archaeological Museum.[3] The majority of the bones are from the eastern necropolis of the ancient city of Nea Paphos, located outside the city wall near the eastern seafront. This necropolis was discovered during the construction of hotels in the 1980s and was excavated under the direction of Demetrios Michaelides, then Paphos District Archaeological Officer. A minimum of 275 individuals is represented among the 31 Paphian tombs studied.[4] Domurad (1985, 1986, 1988) previously analysed the human remains of a small number of the tombs. The present author's analysis was conducted on a tomb-by-tomb basis (to avoid inadvertent commingling) between 1990 and 1995 both in Paphos and in Nicosia at the Cyprus American Archaeological Research Institute.

The human skeletal series from Corinth comprises one of the largest known collections of human remains in Greece dating to the Roman and Late Roman periods. Although some Hellenistic remains are included in the analysis, the majority of the remains are Roman in date. The Corinthian material analysed for this study comes from 33 lots excavated by the American School of Classical Studies at Athens between 1960 and 1963.[5] Unlike the bones of the Paphos series, most of which derive from a single necropolis, the human remains from Corinth are from tombs excavated all around the ancient city. A minimum of 94 individuals is represented among the 33 Corinthian bone lots studied. Angel previously analysed some human skeletal material from Corinth (N. Bookides, personal communication 1993), but unfortunately never published his results. Wesolowsky (1973) analysed Late Roman remains from Lerna Hollow at Corinth. Burns (1979, 1982) has studied Late Roman dentition at Corinth, while currently Barnes is examining human remains from the site's Frankish levels. The present author's analysis was conducted during 1993–94 both in Corinth and in Athens. Unlike the peaceful occupation of Cyprus by the Romans, Corinth was sacked in AD 146, but it is generally believed to have been repopulated by local inhabitants (Thelemis 1987).

Determination of the condition of the remains was subjective, with rankings assigned from 'poor' to 'good'. No remains from either site were found to be in an 'excellent' state of preservation. Bones that could not be identified were ranked 'poor'. In general, if a complete long bone was present or could be reconstructed the remains were deemed to be in 'good' condition. The majority of the remains, however, being somewhere between 'poor' and 'good', were ranked as 'fair'. The minimum number of individuals (MNI) at each site was based upon duplication of the same bone and/or the presence of bones from individuals of different ages or sexes. Furthermore, the MNI was analysed by tomb or occasionally by distinct contexts within tombs. Sex determinations were based predominantly upon morphological assessments of the skeletal remains (Krogman 1962; Bass 1971; Stewart 1979), since the material's state of preservation and completeness severely limited the usefulness of metrical observations. Furthermore, sex determinations were established on the basis of more than one feature and were not attempted for immature remains.

Morphological means were also used to estimate age at death. Age assessment of immature individuals was based upon the dental eruption and developmental sequence established by Schour and Massler (1944) as well as by the timing of epiphyseal fusion employed by Angel et al. (1986). Foetal and neonatal individuals were aged by long bone diaphyseal length measurements according to Fazekas and Kósa (1978). For older children, a similar methodology was adopted according to Johnston (1962), Hinkes (1983), and Weaver (1977) who also includes clavical length in his tables. Adults were aged according to pubic symphyseal (Todd 1920; Gilbert and McKern 1973; Katz and Suchey 1986) or sternal rib morphologies (İşcan et al. 1984, 1985) when present. Cranial suture closure was employed to assist in aging individuals only when other criteria were unavailable (Angel et al. 1986).

Stature was reconstructed for individuals and not for individual bones. The formulae derived by Eliakis et al. (1966) from samples of modern Greeks were employed to estimate the living statures of the ancient Paphians and Corinthians. With respect to dentition, the state of eruption was recorded, as well as the completeness of teeth, ante-mortem or post-mortem tooth loss, and incidence of agenesis.

Palaeopathological lesions were recorded for each individual bone or tooth and described following guidelines provided by the Palaeopathology Association (Rose et al. 1991).[6] Emphasis was placed on the diseases common to Cyprus and Greece (Grmek 1989). The extent of lesions in individual bones was measured and patterns within individuals were noted where possible. Occasionally, a distinct pathology of several bones led to their association with a single individual. In other instances, bone identification was hampered by the destructive forces of a pathology. Although Ortner and Putschar's (1981) palaeopathology reference and other excellent sources were used to diagnose ancient diseases and traumata, many lesions remain undiagnosed. The location of each palaeopathology was entered in a DBaseIV file for potential descriptive statistics[7] to identify, for example, which joint surfaces were most affected by osteoarthritis, which bones had the highest prevalence of fracture and what types of disease and trauma were most common. These results were compared between the two sites with particular attention focused on any observable inter-tomb differences in hereditary diseases; for example, the presence of porotic hyperostosis possibly relating to a congenital haemolytic anaemia. Finally, palaeopathological bones were photographed and select samples also radio-graphed. In addition, bone samples from two individuals, including one with porotic hyperostosis, were tested for β-thalassaemia by Dr Marios Cariolou of the Cyprus Institute of Neurology and Genetics in Nicosia.

COMPARATIVE RESULTS

Comparative results from Paphos and Corinth are presented below, including a brief discussion of preservation, minimum number of individuals, sex, age at death, reconstructed living stature, dentition and dental and osseous palaeopathological lesions of individuals.

Preservation

Since greater palaeopathological data can be gleaned from well-preserved bones than from those poorly preserved, documentation of the condition of the remains is imperative. Bone preservation at Paphos, as also at Corinth, although ranging from 'poor' to 'good', is usually found to be 'fair'. Alkaline limestone soil conditions prevail at both sites, while the respective climates – although relatively cooler and wetter at Corinth – are not vastly different. Basic soil pH in addition to alternating wet winters and hot, dry summers (typical in the Eastern Mediterranean) combine to create poor bone preservation. Completeness of remains ranged from single bones to virtually complete skeletons.

Minimum number of individuals

The palaeopathological study of human remains is limited in cases where discrete individuals may not always be discernible, since patterns of disease or trauma within individuals can therefore be lost. This is unfortunately the situation at both Paphos and Corinth, where multiple interments resulting from tomb reuse is common; Vermeule (1974) has even reported continuous tomb use lasting 500 years for a tomb in Cyprus. Subsamples of the large collections from both sites were selected for analysis and include at least 275 individuals from Paphos and 94 from Corinth.

Sex

Sex determinations were only attempted on adult and, when possible, (post-pubescent) adolescent material. Sex distributions at both sites are summarised in Table 3.1. It should be noted, however, that for the vast majority of remains sex could not be determined. Of single interments, for example, only 8 of 32 (25 per cent) could be sexed at Paphos and 9 of 16 (56 per cent) at Corinth.

Age at death

Age could be estimated for only 93 of the 275 individuals (33.8 per cent) from Paphos. The mean age at death for the 25 Paphian males that could be aged is 34.4 years, while the mean age at death for the 20 Paphian females is comparable at 34.6 years. Age distributions by sex at Paphos are presented in Table 3.2.

The ages for all individuals at Paphos range from 9.5 lunar months to possibly 71 years. Based upon t-tests, no significant differences in mean age were found either within or between the sexes at Paphos and Corinth. It should be noted, however, that samples of discrete individuals of known sex and age are rare at both sites, and it is more common that individual bones have been sexed and aged rather than individuals.

Age at death could be estimated for 44 of 94 individuals (46.8 per cent) from Corinth. Age distributions by sex for individuals at Corinth are presented in Table 3.3. The average age at death for Corinthian males whose age could be estimated is 42.3 years, while the mean age at death for Corinthian females is 39.6 years. Ages at Corinth range from possibly late foetal to 78 years for an adult male.[8]

Stature

Living statures were reconstructed for 23 individuals from Paphos and 9 individuals from Corinth. There are 7 females, 9 males and 7 individuals of indeterminate sex from Paphos, and 5 females and 4 males from Corinth, for whom living stature could be estimated. At Paphos, the range for

Table 3.1 Sex distribution of adults at Paphos and Corinth

	Females			Males			Indeterminate	
	n	%sexed	%	n	%sexed	%	n	%
Paphos	51	43.6	25.4	66	56.4	32.8	84	41.8
Corinth	18	43.9	30.5	23	56.1	39.0	18	30.5

Notes
n = subsample size.
%sexed = utilises sample sizes of 117 at Paphos and 41 at Corinth.
% = utilises sample sizes of 201 at Paphos and 59 at Corinth.

Table 3.2 Age distribution by sex at Paphos

	Late foetal to 3 years	4–11 years	12–20 years	21–30 years	31–40 years	41–50 years	51–60 years	61+ years
Male	—	—	5	8	7	1	4	1
Female	—	—	5	5	4	1	5	—
ind.	22	34	17	3	—	—	—	2

Note
ind. = indeterminate sex.

Table 3.3 Age distribution by sex at Corinth

	Late foetal to 3 years	4–11 years	12–20 years	21–30 years	31–40 years	41–50 years	51–60 years	61+ years
Male	—	—	1	1	1	1	1	1
Female	—	—	—	3	1	—	3	—
ind.	14	15	1	1	—	—	—	—

Note
ind. = indeterminate sex.

females including standard errors is 141.53–174.09 cm with a mean stature of 155.91 cm, while the range for males including standard errors is 164.69–182.71 cm with a mean stature of 171.13 cm. At Corinth, the range for females including standard errors is 144.76–154.67 cm with a mean stature of 148.29 cm, while the range for males including standard errors is 157.49–172.69 cm with a mean stature of 165.76 cm. Using t-tests, no significant differences were found between either mean male statures ($p = 0.12$) or female statures ($p = 0.08$) at Paphos and Corinth.

Dentition

A total of at least 1,363 teeth were recovered from Paphos including complete (494 maxillary/538 mandibular), fragmentary (80 maxillary/163 mandibular), unerupted (19 maxillary/16 mandibular), and deciduous dentition (16 maxillary/37 mandibular). In addition, at least 1,017 adult mandibular and 599 adult maxillary alveoli were recorded at Paphos. Individual complete teeth at Paphos that could be identified (726) are presented in Table 3.4.

A total of at least 852 teeth, or parts thereof, were recovered from Corinth including complete (242 maxillary/313 mandibular), fragmentary (55 maxillary/35 mandibular), unerupted (21 maxillary/62 mandibular),

Table 3.4 Identifiable and complete teeth from Paphos

#1	#2	#3	#4	#5	#6	#7	#8		#9	#10	#11	#12	#13	#14	#15	#16
11	24	33	22	20	34	19	22		24	15	22	16	20	34	17	10

#32	#31	#30	#29	#28	#27	#26	#25		#24	#23	#22	#21	#20	#19	#18	#17
26	36	38	24	17	22	18	10		9	13	23	14	20	43	43	27

Table 3.5 Identifiable and complete teeth from Corinth

#1	#2	#3	#4	#5	#6	#7	#8		#9	#10	#11	#12	#13	#14	#15	#16
5	17	15	7	5	10	8	9		8	8	12	11	9	14	10	9

#32	#31	#30	#29	#28	#27	#26	#25		#24	#23	#22	#21	#20	#19	#18	#17
3	16	24	13	12	15	14	8		6	9	15	13	11	22	16	8

and deciduous dentition (46 maxillary/78 mandibular). In addition, at least 370 adult mandibular and 389 adult maxillary alveoli were recorded at Corinth. A total of only 372 complete adult teeth from Corinth could be identified (Table 3.5).

Palaeopathological lesions

Dental and skeletal palaeopathological lesions are summarised here.[9] Dental palaeopathological lesions capable of spreading systemically, such as caries and periapical abscesses that reach the pulp chamber, can have a large impact on general health. Enamel hypoplasias are also reflective of general health, as they represent permanent records (for as long as the tooth is retained) of growth interruptions during enamel formation.

Dental palaeopathological lesions

At Paphos, dental and jaw palaeopathological lesions include:

- Ante-mortem tooth loss (67 maxillary teeth from 27 maxillae; 84 mandibular teeth from 30 mandibles) (Table 3.6)
- Caries (86 in 44 maxillary and 38 mandibular teeth, including one tooth with 3 separate caries) (Table 3.7)
- Periodontal disease (at least 23 mandibles and 16 maxillae from 30 individuals) and reactive tissue within an alveolus (16 alveoli from at least 6 mandibles and 5 maxillae from minimally 8 individuals)
- Enamel hypoplasia (teeth from at least 17 maxillae and 20 mandibles representing at least 25 individuals)
- Periapical abscess (11 maxillary and 6 mandibular abscesses from 13 individuals)
- Mandibular condyle lipping (6 individuals)
- Impaction (1 maxillary and 4 mandibular third molars from 5 individuals)
- Ante-mortem enamel fracture (1 mandibular and 2 maxillary premolar crowns)
- Osteomyelitis (involvement of a dental alveolus and a maxillary sinus of 1 individual)
- A bony exostosis (unknown aetiology).

At Corinth, dental and jaw palaeopathological lesions include:

- Caries (13 mandibular teeth and 16 maxillary teeth) (Table 3.8)
- Ante-mortem tooth loss (8 maxillary and 19 mandibular teeth) (Table 3.9)
- Enamel hypoplasia (teeth from at least 5 maxillae and 8 mandibles representing minimally 12 individuals)

Table 3.6 Ante-mortem tooth loss at Paphos

#1	#2	#3	#4	#5	#6	#7	#8	#9	#10	#11	#12	#13	#14	#15	#16
4	3	10	5	4	2	2	2	3	3	3	3	7	8	5	6
#17	#18	#19	#20	#21	#22	#23	#24	#25	#26	#27	#28	#29	#30	#31	#32
6	12	15	5	3	2	1	4	4	2	1	2	6	9	6	6

Table 3.7 Number of caries by tooth at Paphos

#1	#2	#3	#4	#5	#6	#7	#8	#9	#10	#11	#12	#13	#14	#15	#16
2	7	2	1	2	0	1	1	1	0	0	1	2	5	2	2
#17	#18	#19	#20	#21	#22	#23	#24	#25	#26	#27	#28	#29	#30	#31	#32
3	7	7	0	0	0	0	0	0	0	0	0	0	4	2	5

Table 3.8 Number of caries by tooth at Corinth

#1	#2	#3	#4	#5	#6	#7	#8	#9	#10	#11	#12	#13	#14	#15	#16
0	1	2	1	1	0	0	0	0	1	0	0	0	0	4	1

#17	#18	#19	#20	#21	#22	#23	#24	#25	#26	#27	#28	#29	#30	#31	#32
0	0	2	1	0	1	0	0	0	0	0	0	0	1	2	1

Table 3.9 Ante-mortem tooth loss at Corinth

#1	#2	#3	#4	#5	#6	#7	#8	#9	#10	#11	#12	#13	#14	#15	#16
0	0	1	1	0	1	0	0	0	0	0	1	4	0	0	0

#17	#18	#19	#20	#21	#22	#23	#24	#25	#26	#27	#28	#29	#30	#31	#32
0	0	3	1	0	1	0	3	1	0	1	0	3	5	1	1

- Periodontal disease (3 maxillae and 8 mandibles from 10 individuals) and reactive tissue within an alveolus (1 maxillary)
- Periapical abscess (3 maxillary and 3 mandibular abscesses from 5 individuals)
- Articular pitting and osteophytic lipping of the mandibular condyles (4 individuals) resulting from trauma and/or osteoarthritis
- Impaction (1 maxillary and 1 mandibular tooth from 2 individuals)
- Ante-mortem enamel fracture (4 incisors: 3 maxillary and 1 mandibular from 2 individuals)
- Osteomyelitis (1 adult mandible with a cloaca).

Skeletal palaeopathological lesions

At Paphos, skeletal palaeopathological lesions include:

- Osteophytosis (minimally 184 observations ranging anywhere from an occipital condyle to a distal foot phalanx of minimally 40 individuals) and additionally osteophytosis with other observations such as plaques (at least 6 individuals), porosity (at least 11 individuals) and osteopenia (at least 2 individuals)
- Porosity of articular surfaces without osteophytosis, perhaps also related to osteoarthritis (60 observations from 28 individuals)
- Evidence of anaemia (30 individuals) in the form of porotic hyperostosis (5 individuals) Figure 3.2 and/or cribra orbitalia (11 individuals) Figure 3.3 and/or cranial vault thickening (20 individuals) and thickening or pitting of 6 other bones from 6 individuals
- Plaque (38 bones from at least 21 individuals possess plaques alone on their articular surfaces without osteophytosis)
- Exostosis (42 observations on at least 16 individuals, including roughened areas on 3 long bone shafts)
- Fracture (possibly 28 bones from 19 individuals)
- Periostitis (26 bones from a minimum of 14 individuals in addition to reactive areas of unknown aetiology of 3 bones from 3 individuals)
- Pitting of the costoclavicular ligament attachment of the clavicle, perhaps from heavy lifting (17 clavicles from 11 individuals)
- Extension of an articular surface (11 bones from a minimum of 10 individuals), perhaps an indicator of age or trauma
- Schmorl's nodes (22 observations from at least 8 individuals), also an indicator of trauma
- Bony spicules (2 humeri from 2 different individuals), also a possible indicator of trauma
- Osteochondritis non-dissecans[10] (5 bones from 5 individuals)

Figure 3.2 Immature left parietal from Paphos with active porotic hyperostosis (P.M. 2518).

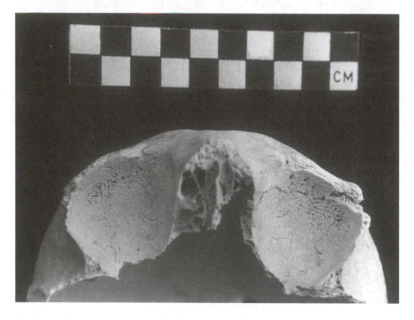

Figure 3.3 Healed cribra orbitalia of adult from Paphos (P.M. 2518).

- Eburnation, pathognomonic of osteoarthritis, with or without plaques and osteophytes (9 bony articular surfaces from at least 5 individuals)
- Osteopenia (9 bones from at least 4 individuals) and osteopenia with porosity (3 bones from 3 individuals)
- Traumatic arthritis (3 observations)
- Ankylosing spondylitis or DISH (Diffuse Idiopathic Skeletal Hyperostosis) of at least 2 individuals
- Slight depressions (unknown aetiology) noted on the articular surfaces of 4 bones from at least 2 individuals, as well as ectocranial depressions (also unknown aetiology) observed on 1 frontal
- An irregular joint surface (2 individuals) (unknown aetiology)
- Osteomyelitis (one unidentified post-cranial long bone fragment, in addition to previously mentioned fragment of maxilla)
- Healed rickets (6 bones from 2 individuals)
- Possible gout in 1 wrist and 1 foot bone from 2 individuals
- Articular facets on the greater tuberosities of 2 right humeri
- Harris' lines observed on 3 bones from possibly 2 individuals
- Pyogenic or septic arthritis of a proximal left ulna, perhaps also associated with a radial fragment
- A growth disorder, perhaps involving the pituitary, observed on 3 diminutive long bones from 1 individual
- A possible periosteal tumour (postero-lateral surface of distal one-third shaft of right humerus)
- A pit (unknown aetiology) on the endocranial surface of an occipital fragment
- Another depression (also unknown aetiology) that appears healed although thickened on the outer cortex of a sub-adult ilium fragment
- What appears to be an endocranial infection of hyperblastic nature (unknown aetiology), near the coronal suture of a frontal
- Porosity (unknown aetiology) of paired sub-adult femora
- A bony protuberance (unknown aetiology) on superior aspect of an acetabulum of right innominate as well as a bony nodule (unknown aetiology), superior and lateral to the base of a right second metatarsal, and a bony build-up (unknown aetiology) between the articulations for the navicular and lunate on a distal left radius
- A misshapen adult left clavicle (unknown aetiology).

Skeletal pseudopathologies at Paphos include:

- Pitting near the articular margins of 4 long bones of a single individual
- A 'tug' lesion of a right fibula at insertion of the soleus muscle (Keats 1988).

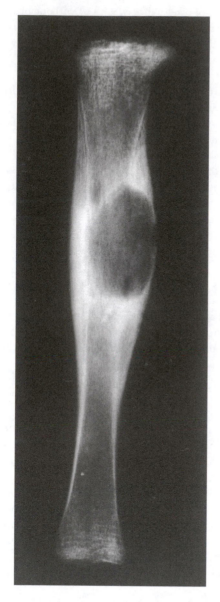

Figure 3.4 Radiograph of subadult tibia with giant cell tumour from Corinth (Corinth 61-10).

At Corinth, skeletal palaeopathological lesions include:

- Osteophytosis (29 observations among 11 individuals) along with plaques (1 individual) and porosity (1 individual) that may be evidence for osteoarthritis
- Possible evidence of anaemia in the form of cranial vault thickening (8 individuals), a thickened rib (1 individual) and cribra orbitalia (5 individuals)
- Entheses (5 individuals), possible evidence of DISH
- Schmorl's nodes (4 individuals)
- Healed fractures (3 individuals)
- Osteomyelitis (2 individuals)
- Osteochondritis non-dissecans (2 individuals)
- Traumatic arthritis from a fractured distal hallux (1 individual)
- Osteoarthritis based upon evidence of eburnation (1 individual)
- An osteochondroma (1 individual)
- A giant cell tumour (tibia of a sub-adult) Figure 3.4
- An osteoma (1 individual)
- A cranial infection (1 individual)
- An active mandibular infection of a sub-adult (1 individual)
- Osteopenia (1 individual)
- Possible healed rickets (1 individual)
- Metatarsal pitting (1 individual)
- And a bowed metatarsal shaft and 4 palaeopathological lesions of unknown identity (1 individual).

A skeletal pseudopathology at Corinth known as a 'tug' lesion has also been identified on a fibula (1 individual) (Keats 1988). See Tables 3.10 and 3.11.

Table 3.10 Summary of dental palaeopathological lesions

	Paphos obs.	MNI	obs./ MNI	MNI/ n = 275 (%)	Corinth obs.	MNI	obs./ MNI	MNI/ n = 94 (%)
Ante-mortem loss	151	42	3.6	15.3	27	12	2.3	12.8
Caries	86	39	2.2	14.2	29	15	1.9	16.0
Periodontal disease	50	38	1.3	13.8	12	11	1.1	11.7
Enamel hypoplasia	37	25	1.5	9.1	13	12	1.1	12.8
Periapical abscess	17	13	1.3	4.7	6	5	1.2	5.3
Condyle lipping	8	6	1.3	2.2	4	4	1.0	4.3
Impaction	5	5	1.0	1.8	2	2	1.0	2.1
Enamel fracture	3	2	1.5	0.7	4	2	2.0	2.1

Notes
MNI = minimum number of individuals.
obs. = observations.

Table 3.11 Summary of osseous palaeopathological lesions

	Paphos obs.	MNI	obs./ MNI	MNI/ n = 275 (%)	Corinth obs.	MNI	obs. MNI	MNI/ n = 94 (%)
Osteophytosis	184	40	4.6	14.5	34	12	2.8	12.8
Porosity	60	28	2.1	10.2	0	0	—	0
Exostosis	39	18	2.2	6.5	1	1	1.0	1.1
Osteoarthritis	9	5	1.8	1.8	1	1	1.0	1.1
DISH	38	17	2.2	6.2	5	4	1.3	4.3
Gouty arthritis	2	2	1.0	0.7	2	1	2.0	1.1
Septic arthritis	2	1	2.0	0.4	0	0	—	0
Anaemia	42	30	1.4	10.9	14	11	1.3	11.7
Rickets (healed)	6	2	3.0	0.7	1	1	1.0	1.1
Osteopenia	20	8	2.5	2.9	1	1	1.0	1.1
Endocrine disorder	3	1	3.0	0.4	0	0	—	0
Harris' lines	3	1	3.0	0.4	0	0	—	0
Fracture	26	19	1.4	6.9	3	3	1.0	3.2
Schmorl's nodes	22	8	2.8	2.9	6	4	1.5	4.3
Traumatic arthritis	5	3	1.7	1.1	1	1	1.0	1.1
CC ligament	17	11	1.5	4.0	0	0	—	0
OND	5	5	1.0	1.8	3	2	1.5	2.1
Metatarsal pitting	3	1	3.0	0.4	3	1	3.0	1.1
Periostitis	26	14	1.9	5.0	4	2	2.0	2.1
Osteomyelitis	1	1	1.0	0.4	2	1	2.0	1.1
Tumours	1	1	1.0	0.4	3	3	1.0	3.2

Notes
MNI = minimum number of individuals.
DISH = diffuse idiopathic skeletal hyperostosis.
CC = costoclavicular.
OND = osteochondritis non-dissecans.
obs. = observation.

DISCUSSION AND CONCLUSIONS

An important aspect in fully understanding states of health in the ancient cities of Paphos and Corinth is a familiarity with environmental conditions and cultural practices that may have affected the peoples living there. At Paphos, for example, where a stream once emptied into the ancient harbour, malarial conditions may have affected the health of Hellenistic and Roman Paphians and occasionally left indications of anaemia upon their bones. Medieval travellers to the area complained of pestilent 'bad air' (Leonard et al. 1998). Angel (1967) was the first to suggest an association between porotic hyperostosis and thalassaemia. There is a relationship known as a balanced polymorphism that exists between anaemias (specifically thalassaemia) and malaria in the Eastern Mediterranean, whereby mutations producing the deleterious thalassaemia genes have been retained by natural selection since heterozygotes or carriers of a single gene are afforded protection from malaria. Inheritance of two thalassaemia genes generally leads to death in childhood, while those not inheriting a single thalassaemia gene remain vulnerable to malaria, the single most common infectious disease (McFalls and McFalls 1984). Those that survive the disease often suffer from depressed fecundity such as possible coital inability, conceptive failure, pregnancy loss and the effects of placental parasitisation (McFalls and McFalls 1984). Those that lived to reproduce were thus often carriers (heterozygotes) of thalassaemia. Despite the fact that malaria was eradicated from the island during the last century, one in seven Cypriots remains a carrier of β-thalassaemia (Angastiniotis et al. 1993). Although less common, Loukopoulos (1990) has identified between 5 and 10 per cent of the modern inhabitants of the region of Corinth as carriers. Additionally, the incidence of α-thalassaemia also remains relatively high in Cyprus, although lower than β-thalassaemia (cf. Hadjiminas et al. 1979).

Furthermore, communicable disease played a much greater role in ancient health from the Neolithic period onwards than it had previously, as people began to live sedentary existences in larger numbers as well as in closer proximity to one another and their domesticated animals. Diseases, called zoonoses, that spread from animals to humans (or vice versa), may have had an influence on human evolution. In Cyprus, the common practice of animals sharing domestic living space with humans was practised at least by the Late Roman period (mid-fourth century AD), as evidenced by a mule found lying still tethered beside a young girl in Room 2 at the earthquake-destroyed city of Kourion (Soren and James 1988). This custom of animals and humans sharing dwellings has persisted in Cyprus into modern times (Christodoulou 1959), leading perhaps to the spread of tuberculosis, echinococcosis and brucellosis. All of these zoonoses have been detected among twentieth-century inhabitants of Cyprus and Greece. Other communicable diseases, such as syphilis and leprosy, have also been identified among modern Cypriots and Greeks and have been alluded to by ancient authors (see Patrick 1967). Yet none of these diseases, including tuberculosis, to date have been detected among human remains dating to Graeco-Roman times in either Cyprus or Greece (Grmek 1989).

In summary, the human skeletal remains are not well preserved from either ancient Paphos (275 individuals, minimally) or Corinth (94 individuals, minimally). The number of individuals per tomb at Paphos ranged from 1 to 82, with an average of 8.9, while the number at Corinth ranged from 1 to 34, with an average of 4.8 (compare with Wesolowsky's 1973 results from the rock-cut tombs from Lerna Hollow with an average of

3.92 individuals per tomb). It is apparent from the two sites' skeletal samples that multiple interments became common at an earlier date in Paphos than at Corinth. It is also evident that tomb reuse, although observed at Corinth, was practiced to a greater extent at Paphos, as evidenced both by dates of tomb use and by numbers of individuals interred.

The percentage of males and females identified at both sites is virtually identical, although the sex of only 117 individuals at Paphos (66 males, 51 females) and 41 individuals at Corinth (23 males, 18 females) can be determined. A far greater percentage of children under the age of 12 years are represented at Corinth than at Paphos (30.9 per cent versus 20.4 per cent, respectively). This latter figure (20.4 per cent at Paphos) is comparable to that from Graeco-Roman inscriptional evidence (20.1 per cent by the author's calculations) recorded by Richardson (1933: 232), but she also states, 'the deaths of small children may not have always been recorded and the group may be larger than we suppose'. Thus, despite the fact that the average age of adults is greater at Corinth than at Paphos for both males (42.3 years versus 34.4 years) and females (39.5 years versus 34.5 years), it appears that more individuals survived childhood at Paphos. For adults, however, a greater life expectancy for both sexes prevailed at Corinth. The skeletal evidence does not indicate a greater-than-expected number of deaths among adult females of childbearing age from complications of pregnancy and childbirth at either Paphos or Corinth.

With respect to stature, ancient Corinthians were on average shorter in comparison with their Paphian counterparts, but it should be noted that results of t-tests demonstrate no statistical significance. It is possible that the living stature of people at Corinth was affected by dietary stress or the prevalence of disease during development. Larger sample sizes are necessary, however, before firm conclusions can be drawn concerning a possible relationship between living stature and health at ancient Corinth.

Prevalences of dental disease do not largely differ between Paphos and Corinth. Ante-mortem tooth loss among individuals from Paphos and caries from those at Corinth represent the predominant dental diseases. Individuals from both Paphos and Corinth incurred greater ante-mortem loss in mandibular teeth, while more posterior teeth were lost ante-mortem among both maxillary and mandibular teeth. Posterior dentition from individuals at both sites also exhibits more dental caries. During the present study, more caries would likely have been detected on permanent dentition if radiography of all teeth had been employed. All caries, with a single exception from Corinth, were found on permanent dentition. The location of caries differs somewhat between the sites. For example, the occlusal surfaces of maxillary teeth from individuals from Paphos display more caries than those at Corinth, while interproximal caries of maxillary teeth at Corinth account for a greater percentage of the caries recorded there. Severity of dental caries also appears to be greater at Corinth, with caries affecting a greater number of tooth surfaces and entire crowns.

Corinthians exhibit relatively more enamel hypoplasias (indicative of interruption in development during enamel formation) when compared to Paphians, suggesting that perhaps more people at Corinth suffered from nutritional deficiencies or constitutional disorders. In addition, 2 of the 12 individuals with enamel hypoplasias at Corinth, after surviving the initial insult causing the condition, died before reaching adulthood.

Two instances of osteomyelitis are detected; 1 in a mandible and the other in a maxilla from 2 adults at Corinth. In one of these individuals, it is possible that the disease, although apparently not in an active state at time of death, had spread systemically. Osteomyelitis is not observed among any jaws from Paphos, although it is detected elsewhere in the skeleton among a single individual from the site. An infant from Corinth also demonstrates an active infection of the mandible that may have been osteomyelitis. When instances of osteomyelitic and periostitic infections are combined at Paphos and at Corinth, the resulting prevalences of bone infection at each of the two sites nearly approximate each other. Overall, based upon the present study, the relationship between dental and general health remains unclear.

Osteophytosis is the most prevalent skeletal palaeopathology found at both Paphos and Corinth, the greatest frequency of which is found in the vertebral column. The majority of observed skeletal palaeopathological lesions, however, including osteophytosis, porosity, exostosis, osteoarthritis, DISH (diffuse idiopathic skeletal hyperostosis), gouty arthritis and osteopenia, are likely age-related or degenerative changes rather than true palaeopathological lesions. No sub-adult material possesses any of these skeletal lesions, nor do these remains contain any evidence of trauma such as fracture, Schmorl's nodes, traumatic arthritis, costoclavicular ligament damage to the clavicle, osteochondritis non-dissecans or metatarsal pitting. All identified fractures appear to be healed, while the cranial fracture of an adult male from Paphos (indicative of a sharp-implement injury likely from a metal blade) also exhibits signs of infection. The only other fractures possibly caused by violence are the fractured nasal bones of an individual from Corinth, although these breaks could equally have been incurred by a fall.

As in the case of dental lesions, the prevalences of skeletal lesions do not differ greatly between the two sites. Although childhood rickets afflicted 2 individuals from Paphos and 1 from Corinth, these individuals survived into adulthood.[11] The one individual with a metabolic disorder from Paphos also reached adulthood. Furthermore, all of the tumours identified at Corinth (3 individuals) and Paphos (1 individual) were benign.

Comparable prevalences of what may demonstrate anaemias exist at Paphos and Corinth, as evidenced by one or more of the following: porotic hyperostosis, cribra orbitalia, cranial vault thickening, or thickening or pitting of associated skeletal elements. No porotic hyperostosis, however, was observed at Corinth. Active forms of porotic hyperostosis and/or cribra orbitalia were found among 3 individuals (all sub-adults, including 1 infant) at Paphos. Three Corinthians (including 1 infant) also demonstrated active forms of cribra orbitalia. Evidence of possible anaemias and infectious lesions, then, represent two types of discernible palaeopathological lesions at Paphos and Corinth that may have increased the mortality of children, and which therefore may have had evolutionary implications. It should also be noted that 2 children from Corinth and 3 from Paphos demonstrate enamel hypoplasias, possibly indicative of malnutrition or a constitutional disorder, and succumbed prior to attaining adult age.

In conclusion, although the health of ancient Paphians and Corinthians was largely similar, subtle differences did exist. Greater infant mortality, relatively shorter statures and greater evidence of stress in the form of enamel hypoplasias characterise the Corinthians when compared to the Paphians during Hellenistic and Roman times. This situation may be related to different political environments at the two cities. Corinth was sacked by the Romans, whereas at Paphos the transition to Roman rule was relatively uneventful. Despite comparable instances of what may be evidence for anaemia, osteomyelitis, and periostitis at the two sites, porotic hyperostosis does not appear at Corinth. The types of anaemia that afflicted residents of Paphos and Corinth, therefore, may have been different. Although iron deficiency anaemia was probably present at both sites, the present study suggests (but only on the basis of negative evidence) that thalassaemia was not present at Corinth as it may have been at Paphos. Klepinger (1992) suggests an increased prevalence of skeletal infectious lesions associated with cases of porotic hyperostosis. Additionally, Giardina et al. (1993: 106) suggest that 'patients with thalassemia major and intermedia are osteopenic and prone to fractures'. Although the prevalences for infectious diseases, osteopenia and fractures are relatively higher among Paphians when compared to Corinthians, these differences are not significant. Unfortunately, preliminary DNA tests for β-thalassaemia, conducted on Paphian bone samples from the present study by the Institute of Neurology and Genetics in Nicosia, Cyprus, have proven inconclusive. Future DNA analysis could perhaps clarify our understanding of anaemias at ancient Paphos and Corinth.

ACKNOWLEDGEMENTS

I would like to thank Karen Stears for her kind invitation to participate in the initially planned volume and Helen King for persevering with the idea.

The dissertation (Fox Leonard 1997) upon which the present work is based was completed in part under the auspices of a J. William Fulbright Grant (Cyprus) and a J. Lawrence Angel Fellowship from the Wiener Laboratory of the American School of Classical Studies at Athens (Greece), for which I am deeply grateful. I am also indebted to D. Michaelides and C.K. Williams, II, for permitting me to examine the human remains from their excavations in Paphos and Corinth respectively, and to W.H. Birkby and R.G. Snyder for their invaluable editorial assistance with the original work. To past and present Directors of the Cypriot Department of Antiquities, A. Papageorghiou, M. Loulloupis, D. Christou and S. Hadjisavvas, and the Greek Ephorea of Palaeoanthropology and Speliology I extend my sincere gratitude for permitting the study to proceed. In addition, the staff both of the Cyprus American Archaeological Research Institute (S. Swiny and M. Stavrou in particular) and the Wiener Laboratory of the American School of Classical Studies at Athens, as well as all those other individuals in Cyprus and Greece who so generously supported my research deserve my special thanks. Lastly, I express my heartfelt appreciation to my husband, John R. Leonard, for his tireless assistance in the completion of this chapter.

NOTES

1 Analysis of cremated human remains not only requires specialised training and experience, but also takes more time and may offer fewer results due to the effects of fire damage to the bones. In addition, evidence of palaeopathological lesions may not survive the cremation process. For these reasons, fewer such analyses are undertaken.

2 The author usually publishes under the name 'Fox', but university regulations required the full legal name (Fox Leonard) on the dissertation.

3 P.M. inventory numbers: 2518, 2519, 2520, 2524, 2528, 2536, 2537, 2545, 2548, 2553, 2584, 2601, 2603, 2605, 2609, 2613, 2614, 2626, 2631, 2632, 2642, 2651, 2652, 2657, 2658, 2659, 2660, 2661, 2662, 2664 and 2668.

4 The basis for determination of minimum number of individuals is discussed under the heading 'Minimum number of individuals' and in the section DISCUSSION AND CONCLUSIONS.

5 Corinth lot numbers: 60-1, 60-3, 61-1, 61-14, 62-1, 62-2, 62-3, 62-4, 62-11, 62-12, 62-13, 62-14, 62-15, 62-17, 62-18, 62-22, 62-23, 62-26, 62-31, 62-35, 62-36, 62-41, 62-42, 62-43, 62-44, 62-45, 62-47, 62-48, 62-49, 63-6, 63-7, 63-8, 63-13.

6 Buikstra and Ubelaker's (1994) *Standards for Data Collection from Human Skeletal Remains*, which are standard guidelines today, were not yet available during the present study.

7 A Minitab statistical package was used for limited statistical analyses including descriptive statistics and *t*-tests.

8 One explanation for the slightly lower mean age of females at Corinth, however, is that 59 years is the upper limit of the spectrum for Gilbert and McKern's (1973) aging method of the pubic symphysis.

9 Limitations of space within the present volume prohibit individual discussion of each palaeopathology. For more complete details see Fox Leonard (1997).

10 See J. Rogers and Waldron (1995: 30), citing D. Burkitt, for this terminology.

11 The sexes of these three individuals are unknown and their pelvic bones were not recovered. It is therefore uncertain whether complications due to childbirth could have occurred in these three cases.

4

HEALTH AND THE LIFE COURSE AT HERCULANEUM AND POMPEII

Ray Laurence

The development of scientific archaeology, with its focus on preserved elements of flora and fauna, has made a considerable contribution to our understanding of antiquity. Nowhere can this be more easily demonstrated than at the sites destroyed during the volcanic events associated with the eruption of Vesuvius, the evidence for which has been reviewed recently by Jashemski and Meyer (2002). Wilhelmina Jashemski's work on medicinal plants found in Pompeii (1999) reveals the potential for this new material to contribute to the history of medicine, alongside studies of the diet of those in Pompeii (e.g. Meyer 1988). In the 1970s and 1980s, work by Jashemski (1979, 1993) and others recovered the nature of Roman horticulture and established its importance within the sphere of life in the city. These studies led to a greater emphasis on the use of scientific techniques at the Vesuvian sites. This interest was given a further stimulus with the setting up of scientific laboratories and an understanding that what had been collected in the past needed to be studied with the new techniques that were now available (Ciarallo and De Carolis 1999).

Nowhere has the impact been greater than in the study of human remains. The find of 139 skeletons in Herculaneum in the early 1980s resulted not only in the first identification of human remains at that site, but also spilled over to Pompeii, leading to a fresh interest in the human bones there. The result of these developments has been a dramatic increase in the range of the skeletal data and the type of analyses conducted. An obvious point needs to be stressed: the skeletal remains from the Vesuvian sites represent a living population, unlike those found in cemeteries. All were alive on 23 August AD 79, and all were dead by 25 August. This chapter will be concerned with presenting the results of the analysis of human skeletal remains. In doing so, it depends on the published reports of the scientists, but goes beyond these by attempting to relate their findings to the interests of Roman social history and, specifically, to aspects of health.

THE DATA SETS

Interest in the human remains at Pompeii dates from the time of the earliest excavations. Not surprisingly, the focus in the nineteenth century was on the metrical analysis of the human skulls to the exclusion of other attributes of the skeleton. This factor led to skeletons being stored not according to their associated bones, but according to bone type. In other words, the skeletons found were disarticulated and all bones of a particular type – for example, femurs – were stored together. This practice did not stop in the twentieth century and was exacerbated by the loss not only of parts of the skeletons, but even a sense of where the bones had been found in excavations prior to the 1960s.

These factors have created a major problem in the Pompeii data set as a whole. Henneberg and Henneberg (2002) returned to study the human bones available from excavations in the past at Pompeii, and were able to identify 500 individuals and 50 complete skeletons. In sorting the bones, the discovery of the skeletal remains of a barbary ape was made (Bailey *et al.* 1999). The overall sample of the bones, however, provides essential information for a large number of individuals.

The human bones excavated from the rear of the House of Julius Polybius provide additional information of a houseful of 6 adults, 6 children and a foetus at term (Ciarallo and De Carolis 2001). In contrast to the other skeletons from Pompeii, these have most of their bones present and were re-articulated to form almost complete skeletons for analysis. In contrast, the site of Herculaneum produced no skeletal evidence, until a unique find located the final place of shelter for a number of individuals, within the arched vaults supporting the upper-terraces close to the Suburban Baths, which in antiquity faced onto the beach: 139 skeletons have to date been studied by Bisel and Bisel (2002), of which 51 are male adults, 49 female adults and 39 children. Their analyses of this sample have already been published and further publication will reveal the health of all of these individuals.

THE SHAPE OF THE BODY IN ANTIQUITY

In considering the health of the ancient body, a number of factors need to be taken into account. Many of these reveal the divergence of the ancient body from our own; this point needs to be appreciated, in order that we might resist the common assumption that our skeletal frame today is in all ways better, due to improved nutrition and health care within the modern West. Bisel and Bisel's paper (2002) compares the skeletal evidence from Herculaneum with that of the USA; a more fruitful comparison might be with other modern populations from non-Western societies.

The major samples from Herculaneum and Pompeii reveal the stature of the ancient adult body. The average height for females was calculated from the data to have been 155 cm in Herculaneum and 154 cm in Pompeii: that for males was 169 cm in Herculaneum and 166 cm in Pompeii. This is somewhat higher than the average height of modern Neapolitans in the 1960s (Bisel and Bisel 2002: 455) and about 10 cm shorter than the WHO recommendation for modern world populations. As for body weight, calculations from the sample from Pompeii would produce males weighing in at 66 kg and females at 50 kg, in line with the Food and Agriculture Organization of the United Nations' expectations of size in temperate climates (Henneberg and Henneberg 2002: 84–5). The overall height and stature found at both sites coincides with the general pattern derived from cemetery sites; for example, at Metaponto (Henneberg and Henneberg 1998, 2001).

The nature of human growth in childhood may have been quite different in antiquity. Today, we expect the adolescent growth spurt to begin at age 9 and to continue in females to about 14 and in males to 16 or 17. The data from Herculaneum reveal a very similar growth curve for females as that found today, ending at about 14, but – in contrast – the male growth curve in antiquity follows that of his female counterpart. However, male growth would not have ceased in antiquity until a male's twenties (Laurence 2000: 446).

A further major difference in terms of the human body of antiquity was the nature of the mouth. Bisel and Bisel (2002: 455) observe that, in most cases, the bite of the Herculaneans was edge to edge. This avoids the very notion of the possibility of crooked teeth. The reasons for this difference are unclear, but they suggest that the need to chew food to a greater degree (if eating with hands, as opposed to knives and forks) and the longer period that children were nursed may have allowed for greater stimulation of jaw growth at an early age.

The general increase in the non-closure of the sacral canal associated with *spina bifida occulta* has been observed in modern populations of the twentieth century. Significantly, the frequency of *spina bifida* at Pompeii was found to be 15 per cent compared to 27 per cent in modern Cambridge amongst those in their twenties (Henneberg and Henneberg 1999a). There is a common association between *spina bifida* and fluoride in water. It is significant that the skeletons in the House of Julius Polybius were found to have fluoride levels in their teeth ranging from 400 to 1,200 parts per million (ppm, compared to Herculaneum, at 500–3,600 ppm), with one individual found to have fluoride levels that were in fact toxic (12,000 ppm). Such a wide variation in fluoride content in teeth points to this individual coming from another region, where drinking water was saturated with fluoride. It is notable that the water drunk at Herculaneum and Pompeii was not the same in terms of its fluoride content (Torino and Furnaciari 2001). Hence, we should not generalize rates of *spina bifida* across the Mediterranean in antiquity, given the variation in the chemical composition of water at different sites. *Spina bifida* need not have dramatically affected a person's life, but may have increased the rate at which lead was absorbed from the environment.

HEALTH AND AGE

Childhood

Bones can be examined to establish periods in which their formation was interrupted; these events are marked with what are known as the presence of Harris stripes. Common reasons for them are a lack of nutrition, or acute illness, in childhood or young adulthood. Nine individuals from the House of Julius Polybius were examined by Torino and Furnaciari (2001). From the analysis of zinc, strontium and calcium, they established that all individuals had an adequate diet, so that the distortion to bone formation which has been found indicates periods of acute illness. Of the 9 individuals, only 1 did not experience any such illness (see Table 4.1).

Significantly, two female adults – unlike their male counterparts – experienced acute illness during their early adult life. This pattern of childhood illnesses found in the house of Julius Polybius is confirmed through the finding of enamel hypoplasia in their teeth (horizontal lines of thinner enamel indicating periods of acute illness or starvation of over two weeks that prevented the assimilation of calcium): 88 per cent of those in the House of Julius Polybius; 80 per cent of the whole Pompeii sample and 50 per cent of the Herculaneum sample (Henneberg and Henneberg 1999b: 53; Bisel and Bisel 2002: 455). The considerably lower level of hypoplasia in the sample from Herculaneum is striking, and suggests that the level of childhood illness in towns on the Bay of Naples was far from standard.

Table 4.1 Acute illness in the House of Julius Polybius (data from Torino and Furnaciari)

Individual	Age in AD 79	Number of incidents	Age incident began	Date incident began
Male 1B	50+	1	1 year 8 months	c.AD 27
Male 4A	45+	2	$2\frac{1}{2}$ and $1\frac{1}{2}$	c.AD 36, 37
Female 1A	45+	3	5, 6 and 15	c.AD 37, 38, 49
Female 5A	c.35	2	$10\frac{1}{2}$ and $11\frac{1}{2}$	c.AD 55, 56
Child 2A	$8\frac{1}{2}$	1	8	AD 79
Child 2B	13	0	—	—
Child 2C	3	2	2 and $2\frac{1}{2}$	AD 77, 77
Child 5B	13	2	1 and 9	AD 67, 75
Child 3D	11	4	$4\frac{1}{2}$, $5\frac{1}{2}$, 7, $7\frac{1}{2}$	AD 73, 74, 75, 76

What is clear, however, is that the acute illness of children was an aspect of life in the household and a feature that would have affected both biological and human development in childhood. It is this factor, rather than poor nutrition, which accounts for the stature of the population; quite simply, people did not grow as fast in antiquity due to childhood illnesses, and as a consequence did not attain their potential stature.

Endemic diseases

The determination of the nature of chronic infection in Pompeii is at an early stage at present. Henneberg and Henneberg (2002: 174–6) identified signs of the inflammation of the periosteum or tissue covering bone surfaces in 141 of the 365 tibiae examined. Some of these may be due to a local trauma, but to find it in 30 per cent of cases would suggest some form of systemic blood-borne disease: most commonly leprosy, tuberculosis or treponemal diseases (including syphilis). Henneberg and Henneberg (2002: 176) attempted to collate their findings from the examination of tibiae with other bone parts, and on four skulls they did discover stellate lesions, the result of healed ulcers caused by a treponemal disease, thus confirming the presence of syphilis in Pompeii. They also found signs of tuberculosis, but no positive evidence of leprosy. We might suggest endemic levels of tuberculosis within the population as a whole and the presence of syphilis in the adult population. A key factor in the high level of tuberculosis-type diseases might have been the presence of malaria. Sallares (2002: 123–40) observes how the interaction of malaria and respiratory illnesses might produce a higher level of disease and death via pneumonia (note that the presence of malaria hinders the development of syphilis, Sallares 2002: 123–4). The observation made earlier, that the incidence of hypoplasia at Herculaneum and Pompeii varied, needs further consideration. We might speculate here: Herculaneum was situated on a site associated in antiquity with good air (Strabo, *Geog.* 5.4.8 = 246C), whereas Pompeii was close to a major river, which was associated with marshland (Strabo, *Geog.* 5.4.8 = 247C; De' Spagnolis Conticello 1994; Ciarallo 2001: 22–32 for reconstruction of the river environment). What may be causing the difference in the incidence of hypoplasia might be the presence or the virulence of malaria at Pompeii, with an absence, or a lower incidence, of malaria at Herculaneum (Sallares 2002: 55–90). As a consequence of the lower incidence or absence of malaria at Herculaneum, the incidence of childhood respiratory illnesses would also have been lower.

Development of the male body

The development of muscle, and the nature of those muscles, is a feature of the study of bones from Herculaneum. A man aged 46, Erc86, displays evidence of massive muscles over the whole body, quite unlike those developed through physical labour, but those associated today with athletes. There is evidence of overworking of the muscles, including scarring and herniations of some vertebrae (Bisel and Bisel 2002: 460–1). This is a man who deliberately shaped his body through exercise. It should be noted there are no signs of wounding on the body, so we should not see this man as a professional fighter or something similar. Instead, he appears to be a civilian developing his own body to an aesthetic ideal of health and activity. There is a marked contrast here with those individuals whose bodies developed through work: a 16 year-old with massive upper-body strength, Erc28, is compared by Bisel and Bisel (2002: 467–8) to the muscle tone of modern fishermen, and a soldier's skeleton, Erc26, reveals a life of exercise and horsemanship. However, these provide the confirmation of Erc86's interest in the development of his own body into a particular shape, rather than through a particular form of work. It is possible to see here the importance of exercise at the baths, as well as the action of cleansing.

Pregnancy and fertility

Thirty-seven skeletons of adult women found at Herculaneum provide us with an insight into fertility. Bisel and Bisel (2002: 451–3) examined the dorsal rim of the pubic symphyses of these individuals for wear or even destruction associated with the birth of children. The mean number of births was 1.69 for this population of women, one which included only 16 women over 40 or beyond child bearing. Even amongst those over 40, the mean number of births was only 1.81. This demonstrates a relatively low birth rate, but it needs to be stressed that the sample examined is not huge. Two women were pregnant: Erc52 and Erc110 (full data in Bisel and Bisel 2002: 465–6). Erc52 was 24 years old and pregnant with her first child in good health. Erc110 was 16 and had not finished growing; in fact the size of her pelvis was too small for the foetus to have passed through. In short, she was lucky to be killed by the pyroclastic surge of AD 79 rather than to have gone through days of labour with no possibility of birth and eventually dying of exhaustion. This is conclusive proof, if it is needed, that the pregnant young bride of antiquity need not have grown sufficiently to give birth.

An interesting example from the sample is Erc98, a woman of about 49 who had given birth to 4 or 5 children. Bisel and Bisel (2002: 466–7) identified her as having the same pelvic abnormalities found in prostitutes in North America. This individual demonstrates the higher end of the range of fertility in Herculaneum; our difficulty is to relate her experience of sex and childbirth to ideas found in literature on abortion and contraception (Riddle 1992, 1997; Frier 1994, 2001). Compared to, say, the fertility of Augustus' daughter, Julia, in her brief marriage to Agrippa, this woman from Herculaneum has given birth to fewer children. We should not necessarily rule out the desire to have children (Flemming 1999). However, in the light of the low birth rate amongst other women found at Herculaneum, we can see her 4 or 5 children as a result of a greater frequency of intercourse with a greater number of male partners. This skeleton of a prostitute may provide a standard by which to test the effectiveness of ancient contraceptive practice.

Degeneration of the body

The characteristic degenerative diseases of the body were found. Arthritis is present in 35 per cent of joints examined in Pompeii (Henneberg and Henneberg 2002: 175). A man aged 51, Erc62, from Herculaneum displays symptoms of acute arthritis of the knees, causing the cartilage to wear away and the bones literally to rub together (Bisel and Bisel 2002: 469–70). Three cases of Paget's disease were identified at Pompeii (Henneberg and Henneberg 2002: 178). Osteoporosis was found to be present amongst the skeletal remains from the House of Julius Polybius (Oriente et al. 2001); the mineral bone density for females was found to be the same as that of today, but that of the males from antiquity was higher than that of today. The authors of this report note that the fracture of a femur with osteoporosis results in death in 15–20 per cent of cases that are not treated with modern medical practice, a rate that tends to increase with age. This factor suggests that, although there is clear evidence of adequate bone setting after fractures, the ability for the body to recover would decline with age.

When considering dental health, the reports on the skeletons from Pompeii and Herculaneum produce rather different results. In the overall sample from Pompeii, deep caries penetrating to the pulp cavity with infection spreading into the root, with the consequent formation of abscesses, was not uncommon (25 per cent of all mouths with 1 or more abscesses). Added to this was the presence in 50 per cent of the individuals of periodontal disease (inflammation of gum and underlying bone). For Pompeii, this produces a picture of a complete lack of dental hygiene and frequent toothache, the only form of treatment being extraction of the occasional tooth (Henneberg and Henneberg 2002: 181–2).

In contrast, Bisel and Bisel (2002: 455) find at Herculaneum a rather more positive view of dental hygiene. Compared to the modern USA, the number of carious teeth and/or abscessed teeth is considerably lower (3.4 per mouth in Herculaneum, 15.7 per mouth for USA). This is accounted for by the absence of sugar in the diet in antiquity, but we should note the use of lead acetate syrup as a sweetening agent for wine (Pliny, *NH* 14.136; Columella, *RR* 12.19.1; Bisel and Bisel 2002: 459–60) that may have resulted in a higher lead concentration in the bones of adult male skeletons, who had greater access to wine. The individuals suffering from slight periodontal disease accounted for 60 per cent, 9 per cent having the acute form. The overall divergence in dental health may in part be accounted for by the fluoride content of water at Herculaneum being considerably higher than that drunk at Pompeii (Torino and Furnaciari 2001). The problem of the loss of teeth and dental decay increases with age, and hence so does the presence of the pain associated with toothache.

In terms of health and illness, it needs to be pointed out that there are dramatic differences between individuals according to their relative nutrition and wealth. We can compare Erc27 and Erc86, both males aged 46 (full details, Bisel and Bisel 2002: 460–1, 468–9). Erc27 is short – 163.5 cm – with spindly flattened bones; he had acute dental problems, having lost 7 teeth, and had 4 caries and 4 abscesses painful enough to cause him to chew only on one side of his mouth. Seven of his thoracic vertebrae were fused, and display osteoarthritis caused by Forestier's disease. His body had been exposed to years of hard labour and had been worked beyond its strength. In contrast, Erc86 stood nearly ten centimetres taller (172.4 cm) with thick and solid bones. His teeth were in good condition with only one abscess. The only odd feature of this man is that his right arm is ten centimetres longer than his left. His body as a whole displayed the physique of an athlete rather than that of a labourer. We might see this man as a healthy member of the leisured class. The contrast in terms of health and the experience of pain between two individuals of the same age could not be greater.

CARE FOR THE SICK

In Table 4.1, the presence of sickness in childhood was established with reference to the House of Julius Polybius. We need now to return to this house with view to understanding the presence of disease and the nature of health care within the Roman household. The house takes its name from that of Gaius Julius Polybius found in electoral graffiti on the façade; in the interior of the house were found painted graffiti referring to a Gaius Julius Philippus, perhaps the brother of Polybius. Julius Polybius stood for election to the magistracy of duumvir and hence is obviously a member of the Pompeian elite; from his name and from that of Julius Philippus, it is clear that they were descended from imperial freedmen (Franklin 2001: 142–8). The skeletal remains were found in two separate rooms at the rear of the house, adjoining the peristyle; the numbering of the skeletons reflects the original boxing up of these finds. Relationships based on Henneberg and Henneberg (1996, 2001) follow from the original notes and sketches made at the time of the excavation (Table 4.2).[1]

What we find in the house are three adult couples with a range of children associated with them, with no real knowledge of who is related to whom or of their status: *paterfamilias*, freeborn, slave and so on. To resolve these matters, ancient DNA (aDNA) was extracted from the skeletons with the hope of matching the genetic relationships across this houseful of persons (Cipollaro *et al.* 1999; Di Bernardo *et al.* 2001). This process has been reported on and demonstrates the value of the technique, but the amount of aDNA was small and the samples had been contaminated, presenting some

Table 4.2 Composition of the skeletal evidence from the House of Julius Polybius

Skeleton	Age	Height (cm)	Gender	Suggested relationship by Henneberg and Henneberg (1996, 2001)
1A	45–55	158–9	F	Partner of 1B
1B	60–70	162–3	M	Partner of 1A
2A	8–9	134	M?	—
2B	12–14	143	M	—
2C	+/−3	115	M?	—
3A	25–30	168–9	M	Partner of 3B
3B	16–18	142–5	F	Partner of 3A. Pregnant with foetus 3C
3C	Foetus	48.9–50.5	—	Mother = 3B
3D	10–12	142	?	—
3E	15–18	160	M?	—
4A	60–70	165–67	M	Partner of 5–6A?
5–6A	30–40	148–53	F	Partner of 4A
5–6B	12–14	152	F?	—

obstacles to greater precision. However, there is some distinction in terms of the room in which they sought refuge; Skeleton 1A was found holding hands with another adult/teenager and in the presence of a single child (Di Bernardo *et al.* 2001: figures 1–6, but note that the measurements of the skeletons on the original excavation sketches seem inaccurate). All the other skeletons were found in the other room. This division might be based on status divisions, but in the circumstances of the eruption, perhaps panic and terror provide a more likely explanation for a move to the shelter of these two rooms.

However, what is clear is that there were regular bouts of illness within this houseful in years immediately prior to the eruption of Vesuvius (Table 4.1).

A major question is: who cared for the sick? Whether the 3 adult couples represent 6 free individuals or 2 free persons and 4 slaves, it is clear that a number of adults would have been available for the nursing of children in trauma. Keith Bradley (1991) has demonstrated, from epigraphic evidence, a role for both men and women in child care generally. Similarly, inhabitants in the house would have cared for the sick. The property is not reported to have contained medical instruments as such (Bliquez 1994). However, the cure of the diseases suggested from the skeletal remains may not have been solved by surgery. The site of Pompeii has revealed 28 properties in which 'medical instruments' have been found. However, the coincidence between 'medical instruments' and those for leather working and other 'craft' activities reduces the number that were probable residences of doctors to four (Bliquez 1994: 81, 96). It is notable that the House of the Medicus Aulus Pomponius Magonimus (8.3.10–12) contained mortars and pestles as well as surgical and gynaecological instruments, and a bleeding cup.

The use of herbs in medicine is well attested in literary texts. The excavations of gardens in Pompeii have provided a remarkable range of these plants that would have been used for the treatment of disease and, in some cases, even prevention (Jashemski 1999). For example, the finding that wormwood (*Artemesia absinthium*) grew as a weed in antiquity (Jashemski 1999: 26) provides substance to the literary references for its use as a mosquito deterrent (Sallares 2002: 48). We might revise the idea of classifying it as a weed, and instead view it as a cultivated herb. The garden of the house of Julius Polybius was productive, containing five large trees and some smaller shrubs (Jashemski 1979: 25–30, 1993: 549–51, 2002: 19–20). Knowledge of medical uses of herbs and vegetables was shared by the elite, as is demonstrated by both Cato and Pliny the Elder, and was applied in the gardens of the houses of Pompeii. This has been graphically demonstrated by Ciarallo's (2002) analysis of a dolia containing the remains of a theriacal compound composed of 54 ingredients, many of which were poisonous and also included parts of reptiles, amphibians, birds and small mammals, as well as 47 plant species. Such theriaca mentioned in Pliny, as used by Mithridates Eupator (*NH* 20.264, 23.149, 25.6–7, 29.24), may have had a more wide-spread application. The combination of poisons and medicinal elements may have produced some relief, especially with the presence of opiates and cannabis. The household not only contained the sick, but also those who had knowledge of remedies that might cure them or do them harm.

ERUPTION AND HEALTH

The events of the 24 and 25 August AD 79 continue to represent one of the most violent volcanic eruptions ever known (Sigurdsson and Carey 2002). Material was thrown upwards from the volcano to a height of between 15 and 30 km, depending on the stage of the eruption. The most destructive forces, known as pyroclastic surges, occurred only when this column collapsed; the overall forces of the eruption are considered to have been 100,000 times that of the bomb that wiped out Hiroshima. The eruption alternated six times between a column and then a collapse, resulting in pyroclastic surges over a period of time from 12 noon on the 24 August at least until 7 a.m. on the following day; the first of these destroyed Herculaneum and the fourth and sixth engulfed Pompeii. Pumice material has been located from the eruption at a distance of 74 km south-east of the mountain. The effect on local agriculture was dramatic, as described by Martial (4.44) and by Statius (*Silv.* 4.4.78–86). Cassius Dio (66.21–4) also noted that airborne material fell at Rome, Africa, Syria and Egypt. The effect in the short term of such a quantity of material in the earth's atmosphere can quite literally block out the rays of the sun, resulting in a negative adjustment of annual global temperature by one or two degrees, affecting all aspects of agriculture and thus production and the economy across the entire Roman world (*contra* Horden and Purcell 2000: 305).

For those that left Pompeii or were, like Pliny the Younger, located at Misenum 30 km away, the dawn of 25 August did not happen (*Epistles* 6.20 and 6.16). The air was saturated with debris and the sun was blocked out, making it impossible to see. Moreover, the ash fall was considerable even near Misenum and caused Pliny to shake his clothes to disperse the build-up of material. Those attempting to flee to safety (the majority of the population of Herculaneum and Pompeii) would have been afflicted with serious breathing difficulties that would have been exacerbated in a population that already suffered from respiratory diseases (e.g. Pliny the Elder's 'experience', see Pliny the Younger, *Epistle* 6.16). The time of year was ripe for disease; in Italy right up to the recent past, August has been the period of the year in which more people die than any other (Scheidel 1996; B.D. Shaw 1996). Those escaping early on may have taken what are the typical goods of all refugees, cooking equipment and food (Cola 1996), further hindering their progress and perhaps explaining why a number of kitchens in Pompeii appear to be out of use (Allison 1992: 92–5 does not consider this factor in discussion of the use of kitchens). Many would not have made it to a safe distance away from the devastating pyroclastic surges whether by land or sea (to date their bodies have not been found). Those who did manage to escape would have experienced health problems similar to those associated with intensive pollution accentuating any respiratory problems.

THE DEMOGRAPHY OF THE ROMAN CITY

The skeletal evidence from Pompeii and Herculaneum provides an indication of the relative pathologies of the urban populations of Campania in the first century AD. The evidence presented via scientific study of the bones shows a difference between two neighbouring cities, in terms of the intensity of respiratory illness (perhaps increased by the presence of malaria at Pompeii) and differences in the fluoride content of the water. In viewing the health of urban populations, there has been a tendency to assume that the most hideous excesses of disease found in the rapidly expanding metropoleis of the nineteenth century would also be present in, for example, ancient Rome (Scobie 1986; Morley 1996). The basis for health and disease in Alex Scobie's (1986) masterful picture of disease at Rome are the literary sources plus cross-cultural extrapolation. While cross-cultural perspectives are very useful in the development of models, in this case the literary sources need to be regarded for what they are; literature of the city, often anecdotal, and written to create an image of dystopia compared to some rural ideal. Such images are easily made real again by historians in the twentieth century writing in a tradition that promoted the Garden Suburb or New Town over the city (Laurence 1997; for critique see Scheidel 2003). Often this process creates a homogenous model, in which all diseases ever known create a dystopia for the past compared to life in the cities of the developed world in the twenty-first century. The danger here is that we simply create a vision of health in the past, which is worse than our own today, rather than under-standing the variation or nature of health and disease in the past. As has been shown above, historians need to see that health could have varied in cities of a similar nature and of a similar size (as shown above for Herculaneum and Pompeii).

In a pioneering paper, Walter Scheidel (2002) showed that the effects of the epidemic often known as the Antonine plague, of AD 165, would have destabilized the population of Egypt and the Mediterranean as a whole. His data, based on Duncan Jones (1996), have been criticized by Bruun (2003; cf. Greenberg 2003), but his findings and theoretical position have considerable relevance to the discussion of the skeletal material from Pompeii and Herculaneum. He suggests (Scheidel 2001: 23–4) that the population of antiquity was far from stable and hence would not have conformed to models based on Coale–Demeny life tables that had formed the basis of previous demographic models (for discussion of these, see Parkin 1992; Saller 1994; Scheidel 2001). The Vesuvian material, unlike skeletal material from cemeteries, is not subject to the biases of burial practice and hence it should be possible to reconstruct the nature of the population at Herculaneum and Pompeii from the data given. In terms of its age structure, the skeletal sample from Herculaneum is not what was anticipated (Bisel and Bisel 2002: 451–4). There are fewer children than expected within the recovered 139 skeletons (39 in total); in a world with a high infant death rate, we would expect to see far more children than this for a stable population to be represented. The argument that the children left prior to the adults, and hence survived, is a weak one given the mixture of adults and children found here. The low birth rate identified (1.69 per female adult) also points to a population that is not reproducing itself. We might conclude from the evidence presented for Herculaneum that the population was undergoing an overall reduction in its numbers. The recovery of skeletons at Pompeii mostly took place in the nineteenth century and, as a result, infants might be significantly under-represented (Henneberg and Henneberg 2002: 171–4). However, in the light of the findings from Herculaneum utilizing techniques of archaeological recovery from the early 1980s, we should not necessarily over-emphasise this factor. Most individuals recovered at Pompeii were adults in the age range of 20–40. Male to female ratio was almost 1 : 1. No comment is made on fertility rates, since the study concerns skulls, hip-bones and mandibles. A number of older people are also identified. This data is combined with Coale–Demeny Life Tables to produce a Life Table that includes the under-represented children. However, the data derived from skeletal evidence can only really inform us of the ages 20–40, rather than a total demographic sample from which a Life Table can be built. Moreover, if we follow Scheidel (2001) and admit that populations in antiquity were inherently unstable, we open the material up to other interpretations. In short, there is no real indication from the evidence that the population, as seen here from the skeletal remains, was stable and reproducing itself – if anything, it represents a population in decline. Further research on the skeletal evidence might confirm this compelling hypothesis. The cause of such a situation might be identified as one or more of the following: the disruption caused by the earthquake in AD 62, only 17 years prior to the eruption of Vesuvius; the high incidence of traumatic disease within the population in the years leading up to AD 79 (see Table 4.1 column 5 given earlier) and the possibility of strategies to reduce reproductive rates.

NOTE

1 Ages in this table follow Henneberg and Henneberg 2001; those in Table 4.1 follow Torino and Furnaciari 2001.

5

HOLDING ON TO HEALTH?

Bone surgery and instrumentation in the Roman Empire

Ralph Jackson

Roman healers of the imperial period were an eclectic group ranging from court physicians to root-cutters and wise women (Nutton 1985, 1992, 1993; Scarborough 1993: 33–40; Flemming 2000). Some styled themselves *medicus* or *iatros* and regarded themselves as part of a medical 'profession' (*professio medici*, Scribonius Largus, *Compositiones*, prooemium; J.S. Hamilton 1986: 213–15), but such titles brought no guarantee of superior treatment.[1] There were no regular courses of medical teaching to be undertaken, no examinations to be passed, no qualifications to be gained, no controlling body and no general agreement on standards or required skills. In effect, there was no restraint on anyone who wished to set up himself (or herself) as a healer, and levels of ability evidently varied widely (Nutton 1993).

For those who sought training, travel to famous centres of medicine was restricted mainly to the wealthy, while book-learning, although highly valued by those such as Galen, required both money and literacy (*On Examining the Best Physicians* 9.3, 9.22; Cavallo 2002). The normal avenue for most prospective healers was probably that of apprentice or assistant to an established practitioner (e.g. Martial, *Epigrams* 5, 9; Jackson 1988: 58ff.). The scope of their healing would have been dictated, in large part, by the size of the community in which they lived and practised. In small towns and sparsely populated regions a healer, of necessity, probably dealt with most, if not all, health matters. But a peripatetic healer or a resident healer in a large town or city, whether a public doctor or a private practitioner, might have the opportunity to concentrate on or restrict himself to particular treatments, diseases or operations. Such specialisation could benefit the patient, either through a healer's long experience of particular diseases through his skill in performing specific, delicate or complex surgery. Certainly, in the greatest cities like Rome, Alexandria and Athens one could find 'specialists' in eye medicine, lithotomy, ear disorders, hernia, fever, rectal treatments, dietetics and hydrotherapy, amongst others (Galen, *On the Parts of Medicine* 2; Baader 1967; Korpela 1984). Elsewhere, in places the size of Pompeii, Rimini and Lyon, for example, the range would not have been so great, although even there, in addition to, or amongst, the 'general practitioners', there might be healers who specialised in surgery or in the most prevalent diseases and disorders – eye complaints, women's diseases and dentistry (Feugère *et al.* 1985; Boyer *et al.* 1990; Bliquez 1994, 1995; Jackson 1996, 2003; Künzl 1998).

In fact, the routine treatment of fractured, dislocated, diseased and injured bone is likely to have comprised a large part of the surgical work of many of those Roman healers who catered to the needs of 'the general public'. However, if diseased bone or flesh wounds went untreated or were unsuccessfully treated the ultimate and distressing consequence might easily be the development of gangrene. Despite the extreme danger of limb amputation the patient would then have had little alternative than to undergo the operation.[2] Fortunate, at least, would have been those operated upon by healers who knew and followed the procedure outlined in the *De medicina* (*On Medicine*) of Cornelius Celsus. For the author appreciated the need to eradicate all of the diseased flesh and bone, and in order to achieve this to cut a little into the sound tissue. Furthermore, he also understood the need to allow an exit for sanies after completion of surgery and closure of the wound, and the method that he advocated corresponded to that still practised at the time of the First World War. Celsus described the operative instrument as a small saw (*serrula; De med.* VII, 33, 2). None has yet been positively identified, but there is no reason to believe that the tool differed greatly, if at all, from the smaller range of bow saws or frame saws used by Roman carpenters. The small, fine-toothed iron saws found in sets of surgical instruments at Stanway, England and Rimini, Italy (Figure 5.1, no. 1) may have been used for amputation as well as for other bone surgery (Jackson 1994: 195, 1997a, 2003: 319; Künzl 1995).

Celsus' work is one of the few surviving classical medical texts to incorporate a section on the treatment of battle wounds, including a description of some of the instruments. For the removal of a missile wedged in a joint, extension by means of straps fastened to the adjacent bones might be sufficient. But when embedded in a bone a projectile could sometimes only be released by the use of a drill and chisel, implements to which we shall return later. More intriguing is the description of two specialised instruments for extracting arrowheads and spearheads. The instrument that Celsus calls the 'Scoop of Diocles' was specifically developed for the removal

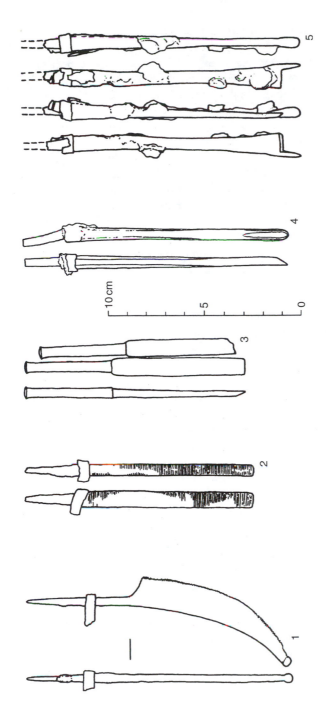

Figure 5.1 Some of the Roman instruments of bone surgery from the *Domus* 'del chirurgo' find at Rimini. 1. Saw-knife; 2. File; 3. Pair of small chisels; 4. Gouge; 5. Lenticular. All iron, except handles of 3 are copper alloy.

of a broad weapon by military surgeons. Celsus says:

> If a broad weapon has been embedded, it is not expedient to
> extract it from the other side lest a second large wound is added
> to one already large. It should therefore be pulled out by a certain
> type of instrument which the Greeks call the Dioclean
> *kyathiskos*... . The instrument consists of a thin piece of iron or
> even of bronze. At one extremity it has two hooks turned down-
> wards on both sides; at the other it is bent double at the sides and
> is slightly inclined at the end towards that part which is bent.
> Moreover, it also has a perforation there. The instrument is low-
> ered – into the wound – alongside the weapon, then, when the
> very bottom of its point has been reached, it is twisted a little so
> that it takes hold of the missile in its hole. When the point is in
> the cavity, two fingers placed under the hooks of the part draw out
> the instrument and missile simultaneously.
>
> (VII, 5, 3, trans. Longrigg 1998: 186–7)

Although his description is clear and detailed, no example of the instrument
has yet come to light (Jackson 1994: 188–9).[3]

The description of the second instrument is less comprehensive and is
complicated by a lacuna in the text:

> Nothing penetrates so easily into the body as an arrow, and it also
> becomes very deeply fixed... . Hence it is more often to be
> extracted through a counter-opening than through the wound of
> entry.... When a passage out has been laid open, the flesh ought
> to be stretched apart by an instrument like a Greek letter []; next
> when the point has come into view, if the shaft is still attached, it
> is to be pushed on until the point can be seized from the counter-
> opening and drawn out... by the fingers or by forceps... Nor is
> the method of extraction different when it is preferred to withdraw
> the arrow by the wound of entry.
>
> (VII, 5, 2, trans. Spencer 1938: 316–19)

Despite the loss of the Greek letter this description of the appearance of the
instrument together with the function ascribed to it, the stretching apart of
the edges of an entry wound or a counter-opening in order to permit the
removal of an embedded arrowhead, have allowed the tentative identification of the instrument as a bivalve dilator. The dilator, in its fully open position, certainly resembles the Greek letter upsilon (Y), and examples are known
from Pompeii (first century AD), Rome, Italy (first or second century AD),

Vechten, The Netherlands, Marcianopolis, Bulgaria (fifth century AD) and Sarmizegetusa/Micia, Romania (Jackson 1991).

The great majority of detailed references to bone surgery, however, are to operations on the skull, for Roman practitioners resolved or treated several diseases of the head by surgery, most dramatically by trepanation. Direct or indirect trauma, caused by accidental injuries or battle wounds, was a classic indication. Such trauma took many forms, from complex fracture, fissuring, perforation or crushing of the cranium to intracranial haemorrhage. Further applications included the removal of carious bone consequent on chronic ulceration of untreated or poorly treated flesh wounds, and the relief of symptoms of intracranial disease, notably hydrocephalus. Trepanation was also recommended as a therapeutic measure in the treatment of epilepsy, even though some medical writers censured the practice.[4] It may also have found an application in the treatment of paralysis, mental disease, or the attempt to relieve acute or chronic head pains. Such head pains, according to the Elder Pliny, were considered to be one of the three most painful diseases of mankind, which together,' he said, were 'about the only diseases that are responsible for suicides' (*NH* 25.23). There were, therefore, many indications for skull surgery, but the written sources suggest that trepanation was never undertaken lightly.

The various accounts of skull surgery in Greek and Roman medical texts demonstrate that a range of tools and instruments would be required to carry out the interventions described. Some of these were evidently, or likely, to be found in a healer's basic instrumentarium, being essential surgical tools; for example, scalpels, fine probes and cauteries.[5] Others, however, were more specialised and were adapted either generally to bone surgery or specifically to surgical interventions on the skull. The written descriptions of instruments are, fortunately, supplemented by examples of the instruments themselves. For, from the early first century AD, distinctive custom-made surgical tools were manufactured and used throughout the Roman world (Jackson 1990, 1997b; Künzl 1996). Furthermore, within the period from the first to the third centuries AD, deceased medical personnel in the Roman Empire were sometimes buried with their instruments or with some of them (Künzl 1983). These favourable circumstances have resulted in a better knowledge of the instrumentation of healers in the Roman Empire than in any other culture or period up to the European Renaissance. Nevertheless, the picture is very far from complete, and our understanding is limited by the differential survival of different types of instrument. Inevitably, those that remain are almost exclusively the more robust and stable metal instruments: of the wide variety of surgical tools and appliances made from organic materials mentioned, for example, in Celsus' *De medicina* virtually none has been preserved (Jackson 1994, 1997b).

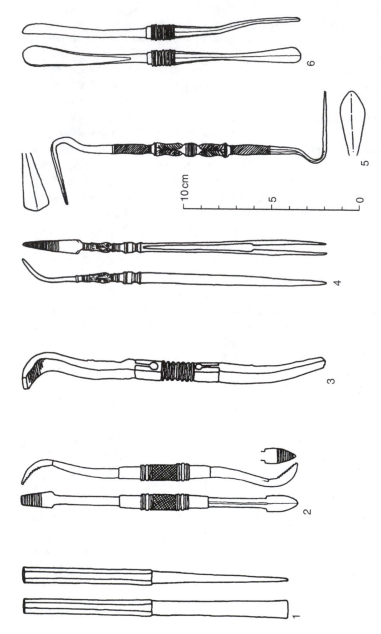

Figure 5.2 Roman instruments of bone surgery. 1. Bone chisel, Italy; 2, 3. Bone levers (elevators), Pompeii; Bingen; 4. Pointed-jawed forceps with elevator, Aschersleben; 5. Double blunt hook (? *meningophylax*), Italy; 6. Combined curette/elevator, London. All copper alloy, except blade of 1, levers of 3 and 6 are iron.

Even metal instruments are subject to differential survival, and those made of iron are much less likely to be preserved in a recognisable form than those of copper and its alloys.

Of course, in addition to problems of survival there are also problems of recognition. Some instruments are so clearly described in the ancient texts as to permit certain identification of examples in the archaeological record. Some others are so similar to their modern or late pre-modern counterparts as also to allow confident identification. Others pose a greater challenge. Thus, there are instruments named in the texts which cannot be equated with surviving artefacts. Conversely, in sets of Roman medical instruments there are often objects whose function is not obvious and which cannot easily be identified with any textual description. In fact, instruments for bone surgery are the commonest identifiable 'specialist' component in the largest apparently complete Roman instrumentaria (Jackson 1995), and examples of all the following categories have been either positively or tentatively identified: crown trepan (*modiolus*), trepanning bow, saw, bone chisel, gouge, lenticular, rasp, file, curette, bone lever, sequestrum forceps, spring forceps and *meningophylax* (Figures 5.1–5.5 and 5.8).

Drawing heavily on Greek sources, notably several Hippocratic treatises such as *On Wounds in the Head, On Surgery, On Fractures*, and *On Joints*, as well as on works by Alexandrian, post-Alexandrian and Roman surgeons, Cornelius Celsus wrote his *De medicina* early in the first century AD. In Book VIII he gave a clear and detailed account of the techniques and tools of skull surgery. Many of the proposed interventions were effectively carpentry of the cranium, and his terminology reflects this: cutting, sawing, drilling, gouging, scraping, rasping, filing, levering and so on. The potentially lethal consequences of a technique that was less than excellent were keenly appreciated, and surgery generally took place only after alternative treatments had been tried.

Sometimes it was the lack of success in treating scalp lesions that resulted in the need for surgery, as, for example, in the case of diseased cranial bone consequent on severe and chronic ulceration (*De med.* VIII, 2, 1–3). Celsus' method was to cut out the ulcer, expose the full extent of the diseased bone and either cauterise it or scrape it away with a scalpel until sound white bone was reached. The scalpel was probably the normal Roman type, combining a copper-alloy handle and leaf-shaped blunt dissector with an iron blade, most commonly of convex bellied form (Jackson 1994: figure 1, nos. 1–2). Few cauteries have been identified in surviving assemblages of Roman surgical instruments, and it seems likely that cauterisation was often achieved through heating the ends of other surgical tools, notably probes (Jackson 1994: 177–9).

If the bone was more seriously diseased or carious, it might require removal to a greater depth of a more substantial quantity of necrotic tissue. In that case, a gouge or curette might be used. A first- or second-century AD dual-purpose iron instrument from London, combines a curette with an elevator (Figure 5.2, no. 6), but all other known examples of the curette are of copper alloy, with a sharp, semi-sharp or toothed rim (Jackson forthcoming a). Those in the instrumentaria from Bingen in Germany (Künzl 1983: 82, figure 56, 14), Colophon in Turkey (Caton 1914: 117, plate IX, 24), and Italy (Jackson 1986: 121–3, figure 1, 6), which date to the same period as the London instrument, were all associated with other instruments of bone surgery. To gauge the depth of penetration of the caries, a fine probe or a drill was recommended, and cauterisation through the drilled holes might follow (*De med.* VIII, 2, 4–5). Generally, however, caries of the skull would have required excision, for which Celsus recommended three types of drill, all operated with a bow and cord or a strap (VIII, 3, 2; Heliodorus in Oribasius, *Medical Collections* XLVI, 11). If the diseased bone was confined to the skull's outer table then use of either a *modiolus* or a *terebra* was appropriate. The *terebra* was a solid-tipped drill of the type used commonly by artisans, but the *modiolus* was a specialised surgical instrument, a crown trepan, the appearance and operation of which Celsus describes in one of the clearest such passages from antiquity. Celsus says:

> The modiolus is a hollow cylindrical iron instrument with its lower edges serrated; In the middle of which is fixed a pin which is itself surrounded by an inner disc.... When the disease is so limited that the modiolus can include it, this is more serviceable; and if the bone is carious, the central pin is inserted into the hole; if there is black bone, a small pit is made with the angle of a chisel for the reception of the pin, so that, the pin being fixed, the modiolus when rotated cannot slip; it is then rotated like a trepan by means of a strap. The pressure must be such that it both bores and rotates; for if pressed lightly it makes little advance, if heavily it does not rotate. It is a good plan to drop in a little rose oil or milk, so that it may rotate more smoothly; but if too much is used the keenness of the instrument is blunted. When a way has been cut by the modiolus, the central pin is taken out, and the modiolus worked by itself; then, when the bone dust shows that underlying bone is sound, the modiolus is laid aside.
>
> (*De med.* VIII, 3, 1–3, trans. W.G. Spencer, 1938)

Just one Roman crown trepanning kit is so far known (Figure 5.3, no. 1; Figure 5.4), that in the famous instrumentarium found in a cremation burial at Bingen, Germany, and dated to the late first–early second century AD (Como 1925; Künzl 1983: 80–5). This instrumentarium, one of the largest yet found, with over 40 instruments, includes several tools of bone surgery.

Figure 5.3 Trepanning kit and folding handles. 1. Bingen, Germany (Photo: Römisch-germanisches Zentralmuseum, Mainz); 2. Unprovenanced (Photo: British Museum); 3. Unprovenanced (Photo: Antikenmuseum Berlin, Staatliche Museen Preussischer Kulturbesitz). Folded length of handles: 1. 19 cm; 2. 20.8 cm; 3. 21.3 cm.

The trepanning kit consists of a folding bow handle and two cylindrical drills (*modioli*), all of copper alloy. The handle has perforations to secure the cord that rotated the drills. The drills, which now lack their wooden stock and head, are tubular, with a toothed cutting edge. They differ slightly in length and diameter, and the teeth vary in number and thickness.

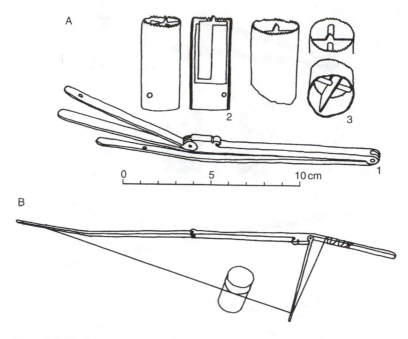

Figure 5.4 The Bingen trepanning kit. A, showing folded handle (1) and construction details of the two *modioli* (2, 3). B, showing the trepan in operation (NB wooden drill-stock not restored). (After Como and Kessler.)

Since the backwards and forwards movement of the bow provided a clockwise/anti-clockwise rotation of the drill, the teeth are symmetrical so that they could cut in both directions. Corresponding to Celsus' description, the drills are provided with a centre-point mounted on a retractable cross-plate.

Six other folding copper-alloy trepanning bow handles have been recorded, one each, of unknown provenance, in the British Museum (Figure 5.3, no. 2) and the Berlin Antikenmuseum (Figure 5.3, no. 3), two from the *domus* 'del chirurgo' find at Rimini (third century AD; Ortalli 2000: 192a; Jackson 2003: 316–17, figure 2) (Figure 5.5), and one each from the instrument finds at Colophon (first or second century AD; Caton 1914: 116–17) and Marcianopolis (early fifth century AD; Minchev 1983; Kirova 2002). The two unprovenanced examples and one of those from Rimini have a stylised snake-head finial, probably to imbue the instrument and its user with the healing powers of Aesculapius.[6] Although Celsus' use of the phrase *modiolus ferramentum* suggests that the crown trepan was an iron instrument, the only

Figure 5.5 One of the fused clusters of instruments from the *Domus* 'del chirurgo' at
Rimini. Most clearly visible are a bone forceps, two folding handles for
bow drills (trepans), and a lithotomy scoop. (Photo: Ralph Jackson.)

recognised certain surviving examples to date, those from Bingen, are of
copper alloy.

Similarly, rare are surviving identifiable examples of crown-trepanned
skulls, partly, no doubt, because of burial practice: cremation was the
Romanus mos from the fourth century BC to the second century AD
(Tacitus, *Annals* XVI, 6; Toynbee 1971: 40), thus erasing most evidence of
pathology and therapy for much of the periods of the republic and empire.
In fact, some of the best evidence for the use of the crown trepan comes not
from the Roman empire or republic but from beyond the frontier, from the
Celtic sites of Katzelsdorf, Guntramsdorf and Dürrnberg/Hallein, Austria
(Urban *et al.* 1985; Breitwieser 2003).[7] The skulls of 3 third – second
century BC inhumations at Guntramsdorf (Graves 5, 6 and 29) and 1 at
Katzelsdorf (Grave 1) yielded a total of 9 circular drilled trepanations
measuring between 17 mm and 20 mm in diameter (compare the Bingen
modioli with diameters of *c.*24 mm and *c.*25 mm). In one case (Katzelsdorf)
an incomplete triple trepanation also preserved the impression of a centre-point.
The earliest evidence for the use of a crown trepan comes from the Dürrnberg,

where the skull of a male inhumation of the first half of the fourth century BC revealed a six-fold trepanation (Breitwieser 2003: 149–50, figure 2). The majority of Celtic trepanations were performed by cutting or scraping, and it is generally assumed (though unproven) that the crown trepan was a Greek or Hellenistic introduction. Certainly, a trepan is mentioned in one of the Hippocratic treatises (*On Wounds in the Head* 21), and, although a proper description is lacking, the reference to examining 'the circular track of the saw' confirms that the instrument was a crown trepan. Of the 7 patients with drilled trepanations at Guntramsdorf and Katzelsdorf, 2 appear to have undergone surgery following cranial injury. Four seem to have survived their operations but, as the survival rate for cutting and scraping trepanations was significantly higher, it may be that, like Galen several centuries later (see in the following paragraphs), Celtic practitioners rejected the crown trepan in favour of safer traditional techniques (Künzl 1995: 222–3; Breitwieser 2003: 149).

Where the carious bone was too extensive to be enclosed by the *modiolus*, Celsus recommended the *terebra*, with which the diseased area was encircled by a series of drilled holes located at the margin of diseased and sound bone. A mallet and chisel were then used to divide the intervening 'bridges' and detach the diseased bone. The chisel was also used to smooth down the edges of the trepanation and the surface of the inner table, if that was not to be removed (*De med.* VIII, 3, 3–6).[8]

Celsus reserved the third type of drill for the removal of deeper carious bone, in the case of the skull for those occasions on which the disease had penetrated both the outer and inner tables. Also called *terebra*, it, too, was a solid-tipped drill, but one with an expansion above the tip in order to provide a more precise control over the depth of penetration. Further descriptions of the instrument are given by Galen in the second century and Paul of Aegina in the seventh century. Galen remarked that 'in order to make less chance of error they have invented drills called *abaptista*, which have a circular border a little above the sharp point of the drill' (Paul of Aegina 6.90; Galen, *On the Method of Medicine* 10.445 K; Milne 1907: 129). No definite example of either type of these bow drills with solid tip has yet been found. The reason is not hard to understand. The drill-bit itself would have been a small, slender iron object in a wooden stock, easily destroyed or altered by corrosion, while the bow was probably of the type used by many Roman artisans, a simple, highly effective, but perishable bow of springy wood and cord (see Figure 5.6). Even more perishable would have been the tiny drill advocated by Archigenes of Apamea (*fl* AD 98–117) for perforating the nasal bone in cases of fistula lachrymalis (Galen, *De compositione medicamentorum secundum locos* 5.2, 12.821 K; Paul of Aegina 6.22). It is possible that one of the poorly preserved iron implements in the Bingen

Figure 5.6 Detail of the tomb relief of the freedmen Philonicus and Demetrius, from Frascati, Italy. Amongst the carpentry tools depicted to the right of Demetrius is an artisan's bow drill. It consists of a loosely strung wooden bow and a spear-shaped iron drill-bit held in a bipartite wooden stock. (Photo: British Museum, Neg. no. XXII, D (42).)

instrumentarium is a *terebra* drill-bit (Künzl 1983: figure 58, no. 9).[9] Certainly, the Bingen find includes an iron gouge and 3 iron chisels in addition to the more distinctively surgical tools – the trepanning kit, a curette, 4 bone levers and a rasp – but, even with their secure medical association, these iron tools can be interpreted in various ways. They might be purpose-made tools of bone surgery, or perhaps carpentry tools acquired by the healer for use in bone surgery, or even carpentry tools used as such to make splints, traction equipment, walking aids and the like.

For skull surgery the instrument most frequently referred to by Celsus is called *scalper* or *scalper excissorius*. From its various recommended applications, this was evidently not 1 but 2 instruments, a chisel and a gouge. In addition to cutting and dividing cranial bone the chisel was used to smooth sharp projections and excise fragments of fractured bones, to reveal fracture fissures, to cut the small pit needed to locate the centre-pin of the *modiolus*, and to smooth the margin of trepanations (*De med.* VIII, 3, 2; 4, 6; 4, 12; 4, 14–16; 10, 7F.). But the chisel had further applications in post-cranial surgery, whether for the division of bone in complex fracture or in distorted union (Paul of Aegina 6.109). For the removal of digits or the division of a rib two chisels were used in opposition (Galen, *On Anatomical Procedures* 8.7, 2.687 K; Paul of Aegina 6.43, 6.93). The *planus scalper* used to level the elevated section of a depressed cranial fracture probably had a flatter and wider cutting edge than the normal chisel. Wide-bladed chisels are known in the instrumentaria from Bingen (first to second century AD; Künzl 1983: figure 58, no. 15) and from Nijmegen, the Netherlands (third century AD; Leemans 1842: plate II, no. 27), while the normal form of *scalper* is probably that seen in instrumentaria from Italy (first to second century AD; Jackson 1986: 124–5, figure 2, nos. 17–18) (Figure 5.2, no. 1), Xanten, Germany (third century AD; Künzl 1986: 494, figure 3), Kallion, Greece (third century AD; Künzl 1983: 40, 42, figure 11, 4), and, in some numbers, from Pompeii (first century AD; Bliquez 1994: 132–3, nos. 94–102). These chisels have a slender iron blade tanged into a copper-alloy handle with a flat or low-domed head. Where identifiable, the blade usually corresponds either to that of a carpenter's general-purpose firmer chisel, which tapers evenly on both faces down to a lightly splayed cutting edge, or to that of a mortise chisel which is bevelled on one side of the cutting edge. The potential full extent of a surgeon's set of bone chisels has recently been revealed in the extraordinary third-century AD find from the Rimini *domus* 'del chirurgo' (Ortalli 2000, 2003; Jackson 2002, 2003). Of over one hundred and fifty surgical instruments more than forty are tools of bone surgery, of which at least ten are chisels. These range from tiny, narrow-bladed instruments to broad, heavy tools and wide, flat-bladed examples. There are two matching pairs (Figure 5.1, no. 3), as also in the finds from Italy and Xanten, recalling Galen's description of the use of a pair of chisels as osteotomes (Galen, *On Anatomical Procedures* 8.7, 2.687 K).

For the manipulation of fractured bones, powerful levers were required, and examples are known both in copper alloy, from Pompeii (first century AD; Bliquez 1994: 131, nos. 91–2) (Figure 5.2, no. 2), Colophon (first to second century AD; Caton 1914: 115, plate X, 15), Wehringen, Germany (third century AD; Künzl 1983: 120–1, figure 96, 1) and Kalkriese, Germany (first century AD; Franzius 1992: 371–3, figure 14, 1, figure 15, 1), and in iron, from Luzzi (first century AD; Guzzo 1974: 472–3, figure 32, no. 99), Xanten (third century AD; Künzl 1986: 493, figure 2, no. 3) and Rimini (third century AD; unpublished). Often, too, they are composite tools consisting of a copper-alloy centre grip with an iron lever mounted at each end, from Pompeii (Bliquez 1994: 131, no. 93, 206, no. A19), Bingen (first to second century AD; Künzl 1983: figure 56, 10–13, 18) (Figure 5.2, no. 3), Nea Paphos, Cyprus (second to third century AD; Michaelides 1984: 317–18, 326–7, figure 1, 21–2), Aschersleben, Germany (second to third century AD; Künzl 1983: 100–1, figure 80, 4–5) and Rimini (unpublished). Frequently, the inner concave face of the lever has a ridged surface to ensure a more secure hold. While some of these may have been used for the elevation of cranial bone they were not exclusive to cranial surgery. The larger examples were doubtless primarily used in the reduction of fractured long bones, for which a range of graded sizes was recommended, while some, at least, may have been used in place of forceps to extract teeth (Hippocrates, *On Fractures* 31; Galen, *Commentary on Joints* 18.593 K; Paul of Aegina 6.106). Curiously, Celsus makes no specific reference to bone levers. Instead, on the one occasion in the *De medicina* where the levering of bone is described, the elevation of depressed skull fragments, Celsus advised use of an instrument called *meningophylax* (*De med.* VIII, 3, 8–9; VIII, 4, 17; Paul of Aegina 6.90).

Precision was critical when the cerebral membranes were to be exposed during the removal of diseased or fractured bone, so it is hardly surprising that a specialised instrument was recommended. Celsus calls it 'a guard of the membrane (*membranae custos*) which the Greeks call *meningophylax*'. He continues:

> This consists of a plate of bronze, its end slightly concave, smooth on the outer side; this is so inserted that the smooth side is next the brain, and is gradually pushed in under the parts where the bone is being cut through by the chisel; and if it is knocked by the corner of the chisel it stops the chisel going further in; and so the surgeon goes on striking the chisel with the mallet more boldly and more safely, until the bone, having been divided all round, is lifted by the same plate, and can be removed without any injury to the brain.
>
> (*De med.* VIII, 3, 8–9, trans. Spencer 1938: 500–3)

The use of 3 instruments, simultaneously, demonstrates that at least 2 medical personnel were involved in this operation, 1, perhaps the assistant or apprentice, manoeuvring the *meningophylax*, while the other divided the bone with mallet and chisel.

The *meningophylax* was primarily a protector and treatment platform, not only in skull operations but wherever vital parts lay beneath the bone to be excised. Paul of Aegina, for example, describes its use in conjunction with a chisel when dividing a fractured clavicle (Paul of Aegina 6.77; 6.93). It would appear to have been a copper-alloy instrument with a plate-like terminal, which was sufficiently narrow, flat and smooth to insert easily and safely between the cranium and the dura mater as soon as a large enough hole had been made. The plate needed a very lightly convex outer face, so as not to injure the membrane, and a flat inner face upon which the cranial bone could be resected. A distinctive type of instrument which fits this description has been found with other tools of bone surgery in several Roman instrumentaria and may be the tool Celsus had in mind. There are single examples from Italy (first to second century AD; Jackson 1986: 124–5, figure 2, 16) (Figure 5.2, no. 5), Bingen (first to second century AD; Künzl 1983: 82, figure 56, 17) and Nea Paphos (second to third century AD; Michaelides 1984: 317–18, 327, figure 1, 20) and two from Rimini (third century AD; unpublished).[10] Each is a robust Z-shaped double-ended blunt hook made of copper alloy. Like so many Roman surgical instruments they probably served several different roles, both in orthopaedics and in other surgical interventions.

So far we have considered cranial disease, but often skull surgery was necessitated by a wound or injury. The first priority after a violent blow to the head was to establish whether or not a fracture had occurred. Celsus, like surgeons today, underlined the importance of securing an accurate, detailed history of patients with head injury (*De med.* VIII, 4, 1–2; Toledo-Pereyra 1973: 367). Questioning the patient, or a witness, to check for post-traumatic symptoms, and to discover the cause of injury or type of weapon and the force of impact, might reveal useful information, but the best plan was to make certain by exploration. Sounding with a fine probe was the initial response, and from all the written evidence it is clear that the tactile sense of some practitioners was extremely highly developed.[11] But, because of the possibility of confusing a fracture with a natural suture it was considered best, in cases of doubt, to open up the wound. As Celsus said, 'Even if it be uselessly incised, the scalp heals without much trouble. A fractured bone unless it is treated causes severe inflammations, and is treated afterwards with greater difficulty' (*De med.* VIII, 4, 7; Spencer 1938: 506–9).

The patient's head was shaved and the scalp cut back, a sponge squeezed out of vinegar being used when necessary to stop haemorrhage. Particular care was to be taken to ensure that the fine membrane covering the skull was incised and retracted with the scalp, for complications were anticipated if it was later lacerated by the chisel or trepan (VIII, 4, 8). At this point it might become clear to the surgeon that the injury, whilst having inflicted

Figure 5.7 The Celsian version of the Hippocratic technique for disclosing a hairline fracture of the skull and distinguishing it from a natural suture. 1. Retract scalp and membrane, apply inky paste; 2. Scrape paste away with chisel. (Drawing: Karen Hughes, after Majno.)

an indentation or roughening of the cranium, had not caused a fracture. It would then be sufficient to scrape and smooth the lesion with a scalpel, chisel or rasp before applying dressings and medicaments. However, if a fracture was still suspected but was not visible, or if there was uncertainty as to whether it was a fracture or a natural suture, the Roman healer could use a Hippocratic technique to reveal it (Figure 5.7). A black inky paste was smeared onto the bared skull, was covered by a plaster and bandaged. After twenty-four hours the paste was scraped off to reveal any cracks which, having been stained black were readily distinguished from natural sutures (VIII, 4, 6; Hippocrates, *On Wounds in the Head* 14).

Even if no fracture was located there might still be reason to consider performing craniotomy if sub-dural or extra-dural haematoma was suspected, as seems to have been the case with a trepanned skull of the third century BC from a necropolis at Contrada Santo Stefano, Gravina (Saponetti *et al.* 1998). Certainly, Celsus warned of the danger of intracranial haemorrhage without fracture (VIII, 4, 7). Conversely, where a fracture was identified, trepanning was not considered inevitable, and Celsus advised an initial treatment with plasters and medicated dressings (VIII, 4, 10–12). If the major sub-cranial blood vessels were avoided (Hippocrates, *On Wounds in the Head* 13), skull operations presented less risk than surgery on many other parts of the body, but infection was a constant danger. Trepanation was therefore regarded very much as a last resort, and Celsus advised extreme caution in the removal of cranial bone. In particular he drew attention to the life-threatening consequences of damage to the dura mater (VIII, 3, 7–8).

Whether the fracture was a split bone or a depressed fracture it was important to cut away the edge of overlying bone with a flat chisel and to remove all readily accessible detached fragments and sharp splinters using a forceps or fingers. The sequestrum forceps recommended for the removal of detached or partially detached cranial fragments was evidently capable of many other functions, including the clamping of blood vessels and the removal of arrowheads or slingshot. It was a stout iron or copper-alloy cross-legged instrument, sometimes interchangeable, it would seem, with the iron dental forceps (Paul of Aegina 6.88; Soranus, *Gynaecology* IV, 63), and two principal varieties have been identified. One has straight, the other curving jaws, in both cases with elongated close-fitting gripping faces, usually with accurately cut ridging to ensure the firmest possible grip. Examples of the copper-alloy curved-jawed type include those found at Pompeii (first century AD) (Figure 5.8, no. 1), Luzzi (first century AD) and Rimini (third century AD), while the straight-jawed variety is known in copper-alloy from Colophon (first to second century AD) (Figure 5.8, no. 2), Rimini (Figure 5.5), Potaissa/Turda, Romania, and in iron from Luzzi and Carnuntum, Hungary (Künzl and Weber 1991). A particularly ingenious example from Rome combines both jaw types in one instrument by means of a loose-hinge assembly (Figure 5.8, no. 3; Jackson forthcoming b).

For retrieving the tiniest detached cranial fragments and splinters a finer forceps would sometimes have been advantageous, notably the spring type forceps with pointed jaws, which resembles the modern anatomical forceps.

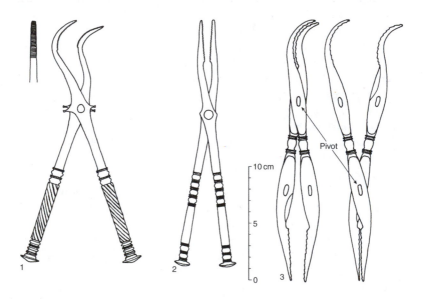

Figure 5.8 Roman instruments of bone surgery. Bone (sequestrum) forceps. 1. Pompeii; 2. Colophon; 3. Rome. All copper alloy.

An example in the extensive third century AD instrument find from Paris (Sorel 1984: 231, figure 133c, top right), and another (Figure 5.2, no. 4) in the second – third century AD surgical kit from Aschersleben (Künzl 1983: 100–1, figure 80, 2), both found with other instruments of bone surgery, were combined with a small elevator whose finely ridged face would have been well-suited to the elevation of cranial fragments. Additional examples of this type come from Gauting, Germany, from Lancaster, England and from Asia Minor, and illustrate the uniformity of surgical instrumentation throughout the Roman Empire.

To return to our patient with a fractured skull: as well as removing bone splinters it was also necessary to resect the sharp ends of inward-projecting pointed fragments over the plate of the *meningophylax*, and to elevate any depressed bone with the same instrument (*De med.* VIII, 4, 13–17; Heliodorus in Oribasius, *Medical Collections* XLVI, 11, 16–17). If the fractured edges had become interlocked an opening had to be made with drill and chisel to allow an exit for any harmful matter. Celsus advised loss of as little bone as possible, and the inner table was to be removed only in those cases where it was unavoidable. Both Celsus (*De med.* VIII, 3, 9–10; 4, 17–18) and the Hippocratic author of *On Wounds in the Head* 21 appreciated the dangers of exposing the brain and the dura mater, either at the time of operating or subsequently, when they were very vulnerable both to physical injury and to infection, either of which would easily lead to death. After the operation, any bone dust sticking to the dura was to be removed, and strong vinegar was sprinkled on to check haemorrhage and disperse blood clots. Then a plaster softened with rose oil cerate was applied to promote new bone growth and was covered with dressings of ointment on lint and un-scoured wool. There followed a detailed account of wound dressing, medication, regimen and precautions for the convalescent patient, and the account finished with a listing of the good and bad signs indicating recovery or death (VIII, 4, 18–22).

Galen also described the post-operative treatment and care of those who had undergone trepanation, questioning the merits of different kinds of plaster. Most doctors of his day, he said, applied gentle, soothing medications, but Galen drew attention to a powerful desiccating plaster called 'Isis', which a venerable old doctor named Eudemus applied directly to the exposed cerebral membrane. Galen had not used it himself and so was cautious, but he noted that Eudemus' patients recovered more often than those of other doctors. He thought he might have tried Eudemus' plaster one day had he not moved to Rome where, as was the custom, he said, he 'left to those who are called surgeons most operations of this kind' (i.e. cranial trepanation; Galen, *On the Method of Medicine* 6.6 (10.454 K); Moraux 1985).

Another indication for cranial surgery was hydrocephalus, although treatment was not always attempted. In a mid-second century AD pseudo-Galenic treatise, four kinds of hydrocephalus were identified:

> one between the brain and the meninges, one between the membranes and the bone, one between the bone and the pericranium, and one between the bone and the skin.... Hydrocephalus under the skin and pericranium we empty by two or three incisions. Those beneath the bone we chisel out. Those between the meninges and the brain do not admit treatment.
>
> (ps.-Galen, *Introduction or the Doctor* 19 (14.783–4 K),
> trans. L.H. Toledo-Pereyra 1973: 368)

In the few distinctive cases of hydrocephalus recognised in the palaeopathological record it has rarely been possible to identify a specific cause because the characteristic changes are in the soft tissues that seldom survive (Roberts and Manchester 1995: 41–3). Now, however, there is an intriguing exception, the early second century AD burial of a young child in the small cemetery of a *villa rustica* at Fidenae, near Rome. Excellent preservation of the skull has revealed not only a large grooved trepanation on the right fronto-parietal (54 × 48 mm), but also pathological traces, which have permitted a probable specific diagnosis (Mariani-Costantini *et al.* 2000). Despite the seemingly low economic status of the Fidenae community, the cranial and post-cranial skeleton provides evidence of prolonged and quite intensive care of the child in the years before the trepanation. The operation, whether performed by a local healer or a surgeon from Rome, seems to have been done as a last resort, which, in any case, was destined only to relieve the symptoms temporarily, and the child died soon after.

For surgery of the skull, Galen preferred gouge and lenticular to drill or trepan. Thus, for cranial trepanation he advocated use of a narrow-bladed gouge to cut a route for the lenticular, and this appears to have been the technique employed in the case of the child from Fidenae which, in place and time, was close to Galen (*On the Method of Medicine* 6.6, 10.445 K; Jackson 2002, 2003: 319). Until recently neither the narrow-bladed gouge nor the lenticular had been identified in any medical find of the Roman period. However, analysis of the instrumentation in the Rimini *domus* 'del chirurgo' assemblage has revealed examples of both instruments (Jackson 2003: 315–19, figure 1, nos. 5–6). Of 3 iron gouges, 1 (Figure 5.1, no. 4) is a fine narrow-bladed example with rounded V-shaped tip, of a gauge virtually identical to the grooving on the Fidenae skull, and we may be sure that it is an example of the 'hollow chisel' so much appreciated by Galen.

Even more significant are four examples of a new type of instrument that may be identified as lenticulars. They are iron chisels with a narrow cutting edge, at one end of which is a blunt projection, lightly convex on its outer face (Figure 5.1, no. 5). They correspond closely to Galen's description of the appearance and function of the lenticular (*On the Method of Medicine* 6.6, 10.445 K). The texts reveal that the instrument was close to its pre-modern counterpart, having a vertical blade with the cutting edge on the leading side and, critically, a solid projecting guard, and the Rimini instruments are close analogues to examples of the later nineteenth century (e.g. Windler 1912: 4–5, no. 80, 514–15, no. 16593). According to Paul of Aegina, who repeated Galen's description:

> The method of operating with a sort of incisor called lenticular is greatly praised by Galen, being performed without drilling after the part has been grooved all round with gouges. If you have once exposed the place, then applying the chisel, which has at its point a blunt, smooth, lentil-shaped knob, but which longitudinally is sharp, when you apply the flat part of the lenticular to the meninges divide the cranium by striking with the small hammer. For we have all that we require in such an operation, for the membrane, even if the operator were half asleep, could not be wounded, being in contact only with the flat part of the lenticular, and if it be adherent anywhere to the calvarium the flat part of the lenticular removes its adhesion without trouble. And behind it follows the incisor or lenticular itself, dividing the skull, so that it is impossible to discover another method of operating more free from danger or more expeditious.
>
> (Paul of Aegina 6.90, trans. Milne 1907: 124–5)

Working from a fractured edge, a gouged groove or a drilled perforation the surgeon divided the cranium by striking the handle of the lenticular with a small mallet. Simultaneously the smooth, blunt projection guarded the brain and safely separated the dura from the cranium. The four Rimini examples all differ slightly in the width of the blade and in the size and shape of the projecting guard, and, like the rest of the assemblage, they give the impression that the Rimini healer was equipped with a very full range of surgical tools, above all those for bone surgery. Of all the tools of bone surgery, virtually the only one lacking from the Rimini find is the *modiolus*, and it is very likely that its absence is significant. A medical writer of the mid-second century AD noted that:

> All kinds of fractures of the skull are treated by chiselling out the fractured parts, cutting clear round the fracture with the chisel (gouge). The ancients used to cut them out with circular trepans which they rotated, later head augurs were employed, which gave starting points for the chisels. For the moderns the chisels (gouges) alluded to above suffice.
>
> (ps.-Galen *Introduction or the Doctor* 19 (14.782–4 K),
> trans. L.H. Toledo-Pereyra 1973: 368)

There may, therefore, have been a move away from use of the crown trepan, and even the drill, in skull operations, and this might help to explain the rarity of *modioli* in the archaeological record. Certainly, the clearest evidence, Celsus' vivid account and the Bingen *modioli*, dates within the first – early second century AD, while the absence of a *modiolus* from the very extensive Rimini instrumentarium surely suggests it had become obsolete by the mid-third century, if not before. Indeed, it is quite possible that the authority of Galen contributed to its demise. The presence of folding trepanning handles in the third-century Rimini assemblage and the early fifth-century Marcianopolis instrumentarium are not problematic, because they could have been used to operate the solid-tipped type of drill in bone surgery on other parts of the body.

To conclude, it is a truism that in early medicine, despite the best efforts of the best surgical practitioners, post-operative infection, largely beyond the healer's control, might easily reverse an otherwise successful operation: 'the operation was a success, but the patient died'. That was as true in Roman times as in other periods. Yet there was some reason for optimism in bone surgery of the Roman Imperial era. The generally excellent operative techniques described in the medical texts had their counterpart in the finely designed and exquisitely crafted surgical tools. If the practitioners of bone surgery had read the relevant texts, if they had access to the sort of instrumentation found in the Rimini *domus* 'del chirurgo', if their operative skills were the best, if the patient was strong and otherwise in good health, and if nature, good fortune and the gods were on their side, the patient had as good a chance of recovery as at any other period up to recent times. But that is still a lot of 'ifs'.

ACKNOWLEDGEMENTS

Versions of parts of this chapter were presented at the Pybus Society of Newcastle University, at the University of Rome 'La Sapienza', at the

International Colloquium on Cranial Trepanation held at Birmingham University, and at the University of Pisa as one of a series of *conferenze* on Graeco-Roman medicine. I am extremely grateful to participants on those occasions for their comments, suggestions and stimulating discussion; to Dr Jacopo Ortalli for his constant and generous support on the Rimini *Domus* 'del chirurgo' project; to Professor Renato Mariani-Costantini and Professor Luciana Rita Angeletti for discussing the Fidenae trepanned skull with me in Rome in March 1999 and for permitting and organising the making of a mould of the trepanation groove; to my Museum colleague Steven Crummy for his valued assistance with the illustrations; as ever, to Ernst Künzl and Larry Bliquez; and, above all, to Helen King for bringing this volume to fruition.

NOTES

1 For guilds (*collegia*) of healers, see for example, Nutton 1995b: 5–7.
2 On the evidence for artificial limbs in antiquity see Bliquez 1996.
3 For the true nature of the celebrated but bogus 'Dioclean Scoop' in the collection of Theodor Meyer-Steineg see Zimmermann and Künzl 1991: 522–4.
4 See Caelius Aurelianus *Tardae passiones* I, 4, 143 (Drabkin (1950: 532–3) where Soranus (second century AD) rejects trepanning of the middle of the skull amongst other therapies for epilepsy recommended by Themison (*floruit c.*50 BC), reputed founder of the Methodist sect.
5 For the constituents of core instrumentaria see for example, Künzl 1983: 10–15; Jackson 1995: 193–4.
6 For the importance of symbols of healing and their applications to surgical instruments see for example, Bliquez 1994: 99ff.; Jackson 1988: 138ff.; Jackson and Leahy 1990.
7 For medicine and surgery in the Celtic world see Künzl 1995.
8 See also Hippocrates, *On Wounds in the Head* 18; Heliodorus in Oribasius, *Medical Collections* XLIV, 8, XLVI 22, 16; Galen, *On the Method of Medicine* 6.6 (10.446 K).
9 It is possible, too, that the 'probe' in the Middle La Tène 'doctor's grave' (grave 7) at Obermenzing, Bavaria (De Navarro 1955, figure 2, 2), an iron tanged implement of similar form and size, is also the drill-bit from a trepan.
10 A similar instrument in the Middle La Tène 'doctor's grave' at Obermenzing (De Navarro 1955, figure 2, 1) may have served the same role as the *meningophylax*.
11 See, for example, Celsus, *De med.* V, 28, 12C–E, on the sounding of fistulae; and Galen, *On Differences between Pulses.*

6

'WITHOUT YOU NO ONE IS HAPPY'

The cult of health in ancient Greece

Emma Stafford

> Health, greatest of the blessed gods, may I live with you
> for the rest of my life, and may you be a willing inmate of my house.
> For if there is any joy in wealth or children,
> or in a king's godlike power over men,
> or in the desires which we hunt with Aphrodite's hidden nets,
> or if any other delight or rest from labours
> has been revealed by the gods to mortals,
> it is with your help, blessed Health,
> that all things flourish and shine to the Graces' murmuring.
> Without you no one is happy.
> (Ariphron, *Hymn to Hygieia* (in Athenaios 15.702))

To a modern reader the term 'cult of health' is not likely to be taken literally, conjuring up images of obsessive adherents of jogging, aerobics and health food rather than religious worship of a real deity called Health. Post-classical images of the goddess herself include the rather shadowy figure receiving libations in Reynolds' portrait of Mrs Peter Beckford (1782, Lady Lever Art Gallery), a self-consciously intellectualised product of the Enlightenment, ranking alongside the abstract goddesses Liberty and Reason of revolutionary France (Warner 1985: 267–93). In nineteenth-century public sculpture, the figure of Health, always shown as a young woman with a snake, likewise appears in contexts which emphasise her allegorical nature. The monument in the central court of the Founder's Building at Royal Holloway, University of London, depicts Thomas Holloway and his wife supported by a base decorated with four seated female figures, each representing an aspect of Holloway's philanthropy, which is more explicitly described in the inscription: the college would develop young ladies' education with such skills as Reading and Writing, while Holloway's Charity also provided a sanatorium nearby, represented by Health. Health is recognisable by her attributes of a snake and *patera*, following an iconography established as early as the beginning of the fourth century BC with statues such as the Hope Hygieia (Figure 6.1). The snake again identifies Health as the entirely appropriate occupant of the *tholos* of

Figure 6.1 The Hope Hygieia. Roman copy of original of 400–350 BC, Los Angeles County Museum of Art (The William Randolph Hearst Collection) no. 50.33.23. Photo: museum.

St Bernard's Well, a spa-water spring provided 'for the benefit of the citizens of Edinburgh' by a nineteenth-century philanthropist beside the Water of Leith in Edinburgh.

Such an intellectual figure is, however, far removed from the Health (Hygieia) to whom Ariphron wrote his hymn around 400 BC. The hymn's literary appeal is attested by citation in writers as late as the Middle Ages (Campbell 1993: 134–7), but Athenaios quotes it in the context of the libations and purificatory ritual performed at the end of a meal, and evidence for the hymn's use in an official cult context in Late Antiquity is supplied by its inscription on a number of *stelai*, all of which date from *c*.AD 200 or later (Sobel 1990: plate 1a; Lee 2000: 25, no. 1.6). One of these forms a pair with another stele at the sanctuary of Asklepios at Epidauros (*IG* IV.1 132; Wagman 1995: 23–7, plate VII), on which hymns to six deities in total are inscribed, each to be sung at a particular hour of the day (Bremer 1981: 210–11; cf. Wagman 1995: 159–78). This kind of liturgical use of the hymn may be a late development, but we have plenty of other evidence from which to build up a picture of Hygieia as a fully realised goddess, worshipped as part of the cult of the healing god Asklepios from at least the fifth century onwards. I have discussed Hygieia elsewhere (Stafford 2000: 147–71) alongside a number of abstract qualities which likewise attained some degree of recognition as anthropomorphic deities, like Persuasion (Peitho) and Peace (Eirene). Unlike these, however, Hygieia does not appear in extant literature or art before her earliest attestation in cult, and she has very little mythological role to provide the kind of personal characterisation which might ease her entry into the sphere of worship. The quality she embodies is also of a different order: as we have seen earlier, *hygieia* is good health, a proper balance of the body's elements, as opposed to the unnatural state of disease, and the prime good without which none of life's other advantages can be enjoyed. Health is one of a number of physiological states to be personified in the ancient world, perhaps most closely paralleled by Sleep (Hypnos/Somnus), who also had strong associations with healing cults (Stafford 2003), and who could even be represented asleep at Hygieia's feet (Lochin 1990: nos. 146–50 *bis*).

AN EARLY HISTORY OF HEALTH

Some have postulated that Hygieia originated in the Peloponnese as an autonomous deity who became associated with Asklepios because of their similarity of function (Croissant 1990: 554). This is based on two passages in Pausanias, both of which in fact already associate Hygieia with Asklepios. Statues of Hygieia and Asklepios are listed amongst a dozen or so which were dedicated at Olympia by Mikythos of Rhegion in fulfilment of a vow on the miraculous recovery of his son from a 'wasting disease' (Pausanias 5.26.2–5). Mikythos was treasurer of the tyrant Anaxilas of Rhegion and later regent for his children, but lived in exile at Tegea after 467 BC (Herodotos 7.170, Diodorus 11.66); fragments of an inscribed base which may have supported part of Mikythos' dedication survive, but even Kaibel's heavy restoration mentions no individual deity by name (*Olympia* V nos. 267–9; Frazer 1898: III, 646–8). Asklepios and Hygieia seem to have been worshipped together at Tegea in the fourth century (see later), however, so it is possible that Mikythos' dedication was influenced by local knowledge of these deities, and such a dedication would certainly reflect later votive practice at Epidauros. Elsewhere Pausanias describes the Asklepieion at Titane, in the northern Peloponnese, as founded by the legendary Alexanor, son of Machaon and grandson of Asklepios himself (2.11.6). The statue of Asklepios was so old that nobody knew who had made it, and it was dressed in a white woollen tunic and cloak, while that of Hygieia was almost hidden by the swathes of 'Babylonian clothing' and masses of women's hair offered to her. Such clothed statues and offerings are certainly suggestive of an archaic cult (Romano 1988), and the account implies that it was still popularly observed in Pausanias' day. That the cult of Hygieia was well established in this locality by the end of the fifth century is suggested by the fact that Ariphron, author of our hymn, came from Sikyon, just a few miles away from Titane.

At Athens, Hygieia's early history is bound up with Athene rather than Asklepios. From the first half of the fifth century we have evidence for a cult on the Akropolis of Athene Hygieia, a striking noun-noun combination paralleled most obviously by the Athene Nike who was worshipped nearby (Stafford 2000: 24). A dedication of c.475 BC by the potter Euphronios, found on the Akropolis (*IG* I³ 824, b.4), is often cited as honouring Athene Hygieia (e.g. Aleshire 1989: 12 and n. 1; Shapiro 1993: 125; Robertson 1996: 47). One commentator ingeniously links this with Euphronios' change of career from painter to potter and suggests that the 'health' desired might have been a cure for long-sightedness (Maxmin 1974). The inscription is very fragmentary, however, and an alternative restoration would make the dedicatee Apollo Paian; in either case it seems just as plausible to read *hygieia* as the concept rather than as an epithet of Athene, in a prayer for health. Less equivocal evidence is provided, however, by a vase fragment also from the first half of the fifth century bearing the graffito 'Kallis made and dedicated this to Athene Hygieia' (*IG* I³ 506). Although not much of the vase survives, the image over which the dedication is inscribed could well be an armed Athene: most of the shield can be seen, decorated with a snake, held against flowing drapery (Graef and Langlotz 1933: 1367, plate 91). We do not hear of Athene

Hygieia again until the 430s, in Plutarch's account of an accident which happened in the course of Perikles' building programme on the Akropolis. A workman engaged on the Propylaia fell from a great height, and was so badly injured that doctors despaired of him, but Athene appeared to Perikles in a dream and prescribed a course of treatment, which rapidly healed the man: 'It was in commemoration of this that he set up the bronze statue of Athene Hygieia on the Akropolis near her altar, which was there before, as they say' (*Perikles* 13. 7–8). The details of the story, with its combination of divine intervention and practical treatment, probably owe much to the author's knowledge of later healing procedures at Epidauros and other Asklepieia, but such a statue was indeed dedicated at around this time. A base found just inside the Propylaia, and still *in situ* next to an altar of the same period, attests a public dedication, rather than a private one by Perikles: 'The Athenians to Athene Hygieia. Pyrrhos the Athenian made this' (*IG* I^3 506). Attempts to identify Pyrrhos' statue with the Hope Athene or with the Athene Promachos (Robertson 1996: 47–8) are not convincing, but it is also mentioned by Pliny (*NH* 34.80) and by Pausanias (1.23.4), who takes care to distinguish between statues of Hygieia 'who people say is daughter of Asklepios' and of Athene 'who also bears the surname Hygieia'. Athene Hygieia appears only rarely after 420 and the arrival of Asklepios with his associate. In the 330s sacrifices to her at the Lesser Panathenaia are recorded as having been funded by taxes levied on the then recently recovered territory of Oropos (*IG* II^2 334.8–10; Humphreys 1985: 208), and Lykourgos' speech *About the Priestess of Athene* detailed activities of the priestesses of Athene Nikê and Athene Hygieia as well as Athene Polias (Mikalson 1998: 24). Elsewhere in Attika Athene Hygieia is only mentioned once, and in passing, by Pausanias (1.31.6) as having an altar at Acharnai. Outside Attika her appearances are extremely rare. A priest of Asklepios at Epidauros makes a dedication to her in the early fourth century AD (*IG* IV 428), and Shapiro suggests than an altar found in the *temenos* of Athene Pronoia at Delphi might be another instance of her cult, its location marked by the inscription HYGIEIAS still conspicuous on the terrace wall (Frickenhaus 1910: 242–7, figure 4; Shapiro 1993: 126, n. 265).

The two strands of development come together with Hygieia's arrival in Athens in the wake of the Epidaurian Asklepios in 420/419 BC. The event is recorded on the Telemachos Monument, found on the site of Asklepios' sanctuary on the south slope of the Akropolis, which gives an exceptionally detailed account of the cult's establishment. Though fragmentary, the monument can be reconstructed as consisting of a tablet carved with reliefs on both sides, supported by a pilaster with inscriptions and reliefs on all four sides (Beschi 1982). On the main relief Asklepios is shown standing, to the right, with a female companion seated on a table, beneath which crouches a dog; a smaller scale figure to the left, his hand raised in a gesture of prayer, must be a human, quite plausibly Telemachos himself. The presence of the dog may be paralleled by the animal's association with the hero elsewhere: Thrasymedes' chryselephantine cult statue of Asklepios at Epidauros had a dog lying at its side (Pausanias 2.27.2), while dogs and 'hunters-with-dogs' (*kynagêtai*) are among the recipients of bloodless sacrifice specified in a fourth-century *lex sacra* from the Peiraieus Asklepieion (*IG* II² 4962 a. 8–10). Parker (1996: 182) suggests that the dogs may be explained by the myth in which the infant Asklepios, having been exposed by his mother, is guarded or suckled by a dog and discovered by a group of hunters. The larger male figure on the relief is recognisable as Asklepios on iconographic grounds, being bearded and semi-draped, but the female is without distinguishing attributes. The identity of both, however, can be inferred from the account of Telemachos' contribution to the cult's foundation inscribed on the one reasonably well-preserved side of the pilaster:

> Telemachos founded the sanctuary and altar to Asklepios first, and Hygieia, the sons of Asklepios and his daughters and . . . coming up from Zea during the Great Mysteries he (Asklepios) was conveyed to the Eleusinion; and having sent for servants at his own expense, Telemachos brought him (Asklepios) here on a wagon, in accordance with an oracle; at the same time came Hygieia; and so the whole sanctuary was established in the archonship of Astyphilos of Kydantidai.
>
> (*IG* II² 4960 fr.a.1–20; *SEG* XXV 226;
> Athens EM 8821)

It has been generally held that Asklepios travelled in the form of a snake, but Clinton has made a good case for the alternative restoration of the inscription adopted here, and suggests that both Asklepios and Hygieia took the more orthodox form of statues, eventually to be put up in the new sanctuary (Clinton 1994: 23–4; *contra* Parker 1996: 178); such 'ancient images (*aphidrymata*)' of Asklepios and Hygieia are indeed referred to in a decree from the Athenian Asklepieion of 52/1 BC (*IG* II² 1046.13–14). This journey from the Peiraieus was commemorated annually thereafter by the Epidauria, held on the 17th Boedromion, a conveniently empty day in the midst of the older festival of the Eleusinian Mysteries (Philostratos, *Life of Apollonios* 4.17; Pausanias 2.26.8; Parke 1977: 63–5). Clinton (1994) demonstrates that the connection with Epidauros was not only emphasised by the festival's name, but also by the regular participation of officials from Epidauros; this he connects with the important role of Eleusinian officials in bringing Asklepios to the Eleusinion, and possibly previously to Zea, which Telemachos' account carefully down-plays, stressing rather that his own part in the proceedings had the approval of Delphi. A second festival, the Asklepieia, was held on the 8th Elaphebolion, the day of the 'Preliminary to the Contest' at the beginning of the City Dionysia, although we have little information on this (Aischines 3.67; IG II² 1496.109–10, 133–5, 150; SEG XVIII.26.11). Asklepios must have been known in Athens long before 420 as a mythological figure, but it is only with Telemachos' formal introduction that the cult begins to be observed. The sanctuary with which it is associated probably remained essentially private for the first 50–75 years of its existence, not receiving state funding until the mid-fourth century (Aleshire 1989: 7–20; see also Garland 1992: 116–35 and Parker 1996: 175–85).

The Hygieia of the Telemachos Monument is one of her earliest Athenian representations as a goddess separate from Athene. Hygieia is attested at Epidauros from c.400 BC and elsewhere in the Peloponnese, as we have seen, she was associated with Asklepios from an earlier date. Clinton (1994: 24, n. 22) argues against the idea of an Epidaurian origin for the Athenian Hygieia on the grounds that the Telemachos inscription implies that her statue only joined Asklepios' after he left the Eleusinion, but even if such a literal interpretation were accepted, it would not necessarily mean that Hygieia came from a local Athenian source. Both the inscription and the relief above it rather associate Hygieia closely with the explicitly imported cult of Asklepios. That sacrifices were still being made to Athene Hygieia in the 330s also undermines the hypothesis that the Hygieia of the Telemachos Monument was in some way a development from the Athenian Athene Hygieia. Nor can it be coincidental that Hygieia appears for the first time in Athenian vase painting in the last two decades of the century. These images and their relationship to the Athenian cult are discussed in detail elsewhere (Shapiro 1993: 125–31; Stafford 2000: 159–63), but a few important points should be noted here. Nearly all of the images are by the Meidias Painter, or in his manner, and present Hygieia divorced from her usual association with Asklepios. Perhaps the most significant is the Meidias Painter's name vase (London E224), which presents Hygieia with Herakles in the Garden of the Hesperides; her presence here is allegorically appropriate, since the Hesperides episode is part of a whole complex of stories associating Herakles with immortality (Stafford 2005), but there may also be a deliberate reference to Athens' recent adoption of her cult, as several Attic heroes are included in the rest of the frieze (Burn 1987: 15–25). For the most part, however, the Meidian Health appears in the company of other personifications of 'good things': Eudaimonia (Happiness), Eutychia (Good Fortune), Eukleia (Good Repute), Harmonia (Harmony), Eunomia (Lawfulness), Pandaisia (Wedding Feast), Aponia (Leisure), Paidia (Play), Peitho (Persuasion), and Erotes variously labelled as Himeros (Desire), Pothos (Yearning) and even Hedylogos (Sweet-Talk). These multiple personifications have been explained as simply promoting a general atmosphere of well-being in an escapist paradise (Burn 1987: 36), but close reading of individual images shows that, rather than being chosen at random, the figures convey carefully constructed allegorical messages (Borg 2005). Thus the figure of Hygieia can be understood as representing both the goddess herself and the benefit of health promoted by Asklepios' new cult, in an iconographic language where the male figure of the god himself would be out of place (Warner 1985; Stafford 2000: 27–35).

THE FAMILY AND OTHER CULT ASSOCIATES

As the wording of the Telemachos Monument – 'Asklepios first, and Hygieia, the sons of Asklepios and his daughters' – implies, in cult terms Health is first amongst a whole family of Asklepios' offspring. She accompanies her father on a high proportion of surviving votive reliefs dedicated at Asklepieia in the late fifth and fourth centuries (Hausmann 1948; Van Straten 1995: 63–71, R1–35). Asklepios himself is always bearded and semi-draped, Hygieia demurely dressed in chiton or peplos and himation, and both divinities, in accordance with the iconographic conventions of the medium, are shown on a much larger scale than their mortal worshippers. One of the earliest of these reliefs, now in a private collection, is said to come from the Athenian Asklepieion (Figure 6.2; Croissant 1990: no. 137; Sobel 1990: II, 60; Hausmann 1948: no. 3). Worshippers approach Asklepios, who holds out a *phiale* in his right hand, and behind him stands Hygieia carrying a small vase, perhaps meant to contain medicine; with her left hand she pulls at her veil in a gesture which has long been associated with the unveiling of the bride, but could just as easily, and more appropriately here, signify a modest covering of the face (Llewellyn-Jones 2003: 96–110). Several fourth-century reliefs also from the Athenian Asklepieion have the combination of a seated Asklepios and Hygieia leaning against a column, *stele* or tree (Athens NM 2557, 1330, 1335; Croissant 1990: nos. 29*, 31, 34; Sobel 1990: plates 4a–b; Van Straten 1981: 85–6, figure 19; Kerenyi 1959: figure 18). On one, worshippers carry offerings of fruit and cakes, while on another, they bring a pig, a variety perhaps to be explained by the fourth-century sacred law from the Peiraieus Asklepieion mentioned earlier (*IG* II^2 4962), which lists a number of healing deities to whom three cakes (*popana*) must be given as a 'preliminary', presumably to be followed by a blood sacrifice (Kearns 1994). The coupling of Asklepios and Hygieia in Athenian cult practice is

Figure 6.2 Hygieia and Asklepios approached by worshippers. Votive relief, *c.*415 BC. Photo: FA Köln, neg. 967/4; private collection.

finally attested by two Hellenistic inscriptions which mention a shared priest (*IG* II² 974, 138/7 BC) and joint sacrifices:

> it is the ancestral custom of the physicians who are in the service of the state to sacrifice to Asklepios and to Hygieia twice each year on behalf of their own bodies and of those they have healed.
>
> (*IG* II² 772.9–13, *c.*250 BC)

Asklepios' sanctuary at Zea in the Peiraieus may have been established by the influential Eleusinian families, the Eumolpidai and Kerykes, perhaps as much as a year before Asklepios' progression into Athens (Clinton 1994: 24, 30, 34). When Aristophanes produced his *Wealth* in 388 BC it would still have been more popular than the privately founded Akropolis sanctuary, making it the more likely setting for the miraculous cure of Wealth's blindness (ll. 653–747), which, for all its burlesque, provides our most substantial surviving account of the process of incubation (Aleshire 1989: 13; Sommerstein 2001: 11–13). When during the night the god does the rounds of his patients, he is attended by his daughters Iaso and Panakeia (ll. 701–3), and it is Panakeia who assists in Wealth's cure (ll. 730–1). Hygieia's absence here is in keeping with the play's high degree of allegory, since her sister's healing capacities (see later) are more appropriate to the context than Health, but it is also just possible that Aristophanes has omitted her out of the kind of respect shown to Eirene in the *Peace* (Stafford 2000: 186–7). It is certainly likely to be Hygieia who appears, in her usual role as Asklepios' companion, on a relief from the Peiraieus Asklepieion of *c*.400 BC (Figure 6.3; Croissant 1990: no. 138; Hausmann 1948: no. 1, plate 1). Unlike the sacrificial scenes of the Athenian reliefs, this shows a scene of healing: a woman lying on a couch is being attended by Asklepios, just as though he were a mortal doctor, while three adults and a child look on. Behind Asklepios stands a rather casual-looking Hygieia, holding a fold of her cloak in a gesture similar to that in Figure 6.1. This might reflect

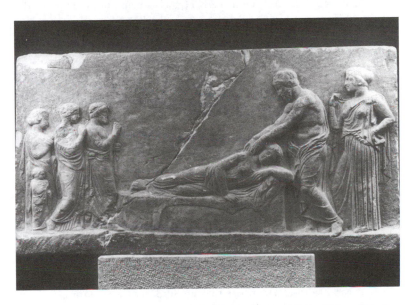

Figure 6.3 Asklepios and Hygieia attend a patient. Votive relief, *c*.400 BC, Peiraieus Museum 405. © Archaeological Receipts Fund.

the visions of the god seen during incubation, as parodied in the *Wealth*, or the domestic context of a real doctor's visit to a patient, with Hygieia here perhaps in the role of female healer or midwife (King 1998: 172–87).

Sometimes associated with the Athenian Asklepieion is the statue of Hygieia once in the Hope collection, an Antonine-period copy found at Ostia, together with the Hope Athene and Asklepios (Figure 6.1; Croissant 1990: no. 160; Waywell 1986: 68–9, figure 10, plate 47). There are good grounds for supposing that the original was an important Attic work of the first half of the fourth century (Croissant 1990: 570), although its identity as Hygieia's cult statue from the Asklepieion is entirely conjectural (Aleshire 1991: 43–4, plate 11). Like the Hygieia of the reliefs, the Hope statue is thoroughly draped in chiton and himation, with her hair bound in a snood. She is identifiable as Health because of the snake draped around her shoulders, which she once fed from a *phiale* in her outstretched right hand; the snake is Asklepios' attribute too, often appearing entwined in his staff or coiled beneath his throne. The snake is not only symbolic of healing, with its ability to slough off its old skin and generate a new one, but frequent references attest to the presence of sacred snakes in sanctuaries of Asklepios. At Epidauros these may have been housed in the tholos (Burford 1969: 67–8), and the fourth-century cures recorded at the sanctuary include several which involve the actual sanctuary snakes, or visions of them (*IG* IV² I.121–3, 17, 33, 39, 44). The snake is Hygieia's constant attribute in the statues which constitute by far the largest body of her representations (Croissant 1990; Sobel 1990). Like the Hope Hygieia, most of these are Roman versions of fourth-century originals, only a handful of which come from identifiable cult contexts. The original of the much-copied 'Broadlands' type, for example, was very probably part of the group sculpted by Timarchos and Kephisodotos the Younger for the sanctuary of Asklepios on Kos around 320 BC (Croissant 1990: 571, nos. 63–83). Other types have been identified with statue groups of Asklepios and Hygieia attributed to the mid- to late-fourth-century sculptor Skopas, in the temple of Athene Alea at Tegea and in the temple of Asklepios at Gortys, where the god was unusually represented as young and beardless (Pausanias 8.47.1, 8.28.1); Hygieia's cult association with Asklepios in Arkadia is the subject of a recent detailed study (Mitropoulou 2001).

The rest of Asklepios' family reflects his own ambiguous nature as a hero-god. He has a rarely mentioned wife Epione, 'the Mild', 2 hero sons, Machaon and Podaleirios, and 3 or 4 divine daughters in addition to Hygieia, Iaso, Panakeia, Akeso and sometimes Aigle. The sons are healing heroes as early as the *Iliad*, where they are leaders of the contingent from Trikka, Ithome and Oichalia (2.729–31), and Asklepios himself is the 'blameless physician' (4.405, 11.518). Most versions of Asklepios' life-story likewise make him formally a hero in that he is son of Apollo by the mortal woman Koronis, and eventually dies, struck down by Zeus' thunderbolt (Hesiod, *Catalogue of Women* frs. 50–2 MW and Pindar, *Pythian* 3.25–60; Edelstein and Edelstein 1945: II, 1–22; Kerényi 1959: 70–86). Heroic status may also be alluded to in the iconography of the Telemachos Monument, given the chthonic associations of the dog featured on both sides of the relief (Beschi 1982: 42), and an Athenian *Heroa* festival is attested in the second century BC (*IG* II^2 974.12, *SEG* XVIII 26.12, 137/136 BC). Asklepios is 'un-heroic', however, in the geographical extent of his cult, and divine status is suggested by his other festivals and his temples, as well as being explicitly attributed to him by some sources (e.g. Pausanias 2.26.8; Edelstein and Edelstein 1945: nos. 232–65 and II, 76–91). Asklepios' acquisition of divine status may be reflected by the addition to his family of the goddess daughters (Edelstein and Edelstein 1945: II, 85–9), who are all named after aspects of Asklepios' work: Hygieia and Panakeia are personifications of abstract nouns meaning 'health' and 'cure-all'; Iaso and Akeso are slight variations on the nouns *iasis* and *akesis*, both meaning 'healing' or 'cure'; even *aigle* means 'light of the sun', suggesting an association between healing and light inherited from Apollo (Kerenyi 1959: 28–9 and n. 15; Barefoot, Ch. 12, this volume). Such a mixture of heroic and divine elements is paralleled only by the hero-god Herakles, who, like Asklepios is firmly a hero in the *Iliad*, but later acquires divine status which is reflected both in cult practice and in his marriage to Hebe (Youth) on Olympos (Stafford 2005).

Hygieia's sisters are first attested in literature no earlier than the second half of the fifth century. A fragment of the Athenian iambic poet Hermippos (fr. 1 West) lists the 2 sons, Iaso, Panakeia and Aigle as being Asklepios' children by Lampetia, daughter of Helios, while the opening invocation of the *Hippocratic Oath* singles out just 2 goddesses for individual mention: 'I swear by Apollo the healer and Asklepios and Hygieia and Panakeia and all the gods and goddesses...'. The Hermippos fragment is cited by the scholia on Aristophanes' *Wealth* (ad 701) while the play itself, as we have seen, mentions only Iaso and Panakeia. A little later, in around 370 BC, the anonymous Erythraean hymn to Asklepios has the same list of the god's children as Hermippos, but makes their mother Epione and adds 'bright Hygieia the glorious' (*Paean Erythraeus* 14–15, 23–4; Edelstein and Edelstein 1945: no. 592, II, 200). Bremer comments, 'This whole catalogue serves a double purpose, that of situating the god in his happy family and thus honouring him, and also that of enumerating the effects of the god's medical powers' (Bremer 1981: 209). Croissant goes too far when he dismisses Hygieia's sisters as 'simples allégories exprimant la fonction médicale d'Asclépios' (1990: 554), since there is some evidence for their cult. The

Telemachos Monument speaks of the Akropolis sanctuary as being founded in honour not only of Asklepios and Hygieia but also of 'the sons of Asklepios and his daughters', while Pausanias describes the sanctuary as worth seeing for the statues of 'the god and his children' (1.21.4). All of the children are invoked in the opening prayer of Herodas' fourth *Mimiamb* (ll. 1–11), which dramatises a sacrifice to Asklepios on Kos in the third century, with Hygieia in first place behind Asklepios and his mother Koronis. Most telling is the children's appearance on votive reliefs, more than twenty of which are catalogued by Hausmann as representing Asklepios with sons/daughters other than Hygieia (1948: nos. 79–89, 123, 147–58). The whole family can reasonably be identified on a relief of *c*.370–360 BC from Thyreatis in the northern Peloponnese, where a standing Asklepios is accompanied by 2 male and 4 female deities (Athens NM 1402; Sobel 1990: II, 44; Krug 1985: figure 50), whereas on a relief of around 340 BC an enthroned Asklepios is surrounded by 4 female figures identified by the accompanying inscription as Akeso, Iaso, Panakeia and Epione (Athens NM 1352, *IG* II^2 4388; Kerényi 1959: figure 23). However, Hygieia remains by far the most frequently mentioned of Asklepios' female relatives in cult-related documents, and can even be described by Aristeides as the 'counterpoise of all the others' (*Orations* 38.22).

Apart from these family links, Hygieia has just a few other cult associates. At Oropos, major cult centre of the healing hero Amphiaraos, Health appears several times either alone or in company with the hero. According to Pausanias (1.34.3) she shared the fourth division of the great altar of the Amphiareion with Panakeia and Iaso, Aphrodite and Athene Paionia (Schachter 1986: II, 60–1). This may well have influenced the Athenian cult of Amphiaraos when Oropos was handed over to Athens after Chaironeia, and Hygieia seems to have had a place in the Athenian Amphiaraion in the 330s: one of the charges against Euxenippos defended in Hypereides' speech (4.19) is that he allowed Olympias, the Macedonian queen-mother, to dedicate a *phiale* to the statue of Hygieia there. It has been argued that Euxenippos was an official of Hygieia's cult at the Amphiaraion, and had set up the cult statue himself (F.W. Mitchell 1970: 24, n. 99; Humphreys 1985: 219). It may be the Oropos Amphiareion which is reflected on a Boiotian *krater* of *c*.400 BC: on Side A, a mature male figure reclines on a couch, offering a *kantharos* of wine to a snake; on Side B (Figure 6.4; Croissant 1990: no. 7*), a goddess holding a staff receives a (smaller scale) mortal woman who brings a tray of offerings and a jug for libations. Though neither figure is inscribed, the male accords with the iconographic type of either Asklepios or Amphiaraos in his healing-hero role, while in the background of Side B hang two disembodied limbs (a leg and what may be an arm), representing the kind of anatomical votives which were commonly offered at healing shrines (Van Straten 1981; Forsen 1996).

Figure 6.4 Hygieia and worshipper in healing shrine. Boiotian red-figure krater, *c.*400 BC, Athens NM 1393. © Archaeological Receipts Fund.

Hygieia would be a particularly appropriate figure to decorate a krater because of her associations with Dionysos. A Dionysos *Hygiates*, 'Dispenser of Health', is attested in Athenaios (2.36a–b), quoting the fourth-century medical writer Mnesitheos (fr. 41 Bertier). The fragment is a passage on the beneficial properties of wine, if taken in moderation, as giving strength to mind and body, and being useful in medicine, for mixing with drugs. It ends with the comment, 'Because of this Dionysos is everywhere called physician (*iatros*)', to which Athenaios adds, 'The Pythia has told some to call Dionysos *hygiates*'. It is not at all clear that either *iatros* or *hygiates* were ever official cult titles – once the medical properties of wine have been adduced it is almost inevitable that the giver of wine should be described as 'doctor' (Bertier 1972: 61) – but H/health does have a broader association with wine-drinking. Ariphron's hymn is sung by the host of Athenaios' symposium immediately after 'making the libation of wine' (15.701f), and in a fragment of Philetairos' comedy *Asklepios* (fr. 1 Kassell-Austin) we hear of a special 'cup of Health' (*Hygieias metaniptris*) used for invoking Hygieia: 'one shook the great cup, full half with wine, half with water, calling on the name of Health' (cf. Antiphanes fr. 147, Kallias fr. 9, and Nikostratos frs. 3

and 18 Kassell-Austin, and Kallimachos fr. 203.20–22 Pfeiffer). Pollux explains that this *metaniptris* was actually a regular shallow drinking-cup (*kylix*), but took its name from the fact that it was used 'after washing the hands' (*meta nipto*), adding that 'it was sacred to Hygieia, just as the *krater* was sacred to Zeus Soter' (6.100). Thus the universal modern toast 'your health' (*ygeia sas* in modern Greek) would seem to have good classical roots in the worship of Hygieia.

CONCLUSION

Our evidence for Hygieia's existence before 420 BC is not conclusive, but does seem to suggest that she originated in the Peloponnese in connection with the cult of Asklepios; when this cult was imported into Athens in 420, Hygieia naturally came too. Her entry into the Athenian pantheon may have been facilitated by the pre-existence of the cult of Athene Hygieia, but Athene's complete separation from Hygeia in Attic iconography after 420 suggests that any perceived link between the two did not persist. It is possible that Hygieia originated purely in iconographical invention, as a useful means of representing Asklepios' 'product': while *hygieia* is in any case grammatically feminine, the relative anonymity of the female form serves to convey her meaning more directly than the male form of her brothers Podaleirios and Machaon – since no stories are attached to her, and she has virtually no existence outside Asklepios' cult, there is nothing to distract the viewer from her significance as 'health'. For a non-mythological figure, however, Hygieia achieved astonishing success. From the fourth century BC onwards Hygieia was present in the form of statues or votive reliefs, and invoked in inscriptions, in sanctuaries of Asklepios all over the Greek world. She came to Rome as part of the cult of Aesculapius in 293 BC (Livy 10.47.6–7, with summary of book 11; Ovid, *Metamorphoses* 15.626–744), where she continued to flourish long after she was officially identified with and absorbed by the Italian *Salus* in 180 BC (Livy 40.37.1–3; Axtell 1987: 13–15), and evidence of her worship in the imperial period has been found in places as far apart as Rouen and Ptolemais.

This can only be due to the importance attached to the concept she embodies. That Asklepios' cult embraced the maintenance of good health as well as the curing of sickness is demonstrated by the fact that he was regularly worshipped by the healthy (Edelstein and Edelstein 1945: II, 182–4): Athens' two annual festivals in honour of Asklepios were celebrated by the whole city, and Epidauros' quadrennial Asklepieia, held nine days after the Isthmian Games, included athletic and dramatic contests. Asklepios' daughters may be understood as representing both these aspects of the god's work: Iaso, Akeso and Panakeia are the processes of healing, but Hygieia is the continuing state of good health which everyone hopes to achieve.

> Then if Health is greatest of the gods, her work, the enjoyment of health, is likewise to be put before the other goods.
>
> (Lucian, *De lapsu* 6)

ACKNOWLEDGEMENTS

I am grateful to Karen Stears for making me think about Hygieia in the first place, and to Rebecca Flemming and Caroline Humphries for ideas and references.

7

HYGIEIA AT DINNER AND
AT THE SYMPOSIUM

John Wilkins

Hygieia was a goddess honoured both in public sanctuaries and in the home. She was also good health personified, the objective of nearly if not all human beings, whether laymen or doctors. An important means to achieving that objective was through diet, for Galen tells us that dietetics was the most useful branch of medicine (*On the Powers of Foods* 1.1). The aim of this chapter is to explore the broad cultural perspective within which the Greeks combined the objective of good health (*hygieia*) with honouring the goddess (Hygieia) in cult and literature.

Ancient dietetics strove at all times to maintain good health (*hygieia*) by good practice and preventative means, by nourishing the body, by maintaining a balanced diet and by rectifying any imbalance of humours through adjustments in the diet. Thus there are Hippocratic treatises entitled *Regimen I–IV, Regimen in Good Health [peri diaites hygieines], Regimen in Acute Diseases, Humours* and *Nutrition*; Diphilos of Siphnos wrote a *Suitable Foods for the Sick and the Healthy*; Plutarch wrote his *Advice on Good Health [Hygieina Praecepta]* and Galen wrote for the sick and the healthy in his *On the Maintenance of Good Health [Hygieina], On the Powers of Foods, On the Thinning Diet* and in other works. It is possible to study the role of diet in good health alongside other cultural aspects of Hygieia in a text combining extensive quotation from medical authors with a wide range of sympotic practice, namely the *Deipnosophistai* of Athenaios of Naucratis. Athenaios composed this work at the end of the second century AD or the beginning of the third and it provides a complex synthesis of many aspects of Greek culture, in particular those which concern food and drink. Athenaios surveys topics relating to the dinner and the symposium, broadly in the order dictated by those social events. Lists of foods are provided, covering such foods as vegetables, meats, fruits, fish, breads and cakes. There are also sections, sometimes whole books, devoted to drinking cups, luxury, courtesans, music, games, perfumes and garlands. These foods and other aspects of culture are illustrated by a mixture of quotation and anecdote. Quotations are drawn from comedy, medical authors, historians and cultural historians, ethnographers and technical authors such as Aristotle on animals and Theophrastus on plants.

Athenaios is not an easy author to read. He fits only loosely into literary categories; he writes within the genre of sympotic literature, as does Plato, but in a rambling and discursive manner. In no sense is he a canonical author, being given only half a column in the third edition of *The Oxford Classical Dictionary* (1996: 202). Critics have sometimes asserted that he seems to be barely in control of his material (D. Braund and Wilkins 2000). Despite these reservations, the *Deipnosophistai* remains one of the great storehouses of Greek culture, and in it Hygieia, both the goddess herself and good health in the abstract, plays an important part.

Most prominently, at the end of the book (15.702a–b), Larensis, the semi-fictional host of the feast Athenaios has been describing, sings the hymn to the goddess Hygieia composed by Ariphron of Sicyon in the fifth or fourth century BC. She is the personified goddess of Health, the most honoured of the immortal ones:

> Hygieia, most honoured of the blessed gods, may I live with you for what is left of my life and may you live with me and favour me! If there is any delight in wealth or in children or in royal power which brings mortals to the level of gods or in the desires which we chase in the hidden nets of Aphrodite, or if the gods send any other delight for mortals or respite from labours, it is with you, blessed Hygieia, that all flourishes and shines in the songs of the Charities. Without you no man prospers.

The hymn was well known and was inscribed on stone at Epidaurus and elsewhere in the fourth century BC. The goddess had appeared earlier in the *Deipnosophistai*, either personified or in abstract formulae. She was linked with Dionysos by the Pythian priestess at Delphi in his form as Dionysos Hygiates (2.36b). Barley-cakes offered to the gods at sacrifices were called *hygieiai* (3.115a). In book 15, Athenaios discusses Hygieia as the goddess addressed at the beginning of the symposium along with Zeus the Saviour and the Agathos Daimon or 'Good Spirit'. In illustration, he quotes fragment 93 (KA) of the comic poet Eubulos,[1] which presents the god Dionysos describing one of his symposia: 'I mix just three bowls [of wine and water] for sensible people. One for good health, which they drink first. The second for love and pleasure. And the third for sleep. When they've drunk this, wise guests go home . . .'.[2] The god's words resemble the formal procedure at the start of the symposium (the drinking session after the meal or *deipnon* has been eaten), in which cups of neat wine were offered to certain gods before the human drinkers began to share the wine mixed with water. Athenaios comments:

> most of them called for a cup of the Good Spirit, others of Zeus the Saviour, others of Hygieia, some naming one of them, others another. We thought it a good idea to draw up a list of the poets who mentioned these mixtures [and their gods], which I shall now relate... Nicostratos [the comic poet] writes in *Pandrosos* (fr. 18 KA),
>
> A: Me too, darling. Pour him out a cup for Hygieia.
> B: You take one for Hygieia too. Come then. Good luck to us.
>
> (15.692f.)

Later in the symposium a *skolion* or drinking song to Hygieia is quoted, among many others. This is one of the best known and most quoted:

> To have Good Health is the best thing for a mortal.
> Second is to be born handsome in appearance.
> Third best is to have uncomplicated wealth.
> The fourth thing is to enjoy our youth with our friends.
>
> (15.694e)

In short, Hygieia is well integrated into the Greek symposium as one of the gods and goddesses asked to oversee the proceedings. The goddess represents well-being, and, as Ariphron put it, she is associated with wealth, children and power. The combination of Good Health (Hygieia) with Wealth (Ploutos) was ancient and popular, according to Aristotle (*Rhetoric* 1394b13). This popular tradition appears also in the beautiful dream of Kleon/Paphlagon in the *Knights* of Aristophanes (1090–01), in which Athene bathes the demos (the Athenian people) with a bath ladle full of *Plouthygieia* (wealth–health). This tradition is seen too in the Boeotian festival in which famine was driven out of the community and Ploutos and Hygieia welcomed in.[3]

These are broad cultural aspects of Hygieia. I turn now to Hygieia in the more narrowly defined medical sense of the good health of the body which was normally achieved by diet. The role of dietetics in medicine had been established centuries before this date, probably in the fifth century BC by followers of Hippocrates and Pythagoras.[4] The Hippocratic treatise *On Ancient Medicine* (3) identifies diet as a central feature in the development of the art of medicine: 'The doctor's art would not have been discovered in the first place nor would it have been researched, for there would have been no call for it if the sick among mortals benefited from a way of life and a way of taking their food which was the same as the way in which the healthy eat, drink and lead their lives and there were not other things that were better for the sick. As it is, necessity herself has caused us to seek out and discover the art of medicine because the same things did not and do not suit the sick as suit those in good health.' The Hippocratic *Regimen 1* (1–2) makes it clear that the role of diet was heavily theorised and contested, certainly by the fourth century BC. Apparently important names in the development of the science of dietetics were Herodicos, Praxagoras and Chrysippos.[5] Athenaios has pre-served much important material from this area of medicine, in particular extensive quotation from Diocles of Carystos (who is probably to be dated to the fourth century BC; Van der Eijk 2000), Diphilos of Siphnos (whom Athenaios places at the court of Lysimachos in the early third century BC) and Mnesitheos of Athens (probably fourth century BC; Bertier 1972). We shall see shortly that these authors demonstrate that, by the Hellenistic period, nearly all the elements of the human diet had been placed into an elaborate system which listed the effects of the foods on the human body and located them within the theory of humours which had been developed by the Hippocratic doctors during the fifth and fourth centuries BC. These texts only exist in fragmentary form through citation by Athenaios and other specialist authors, and medical authors such as Galen and Oribasius.

Athenaios provides another valuable service. In his pursuit of arcane authors and works in addition to the great authors of antiquity, he quotes minor texts on exotic topics. Thus we discover that Herophilos, the great Hellenistic doctor, wrote on perfumes, while the less well known Philonides wrote on perfumes and garlands. Numenios of Heraclea wrote on banquets and Andreas on popular superstitions. Many of these doctors wrote on what we would term cookery. The great Erasistratos of Iulis is quoted for a meat recipe comprising roast meat boiled in blood, honey, cheese, salt, cumin, silphium and vinegar (7.324a). Many more doctors are mentioned on the subject of a related sauce, the famous *karukê*. Athenaios lists them at 12.516d: 'The Lydians were the first to discover *karukê* on the preparation of which the compilers of cookery books have spoken, Glaucos of Locri, Mithaecos, Dionysios, the two Heracleidae of Syracusan origin, Agis, Epainetos, Dionysios, Hegesippos, Erasistratos, Euthydemos and Crito, and in addition to these Stephanos, Archytas, Akestios, Akesias, Diocles and Philistion. These are the writers of cookery books known to me.' Of these authors, Philistion, Diocles of Carystos, at least one of the Heracleidae and Erasistratos are almost certainly to be identified with homonymous medical writers. Further, Diphilos of Siphnos wrote on salt fish as well as on dietetics and Heracleides of Tarentum commented on the order of the meal (2.53c) and on whether the *tragemata* (dessert) should come first rather than at the end.

It is clear from Athenaios as well as from other authors that cookery was not rigidly separated from dietetics in the way that Plato proposes in his *Gorgias*. Plato's separation of the useful art of medicine from the meretricious art of cookery does not appear to be followed by medical authors. Ancient dietetics itself came under attack from a different perspective in Edelstein (1967). His view was that a life of idleness was required to follow the dietary prescriptions of the doctors and that no working person could afford the time required for devotion to all the instructions, although he conceded that ideas of a good diet and good health – Hygieia – appear to have been widespread and popularly based in antiquity. We have seen as much in the examples above from Boeotia and from notions of Health and Wealth as the aim of all.

According to Edelstein (1967: 305–6), the ancient reader of treatises on diet, if he took the advice seriously, tended to the kind of valetudinarianism that Plato ridiculed at *Republic* 406a5–e3. He assumes that such treatises were followed to the letter. Edelstein also comments on the notion that doctors were called upon in health as much as in sickness, but here he writes within the prejudices of his own time; the essay was first written in 1931. He ignores the notion of a good diet that is now considered essential to health (whether within conventional or complementary medicine). It is now far from outlandish to imagine that such conditions as diabetes, for example, some cancers and heart disease may be triggered by certain foods. Edelstein also ignores the modern pursuit of diets which people follow at great cost to themselves in order to maintain a particular body weight through proprietary brands, quite independently of the medical profession. Ancient dietetics appears to have applied itself to the standard dietary foods and not to have proposed special food such as crispbreads and low fat yoghurt.

We should probably reformulate the last point, however. Since the ancient doctors were working within the standard diet, individuals were at liberty to act independently of the medical profession or to take advice. That advice shows, at least in the testimony of Hippocrates and Galen, that there were special preparations in the sense that methods of cooking and mixing with other foods are crucial. A crispbread, after all, is no more than specially prepared wheat or rye. In this sense, ancient preparations do resemble the modern products mentioned earlier and others such as margarine that claims to reduce cholesterol and honey that claims to boost energy.

If we ask about special preparations which fall outside the normal diet, such as a Hippocratic report on a prescription including boiled puppy (*Epidemics* 7.72), these usually prove in fact to belong to the normal diet, which included fox, puppy and hedgehog (*Regimen* 2.46). Galen is particularly revealing on foods at the margins of the human diet, such as donkeys, camels, lions, wild plants and vetches (Wilkins 2003).

Now I would like to consider Hygieia, good health, within the context of diet, and only in terms of food. I deliberately exclude other important aspects of regimen, such as physical exercise and bathing. Three questions arise from Edelstein's essay:

1   To what extent were ancient treatises on diet prescriptive and to what extent descriptive, reflecting the diet as eaten?
2   Do ancient dieticians ever give thought to the poor, to the artisan, to those outside the wealthy elite?
3   If so, does the diet of the poor citizen enter Athenaios' presentation of dietetics?

Plato's moral objections to misplaced interest in eating for pleasure deserve our attention since they are taken up by Athenaios, who quotes part of the relevant section of *Gorgias*. Athenaios was writing in a tradition that drew on both Plato and the Stoic tradition, according to which luxury, self-indulgence and the pursuit of pleasure were to be deprecated. In *Gorgias* 517–18, cookery is compared unfavourably with medicine in the treatment of bodily disorders, since 'medicine knows what is good and bad as concerns food and drink for promoting the excellence of the body, while the other skills (such as cookery) do not know'. This is an important but misleading distinction. If we set aside what the baker knows and what the doctor knows – and these are indeed separate areas of knowledge – then we can say that the baker's bread can contribute to the maintenance of good health, if appropriate to that person. It is also asserted in *Gorgias* (451e) that the cook will make a man fat, and will only feed him on what he likes and will win his approval. Athenaios quotes this passage, along with Plato's comments on the excessive dining of the Sicilians (in the seventh *Epistle*) and on the dangers of pleasure (in the *Philebus*).

In the *Republic* (371d), a vegetarian diet is proposed for the citizens, which they will enjoy with pleasure, peace and Hygieia, says Socrates. This healthy city is contrasted with the bloated city 'that we now have'. The bloated city will not be 'healthy' (*hygiês*) but 'swollen' (*phlegmainousa*). Now, Plato's ideal diet is close to the diet of the Attic peasant farmers (Gallo 1989; Garnsey 1999). The qualities that he ascribes to this ideal, namely pleasure, peace and Hygieia, were said by Aristotle to be important to the masses (see earlier). The swollen city of *Republic* and *Gorgias* thus appears to reflect the city of the wealthier citizens, the very idle rich whom Edelstein believes were the main consumers of treatises on dietetics. This Platonic perspective will help us to place the advice carried in the dietetic passages quoted by Athenaios. We shall consider too the question of the taste of food. Does a morally good diet necessarily exclude pleasure and a pleasant taste? It is not completely excluded from Plato's ideal state which allows a pleasurable atmosphere (*hedeos sunontes*). Similarly, in Plutarch's *Advice on Good Health*, much is said on the subject of simple foods, after Pythagoras and Epicurus, and of not submitting to appetite. A pure and unspoilt appetite makes everything, to a healthy body, pleasant. So much for the moralists. Do the dieticians exclude the pleasure of eating? Taste, as we shall see, is an important component, as are flavour and pleasure, provided there are not considerations of utility and the like which override these.

The advice that we are about to see in Diphilos and Mnesitheos is largely descriptive. The qualities of the cereal or fish are given in considerable detail, since it was for the physician to determine what was required by any particular patient. In a sense, a special diet was needed in every case, according to the individual concerned and other factors such as the time of year, age and sex. There is more focus on what might be consumed by the wealthy than by the poor, but the whole diet is described. We should note at the outset that Athenaios is only really concerned with the diet necessary for a person enjoying good health. The special needs of the sick are generally omitted in the passages he selects from Diphilus and others. The standard diet is exemplified by the discussion on cereals at 3.115c–116a.

THE CEREAL BASE OF THE DIET

The report on what the medical authorities have to say on bread (115c) is given by the character Galen (who appears to be modelled on the historical author): 'Galen said, "We shall not dine until we have heard what the sons of the Asclepiadae have said about bread and cakes and barley meal. Diphilos of Siphnos in *Suitable Foods for the Sick and the Healthy* says that bread made from wheat is more nourishing than its barley equivalent, more easy to digest and altogether better."' There is thus a sequence of bread from finest wheat flour (*semidalitês*), bread from ordinary wheat and then bread of unbolted flour made from unsifted meal. These [wheat breads] are believed to be the more nourishing. Philistion of Locri is cited as an authority for the claim that bread from the most refined flour is more given to promoting strength in the body than bread made of coarse flour. He places the latter second; third is bread from ordinary wheat flour. On the other hand, bread made from highly refined flour (*guris*) has bad flavour (or bad juices) and offers little nourishment. All fresh bread is easier to digest than dried bread and more nourishing and with better juices, as well as producing more air and assimilating better. Dried breads are filling and hard to digest. Old and heavily dried bread offers little nourishment, binds the bowels and has bad juices (or flavour). The detail goes on, with more medical authorities brought in. The fictional Galen's summary of Diphilus and Philistion on bread makes interesting reading. The dieticians follow the categories of bread as it was eaten, wheat according to the grades of flour, followed by barley which was normally not made into bread at all but into barley-cake or *maza*. There are several criteria to be considered: nourishment provided by the cereal, ease of digestion, strength imparted to the body, qualities of juice or *chyle* produced in the body, and even the amount of air produced. Philistion appears to be writing in the school of the 'Pneumatics' who considered the action of air, or *pneuma*, in the body to be crucial (e.g. Longrigg 1993: 162–76). If we map the classification of breads by Diphilus and Philistion on to the Greek diet, it rapidly becomes evident that the doctors favoured the diet of the rich over the diet of the poor, for the rich were much more likely to eat wheat over barley and better grades of flour over poorer, while the majority of the population consumed barley-cakes, and for much of the year barley-cake dried in the sun into bricks for winter consumption (Sallares 1991; Foxhall and Forbes 1982). There are exceptions to this – Archestratos of Gela, for example, praised a range of barley-cakes to the gourmet eater (Archestratos, fr. 4; Wilkins and Hill 1994: 40–1; fr. 5 in Olson and Sens 2000: 21–37) – but the doctors from the Hippocratics to Galen consistently favoured wheat over barley, and even the idealised vegetarian diet in Plato's *Republic* allowed wheat loaves as well as barley-cakes. As far as the cereal base of the diet was concerned (by far the greatest part of the calorie intake of all Greeks), the rich, in the opinion of the doctors, had a much more healthy diet.

FRUIT AND VEGETABLES

The doctors classified fruit and vegetables in the same system as the one we have followed for cereals. Once again, Athenaios reports their findings. I give four examples:

> Mnesitheos of Athens in his book *On Edible Foods* says, 'when it comes to Euboean nuts or chestnuts (they are known by both names) their breaking down in the stomach is difficult and digestion (*pepsis*) is attended with wind. However they fatten the system, if the eater can manage them. Almonds and Heracleot nuts and Persian nuts and others of the same kind are inferior to them. It is important that none of this class is eaten uncooked, apart

from green almonds. Some should be boiled, others...roasted. Some of them are naturally oily, such as dried almonds and Zeus' acorns, while others are tough and astringent, such as beech-nuts and all of that kind. Heating removes the fat from the oily varieties, and that is the worst part. The tough and astringent varieties soften if a slow and gentle heat is used.

(2.54b–c)

On apples, Athenaios quotes Diphilos, among others:

green and unripe apples have bad juice and are bad for the stomach. They rise to the top of the stomach, they generate bile, they create disease and cause the patient to shiver. When they are ripe, the sweet ones have good juice and are easily excreted because they have no binding quality; bitter apples however have bad juice and are binding.

(3.80e–f)

On mallows, a plant dismissed in many texts as fit only for the poor, Athenaios summarises Diphilos as follows

the mallow has good juice, softens the bronchial tubes, and dissolves the bitter humours at the top of the stomach. He says that it is suitable for irritation of the kidneys and the bladder, is easily passed and is nourishing, though the wild variety is better than the cultivated.

(2.58e)

On wild plants, Athenaios quotes from the first book of the *Hygieina* (*On Health*) of Diocles of Carystos: 'wild plants that may be boiled are lettuce (the black variety is the best), cress, coriander, mustard, onion (the varieties to use are the *askalonion* and the *geteion*), garlic, clove-garlic, cucumber, melon and poppy' (2.68d–e). Shortly afterwards he says, 'the melon is better for the heart and easier to digest. The cucumber when boiled is soft, innocuous and diuretic. The melon is more laxative if boiled in honey' (fr. 196 Van der Eijk).

These are foods available to all at low price. Edelstein may be right to believe that this advice was designed for doctors and rich hypochondriacs but the doctors' attention to such foods allows us to evaluate by their criteria foods available to all citizens. Furthermore, vegetables and wild vegetables in particular enjoy a low reputation in many texts. Clearly they were not beneath the attention of the dieticians.

FISH

If vegetables enjoyed a poor reputation among many authors (but not, of course, in Athenaios and the medical authors), the reverse may be said of fish. This is the food that is thought to have appealed to the ancient gourmet above all, and to have commanded the highest prices. The ancient evidence has been discussed recently by Dalby (1995), Davidson (1997) and Wilkins (2000). This is not to say that fish had no part to play in a healthy diet. The testimony of Athenaios is interesting in this regard. In his seventh book, he lists fish alphabetically and notes mention of them in comic, zoological and some medical texts. The main evidence for their place in a healthy diet is however reserved for the next book where two lengthy excerpts from Mnesitheos and Diphilos are given (8.355b–358c). The classification of fish by the doctors follows both zoological and dietary criteria. I give two quotations:

> Diphilos of Siphnos in his book *Suitable Foods for the Sick and the Healthy* [says] that of the sea fish, the rock fish are easy to digest, of good juice, purgative, light and of little nourishment, while the pelagic fish are difficult to digest, very nourishing and difficult to assimilate. Of the rock fish, both male and female *phukes* (possibly one of the wrasse; Thompson 1947: 276–8) are very tender little fish, free from smell and easy to digest. The sea-perch is similar but differs a little according to locality. ...The parrot-wrasse (*skaros*; Thompson 1947: 238–41) has tender flesh, is flaky, sweet, light, easy to digest and assimilate and loosens the bowels. A recently-caught fish is suspect since this fish feeds by hunting sea-hares[6] and so their innards may cause 'cholera'. ... The sea perch has good juices and plenty of them, is viscous, difficult to digest, very nourishing and diuretic. Its head meat is viscous and easy to digest, the body is difficult to digest and heavier, while the tail is more tender. The fish gives rise to phlegm [one of the four humours] and is hard to digest. ... The gilt-head bream is acrid, of tender flesh, without smell, good to taste and diuretic. When it is boiled it is not indigestible but when fried it is difficult to digest. The red mullet is good to taste but is fairly astringent, hard to digest and restricts the bowels, particularly when cooked over charcoal. ... The *box* (Thompson 1947: 36–7) if boiled is easy to digest and assimilate, releases moisture and is good for the bowels. Cooked on charcoal, it is sweeter and more tender. ... Small fry are heavy and difficult to digest (the white variety is called *kobitis*). Boiled small fish are of the same class. ... The electric ray is

difficult to digest, though the head meat is tender and of a good taste and even digestible. The rest is not.

(8.355b)

A further section reads:

> Mnesitheos of Athens in his book *On Edible Foods* says...the shoaling fish offer food that is pleasing because they are fat but that is also heavy and hard to digest. For this reason, they are best salted and these make the best kinds of preserved fish. ...Small fry and anchovies and sardines and the other fish that we eat bones and all make for a windy digestion but give nourishment which is moist. Since digestion in this case is uneven, with the flesh digested very quickly and the bone dissolved slowly (for small fry are in themselves bony) each part gets in the way of the other in digestion. As a result wind arises from digestion and humours arise from this food. They are better boiled. ...Every dish of fish is easier to digest if it is prepared simply.

(8.357a)

These two extracts, which I have heavily excerpted, cover a wide range of fish which share much with the classification of Aristotle in his *History of Animals* and with writers on cookery such as Archestratos of Gela, who shows particular interest in wrasse, bream and the head meat of fish. The division of fish into rockfish and pelagic fish and the category of shoaling fish are found in Aristotle, while the inferior flesh of the electric ray is found in Archestraus fr. 48 Brandt (= 49 Olson and Sens). As we saw in the survey of vegetables and cereals, the doctors include foods that were available to the poor, such as small fry and anchovies (Wilkins 2001). Once again, they review the nutritional qualities of a large section of the diet and, while many species under discussion were likely to command high prices and to be found on the tables of the better off, their focus on good health gives an impressive counter-balance to all the other texts which emphasise the cost and luxury of such dishes. The doctors appear to be aware of such considerations – Mnesitheos, for example, counsels against all elaboration – but are relatively uninterested in them. The doctors thus enable us to classify the diet of all citizens according to ancient theories of nutrition, even if only the better off were able to pay for such advice and adjust their diets accordingly. These texts on fish bear some comparison with the cookery books, in so far as they tolerate taste and pleasure, and take much account of variety and season. They are also much more concerned in general with the diet required for the healthy rather than for the sick.[7] It appears to be left to the doctor to determine adjustments required in illness.

The texts on nutrition also allow Athenaios to cover a wider range of thought on eating than the luxurious diets and pastimes of the rich, which might appear to fill so many pages of the *Deipnosophistai*. It is undoubtedly the case that much of his evidence, since it draws on literary sources, is concerned solely with the lives of the better off, but our theme of Hygieia has enabled us to see that both at the symposium and in dietetics, Good Health was of interest, at least in theory, to all. The better off were simply better placed to attain that goal, as they are in most cultures, particularly our own.

GALEN

In order to sharpen our picture of eating and Good Health in Athenaios, I turn, finally, to our author's older contemporary, Galen, who died in the early third century AD, and has already been quoted as a semi-fictional speaker in the *Deipnosophistai*. Like Athenaios, he was a Greek speaker who worked and wrote within the culture of the Roman Empire. Like Athenaios, he had to come to terms with the power of Rome, and spent some of his time as physician to the emperor Marcus Aurelius and other periods in his native Pergamum. Unlike Athenaios, he was a systematic thinker and a medical practitioner. He was also a great traveller who applied personal observation to theory and belief. In his work on nutrition, he brings a great deal of personal experience to bear in a way that is not found in Athenaios.

The comprehensive coverage of Galen in *De alimentorum facultatibus* (*On the Properties of Foods*) is striking. He considers first cereals, then other plants and finally land animals, fish and birds and takes much account of season and what the animal is fed on; for example, animals are best when fed on spring grasses (6.665 K) and when young (6.704 K); goats are best eaten cold and in summer (15.880 K; see further Lopez-Ferez 1988). Galen has much on the diet of the poor. Peasants add cheese to flat breads on festival days. All suffer (6.486 K, p. 80 Grant). Country folk and city dwellers make flat cakes in no time (6.491 K, p. 82 Grant); they eat boiled wheat which is bad for digestion (6.498 K, p. 85 Grant); they use crushed barley when bread is short – this affords little nourishment (6.507 K, p. 89 Grant); no one eats *zeia* and is healthy. The smell is unpleasant but they get used to it (6.513 K, p. 91 Grant). Bread from *bromos is* consumed only if the population is threatened by famine (6.523 K, p. 95 Grant). *Lathyroi* (chickling) are used a great deal by countryfolk in Asia and are relatively nourishing (6.540 K, pp. 102–3 Grant), while men do not eat bitter vetch (*orobos*). It is suitable for cattle and unpleasant to taste, with bad juices. In times of famine, as Hippocrates observed, they are forced to eat it (6.546 K, p. 105 Grant).

In addition to comment on the poorer citizen, Galen's survey also embraces the seasonal factors and aspects of cooking and pleasure that we have explored above. The flesh of pigs is sweeter, more nourishing and easier to cook if they have been castrated (6.676 K, p. 160 Grant); the liver of all animals has a thick juice and is hard and slow to digest. Much better both for pleasure and for other reasons is the 'fig' liver, so called because the animal is fed on dried figs prior to slaughter. It is sweetest in the case of the pig (6.679 K, p. 162 Grant). As for fish, the taste as it is eaten will instantly reveal which is the better grey mullet (*kephalos*). Its flesh will have a better bite, and it will be sweeter and less fat (6.712–13 K, p. 175 Grant). The red mullet is valued for the pleasure it gives when eaten (6.715 K, p. 176 Grant). Pleasure is afforded even by millet (for peasants who are used to it, 6.524 K, p. 96 Grant) while rice is unpleasant to eat (6.525 K, p. 96 Grant). Galen's discussion of lentils (6.528 K, pp. 97–8 Grant) is redolent of Hippocratic doctrine – which Galen follows closely. For all foodstuffs, the geographical location is crucial, together with the season and the climate in which they are consumed. In autumn, care must be taken to avoid foods that dry the body and turn into black bile, but such foods should be safe in winter, just as cooling and moistening foods are required in summer. In spring a middling food is needed. An example of such a food is a preparation by Heracleides of Tarentum who used to give a dish that combined beets and lentils to the well and the sick, this being a middle dish composed of opposites. On lentils specifically, Galen declares that their juice is not astringent, that they can be boiled in water to make a laxative and that flavouring them with savoury, pennyroyal and dill or leek makes them more tasty and digestible. The way that cooks prepare lentils with reduced wine (*siraion*) is however very bad. On fruit and vegetables, Galen notes that apples may be prepared for their sweetness or for usefulness (6.596 K, p. 126 Grant). This division, which recalls Plato's views in *Gorgias*, is seen also in his discussion of spices (6.638–9 K, p. 144 Grant). Spices are read about in cookery books, which are in a sense the common property of doctors and cooks. These professions have different aims and objectives. Doctors aim at utility in foods rather than pleasurable qualities. Cautious flavouring with spices can lead to both better flavour and better digestion, but some cooks use these flavourings too much and produce indigestion rather than good digestion. Pleasure is normally permitted in this treatise, provided medical outcomes are not compromised. Thus *intibi* (endives) have the same strength as lettuce but lack pleasurable eating and the other qualities described in lettuces (6.628 K, p. 139 Grant).

Comparison with Galen suggests that the dieticians in Athenaios used less personal observation and were less interested in the social context of eating.[8] By Athenaios' report at least, they appear to be less interested than

Galen in the inferior grains and pulses. On the other hand, they give a comprehensive survey of categories of food and demonstrate that medical authors did not follow Plato's objections to prepared foods or taste, provided the nutritional outcome was unimpaired. If we are concerned with what was eaten and how this might be fitted into a programme of good health, then these texts have much to offer. They systematise and attempt a comprehensive coverage. What Athenaios and Galen can contribute to the present volume, meanwhile, in addition to their preservation of some of the words of the Hellenistic doctors, is a cultural overview of Hygieia, Good Health, in their own second/third century AD and over the previous 600 years of Greek culture. This overview, that takes in literature, philosophy, history and medicine, may be placed beside the complex associations of Hygieia at the turn of the fifth and fourth centuries BC. This was the period when Ariphron composed his influential hymn; the religious underpinning of good health was expanding in the building of new sanctuaries of Asklepios; scientific medicine was expanding in the treatises of the Hippocratic doctors; the goddess was honoured on the thousands of occasions when people met at symposia and Plato was exploring good and bad approaches to physical and psychic health. Good health was a major cultural preoccupation, and far too important to be left to hypochondriacs.

NOTES

1 Hunter 1983, in his commentary on Eubulus, cites a number of other literary references to libations for Hygieia at the start of the symposium, including Critias fr. 6 West, on Spartan drinking.
2 The fragment goes on to list the unhealthy consequences for guests who go as far as the tenth bowl.
3 The compound noun wealth–health appears to be a coinage of Aristophanes; he used it also at *Birds* 731 and *Wasps* 677. On the Boeotian festival, see Plutarch, *Table-Talk* 6.8.1 = *Mor.* 693f.
4 For an overview see Edelstein 1967; Lonie 1977; Vallance 1996: 468. Longrigg 1998: 146–56 summarises relevant texts and bibliography. On Pythagoras see Iamblichus, *Life of Pythagoras* 163 (quoted by Longrigg).
5 Porphyry, *Homeric Enquiries* (on *Iliad* 11.515), 165.12 Schrader. See further Nutton 1995a; Longrigg 1998.
6 Thompson 1947: 142–3 notes 'the sea-hare was celebrated in antiquity as extremely poisonous and of magical qualities'.
7 Comparison with all the fragments of Mnesitheos known to us (not merely those cited by Athenaios) and with Dieuches (a doctor only mentioned in passing by Athenaios) is possible in Bertier 1972. Mnesitheos appears to concern himself primarily with the healthy, Dieuches with the sick.
8 Scarborough 1970 describes Diphilos as an 'academic'!

8

WOMEN'S HEALTH AND RECOVERY IN THE HIPPOCRATIC CORPUS

Helen King

'Is women's health the absence of disease, or is it something more?' This question, provoked by the World Health Organisation (WHO) definition of health discussed briefly in the Introduction, was posed at the beginning of the first section of a recent collection of pieces on women's health (Ruzek *et al.* 1997: 3). Work to date on Hippocratic gynaecology has tended to focus on diseases, rather than on health (e.g. Hanson 1989; Dean-Jones 1994; Demand 1994; King 1998). There is a very good reason for such an emphasis; the bulk of the Hippocratic *Gynaikeia* concerns the symptoms exhibited by the sick female body, and recommendations for how to treat them, so that the usual English translation of the title is not the neutral 'Women's matters', but rather *Diseases of Women*. Here I want to examine Hippocratic gynaecology from the perspective offered by the concept of health, and to assess the view of health for women which is implicit in the texts. To do this, I will use models from the sociology of medicine to help formulate questions; these models are based on Western biomedicine, so that it is more appropriate to use them to raise questions than to assume that they provide answers.

One particular question of interest here concerns the differences between what is defined as 'health' for men and what counts as 'health' for women. In the 1970s, as a consequence of the feminist movement, challenges were mounted to the idea that health is the same for all. In America, the National Women's Health Network was established in 1975. The Society for Women's Health Research currently argues that women's difference from men is not only social and cultural, but physical, with gender differences present in bone, in the reaction to certain drugs, and in the function of the immune system. Its website announces that 'Sex differences exist in virtually every system in the body.'[1] In the modern West, disease can be gendered in a way that adversely affects women's health. For example, lung cancer and coronary heart disease are regarded as 'men's diseases' (Narrigan *et al.* 1997: 553). Although women's mortality from coronary heart disease is as high as that of men, it is wrongly believed that cancer poses a greater risk to them, and so female patients may ignore the symptoms of heart disease, while their doctors in turn may be reluctant to send them for tests. They may be therefore be diagnosed only at an advanced stage of the disease (Villablanca 2000). Furthermore, in pharmaceutical research, there is a long tradition of seeing men as the norm, and women as a variation on that norm (Stanton *et al.* 2000: 616–17). The way in which drug trials are conducted as controlled experiments, with variables reduced as far as possible, means that it is normal practice to use as a sample an all-male group. For example, research showing that aspirin can prevent heart disease was carried out on a sample of 22,000 subjects: all men (Narrigan *et al.* 1997: 573–4, n. 1). Women's exclusion from drug trials is also defended on the grounds that they may be pregnant – so that there is a risk of an unborn child being affected by the drugs being tested – and that their hormonal cycle in any case makes them too variable (Narrigan *et al.* 1997: 555); yet, of course, they will eventually be prescribed the drugs which have only been tested on men.

As these examples show, recent work on women's health has emphasised that it involves far more than reproductive matters (Boswell and Poland 2003); in this chapter, my focus will be on the relationship between reproductive and more general health in the Hippocratic texts on the diseases of women. I will argue that, although these texts regard pregnancy and childbirth as signs of health and forms of therapy, they are by no means as rigid as one may expect in assuming that female health must necessarily involve being able to give birth.

DEFINING HEALTH

At what level should we take the Hippocratics' direct and oblique references to what is considered healthy in a female patient? In order to answer this question, we need to raise some prior issues; in particular, what for these texts is 'health'?

The ancient Greeks saw health primarily in terms of balance; as Temkin (1977: 272) pointed out, when the pre-Socratic philosopher Alcmeon defined health in this way, his term for balance – *isonomia* – was also that used for equality of political rights, so that health became a sort of democracy and disease was a 'monarchy' in which one of the qualities predominated at the expense of the others (DK 24 B 4; see further Vlahogiannis,

Ch. 10, this volume).[2] Health as balance was intrinsic not only to Galenic medicine, through the many centuries in which Galen's view of the body as a mixture of fluids dominated the Western medical tradition, but also to those individuals who perceived themselves as putting forward a new message within that tradition. For example, in his *Essays on the Preservation and Recovery of Health* (1704), where he argued for the virtues of water over the 'new' drinks of cider, fortified wine, coffee and tea, Thomas Curteis defined health, 'the most valuable of temporal blessings' (1704: 1), as 'A due Symmetry, Temperament, and regular impulsive Energy, of the Blood, Spirits, and their subservient Fluids; actuating and enabling all the Parts of our Bodies to an uninterrupted Discharge of their respective Functions' (1704: 2).

But health could also be understood in terms of monarchy: the rule over oneself that is represented in the pseudo-Hippocratic letters as something out of the reach of women, and not to be bought by kings (*Pseudepigrapha* 13). The body must 'rule over' the foods it takes in; the verb *krateein* is used in, for example, the Hippocratic *Places in Man* 44, where we are told that one should give only that food which the body can master/digest. Some foods are mastered by the body quickly, others slowly (*Epidemics* 6.5.15), and it is those foods the body cannot master which cause pain, disease and death (*On Ancient Medicine* 3, Loeb I, 16–20 and 14, Loeb I, 36–8).

In Western medicine from the early modern period onwards, it was health which became 'democratised'. Texts on health from the seventeenth century onwards often carry an explicitly political message; by advising their readers to 'Use moderation and temperance, and defie the Physician' (Harris 1676: 162), and showing 'that every Man is, or may be, his own best physician' (Flammand 1697), they argue that the sick have no need of expensive doctors. Such texts as Cornwell's *The Domestic Physician; Or, Guardian of Health*, published in 1784, start with the Galenic definition that medicine is the art of preserving health, and then go on to list for the lay reader 'in the most familiar manner, the symptoms of every disorder incident to mankind; together with their gradual progress, and the method of cure'. The message of *Medicina Flagellata: Or, the Doctor Scarify'd, With an Essay on Health, or the Power of a Regimen* (1721) is that the reader can dispense with the need for doctors by following 40 'General Maxims for Health'; listed on pages 161–73, these include 'Whoever eats or drinks too much, will be sick.' 'Health' manuals focus on regimen, particularly on food, which 'preserves and supports our health', rather than on medicine, which 'restores our health' (Flammand 1697: 73). They list the symptoms of ill-health in order to argue that, through the use of instinct and reason, we can know when we are about to fall ill, and then cure ourselves; their hero is not Hippocrates or Galen, but Cato the Censor, who acted as physician to himself and to his family (e.g. Flammand 1697: 3). Plutarch described the home remedies used by Cato, who wrote his *De agri cultura* in around 160 BC; according to the evidence that survives, Cato's views on medicine were that Greek doctors can seriously damage your health, and that true medicine lies in the book of remedies (*commentarius*) kept by the Roman *paterfamilias*, the head of household. Pliny states that Cato had 'a notebook, by the aid of which he treated his son, servants, and household' (*NH* 29.7.14–29.8.16). Plutarch goes further than Pliny, making Cato into the compiler, not just the possessor, of this book: he 'had compiled a notebook (*hypomnema*) of recipes and used them for the diet or treatment of any members of his household who fell ill' (*Life of Cato* 23). Here, then, the early modern praise of Cato is part of a message that the means to health should be in the hands of the patient, not of the doctor.

WOMEN'S HEALTH

Today, women's life expectancy in the developed world is greater than that of men. This is a contrast to the past; Arnott (Ch. 1, this volume) notes that life expectancy for men fell in some parts of Minoan Crete while women's remained more stable, but that women could still expect to live for 3–6 years less than men. Medical sociology has drawn our attention to a range of issues focused on the gender of the patient. Do women in contemporary Western society feel ill more than men do? Are they more likely to be labelled as having a disease?

It is a commonplace that women today make more use than men of health services. Even when medical conditions associated with childbirth are excluded, women report more physical and mental illness than men (Nathanson 1975). In medical literature this behaviour is not, however, taken as evidence that women have a more responsible attitude to their health than men have, but is instead traditionally seen as confirming the view that women are sicker and more dependent (Weisensee 1986: 19); indeed, women apparently internalise this, and believe themselves to be sicker than men (Weisensee 1986: 22). Why do women visit the doctor more? The statistics are clear, but their interpretation is vigorously debated. Is it because it is more acceptable for women to be ill; that, while 'the ethic of health is masculine', the sick role is seen as feminine? Or is it because they are indeed more ill than men, because of particular stresses they suffer, or because of exposure to children's illness? Or is it because doctors are more likely to dismiss women's ailments as trivial, making more visits necessary before the patient is taken seriously (Weisensee 1986: 20–1)? The problem underlying all this material is the difficulty of deciding what is really going on: are women more likely to *feel* ill, or more likely to *be diagnosed* as having a disease?

Moving from illness and disease to health, a study of white middle-class Americans carried out in the early 1990s attempted to discover whether men and women conceptualised their own health differently. In true WHO style, both sexes saw health as a state of well-being encompassing physical, mental and emotional aspects, and both referred to 'balance' as a key concept. They thought of health as something precarious which one had to work at, by making decisions about food, sleep and exercise. For the student of ancient medicine, this modern lay approach shows striking similarities with the humoral system. However, men were more likely to talk about control of their health and their bodies, while women seemed to think of their bodies as having their own momentum: 'my body just wants to keep eating'. The study therefore concluded that men think of themselves *as* their bodies, while women think of their bodies as objects (Saltonstall 1993). I would argue that this distinction could be seen as an internalisation by women of men's view of them as 'the other'. Men see women's bodies as 'other': women absorb this, just as they absorb the construction of their bodies as sicker than those of men, and in constructing themselves women maintain a critical distance from their own bodies. A study of the 'wellness revolution' in contemporary America showed that women worked out in order to become thin, while men worked out in order to become stronger and more muscular; women wanted to become smaller, men bigger (Conrad 1994: 395–6). This would suggest that men's and women's experiences of themselves as embodied are radically different.

However, there is also a danger in thinking of 'women' as an undifferentiated group. While arguing for a concept of 'women's health' focused on those diseases found almost exclusively in women (e.g. breast cancer), or more common in women (e.g. osteoporosis) or which present differently (e.g. heart disease), the authors of the collection *Women's Health: Complexities and Differences* also stress 'the diversity of women's health needs' (Ruzek *et al.* 1997: 3); there is no 'standard woman', and any attempt to improve women's health needs to take into account ethnic and social factors.

HIPPOCRATIC HEALTH

Turning now to the Hippocratic corpus, a few remarks about Hippocratic attitudes to health in general are necessary before looking at the representation of female health in the gynaecological texts. Today health is seen as a positive condition; not merely the absence of disease, but as multidimensional and dynamic, 'a process rather than a state' (Weisensee 1986: 30). It also carries strong moral implications; we exercise not only to feel and look good, but to *be* good, jogging for 'personal and social redemption' (Conrad 1994: 388–9).

There is an ancient Greek medical tradition of seeing health not as a static norm, but as an acquired condition which has to be worked at; a process in a wider historical sense. This is the position taken by *On Ancient Medicine* 3 (Loeb I, 16–20), which suggests that primitive mankind suffered as a result of eating the same strong, raw foods as the animals. Only a proper recognition of difference from the rest of the animal kingdom led to the gradual development of an appropriate diet – and of health – for humanity.

Not all Hippocratic texts consider health as a process. The main interest in the texts is not in the question, 'How do I achieve health?' but rather in the question, 'From what do diseases arise?' Nevertheless, the writers are interested in health as well as in disease. *Regimen in Acute Diseases* 9 (Loeb II, 70) says that medicine can bring security to the healthy, and in chapter 28 (Loeb II, 84) the author recommends studying healthy people, to see how their condition changes if they alter their regimen; for example, by having lunch when they are unaccustomed to it. *Regimen in Health* is directed at the *idiôtês*, the layman, and advises him how he should control his diet, according to the season and his own physique, in order to remain in the best of health.

The role of the doctor is to convert disease into health, although Hippocratic writers disagree on how far their powers here extend. The author of *Regimen in Acute Diseases* 9 (Loeb II, 7) claims that the medical *technê* can bring health in all diseases. But *Prognostics* 1 (Loeb II, 6) observes that 'it is not possible to make healthy all who are ill'. *Diseases* 1.5 (Loeb V, 108) points out that some diseases would get better of their own accord, even if the doctor were not there, while chance, *tychê*, plays an important role in medicine (*Diseases* 1.8; Loeb V, 114).

However, the Hippocratic writers show more confidence in the scope of their art when considering its universal applicability. Like medical writers today, who generally suggest that health and disease are universally definable conditions, so that presenting a particular set of indicators – physical or psychological symptoms – makes a person 'sick' regardless of the society within which that person lives, the Hippocratics generally do not believe in cultural variation in disease. Their theories are universally applicable: the same symptoms have the same meaning 'in Libya, in Delos and in Scythia' (*Prognostics* 25; Loeb II, 54). The Hippocratic writers would have little sympathy with modern socioculturalists, who look at the different standards by which different societies judge normality and pathology (Kellert 1976: 222). One South American tribe suffers so extensively from the skin disorder dyschromatic spirochetosis that anyone who does not have it is seen as abnormal, and excluded from marriage (Mechanic 1968: 16, cited by Kellert 1976: 223). Other cultures have been found to regard measles not as a disease, but as a normal rite of passage into adulthood. The Hippocratics, however, regard the different systems they propose as universal in scope, because they are founded on the basic biological structure common to all human beings.

For a woman, what do the Hippocratic texts regard as 'health'? In these works, 'health' is not a code word for democracy or an expression of freedom from the need for doctors; on the contrary, the discussion of health in the gynaecological texts often takes place to bolster the doctor's prestige as carer, with a large proportion of the references to 'being healthy' in *Diseases of Women* providing variations on 'if she is cared for (usual verb, *meledainein*) she is quickly healthy' (*Diseases of Women* 1.2, Littré 8.16; 1.8, L 8.34; 1.9, L 8.40; 1.29, L 8.72 etc.). The normal opposition here is not health/disease but health/death: 'but if not cared for, she will die' (*DW* 1.4, L 8.26; 1.8, L 8.36). This opposition is not exclusive to the gynaecology of the corpus; Galen (17A.611 K) explains the shorthand symbols found in some manuscripts of *Epidemics* 3, noting that case histories always end Y or Θ respectively meaning *hygieia*, 'recovery of health', or *thanatos*, 'death'. When the focus is on *disease*, the outcome of the case can only be one of two options; either health, or death.

Thus the very idea of 'health' here implies medical intervention. This is particularly true where women are concerned, because women are seen as physically more at risk of disease than are men. Health is balance, but women's bodies are always in flux between excess and evacuation, and this process is always at risk of interruption because of the fragility of the main organ responsible for maintaining the balance, the womb, which can tilt, close, gape open or retreat up the body (King 1998: 33–5). For Hippocratic men, the evidence for the restoration of women's 'health' is demonstrated in the return of the regular bleeding upon which Hippocratic medicine insists.

The definition of women's health is very closely and explicitly linked to women's reproductive functions. Health is shown by regular monthly menstruation (*Seven Months' Child* 9, L 7.448); it is defined as the production of menstrual blood which flows like that of a sacrificed beast, and which clots quickly (*DW* 1.6, L 8.30; *Nature of the Child* 18, L 7.502; cf. *DW* 1.72, L 8.152). The correct quantity of blood loss per month, 'if she is healthy', is 2 Attic cotyls in 2 or 3 days. This figure recurs in Soranos, although as a maximum rather than as the norm (*DW* 1.6, L 8.30; Soranos, *Gynaecology* 1.20). Lesley Dean-Jones (1994: 90–1) has pointed out that another section of *Diseases of Women* takes two cotyls as the most that the womb can hold, outside pregnancy, so that when the womb needs to be washed out this is given as the maximum amount of fluid one should pour in. In fact, the capacity is 2–3 fluid ounces. The assumption behind the figure of two cotyls for the amount to be lost each month is thus that the container which is the womb fills completely each month and must empty itself completely.

In addition to regular and heavy menstrual bleeding, sexual intercourse is presented as essential to health; *Generation* 4 (L 7. 476) explains that women are healthier if they have sex. Pregnancy is also 'healthy'; in a number of pathological conditions – including a tilted womb, and 'the whites' – the description ends with, 'if she becomes pregnant, she is healthy' or with variations on this theme, such as 'if she conceives' or 'if she bears a child' (*DW* 1.37, L 8.92; 1.63, L 8.130; 2.119, L 8.260 etc.: *DW* 2.162, L 8.342: *DW* 1.59, L 8.118). The different stages of pregnancy and childbirth are not equivalent, but are credited with distinct powers; becoming pregnant is evidence of health, because it shows that the womb must be in place, open and receptive, while giving birth purges, as in a description of water on the womb which states, 'if she carries a child to full term, she evacuates everything, and becomes healthy' (*DW* 2.175, L 8.358). It is also possible to substitute drugs for the natural purge of childbirth; what matters most appears to be not the successful pregnancy, but the release of retained matter from the womb to make the woman *hygiês* again (*DW* 1.60, L 8.122; 2.133, L 8.284; 2.170, L 8.350).

In these texts, it does however seem possible to be healthy while infertile: to be healthy as a person, while having an unhealthy womb. The phrase 'the health of the body and of the womb' (*DW* 3.217, L 8.418; *Superfoetation* 29, L 8.494) suggests the separation of the woman from her womb; instead of the modern 'my body just wants to keep eating' perhaps we should envisage an ancient Greek woman saying 'my womb just wants to have a baby'. The use of the phrase 'healthy *and* fruitful' (*hygiês kai phoros, DW* 1.40, L 8.98) could be taken in either of two ways. It may be a simple doublet – fruitfulness being seen as the consequence of health – but it may also open up the possibility of the woman who is healthy but *not* fruitful. It is the second suggestion which can best be supported from other passages in the gynaecological texts. For example, in a woman suffering from excess phlegm in her body, a Hippocratic author notes that, even if the disease has become chronic, she will recover (*hygiainei*) if treated; there is little danger of death, but she will not be able to become pregnant (*DW* 1.9, L 8.40). In considering the possibility of health in the absence of fertility, three categories are used. First, there is the woman who cannot conceive, although her womb is basically healthy, because it is 'weak'. The remedy given here is to strengthen the womb, treating it 'until it appears to be healthy', but also paying attention to the health of the whole body (*DW* 1.12, L 8.48; 2.119, L 8.260). As a second possibility, the writers envisage the woman who recovers from illness, who thus becomes 'healthy' once again, but is not able to conceive, as in *Diseases of Women* 1.9, or in 1.65, where the description of treatment for a woman suffering from severe ulceration of the womb ends, 'By doing these things, she becomes healthy: but she is no longer fertile'

(*DW* 1.9, L 8.40; 1.65, L 8.134). This situation is also expressed by saying that the woman 'will be healthy, but sterile': *hygiês estai, aphoros de*. The use of 'but' suggests that female health would normally be thought to include fertility. This situation occurs most frequently after severe ulceration (*DW* 1.2, L 8.20; 1.65, L 8.134; 1.67, L 8.140) but it is also a danger after a complete uterine prolapse, when the condition is described as one to which women who have never given birth are particularly susceptible (*DW* 2.145, L 8.320). Third, and undermining any idea of health and disease as simply either/or, in a discussion of dealing with the particularly intractable condition called 'the white flux', affecting the whole body, treatments are listed to dry out the body in a range of ways, but the writer adds, 'by doing these things, they become healthy, but not completely: however, their life is made easier' (*eupetesteron de diagousin*, *DW* 2.116, L 8.252).

Health, then, is normally shown by conception and childbirth, although it is accepted that some women can be healthy in the body, while not in the womb. Although individual variation is also accepted in some Hippocratic discussions of menstrual blood loss, there is however much less leeway given to women here. Writers of some parts of *Diseases of Women* consider that bleeding for more or less than the canonical 2–3 days a month constitutes disease (*epinosos*, *DW* 1.6, L 8.30). Others take into account the individual *physis* of each patient, based on visible signs: the fair and the young are wetter and more liable to flux, while darker, older women have firmer flesh (e.g. *DW* 2.145, L 8.320; *Nature of Woman* 1, L 7.312). However, as another passage of the gynaecology puts it, 'Generally, most treatment is the same for all women' (*DW* 1.11, L 8.44). Furthermore, all women have to bleed every month without fail, or they will call down upon themselves the full Hippocratic battery of treatments to draw out the hidden blood; the beetle pessaries and fumigations.

I have argued elsewhere (King 1995a) that, if we take our definitions of health as universally valid, then it is possible to argue that women's health was defined by the Hippocratics in such a way that it could never be attained. Data from rural Sri Lanka, pre-contact Australia and eighteenth century England and Wales all suggest that menstruation was normally both scanty and infrequent. So, either ancient Greek women persistently failed to meet the standards set for them, and thus ran the risk of being defined, in terms of their own culture, as very sick indeed; or, they really did bleed to such an extent that, by our cultural definitions, they *were* very sick indeed.

At this point we have to decide on the status of the Hippocratic texts. They are clearly normative; they set limits, and judge health accordingly. They are also clearly trying to establish the authority of their writers. Do they, in any way, reflect real medical practice? There is no alternative here to speculation. So – can we suggest that in ancient Greek culture too there was a mismatch between the patient's view of health – 'I feel fine' – and the doctor's view – 'You have a disease'?

Why would an ancient Greek woman decide she was sick? She lived within a very special cultural context, in which Hesiod's Pandora remained the origin of 'the race of women' (Loraux 1978) and where, by definition, women could never meet the ideal for humanity, the adult free-born Greek male. Would she accept the Hippocratic medical model which says she is a tube and jar concoction, accumulating and evacuating blood? She was told that her flesh was of a looser texture than that of a man, so that it absorbed more fluid from her diet and converted it into an excess of blood. She was told that her body developed more spaces inside during puberty, and that the flesh was further 'broken down' by the process of giving birth. She was told that she must bleed heavily each month, otherwise the blood would build up and rot, or put pressure on her vital organs. Believing such things would encourage her to report the absence of bleeding as a very serious sign. But then if she knew what the treatment would be – beetle pessaries, three-day long fumigations with vapour from a jar containing a dead puppy being passed through a reed up her vagina – we may feel that she would be very unlikely to report the absence of bleeding (*DW* 2.230, L 8.440). If she had fully internalised the Hippocratic model of her body, one missed period in the absence of conception was a serious symptom and should be reported at once. If, however, she otherwise felt healthy, would she bother?

Our imaginary woman should, however, always be under the control of a male *kyrios*; her father, husband or brother. It may have been his decision rather than hers as to whether medical attention was deemed necessary. The dominant cultural model of male and female held that only men could be healthy because only men could exert the control necessary over every aspect of their lives. Women's bodies were unbalanced even by definition, and they could not regulate their regimen in the way men could. *Regimen in Health* mentions women only once, in chapter 6 (Loeb IV, 52), where they are advised to keep to a dry diet because of their soft, spongy flesh. Their ability to control their health is thus limited by their basic physical constraint of wet spongy flesh, as well as by their position under the control of a male *kyrios*.

However, I do not believe that we should overstate the subservient position of ancient Greek women. I have discussed elsewhere (King 1995b) how Hippocratic medicine incorporates mechanisms by which women can 'play the system', turning around Hippocratic doctors' grand ideological statements about women's bodies and using them for their own ends. Because they share the cultural belief that women are supposed to 'know' whether or not they have conceived from an act of intercourse, doctors cannot challenge a woman who has not menstruated for some time but rejects the suggestion that she could be pregnant. The Hippocratic theory of 'critical days', which explicitly covers conception, miscarriage and child-birth, regards as the most important days in any bodily process the first and seventh; uneven days are thought to be dangerous and, among even days, 14, 28 and 42 are significant, as are multiples of 3 and 4 (*Seven Months' Child* 9, L 7.446–8). A woman who thinks she is miscarrying can avoid awkward questions about culpability by stating, for example, that it is 'the seventh day' since she felt herself conceive. In therapy, the woman patient's knowledge of her internal anatomy is trusted; if asked by the Hippocratic practitioner whether her womb is still tilted, replying that it is not will end the possibly painful treatment (*DW* 2.133, L 8.284–6).

In conclusion, then, not only do different societies have different concepts of 'health', but within any social group men and women may have different experiences of the body. A doctor's construction of health may differ from that of the patient, one diagnosing 'disease' while the other insists on feeling well. We have no way of knowing whether the female patients of the Hippocratic corpus bought into the model of the healthy body – a model by our standards deeply unhealthy – held out to them by Hippocratic medicine. But modern analogies would suggest that the decision to seek medical help depends on whether one is able to do all that one has to, or wants to, do, and that the social cost of seeking help is weighed up against the social cost of doing nothing. Here it is possible that conception was one of the focal points where doctors' and patients' views met. Failure to conceive, in a society in which giving birth was essential to being a fully mature woman, or *gynê*, could have been one experience which led a woman to seek help. A Hippocratic explanation, like that of 'ulcers in the womb', the treatment programme provided for the condition, and the outcome of being 'healthy, but infertile' did, at least, provide an answer to a distressing situation. Here, health can exist despite the infirmity of an important part of the body. Contemporary definitions of health in terms of ability to cope within one's social networks (e.g. Kellert 1976: 223) would suggest that other focal points may have existed where a woman could not fulfil her duties. For example, in the Hippocratic description of 'the white flux' already discussed, the list of symptoms includes visual disturbances, and feet so swollen that the woman was 'unable to walk'; although here the Hippocratic author states that she could not be cured, the treatments given are at least able to make a female patient's life 'easier' (*eupetesteron*, *DW* 2.116, L 8.252). Comparing the ancient materials with early modern and contemporary concepts of health can offer a new set of perspectives from which we can interrogate the Hippocratic texts, and can help us to think about the social and cultural dimensions of ancient Greek medicine.

ACKNOWLEDGEMENTS

Earlier versions of this chapter were delivered at the conference in Exeter in 1994 organised by Karen Stears, and as 'Women's health: the state of play in Classics and History' at a conference organised by Monica Green, 'Defining women's health: an interdisciplinary dialogue', University of Harvard, 2002. A section was presented as 'Rule and self-rule in the Hippocratic corpus' at a panel organised for the American Association for the History of Medicine, Buffalo, 1996 by Heinrich von Staden. I would like to thank all those who have contributed to its development.

NOTES

1 http://www.womens-health.org/ accessed 14 May 2004.
2 On the 'entrance of political language into the emerging discourse of medicine', see Vegetti 1983: 459. On Alcmeon, Tracy 1969: 23–4; Cambiano 1983: 441–4. On the textual problems of the Alcmeon fragment, Schubert 1997, with discussion by Jouanna.

9

DRAMA AND HEALING

Ancient and modern

Karelisa Hartigan

Within the past several decades, the idea that medicine and art, especially dramatic art, can work together in the healing process has attracted the interest of those in the medical profession. While a story and movie such as *Patch Adams* called attention to the concept, for many years doctors have realised the therapeutic value of the arts for patients of all ages and with all types of illness. Many of these doctors understood that the bond between art and medicine is not a recent idea; its roots lie with the ancient Greeks.

Aristotle's well-known statement that drama produces an emotional catharsis has continued validity and plays a role in the contemporary belief in the healing power of drama and the other arts. While Aristotle's statement described the normal response of a typical and healthy theatre audience, its message is equally applicable to those who need to be healed.

Recent studies in medicine underscore and expand Aristotle's dictum. As the evidence from the new and growing field of psychoneuroimmunology (PNI) indicates, good mental and emotional health lead to better bodily health (Graham-Pole *et al.* 1994: 19).[1] PNI studies the interaction among the psychological, neurological and immunological systems, trying to elucidate how the immune and nervous systems work with the psyche to help fight disease. In the initial work, PNI research focused on the material side of these interactions, which are easier to study: now, those involved in PNI are looking at how psychosocial components may influence immunity and its effects on health. While the importance of the psychological system in PNI is still difficult to define, clinical observations have shown how a positive mental condition assists the healing process (Martin 1997).[2]

Placebo studies have also received serious medical attention in recent years. Although giving a placebo is not done as an actual dramatic performance, the doctor administering it is involved in creating an artificial world by his or her pretended action. However, the doctor acts in a real situation. The placebo response may be defined as 'A change in the body (or the body–mind unit) that occurs as the result of the symbolic significance which one attributes to an event or object in the healing environment' (Brody 2000: 9).[3] The doctor is an active agent in the so-called 'placebo effect', with the relationship between doctor and patient affecting the healing process. The patient believes the doctor can and will help his pain, and thus the attitude with which the doctor gives a placebo is important (Spiro 1986).[4]

In a recent placebo study, it was discovered that even 'fake' surgical procedures could cure an ailment when the patient believed he had undergone actual surgery. The author of the study describes the reason for placebo cures by pill or process:

> What all explanations have in common . . . is the element of expec-
> tation, the promise of help on the way that can only be imparted
> by another human being. . . . Hope can help soften the experience
> of illness, though it cannot cure the underlying disease . . .
> a compassionate and optimistic physician can be a walking placebo.
>
> (Talbot 2000)

This study also used role-playing: an anaesthetist visited one group of patients the night before their operation in a brusque quick manner, and visited another group in a gentle sympathetic manner, having lengthy discussion with them. The second group 'required only half the amount of pain killing medication and were discharged an average 2.6 days earlier'.[5] The best studies of the placebo effect now argue that the doctor who gives out the inert pill is not writing off the patient's complaint. Rather, he understands that his attitude toward a patient's pain joins with the patient's need to believe that it can be cured; this combination leads to the remarkable number of successful placebo 'cures' (Shapiro and Shapiro 1997; Peters 2001).

Those who believe that art can assist a patient in attaining a more positive mental outlook add a further component to the answers sought by those involved in PNI research. One of the leaders in the field of art for healing is Dr John Graham-Pole at the University of Florida, where he is a founding director of the Arts-in-Medicine (A.I.M.) programme. According to Graham-Pole, 'Art is therapeutic because it lets us shed pent-up feelings – both in the creator and, if effective, in the observer' (Graham-Pole et al. 1994: 19). When negative emotions are displaced, a person can view the existing situation more clearly and effectively.[6] Here, I discuss how a form of drama is used at Shands Hospital at the University of Florida. I then suggest how drama was a part of the rituals performed at the sanctuaries of Asklepios in the ancient Greek world.

It is through the assistance of Dr John Graham-Pole that I became involved in the A.I.M. programme at Shands Hospital. There I have been able to observe the interaction of terminally ill patients with artists who create in various media: music, painting and especially theatre. The latter realm is particularly effective in the healing of illness, both physical and psychological.

The form of drama we use is 'Playback Theatre'. Invented in 1974 by Jonathan Fox, who was inspired by early oral narrative (such as that of Homer) and believed it could be vital once again. Playback Theatre is non-scripted theatre, an oral composition, but without even the formulae of Homeric epic. In this form of drama, actors establish a framework in which the story dramatisation takes place. Stories are gleaned from the audience and then played back to that audience (Fox 1994). Playback Theatre is most commonly practised in the public arena, as a community experience. It was used extensively, for example, in New York City and elsewhere after 11 September 2001. It is also used in educational settings, and occasionally when a social statement needs to be made. It is performed by actors, but actors who have a greater interest in their audience than in their own stage presence – in the outcome of the performance, not its polish or theatrical effect. It is entirely improvisational, non-scripted drama. From these ideas, as developed by Jonathan Fox and his assistant Jo Salas, regional groups have taken Playback Theatre around the world, first in Australia, then in the Scandinavian countries, and now in most of Europe and Israel.

It is important here to distinguish between Playback Theatre, Psychodrama and Drama Therapy. The use of drama in healing has been extensively studied and practised during the last 30 years. The belief that cures could come through enactment has attracted psychologists and people in theatre in both America and England. Their study frequently includes anthropological work, for in cultures more closely tied to shamanism and ritual, drama has long played a role as part of the healing process.

Dramatherapy (one word, coined by Peter Slade, for England) and Drama therapy (two words, as used in America) focus on the patient in need of psychological assistance. Psychodrama and drama therapy are not identical, but are similar in that both use the patient as the actor; it is the patient who must come to realise his or her situation through an enactment. Leaders in the field include Sue Jennings in Europe, J.L. Moreno in Europe and America and R. Landy in America among many others. Drama therapy is a recognised part of the curriculum in England, and has a national organisation in the United States.

Those who do psychodrama are specially trained in psychology if not in drama. The practitioners of drama therapy have training in both fields: theatre and psychology. It is used exclusively in a therapeutic context: those who participate are in need of cure. The vast amount of literature on drama therapy and psychodrama focuses upon the catharsis brought in the patient when he or she comes to terms with the psychological situation.

As Sid Homan has written, the world of the hospital and that of the theatre complement each other, each starkly real: real men and women act out significant moments in life and death. Reality and fiction blur on the stage, however, while in the hospital only reality is present. Homan works, however, to make that reality more bearable for those trapped within it. By creating fictions for them to act out, he opens them up to a world beyond their suffering and pain. Improvisational theatre allows patients, especially young patients, to direct their energy to something positive, even if it is an enactment of their unhealthy situation. The excitement of doing, of creating, does more to lift the spirit than the kindest of ministrations. Homan also conducts drama workshops for physicians, asking them, for example, to act out how they will tell a patient unexpectedly bad news. In this way, he argues, they can view their actions before they are completed; the rehearsal will help the doctor connect more sympathetically with his terminally ill patient (Homan 1994).

In his study, *Catharsis in Healing, Ritual and Drama*, T.J. Scheff follows similar lines. He writes that in cathartic drama (that which is neither too Apolline, that is, too devoted to thought, nor Dionysian, too devoted to emotion), the audience can share the emotions of the actors. 'In dramas of the cathartic type, with the audience being included in a shared awareness with one or more of the characters...the effect is subtle but powerful. Dramatic scenes move an audience because they touch upon repressed emotions...they need not be exactly equivalent to an individual's experience; certain events are universal' (1979: 152–7). To create scenes giving most opportunity for discharging distressful emotion, Scheff writes, the scene must touch upon repressed emotions that are shared by most members of the audience and are so constructed that the audience is involved, but not overwhelmed.

Playback Theatre, on the other hand, takes a different approach. Here drama is used to retell a person's story: the teller becomes audience of his or her own story. The link here is between narrative and drama, oral performance doubly told: first by the individual, then by the actors. The stories are enacted in an atmosphere of respect, empathy is a major goal, and the healing comes in the sense of community that is generated when an individual's story is shared with others.

The use of Playback Theatre in the hospital setting, as practised at Shands Hospital at the University of Florida, is unique (Figure 9.1). Paula Patterson, a trained drama therapist who has completed the programme for teaching Playback Theatre, introduced the idea, bringing the art of this

Figure 9.1 Reflections drama group in action; Mary Lisa Kitakos-Spanos, Lauryn Arce, Nancy Lassiter, Adria Klausner, Michael Godey, in Charlie's Corner, common room for Cancer and Heart Transplant Unit at Shands Hospital, University of Florida.

non-scripted theatre to the hospital's public areas and then to a patient's bedside. The idea of Playback Theatre, that the audience is the centre of attention, is special in the hospital setting. There the patient tells his or her story, and the narrative is given dramatic form by the acting troupe. While the actual enactment is no different than in the community performance, the atmosphere is more highly charged when the teller is a patient. The emotional context is deeply moving for both audience and actor. Patients see their story – their suffering – in a new way. The actors report that the performances they give for the patients are more fulfilling than those they do in a regular theatre.

In the process as used by 'Reflections', the drama troupe at Shands Hospital, the patients relate a problem, a story or a significant event of their life. The troupe then improvises an enactment of that event, guided by a series of dramatic methods. In **Story Tableau**, a series of 3–4 snap-action tableaus are formed to illustrate the story's theme. The Director gives a single sentence expressing each part of the story's idea and the cast members form a unified tableau of that idea. In **Fluid Sculpture**, a mini-dance or swirling motion tells the key points of the patient's story. In **Sound Sculpture**, a line of actors, hands joined, run a series of thoughts illustrating the story's theme up and down the line, with the climax at the turning point of the line. These ideas are often expressed in song. **Action Haiku** is a form in which two actors work together, one speaking, the other moulding, to create an instant expression of a theme. In **String of Pearls**, the first and last ideas of a story are expressed, with pearls added by the other members: when all sentences are strung together, the story has been told as a strand of pearls. In the most developed form, an entire story is enacted. The story must have three parts: beginning, middle and end, with each act highlighting one aspect of the teller's story. Once a patient has told a story, the troupe leader (immediately) determines which method will be used, and the actors immediately create a set of scenes, sentences or songs that capture the essence of the patient's story. The actors express the pain, if that has been told, but also suggest a healing.

The theory behind Playback Theatre, when done in a hospital setting, is three-fold: first, an individual, but especially a patient, needs to tell his or her story at this time when identity itself has been so assaulted; second, the story is told in an atmosphere of respect, something frequently lacking in a hospital;[7] third, and most important, is the aesthetic element of the process, 'when life is distilled into art'. When an individual's experiences are reflected in aesthetic form, that experience is given new meaning and through that meaning a sense of reassurance – part of the healing process (Salas 1996: 111–12).

In seeing his story performed, the patient can come to terms with it; the personal issue becomes generalised by the players' re-enactment, as the scene takes the suffering away from the patient, alleviating it by elevating it to a more impersonal level. Even when performed at the bedside, the effect on the patient is immediately noticeable. Scheff's advice (quoted earlier) is important for Playback Theatre done in the hospital setting, both in theory and as the Reflections' own troupe experience has shown.

Although I am now a member of the drama troupe, I first attended a performance by Reflections in the Bone Marrow Transplant Unit (BMTU) as an observer. One patient was clearly having a very bad day, and her dream was so simple: to be healed and away. The group acted a 'Sound Sculpture' that managed to offer hope and brought an evident sense of peace to this suffering woman. The patients were startled at how clearly the actors expressed the emotions they were feeling and the events they had described. Each patient seemed to have already a positive outlook – these would be the survivors – and the actors by their talent and their caring had brought a ray of hope to these people, who came to watch masked and plugged into their medical machines. One patient, upon leaving the hospital after his course of therapy, stated his belief that the drama had done as much for his healing as had the care of the doctors and the medicines he received.

Reflections most often performs in the public lounge on the heart-transplant floor. Ambulatory patients come together to tell their stories, see them enacted and share their common emotions. One day, a patient who had suffered a stroke and was now awaiting a heart transplant came to the lounge angry about his handicapped and now limited life. Our 'String of Pearls' version of his story recognised his frustration and pain, but also looked to the new life a new heart would bring. He was visibly moved and visibly encouraged. That same day a woman whose operation had gone wrong and forced her return to the hospital attended the 'show'. She was in despair: who would tend her seven fatherless children if she did not get well? How would she cope? She had no family to visit her. The actors offered her a 'River' of compassion and hope; they also brought her art and journal supplies. Her tears finally dried and she left the lounge with a smile, escorted by those who had shown her that someone honoured her and cared for her pain.

On other occasions, our drama troupe takes the performance to the bedside. There, too, the magic works. For example, one patient visited was a middle-aged man awaiting a heart transplant. From the few clues he gave about his life, the actresses began their work. A 'Story Tableau' of his enjoyment of camping and the possibility of doing that with his new-born daughter brought the first look of hope to his face. As we left, it was clear that, at least for the moment, he was thinking beyond his operation to the new life he would be able to create.

On another day of bedside theatre, we played to an African-American woman whose strength of character was evident even during her time of sickness. Her daughters, all successful, were gathered together in her room. We did a simple 'Alphabet Game' about the family interaction, how this matriarch had guided and shaped their lives. Somehow we found the right words to describe her and her family, and there was not a dry eye in the room: 'You hit it perfectly!' the women exclaimed. When by chance one daughter, in charge of the hospital recovery room, saw me there many months later, she still remembered the memories we had evoked that day we played theatre in her mother's room.

When I first learned about the therapeutic benefits of arts in medicine I was both intrigued and sceptical. An interesting idea, but could it work? Personal observation and participation, however, has changed my mind. The patients, who have terrible illness and must wait so long for the hoped-for operation, are wonderfully receptive to the sort of emotional catharsis that the drama troupe brings. Equally positive results arise from art, music, or dance performances; art seems to be particularly effective, when the patient's own creative abilities direct his or her attention away from the immediate suffering. But drama, in which verbal and physical expression is given to the patients' dreams and fears, does more than distract: it offers a larger view and opens up a realm of possibilities.

As a scholar and student of drama, I found this means of bringing hope to a patient intriguing in another way. Playback Theatre in the hospital setting seemed a reversal of the usual response to a theatrical performance, where we (a healthy audience) empathise with the experience of the characters and make the general more personal. In the hospital setting, the personal is, through the drama enactment, made more universal. For both hospital patient and theatre audience, then, the catharsis Aristotle described as arising from drama occurs and leads to a healthier soul.

Looking back from these current ideas on the interaction between drama and healing, can they shed new light on the ancient Greek past? The conception of the god Asklepios himself, it has been noted, was very similar to that of a doctor (Edelstein and Edelstein 1945: 112, n. 4). Hippocrates wrote that the art of medicine (a *technê*) had three parts: 'the disease, the patient and the physician'. As the doctor is the servant of the art, 'the patient must cooperate with the physician in combating the disease'. These views are reflected in much current medical literature (e.g. Spiro 1986: 35). Can an examination of our modern concepts of the relationship between art, especially drama, and health help us better understand what went on at the many sanctuaries of Asklepios; in particular, can they suggest what the patient saw performed in the theatres of the Asklepieia? It is noteworthy that theatres, or at least odeia, stand in or are adjacent to the majority of the Greek sanctuaries dedicated to the god of healing. In the following pages I consider the evidence from archaeology, art and text to argue that drama and its role in restoring health played a part in the dream therapy practised in the Asklepieia of the ancient Greek world, and offer a suggestion as to what went on in the dramatic spaces of these ancient healing sanctuaries.

First, a few words about Asklepios himself. He was said to be the son of Apollo by a mortal woman. In most accounts, that woman was Coronis, daughter of the Thessalian prince Phlegyas. Coronis did not remain faithful to her immortal (and thus absent) lover, but took up with a local peasant, Ischys. Told of her infidelity by a raven (or crow), Apollo in quick anger killed her, or had his sister Artemis do the deed. But then, overcome by grief for his hasty action, he snatched the unborn child from the funeral pyre and gave the baby to Chiron the wise centaur to raise. In many accounts, it was Chiron who instructed him in the arts of healing; in others, Asklepios learned medicine from his father.

The place of the divinity's birth and first cult varies in location depending upon the story's teller. The oldest account places his early life and first healing site in northern Greece, in Trikka (modern Trikkala), although there is little textual or archaeological evidence for this version. The ambiguity of Asklepios' origins rests partially upon the fact that he was a hero before he was a god, and thus would have an origin story more appropriate to a mortal than a divinity. In the *Iliad* Asklepios is a king, but important only as the father of the healer-warriors, Machaon and Podaleirios, who led the forces from Trikka. As in the Homeric text Asklepios' importance rests upon his medical, not his political or military skill, his sons thereby gain respect in the healing realm: 'Machaon and Podalirius are physicians rather than warriors, craftsmen rather than kings' (Edelstein and Edelstein 1945: II, 9; cf. Kerényi 1959: 87–100). While there is considerable debate and conflicting information about these two healers, my concern here is with the hero who became god of healing.

A different version of the divinity's birth was told at Epidauros. In that account, Coronis gave birth to the child when visiting the area with her father. Ashamed, she abandoned the infant on the slopes of Mt Myrtium, but divine or fated offspring cannot die. Thus goats nursed the child and the herd dog guarded him. The story unfolded rather differently from that of Romulus and Remus, found and raised by Faustulus. For when the local shepherd discovered the baby Asklepios, he was frightened away by lightning flashing about the child's head, and left the infant to be raised by the goats and dog, under the protection of Apollo. In the traditional version, in time the youth came to his father's sanctuary in Epidauros, where the Olympian was known as Apollo Maleatas, and joined him in curing illness via dreams (Walton 1894; Kerényi 1959).

In early accounts, Asklepios heals by such means as other physicians; he is just better at it, and is honoured for his skill. He is a culture hero, celebrated for his *technê*. In the course of time, his legend accrues details differing from those of other heroes: when he goes too far in his healing and restores a man to life, he is hurled to death by Zeus (cf. Pindar, *Pythian* 3.8–46). But Asklepios as culture hero cannot be so easily forgotten, so soon he earns veneration as a chthonic god. At some point he is restored to life and elevated to divine status.

Asklepios, the prototype of the good doctor, the one who protects from death by disease and restores mortals to health, was frequently designated as *daimôn*, a distinction which in his case marks him as a 'terrestrial god', neither an Olympian nor a chthonian (Edelstein and Edelstein 1945: II, 82–6). His attendants are his family, each a personification of an abstract iatric concept, for example, Iaso, Panacea, Hygieia, the latter the most important of his daughters (Stafford, Ch. 6, this volume). Asklepios never attained a place on Mt Olympus, but nor was he a regional deity with an identifiable tomb (as, for instance, Amphiaraos and Trophonios); he was worshipped throughout the ancient world. By the end of the sixth century BC, Asklepios was revered both among physicians and those he had cured as the god of healing.[8]

He was honoured as a god in an ever-increasing number of sanctuaries around Greece. With his staff and coiled serpent, he healed those who came to his temples; because of his care and concern for human suffering he would become the greatest challenger to Jesus and His teaching (Edelstein and Edelstein 1945: II, 132–8). As has been noted, the destruction of Epidauros, Asklepios' most important site, is clearly deliberate (Tomlinson 1983: 33), while in other locations, for example in Athens and Peiraieus, a church of healing saints arose on the foundations of his temple (e.g. M. Dillon 1997: 247, n. 129; cf. Montserrat, Ch. 14, this volume).

The divine physician, although worshipped throughout the Greek world, is most closely associated with Epidauros, where most post-Homeric texts place the Coronis story. The Asklepieion there, established in the later years of the sixth century BC, became the primary centre for the cult, the main destination of pilgrimage and the major colonising site: from here the Asklepieia at Athens, Pergamon and Rome (among others less famous) were founded. The cures at Epidauros and elsewhere took place in an *abaton*, a specially designated place to sleep. At Epidauros the *abaton* was beside the god's temple; there the patients slept and awaited the nocturnal visit and healing acts by Asklepios or his sacred animals, the serpent or the dog. But at the Epidaurian sanctuary the most famous structure is the theatre built by Polykleitos of Argos in the later fourth century BC, adjacent to the god's sanctuary, and best known today for the festival of dramatic performances held there every summer. What role did the theatre originally play in the sanctuary?

There were nearly 300 sanctuaries to Asklepios throughout the Greek world, with some archaeological evidence for about half of these; of those with more extensive remains, a theatre or an odeion forms part of the site. At Pergamon, itself centred around a magnificent theatre, a fine odeion stands within the extensive sanctuary to Asklepios. At Dion in northern Greece, where again a fine theatre forms part of the main city, there is an odeion within the god's cult area (here, unusually, located in the public baths). At Oropos, the Amphiaraion is adorned with an attractive little odeion adjacent to the stoa where the sick awaited healing ministrations (Petracos 1995). One of the major identifying structures at Messene/Ithome is the theatre within the sanctuary to Asklepios. And the list could go on (cf. Semeria 1986). The archaeological evidence, then, suggests that the Greeks routinely constructed theatres as a part of a healing sanctuary. The site of the Asklepieion in Athens is also worthy of consideration: why was the new home for the cult of the healing god placed immediately beside the theatre of Dionysos on the south slope of the Acropolis?

Several inscriptions from these Asklepieia record that a portion of the sacrificial offering is to be distributed to 'the members of the chorus' *IG* IV² 40 (= Edelstein and Edelstein 1945: I, 561); *IG* IV² 41 (= Edelstein and Edelstein 1945: I, 562); *IG* II² 974 (= Edelstein and Edelstein 1945: I, 553). Further inscriptional evidence and a tantalisingly few literary sources seem to indicate that some type of dramatic performance may have been a part of the rituals performed at the god's site; for example, Athenaios (*Deipnosophistae* 11.485b = Edelstein and Edelstein 1945: I, 611), describes a scene in a play 'in which a physician, possibly Asklepios himself, is the main character', and alludes to 'the use of flutes' in the *Asclepius* of Telestes (Athenaios 14.617b = Edelstein and Edelstein 1945: I, 613). Were these plays staged for therapeutic reasons? Did the ancient Greeks believe that drama could assist the healing process? As neither tragedy nor comedy was created for entertainment only, drama was neither offered to divert and amuse those who came in attendance with the sick, nor to amuse the patients themselves.[9] While in the modern medical school interns and medical students are brought to the theatre (significantly named) to watch a new and advanced procedure performed (significant verb) by an expert, we have no evidence that this was a common practice by the local *iatros*. Might one suggest, then, that ambulatory patients were brought to the theatre or odeion to assist their recovery?

While no particular extant testimony suggests the purpose of these theatres and odeia, it would seem that a primary function would be for the celebration of cures. Paeans were sung for Asklepios, and they would have to be performed somewhere. As epinicians were sung in the theatre at Delphi (or in the sphendome of the stadium), so a choral performance to offer appropriate thanks to the healing god needed a venue in which to sing. At smaller sanctuaries like that at Oropos, a simple (yet elegant) odeion would suffice. At Messene, Dion or Pergamon, a concert hall within the Asklepieion itself provided an appropriate location.

At Epidauros, the premier healing site, providing medication and ministration for hundreds of patients, a larger theatre was necessary. Paeans would have been sung to the god at the opening of any festival there. As the sanctuary also became the setting for an athletic contest, victory hymns could be sung at the theatre as well.

But the large theatre at Epidauros could also be used for healing performances. While inscriptional evidence at the sanctuary is to date entirely confined to dream cures, there is no reason to doubt that the methods recorded elsewhere were not in use there. The site has no other public gathering space. The dining hall (*estiatorion*), formerly identified as the gymnasium, would have been suitable for private meals and even ritual dining, but not the enactment or celebration of cures. It is instructive that, when the Romans took over the sanctuary, they built a small odeion within the dining hall, recognising, perhaps, the need to have a performance site within the confines of the temenos itself, as at Pergamon, Dion or Messene.[10]

In the absence of early literary evidence, there are two possible sources for the purpose of these theatres: inscriptional and artistic evidence, and comparison with ideas from contemporary art and therapy studies. Numerous reliefs portraying the god and attendant family show the deity standing over a sleeping patient, extending a hand in an apparently healing gesture. As it is well known that Asklepios thus appeared to the patient during the dream-therapy process, it has always been assumed that the sculptured reliefs commemorated that moment. But can we be so sure?

To my knowledge, neither vase paintings nor sculpture in the ancient world illustrated dreams or, indeed, any imaginary events. While we might consider a statue of Zeus carrying off Ganymede or a vase painting of Theseus slaying the Minotaur to be fanciful artefacts, these were images of the stories in which the ancient artist and his audience believed. When art illustrated art, it was the art of theatre. While many vase paintings are independent creations, there is little doubt that numerous scenes on pottery reflect those presented on stage (Baldry 1968; Trendall and Webster 1979). Other art work echoes festival events, such as practice for and participation in the various athletic contests and the crowning of the victors, the Parthenon frieze, the most famous example of processional art, which portrays the participants (mortal and divine) in the Panathenaic festival and the many illustrations of the rituals, visible yet elusive, of the Eleusinian Mysteries.

The cult of Asklepios is connected to that celebrated at Eleusis: when the god was first brought to Athens (probably from his sanctuary at Zea in the Peiraieus), he was given 'temporary accommodation' at the Eleusinion in Athens (Garland 1992: 123–4). The introduction of the cult coincided with the nine-day Eleusinian festival, and the fourth day was later termed 'Epidauria' and was designated for those who arrived after the festival had begun. More importantly, several aspects of the Eleusinian ritual were echoed in that of Asklepeios. Both had a *hierophantês*, the priest who revealed holy objects. A drink of honey, wheat, mint and oil was consumed by the initiates at Eleusis in remembrance of Demeter and by the sick at Epidauros in honour of Hygieia. Some have suggested that the six male figures greeting the goddesses on a votive relief at the Athenian Asklepieion are members of the medical profession (*IG* II^2 4359; Garland 1992: 124). Finally, it is generally agreed that the culminating rituals at Eleusis involved some type of dramatic performance.

While the actual events and revelations of the *drômena, legomena* and *deiknymena* of the Eleusinian *teletê* remain unknown, most scholars agree that the pageant (*drômena*) was an enactment of the abduction and return of Persephone. The site of Eleusis supports this interpretation, with one cave suitable for Hades' seizure of the maiden, the other with its secret stairway and opening for Persephone's return. The text (*legomena*) is as lost to us as any Asklepieion scripts, but the many images of wheat, poppies and enthroned goddesses suggest the objects and vision of the final revelation (*deiknymena*). And the Niinnion tablet, now in the museum at Eleusis, showing the procession (*pompê*) to Eleusis, offers another example of processional art. Similar enactments can easily be imagined as part of the rituals for Asklepios, these being performed in the sanctuary theatres.

From this background, why must we assume that the sculpted stories of interaction with Asklepios must represent a patient's dream vision? As noted above, the cures at Epidauros and elsewhere took place in an *abaton* within the sanctuary, usually near the god's temple; there the patients slept and awaited the god's nocturnal visit. The inscriptions record the animal ministrations, but the sculptures present the deity, sometimes accompanied by his sacred snake. I would therefore argue that, in the tradition of theatrical and festival art, Asklepieion art portrays actions performed at pre-cure pageants.

Sometimes insight from those outside the field of Classics can assist in understanding the ancient evidence. In her study, *Imagery in Healing. Shamanism and Modern Medicine*, Jeanne Achterberg speculates about what these rituals may have entailed and meant to this audience: 'Since the temples were established well after Asclepius' lifetime, the rituals were performed by physician/priests, dressed as Asclepius, accompanied by a retinue representing his family.' She suggests that the group performed, or acted, rituals for healing:

> In the semidarkness, in the presence of the earthly representatives of healing deities, with music playing in the background, and surrounded by all the pomp and circumstance of the magnificent shrines, whatever innate healing ability the patients possessed in the face of their grave illnesses was greatly enhanced. It was a perfect situation for the imagination to go to work; and go to work it apparently did.
>
> (Achterberg 1985: 55)[11]

Having seen such a performance in the theatre or odeion, in the company of fellow patients, the sick would then move to perform the requisite personal rituals and retire to the *abaton* or other sleeping quarters. To see a dramatic presentation always heightens the senses; for the ancient Greek, for whom any such event would be even more emotionally charged through the connection between drama and divinity, the viewing of an enactment of a healing ritual would prepare the mind to receive healing dreams sent by the god. At dawn, the patient would awake and record the vision seen while asleep, a vision prompted by a dramatic performance late the day before.

As I noted above, one of the inscriptions from Epidauros records the division of the sacrificial offering (*IG* IV^2 I.40). The first portion goes to the god, the second to the financial officials and the fourth to the *phrouroi* or military. The third portion is allotted to the *aiôdoi*, the choristers. Burford (1969: 14, n. 2) records this information, but states that the function of the *aiôdoi* 'is not clear'. I would, however, suggest that these choristers, in addition to singing paeans of thanksgiving, played a role in the pre-dream cure drama. Thus, their residence at the sanctuary is given further validity and importance. The priests and choir members, playing Asklepios and his family, would speak traditional lines underscored with ritual gestures. The plays would not have needed to be long to have an effect on the ailing audience. As the sudden display of holy objects in a blaze of light at the Eleusinian Mysteries aroused powerful emotions, offering witnesses the belief that their lives now, and in the future, would be better, so those who watched the enactment of Asklepios' healing ministrations could easily believe the deity and his attendant animals would bring health for their ailments. The impact of the performance led to the healing dream.

We have a single text that builds its humour from this theory. Aristophanes' scurrilous Karion in *Ploutos* (652–748) gives us the best record of the rituals performed before retiring. His audience would also have recognised that what he said was true. But Karion continues his story by reporting events that occurred during the 'dream-cure'. He claims that it is the temple attendants who approach and 'heal' the patients. The humour lies in the very suggestion that the drama enacted before bedtime is continued within the *abaton*. While the sceptical few may have thought that Karion got it right, most patients at the *abaton* of an Asklepieion would have believed it was the god himself who came to heal and cure. As the Eleusinian hierophant revealed the sacred objects, so the actor playing Asklepios inspired a dream in which the god's hands cured a patient's medical complaint.

Galen wrote about the role of drama in a healing context, indicating that he realised the connection between health and emotion. He suggested, for example, that as a cure for those who 'were ill through the disposition of their souls... Asklepios ordered not a few to have odes written as well as to compose comical mimes and certain songs' (Galen, *De Sanitate Tuenda* I.8.19–21 = Edelstein and Edelstein 1945: I, 413). In *Deipnosophistae* (11.485b; 11.487a; 14.617b), Athenaios records several texts entitled 'Asklepios', which suggests that dramas about the god existed, and we know the name of an actor who made the role famous, a man by the name of Telestes (Suidas, *Lexicon* s.v.).

We have long wondered why the patients at the Asklepieia so readily received (and accepted) their dream visions. It has been argued that, as they came ready to believe, and saw the images of the god within the sanctuary and the cure tablets displayed there, the very atmosphere of the sanctuary would inspire their dreams. If, as I suggest, the patients were prepared for the god's visit not only by expectation but also by the emotions aroused by a drama enacting a cure, they would be far more likely to dream of the god's visit. They would also awake expecting to have been cured or to have been told the remedy necessary to drive away their illness and regain their health. The author of the Hippocratic treatise *Regimen* – or *On Dreams* – 4.88 (Loeb IV, 424) credited a healing power to dreams. In sleep, he writes, when dreams 'take on a character contrary to daytime activities and involve a conflict with them, they constitute a sign of bodily disturbance'. He goes on, then, to discuss a variety of regimens appropriate to the dream's visions.

While no pre-cure scripts have yet been found, we have a fairly good record of the paeans sung at the theatres or odeia within an Asklepieion. These songs would have been sung on two occasions: first, at the time of local festivals for Asklepios; second, after the patients' cures had taken place. Perhaps the most famous paean is that reputedly composed by Sophocles (*IG* II^2 4510), some eight fragmentary verses inscribed on the Sarapion monument:

> O far-famed daughter of Phlegyas, mother of the god who wards off pains…the unshorn [Phoebus] I begin my loud-voiced hymn…accompanied by flutes…the helper of the sons of Cecrops…may you come…the golden-haired [?] him, the Olympian.
>
> (trans. Edelstein and Edelstein 1945: 324)

This earned Sophocles the title *Dexion*, and led to the belief that it was the tragic poet who not only welcomed the cult of Asklepios into his home but also established the sanctuary for the god on the south slope of the Acropolis. Sophocles may well have welcomed the cult to Athens or Colonus but, as inscriptional evidence has ascertained, it was one Telemachos who so placed the god's sanctuary in the location described by Pausanias (Burford 1969: 51; Aleshire 1989: 7–11). On the basis of *IG* II^2 4960 and *SEG* XXV.226, we know it was Telemachos, not Sophocles, who brought Asklepios to Athens in 420/419 BC. And, at the time of the cult's establishment, it was a private, not a state cult. As Sara Aleshire argues, after an exhaustive analysis of the archaeological evidence and the limits of the temenos by its peribolos wall have been determined:

> *TO ASKLEPIEION TO EN ASTEI*, then, was located on the
> eastern terrace, between the eastern peribolos of the Pelargikos
> and the NW arc of the Temple of Dionysus and fitted in between
> the Peripatos and the Akropolis rock. [It] consisted originally of
> a single small temple and the bothros, which functioned as a reser-
> voir or (perhaps less likely) as a sacrificial pit.... At least as early
> as 300 BCE a stoa was constructed to serve as the abaton for the
> sanctuary, the bothros and the sacred spring were carefully integrated
> into the plan of this building.
>
> (Aleshire 1989: 34; Garland 1992: Ch. 6)

The existence of the spring was important for the location of a healing
sanctuary, but there are other springs on the Acropolis and elsewhere in
Athens.

I would argue that the choice of this site is related to its proximity to the
Theatre of Dionysos. We know that the theatre was used occasionally for
meetings (witness Andocides' report in *On the Mysteries* I.38.4); why could
it not have been used for healing performances offered in connection with
incubation at the Asklepieion? This would suggest that the location of the
Asklepieion in Athens was neither random nor determined by geography,
but depended on its proximity to the extant theatre.

The paeans recorded on the Sarapion Monument are three of the many
hymns of praise known from Asklepieia. The Edelsteins collected the
greater part of those known from many sanctuaries around the Greek world,
Aleshire discussed the paeans found in Athens, and, most recently, Louise
Wells (1998) has presented the language of healing in inscriptions from
Athens, Kos and Pergamon. Robert Wagman (1995) has published the
lesser known hymns and fragments from Epidauros; his work focuses on
hymns to Pan and 'The Mother of the Gods' (among others), which raises
further questions as to the role of other divinities in the cult of healing.

Theatres or smaller performance spaces, then, were included as part of
a healing sanctuary because of the role of song and drama in the healing process.
As the Arts-in-Medicine programme at Shands Hospital at the University of
Florida has shown, art in all its forms, and especially drama, can help a patient
on the road to healing. Modern studies demonstrate how pain can be alleviated
by the patient's belief in a doctor's skills; in a world where medicine was largely
confined to herbs, bandaging and prognosis, it was natural that many people
would turn to Asklepios, the divinity whose rites began with drama and whose
cures began with dreams (Edelstein and Edelstein 1945: II, 139–80).[12]

NOTES

1 Psychoneuroimmunology (PNI) studies the connection between the brain and the immune system. Those involved in this research believe that psychological experiences such as stress and anxiety can influence immune function, which in turn may have an effect on the course of a disease. See Ader and Cohen 1991; Brody 2000.

2 Martin (1997) is a well-documented account of the relationship between the brain and healing. Other information on PNI cited here is from Internet: http://home.tiscalinet.ch/kmatter/psychone.htm#_Toc442256827.

3 Brody defines *placebo* thus: 'In therapeutic healing, a placebo is a treatment modality or process administered with the belief that it possesses the ability to affect the body only by virtue of its symbolic significance' (2000: 14).

4 Cf. Lloyd 1978: 60, 'While most of the anatomical, physiological and pathological doctrines in the Hippocratic writings have long since been superseded, the ideal of the selfless, dedicated and compassionate doctor they present has lost none of its relevance in the twentieth century.' Plato, too, urged an honest and caring relationship between doctor and patient. In *Laws* IV.720, he writes, 'The [physician] treats his patients' disease ... from the beginning in a scientific way, and takes the patient and his family into his confidence. ... He does not give his prescriptions until he has won the patient's support, and when he has done so, he steadily aims at producing complete restoration to health by persuading the sufferer into compliance.'

5 Talbot's article (2000) is frequently cited as a key study of the placebo effect; see also a study by Dr Bruce Moseley of Baylor College of Medicine in Houston, showing that arthroscopic procedures for arthritis on the knee had no better result than placebos. When patients awoke from sham surgery, 'at every point over the next two years, those who had the fake surgery could climb stairs and walk slightly faster on average than those who had gotten real operations' (msnbc.com/news, July 2002). Clearly the belief that arthroscopic surgery had been done was as effective as the actual procedure.

6 Distancing on the part of medical personnel has an effect on the patient, who is always in some state of fear or grief. If medical personnel, to protect their own psyches, cannot overcome the distancing they have developed, the patient can feel rejected and/or unimportant. The training of both medical and psychiatric doctors needs to be redone to create a balance between care and caution. On the subject of distancing, see Scheff 1979: 208.

7 As one study of the placebo effect comments, 'One of the most tragic effects of major illness is the sense – the realistic sense – of loss of control over one's life, and over one's environment ... The seriously ill patient is deliberately rendered helpless, denied control over anything that has to do with his illness or his care.' F.A. Ruderman, 'A placebo for the doctor', *Commentary*, May, 1980: 54–60, cited by Spiro 1986: 111.

8 We know that doctors had statues of Asklepios in their homes. Theocritus wrote an epigram on a statue of Asklepios taken to the home of Nicias, 'healer of all sickness' (Edelstein and Edelstein 1945: I, T.501), and his *Idyll* XI (on Polyphemus' cure for love) is addressed to this same physician Nicias.

9 The idea persists in common thought, however. For instance, in an otherwise very good guidebook to Turkey, Yenans (1998: 356) writes of the sanctuary at Pergamon: 'The Theater is a small building in Roman style ... mainly used

for performances to entertain the patients when not receiving treatment.' Surprisingly, Jones, in his careful analysis of Aelius Aristides' time at the Asklepeion at Pergamon and the site itself, offers no suggestion as to what type of plays were performed in the theatre: '... the theater, which was doubtless as important for lectures and show speeches as for plays' (1998: 72).

10 The construction of this odeion within the *estiatorion* promoted the idea that the dining hall was a gymnasium, as a similar concert hall had been constructed into the gymnasium at the Athenian Agora.

11 While I think the ritual performance did influence the patients' dreams, Achterberg errs by writing as if there were hard evidence for what she describes. As I point out here, most scholars do not consider what purpose the ever-present theatre/odeion served.

12 As Brody reiterates, the very idea of the placebo response remains a mystery: 'It is critical for us to retain a sense of awe and wonder when we contemplate this intricate connection of mind and body.... If it *is* going to work for us, it will be partly to the extent that we continue to view it as mysterious' (2000: xix).

10

'CURING' DISABILITY

Nicholas Vlahogiannis

Sometime during his travels in the second century AD, the Greek writer Pausanias visited the Asklepieion sanctuary at Epidauros. Nestling among the surrounding mountains, the sacred grove had long been considered the healing god's pre-eminent shrine and hospital. Pausanias admired the *tholos*, theatre and temple and the ivory and gold cult statue of Asklepios carved by Thrasymedes of Paros. Within the enclosure, he stopped to read six ancient stone tablets inscribed in Doric (2.27). The geographer Strabo had seen them two centuries earlier, and reported other such tablets at Kos and Trikka (*Geog.* 8.16.15). The inscriptions were dedications by men and women honouring Asklepios for curing them of physical disabilities and debilitating diseases.

Health (*hygieia*) was high on the Greek agenda. Good health, the soundness of body and mind, were regarded as a gift of the gods, and the basis of physical prowess. In Plato's definition of goodness, or good things (*agatha*), health ranked first among the human or earthly good, ahead of beauty (*kalos*), physical success (*ischus*), and wealth (*Laws* 631b–d). Health was absence of illness and disease (*astheneia, nosos*); it was, physically and metaphorically, the force of life. According to Alcmeon, the younger contemporary of Pythagoras, health stood for the *isonomia*, or balance, of the bodily powers of moistness and dryness, cold and heat, bitter and sweet, and so forth (DK 24 B 4), while disease was the control of one (*monarchia*) over the others.

In recent decades anthropologists and sociologists, and now historians, concerned with the body and medicine have increasingly focused on issues concerning pain, disease and illness (Kleinman 1980; Good 1994; Helman 1994; Longmore and Umansky 2001b). Disease is considered a disturbance of the organism, or an atypical functional deficiency, while illness is a social and evaluative concept that connotes undesirable deviation from the accepted norms of health and appropriate behaviour. Both disease and illness however also mark out, and stigmatise, the patient as different, and can carry a smear that is commensurable with the devaluation of the self (Turner 1984: 236–7). Philoctetes is banished to nine years of loneliness on Lemnos because of the wound on his foot (Worman 2000). Here the illness is matched with wilderness and separation (Parham 1990: 12–20). In antiquity, disease was the embodiment of evil, which changed with shifts in cultural and political values: Pandora's box in the archaic period (Hesiod, *WD* 101–2); the beggar confronted by Apollonius in second century AD Ephesus (Philostratos, *VA* 4.10).

Physical and mental disability, whether a physical handicap like lameness, congenital deformity like dwarfism or polydactylism, or symptom of disease like polio, is present in every society (Titchkosky 2003: 46–8). It is a condition imbued with culturally determined interpretations of that circumstance. It is considered a permanent state because of the incapacity involved, but it is neither an illness nor a disease. Yet it is equated with disease, and so is invested with cultural traits that are predicated on the values that are placed on the body. The body is who we are: it is a tangible frame of our self in an individual and collective experience (Comaroff 1985: 6–7; Gold 1998: 369–70). Therefore, visible signs of disability mark out the disabled from other members in the community, turning the disabled person's private body public: an object of consideration, interpretation, communication and social construction (L.J. Rogers and Swadener 2001). How disability was explained is also pertinent to the understanding of body and disability. In antiquity, physical and mental disabilities were the result of many varied causes and situations, be they congenital, accident, occupational hazard, misadventure on the battlefield, disease or old age (Brothwell and Sandison 1967; Grmek 1989). Ancient Greek literature, however, reflecting a common mentality, locked disability firmly into punishment – by the gods, by communities and by individuals – for the transgression of the ordered condition, to the degree that disability served as a metaphor for punishment (Vlahogiannis 1998). Thus, when applied to disability, *hygieia* constitutes both familiar and broader connotations, be they physiological, social, religious or psychological. It confronts the semantics of disability: whether disability is simply a physical condition, or whether it is a disease or illness; whether a disabled person is healthy or unhealthy; whether the disabled can be cured and whether the status of a cured person changes from 'cursed' or 'punished' to 'blessed'.

In *Mythologies*, Roland Barthes used the example of a French Black-African saluting the French flag to illustrate his concept of 'signifier' and 'signified'. Considered as an individual icon, he suggested, the image had little potency. But as a historical image it conveyed the broad messages of colonialism, imperialism and ethnicity that are open to interpretation and appropriation by anyone concerned with this issue (1973: 116–20). The signifier/signified model can also be applied to explain how society generally understood and responded to persons suffering a disability: the physically incomplete body; the state of permanence; the stigmatisation that comes with difference; the community fear of the unknown and the seeming lack of individual value (D.T. Mitchell and Snyder 1997: 2–6). These broad categories are not intended to ignore individual situations or specific conditions, or to deny exceptions to broad social attitudes. Here, rather, they serve as the basis of asking the corresponding question: if a disabled person is cured through divine intervention, does the social position of that person improve?

TOWARDS A DEFINITION OF DISABILITY

In the World Health Organisation (WHO) definition, as we have already seen in the Introduction to the present volume, 'health' is 'a state of complete physical, mental and social well-being and not merely the absence of disease or infirmity'. In this sense, the International Disability Foundation estimates that 10 per cent (514 million) of the current world population is disabled, with the majority living in developing and Third World countries (Priestley 2001: 3). Its categorisation of disability included physical infirmities, communicable and non-communicable diseases, mental disorders, trauma and injury (Satapati 1988). To this can be added the opening sentences of an important study of disability in a cultural context: 'Impairment of the mind, the senses, and the motor functioning of the body are universal. Everywhere there are people with biological defects that cannot be cured and that inhibit, to some extent, their ability to perform certain functions' (Ingstad and Whyte 1995: ix). That is, being disabled extends beyond being ill: it constitutes permanency, incurability and a hindrance to performing daily functions.

It is plausible to suggest that the degree of disability in the ancient world was also very high, as can be seen from the diverse literary, epigraphic, iconographic, archaeological and skeletal evidence. However, establishing a generic definition of disability that the ancient Greek world understood is not a straightforward matter, especially if we limit ourselves to medical or biological categories of limb, sense and mind (cf. Garland 1995; M.L. Edwards 1997a). Rather, establishing a generic social and cultural definition of disability involves considering physical conditions, medical and social understandings of causation and social attitudes. It encompasses questions of cultural and constructed identities, and the interpretation and representation of body within the parameters of body normality and abnormality, that cast the disabled body in terms of 'lacking'. The body as a functional tool of community production, procreation and military survival was necessarily the basis of any understanding of definitions of, and attitudes towards, disability. The disabled was placed in opposition to the able-bodied, a contrast of physical states that focused on negation – *dunatos/adunatos* (able/disable; *firmus/infirmus*); physical negatives which collectively absorbed and reflected social, political, religious and moral connotations (Reckford 1998: 346–8; Vlahogiannis 1998: 23–8; Titchkosky 2003: 50–2).

Another factor linked to negative connotations of the disabled body is the Greek comprehension of, and explanation for, disabilities. Notwithstanding the probable large numbers of disabled persons in the ancient world, and the many different causes for them, Greek thinking consistently ascribed religio-moral values to the cause, brought about by the human tendency to place guilt and attribute blame. That is, however a disability might have happened, the ancient Greek mind, steeped in superstition and the numinous religious experience, understood physical misfortune such as disease, extreme illness or disability as divine intervention, and as evil. Philoctetes' 'foul-smelling, suppurating, agonizing foot-wound' (Leder 1990: 1), caused by a snakebite because he had inadvertently wandered near the shrine of Chryse (Gantz 1993: 589–90), reminds us that the sufferer did not even have to be guilty of a crime or sin to be punished by the gods (Soph., *Philoctetes*; Leder 1990). Apollo brought plagues (*Il.* 1.456; Soph., *Oedipos Tyrannos*); Zeus brought blindness (*Il.* 6.193), infertility (*Il.* 9.454–6) and mental disorder (*Il.* 6.234, 9.377), as did Athene (*Od.* 20.345–9). This theme of divine punishment permeates through antiquity, in mythology, historical accounts and personal testimonies. Even the advent of 'scientific medicine' among the Hippocratic authors of the sixth and fifth centuries BC, who sought to demystify medicine with alternative views based on nature, could not shift the socially and religiously ingrained opinion that all ills were brought about by the gods. Therefore, while some occurrences of disease, illness or disability – such as the blindness that struck Epizelos the gallant Athenian hoplite at Marathon (Hdt. 6.117; King 2001b) – were inexplicable, most were understood or constructed as divine punishment for a known or unknown sin or ritualistic or moral transgression. The blinding of Oedipus, Orion and others, were punishments linked to violations, usually sexual, that over-stepped the limits and boundaries set by the gods. Orion, the son of Poseidon, had raped the daughter of his host Oenopion (Gantz 1993: 271–3; a theme in many of Parthenius' *Erotika Parthemanta*), while Oedipus had committed incest. Even when a natural cause could explain an incident, an explanation involving the supernatural often replaced it. Thus Philip of Macedon's blindness, well attested in sources as having occurred in battle, was rewritten by tradition as punishment by the god Amon (Plut., *Alex.* 30). Divine intervention was also the causal explanation for many 'historical' incidents of debilitating injuries (Vlahogiannis 1998: 28–32).

Being struck with a permanent disability would alter how one lived and functioned, and how one was perceived and received, as an individual and member of a community. According to Dionysus of Halicarnassus (*RA* 2.15.1–2) and Plutarch (*Lyc.* 16.1–3) early Roman and Spartan societies killed their deformed children, while Plato (*Theaetetos* 160c; *Rep.* 460c) and Aristotle (*Pol.* 1335b20) condoned the practice for their ideal societies (M.L. Edwards 1996). Dwarfs were ridiculed as being of inferior intelligence (Arist., *PA* 686b20–5), but supposedly endowed with large sexual organs (Arist., *HA* 577b). The citizens of Sybaris kept them as curiosities (Ath., 518e; cf. Plut., *Mor.* 520c), whereas the Emperor Augustus feared them as bearers of bad luck (Suetonius, *Aug.* 83; Dasen 1993; Vlahogiannis 1995). Philoctetes suffered indescribable pain and became a social outcast, having been abandoned by his shipmates on Lemnos. Indeed, Sophocles' version of the myth serves as a metaphor for illness as a period of exile from the accustomed world (Leder 1990: 1; Worman 2000: 2). Social exile and lives as beggars were also the fate of Oedipus and Bellephoron (Pindar, *Isthm.* 7.60–8). Thus, besides the emotional and physical effects, the disability each individual suffered had the potential of stigmatisation and marginalisation by placing the sufferer outside society and civilisation.

'CURING' DISABILITY

Any discussion of disability in the ancient world – its incidence, causation, effect of lifestyle and healing – is based on the collective, but still vague, impression left by a myriad of usually unrelated snippets of information that often only touched on the issue in passing. The Hippocratic and other medical texts, recognising the futility of attempting to cure the incurable (Von Staden 1990: 75–6), warned against trying or offered little guidance (*On the Art.* 8; *Joints* 63.4). Some conditions were treatable, and treated, whether through corrective manipulation, drugs, surgery or luck (Garland 1995: 122f.). The Hippocratic tradition might have been disdainful of the involvement of the divine in health, but Greek medicine was more complicated than simple claims for rationality based on scientific principles of empirical observation. In reality, ancient medicine did not separate such phenomena as 'religion', 'science', 'folklore' and 'philosophy' from medical theory and practice, but was a blend of natural, divine, herbal and practical elements. The attempt to differentiate between them, in order 'to extract some concept called "scientific Greek medicine" and to isolate it from other medical phenomena in the total picture says much about contemporary society, little about ancient culture' (Oberhelman 1990: 141). The advent of deductive reasoning may have introduced philosophical rationality to medical thinking, by claiming to reject the supernatural, magical and superstitious, but its own prescribed methods of treating the ill were as fanciful as those of the practitioners they criticised. To quote Geoffrey Lloyd, 'Hippocratic pro-phylactic recommendations were generally of more help than the treatments they prescribed for their patients once sick. Those treatments were often ineffectual... and they were sometimes more dangerous than the condition they were used to remedy, whether it... (be) drugs... or surgical procedures' (1987: 18–19; cf. Longrigg 1993).

On the whole success was limited, and the reputation of physicians in the popular imagination of antiquity was hardly compelling (Hunter 1983: 135f.; cf. Nutton 1985), as can be seen from the Hellenistic epigramma-tists' general satirisation of physicians who used bizarre and extreme methods to cure disabilities. Consider the case of Diodorus who suffered from a crooked back and sought medical treatment from Socles. His solution was to weigh Diodorus down with heavy stones, killing his patient in the process (*Anth. Pal.* 11.120; also 11.121). The treatment of these medical cases in verse, however, suggests that, despite the seeming futility, patients visited these practitioners hoping for a cure. Thus while we can never know how Diodorus described or regarded himself and his physical condition, or how much it hampered him, we can presume that he wanted a straight back (and to live) – although in this instance, it was clearly beyond the practitioner's capabilities.

Diodorus wanted to be cured, and, so too, presumably, did most people suffering illness, disease or disability. But if the gods were responsible for causing disability, then they too cured you. Thus while Diodorus sought the assistance of Socles, more turned to the gods. And ancient texts are littered with a plethora of reports detailing the miraculous healing of persons suffering some disability, both in human and mythological contexts.

Magical incantations, prayers for help, amulets, charms and votives, magic potions and so forth, were prevalent in Greek and Roman public and private life (Pind., *Pyth.* 3.47–54). They reflected everyday basic fears and aspirations, be it an athletic victory, success in love, revenge, wealth, power, protection of a tomb or a cure for illness or injury. If a curse was being invoked, a disability was often the evil incurred. Magic also underpinned basic faith and belief in the power of healing: that is, the power of the divine to intervene and perhaps fulfil the wants of individuals, whether harmful or helpful (Faraone and Obbink 1991: 3–12; Kotansky 1991: 107; Gager 1992). Appeals for help, and expressions of gratitude, were often accompa-nied with votives shaped to represent an ailing part of the body, sometimes inscribed with a simple message (Plut., *Mor.* 706e). All types of medical complaint were covered, confirming both the general prevalence of disease and disability, and the general belief in divine help (Van Straten 1981).

The large number of eye votives found at the Athenian shrine of Asklepios point to its popularity with suppliants suffering from problems with sight (Aleshire 1989).

Prayers, representing need and a wish for divine help, were declarations of belief and a token of piety, expressing a contract with a god, and a response to divine action (Versnel 1981; Pulleyn 1997). Similarly votives, dedications to the gods, represented vows of individuals or the community, expressing a typical 'if..., then...' agreement. As offerings, the supplicant was seeking communication with the gods, the offering of an exchange, which the gods might or might not recognise (Burkert 1987: 14).

Ancient sources also abound with references to miraculous healings. Miracles can be defined as extraordinary events that lie outside the explanation of human power and the laws of nature. By definition they defy the normal boundaries of human existence and the natural order, and challenge a genuinely historical analysis (Van Dam 1993: 84). They usefully explained extraordinary, inexplicable cures. While ancient medicine involved observation and diagnosis of human ailments, miraculous healing came through appeal to and action of the gods. It differed, however, from magic, which used verbal and ritualistic techniques to bring about the desired end (Kees 1986: 3).

Testimonies such as those that Pausanias saw at Epidauros confirm that belief in miraculous punishment and healing was commonplace, and was not challenged by a society accustomed to it. However, if disability represented divine punishment, were miraculous healings understood as supernatural reward?

In general, miraculous cures are seldom part of a specific discussion about disability, but are reported within the wider narrative with varying degrees of detail or comment. Thus, the Egyptian god Sarapis allegedly restored the sight of the Athenian statesman and philosopher Demetrius of Phaleron (DL 5.76). Isis, another Egyptian deity, was also renowned for her skills in healing sight (DS 1.25). 'Pheros', who was blinded by the Egyptian gods for spearing the Nile in anger, was healed ten years later after an oracle advised him to wash his eyes with the urine of a wife who had remained faithful to her husband (Hdt. 2.111). The intervention of Athene Hygieia in the recuperation of the injured craftsman who had fallen from the Acropolis Propylaia saved his life (Plut., *Per.* 13.8; Pliny, *NH* 22.44). An elderly lame woman was healed by the hot springs of Etna (*Anth. Pal.* 6.203). Water played a significant role in healing, not only in purification, getting the supplicant ready, but also as a healing agent.

Herodotos' account of the healing of Croesus' *kofos* son is more detailed. Nameless, silent all his life, and shunned by his father because of his disability, this son stood in stark comparison with Atys, the handsome and manly elder brother whom Croesus adored (Hdt. 1.34, 38; on *kofos*,

McNeal 1986: 123–4). Here, the younger brother served as the contrasting doublet to Atys; which, in Herodotos' wider narrative detailing Croesus' demise saw the cherished son killed in a hunting accident, and the Lydian empire crushed. Defeated by Cyrus' army, and on the verge of being killed by an enemy soldier, Croesus was saved only by the miraculous and timely 'cure' of his *afonos* son, whose first words stopped the Persian killing the king. Here, Herodotos seemed to echo a second tradition that represented the prince as a 'fine young man' who had not been ignored by his father. In his concern, Croesus had even appealed to the Delphic Oracle in search of a cure. On one level, the incident may simply suggest that the younger son had hitherto chosen not to speak. On another level, it complied with Herodotos' didactic moralism, and served the interests of the Delphic Oracle: the miracle happened only after Croesus' engrossed hubris had been crushed and replaced by meekness and emotional surrender (1.84–5; see M.L. Edwards 1997b).

In the same vein is Herodotos' narration of the treatment of the Phocean prisoners of war by the Tyrrhenean Agyllans in *c.*535 BC. Having resettled in Corsica after they left Asia Minor, the Phoceans inevitably came into conflict with the Phoenicians over trading interests in the Western Mediterranean, culminating in military confrontation. The disastrous sea battle of *c.*535 BC cost the Phoceans much of their navy and manpower, while captured prisoners were divided among the Phoenicians and their allies, the Agyllans. As Herodotos tells us, the Agyllans stoned their prisoners to death, and in the process incurred the wrath of the gods. As punishment, any human or animal that passed the place where this outrageous act had occurred was struck with a paralysing stroke. Forgiveness came only after the Agyllans had consulted the Delphic Oracle and instituted an annual funerary ceremony and games in honour of their victims (Hdt. 1.167).

It is pertinent that these tales related by Herodotos had assumed an inherent pattern that had already appeared in the Homeric *Iliad* (1.456): recognition of the problem, repentance and retribution (Jones 1990: 12). Aspects of this *topos* can be identified a millennium later in Philostratus' fascinating but dubious biography of the itinerant philosopher and holy man Apollonius of Tyana. Pure of soul and without sin (3.42) and taught the skills of healing by Asklepios (1.8), Apollonius was credited with many and varied miraculous feats, including healing the disabled (3.40; 4.11). It is now well understood that miracle working involving religious feats formed a common motif in literature (Anderson 1986: 140), and part of the competition between paganism and Christianity over who was the greater healer, Asklepios or Jesus Christ (Temkin 1991: 75–82). For this reason, the story of the rich supplicant who had lost an eye is compelling.

According to Philostratus' narrative, this supplicant approached Asklepios with sacrifices and rich offerings to have his eye restored. Suspicious of a man who was offering gratitude before the customary stay in the temple, or the cure, the cult priests were reluctant to help. After some deliberation, Apollonius decided that the affliction was due to a sinister reason, and that the supplicant was hoping to avoid punishment for some cruel deed. That night, Asklepios appeared before the supplicant and ordered him away, noting that he deserved to lose his other eye too. Inquiries by priests revealed that the petitioner had been having an affair with his stepdaughter, and that his wife, surprising them in bed, had stabbed his eye out with a brooch-pin (1.10). Thus blindness followed a sexual crime; and the illness or disability is represented as a public manifestation of the private or hidden sin; here, adultery with the stepdaughter. Retribution came with the supplicant's entreaties to Asklepios, which the healer rejected.

Of course the key figure in Philostratus' story is Asklepios. Numerous traditions surrounded the elevation of Asklepios from Homeric hero to the Greek world's pre-eminent god of healing who also raised the dead (see Hartigan, Ch. 9, this volume). Taught the art of healing by the centaur Chiron, he was rewarded with divinity for his work. His wife, sons and daughters were also involved in healing. Standardised iconographic representations depict a bearded, mature god, bearing a calm expression. A snake is entwined around his staff. His principal sanctuary was at Epidauros, where his cult appears to have replaced the older cult of Apollo Malaetas. By the fifth century BC, Asklepios was evolving as the major healing deity in the Greek world, and paralleled the evolving Hippocratic tradition and increasing appearance of public physicians. By the second century AD, the cult's popularity in the Graeco-Roman world had grown to over 300 known sanctuaries (Garland 1992: 16–22; Gantz 1993: 91–2).

The popularity and confirmation of the deity's healing prowess and growing reputation can be seen in the increasing number, size and wealth of the sanctuaries throughout the Greek world; the enormous number of votive offerings found in the sanctuaries and the famous epigraphic dedications from Epidauros. From c. 500 BC, when the sanctuary at Epidauros had become associated with Asklepios, the sanctuary became renowned as a place of miracle healing. The stories of miracle healing acted as a self-perpetuating catalyst, extending the reputation of the sanctuary, and of the powers of Asklepios, and in turn, attracting further suppliants.

The extant inscriptions, carved on two stone tablets dating to the fourth century BC, list the gratitude of 43 suppliants who had made the pilgrimage from 22 different Greek states, and as far afield as Thessaly, Cnidus and Troezen (Edelstein and Edelstein 1945: I, 221–9, T 423). Each entry recorded the name, age, gender and origin of the patient, the medical complaint, an account of the cure, and whether it was Asklepios or one of his agents, the snake, dog (cf. Paus. 2.27.2) or temple priest, who administered the healing. In most cases, the supplicant's physical situation seemed hopeless, and would appear to have been outside the ability of trained physicians, such as the supplicant with an empty eye socket (T 423: 9). Other conditions included lameness, stigmata, irregular pregnancies, paralysis, muteness, war wounds, leeches, malignant tumour, dropsy, tapeworm, lice, migraine, consumption, baldness and even a broken drinking goblet.

The healing process began with purification rites, followed by a night spent in the large dormitory. It was during the period of incubation that the god visited suppliants in a dream and proposed a cure. The miraculous healings might involve the god directly, such as when Asklepios cured a man with a stomach abscess by cutting open the abdomen and removing it. Other times divine help came via the god's agents, namely his snake, such as occurred to Nicasibula of Messene, who dreamt she was impregnated by the snake, and within a year bore twins (T 423: 42). Sacred dogs are twice recorded healing young boys. One cured the blind Lyson of Hermione while he was wide awake (T 423: 20), another a boy from Aegina who had a growth on his neck. In this case the dog licked the wound, again while the patient was awake, and he too was cured (T 423: 26). On occasions, a short postscript added personal information that was or was not necessarily linked to the cure but enhanced the god's reputation. One example recorded how Hagestratus was both cured of headaches, and taught 'the lunge' which he probably used to win the pancratium at the Nemean games (T 423: 29). Another interesting feature of the texts is the incredulity of some witnesses, particularly with cases that seemed beyond help: they were rebuked or punished.

Asklepios' miracles were impressive because they seemed to reveal the reality of divine power and providence. Whether these dedications represented authentic case-studies, or fabrications by the Epidaurean priesthood, is a moot point (Temkin 1991: 81; Garland 1992: 123, n. 3; Nutton 1993: 8). What they were advertising were not life-stories, but the infallibility of the god: every case was successful. They were promoting the cult and sanctuary. Yet what is lacking from these dedications are exclamations of excitement, joy, celebration, wonderment, praise in the glory of the god for the altered physical state or a sense of blessing in the curing (cf. Versnel 1981: 42–62, on prayers of gratitude; also Pulleyn 1997). An example of this is the parable about a champion cock from Tanagra with a mutilated foot. Cured by Asklepios, the cock strutted about proudly flapping its wings, taking long strides, shaking its chest, glorying in its healing, and its re-found strength (Edelstein and Edelstein 1945: I, 265–6, T 466). Another feature missing from these dedications is a moral tone. The only exceptions are the occasions when the god punished incredulity and failure to honour any undertakings to make a contribution to the god's efforts. This was not the case with the second and third centuries AD propitiatory inscriptions and dedications from Lydia and Phrygia. While not knowing the outcome of their prayers, these dedications reflected the popular mentality already seen in literary texts, that their afflictions were divine punishments, and that cure could be achieved through expiation. Consequently, the dedications acknowledge the sin, and promise repentance in the form of payment (Chaniotis 1995).

PRIVILEGING THE 'BLESSED'

The early history of Christianity saw the elevation of Jesus Christ to the status of miracle healer in competition with Asklepios, who was enjoying a broad following among the poor. Early Christian miraculous healings were understood as forgiveness and a blessing by God. As we have seen, the popular imagination of ancient Greece considered disability as divine punishment. What is not clear, however, is whether disabled persons who were miraculously healed regarded their cure as a reward and a blessing. One of the earliest comments on this theme is the story of the 'just' and 'unjust' cities in Hesiod. A just city, Hesiod recorded, was rewarded with a blessed, healthy and productive community, while the unjust city was blighted with infertility and abnormal births (Hesiod, *WD* 225–47; West 1978: 213–15). Although in the scenario portrayed here the reward is in direct correlation to proper behaviour, and therefore is slightly different to the question that I am posing, the concept of reward was complex.

As we have seen, historical and quasi-historical texts reflect the sense of retribution, but little of the obverse. Where we do find a sense of reward is in mythological incidents of divine punishment that are counterbalanced, not directly with healing, but with a compensatory reward or blessing that involved an extraordinary quality, or art. The disabled Hephaestos serves as an excellent example. Hated and shunned by his mother Hera, and ridiculed and cuckolded by Aphrodite and her lover Ares, he is blessed with exquisite skill and grace, in a trade of metalworking that causes disability and stereotypically is represented by lame workmen (Detienne and Vernant 1978: 270–3).

Greek mythology's best-known example of a compensatory reward is the seer Teiresias who also served as an example of the innocent victim. The popularity of the myth is attested by the numerous traditions explaining his fate. Callimachos' version has Teiresias unintentionally stumbling on Athene bathing naked (*Hymn to Athena* 5.75–136). Despite his innocence, ancient laws laid down by Kronos demanded that transgressions of the natural order must be punished: that is, Athene has no option but to punish him with blindness, which can be regarded as emasculation. Athene, acknowledging Teiresias' innocence, compensated him with the art of divination, and the ability to move in a cosmological space, outside society (Apoll., *Bibl.* 3.6.7; on emasculation, Devereux 1973; Loraux 1995: 211–16).

Teiresias was blessed with the art of divination, as were a number of other seers, notably Evenius, who also had been punished with blindness (Hdt. 9.93–5), Orphioneus, Phineus and Phormio (Grottanelli 2003: 214–15). A more common image is the blind poet. Demodocus, for example, the poet in the court of Alcinous had been blinded by the Muses but compensated with great mastery of song (*Od.* 8.44–5, 62–4). As Richard Buxton has noted, poets, together with seers and those 'blessed with madness' (*mania*), were linked by the Greek imagination to a universal stereotype associating blindness and divination with extraordinary powers, a sixth sense, second sight or insight (1980: 20–1). The privileging, however, also confirmed an occurring ambivalence in classical literature associated with disability. The social and cultural status of blindness, and its link with the sacred, emphasise that the manifestations of some disabilities were attributed to realms beyond human knowledge or social control. Just as the blind beggar is outside society, so too are the 'blessed'. They remain on the margins of society and outside society, because of their extraordinary quality, or their privileging – perhaps in the same way that a king assumed the function of a *pharmakos* (scapegoat) (Bremmer 1980, 1983; Girard 1986).

CONCLUSION

Over the centuries, Strabo, Pausanias and countless others read the testimonies of suppliants at the various Asklepian sanctuaries. Some readers were incredulous; but most believed that the healing god miraculously cured disabilities and other ailments outside the scope of human medicine. In the popular imagination, gods caused disabilities and other extreme ailments and cured them. It is a mark of the value that society places on the able-body that the popular imagination also constructed afflictions of disability as divine punishment which in time became ascribed with socio-religious connotations and positioned the afflicted on the margins of society. In mythology those healed by divine intervention or privileged with compensatory powers are also marginalised, marking the reality that, while humans might hope, the curing of disability was outside common experience.

11

THE SALUBRIOUSNESS
OF THE ROMAN CITY

Neville Morley

CITIES OF DARKNESS AND LIGHT

The ancient Greeks regarded illness as a disturbance of the natural balance between the internal and external environments of the person, while the Romans made a contribution to public health through the provision of good water supplies, roads and housing. It was not, however, until the nineteenth century that the individual's environmental and living conditions became the focus of medical attention in a scientific and modern way.

(Davies and Kelly 1993: 1)

How healthy was the Roman city? Even a brief consideration of the question tends to emphasise the extent of our ignorance. How is 'health' to be defined and measured – purely in terms of morbidity and mortality, the incidence of disease and its effects on the population, or drawing on holistic concepts that see health as more than the simple absence of disease?[1] In either case, the ancient evidence seems inadequate to support anything other than tentative generalisations; as usual, we have to bemoan the lack of ancient statistics, the sole consolation being that the reasons for this lack may tell us something about the differences between ancient and modern attitudes to public health in the city. Most alarmingly, however, a survey of existing literature on the subject reveals two traditions of writing about the Roman city, which are diametrically opposed in their conclusions.

For many writers on both ancient and modern urbanism, the Roman city provides a model of how the urban environment may be made healthy and pleasant (Laurence 1994: 12–16). Drawing above all on archaeological evidence, but also on writings such as the architectural treatise by Vitruvius, they offer a vision of cities that were founded only after careful consideration of the site, planned and laid out in accordance with clear principles, and provided with extensive public facilities for the comfort, convenience and health of their inhabitants (Kolb 1995: e.g. 577–8; Scheidel 2003: 160, n. 7). The contrast with most nineteenth- and twentieth-century cities – seen to be dangerous, unhealthy and above all chaotic – is deliberate, intended to encourage the adoption of new policies for urban renewal or public health. For advocates of the planned city, as for the proponents of the holistic and ecological 'Healthy Cities' initiative, the Roman example adds the prestige of classical precedent to the scientific logic of their arguments. We may be offered an optimistic narrative of progress, in which the Roman city is one stage on the road to today's enlightened attitudes, or a nostalgic account in which it stands as an example of what cities ought to be in contrast to the soulless modern metropolis, an approach associated with the 'New Urbanism' of architects like Leon Krier. This view of the Roman city as pleasant and healthy is echoed in many visual representations of Roman life, which emphasise light, space, cleanliness (white togas, marble surfaces) and flowing water.[2]

There is an equally long tradition of seeing the Roman city, and above all the city of Rome itself, as an urban dystopia, a place of darkness and death (Laurence 1997).[3] Such writers may also draw on archaeological evidence (e.g. the siting of latrines adjacent to kitchen areas), but their main inspiration is literary; not so much the sober treatises on town planning and water supply as the impressionistic portrayals of urban life by Horace and especially Juvenal, and the passing comments of a multitude of other authors. Rome is portrayed as an over-crowded, filthy slum, its streets choked with rubbish and roamed by dogs, muggers and vultures; the lives of the majority of its population are seen to be squalid, miserable and, above all, short. In some cases, this negative view of life in the Roman city is part of a wholesale rejection of urbanism in both its ancient and modern forms; in others, there is an explicit contrast with the cities of the modern world and the vastly improved living conditions of the majority of their inhabitants compared with the majority of Romans.[4] It may perhaps also be related to the rejection of Rome as a model for society, with the growing awareness from the late eighteenth century of the potential power of modern technology; as David Hume put it, 'All our later improvements and refinements, have they done nothing towards the easy subsistence of men, and consequently towards their propagation and encrease?' (Hume 1882: 412).[5]

Such divergent views of the Roman city are possible because of the limitations of the ancient sources, which can easily be evaluated and interpreted in different ways according to the preconceptions of the historian. Our knowledge of the monumental landscape of Rome is detailed and more or less fixed, but there is limited evidence and hence little agreement on the wider context, the setting for those monuments; as Hermansen put it in his discussion of accounts of the population of Rome, 'von Gerkan sees Rome as a serene group of upper-middle-class residences, very remote from medieval conditions, while Calza and Lugli believe in a slummy metropolis' (Hermansen 1978: 167). The recommendations of Vitruvius on town planning, which focus on the need to ensure *salubritas* for the city's inhabitants, may be taken as representative of Roman concerns, or they may be treated with suspicion on the grounds that they are prescriptive rather than descriptive – after all, we do know that his warnings against the use of lead water pipes were ignored (Vitruvius 8.6.10; Hodge 1981). An anecdote in Suetonius' life of Vespasian about a dog carrying a human hand from the street into a dining-room may be dismissed as fictional and hence irrelevant, or cited as evidence for conditions in Rome on the grounds that it must have seemed plausible to Suetonius' audience that such a thing *might* happen (Scobie 1986: 418; Laurence 1997: 12). As for the archaeological evidence for living conditions, the basic problem has always been that we have no idea how many people lived in a typical Ostian *insula*; depending on one's preconceptions, they can be seen as elegant and spacious apartment blocks or overcrowded tenements (Vitruvius 2.8.7; Packer 1971; Morley 1996: 34; Laurence 1997: 13). Since the evidence is so malleable, and since our culture has always had an ambivalent attitude towards cities and what they represent, it is scarcely surprising that such different accounts of Roman cities have emerged.

What, then, can we hope to say with any certainty about the health or otherwise of the Roman city? It has been argued that any attempt to evaluate urban living conditions is doomed to failure; merely a rhetorical exercise, following the tradition of the Romans themselves, which can never hope to account for the city's labyrinthine complexity.[6] This seems unduly nihilistic. For all that different inhabitants of a city may experience and imagine it in different ways, they all live within a particular material environment, which regularly shapes and restricts their actions. As far as health is concerned, it is most helpful to think of this environment as an ecosystem, considering the relationship between humans and other inhabitants of the city – above all, pathogenic micro-organisms (Sallares 1991: 3–6; Scheidel 2003: 158). Of course the evidence is scarcely adequate for this sort of study, but modern research on the behaviour of pathogens nevertheless allows us to put forward hypotheses about the nature and dynamics of the urban ecosystem (Wills 1996; for detailed examples, see e.g. B.D. Shaw 1996; Sallares 2002; Scheidel 2003). We can then go on to consider how the Romans thought about and tried to respond to the hazards posed by this environment.

The urban ecosystem

Clearly we are in no position to discuss the incidence of disease in the Roman city in absolute terms; we can, however, try to establish its relative morbidity compared with cities in other periods and with the countryside. We need to consider what pathogens were faced by the different populations, how far the urban environment assisted or hindered the survival and reproduction of these pathogens, and how far there were effective remedies available to counter the effects of disease.

First, we need to try to establish the identity of the non-human inhabitants of the ancient urban ecosystem. There are considerable problems in identifying diseases in the past, whether using ancient medical writings or skeletal evidence; indeed, even today doctors may disagree as to what pathogen caused a particular outbreak.[7] However, through a combination of different kinds of evidence, along with the 'proxy' evidence of gravestones that indicate seasonal patterns of mortality (often associated with particular pathogens), a broad picture can be developed (Scheidel 1994; B.D. Shaw 1996). Unlike the majority of the inhabitants of the modern West, the Romans faced a number of diseases traditionally seen as mass killers: malaria (Sallares 2002; Scheidel 2003), tuberculosis and perhaps smallpox (cf. Morley 1996: 42–3; Scheidel 2003: 172). With the exception of smallpox, of course, these remain problems for most cities in the modern Third World, many of which, especially in Africa, have to contend with the additional burden of the devastating HIV/AIDS epidemic. Comparisons of ancient and modern cities tend without thinking to take the modern European or American conurbation as their model, as if to accentuate the contrast and present the triumphs of modern medicine and hygiene in the best possible light.

The Romans were spared a number of diseases that crossed from Asia into Europe in subsequent centuries. It seems that bubonic plague did not succeed in crossing the 'epidemiological barriers' of steppes and desert that separated Europe from Asia until the sixth century AD (McNeill 1977: 106–7).[8] Typhus and Indian cholera (Wills 1996: 105–30) arrived in Europe with devastating effect in the fifteenth and nineteenth centuries respectively; it is pure speculation as to whether the extensive trade links between Rome and the East might in fact have introduced these pathogens to Europe in the previous millennium (much as bubonic plague crossed Europe in waves, with outbreaks separated by centuries; Gottfried 1983; Slack 1985; Wills 1996: 53–89). It is possible, although impossible to determine, that the Romans may have been faced with other pathogens which have since either died out or mutated into less harmful forms. Otherwise it appears that they were exposed to a smaller number of diseases than the inhabitants of medieval or early modern Europe. Undoubtedly the mix varied across regions; Rome was dominated by hyperendemic malaria, with periodic epidemics of other diseases, while Alexandria was plagued with leprosy (Galen, 11.142 K; Scheidel 2003: 170–1).

However, the number of pathogenic species in the environment was not the only relevant factor. A key feature of the urban ecosystem, at least in the great cities, was the high level of immigration: this brought a regular influx of new diseases which might, temporarily at least, compete successfully with endemic species to spread through the population as an epidemic, and it also brought in a constant supply of new hosts who had not acquired resistance in childhood for the endemic diseases (Morley 1996: 43–6, 2003; Scheidel 2003: 175–6). The Romans' efforts in establishing communications across the whole empire and beyond eased the passage of pathogens around Europe, but drew most of them to Rome. A world of more restricted communication and smaller cities – medieval Europe, for example – remained vulnerable to severe epidemics, but suffered from fewer endemic diseases; the early modern growth in population and expansion of trade and travel together created an environment more like that of the Roman period (McNeill 1977; Kiple 1993).

The most interesting – and, for understanding the ecology and demography of the Roman Empire as a whole, the most important – comparison is that between the health of the Roman city and that of the Roman countryside, and that of the city of Rome as opposed to other, smaller cities. I have argued elsewhere that mortality in the city of Rome was higher than elsewhere in Italy – the 'urban natural decrease', an excess of deaths over births, familiar from other pre-industrial cities – not because its inhabitants were exposed to a wholly different set of pathogens but because they were exposed to them on a more regular basis (Morley 1996: 42–3). Because of the size of the metropolis, a number of diseases could become endemic rather than epidemic; its inhabitants were constantly at risk of infection, whereas those outside were at risk only periodically when a disease spread out into the countryside (Manchester 1992: 8–14). At the same time, the capital was able to attract vast numbers of migrants, to feed the pathogens. Further, as Rome was the destination for so many ships bringing cargoes from distant corners of the empire and beyond, it can also be argued that it was likely to be infected first, and most severely, by any newly imported pathogen.

How far might this be true of other cities? The 'density-dependent', urban diseases can become endemic only if the city population is large enough, the critical point being determined by the number of live births per week. Measles requires a population of about half a million to become endemic, which applies at most to just a few cities in the empire, like Alexandria and Constantinople. Smallpox, tuberculosis and mumps all require populations of several hundred thousand, which also rules out all but a few major centres. The ecosystem of empire therefore involved a small number of disease 'strongholds' scattered around the Mediterranean, from which the pathogens would make periodic forays to smaller cities and into the countryside. Generally, smaller cities were less unhealthy than the great conurbations. However, 'urban natural decrease' has been observed in early modern towns with as few as 1,500 inhabitants; we cannot assume that, because most Roman cities were significantly healthier places to live than the capital, they were necessarily as healthy as the countryside.[9]

This may be accounted for by the fact that urban living conditions, even when the city is relatively small, increase the chances of infection by providing pathogens with a hospitable environment for reproduction. Those organisms which live directly off humans and spread by contact, ingestion or inhalation need as large and densely settled a population as possible to prosper. City dwellers, even those in small centres, tend to have contact with a much larger number of people than those living in the country, aiding the spread of infection; further, people travelling from elsewhere (and so acting as potential carriers of disease) were more likely to visit the city than the country (cf. Morley 1997). The city has an enormous waste-disposal problem for which the sewage system was scarcely adequate, running the risk of contaminating food and water; farmers had space to store waste products well away from the house before spreading them on the fields (Varro goes into considerable detail on the ideal location of privies and manure-pits, and recommends that humans and animals should have separate water-sources; *RR* 1.11.2, 1.13.4). Modern experience suggests that farmers who keep their animals in separate buildings (as recommended by the agronomists) are less likely to suffer from malaria, since the mosquitoes concentrate on the animals (see Wills 1996: 167, on Denmark in the early twentieth century). Poorer farmers who slept in the same building as their animals, but more particularly town dwellers, had no such protection.

A number of ancient writers observed that the town was less healthy than the countryside, and not only as part of the rhetorical tradition of comparing the two (Quintilian, *Institutes* 2.4.24; Juvenal, *Satire* 3; S.H. Braund 1989). Celsus notes that 'the weak, amongst whom are a large portion of townspeople (*urbani*) and almost all who are fond of letters, need greater precaution, so that care may re-establish what the character of their constitution or their residence or their study detracts' (1.2.1). Describing an epidemic in 463 BC, Livy (3.6.2) suggests that, while the pestilence affected both city and country, it spread most dramatically when the country people fled to the city and were crowded together in narrow quarters (cf. Amm. Marc. 14.6.23). Finally, we should remember the elite custom of seeking *salubritas* precisely by getting out of the city, to a villa in the *suburbium* or to the Bay of Naples, during the hot summer months (Seneca, *Ep.* 104; Champlin 1982/85; D'Arms 1970). We have no evidence as to whether the elites of other towns did the same; from what we can surmise of the nature of the urban environment, they would have been well advised to do so.

Much of this is, of course, true of any city: a concentration of people provides a hospitable environment for the reproduction of parasitic micro-organisms. Modern western cities have achieved a limited reduction in the numbers of rats, cockroaches and other creatures which feed off human waste and which are potential carriers of disease; improved sewage systems, sanitation and the use of chemicals for water purification and cleaning have reduced the likelihood of food or water becoming contaminated (although at the same time as industrial food production methods have increased it). The Roman system for waste disposal was, by comparison, rudimentary and potentially hazardous (Scobie 1986). However, it did ensure that the streets (if not the houses) were cleaned regularly, reducing to some extent the likelihood of infection and also reducing the population of rats and other scavengers by removing part of their food supply. The baths may not have been particularly hygienic, but regular washing would reduce the populations of human parasites, which might carry disease. The fact that even the city of Rome does not seem to have had a major problem with rats – one generic term for 'vermin' was, oddly enough, *serpentes* – may explain the apparent absence of bubonic plague until the time of Justinian.[10] Finally, the constantly flowing fountains and basins supplied by aqueducts provided a much healthier water supply than wells or rivers (Wills 1996: 107, 109–16). Outside the city, the Romans' attempts at draining marshland might have done something to reduce the incidence of malaria, although it is equally possible that their activities in clearing woodland for agriculture actually resulted, through the erosion of hillsides and the deposition of the silt at river mouths, in the creation of new habitats for mosquitoes (Hughes 1994: 189).

Overall, therefore, living conditions in the typical Roman city were quite possibly healthier than those of the Middle Ages or early modern period, and certainly better than those in many parts of modern Third World cities. To some extent this was even true of the city of Rome, but the sheer number of people crowded into the city, and the level of immigration, made this only a relative advantage; the lives of its inhabitants were dominated by disease, and as a result 'life in Rome was probably nastier and certainly shorter than many historians are likely to appreciate' (Scheidel 2003: 158).

THE HUMAN RESPONSE

The great advantage of the inhabitants of the modern West in their relationship with pathogenic micro-organisms lies not so much in their limited (and now deteriorating) successes in making the urban environment less hospitable to disease than in their ability to deploy medical technology to limit the effects of infection. Programmes of immunisation have lowered dramatically the world-wide incidence of diseases like measles, mumps and diphtheria, and have effectively eradicated smallpox; not only can many of those infected now be cured, but doctors are able to take steps to prevent an epidemic as soon as the first few cases are identified.[11] Even in the Third World, outbreaks of plague or cholera now have surprisingly low death tolls, unless the situation is complicated by war, famine or political upheaval. Of course, smallpox and tuberculosis have been succeeded in the West by heart disease and cancer, the incidence of 'environmental' ailments like asthma and other allergies is increasing dramatically, the misuse of anti-biotics has created strains of resistant pathogens and it is debatable how far the modern western urbanite is mentally and socially 'healthy'; but purely in terms of life expectancy, even after contracting most diseases, the modern world has a clear advantage over the Romans.

It is a truism that ancient medicine did not develop a proper theory of contagion; recent studies attribute this to the fact that physicians empha-sised prognosis and therapy rather than aetiology, and that contagion was associated with religious pollution (and hence religious remedies) rather than medicine proper (Longrigg 1992; Flemming 2000: esp. 102–9; Laskaris 2002: 149–55). From the modern perspective, therefore, ancient responses to disease could only be limited and ineffectual. It is of course a distinctively western approach to focus exclusively on the pathogen rather than on the patient's overall state of health that had left him vulnerable to infection, or on the environment that had fostered disease (cf. Kapchuk 1983; Kendall 2002: 8–9). Ancient medicine was 'holistic' in its approach, focusing on the balance of different humours within the individual and the influence of the environment. On this latter point, physicians were well aware that cities might be unhealthy. Celsus' observation that *urbani* could be debilitated by the place of residence has already been quoted (1.2.1); Galen remarked that there was no need to consult books when one could find exemplary specimens of semitertian fever on any given day on the streets of Rome (Galen 7.135 K), while Herodian provides an acute summary of the capital's particular problems: 'Just at this time a plague struck Italy, but it was most severe in Rome, which, apart from being normally overcrowded, was still getting immigrants from all over the world' (1.12; generally, Nutton 2000: 66–7).

The aim of the doctors was to treat the individual, even in an unhealthy situation (although the best cure was often to remove to a less unhealthy situation), rather than to embark on initiatives to improve the quality of the environment (Nutton 2000: 71). Other Roman writers, however, sought to draw on their insights to promote 'public health'. Vitruvius (1.1.3, 1.1.10) goes into considerable detail about the causes of illness and the ways in which the architect may try to remedy them; indeed, he suggests that the ideal architect should know all about medicine (as well as mathematics, history, philosophy, astronomy and law). The cause of sickness is an imbalance of the elements of the body, resulting from excessive heat or cold, excessive moisture or dryness. The main task of the architect is therefore to select an appropriate site, from the point of view of both locality and aspect, and to lay out the buildings so as to reduce the effects of noxious winds; finally, he should ensure that the water supply is healthy (1.4, 1.6, 8 preface, 8.3). Such advice was clearly of limited use for existing cities which had already been built in pestilential regions; but it would be interesting to investigate further how far Vitruvius' comments were descriptive of regular practice in the new Roman foundations in the west of the Empire, rather than purely prescriptive and theoretical (Grew and Hobley 1985; Owens 1991; Laurence 1994: 12–19).

Vitruvius can be claimed as a pioneer of the 'green city' concept, though his reasons for advocating that the spaces between colonnades should be planted up are not those of modern environmentalists: 'walks in the open air are very healthy, first for the eyes, because from the green plantations, the air being subtle and rarefied, flows into the body as it moves, clears the vision and so by removing the thick humour from the eyes, leaves the glance defined and the image clearly marked. Moreover, since in walking the body is heated by motion, the air extracts the humours from the limbs, and diminishes repletion, by dissipating what the body has, more than it can carry' (5.9.5). Rome did contain a number of parks – Ovid describes the gardens of Maecenas as having made the Esquiline *salubris* – but it is arguable how far they were constructed with Vitruvius' advice in mind (Ovid, *Sat.* 8.14; cf. Robinson 1992: 116–17). Pleasure gardens were more often associated with luxury, especially imperial luxury, trying to turn the city into a private park (Suet., *Nero* 31; Pliny, *NH* 19.50; Purcell 1987; C. Edwards 1993: 139–40, 148–9). They may have improved the quality of life in the city, at least for a few of its inhabitants, but they are unlikely to have had a significant impact on the level of mortality.

More significant from a practical point of view are the comments of Frontinus, *curator aquarum* under Nerva and Trajan, that his duties concerned 'not merely the convenience but also the *salubritas* and even the security of the city' (*Aq.* 1). A similar phrase is found in the comments of

Roman jurists concerning the legal obligation to allow the clearing and repair of drains: 'Both pertain to the *salubritas* of citizens and to safety. For drains choked with filth threaten pestilence of the atmosphere and ruin, if they are not repaired' (*Digest* 43.23.1.2). This is clear evidence that the Roman authorities considered the public health of the city as their responsibility.[12] However, their activities seem to have been limited largely to maintaining existing services. In part, perhaps, this was because urban renewal on the grand scale became associated with megalomaniacs like Caesar and Nero, but there was also a limit to what could be done in Rome (Suetonius, *Div. Iul.* 44; Cicero, *Att.* 13.20, 13.33; Suet., *Nero* 16, 38). Tacitus even says that some people complained that the city had been more salubrious before Nero's reforms, because the narrow streets had protected them from the sun (*Ann.* 15.43). As Vitruvius noted, the way to ensure that a city would be healthy was to found it in the correct place. Rome had already been founded (opinions differed as to whether its site had been carefully chosen or was on the contrary a matter of necessity rather than choice; Cicero, *Rep.* 2.11; cf. Strabo, 5.3.2), so there was little else they could do.

Thus Frontinus' answer to the city's problems is simply to increase the volume of the water supply, by building new aqueducts or by stamping out abuses in the system, 'so that the public fountains may flow as continuously as possible' (*Aq.* 88, 103–4). This will improve the city air by removing the causes of the *gravius caelum* for which it was *infamis* (*Aq.* 88). As a secondary measure he aims to improve the purity and palatability of the water supplied so as to enhance its *vitalitas*. He does classify the waters of the different aqueducts according to their salubriousness, on the basis of their colour, taste and clarity (*Aq.* 11, 15, 89–90). The purest water is designated for drinking only, the worst is used for irrigation and 'other mean usages of the city' – but even this latter water, like that of the Aqua Alsietina, is used in fountains when other supplies are short, so clearly it was not regarded as harmful but merely unpleasant (*Aq.* 11, 92). As with Vitruvius' advice regarding gardens, these measures might improve the overall quality of life in the city for some people, but was unlikely to affect their chances of contracting disease.

Most Roman authors who comment on the healthiness or otherwise of the city approach the subject in a less 'scientific' manner; it is simply accepted that city life is less healthy than country life, and the solution to this is to move to the country (e.g. Columella 1 preface 15–20). To some extent, this is no more than a rhetorical commonplace, part of an attempt to present the city in the worst possible light; it draws, among other things, on the idea that there was a direct link between virtue and good health, luxury and sickness.[13] However, since we have seen plenty of reasons for supposing that the city was indeed less healthy than the country, it can plausibly be suggested that the fact of high urban mortality aided the moralists' attempts to characterise all aspects of urban civilisation as inimical to the truly good life. The Roman elite did not retire to suburban villas in the summer simply because of an ideological preference for the country.

In other respects, too, the rhetoric of Juvenal's third satire, whether or not it is to be read as a parody of this sort of moralising, may be seen to be responding to the consequences of Rome's excessive mortality; in its hostility towards immigrants (with no understanding of why Rome should be full of immigrants) and its overwhelming fear of death, either actual (due to fire, muggers or falling marble) or metaphorical (loss of identity in the crowd, erosion of social distinctions; Juvenal, *Satire* 3: 58–65, 190–211, 242–8, 257–61, 278–308; cf. Morley 2003: 153–4). The Roman *plebs'* love of gladiatorial games might be explained in part as a response to the peculiar conditions of urban, or at any rate metropolitan, life; its brevity and fragility in the face of a range of pathogens (Hopkins 1983; on comparative responses to disease, see also Slack 1985: chapters 2 and 11; Ranger and Slack 1992). On the other hand, perhaps it was only the rich, who could afford to escape the city regularly, who conceived of it as a place of pestilence in contrast to the salubrious countryside; for many of the population, especially those who had chosen to migrate there, the city might be seen in far more positive terms, regardless of its level of mortality. Disease was seen as something beyond human control – a matter either of the will of the gods, or of the inevitable 'sickly season' (*grave tempus*) – not as something which might be prevented by human means (cf. Livy, 3.6.8, on the passing of the plague of 463).

CONCLUSION

If we hope to understand the past, we can scarcely avoid some degree of comparison with our own world. By modern western standards, the Roman city was unhealthy and dangerous, not somewhere we would wish to live. To see it as an ideal form of urbanism it is necessary to take theoretical accounts of how the city *should* be – Vitruvius and the law codes – as unproblematic representations of reality, and to concentrate on the surviving architecture rather than the people (not to mention the rodents, dogs, insects and microbes) who inhabited it. This is not to say that all Romans would have experienced the city as hazardous; many would survive their illnesses or even escape infection altogether, and we simply have no way of knowing how the mass of the population thought about city life. Nevertheless, the basic fact of urban civilisation in the Roman Empire is that the city formed an ecosystem which supported large populations of pathogenic micro-organisms, feeding off the humans and periodically bringing about the deaths of their hosts.

However, comparison with the modern city and modern standards of public health is not the whole story; compared with other pre-industrial cities, the Roman city was indeed a model of urbanism. The *insulae* may have been cramped and insanitary, the baths may have been less healthy than is normally imagined, but at least the Roman town dweller benefited from copious water supplies, regular clearing of rubbish from the streets and a minimum expected standard of personal hygiene. Perhaps our image of the Roman city needs more dirt and grubbiness on the polished marble and freshly pressed togas, but the reality is still a long way removed from the squalor of the typical medieval or early modern city.

NOTES

1 See T. Hancock, 'The Healthy City from concept to application', in Davies and Kelly 1993: 14–24, drawing on the WHO 1946 definition: 'a state of complete physical, mental and social well-being, not merely the absence of disease or infirmity' (see earlier, Introduction). Hancock also notes that, for the most part, the data for measuring 'health' in these terms simply do not exist.

2 Seen clearly in many of Alma-Tadema's paintings (Liversidge and Edwards 1996: e.g. 132–8, 152–4, 165–70) and the Asterix books (especially *Asterix and the Laurel Wreath*), but also in film: Wyke 1997: illustration 6.5 on p. 168.

3 In fiction, see, above all, the Falco novels of Lindsey Davies.

4 On traditions of writing about cities in general see Williams 1973. A good example of an explicit contrast between ancient and modern is Scobie 1986.

5 Compare Marx's use of Rome – not specifically the city of Rome – to highlight modernity's failures: 'On the one hand, there have started into life industrial and scientific forces, which no epoch of the former human history had ever suspected. On the other hand, there exist symptoms of decay, far surpassing the horrors recorded of the latter times of the Roman Empire' (Marx and Engels 1980: 655).

6 Laurence 1997: 14–18, drawing on Raban 1974; another perspective on Raban's book is offered by Harvey 1988: 3–9. On Laurence, see Scheidel 2003: 159–60.

7 Identification of ancient diseases: Zivanovic 1982; Grmek 1989; Sallares 1991: 221–93. On the problems of identifying the cause of the Indian plague of 1994, Wills 1996: 90–102.

8 However, similar symptoms are described by Hippocrates, *Epid.* 3.3, cited by Hughes 1994: 187. General discussion in Sallares 1991: 263–70.

9 Urban natural decrease in early modern Europe: J. de Vries 1984: 179–97. See also Wear 1992: 127–32, on seventeenth- and eighteenth-century discussions of the contrast between healthy country and unhealthy city.

10 *Mus* covers both rats and mice, which may suggest that rats were not identified as a significant problem in themselves. It has even been suggested that there

were no rats in the ancient Mediterranean, though there is an unpublished claim of one in second-century BC Pompeii: Sallares 1991: 263–4. Cicero, *De Off.* 3.54 refers to a house which is infested with *serpentes*.

11 Although the recent example of the SARS virus shows the problems of implementing the desired strategy in the face of the demands of the global economy and political intransigence; Leung and Ooi 2003.

12 The laws relating to public health in Rome are detailed at length by Robinson 1992: 111–29; see also her discussion of how far the city was administered according to a coherent plan, 14–32.

13 Celsus, *Prologue* 4–5, argues that, although people of Homer's time had no understanding of the causes of disease and no remedies, they were nevertheless generally healthy because of their good habits; Vitruvius, 1.4.4, suggests that excessive moisture may dissolve virtues in the body and chilling winds may infuse vices; Columella, 1 preface 17, 'The consequence of [urban life] is that ill health attends so slothful a manner of living; for the bodies of our young men are so flabby and enervated that death seems likely to make no change in them.'

12

BUILDINGS FOR HEALTH

Then and now

Peter Barefoot

It is not enough for the physician to do what is necessary, but the patient and the attendants must do their part well, and the environment[1] must be favourable.

(Hippocrates, *Aphorisms* 1)

For most of the years that I was in practice as an architect, I was involved in the design of hospitals, or rather parts of hospitals, including patients' wards, day centres and facilities for therapy of various kinds. The brief given by the health authority was always precise and specific on matters of floor space, equipment, technology and detail, but silent on the general quality of the environment. There was something lacking here; I became interested in the way such factors as colour, light and air could be considered in the interests of the patient. I thought of a name for this desirable but undefined quality: locotherapy, or cure through the environment. Seeking support for further study of this aspect of health care, I was lucky enough to receive funding from the Guild of St George (a charity founded by John Ruskin) and from the RIBA to study, respectively, the needs of children in hospital with cancer, and the design of wards for psychiatric care in District General Hospitals. This research was carried out concurrently with the design and then construction of two such wards, together with day care facilities, at St Bartholomew's Hospital in London.[2] After these projects were completed, I became interested in the history of buildings for health care and, having always had a love of Greek classical architecture, it occurred to me to look at the shrines for health in ancient Greece. In 1991 I started a study of *asklepieia* and similar buildings to see if there was anything to learn from the Greeks that could be of use or inspiration to a hospital architect today. What follows are notes of my impressions of places visited and my conclusions.

Before the temples were built, healing was a sacred art, often associated with a cave or a spring, where a practitioner administered strange remedies, or gave advice on therapies or ritual to cure the sick, in return for payment or a sacrifice. In ancient Greece, the god Asklepios was the best-known healer; the legends tell of him visiting patients, or even their proxies, in their sleep, in shrines held sacred to him and his art. Many descriptions of these rites survive (Edelstein and Edelstein 1945: II, T. 4.82–626). The cure involved his appearance in their dreams as himself or sometimes in the form of a serpent, whose touch could heal. With his legendary helpers, Hygieia personifying physical and mental health, and Panacea ('she who cures everything'), the god offered a virtual health service, to cure disease and to maintain health.

How medicine has changed since then! A study of the shrines where these strange rites were performed is hardly likely to be of immediate benefit to the architect of hospitals today. Later, the art of medicine progressed from a strange cult to the more rational approach of Hippocrates and his followers. The design and, in particular, the siting of the buildings in the Asklepieia become more sophisticated, and to have a quality worth investigating. This I suggest becomes of interest, and I hope of inspiration, to the designer of today, when seen in the context of the legendary god, Asklepios, and the alternative, by then concurrent, ideas of Hippocrates and his followers. There is a paradox here, realised visually in a large mosaic paving from a Roman house of the second or third century AD, found during the Italian excavations of 1935–43, and now in the archaeological museum on the island of Kos. It shows the legendary meeting of Asklepios with Hippocrates, as the latter disembarks from a boat in the harbour, overlooked by a Coan (Verbanck-Piérard 1998: 160, 282). On the one hand, the faith and magic of the god: on the other, the medicine and the reason of Hippocrates. Both sought a balance of the forces of nature (Figure 12.1).

There were many shrines of Asklepios in ancient Greece; perhaps several hundred. The largest and best known were at Kos, Epidauros and Pergamon. In each place, the original focal point seems to have been the sacred spring; later, the dominant building was the temple, or temples. Other buildings might include the *palaestra*, the *abaton* or *enkoimeterion*, where patients awaited their god and/or cure, and sometimes a curious circular building or *tholos*. In the larger centres, these structures were often associated with a gymnasium, theatre or stadium, leading one to the idea of health being a state of equilibrium for the whole man – body and mind. The shrine at Epidauros is close to both the stadium and the gymnasium, and not far from the better-known theatre with its amazing acoustic quality (see Hartigan, Ch. 9, this volume).

I would like now to look at four Asklepieia in more detail. The first, at Kos, is the largest shrine for health on the Greek islands. Even today, it is an impressive sight; three extensive terraces face northeast, with a superb

Figure 12.1 Contemporary statue in the International Hippocratic Foundation conference centre on Kos; sculptor, Nikos 1988 © The International Hippocratic Foundation.

view over the gardens and orchards of the city across the water to Halicarnassus. The site must have been chosen with great care, above a spring and below a sacred grove. It is some 4 km away from the noise and activity of the city and, unusually, not near a theatre or gymnasium. Construction of the three temples, the portico on the upper and lower terraces and the Roman baths, extended over a long period, from the early third century BC to the late third century AD. Unlike a hospital complex today, it seems that the initial choice of a superb site, and the construction of the terraces linked by formal stairways of some grandeur, may have been made with the intention of allowing space for the many later additions. Even the enrichment of the Imperial period and the apparent scattering of the later buildings lost little of the quality of the original setting. It could even be said to enhance what has been called its baroque character, but it was a baroque surrounded by, and subservient to, nature (Figure 12.2).

Each terrace had its own distinct character. Entering the lowest level, through the entrance to the Asklepieion in the south side of the portico, one's view of the main buildings ahead is at an angle, framed on each side by the east and west wings of the portico. Beyond the temples is the sacred grove; below them an impressive arcaded retaining wall with the basins and a fountain fed by sulphurous spring water. The stone steps themselves are worthy of comment; dramatic in overall height and width, they are also designed with perfect proportion in their ratio between rise and tread and to human scale. The possible use of a particular formula here minimises the effort needed to ascend or descend. Approaching the middle level, the temples, *abaton* and altar are sited at subtle angles; there is no formal centre line, and each building is seen to best advantage as the visitor progresses upwards. The portico is reversed on the upper level, framing the view downwards to the sea; it was here that the cooling sea breeze would best be felt on a hot day, along with the scents of wild flowers in the sacred grove.

It is legendary that the first ideas of rational medicine were formed on Kos by Hippocrates, with the patronage of the god Asklepios, as idealised in the Roman mosaic mentioned earlier. Perhaps tourism has kept this delightful idea alive; in the city below the Asklepieion there is a plane tree, or maybe a clone of it, where Hippocrates or his co-authors may perhaps have held medical seminars; now T-shirts printed with the Hippocratic oath are on sale in the shade of the tree. Both the legend and an interest in historic medicine inspired today's International Hippocratic Foundation to

Figure 12.2 The three terraces of Kos today.

found a School of Medicine near the Asklepieion; an impressive range of conference rooms has already been completed, and the Foundation's President, Professor Spyros Marketos, occasionally stages a dramatic performance on the terraces, re-enacting with some music and much imagination a colourful version of the ceremony of the Hippocratic oath, with its tributes to Asklepios and his family (Figure 12.3).

The Coan Asklepieion was eventually destroyed by earthquake, the Anatolian hordes and the knights of St John, but what remains is evidence of the love of water, clean air and nature, enhanced by a subtle and asymmetric siting of the individual buildings, their relationship to each other, to the massive altar and to the sacred grove.

My second example is at Corinth. Well outside the main part of the city, there is a much smaller shrine than at Kos. It is just within, and indeed forms part of, the city wall. Again, the presence of water led to its foundation; on a lower level below the shrine there are basins filled by reservoirs in the rock. Perhaps the anxious patient would bathe first in the sea, as happened to Ploutos in Aristophanes' play, *Ploutos* (Wealth). A cure for the god in human form was described by Karion, a slave, who comments 'first of all we

Figure 12.3 An imaginative recreation of the Hippocratic Oath ceremony, staged by the International Hippocratic Foundation; 7 pairs of young girls bearing libations were preceded by 2 boy flautists, and followed by the qualifying student, who read his solemn oath to the audience below.

took him to the sea, and bathed him there...then we went to the precincts of the gods' (*Ploutos* 656–7, 659) where further ritualistic bathing might follow. The ramps and the lower courtyard are unusual features; there is a small ramp for the temple entrance, perhaps intended for the disabled patient; another ramp, 30 metres in length, leads down to the lower court-yard. On one side of this open area are three small rooms. Their purpose is unclear; they are similar to rooms found in the sanctuary of Demeter and Persephone, to the south of the city, and Mabel Lang (1977) has suggested that they could have been used for dining, perhaps each one for different ill-nesses or even for special diets. Whatever their function, these lower rooms would have been cooled by the thermal breeze; on hot summer days, warm air rises above the hills to the south, to be replaced by cooler air which would swirl into the open basement area (Figure 12.4).

Both water for cleansing and the quality of the air could be described as essential features in the healing process. The extent and indeed the type of cure offered, or at least the part of the body to be healed by the priest or doctor, can be seen today in the museum, which has collected and displayed a vast number of votive offerings found on the site: replicas of arms, legs and various organs, modelled in clay, fired to order by a local potter, or bought off-the-peg, then donated by the discharged patient, who had also, no doubt, contributed to the offertorium box found near the entrance.

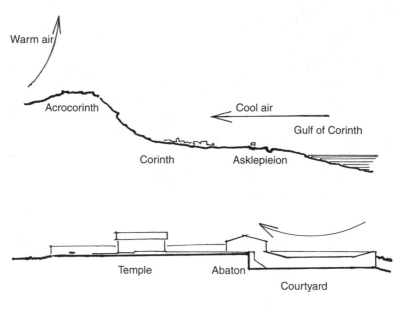

Figure 12.4 The micro-climate of Corinth.

My third example is near Oropus, on the northeast coast of Attica, about 50 km from Athens. Many of the shrines for health or cure fell into disuse after the Roman occupation, perhaps as a result of their disbelief in the Greek healers, but here and at Kos they continued to attract visitors into a much later period. The healing shrine at Oropus was dedicated not to Asklepios, but to Amphiaraos, who in legend was saved by Zeus, after the 'Seven against Thebes' campaign. It was dedicated also to Hygieia. The complex is unusual in form; the main buildings extend along the banks of a steep ravine, with none of the grandeur of Kos or the exposure of Corinth. Gaps in the pine trees along the approach road give occasional views over the Evian Gulf, towards Amarinthos. In spring, the grass banks are covered with wild flowers. Levi (1979: 97) comments that the 'gorge still has the air of a place for sacred sleep' and Pausanias (1.34.3) notes that, although the sacred spring was near the shrine, the water was not used for ritual or sacrifice, but patients would, more commercially, drop coins of gold or silver into the pool. This symbolic gesture continues today; in many of our larger children's hospitals, a fountain plays near the main entrance, and coins are still thrown. There is also evidence at Oropus that payment for admission was acknowledged in the form of a lead tablet inscribed with the profiled heads of Amphiaraos and of Hygieia.

The buildings on this site include two temples. One was adjacent to a fountain and to the altar, and there, according to Pausanias (1.34.3), they sacrifice a ram and sleep on the fleece, waiting for the revelation of a dream. There is a line of statues (twenty five pedestals have been found, mostly Roman), a small theatre, and an *enkoimeterion* in the form of a long stoa which runs parallel to the glade bordering the stream, and beyond that, the Roman baths. There is accommodation for visitors on the opposite bank, now covered by trees, and a remarkable *klepsydra* or water clock, which seems to suggest that there may have been a daily routine to be followed. Today, and no doubt when the shrine was in use, there is once more an overall feeling of peace and union with nature. This shrine probably gives a better idea of how the surroundings looked when it was in use than those on the islands, where man and the goat have destroyed most of the vegetation.

Finally, to Athens, where the chosen site for the shrine to Asklepios was towards one end of a series of buildings devoted to the arts. The sunlit south slope of the Acropolis, sometimes called Europe's first cultural centre, had been chosen for a variety of buildings for drama, ceremony and choragic monuments. The building for health fits neatly between the theatre of Dionysos and the later stoa of Attalos, where theatregoers might well have mingled with patients seeking a cure. As elsewhere, there is natural spring water from the ancient rock itself. The essential elements appeared again in the choice of site and its planning; the south aspect, with a distant view to the sea, now obscured by new buildings and pollution of the atmosphere, beyond pine-covered slopes, now replaced by the housing suburbs of Peiraieus. Said to be founded by a private citizen, with a small temple dedicated to Asklepios and Hygieia, the patient seeking cure here would seem to have had a choice of admission to the Doric or the Ionic wing, each used as an *enkoimeterion*, where healing was attempted with the aid of the gods. A stone-lined pit at one end of the complex could have been used for snakes, creatures frequently associated with Asklepios in imagery and in literature; there are many references in the Edelsteins' source collection (1945: I, 360–9). As far as I know, the snake legend survives today only in the form of a logo, twined round the god's staff, to identify a place of healing.

Even after destruction by the barbarians, the Athenian site was respected as a healing sanctuary; a Byzantine Church was dedicated there to the physician saints, Cosmas and Damian. There is a parallel here with Rome; the first temple dedicated there to Asclepius (to use the Latin spelling) was built on Isola Tiberina, an island referred to by Ovid as that chosen by the god when he was brought to Rome in his form as a snake (Ovid, *Metamorphoses* [1987] trans. A.D. Melville, Oxford University Press, p. 374, 29–40). A church dedicated to St Bartholomew was later built on the island, and a hospital founded by the Brothers of St John of God, the Ospedale Fatebenefratelli, was built over the ruins of the temple, and still functions today; the visitor may still detect the carving in stone, just above the water level of the Tiber, of Asclepius with his staff and snake.

Here then were four different centres of healing. Today, the genius of most of these places is still apparent, in that they are pleasant to the senses, near water, and surrounded by open spaces, and on most of these sites one can still enjoy sunshine, cool air and a view of sea or river and landscape. When they were built, it was thought by some early philosophers that there were four elements: fire (or sunlight), air, earth and water. This idea goes back at least to Empedokles, and at much the same time, there was a reference to the four elements in Sanskrit literature in the fifth century BC (Mascaro 1962: 74). These simplistic ideas were expanded in Islamic and medieval medicine, but without wishing to go any further towards the various 'balances' sought with reference to the 'humours' of early medicine, I do find the idea of sunshine, clean air, water and landscape a helpful summary of the non-medical essentials for a pleasant environment for healing, underlining the point that the return to good health is not just a matter of medication or surgery.

So, of what value could these studies be to the architects and designers of modern hospitals? We can look back first to two particular times of change in ideas of design in the last hundred and fifty years. In the nineteenth century, the then-prevalent ideas of hospital planning were given harsh criticism by Florence Nightingale (1820–1910). Better known in England for her work in the Crimea, she spent many years in observation and care of the sick, and in her book *Notes on Nursing* (1859), she campaigned for many of the features which I have tried to identify in ancient Greece, such as the need for fresh air and good light; even the view from the patient's window is important – they should be able, without raising themselves or turning in bed, to look out of the window from their beds, to see sky and sunlight at the very least (1860: 84–7). Thus was the Nightingale ward conceived, as pavilions with windows on either side, cross-flow of air and beds at right angles to the long walls, giving outward views for the patients.

Nightingale's comments found a kind of echo in Pennsylvania, USA, between 1972 and 1981. Fully described under the heading 'View through a window may influence recovery from surgery' (Ulrich 1984), the study compared the recovery after cholecystectomy of 23 patients assigned rooms with a view to a natural scene, with a control group of the same size whose view was that of a brick wall. Not surprisingly, those with the 'room with a view' were found to have had 'shorter post-operative stays, received fewer negative comments in nurses' notes, and took fewer potent analgesics than those without the view'.

The Nightingale ward became the standard, at least in the United Kingdom, but after the Second World War developments in medicine had progressed so far that further changes in ward design became essential. In the late 1940s, research was carried out to devise new plans suited to the advanced technology of medicine in both medical and surgical wards, but in their application many of those basic needs of light, air and views of sky and nature, were forgotten. There were exceptions, and I would like to close the argument of this chapter with illustrations of hospitals where attempts have been made to provide a healing environment. I have chosen 4 examples, and comment on them with reference to the 4 elements.

- Sun: a drug dependency unit in the St Pau Hospital at Barcelona. The day room used by patients undergoing an intense 28-day course faces an open terrace; the symbolic opening to a better life ahead. The whole unit is a conversion of an innovative design of around 1900; the architect of the original building was Dominic y Montana, a contemporary of Antonio Gaudi, and the style was a flamboyant *art nouveau*. The aim of the conversion was to restore the best of the original design, and to provide a pleasant environment for the residents, who are required to follow a particularly rigorous regime. A space to be enjoyed, and good food, were part of the therapy.
- Air: Philadelphia Children's Hospital occupies a downtown city block; the interior is planned around a central atrium, and hospital corridors

look down on to an open floor, rich with planting, colour and activity. Something of the world outside has been successfully introduced into the closed environment of the hospital, and this is helped by the atmospheric quality (Figure 12.5).

- Water: in many hospitals today, the sight and sound of water is still apparent; a common feature is the 'wishing well' or pool of health, where coins are still thrown as they were at Oropus. There are wishing wells at Philadelphia (shown here), Boston Children's Hospital and many others.
- Earth: as nourishment for plants, is the fourth element. In recent years it has become apparent that the sight, feel and smell of plant life can help to speed recovery. In the new Children's Cancer Unit at St Bartholomew's Hospital in London, I was able to provide a roof terrace with plants and play balcony in the extension to a ward above a nineteenth-century wing of this city hospital. There is a long historical link between Asklepios and St Bartholomew's Hospital. In my comments on Athens and Rome, I mentioned the first part of this link, from Kos to the Tiber Island, but it is perhaps of interest that St Bartholomew's hospital was founded in memory of Rahere, an English court servant who travelled to Rome and whose illness was cured at the hospital on Tiber island. Then the link continues into the twentieth century, when 2 wards were remodelled for children, and 1 for psychiatry.

Figure 12.5 Air: Philadelphia Children's Hospital.

In conclusion, I believe that what I have called locotherapy was used, deliberately or unconsciously, in the places I have described, and in many others in the classical world. This idea is of value to hospital designers today alongside the functional and complex technical requirements of modern medicine and nursing care. Architects would do well to visit the asklepieia and other health centres of ancient Greece; they would find inspiration there, and a strong suggestion that the return to good health is not just a matter of medication or surgery, but the environment must play its part as well.

ACKNOWLEDGEMENT

I would like in particular to acknowledge with thanks the help and encouragement of Spyros Marketos, Professor of Medicine and President of the International Hippocratic Foundation of Kos.

NOTES

1 This is from the first aphorism, Loeb IV, 98 (trans. Chadwick and Mann, in Lloyd 1978: 206), but I have used the word 'environment' rather than 'circumstances' for *exôthen* in the original, which seemed appropriate in the context of this chapter.
2 A fully-illustrated article based on my report Children in Hospital for the Guild of St George was later published in Italian in the medical quarterly journal *Technologie per la Sanitá* (May 1992): Progetto LM, Bologna, pp. 66–9, and the report to the RIBA was published as Barefoot 1991.

13

THE HEALTH OF
THE SPIRITUAL ATHLETE

Gillian Clark

'These men are competing in the greatest contest of all, are they not? Would the condition of present-day athletes in training be right for them?'

'Maybe.'

'But it is soporific and precarious for health. Don't you see how athletes sleep through their lives, and if they lapse even a little from their training programme, get seriously ill?'

Plato's comment (*Rep.* 403e–404a) on the training of guardians, the elite class of warriors and philosophers who rule his ideal state, helped to inspire philosophical and Christian tradition with the metaphor of the spiritual athlete. This athlete's 'greatest contest' is for the integrity of the soul, and he or she must be always in training, *askêsis*, for the fight against the onslaughts of desire. The training is both for soul and for body, but it is the training of the body that has pre-empted the name of asceticism.

You know how all the runners in the stadium run, but one gets the prize? Every competitor practises self-control in all things, they for a perishable crown but we for an imperishable. I run as if everyone was watching, I fight and do not shadow-box. I treat my body hard and make it serve me, for I have announced contests for others and do not want to be disqualified myself.

(Paul, *I Corinthians* 9.25–7)

Late-antique asceticism attracted much scholarly interest in the body-conscious 1980s and 1990s (e.g. P.R.L. Brown 1988; Wimbush 1990; Wimbush and Valantasis 1995; Grimm 1996; T. Shaw 1998). Even when people find it hard to sympathise with either the motive or the method, they can recognise the appeal of rigorous training programmes to prepare for the Olympics of the soul (Porphyry, *On Abstinence* 1.31.3). Preoccupation with the functioning and appearance of the body, and attempts to assess its requirements for food, drink and sex and modify them to something nearer the ideal, are very familiar. But whereas the modern workout aims at peak physical performance which manifests as energy, strength, beauty and health, the spiritual athlete aimed at peak intellectual and spiritual performance undistracted by the demands of the body. This chapter asks whether, and in what sense, the spiritual athlete was healthy. Did ascetics accept, for the sake of spiritual health, the risks to physical health entailed by their lifestyle, or even welcome physical illness as a means of spiritual growth? Alternatively, did they expect the ascetic lifestyle to benefit physical as well as spiritual health, or think that the health of the spiritual athlete, like the health of the physical athlete, differs from the health of ordinary people?

These questions find some answers in the life and work of Porphyry of Tyre, an influential Platonist philosopher of the later third century AD. He chose philosophy in preference to the career of the dutiful citizen who creates wealth and procreates children. He left his native city, the ancient and glamorous Tyre in Phoenicia, to study in Athens; then (in AD 263) he went on to Rome to work with Plotinus, whose writings he later edited and arranged as the *Enneads*. In his preface to the *Enneads*, 'On the life of Plotinus and the order of his writings', Porphyry depicts Plotinus as celibate, vegetarian and frugal in diet, sleeping little, and subordinating his physical health to his principles (*Life* 2.1–15, 8.20–4). Plotinus had chronic health problems, including poor eyesight (*Life* 8.1–4), which made it impossible for him to revise what he had written. But he refused the wonder-drug theriac because, as its name *thêriakon* acknowledges, its many ingredients included derivatives from wild animals, *thêria*. One of these, an innovation by Nero's doctor, was viper's flesh; Porphyry noted an anti-vegetarian argument that it had saved the sight of people going blind (*Abst.* 1.17.1). Plotinus also said that an enema was unsuitable treatment for an old man. He would not go to the public baths, but used his own masseurs, and did not trouble to replace them when they died in an epidemic. The lack of daily massage, Porphyry says, allowed the development of the painful and distressing illness that killed him: this probably reports the judgement of his student and doctor Eustochius. Porphyry calls the illness *kunanchê*, 'quinsy', an extreme swelling of the throat that inhibits speech and breathing. It is notoriously difficult to make modern diagnoses from ancient descriptions, but Plotinus may have had a form of tuberculosis (Grmek 1992).

The students of Plotinus made their own decisions on how to combine the philosophic life with the demands of their families, professions and cities (G. Clark 2000b). Porphyry was at one end of the range: vegetarian, probably celibate, and resolutely distant from civic life. He argued forcefully in *On Abstinence*, written for a fellow-student who was a lapsed vegetarian, that the philosophic life requires a light, meatless diet, and that you cannot become involved in the round of dinner-parties and political deals without distracting your soul from its true concerns. Some people prefer to slumber comfortably through their lives, but the philosopher wants to stay alert, resisting the soporific effect of the material world (*Abst.* 1.27). Porphyry married, but relatively late, and (as he told his wife in *To Marcella* 1) not in the hope of children, but in order to protect the widow and children of a fellow-student. *On Abstinence* never considers the choices, or lack of them, open to women; Porphyry takes it for granted that the philosopher is male and subject to male distractions, whether from public life or from female bodies. The usual argument of high-minded philosophers, whether Platonist or Stoic, was that the only proper use of sex is within marriage for procreation; this doctrine was not a Christian invention. But Porphyry argued (*Abst.* 4.20.4–5) that all sexual intercourse is contamination. If it results in conception, soul is contaminated with body, and if it does not, living body is contaminated with dead seed. He acknowledged (*Abst.* 1.41.4) that concessions must be made to physical existence: some people must reproduce, and everyone, even the philosopher, has to eat.

Sex is unproblematic, according to this argument, because it is simply not necessary unless you want children. Sexual desire in any other context is probably brought on, and certainly increased, by excessive eating and drinking. Porphyry in fact says little about sex, except to use it as an extreme case when dismissing an argument that what you do to the body does not affect the soul (*Abst.* 1.41.2): 'if you can be concerned with the immaterial while eating gourmet food and drinking vintage wine, why not when having intercourse with a mistress, doing things it is not decent even to name?' It is puzzling that he does not comment, as Christian ascetic texts so often do, on the strength and persistence of sexual desire, since he makes the point that true detachment entails progress from not doing something to not even wanting to do it (*Abst.* 1.31.5). Perhaps he was temperamentally like Augustine's friend Alypius (Augustine, *Conf.* 6.12.22), who just did not see why Augustine was so addicted to sex. More important, Porphyry had a different perspective on the problem of embodied existence. Christian ascetic texts present sexual desire as the mark of mortality, because this desire was the immediate consequence of the human fall away from God that made us mortal. Our fallen state is manifest in our gendered and reproductive bodies, in which sexual response and fertility are outside rational control, conception cannot happen without desire, and both conception and childbirth violate the mother's bodily integrity (G. Clark 1996). But for

Porphyry, the mark of mortality is eating (G. Clark 2001). The gods do not need to eat as we do, but our mortal bodies are always in flux, losing something that must be replaced (*Abst.* 2.39.2).

> If only it were possible to abstain without problems even from crops as food, if there were not this corruptible part of our nature! If only, as Homer says [*Il.* 5.341–2], we had no need of food or drink, so that we might really be immortals! The poet rightly shows that food is a provision not only for life but also for death; so if we did not need this food, we should be the more blessed inasmuch as more immortal. But as it is, being in the state of mortality, we unwittingly make ourselves (so to speak) even more mortal by taking in this food.
>
> (*Abst.* 4.20.13–14)

Augustine, who found sexual desire more problematic than Porphyry did, also understood (*Conf.* 10.31.44) the problem of food. People must eat to stay alive, but what and how much must they eat? Porphyry says (*Abst.* 1.38.1) that the philosopher should ask not 'is this a permitted food?' but 'do I need this?' Augustine says that food should be like medicine, taken to keep you well, but how can you tell the difference between what you really need and what you just feel like eating? Life would be so much simpler, Porphyry mused (*Abst.* 4.20.15), if it were possible to use the 'hunger suppressant' discovered by Pythagoras; he seems to have no confidence in the recipes given in his life of Pythagoras (34). In his (unacknowledged) source, Plutarch's *The Seven Sages at Dinner*, Solon comments (*Mor.* 158c), perhaps ironically, that it would really be better not to eat at all.

 Why, indeed, should the philosopher trouble to stay alive? Plato said (*Phaedo* 67e) that philosophy is preparation for death, that is, for the release of the soul from the body. In the meantime, the body is a nuisance, because we have to feed it (*Phaedo* 66b), and it is liable to illness, desires and general turmoil; but we must wait for God to say that we may leave (*Phaedo* 62b). *On Abstinence* argues for detaching the soul, as far as possible, from the concerns of the body. Porphyry accepts that suicide will not work, because violent death ties the soul to the body instead of liberating it (*Abst.* 1.38.2), just as violent detachment always leaves something attached. But this teaching (ascribed in 2.47.1 to 'the Egyptian', that is Hermes Trismegistus) would not necessarily rule out slow suicide by detachment from bodily concerns. That could happen by disregard of physical health, as in the case of Plotinus, or by consistently answering 'No' to the question 'do I need to eat this?' Stoic philosophers argued that in some circumstances the wise man may make a rational choice of death: could not the wise man exercise a rational preference for the unimpeded activity of the soul, and die without violence?

In the *Life of Plotinus* (11.11–19) Porphyry says that he considered 'taking himself out' from life. Plotinus found out and dissuaded him, saying that his eagerness came not from a secure intellectual state but from a melancholic illness (he may, in modern terms, have been manic-depressive), and he needed a holiday. So Porphyry went to Sicily, and was away when Plotinus died. The *Life of Plotinus* does not suggest that Plotinus was a suicide by self-neglect, but it does include an oracle (*Life* 22), probably composed by Porphyry himself, which presents death as the triumphant escape of Plotinus' soul. Porphyry's commentary on the oracle says that Plotinus 'did everything to be freed and to escape from the bitter wave of blood-drinking life here' (*Life* 23.6–8). Book 4 of *On Abstinence* offers a more dramatic example. Porphyry's sequence of ascetic spiritual elites, who make their own contribution to different societies, culminates in the Samaneans of India, a group self-selected by vocation.

> Their attitude to death is such that they unwillingly endure the time of life as a kind of necessary service to nature, and are eager to liberate their souls from their bodies. Often, when they are perceived to be in good health, with no evil pressing upon them or driving them on, they exit from life, though they give the others notice. No one will try to stop them, but everyone congratulates them and charges them with messages for their relatives among the dead.
>
> (4.16.1–2)

This is direct transcription from the speech of the Jewish leader Eleazar, as presented by Josephus (*Jewish War* 7.352–7). There was no further hope of resistance to Roman troops, and Eleazar used the tradition of Indian sages (Stoneman 1994, 1995) to hearten the defenders of Masada for mass suicide.

But Plotinus did not encourage his students to think themselves Samaneans (J. Dillon 1994). A fragment of discussion (*Ennead* 1.9), written before Porphyry's arrival in Rome, shows Plotinus refusing to endorse suicide, on the same grounds that he used to dissuade Porphyry: there is almost always an element of passion, that is, strong emotion which damages the soul. It is better to wait for death, even if one is aware of going mad (this was one of the five reasons for 'rational withdrawal' given by the Stoics), for the soul can scarcely be helped by taking drugs for its release. The treatise on *eudaimonia*, well-being (*Ennead* 1.4), was placed earlier in the *Enneads* by Porphyry, but was written later, perhaps at a time when Plotinus' physical health was worsening. Its allusions to the option of suicide are always followed by a comment that the good man need not make this choice, but the choice remains open. 'He must give to this [common life of body and soul] as much as is needed and he can, but he himself is other than it and is not prevented from letting it go. He will let it go in nature's good time, and he also has the authority to make decisions about it' (*Ennead* 1.4.16.18–21). The body is like a musician's instrument: when it can no longer be used, the musician will change to another, or sing on without. 'Yet the instrument was not given him in the beginning without a purpose, for he has already used it many times' (*Ennead* 1.4.16. 28–30).

Porphyry begins his *Life* by saying that Plotinus seemed ashamed of being in a body, but it does not follow that Plotinus wanted his instrument to suffer (S.R.L. Clark 1996). He regarded health as natural to us, and illness as alien and distracting. 'Illness makes a greater impact, but health, quietly being with us, brings greater understanding of itself; for health sits beside us like something that belongs and is united with us, whereas illness is alien and does not belong' (*Ennead* 5.8.11.27–30). He had nothing against medical treatment that did not conflict with his principles. One of his objections to gnostics (*Ennead* 2.9.14) was that they ascribed illnesses to demons and claimed to purify their bodies by incantations. Sensible people, he said, know that most illness is caused by exhaustion, over-eating, deficiency, sepsis, or some other change originating inside or outside the body, and that it is treated by purgatives and medicines, blood-letting and fasting. In his discussion of well-being, he envisaged disregard of the body, but not to the point of self-harm:

> Well-being is certainly not the size and good condition of the body. Nor is it good sense-perception: advantage in such things tends to weigh someone down and pull him towards them. But when there is a sort of counterbalance towards the best, it can diminish the body and make it worse, so that this person can be shown to be other than his external appearance. Let the man who belongs here [in the material world] be handsome and tall and rich and lord of all mankind, because he does belong here; but we must not envy him such things, for they delude him. The wise man perhaps will never have had them, and if he does, he himself will lessen them if he cares for himself. He will lessen and gradually wither away the advantages of his body by neglect, and will renounce public office. He will protect the health of his body, but will not want to be entirely without experience of illness, or indeed without experience of pain. When he is young, he will want to learn about these even if they do not happen, but when he is old he will not want either pains or pleasures to obstruct him, or anything of this world whether agreeable or the opposite, so that he does not have to consider the body.
>
> (*Ennead* 1.4.14.1–26)

Selective quotation from this passage could suggest that Plotinus advocated making the body worse, eliminating physical advantages by neglect, and cultivating illness in youth. But the full text makes it clear that it is a question of where one's attention is directed. Health is useful, but preoccupation with body is always a distraction from what matters. 'We might say that a healthy person among other healthy people is there for them, giving himself to them either in his action or in his contemplation, whereas an ill person concerned with the care of the body is there for the body and living for it' (*Ennead* 4.3.4.33–8).

Porphyry, like Plotinus, thinks that the philosopher will accept some impairment of physical health as a consequence of his commitment to philosophy. 'Plato chose to live at the Academy, a place not just lonely and remote from the town, but, so they say, unhealthy' (*Abst.* 1.36.1). This does not mean that Plato wanted to be ill: he wanted quiet, away from the city and its distractions. The philosophic life is not in itself unhealthy. The philosopher will not have the robust strength of those who work with their bodies, but then he does not need it; in fact, it would be bad for him. Soldiers, physical athletes and even orators may need to eat meat, but for the philosopher, meat eating is expensive and over-stimulating.

> Health is maintained by the very same things through which it is acquired; and it is acquired by a very light and fleshless diet, so that must be how it is sustained. If inanimate foods do not help to build the might of Milo [a wrestler of legendary strength], neither do they in general increase physical strength. But the philosopher does not need either might or increased physical strength, if he is to apply himself to contemplation, not to action and riotous living. It is not surprising that ordinary people think meat-eating contributes to health, for they are just the people who think that enjoyment and sex preserve health, whereas these things have never profited anyone, and one must be content if they have done no harm.
>
> (*Abst.* 1.52.1–3)

What the philosopher needs is not physical vigour but stamina, sustained endurance for the hard work of self-discipline and contemplation. But it is not just a question of accepting relative weakness. The philosopher's physical health will benefit, perhaps dramatically, from his ascetic lifestyle:

> One must safeguard health, not from fear of death, but so as not to be hindered in pursuit of the goods which come from contemplation. Health is best safeguarded by the undisturbed condition

of the soul and the maintenance of thought directed to that which really is. This has considerable effect even on the body, as friends of ours have shown by experience. They had such severe arthritis in hands and feet that for eight whole years they had to be carried about, and they shook it off at the time when they quit their possessions and looked to the divine. Bodily illness was dismissed together with possessions and worries; so we can see that a certain condition of the soul has a great effect on the body, with regard to health and to everything else. In most cases, reduction of food also contributes to health.

(*Abst.* 1.53.2–4)

The 'friends' are generalised from one impressive case, Rogatianus, a senator and student of Plotinus. Porphyry says in the *Life of Plotinus* (7.32–46) that he was cured by eating only every other day. He had also (as Plotinus advised in his *Ennead* on well-being) refused public office: he would not act as praetor even when the lictors came to summon him, and he moved from friend to friend instead of being available in his own great house.

Porphyry's other examples of asceticism that benefits health come from non-Greek philosophical communities. These groups supplied for the late-antique imagination what Zen monks and advanced yogis supply for the late twentieth-century west. Egyptian priests (according to Chaeremon the Stoic, himself a priest) eat a restricted diet at all times, and at their times of purification a very restricted diet, excluding bread, oil, vegetables, pulses and all animal foods; they also abstain from intercourse with their wives. But 'without taking walks or using passive exercise, they remained free from illness and vigorous in comparison with average strength. In the course of the rituals they undertook many heavy tasks and forms of service which are too much for everyday strength' (*Abst.* 4.8.1). Essenes (according to Josephus) work without a break from sunrise to the fifth hour, then bathe and pray before eating a meal of bread and one dish, then pray again and work until dinner. They do not marry, but adopt children. They are serene because their food and drink is exactly matched to their needs (*Abst.* 4.12.1–5). These people are strong and healthy because they do not impede their bodies with the kind of food which can only cause physical as well as spiritual problems: that is, 'animate' food, flesh food which has once had a soul, rather than 'inanimate' plant food.

Find me someone who is eager to live, so far as is possible, in accordance with intellect and to be undistracted by bodily passions, and let him demonstrate that meat-eating is easier to provide than dishes of fruits and vegetables; that meat is cheaper to prepare than inanimate food for which chefs are not needed at all; that, compared with inanimate food, it is intrinsically pleasure-free and lighter on the digestion, and more quickly assimilated by the body than vegetables; that it is less provocative of desires and less conducive to obesity and robustness than a diet of inanimate food. But if no doctor, no philosopher, no trainer, no layman ventures to say this, why do we not voluntarily detach ourselves from this bodily burden? Why do we not liberate ourselves, by this detachment, from many constraints? A person who has accustomed himself to being satisfied with the minimum has got rid not just of one thing, but of thousands: excess of riches, the service of too many slaves, a mass of belongings, a condition of somnolence, intensity and frequency of illness, need for doctors, provocation of sexual desire, thick exhalations, much residue, heavy chains, robustness which prompts action, an Iliad of evils. An inanimate, simple diet, available to all, takes these away from us, offering peace for the reasoning power which provides us with security.

(Abst. 1.46.2–47.3)

On Abstinence may seem excessively preoccupied with the body and what goes into it, but Porphyry's position is essentially the same as that of Plotinus. He is arguing for a lifestyle that, once achieved, will free the soul from bodily distractions. The process of achieving it is useful training in moral effort and in the discrimination that is required to control greed and to distinguish the real needs of the body from passing fancies. Every victory over desire strengthens the rightful position of reason as the ruling power in human beings. Porphyry's philosopher would follow the ascetic lifestyle even if it hurt, just as he would endure the cautery and purgatives of necessary medical treatment, but in fact this therapy for the soul will do him nothing but good (Abst. 1.56.3).

There were several doctors among the students of Plotinus: Eustochius who treated Plotinus in his last illness, Zethus from Arabia, Paulinus from Scythopolis in Palestine. Would they have agreed with Porphyry that the ascetic life is healthy? Doctors of course varied in their opinions, but the most likely medical response to questions of food intake and sexual activity was 'it depends who you are and what you are doing'. Hippocrates and Galen were basic for late-antique medical training (Temkin 1991), and many educated people who did not train as doctors found them philosophically interesting; for instance, about the physical correlates of human emotion. Hippocratic medicine offered an impressively coherent account of the relationship between food and sex (Dean-Jones 1994; King 1998; Flemming 2000).

According to Hippocratic theory, what human beings use for reproduction is blood that (like excess calories) is surplus to the requirement of maintaining the body. The surplus will naturally vary with food intake and exercise. In the male, physical exercise, which includes public speaking, burns off most of the surplus. The rest is refined into semen, which takes up less space than blood, or is absorbed by glands. But in the female, there is more surplus because female flesh is looser and spongier, absorbing more moisture from the food intake; the surplus remains as blood; and though strenuous exercise has an observable effect, female lifestyle is typically more sedentary. So the surplus will cause pressure and obstruction unless it is either used for reproduction or shed, with other harmful residues, in regular menstruation. The most likely reason for menstrual problems is sexual inactivity. A dry womb may shift in search of moisture; its mouth may close so that the menses cannot escape; and the channels of the body may be constricted, especially in virgins and in widows who were used to sexual intercourse. These problems decrease as a woman grows older and drier, but in her fertile years, the reproductive system is both her main line of defence against illness and the most likely cause of it, and it needs to be kept in good working order by intercourse and childbearing.

Celibacy, according to Hippocratic medicine, will probably endanger the health of the female (but see King, Ch. 8, this volume). There is no reason for the celibate male to be unhealthy provided he is not also physically inactive and greedy. Physical athletes were told that sex interferes with training and performance, so it must be possible for an active adult male to be healthy when celibate; and the spiritual athlete, the physically inactive philosopher, will in any case be careful about what he eats and drinks. Celibacy may, indeed, be good for the health of the male, because ejaculation makes demands on the male body. People ask, Galen says, why sexual intercourse is so debilitating. His answer (*On Semen* 1.14–16) uses the results of dissection to confirm Aristotle (*GA* 1): semen is found not only in the testicles, but also in the spermatic veins and arteries. If these are drained of semen by excessive sexual activity, they draw it from other parts of the body by (in effect) osmosis. This weakens the whole body, because semen is nourishment for blood vessels; moreover, with the semen goes *pneuma*, vital heat.

> So it is not surprising that those who over-indulge in sex are weaker as a result, because the entire body is deprived of the purest part of both substances [seminal fluid and *pneuma*], and also because there is an access of sexual pleasure, which is capable by itself of relaxing the vital tone. People have, before now, died from too much pleasure.
>
> (*On Semen* 1.16.31)

But people do vary. The *Medical Collections* made by Oribasius, court doctor to the emperor Julian, include a section on sex. Here Galen is cited for the opinion that sexual activity can be healthy, provided it is properly timed and not excessive and provided the parties were not already unwell, but abstinence may cause problems.

> Some people, from youth on, become ill as soon as they have inter-course. Others, if they do not have frequent intercourse, get headaches and nausea and fever, lose their appetites and have digestive troubles. I have known some people who are of this nature, and then become sexually continent, to end up torpid and difficult to rouse, and some to be unreasonably gloomy and despondent like melancholics, but these things stopped quickly on resumption of intercourse. Taking this into account, I think retention of sperm does serious harm to those whose seed is natu-rally unwholesome and abundant, and whose life is inactive, and who had previously had plenty of intercourse, but then [lacuna . . .] strong and young.
>
> (Oribasius 6.37, CMG VI.1.1 pp.187–8)

Is that a medical description of a Christian ascetic lamenting his sins? But in most cases male celibacy will not damage health, provided that exercise and food intake are monitored.

Some doctors said the same about female celibacy. Soranus (*Gynaecology* 1.27–33) reports medical debate, in the late first or early second century, on whether menstruation is itself a manifestation of illness, and on whether female virginity is healthy. Some say that menstruation is nature's provision for disposing of the surplus which men eliminate by exercise, but this is unconvincing, both because nature could have provided for the surplus not to be formed, and because nature does not make the provision until the woman is ready for childbearing. So menstruation is for childbearing, not for health; but some doctors wrongly interpret menstruation as a condition of ill-health (ulceration of the uterus) irrelevant to conception. Soranus, characteristically, allows for human variation: some women are healthier if they menstruate, others are weakened, but menstruation is generally dis-ruptive and therefore bad for the health. Women who do not menstruate at all are often robust and mannish.

Soranus reports a further debate about women, and men, who are not sexually active. Some doctors, he says, say that desire makes you ill and that loss of seed, whether from male or from female, is debilitating. Men who remain chaste are bigger, stronger and healthier, and this should apply to women too because pregnancy and childbirth are debilitating. But others say that desire makes virgins ill, that occasional (but not excessive) emission of seed is beneficial, and that intercourse relaxes the uterus and assists menstruation, whereas women who do not have intercourse suffer from retained menses and obesity. Soranus, again, thinks that intercourse is usually disruptive and therefore bad for the health. For some women, intercourse is beneficial; in particular, widows who are accustomed to intercourse may be advised to remarry. But life virgins can be perfectly healthy unless they become obese from a sedentary life of guardianship. This is presumably the guardianship of a sacred place, such as the temple of Vesta at Rome, or a few sanctuaries near Soranus' birthplace, Ephesus in Asia Minor: Soranus could have met Christian ascetic women, but they practised strict fasting. The *Gynaecology* is a textbook for midwives, so Soranus has no detailed discussion of male celibacy, but the same general principles apply.

Late-antique medical opinion, then, had no need to oppose the philosophic claim that the spiritual athlete is in good health, although it is a different variety of good health from that of people who work with the body as soldiers and physical athletes and orators. For some men, celibacy may be difficult or even dangerous, but for most it is manageable or even beneficial with due attention to diet and exercise. A man who takes little exercise should avoid stimulating foods, especially meat, and should restrict his food intake; and this is exactly what the philosopher would do for the sake of his soul. For women, long-term celibacy might be considered a health risk, but at least some doctors took diet and expenditure of energy into account. Celibate women could reasonably expect that fasting would reduce not only sexual desire but also sex-related health problems; but in practice, non-Christian philosophers did not consider the option of lifelong female celibacy. With the famous exception of Hypatia (daughter of Theon the mathematician) who refused marriage, the women who counted as philosophers were wives of philosophic men. They lived in accordance with the traditional expectation that women should be faithful to their husbands and should control their appetites for food and sex, but were celibate only when they had completed their families. Porphyry's philosophic wife Marcella had seven children by her first marriage (and was not very well, *Marcella* 1).

On Abstinence is the fullest extant text of philosophic asceticism, and the most austere. Porphyry's solitary philosopher, seeking God 'alone to the alone' and rigorously avoiding contamination of body and soul, is a long way from the life of most students of Plotinus, with their friends and families and political commitments. He is also a long way from the role models of Christian asceticism. Antony of Egypt practised strict fasting, declaring with Paul 'when I am weak, then I am strong' (*Life of Antony* 7), and withdrew to total solitude in the desert. But his admirers noted that in extreme old age he was in good health, not emaciated but maintaining his body in perfect balance on its minimal intake of food (*Life of Antony* 93). After the pioneering phase of asceticism, Christians were generally advised against excessive fasting, and were encouraged to follow the rules of a community: but their heroes and heroines could still be praised for being, by everyday standards, obviously ill. In two letters (45, 46) ascribed to Basil of Caesarea, a starved male body is presented as heroic, and a woman pale with fasting is said to have a special beauty. Basil himself did permanent damage to his digestive system by extreme fasting in youth. So did John Chrysostom. This forced them both to abandon the strict ascetic life and was a constant distraction during their years as bishops, but their biographers still find it admirable.

'Make yourself ill' was not a Christian command (Temkin 1991: 149–69; Amundsen 1996: 83–93). Illness could be interpreted as an opportunity to repent, as a share of the suffering of Christ, as a demonstration that bodily pain is insignificant compared to spiritual health, or as a fight against demonic attack. Saints could therefore see it as a means of spiritual growth, but that was not to say that illness is good in itself. Christians, like non-Christians, regarded illness as alien, to be healed, if possible, by doctors or by prayer. But Christians who, like Paul, attempted to 'treat my body hard and make it serve me' were prepared to accept serious impairment of health in their drastic attempts to bring the body, especially its sexual responses, under control. Both the efforts and the ill health could only demand more attention for the body. Why not, like Plotinus and Porphyry, concentrate on the soul, minimise the needs of the body by gentle and consistent detachment, but allow the body what it must have?

> We must feed everything in us, but endeavour to fatten what is superior in us. Now the food of the rational soul is that which maintains it in rationality; and that is intellect. So it must be fed on intellect, and we must strive to fatten it on that, not to fatten our flesh on meat. For intellect sustains our everlasting life, but when the body is fattened it starves the soul of the blessed life and enlarges the mortal part, distracting and obstructing the soul on its way to immortal life.
>
> (*Abst.* 4.20.10–11)

Early Christian asceticism can be seen as an extension of philosophic asceticism. It could go further because philosophic confidence in the power of reason was replaced by confidence that the Christian ascetic is directly in contact with God by prayer, and is supported through trials by identification with the suffering of Christ and with the specifically Christian history of martyrdom. It did not need to compromise with the social demand to perpetuate families and cities. But surely going further was counter-productive? Christian asceticism has often been seen as collective Christian neurosis, a religious legitimation of suicidal anorexia, perhaps enhanced by a kind of survivor-guilt after the heroic days of martyrdom. A different range of explanation invokes a different Christian perspective on the relationship of body and soul. For a Platonist philosopher, the soul is temporarily assigned to a material, desire-ridden body. This body must be given some attention because it affects and impedes the soul, and also because the soul is properly concerned for it. But it can be trained to cause the minimum of trouble while it lives, and it will eventually die and be discarded. For a Christian, the physical suffering of Christ, and of the martyrs, is not finally insignificant: it shows that even the fallen material body may be transformed by a soul united with God. So whereas the non-Christian spiritual athlete trained to overcome the limitations imposed by the body, the Christian spiritual athlete worked on the body as well as the soul, and spiritual health, for the committed Christian, came at a higher physical cost.

ACKNOWLEDGEMENTS

Rebecca Flemming and Helen King commented on the conference (1994) version of this chapter. It has changed considerably in the intervening years, and I have continued to learn from their work. All translations are my own unless otherwise stated, but I am indebted to the translation of Plotinus by Hilary Armstrong (Loeb 1966–88).

14

'CARRYING ON THE WORK OF THE EARLIER FIRM'

Doctors, medicine and Christianity in the
Thaumata of Sophronius of Jerusalem

Dominic Montserrat

INTRODUCTION

The first part of my title is drawn from a book review by no less a cultural pundit than E.M. Forster, published in the *Egyptian Mail* on 29 December 1918 during his little-known time as a jobbing journalist in Alexandria. As far as I am aware, it has never been reprinted since. The book he was reviewing was *Canopus, Menouthis, Aboukir* (Faivre 1918), a guide to the ruined sites at Canopus and Menouthis (modern Abuqir), a few miles outside Alexandria. Although not much is left to see on the ground, in the sixth and seventh centuries the shrine at Menouthis was one of the most important pilgrimage centres in the east, with a great reputation for miraculous cures. Its martyred saints, Cyrus and John, were invoked particularly to help with eye diseases. Healing was brought about through the practice of incubation, or sleeping in the shrine as close as possible to the entombed bodies of the martyrs, who channelled the divine healing power down to earth. This practice had a long history at Menouthis. In the Roman period, there had been a healing temple of Isis on the site (the Egyptian form of Menouthis means 'place of the divinity'), where cures were effected in exactly the same way as in the Christian period – hence Forster's joking reference to Cyrus and John 'carrying on the work of the earlier firm'. Perhaps because of its importance as a healing centre, the sanctuary at Menouthis played an important part in the rivalry with paganism (the Isis shrine still seems to have been functioning as late as the last decade of the fifth century AD) and subsequently in Christian doctrinal controversies.

Seventy of the miraculous cures attributed to SS Cyrus and John at Menouthis are recorded in detail by Sophronius, later Patriarch of Jerusalem (*c*.AD 569–638) in the long miracle cycle known as the *Thaumata* (henceforward cited as *PG* 87.3).[1] Sophronius had himself been cured of an eye disease by the saints and his *Thaumata*, composed around AD 610–620, is an extraordinary text. It is simultaneously a piece of sectarian propaganda (Sophronius was robustly pro-Chalcedonian and viewed the schismatic Egyptian Monophysite church with horror) and a literary *ex voto* thanking the saints of Menouthis for his cure in the most fulsome terms. The *Thaumata* have been under-used by scholars, perhaps through a combination of Sophronius' religious agenda and his difficult Greek (Chadwick 1974; Timm 1984; Montserrat 1998): he is not known as Sophronius the Sophist for nothing. This neglect is regrettable, for the *Thaumata* provide striking information on so many topics relating to health: on ideas about disease and the body; on medical treatments and prescriptions; on the aspirations and experiences of individual sick pilgrims; on the relationship between rational medicine and faith; and also on the continuity of holy space in healing contexts. In this chapter I propose to examine the ways in which the relationship between healing, Christianity and paganism at Menouthis are presented in Sophronius' *Thaumata*, bearing in mind how the Christian saints carried on 'the work of the earlier firm'. In this context of a Christian veneer over a pagan healing shrine, the role of doctors and the medical profession in the *Thaumata* seems particularly interesting. Are they representatives of a dangerous paganism, never far from the surface at this shrine? A pietist like Sophronius might be expected to be opposed to rational medicine, and indeed he generally presents physicians negatively, either as incompetents over-reliant on the empty teaching of pagan medical writers or quacks only interested in the patient's cash. But suspicion of doctors runs throughout Hellenistic and Roman sources, so Sophronius' attitude does not characterise a purely Christian position (Crisafulli and Nesbitt 1997: 44–56). And, while adopting the conventional stance that Christ is the only true healer and human powers are pusillanimous compared to his, Sophronius nonetheless assumes that the incurable cases who seek divine help for their diseases have already sought assistance from conventional medicine (albeit unsuccessfully). This becomes more significant given the problematic political status of the Menouthis shrine, which for much of the fifth century was a football in the dynastic and sectarian struggles of the patriarchs of Alexandria (Montserrat 1998: 259–66). A closer examination of the role of doctors in Sophronius' narrative is therefore potentially rewarding for the history of how medicine and the pursuit of good health could become issues of religious, cultural and political significance, going far beyond the concerns of the individual afflicted body.

THE SAINTS, THEIR SHRINE AND ITS POWERS

According to the *Vita* of SS Cyrus and John attached to Sophronius' *Thaumata* (*PG* 87.3: 3680ff.), the saints of Menouthis were martyrs in Egypt during the persecution of Diocletian in the early fourth century, Cyrus being, significantly, a doctor, and John a soldier. Cyrus is presented very much as the senior partner of the team (see the discussion of miracle 33 later, p. 239). SS Cyrus and John are thus another instance of the ancient tendency to conceive of healing divinities as dualities. The sons of Asclepius, Machaon and Podaleirios, probably formed the prototype for several pairs of healing saints in Late Antiquity: apart from the most famous, SS Cosmas and Damian, there are also SS Pantalaemon and Hermolaus, Sampson and Diomedes, Mocius and Anicetus, and Thalelaius and Tryphon, all of whom are invoked as intercessors alongside Cyrus and John in the Greek orthodox *euchologion* for healing the sick (Konstantelos 1985: 383). Indeed, SS Cyrus and John show many parallels with SS Cosmas and Damian. There is Cyrus' medical background before his conversion and martyrdom, and also their shared epithet, *anargyroi*, literally 'silverless ones', that is doctors who demand no fees from the patient. Lest SS Cyrus and John be seen as a cut-price version of the older and more famous saints, however, Sophronius seems anxious to stop people making too much of the comparisons between them: in one of the miracles he uses their similarity as proof of the healing power of Christ, the common source of the miracles of both SS Cyrus and John and Cosmas and Damian. 'Nobody need be surprised if these saints perform exactly the same miracles as each other: Cyrus and John, and Cosmas and Damian, draw their cures from a single well, namely Christ our Lord, and each of them has and honours one master, him who grants us the cures through them and brings about the many different wonders' (*PG* 87.3: 3520, miracle 30).

Although supposedly martyred under Diocletian, there is no evidence for the cult of Cyrus and John at all before the early fifth century, when their remains are apparently moved from Alexandria out to Menouthis by patriarch Cyril of Alexandria, sometime during the first half of the reign of emperor Theodosius II (AD 408–450). The date of the establishment of SS Cyrus' and John's cult at Menouthis, and the significance of this for the Christianisation of Egypt, have been frequently debated, without much consensus emerging. There are essentially two theories: that their shrine was established by Cyril of Alexandria sometime in the early part of his patriarchate, but at any event before AD 429; or that it was established in the last years of the patriarchate of Peter Mongus, *c*.AD 489, in connection with the ending of formal Isiac worship there. The most likely story seems to be that the shrine was indeed established during the reign of Theodosius, but fell into abeyance after the family of patriarch Cyril lost influence when he was succeeded by Dioscorus in AD 444. After being deprived of funds for almost 50 years, the shrine was revived in the last decade of the fifth century to combat the vital paganism that still persisted there (e.g. Wipszycka 1988: 138–42; McGuckin 1993, 1994: 16–20; Takacs 1994; Haas 1997: 169–70, 327–9). Whenever it was established, by the time that Sophronius completed the *Thaumata* around 620, the shrine had developed a particular reputation for curing eye diseases. These were a perennial problem given the climate of Egypt (Savage-Smith 1984; Marganne-Mélard 1994: 1–33), and ten of the individual cures Sophronius relates are of eye problems (miracles 2, 9, 24, 28, 37, 47, 51, 65, 69, 70).

Sophronius makes it quite clear that most of the people who came to the shrine had sought conventional medical assistance first. Of course, this is partly included to make the miraculous healing powers of Christ working through Cyrus and John more marvellous, and so tacitly to work for Sophronius' pro-Chalcedonian agenda. The uselessness of the doctors is also presented as something of a revelation to the sick person. Miracle 27 is a typical example of the kind of conventional treatments that were tried before a pilgrimage to Menouthis, and the sick person's reaction to their failure. Theodore sought treatment from the lay doctors of Alexandria for his agonising stomach pains, but they had been unable to cure him.

> But he returned from them just as he had first gone, not helped in any way at all by the doctors, and having gained nothing from them except the knowledge of their uselessness. Knowing now that all of them were powerless to treat his disease, and giving up hope of being released and saved by them, he turned to the martyrs Cyrus and John, who are the real helpers (*arôgous*) powerful to save, and he lay down in their basilica (*sêkos*) awaiting their help.
>
> (*PG* 87.3: 3498ff.)

While Sophronius is at pains to stress the international appeal of the shrine at Menouthis, most of the people whose miraculous cures he records in the *Thaumata* are Egyptians, with the majority (35 out of 70) from Alexandria itself, which was only a few miles away. Most of the pilgrims from outside Alexandria lived at places within fairly easy reach of the shrine, with only two having travelled from more distant parts of Egypt where Chalcedonian elites might be expected to hold little sway. The preponderance of Alexandrian pilgrims, an appreciable number of whom were rich or otherwise socially prominent, suggests that an important constituency of the shrine was among the Chalcedonian élite of Alexandria – or at least those were cures that Sophronius got to hear about. But the cult at Menouthis also overarched and transcended boundaries, since orthodox believers, heretics, pagans and Jews all sought and obtained healing there.

All these pilgrims hoped to be cured through the practice of incubation, long-established in Greek religion and practised at Menouthis at least since the first century BC (Strabo XVII 1.17). To obtain the closest possible proximity to the martyrs' relics, incubation took place in various parts of the basilica itself. Miracles outside the shrine, without any incubation, were exceptional. Sophronius records only two such cases: miracle 8, where the saints rescued Christodorus, the steward of their shrine, from drowning on nearby Lake Mareotis by pacifying the winds, and that of Theopompus (miracle 14), who arrived at the shrine too weary from his journey to drag himself into the basilica. He decided to sleep outside the church within the shrine enclosure and try to get into the church the next day, but was rewarded with a dream of the martyrs the same night. Indeed, a curious feature of the miraculous cures in the *Thaumata* is how strongly they are connected with the physical presence of the martyrs and their devotees *in Menouthis itself*. Other major thaumaturgic saints of this period, such as St Menas (at Abu Mena, not far from Menouthis) and St Artemius in Constantinople, are much more mobile than SS Cyrus and John, and their miracles take place in different and widely scattered locations, as though they were imagined to be not so closely tied to their shrines (Drescher 1946: 108–25, 150–9; Crisafulli and Nesbitt 1997: xii–xv). In contrast, SS Cyrus and John nearly always operate out of their shrine complex. Virtually all their cures are bestowed on individuals who have slept in their shrine, where the cure is revealed to them. On the rare occasions when the saints appear to people outside their shrine, it is not to cure them there and then, but to bid them come to Menouthis to be healed, as in miracles 9 and 29. Only miracle 8 actually happens somewhere other than Menouthis itself; and this is on Lake Mareotis, not far from Menouthis. Thus the spiritual power of SS Cyrus and John, while specifically stated to be universal in miracle 60 (*PG* 87.3: 3635), is at the same time inextricably tied to their home locale. This is perhaps surprising since, as Sophronius puts into the mouths of the saints themselves in miracle 42, Cyrus and John have no intrinsic healing power of their own. They do not decide who will be cured, but merely channel the healing power of Christ, who makes the decisions (*PG* 87.3: 3585; see also *PG* 87.3: 3520 quoted earlier).

Within the shrine complex itself, the limited space of the basilica obviously became very crowded, and the general picture Sophronius conveys is of the shrine being filled at night with rows of expectant pilgrims. So in miracle 62 Rhodope from Antioch, while sleeping in the basilica, sees a vision of SS Cyrus and John passing among the ranks of sick pilgrims, apportioning cures (*PG* 87.3: 3640). Overcrowding also appears in miracle 37, where John, a sub-deacon from Cynopolis in middle Egypt, is cured of cataracts.

The basilica was so full of pilgrims that he was forced to sleep in a part of the church Sophronius calls the *hierateion*, 'where all the pilgrims stay who cannot find another place because of the crowd of sick who are there' (*PG* 87.3: 3564). Presumably money could be useful to get away from these throngs and secure the most potent place for incubation, next to the entombed bodies of the martyrs themselves. This is the implication behind miracle 24, the healing of two women named Juliana. One was rich, and used her wealth to install herself near the tomb of SS Cyrus and John, lying comfortably on a bed, while the poor woman had to sleep on the ground outside the gate. Of course the saints healed the poor Juliana first, and the rich one only after she had abased her worldly self by emulating her poor namesake (*PG* 87.3: 3492).

Unlike St Artemius and SS Cosmas and Damian, SS Cyrus and John never perform surgery, and rarely even touch the bodies of the pilgrims. Most of their cures were wrought through dream appearances to the afflicted pilgrims, in which they would either heal them there and then or prescribe a remedy which was to be taken on waking. Occasionally, the saints themselves give the medication in the dream or waking vision. So in miracle 25, a woman called Elpidia was cured of haemorrhages after dreaming that Cyrus and John had given her wine infused with bay leaves to drink (*PG* 87.3: 3496), and in miracle 4 Isidore was relieved of his lung condition after eating a piece of lemon received from the saints: he then vomited up the worm which was consuming his lung and causing the sickness (*PG* 87.3: 3431). These cures are the exception rather than the rule, however; most of the visitors to the shrine were cured after the apparition of the saints in their sleep, and in these cures the agent of healing is usually something that one would not necessarily call medical as such. Generally the sick people are told to ingest or apply to their bodies something which has come into contact with the sacred bodies of the martyrs, the earthly conduits for the heavenly. This might involve drinking or bathing in the water of the spring at their shrine, or the oil and wax from the lights that burned around their tomb: Sophronius was himself cured of his eye complaint by an ointment made from the wax of one of these candles (*PG* 87.3: 3672).

A range of other complaints, however, are cured by prescriptions which have a closer relationship to late antique pharmacopeias, especially as evidenced from the papyrological documentation. A recently published fourth century AD medical book on papyrus consists entirely of recipes for plasters or poultices applied to wounds, ulcers, ruptures of sinews or tendons, surgical incisions and fractures. Many of the recipes in this text, as the editor demonstrates in her commentary, are closely related to ones in Galen, Aetius of Amida, Oribasius and later Paul of Aegina, who stayed on in Alexandria after the Arab conquest: they are made of ingredients such as animal lard, wine and *materia medica* (Youtie 1996 *passim*). In line with texts like this, Cyrus and John recommended flesh-based plasters for a wide range of ailments: a poultice of sea-fish pounded in local wine for a woman's wounded hand (*PG* 87.3: 3448, miracle 9); salt quail applied to the foot for lameness (*PG* 87.3: 3588, miracle 43); anointing a decoction of calves' flesh in wine all over the body of a man who had fallen victim to demonic possession (*PG* 87.3: 3629, miracle 57). Another pilgrim, Joannia from Hierapolis in Syria, came to the shrine after being poisoned by her jealous sisters-in-law, which resulted in her suffering terrible physical spasms that the local doctors were unable to cure (*PG* 87.3: 3657, miracle 68). At Menouthis, a bath and a poultice of lentils applied to her stomach was prescribed, and she duly evacuated the poison. Purging the body through various emetics recurs frequently in the *Thaumata*. Miracle 44 tells the story of a nun called Anna, poisoned after swallowing a kind of small lizard (*samamithion*) which entered her intestines and caused her appalling pain (*PG* 87.3: 3589ff.). She was eventually conveyed to the shrine of Cyrus and John, 'for they could not find any other doctor with enough power against such a disastrous malady'. The saints advised her in a dream to drink quickly three large measures of wine unmixed with water, which she duly did, and of course vomited up the lizards along with the rest of her stomach contents.

In certain circumstances, the doctor's cure might even be preferable to what the saints could do, although Cyrus and John do not necessarily share this opinion. An ordinary doctor might be the first port of call if emergency help was required, and it was impossible to wait for the saints to act (some of the pilgrims waited as long as eight years to be healed). In miracle 67 (*PG* 87.3: 3652ff.) George, a pilgrim from Cyprus, believed himself to be possessed by a demon. Despairing of a cure, he attempted suicide, slashing his throat repeatedly with a knife. Sophronius describes vividly the dreadful wound and the panicked reaction of the shrine's personnel:

> When the door-keepers and those who were tending the shrine of the saints saw what had happened, they were not a little alarmed, lest they be charged and blamed for not preventing the man who was possessed by an evil demon from doing what he had. Fearing that they would be in trouble, lest the man die and they be in danger because of it, they ran off to the neighbouring villages calling for doctors, in case it was possible to sew the wound up and save him. They found only one doctor in the entire estate of Heracleus, and led him to the martyrs' shrine entreating him with many prayers. When he saw that the wound seemed to be fatal, he left without performing the task, filled with great fear and astonished that George had not yet died after inflicting such a wound on himself. (In fact, he was able to inhale and exhale through it, and nourishment made its exit from it in the same way.)

The local doctor was evidently very uncertain what kind of reception he was going to get at the shrine: maybe he suspected some kind of trickery or even an ambush. In the night, SS Cyrus and John appeared to the steward of the shrine and ordered him to give George an appropriately Christian cure: oil and wine was to be poured on the wound, like the oil and wine that saved the robber crucified alongside Christ. Then the saints, 'imitators of Christ', as Sophronius calls them here, punished the door-keeper who had brought the doctor to the shrine, whipping him and shouting at him:

> Don't you know that our church has become the hospital of the entire world?
> Don't you know that Christ has appointed us to be the doctors of the faithful?
> Why, then, did you lead into our church another doctor, who knows nothing of our kind of healing (*iatreias hêmeteras deomenon*)?

The door-keeper's instinctive reaction to call a doctor in an emergency carried little weight with the saints. Needless to say, George was eventually cured of both his wound and the demon that possessed him.

So the relationship of the cures effected by the saints of Menouthis to contemporary medicine is not entirely clear cut. On the one hand, Sophronius consistently presents pilgrimage to their shrine as a last resort, after conventional medicine has failed, and he describes many cures based primarily on faith in the miraculous powers of the saints; but on the other hand, he also describes plenty of cases of healing at the shrine brought about through means that can be accommodated within conventional medicine as it was practised at the time. Indeed, the opponents of the shrine alleged that the supposedly miraculous cures were actually brought about by medical means (*PG* 87.3: 3516: see discussion of miracle 30 later, p. 239–40). There is some evidence for this in the text, with the cures based on purging and emetics perhaps reflecting something of humoral theories of disease, for instance; and miracle 67 shows how the practices of earthly doctors are sometimes preferable to heavenly miracles.

DOCTORS, SAINTS AND MIRACLES

Sophronius certainly presents the Alexandrian doctors as an unscrupulous and mercenary lot. They are irredeemably tainted by their dependence on the pagan ideas of Galen, Hippocrates and Democritus, whom Sophronius calls 'nature's bastard brother' (*ho adelphos ho nothos tês phuseôs: PG* 87.3: 3464, miracle 13); they exploit the patients when they are at their most vulnerable. A characteristic example of this is narrated in miracle 40 (*PG* 87.3: 3577ff.). John (who lived near Egypt's other great healing shrine, that of St Menas) was prostrated by an agonising kidney disease, and went to Menouthis for a cure, but none was forthcoming. Losing patience with the saints, he encountered a doctor (Sophronius dismissively calls him by the diminutive *iatriskos tis*, 'some little quack'), who offers John a cure for a high price, three *nomismata*. John is so desperate to be relieved of his pain that he is about to pay up, but SS Cyrus and John intervene and cure him – for a price. John is charged with donating the same sum as the doctor's fee to the shrine. Conventionally, Sophronius presents this as a punishment for John's lack of faith in the efficacy of the saints.

Yet while Sophronius advocates suspicion of doctors, he also places his healing saints in a close relationship with the medical profession. The miracles of Cyrus and John constantly have to answer the claims of rational medicine. Democritus, Hippocrates and Galen are spectral presences which flit in and out of Sophronius' narrative, and he keeps reminding the reader that the miracles are a superior form of cure to their medicine: yet it is noticeable that their names crop up more often in the *Thaumata* than in any other comparable late antique miracle cycle (Crisafulli and Nesbitt 1997: 143, 151). The relationship of Hippocrates and Galen to SS Cyrus and John's cures is addressed in miracle 15, where another pilgrim named John is apparently cured of elephantiasis, 'a condition worse and more painful than all physical ailments'. Sophronius says (*PG* 87.3: 3469) that 'I will describe the remedy through which the saints were able to cure such sickness so easily, lest the interfering (*periergoi*) doctors claim that this was something Hippocratic not brought about by the saints, and announce that Hippocrates or Galen was the cause of the cure, rather than the saints who really accomplished it.' Sophronius may be keen to appropriate John's case for the saints, not only because of the particular severity of his illness but also the bizarre nature of their remedy (they recommended administering a glass embrocation).

It is still notable, however, that SS Cyrus and John are often presented as doctors, albeit superior kinds of doctors who take no fee and tend to the souls of the sick as well as their bodies. Some of this may be explicable in terms of St Cyrus' own background as a doctor before he was converted to Christianity and martyred under Diocletian. Sophronius gives few details about this in the short *Vita* of the saints attached to the *Thaumata* (*PG* 87.3: 3680). St Cyrus trained in his native city of Alexandria, the city synonymous with doctors and medical studies more than any other in antiquity (Duffy 1984b: 22). St Cyrus, however, was concerned for his patients' spiritual welfare, 'not consoling them with the words of Galen, Hippocrates and the other writers of that sort, but with the words of the prophets, the apostles and evangelists, leading them on to good health and life. He is also said to practice medicine without its *gnômê*. *Gnômê* is often used in a pejorative sense by patristic writers, to describe the opinions or doctrines of heretics, though here it could mean something like acquiring a set of opinions through training. The question of *gnômê* comes up in miracle 69, again in connection with a suitably Christian way of practising conventional medicine. In this account, yet another John (a Roman) had been treated by a crowd of doctors who had done nothing to help his eye disease: Sophronius goes into some detail about John's tribulations at their hands. John was by now very badly off, and he therefore 'sought one who would have the *gnômê* of doctors and yet not require money, and not only that, but one who would support the patient' (*PG* 87.3: 3661).

Apart from the question of their training, the saints can even look and behave like ordinary doctors. Miracle 33, the curing of Cosmiana from injuries she sustained after falling off an ass, is interesting in this context. Cosmiana had hurt herself while travelling to Menouthis: she was not sick, but merely wanted to make a pilgrimage to the site and see the holy relics. In spite of her accident, she decided to continue her journey and seek help from the saints. As she lay in the basilica in the usual way, the saints appeared to her at night in the garments of doctors (*schêmasin iatrôn: PG* 87.3: 3533), and asked, 'What is your sickness?', and she replied to the saints, 'You are to blame, since you who bring about good health for others who are infirm have wrecked good health for me alone.' Smiling, the man who was apparently the superior and worthy of having a pupil said to his student, 'Come here, and free her from her affliction more quickly.' This was brought about by a slap on the jaw. Only after Cosmiana woke up and found that she was cured did she realise that it was not a doctor and medical student she had seen, but SS Cyrus and John in disguise. In spite of its pious trappings, this anecdote may well preserve a vignette into how doctors trained their students, as John Duffy (1984b: 24) has suggested. Here, SS Cyrus and John seem not to have completely relinquished their links with conventional medical training in nearby Alexandria. But the miracle where the reader is presented most forcefully with the relationship between the Alexandrian medical establishment and the saints of Menouthis is miracle 30, the cure of Gesius the pagan *iatrosophistês*. This miracle is particularly interesting, because of Gesius' mythical status as a symbol of the unredeemed pagan in Egyptian conflicts between Christianity and paganism. The author of the *Vita* of Shenoute, Egypt's most important saint in the fifth century, chose to call Shenoute's stubbornly pagan adversary Kesios, the Coptic form of Gesius (Cameron 1964; Besa, *Life of Shenoute*, Behlmer 1993: 11–15, esp.14). Sophronius' use of this archetype here immediately makes the story have a wider applicability to the religious and doctrinal divisions of Egypt.

The story of Gesius, one of the longest accounts in the *Thaumata*, goes as follows. Gesius was an Alexandrian *iatrosophistês*, 'an extremely wise sophist, not in the teaching of rhetoric (though he wore the philosopher's cloak), but as a foremost practitioner of the medical profession and a well-known teacher of its precise methods at that time' (*PG* 87.3: 3513). Unsurprisingly, given this background, Gesius is a crypto-pagan, an accusation often levelled at iatrosophists (Epiphanius, *Panarion* 64.67.5 and 66.10; Dawson 1923). Gesius submitted to baptism following an imperial decree, but quoted an appropriate line of the *Odyssey* as he emerged from the font: 'Ajax perished utterly when he drank of the salt sea-water.' Thereafter Gesius lost no opportunity of mocking Christians, and the shrine at Menouthis was an obvious and convenient target for his opprobrium. Most interestingly, he claims that all the cures there have sources in conventional medical wisdom:

> He mocked the martyrs Cyrus and John, saying that they cured people's illnesses through medical knowledge (*ek technês iatrikês*) rather than through some divine and most high power. For when he learned about the remedies they prescribed for the sick (which I have already described), he maintained that they came from the teachings of the doctors: he said that one remedy was Hippocratic, while another was in other medical writers, and he called something else Galenic, announcing that it was found in such-and-such a passage. He remembered that another remedy was in Democritus, and he said he recognised clearly the chapter-heading, and the place where it was.
>
> (*PG* 87.3: 3516)

But soon Gesius himself fell ill, with stiffness and pain in the neck and shoulders. He could not move, nor do anything to heal himself, and his fellow-physicians were powerless too. Eventually he was forced to go to Menouthis and ask for help from SS Cyrus and John. They duly appeared and made various humiliating demands on him, such as wearing a pack-saddle and bell round his neck like a beast of burden. Gesius at first refused to be demeaned, but had to capitulate and was finally cured. After this, the saints appeared a final time to taunt him about his reliance on the canonical medical authorities: 'Tell us where Hippocrates set down the remedies for your sickness? Or what about Galen, who is so marvellous according to you? Where does Democritus say anything, or any of those other famous doctors you remembered?' (*PG* 87.3: 3520).

CONCLUSION

It is conventional wisdom that in Late Antiquity 'the medical-saints were antagonistic to the physicians and looked upon them as inferior competitors with their miraculous powers' (Magoulias 1964: 128). Yet, as John Haldon has demonstrated (in Crisafulli and Nesbitt 1997: 44–56), the picture is more complex than a dualistic conflict between (pagan) medicine and (Christian) faith, with good health the football that is kicked about between them. This seems to be particularly true at Menouthis, given the status of the shrine and the history of its presiding saints. Sophronius' constant references to the medical profession and its presiding *genii*, especially Hippocrates and Galen, suggest that he was somewhat uneasy about medicine in Alexandria, the city which provided the main pilgrim constituency of the shrine. Alexandria was the ancient city most associated with doctors and medical training, and because of this connection perhaps Sophronius felt that he needed to emphasise the role of faith more strongly. Then there is the question of St Cyrus' past as a doctor who had undergone conventional training: just who, in Forster's words, was 'carrying on the work of the earlier firm'? SS Cyrus and John certainly did not abandon all the accoutrements of doctors after they went up to a higher plane. Even their status as selfless *anargyroi* may be questioned, since the saints often receive something in return for their free medical services. The *Thaumata* describe some of the impressive *ex votos* left by grateful pilgrims (e.g. *PG* 87.3: 3505ff., miracle 28), and there were also the less tangible manifestations of thanks, such as loyalty to the place and support for its various services.

Sophronius wrote the *Thaumata* at a time when the Byzantine world was about to undergo great changes. Within a few years of their completion, Egypt had officially become Muslim, and pilgrimage to its shrines began to decline. In the larger Byzantine world, the cult of healing saints and the tension it implied between 'rationalist' and 'anti-rationalist' ways of looking at the world became an important focus of the Iconoclast movement that was to blow up early in the next century. Yet while it is tempting to read the *Thaumata* in the context of these political upheavals, it is also important to think of the experience of healing at Menouthis on the level of the individual afflicted body. Political considerations become less important when individual aspirations for good health are reinstated into the historical reconstruction. As the sick travelled to the healing shrine, sanctified by generations of religious usage, their journey brought them from the margins of secular society to the centre of a temporary community travelling towards the sacred. On arrival, the sick pilgrims found themselves the focus of attention in the public places and religious rituals, where ill health and human physical imperfection were, for once, placed in an exalted position as vessels for the spiritual power which brings the heavenly down to earth.

NOTE

1 The text of Sophronius used is that edited by J.-P. Migne, *Patrologiae Cursus Completus, Series Graeca* (= *PG* 87.3), incorporating textual emendations suggested by Fernandez Marcos (1975) and Duffy (1984a).

BIBLIOGRAPHY

Achterberg, J. (1985) *Imagery in Healing. Shamanism and Modern Medicine*, Boston, MA and London: Random House.

Ader, R. and Cohen, N. (1991) *Psychoneuroimmunology*, 2nd edition, San Diego, CA: Academic Press.

Agelarakis, A. (1987) 'Report on the Mycenaean human skeletal remains at Archontiki', *Ossa*, 13: 3–11.

—— (1995) 'An anthology of Hellenes involved with the field of physical anthropology', *International Journal of Anthropology*, 10: 149–62.

—— (1997) 'Greece', in F. Spencer (ed.) *History of Physical Anthropology. An Encyclopedia*, Vol. 1, New York and London: Garland Publishing.

—— (2000) 'Aspects of demography and paleopathology among the Hellenistic bderetes in Thrace, Greece', *Eulimene*, 1: 13–24.

Aleshire, S.B. (1989) *The Athenian Asklepieion: The People, Their Dedications and the Inventories*, Amsterdam: J.C. Gieben.

—— (1991) *Asklepios at Athens: Epigraphic and Prosopographic Essays on the Athenian Healing Cults*, Amsterdam: J.C. Gieben.

Allison, P.M. (1992) 'The distribution of Pompeian house contents and its significance', PhD thesis, University of Sydney.

Amundsen, D.W. (1996) *Medicine, Society and Faith in the Ancient and Mediaeval Worlds*, Baltimore, MD: Johns Hopkins University Press.

Anderson, G. (1986) *Philostratus: Biography and Belles Lettres in the Third Century A.D*, London and Dover, NH: Croom Helm.

Angastiniotis, M., Sophocleous, T., Kyrri, T.A., Loizidou, D., Ioannou, P., Cariolou, M., Georghiou, D., Drousiotou, A., Kalogirou, E., Vasiliades, P. and Kouspou, G. (1993) 'Community control of thalassaemia in Cyprus' (abstract), *5th International Conference on Thalassaemias and the Haemoglobinopathies, March 29–April 3, 1993*, Nicosia, Cyprus, Geneva: World Health Organisation, 77.

Angel, J.L. (1942) 'A preliminary study of the relations of race to culture, based on ancient Greek skeletal material', PhD thesis, Harvard University.

—— (1944a) 'A racial analysis of the Ancient Greeks: an essay on the use of morphological types', *American Journal of Physical Anthropology*, 2: 329–76.

—— (1944b) 'Greek teeth: ancient and modern', *Human Biology*, 16(4): 283–97.

—— (1945) 'Skeletal material from Attica', *Hesperia*, 14: 280–3.

244

BIBLIOGRAPHY

Angel, J.L. (1946a) 'Race, type and ethnic group in ancient Greece', *Human Biology*, 18: 1–32.

—— (1946b) 'Social biology of Greek culture growth', *American Anthropologist*, 48: 493–533.

—— (1947) 'The length of life in ancient Greece', *Journal of Gerontology*, 2: 18–24.

—— (1949) 'Constitution in female obesity', *American Journal of Physical Anthropology*, 7: 433–72.

—— (1964a) 'Osteoporosis: thalassemia?', *American Journal of Physical Anthropology*, 22: 369–74.

—— (1964b) 'The reaction area of the femoral neck', *Clinical Orthopedics*, 32: 130–42.

—— (1965) 'Old age changes in bone density: sex and race factors in the United States', *Human Biology*, 37: 104–21.

—— (1966) 'Porotic hyperostosis, anemias, malarias and marshes in the prehistoric Mediterranean', *Science*, 153: 760–3.

—— (1967a) 'Porotic hyperostosis or osteoporosis symmetrica', in D.R. Brothwell and A.T. Sandison (eds) *Diseases in Antiquity: A Survey of the Diseases, Injuries and Surgery for Early Populations*, Springfield, IL: Charles C. Thomas, 378–89.

—— (1967b) 'Porotic hyperostosis, anemias, malarias and marshes in the prehistoric eastern Mediterranean', *Science*, 153: 760–3.

—— (1968) 'Ecological aspects of paleodemography', in D.R. Brothwell (ed.) *The Skeletal Biology of Earlier Human Populations*, Symposia of the Society for the Study of Human Biology, Vol. 8, London: Pergamon Press, 263–70.

—— (1969a) 'Paleodemography and evolution', *American Journal of Physical Anthropology*, 31: 343–53.

—— (1969b) 'The bases of paleodemography', *American Journal of Physical Anthropology*, 30: 427–37.

—— (1971) *The People of Lerna: Analysis of a Prehistoric Aegean Population*, Princeton, NJ: American School of Classical Studies at Athens.

—— (1972a) 'Ecology and population in the eastern Mediterranean', *World Archaeology*, 4: 88–105.

—— (1972b) 'Human skeletons from grave circles at Mycenae', in G.E. Mylonas (ed.) *Taphikos Kyklos B ton Mykēnōn*, Athens: Archaeological Society, 379–97.

—— (1974) 'Patterns of fractures from Neolithic to modern times', *Anthropologiai Kozlmenyek*, 18: 9–18.

—— (1975) 'Paleoecology, paleodemography and health', in S. Polgar (ed.) *Population, Ecology and Social Evolution*, The Hague: Mouton Press, 167–90.

—— (1977) 'Anemias of antiquity: Eastern Mediterranean', *Porotic Hyperostosis: An Enquiry*, Paleopathology Association Monograph 2, 1–5.

—— (1978) 'Porotic hyperostosis in the Eastern Mediterranean', *Medical College of Virginia Quarterly*, 14: 10–16.

—— (1982) 'Osteoarthritis and occupation (ancient and modern)', in V.V. Novotny (ed.) *Second Anthropological Congress of Ales Hrdlicka*, Pragensis: Universitas Carolina, 443–6.

—— (1984) 'Health as a crucial factor in the changes from hunting to developed farming in the eastern Mediterranean', in M.N. Cohen and G.J. Armelagos (eds) *Paleopathology at the Origins of Agriculture*, Orlando, FL: Academic Press, 51–70.

244

Angel, J.L. and Caldwell, P. (1984) 'Death by strangulation: a forensic anthropological case from Wilmington, Delaware', in J.E. Buikstra and T. Rathburn (eds) *Human Identification. Case Studies in Forensic Anthropology*, Springfield, IL: Charles C. Thomas, 168–75.

Angel, J.L. and Bisel, S.C. (1985) 'Health and nutrition in Mycenean Greece. A study in human skeletal remains', in N.C. Wilkie and W.P.D. Coulson (eds) *Contributions to Aegean Archaeology*, Minneapolis, MN: Centre for Ancient Studies, University of Minnesota, 197–209.

——(1986) 'Health and stress in early Bronze Age population', in J.V. Canby, E. Porada, B.S. Ridgway and T. Stetch (eds) *Ancient Anatolia: Aspects of Change and Cultural Development. Essays in Honor of Machteld J. Mellink*, Madison, WI: University of Madison Press, 12–30.

Angel, J.L., Suchey, J.M., İşcan, M.Y. and Zimmerman, M.R. (1986) 'Age at death estimated from the skeleton and viscera', in M.R. Zimmerman and J.L. Angel (eds) *Dating and Age Determination of Biological Materials*, London: Croom Helm, 197–220.

Angel, J.L., Kelley, J.O., Parrington, M. and Pinter, S. (1987) 'Life stresses of the free black Community as represented by the First African Baptist church, Philadelphia, 1823–1841', *American Journal of Physical Anthropology*, 74: 213–29.

Anon. (1721) *Medicina Flagellata: or, the Doctor Scarify'd, with an Essay on Health, or the Power of a Regimen*, London: J. Bateman and J. Nicks.

Aristophanes (1994) *Ploutos/Wealth*, trans. K. McLeish and J.M. Walton, London: Methuen.

Arnott, R. (1996) 'Healing and medicine in the Aegean Bronze Age', *Journal of the Royal Society of Medicine*, 89: 265–70.

—— (2004) *Disease, Healing and Medicine in the Bronze Age*, Studies in Ancient Medicine, Leiden: E.J. Brill.

Arnott, R., Finger, S. and Smith, C.U.M. (eds) (2003) *Trepanation: History, Discovery, Theory*, Lisse: Swets and Zeitlinger.

Aston, E. and Savona, G. (1991) *Theater as Sign-System*, London and New York: Routledge.

Athanassakis, A.N. (1977) *The Orphic Hymns: Text, Translation and Notes*, Baltimore, MD: Johns Hopkins University Press.

Axtell, H.L. (1987 [1907]) *The Deification of Abstract Ideas in Roman Literature and Inscriptions*, New York: Aristide D. Caratzas [originally University of Chicago Press].

Baader, G. (1967) 'Spezialärzte in der Spätantike', *Medizinhistorisches Journal*, 2: 231–8.

Bailey, J.F., Henneberg, M., Colson, I.B., Ciarallo, A., Hedges, E.M. and Sykes, B. (1999) 'Monkey business in Pompeii – unique find of a juvenile Barbary Macaque skeleton identified using osteology and DNA techniques', *Molecular Biology and Evolution*, 16: 1410–14.

Baldry, H.C. (1968) *Ancient Greek Literature in its Living Context*, New York: McGraw-Hill.

Barefoot, P. (1991) *Psychiatric Wards in District General Hospitals*, East Bergholt: Peter Barefoot.

Barnes, E. and Ortner, D.J. (1997) 'Multifocal eosinophilic granuloma with a possible trepanation in a 14th century Greek young skeleton', *International Journal of Osteoarchaeology*, 7: 542–7.

Barthes, R. (1973) *Mythologies*, trans. A. Lavers, London: Granada.

Bass, W. (1971) *Human Osteology*, Columbia, MI: Missouri Archaeological Society.

Becker, M.J. (1975) 'Human skeletal remains from Kato Zakrto', *American Journal of Archaeology*, 79: 271–6.

Behlmer, H. (1993) 'Historical evidence from Shenoute's *De extremo iudicio*', Sesto Congresso internazionale di Egittologia, Turin.

Behr, C.A. (1968) *Aelius Aristides and the Sacred Tales*, Amsterdam: Adolf Hakkert.

Behrens, G. (1939) 'Schädeltrepanation in römischen Bingen', *Saalburg-Jahrbuch*, 9: 4–5.

Bertier, J. (1972) *Mnésithée et Diechès*, Leiden: E.J. Brill.

Beschi, L. (1982) 'Il rilievo di Telemachos ricompletato', *Athens Annals of Archaeology*, 15: 31–43.

Bessios, M. and Triantaphyllou, S. (2002) 'Omadikos tafos apo to Voreio nekrotafeio tis archaias Pydnas', To *Archaeologiko Ergo stin Makedonia kai Thraki*, 15: 385–93.

Betancourt, P. (1976) 'The end of the Greek Bronze Age', *Antiquity*, 50: 40–7.

Bett, R. (1997) *Sextus Empiricus, Against the Ethicists (Adversus Mathematicos* XI), Oxford: Clarendon Press.

Bhasin, M.K., Walter, H. and Danker-Hopfe, H. (1994) *The People of India. An Investigation of Biological Variability in Ecological, Ethnoeconomic and Linguistic Groups*, Delhi: Kamla-Raj Enterprises.

Bisel, S.C. (1980a) 'Human bone mineral and nutrition in Nichorian individuals of post-Mycenaean periods', in W.A. McDonald (ed.) *Excavations at Nichoria in Southwest Greece, Vol. II, The Bronze Age Occupation*, Minneapolis, MI: University of Minnesota Press, 264.

—— (1980b) 'A pilot study in aspects of human nutrition in the eastern Mediterranean', PhD thesis, University of Minnesota.

—— (1992) 'The human skeletal remains', in W.A. McDonald and N.C. Wilkie (eds) *Excavations at Nichoria in Southwest Greece, Vol. II, The Bronze Age Occupation*, Minneapolis, MI: University of Minnesota Press, 345–58.

Bisel, S.C. and Angel, J.L. (1985) 'Health and nutrition in Mycenaean Greece: a study in human skeletal remains', in N. Wilkie and W.D.E. Coulson (eds) *Contributions to Aegean Archaeology: Studies in Honor of W.A. McDonald*, Minnepolis, MI: Center for Ancient Studies, University of Minnesota, 197–210.

Bisel, S.C. and Bisel, J.F. (2002) 'Health and nutrition at Herculaneum: an examination of human skeletal remains', in W.F. Jashemski and F.G. Meyer (eds) *The Natural History of Pompeii*, Cambridge: Cambridge University Press, 451–75.

Black, F.L. (1974) 'Evidence for persistence of infectious agents in isolated human populations', *American Journal of Epidemiology*, 100: 230–50.

—— (1975) 'Infectious diseases in primitive societies', *Science*, 187: 515–18.

Blacking, J. (ed.) (1977) *The Anthropology of the Body*, London and New York: Academic Press.

Blatner, A. (1988) *Acting-in. Practical Applications of Psychodramatic Methods*, 2nd edition, New York: Springer Publishing.

Bliquez, L.J. (1994) *Roman Surgical Instruments and Other Minor Objects in the National Museum of Naples*, Mainz: Philipp von Zabern.

—— (1995) 'Gynecology in Pompeii', in Ph. J. Van der Eijk, H.F.J. Horstmanshoff and P.H. Schrijvers (eds) *Ancient Medicine in its Socio-cultural Context*, Vol. 1, Amsterdam and Atlanta, GA: Editions Rodopi (= Clio Medica 27), 209–23.

—— (1996) 'Prosthetics in classical antiquity: Greek, Etruscan and Roman prosthetics', in W. Haase and H. Temporini (eds) *Aufstieg und Niedergang der römischen Welt* (*ANRW*) II 37.3, Berlin and New York: Walter de Gruyter, 2640–76.

Boddington, A., Garland, A.N. and Janaway, R.C. (eds) (1987) *Death, Decay and Reconstruction. Approaches to Archaeology and Forensic Science*, Manchester: Manchester University Press.

Bodson, L. (ed.) (1988) *Anthropozoologica: L'animal dans l'alimentation humaine. Les critères de choix*, Paris: Musée d'Histoire Naturelle.

Borg, B. (2005) 'Eunomia or "make love not war"? Median personifications reconsidered', in J.E. Herrin and E.J. Stafford (eds) *Personification in the Greek World: From Antiquity to Byzantium*, London: Ashgate.

Borobia Melendo, E.L. (1988) *Instrumental medico-quirurgico en la Hispania romana*, Madrid: Impresos Numancia, S.A.

Bostanci, E. (1964) 'An examination of a Neanderthal type fossil skull found in Chalcidique Peninsula', *Belleten (Turk Tarih Kurumu)*, 28: 373–81.

Boswell, G. and Poland, F. (eds) (2003) *Women's Minds, Women's Bodies: Interdisciplinary Approaches to Women's Health*, Basingstoke and New York: Palgrave Macmillan.

Bourbou, C. (1998) 'More evidence on the association of DISH and upper class individuals from the Hellenistic Crete', *Paleopathology Association Newsletter*, 101: 7–10.

—— (2000) 'Paleopathological study and analysis of the population', in P. Themelis (ed.) *Protobyzantine Eleutherna*, Vol. 1, Rethymno: Crete University Press, 291–319.

—— (2001a) 'Pathological conditions of the lower extremities in two skeletons from early Byzantine Greece', in M. La Verghetta and L. Capasso (eds) *Proceedings of the XI European Meeting of the Paleopathology Association*, Chieti, Italy: Edigrafital S.p.A, 22–8.

—— (2001b) 'Infant mortality: the complexity of it all!', *Eulimene*, 2: 187–203.

—— (2003a) 'Health patterns of proto-Byzantine populations (6th–7th centuries AD) in South Greece: the cases of Eleutherna (Crete) and Messene (Peloponnese)', *International Journal of Osteoarchaeology*, 13: 303–13.

—— (2003b) 'The interaction between a population and its environment: probable case of subadult scurvy from early-Byzantine Greece', *Eres, Arquelogia/Bioantropologia*, 11: 105–14.

—— (2004a) *The People of Early Byzantine Eleutherna and Messene (6th–7th centuries AD): A Bioarchaeological Approach*, Athens: University of Crete Press.

—— (2004b) 'A survey of neoplastic diseases in ancient and medieval Greek populations', *Eulimene*, 5: 181–8.

—— (in press) 'Biological Status in Hellenistic and Roman elites in Western Crete (Greece)', *Eres*.

Bourbou, C. and Richards, M. (forthcoming) 'Dietary patterns in Middle Byzantine (11th century AD) Crete. The evidence of Stable Isotope Analysis'.

Bourbou, C. and Rodríguez-Martín, C. (2003) *Bioarqueología de poblaciones insulares: estudio comparativo entre Mediterráneo y Atlántico (Creta–Tenerife)*. *Un informe preliminary*, Vol. 1, Barcelona: Actas de XII Congreso de la Sociedad Española de Antropología Biológica, 78–87.

Bowman, J. (1992) *Kos. General Guide*, Athens: Efstadiadis.

Boyd, D.W. (1900–01) 'Skulls from cave burials at Zakro', *Annual of the British School at Athens*, 7: 150–5.

Boyer, R. *et al.* (1990) 'Découverte de la tombe d'un oculiste à Lyon (fin du IIe siècle après J.-C.). Instruments et coffret avec collyres', *Gallia*, 47: 215–49.

Bradley, K.R. (1991) *Discovering the Roman Family: Studies in Roman Social History*, Oxford: Oxford University Press.

Braund, D. and Wilkins, J. (eds) (2000) *Athenaeus and His World*, Exeter: Exeter University Press.

Braund, S.H. (1989) 'City and country in Roman satire', in S.H. Braund (ed.) *Satire and Society in Ancient Rome*, Exeter: Exeter University Press, 23–48.

Breitinger, E. (1939) 'Die Skelette aus den submykenischen Gräbern', in W. Kraiker and K. Kübler (eds) *Kerameikos I*, Berlin: Walter de Gruyter, 223–61.

—— (1964) *Der Neanderthaler von Petralona*, Vortrag VII International Congress of Anthropology and Ethnography, Moskau.

Breitwieser, R. (2003) 'Celtic trepanations in Austria', in R. Arnott, S. Finger and C.U.M. Smith (eds) *Trepanation: History, Discovery, Theory*, Lisse: Swets and Zeitlinger, 147–53.

Bremer, J.M. (1981) 'Greek hymns', in H.S. Versnel (ed.) *Faith, Hope and Worship: Aspects of Religious Mentality in the Ancient World*, Leiden: E.J. Brill, 193–215.

Bremmer, J.N. (1980) 'Medon, the case of the bodily blemished king', *Perennitas. Studi in onore di Angelo Brelich*, Rome: Edizione dell'Ateneo, 67–76.

—— (1983) 'Scapegoat rituals in ancient Greece', *Harvard Studies in Classical Philology*, 87: 299–320.

Breslow, L. (2000) 'The societal context of disease prevention and wellness promotion', in M.S. Jamner and D. Stokols (eds) *Promoting Human Wellness: New Frontiers for Research Practice and Policy*, Berkeley, CA: University of California Press, 38–43.

Bridges, P.S. (1990) 'Osteological correlates of weapon use', in J.E. Buikstra (ed.) *A Life in Science: Papers in Honor of J.L. Angel*, Kampsville, IL: Center for American Archeology, Scientific Paper 6, 88–98.

—— (1991) 'Degenerative joint disease in hunter-gatherers and agriculturists from the southeastern United States', *American Journal of Physical Anthropology*, 85: 379–91.

Brody, H. (2000) *The Placebo Response*, New York: HarperCollins.

Brongers, J.A. (1969) 'Ancient Old-World trepanning instruments', *Berichten Rijksdienst Oudheidkundig Bodemonderzoek*, 19: 7–16.

Brothwell, D.R. (1974) 'Osteological evidence of the use of a surgical modiolus in a Romano-British population: an aspect of primitive technology', *Journal of Archaeological Science*, 1: 209–11.

Brothwell, D.R. and Sandison, A.T. (eds) (1967) *Diseases in Antiquity: A Survey of the Diseases, Injuries and Surgery of Early Populations*, Springfield, IL: Charles C. Thomas.

Brown, P.J., Inhorn, M.C. and Smith, D.J. (1996) 'Disease, ecology and human behaviour', in C.F. Sargent and T.M. Johnson (eds) *Medical Anthropology. Contemporary Theory and Method*, London: Praeger, 183–218.

Brown, P.R.L. (1988) *The Body and Society: Men, Women and Sexual Renunciation in Early Christianity*, London: Faber.

Brown, T. and Brown, K. (1992) 'Ancient DNA and the archaeologist', *Antiquity*, 66: 10–23.

Bruce-Chwatt, L. and de Zuluetta, J. (1980) *The Rise and Fall of Malaria in Europe: A Historico-Epidemiological Study*, Oxford: Oxford University Press.

Bruun, C. (2003) 'The Antonine Plague in Rome and Ostia', *Journal of Roman Archaeology*, 16: 426–33.

Bryson, R.A., Lamb, H.H. and Donley, D.R. (1974) 'Drought and the decline of Mycenae', *Antiquity*, 48: 46–50.

Buikstra, J.E. (ed.) (1990) *A Life in Science: Papers in Honor of J.L. Angel*, Kampsville, IL: Center for American Archeology, Scientific Paper 6.

—— (1991) 'Out of the Appendix and into the dirt: comments on 13 years of bioarchaeological research', in M.L. Powell, P.S. Bridges and A.W. Mires (eds) *What Mean these Bones?*, Tuscaloosa, AL: University of Alabama Press, 172–88.

—— (1998) 'Bioarchaeological approaches to Aegean archaeology', in S. Pike (ed.) *Selected Papers from a Workshop on Excavation and Treatment of Finds. Balancing the Constraints of Excavation with Conservation and Analytical Potential*, Athens: Wiener Laboratory Publication No. 4.

Buikstra J.E. and Hershover, L. (1990) 'Introduction', in J.E. Buikstra (ed.) *A Life in Science: Papers in Honor of J.L. Angel*, Kampsville, IL: Center for American Archeology, Scientific Paper 6, 1–16.

Buikstra J.E. and Ubelaker, D.H. (eds) (1994) *Standards for Data Collection from Human Skeletal Remains*, Fayetteville, AR: Arkansas Archaeological Survey Research Series 44.

Buraselis, K. (2000) *Kos. Between Hellenism and Rome*, Philadelphia, PA: American Philosophical Society.

Burford, A. (1969) *The Greek Temple Builders at Epidauros*, Liverpool: Liverpool University Press.

Burkert, W. (1985) *Greek Religion*, trans. J. Raffan, Cambridge, MA: Harvard University Press (original German 1977).

—— (1987) 'Offerings in perspective: surrender, distribution, exchange', in T. Linders and G. Nordquist (eds) *Gifts to the Gods: Proceedings of the Uppsala Symposium 1985*, Uppsala: Academiae Uppsaliensis, 43–50.

Burn, L. (1987) *The Meidias Painter*, Oxford: Oxford University Press.

Burns, P. (1979) 'Log–linear analysis of dental caries occurrence in four skeletal series', *American Journal of Physical Anthropology*, 51(4): 637–47.

—— (1982) 'A study of sexual dimorphism in the dental pathology of ancient peoples', PhD dissertation, Department of Anthropology, Arizona State University, Tempe, AZ.

Buxton, R. (1980) 'Blindness and limits: Sophokles and the logic of myth', *Journal of Hellenic Studies*, 100: 22–37.

Caffey, J. (1937) 'The skeletal changes in the chronic hemolytic anaemias', *American Journal of Roentgenology and Radium Therapy*, 37: 293–324.

Callahan, D. (1982) 'The WHO definition of health', in T.L. Beauchamp and L. Walters (eds) *Contemporary Issues in Bioethics*, 3rd edition, Belmont, CA: Wadsworth, 80–5 (first published 1973).

Cambiano, G. (1983) 'Pathologie et analogie politique', in F. Lassere and Ph. Mudry (eds) *Formes de Pensée dans la Collection Hippocratique*, Actes du IVe colloque international hippocratique, Lausanne, 21–25 septembre 1981, Geneva: Librairie Droz, 441–58.

Cameron, A. (1964) 'Palladas and the fate of Gessius', *Byzantinische Zeitschrift*, 57: 279–92.

Campbell, D.A. (1993) *Greek Lyric* V, Cambridge, MA: Harvard University Press.

Campillo, D. (1993) 'Healing of the skull bone after injury', *Journal of Palaeopathology*, 3: 137–49.

Capasso, L. (1995) 'The origin of human malaria', in *Proceedings of the 9th European Meeting of the Paleopathology Association, Barcelona 1–4 September 1992*, Barcelona: Museu D'Arqueologia de Catalunya, 91–102.

Capasso, L. and Capelli, A. (1995) 'A trephined skull from central Italy (Alba Fucens, Abruzzo), dated to Roman times (1st–2nd century AD)', *Proceedings of the 9th European Meeting of the Palaeopathology Association*, Barcelona: Museu d'Arqueleogia de Catalunya, 103–6.

Carpenter, R. (1966) *Discontinuity in Greek Civilisation*, Cambridge: Cambridge University Press.

Carr, G.H. (1960) 'Some dental characteristics of the Middle Minoans', *Man*, 60: 119–22.

Cassady, M. and Cassady, P. (1982) *Theatre: A View of Life*, New York: Holt, Rinehart & Winston.

Caton, R. (1914) 'Notes on a group of medical and surgical instruments, found near Kolophon', *Journal of Hellenic Studies*, 34: 114–18.

Cavallo, G. (2002) 'Galeno e la levatrice. Qualche riflessione su libri e sapere medico nel mondo antico', *Medicina nei Secoli*, 14: 407–16.

Chadwick, H. (1974) 'John Moschus and his friend Sophronius the Sophist', *Journal of Theological Studies*, n.s. 25: 41–74.

Champlin, E. (1982/85) 'The suburbium of Rome', *American Journal of Ancient History*, 7: 97–117.

Chaniotis, A. (1995) 'Illness and cures in the Greek propitiatory inscriptions and dedications of Lydia and Phrygia', in Ph.J. Van der Eijk, H.F.J. Horstmanshoff and P.H. Schrijvers (eds) *Ancient Medicine in its Socio-cultural Context*, Vol. 2, Amsterdam/Atlanta, GA: Editions Rodopi (= Clio Medica 27), 323–44.

Charles, R.P. (1958) 'Étude anthropologique des nécropoles d'Argos. Contribution à l'étude des populations de la Grèce antique', *Bulletin de Correspondence Hellenique*, 82: 258–313.

—— (1963) 'Étude anthropologique des nécropoles d'Argos. Contribution à l'étude des populations de la Grèce antique', École Français d'Athènes, Vol. III, *Études Péloponnésiennes*, Paris: J. Vrin.

—— (1965) 'Le Neanderthalien de Petralona en Chalcidique (Grèce)', *Cahiers Ligures de Préhistoire et d'archéologie*, 14: 182–94.

Christodoulou, D. (1959) *The Evolution of the Rural Land Use Pattern in Cyprus*, The World Land Use Survey Monograph 2: Cyprus (L.D. Stamp, ed.), Herts, England: Geographical Publications.

Ciarallo, A. (2001) *Gardens of Pompeii*, Los Angeles, CA: J. Paul Getty Museum.

—— (2002) 'About an ancient medical mixture found in Pompeii', in J. Renn and G. Castagnetti (eds) *Homo Faber: Studies in Nature and Science at the Time of Pompeii*, Rome: "L'Erma" di Bretschneider, 153–67.

Ciarallo, A. and De Carolis, E. (1999) *Pompeii: Life in a Roman Town*, Milan: Electa.

—— (2001) *La casa di Giulio Polibio: Studi Interdisciplinari*, Tokyo: University of Tokyo.

Cipollaro, M., Di Bernardo, G., Forte, A., Galano, G., De Masi, L., Galderisi, U. Guarino, F.M., Angelini, F. and Cascino, A. (1999) 'Histological analysis and ancient DNA amplification of human bone remains found in Caius Iulius Polybius house in Pompeii', *Croatian Medical Journal*, 40: 392–7.

Clark, G. (1996) 'The bright frontier of friendship: Augustine and the Christian body in late antiquity', in R. Mathisen and H. Sivan (eds) *Shifting Frontiers in Late Antiquity*, Aldershot: Variorum, 212–23.

—— (2000a) *Porphyry: On Abstinence from Killing Animals, Translation and Commentary*, London: Duckworth.

—— (2000b) 'Porphyry and Iamblichus: philosophic lives and the philosophic life', in T. Hägg and P. Rousseau (eds) *Greek Biography and Panegyric in Late Antiquity*, Berkeley, CA: University of California Press, 29–51.

—— (2001) 'Fattening the soul: Christian asceticism and Porphyry on abstinence', *Studia Patristica*, 35: 41–50.

Clark, S.R.L. (1996) 'Plotinus: body and soul', in L. Gerson (ed.) *The Cambridge Companion to Plotinus*, Cambridge: Cambridge University Press, 275–91.

Clarke, B. and Aycock, W. (eds) (1990) *The Body and the Text: Comparative Essays in Literature and Medicine*, Lubbock, TX: Texas Tech University Press.

Clinton, K. (1994) 'The Epidauria and the arrival of Asclepius in Athens', in R. Hägg (ed.) *Ancient Greek Cult Practice from the Epigraphical Evidence*, Stockholm: Svenska Institutet i Athen Jonsered/P. Aström, 17–34.

Cockburn, A. (1963) *The Evolution and Eradication of Infectious Diseases*, Baltimore, MD: Johns Hopkins University Press.

—— (1967) 'The evolution of human infectious disease', in A. Cockburn (ed.) *Infectious Diseases*, Springfield, IL: Charles C. Thomas, 84–107.

Cohen, M.N. (1989) *Health and the Rise of Civilisation*, New Haven, CT: Yale University Press.

Cohen, M.N. and Armelagos, G.J. (eds) (1984) *Paleopathology at the Origins of Agriculture*, London and Orlando, FL: Academic Press.

Cola, R.M. (1996) 'Responses of Pampanga households to Lahar warnings: lessons from two villages in the Pasig-Potrero River watershed', in C.G. Newhall and

R.S. Punongbayan (eds) *Fire and Mud: Eruptions and Lahars of Mount Pinatubo, Philippines*, Seattle, WA: University of Washington Press.

Coldstream, J.N., Callaghan, P. and Musgrave, J.H. (1981) 'Knossos: a geometric tomb on lower Gypsades', *Annual of the British School at Athens*, 76: 141–65.

Coluzzi, M., Sabatini, A., della Torre, A., Di Deco, M. and Petrarca, V. (2002) 'A polytene chromosome analysis of the Anopheles gambiae species complex', *Science*, 298: 1415–18.

Comaroff, J. (1985) *Body of Power, Spirit of Resistance: The Culture and History of a South African People*, Chicago, IL: University of Chicago Press.

Como, J. (1925) 'Das Grab eines römischen Arztes in Bingen', *Germania*, 9: 152–62.

Compton, M.T. (2002) 'The association of Hygieia with Asklepios in Graeco-Roman Asklepieion medicine', *Journal of the History of Medicine and Allied Sciences*, 57: 312–29.

Conrad, P. (1994) 'Wellness as virtue: morality and the pursuit of health', *Culture, Medicine and Psychiatry*, 18: 385–401.

Cook, R. and Cook, K. (1968) *Southern Greece: An Archaeological Guide*, New York: Frederick Praeger.

[Cornwell, B.] (1784) *The Domestic Physician; Or, Guardian of Health*, London: The Author, J. Murray, etc.

Corvisier, J.-N. (2001) 'Les "Préceptes de santé" de Plutarque et leur place dans la literature comparable', in J.-N. Corvisier, C. Didier and M. Valdher (eds) *Thérapies, médecine et démographie antiques*, Artois: Presses Université, 137–56.

Corvisier, J.-N., Didier, C. and Valdher, M. (eds) (2001) *Thérapies, médecine et démographie antiques*, Artois: Presses Université.

Crisafulli, V.S. and Nesbitt, J.W. (1997) *The Miracles of St Artemios*, Leiden: E.J. Brill.

Croissant, F. (1990) s.v. 'Hygieia', in *Lexicon iconographicum mythologiae classicae* V, Zürich and Munich: Artemis Verlag, V, 554–72.

Curteis, T. (1704) *Essays on the Preservation and Recovery of Health*, London: Richard Wilkin and Henry Bonwick.

Dalby, A. (1995) *Siren Feasts*, London and New York: Routledge.

D'Arms, J.H. (1970) *Romans on the Bay of Naples*, Cambridge, MA: Cambridge University Press.

Dasen, V. (1993) *Dwarfs in Ancient Egypt and Greece*, Oxford: Clarendon Press.

Davidson, J. (1997) *Courtesans and Fishcakes*, London: Harper Collins.

Davies, J.K. and Kelly, M.P. (eds) (1993) *Healthy Cities: Research and Practice*, London and New York: Routledge.

Davis, L.J. (ed.) (1997) *The Disability Studies Reader*, London and New York: Routledge.

Dawson, G.G. (1935, repr. 1977) *Healing: Pagan and Christian*, London: Society for Promoting Christian Knowledge.

Dawson, W.R. (1923) 'Egyptian medicine under the Copts in the early centuries of the Christian era', *Proceedings of the Royal Society of Medicine*, 17: 56ff.

Dean-Jones, L. (1994) *Women's Bodies in Classical Greek Science*, Oxford: Oxford University Press.

De Franciscis, A. (1988) 'La casa di C. Iulius Polybius', *Rivista di Studi Pompeiane*, 2: 16–36.

Demand, N. (1994) *Birth, Death, and Motherhood in Classical Greece*, Baltimore, MD: Johns Hopkins University Press.

De Navarro, J.M. (1955) 'A doctor's grave of the middle La Tène period from Bavaria', *Proceedings of the Prehistoric Society*, 21: 231–48.

Deneffe, V. (1893) *Étude sur la trousse d'un chirurgien gallo-romain du IIIe siècle*, Antwerp: H. Caals.

De' Spagnolis Conticello, M. (1994) *Il pons sarni di scafati e la via Nuceria-Pompeios*, Rome: "L'Erma" di Bretschneider.

Detienne, M. (1989) *Dionysos at Large*, Cambridge, MA: Harvard University Press.

Detienne, M. and Vernant, J.-P. (1978) *Cunning Intelligence in Greek Culture and Society*, trans. J. Lloyd, Hassocks (Eng.): Harvester Press.

Devereux, G. (1973) 'The self-blinding of Oidipous in Sophokles' *Oidipous Tyrannos*', *Journal of Hellenic Studies*, 93: 36–49.

Di Bernardo, G., Galano, G., Galdersi, U., Cascino, A., Guarino, F.M., Angelini, F. and Cipollaro, M. (2001) 'Analisi dei reperti ossei della Casa Grado di conservazione ed amplificazione del DNA antico', in A. Ciarallo and E. De Cariolis (eds) *La casa di Giulio Polibio: studi interdisciplinari*, Tokyo: University of Tokyo, 112–24.

Dickinson, O.T.P.K. (1974) 'Drought and the decline of Mycenae: some comments', *Antiquity*, 48: 228–30.

Dillon, J. (1994) 'Singing without an instrument: Plotinus on suicide', *Illinois Classical Studies*, 19: 231–8.

Dillon, M. (1977) *Pilgrims and Pilgrimage in Ancient Greece*, London and New York: Routledge.

Dodd, D.B. and Faraone, C.A. (eds) (2003) *Initiation in Ancient Greek Rituals and Narratives: New Critical Perspectives*, London and New York: Routledge.

Domurad, M. (1985) 'The human remains', Appendix in D. Michaelides and M. Sznycer, 'A Phoenician graffito from tomb 103/84 at Nea Paphos', *Report of the Department of Antiquities*, Cyprus, 256.

—— (1986) 'The populations of ancient Cyprus', PhD dissertation, Department of Classics, University of Cincinnati, Cincinnati, OH.

—— (1988) 'The human remains', Appendix in D. Michaelides and J. Mlynarczyk, 'Tombs P.M. 2520 and P.M. 2737 from the eastern necropolis of Nea Paphos', *Report of the Department of Antiquities*, Cyprus, Part 2, 169–70.

Drabkin, I.E. (ed. and trans.) (1950) *Caelius Aurelianus On Acute Diseases and On Chronic Diseases*, Chicago, IL: Chicago University Press.

Drancourt, M., Aboudharam, G., Signoli, M., Dutour, O. and Raoult, D. (1998) 'Detection of 400-year-old *Yersinia pestis* DNA in human dental pulp: an approach to the diagnosis of ancient septicemia', *Proceedings of the National Academy of Science*, 95: 12637–40.

Drescher, J. (1946) *Apa Mena. A Selection of Coptic Texts Relating to St. Menas*, Cairo: Publications de la Société d'archéologie copte.

Drews, R. (1993) *The End of the Bronze Age: Changes in Warfare and the Catastrophe ca. 1200 BC*, Princeton, NJ: Princeton University Press.

Driessen, J. and Macdonald, C.F. (1997) *The Troubled Island: Minoan Crete Before and After the Santorini Eruption*, Liège and Austin, TX: Université de Liège and the University of Texas at Austin (Aegaeum 17).

Duckworth, W.L.H. (1902–3) 'Ossuaries at Roussolakkos', *Annual of the British School at Athens*, 9: 350–5.

—— (1904) *Archaeological and Ethnological Researches in Crete 2. Report On Anthropological Works in Athens and Crete*, Report of the 73rd Meeting of the British Association for the Advancement of Science, Southport, London: John Murray, 404–11.

—— (1913) *Archaeological and Ethnological Researches in Crete Part II: The Craniology of the Ancient Inhabitants of Palaekstro and its Neighbourhood*, Report of the 82nd Meeting of the British Association for the Advancement of Science, Dundee, London: John Murray, 227–47.

Duffy, J. (1984a) 'Observations on Sophronius' miracles of Cyrus and John', *Journal of Theological Studies*, n.s. 35: 70–90.

—— (1984b) 'Byzantine medicine in the sixth and seventh centuries: aspects of teaching and practice', *Dumbarton Oaks Papers*, 38: 22–7.

Dumont, J. (1988) 'Les critères culturels du choix des poissons dans l'alimentation grècque antique: le cas d'Athénée de Naucratis', in L. Bodson (ed.) *Anthropozoologica: L'animal dans l'alimentation humaine. Les critères de choix*, Paris: Musée d'Histoire Naturelle, 99–113.

Duncan Jones, R.P. (1996) 'The impact of the Antonine Plague', *Journal of Roman Archaeology*, 9: 108–36.

Edelstein, E.J. and Edelstein, L. (1945) *Asclepius: A Collection and Interpretation of the Testimonies*, 2 vols, Baltimore, MD: Johns Hopkins University Press.

Edelstein, L. (1967) *Ancient Medicine*, Baltimore, MD: Johns Hopkins University Press.

Edwards, C. (1993) *The Politics of Immorality in Ancient Rome*, Cambridge: Cambridge University Press.

Edwards, C. and Woolf, G. (eds) (2003) *Rome the Cosmopolis*, Cambridge: Cambridge University Press.

Edwards, M.L. (1996) 'The cultural context of deformity in the ancient Greek world: "Let there be a law that no deformed child shall be reared" ', *The Ancient History Bulletin*, 10: 79–92.

—— (1997a) 'Constructions of physical disability in the ancient Greek world: the community concept', in D.T. Mitchell and S.L. Snyder (eds) *The Body and Physical Difference: Discourses on Disability*, Ann Arbor, MI: University of Michigan Press, 35–50.

—— (1997b) 'Deaf and dumb in ancient Greece', in L.J. Davis (ed.) *The Disability Studies Reader*, New York: Routledge, 29–51.

Eisenberg, L. (1977) 'Disease and illness: distinctions between professional and popular ideas of sickness', *Culture, Medicine and Psychiatry*, 1: 9–23.

Eliakis, C., Eliakis, E. and Iordanidis, P. (1966) 'Détermination de la taille d'après la mensuration des os longs', *Annales de Médecine Légale*, 46: 403–21.

Eliopoulos, C. (1998) 'The problem of standardization in palaeopathological lesion recording: an interobserver error study', MSc thesis, University of Sheffield.

Emunah, R. (1994) *Acting for Real. Drama Therapy Process, Technique, and Performance*, New York: Brunner/Mazel.

Faivre, J. (1918) *Canopus, Menouthis, Aboukir: Pagan Memories, Christian Memories, Battle Memories*, Alexandria: Alexandria Archaeological Society.

Faraklas, N. (1972) *Epidauros. The Sanctuary of Asclepios*, Athens: Lycabettus Press.

Faraone, C.A. and Obbink, D. (eds) (1991) *Magika Hiera: Ancient Greek Magic and Religion*, New York: Oxford University Press.

Fazekas, I.G. and Kósa, F. (1978) *Forensic Fetal Osteology*, Budapest: Akadémiai Kiadó.

Fernandez Marcos, N. (1975) *Los Thaumata de Sofronio: contribucion al estudio de la incubatio cristiana*, Madrid: Consejo superior de investigaciones cientificas.

Festugière, A.J. (1960) *Personal Religion Among the Greeks*, Berkeley, CA: University of California.

Feugère, M., Künzl, E. and Weisser, U. (1985) 'Die Starnadeln von Montbellet (Saône-et-Loire). Ein Beitrag zur antiken und islamischen Augenheilkunde', *Jahrbuch des römisch–germanischen Zentralmuseums*, 32: 436–508.

Flammand, M. (1697) *The Art of Preserving and Restoring Health*, English translation of French original, London: R. Bentley.

Flemming, R. (1999) 'Quae corpore quaestum facit: the sexual economy of female prostitution in the Roman Empire', *Journal of Roman Studies*, 89: 38–61.

—— (2000) *Medicine and the Making of Roman Women: Gender, Nature, and Authority from Celsus to Galen*, Oxford: Oxford University Press.

Fornaciari, G., Mezzetti, M.G. and Roselli, A. (1991) 'Trapanazione cranica del IV secolo a.C. da Pontecagnano (Salerno)', *Studi Etruschi*, 56: 285–6.

Forsen, B. (1996) *Griechische Gliederweihungen. Eine Untersuchung zu ihrer Typologie und ihrer religions- und sozialgeschichtlichen Bedeutung*, Helsinki: Papers and Monographs of the Finnish Institute at Athens, Vol. 4.

Foster, G.V., Kanada, K. and Michaelides, D. (1988) 'A Roman surgeon's tomb from Nea Paphos. Part 2: Ancient Medicines: by-products of copper mining in Cyprus', *Report of the Department of Antiquities*, Cyprus, Part 2, 229–34.

Fox, J. (1994) *Acts of Service. Spontaneity, Commitment, Tradition in the Nonscripted Theatre*, New Paltz, NY: Tusitala.

Fox, J. and Heinrich Dauber (eds) (1999) *Gathering Voices. Essays on Playback Theatre*, New Paltz, NY: Tusitala.

Fox Leonard, S. (1997) 'Comparative health from paleopathological analysis of the human skeletal remains dating to the Hellenistic and Roman periods from Paphos, Cyprus and Corinth, Greece', PhD thesis, University of Arizona.

Foxhall, L. and Forbes, H. (1982) 'Sitometreia: the role of grain as a staple food in classical antiquity', *Chiron*, 12: 41–90.

Franklin, J.L. (2001) *Pompeis difficile est. Studies in the Political Life of Imperial Pompeii*, Ann Arbor, MI: University of Michigan Press.

Franzius, G. (1992) 'Die Fundgegenstände aus Prospektion und Grabungen in der Kalkrieser-Niewedder Senke bei Osnabrück, 349–383', in W. Schlüter, 'Archäologische Zeugnisse zur Varusschlacht?', *Germania*, 70: 307–402.

Frazer, J.G. (1898) *Pausanias's Description of Greece* (6 vols), London: Macmillan.

Frickenhaus, A. (1910) 'Heilige Stätten in Delphi', *Mitteilungen des Deutschen Archäologischen Instituts, Athenische Abteilung*, 35: 235–73.

Frier, B.W. (1994) 'Natural fertility and family limitation in Roman marriage', *Classical Philology*, 89: 318–33.

Frier, B.W. (2001) 'More is worse: some observations on the population of the Roman Empire', in W. Scheidel (ed.) *Debating Roman Demography* (*Mnemosyne* supplement 211), Leiden: E.J. Brill, 139–60.

Fürst, M.C. (1930) *Zur Anthropologie der prähistorischen Griechen in Argolis*, Lunds Universitets Årsskrift N. F. Avd 2, Bd 26, Nr 8.

—— (1932) *Über einen neolithischen Schädel aus Arkadien*, Lunds Universitets Årsskrift N. F. Avd 2, Bd 28, Nr 13.

Gager, J. (1992) *Curse Tablets and Binding Spells from the Ancient World*, New York and Oxford: Oxford University Press.

Gaitzsch, W. (1981) 'Ziegelstampfe oder Trepan? Ein chirurgisches Instrument aus Niederbieber', *Das Rheinische Landesmuseum Bonn*, 2/81: 22–3.

Gallo, L. (1989) 'Alimentazione urbana e alimentazione contadina nell' Atene classica', in O. Longo and P. Searpi (eds) *Homo Edens*, Verona: Diapress/Documenti, 21–30.

Gantz, T. (1993) *Early Greek Myth: A Guide to Literary and Artistic Sources*, Baltimore, MD and London: Johns Hopkins University Press.

Garland, R. (1992) *Introducing New Gods: The Politics of Athenian Religion*, London: Duckworth.

—— (1995) *The Eye of the Beholder: Deformity and Disability in the Graeco-Roman World*, London: Duckworth.

Garnsey, P. (1999) *Food and Society in Classical Antiquity*, Cambridge: Cambridge University Press.

Garvie-Lok, S. (2001) 'Loaves and fishes: a stable isotope reconstruction of diet in Medieval Greece', PhD thesis, University of Calgary, Alberta, Canada.

Gejvall, N.G. and Henschen, F. (1968) 'Two late skeletons with malformations and close family relationships from ancient Corinth', *Opuscula Atheniensia*, 8: 179–93.

Germanà, F. and Fornaciari, G. (1992) *Trapanazioni, craniotomie e trauma cranici in Italia*, Pisa: Giardini.

Giardina, P.J., Gertner, J.M., Schneider, R., Simmons, B.H. and Rodriguez, A. (1993) 'Abnormal bone metabolism in thalassemia [abstract]', *5th International Conference on Thalassaemias and the Haemoglobinopathies, March 29–April 3, 1993*, Nicosia, Cyprus, Geneva: World Health Organization, 106.

Gilbert, B.M. and McKern, T. (1973) 'A method for aging the female *os pubis*', *American Journal of Physical Anthropology*, 38(1): 31–8.

Girard, R. (1986) *The Scapegoat*, trans. Y. Freccero, London: The Athlone Press.

Gold, B.K. (1998) ' "The house I live in is not my own": women's bodies in Juvenal's *Satires*', *Arethusa*, 31: 369–86.

Good, B.J. (1994) *Medicine, Rationality and Experience: An Anthropological Perspective*, Cambridge: Cambridge University Press.

Gordon, D. (1976) *Health, Sickness, and Society: Theoretical Concepts in Social and Preventive Medicine*, St Lucia, Queensland: University of Queensland Press.

Gottfried, R.S. (1983) *The Black Death: Natural and Human Disaster in Medieval Europe*, London: R. Hale.

Gräf, B. and Langlotz, E. (1933) *Die antiken Vasen von der Akropolis zu Athen* II, Berlin: L. Walter de Gruyter and Co.

Graham-Pole, J. (2000) *Illness and the Art of Creative Self-Expression*, Oakland, CA: New Harbinger Publications.

Graham-Pole, J., Rockwood Lane, M., Kitakis, M.L. and Stacpoole, L. (1994) 'Creating an Arts Progam in an academic setting', *International Journal of Arts Medicine*, 3: 17–25.

Grammenos, D. and Triantaphyllou, S. (eds) (2004) *Anthropologikes meletes apo tin Voreia Ellada*, 1, Thessaloniki: Archaeological Institute of Northern Greece.

Grant, M. (2000) *Galen on Food and Diet*, London and New York: Routledge.

Grauer, A.L. and Roberts, C.A. (1996) 'Paleoepidemiology, healing and possible treatment of trauma in the medieval cemetery population of St. Helen-on-the-Walls, York, England', *American Journal of Physical Anthropology*, 100: 531–44.

Gray, K.C. (as Calnan, K.A.) (1992) 'The health status of Bronze Age Greek women', PhD thesis, University of Cincinnati.

—— (1994) 'The health status of Bronze Age Greek women', *American Journal of Archeology*, 98: 340 (summary of paper read to the 95th Annual Meeting of the Archeological Institute of America, December 1993).

Greenberg, J. (2003) 'Plagued by doubt: reconsidering the impact of a mortality crisis in the second century AD', *Journal of Roman Archaeology*, 16: 413–25.

Grew, F. and Hobley, B. (eds) (1985) *Roman Urban Topography in Britain and the Western Empire*, London: Council for British Archaeology.

Grimm, V. (1996) *From Feasting to Fasting: The Evolution of a Sin*, London and New York: Routledge.

Grmek, M.D. (1983) *Diseases in the Ancient Greek World*, Baltimore, MD and London: Johns Hopkins University Press.

—— (1989) 'Les maladies et la mort de Plotin', in L. Brisson (ed.) *Porphyre: La Vie de Plotin*, tome II, Paris: J. Vrin, 335–53.

Grottanelli, C. (2003) 'Evenius becomes a seer (Herodotus 9.93–5): a paradoxical initiation?', in D.B. Dodd and C.A. Faraone (eds) *Initiation in Ancient Greek Rituals and Narratives: New Critical Perspectives*, London and New York: Routledge, 203–18.

Groube, L. (1996) 'The impact of diseases upon the emergence of agriculture', in D.R. Harris (ed.) *The Origins and Spread of Agriculture and Pastoralism in Eurasia*, London: UCL Press, 101–29.

Grove, A.T. and Rackham, O. (2001) *The Nature of Mediterranean Europe: An Ecological History*, New Haven, CT: Yale University Press.

Gurdjian, E.S. (1973) *Head Injury from Antiquity to the Present with Special Reference to Penetrating Head Wounds*, Springfield, IL: Charles C. Thomas.

Guzzo, P.G. (1974) 'Tomba 17', in id., 'Luzzi Località S. Vito (Cosenza) – Necropoli di età romana', *Notizie degli Scavi*, 28: 449ff., esp. 469–75.

Haas, C. (1997) *Alexandria in Late Antiquity*, Baltimore, MD and London: Johns Hopkins University Press.

Habicht, C. (1985) *Pausanias' Guide to Ancient Greece*, Berkeley, CA: University of California Press.

Hadjiminas, M., Zachariodis, Z. and Stamatoyannopoulos, G. (1979) 'α-thalassaemia in Cyprus', *Journal of Medical Genetics*, 16: 363–5.

Hägg, R. (1994) (ed.) *Ancient Greek Cult Practice from the Epigraphical Evidence*, Stockholm: Paul Åströms.

Hägg, R. and Nordquist, G.C. (eds) (1990) *Celebrations of Death and Divinity in the Bronze Age Argolid*, Proceedings of the 6th International Symposium of the Swedish Institute of Athens, 11–13 June, 1988, Stockholm: Svenska Institutet.

Haldane, J.B.S. (1957) 'Natural selection in man', *Acta Genetica et Statistica Medica*, 6: 321–2.

Halstead, P. (1977) 'The Bronze Age demography of Crete and Greece – a note', *Annual of the British School at Athens*, 72: 107–11.

Hamilton, J.S. (1986) 'Scribonius Largus on the medical profession', *Bulletin of the History of Medicine*, 60: 209–16.

Hamilton, M. (1906) *Incubation. The Cure of Disease in Pagan Temples and Christian Churches*, London: Simpkin, Marshall, Hamilton, Kent and Co.

Hankinson, R.J. (1991) (trans.) *Galen, on the Therapeutic Method*, Oxford: Clarendon Press.

Hanks, P. (1979) *Collins Dictionary of the English Language*, London and Glasgow: Collins.

Hanson, A.E. (1989) 'Diseases of women in the *Epidemics*', in G. Baader and R. Winau (eds) *Die Hippokratischen Epidemien: Theorie-Praxis-Tradition, Verhandlung des Ve Colloque International Hippocratique, Berlin 10–15.9.1984, Sudhoffs Archiv*, Heft 27, Stuttgart: Franz Steiner, 38–51.

Harris, J. (1676) *The Divine Physician*, London: H.B. for William Whitwood.

Harvey, D. (1988) *The Condition of Postmodernity*, Oxford: Blackwell.

Hasluck, M.M. and Morant, G.M. (1929) 'Measurements of Macedonian men', *Biometrika*, 21: 322–36.

Hassel, F.J. and Künzl, E. (1980) 'Ein römisches Arztgrab des 3. Jahrhunderts n. Chr. Aus Kleinasien', *Medizinhistorisches Journal*, 15: 403–41.

Hausmann, U. (1948) *Kunst und Heiltum: Untersuchungen zu den griechischen Asklepiosreliefs*, Potsdam: E. Stichnote.

Hawes, C.H. (1909–10) 'Some Dorian descendants', *Annual of the British School at Athens*, 16: 258–80.

—— (1911) *Archaeological and Ethnological Researches in Crete. Appendix I. A Report On Cretan Anthropometry* (Report of the 80th Meeting of the British Association for the Advancement of Science, Sheffield), London: John Murray, 404–11.

Helman, C.G. (1985) 'Disease and pseudo-disease: a case history of pseudo-angina', in R.A. Hahn and A.D. Gaines (eds) *Physicians of Western Medicine: Anthropological Approaches to Theory and Practice*, Dordrecht: D. Reidel, 293–331.

—— (1994) *Culture, Health and Illness: An Introduction for Health Professionals*, Oxford: Butterworth Heinemann.

Henneberg, M. and Henneberg, R.J. (1996) 'Skeletal material from the house of C. Iulius Polybius in Pompeii, AD 79', *Human Evolution*, 11: 249–59.

—— (1998) 'Biological characteristics of the population based on skeletal remains', in J.C. Carter (ed.) *The Chora of Metaponto: The Necropoleis*, Austin, TX: University of Texas Press, 503–59.

—— (1999a) 'Variation in the closure of the sacral canal in the skeletal sample from Pompeii, Italy, 79 AD', *Perspectives in Human Biology*, 4: 177–88.

—— (1999b) 'Human skeletal material from Pompeii', in A. Ciarallo and E. De Carolis (eds) *Pompeii: Life in a Roman Town*, Milan: Electa, 51–3.

—— (2001) 'Analysis of human skeletal and dental remains from Metaponto (7th–2nd C BC)', in *Problemi della 'Chora' Coloniale dall'Occidente al Mar Nero* (Atti del quarantesimo convegno di studi sulla Magna Grecia Taranto, 29 settembre–3 ottobre 2000), Taranto: Istituto per la storia e l'archeologia della Magna Grecia, 461–84.

—— (2002) 'Reconstructing medical knowledge in ancient Pompeii from the hard evidence of bones and teeth', in J. Renn and G. Castagnetti (eds) *Homo Faber: Studies On Nature, Technology and Science at the Time of Pompeii*, Rome: "L'Erma" di Bretschneider, 169–87.

Hermansen, G. (1978) 'The population of imperial Rome: the regionaries', *Historia*, 27: 129–68.

Herrmann, B. (1992) 'Gräberfelder der Siedlung Kastri, Thassos. Identifikation der Skeletreste', in Ch. Koukouli-Chrysanthaki (ed.) *Protoistoriki Thasos: Ta nekrotafeia tou oikismou Kastri. Meros B*, Athens: Ekdosi tou tameiou Archaeologikon Poron kai Apallotrioseon, 739–51.

Hill, M.C. and Armelagos, G.J. (1990) 'Porotic hyperostosis in past and present perspective', in J.E. Buikstra (ed.) *A Life in Science: Papers in Honor of J.L. Angel*, Kampsville, IL: Center for American Archeology, Scientific Paper 6, 52–63.

Hinkes, M. (1983) 'Skeletal evidence of stress in subadults: trying to come of age at Grasshopper Pueblo', PhD dissertation, Department of Anthropology, University of Arizona, Tucson, AZ.

Hodge, A.T. (1981) 'Vitruvius, lead pipes, and lead poisoning', *American Journal of Archeology*, 85: 486–91.

Homan, S. (1994) 'The "theatre" in medicine', *International Journal of Arts Medicine*, 3: 26–9.

Hooton, E.A. (1930) *The Indians of Pecos Pueblo. A Study of their Skeletal Remains*, New Haven, CT: Yale University Press.

Hope, V.M. and Marshall, E. (eds) (2000) *Death and Disease in the Ancient City*, London and New York: Routledge.

Hopkins, K. (1983) 'Murderous games', in K. Hopkins (ed.) *Death and Renewal*, Cambridge: Cambridge University Press.

Horden, P. and Purcell, N. (2000) *The Corrupting Sea: A Study in Mediterranean History*, Oxford: Basil Blackwell.

Hughes, J.D. (1994) *Pan's Travail: Environmental Problems of the Ancient Greeks and Romans*, Baltimore, MD: Johns Hopkins University Press.

Hume, D. (1882) 'On the populousness of ancient nations', in T.H. Green and T.H. Grose (eds) *Essays: Moral, Political and Literary*, Vol. 1, London: Longmans, Green & Co., 381–443.

Humphreys, S.C. (1985) 'Lycurgus of Butadae: an Athenian aristocrat', in J.W. Eadie and J. Ober (eds) *The Craft of the Ancient Historian: Essays in Honour of Chester G. Starr*, Lanham, MD: University Press of America, 199–236.

Hunter, K. (1983) 'The Satiric Images: healers in literature', *Literature and Medicine*, 2: 135–47.

Ingstad, B. and Whyte, S.R. (eds) (1995) *Disability and Culture*, Berkeley, CA: University of California Press.

Ingvarsson-Sundström, A. (2003) 'Children lost and found: a bioarchaeological study of Middle Helladic children in Asine with a comparison to Lerna', PhD thesis, Uppsala University.

İşcan, M.Y., Loth, S.R. and Wright, R.K. (1984) 'Age estimation from the rib by phase analysis: white males', *Journal of Forensic Sciences*, 29: 1094–104.

İşcan, M.Y., Loth, S.R. and Wright, R.K. (1985) 'Age estimation from the rib by phase analysis: white females', *Journal of Forensic Sciences*, 30: 853–63.

İşcan, M.Y. and Kennedy, K.A.R. (eds) (1989) *Reconstruction of the Life from the Skeleton*, New York: Alan Liss.

Jackson, R. (1986) 'A set of Roman medical instruments from Italy', *Britannia*, 17: 119–67.

—— (1988) *Doctors and Diseases in the Roman Empire*, London: British Museum Press.

—— (1990) 'Roman doctors and their instruments: recent research into ancient practice', *Journal of Roman Archaeology*, 3: 5–27.

—— (1991) 'Roman bivalve dilators and Celsus' "instrument like a Greek letter..." (*De med.* VII, 5, 2B)', in G. Sabbah (ed.) *Le Latin medical: la constitution d'un langage scientifique*, St. Étienne: Centre Jean Palerne, *Mémoires*, 10: 101–8.

—— (1993) 'Roman medicine: the practitioners and their practices', in W. Haase and H. Temporini (eds) *Aufstieg und Niedergang der römischen Welt* (*ANRW*) II 37.1, Berlin and New York: Walter de Gruyter, 79–101.

—— (1994) 'The surgical instruments, appliances and equipment in Celsus' *De medicina*', in G. Sabbah and Ph. Mudry (eds) *La Médecine de Celse: Aspects Historiques, Scientifiques et Littéraires*, St. Étienne: Centre Jean Palerne, *Mémoires* XIII: 167–209.

—— (1995) 'The composition of Roman medical instrumentaria as an indicator of medical practice: a provisional assessment', in Ph.J. Van der Eijk, H.F.J. Horstmanshoff and P.H. Schrijvers (eds) *Ancient Medicine in its Socio-cultural Context*, Vol. 1, Amsterdam/Atlanta, GA: Editions Rodopi (= Clio Medica 27), 189–207.

—— (1996) 'Eye medicine in the Roman Empire', in W. Haase and H. Temporini (eds) *Aufstieg und Niedergang der römischen Welt* (*ANRW*) II 37.3, Berlin and New York: Walter de Gruyter, 2228–51.

—— (1997a) 'An ancient British medical kit from Stanway, Essex', *The Lancet*, 350: 1471–3.

—— (1997b) 'Medical instruments in the Roman World', *Medicina nei Secoli*, 9: 223–48.

—— (2002) 'A Roman doctor's house in Rimini', *British Museum Magazine*, 44: 20–3.

—— (2003) 'The Domus "del chirurgo", at Rimini: an interim account of the medical assemblage', *Journal of Roman Archaeology*, 16: 312–21.

—— (forthcoming a) *Greek and Roman Surgical Instruments and Medical Objects in the British Museum*, London: British Museum Press.

—— (forthcoming b) 'Some recent discoveries of Roman surgical instruments', in L.Melillo Corleto (ed.) *Storia della medicina, scienza dell'uomo*, Naples: Istituto Universitario Orientale.

Jackson, R. and Leahy, K. (1990) 'A Roman surgical forceps from near Littleborough and a note on the type', *Britannia*, 21: 271–4.

Jacobsen, T.W. and Cullen, T. (1990) 'The work of J.L. Angel in the eastern Mediterranean', in J.E. Buikstra (ed.) *A Life in Science: Papers in Honor of J.L. Angel*, Kampsville, IL: Center for American Archeology, Scientific Paper 6, 38–51.

Jamner, M.S. and Stokols, D. (eds) (2000) *Promoting Human Wellness: New Frontiers for Research Practice and Policy*, Berkeley, CA: University of California Press.

Janko, R. (1996) 'Ayios Stephanos: a Bronze Age village in Laconia', *Bulletin of the Institute of Classical Studies*, 41: 139 (summary of a paper read to the Mycenaean Seminar on 6 December 1995).

Jashemski, W.F. (1979) *The Gardens of Pompeii*, Vol.1, New Rochelle, NY: Caretzas Brothers.

—— (1993) *The Gardens of Pompeii*, Vol. 2, New Rochelle, NY: Caretzas Brothers.

—— (1999) *A Pompeian Herbal*, Austin, TX: University of Texas Press.

—— (2002) 'The Vesuvian sites before AD 79: the archaeological, literary and epigraphic evidence', in W.F. Jashemski and F.G. Meyer (eds) *The Natural History of Pompeii*, Cambridge: Cambridge University Press, 6–28.

Jashemski, W.F. and Meyer F.G. (2002) *The Natural History of Pompeii*, Cambridge: Cambridge University Press.

Jennings, S. (1990) *Dramatherapy with Families, Groups and Individuals Waiting in the Wings*, London: Jessica Kingsley Publishers.

Johnson, D.R. (1991) 'The theory and technique of transformations in drama therapy', *The Arts in Psychotherapy*, 18: 285–300.

Johnston, F.E. (1962) 'Growth of the long bones of infants and young children at Indian Knoll', *American Journal of Physical Anthropology*, 20(3): 249–54.

Jones, A.H. (1990) 'Literature and medicine: traditions and innovations', in B. Clark and W. Aycock (eds) *The Body and the Text: Comparative Essays in Literature and Medicine*, Lubbock, TX: Texas Tech University Press, 11–24.

Jones, C.P. (1998) 'Aelius Aristides and the Asclepicion' in H. Koester (ed.) *Pergamon: Citadel of the Gods: Archaeological Record, Literary Description, and Religious Development*, Harvard Theological Studies 46, Harrisburg, PA: Trinity Press, 63–76.

Jurmain, R.D. (1991) 'Paleoepidemiology of trauma in a prehistoric Central Californian population', in D. Ortner and A. Aufderheide (eds) *Human Paleopathology. Current Syntheses and Future Options*, Washington, DC: Smithsonian Institution Press, 241–8.

—— (1999) *Stories from the Skeleton. Behavioural Reconstruction in Human Osteology*, Amsterdam: Gordon and Breach.

Kalcyk, H., Neinrich, B. and Knauss, J. (1986) 'Die Melioration des Kopaisbeckens in Böotien', *Antike Welt*, 17: 15–38.

Kapchuk, T. (1983) *The Web That Has No Weaver: Understanding Chinese Medicine*, New York: Congdon and Weed.

Karali, L. (1987) *Assumetra xaraktiristika se krania Epoxis Xalkou, Klasikon kai Mesaionikon xronon, apo th sullogi tou Anthropologikou Mouseiou tou Panepistimiou Athinon* (Archive Paper), Athens: University Anthropological Museum.

Karali, L. (1999) *Shells in Aegean Prehistory*, British Archaeological Reports International Series 761.

Karali, L. and Tsaliki, A. (2000) 'Athens University: Projects of study and curation of organic archaeological remains', Poster presented at the British Association of Biological Anthropology and Osteoarchaeology 2nd Annual Conference, University of Bradford.

—— (2001a) 'Paleoanthropological remarks on skeletons from Neolithic Cyprus', in M. La Verghetta and L. Capasso (eds) *Proceedings of the XII European Meeting of the Paleopathology Association*, Chieti, Italy: Edigrafital S.p.A, 135–8.

—— (2001b) *Four chamber tombs at Audemou–Kamares, Cyprus (ca 2000–1700 BC) – Osteological analysis*, Ancient Cyprus web project (http://www.ancientcyprus. ac.uk/papers/audemouosteo.asp), date of access: 25/7/2003.

Karlen, A. (1996) *Plague's Progress*, London: Indigo (first published as (1995) *Man and Microbes: Diseases and Plagues in History and Modern Times*, New York: Jeremy P. Tarcher).

Karolyi, L. (1968) 'Das Trepanationsproblem. Beitrag zur Paläoanthropologie und Paläopathologie', *Homo*, 19: 90–3.

Katz, D. and Suchey, J.M. (1986) 'Age determination of the male *os pubis*', *American Journal of Physical Anthropology*, 69: 427–35.

Katzenberg, M.A. (2000) 'Stable isotope analysis: a tool for studying past diet, demography and life histories', in M.A. Katzenberg and S.R. Saunders (eds) *Biological Anthropology of the Human Skeleton*, New York: Wiley-Liss, 305–27.

Kearns, E. (1994) 'Cakes in Greek sacrifice regulations', in R. Hägg (ed.) *Ancient Greek Cult Practice from the Epigraphical Evidence*, Stockholm: Svenska Institutet i Athen Jonsered/P. Aström, 65–70.

Keats, T. (1988) *An Atlas of Normal Roentgen Variants that May Simulate Disease*, Chicago, IL: Yearbook Medical Publishers.

Kedem-Tahar, E. and Felix-Kellermann, P. (1996) 'Psychodrama and drama therapy: a comparison', *The Arts in Psychotherapy*, 23: 27–36.

Kees, H. (1986) *Medicine, Miracle and Magic in New Testament Times*, Cambridge and New York: Cambridge University Press.

Kellert, S.R. (1976) 'A sociocultural concept of health and illness', *Journal of Medicine and Philosophy*, 1: 222–8.

Kendall, D.E. (2002) *Dao of Chinese Medicine: Understanding an Ancient Healing Art*, Oxford: Oxford University Press.

Kennedy, K.A.R. (1989) 'Skeletal markers of occupational stress', in M.Y. İşcan and K.A.R. Kennedy (eds) *Reconstruction of Life from the Skeleton*, New York: Alan Liss, 129–60.

—— (1990) 'A life in science: J. Lawrence Angel as colleague and friend', in J.E. Buikstra (ed.) *A Life in Science: Papers in Honor of J.L. Angel*, Kampsville, IL: Center for American Archeology, Scientific Paper 6, 201–10.

Kent, S. (1986) 'The influence of sedentism and aggregation on porotic hyperostosis and anaemia: a case study', *Man*, 21: 605–36.

Kerényi, C. (1959) *Asklepios: Archetypal Image of the Physician's Existence*, trans. R. Manheim, New York: Pantheon Books.

King, H. (1995a) 'Medical texts as a source for women's history', in A. Powell (ed.) *The Greek World*, London and New York: Routledge, 199–218.

—— (1995b) 'Self-help, self-knowledge: in search of the patient in Hippocratic gynaecology', in R. Hawley and B. Levick (eds) *Women in Antiquity: New Assessments*, London and New York: Routledge, 135–48.

—— (1998) *Hippocrates' Woman: Reading the Female Body in Ancient Greece*, London and New York: Routledge.

—— (1999) 'Comparative perspectives on medicine and religion in the ancient world', in R. Porter and J. Hinnells (eds) *Religion, Health and Suffering*, London: Kegan Paul, 276–94.

—— (2001a) *Greek and Roman Medicine*, London: Bristol Classical Press.

—— (2001b) 'Recovering hysteria from history: Herodotus and "the first case of shell shock"', in P. Halligan, C. Bass and J. Marshall (eds) *Contemporary Approaches to the Study of Hysteria: Clinical and Theoretical Approaches*, Oxford: Oxford University Press, 36–48.

Kiple, K.F. (ed.) (1993) *The Cambridge World History of Human Disease*, Cambridge: Cambridge University Press.

Kirova, N. (2002) 'Specialized medical instruments from Bulgaria in the context of finds from other Roman provinces (I–IV c. AD)', *Archaeologia Bulgarica*, 6: 73–94.

Kleinman, A. (1980) *Patients and Healers in the Context of Culture: An Exploration of the Borderland between Anthropology, Medicine, and Psychiatry*, Berkeley, CA: University of California Press.

Klepinger, L. (1992) 'Innovative approaches to the study of past human health and subsistence strategies', in S.R. Saunders and M.A. Katzenberg (eds) *Skeletal Biology of Past Peoples: Research Methods*, New York: Wiley-Liss, Inc.

Knell, A.J. (ed.) (1991) *Malaria*, Oxford: Oxford University Press (for The Wellcome Trust).

Kolb, F. (1995) *Rom: die Geschichte der Stadt in der Antike*, Munich: C.H. Beck.

Konstantelos, D.J. (1985) 'Clerics and secular professions in the Byzantine Church', *Byzantina*, 13: 375–90.

Korpela, J. (1984) 'Fachärzte in der antiken Stadt Rom', *Hippokrates*, 1: 27–38.

—— (1987) *Das Medizinalpersonal im antiken Rom: eine sozialgeschichtliche Untersuchung*, Helsinki: Annales Academiae Scientiarum Fennicae Dissertationes Humanarum Litterarum 45.

Kotansky, R. (1991) 'Incantations and prayers for salvation on inscribed Greek amulets', in C.A. Faraone and D. Obbink (eds) *Magika Hiera: Ancient Greek Magic and Religion*, New York: Oxford University Press, 107–37.

Koumaris, J.G. (1930) 'The sagittal cranial index in Greek skulls', *Proceedings of the Greek Hellenic Society*, 7: 18–40.

—— (1931) 'Anthropological report on crania from the excavations at Aghios Kosmas' (preliminary report), *Proceedings of the Greek Anthropological Society*, 8: 45–53.

—— (1961) 'Le caractère autochthone du people Grec. Cahiers Ligures de Préhistoire et d'archéologie', *Sections Françaises de l'Institut International d'Études Ligures*, 10.

Kritzas, Ch.B. (1972) *Archaiologikon Deltion*, 27: 198–201 (Volume B'1 Chronika: Argos).

Kritzas, Ch.B. (1988) 'Health and diet in Minoan times', in R.E. Jones and H.W. Catling (eds) *New Aspects of Archaeological Science in Greece*, Occasional paper 3 of the Fitch Laboratory of the British School at Athens, Athens: British School at Athens, 47–54.

—— (1992) 'Part II: the burials', in B. Hallager and P.J.P. McGeorge, *Late Minoan III Burials at Khania*, Göteborg: Paul Åströms Förlag (SIMA XCII), 29–44.

Krogman, W.M. (1962) *The Human Skeleton in Forensic Medicine*, Springfield, IL: Charles C. Thomas.

Krug, A. (1985) *Heilkunst und Heilkult. Medizin in der Antike*, Munich: Beck.

—— (1992) 'Archive in Heiligtümern', in A. Krug (ed.) *From Epidauros to Salerno*, PACT 34/Journal of the European Study Group on Physical, Chemical, Biological and Mathematical Technology Applied to Archaeology, 187–200.

Krukof, S. (1971) 'Les ossements humains', *Bulletin de Correspondence Hellenique*, 95: 725–6.

Künzl, E. (1983) *Medizinische Instrumente aus Sepulkralfunden der römischen Kaiserzeit. Unter Mitarbeit von Franz Josef Hassel und Susanna Künzl* (Kunst und Altertum am Rhein 115, Köln und Bonn) = ibid., *Bonner Jahrbücher*, 182(1982): 1–131.

—— (1986) 'Operationsräume in römischen Thermen', *Bonner Jahrbücher*, 186: 491–509.

—— (1995) 'Medizin der Kelten. Ein archäologischer Forschungsbericht', in R. Bedon and P.M. Martin (eds) *Mélanges Raymond Chevallier. Vol. 2: Histoire et archéologie* Tome 2, Tours: Centres de Recherches A. Piganiol, 221–39.

—— (1996) 'Forschungsbericht zu den antiken medizinischen Instrumenten', in W. Haase and H. Temporini (eds) *Aufstieg und Niedergang der römischen Welt* (*ANRW*) II 37.3, Berlin and New York: Walter de Gruyter, 2433–9.

—— (1998) 'Instrumentenfunde und Ärzthäuser in Pompeii: Die medizinische Versorgung einer römischen Stadt des 1. Jahrhunderts n. Chr.', *Sartoniana*, 11: 71–152.

—— (2002) *Medizin in der Antike. Aus einer Welt ohne Narkose und Aspirin*, Stuttgart: Theiss.

Künzl, E. and Weber, T. (1991) 'Das spätantike Grab eines Zahnarztes zu Gadara in der Dekapolis', *Damaszener Mitteilungen*, 5: 81–118.

Kurtz, D.C. and Boardman, J. (1971) *Greek Burial Customs*, Ithaca, NY: Cornell University Press.

Laffineur, R. (ed.) (1987) *Thanatos: les coutumes funéraires en Égée à l'Âge du Bronze*, Liège: Aegaeum I.

Lagia, A. (1993) 'Differential diagnosis of the three main types of anaemia (thalassaemia, sickle cell anaemia and iron deficiency anaemia) based on macroscopic and radiographic skeletal characteristics', MSc thesis, University of Bradford.

—— (1997) 'Widespread skeletal manifestations of osteoblastic and of osteolytic metastatic carcinoma: evidence from two modern cases', paper presented at the Annual Meeting of the Paleopathology Association, St. Louis, MI.

—— (1999) 'Elements of everyday life. The human skeletal remains from Roman Tomb Nr 1 at the Kerameikos cemetery', *Athenische Mitteilungen*, 114: 291–303.

——— (2000) 'Kerameikos Grabung 1999. Preliminary analysis of the human skeletal remains', *Archäologische Anzeuger*, 3: 481–93.

——— (2002) 'Ramnous, the stone-cist burial Nr 8: mortuary behaviour in the light of the taphonomic and anthropological analysis', *Eulimene*, 3: 202–22.

Lagia, A. and Kontanis, E. (1997) 'The skeletal manifestations of acromegaly based on a modern case from the Wiener Laboratory Human Skeletal Collection', paper presented at the 4th Annual Meeting of the Midwest Bioarcheology and Forensic Anthropology Association, 4–5 October 1997, Chicago, IL.

Lagia, A. and Ruppenstein, F. (1999) 'Assessing community attitude from human skeletal remains: the burial of a child with a congenital anomaly of the spine from the Submycenean cemetery of Kerameikos', paper presented at the 26th Annual Meeting of the Paleopathology Association, Columbus, OH.

Lagia, A., Moraitis, K., Elipoulos, C. and Manolis, S. (2000) 'Sex and age determination from the skeleton: application and evaluation of modern methods in Greek populations', paper presented at the 22nd Panhellenic Conference of the Hellenic Association of Biological Sciences, Skiathos Island.

Landy, R.J. (1986) *Drama Therapy. Concepts and Practices*, Springfield, IL: Charles C. Thomas.

——— (1993) *Persona and Performance: The Meaning of Role in Drama Therapy and Everyday Life*, New York: Guilford Press.

Lang, M. (1977) *Cure and Care in Ancient Corinth*, Princeton, NJ: American School of Classical Studies.

Laskaris, J. (2002) *The Art is Long:* On the Sacred Disease *and the Scientific Tradition*, Leiden: E.J. Brill.

Laurence, R. (1994) *Roman Pompeii: Space and Society*, London and New York: Routledge.

——— (1997) 'Writing the Roman metropolis', in H. Parkins (ed.) *Roman Urbanism: Beyond the Consumer City*, London and New York: Routledge, 1–20.

——— (2000) 'Metaphors, monuments and texts: the life course in Roman culture', *World Archaeology*, 31: 442–55.

Leder, D. (1990) 'Illness and exile: Sophocles' *Philoctetes*', *Literature and Medicine*, 9: 1–11.

Lee, A.D. (2000) *Pagans and Christians in Late Antiquity: A Sourcebook*, London and New York: Routledge.

Leemans, C. (1842) 'Romeinse steenen doodkisten, bij Nijmegen in den zomer van 1840 opgedolven, en thans, met de daarin gevonden voorwerpen, bewaard in het museum van oudheden te Leijden', *Nijhoffs Bijdragen*, 235ff.

Leonard, J.R., Dunn, R.K. and Hohlfelder, R.L. (1998) 'Geoarchaeological Investigations in Paphos Harbor, 1996', *Report of the Department of Antiquities*, Cyprus, 141–57.

Leung, P.C. and Ooi, E.E. (eds) (2003) *Sars War: Combatting the Disease*, River Edge, NJ: World Scientific.

Levi, P. (1979) (trans.) *Pausanias' Guide to Greece*, 2 vols, Harmondsworth: Penguin Books.

Levitt, R. (1976) *The Reorganized National Health Service*, London: Croom Helm.

Lewis, M.E., Roberts, C.A. and Manchester, K. (1995) 'Comparative study of the prevalence of maxillary sinusitis in later Medieval urban and rural populations in Northern England', *American Journal of Physical Anthropology*, 98: 497–506.

Linders, T. and Nordquist, G. (eds) (1987) *Gifts to the Gods: Proceedings of the Uppsala Symposium 1985*, Uppsala: Academiae Uppsaliensis.

Lisowski, F.P. (1967) 'Prehistoric and early historic trepanation', in D. Brothwell and A.T. Sandison (eds) *Diseases in Antiquity*, Springfield, IL: Charles C. Thomas, 651–72.

Liston, M.A. (1993) 'The human skeletal remains from Kavoussi, Crete: a bioarchaeological analysis', PhD thesis, University of Tennessee, Knoxville, TN.

Little, L.M. and Papadopoulos, J.K. (1998) 'A social outcast in early Iron Age Athens', *Hesperia*, 67: 375–404.

Liversidge, M. and Edwards, C. (eds) (1996) *Imagining Rome: British Artists and Rome in the Nineteenth Century*, London: Merell Holberton.

Llewellyn-Jones, L. (2003) *Aphrodite's Tortoise: The Veiled Women of Ancient Greece*, Swansea: Classical Press of Wales.

Lloyd, G.E.R. (ed.) (1978) *Hippocratic Writings*, Harmondsworth and New York: Penguin.

—— (1987) *The Revolutions of Wisdom*, Berkeley, CA: University of California Press.

—— (2003) *In the Grip of Disease: Studies in the Greek Imagination*, Oxford: Oxford University Press.

Lochin, C. (1990) s.v. 'Hypnos/Somnus', in *Lexicon iconographicum mythologiae classicae* V, Zürich and Munich: Artemis Verlag, 591–609.

Longmore, P.K. and Umansky, L. (eds) (2001a) *The New Disability History: American Perspectives*, New York: New York University Press.

—— (2001b) 'Introduction: disability history: from the margins to the mainstream', in P.K. Longmore and L. Umansky (eds) (2001a) *The New Disability History: American Perspectives*, New York: New York University Press, 1–29.

Longrigg, J. (1992) 'Epidemics, ideas and classical Athenian society', in T. Ranger and P. Slack (eds) *Epidemics and Ideas: Essays on the Historical Perception of Pestilence*, Cambridge: Cambridge University Press, 21–44.

—— (1993) *Greek Rational Medicine: Philosophy and Medicine from Alcmaeon to the Alexandrians*, London and New York: Routledge.

—— (1998) *Greek Medicine from the Heroic to the Hellenistic Age: A Source Book*, London: Duckworth.

Lonie, I.M. (1977) 'A structural pattern in Greek dietetics and the early history of Greek medicine', *Medical History*, 21: 235–60.

Lopez-Ferez, J.A. (1988) 'L'animal dans l'alimentation humaine selon Galien', in L. Bodson (ed.) *Anthropozoologica: L'animal dans l'alimentation humaine. Les critères de choix*, Paris: Musée d'Histoire Naturelle, 91–4.

Loraux, N. (1978) 'Sur la race des femmes et quelques–unes de ses tribus', *Arethusa*, 11, 43–87; English, 1993, in *The Children of Athena: Athenian Ideas about Citizenship and the Division between the Sexes*, trans. C. Levine, Princeton, NJ: Princeton University Press.

—— (1995) *The Experiences of Tiresias: The Feminine and the Greek Man*, trans. P. Wissing, Princeton, NJ: Princeton University Press.

Loukopoulos, D., Hadji, A., Papadakis, M., Karababa, P., Sinopoulou, K., Boussiou, M., Kollia, P., Xenakis, M., Antsaklis, A. and Mesoghitis, S. (1990) 'Prenatal diagnosis of thalassemia and of the sickle cell syndromes in Greece', *Annals of the New York Academy of Sciences*, 612: 226–36.

Lovejoy, C.O. and Heiple, K.G. (1981) 'Analysis of fractures in a skeletal population with an example from the Libben site, Ottawa County, Ohio', *American Journal of Physical Anthropology*, 55: 529–41.

Lovell, N.C. (1997) 'Anaemia in the ancient Indus Valley', *International Journal of Osteoarchaeology*, 7: 115–23.

McFalls, J.A. and McFalls, M.H. (1984) *Disease and Fertility*, Orlando, FL: Academic Press, Inc.

McGeorge, P.J.P. (1987) 'Biosocial evolution in Bronze Age Crete', in *EILAPINĒ: Tomos timē tikos gia ton Kathēgētē Nikolao Platōna*, Heraklion: Bikelaia Bibliotheke, 406–16.

—— (1988) 'Health and diet in Minoan times', in R.E. Jones and H.W. Catling (eds) *New Aspects of Archaeological Science in Greece. Proceedings of a Meeting held at the British School at Athens, January 1987*, Athens: British School at Athens, Occasional Paper 3 of the Fitch laboratory, 47–54.

—— (1990) 'A comparative study of the mean life expectation of the Minoans', *Pepragmena tou 6th Diethnous Krētolikou Eunedpiou (Chania 1986)*, Chania, Philologikos Sullogos 'O Chrysostomos', 419–28.

—— (1992) 'Part II: The burials' and 'Conclusion', in B.P. Hallager and P.J.P. McGeorge (eds) *Late Minoan III Burials at Khania. The Tombs, Finds and Deceased in Odos Palama*, Studies in Mediterranean Archaeology Vol. 92, Goteborg: Paul A. Stroms Forlag, 29–47.

McGuckin, J.A. (1993) 'The influence of the Isis cult on St. Cyril of Alexandria's Christology', *Studia Patristica*, 24: 291–9.

—— (1994) *St. Cyril of Alexandria: The Christological Controversy*, Leiden: E.J. Brill.

McKeown, T. (1988) *The Origins of Human Disease*, Oxford: Blackwell.

McKinley, J. and Roberts, C.A. (1993) *Excavation and Post-excavation Treatment of Cremated and Inhumed Human Remains*, Birmingham: Institute of Field Archaeologists Technical Paper 13.

McNeal, R.A. (ed.) (1986) *Herodotus, Book 1*, Lanham, MD: University Press of America.

McNeill, W.H. (1977) *Plagues and Peoples*, Oxford: Blackwell.

McNiff, S. (1992) *Arts as Medicine: Creating a Therapy of the Imagination*, Boston, MA and London: Shambhala.

Magou, H., Panagiaris, G., Manolis, S. and Zafeiratos, C. (1997) 'Identification of chemical elements in excavated human bones of ancient cemeteries from Greece', *Physical, Archaeometric and Chemical Techniques Applied to Archaeology*, 45: 97–110.

Magoulias, H.J. (1964) 'The Lives of the Saints as sources of data for the study of Byzantine medicine in the sixth and seventh centuries', *Byzantinische Zeitschrift*, 57: 127–50.

Majno, G. (1975) *The Healing Hand: Man and Wound in the Ancient World*, Cambridge, MA and London: Harvard University Press.

Malama, P. and Triantaphyllou, S. (2003) 'Anthropologikes plirofories apo to anatoliko nekrotafeio Amfipolis', *Archaeologoko Ergo Stin Mekdonia Kai Thrakis*, 15 (2001): 127–36.

Malamis, G. and Manolis, S.K. (1994) 'Genetic history of the European populations and inherited diseases', *Proceedings of the 16th Conference of the Greek Society of the Biological Sciences*, 10: 35–9.

Manchester, K. (1992) 'The palaeopathology of urban infections', in S. Bassett (ed.) *Death in Towns: Urban Responses to the Dying and Dead, 100–1600*, Leicester: Leicester University Press, 8–14.

Manginis, G., Karali, L., Tsaliki, A. and Vavouranakis, G. (2001) 'An interdisciplinary approach towards burial practices in Prehistoric Bronze Age Cyprus: artifactual and osteological material from Audemou-Kamares', poster presented at the British Association of Biological Anthropology and Osteoarchaeology 3rd Annual Conference, University of Durham.

Manolis, S.K. (1991a) 'Anthropological research on the composition of Bronze Age populations from Southern Greece', PhD thesis, University of Athens.

—— (1991b) 'Area of Kandou-Alassa (Cyprus) Anthropological study. Appendix', in P. Flourentzos (ed.) *Excavations in the Kouris Valley I. The Tombs*, published for the Republic of Cyprus by the Department of Antiquities, Cyprus, 67–8.

—— (1996) 'The Hellenic late Pleistocene fossils', *Anthropologie*, 34: 89–97.

Manolis, S.K. and Mallegni, F.F. (1996) 'The Gravettian fossil hominids of Italy', *Anthropologie*, 34: 99–108.

Manolis, S.K. and Neroutos, A.A. (1997) 'The Middle Bronze Age burial of Kolona at Aegina island, Greece: study of the human skeletal remains, Appendix 1', in I. Kilian-Dirlmeier (ed.) *Das Mittelbronzezeitliche Schachtgrab von Ägina*, Rhein: Verlag Philipp Von Zabern-Mainz, 169–75.

Manolis, S.K., Papagrigorakis, M. and Zafeiratos, C. (1994) 'Trepanations in Greece: observations on a mid-Bronze Age skull', *Homo*, 45 (Supplement): 80.

Manolis, S.K., Neroutos, A., Zafeiratos, C. and Daponte, A. (1995) 'Secular changes in body formation of Greek students', *Human Evolution*, 10: 199–204.

Marganne-Mélard, M.-H. (1987) 'Les instruments chirurgicaux de l'Égypte gréco-romaine', in *Archéologie et médecine: Actes du colloque 23–24–25 octobre 1986*, CNRS, Mus. Arch. d'Antibes: Juan-les-Pins, 403–12.

—— (1994) *L'ophthalmologie dans l'Égypte gréco-romaine d'après les papyrus littéraires grecs*, Leiden: E.J. Brill.

—— (1998) *La chirurgie dans l'Égypte gréco-romaine d'après les papyrus littéraires grecs*, Studies in Ancient Medicine, no. 17, Leiden: E.J. Brill.

Margetts, E.L. (1967) 'Trepanation of the skull by the medicine-men of primitive cultures', in D. Brothwell and A.T. Sandison (eds) *Diseases in Antiquity*, Springfield, IL: Charles C. Thomas, 673–701.

Mariani-Costantini, R., Catalano, P., di Gennaro, F., di Tota, G. and Angeletti, L.R. (2000) 'New light on cranial surgery in ancient Rome', *The Lancet*, 355: 305–7.

Martin, P.R. (1997) *The Healing Mind. The Vital Links between Brain and Behavior, Immunity, and Disease*, New York: St. Martin's.

Marx, K. and Engels, F. (1980) *Collected Works*, Vol. XIV, London: Lawrence and Wishart.

Mascaro, J. (1962) (trans.) *The Bhagavad Gita*, London: Penguin Books.

Maxmin, J. (1974) '*Euphronios epoiesen*: portrait of the artist as a presbyopic potter', *Greece and Rome*, 21: 178–80.

Mazzini, I. (1994) 'La chirurgia celsiana nella storia della chirurgia Greco-romana', in G. Sabbah and Ph. Mudry (eds) *La Médecine de Celse: aspects historiques, scientifiques et littéraires*, St. Étienne: Centre Jean Palerne, *Mémoires* XIII: 135–66.

Mechanic, D. (1968) *Medical Sociology: A Selective View*, New York: Free Press.

Meier, C.A. (1967) *Ancient Incubation and Modern Psychotherapy*, trans. M. Curtis, Evanston, IL: Northwestern University Press.

Merbs, C. (1983) *Patterns of Activity Induced Pathology in a Canadian Inuit Population*, Ottawa, ON: National Museums of Canada.

Meyer, F.G. (1988) 'Food plants identified from carbonized remains at Pompeii and other Vesuvian sites', in R.I. Curtis (ed.) *Studia Pompeiana et Classica*, Vol. 1, New Rochelle, NY: Caratzas, 183–230.

Michaelides, D. (1984) 'A Roman surgeon's tomb from Nea Paphos', *Report of the Department of Antiquities*, Nicosia, Cyprus, 315–32.

Michler, M. (1969) *Das Spezialisierungsproblem und die antike Chirurgie*, Bern-Stuttgart-Vienna: Verlag Hans Huber.

Mikalson, J.D. (1998) *Religion in Hellenistic Athens*, Berkeley, CA: University of California Press.

Milne, J.S. (1907) *Surgical Instruments in Greek and Roman Times*, Oxford: Clarendon Press, repr. Chicago, IL: Ares Publishers Inc. 1976.

Minchev, A. (1983) 'Roman medicine in Marcianopolis', in *Concilium Eirene XVI, Proceedings of the 16th International Eirene Conference Prague 1982*, Prague: Kabinet pro studia řecká, řimská a latinská CSAV, 143–8.

Mitchell, D.T. and Snyder, S.L. (eds) (1997) *The Body and Physical Difference: Discourses on Disability*, Ann Arbor, MI: University of Michigan Press.

Mitchell, F.W. (1970) *Lykourgan Athens: 338–322* (*Lectures in Memory of Louise Taft Semple*, 2nd series), Cincinnati, OH: University of Cincinnati.

Mitropoulou, E. (2001) *Latreia Asklepiou kai Hygeias sten Arkadia*, Athens: Georgiades.

Mol, A. and Berg, M. (1994) 'Principles and practice of medicine: the co-existence of various anemias', *Culture, Medicine and Psychiatry*, 18: 247–65.

Montserrat, D. (ed.) (1998) *Changing Bodies, Changing Meanings: Studies on the Human Body in Antiquity*, London and New York: Routledge.

Moore, P. (1565) *The Hope of Health*, London: J. Kingston.

Moore-Jansen, P. and Jantz, R.L. (1989) *A Data Base for Forensic Anthropology: Structure, Content and Analysis*, Report of Investigations No. 47, Knoxville, TN: University of Tennessee, Department of Anthropology.

Moraitis, K. (1998) 'The use of modern forensic principles to understand animal scavenging activity and disposal of human bones from the Late Bronze Age settlement at Runnymede Bridge, UK', MSc thesis, Department of Archaeological Sciences, University of Bradford.

Moraitis, K. and Koutselinis, A. (2000) 'Animal scavenging activity of human bones and mortuary practices in the late bronze Age settlement at Runnymede Bridge, UK', paper presented at the International Archaeological Symposium on Mediterranean burial practices and traditions from 1100 BC to AD 400, Rhodes, Greece.

Moraitis, K., Spiliopoulou, C. and Koutselinis, A. (2000) 'Forensic anthropology: a new scientific branch in the service of justice', *Police Review*, December 2000: 756–9 (in Greek).

Moraux, P. (1985) *Galien de Pergame, Souvenirs d'un médecin*, Paris: Les Belles Lettres.

Morley, N. (1996) *Metropolis and Hinterland: The City of Rome and the Italian Economy 200 BC–AD 200*, Cambridge: Cambridge University Press.

—— (1997) 'Cities in context: urban systems in Roman Italy', in H.M. Parkins (ed.) *Roman Urbanism: Beyond the Consumer City*, London and New York: Routledge, 42–58.

—— (2003) 'Migration and the metropolis', in C. Edwards and G. Woolf (eds) *Rome the Cosmopolis*, Cambridge: Cambridge University Press, 147–57.

Morris, I. (1987) *Burial and Ancient Society: The Rise of the Greek City State*, Cambridge: Cambridge University Press.

—— (1992) *Death-ritual and Social Structure in Classical Antiquity*, Cambridge: Cambridge University Press.

Moseley, J.E. (1965) 'The palaeopathologic riddle of symmetrical osteoporosis', *American Journal of Roentgenology, Radium Therapy and Nuclear Medicine*, 95: 135–42.

Motulsky, A.G. (1960) 'Polymorphisms and infectious diseases in human evolution', *Human Evolution*, 32: 28–62.

Mudry, P. (1985) 'Médecins et spécialistes. Le problème de l'unité de la médecine à Rome au premier siècle ap. J.–C.', *Gesnerus*, 42: 329–36.

Murray, J.E. (2003) 'Social insurance claims as morbidity estimates: sickness or absence?', *Social History of Medicine*, 16: 225–45.

Musgrave, J.H. (1976a) 'A new figured crater from Knossos. Appendix: the human remains from Tekke Tomb "E", Heraklion, Crete', *Annual of the British School at Athens*, 71: 126–9.

—— (1976b) 'The human remains from an early Christian osteotheke at Knossos. Appendix A: the human remains', *Annual of the British School at Athens*, 71: 40–6.

—— (1980a) 'The human remains from the cemeteries. Appendix C', in M.R. Popham, K.H. Sackett and P.G. Themelis (eds) *Lefkandi 1: the Iron Age*, B.S.A. Supplement 11, London: Thames and Hudson, 429–46.

—— (1980b) 'By strangers honor'd: a statistical study of ancient crania from Crete, Mainland Greece, Cyprus, Israel and Egypt', *Journal of Mediterranean Anthropology, and Archaeology*, 1: 50–107.

—— (1985) 'The skull of Philip II of Macedon', in S.J.W. Linsey and B. Matthews (eds) *Current Topics in Oral Biology*, Bristol: University of Bristol Press, 1–16.

—— (1990) 'The cremated remains from Tombs II and III at Nea Mihaniona and Tomb Beta at Derveni', *Annual of the British School at Athens*, 85: 301–25.

Musgrave, J.H. and Popham, M. (1991) 'The Late Helladic IIIc intramural burials at Lefkandi, Euboea', *Annual of the British School at Athens*, 86: 273–96.

Narrigan, D., Zones, J.S., Worcester, N. and Grad, M.J. (1997) 'Research to improve women's health: an agenda for equity', in S.B. Ruzek, V.L. Olesen and A.E. Clarke (eds) *Women's Health: Complexities and Differences*, Columbus, OH: Ohio State University Press, 551–79.

Nathanson, C.A. (1975) 'Illness and the feminine role', *Social Science and Medicine*, 9: 57–62.

Nightingale, F. (1860) *Notes on Nursing*, London: Harrison, republished 1969, Appleton-Century-Crofts, USA.

Nordenfelt, L. (1993) 'Concepts of health and their consequences for health care', *Theoretical Medicine*, 14: 277–85.

Nutton, V. (1985) 'Murders and miracles: lay attitudes towards medicine in classical antiquity', in R. Porter (ed.) *Patients and Practitioners. Lay Perceptions of Medicine in Pre-industrial Society*, Cambridge: Cambridge University Press, 23–53.

—— (1992) 'Healers in the medical market place: towards a social history of Graeco-Roman medicine', in A. Wear (ed.) *Medicine in Society. Historical Essays*, Cambridge: Cambridge University Press, 15–58.

—— (1993) 'Roman medicine: tradition, confrontation, assimilation', in W. Haase and H. Temporini (eds) *Aufstieg und Niedergang der römischen Welt* (*ANRW*) II 37. 1. Berlin and New York: Walter de Gruyter, 49–78.

—— (1995a) 'Galen and the traveller's fare', in J. Wilkins, D. Harvey and M. Dobson (eds) *Food in Antiquity*, Exeter: Exeter University Press, 359–70.

—— (1995b) 'The medical meeting place', in Ph.J. Van der Eijk, H.F.J. Horstmanshoff and P.H. Schrijvers (eds) *Ancient Medicine in its Socio-cultural Context*, Vol. 1, Leiden: E.J. Brill (= Clio Medica 27), 3–25.

—— (2000) 'Medical thoughts on urban pollution', in V.M. Hope and E. Marshall (eds) *Death and Disease in the Ancient City*, London and New York: Routledge, 65–73.

Oberhelman, S.M. (1990) 'The Hippocratic Corpus and Greek Religion', in B. Clark, and W. Aycock (eds) *The Body and the Text: Comparative Essays in Literature and Medicine*, Lubbock, TX: Texas Tech University Press, 141–60.

Olson, S.D. and Sens, A. (2000) *Archestratos of Gela*, Oxford: Oxford University Press.

Oriente, P., Del Puente, A., Lorizio, R. and Brunetti, A. (2001) 'Studio della densità minerale ossea negli scheltri di età romana rinvenuti in Pompei nella casa di Polibio', in A. Ciarallo and E. De Cariolis (eds) *La casa di Giulio Polibio: studi interdisciplinari*, Tokyo: University of Tokyo, 107–10.

Ortalli, J. (2000) 'Rimini: La domus "del chirurgo"', in M. Marini Calvani, R. Curina and E. Lippolis (eds) *Aemilia: La cultura romana in Emilia Romagna dal III secolo a. C. all' età costantiniana*, Bologna: Marsilio, 512–26.

—— (2003) 'Rimini archeologica/The archaeology of Rimini', in L. Braccesi (ed.) *Rimini imperiale (II–III secolo)/Rimini in the Roman Empire (II–III centuries)*, Rimini: Musei Comunali Rimini, Le Guide/I, 69–116.

Ortner, D.J. and Putschar, W.G.J. (1981) *Identification of Pathological Conditions in Human Skeletal Remains*, Washington, DC: Smithsonian Institution Press.

Ortner, D.J. and Kelley, J.O. (1988) 'J. Lawrence Angel (1915–1986)', *American Anthropologist*, 90: 145–8.

Owens, E.J. (1991) *The City in the Greek and Roman World*, London and New York: Routledge.

Packer, J. (1971) *The Insulae of Imperial Ostia and Rome* (MAAR 31), Rome: American Academy at Rome.

Paidoussis, M. and Sbarounis, C.N. (1975) 'A study of the cremated bones from the cemetery of Perati (LH IIIC)', *Opuscula Atheniensa*, 11: 129–59.

—— (1979) 'Meleti epi oston kauseos ek tou nekrotafeiou tis Peratis', *Praktikia tis Ellinikis Anthropologikis Etaireias*, 48: 1–54.

Panagiaris, G., Hassiacou, A. and Manolis, S.K. (1997) 'The ecological influence on human microevolution and culture: a study of Ancient Greek populations around Mount Pindos', in A. Sinclair, E. Slater and J. Gowlett (eds) *Archaeological Sciences 1995. Proceedings of a Conference on the Application of Scientific Techniques to the Study of Archaeology, Liverpool*, Oxford: Oxbow Monograph 64, 369–76.

Pandermalis, D. (1997) *Dion, The Archaeological Site and the Museum* [Site Guide], Athens: Adam Editions.

Papadopoulos, J.K. (2000) 'Skeletons in wells: towards an archaeology of social exclusion in the ancient Greek world', in J. Hubert (ed.) *Madness, Disability and Social Exclusion. The Archaeology and Anthropology of Difference*, London and New York: One World Archaeology, 96–118.

Papagregorakis, M. and Syropoulos, M. (1988) 'Cephalometric findings of the skull of the Petrolana man', *Anthropologica Analecta*, 49: 47–53.

Papathanasiou, A. (2001a) 'Health and subsistence of a Neolithic population: a case study from Aleptrypa Cave, Greece', paper presented at the 70th Annual Meeting of the American Association of Physical Anthropologists, Oakland, California.

—— (2001b) *A Bioarchaeological Analysis of Neolithic Alepotrypa Cave, Greece*, British Archaeological Reports, International Series 961.

Papathanasiou, A., Larsen, C.S. and Norr, L. (1995) 'A bioarchaeological analysis of a Neolithic ossuary from Alepotrypa Cave, Diros, Greece', paper presented at the 64th Annual Meeting of the American Association of Physical Anthropologists, Oakland, California.

—— (2000) 'Bioarchaeological inferences from a Neolithic ossuary from Alepotrypa Cave, Diros, Greece', *International Journal of Osteoarchaeology*, 10: 210–28.

Pappa, M., Valamoti, T., Gerousi, T., Lachanidou, N., Skourtopoulou, K. and Triantaphyllou, S. (1998) 'Neolithikos oikismos Makrigialou: Prota apotelesmata tis meletis ton anthropinion oston', *Archaeologiko Ergo tin Macedonia ke Thraki*, 10: 239–77.

Parham, S.F. (1990) 'Philoctetes' wound', *Literature and Medicine*, 9: 12–20.

Parke, H.W. (1977) *Festivals of the Athenians*, Ithaca, NY: Cornell University Press.

Parker, R. (1996) *Athenian Religion: A History*, Oxford: Clarendon Press.

Parkin, T.G. (1992) *Demography and Roman Society*, Baltimore, MD: John Hopkins University Press.

Patrick, A. (1967) 'Disease in antiquity: Greece and Rome', in D. Brothwell and A.T. Sandison (eds) *Diseases in Antiquity*, Springfield, IL: Charles C. Thomas, 238–46.

Pendzik, S. (1994) 'The theatre stage and the sacred space: a comparison', *The Arts in Psychotherapy*, 21: 25–35.

Perlès, C. (2001) *The Early Neolithic in Greece*, Cambridge: Cambridge University Press.

Peters, D. (ed.) (2001) *Understanding the Placebo Effect in Complementary Medicine: Theory, Practice and Research*, Edinburgh: Churchill Livingstone.

Petracos, B.C. (1995) *The Amphiareion of Oropos* [Site Guide], Athens: Clio Editions.

Pierret, J. (1993) 'Constructing discourses about health and their social determinants', in A. Radley (ed.) *Worlds of Illness. Biographical and Cultural Perspectives on Health and Disease*, London and New York: Routledge, 9–26.

Pike, S. (1997) 'The Wiener laboratory', *Paleopathology Association Newsletter*, 100: 8–9.

Pitsios, Th. (1978) *Anthropological Study of the People of the Peloponnese: The Origin of Peloponnesians*, Athens: Library of the Anthropological Society of Greece 2.

—— (1979) 'Paleoanthropological finds of Inner Mani', *Anthropos*, 6: 98–105.

—— (1985) 'Paleoanthropological research in the site of Apidima of Mesa Mani II', *Archaeologia*, 15: 26–33.

—— (1993) 'Educational research content of physical anthropology', *Anthropologia*, 1: 33–41.

—— (1994) 'The museum of anthropology at the University of Athens: history and reconstruction of the museum', *Anthropologia*, 2: 5–17.

Pitsios, Th. and Liebhaber, B. (1995) 'Research conducted at the site of Apidima and the surrounding region – Taenarios man', *Acta Anthropologica*, 1: 175–9.

Polunin, I. (1977) 'The body as an indicator of health and disease', in J. Blacking (ed.) *The Anthropology of the Body*, London and New York: Academic Press, 85–98.

Porter, R. (1985) *Patients and Practitioners: Lay Perceptions of Medicine in Pre-industrial Society*, Cambridge: Cambridge University Press.

Potter, P., Maloney, G. and Desautels, J. (eds) (1990) *La Maladie et les Maladies dans la Collection hippocratique, Actes du VIe colloque internationale hippocratique*, Quebec: Editions du Sphinx.

Poulianos, A.N. (1967) 'Isterominoikon kranion ek tou tafou "H" Katsamba', in S. Alexiou (ed.) *Isterminoikiou tafoi Limenos Knossou (Katsamba)*, Athens: Vivliotheki tis en Athinais Arkhaiologikis Etaireias No. 56, 84–5.

—— (1968) *The Origins of the Greeks*, Athens: Morfosi.

—— (1971a) *The Origin of the People of Crete*, Athens: Vivliotheke Anthropologikis Etaireias (No. 1).

—— (1971b) 'Petralona. A Middle Pleistocene cave in Greece', *Archaeology*, 24: 6–11.

—— (1976) *Arcanthropus Europaeus Petraloniensis*, Université de Bordeaux: Colloque de Taxonomie Anthropologique, Bordeaux.

—— (1977) 'The most ancient (known to date) traces of fire used by man in Petralona (preliminary study)', *Anthropos*, 4: 144–6.

—— (1983a) 'On the stratigraphy and dating of Petralonian Man', *Anthropos*, 10: 49–52.

—— (1983b) 'Faunal and tool distribution in the layers of the Petralona Cave', *Journal of Human Evolution*, 12: 743–6.

Powell, J.E. (1989) 'Metric versus non-metric skeletal traits. Which is the more reliable indicator of genetic distance? With special reference to crania from ancient Greece and Egypt', PhD thesis, University of Bristol.

Powell, O. (2003) *Galen: On the Properties of Foodstuffs*, Cambridge: Cambridge University Press.

Prag, A.J.N.W., Musgrave, J.H. and Neave, R.A.H. (1984) 'The skulls from Tomb II at Verginia. King Philip of Macedon', *Journal of Helladic Studies*, 104: 60–78.

Preka-Alexandri, K. (1988) 'Anthropologiki proseggisi taphikon envrimaton Kerkiras', *Anthropologika Analekta ex Athinon*, 49: 55–64.

Priestley, M. (ed.) (2001) *Disability and the Life Course: Global Perspectives*, Cambridge: Cambridge University Press.

Pullen, D.J. (1985) 'Social organization in early Bronze Age Greece: a multidimensional approach', PhD thesis, University of Indiana.

—— (1990) 'Early Helladic burials at Asine and early Bronze Age mortuary practices', in R. Hägg and G.C. Nordquist (eds) *Celebrations of Death and Divinity in the Bronze Age Argolid*, Proceedings of the 6th International Symposium of the Swedish Institute of Athens, 11–13 June, 1988, Stockholm: Svenska Institutet, 9–12.

Pulleyn, S. (1997) *Prayer in Greek Religion*, Oxford: Clarendon Press.

Purcell, N. (1987) 'Town in country and country in town', in E.B. MacDougall (ed.) *Ancient Roman Villa Gardens*, Washington, DC: Dumbarton Oaks, 187–203.

Raban, J. (1974) *Soft City*, London: Fontana.

Ranger, T. and Slack, P. (eds) (1992) *Epidemics and Ideas: Essays on the Historical Perception of Pestilence*, Cambridge: Cambridge University Press.

Raviglione, M.C., Snider, D.E. and Kochi, A. (1995) 'Global epidemiology of tuberculosis. Morbidity and mortality of a worldwide epidemic', *Journal of the American Medical Association*, 273: 220–6.

Reckford, K.J. (1998) 'Reading the sick body: decomposition and morality in Persius' Third Satire', *Arethusa*, 31: 337–54.

Resnick, D. (1995) *Diagnosis of Bone and Joint Disorders*, London: W.B. Saunders.

Richardson, B.E. (1993) *Old Age among the Ancient Greeks*, Baltimore, MD: Johns Hopkins University Press.

Riddle, J.M. (1992) *Contraception and Abortion from the Ancient World to the Renaissance*, Cambridge, MA: Harvard University Press.

—— (1997) *Eve's Herbs: A History of Contraception and Abortion in the West*, Cambridge, MA: Harvard University Press.

Riley, F.R. (1999) *The Role of the Traditional Mediterranean Diet in the Development of Minoan Crete*, Oxford: British Archaeological Reports (International Series S810).

Riley, J.C. (1997) *Sick, not Dead: The Health of British Working Men during the Mortality Decline*, Baltimore, MD and London: Johns Hopkins University Press.

Roberts, C.A. and Manchester, K. (1995) *The Archaeology of Disease*, Gloucester: Sutton Publishing and Ithaca, NY: Cornell University Press.

Roberts, C.A. and Cox, M. (2003) *Health and Disease in Britain. Prehistory to the Present Day*, Gloucester: Sutton Publishing.

Roberts, C.A. and McKinley, J. (2003) 'Review of trepanations in British antiquity focusing on funerary context to explain their occurrence', in R. Arnott, S. Finger and C.U.M. Smith (eds) *Trepanation: History, Discovery, Theory*, Lisse: Swets and Zeitlinger, 55–78.

Roberts, C.A., Lewis, M.E. and Boocock, P. (1998) 'Infectious disease, sex and gender. The complexity of it all!', in A. Grauer and P. Stuart-Macadam (eds) *Sex and Gender in Paleopathological Perspective*, Cambridge, Cambridge University Press, 93–113.

Robertson, N. (1996) 'Athena's shrines and festivals', in J. Neils (ed.) *Worshipping Athena: Panathenaia and Parthenon*, Madison, WI: University of Wisconsin Press, 27–77.

Robinson, O.F. (1992) *Ancient Rome: City Planning and Administration*, London and New York: Routledge.

Rocca, J. (2003) 'Galen and the uses of trepanation', in R. Arnott, S. Finger and C.U.M. Smith (eds) *Trepanation: History, Discovery, Theory*, Lisse: Swets and Zeitlinger, 253–71.

Rogers, J. and Waldron, T.W. (1995) *A Field Guide to Joint Disease in Archaeology*, Chichester, England: John Wiley & Sons.

Rogers, L. (1930) 'The history of craniotomy: an account of the methods which have been practiced and the instruments used for opening the human skull during life', *Annals of Medical History*, N.S. 2(5): 495–514.

Rogers, L.J. and Swadener, B.B. (eds) (2001) *Semiotics and Dis/ability: Interrogating Categories of Difference*, Albany, NY: State University of New York Press.

Romano, I.B. (1988) 'Early Greek cult images and cult practices', in R. Hägg, N. Marinatos and G.C. Nordquist (eds) *Early Greek Cult Practice*, Stockholm: Svenska Institutet i Athen Jonsered/P. Aström, 127–34.

Rose, J.C., Anton, S.C., Aufderheide, A.C., Eisenberg, L., Gregg, J.B., Neiburger, E.J. and Rothschild, B. (1991) *Skeletal Database Committee Recommendations*, Detroit, MI: Paleopathology Association, 1–12.

Rothaus, R.M. (2000) *Corinth: The First City of Greece. An Urban History of Late Antique Cult and Religion*, Leiden: E.J. Brill.

Runco, M.A. and Richards, R. (eds) (1997) *Eminent Creativity, Everyday Creativity, and Health*, Greenwich, CT: Ablex Publishers.

Ruzek, S.B., Olesen, V.L. and Clarke, A.E. (1997) *Women's Health: Complexities and Differences*, Columbus, OH: Ohio State University Press.

St Hoyme, L.E. (1988) 'Obituary: J. L. Angel, 1915–1986', *American Journal of Physical Anthropology*, 75: 291–301.

Salas, J. (1996) *Improvising Real Life*, 2nd edition, Dubuque, IA: Kendall/Hunt.

Sallares, R. (1991) *The Ecology of the Ancient Greek World*, London: Duckworth.

——(2002) *Malaria and Rome: A History of Malaria in Ancient Italy*, Oxford: Oxford University Press.

Saller, R.P. (1994) *Patriarchy, Property and Death in the Roman Family*, Cambridge: Cambridge University Press.

Salo, W.L., Aufderheide, A., Buikstra, J.E. and Holcomb, T.A. (1994) 'Identification of *M. tuberculosis* DNA in a pre-Columbian mummy', *Proceedings of the National Academy of Science*, 91: 2091–4.

Saltonstall, R. (1993) 'Healthy bodies, social bodies', *Social Science and Medicine*, 36: 7–14.

Samuels, M. and Lane, M.R. (1998) *Creative Healing. How to Heal Yourself by Tapping Your Hidden Creativity*, San Francisco, CA: HarperCollins.

Saponetti, Sublimi S., Scattarella, V. and Volpe, G. (1998) 'Cranial trepanation in an individual of the Hellenistic age (III century BC) from the necropolis of Contrada Santo Stefano (Gravina, Bari, Italy)', *Journal of Palaeopathology*, 10(3): 121–5.

Sassatelli, R. (2003) 'Beyond health and beauty: a critical perspective on fitness culture', in G. Boswell and F. Poland (eds) *Women's Minds, Women's Bodies: Interdisciplinary Approaches to Women's Health*, Basingstoke and New York: Palgrave Macmillan, 77–88.

Satapati, P.R. (1988) *Rehabilitation of the Disabled in Developing Countries*, Frankfurt am Main: AFRA-Verlag.

Savage-Smith, E. (1984) 'Hellenistic and Byzantine ophthalmology: trachoma and sequelae', *Dumbarton Oaks Papers*, 38: 169–86.

Scarborough, J. (1970) 'Diphilus of Siphnos and Hellenistic medical dietetics', *Journal of the History of Medicine and Allied Sciences*, 25: 194–201.

—— (1993) 'Roman medicine to Galen', in W. Haase and H. Temporini (eds) *Aufstieg und Niedergang der römischen Welt (ANRW)* II 37. 1, Berlin and New York: Walter de Gruyter, 3–48.

Scattarella, V., Saponetti, Sublimi S., Cuscianna, N. and Gattullis, A. (1996) 'A case of skull trephination from late Imperial Rome', *Journal of Paleopathology*, 8: 85–8.

Schachter, A. (1986–94) *Cults of Boiotia (BICS Supplement* 38), London: Institute of Classical Studies.

Schadewaldt, H. (1970) 'Schädeltrepanation in Africa', *Medizinhistorisches Journal*, 5: 289–98.

Scheff, T.J. (1979) *Catharsis in Healing, Ritual, and Drama*, Berkeley, CA: University of California Press.

Scheidel, W. (1994) 'Libitina's bitter gains: seasonal mortality and endemic disease in the ancient city of Rome', *Ancient Society*, 25: 151–75.

—— (1996) *Measuring Sex, Age and Death in the Roman Empire. Explorations in Ancient Demography (Journal of Roman Archaeology* Supplement 21), Ann Arbor, MI.

—— (2001) 'Progress and problems in Roman demography', in W. Scheidel (ed.) *Debating Roman Demography (Mnemosyne* Supplement 211), Leiden: E.J. Brill, 1–82.

—— (2002) 'A model of demographic and economic change in Roman Egypt after the Antonine Plague', *Journal of Roman Archaeology*, 15: 97–114.

—— (2003) 'Germs for Rome', in C. Edwards and G. Woolf (eds) *Rome the Cosmopolis*, Cambridge: Cambridge University Press, 158–76.

Schour, I. and Massler, M. (1944) *Development of the Human Dentition* (chart), American Dental Association.

Schouten, J. (1967) *The Rod and Serpent of Asklepios: Symbol of Medicine*, Amsterdam: Elsevier Publishing.

Schubert, C. (1997) 'Menschenbild und Normwandel in der klassischen Zeit', in H. Flashar and J. Jouanna (eds) *Médecine et Morale dans l'Antiquité* (Entretiens sur l'Antiquité Classique, XLIII), Vandoeuvres-Genève: Fondation Hardt, 121–43.

Scobie, A. (1986) 'Slums, sanitation and mortality in the Roman world', *Klio*, 68: 399–433.

Semeria, A. (1986) 'Per un censimento degli *Asklepieia* della Grecia continentale e delle isole', *Annali della Scuola Normale Superiore di Pisa*, 16: 931–58.

Shapiro, A.K. and Shapiro, E. (1997) *The Powerful Placebo: From Ancient Priest to Modern Physician*, Baltimore, MD: Johns Hopkins University Press.

Shapiro, H.A. (1993) *Personifications in Greek Art: The Representation of Abstract Concepts 600–400 B.C.*, Zurich: Akanthus Press.

Shaw, B.D. (1996) 'Seasons of death: aspects of mortality in imperial Rome', *Journal of Roman Studies*, 86: 100–38.

Shaw, T. (1998) *The Burden of the Flesh: Fasting, Gender and Embodiment in Early Christian Ascetic Theory*, Minneapolis, MI: Fortress Press.

Sigurdsson, H. and Carey, C. (2002) 'The eruption of Vesuvius in AD 79', in W.F. Jashemski and F.G. Meyer (eds) *The Natural History of Pompeii*, Cambridge: Cambridge University Press, 37–64.

Simon, B. (1978) *Mind and Madness in Ancient Greece. The Classical Roots of Modern Psychiatry*, Ithaca, NY: Cornell University Press.

Siraisi, N.G. (1990) *Medieval and Early Renaissance Medicine: An Introduction to Knowledge and Practice*, Chicago, IL: University of Chicago Press.

Slack, P. (1985) *The Impact of Plague in Tudor and Stuart England*, London and New York: Routledge, Kegan and Paul.

Smith, T. (1934) *Parasitism and Disease*, Princeton, NJ: Princeton University Press.

Spiro, H.M. (1986) *Doctors, Patients and Placebos*, New Haven, CT: Yale University Press.

Sobel, H. (1990) *Hygieia: die Göttin der Gesundheit*, Darmstadt: Wissenschaftliche Buchgesellschaft.

Sommerstein, A.H. (2001) *Aristophanes: Wealth*, Warminster: Aris and Phillips.

Sorel, P. (1984) 'Une trousse de médecin du IIIe siècle trouvée à Paris', in *Lutèce: Paris de César à Clovis*, Paris: Société des amis du Musée Carnavalet, 21–2, 226–32.

Soren, D. and James, J. (1988) *Kourion: The Search for a Lost Roman City*, New York: Doubleday.

Spencer, W.G. (1935, 1938) *Celsus*, De medicina, Loeb Classical Library, 3 Vols, Cambridge, MA and London: Heinemann.

Stafford, E.J. (2000) *Worshipping Virtues: Personification and the Divine in Ancient Greece*, London: Classical Press of Wales/Duckworth.

—— (2003) 'Brother, son, friend and healer: sleep the god', in K. Dowden and T. Wiedemann (eds) *Sleep* (Nottingham Classical Literature Studies Vol. 8), Bari: Levanti Editori, 71–106.

—— (2005) 'Vice or Virtue? Herakles and the art of allegory', in L. Rawlings (ed.) *Herakles/Hercules in the Ancient World*, Swansea: Classical Press of Wales.

Stanton, A.L., Danoff-Burg, S. and Gallant, S.T. (2000) 'Enhancing women's health: current status and directions in research and practice', in M.S. Jamner and D. Stokols (eds) *Promoting Human Wellness: New Frontiers for Research Practice and Policy*, Berkeley, CA: University of California Press, 615–42.

Steinbock, R.T. (1979) 'Lead ingestion in ancient times', *Paleopathology Newsletter*, 27: 9–11.

Stewart, T.D. (1979) *Essentials of Forensic Anthropology*, Springfield, IL: Charles C. Thomas.

Stoneman, R. (1994) 'Who are the Brahmans? Indian lore and Cynic doctrine in Palladius *De Bragmanibus* and its models', *Classical Quarterly*, 44: 500–10.

—— (1995) 'Naked philosophers: the Brahmans in the Alexander historians and in the Alexander Romance', *Journal of Hellenic Studies*, 115: 99–114.

Stravapodi, E. (1993a) 'An anthropological assessment of the human findings from the cave and the cemetery', in A. Sampson (ed.) *Skoteini, Tharrounia. The Cave, the Settlement and the Cemetery*, Athens: TAPA, 378–91.

—— (1993b) 'Meleti tou anthropologikou Ylikou ton Tafon tis Perioxis Kaloyerovrisis', in A. Sampson (ed.) *Kaloyerovrisis. A Bronze Age Settlement at Phylla, Euboea*, Athens: TAPA, 161–2.

Stravapodi, E., Manolis, S.K. and Kyparissi-Apostolika, N. (1999) 'Paleoanthropological findings from Theopetra Cave in Thessaly. A preliminary report', in

BIBLIOGRAPHY

G.N. Bailey, E. Adam, E. Panagopoulou, C. Perrlés and K. Zachos (eds) *The Palaeolithic Archaeology of Greece and Adjacent Areas. Proceedings of the ICOPAG Conference, Ioannina, September 1994*. British School at Athens Studies, 3: 271–83.

Stuart-Macadam, P. (1992) 'Anemia in past human populations', in P. Stuart-Macadam and S. Kent (eds) *Diet, Demography and Disease*, New York: Aldine de Gruyter, 151–79.

Sublimi Saponetti, S., Scattarella, V. and Volpe, G. (1998) 'Cranial trepanation in an individual of the Hellenistic Age (III century BC) from the necropolis of Contrada Santo Stefano (Gravina, Bari, Italy)', *Journal of Paleopathology*, 10: 121–5.

Tabanelli, M. (1958) *Lo strumento chirurgico e la sua storia*, Forli: Romagna Medica.

Takacs, S. (1994) 'The magic of Isis replaced, or Cyril of Alexandria's attempt at redirecting religious devotion', *Poikila Byzantina*, 13: 491–507.

Talbot, M. (2000) 'The placebo prescription', *The New York Times Magazine* (January 9): 44.

Tayles, N. (1996) 'Anemia, genetic diseases and malaria in prehistoric mainland Southeast Asia', *American Journal of Physical Anthropology*, 101: 11–27.

Taylor, G.M., Rutland, P. and Molleson, T. (1997) 'A sensitive polymerase chain reaction method for the detection of *Plasmodium* species DNA in ancient human remains', *Ancient Biomolecules*, 1: 193–203.

Temkin, O. (1977) 'Metaphors of human biology', in *The Double Face of Janus and Other Essays in the History of Medicine*, Baltimore, MD: Johns Hopkins University Press, 271–83; first published in R.C. Stauffer (ed.) *Science and Civilization*, Madison, WI: University of Wisconsin Press, 169–94.

—— (1991) *Hippocrates in a World of Pagans and Christians*, Baltimore, MD: Johns Hopkins University Press.

Themelis, P.G. (1987) *Ancient Corinth*, Athens: Editions Hannibal.

Thompson, D.W. (1947) *A Glossary of Greek Fishes*, Oxford: Oxford University Press.

Tick, E. (2001) *The Practice of Dream Healing: Bringing Ancient Greek Mysteries into Modern Medicine*, Wheaton, IL: Quest Books.

Timm, S. (1984) *Das christlich-koptische Ägypten in arabischer Zeit*, Teil I Wiesbaden: Reichert, 438–46 s.v. Buqir.

Titchkosky, T. (2003) *Disability, Self, and Society*, Toronto, ON: University of Toronto Press.

Todd, T.W. (1920) 'Age changes in the pubic bone: I. The male white pubis', *American Journal of Physical Anthropology*, 3: 285–334.

Toledo-Pereyra, L.H. (1973) 'Galen's contribution to surgery', *Journal of the History of Medicine*, 28: 357–75.

Tomlinson, R. (1983) *Epidauros. An Archaeological Guide*, Austin, TX: University of Texas.

Torino, M. and Furnaciari, G. (2001) 'Paleopatologia degli individui nella casa di Guilio Polibio', in A. Ciarallo and E. De Cariolis (eds) *La casa di Giulio Polibio: studi interdisciplinari*, Tokyo: University of Tokyo, 93–106.

Toynbee, J.M.C. (1971) *Death and Burial in the Roman World*, London: Thames and Hudson.

Tracy, T.J. (1969) *Physiological Theory and the Doctrine of the Mean in Plato and Aristotle*, The Hague and Paris: Mouton.

Trautmann, J. (ed.) (1981) *Healing Arts in Dialogue: Medicine and Literature*, Carbondale, IL: Southern Illinois University Press.

Trendall, A.D. and Webster, T.B.L. (1979) *Illustrations of Greek Drama*, London: Phaidon.

Triantaphyllou, S. (1997) 'Appendix. Neolithikos Makrigialos: prota apotelesmata tis meletis ton anthropinon oston', *Archaelogiko Ergo stin Mekedonia kai Thraki*, 10 A: 273–5.

—— (1998a) 'Prehistoric populations from northern Greece: a breath of life for the skeletal remains', in K. Branigan (ed.) *Cemetery and Society in the Aegean Bronze Age*, Sheffield: Sheffield Academic Press, 150–64.

—— (1998b) 'I Neolithiki Tafi apo tin Anaskafi D. E. Thessalonikis. Apotelesmata tis osteologikis exetasis', *Thessalonikeon Polis*, 2: 14–17.

—— (1998c) 'An early Iron Age cemetery in Pydna, northern Greece: what do the bones tell us?', *Annual of the British School at Athens*, 93: 353–64.

—— (2000) 'Prehistoric Makrigialos: a story from the fragments', in P. Halstead (ed.) *Neolithic Society in Greece*, Sheffield: Sheffield Academic Press, 116–23.

—— (2001) *A Bioarchaeological Approach to Prehistoric Cemetery Populations from Central and Western Greek Macedonia*, British Archaeological Reports International Series 976.

Triantaphyllou, S. and Chamberlain, A.T. (1996) 'An obstetric fatality from Northern Greece', poster presented at the 23rd Annual Meeting of the Paleopathology Association, Durham, NC.

Tsaliki, A. (1996) 'Environmental material from Neolithic and Chalcolithic sites in Cyprus, with emphasis on burial', undergraduate thesis, Department of Archaeology, University of Athens (in Greek).

—— (1997) 'Investigation of extraordinary Greek human body disposals with special reference to necrophobia: research outline towards a PhD', *British Section of the Palaeopathology Association Newsletter*, 20: 5–6.

—— (2000) *Environmental Remains and Burials from Neolithic and Chalcolithic Cyprus*, Ancient Cyprus Web project (http://www.ancientcyprus.ac.uk/papers/Tsaliki1/page1.html). Date of access 16/10/2003. Greek with English abstract.

—— (2001) 'Vampires beyond legend: a bioarchaeological approach', in M. La Verghetta and L. Capasso (eds) *Proceedings of the XII European Meeting of the Paleopathology Association*, Chieti, Italy: Edigrafital S.p.A, 295–300.

—— (2002a) 'The Capestrano Warrior: artistic caprice or disease?', *Paleopathology Association Newsletter*, 119: 3–11.

—— (2002b) 'The fauna and flora in Prehistoric Cyprus', *Archaeologia & Tekhnes*, 83: 91–6 (in Greek with English abstract).

—— (2003a) 'Evidence of platycnemia 5,000 years b.p. at Sifnos, Greece', *British Association of Biological Anthropology and Osteoarchaeology (BABAO) Annual Review*, 4: 13–14.

—— (2003b) 'Study of ancient skeletal remains from Greece and Cyprus', in S. Lucy (ed.) *Universities of Durham and Newcastle Archaeological Reports*, 24 (2001–2): 71–5.

Tsaliki, A. (2004a) 'Spine pathology and disability at Lesbos, Greece', *Palaeopathology Association Newsletter*, 125: 13–17.

—— (2004b) Animal and human bores in archaeological assemblages (in Greek with English abstract), *Archaeologia & Technes*, 92: 83–8.

—— (in press) 'Ancient human skeletal remains from Sifnos: an overview', Proceedings of the 2nd International Sifnean Symposium, June 27–30, Athens: Society for Sifnean Studies.

Turner, B. (1984) *The Body and Society: Explorations in Social Theory*, Oxford: Basil Blackwell.

Tzedakis, Y. and Martlew, H. (eds) (2002) *Minoans and Myceneans. Flavours of their Time*, Athens: Kapon Editions.

Ubelaker, D.H. (1982) 'The development of American paleopathology', in F. Spencer (ed.) *A History of Physical Anthropology 1930–1980*, London: Academic Press, 337–56.

—— (1990) 'J.L. Angel and the development of forensic anthropology in the United States', in J. Buikstra (ed.) *A Life in Science: Papers in Honor of J.L. Angel*, Kampsville, IL: Center for American Archeology, Scientific Paper 6, 201–10.

Ulrich, R.S. (1984) 'View through a window may influence recovery from surgery', *Science*, 224: 420–1.

Urban, O.H., Teschler-Nicola, M. and Schultz, M. (1985) 'Die latènezeitlichen Gräberfelder von Katzelsdorf und Guntramsdorf, Niederösterreich', *Archaeologia Austriaca*, 69: 13–104.

Vallance, J.T. (1996) 'Dietetics' in *Oxford Classical Dictionary* (3rd edition), Oxford: Oxford University Press.

Van Dam, R. (1993) *Saints and the Miracles in Late Antique Gaul*, Princeton, NJ: Princeton University Press.

Van der Eijk, P. (2000) *Diocles of Carystus*, Leiden: E.J. Brill.

Van Klinken, G.J. and Triantaphyllou, S. (1997) 'Dependence on legume protein in Neolithic Makrigialos, Macedonia, Greece', paper presented at the 5th Advanced Seminar on Palaeodiet, Valbonne, France.

Van Straten, F.T. (1981) 'Gifts for the gods', in H.S. Versnel (ed.) *Faith, Hope and Worship: Aspects of Religious Mentality in the Ancient World*, Leiden: E.J. Brill, 65–151.

—— (1995) *Images of Animal Sacrifice in Archaic and Classical Greece*, Leiden: E.J. Brill.

Vavouranakis, G., Karali, L., Manginis, G. and Tsaliki, A. (2002) 'Funerary rites of passage in PreBA2 Cyprus: the evidence from Audemou – Kamares', paper presented at the American School of Oriental Research Annual Meeting, November 20–24, Toronto, ON, Canada.

Vegetti, M. (1983) 'Metafora politica e immagine del corpo negli scritti ippocratici', in F. Lassere and Ph. Mudry (eds) *Formes de Pensée dans la Collection Hippocratique, Actes du IVe colloque international hippocratique*, Lausanne, 21–25 septembre 1981, Geneva: Librairie Droz, 459–69.

Verbanck-Piérard, A. (1998) *Au Temps d'Hippocrate. Médecine et société en Grèce antique*, Mariemont: Musée Royal de Mariemont.

Vermeule, E.T. (1974) *Toumba tou Skourou: The Mound of Darkness*, Cambridge, MA: Harvard University Press.

Versnel, H.S. (1981) 'Religious mentality in ancient prayer', in H.S. Versnel (ed.) *Faith, Hope and Worship: Aspects of Religious Mentality in the Ancient World*, Leiden: E.J. Brill, 1–64.

Villablanca, A.C. (2000) 'Cardiovascular disease in women: exploring myths and controversies', in M.S. Jamner and D. Stokols (eds) *Promoting Human Wellness: New Frontiers for Research Practice and Policy*, Berkeley, CA: University of California Press, 643–75.

Virchow, R. (1872) 'Altgriechische Schädel von der Piräusstrasse in Athen', *Zeitschrift für Ethnologie*, 4, Verhandlungen, 146–52.

—— (1873) 'Über altgriechische Funde', *Zeitschrift für Ethnologie*, 5, Verhandlungen, 114–18.

—— (1891) 'Schliemann's letzte Ausgrabung', *Sitzungsberichte der Königlich Preussischen Akademie der Wissenschaften zu Berlin*, 819.

—— (1893) 'Über griechische Schädel aus alter und neuer Zeit, und über einen Schädel von Menidi der für den des Sophokles gehalten wird', *Sitzungsberichte der Königlich Preussischen Akademie der Wissenschaften zu Berlin*, 686–99.

Vlahogiannis, N. (1995) Review of V. Dasen, *Dwarfs in Ancient Egypt and Greece*, *Medical History* 39, 119–20.

—— (1998) 'Disabling bodies', in D. Montserrat (ed.) *Changing Bodies, Changing Meanings: Studies on the Human Body in Antiquity*, London and New York: Routledge, 13–36.

Von Staden, H. (1990) 'Incurability and hopelessness: the Hippocratic Corpus', in P. Potter, G. Maloney and J. Desautels (eds) *La Maladie et les Maladies dans la Collection hippocratique, Actes du VIe colloque internationale hippocratique*, Quebec: Editions du Sphinx, 75–112.

Vries, J. de (1984) *European Urbanization 1500–1800*, London: Methuen.

Waage, F.O. (1949) 'An Early Helladic well near Old Corinth', in *Commemorative Studies in Honor of Theodore Leslie Shear*, supplement VII, *Hesperia*, Cambridge, MA: American School of Classical Studies at Athens, 415–22.

Wade, W. (1983) 'The burials', in W.A. McDonald, W.D.E. Coulson and J. Rosser (eds) *Excavations at Nichoria in Southwest Greece*, Vol. III, Minneapolis, MI: University of Minnesota Press, 398–404.

Wagman, R. (1995) *Inni di Epidauri*, Pisa: Giardini Editori.

Waldron, T. (1994) *Counting the Dead. The Epidemiology of Skeletal Populations*, London: Wiley.

Wall, S.M., Musgrave, J.H. and Warren, P. (1986) 'Human bones from a late Minoan IB house at Knossos'. *Annual of the British School at Athens*, 81: 333–88.

Wallace, P.W. and Orphanides, A.G. (1990) *Sources for the History of Cyprus Vol. I: Greek and Latin Texts to the Third Century A.D.*, Cyprus: Konos Press.

Walton, A. (1894) *Asklepios. The Cult of the Greek God of Medicine* (reprinted 1979), Chicago, IL: Ares.

Warner, M. (1985) *Monuments and Maidens: The Allegory of the Female Form*, London: Weidenfeld and Nicolson.

Warren, B. (ed.) (1984) *Using the Creative Arts in Therapy*, London: Croom Helm and Cambridge, MA: Brookline Books.

Waywell, G.B. (1986) *The Lever and Hope Sculptures*, Berlin: Gebr. Mann Verlag.

Wear, A. (1992) 'Making sense of health and the environment in early modern England', in A. Wear (ed.) *Medicine in Society: Historical Essays*, Cambridge: Cambridge University Press, 19–47.

Weaver, D.S. (1977) 'New methods for the determination of sex, age and rates of growth of infant and child skeletal remains in prehistoric American Indian populations', PhD dissertation, Department of Anthropology, University of New Mexico, Albuquerque, NM.

Weisensee, M. (1986) 'Women's health perceptions in a male-dominated world', in D.K. Kjervik and I.M. Martinson (eds) *Women in Health and Illness: Life Experiences and Crises*, Philadelphia, PA: W.B. Saunders, 19–33.

Weisman, C.S. (1998) *Women's Health Care, Activist Traditions and Institutional Change*, Baltimore, MD: Johns Hopkins University Press.

Wells, C. (1965) 'Osteogenesis imperfecta from an Anglo-Saxon burial ground at Burgh Castle, Suffolk', *Medical History*, 9: 88–9.

Wells, L. (1998) *The Greek Language of Healing from Homer to New Testament Times*, Berlin and New York: Walter de Gruyter.

Wesolowsky, A.B. (1973) 'The skeletons of Lerna Hollow', *Hesperia*, 42: 340–51.

West, M.L. (1978) *Hesiod, Works and Days: edited with prolegomena and commentary*, Oxford: Clarendon Press.

White, L., Tursky, B. and Schwartz, G. (eds) (1985) *Placebo. Theory, Research and Mechanisms*, New York: Guilford Press.

Wilkins, J. (2000) *The Boastful Chef: The Discourse of Food in Ancient Greek Comedy*, Oxford: Oxford University Press.

—— (2001) 'Les poissons faisaient-ils partie de la diète antique?', in J.-N. Corvisier, C. Didier and M. Valdher (eds) *Médecine et Démographie dans le Monde Antique*, Arras: Artois Presses Université, 183–91.

—— (2003) 'Foreword', to O. Powell, *Galen: On the Properties of Foodstuffs*, Cambridge: Cambridge University Press, ix–xxi.

Wilkins, J. and Hill, S. (1994) *Archestratus: The Life of Luxury*, Totnes, Devon: Prospect Books.

Wilkins, J., Harvey, D. and Dobson, M. (eds) (1995) *Food in Antiquity*, Exeter: Exeter University Press.

Williams, R. (1973) *The Country and the City*, London: Hogarth Press.

Wills, C. (1996) *Plagues: Their Origin, History and Future*, London: Harper Collins.

Wimbush, V.L. (1990) (ed.) *Ascetic Behavior in Greco-Roman Antiquity: A Sourcebook*, Minneapolis, MI: Fortress Press.

Wimbush, V.L. and Valantasis, R. (1995) (eds) *Asceticism*, New York: Oxford University Press.

Winberg, E.G. (1974) 'Iron and the susceptibility to infectious disease', *Science*, 184: 952–6.

Windler, H. (1912) *Haupt-Katalog 50: Chirurgie-instrumente, Krankenhaus-möbel, Bandagen, Apparate zur Orthopädie, Sterilisation und Krankenpflege*, Berlin/St. Petersburg: Windler.

Wipszycka, E. (1988) 'La christianisation de l'Égypte aux IVᵉ–VIᵉ siècles. Aspects sociaux et ethniques', *Aegyptus*, 58: 117–65.

Wood, J.W., Milner, G.R., Harpending, H.C. and Weiss, K.M. (1992) 'The osteological paradox. Problems of inferring prehistoric health from skeletal samples', *Current Anthropology*, 33: 343–70.

Worman, N. (2000) 'Infections in the sentence: the discourse of disease in Sophocles' *Philoctetes*', *Arethusa*, 33: 1–36.

Wyke, M. (1997) *Projecting the Past: Ancient Rome, Cinema and History*, London and New York: Routledge.

Xirotiris, N.I. (1980) 'The Indo-Europeans in Greece. An anthropological approach to the population of the Bronze Age', *Journal of Indo-European Studies*, 8: 201–10.

—— (1981) 'Anthropologie des Äneolithikums und der Frühbronzezeit in Mittel- und Südosteuropa', *Sloveska Archaeologia*, 29: 235–41.

—— (1982) 'Apotelesmata tis anthropologikis exetasis ton kamenon oston apo ti Soufli Magoula kai tin Platia Magoula Zarkou', in K. Gallis (ed.) *Kafseis nekron tin Neolothiki epochi sti Thessalia*, Athina: Dimosievmata tou Archeologikou Deltiou 30 T.A.P, 190–9.

—— (1986) 'Die Ethnogenese der Griechen aus der Sicht der Anthropologie', in W. Bernhard and A. Kandler-Palsson (eds) *Ethnogenese europäischer Völker: aus der Sicht der Anthropologie und Vor- und Frühgeschichte*, Stuttgart: Gustav Fischer, 39–53.

—— (1992) 'Anthropologiko iliko tafou B3', in Ch. Koukouli-Chrysanthaki (ed.) *Protoistoriki Thasos: Ta nekrotafeia tou oikismou Kastri, Meros B*, Athens: Ekdosi tou tameiou Archaeologikon poron kai Apallotrioseon, 752.

Yenans, S. (1998) *Turkish Odyssey*, Istanbul: Astir Matbaacilik.

Youtie, L.C. (1996) *The Michigan Medical Codex*, Atlanta, GA: Scholars Press.

Zimmermann, S. and Künzl, E. (1991) 'Die Antiken der Sammlung Meyer-Steineg in Jena I', *Jahrbuch des römisch-germanischen Zentralmuseums Mainz*, 38: 515–40.

Zivanovic, S. (1982) *Ancient Diseases: The Elements of Palaeopathology*, London: Methuen.

INDEX

eBooks – at www.eBookstore.tandf.co.uk

A library at your fingertips!

eBooks are electronic versions of printed books. You can store them on your PC/laptop or browse them online.

They have advantages for anyone needing rapid access to a wide variety of published, copyright information.

eBooks can help your research by enabling you to bookmark chapters, annotate text and use instant searches to find specific words or phrases. Several eBook files would fit on even a small laptop or PDA.

NEW: Save money by eSubscribing: cheap, online access to any eBook for as long as you need it.

Annual subscription packages

We now offer special low-cost bulk subscriptions to packages of eBooks in certain subject areas. These are available to libraries or to individuals.

For more information please contact webmaster.ebooks@tandf.co.uk

We're continually developing the eBook concept, so keep up to date by visiting the website.

www.eBookstore.tandf.co.uk

The
ROSENBERG
LETTERS

Garland Reference Library of the Humanities
(Vol. 1184)

Photo courtesy of Michael and Robert Meeropol.

The
ROSENBERG LETTERS

A Complete Edition of the
Prison Correspondence of
Julius and Ethel Rosenberg

♣Edited by
Michael Meeropol

GARLAND PUBLISHING, INC.

New York & London

1994

Library of Congress Cataloging-in-Publication Data

Rosenberg, Julius, 1918–1953.
    [Correspondence.   Selections]
    The Rosenberg letters : a complete edition of the prison
correspondence of Julius and Ethel Rosenberg / edited by
Michael Meeropol.
       p.   cm. — (Garland reference library of the
humanities ; vol. 1184)
    Includes bibliographical references.
    ISBN 0–8240–5948–4 (acid-free paper)
    1. Rosenberg, Ethel. 1915–1953—Correspondence.
2. Rosenberg, Julius, 1918–1953—Correspondence.
3. Communists—United States—Biography.   4. Prisoners—
United States—Biography.   I. Rosenberg, Ethel, 1915–1953.
II. Meeropol, Michael.   III. Title.
HX84.R578A4   1994
364.1'31'092—dc20   93–40860
[B]   CIP

Printed on acid-free, 250-year-life paper
Manufactured in the United States of America

To Annie

Contents

Preface

The effort to bring my parents' correspondence before the public began as early as 1951 while they were imprisoned on death row in Sing Sing. My parents had direct contact only with prison personnel, attorneys, family, and my mother's psychiatrist. By fall of 1951, they realized that the only way to reach their fellow citizens on whom they were counting for political support was through their letters. A few letters were published in the *National Guardian* following William A. Reuben's series, "The Rosenberg Case: Is This the Dreyfus Case of Cold War America?" which ran from August through October. The decision to publish a book of the letters was made sometime in the Fall of 1952, but the actual publication was delayed until June of the next year. The official date of publication of *Death House Letters of Ethel and Julius Rosenberg* was during the first week of June in 1953. The last letter published in that first edition was written March 19, 1953. It is doubtful that my parents ever saw the printed edition since they made no reference to it in any of the June letters. A more complete edition, *The Testament of Ethel and Julius Rosenberg,* was published in 1954 with letters, including the very last one, omitted from the 1953 edition. As described in the text, the letters were collected by their lawyer and friend, Emanuel Bloch, who created the publishing company (JERO Publishing Company) which owned the copyright to the letters. With his untimely death in 1954, his assistant and fiancée, Gloria Agrin, took possession of the letters, and they were retained by her until Walter and Miriam Schneir began research for their book *Invitation to an Inquest.* A number of the letters were excerpted and published in that work. During the course of their research, the Schneirs stored the original letters in a bank safety-deposit box until Robert and I took possession of them as we began to put together the first edition of *We Are Your Sons* (Boston: Houghton-Mifflin, 1975). We acquired a few more original letters from family, and then in 1977 received a batch of letters that our parents had sent to us at the Hebrew Children's Home in the Bronx where we lived from November 1950 to June 1951. The director of the home had saved the letters and they were discovered by the man who took over his position some time in the 1950s. After reading a letter we had published in the *New York Times,* he contacted us and gave us those letters. At this point, we believe that we have all the letters (originals or, in some cases, typed copies made as the first book was being prepared) that have survived the years. As we noted in *We Are Your Sons,* anyone in possession of any other letters should approach us through our publisher.

We have always believed that a complete edition of the letters would be useful for people interested in gaining as full an understanding as possible of our parents as human beings. I was about to begin this project as Ilene Phillipson's *Ethel Rosenberg: Beyond the Myths* was published.[1] In our view, Phillipson wrote a mean-spirited and poorly researched book. She portrayed our mother as a woman who might have died willingly because she knew she was a bad mother and who might have believed that Robert and I would be better off if she were absent. This notion is totally at variance with the memory of the one surviving mental health professional, Dr. Elizabeth Phillips (interviewed at length for the second edition of *We Are Your Sons* [Urbana IL: University of Illinois Press, 1986], also interviewed by Phillipson), who worked personally with our mother. With the publication of this complete edition, our parents speak for themselves.

I am grateful to Garland Publishing for accepting this project and remaining true to the goal which has been to produce a full and complete edition of the letters. The letters had to be transcribed from the originals

---

[1]We originally cooperated with Phillipson, giving her permission to read all the letters, including the unpublished ones. In order to protect our ability to publish a full edition of the letters, we only gave permission after Phillipson signed an agreement prohibiting quotation from any of the letters without explicit permission. The agreement read in part

> It is understood and agreed that in making these letters available to you, that the same does not constitute the right to copy, print, publish or disseminate any of those letters or any part thereof, and verbatim excerpts or any letter in its entirety will not be used without the express written consent of . . . Michael and Robert Meeropol. (Marshall Perlin to Ilene Phillipson, 25 January 1985. Original, signed by Phillipson, in possession of Marshall Perlin, P.C.)

In view of this agreement, it is difficult to believe that Phillipson would be surprised to find it impermissible to publish extensive excerpts of the letters.

with all self-editing (crossed out words or phrases, inserts) revealed and with all misspellings and grammatical mistakes included. The Garland editor, Paula Ladenburg, has been very helpful in suggesting ways to minimize the interference that this inclusion creates. She has also been very helpful in guiding what I should include and not include in the introduction. Although my original intent was that this volume focus exclusively on the letters, she encouraged me to restate my brother's and my views about what research into the case has uncovered as well as what we believe to be the truth about the case. After all, the last such comprehensive statement was published seven years ago and significant events have occurred since that time. Finally, I am pleased that she and Garland agreed that in addition to the letters, the two petitions for executive clemency would be published in their entirety. In fact, we have decided to begin the book with the first petition because it included my parents' and Manny Bloch's comprehensive statements in defense of themselves as well as a summary of what they perceived to be the issues in the case.

When Garland took on the project, Robert was planning the creation of the Rosenberg Fund for Children, a public foundation that "provides for the educational and emotional needs of children in this country whose parents have been targeted because of their progressive activity."[2] In effect, this organization aims to do for other children what was done for Robert and me as a result of the Rosenberg Children's Trust Fund. That fund financed summer camp, music lessons, and most importantly, tuition at Elisabeth Irwin High School and Little Red School House.[3] The fund also covered our college tuition. With Robert focused on the creation of the fund, I took over the task of preparing the book of letters.

The one omission from the record is evidence of the interaction between my mother and her psychiatrist. I interviewed the psychiatrist in 1974 and the interview is discussed in *We Are Your Sons*.[4] During the interview he mentioned that he had a number of letters my mother had written to him. I did not ask him for them, nor did he offer them to me. While transcribing the letters for this book, I discovered one of my mother's letters to the psychiatrist. This led me to call his widow, a doctor herself, to ask if I might see the letters. She refused, citing doctor-patient confidentiality. I have consulted with my sister-in-law, Dr. Kathryn Basham, who is a psychiatric social worker, and she has advised me that without the full context of the doctor-patient relationship, a context that only the patient or the

[2]For more information, contact Rosenberg Fund for Children, Suite 408, 1145 Main Street, Springfield, MA 01103.
[3]For details, see *We Are Your Sons,* pp. 171–74, 266–67, 277–79.
[4]See *Sons,* p. 38–39, 71, 94, 148, 149.

doctor can truly provide, a single letter or even a group of letters might be misleading. Thus, I have chosen not to include the one letter in our possession, nor have I pursued the issue with the psychiatrist's widow.

While preparing this edition, I became fully aware of how heavily edited were the original editions of *Death House Letters* and *The Testament of Ethel and Julius Rosenberg*. A number of the original letters are no longer available, and I have had to work from typed versions prepared in 1952 and 1953. Having no alternative, we have treated them as accurate. Though in one or two instances, I have called the attention of readers to the editing of particular letters, I have made no attempt to systematically investigate how the two original published versions differ from the originals. Even in some of the letters included in *We Are Your Sons,* which were selected from the originals rather than the previously published versions, I noticed some discrepancies with the originals.

Abbreviations in the text are there to guide readers to mistakes and editorial changes my parents made themselves. Misspellings are followed by [*sic*]. Where words have been crossed out, the abbreviation is CO. If the words crossed out are legible, I bracket the word and add CO. For example, on the first page of the first letter the reader will see ["until" CO]. This means that in the original the word "until" is initially in the text and then crossed out. Where words are inserted, the bracketed abbreviation precedes the word or words inserted. In the sentence following the bracketed reference to "until," we read [N4WI], which indicates that the next four words in the text were inserted by my father. Sometimes these two need to be combined. Four lines later in the first letter, the following appears: ["only" inserted, then CO].

Since their first publication, the letters have been controversial. Some readers have seen the letters as a moving testament to love of life, truth, and progress, as well as to love of family. The letters have also been dismissed as the raving of "Stalinist soldiers."[5] In a 1983 analysis, Ronald Radosh and Joyce Milton claimed that the letters reveal a "contempt for their countrymen . . ." displayed by "rigid self-righteous ideologues . . . reveling in the knowledge that they were earning for themselves a place in history." Now the complete letters are published—exactly as they were written, to the extent possible—for anyone who wants to read them and judge for him or herself. My parents' politics and family relationships, their hopes and frustrations, are all present to be read and studied.

---

[5]For a detailed analysis of the various interpretations of the letters, see Andrew Ross, "Reading the Rosenberg Letters," in *No Respect: Intellectuals and Popular Culture* (NY: Routledge, 1989), pp. 15–41. The major critical analyses of the letters are discussed and footnoted in that chapter.

If there is one theme that has struck me most deeply in reading and transcribing these letters it is my parents' desire to maintain dignity. Throughout the trial, during their years in Sing Sing, and as they faced death, they struggled to maintain that dignity. One juror, in an interview, described them as "emotionless" when they testified.[6] Morton Sobell remarked how calmly my mother endured her outrageous cross-examination, and wondered why she didn't permit herself to become upset or angry.[7] Her calm was, I believe, part of her struggle for dignity. In a speech in Detroit on September 22, 1953, Emanuel Bloch remembered my mother telling him that she shivered from head to foot when she thought of getting into the electric chair and having electric current run through her, but she said she would "die with dignity." I read the letters when Robert and I wrote *We Are Your Sons,* but this careful re-reading has brought my parents closest to me since I lived with them. I hope these letters will also help them live for their four grandchildren, Ivy, Greg, Jenn, and Rachel. People throughout the world have learned about them through poems, paintings, novels, plays, movies, and histories. Their letters have survived the years and I believe that they will help the reader gain insight and understanding. I believe they will help the reader feel their love. I hope the reader will, perhaps, want to return that love.

Michael Meeropol
Springfield, Massachusetts
September 1993

---

[6]See Ted Morgan, "The Rosenberg Jury," *Esquire* (May, 1975).
[7]See Morton Sobell, *On Doing Time* (NY: Charles Scribner's Sons, 1974), pp. 222–39.

Acknowledgments

This project has been a long labor of love that could not have been possible without the steadfast support of my family, Ann, Ivy, and Greg. Ann has always been there for me with her encouragement and strength. This fall, she read the Preface, improving its prose immeasurably. Ivy researched a number of newspaper articles from the 1950s. My brother, Robert, encouraged me along the way and, toward the end, gave generously of his time to read and comment upon the Introduction.

As always, whatever success I have achieved as a student of history has been significantly enhanced by my long, deep friendship with Jerry Markowitz. A fine historian, he has been a friend and sometime collaborator on this and other historical issues for over thirty years.

I am also indebted to my editor at Garland Publishing, Paula Ladenburg, for her encouragement with the Introduction. She believed that my brother's and my perspective on our parents' case, seven years after the last edition of *We Are Your Sons,* should be part of the book of letters.

Marshall ("Mike") Perlin, my attorney and friend of twenty years, who has been associated with the case as an attorney since June 19, 1953, read the Introduction and made several important suggestions. Most of the material referred to in the footnotes, and most of the evidence alluded to in the Introduction is the fruit of the labor that Mike and his associates, Max Millman, Bonnie Brower, Samuel Gruber, and David Rein engaged in over many years. The happy confluence of the strengthening of the Freedom of Information Act in 1974 and the revival of interest in the case at that time provided the opening for the lawyers, my brother and me, and active political groups, the National Committee to Reopen the Rosenberg Case and the Fund for Open Information and Accountability, to force the release of previously secret government documents on the case. Mike remains a stalwart defender of my parents as he was for Morton Sobell during most of his incarceration. The importance of what he and his associates were able to wrest from the clutches of the U.S. government cannot be too strongly emphasized.

The work on transcription and footnoting took fully two years longer than originally anticipated, and I am extremely grateful for the extraordinary amount of work that Ms. Ladenburg put into this aspect of editing. She made my notations and analyses of the main text of letters as unobtrusive as possible, allowing the letters to remain central and accessible to the reader.

J. Kevin O'Brien of the F.B.I. FOIA-Privacy Section tracked down a number of sources among the documents released to my brother and me pursuant to our Freedom of Information Act lawsuit. I thank him for the courtesy he extended me.

I remain solely responsible for the errors that may remain despite the best efforts of those who have read and commented upon the manuscript.

I must thank everyone who has made it possible for my brother and me to lead the lives we have led instead of the lives the government wished for us.[1]

The movement that attempted to save my parents' lives did succeed in saving my brother and me in 1954 and after. We have tried to give something back during our adulthood. *We Are Your Sons*, the Rosenberg Fund for Children, and this book are all part of that effort. And the struggle continues.

---

[1]As this book went to press, Robert and I received some pages from *Inadmissible Evidence*, Evelyn Williams' autobiography (NY: Lawrence Hill Books, 1994). She is an African-American lawyer who defended, among others, Assata Shakur, alleged member of the Black Liberation Army. Before becoming a lawyer, Ms. Williams had been the probation officer assigned (in 1954) to report on whether Robert and I should be permitted to live with our grandmother or be institutionalized to "protect" us from publicity and "misuse" by those who had tried to save our parents' lives. (See *We Are Your Sons* [Urbana, IL: University of Illinois Press, 1986], pp. 246–55.) She tells of being threatened with the loss of her job by a Children's Court Judge if she did not agree to recommend institutionalization (p. 33).

Introduction

Ever since my parents' arrests in July and August of 1950, it has been apparent that the interest shown in their case and the attitudes of people toward the issues involved have reflected contemporary political trends. Thus, in the period between the arrest and execution, the politics of the Cold War, the Korean War, and McCarthyism were crucial backdrops to the specifics of the case. Decisions on what (if anything) to do about it were shaped by the current political reality. In 1950, that reality, as defined by our leaders and accepted by the vast majority of the people, was the fact that, in the words of trial judge Irving R. Kaufman, "this country is engaged in a life and death struggle with a completely different system."[1] This meant that anyone who would provide important aid to that other system—and anyone who appeared to share the political beliefs of people who would do such a thing—was deserving of hate and fear from ordinary citizens. The majority of Americans seem to have approved of the sentence of death and ultimately of the executions of my parents, even as some had doubts and many opposed the punishment as too severe while not doubting guilt or the heinous nature of the crime.

In that context, it is interesting to consider the various stages in the struggle over which version of the history of this case will come to be accepted, both in the United States and abroad. Until four months after the

---

[1] *U.S. vs. Rosenbergs, Sobell, Yakovlev and Greenglass* (Cr. No. 134-245). The full trial transcript was reprinted from the submission to the United States Supreme Court which was filed along with the first petition for a writ of *certiorari* on June 7, 1952. The page references are to the printed copy which the National Committee to Secure Justice in the Rosenberg Case duplicated and sold in an effort to acquaint the public with the flimsiness of the prosecutor's case. Henceforth, the transcript will be referred to as "Record." The quote from Judge Kaufman is on p. 1613.

trial, not one voice was raised outside of my parents' testimony in the courtroom in favor of the view that they were not guilty. The left had been successfully marginalized by the defeat of former Vice President Henry Wallace
and the Progressive Party in the 1948 election, the purging from unions of
alleged Communist influence, the beginning of the Korean War, and the
indictment of the Communist Party under the Smith Act. The communist
and fellow-traveling left did not respond to the case. They made a tactical
decision to defend the right of the Communist Party to function as a legal
political party by attempting to win the Smith Act cases. They also focused
on the rights of individuals to refuse to answer questions about their political associations when called by Congressional committees.[2] They chose not
to associate themselves with the defense of people accused of espionage. An
historian close to the Communist Party told me many years later that this
was analogous to the rule the NAACP set in the 1930s, '40s, and '50s that
it would not get involved in defending black men accused of rape. Meanwhile, the non-communist left ignored the case—unwilling, it appears, to
support communist defendants who, for all they knew, might be guilty and
not deserving of support.

At the trial, David and Ruth Greenglass, my mother's brother and
sister-in-law, testified that while David worked as a G.I. machinist at the
Los Alamos facility where the first atom bombs were built, my father and
mother persuaded Ruth to enlist him as an espionage agent for the Soviet
Union. He testified that through snooping around and asking questions he
figured out enough information about what was going on to pass sketches
of certain experimental set-ups and molds used in creating the shaped charges
(explosive lenses) that would be used to focus shock waves toward a central
point so that the fissionable material making up the core of the bomb would
collapse inward (implode) and reach critical mass. He also claimed that he
was able to draw a cross section of the implosion bomb and provide a
theoretical description. He testified that he drew the latter sketch in my
parents' living room and gave both it and written descriptive material to my
father. He also said he gave some other sketches and information to Harry
Gold, who arrived at his apartment in Albuquerque in June of 1945. Gold
testified that he had been a spy working as a courier with Dr. Klaus Fuchs, a
German-born British physicist who had worked on the bomb at Los
Alamos. Gold said that on one occasion he had traveled to Albuquerque and
received sketches and written material from Greenglass. Though saying he
never met either of my parents, he did claim, as did Greenglass, that the
recognition signal they used was "I come from Julius." They also both

---

[2]For good summaries see Cedric Belfrage, *The American Inquisition* (NY: Bobbs-
Merrill, 1973) and David Caute, *The Great Fear* (NY: Simon and Schuster, 1978).

testified that the cut side of a Jello box was matched upon their meeting. David and Ruth Greenglass had testified that Julius Rosenberg cut the Jello box in half, gave one half to the Greenglasses, and kept the other. This was the crux of the government's case as presented at the trial. The jury believed it and voted to convict.

The controversy over my parents' case within the United States began with a series of articles by William A. Reuben in the *National Guardian*, beginning in August of 1951. In those first halting steps toward opposition, much of the government's case was accepted. Reuben based his entire effort on the trial record and emphasized that nothing but accomplice testimony without any independent corroboration convicted my parents. His contention and that of the whole defense effort up to the executions was based on the view that the Greenglasses and Harry Gold were indeed spies, but that the Rosenberg connection to these spies was not proven. In addition, the unfairness of the way Judge Kaufman conducted the trial as well as the extreme nature of the death sentence became focal points for the effort to save the Rosenbergs that began in the fall of 1951 and grew to a fairly substantial protest, especially overseas, by the time of the executions.

The strength of domestic anti-communism rendered our parents' defenders unwilling to admit publicly what we learned for certain in the 1970s, that they were Communist Party members. Our parents strongly identified with the Popular Front politics of the New Deal, unions, civil rights for African-Americans, the wartime alliance with the Soviet Union, and the need for accommodation rather than conflict with Soviet interests and the rising nationalistic (and often communist) movements in the rest of the world, but attempted to keep their personal politics out of the trial by availing themselves of the privilege against self-incrimination under the Fifth Amendment. This played right into the prosecution's strategy. The prosecution called them communists and in those days "Fifth Amendment Communists" were those who refused admit that they were communists. From the moment of their arrests, through their executions, and even continuing through the 1960s, supporters of my parents insisted they didn't know whether or not they were communists. When I interviewed people for *We Are Your Sons* (Boston: Houghton-Mifflin, 1975) relatives professed not to know whether they were in fact communists. Morton Sobell, their co-defendant, who proclaimed his own membership in the Communist Party in his book *On Doing Time* (NY: Charles Scribner's Sons, 1974), once said, "One just didn't discuss those things." Carl Marzani, a public communist who had employed my mother as a secretary in the early 1940s, stated on the television documentary *The Unquiet Death of Ethel and Julius Rosenberg* that he, himself, didn't know whether they were communists.[3]

This is testimony to the extraordinary success of McCarthyism in defining the limits of responsible debate. Communism was defined as "un-American." The committee of the House of Representatives that held center stage for most of this period as an exposer of communists was aptly called the House Un-American Activities Committee. Once someone was defined as "un-American," it was a very short step to agreeing that the privileges of being an American (such as the protections of the Bill of Rights) did not apply to them. Thus, the initial movement to save my parents debated the appropriateness of the death penalty and argued that spies, the Greenglasses, had perjured themselves to finger innocent individuals to reduce their sentences. But it was not acceptable to admit to being communists and attempt to convince the American people that communists still deserved the protections of the Constitution and the presumption that one is innocent until proven guilty. It also would not have been acceptable to accuse the government of framing innocent people in order to pursue the Cold War. My father's statements to that effect in his letters were not among those published in 1953 and 1954.

The attitude of my parents' defenders began to shift in 1954. William Reuben argued in *The Atom Spy Hoax* (NY: Action Books, 1954) that all individuals accused of spying for the Soviets in the case, beginning with Klaus Fuchs, were in fact innocent. This view was echoed by John Wexley in *The Judgment of Julius and Ethel Rosenberg* (NY: Cameron and Kahn, 1955). Only Malcolm Sharp in *Was Justice Done* (NY: Monthly Review Press, 1956) argued the original defense position that there was a conspiracy that included Gold, Greenglass, and Yakovlev but not my parents.[4] With the publication of Wexley's book, the historiography solidified into two camps: those who believed that the government was more or less correct in its charges and those who believed that the Rosenberg-Sobell case was a fraud. The pro-government side was restated by Jonathan Root in *The Betrayers* (NY: Coward-McCann, 1963).

In 1965, Walter and Miriam Schneir published *Invitation to an Inquest*[5] which set the stage for one of the most concerted legal efforts to overturn

---

[3]See Alvin H. Goldstein, *The Unquiet Death of Ethel and Julius Rosenberg* (NY: Lawrence Hill & Co., 1975).

[4]Sharp had joined the defense team in May of 1953. He strongly criticized the arguments of Reuben and Wexley in a book review included in his book.

[5]Original edition (NY: Doubleday, 1965). Most recent updated and expanded version (NY: Pantheon, 1983). All future references unless otherwise specified will be to this most recent edition.

the original convictions.[6] Agreeing with Wexley that Harry Gold and the Greenglasses were not spies and falsely confessed as part of a government frame-up, but disagreeing with Wexley about Fuchs, the Schneirs helped set the tone for the next round of debate that erupted in the 1970s in the wake of Watergate. The Schneirs attacked the core of the government's case. Their initial research led them to conclude that the documentation showing that Harry Gold had been in Albuquerque in June of 1945 was forged by the F.B.I. Wexley had made the same charge, basing his view on Gold's inability to make train connections from Albuquerque to New York, as he had testified at the trial. The Schneirs used photostats of two hotel registration cards, one from June, 1945, the other from September, to call into question the authenticity of the June card. Reviewers did not ignore the book as they had Reuben's and Wexley's, but despite praise for the systematic and thorough way in which the Schneirs approached the subject, most reviewers recoiled in horror from the idea that our federal government would frame innocent people and forge documents. The Schneirs' conclusions were considered so out of the mainstream that when Louis Nizer turned a movie script into a best-selling narrative (*The Implosion Conspiracy* [NY: Doubleday, 1973]) he felt confident enough to ignore their arguments.

The lawyers for co-defendant Morton Sobell, who had been convicted along with my parents but sentenced to thirty years in prison, filed a motion for a new trial based in part on the Schneirs' research but also on a challenge to the heart of the government's case, that my parents had stolen the "secret of the atomic bomb." Though the judges continued to rule against the defense, the material developed in that motion made it impossible for government apologists to ever again make that claim. I can do no better than to quote a summary of the conclusion that became inescapable to Marshall Perlin, the attorney who represented Morton Sobell at that time and then went on to represent my brother and me in a copyright lawsuit against Louis Nizer and then in the long, arduous Freedom of Information Act lawsuit against eleven government agencies for material on our parents' case. ". . . the fraud that made a fair trial impossible and which was used to justify the death sentence was the claim of the theft of the secret of the bomb represented by [Greenglass' cross-section sketch] and Greenglass' description and the prosecution's claims in opening and closing statements. . . . The heart of the government's fraudulent case was how to prove not merely the guilt of the Rosenbergs but the effect and importance of what they did. Assuming *arguendo* their guilt, if there was an honest appraisal of [Greenglass' sketches] the best you can say is that there was a meaningless

[6]See *Morton Sobell vs. U.S.* 66 Civ 1328 U.S. District Court SDNY. See also Record on Appeal Docket #31259 U.S. Court of Appeals for the 2nd Circuit.

transmission of information which technically might have been sufficient as a matter of law for a conviction. . . ."[7] but which clearly could never have justified the death penalty.

With the Watergate revelations, the American public awakened to the fact that our government could frame people, as well as lie, forge, and cheat. The anti-Vietnam War movement had done much to expose official governmental mendacity. Watergate gave the "innocence" of the American public the *coup de grace*. This provided a new context for those who became interested in issues such as our parents' case. The documentary *The Unquiet Death of Ethel and Julius Rosenberg,* which ran on public television in 1974, raised new questions. Even an uncritical dramatization of the trial on ABC television that year raised doubts among the public. Now, suddenly, people who thought about the case didn't insist that the Schneirs and others prove my parents' innocence. Instead they wanted to know how government officials could continue to ignore our charges.

As summarized in the speeches my brother and I began to give in 1974 (speeches we have continued to give in modified form to this day), the charge of frame-up was based on a number of successful refutations of crucial elements in the prosecution's case as presented at the trial:

1) There was no secret of the atom bomb and arguments to the contrary by the prosecution perpetrated a major fraud on both the jury and the public.[8]

2) David and Ruth Greenglass were caught in major perjuries by researchers investigating the case after the convictions. Among the lies were:

a) The story of an alleged piece of Soviet spy equipment in my parents' apartment, a console table. The story told by my parents that it was an ordinary table purchased at Macy's later was confirmed but Judge Kaufman refused to let that be grounds for a new hearing.[9]

b) The story of the Greenglasses allegedly having had passport photographs taken. The photographs introduced as government exhibits were not passport photographs.[10]

---

[7]Letter, Marshall Perlin to Michael Meeropol, 15 November 1993.
[8]This was fully spelled out in Gerald E. Markowitz and Michael Meeropol, "The 'Crime of the Century' Revisited: David Greenglass' Scientific Evidence in the Rosenberg Case." *Science and Society* 44 (1980): 1–26.
[9]See Robert and Michael Meeropol, *We Are Your Sons,* 2nd ed. (Urbana, IL: University of Illinois Press, 1986), pp. 187–89, 192–97, 404–6. Hereafter referred to as *Sons.*
[10]See Schneir and Schneir, pp. 350–55.

c) The story of a deposit of $400.00 right after Harry Gold allegedly visited them. There were numerous other deposits indicating black marketeering and thievery rather than espionage.[11]

3) Harry Gold's visit to Albuquerque in June of 1945 is documented by a forged hotel registration card.[12]

By fall of 1975, we knew as a result of a Freedom of Information Act request that the phrase "I come from Julius" was not mentioned by either Harry Gold or David Greenglass in sworn testimony taken months after their arrests.[13]

The supporters of the government did not sit quietly by and allow us full center stage. A former federal judge, Simon Rifkind, possibly at Kaufman's request, had written letters to newspapers as early as 1969 attacking what he considered irresponsible arguments in the play *Inquest* that my parents were innocent. In 1974 he was able to publish an attack on both the public television documentary and the ABC dramatization of the trial in *TV Guide* as part of a series of viewpoint articles. Entitled "Why is TV Turning Soviet Spies into Folk Heroes?" the article introduced a number of themes that traditionally have been used to support the government's case. These were: my parents' attorney pronounced the trial "fair," the case was meticulously scrutinized by appellate courts, and anyone who still wished to generate sympathy for people who had had the full benefit of the American legal system was in effect stating that the system is rotten to the core. In emphasizing the extent of appellate scrutiny, Rifkind restated a trick Louis Nizer had used in an appendix to *The Implosion Conspiracy*. Nizer had added up the number of judges who sat whenever motions were filed in the case. Thus he counted the same nine justices on the Supreme Court who dealt with nine separate applications as 81 judges. That prestidigitation, coupled with additional multiple counting of three-judge appeals panels enabled him to balloon the number to 112 judges. Nizer then stated that not one of them,

---

[11]See Schneir and Schneir, p. 393.

[12]See Schneir and Schneir, pp. 378–90, 455–50.

[13]References to F.B.I. documents related to my parents' case are by file name, file location, and document number. JR is Julius Rosenberg, DG is David Greenglass, HG is Harry Gold. HQ is F.B.I. headquarters, NY is the New York field office of the F.B.I., Phila. is the Philadelphia field office of the F.B.I. Thus a reference to JR NY 1255 means the Julius Rosenberg file from the New York field office, number 1255. All documents are available in the F.B.I. reading room in Washington, D.C. Our own personal collection has been donated to Columbia University Law School and is available in that library. The Gold and Greenglass statements are in HG HQ August 3, 1950 and DG HQ 332.

even those who voted for stays or *certiorari*, ever questioned the fairness of the trial.[14] Rifkind restated this point in his article.

Since we had already given our first interviews in the summer of 1973, I attempted to get equal space in *TV Guide* with an answer that pointed out the fraudulent nature of the "112 judges" point and others, but I was not permitted. Later we learned that the *TV Guide* article was known to Judge Kaufman and the F.B.I. even before it was published. The F.B.I. distributed it to all of their field offices to use in responding to public inquiries about the case, which were quite widespread in the spring and summer of 1974. After the first public rally of the newly formed National Committee to Reopen the Rosenberg Case in June of 1974, Rifkind published a version of his article on the op-ed page of the *New York Times* as well as elsewhere in the country.

There was quite a lot of public interest in the case at that time, as evidenced by the invitations we received to speak, by the advance we received for the first edition of *We Are Your Sons,* and by the turnouts at various rallies organized in different parts of the country. In the Los Angeles area, our rally was sabotaged when an individual (who was never caught) set off a tear-gas bomb a few minutes into the program, causing a two-hour delay. We made a Freedom of Information Act request in February of 1975 in order to, we hoped, blow the lid off the frame-up. We expected that public attention would make our request irresistible, but even if the government did resist, we hoped public attention would increase the likelihood that the courts would rule in our favor. We were partially right. Public pressure and some very persistent legal efforts by our lawyers forced the release of over 180,000 pages of (mostly F.B.I.) documents by January of 1978. Unfortunately, we failed to win the release of perhaps 500,000 or more additional documents and those that were released had sections blacked out claiming one or another of the FOIA exemptions.[15]

The fall 1975 releases revealed the new "line" of the government's defenders. The government released files showing that there had been a jailhouse informer, one Jerome Eugene Tartakow, who was supplying the FBI with details of conversations he had allegedly had with my father before and during the trial. The informer alleged that my father confessed that he was indeed a Soviet spy and also gave details about the espionage ring beyond what was disclosed by David Greenglass' testimony at the trial.[16] From that moment forward a major issue for all students of the case has been: How

---

[14]See Nizer, pp. 493–95.

[15]At last count our attorney Marshall Perlin estimates that we have received approximately 300,000 pages with about 500,000 still withheld.

[16]For an early F.B.I. account of Tartakow, see JR HQ 639.

much of Tartakow's information contained in the F.B.I. documents is to be believed?

Initial newspaper stories mostly supported the view that the Tartakow revelations were strong evidence that our parents were guilty. Slowly, the skepticism about Tartakow based on our and others' vigorous disputations began to seep into the public debate.[17] In 1979, Ronald Radosh and Sol Stern, self-described members of the "democratic left" (which usually meant anti-communist), published an article in the *New Republic* entitled "The Hidden Rosenberg Case." Stern and Radosh argued that Tartakow was believable enough to conclude that our father was guilty. They also used some FBI documents to argue that our mother was framed. This "split the difference" verdict was later modified when Radosh and his new collaborator Joyce Milton published *The Rosenberg File,* which rehabilitated virtually all elements of the government's case. The book built on the work of Stern and Radosh to flesh out their views on the "other spy ring," individuals who were never officially charged in the trial but were mentioned as possible espionage affiliates of my father: Alfred Sarant, Joel Barr, Michael and Ann Sidorovich, and William Perl. The details of the issues that divide Radosh and Milton on one hand and those adhering to "innocent and framed" on the other can be followed in the new chapters in the 1983 edition of *Invitation to an Inquest,* in the second edition of *We Are Your Sons,* and in various letters to the editor columns in the fall of 1983.

With the publication of *The Rosenberg File,* establishment historian Arthur Schlesinger, Jr. stated that all questions about the case had been answered. Columnist George Will pronounced the case "closed," both in his column and on national television. Yet despite that, Radosh and Milton were effectively confronted by Walter and Miriam Schneir in a debate staged at New York City's Town Hall in October of 1983 before a packed house. The debate was continued on an ABC News *Nightline* program.[18] I believe that anyone who takes the time to read the various rebuttals and check the footnotes will come to the same conclusion I did in the new edition of *We Are Your Sons:*

[17]For our first response see *New York Times* (8 January 1976): 31.
[18]See Radosh and Stern, "The Hidden Rosenberg Case," *New Republic* (23 June 1979): 13–25; "The Rosenberg Letters," *New Republic* (4–11 August 1979): 27; Radosh and Milton, *The Rosenberg File* (NY: Holt, 1983); Schneir and Schneir, "New Light on the Rosenberg Case: An Interview with Michael and Robert Meeropol," *Socialist Review* 13 (1983): 71–96; Meeropol and Meeropol, *We Are Your Sons,* 2nd ed. (Urbana, IL: University of Illinois Press, 1987), Ch. 15; "Were the Rosenbergs Framed?" Transcript of a debate at New York City's Town Hall, 20 October 1983 (this transcript is available from *The Nation*); "The Rosenbergs: A Thirty Year Debate," *Nightline,* Show #639, 20 October 1983: 9.

If one wishes to be generous, one can say [*The Rosenberg File*] is a terribly flawed work that avoids all evidence that would tend to contradict its conclusions. If one wishes to be harsh, one can say that it is based on deliberate misrepresentation of the material.[19]

The book, in my opinion, is an intellectual fraud.[20]

Meanwhile a member of the original F.B.I. team, Robert J. Lamphere, a man who by his own admission would have had to be at the center of any frame-up, had been quietly preparing his own version. Relying, he claimed, on his memory, he put together a memoir entitled *The FBI-KGB War*.[21] In it he describes the F.B.I.'s utilization of intercepted cables between the KGB and Soviet agents in the West to catch a number of spies, including my parents. He left the F.B.I. in 1955 and the only documentation used in his book was material released by the FBI pursuant to my brother's and my FOIA lawsuit. That material contains not one word of KGB messages. However, some F.B.I. documents do contain the F.B.I.'s characterization of material that may or may not come from the KGB cables (we must take Lamphere's word that they do).

For instance, Lamphere refers to an alleged KGB cable that refers to someone described in an F.B.I. document thusly:

> Christian name, ETHEL, used her husband's last name; had been married for five years (at this time); 29 years of age; member of the Communist Party USA, possibly joined in 1938; probably knew about her husband's work with the Soviets.[22]

We are left with Lamphere's word that this referred to someone involved in espionage. Lamphere asserts that "the details in [this] message fit Ethel Rosenberg's background precisely."[23] In fact, aside from the fact that the U.S. government later framed my mother as a spy, the other elements of the description would fit any married American Communist named Ethel who

---

[19]*Sons*, p. 398

[20]See Gerald E. Markowitz, "How Not to Write History: A Critique of Radosh and Milton's *The Rosenberg File*," *Science and Society* (Spring 1984); Edward Pessen, "The Rosenberg Case Revisited: A Critical Essay on a Recent Scholarly Examination," *New York History* (January, 1984).

[21]See Robert J. Lamphere and Tom Schachtman, *The FBI-KGB War* (NY: Random House, 1986).

[22]Lamphere, p. 95–96

[23]Lamphere, p. 185–86

was twenty-nine years old in 1945. Also, we are unsure as to whether the lines "probably knew about her husband's work with the Soviets" are the F.B.I.'s or the KGB's. Since this is the only fragment potentially related to my parents, Lamphere makes the most of it. Assuming this fragment does refer to my mother, what other explanations for this reference could there be? One possibility is that the KGB cables included biographies of potential recruits. It might even include biographies of people to be avoided—for example, because their involvement in Communist political activities would make them subject to suspicion. Except for Lamphere's assurance, out of context of the entire F.B.I. document of which the above quote is a small fragment, it is impossible to come to any conclusion as to what this means.

And then there is another possibility. The KGB operative reporting the various people involved in his ring might be padding his contacts to gain favor at home. Agents are capable of exaggerating and even altering information for the benefit of superiors. F.B.I. documents that purport to describe what went on between an witness and an FBI agent are not necessarily accurate portrayals of what actually occurred. For example, there are two different versions of the FBI's first interview with Ruth Greenglass that present quite different pictures.[24] Lamphere's uncritical use of KGB cables is his only basis for the conviction of my parents before the bar of history.

Everything else in his book is a rehash of the trial testimony with some information taken from Radosh and Milton's book as well. There is also a glaring omission. Lamphere surmises that Morris and Lona Cohen, two Americans who disappeared from New York around the time of my parents' arrests and later reappeared when they were arrested in England as Peter and Helen Kroger, acted "as 'cut outs' so that Julius Rosenberg would never be able to identify the man who was directing his network's activities."[25] In fact, Morris and Lona Cohen were couriers between Yakovlev and a scientist, code-named Perseus, at Los Alamos who, unlike Klaus Fuchs, was never caught. The Cohens were traded to the Soviets in 1965. Lamphere's diagram in the picture section of his book doesn't even include Morris and Lona Cohen. This despite the fact that Klaus Fuchs explicitly told the F.B.I. (and the person he told was probably Lamphere) that he knew from the nature of the questions he was being asked by his Soviet contacts that the Soviets were receiving other scientific information from inside the

---

[24]See *Sons*, p. 435, which compares the F.B.I.'s descriptions of their first interview with Ruth Greenglass with Ruth's own version prepared for her attorney. See also Report of Agent John W. Lewis, DG HQ 193: 38 and NY to Washington, JR NY 1636 In., 1 May 1953.
[25]Lamphere, p. 278

Los Alamos project. Since Lamphere knew what Fuchs had said, it is revealing that he did not put two and two together and include the Cohens as contacts between Yakovlev and the uncaught scientist(s). Perhaps he was hiding something from his readers.[26]

In 1990, the third volume of former Soviet leader Nikita Khrushchev's memoirs, *Khrushchev Remembers: The Glasnost Tapes,* was published. Included in that volume were two joined fragments that stated:

> I will share a secret with you: we got some assistance on a number of issues through some good people who helped us to master the production of nuclear energy faster and to produce our first atomic bomb. These people suffered; they were people committed to ideas. They were neither agents nor spies for the Soviet Union. Rather, they were people sympathetic with our ideals. They acted on their progressive views, without seeking any payment. I say progressive because I believe they were not Communists. They did what they could in order to help the Soviet Union to arm itself with the atomic bomb and thus to stand against the United States of America. That was the issue of the times.
>
> This does not diminish the merits and initiative of our own scientists, but one must not discount the help that was provided to us by our friends. The names of those friends are known to thinking people and to those who follow events in the newspapers. Those friends suffered; they were punished. But their names are known.
>
> Let this be a worthy tribute to the memory of those people. Let my words be like words of thanks to those people who sacrificed their lives and who provided help to the Soviet state for that great cause when the United States was ahead of us and was blackmailing us. Finally, exerting all our strength and all our capacities, we built the atomic bomb; but it must be understood that we did it to become equal.

---

[26]For Morris and Lona Cohen, see Michael Dobbs, "How Soviets Stole U.S. Atom Secrets: Pieces in a Puzzle," *Washington Post* (October 4, 1992): 1, 36.

Since I was present at the talks that Stalin had in a limited circle when he mentioned the Rosenbergs with warmth, I feel it is my duty to speak of them now. I cannot specifically say what kind of help the Rosenbergs provided us, but both Stalin and Molotov were informed. Molotov knew because he was then the minister of foreign affairs. I heard from both Stalin and Molotov that the Rosenbergs provided very significant help in accelerating the production of our atomic bomb.[27]

The knee-jerk media response that occurred when Tartakow's identity became public occurred again. The major news media assured people that Khrushchev was in a position to know and had no reason to lie.[28] We responded with a submission to the *New York Times* op-ed page, while Walter Schneir wrote a detailed analysis for *The Nation*.[29] There were three issues for my brother and me. First, the individual who did the voice print analysis which proved that the first two volumes of *Khrushchev Remembers* were transcripts of tapes of Khrushchev's voice was unable to verify the voice on the quoted portion of this new tape as Khrushchev's. This is strong evi-dence that the statement in the book is cobbled together from different reels of tape. Thus, it is quite possible that the early paragraphs in the quoted passage, even if stated by Khrushchev, were not meant to refer to my parents. We do not know if Khrushchev actually spoke the paragraphs that do explicitly refer to my parents. Second, the story Khrushchev tells is published from a transcript that was made in 1989 of a tape recording made around 1973 about conversations Khrushchev supposedly remembered from 1953. And all involved, the people Khrushchev quoted as well as Khrushchev himself, are dead.

---

[27]*Khrushchev Remembers: The Glasnost Tapes*, foreword by Strobe Talbot, trans. and ed. Jerrold L. Schechter with Vyacheslav V. Luchkov (Boston: Little, Brown, 1993), pp. 193–94. Note that the first paragraph refers to people who clearly were not my parents. Perhaps this is a reference to the scientist Perseus. See below, xxxi.

[28]See, for example, Esther Pessin, "Yesterday's stunning revelation seems to establish the Rosenberg's guilt beyond a reasonable doubt," *New York Post* (25 September 1990): 3; "Red Scares and False Alarms," *New York Times* (editorial) (10 October 1990).

[29]See Walter Schneir, review of *Khrushchev Remembers: The Glasnost Tapes* in *The Nation* (3 December 1990). See also Meeropol and Meeropol letter to the *New York Times*, "Doubts on Khrushchev's Rosenberg Comment," 11 December 1990.

Our third point assumes for the sake of argument that Khrushchev did make those statements. The reference to the "great help" my parents had been to the Soviets in building their atom bomb is wrong. Even Radosh and Milton's book doesn't make that claim. So how could Khrushchev have gotten it so wrong? Possibly he just mis-remembered the conversations he had overheard. Perhaps they were referring to Fuchs or to Morris and Lona Cohen. Perhaps the references to my parents were about their being good communists and unwilling to help the U.S. government create a massive show trial. We cannot speculate as to what Khrushchev *actually* heard from Stalin and/or Molotov, but we can be absolutely certain that even if the government's case was totally correct about my parents and David Greenglass, the material they supposedly transmitted had no possible impact on the Soviets' ability to build the atom bomb, especially in the context of what Fuchs accomplished.[30]

Support for this view was expressed by a rather unlikely source, General Leslie Groves, the commander of the Los Alamos installation where the Manhattan Project was located during World War II. In the spring of 1954, the Atomic Energy Commission was deciding whether or not to lift the security clearance of Dr. J. Robert Oppenheimer, a top scientist who had many left-wing associates in the 1930s. In the course of his testimony, Groves gratuitously made the following statement:

> I think the data that went out in the case of the Rosenbergs was of minor value. I would never say that publicly. Again, that is something, while it is not secret, I think should be kept very quiet because irrespective of the value of that in the over-all picture, the Rosenbergs deserved to hang and I would not like to say anything that would make people say General Groves thinks they didn't do much damage after all.[31]

My brother and I believe that there is much more to this statement than the corroboration of the fact that the government at the trial exaggerated and

---

[30]For some detailed evidence in support of this argument, see Joseph Sharlitt, *Fatal Error* (NY: Scribner's, 1989), pp. 202–48. See also "Affidavit of Phillip Morrison" and "Affidavit of Henry Linschitz," *Morton Sobell vs. United States of America* 66 Civ 1328, United States District Court for the Southern District of New York. See also Markowitz and Meeropol.

[31]United States Atomic Energy Commission, *In the Matter of J. Robert Oppenheimer,* Vol. 4 (Washington, D.C.: April 15, 1954), p. 570. This section of the transcript was classified and deleted from the published transcript, p. 175. The deleted section was released to my brother and me as a result of our FOIA lawsuit and enclosed in a letter, Richard G. Hewlett to Marshall Perlin, 23 February 1979. Quoted in Markowitz and Meeropol, p. 1.

even falsified the accuracy and significance of the Greenglass scientific evidence. Why did our parents "deserve to hang," if the information Greenglass stole was "of minor value"? They were communists who could, because they were related to David Greenglass, be successfully connected with atomic espionage, yet they resisted. If they were to "fully cooperate" (see below, 676ff), they would expand the group of spying communists, perhaps to include top communist officials in the espionage ring. But they "deserved to hang" because they resisted.

According to Emanuel Bloch, after the death sentence was pronounced, my father made the following comments to him, Bloch's father, and Ethel:

> This death sentence is not surprising. It had to be. There had to be a Rosenberg Case. There had to be a Rosenberg Case because there had to be an intensification of the hysteria in America to make the Korean War acceptable to the American people. There had to be a hysteria and a fear sent through America in order to get increased war budgets. And there had to be a dagger thrust in the heart of the left to tell them that you are no longer gonna give five years for a Smith Act prosecution or one year for Contempt of Court, but we're gonna kill ya.[32]

In January of 1953, my father reacted to Judge Kaufman's refusal to reduce the sentence by saying his opinion should be called "Alleged Communists or pro-Communists are better off dead." Here and elsewhere he demonstrated understanding that the case was political and that the death sentence served a dual purpose: to attempt to coerce a confession and cooperation out of them and to sanitize America, cutting out the "cancer" of communism from the country with death sentences and threats of death sentences.

In the years since the break-up of the Soviet Union, Russia has become a cornucopia of Cold War memories and stories. Individuals have attempted to tell of their activities, sometimes for money, sometimes just for the sake of "history." Among the individuals who have been speaking about their roles as Soviet intelligence agents in the United States is the Soviet national who was indicted along with our parents, the man known as "John," A. Yakovlev (né Yatskov) for whom Harry Gold was allegedly working. Before he died, Yatskov gave some interviews to American journalists and one of the interviews was utilized for a major story in the *Washington Post* called "How Soviets Stole U.S. Atom Secrets." Much of the focus of the article is

---

[32]*Sons,* 1st ed. (Boston: Houghton-Mifflin, 1975), p. 352.

on Morris and Lona Cohen. Their role in atomic espionage was the center-piece of Yatskov's interview. It appears they had been the link between the Soviets and a still-unknown scientist at Los Alamos, code-named Perseus. The prominent role played by these individuals suggests a possible new motive for the manufacture of the case against my parents. The FBI may have been covering up its failure to prevent significant espionage from taking place right under its nose. In early March of 1950, J. Edgar Hoover informed Rear Admiral Sidney Souers, Special Consultant to President Harry S. Truman, of Fuchs' January 30 confession. In that report is a tantalizing piece of information:

> The [Soviet] agent . . . asked Fuchs what he knew about the electro-magnetic method as an alternative means of separating the uranium isotopes. This very much surprised Fuchs who, at the time, knew nothing of any work on this method and had never considered it. . . .

> During 1947 Fuchs was asked on one occasion by the Russian agent for any information he could give about "the tritium bomb." He said that he was very surprised to have the question put to him in those particular terms and it suggested to him (as had the earlier request for information about the electro-magnetic isotopes separation process) that the Russians were getting information from other sources. . . .

> During the latter part of 1948 he [Fuchs] was asked on one occasion for a specific Chalk River report . . . which he had never seen. He was also told that "there is a report on mixing devices" and was asked whether he could get it. He had not . . . seen this report.

> He was also asked about the solvent extraction process. . .

> All these questions confirmed his opinion that the Russians had access to information from another source or sources.[33]

---

[33]Hoover to Souers, March 2, 1950, National Security Council, Atomic, Russia File, Harry S. Truman Library, quoted in Robert C. Williams, *Klaus Fuchs, Atom Spy* (Cambridge: Harvard University Press, 1987), pp. 189, 192–93.

When Hoover realized that there was another leak out of the U.S. atomic weapons project he must have been desperate to demonstrate his spy-catching ability, no matter what. The first paragraph in the quote refers to Fuchs' activities between 1942 and December of 1943. Thus it is impossible for the alleged activities of David Greenglass to have been the source of the questions Fuchs was asked at that time because Greenglass' alleged activities did not commence until 1944.[34] But for Hoover that was immaterial. Any communist or associate of communists would be fair game for the "development" of a case. We believe the genesis of the Rosenberg-Sobell case is the inability of the F.B.I. to catch the people referred to in the above quoted passages. For Lamphere, this is a fact that his otherwise photographic memory conveniently omits. For the FBI, creating the Greenglass testimony that identified my father as the head of a spy ring that stole important secrets from Los Alamos permitted them to avoid admitting that they had failed to catch the real spy and his couriers from Los Alamos.[35]

But there is another aspect of the Yatskov interview that bears comment. Yatskov has stated that he did, in fact, control the activities of Harry Gold and that Gold was, indeed, a Soviet courier, acting as a liaison between Yatskov and Fuchs. This point was seized upon by Ronald Radosh in a recent series of articles. Yatskov's "admission," according to Radosh, seals the guilt of my parents because our side has always argued that Gold was a "Walter Mitty" type—a man with a vivid imagination who fantasized all sorts of things, who lied for the sheer creative joy of it, and who was, in the words of the documentary *The Unquiet Death of Ethel and Julius Rosenberg*, a "weak link" in what the prosecutors described as a "perfect chain" from Fuchs to Gold to the Greenglasses and then my parents.[36]

Now it is certainly true that I have always believed that Gold was not a spy. I am still not ready to abandon that view, solely because one former Soviet espionage agent has given some press interviews. Instead, my brother and I have made a strong effort to get Russian intelligence, the successor organization to the Soviet KGB, to release documents from their files about our parents, should any such files exist. We sought the good offices of one of our Senators, who wrote a letter to Mr. Primakov, then

---

[34]See Record, pp. 422–27. In the *Washington Post* article there is further confirmation of that fact. Igor Kurchatov, the so-called father of the Soviet atomic bomb, wrote in his notes that important intelligence arrived from the United States on March 22, 1943. (See Dobbs, p. 36)

[35]This might explain why, when the Cohens were captured in Great Britain, the U.S. government made no effort to have them extradited to stand trial here.

[36]See "The Guilt of the Rosenbergs: An Exchange," *The New York Post* (June 245, 1993): 32.

head of Soviet intelligence, as well as to General Volkogonov. The latter was the man who researched whether American POW's from the Vietnam War were ever in the Soviet Union, as well as whether or not Alger Hiss had been a Soviet spy. We hoped he would be willing to conduct a similar effort. Our hopes were not realized. We received a response through our Senator that stated that it is the policy of Russian intelligence not to release any material about their previous activities. We think it is impossible, without documentation, to be certain whether the recollections of Yatskov or other former Soviet intelligence agents are accurate and complete. So we are skeptical about the new "revelations" emanating from the former Soviet Union, especially when they are uncorroborated oral testimony. This is the same stance I urge in response to Lamphere's work, until the F.B.I. and the rest of the government choose to release details of the alleged deciphering of KGB cables.

However, let us for the sake of argument assume that Yatskov accurately reports that Gold was a Soviet courier. While that forces my brother and me (and the Schneirs) to abandon our view that Gold was not a spy, it does not mean that Gold is telling the entire truth about the alleged meeting with David Greenglass in Albuquerque. It does not even prove that Gold met Greenglass in Albuquerque. All it shows is that Gold was a spy. I find it hard to imagine how anyone could seriously accept Radosh's assertion that Yatskov's statements about Gold prove my parents' guilt. In fact, all they really do is force those of us who used to scorn the original defense view that Gold and the Greenglasses were spies but my parents weren't to wonder if the view adopted by Emanuel Bloch, my parents, and Malcolm Sharp, in opposition to Wexley and Reuben, might not be closer to the truth than we imagined. Of course, future reports from the former Soviet Union as to whether David Greenglass was in fact a spy may shed additional light upon this issue. The important thing to bear in mind as memoirs emerge in the former Soviet Union is that, absent documentation, these "oral histories" must be approached very skeptically, whatever position they bolster. Former KGB agents have their own agenda (financial, political, and others that we who live in a different culture may not be able to fathom). We believe, and have always believed, that full disclosure of all documents by both governments is the best way to get to the bottom of what Soviet espionage actually accomplished in the U.S. during World War II. When that picture emerges, we will, perhaps, be able to close the historical book on the factual aspects of our parents' case.

An extraordinary event unfolded at the Waldorf-Astoria Hotel in New York City on August 9 and 10, 1993. The American Bar Association Litigation Section, as part of its "Trials of the Century" series, retried my

parents with new lawyers, a real federal judge, and two juries of six New
Yorkers each. As with previous exercises such as the retrial of Lee Harvey
Oswald for the assassination of President John F. Kennedy, its point, from
the ABA's perspective, was to showcase litigation strategies, criminal law
procedure, and the litigation talents of the two "sides" for the conventioneers
and for the general public. In the year when Oswald was being "tried," *USA
Today* ran five separate articles before, during, and after the event, emphasizing the significance of the exercise in the light of the controversy generated by Oliver Stone's film *JFK*. When I heard about the planned retrial of
my parents I immediately put myself at the disposal of the defense team. I
wanted to make sure that every piece of evidence that had been wrung from
the F.B.I. through our FOIA lawsuit as well as material developed by the
Schneirs and others would be available to these lawyers as they attempted to
"defend" my parents against the charge of conspiracy to commit espionage.
Marshall Perlin and Walter Schneir also gave generously of their time and
provided documents to the defense.

The rules set out by the ABA Litigation Section were quite interesting.
The exercise was to take place as if the original trial had occurred but now a
retrial was going on. Everything uncovered about the case by the Schneirs
(Harry Gold's conversations with his attorneys, for example[37]) and everything in the F.B.I. and other government files could be utilized to cast doubt
on the veracity of the prosecution witnesses. I pointed out promising areas
of research to the team of defense attorneys and they spent hundreds of hours
becoming experts on the case and prepared for it as they would for a real
trial. Meanwhile, the new set of prosecutors consulted with Ronald Radosh
and attempted to develop information from the F.B.I. files that would bolster Harry Gold's *bona fides* as a real spy with direct evidence supporting his
testimony that he actually had gone to Albuquerque and met with David
Greenglass on June 3, 1945.[38] This would be necessary should the new
"defense team" choose to use the Wexley/Schneir thesis that Gold was not a
spy but a pathological liar, as my brother and I called him. They even
proposed a stipulated "testimony" from Yatskov based on his interview with
the *Washington Post*. That testimony, which became part of the record of
the retrial, stated that Yatskov was Gold's control but also stated that he
never met or knew my parents.[39]

Since my parents and Harry Gold were dead and neither the real David
and Ruth Greenglass nor Max Elitcher were available (it would have been

[37]See Schneir and Schneir, pp. 397–403.
[38]For the lines they were preparing to pursue, see Radosh and Milton, pp. 455–
70.
[39]See Dobbs, p. 36.

interesting if the team of lawyers for the government had attempted to interview the Greenglasses and Elitcher to clear up some of the contradictions between what was in the F.B.I. files and what they said at the trial, but as far as I know they talked only to Ronald Radosh), the two sets of lawyers hired actors to play the parts of witnesses and defendants. The lawyers "prepped" their clients just as they would real clients. The difference is that the lawyers had to surmise how their clients would respond to difficult questions on cross examination that the real individuals had never been asked. For example, how should an actor playing Harry Gold respond to questioning regarding the contradiction between his statement in August of 1950 that he brought greetings from "Ben in Brooklyn" and his testimony at the trial that he said "I come from Julius"? As it turned out the new prosecution team's strategy was to have Greenglass not even specify the code that was used and have the actor playing Gold state that in the past he had thought the greeting was from Ben or from Julius but "today" he was not sure what man's name it was.

The actors playing my parents were told by the defense teams not to take the Fifth Amendment when asked about being communists but to forthrightly state that they had indeed been communists. The actress who played my mother stated in the retrial that the 1938 slogan of the Communist Party had been "Communism is Twentieth Century Americanism" and that she had believed that.[40] She explained the lessening of political activity after 1943 as stemming from her primary devotion to being a mother after my birth. "When a choice comes between a diaper and a meeting, I choose the diaper, and I always have."[41] The result of the refusal to treat the charge of communism as a contagious disease from which one needed to be immunized by the Fifth Amendment worked with the jury. The jury's refusal to see communism as evidence of a proclivity to be spies[42] was apparent in the interviews they gave to the media after they rendered not guilty verdicts.[43]

---

[40]"In the Matter Of: *United States of America v. Julius Rosenberg and Ethel Rosenberg.*" August 9, 1993. Noon and Pratt Min-U-Script (available from Noon and Pratt (800) 362-2520, Original File aba08093.v1, 466 pages): 327.

[41]ABA: 350. See also *Sons,* pp. 95–96, 399–403 for my evidence and speculation on this issue.

[42]"The Communist Party being part of the Communist International only served the interests of Moscow, whether it be propaganda or espionage and sabotage." This from Elizabeth Bentley's testimony, Record: 978.

[43]This led Ronald Radosh to blast the "ignorance" of the jury about the "true nature" of American Communism in the 1940s and 1950s. See Ronald Radosh, "The ABA Acquits the Rosenbergs with Poor History and PC," *Wall Street Journal* (18 August 1993).

Unable to use communism as a club to destroy my parents' credibility before the jury, the new prosecutors had hoped to use the testimony of the jailhouse informant Jerome Eugene Tartakow. Had the judge permitted it, the jury would have been faced with another credibility issue. It would not only have been the word of my parents against the Greenglasses (with Gold's credibility playing a supporting role), but now the juries' decisions would have hinged on their willingness to believe either Tartakow or my father. I would have relished the challenge of using the F.B.I. files to show contradictions in Tartakow's statements. However, the defense team chose to use a legal precedent excluding testimony about what defendants have said to individuals who acted as "government agents" in soliciting the statements. Both teams wrote detailed motion and rebuttal papers, and Judge Marvin Aspen, a sitting federal judge for the Northern District of Illinois, rendered a decision that excluded all of Tartakow's "testimony" from the mock trial. A side effect of this was that the testimony of the photographer Ben Schneider was also not admissible because in legal terms it was "fruit of the poisoned tree." The F.B.I. documents clearly indicate that Tartakow was the reason they "found" Schneider, who testified as a seemingly disinterested witness that my parents had taken passport photographs. Since this was in direct contradiction to my parents' statements on the witness stand, many believe this significantly impressed the jury by damaging my parents' credibility.[44]

The judge's rulings about Schneider and Tartakow raise an interesting question about the difference between "legal guilt" and "historical guilt." Legal guilt exists when one is proven guilty beyond a reasonable doubt in a court of law. In that respect, the destruction of all aspects of the government's case by subsequent research which was then confirmed by the ABA mock trial should give us all pause. When the prosecution's case has been proven false and fraudulent the presumption of innocence must reassert itself. The refusal to, *as a matter of law,* permit the jury to listen to Tartakow's testimony is based on the valuable common sense idea that such individuals have such a tremendous incentive to create stories supportive of the government's case that their testimony should not be permitted to influence a jury. It may sound trite, but our entire system of justice is predicated on the idea that it is better for ten guilty people to go free as a result of the Constitutional protections we all enjoy than to ignore those protections and perhaps convict one innocent person. Though it was only a mock trial, the refusal of the judge to permit Schneider to testify because he was "fruit of the poisoned tree" (namely Tartakow) reminds us all that those rules are not there to be broken whenever the government *really* wants a conviction. One of the attorneys working with the defense made an

---

[44]For my view on the Schneider issue, see *Sons,* pp. 423–25.

important point about the issue of "legal guilt" in a letter to me one month
after the ABA mock trial.

> Law students are taught that while a defense attorney has
> the obligation to do whatever is ethically possible to
> secure an acquittal . . . the government's obligation is
> quite different. Prosecutors have an express ethical obli-
> gation to "justice." It is this notion that attempts to level
> the playing field on which the government brings its awe-
> some powers to bear against a [lawyer] . . . with limited
> assets; it is this obligation that ultimately resulted in
> dramatic changes to our criminal procedure laws that now
> require the government to share exculpatory information
> with defense counsel. The mock trial of your parents clear-
> ly demonstrated what those of us who practice criminal
> defense law have learned the hard way: In the hands of
> unprincipled prosecutors the government's obligation to
> justice is reduced to hollow words in a law student's
> textbook.
> . . . the evidence that the original jury heard and used as a
> basis to convict was cooked up by the Greenglasses and
> Harry Gold. On that basis alone, I will always tell people
> who ask that your parents were innocent.[45]

Nevertheless, as a student of history and as someone concerned not with
the technical "victory" at the ABA mock trial but with the judgment of our
country about my parents, I admit that I would have wished to have the
information I used in *We Are Your Sons* to refute Radosh and Milton's
belief in Tartakow's credibility put to the test before the two juries at the
ABA retrial. Similarly I would have been interested to see whether this jury
would have doubted Schneider if the perjury he committed at the original
trial had been revealed to them.[46]

As this book goes to press, the American Bar Association retrial has
generated a bit of publicity, but interestingly, there was no news coverage
on the major television networks, no news stories in *USA Today,* the *New
York Times,* the *Wall Street Journal,* nor the *Washington Post.* Court TV
ran specials and C-SPAN ran the panel discussion that followed the event, at
which I, Marshall Perlin, Sidney Zion (journalist and co-author of *The
Autobiography of Roy Cohn*), Ronald Radosh, and the only surviving

---

[45]Letter, Stephen P. Shea to Michael Meeropol, 7 September 1993.
[46]For Schneider's perjury, see Record: 1437; Schneir and Schneir, pp. 180–83.

prosecutor, James Kilsheimer, participated. During that panel discussion, a question from the audience brought up the fact that the American Bar Association committee that had supposedly investigated the charges against Judge Kaufman had kept its report "exonerating" the judge secret.[47] This prompted the chair of the panel, Jerold Solovy, the Head of the ABA Litigation Section, to promise to intercede with the new president of the ABA to get that report released. He has since made that request. Since I know that the report is a whitewash, I would be very interested in getting a crack at analyzing what it ignores in order to reach its conclusion.

Meanwhile, the Arts and Entertainment Network ran a special in November, 1993, and there have been a number of discussions on radio shows. It remains to be seen if this flurry of interest will prompt anyone in the government to release more of the currently withheld documents and/or launch a Congressional investigation with subpoena power. It has been over a decade since I asked in 1982 for such an investigation. I won't hold my breath.

The reason I am not very sanguine about a full reopening of the case is that, again, my parents' case was first and foremost about politics. The *Columbia Law Review,* in a detailed analysis of some of the legal issues in the case, called it "the outstanding 'political' trial of this generation."[48] Putting the word "political" in quotes was perhaps their way of distancing themselves from characterizing it as a political case, a not surprising desire given that the article was written in 1954 at the height of the McCarthy period. Today, with the hind-sight of over forty years of history, it is clear, as the statement by General Leslie Groves demonstrates, that the case has always been about politics, not espionage. The government behaved the way it did because *it did not matter if real spies were caught or if communists were framed as spies.*

Judge Kaufman summed up the political goal as he prepared to sentence our parents to death:

> It is so difficult to make people realize that this country is engaged in a life and death struggle with a completely different system. This struggle is not only manifested externally between these two forces but this case indicates quite clearly that it also involves the employment by the enemy of secret as well as overt outspoken forces among our own people. All of our democratic institutions are,

---

[47]See *Sons,* pp. 382–84; see *New York Times* (23 September 1983): B4 for a news story on the report.
[48]*CLR:* 219

therefore, directly involved in this great conflict. I believe that never at any time in our history were we ever confronted to the same degree that we are today with such a challenge to our very existence.[49]

This case forged the essential link between domestic radicalism (communists and "fellow travelers" and anyone who could be smeared for sounding like or agreeing with communists about anything) and grave danger to the nation's security. American public opinion became mostly monolithic as a result of the successes of the McCarthy period in defeating the left and cowing dissenters. The government's victory was achieved by convincing the general public that the left was un-American, a bunch of would-be if not actual traitors. Convincing the public was the major success that the American government achieved with the conviction and executions of my parents.

Had my parents wanted to "fully cooperate," they would have had to put other people exactly where they were and add further "evidence" to the testimony introduced at the trial that their love of communism was so great they were willing to betray their country. Thus, David and Ruth Greenglass testified about my parents' preference for "Russian Communism" over the American form of government.

> In order to connect Party membership and activities with motive for espionage, the Government put Elizabeth Bentley on the stand. She testified that the American Communist Party was part of the Communist International, serving only the interest of Moscow, whether though "propaganda or espionage or sabotage," and carrying out the directives of Moscow; that the members were instructed to do everything possible to aid Russia; and that those who disobeyed instructions were expelled from the Party.[50]

My parents refused to play the roles written for them by the government. Instead, in a naive way, particularly my father believed that the American system of justice and fair play would ultimately vindicate him. He was wrong, but it was actually a pretty close issue. The research of Michael Parrish about the Supreme Court deliberations on the case indicates that at one point at the May 25, 1953 conference, there were four votes for

---

[49]Record, pp. 1613-4
[50]*CLR:* 226

certiorari and the Court was already beginning to make plans to receive briefs during the summer.[51] Unfortunately, Justice Jackson, who had only offered to vote for *certiorari* to keep a damaging memo by Justice Douglas from being published as a dissent, withdrew that offer when Douglas withdrew the memo. Meanwhile, Emily Alman, who together with her husband David was a mainstay of the Committee to Secure Justice in the Rosenberg Case, has told me that members of Congress who were supportive of the clemency effort said that the supporters of my parents came "that close" to getting enough pressure on President Eisenhower to convince him to intervene.

Whatever comes out, should the American and Russian governments relent and release all information in their files, the role my parents were asked to play by being offered the choice to "talk or die" was at bottom a *political* role. They made not only a personal decision but a *political* decision not to name names and put others in their places. My brother and I have always believed and continue to believe that that was what *any decent person* should have done.

---

[51]For details see Michael Parrish, "Cold War Justice: The Supreme Court and the Rosenbergs," *American Historical Review* 82 (1977): 823–25.

First Petition for Executive Clemency

Identical petitions were filed by each of my parents. Below, we print the petition filed by my mother on January 9, 1953.

The President of the United States:

Your petitioner, ETHEL ROSENBERG, a federal prisoner, No. 110510, confined in the Sing Sing Prison at Ossining, New York, hereby respectfully prays your Excellency to grant her Pardon or Commutation of Sentence for reasons herein set forth.

THE FACTS

Petitioner states that the facts in her case are as follows: I pleaded not guilty to the crime charged against me. I have proclaimed my innocence at all times and defended it at my trial by producing evidence on my behalf and testifying in my own defense. I am guilty of no wrong-doing, and I assert here before you, Mr. President, and before God and all men, that the whole truth is that I am innocent.

My husband, JULIUS ROSENBERG, and myself were convicted, together with Morton Sobell, a co-defendant, of having conspired with Anatoli Yakovlev, a Soviet national, Harry Gold, and David and Ruth Greenglass, during World War II and for some years thereafter, to transmit information "relating to the national defense" to the Soviet Union, with the intention to advantage that nation, although not to injure the United States.[1]

---

[1]See Record, p. 2

CASE FOR THE PROSECUTION

The spy plot unfolded by the Greenglasses, Ruth corroborating David with studied rehearsal, is predicated upon the following recital. (1) In November, 1944, prior to her departure to visit David at his station in New Mexico, Ruth was solicited by us to induce David to transmit specific information concerning the Los Alamos project: "location, personnel, physical description, security measures, camouflage and experiments."[2] Ruth was asked to memorize the data and, on return, relay the information to my husband for ultimate transmittal to the Soviet Union. At Albuquerque, David, after an ephemeral refusal, gave Ruth the requested data, readily known to him despite its secrecy. (2) In January, 1945, David, on furlough, delivered to my husband in New York a fuller written report on the project, including a sketch of a lens mold used in the atomic experimentations. (3) A few nights later, the Greenglasses were introduced to a Mrs. Sidorovich at a social visit to our home. After the departure of this woman, when the Greenglasses and we were alone with each other, my husband described her as a potential courier to collect information from David in New Mexico. To perfect identification of the actual messenger, the side of a Jello-box was cut into two parts, one part of which was kept by Ruth and the other, retained by my husband, was to be on the person of the emissary. At this meeting, I admitted I aided Julius in his espionage work, as a typist. (4) In June, 1945, Harry Gold arrived at the Greenglass apartment in Albuquerque with the salutation "I come from Julius" and produced a portion of the side of a Jello-box that matched the one kept by Ruth. Gold testified his part of the side was given to him by his Soviet superior, Yakovlev. David delivered to Gold information about personnel at the project who were potential recruits for espionage and another sketch of a section of the lens mold, indicating the principles of implosion used in this phase of bomb construction. (5) In September, 1945, on another furlough, in New York, David turned over to my husband a sketch of the cross-section of the atom-bomb and a 12-page exposition covering the functions of its component parts, both of which, despite his stunted educational background, he claims to have composed from memory of scraps of oral information gleaned at the project. While I typed the material, my husband confided he had pilfered a proximity fuse for the Soviet Union from a factory at which he was employed. (6) In the post-war years, David and my husband were co-entrepreneurs in a machine shop business. In the course of this relationship and in sharp contrast to the acrimony that had developed between the Greenglasses and my husband, David described himself as the repository of my husband's confidences that

---

[2]See Record, p. 680

he still was active on behalf of the Soviet Union and had been rewarded for his efforts by gifts and a certificate from the Soviet Government granting him special privileges in Russia. (7) In 1950, after the arrest, in England, of Dr. Klaus Fuchs, an English scientist, accused of stealing atom-bomb information at Los Alamos for the Soviet Union, my husband urged David to flee the country and promised to subsidize the flight. He renewed his imprecations after Gold's arrest and with a clairvoyance that jars the sophisticated mind, predicted that David "would be . . . picked up between June 12th and June 16th."[3] My husband gave David $1000 to prepare for the journey, adding that he and his family were likewise intending to escape. When they accepted the $1000, David and Ruth had already decided to remain in the country and co-operate with the Government. Their subsequent taking of family passport photos, suggesting their preparations for flight, indicates less their remorse and desire for atonement, than a calculated maintenance of avenues for escape from retribution. About a week later, Julius primed David on flight plans and gave him an additional $4000 for flight purposes. Their disingenuousness was more fully exposed by their sedulous secretion of the contraband $4000 from the F.B.I. for their own use,* even after David's professed prompt confession.

The lack of supporting oral testimony was not compensated by the quality of documentary corroboration. The exhibits relating to the crux of the conspiracy—the Jello-box, sketches of the lens mold, cross-sections of the atom-bomb—were replicas which were prepared for trial purpose by David after his arrest or during the trial; they have no probative weight independent of the veracity of his parole testimony. The other exhibits were "puff," dealing with non-controverted matters.

The other Government evidence has already been relegated to insignificance by the Court of Appeals. This testimony follows:

Max Elitcher, a Navy Department senior engineer and a casual acquaintance of my husband in college days, testified he attempted, on several occasions, to interest him in espionage. The initial overture is alleged to have been made directly within a few minutes of a visit, the first communication between my husband and him in six years.[4] His continued wooing of Elitcher over a period of four years, is likewise improbable in the face of the admitted facts that Elitcher never promised to pass nor ever passed any information to anyone. Elitcher's pliant obeisance to officialdom and his

---

*This $4,000 was given to O. John Rogge, the attorney for the Greenglasses, as a fee, the day after David's apprehension.

---

[3]See Record, p. 709
[4]See Record, p. 207

resultant trial testimony is illumined by the witness' admission of fear, bordering on panic, when the authorities implied the presentation against him of espionage and well-founded perjury charges. His hope for immunity was rooted in reality; he was never prosecuted for any crime.

Elizabeth Bentley, a notorious and self-styled Soviet agent unconnected with the instant alleged conspiracy, supplied testimony, whose legal purport is still obscure, that she received certain telephone calls in years prior to the inception of the charged conspiracy from a person who described himself as "Julius."

Harry Gold served to corroborate the enmeshment only of the Greenglasses. His testimony reveals that he neither knew us to be in the conspiracy, nor indeed, that he had ever met us.

The ability of these subsidiary witness to corroborate, at all, our participation in the conspiracy charged, was dependent on resort to flimsy circumstantial evidence. The accomplice, Gold, who had direct contact with the "Russians," could supply the sole link of us with them, only by the inference from the wanderings of one side of the Jello-box. Neither Gold nor Bentley knew the actual person to whom they referred as "Julius." The proposition which the prosecution advanced that it is inferable from the identity of "Julius" with my husband's given name, Julius, that he was "Julius," is negatived by the direct testimony of these same witnesses that the practice of trained and experienced spies, including themselves, was to take care to use assumed names.

Evidence treating with our alleged political views and associations threaded the record and constrained us to put them in issue. This proof was urged and received on the theory that the "communist" character of the views and associations was relevant to show motive but was submitted to the jury solely on the requisite statutory intent "to advantage" the Soviet Union.

To lay the foundation for the admission of this evidence, the prosecution imported Elizabeth Bentley to double in brass. In stating her qualifications as an "expert," she spread before the jury her lurid career of an earlier period. Only the unsavory details of her personal misdeeds make the connection, which was the design of this testimony, between membership in the Communist Party and militarily advantaging the Soviet Union. Her "expert" testimony is neither a generalization that extends the applicability of her experience to all Party members or a specification to reach us.

The Government, under the aegis of the trial court, made "communism" the whipping boy of the proceedings. It was featured in the prosecutor's opening[5] and recurred, whether aptly or not, with unmitigated persistence,

---

[5] See Record, pp. 180–81

during the entire course of the trial. The Government, on this subject, following the tactic of re-asking questions already asked and answered, and pressing lines of interrogation that it came to know would draw assertions of the Fifth Amendment privilege, which, when raised, went unchallenged, displayed a seemingly greater interest in asking the questions than in receiving the answer. In his summation, the prosecutor again invoked "communism" to bind his fragmented evidentiary structure, and, on this behalf, excoriated us as "traitors."

CASE FOR THE DEFENSE

My husband and I testified in our own defense. We denied, generally, and in detail, every part of the evidence introduced by the Government to connect us with a conspiracy to commit espionage. We showed that, during the years in question, we lived a steady, normal existence. Even as late as May, 1950, during the period when the Government claimed we were preparing for flight, my husband depleted our meager cash reserves and obligated himself, on a long term basis, to buy out the holder of the preferred stock of the business in which he was engaged, to gain its absolute ownership and control.

Upon the birth of our two sons, I ceased my outside employment, and discharged the responsibility of mother and housewife. My husband, a graduate engineer, held a regular succession of low-salaried positions until his entrance into the machine shop enterprise with David Greenglass. The modesty of our standard of living, bordering often on poverty, discredits David's depiction of my husband as the pivot and pay-off man of a widespread criminal combination, fed by a seemingly limitless supply of "Moscow gold."

Our knowledge of the existence of the atom-bomb came with its explosion at Hiroshima, and David's connections with it at Los Alamos, from his revelations to us on his discharge from the Army in 1946.

We knew neither Gold nor Yakovlev, our alleged co-conspirators, nor Bentley—facts which the Government did not controvert.

Our relations with Sobell, our co-defendant, were confined to sporadic social visits. Following a complete six-year break, after graduation from college, our ties with Elitcher assumed similar, but even more tenuous, character.

Our relationship with the Greenglasses, both during and after the war, was on a purely familial and social level, the cordiality becoming strained to the breaking, however, with the advent of bitter quarrels which arose in the course of our post-war business ties.

In 1950, my husband was negotiating to purchase David's stock in our co-enterprise, David having abandoned active participation in the business a few months before. The bargaining was heated and protracted. Finally, in May, they arrived at an understanding. The stock was assigned and the purchase price fixed, although the time of its payment remained in dispute. In the middle of May, David, agitated, asked my husband for a few thousand dollars. When he refused because his debt on the purchase price of the stock was not due and because, in any event, he did not have the money, David asked him, as an alternative, to procure a small-pox vaccination certificate from his doctor and to ascertain the injections required to enter Mexico.

Rebuffed by David in his inquiries about the source of David's apparent troubles, my husband, remembering Ruth's concern in the war years that David had stolen things from the Army, attributed David's plight to this account. The pull of family ties prevailed over the strained relationship and he felt under moral obligation to lend comfort to David. He found out from his doctor the information about travel to Mexico but was unsuccessful in obtaining the desired certificate. David, so informed by him, stated he himself would take care of the matter.

Near the end of May or early June, David, in a more agitated state, repeated his request of him for a "couple" of thousand dollars, and, when he refused, told him: "You are going to be sorry." In short, no monies were given to David for flight or any other purposes. Nor did my husband or I make any preparation to flee this country. He continued to conduct his business in a normal way and the pedestrian routine of living of our family continued even to the day of our arrests.

REASONS FOR CLEMENCY

Petitioner respectfully prays that she be granted a pardon or commutation of sentence for the following reasons:

FIRST: The primary reason I assert, and my husband with me, is that we are innocent.

We stand convicted of the conspiracy with which we were charged. We are conscious that were we to accept this verdict, express guilt, penitence and remorse, we might more readily obtain a mitigation of our sentence.

But this course is not open to us.

We are innocent, as we have proclaimed and maintained from the time of our arrest. This is the whole truth. To forsake this truth is to pay too high a price even for the priceless gift of life—for life thus purchased we could not live out in dignity and self-respect.

It should not be difficult for Americans to understand this simple concept to be the force that gives us strength—even in the face of imminent death, knowing well that the abandonment of principle, might, alone, save our lives—to adhere to the continued assertion and profession of our innocence. Our citizenry has a fine heritage of the right of the individual to protect his good name. Our country has a proud history of struggle to defend right and justice. Many of its finest sons, throughout the years, have defended this birthright with their lives, and been honored for their courage. It is difficult, rather, to come to believe that this country would shed this cherished tradition, and accept the word of those who betray themselves to curry favors.

Yet, we have been told again and again, until we have become sick at heart, that our proud defense of our innocence is arrogant, not proud, and motivated not by a desire to maintain our integrity, but to achieve the questionable "glory" of some undefined "martyrdom."

This is not so.

We are not martyrs, or heroes, nor do we wish to be. We do not want to die. We are young, too young, for death. We long to see our two young sons, Michael and Robert, grown to full manhood. We desire with every fibre to be restored sometime to our children and to resume the harmonious family life we enjoyed before the nightmare of our arrests and convictions. We desire someday to be restored to society where we can contribute our energies toward building a world where all shall have peace, bread and roses.

Yes, we wish to live, but in the simple dignity that clothes only those who have been honest with themselves and their fellow men. Therefore, in honesty, we can only say that we are innocent of this crime.

SECOND: We understand, however, that the President, like the courts, considers himself bound by the verdict of guilt, although, on the evidence, a contrary conclusion may be admissible.

You may even harbor a personal conviction of our culpability. But many times before there has been too unhesitating reliance on the verdict of the moment and regret for the death that closed the door to remedy when the truth, as it will, has risen. Borchard, *Convicting the Innocent*, Yale University Press (1932).

Here the prosecuting authorities have constantly purveyed the self-serving characterization of their case against us as "overwhelming." Even the face of the record, in the present posture of the proceedings against us, must warn against the facile acceptance of this description when weighing the balance between life and death.

We say to you, Mr. President, that the character of evidence on which we were convicted, and the force of the impact of certain circumstances in our case upon the mind of the jury, cannot assure the reasonable mind that this verdict was not corrupt.

You have the advantage of viewing the whole, removed from the proximity, in time, of the conflict of a "passion-rousing" trial. You, in the searchings of balanced mind and conscience, must determine whether this is a verdict so certain in its rectitude that this great nation can afford, in not staying the hand of the executioner, to risk its universal reputation for decency and justice.

Our arrests took place in the summer of 1950, when the general public fear engendered by the announced mastery of the atom-bomb by the Soviet Union was aggravated by the increased international tensions occasioned by the Korean War. Already the public had been attuned to turn this fear into anger against persons called responsible for the loss of our monopoly.

From the time of the arrest of Dr. Klaus Fuchs, in England, fourteen months before our trial and continually to the time of the trial, the public was given to understand that the mastery thus achieved resulted solely from the delivery to Russia of our most closely guarded atomic secrets, by Fuchs and his American confederates. They were told that not only had this country lost its vaunted atomic monopoly, but that the Soviet Union had already acquired a superiority in atomic armament, which made attack on us possible, and, in the then posture of international relations, imminent. They were told that this nation and our city, in particular, were open to easy attack to which there was no real defense, an attack which could desolate New York City, annihilate hundreds of thousands of its inhabitants, and inflict untold sufferings upon the survivors.

When we were arrested as spies for the Soviet Union, labeled as "Communists," charged, in the main, with theft of atomic-bomb information from the Los Alamos Project, the mere accusation was enough to arouse deep passions, violent antipathies, and fears, as profound as the instinct of self-preservations. Our "guilt" of the accusation, and our alleged association of confederates, once removed, of Fuchs, was broadcast and confirmed to the public—before trial and out of court—by the F.B.I. and prosecuting officers of the Government, buttressed by the weight of the tremendous prestige which they publicly enjoy.

It was hammered home, and kept alive by a virtual avalanche of publicity which saturated the communal mind with a consciousness that our country was imminently in danger of atomic attack and devastation by the Soviet Union, which had acquired the bomb by reason of its having obtained the "secret" from an espionage apparatus, ideologically motivated, of which we were "aggressive" members.

From this community, the jurors who tried us were chosen.

During our trial, one, William Perl, inferred to be a spy, was indicted for perjury committed some seven months earlier in having denied he knew my husband, the co-defendant Sobell (who stood trial with us), and certain persons whose names were prominently and invidiously mentioned at the trial. To this very day, Perl, although he has pressed for a trial, has not been brought to trial, upon the Government's adamant refusal to do so.

Even the Court of Appeals, in its decision affirming the denial of our application under Section 2255 (as yet not officially reported)[6] assumed, on the facts shown, that the Perl indictment had been deliberately "timed" by the prosecution to prejudice us. It censured the Government, commenting: "Such assumed tactics cannot be too severely condemned."

On the morning of the return of the Perl indictment, after David Greenglass had completed his testimony and Ruth Greenglass was still on the stand, the then United States Attorney, Irving H. Saypol, issued a statement never denied, as follows:

> "Mr. Saypol said also that Perl had been listed as a witness in the current espionage trial. His special role on the stand, Mr. Saypol added, was to corroborate certain statements made by David Greenglass and the latter's wife, who are key Government witnesses at the trial."[7]

Of this statement the Court said: "Such a statement to the press in the course of a trial we regard as wholly reprehensible."

The Court conceded that the "reprehensible" conduct of the prosecutor resulted in prejudice to us so irremediable that, were it not for certain technical legal considerations which seemed to satisfy that Court,* a new trial should have been granted. Courts before have overturned convictions procured by prosecution unfairness, in recognition of the undue influence

---

*The Court considered that the prejudice was vitiated by our counsel's failure to move for a mistrial. But it is noteworthy that omission to do so move was induced by a representation of the prosecutor, discovered subsequent to the trial to be false, namely that the Perl indictment had been procured in the regular course of the administration of criminal justice, and not for ulterior purposes.

---

[6]Note this was as of February 9, 1953. The Appeals Court decision had been reported in the newspapers December 31, 1952. See also letter of January 1, 1953, p. 533 below.

[7]"Columbia Teacher Arrested, Linked to 2 on Trial as Spies," *New York Times* (March 15, 1951): 1.

thereby produced on the jury's mind, e.g., *Berger v. United States,* 295 U.S. 78 (1935).

Our great respect for the independence of the human mind and spirit cannot, under these circumstances, permit the conclusion that our jurors were so endowed with a sense of detachment, so clear in their introspective perceptions of their own mental processes, that they might exclude even the unconscious influence of preconceptions of our guilt or antipathy toward us.

Should this not temper reliance—to death—on this verdict of a jury, in which the unconscious influence of the enveloping atmosphere may have overridden the overt desire to be fair and seduced it into a more ready acceptance of the prosecution's evidence as against our defense?

The persistent intrusion into our trial of "evidence" of our alleged "communist" beliefs and associations, must have been a further extraneous factor tending to blunt objectivity, juvenate the political passions and prejudices of our times, and utterly impair that sense of detachment already so burdened by pretrial influences. Although the Court of Appeals held this evidence to have been properly admitted, it acknowledged that "such evidence can be highly inflammatory in a jury trial. This Court and others have recognized the Communist label yields marked ill-will for its American wearer." It further noted that the admonition of the trial judge to the jury "not to determine guilt or innocence of a defendant on whether or not he is a Communist" might be "no more than an empty ritual without any practical effect upon the jurors . . ." It is therefore, not unreasonable to assume that any gap or inadequacy in the proof of the substantive crime may well have been filled by the conjunction of our "communism" with the extant political fixation that domestic communists merit a suspicion of infidelity to their native land. Indeed, the intermingling of the "communist" evidence along with the evidence on the substantive charge makes it difficult to determine whether the verdict was the product of a sober estimation of our culpability or a triumph of political prejudice.

Can one be secure—to death—in accepting a verdict that may have been, in large part, a response to the fears, the passion, the political clamour of the passing day?

THIRD: The Government's case against us stands or falls on the testimony of David Greenglass and Ruth, his wife, and even the Court of Appeals, in affirming this judgment, has explicitly so declared. *United States v. Rosenberg,* 195 F. 2nd 583 (C.A. 2nd, 1952). How firm is a verdict predicated upon the testimony of "accomplices," trading their Judas-words for a few years of their miserable lives? Even the rigorous canons of the law recognize that the overriding motive for falsehood requires that the accusations of a trapped criminal, testifying to mitigate or avoid his own punishment, be taken with care and caution, and brand a prosecution founded on such evidence as "weak" and suspect.

We have never been able to comprehend that civilized and compassionate consciences could accept a smiling "Cain" like David Greenglass—or the "serpent," Ruth, his wife—who would slay not only his sister, but his sister's husband, and orphan two small children of his own blood.

We have always said that David, our brother, knowing well the consequences of his acts, bargained our lives away for his life and his wife's. Ruth goes free, as all the world now knows; David's freedom, too, is not so far off that he will not have many years to live a life—if we should die— that perhaps, only a David Greenglass could suffer to live.

Sometimes only history uncovers the infamy that would have made contemporaneous generations cringe with shame that they had victimized the later vindicated innocents. But here, already, in spite of the self-interest of our accusers to maintain intact the structure of the case against us, cracks appear through which the truth is slowly seeping.

David had testified at our trial that at the moment of his apprehension he had not "conscientiously withheld" anything from the authorities. Yet within a day after sentence was passed upon us, we had, from the very lips of our chief prosecutor, the unwitting confirmation of our contention that David's "confession," implicating us, came later as the contrived *quid pro quo* in the bargain for his life and freedom for his wife. Only later, according to Saypol, in his remarks on the Greenglass sentence, ". . . through Ruth Greenglass, his wife, came the subsequent recantation . . . their cooperation and the disclosure of the facts by both of them."

When David in his trial testimony sponsored sketches of mechanisms—including the cross-section of an atom bomb—drawn as accurate replicas, from the memory without outside aid, of those he asserts were transmitted to us and others, five years before, this was to us a mark of the fabricated nature of his tale. We knew David to be, even as a simple machinist, an incompetent, and otherwise, a scientific illiterate. Now we are buttressed by the attestation of disinterested scientists of note, who, understanding the nature of David's capacity, indicate that David's word that he made the replicas introduced at the trial, from memory, unaided, could be no closer to the truth than if he had testified that he, as a mortal, was able to and did, run at supersonic speed.

Tenuous explanations and half-denials of these perjuries by the Government, and its knowledge of them, may still have the ring of outward plausibility, because the full proof to expose the lies remains locked in files not now subject to process, and in the hearts of the Greenglasses, who still have much to lose by recanting their falsehoods.

Yet, in one instance, where the possibility existed for full independent proof of the perjury, the Government was constrained to concede it. Ben Schneider, a photographer, the Government's "surprise" witness on the sensitive question of flight, was permitted to testify falsely that he had not seen us, from the time he said he took passport photos of us, until the moment he took the stand to testify. The Government admitted, after we had brought this to light, that the day prior an F.B.I. agent, at the direction of Saypol and in violation of the order of the trial court excluding all witnesses, brought Schneider into the courtroom, behind the rail, to identify us. This secret and unlawful intrusion, in aid of his subsequent testimonial identification, unrevealed to the Court or the jury, served to avoid the destruction of his probity that rested on the certainty of his identification.

The Government, ill-becoming its responsibility in the face of death, cavalierly dismissed its conduct and the Schneider perjury as a "quibble." The Court of Appeals refused us relief on the legal ground that it believed that Schneider had not meant to lie, and that, as to Greenglass, we have not, as yet, produced enough evidence to nail his lies.

In the face of death, however, can minds close themselves to the consideration that these facts may represent the first tears in the tangled web in which we have been caught up? Do they not hold the promise that, in the inexorable operation of time and conscience, all may be unraveled to set us free? Are they not, at least, that contradiction of the certainty of the verdict that argues for the preservation of life to maintain the opportunity for vindication? Where one doubt exists, the common conscience of man could call the taking of life an injustice and defiance of decency and humanity.

FOURTH: Only one tribunal, the sentencing court, has asserted the correctness of our sentences to death, and only one court has confirmed it: the sentencing court. In other words, only one human being in a position of power has said we ought to die.

Although our case was appealed to the higher courts, the appellate tribunals, denying their power to review the discretion of the sentencing judge, have not, on the assumption of our guilt, ruled on the propriety of the sentences of death.

You, Mr. President, are the first one who is empowered to review these sentences—and the last one.

The sentences imposed upon us were unprecedented. Never before in the entire history of the United States has a civil court, either in peace or war, decreed a sentence of death for the crime of espionage. For that most grave of all crimes, treason, only two death sentences have been imposed since the adoption of the Constitution and no execution has taken place. In the midst of the last war three persons were charged with, tried for, and convicted of treason for adherence to an enemy that was despicable to the entire world for a wantonness unparalleled in human history. No one of these was executed for his crime.*

Ours were not sentences made mandatory by the provisions of the espionage statute under which we were convicted. To tailor the punishment to fit the crime, the sentencing judge was free to impose punishment ranging from one day to thirty years of imprisonment and also death. Instead he tailored the crime to fit the punishment.

The maximum penalty was imposed in the belief that our crime was of "the highest degree." The opinion had no basis in fact and is premised on unfounded assumptions, and the judge remained impervious to the force of any facts advanced to demonstrate that he was in error.

He had stated, in his sentencing remarks:

> "The evidence indicated quite clearly that Julius Rosenberg was the prime mover in this conspiracy. However, let no mistake be made about the role which his wife, Ethel Rosenberg, played in this conspiracy. Instead of deterring him from pursuing his ignoble cause, she encouraged and assisted the cause. She was a mature woman—almost three years older than her husband and almost seven years older than her younger brother. She was a full-fledged partner in this crime."

Within a week after the imposition of sentence upon us, the Senate-House Joint Committee on Atomic Energy had published a study based

---

*During hostilities: United States v. Cramer, 137 F. 2nd 888 (C.C.A. 2nd, 1943) rev'd 325 U.S. 1 (45 years and $10,000); Haupt v. United States, 330 U.S. 631 (life imprisonment and $10,000); Stephan v. United States, 133 F. 2nd 87 (C.C.A. 6th, 1943), cert. den. 318 U.S. 781 (death sentence imposed but not executed).
After cessation of hostilities: Chandler v. United States, 171 F. 2nd 921, cert. den. 336 U.S. 918 (life imprisonment and $10,000); Best v. United States, 184 F. 2nd 131 (C.A. 1st, 1950) (life imprisonment and $10,000); United States v. Burgman, 87 F. Supp. 568 (D.C., D.C., 1949), aff'd 188 F. 2nd 637 (imprisonment, term not mentioned). The two women in the group, better known as "Axis Sally" and "Tokyo Rose," were given minimal prison sentences. Gillars v. United States, 192 F. 2nd 962 (App. D.C., 1950) (10 to 30 years imprisonment and $10,000); D'Aquino v. United States, 180 F. 2nd 271 (C.A. 9th, 1950) (10 years imprisonment and $10,000).

upon all the secret and public evidence made available to it, including the testimony given at our trial. *Report on Soviet Atomic Espionage,* Joint Committee on Atomic Energy, 82 Cong., 1st Sess. (U.S. Gov't Printing Office, April, 1951). This Committee rated Fuchs, May and Greenglass (along with British Bruno Pontecorvo) as the only important atomic espionage agents, and subordinated us to a minor place. *Accord: The Shameful Years,* House Comm. on Un-Am Activities (U.S. Gov't Printing Office, 1952).

The judge's reconsideration ignored the findings of these Congressional Committees. He continued to defend the sentences by reiterating:

> The Rosenbergs were not minor espionage agents; they were on the top rung of this conspiracy. . . . and at all times Ethel Rosenberg, older in years, and wise in communist doctrine, aided and abetted and advised her husband.

Only prison sentences were meted out to those, according to the Government, more culpable or more capable of doing greater harm: Dr. Klaus Fuchs, in England, 14 years; Allan Nunn May, in England, 10 years (*Report on Soviet Atomic Espionage, op. cit. supra*), released recently after serving less than 7 years of his term; David Greenglass, 15 years; Harry Gold, 30 years. Ruth Greenglass, David's wife, a co-conspirator, though not a defendant, was never indicted for her crime and is presently a free woman.

The sentencing judge refused to consider these lesser sentences as bearing on a proper exercise of his discretion here.

He dismissed, as irrelevant to his concern, the Fuchs and May sentence, in England, by asserting that their influence would be tantamount to binding an American court to adopt the law of England. While it is true that our laws, dealing with espionage, confer power to exact severer penalties, it should not follow that the wider power justified the abandonment of restraint in its exercise. The temper of the British people, in the same status and political position as the United States, did not yield to panic over the dis-closures of the Fuchs and May affairs. Three days after Fuchs' arrest, the *New York Times* (February 5, 1950, p. 2), under a London dateline, reported: "BRITAIN UNEXCITED OVER FUCHS' ARREST." When May was recently freed, the same paper (December 30, 1952, pp. 1, 4) reported England's understanding that, in 6 years and 8 months, May had "paid for his crime" and concern that he be accorded "civilized" treatment. It is right to test the judgment of this country against the judgment of England, a sister nation, traditionally our partner in democratic ideals and moral standards. It is not amiss to indicate that many, in the Western European and English-speaking nations of the world, regard our death sentences as an hysterical capitulation to the pulls and tensions of the times.

We are told that the "confessions" and "cooperation" of Greenglass and Gold and others earned them more lenient sentences. While this is recognized practice, the coercive power of sentence beyond that justified by the nature of the criminal act cannot legitimately be made to substitute for the proscribed "thumbscrew and rack" to secure confessions which cannot in truth and good conscience be forthcoming.

But we are told that our lives ought to be forfeited because we have not "seen fit to follow the course of David Greenglass and Harry Gold." Our sentences cannot be accounted for by the normal divergence of treatment between those who "cooperate" and those who do not, but, stretched beyond the limits of life, are revealed as the instruments of coercion.

That such was the illegitimate design of the sentences becomes clear, when the nature and character of the crime with which we were charged is rationally evaluated.

The conspiracy was allegedly conceived at a time when the Soviet Union was a war-time ally, respected, aided and extolled by the Government of the United States and its public and private leaders. Nevertheless, the Court stated on sentence:

> Citizens of this country who betray their fellow countrymen can be under none of the delusions about the benignity of Soviet power that they might have been prior to World War II. . . . Indeed, by your betrayal you undoubtedly altered the course of history to the disadvantage of our country. No one can say that we do not live in a constant state of tension. We have evidence of your treachery all around us every day—for the civilian defense activities throughout the nation are aimed at preparing us for an atom-bomb attack.

It commented further:

> Nor can it be said . . . that the power which set the conspiracy in motion . . . was not openly hostile to the United States at the time of the conspiracy.

These remarks, conjoined with the Court's limitation of the period of Soviet "benignity" to a time "*prior* to World War II," warped history to attribute to us hostile mind *in limine*. Common knowledge of our war-time alliance with the Soviet Union, of course, contradicts this interpretation of events.

The Judge urges that our then alliance with the Soviet Union has no bearing on an evaluation of the intent with which the alleged criminal act was committed—a factor always relevant on sentence. That an individual has no right, as he says, to determine to reveal "secret" military information to any nation, including an ally, or that, no matter who the beneficiary, such an act is criminal, is axiomatic. But for the Court to say: "No one was more aware than the defendants of the true nature of an 'ally' which would take these furtive steps to set up an extensive espionage network . . ." is to prove the intent from the fact of espionage itself. On this thesis, espionage, under the law, can be committed with but a single intent, contrary to the explicit distinction made in the statute, which speaks, in the disjunctive of "intent to injure" the United States *or* "intent to advantage" a foreign nation. Nor can the use of *Gorin v. United States,* 312 U.S. 19 (1941), be interpreted to obliterate the express statutory difference of intent. In the later decision of *United States v. Heine,* 151 F. 2nd 813 (C.C.A. 2nd, 1945) cert. den. 328 U.S. 833, Judge Learned Hand, writing for the court specifically states:

> ". . . It is possible to think of many cases where information might be advantageous to another power, and not injurious to the United States . . ." (at p. 815.)

To avoid the necessity, in the context of the current world scene, for taking into consideration the distinction made in the intent provisions of the statute, the sentencing judge diverts by stating that the Espionage Act, under which we were convicted, "was enacted in 1917, at a time when the atom bomb was not existent." Yet Congress, dealing with the specific subject of atomic espionage, the Atomic Energy Act of 1946, passed after the decision of the *Gorin* and *Heine* cases, expresses its legislative design to retain the distinction between "intent to injure" and "intent to advantage." In this Act, Congress did not see fit to prescribe the death penalty for atomic espionage except where there exists "intent to injure" the United States. (Atomic Energy Act of 1946, 42 U.S.C. Section 1816.)

The indictment on which we were tried did not charge an "intent to injure" the United States, as it can be assumed it would have, were the Government in possession of evidence to establish such an intent. And, indeed, the record is bare of any such proof.

The finding thus arrived at that we had an "intent to injure" the United States changed the quality and gravity of the offense. Yet it was on the basis of the intent thus artificially transmuted from "intent to advantage" to "intent to injure" that the sentences were inflicted, where, at the outset, fair play would dictate that sentencing discretion be exercised to favor the well-intentioned state of mind.

Reason understands that this crime, if disposed of at the time it was laid, would not have incurred a harsh or vindictive sentence. These sentences cannot find vindication on the ground of the continuance of the alleged conspiracy into the "cold war" period. Were this the criterion it would have been reasonable to expect a sentence other than death for one of us, Ethel Rosenberg, as to whom the record is bare of post-war involvement. And, more importantly, as to both of us, as suggested by Frank, J., concurring in the Court of Appeals, a persuasive consideration was "the fact that the evidence of the Rosenbergs' activities after Germany's defeat (as well as of their earlier espionage activities) came almost entirely from accomplices."

Judge Frank may well have added that evidence of my husband's alleged post-war involvement consisted of no overt act, but was confined solely to admissions he allegedly made to David Greenglass, and even as to these admissions, there was no corroboration.

During 1944 and 1945, we were not at war with the Soviet Union, nor, since that time, have we been at war with that country. To insist that our alleged crime, in terms of the extent of punishment, was "war-time" espionage, is such adherence to the letter of the law, in derogation of its spirit, of reality, and of common sense, that exposes itself as legal sophistry. The sentencing judge, by citing as precedent the sentences imposed by a military court upon German spies and saboteurs who slipped into this country in 1942, seeks to evade the validity of the extenuating effect of our war-time alliance with Russia. The analogy is inapposite and misleading. These spies were working for Germany—our major—enemy with whom we were then at war.

The true precedent, which you have set, Mr. President, and which the judge ignored, buttresses the common understanding that death was meant to punish war-time espionage in war-time and not after the termination of hostilities. Of the German saboteurs who were tried and sentenced to death during the war, two—William Curtis Colepaugh and Erich Gimpel—who had not been executed by the time of the close of hostilities, were granted commutations of their sentence by President Truman, on June 23, 1945.

The purported reliance, in this case, upon the continuation of the alleged criminal acts into the post-war years, as the justification for the severity of the sentence is also logically self-defeating. Certainly, even in the technical legal sense, the alleged post-war acts are not "war-time" espionage. And, by the court's own admission, it would have been powerless, under the statute, to impose a death penalty for such acts.

The basic inequity, in measuring the severity of the punishment on the gauge of extant political circumstances persists. The sense of fairness must be shocked by the exaction of a retribution for subsequent events and reversed political relations over which we had neither control nor the clairvoyance to foretell.

The sentencing judge cojoined us with this fabricated malevolence he attributes to us, a weird and aggravated estimate of the importance and proximate consequences of our alleged crime, to extenuate the unreasonableness of his sentence. He stated:

> "I believe your conduct in putting into the hands of the Russians the A-bomb years before the best scientists predicted Russia would perfect the bomb has already caused, in my opinion, the Communist aggression in Korea, with the resultant casualties exceeding 50,000 and who knows but that millions more of innocent people may pay the price of your treason. Indeed, by your betrayal you undoubtedly have altered the course of history to the disadvantage of our country."

Patently, these statements are unmitigated fiction. Their judicial pronouncement cannot serve to square their unreality with the facts of life. No one, other than the trial judge, has even pretended that the atom-bomb material allegedly transmitted in the course of the instant conspiracy, was of any substantial value to the Soviet Union.

As a general proposition, Dr. Harold C. Urey, one of the directors of the atomic bomb project, has affirmed that:

> "Any spies capable of picking up this information will get information more rapidly by staying at home and working in their own laboratories." *New York Times,* March 3, 1946, 0. 12.

Specifically in relation to this case, the Government itself, after the trial, conceded that: "Greenglass' diagrams have a theatrical quality," and because he was not a scientist, "must have counted for little." *Report on Soviet Atomic Espionage,* Joint. Comm. on Atomic Espionage, 82nd Cong., 1st Sess. (U.S. Gov't Printing Office, April, 1951). Reflections on the lack of value of the information allegedly transmitted here persist in scientific critiques. See: *Time*, March 29, 1951;* *Life*, March 26, 1951;** *Scientific American*, May, 1951.*** See also: Urey, *N.Y. Times*, March 3, 1951.****

It is perfectly clear that such valueless information could have had little effectiveness "in putting into the hands of the Russians the A-bomb," even had they not possessed the "secret."

It is universally conceded, propaganda to the contrary notwithstanding, that there was no basic "secret" concerning atomic weapons. Dr. J. Robert Oppenheimer, *N.Y. Times*, January 15, 1951; *Atomics*, September, 1949; Letter of Harold C. Urey to *N.Y. Times*, May 11, 1950. This concession extends as well to "know-how." The United States Atomic Energy Commission itself has supported this view, as quoted in an International News Service release datelined Washington, D.C., December, 1949:

> "The Atomic Energy Commission Friday bared secret documentary proof that Russia has known the scientific secrets of *Atom-bomb manufacture* since 1940, the year the United States began attempts to develop the missile." (Emphasis ours)

James R. Newman, a former counsel to the Atomic Energy Commission, in an article published in the Yale Law Journal [*Control of Information Relating to Atomic Energy*, 56 Yale L.J. 769, 780-1(1947)] stated:

> "The general principles underlying all processes are likely to be widely known being derived usually from some discovery of basic science. For example, the successful gaseous diffusion method of separating U-235 was based on identical principles enunciated by Lord Rayleign as early as 1896. Thus, it is only the latest improvement or modification of an existing technique which can be held in camera, and then only for an indeterminate but usually

---

*". . . some of his [Greenglass'] testimony made little scientific sense."
**". . . Greenglass' implosion bomb appears illogical, if not unworkable."
***". . . What the newspapers fail to note was that without quantitative data and other necessary accompanying information, the Greenglass bomb was not much of a secret."
****". . . Detailed data on the atom bomb, he declared, would require 'eighty to ninety volumes of close print' which only a scientist or engineer would be able to read."

brief period. Moreover, there is no likelihood whatever with all our preeminence in technology, that the disparity between the level of our technical competence and that of other industrialized countries—at least half a dozen could be named (e.g. Great Britain, Canada, Russia, France, Sweden, Czecho-Slovakia)—is such that the latter would be more than, at most, a few years behind us. Indeed there is abundant evidence that other nations frequently develop technological methods and processes distinctly superior to ours in a variety of fields.

"Even wholly new processes are likely to be already known or simultaneously discovered in other countries. For intellectual progress, especially in the sciences, is more or less uniform in countries which for generations have shared the same cultural climate. Only a small fragment of our scientific ideas are likely to be original, and that fragment is likely to be of little value by itself. One would not assume that biological evolution functions differently in Des Moines, Copenhagen and Moscow. The likelihood of marked differences in the evolution of scientific thought corresponding to geographical differences is equally small. Doubtless, some nations show especial aptitudes in one field, some in another, but the community of science has long been international and the objects of its search are universal.

"Finally, the cosmopolitan character of the atomic energy project should not be forgotten. This work was the product of the scientific brains of several of the allied nations, and participating scientists inevitably acquired a considerable measure of the specialized and technical knowledge required to produce the bomb. It must be assumed that any 'secrets' known by these scientists, many of whom have returned to their own countries, have been disclosed to fellow-workers in nuclear physics in other parts of the world."

The decisive factor, in terms of the extent of the time lag between our possession of the bomb and its development by the Soviet Union, was the degree of the industrial strength and technology of the Soviet Union, not its scientific knowledge. That time lag was given, by experts, an outside limit of five years. Dr. Irving Langmuir, *N.Y. Times*, October 9, 1945, p. 9; Newman, *Control of Information Relating to Atomic Energy*, 56 Yale L.J.

769 (1947); *Report on Soviet Atomic Energy,* op cit., supra, at pp. 7, 12–14. On this topic, Dr. Urey commented:

> "In my opinion if we published all our data in detail we would not shorten the five . . . years of General Grove's estimate by very much. It takes time to build plants, and it takes time to operate them." Address, reprinted in *Science,* November 2, 1945.

How else can it be explained that it was only a few months ago that Great Britain finally succeeded in detonating a nuclear weapon, although its top scientists (including J.C. Penney, second under Fuchs at Los Alamos, and now head of Britain's Atomic Energy Commission), were working openly hand in hand with American scientists, legitimately had all information available to them, and would have been more able to carry back to their own countries the results of discoveries in this country, than the untutored Greenglass to pass on effective "information" to the Soviet Union.

Scientific judgment undermines the validity of the trial judge's claim that our alleged conduct did or could have, put "into the hands of the Russians the A-bomb years before our best scientists predicted Russia would perfect the bomb."

The judge, obdurately holding to his irrational consideration that the information allegedly here communicated, alone, led to Soviet success in achieving perfection of the atom bomb, re-affirmed our death sentences. The repeated publication of this false myth by a member of our judiciary, not only endangers our lives, but is a disservice to the welfare of our nation, by perpetuating a state of unfounded terror at the loss of the "secret" of atomic weapons.

> ". . . terror at the loss of the 'secret' is a tribal fear which once gaining ascendancy in our minds, must inevitably weaken rather than strengthen our defensive power as a nation. Preoccupation with the 'secret' instead of the thing itself will stifle scientific research from which our real strength is derived, will strengthen the pernicious misconception that we have a monopoly of knowledge in the science of atomic energy and will beguile us into embracing the fatal fallacy that we can achieve security for ourselves by keeping our knowledge from others." (Newman, *op. cit., supra* at 782–3.)

If the trial judge displayed irresponsibility, in blinding himself to the facts and capitulating to the popular myth of atomic monopoly, he threw all rationality and judicial temperance to the winds when he judged us to have "caused . . . the Communist aggression in Korea, with the resultant casualties, exceeding 50,000 . . ., " and thus to have committed a "crime worse than murder," where the murderer "kills only his victim."

This, of course, was so patently ridiculous, that even the judge could not continue to maintain this position since informed opinion knows that a great nation is not thrown into war by the single act of two of its humblest citizens, but by a complex of factors—social, political, and economic.

But fixed in his determination to uphold our death sentences—whether reasonably or unreasonably—he still asserts that our alleged "crime was worse than murder," on an equally infirm thesis. Now it is so stated because: "the murderer kills only his victim while the traitor violates all the members of his society, all the members of the group to which he owes allegiance." We are no longer accused of killing people; now we are accused of being "traitors."

The fact is neither are we traitors, nor did or could the Government have charged us with treason. Any doubts on this score were specifically resolved to the contrary by the Court of Appeals' decision on rehearing in our case. 195 F. 2nd, 609. Neither may we be sentenced for treason. The strictures of the Constitution, wisely drawn because of the historic abusive use of treason, do not countenance such artless circumventions.

Condemnation to death should not be made into a game of fishing for reasons to uphold a predetermined doom.

FIFTH: All of the factors in our case militate against death sentences.

No sentences so irrevocable should in justice be here executed. Our asserted innocence is buttressed by the doubt of the fairness of our verdicts, a misgiving generated by external influences upon, and the internal weakness of the case.

No sentences of death are merited here. Our alleged crime was not treason. There was no charge of traffick with an enemy. We were sentenced while this country was at peace. There was no charge of intent to injure this country, and none was proved. Science disputes any aggravated injury to the welfare or security of the nation.

We submit, Mr. President, that the deterrent efficacy of the sentence was directed at something other than the vindication of the breach of law ascribed to us.

We submit, Mr. President, that life, even in jail, was denied to us in the belief, as the judge himself declared: ". . . if the Rosenbergs were ever to attain their freedom, they would continue their deep-seated devotion and allegiance to Soviet Russia . . ." There is no such crime in our constitutional scheme of things as a "crime of the mind and heart" alone. Punishment may serve only as a deterrent to the recurrence of criminal acts. When the coercive cruelty of punishment is used, literally, to kill ideas, whatever they may be, Government becomes the instrument of tyranny. Our democracy must reject even the hint of this abuse of power.

It may be easy to execute us. But can this nation afford to appear fearful of the impact of ideas upon our security by the display of a show of strength to forfeit two insignificant lives?

The facts of our case have touched the conscience of civilization. The compassion of men sees us as victims caught in the terrible interplay of clashing ideologies and feverish international enmities. Adjudged war criminals, guilty of mass murders and the most ghastly crimes, are daily being delivered to freedom, while we are being delivered to death. Our sentences represent a reversion to barbarism from which humanity recoils in horror.

We have suffered deeply for the past two years. Torn from our children, and in the shadow of death, we have been isolated, like caged animals, from the mainstream of life.

We are husband and wife. We are firmly united by the ties of marriage, the love we bear our two fine sons and one another.

We have never known the ease of riches or even comfort. At times we have felt the pangs of want. We come from a humble background and we are humble people. Were it not for the criminal accusations against us, we would have lived out our lives simply, like most people, unknown to the world, except for the few whose lives crossed ours.

We seek relief from sentences that would produce the unutterable tragedy of the destruction of our small family and set a precedent for the abandonment, in America, of the civilized appreciation of the worth of human life.

We appeal to your mind and conscience, Mr. President, to take counsel with the reason of others and with the deepest human feelings that treasure life and shun its taking. To let us live will serve all and the common good. If we are innocent, as we proclaim, we shall have the opportunity to vindicate ourselves. If we have erred, as others say, then it is in the interest of the United States not to depart from its heritage of openheartedness and its ideals of equality before the law by stooping to a vengeful and savage deed.

Ethel Rosenberg
Julius Rosenberg

Chronology

1950

Feb. 3   Klaus Fuchs, German-born British scientist, confesses in England to having given atomic information to the Soviet Union.

February   David Greenglass, brother of Ethel Rosenberg and formerly a machinist employed at the Los Alamos Atomic Project while in the army during World War II, visited by the FBI and questioned about persons he might have known while stationed at Los Alamos and about some uranium missing from the project.

May 23   Harry Gold, a Philadelphia chemist, states that he had been the American courier for Fuchs in 1944–45.

June 15   David Greenglass signs a confession stating that he was an accomplice of Gold in 1945.

June 16   Julius Rosenberg, brother-in-law and former business partner of David Greenglass, questioned by the FBI, but not arrested. Retains Emanuel Bloch as counsel.

June 25   Korean War begins.

July 17   Julius Rosenberg arrested on charges of having recruited David Greenglass into a Soviet spy ring in late 1944.

Aug. 11   Ethel Rosenberg arrested on the charge of conspiracy to commit espionage with her husband, Greenglass, and Gold.

Aug. 16–18   Morton Sobell, former classmate of Julius Rosenberg,
             kidnapped from his Mexico City apartment, allegedly
             deported to the United States, and arrested by the FBI
             on the charge of having been part of the same espionage
             ring as the Rosenbergs.
Dec. 9   Harry Gold sentenced to thirty years in prison.

1951

Mar. 6–29   Julius had been imprisoned for eight months, Ethel
             Rosenberg and Morton Sobell for seven, when their
             trial began before Judge Irving Kaufman. The jury
             heard two weeks of testimony before returning a guilty
             verdict.
April 5   Morton Sobell sentenced to thirty years in prison. Julius
             and Ethel Rosenberg sentenced to death, executions set
             for May 21, 1951 (automatically stayed pending
             appeal).
April 6   David Greenglass sentenced to fifteen years in prison.
April 11   Ethel Rosenberg transferred to Sing Sing prison in
             Ossining, NY, and housed as the only woman prisoner
             in the Condemned Cells, thus preventing contact with
             Julius and family.
May 16   Julius Rosenberg transferred to Sing Sing's Death
             House.
August–   The *National Guardian,* a small left-wing news
September   weekly, publishes a series of articles concluding that the
             Rosenbergs are innocent and demanding a new trial.
November   The National Committee to Secure Justice in the
             Rosenberg Case is formed.

1952

Feb. 25   Convictions of the Rosenbergs upheld by United States
             Circuit Court of Appeals, Judge Jerome Frank writing
             the unanimous opinion. Sobell conviction affirmed,
             Judge Frank dissenting.

Oct. 13	The Supreme Court denies *certiorari,* refuses to review the case or pass on the merits of the appeal. Justice Hugo Black dissents.
Nov. 17	Supreme Court refuses to reconsider its original ruling; Justice Black again dissents.
Nov. 21	Judge Irving Kaufman sets the second execution date for the week of January 12, 1953.
Dec. 10	Motion for hearing based on evidence of perjury and prejudicial publicity heard by Judge Sylvester Ryan. Motion denied; stay of execution denied.
Dec. 30	Judge Kaufman hears motion to reduce sentence.
Dec. 31	The Court of Appeals upholds Ryan's denial of a hearing.

1953

Jan. 2	Judge Kaufman refuses to reduce sentence.
Jan. 5	Court of Appeals denies stay of execution.
Jan. 10	Petition for executive clemency submitted to the President; executions stayed five days after determination is made.
Jan. 21	Tessie Greenglass visits her daughter at Sing Sing in an effort to induce her to confess and back her brother David's story.
Feb. 11	President Eisenhower denies clemency.
Feb. 16	New execution date set for week of March 9.
Feb. 17	Court of Appeals stays executions so the Supreme Court can consider a new petition for a review.
May 25	Supreme Court again refuses *certiorari,* Justices Hugo Black and William Douglas dissenting.
May 29	Judge Kaufman sets new execution date for week of June 15.
June 2	John V. Bennett, Director of the Bureau of Prisons, visits Sing Sing and personally offers Julius and Ethel Rosenberg their lives if they will "fully cooperate."
June 8	Judge Kaufman hears arguments for new hearing charging that newly discovered evidence proves perjury

	and subornation of perjury. Kaufman immediately denies motion, refuses to stay the executions.
June 9	Appeals Court orders Rosenbergs' lawyers to argue their appeal from Judge Kaufman's ruling on the spot.
June 11	Appeals Court affirms Judge Kaufman's decision; denies stay.
June 15	Supreme Court refuses stay of execution so a new petition for *certiorari* might be filed to appeal Kaufman's June 8 decision. Vote is 5 to 4, Justices Black, Douglas, Frankfurter, and Jackson dissenting. Application for stay made to Justice William Douglas.
June 16	Another application for a stay made to Justice Douglas via a "next friend" brief based on the view that the Atomic Energy Act of 1946 should have applied to the case.
	Clemency petitions filed with the Pardon Attorney at the Justice Department.
June 17	Justice Douglas grants stays of execution until the lower courts can decide the new issue raised in the "next friend" brief.
	Acting on the request of Attorney General Brownell, Chief Justice Fred Vinson recalls the court into special session to consider the point on which Douglas granted the stay.
June 18	Oral arguments before the Supreme Court.
June 19	Supreme Court vacates Douglas' stay, Justices Hugo Black, William Douglas, and Felix Frankfurter dissenting. That afternoon, defense lawyers argue for a stay of execution with the Court of Appeals in New Haven, CT.
	Eisenhower again denies clemency.
	Julius and Ethel Rosenberg are executed.

The
ROSENBERG
LETTERS

1950

The earliest letters available date from the period right after my father's arrest. We believe that there was at least one letter, mostly concerned with my father's business, sent by my father which arrived at our home on July 20. We have no way of knowing if my mother wrote to him before July 20.

The letters from our father in this early period were on special forms provided at the prison, the Men's House of Detention on West Street. The heading had four lines to be filled in as follows:

From Julius Rosenberg

July 20, 1950

To Mrs Ethel Rosenberg[1]
10 Monroe St. NY 2 N.Y.

Dearest Wife & Two Boys.—I am feeling well and getting along. My day {Eleanor}[2] starts at 6:30 A.M. make the bed, get dressed washed etc. Breakfast about 7:30. Stewed fruits, cereal, cake & coffee. I am assigned to 2nd floor detail & after each meal we sweep down the corridors and swab the floors. Then I set down with a book and do some reading. 11:30 AM lunch—kidney stew, succotash, browned potatoes, cake[,] lemonade. Then we have two one hour periods on the roof in the sunshine. Ping pong, hand ball and just chewing the fat with the men. I met some nice guys here and they've been keeping me in cigarettes, cookies & oranges. ["until" CO] This Friday when the Commissary opens [N4WI] I'll get my own. One of the

---

[1]The words From and To were printed on the sheet and the words Date and Address were printed in parentheses under the lines provided for those entries.

[2]"My Day" was a syndicated column by former First Lady Mrs. Eleanor Roosevelt published throughout the 1950s.

3

guys lent me "The Wall" by John Hershey [*sic*] I am up to page 45 at this
writting [*sic*, N2WI] Good book. 5:00 P.M supper—Jellied soup. (n.g.)
pork beans; corn bread, salad chocolate drink. It is now 5:30 P.M. After this
letter I'll go up on the roof for one hour tonight, do some reading possibly
play a game of cards, shower and to bed at 10:00 P.M. I am allowed to send
you ["only" inserted, then CO] 3 letters a week. You'll explain to the family
that you will be the source of all information coming from me.[3] I received a
receipt for the $10.00 you sent in for me. Tomorrow I'll get a lock for my
locker, toothbrush, comb & brush, razor, blades, shaving brushes, fruitt
[*sic*] cookies & candies[.] We are allowed $2.50 a week for such items. This
afternoon before supper I had a talk with the visiting Rabbi. He's a nice guy
& if the front office will permit him he ["h" in previous word written over
illegible letter] will call my Mom and tell her I'm alright I hear your brother
David was shipped off to the "Tombs."[4]

---

[3]This sentence probably is as good an indication we have that this was the first
letter he was able to send.

[4]David and Ruth Greenglass' cooperation with the FBI was an on-going process.
Between Greenglass' arrest on June 16 when he signed a rather vague statement
implicating our father and his wife Ruth in espionage and the early part of July
when he and Ruth gave detailed statements to the FBI about our father's alleged
activities there were a lot of negotiations which resulted in the original
indictments against David in Albuquerque, NM, being dropped and superseded by
indictments in New York. The idea of indicting Ruth was quietly shelved. On the
morning of July 17, 1950, a long memorandum was sent by J. Edgar Hoover to
the Justice Department that contained sufficient details of our father's alleged
activities to convince the Justice Department to order our father's arrest. Once he
was arrested, it was essential that David be moved to a different prison. The
Tombs in New York was the home of the well known "singing quarters" where
cooperating witnesses were housed as their stories were developed. Harry Gold,
an important witness in the case, was also housed in the Tombs and there is at
least one documented instance in the FBI files so far released of Gold and
Greenglass being interviewed at the same time by the FBI to iron out differences
in their stories. As you will see below, both our parents' attorney, Manny
Bloch, and our father surmised that such collusion had occurred, even without
seeing the proof in the FBI files. See John Wexley, *The Judgment of Julius and
Ethel Rosenberg* (NY: Cameron & Kahn, 1955), pp. 640–42. Interoffice memos
of the law firm which represented David and Ruth Greenglass document some of
the early negotiations. See also *U.S. v. Rosenbergs, Sobell, Yakovlev and
Greenglass* (Cr. No. 134–245), p. 1623 where the prosecutor noted that at the
arraignment, even after signing the June 16 statement, David Greenglass' lawyer
"protested his innocence." (This record was reprinted from the submission of the
transcript to the U.S. Supreme Court which was filed along with the first petition
for a writ of *certiorari* on June 7, 1952. All page references are to the printed
copy that the National Committee to Secure Justice in the Rosenberg Case
duplicated and sold in an effort to acquaint the public with the flimsiness of the
prosecution's case. This printed transcript is available in many libraries in the

When you have a chance tell my lawyer to see me at his earliest convience [sic]. I hope the business will not cause you much trouble and I'd like to have a report on the billing & expenses each week you see me. If ["it's possible for my" CO] they can make it ask my Brother & Sister to come. To Michael. I want you to remember all the games we play together, baseball, checkers cards cowboys and when you play them with your Mommie ["remember" CO, NWI] remember I'm enjoying them too. Of course I miss you but you must understand Daddy is occuppied [sic] elsewhere and make the best of the situation. Play as much as possible with your brother and be nice to him. I particularly remember the times you've phoned me at my place.[5] How nice it was to hear your voice. To Robert. "Is that my Robbie this is your Daddy" just like on the phone call to the shop. don't forget his lucky ride every night Mommie. Of course don't forget a trip with the boys now and then. I hope I'm not going off the deep end and giving you a tough job with them. There are many times my mind wanders but with a couple of kids ["y" CO] like ["you" CO] I've got and ["your" CO, NWI] a wonderful ["mommie" CO, NWI] wife I feel much better. Send my love to your mother & family, my mother & my family & regards to all our friends. With all my love and constant thoughs [sic] of you I am looking forward to seeing you this Sunday.[6] Hugs & kisses to my boys and all my affection to you

    Julius

Ethel to Julius

Thursday, July 20, 1950

Dearest Julie,

    Finally got your letter this morning. First to take up the practical matters. Got over to the shop this afternoon and although at first I had thought to take things up with you on Sunday, I think we would waste less time if you had a picture of the situation there beforehand. What I did today was go over your letter bit by bit with Charlie and make notes of his replies

---

U.S., particularly in law school libraries. Henceforth, the transcript will be referred to as "Record.")

[5]His business, the Pitt Machine Products Company, located at 370 E. Houston Street, was a machine shop specializing in small engine repairs and parts sales. He had gone into partnership with his brother-in-law David as well as two silent partners and until his arrest was attempting to pay them off and buy their share of the business out.

[6]July 23.

alongside.[7] So here goes. He is going to get that Carbide Milling Cutter. He's working on the valves and Danny is working on the Lo-Man job. Precision Milling & Depressing job is done—Charlie is waiting for them to pick stuff up after which they will be billed as per your instructions. The MRM bushings were cancelled Tuesday morning. So were the drills so you don't have to worry about them being returned. Incidentally, Dun & Bradstreet came in wanting info. from Charlie which of course he was unable to give them. Letters have already been sent out to their subscribers cutting you off from any more credit. Charlie spoke to Du-Fast the [illegible] who said he must be paid C.O.D. as he had parts ready so Charlie called customer to whom parts were to go to & the customer agreed to take parts. When we bill, we'll deduct handling charges. The accountant will be in next week to work on Social Security taxes.—I'll be in the shop tomorrow early in A.M. and will make calls to various accts. & try to get them to pay up. As for the parts you mention having to do with Templet, when 4 parts were finished, Continental picked up same and made arrangements to work directly with Templet—a cancellation in effect and Charlie doesn't know how to bill them for whatever work we did do. Concerning [two illegible names] Bros. part you mention is simply unobtainable anywhere, Singer included—As for Coil Winders, what would you consider a satisfactory offer for the electrical test equipment—Would suggest that you make notes on paper concerning the fore-going items so all you will have to do is read same off to me when I see you.

Now as to Aristocrat, he is going to write a few suggestions [N3WI] out on paper concerning his work tomorrow morning which I will be able to transmit to you. He spoke some to me today also to the effect that he wishes you would continue with his stuff. Seemed quite put out and although I explained to him that we won't hold it against him if he can't pay right now, he still must realize that he can't expect us to put out more money for new work—Charlie too had a fly in his nose because he feels that there should be some more definite understanding well in advance of the finish of the work—I assured him that if and when we decided to close the doors, he'd receive enough notice not to be left jobless suddenly and unexpectedly—Personally, my feeling is it is imperative to sell the shop— It is ridiculous to temporize. The sooner we stop wasting time and start moving toward that end the sooner will we realize some benefit—I'm hoping to see Bloch concerning same before I speak with you. You should be thinking same over so we can discuss it intelligently on Sunday—

---

[7]This pretty much establishes the existence of a letter written by our father prior to the July 20 letter above.

Gladdy has responded extremely well to the new treatment, so much so that Bernie sounded really elated[8]—It knocked the temp from somewhere bet. 103 & 104 down to normal at once—and she's feeling a lot stronger. Oh, how wonderful it would be if a real cure could be effected. So far, she hasn't found out about you which is all to the good. Bernie is going to see Sharon[9] this week-end and will try to visit the kids and my self as soon as possible after he gets back. Poor Mike, he simply can't see why he shouldn't be permitted to see you or at least talk to you by phone. And he keeps repeating that I shouldn't neglect to tell you how much he misses you and loves you. Robby too, asks for you constantly and I have all I can do not to break down continuously—Please, darling, do take care of yourself and be assured of how much I am trying to justify your faith in me. I miss you terrible, though, and can't tell you enough how much I love you—

See you Sunday—Ethel

Julius to Ethel [pencil]

July 24, 1950

Dearest Honey Wife,—There was so much to tell you and talk about before I saw you but somehow, when I saw you yesterday words came hard and all I could seem to talk about was the business. After you left and until I fell asleep I thought of how you looked and what you said. Eth, believe me I did not want to convey the idea to you that I am hard and that you were weak to cry and feel so badly. It will take more than my inadequate words to convey to you my profoundest feelings and love for you. It is so much more difficult because of the kind of relationship we have. You looked so pretty and your dress looked so well on you. I am sure you were able to get some of the good feeling [N3W1] I obtained from seeing & talking to you. Thinking of this I am suggesting that you become the secretary and active participant in my legal defense. That is, you should be present at all important confidential conferences between my lawyer and myself. You realize that you will be an important witness in my case. ["and" CO] The best results are obtained by a very complete preparation of my defense before I go to trial. You will take this up with Mr. Bloch. Concerning visiting come at the earliest possible hour and waste the time before visiting with the necessary red tape inspection so that we can have the full time allotted to

---

[8]Bernard Greenglass, our mother's middle brother, was married to Gladys, who was dying of Hodgkin's disease.

[9]Bernard and Gladys' daughter, who was staying with one of his in-laws, a woman named Jean whose last name we don't know.

me. Before I go further I want you to understand that you've reacted better than was to be hoped for considering the adverse conditions you are presently facing. Give these instructions to Charlie. Bill Air-Duct installation $291.50 less handling costs {not to exceed $10.00}. Bill Continental for 155 assemblies $4.00 ea. {He is being allowed no more than 25¢ for assembly} we will handle Templet's bill as they owe us a considerable balance. Offer Coil Winders the test Equipment with a 30% discount from the price a legitimate outfit, such as Newark Sales or others that are located at Cortlinat [*sic*] Street would charge. Sell Aristocrat all the small heads we have at 30¢ ea. He can take all the stainless steel & aluminum for his job at a 10% discount off our cost. I want us to keep my personal tools such as, slide rule, drawing instrument micro-meters, scales etc and the parts [N2WI] and tools for the jumping booster bars. Try to make some progress in selling the shop but dont [*sic*] be too hasty. Sweet Michael boy, I know how much you love me and it always makes me feel better to hear you keep on saying it and asking about me. I am very happy we were able to spend such nice times together, at such places as South Beach Amusement Park, Central Park and Prospect Park. Sometimes I think of the nice baseball games we played in the East River Drive Park. I could just close my eyes and see you bang that ball way over my head for a home run. Don't you worry we'll be playing games again as soon as I can straighten out this trouble I'm in. When it comes to my Robbie all I can say I miss him as much as I miss his big brother and mommy. I can just imagine him sitting with his trucks, cars, blocks and tracks in his room playing with them and then rushing in to yell, "Come see what I made." No I can not forget all those joys and they give me sustenence [*sic*]. All my love, hugs and kisses to you my wife and to you my boys. Regards to our families—love—
xxxxxxxxxxxxxxxxxxx   Julius

Ethel to Julius [ink]

                                                  Tuesday July 25, 1950
Dearest honey,
    This will of necessity have to be brief as it is now close to 1:00 A.M. and my eyes ache for lack of sleep. Just got through hanging the clothes as Mike didn't get to sleep until 11:30 PM. Have an awful lot scheduled till I get to see you again. Was supposed to discuss matters with Templet today but never got around to it—The accountant is coming in Thursday morning about the taxes—Got a call from someone concerning Pitt's future which did not sound phony to me—However, I made no commitments of any kind and will simply turn over the name and address to Mr. Bloch when I see him—for possible future investigation—Phoned MRM and Lo-Man

yesterday and this morning 2 checks arrived which I at once deposited—
Received a number of bills [NWI] (Pitt) 2 of which are telephone bills—July
1–$8.75—July 16–$16.87—Don't know if the 2nd bill includes the first—
I see an item on second bill which says $8.83—would that be the $8.75 of
the first bill—Anyway, how long can I wait to pay bills? There's one for
insurance from Sid Tool for $15.22—a few others that are very small in
amount.

Billed Lo-Man today for 135 pcs. which comes to a sizeable amount—
The foregoing should give you some picture of the things—I spoke to
Harry—Said he's looking someone up for me who might be helpful about
Pitt's future—Is there some way of helping him to realize some money
without too great an expenditure on our part—Try to think thru on this so
we can talk on Sunday—Love you darling—miss you & can't wait till
Sunday—Best from your 2 kiddies who never stop asking for you—Why
haven't I heard from you yet—Hope everything's OK with you—It's all so
strange without you, my dear one—I love you, Sweetheart—Goodnight
Ethel

[Next five letters in pencil.]

Julius to Ethel

July 26th 1950

Dearest Honey—9:00 P.M. The guards just collected our pinnocle [*sic*]
cards, my partner and I, we lost three straight games, woe is to us. I spend a
bit of time now and then playing cards to pass the time away. I finished a
very good book to-day "Barbed Wire Surgeon" by Dr Alfred A. Weinstein. It
deals with the miserable life of American prisoners under the Japanese from
Bataan to Japan. The book is well written, good and I highly recommend it
to you. I also want to take this opportunity to suggest you try to get ahold
of the "Wall" by John Hershey a diary of events including the life of the
Warsaw Ghetto. It certainly is worth reading. I am getting a splendid opportunity to catch up on my reading but somehow I would prefer doing it in
pleasanter surroundings. I keep hunting through the library for good books.
Since Thursday I've been receiving the New York Times daily which keep
me informed on current events and baseball results.[10] Sometimes we have a
broadcast of a local ball game, a news commentator or even an evening

---

[10]Our father was an avid Brooklyn Dodgers fan. He and many other leftists were
Dodger fans because the Dodgers had broken the color bar by bringing Jackie
Robinson into the major leagues.

program. During the day we hear some popular recordings over the public address system. The commissary we are able to purchase is very necessary as it fills in the evening with a piece of chocolate or a cookie. I bought some Hershey bars, Ritz Crackers, fig newtons & chocolate snaps. If I'm lucky I'll try to get a dozen oranges next Friday. I am on the 2nd floor of the Detention House in a cell block occupied by ten inmates. There are 5 double tier beds. I occupy the upper deck of one of these. At night time its nice and cool in our cell and I have to use an army blanket over my sheets to keep warm. We are issued a "t" shirt[,] 1 pair of pants, underpants, a pair of socks & a towel. There are three of us sitting around a table writting [sic] letters and one of the men asked me, "What do you write one that you love?["] I promptly replied, "Tell her my mouths watering for you." That brings me to the point that I miss you very much and can't seem to understand that I am living through a situation away from you and the children locked up in this place. I hunger for news from my two boys I can't seem to write enough to them. You take it upon yourself to inform them that I'm well, in good spirits and always thinking about them. Try to send me pictures of you and the kids they don't have to be all together. Don't be afraid to send me 3 or 4 of them. I hope Glady [sic] is feeling much better for now. I want you to remember me to our families and friends and send my best regards to them. Incidentally don't talk to anyone about my case but the lawyer. See if its possible for you to write me as much news as possible concerning you, the kids our family and general gossip. With all my love, hugs, kisses and constant thoughts of you I await this coming Sunday visit.

xxxxx
Julius

Julius to Ethel

July 28, 1950

My Darling—It's now Friday—2:30 P.M. I just finished sunning myself for 2 complete hours my body is quite red and I'm starting to develop a real "Florida" suntan. I had a visit from my lawyer this morning and I am certain by the time you receive this letter he will have discussed with you all that transpired. I was very much disturbed to hear that you're worried because you didn't receive any mail from me. In the first place I've been putting off writting [sic] to you until I get your letter but somehow the time has been passing and no letter from you. I'll try to hold up my end and write you at least three times a week. You should know that all my letters are carefully censored which caused a three to four day delay in letters. I just received a letter from my brother Dave and its [sic] dated 7-24-50. Please call my brother and inform him of all news about me. Thank him for writting [*sic*] tell him to keep 'em coming. I am always glad to hear about my family. How they all are? What they're doing? News concerning my sister Ethel & her clan, Lena & her gang & my mother. Send them all my love and best wishes. Keep in touch with my mother as possible. Dave tells me my mother has been given pills to keep her blood pressure down. It is good to get news of Dave's "problems" concerning his house, beds and vacation. This stuff brings me close to home. Of course, my thoughts are constantly of you and the children. It was quite difficult to fall asleep last night so a bunk mate and I chewed the fat till 1:00 in the morning. My schedule is pretty routine now Sleep, Eat, read and gab. Monotonous but I'm existing. I almost forget our evening pinnocle [*sic*] games. I'd like to get more home news from you. What Mike does with his time? How is he progressing at Day Camp? All about his comic books, building, coloring work & his television programs & his radio programs. Most of all whats [*sic*] he saying these days? I want to be in on his growing up. I want to hear the same kind of news about my Robbie. I was just interrupted and I had to swab down the 2nd floor corridors. I am sitting in a pool of sweat and as soon as I finish this letter its in the shower for me. It is very necessary for both of us Eth to keep on writting [*sic*] as much as we're allowed to. I want to reiterate I expect you to take an active part in my defense and I ask that you be present at all confidential meetings with our legal counsel. I understand its [*sic*] difficult for you to seek recreation, but it would give me a big moral [*sic*] boost to hear you managed a movie or something similar. All my love to my dearest and [NWI] my two honey buns—xxxxx Daddy Julius

Julius to Ethel

July 31st 1950

My Darling —9:30 P.M. The Playing cards have been collected & we're locked up for the night and we are now listened [*sic*] to the Dodger ball game. I received your letter of the 25th of July, as soon as I got back from Foley Square.[11] Note the 6 day delay. Concerning your questions on the bills. They are due in 30 days but in this case we can go a little beyond this time. Look through the checkbook and note the previous checks to see which are due to the Telephone CO. and other firms. Before sending any checks make certain there is a reserve in the bank to cover at least one payroll in advance.

---

[11]Foley Square is the Federal District Court House in lower Manhattan where the trial took place. He was there for some kind of court appearance.

It was very refreshing to see you looking so well and so nicely dressed this morning. I can also thank you for your excellent taste in making my selections.[12] At present I am thinking about your parting remark & it makes me feel good. Eth, I believe that we should use some moderation as to when it is necessary for you to be present[13] as it may take too much out of you. However, lets [*sic*] leave it to your and Mr[.] Blochs [*sic*] discretion. I am very sorry we did not have an opportunity at this hearing to talk about the kids as I am very much concerned about Michael's health. I would like you to have him send me a letter about his experiences with his Uncle Bernie and Cousin Sharon in the country. His cold must have deprived him of a chance to go swimming. I hope an opportunity presents itself for you to take the boys to the beach. Now that summer school is out the little one must be leading you a merry chase. I would like to make a repeat request for photos of you and my boys. That reminds me see if you can get the F.B.I. to return the stuff they took from our house such as watchs [*sic*], pictures[,] books and the typewritter [*sic*].[14] I want you to convey my thanks to Bernie for taking Michael for the weekend and send him and Glady my best wishes. Don't fail to send my regards to your mother and let me know how she's been feeling. Keep me posted on my mother's health. Send her my wishes for a speedy recovery and all my love. Tell her it isn't appropriate for a Grandmother like her to behave in this manner after all everybody is counting on her. Call my sister and let her know what's what. I am trying to keep away from telling you how much I miss you but its no use. Things are so different without you and the kids and only the passing of time and the looking ahead seems to make any sense. All my thoughts are constantly of you and the children & how we spent our time together. Love, more love and hope.
Julius

Julius to Ethel

August 4, 1950

Dearest Honey Wife—Friday—I just had some baked fish, baked potatoe, string beans and watermellon [*sic*] a good lunch. My attorney visited me

---

[12]Probably referring to the clothes she picked out for him to wear to the court appearance.

[13]At court appearances. Note this indicates no intimation on either of their parts that she would be arrested also.

[14]The typewriter and a couple of photographs were returned in 1975 but the FBI admitted destroying a significant number of family photographs that had been in their possession since 1950.

before lunch. It is always good to have a visit from him to discuss the case
and get the latest news on things concerning you and the kids. I am so glad
to hear that you are in good spirits and conducting yourself in a very noble
manner. Remember darling that you are a big factor in my moral [*sic*]. I
love you very much and miss you more than my written words can express.
There are many moments during the day that I think of you and the kids,
exactly what you're doing and how you're managing. Eth, try to write me in
detail about you and the kids. Yesterday, it was raining and since we
couldn't have a roof period we saw movies. The wrestling bouts were quiet
[*sic*] funny and it had the men roaring in the isles [*sic*]. They showed one
match between two women wrestlers & you could just imagine the
comments that this evoked. On the whole the movies were a bit of a
diversion as it helped pass the time. My work on the second floor detail is
improving constantly. My form, style and touch is very professional indeed
[NWI] especially when it comes to sweeping and swabbing the corridors.

I made commissary today and managed to buy a dozen oranges. By the
way make sure to send me another ten dollar money order to cover next
months [*sic*] commissary allowance. I'm going to ask one of the men to
give me a haircut this afternoon in order for me to look well for your next
visit. Darling those half hour visits are so short yet the're [*sic*] the
highpoint of my existance [*sic*] at this place. I just had me an orange and
now i'm [*sic*] munching on a milky way, "some vacation," eh! At this
moment I'm thinking of all the places i'd [*sic*] like to be at and what i'd
[*sic*] be doing now. Incidently [*sic*], in all my concern over you and the kids
I clean forgot to have you send my best regards to the boys working in the
shop. Tell my sister Ethel to get around to send me a letter about herself,
her family, her house and all the news she could send me. You could say the
same to my sister Lena. Let's know what Melvin[15] is doing & all about his
plan for school etc. Tell your mother to have some one write a letter for her
to me. I'd like to hear from her. I hope by the time this letter reachs [*sic*]
you Glady will be out of the Hosp and feeling much better. Send my best
wishes to all our family and friends especially to both our mothers. I am
feeling fine and in the best of health and loving you more and more. A big
hug and many kisses to my darlings.
Daddy—Julius

---

[15]Lena's son

Julius to Ethel

August 7, 1950

My Darling—It's now 4:30 P.M. supper is over and the evening begins. Your short visit yesterday brightened things up considerably. I hope when this letter reaches you your cold will be all gone and you'll be back in tip top shape again. Now more than ever you must be careful of your health [NWI] especially for the kids [*sic*] sake. I spent an interesting afternoon playing chess with an expert. With outside help I was able to attain a draw. I now have a splendid opportunity to learn to play a good game of chess and bridge. NOTE don't fail to send a check to the New York Times for a subscription. I also want to remind you about next months [*sic*] commissary allowance. Its now 9:30 P.M. I spent over two hours on the roof chewing the fat with the men and playing Gin Rummy. The cards have just been collected ending our pinnochle [*sic*] game and the radio is on blaring forth a "Giant" baseball game.

To my two shudderwink boys—Your daddy loves you both very much and misses you. I want you boys to behave properly and play nicely so that your mommy can report to me that you are doing all right by her. Michael send me one of your crayon drawings and write me a letter about how you are and what you're doing. I would also appreciate something from my Robbie. If you wish you can send a message along with your mommy when she comes to visit me next time. I am very proud of my sweet fellows and hope to see you both soon.

Eth, I guess my brother will be going on vacation soon. Tell him to write me before he goes as to his plans and what he intends to do. If it's possible for him I'd like him to take time to see me before he leaves. Send my best regards to his wife and his in-laws. I hope by now they've been able to get set in their new surroundings ["by now" erased] and that his mother-in-law was successful in obtaining a job. Ask my brother if he could help you dispose of the shop. I am sure if you're able to talk to him about it he'll help you. Send my thanks to your mother for watching the kids this Sunday and send her my best wishes. Regards to both our families and get them to write. Explain to my sweet mommie that I'm feeling fine and in the best of health and that its not necessary for her to get sick over my situation. Send my love to my mother and calm her down. Well I'm going to retire now. Good night my love. Sleep is very welcome at this point and I'll write again in two days xxxxxx Love xxx
    Julius

Julius to Ethel [ink]

August 9, 1950

My Sweet Wife—Since my handwritting [*sic*] is so atrocious I bought me a pen in the commissary to remedy the situation. I had an attorney visit yesterday and he brought me up to date on all developments. I still feel that your first concentration should be on liquadating [*sic*] the business at a satisfactory price. I received a letter from you dated Aug 2nd and one from my Michael dated July 28th on the 9th of Aug.[16] Your letters are so heartening and I feel so good to receive them. Your letter touched me deeply and a warm feeling of love welled up in me. Honey, I don't know if you read the letter that Michael sent me ["but" CO, NWI] Nevertheless I want you to understand as I read it I could picture Michael right there besides me saying those things. Its so much like him and I'm so proud of him, I showed the letter to many of my friends here and they got a kick out of it. Hooray for Hop Along Cassidy. Keep on sending me more stories and more letters the're [*sic*] wonderful to receive. I'm sorry I'm limited by space, otherwise, I would write my boy a story. You'll see my boy I'll make up this time to you and tell you lots and lots of stories about space ships, cowboys and all the adventures you like to hear about. I miss my two boys ["the opportunity" CO, N3WI] so much that all my ideas are concentrated on what I'm going to do with them when I get home. We received a notice from the front office, to the effect, that visiting will be permitted during the week if it works a hardship on people visiting weekends. Since you find it so difficult to get some one to watch the kids weekends, by all means, make arrangements to come here some mornings somewhere near 9:00 AM if its [*sic*] possible or any time thats [*sic*] set aside that you can manage. I am going to send my sister Ethel a letter which I'll ask her to pass around to Lena, Dave and you. I miss the New York Times and I hope by the time you visit me I'll be receiving the paper again. The news you sent me about my mother if [*sic*] very encouraging and I wish she'll continue to improve in health so that she can be of some help ["to you" CO] with the children. I know she wants to help you and it will make her feel much better to be of some assistance to you. Send her my love and best wishes. I'd like to receive some news about Sharon, Glady[,] Bernie how'r ther'e [*sic*, "t" written over "e" in previous word] managing in the country and whats [*sic*] doing with Glady's health. Send them and all of our loved ones my regards. The lights will be out in a few minutes. Love and kisses and many hugs
xxxxx Julius

---

[16]Neither of these letters is available.

Given the delays caused by censoring it is almost certain that this letter and possibly the one dated July 7, 1950 were not received by my mother before her arrest on August 11. This letter was written before our father found out about our mother's arrest.

From Julius Rosenberg   August 11, 1950
To Mrs Ethel Goldberg   53-47 65 Place Maspeth, L.I.

Dear Ethel,
    I find myself in a predicament, by force of circumstances, without being guilty of any crime. Even since childhood I can remember the close family relationship and loving cooperation that has always existed among our relatives. In these days of stress more than ever your help is needed. At a time when Ethel is so taken up with our children and my defense, she may be forced to go to work. I know you're not millionaires but all practical help, moral support and love is needed by my wife and children. In the past, when necessity called, my wife and I were never found wanting, on the contrary, we contributed to the best of our abilities. I want you to understand I am not begging nor am I demanding, however I am asking you to stand by me, my wife and children.
    I am limited to three letters per week, therefore, I would appreciate it if you let Lena, Dave and my wife read this letter. Any news you can send me about you, your husband and children will be most welcome ["more so" CO] as I hunger to hear from my family and letters help the time pass pleasantly. Send my best wishes to Oscar [her husband]. Congratulations are in order for your daughter Deanna for her successful graduation. All my love and regards to Seymour, Sharon and of course you my beloved sister.
    Your Brother
    Julius

P.S. To Mamma, Dave and Lena,
    I am sending my letters to my wife who will communicate them to all of you. I sent this letter to Ethel as she lives near you my dear brother and very often she and her family drive down to visit with my sweet mommie and darling sister Lee. If my correspondence were not limited ["and" CO] I would send each of you my dearests personal letters but I am sure you will all understand I am doing my best considering the restrictions I am under send my love to your respective husband, wife and my niece and nephew.
    As for myself I'm in the best of health and hope to hear the same from you. To a great extent my moral [*sic*] depends on my family. I want you to

know it is very high and I'm positive I can count and [*sic*—probably meant "count on"] each and every one of you to help continue to keep it that way.

All my love,

Julius

Hugs & kisses xxxxx.

On August 11, after concluding her second Grand Jury appearance during which she invoked the Fifth Amendment in answer to questions almost identical to those she had been asked a week earlier, our mother was arrested and held on $100,000 bond, the same bail set for our father. We had been looked after by a babysitter for that day and there had been no contingency arrangements made, although my mother had begun to think about the need to do this because of the intense questioning she had been subjected to at the first Grand Jury appearance. Our father's letter of August 12 is written in pencil on small note paper, not on the usual prison 8 x 11" lined paper.

Aug. 12, 1950

Dearest ["Wife" CO] Ethel
10 Greenwich St.[17]

I heard the news over the radio last night and after strenuous efforts to see you or contact you I've been given permission to write this letter. Let me know ["at once how you're" CO, N4WI] as soon as possible how you are feeling. How are the children? Has any provision been made for them? I am fine and alls [*sic*] well. I expect the lawyer to see me this morning and I'll instruct him to send you commissary money, newspapers and all the little things he can do to make it easier. Tell me your plans for the children and I'll try to have the lawyer arrange a meeting for us to decide on the children. Keep a stiff upper lip. All my love.

Your

Julius

---

[17]Address of the Women's House of Detention.

[On the back of the first page is the following:]

one of you. All my love,—Julius

CH 2–8679 Home
BE 3–2444 fathers off.
Emmanuel [*sic*] H. Bloch
270 Bway
Attorney—Bway—near Chambers St
N.Y.C.
WO 2–6851 off.

Subpoenad [*sic*] by Grand Jury Aug 14—11:o'clock.—See me at once
    Julius Rosenberg[18]

[The next letter is written in pencil on small paper stamped "House of Detention" and "Censored By" at the top.]

August 12, 1950

My dearest darling Julie,

By now you must know what has happened to me. Darling, I wish I could say that I am cool, calm and collected but the fact is that although, contrary to newspaper reports, I have not been hysterical at any time, I have shed many anxious tears on behalf of the children and have been feeling badly that I won't be seeing you on Sunday. My heart cries aloud for you and the children. Now indeed it is harder to be inside than out because each of us knows the other is not free to care for our dears. How unfortunate it was that I never got around to discussing arrangements for them with the proper people. I had been planning to do that very thing this week so that the kids should be subjected to as little strain as possible in the event I was detained—and I must confess my mind [NWI] does leap ahead to the frightening possibilities for them. However, I guess I will feel lots better after I see Mr. Bloch and ask him to get in touch with those people who can help us in the matter of the care of the children—By all means sweetheart, if you have any ideas about this and/or any of our other problems, please communicate with our lawyer and also write me about same. Oh, my dear husband, how precious were those last few hours I was permitted to spend

---

[18]I surmise that this is an instruction to the prison people to get this message to attorney Emmanuel Bloch and that these phone numbers and address directions are ways they might carry out his request. It is puzzling as to why it is on the back of the note to our mother.

with you—Do you suppose I'll get to see you sometime in the near future? Am going to shower now. Will continue later—

It's now 8:00 P.M. and we are locked in for the night. My wet underthings are hanging on a wooden rack at the back of my cell. The window faces out on Greenwich Ave, I believe, and from my window I can see the windows of a large apartment house across the street.

As for food here, there isn't much variety but it's edible. Besides there's the commissary which makes available oranges, candy, sandwiches and milk besides comb, toothbrush, paste, etc.

It seems that I'm only permitted to write you once a month but today I spoke with Captain Hubbard who said she would consider my request for more frequent correspondence.

Sweetheart, I talk with you every night before I fall asleep and cry because you can't hear me. And then I tell myself that you too must be choking with the same frustration and wondering if I can hear you. Darling, we mustn't lose each other or the children, mustn't lose our identities. I try to think of the good, fine life we've led all these years and I am agonized with my longing to go on leading it.

All my love and my most devoted thoughts to you my dearest loved one. Please write me as soon as you can. I love you.

Ethel

From Julius Rosenberg [ink]   August 14, 1950
To Michael Allen Rosenberg   10 Monroe St. NY 2 N.Y.

Dear Michael,

Hi son how are you getting along and how do you feel? As for me all's well and I'm doing nicely. I received both your letters and they were sweet. Keep up the good work. You, your brother Robert and your mother are always in my mind. I love ["you" CO] all of you very much and I am glad to hear that you are managing so nicely.

You remember that Lone Ranger story about how his little nephew[19] though all alone managed so well. He was able to do this because he cooperated with the one who was put in charge of him and even as he learned new things he enjoyed himself doing it. I am so glad you are able to play with your clay, blocks crayons and toys and get so much out of it. These things are just like the tools your Daddy used in the shop to do his work with, only your tools are your playthings.

---

[19]Dan Reed, a character in the Lone Ranger series who rode Silver's son Victor.

I was so impressed with your Hop Along Cassidy story that I'll write you one "Crime of the Bar-Q". One day as two cowboys Michael and Robert were riding along the trail to the Bar-Q ranch to see the boss man Mr. Jones, they heard shots coming from the direction of the ranch house. "Lets Go!" yelled Mike to Robert "Giddap" roared Robert as they dug their spurs into their pintos and they raced forward. Rounding a bend in the road they saw three men swiftly mounting their horses to make a get-a-way. Michael drew his six shooter and fired from the hip "Bang Bang". One of the outlaws fell off his horse shot through the head. As their horses came up to the door of the ranch house they heard, "Help, Help. I'm wounded." They rushed into the house and found Mr. Jones lying on the floor badly wounded. "Quick Robert ride to Doc Thomas and bring him back at once. I'll stay here with rancher Jones," said Michael—"Who were those hombres and what did they want?" asked Michael. Jones replied "The Adams gang robbed me of $100,000 cattle money" "don't worry we'll get those owl hoots for you." After making sure that Jones was out of danger & Doc Thomas was on hand, Mike and Robert carefully trailed the remaining two outlaws to their hideout. While the outlaws slept Mike and Robert surprised them and took them prisoners and so ended the "Crime of the Bar-Q."

Give your brother a big hug and kiss for me. Darling I want you boys to remember your Daddy is always thinking of you and wants to hear all about you. See if you can write again real soon ["again" CO]. If I have the time I'll try to make up a story about a space ship and a trip to one of the planets. Now be good, have a lot of fun and keep on playing. I hope to see you soon.

P.S. Love & Kisses & Hugs.   With all my love,
xxxxxxxxxxx   Your Daddy Julius

[Next eleven letters in pencil.]

                                                  Aug. 15, 1950
Dearest Michael boy,

I am so sorry you had to wait so long to hear from me. I am also sorry that I didn't have more time to speak to you on the phone after I was arrested.[20]

Believe me, sweetie, I think of you and Robby all the time and I know how you must be missing your Mommy and Daddy. I know also that it's

---

[20]See Robert and Michael Meeropol, *We Are Your Sons: The Legacy of Julius and Ethel Rosenberg* (Urbana, IL: University of Illinois Press, 1986), 2nd ed., p. 15 for a description of what went on during that conversation.

harder for you to do the usual things when the person you're used to isn't around to help you do them. When you're having a hard time of it, try to remember that I am wishing like anything that I were there taking care of you and that I am also hoping you are cooperating as much as possible with the people who are there in my place. For instance, you can make things easier by telling them where your clothing is, what you and Robby are used to eating and how you're used to having things done generally. In the meantime, Mr. Bloch has already called Mrs. Phillips [21] and when she comes to see me, we will work out the best kind of arrangements possible for you and Robby. So be as happy as you can and try not to mind too much, darling. Your Mommy and Daddy have not forgotten about you. All my love to my dearest boys.

Ethel to Julius

August 20, 1950

Dearest Sweetheart,

It's 7:15 and I'm in the Recreation Room. I've showered and washed my things and hung them to dry. At 7:30 I'll be heading for my "house" (that's what the girls call their cells), and at 8:00 they'll lock each of us in for the night. Lights out by 9:00 and up the next morning at 6:30.

Before I go any further I want you to know that I received ["your second letter" CO] two letters from you.[22] You must write me telling me whether or not you ["have" CO] received the one I wrote you. Then I'll know that the kind I wrote you is acceptable. ["and" CO, NWI] Altho Captain Hubbard has granted me permission to write you once a week, this is no guarantee that the letters will be allowed through.

Darling, I'm thinking of your second letter which came when I was in the sorest need of it. In the main, I would say that I'm taking the situation fairly well, but there are times when I'm terribly blue and depressed. Saturday was just such an unhappy day. Sunday was a little better because a good part of the morning was spent at Protestant and Christian Science services. Right after breakfast, these services are held and by the time we return, it's close to 11:00 A.M. I like it because it constitutes a diversion which is also personally enjoyable because it gives me an opportunity to

---

[21] I had begun to see Mrs. Elizabeth Phillips, a social worker with the Jewish Board of Guardians, in 1950 due to some difficulties my mother was having raising me. For details, see *Sons*, pp. 94–96.

[22] Only one letter from our father to our mother between her arrest and April 10 has survived as far as we know.

sing.[23] Incidentally, it took them just a few days to realize that I could sing so almost every night now I receive various requests. One morning, at breakfast, I was pleasurably surprised to hear a number of girls in corridors other than my own, away across the hall, express their appreciation.

Last Friday I attended the Jewish Services which were all too short. Too bad there was no singing, but the Rabbi intoned the prayers so beautifully that I couldn't help but enjoy it.

During the week there is a lot more to take up one's time. There's visiting, Commissary, an hour on the roof in the afternoon and yesterday just as I came down, I was told to go to Social Service and there Mrs. Phillips sat awaiting me, bless her. She told me that a very good home-maker is now helping my mother and that Michael has been coming to see her (Mrs. Phillips) very willingly. Last week she took him home in a cab after getting him a sandwich he asked for. Hope I get to talk to you in court today, darling.

love you — Ethel

Ethel to Julius

Aug. 29, 1950

My dearest darling Julie,

I am hoping that by now you have received my second letter. By now I know that my first one finally reached you.

Oh, darling, even though we were able to spend some time together the day we went to court, it seemed to me when I had returned here that there were so many other ways I might have expressed my feelings to you, so many other things I might have said. So let me say them now, my dear one. And yet I couldn't ever say enough what pride and love and deep regard for you as an individual I feel. ["toward you" CO] What you wrote me about ourselves as a family and what that family means to you made my eyes fill. And yet, at the same time, there came to me such an abiding sense of faith and joy, such a sure knowledge of the rich meaning our lives have held that I was suddenly seized with an overwhelming desires to see you and say it to you and kiss you with all my heart.

Sweetheart, we must go on pouring out all that we feel toward each other in our letters as I know how this strengthens the deep bond between

---

[23]Our mother had had ambitions of being a singer and an actress. She had taken voice lessons and joined a competitive entry chorus as well as an amateur acting troupe, and had met our father at a fund-raising New Year's Eve party for a union where she was to sing. For details of their early lives see Virginia Gardner, *The Rosenberg Story* (NY: Masses and Mainstream, 1954).

us, that bond you described so well in your last writing. How frustrating it is, though, when we have been accustomed to day-to-day association to have only this means of communication! I treasure the time we spent together last Wednesday (which already seems so long ago) and can't wait for our next meeting.

I saw Mr. Bloch on Monday and took up a number of things with him. On Tuesday, your sister Lena and your mother came to see me. Only Lena was permitted to visit me, but I waved to them both through a window while I was awaiting the elevator to take me back upstairs and I know it reassured your mom to see that I looked my own healthy, cheerful self. In the main, darling, I am healthy and cheerful, so please try not to worry so much about me. It distressed me when Lee told me she had seen you Sunday and that you had been concerned for me. Incidentally the clinic doctor examined [N2WI] my back[24] last week & sent a report to the [NWI] head doctor. It ["sh" CO] shouldn't take too much longer before I get to see her and ask for help.

Honey, I had better finish up now as I want to catch the morning mail. First, however, let me congratulate you properly my "lord and master" on your prowess as a chess player. But your wife is no slouch either. Don't dare tell her, but I am knitting a lovely green sweater for Mrs. Phillips! Now, how's that! Love you, sweetheart,

Your Ethel—

Ethel to Julius

Sept. 8, 1950

Dearest Julie,

I was so delighted to receive your letter of the 30th I was ready to dance. You see, I hadn't heard from you in 10 days and was beginning to get a bit anxious. Incidentally, I asked the proper person why it's [NWI] been taking my letters so long to get to you and she informed me that they were not holding the mail up on this end at all. If I were you I would check where you are; after all I am only permitted to write you once a week and I don't see why there should be all this delay for one measly letter per week.

Sweetheart, your sister Ethel saw me a second time ["yes" CO, NWI] on Wednesday. Did she get to see you as she had planned? And did Lena get to see you Thursday after she had visited me? They have both been perfectly swell with letters, visits and money.

---

[24]Our mother had suffered a curvature of the spine and in fact had been hospitalized after my birth and had had to be assisted by a housekeeper in the mid-1940s. See Record, p. 1296 for some details.

Speaking of money reminds me. Did Mr. Bloch mention my suggestion concerning Michael's education. In a way it's a little too early to
mention it; ["but" CO] after all, we don't know where the children will be
placed and there might not be the kind of school we wish for Mike
available. Still, I'd like to feel [N4WI] we can depend on some relative or
other for the necessary financial aid. When Mrs. Gluck[25] comes to see me
next week, I will take this matter up with her a little more in detail and she
can then discuss it with you intelligently.

Darling, of course I understand about foster-shelter and am in complete
agreement with you on the subject. I, too, have been very much distressed,
indeed incensed over the kind of pressure our sweeties are being subjected to,
and can't wait for the situation to change.[26] I have been making notes
concerning the various needs of both children and ["all" CO] the kind of
handling they have been accustomed to, on the recommendation of Mrs.
Gluck, ["This" CO] and have found it a very satisfying way to spend some
of my time. Some of the desperate need I feel at times to be with them and
care for them in my accustomed way is relieved as I write; the knowledge
that our wishes concerning them are not only respected but sought after is
heartening. And yet the reality of the cold stone walls is one that will not be
denied. My brain shrieks aloud in its desperate attempt to make itself heard
to my dear ones. Would that [NWI] the visit [N3WI] with the children you
speak of so easily could be as easily accomplished. Do I need to tell you
how dearly I should love to see them. And do you need to tell me to [N2WI]
what degree you share these feelings. Of course, do all that it is in your
power to do to make any arrangement possible.

As to books, materials and other things I might desire to make me
happy which you would like to send me, and/or which you would suggest I
request on my own—My dear, sweet husband—don't you know yet that we
are in jail? And my jail from all I have heard tell is on the strict side when it
comes to requests of this sort. However, let me assure you that I am most
appreciative of the sentiment expressed and duly grateful. What I am really
trying to say, my precious idiot, is that I am just slightly crazy about
you—and love you with all my heart, believe me. As many times as I have
said it to you in the past, it seems to me now [NWI] somehow that I never
[NWI] really said it nearly enough!

---

[25]A social worker from the Jewish Child Care Agency—this organization
operated children's shelters, one of which, the Hebrew Children's Home, was the
institution to which Robby and I were sent in November.
[26]This is obviously in reference to Greenglass family pressures. For details, see
Sons, pp. 19–25.

Dearest, they'll be putting the lights out soon and then I'll be alone with you. So I pretend, anyway—and it's sweet and painful together. Oh, honey, how I miss you and long to be in your arms where I belong. Goodnight, darling.—

Ethel to Julius

Sept. 12, 1950

Love, since I began writing you, I received two more letters from you. The one you wrote Labor Day came, oddly enough, before the one dated Sept. 1. So now I know you have my last week's letter and I can now finish this one I'm writing you. Oh, dearest, I'm glad I waited to get that [NWI] earlier letter (Sept. 1) which came later than the Labor Day one because it was just after I had gotten back from a visit with Mr. Bloch and another from my brother Sammy that it was given me, and I was sorely in need of comfort by then. Oh, sweetheart, to think our sweet lovely Gladdy is gone! Even though I'd been expecting it to happen these past weeks, I was so shocked when the lawyer told me, I was hard put to it to concentrate on all the [NWI] other things we had to discuss. I don't think I even [NWI] really believe it, yet; I guess that is because I wasn't with her and didn't see the gradual change from life to death. So the fact of her death hasn't quite registered and my grief is numb within me, even though my eyes ache with weeping.

Of Sammy's visit I wish only to say at the present moment, that even though it was disturbing in some ways (he was incidentally most cordial, even warm toward me) it [NWI] only proved my own faith to me once more.[27] What then was my joy, on receiving your letter, to find my own

---

[27] Sam Greenglass was not so "cordial" in the following letter he wrote her only a week later:

Dear Sis,

Today I visited Mom—I also saw Robert and Michael. I told Michael that I had spoken to you. His first words to me were, "my mother is innocent"— "She would not do anything that was wrong"—Well, you certainly built up a lot of faith in this poor child— How can you have the bitter thought on your conscience to let this child down in such a horrible way.

When a stranger walks into the house—his first question is "Is she from the child welfare or is she an investigator—. I don't want to go to a foster home—I want to stay here."

How can mom keep those two children— They are wearing her away very quickly—I must say you have done and are still doing a very wonderful job— There is not much more disgrace you could bring to your family—but now your great problem seems to be—to get rid of them—one at a time—First

deepest feelings as inspirationally, as profoundly and as genuinely expressed as I have indeed striven to express them to you. I hugged the letter to me and burst into grateful yet achingly lonely tears. Thank you, dearest husband, for your precious gift. I shall hug your beautiful words to me when the longing to see you and talk to you gives me pain. Love you— Ethel

---

Mom—then Chuch [Tessie Greenglass' sister, Chutcha, who lived with her]— The Children in a foster home—your brother in jail— What an excellent job— Pride yourself— And you no doubt have the outlandish courage to think of yourself as a mother! What kind of metal are you made of?

Why dont [sic] you chuck this whole crazy idea of yours and expose all the information you can so that possibly your mother and your two children can look forward to seeing you in your proper role—as a mother to your children.

I still implore you again—for this inhuman idea of yours—you want to sacrifice your entire role in life—to society and to your children to play the martyr—a martyr to whom—to a foreign ideology that will eventually be barred from all corners of the earth.

Certainly there must be some iota of human feeling left in you. Your obligation to your one remaining parent is naught. To a woman like Chucha— who has been the spearhead of every horrible remark made by you—who in turn does so much for you and your children [Manny Bloch remembered it differently. He claimed that the day after Ethel was arrested, Tessie had called his father Alexander Bloch and threatened to dump "these brats" at the nearest police station. (Recording of a speech given by Emanuel Bloch in Detroit, Michigan, on September 22, 1953.) For the reaction of Bernard Greenglass' sister-in-law, see *Sons*, p. 24.]— That undoubtedly I could never tolerate—after all those insulting slurs I'd be damned if I'd ever look upon your children—yet she is giving them a new springboard in life in spite of you. The children cling to her for protection, for love, for warmth,—for comfort. There are good people on this earth and she is one of them. As for me, I wouldn't touch them (those kids) with a tenfoot pole—I wouldn't lift a finger—if it weren't for Mom and Chucha,—and their greatest thought is only for the children to have a natural upbringing in the care of their mother.

Since this entire incident began—I have done things that I never would have given myself credit for—I have even gone to see you— In my lousy heart there is only contempt for you and your kind—but spurred on by the emotions and a mother and an Aunt who unselfishly give of their lives so that poor defenseless and innocent children can have a temporary shelter and comfort and protection—

For these I ask again—give up this wild ideology—come down to earth, give yourself a fighting chance (I may be able to help you) so that someday you may possibly be a mother to your two children—and not a number in some jail—rotting away for years— I mention again that I may be able to help you but I must have your co-operation
     your brother
     Sam

The following letter is available only in a fragment that begins in the middle. It is undated but since Yom Kippur was September 21 in 1950, it was probably written sometime in late September.

. . . and was feeling better.

After lunch, I spent time with a couple of very fine, intelligent Jewish girls up on the roof, whose company I am unable to otherwise avail myself of, since they are not on my floor. Fortunately, I have also made friends with a few girls in my own corridor, who are so sweet & who have come to mean so much to me that I shall miss them sorely when they leave.

At 3:00 P.M. Yom Kippur Services started with a very moving rendition of Kol Nidre on the organ.[28] The combination of sad music, the loss of our lovely Gladdy, and our enforced separation from the children caused the tears to flow freely, after which I felt relieved and settled down to read responsively with the rest of the Congregation, and a girl who was leading us with the absence of our Rabbi.

The one thing that spoiled the day for me were the beans they served for dinner, and which I, like you, did not dain [*sic*] to eat. I made up for it, however, by devouring a nice hunk of layer cake and a pint of milk about an hour before retiring. It is something to see my bed the next morning; it looked like a tornado hit it, that tornado, of course, being your precious wife who has been fighting with the blankets all night and generally behaving like a whirling dervish. Dearest, I am simply marking time till Monday when I'll see you again. Love you, love you, love you—dear husband—Your Ethel

Ethel to Julius

Sept. 29, 1950

My dear sweetheart,

From the above date, you will note that my birthday has come and gone. Darling, it was so sweet of you to try to brighten the darkness for me. With all that you have to plague your mind and spirit, you still managed to so arrange things that your wife would receive not only an exquisitely lovely card but a wonderfully expressive telegram. I am rich indeed in your steadfast, unfailing love. Its precious warmth penetrates these cold stone

---

[28]One of the more bizarre charges made by the prosecutor, Irving Saypol, many years after my parents' execution, was that after their arrest, the FBI found records with pornographic songs and some sacrilegious recordings, including a tasteless ridiculing version of the Kol Nidre. This line and the direct testimony of the Jewish Chaplain at Sing Sing about my parents' attitudes towards Judaism and organized religion should indicate that Saypol is lying.

walls and makes me better able to endure the heartbreak of our own personal separation and that of our dear children from us. Each morning before rising, I fight down a rising sense of desperation, an ineffably bitter longing to see them, an insane impulse to shriek aloud for them and for you. How is it, how is it, my reeling brain demands that we must be apart! And then I remember, for instance, how you looked, how you sounded last Monday at Court, and am conscious of a deep humility which serves not to lessen my pride in my own self, but rather to feed and strengthen it. I am happy to be humble before your manly maturity and strength of purpose, proud to walk beside you and love you, my tender, handsome husband!

Can't write any more now, will answer your letter of Sept. 19 a few days later.[29] You know I kind of have to spread my quota of 1 letter per week.

P.S.1 Got a letter from the children yesterday and a card sent in their name by my dear Bernie. The handwriting and selection are unmistakably his.
P.S.2 It was wonderful to see Michael's name in his own writing but it hurt to know that my dear Gladdy would send no birthday greetings ever again.

Lovingly,
Ethel

The following letter is undated but undoubtedly was written late in October of 1950. The issue addressed in this letter is how to deal with the fact that our mother had been seeing a psychiatrist. She had come to him in a state of anxiety and she had needed someone to hold on to while she sought to discover the sources of her problem. She had had difficulties with me and that was why she arranged for me to begin seeing Mrs. Phillips. In an interview with me, the Doctor made clear that her problems with me were symptomatic of what he called "problems with her core family."[30]

Dear Mr. Bloch,

I called you to come here because I find all attempts to minimize my emotional needs indeed all my efforts to pretend these needs are non-existent at the time of our joint consultations, are to no avail. However, since I find myself shy about expressing myself at these consultations (giving myself the easy out that I am wasting time that rightfully belongs to the prepar-

---

[29]This letter has not survived.
[30]See *Sons*, pp. 38f which reproduces information from the tape of an interview I conducted with her psychiatrist in 1974.

ation of the defense) and since despite my clear understanding of the seriousness of our situation and the exigencies of the defense, I am still unable to
stamp out my true feelings concerning the question of Dr. M.,—I feel that a
much more frank and extensive discussion, and proper appraisal concerning
same is in order.

To begin with, I am not at all satisfied that I understand just what you
brought out to Dr. M. concerning my feelings and I am also not at all
satisfied that what you did bring out was what I expected you would bring
out. By the same token, I am not satisfied as to what he then brought out to
you about me and that it was what I wanted him to bring out. Certainly I
told you myself that I didn't expect to break down, certainly I told you
myself that I had made "remarkable progress" under treatment, & certainly I
told you also that my problems stemmed from way back in my childhood
not from more recent date. To find these things out, I should have thought
was not the sole purpose of your interview with him but rather to ascertain
of what benefit or harm, for that matter, could further treatment possibly be
to me and the case as a whole. To have reached some understanding about
this would have necessitated your giving him a fairly detailed picture of the
case up to now, pointing out the nefarious role my brother D and other
members of the family are playing, what kind of a person they are making
me out to be and what possible capital you figured the opposition might
make of my having undergone psychiatric treatment. It would also have
necessitated his giving you a fairly detailed picture of what actually constituted my problems, in what direction I was moving in order to solve them,
in what way and up to what point psychoanalysis had loosened certain
blocks for me and why I am therefore finding it so difficult now to reconcile
1) my development up to the time I stopped going to him 2) the enforced
clamp on that development since my incarceration and 3) the conflicts
engendered thereof.

If, on the basis of this type of discussion between you and if, after
further discussion concerning ways and means of actually effecting contact
(and I have a few ideas myself on this score) between Dr. M. and myself, it
is still considered inadvisable, I will abide by the decision we have all had
fair opportunity to make. Personally, however, I feel there is much more of
a decision involved here even than that of whether or not my association
with Dr. M. should continue, vitally important though this is to me. I am
referring now to what your Dad[31] so aptly pointed out in response to your

---

[31]Emmanuel Bloch had been retained as an attorney by our father on June 16,
1950, the day of David Greenglass' arrest when, after twelve hours of interrogation, he signed a statement implicating our father in espionage. The FBI had
immediately questioned our father, telling him what they had gotten Greenglass

concern that the prosecution might cash in on the knowledge of my being under the care of a psychiatrist. He said very calmly, "They will do these things anyway, which ever way you behave." What I am getting at is that it's high time we thought in terms of what line we are to take ourselves concerning my psychiatric treatment. What picture should we prepare ourselves to paint for the jury's consumption, if we are called upon for any picture. And it is exactly in this regard that I deem such a discussion as I have outlined above so imperative. Then, once we have established this line (whatever it might be) in our own minds we may find that working out the desired plan is not nearly so impossibly difficult nor so dangerous at all.

Now let me remind you of the note I scribbled just before we parted company last Friday, mentioning Mrs. Phillips. When, during my last visit with her, I begged her to go to Dr. M. about me, ["and" CO] she convinced me that it was far wiser because of the case for me to make my wishes concerning Dr. M. known to you and have you go to see him instead. However, she did promise that should such help from her be needed after you had seen him, it would definitely be forthcoming. To this end, I wrote her, asking her to visit me about further plans. I would like you at this point to read her reply. Of course, she is absolutely right except for one thing. There is a time element involved here which simply has to be considered. First of all, it was Mrs. Phillips that I had been seeing regularly from March of this year on up to perhaps a month ago. Secondly, ours has been that kind of felicitous relationship that has allowed for complete mutual freedom of expression, especially since my imprisonment when she became a substitute to me for Dr. M., receiving the fullest confidences concerning everything about me from ["the" CO] my fears for the kids and my hurt over my family's rejection of me, to the difficulties of adjusting to a stultifying existence and my overwhelming need to go on with Dr. M. Add to this our intense interest in social work, child psychology and psychiatry, and our mutual literacy on these subjects, & you will begin to realize why I am so anxious for her to see Dr. M. for me. When she had refused to do this the first time I made this request, I could see the point she was making that somehow, sometime, I had to begin to learn to ask my attorneys for help,

---

to tell them and in effect inviting him to become a "cooperative witness" by confessing to espionage right then and there. He did not and met Emanuel Bloch that night. (For attorney Bloch's initial thoughts on the situation, see *Sons*, p. 234n.). When our mother was arrested, Emanuel Bloch's father Alexander was the person present at her arraignment and that was how he became a member of the defense team. In the trial, though the attorneys all worked together, Alexander Bloch officially represented our mother as her attorney.

no matter how ashamed or how self-conscious I felt about it.[32] Well, I accomplished this to some degree by convincing you that you had to go. Getting back to the letter she wrote, advising me to go on convincing you, naturally she can't possibly know that the "more permanent plan" she speaks of isn't in the offing at all, nor can she know that the reason it isn't in the offing is because Mssrs. Bloch & M_____ decided it wasn't such a pressing matter after all! Now, that I could get to share my feelings with you a lot more fully, I don't deny, but it stands to reason that you simply can't become aware of and completely understand all that it took Mrs. Phillips so many months to learn unless you too took that time to study the matter. And since, as I said before, speeding things along is of the essence, obviously every short-cut that presents itself to us should be taken full advantage of. This is what I would therefore like you to do for me so that we can give the matter the shove that it needs for it to start moving to some decent solution [an arrow was drawn to the top of the page to insert the next six words] in some reasonable period of time. Please phone (from outside) Mrs. Phillips, giving her the gist of what I have written, and urge her to come to see me Monday or Tuesday of next week. Explain to her that this "one visit" will not stand in the way of the relationship that is beginning to grow between us (it already has a pretty firm footing) nor is it for the purpose of emotional release in the continued absence of Dr. M_____, but that there are informational aspects to this matter which I daren't discuss with her by mail. After all remind her that she did promise me that if I made the first move by bringing the entire matter boldly to your attention and you gave your consent to do something about it, she would stand ready to help me if I called upon her. Besides, as I mentioned in my letter to her there is something I want to give her which wasn't ready for her the last time she saw me[33] & I can't give it to her unless she comes to see me.

Please save this writing for your next appointment with Dr. M. or perhaps we ought to mail it to Mrs. Phillips as I will be asking her to phone him to have him come to the JBG[34] ["to bring" CO] so that she can bring him up to date on what goes with me & she could let him read it then. I could also give her the letter I will be writing to him so that he will

---

[32]Mrs. Phillips told me recently that the reason she refused to go see Dr. Miller was not for the reasons indicated here but mostly for the simple reason that Dr. Miller refused to see her (Mrs. Phillips).

[33]Perhaps this refers to the sweater alluded to in the letter of August 20 above.

[34]Jewish Board of Guardians, where Mrs. Phillips worked.

have a very complete picture by the time he meets with you again. What do you think?[35]

Ethel to Julius

Oct 5, 1950

Julie darling,

Since we saw each other yesterday, I've been walking around in a fog. It was difficult even when I was back in my cell for the count and had changed into my usual duds to realize that I was no longer with you. Oh, my dearest, how invitingly that sweet life I lived with you beckons to me! The all too short periods of time we occasionally spend together only serves to sharpen my already bitter hunger for you and yet the joy I experience is well worth the pain I must taste. Do you know how very dear you are to me, sweetheart! And do you know what a treat your letters are, and how good it makes me feel when you praise mine to you so glowingly. Believe me, it gives me untold happiness to know my words express your own deep feelings as well as mine. Honey, believe me, your sweet words do no less for me; and then, there wells in me the never-ending wonder of the miracle of a man and a woman and the love that is between them, and my delight in our relationship knows no bounds.

Sweetie, they'll be taking the mail soon and I'm already so late with my one letter this week, I don't want it to be any later. Miss Bodek[36] visited me on Thursday; from all she said about the shelter, I am inclined to feel much encouraged about the children's future situation. She is seeing them today and will try to see you Monday. Many kisses, and all my love until I see you, dearest

Your Ethel—

---

[35]There is no indication in the correspondence of what the resulting decisions were, but Dr. Miller did not begin to visit our mother until she was transferred to Sing Sing in April of 1951.

[36]From context this person is obviously from the Jewish Child Welfare agency which ran the shelter where Robby and I were sent after living for a couple of months with our maternal grandmother, Tessie Greenglass.

Ethel to Julius

Oct 19, 1950

My dear one,

I sit and I look at the words and it grows more and more difficult for me to write some more words. You see, sweetheart, with those words, I am at once transferred to your arms and am murmuring them (and others equally appropriate) as my body fuses with yours. Oh, how reluctant I am to shake myself loose from my delicious dream, how loath to thrust from me the imagined sight and sound of us lying together! In the absence of this normal association between husband and wife, however, through which all those sweet feelings which words cannot encompass are expressed, I am the more persuaded to capture them and imprison them here on this page with my pencil, as one impales butterflies on a board with pins, after one has released them from a box against which they had long been beating their disconsolate wings.

Saturday, Oct. 21, 1950

Friday has come and gone and with it our long anticipated ["and" CO] eagerly awaited and mutually enjoyed first regular visits with our lawyers. Sweetheart, life takes on new hope, new meaning, every time I see you. Painful as each regretful good-bye must of necessity be, under the circumstances, there is for me a sense of taking hold, of coming to grips with these very circumstances, that stimulates and refreshes and nourishes.

Honey, this masterpiece will have to be continued another time or it will miss the mail and won't get moving to you till Monday morning.

Consider yourself passionately kissed— Your loving wife—

Ethel to Julius

Wednesday, Oct. 25, 1950

My dearest boy,

I feel so remiss over my emotional behavior today; please forgive me, this situation in playing havoc with my tender mother's feelings. Think of it, it will be eleven weeks this Friday that I last saw our children. Unbelievable, unthinkable, heart-stopping! What [NW] have we done to deserve such unhappiness. All our years we lived decent constructive lives; it's only fitting, therefore, that we should be properly "rewarded"!

Friday, Oct. 27, 1950

Just got back from our regular visit and was delighted to be handed a letter from you. Darling, it hurts me to know you miss us because I know how it is with myself. How I wish it were possible for me to impart some special strength to you that would render you less vulnerable to pain!

Saturday, October 28, 1950

I awoke at 4:30 this morning to hear a mouse squeaking almost in my ear it was so close. A few hard bangs on the spring and he scampered out into the corridor where he proceeded to protest loudly, but to no avail. No one else seemed anxious to invite him in. The damage was already done however, because try as I would I could not get back to sleep. Immediately, my mind seized upon one thing and another so that by the time I arose my brain was spinning with ideas which I had every intention of working through and using in whatever ways I might find for your greatest possible good. What set me off I do not know but after breakfast I found myself about to write [NWI] only sporadically. Usually I am able to prevent thoughts of the children and our shattered home from taking full possession of me but early as it was, there were enough signs [NWI] to warn me that to-day I would be fighting a losing battle. Already, I had wept a few forlorn tears as I [NWI] had tried to concentrate but noisy interruption [NWI] had finally caused me to leave my room. When I returned to it after lunch, I buried myself in my newspaper while a drumming headache began to annoy me. On the roof I played one of my rare games of catch with a couple of girls in a desperate attempt to shake it. All [N2WI] in vain! For several hours thereafter I was on an uncontrollable crying jag and my head felt as though it might burst asunder. My best friend, for whom I had done the very same that morning when she was down with a headache [N3WI] ministered to me with cold compresses and stern admonitions to stop crying and causing it to get worse instead of better. As you can see, it was just one of those delightful days in jail!

Sunday, Oct. 29, 1950

I wish I could say I'm feeling fine this morning, but such is not the case. My head is still throbbing painfully and my eyes ache, but I am a good deal calmer and expect to get through the day with less emotional upset. I have plans for keeping myself busy all afternoon and this time I think I'll succeed.

Dearest, I'm happy for you because you will be called for your weekly visit soon. My buddy just finished giving me a shampoo and my scalp is tingling. Altogether, I feel a good deal refreshed and ready to dig in for some solid writing.

Sweetheart, do you know how dear you are to me. Oh, please, honey be strong for me, I need you so to be strong for me. Lovingly,—Ethel. xxxxxxxxx

After we were moved to the Hebrew Children's Home in the Bronx (see Sons, *pp. 24–33), both our parents began to write to us there. Unlike any letters they may have written between August and November, a number of these have survived.*

From: Julius Rosenberg [ink]

Nov. 2, 1950

Master Michael Rosenberg
c/o Hebrew Children's Home
1682 Monroe Ave, Bronx, N.Y.

My Darling Son,

I am very happy to know that you and your brother are now living at this fine home in the Bronx. You no doubt know that your mother and father made the arrangements with Mrs. Gluck [a social worker with the Jewish Board of Guardians] for you and Robert to be at this place. Here, there are people whose job it is to take care of children and besides men like Mr. Witover[37] understand and love boys like you and is able to help you and see to it that everything is all right. Aunt Lena was over to see me and told me of your visit to the shelter yesterday, all that you are doing and what you are saying. I am very anxious to hear about you and any news she brings is most welcome. Your mother and I are keeping in close touch with Mr. Witover and we'll watch over our dear boys and make sure that all is done to make you comfortable and happy during the time we are unable to be with our loved ones. We will write to you and if it is possible try to have you fellows visit us. In the meantime your Uncle Dave [Note: this is always Julius' brother David Rosenberg], Aunt Lena, Aunt Ethel, Bubbie Sophie

---

[37]Mr. Bernard Witover was the director of the Shelter. He collected many of the letters sent by our parents to us and left them in his desk when he either retired or moved on to other work. His successor saved the letters and gave them to us as described in the preface.

and your cousins will come to see you.[38] I want you and your little brother to know we love you with all our hearts and miss you very much. Twice a week I am able to see your mother at court and we spend a great deal of our time talking about our sweet children and making plans to finish up with our Court case so that we can all be together again. Mr. Emanuel Bloch our lawyer will be over to see you. He will tell you all about us and deliver to you a personal message. This man is defending us and he wants to be your friend and I am positive ["you w" CO] once you know him you'll get along swell with him. As for me I'm well and getting along fine. I'm sure that it wont [*sic*] be long before you'll get used to your new home. Darling don't worry about a thing. If anything bothers you go to the man in charge and he will take care of you. We have told these people all about you what you like and dislike and they will do all they can to make you happy. Please write me and tell me how you are getting along. A big hug and a kiss for Robbie. All my love
Your daddy
Julius
xxxxxxxxxxxxxxxxxxxxxxxxxxxxxxxxxxxx [whole letter filled with x's]

[This first letter from our mother was sent Special Delivery. Unless otherwise noted, the following letters are in pencil.]

                                                        Nov. 4, 1950
Dearest Michael,
      Your sweet Bubbie [Grandmother in Yiddish] Sophie came to see me on Thursday and told me you were leaving for the new place. Then I received a letter from Mrs. Gluck giving me the name and address, so that I would be able to write to you and Robby.
      Yesterday, I saw your dear Daddy and both of us talked about our two boys that we love and miss so much. He told me that he had already sent you a letter so I guess you must have it by now.
      Honey boy, I know things must be strange for you. I am a grown-up and yet it was hard for me, too, to get used to new surroundings and new people and a new routine. So don't expect too much of yourself at first. It will take a little while until you are comfortable about things and the people around you understand that children get used to new things little by little,

---

[38]Note there is no mention of visits from the Greenglass side of the family. The family split had by now become a chasm. Our parents even forbade Tessie Greenglass' sister "Chutcha" from picking us up at the shelter. When Tessie Greenglass would take us for weekends, Chutcha would meet us outside.

not all at once. So, if something bothers you, tell them about it just as you would tell me or Daddy if we were there, and they will help you.

Oh, I almost forgot to tell you. Daddy showed me the letter you had written him with the Cowboy story, and I certainly did enjoy it! And then both of us spoke to Mr. Bloch, our lawyer, about the two wonderful children we have and he promised to visit you as soon as he is permitted to do so.

Good-bye for now, darling. Kiss 'Obby for 'Ulius[39] and me. Wouldn't Mr. Witover laugh about Grekhalkis & Grekmais! Many, many kisses to my sweethearts—Mommy

Ethel to Julius

Nov 5, 1950

My dearest one,

It seems so long ago that it was Friday and we were together. Maybe that's because we had even less time than usual to talk over our personal affairs. Those extra few minutes in the van have come to mean so much to me that I am terribly disappointed when we are deprived of them. And this time, they rushed you out so fast there was no chance for anything but one hurried kiss and you were gone.[40]

---

[39]'Ulius was a character in stories I would sometimes dictate to my mother while she typed them out. We would play with the name Julius: Juluis, Julisu, 'Ulius, etc. Once when I was typing just letters my mother discovered a word that one could actually pronounce because it had vowels in it. That "word" was "greghalkis" which became the name of a character in one of the stories. "Grekmais" was perhaps a character "discovered" similarly.

[40]These trips in the van for weekly court appearances and joint consultations with their attorneys gave them a few precious moments of privacy. The intensity of those moments is captured by the following interview conducted by Virginia Gardner with one of our mother's fellow prisoners and printed in *The Rosenberg Story*:

It was Anna [the names in Gardner's book are pseudonyms] who told the most graphic story of the relationship between Ethel and Julius. . . . She told first of how Ethel never tired of talking about Julie. "Nothing she said was phony, but I just couldn't believe that any marriage was all she said hers was. But I'm telling you, after what I saw in that pie-wagon (prison van), jolting along the streets on the way to Foley Square, why, I know that Romeo and Juliet weren't even in it."

The big van in which they took prisoners to court had called at the West Street jail first, and there the men were loaded into it. "Julie had the seat I learned later the men always reserve for him—next to the grating which separated men from women. It was a pretty large open steel mesh screen.

Sweetheart, have I told you yet that I love you? I want you so badly sometimes that it feels as though I can't bear to be apart from you one more day. And yet I know to-morrow I will still be without you, and the day after that, and the day after that!

Darling, I enjoyed your latest writing so much. I had to smile over your description of our Michael rascal leading his adoring Uncle Dave from store to store. Bless them both, I can't wait to find out how they are doing in their new surroundings. Incidentally, Saturday morning I hit on the idea of sending them a letter via Special Delivery, as I had already missed the morning pick-up and I knew that they probably wouldn't get it until the middle of the week.

Sweetie, I'm in a hurry this morning. So, it seems, is everybody else. A long week-end is over, and I am sitting on my bed, watching a scene of terrific activity out in the corridor and waiting my turn to knock myself out with the mop. I have so much to tell you, my darling, it will be endlessly long till Wednesday. In the meantime, I try to picture you and what you might be doing at this hour or that. My favorite picture is the one, of course, where we've shut everyone and everything out at last and are alone together. Dearest one let's bring it about somehow! Lovingly, Ethel.

Nov. 9, 1950

Dear Hop-a-long Michael,

I thought you might like to know that your uncle David has sent me snapshots of you and Robby. In one of them, you are standing with your hands on your hips, looking tough, and Uncle Dave called that your Hop-a-long Cassidy picture but without the outfit.

I showed all of them to your Daddy yesterday and both of us smiled to see our two sweet children looking so cute, but we also had to wipe our eyes because we wanted so much to really see you, not just your pictures.

Then another nice thing happened. A lady by the name of Mrs. Epstein came to see me yesterday. She said she had already seen you and Robby, and had just come from a visit with Daddy. So now she is acquainted with us all and will be our friend and help us with our problems.

"The women who were going to court that day held back and let Ethel take her seat. I sat down opposite her. It was dark in the van. I didn't even know at the time where Julie was, for you couldn't see any faces. Then I struck a match to light a cigarette.

"I'll never forget what that match lit up. Julie and Ethel, kissing each other through that darned screen. I didn't even wait to get a light, I blew it out." Gardner, p. 78.

I received a letter from Aunt Lena and was so glad to hear that you and Robby sleep next to each other, just like you did at home. When I lie in bed before I fall asleep, I pretend that I see you both, kiss you good-night and tuck you in the way I used to. And I say to my two dears even though you can't actually see me or hear me, "Don't mind, things well work out, Mommy and Daddy are looking after you and loving you all the time, so hush now and rest well till morning—"
Many kisses
Mommy

November 10, 1950

Hello Boys,
Today is Friday and I went to court this morning. Down there I saw your mother and we both decided to write our darling fellows each and every day if it is possible. My brother your Uncle Dave sent me some snapshots of my Michael and Robert and now I can look at your pictures as often as I like. They are very nice pictures and I'm very happy to have them. You understand I'm proud of my sons and I love them very much. Miss Epstein of the Jewish Child Care was over to see me and we talked about you boys. She is going to be seeing you, get to know you and do all she can to help you. As for you Michael, you know by now that everytime there is a change it takes a while before one gets used to the new place.
It is now 9:00 oclock at night and I'm listening to the radio and watching a card game. That reminds me of all the fun we had together playing cards. I hope you are able to spend some time playing games and getting to know some of the other children. I am keeping in close touch with Mr. Witover and Miss Epstein and I'm trying to do all I can to make you happy. I'm well and getting along as best I can but of course I miss you my two sweethearts very much. I made many friends at the place I'm staying and I work in the clothing room. I give out clean clothes to all the men in this house and there are over two hundred people here. There is a roof here and I can play handball and ping pong there. In the evening I play cards and chess. There are nice books that I am able to read. I am sure that you also have many opportunities to enjoy yourself and play. I want you and your brother to know that I love you both with all my heart. Hugs and kisses all you can take. The lights will be going out soon so good night for now.
Your Daddy
Julius
xxxxxxxxxxxxxxxxxxxxxxxxxxxxxxxxx[he filled the page with kisses]

Nov. 10, 1950

Dear Michael,

Today I saw Daddy and as usual we spoke of you and Robby. We promised to write you several times a week. Oh, how we are both looking forward to hearing from you.

Last night, before everyone went to sleep, I was telling a very nice girl that I know here, all about you and Robby. I remembered how you would jump on Daddy when he came home in the evening, pull him to the piano and play "Home on the Range." And then I recalled how Robby would talk about his ferry boats and tug boats because the terrace apartments and the incerators [sic] put together looked like boats to him.

I'll bet there is a piano where you are; it suddenly came to me that there must be, just as I was falling asleep. If there is, it will be like meeting an old friend you haven't seen for a long time, a friend in whose company it is very pleasant to be.[41]

I guess I will be saying good-bye now because this is Saturday morning and mail goes out very early today. Oh, I almost forgot to ask if you had received my Special Delivery letter. Aunt Lena did not mention it to me.

Give my usual kiss to my dear Robby and my dear Michael.

All my love to both of you.

xxxxxxxxx   Mommy

November 11, 1950

Hello My Sweethearts,

Today is Saturday. I don't do any work but read relax and play games. Sometimes chess other times cards[.] When I was home this was the day we always spent together. How well do I remember how we played baseball. I would pitch and you would sock the ball way over my head for a home-run. Michael you are a good hitter and I am sure that if you play with the other boys at the home you will do quite nicely. Yes sir any team that picks you to play on it will do all right for itself. I am told by the people who have been to see you in your new home that you and Robert are together and sleep next too [sic] each other. That is fine and I can see that Mr. Witover will do all he possibly can to make you feel comfortable and happy. I know that Robbie loves you very much looks up to his wonderful brother and it is good that he can be with you. After breakfast one of my friends gave me a haircut. Then I took a shower, put on clean clothes and I feel fresh and in good spirits while I write my two darlings this letter. All the men who live with me have seen your pictures and they tell me how lucky I am to have

---

[41]For more on this issue, see *Sons*, p. 116.

two such swell boys. I spend quite a bit of time telling them of how we used to play cowboys, hide and seek, baseball and all about the different trips we took to Central and Prospect Park. The radio is on blaring loudly reporting a college football game and its so noisy I can't concentrate on this letter. Since you want to know how I pass the time I'll write you some of ["the" omitted] things that I do. Of course, if you want to I'd like you to write me all about yourself. Any news from you is always welcome. You children are the real joy in my life and my greatest pleasure. I love you very much and I'm very happy to be your father. Yes you are lonesome my dearests but I can't do anything at this time. I can only tell you that in the future we will all be together as we have in the past. You must always believe that. Tomorrow is visiting day for both of us and I'll write you and tell you of mine. Until then good-bye for now my loved ones.
Your Daddy
xxxxxxxxxxxxxxxxxxxxxxxxxxxxxxxxxxxxxxxxxxxxxxxxxxxx Julius xxxx

November 12, 1950

Hello My Darling Sons,
Today is Sunday. It always has been our day at the Federal Dention [*sic*] House which is my temporary home[.] it [*sic*] is a day of rest and nobody works. To the me ["n" omitted] here it's like a holiday as their families can visit them. In the evening we are treated to a moving picture. Your Grandma Sophie and Uncle Dave were over to see me today and they said that they saw you boys this morning. I was very glad to hear that you were both feeling fine and you looked so well. They described the nice clothes you and your brother wore and how well you looked in them. Naturally, they were proud of you and it gave me great pleasure to hear such good news about you. It's Monday now and I just received a letter from Aunt Lena and she told me all about her visit to your lovely home. She also said you saw a moving picture while Robbie took his afternoon nap. From all I've heard about your home ["I'm" CO] I'm more than positive you'll be comfortable. As for me I've been very busy with my work here. The man who works with me in the clothing room is sick and I have to do both of our jobs for the time being. Time passes quickly and I'm not able to do much writting [*sic*]. I want to send all my love to my two dearest sweethearts. I think of you all the time and with all of my ability I'm trying to finish up my case so that I can be with my fellows and their mommie as soon as possible. I want to assure you that everything will turn out right. So be patient and try hard to play and have fun since your mother and I, Mr. Witover and Miss

Epstein will look out for you and try to make you happy. It is time to go to bed now so goodnight and goodbye ["for" CO] until tomorrow.
Love and Kisses
Your Daddy—Julius
xxxxxxxxxxxxxxxxxxxx[whole page filled becoming illegible by end]

Nov. 14, 1950

Dear Children,

I was so happy to receive Michael's letter. You certainly have nice stationery. So many moving pictures at one time my you must of [*sic*] had a wonderful time there. From what your Aunt Lena told me I guess you'll be able to see pictures at regular intervals. I can tell from ["what" CO] that letter you said about food that you are making a lot of progress and you are trying awfully hard.[42] Don't worry honey it wont [*sic*] be long before you get accustomed to the meals of your home. I'm proud of you I knew you would be able to take new things in your stride just like the cowboy heroes you like so much such as Hop Along Cassidy Tom Mix and Bill Boyd. As for Robert's [*sic*] crying, darling he is quite young and isn't able to understand whether it be a letter from me or an explanation from a grown up to him they are just words. It is hard for him to grasp the fact that it is best for both of you, at this time, to be at this temporary home. You remember how we used to play hide and seek, cowboys, cards and in this manner only, could we make him feel secure and comfortable. Mr. Witover, Miss Epstein and the counselors will be able to help him by involving him in play that he likes ["such as cards" CO] especially with other children. You will see that once Robert gets into the swing of playing with the materials available at your home like blocks, paints, toys, chalk he'll feel quite at home and adjust rapidly. Also when he sees how well you are making out it will also help him. Remember my boy the people in charge understand you and are working to see that you are happy. Explain to your brother that my ["first" CO] first interest in life are you children, I love you with all my heart. Even though I am not able to be with you or see you at this time you can rest assured that in the future we'll all be together. Yes my boy you are so right I do worry that my sweethearts are homesick and not completely happy but I know my fellows and I am certain everything will turn out just right. Be well and try hard to play and be happy. I am always thinking of you. All my love.
Your own Daddy—Julius
Kisses xxxxxxxxxxxxxxxxxxxxxxxxxxxxxcxxxxxxxxxxx[page filled]

---

[42]See *Sons*, pp. 26–27 for my difficulties with eating.

Ethel to Julius
                                              Tuesday, Nov. 14, 1950
Dearest boy,

I am behind with my letter to you this week. Somehow, when our Friday visit is over and done with, the walls really take over, and I feel like the week-end has swallowed me.

To-day, I wistfully got dressed as for court, got all my business attended to, and sat myself down with my favorite people to await word from the Marshal. At 10:30 A.M. I was informed I wasn't due to go after all. So, off went the clothes back onto the hangers, down went the sheets back on the bed! And off strode your disgruntled wife away over across the corridor to another cell, in a huff, feeling like an awful dope! After griping and chewing the fat a while, I decided to "enjoy" the rest of the day.

After lunch, the up and coming athletic star of this here jail went up on the roof and hit three home runs. You should see the two teams; strictly from hunger![43] We do more laughing than anything else. Actually, though, it's wonderful to punch a ball and run and enjoy wind and sun.[44] I look at the diminished faces and know a keen delight and a sharp pang. How good, how sweet, the warm feeling of simple pleasure shared. How strange, how painful to share it in this building of wall and bar.

                                              Nov. 15, 1950.

Dearest, I enjoyed seeing you today so much. You are my strength and my comfort, my dear friend and my dear love.

                                              Nov. 17, 1950.

It seems I manage to write all of two lines between my visits with you, Sweetheart. Again it was wonderful though over all too soon.

I have received permission to have the few items of warm clothing I mentioned to you brought in. Your wife is getting to be a silly vain female; so help me I'll burst until you can see my latest hat and bag ensemble. The hat, which is already finished has evoked many "oh's" and "ah's" from all and sundry. But it is your approval I anticipate with such impatience and

---

[43]This is an English version of a Yiddish idiomatic expression designed to emphasize the judgment of the speaker that some activity is quite ludicrous.
[44]Urban athletic activity which was being replicated on the roof of the women's prison often depended on using a Spalding rubber ball (called in New York slang a "spaldine") in a game like baseball. You hit it with your fist (punchball—as Ethel was doing) or with a stick (stickball) off a curb or the side of a building, etc.

eagerness. I want to see your eyes light up with undisguised love and pleasure at the sight of me looking smart and snappy. I want to hear you say all kinds of sweet things and tell me you love me. In a word, I want them to give me back my husband; let them live alone and like it! I'm fed to the teeth with it!

Gosh, it would be such fun to play a game of ping pong with you for a change. In your absence, of course, I am forced to make the best of things and play with whoever will. The one saving grace ["in here" CO] of this place I must say, over and over again, is the fact that there are such genuinely nice folks in here.

Honey, let's go home. I miss you and the kids so dreadfully, what shall I do. Hold me close to you to-night — I'm so lonely —

Many, many kisses—Ethel

Nov. 16, 1950

Good Morning, dear children,

It's a bright, lovely day and I am feeling fine. Thank you so much for your wonderful letter. It was a treat to hear about all the interesting things you are doing.

I understand how you feel about Robert's crying but I am absolutely sure it will let up soon.

I saw Daddy and Mr. Bloch yesterday and gave them both your regards. Your Daddy looks just the same as he ever did with his pleasant smile and nice suit. As for myself, I wear a nice skirt and blouse and a pretty green [NWI] wool hat that another sweet Mommy who is here with me, crocheted for me. What is crocheted? Well, you work the wool with a needle that has a hook on the end of it. It's like knitting, except that a knitting needle doesn't have this hook.

This same lady has begun to make another hat for me in gray and white wool. The white is to make the gray look snowy so your mommy can pretend to be Jack Frost. I am remembering right now, how my dear Michael would say, "Oh, Mommy, you look just like a queen." And I'm thinking how Robby used to touch me and say "Pretty"!

Did you know, honey, that I am becoming a fine baseball player? The other day I hit three home runs for my team. We don't have bats in here, so all we can do is punch the ball, but it's lots of fun anyway, and everybody laughs until their tummies hurt. We play up on the roof of the building where there is a beautiful view of the city. We see the Empire State & and

Palisades[45] and even the place where Daddy is staying near the waterfront. Right along that waterfront is the Henrik [*sic*] Hudson Highway. Did you ever hear of it before?

And how is Michael's 'Obby? you look so sweet in the snapshots, 'Obby, that I could eat you up! Yummeldy! And tell me, boykele,[46] whom do you like? Miss Kirsh and Miss Cielei [or Cielci, the next to last letter is unclear] and Mr. Witover and who else? why, Mommy and Daddy of course! And cars and trucks and trains and fire engines and airplanes and boats—and a BUS—and a TAXI!

Michael, dear, what a nice surprise—I mean the brown sugar. Do you know I am making a list of every new thing you learn about and enjoy. Do you suppose it would get so long after a while that it would be too big for my room like that goldfish in the story? I can see it now, creeping out from under the door and hanging out of the window!

Next time you write, I hope you will be able to tell me you have started school. Will Robby be going to the same one or is the kindergarten in the Home itself? The end of the page and the end of the line—All off!

Many hugs & kisses. Mommy

November 16, 1950

Dear Michael,

Yesterday I went to court and I was with your sweet mommie. She looked so well, was in good spirits and was feeling fine. There we spent the time with our lawyers preparing our defense. As usual whenever we get together we naturally make plans for our two dears and talk about you at great length. Your mother told me all that she heard about you from the people who visited her and also about the nice letter you sent her. I in turn informed her of the latest news I knew about you children. Even though we know it's going to be a little hard for you boys at first we are convinced, more so, on the basis of the progress you have made to date that in short order you will be able to manage nicely. Since you're living in the Bronx, now, I've been remembering all the wonderful times we had together especially in Bronx Park. Do you recall all the fun we had on that train ride along the paths as we passed the animal exhibits. Then we would take a

[45]Looking west over the Hudson River from Manhattan, the Palisades are bluffs overlooking the river on the New Jersey side, beginning opposite 100th Street and continuing to the northern tip of Manhattan and beyond.

[46]"ele" is a Yiddish suffix that literally translates as "little" but it connotes a loving feeling or at least a positive warm feeling about the noun so extended or the person so described. When necessary for ease of pronunciation, a consonant is added between the root word and the suffix, e.g., "boykele."

trip, through the childrens [*sic*] zoo. If it's possible I am going to ask your darling Bubbie Sophie to arrange a trip for you and Robbie to Bronx Park on one of her Sunday visits to you. I'm positive you will have a splendid time and I'll have the added pleasure of hearing all about it when they come to visit me. Today I spent most of my time reading a very interesting book and talking about books[.] I hear that when you were over to visit your grandma you busied yourself reading comic books to the extent of not being able to talk to anyone[.] As soon as you get back to school honey and improve your reading ability you will derive a great deal of satisfaction from the new adventures and stories you will be able to read. I know of everything that's happening to you and I am watching your improvement and I want you to understand that it is the job of the grownups to worry about you. Please tell your brother I miss him and you very much and I send all my love and kisses for now. As always your own daddy—Julius xxxxx

November 20, 1950

Dear Michael,

Its [*sic*] Monday night 8:30 P.M and I'm listening to a radio program called the Firestone Hour. The music is very beautiful and it serves as a very delightful background as I write this letter. I just finished a couple of hours playing a card game called contract bridge. I like the game and playing it helps the time pass pleasantly. It was wonderful to get a second letter from you so soon. As for photographs of myself and your mother I don't happen to have any, nor am I able to take any just now. However, I will ask your Grandmother Sophie and if she has any she will send them on to you. I am glad to hear that you are able to play with puzzles and checkers and these games are fun and they help you relax and have a good time. Keep it up darling you are doing swell. I also saw a moving picture this weekend and it was called "Side Street". It was fairly entertaining and I enjoyed it. So you see both you and I are able to manage quite nicely. Of course, I want to assure you that this arrangement is only temporary and you fellows mommy and I have to make the best of this situation. My Sister your Aunt Ethel was over to see ["me" omitted] this Sunday and told me that you have already started school. You learn very quickly and write a letter [omitted word or words, perhaps "and with"] help from the counselor and Mr. Witover you will catch up to the other children in the class. She also said that Aunt Lena, Bubbie Sophie and Linda went to visit you this Sunday and they'll see me later in the week and tell me all about it. I hope you are able to explain to Robbie some of the things I wrote you so that he too can understand[.] I miss you both very much and I think of you constantly. When I came to the part in your letter about football, I just lay back and closed my eyes and the whole picture of us playing in the playground flashed through my mind. We had a lot of fun and we sure enjoyed ourselves. Believe me honey we'll be together again soon and it will be just like before and even more so because I'll make up to you for all the lost time. I love you boys very much and I too am impatient for us to be together as one happy family again. Just know that even if we can't be with you, we think of you and are trying with all our might to be with you as quickly as possible. Your own Daddy—Julius.—Love & Kisses all I can send xxxxx

Nov. 24, 1950

Dearest children,

It's Saturday and the wind is whistling around the building. The rain is coming down hard and I am wondering what you might be doing this minute. Well, I imagine you must be getting ready to eat breakfast as it isn't even eight o-clock. I have already showered, dressed and had mine, swept my room and made my bed. Soon we will order newspapers for the week-end & buy candy and cake and apples and oranges and stamps and toothpaste from a lady who sells these things to us from a little stand on wheels which we call the commissary. She wheels this commissary in and out of the elevator and onto the various floors.

On Friday, two ladies come with a rolling library. This is really a two shelf book case [N3WI] also on wheels, open on both sides, stocked with books of all kinds from which we may choose four at a time, if we like. I have already read several good ones, but the one I liked most was about a Mommy who discovered a substance known as Radium, which has been most helpful in curing disease. This Mommy's name was Marie Curie and her husband who worked with her and was partly responsible for this discovery was Pierre Curie, the great French scientist.

I will send another letter soon. Now I must run to make the morning mail. Love & kisses—Mommy

Ethel

November 25, 1950

Dear Michael,

It's Saturday now and the Thanksgiving Day holiday has come and gone. I hope you had a good time and ate some delicious turkey. The only thing I can be thankful for is that you and your brother are both well and are being taken care of. At the Federal Detention House we had a real celebration. I am sending you a copy of the menu which included twenty-two dishes and they were certainly very good. Besides this feast we were entertained by a movie in the evening. Your Grandmother Sophie was over to see and she raved about how wonderful you fellows are doing. Of course, I agreed with her but I still like to hear her [inserted word CO] talk about it. It is nice to hear that you have both made such excellent progress in adjusting to your new surroundings. She told me how well you are dressed, all about the things you eat and enjoy and also about your going back to public school. Keep up the good work you are doing swell. I told my family to visit me week days and Saturdays so that Sundays will be left over for them to make it Mike and Robbie Day. I saw mommy in court yesterday and we talked about our two dears and made arrangements to tell Miss Epstein and Mr. Witover our ideas and plans for you. Oh yes, I asked your Bubbie for a picture of us and she said she will give you one. When I ate the turkey I recalled the songs you sang about a pumpkin and turkey running away on Thanksgiving Day. Honey I'd like to know if you have a record player at the shelter and if it's possible for you to hear records. I also want you to know that I am constantly receiving reports on whats [*sic*] going on with my children and every time I receive a visit from my family or lawyer I discuss you sweethearts. So you see your mother and I are concentrating on your welfare and our case. All our plans and hopes are that we will be together again soon so that we can enjoy life as one family. My sons you mean the world to me and I love you with all my heart—Your Daddy— Julius

Dec. 4, 1950

Dear pussy Cats,

It seems I haven't spoken to my children for such a long time. So now let's have a nice visit.

Mrs. Epstein came to see me last week and told me that you were going to school and getting along nicely. Could you possibly tell me what kind of a school it is and something about your teacher and your school-mates. I am looking forward to all the latest news concerning both you and Robby. Is he perhaps also attending school, or I guess I should say kindergarten.

By the way, regards also from Mrs. Phillips who asked about you specially and sent her best wishes to you.

I heard from Aunt Lena that both of you had gone to Aunt Ethel for the day, this last Sunday. I can imagine what a time you kids had with the television set there. How are Deanna, Seymour and Sharon? Does Sharon talk much yet? I guess she went for you and Robby in a big way. Little girls usually like boys to play with and make a big fuss over them.

Do you know what I thought of the other day? I remembered how Daddy and I used to call you, Michael, our "boopkie bunny!" And then I remembered those funny words you used to say like, "baukle shop." Have you made up any more funny songs about "the lion on the leader's head" and "next comes the boil and boiling coffee" and "every five minutes he gives the lion a bone." I was lying in bed one night laughing like anything about that song. You see how it is, sweetie—There is always something I'm recalling about you or Robby.

Oh, you never did tell me whether or not there is a piano at the Home. And how about a record player? I know there is a radio which the older children are permitted to listen to before their bedtime.

I should dearly love to see both of you. Do you remember the snapshots Uncle Davy took of you and Robby? Well, I've taken one of them (showing both of you together) and pasted it on to an empty toilet paper holder with scotch tape. The holder which is actually a cardboard cylinder stands on the sill like a frame with the picture fastened to it at top and bottom. It's the last thing I look at before I creep into bed [N2WI] at night and the first thing I run to look at when I jump out of bed in the morning.

Last night a mouse squeezed himself into my room and squeeked [sic] in disappointment because he could find no food. So up he went on the sill & knocked off a book and the picture, if you please. Some nerve! I threw a shoe at him and he scurried away in fright! Love and many kisses.

Mike's xxxxxxxxxxxxxxxxxxxx Robby's xxxxxxxxxxxxxxx Mommy

                                                    December 11, 1950

Michael Darling,

A couple of days ago I received a letter. When I opened the letter I was surprised to see you had written it yourself. I experienced a great deal of pride and joy to receive news about you directly from your hand. Your handwritting [sic] is good and your sentences are easily understood. Honey you are growing up and learning and I'm so happy about it. As for public school, I had no doubt that you would catch up quickly but I had no idea my sweet boy could make such rapid progress. Why in a couple of weeks you are in the 3rd grade and already up to the rest of the class. Your Aunt Lena told me that your teacher even thought you could make out well in the 4th Grade. The fact that you are in the same class with your friends from the shelter makes it pleasanter and since you say that school seems to take only two minutes I know you like it. What I hear from you, Grandma Sophie and Aunt Lena about your eating habits I am convinced you have discovered the secret of trying new things to determine what you really like. Isn't it fun to know that in this manner you don't miss the pleasure of eating new and good foods? Only a month ago you were concerned about school, eating, and

sleeping at your new home and everything turned out as we told you it would. You manage very nicely, have made many new friends, and the people at the shelter like you very much. It was wonderful to hear about the splendid day you and your brother spent at Aunt Ethel's house last Sunday. Your wonderful mother and I are making further arrangements for interesting Sunday visits for you boys. Whenever I get a visit from my family, we spend most of our time hearing glowing reports about our two sweet boys. Of course, when I see your mother you are the principal topic of our conversation and the center of our thoughts. All of us love you so much and we're proud of our fellows. Now that you are back in school and your reading is improving I suppose you spend a lot of time seeking new adventures in books. As for myself I've been doing a great deal of reading which is very satisfying. Chanukah with its candles, games, parties and songs has come and gone. I know you had fun and I remember the wonderful holiday we spent last year, lighting the candles, singing songs and exchanging presents. Since I am unable to be with you and spend time with you something very dear to me is lacking and I miss you very much. However since I know we are all making the best of the situation and that the present state of affairs is only temporary my spirit and hope is high. My sons you represent the best in life to me and I hold you close to my heart. I am always thinking about you. Hugs and Kisses.
xxxxxxxxxxxxxxxxxxx
All my love.
Your Daddy
Julius

                                                          Dec. 11, 1950
Dearest kitty Cats,
    I have been hearing so many nice things about you, I just felt like writing.
    I know that you had a very enjoyable Saturday and Sunday, with toys and lolly pops and ice-cream. Michael, dear, how I should have loved to see you in the Chanukah play. What kind of a part did you have and did you like it? And did Robby see you in it? And what did he have to say?
    Oh, I mustn't forget to tell you I saw the printed letter you sent Daddy. My, but you are progressing by leaps and bounds. And your report card is excellent, especially when you had started to attend school so much later. I want to thank you also for that letter you wrote me at Aunt Ethel's house. It was so wonderful to see my boy Michael's printing and what you had to say pleased me so much. And Daddy—well, he just couldn't get over it, he was so delighted!

Schoene Kinder [Yiddish, for "dear children"], it hurts not to be together during the holidays, as we all used to be. But on the other hand it makes us work all the harder so that sometime in the future this can actually happen. I know you are learning more and more that even though things can get very unhappy, there are always some good people who go right on loving and helping, no matter what! Merry Chanukah, Merry Christmas & Happy New Year to my dearest Michael and Robby, from your Mommy who loves you, no matter what day, month or year it is, no matter where she is— xxxxxxxxxxxxxxxxxxxxxxxxxxxxxx

In addition to these mentions of the Chanukah holiday, the family exchanged Christmas cards. I made a card for each parent and they sent one with a Santa Claus on the front saying "Hi!" and, on the inside, in my father's handwriting "To Michael & Robert" with the card's message "Merry Christmas Happy New Year." It was signed in his handwriting "Love Mommy & Daddy."

Dec. 16, 1950

Dear Children,

It is Saturday morning again and I am looking forward to receiving a letter from you today.

I saw both Bubbies last week—one came Monday and the other one Wednesday—and each brought pleasant news of you and Robby.[47]

When I saw Daddy he informed me that Aunt Ethel had visited him and described the Sunday she had had you at her house. I was delighted to hear that you had played some things you still remembered on her piano. I guess one song was "Home on the Range."

Aunt Lena was telling Daddy how glad you were to see her Sunday at the Chanukah party and how "you cried inside of you" when she had to leave. Sweetheart, you said for me exactly how I feel myself all the time I am away from my two dear boys. Of course, I wish none of us had to cry because we are apart either inside of us or outside, but it is comforting to know that all of us are affected the same way and all of us care about ["what is" CO] how the others are feeling. In the same way, Daddy and I am happy when you and Robby are happy.

Sweetie, they are calling for the mail now so I'll stop but I'll be writing you again soon as usual. Many kisses to my dear Michael & Robby.

xxxxxxxxxxxxxxxx Lovingly, Mommy

---

[47] See *Sons*, p. 26 for what Tessie Greenglass was really doing.

Dec. 18, 1950

Dearest children,

This is your Mommy again writing to Michael and Robert for a change. I know that you can't possibly keep up with my letters because there isn't always time for someone to answer them, but don't let that bother you. Much as I enjoy hearing from you, I understand you can't write me as frequently as I can write you.

Dec. 20, 1950

Yesterday, I was in court and was delighted to see the picture letter you [NWI] had sent Daddy. Yes, my honeybunch's drawing is as fine as it ever was and we both enjoyed seeing it very much, indeed. You know it was sweet of you to tell Daddy to give your regards to "his dearest wife". Being Daddy's wife also means I am Michael and Robby's Mommy who loves them.[48]

I hope to see Mrs. Epstein this week or next. Have you been seeing her every week? And does Robert visit with her a bit, too.

Bubbie Sophie was telling me that you have been learning all about the blessings for various food. Good for you, dear; there are so many interesting things to discover and enjoy.

By the way, what's your teacher's name and what sort of school is it?

As usual, they are calling for mail so I'd better stop now. All my love to you and Robby. And give him some of these many kisses—xxxxxxxxx
Mommy

---

[48]Behind this seemingly positive response one can sense the hurt of being referred to as Julius's "wife" in a letter rather than "mommy."

1951

The first letters available between our parents for 1951 begin after their trial was over. There continued to be letters to Robby and me until May.

Jan. 3, 1951

Dearest Michael,

I want to thank you with all my heart for your wonderful letters you have been sending me. You see, darling, when a small boy (not so small, but still not a great big boy) like you takes the time and effort to do that, it means he must love his mother an awful lot, and that of course makes his mother very happy.

I know that this past week you had a holiday from school and so you had more of a chance to print the letters yourself. If you find less opportunity to do this after you return to school and someone else answers for you, I will be just as delighted. But I still want you to know how much I appreciate the special thoughtfulness you show when you try to write me yourself. I love you very much, Michael dear, and miss you in the same way you miss me.

Honey, I was so glad to hear that you had such an enjoyable visit with Uncle Bernie one Sunday at Bubbie Tessie's house and that you spent another enjoyable Sunday at Aunt Ethel's. Robby must have just gone wild about the electric train. It must have been a lot of fun for both of you.

I was sorry to hear about the sick-room and hope that you are completely well now. I am kind of curious, you know, about this room. Suppose you tell me a little about it next time.

I will write again in a few days, so good-bye for now with many many hugs and kisses to Robby and yourself.

Your loving Mommie.

53

January 8, 1951

My Dearest Sweetest Honey Bunnys I have been very busy going to court and taking care of many things that I have neglected writting [*sic*] you. Do not think that I have forgotten about you fellows. For, on the contrary, I read all the letters that you send your mother and me; then too your Aunts Lena and Ethel send me reports on what's going on with you. Whenever, [*sic*] I receive visits I hear all the details on how you are making out. First let me state that I miss you two darlings very much and I hope in this New Year we will be able to look forward to once again being together. This by right is ours and both your Mommy and I and you our beloved sons are trying with all our might to accomplish this. My love for you boys is even greater and gives me added strength courage and faith. When I hear how well you are learning, growing and getting along I am very proud of you and feel that I am so lucky to have two such wonderful children. This weekend I received another letter from you and it warms my heart to hear that you have such swell times at your Aunt Ethel's house. You certainly had a lot of fun playing with Seymour's new electric trains and as soon as it is possible I wil [*sic*] try to get you the same set with automatic uncoupling, remote control and smoking engine. I am sure we'll both have a lot of fun setting them up together. I'd like to hear more about your activities at the shelter. What do you do in the evenings and afternoons after school? How do you spend your Saturdays? Tell me a little bit about your school. I want to know about your playing and studying. If you have the time let me know how Robbie is doing. All the reports about you children are fine and as good as can be expected considering the circumstances. Grandma Sophie describes you boys to me with the saying "You will not be able to recognize them." She states, "Michael is a little gentleman, neatly dressed well mannered and above all growing up like any other healthy normal boy.["] As for your brother Robert I am told he acts like any other four year old.[49] So you see I am well acquainted with your progress but I still want to know more because you boys mean so much to me. I see your mother regularly now and we talk about your welfare in great length. You our dearest ones are constantly in our minds and we are impatient for an early reuniting of our family. I hold you close and kiss you with all my heart. Be well, I love you very much—Your Daddy—Julius xxxxx

---

[49]Robby would not actually turn four until May.

Jan. 8, 1951

Dearest Michael,

In my last letter I forgot to ask you what you did during the Christmas vacation. I know you were due to go to a party given by the sailors of some aircraft carrier. I am curious as I can be about it. Just what happened there?

Were there any other trips you took or things you did? I would certainly enjoy hearing about them.

And how did Robby spend the holiday? Did he go along on the ship or was something else planned for the kindergarten group?

I hope that whatever you children did, the time passed pleasantly and you went back to school happily.

What are you learning in school? And do you have any classmates that you are particularly friendly with? You know, I don't even know your teacher's name. Or Robby's teacher's name.

I guess I have asked you an awful lot of questions. You don't have to worry about answering them all at once, honey. Whenever you get around to it will be perfectly all right, but of course, I love to hear from you as often as possible.

I will send your regards and Robby's to Daddy when I see him tomorrow.

Mail is here—Love
Mommie—

Jan. 15, 1951

Dearest boy Michael,

I just have to sit down and write you before I go to sleep, so that I'll be sure to make the morning mail. Your Daddy will be delighted when I tell him I managed to write you before going to court to see him. And of course I will give him your love and Robby's.

Pussy cats, how I miss you both. To-day Somebody [*sic*] happened to mention seedless grapes and all of a sudden I could see you and Robby gobbling big plates of them at a terrific speed.

Oh, I just remembered what Aunt Lena told me last week. I'm talking about your telephone call to her house. Gosh, were they pleasantly surprised to hear your voice.

Did you know that Mrs. Epstein visited me last week right before she went to see you. I am so happy when she comes because then I can hear all about you and send you children my love through her.

Always, I must ask the Same [*sic*] questions. What are you doing at school?—How are you feeling? Daddy and I wish with all our hearts that you and Robby are enjoying yourselves at the home as much as it is possible for you to do so without us.

Good-bye, darling, for now. I'll be writing you again soon. All my love, hugs and kisses to my sweet, dear boys—Mommie xxxxxxxxxxx

                                                          Jan. 22, 1951

Dearest Michael & Robby,

What a lovely day to write my children! The sky is blue, the sun is shining and I'm just in the mood to visit with you.

And now that I've entered the room where shall I sit? Oh, this chair will do fine, this one with the broad arms so you can each perch alongside of me. Oh, oh, look out—you're both falling off right on top of me. Help, I'm choking you're hugging me too hard! But I love it!

I had to stop writing because Aunt Ethel was downstairs waiting to see me. She is planning to have you at her house again on Sunday and will do all she can to make your stay there pleasant.

What did you do this past Sunday? Did Uncle Bernie pick you up again or did Bubbie Tessie come for you herself? And what happened when you got to her house? Was there anything particularly interesting that you did?

I am feeling well but miss you and Robby very much. The other day I began to laugh all of a sudden because something Daddy said reminded me of that dog story he used to tell about the College of curs and what fun we all had listening to it.

Do you ever play you are Bill Coal, the engineer and doesn't Robby still call himself "Hop-a-long Cassery"? Love you both and look forward to the time we can all see one another again.

Many hugs and kisses—Mommie

[Next letter written on smaller, unlined paper.]

                                                          Feb. 2, 1951

Dearest Michael,

First, I want to thank you for all your wonderful letters. There was one you wrote from Bubbie Tessie's house about the rubber knife that was lost so quickly. Then there was the one you wrote while visiting Aunt Ethel in which you told me about the cavalry movie and the delicious chicken dinner you and Robby ate. Now I have before me the letter you sent Daddy; we both enjoyed it very much.

I saw Mrs. Epstein last week and she told me all about you and Robert. Daddy & I feel sure that you will get to like the foster home after a while the same as you did the shelter where you are now staying.[50]

This is going to be a very short letter because I didn't write you all week and I want to make sure you get this on Monday. I will write you again next week to make up for it.

In the meantime, sweetheart, I love you and miss you both and send you my best wishes for a pleasant week.

xxxxxxx

Mommie

February 5th, 1951

Dear Michael,

It's about 10:00 o'clock Monday and I just awoke from an early morning nap. There are four of us men sitting in our room and each and everyone of us is doing something, and above all it is nice and quiet. One of the fellows is doing a crossword puzzle, another is reading a newspaper, the third is making picture frames out of the silver wrappings from cigarette packs and I'm writting [sic] to my sweetest honey bunch. I am healthy and my main concern is you boys and the fact that we are separated. I miss being with you and it is because of all the wonderful letters that you send mommy and me that we are able to feel much better. That is so because we hear quite a bit of good news about you especially from Miss Epstein. I love you very much and I long to hold you in my arms to hug you close and shower you with kisses. It is nice to know that on the whole you are getting along and it is only natural for a boy your age finding himself at a temporary shelter to have some problems. That is why we your parents and Miss Epstein your social worker are making arrangements for you fellows to live with a foster mother and father untill [sic] we can all be together again. I am so happy to hear how much you like school and I am especially gratified at the substantial progress you have made in eating new foods. That shows you are improving and things will keep on getting (an erasure follows, "to bet") better. Darling you must never for even one minute doubt that in time all of us will be together again as in the past and we will once again be one big happy family. Often I sit and recall all the fun we had together and remember many things we did such as; [sic] build with your

---

[50]Since Sophie Rosenberg was still not feeling strong enough to take us into her home, and the other (Rosenberg) relatives were busy with their own families (and frightened, also—see *Sons*, p. 25), our parents began to make arrangements to have us placed in a foster home.

erector set, play cards & play many different cowboy and story games. Sweetheart I hold these beautiful memories dear and they are the promise that we will be able to make up for all we missed. Aunt Ethel described in great detail the pleasant Sunday you spent at her house. Boy it must have been sweet to ride in that brand new car. That's the way to spend a day, good food, lots of play and fun and around you people who love you and do all to make you happy and comfortable. Winter didn't give you much chance to be outdoors. However improving weather will change that. I just as well as you am looking forward to brighter better days. All my love

xxxxxxxxxxxxxxxxxxxxxxxxxx Your own Daddy Julius

Feb. 17, 1951

Dearest Michael,

Daddy and I had a wonderful time reading the two letters you wrote while at Aunt Lena's house.

Sweetheart, it makes us very happy to learn that you are doing so well in school. Pussy cat, how I should love to be with you and to be receiving the report card and signing it the way I always did.[51] Daddy's face is one great big smile when we recall the sweet times we spent with you and Robby. We thank you for the "good luck" you wished us.[52] Believe me, we will do all that is we possibly can to be with you again.

In the meantime, we want you to know we think we have the two bestest boys in the whole world and love them more than anything else in the whole world.

Now, boykele Robby,—so you have a red locomotive. Is it the same big wooden one you used to ride about on at 10 Monroe St. or a different one? Choo, choo, everybody get out of the way, here comes Engineer Hop-a-long Robby!

Choo, choo, here comes the mail car and there goes Mommy to load it with this great, big, heavy letter to Michael and Robby. All aboard! Hurry up, mail car, and get it to them fast, fast, fast—chug chug, chug, chug, too-oo-oo-t!

Love and kisses xxxxxxxxxxxxxxx

Mommy

xxxxxxxxxxxxxxxxxxxxxxxx [letter filled up with x's]

---

[51] In the New York public schools in those days, reports were not mailed home to parents but brought home to be looked at, signed by a parent or guardian, and then returned to school.

[52] A reference to the upcoming trial, which began on March 6.

Feb. 24, 1951

Dearest Michael,

I understand from Uncle Bernie's latest letter to me that you spent a very pleasant Sunday at Bubbie Tessie's house last week. I am always happy to know that you and Robby are happy.

Thank you so much, darling, for the Valentine you were trying so hard to make for me. Even though it didn't get to me, I appreciate your thinking of me more than I could even tell you. You must simply pretend that I am giving you a great big Mommy hug and kiss for it.

I hear that you are doing exceptionally well in reading and I find myself wondering just what book or books you are studying. Anyway, whatever it is, isn't it just the most fun to be able to read? What a wonderful thing to open a book and to be able to understand what [NWI] all those black letters are saying to you!

And what is my dear Robby doing? Singing a song, perhaps, with Michael—like Ibashe or Johnny with the Bandy Legs, or Waltzing Matilda[53]—Do you remember "The Little Cowboy" and "Fire, fire, fire, here comes Robert fireman to siss the fire out"!

Time to put the letter out so both my children will be able to hear their Mommy say she loves them ever so much. Many songs and many hugs and many kisses—Mommy.

March 1, 1951

Dearest Michael boy,

I am hoping that this letter will reach you by Saturday to kind of give you a treat after a week of school.

I understand that the chickens are "poxing" at your house. Tell them to hurry up and get over with it so you and Robby can have your usual Sunday visit. Tell them your Daddy says they're "holding up the wheels of progress"!

March 2, 1951

Pussy cat, here it is Friday night and I'm not ready to send this letter out yet. Please forgive me, darling; at least you will get it by Monday.

And what have my two dear boys been doing with themselves this week? It would be so wonderful to get just a tiny, wee bit of a letter from

---

[53]These were songs from an album of 78 rpm records called "Songs from the United Nations." "Johnny with the Bandy Legs" is from South Africa and "Waltzing Matilda" is, of course, kind of a national song of Australia.

you, Michael; your last one wishing us both luck was so sweet and so welcome.

My lovely children, I am hoping, and so is Daddy, of course, that we [NWI] really will have the luck you wished us. Certainly we will do all we can to make things come out the way we all want them to, and Mr. Bloch and his father are working very hard to help us do just that.

In the meantime, sweetheart, happy birthday for March 10th when my precious blue-eyed blonde is 8 years old, and all our love! And much love and many kisses to my darling Robby boyle [Yiddish, not a misspelling]. Robby dear, you had a hair-cut didn't you sweetie—Mommy & Daddy love you both so much.

The trial lasted from March 6 to March 29, 1951 (with weekends off) when our parents and co-defendant Morton Sobell were convicted.[54] On April 5, our parents were sentenced to death by Federal Judge Irving R. Kaufman. The sentencing speech is a masterpiece of mendacity and Cold War hysteria. The first lie occurred at the beginning when he claimed he had refrained from asking the government for a sentence recommendation. FBI documents indicate that before the defense had even presented its case, Raymond Whearty, a high official in the Department of Justice, "knew" Kaufman would sentence Julius Rosenberg to death "if he doesn't change his mind."[55]

---

[54]For detailed analyses of the trial, see Walter and Miriam Schneir, *Invitation to an Inquest* (NY: Pantheon, 1983), pp. 119–67 and Morton Sobell, *On Doing Time* (NY: Scribner's, 1974), pp. 129–249. For pro-government analyses of the trial, see Louis Nizer, *The Implosion Conspiracy* (NY: Doubleday, 1973), pp. 33–348 and Ronald Radosh and Joyce Milton, *The Rosenberg File* (NY: Holt, 1983), pp. 170–274.

[55]Belmont to Ladd, JR HQ 894, March 16, 1951. The Whearty statement is one of a number of revelations from FBI documents collected and published in 1976 as *The Kaufman Papers*. This pamphlet is still available from the National Committee to Reopen the Rosenberg Case. The original 1976 publication consisted of thirty FBI documents. Since that time, more documents pertaining to the issue of Kaufman's improper, unethical, and at times even illegal activities have come to light. Hereinafter, references to "Kaufman documents" will cite them by FBI file, serial, and document number except in those cases where the document number is indecipherable. Those released with the initial Kaufman papers will be designated with the addendum [K]. The complete text of *The Kaufman Papers* as well as some additional documents were read into the Congressional Record at a hearing in 1982. See U.S. Congress, *Hearings before the Sub-Committee on Criminal Justice of the Committee on the Judiciary, House of Representatives, 97th Congress, First and Second Sessions on Federal Criminal Law Revision,* Serial No. 132 Pt. 3, App. 2, "The Death Penalty (Rosenberg Case)" December 16, 1982, pp. 2255–486 (hereinafter cited as

The documents prove that Kaufman's statement from the bench was a lie. He spoke to Assistant U.S. Attorney Roy M. Cohn, two other judges, and prosecutor Saypol asking for sentencing recommendations. Asking prosecutors without the presence of the defense attorney is a violation of the canons of judicial ethics. The reason for this is so that any evidence that prosecutors might bring to bear upon the judge can be rebutted by defense counsel.[56] *He then concluded that the Rosenbergs' actions had put the atom bomb into the hands of the Russians "years before our best scientists predicted Russia would perfect the bomb,"*[57] *which was in flagrant contradiction to views expressed by countless scientists right after World War II that it would take the Soviets about four years to develop their own bomb.*[58] *When the Soviets did explode the bomb, President Harry Truman stated "Nearly four years ago I pointed out that 'scientific opinion appears to be practically unanimous that the essential theoretical knowledge upon which the discovery is based is already widely known'." General Dwight Eisenhower echoed Mr. Truman's sentiments.*[59] *The* New York Times *editorialized that ". . . there is no valid reason for surprise at this development. . . . Only those Americans who failed to pay attention to what was said of the atomic bomb by . . . the men who made it—could ever have believed that we possessed a permanent and exclusive monopoly . . ."*[60]

After blaming our parents for giving the Russians this weapon, he charged them with encouraging the communists to begin the Korean War[61] *and placing millions of innocent people at risk because of their "treason." Thus, in one sentence, he succeeded in lying about the scientific "secrets" of atomic energy, the cause of the Korean War, and the nature of the crime for which our parents have been convicted. Only on the cause of the Korean War could Kaufman have pleaded innocent, though logic should indicate that if the Soviets had planned it they would hardly have been absent from the U.N. Security Council when the U.S. was able to get United Nations approval for a "police action" in Korea to resist the alleged invasion from*

Hearings). *The Kaufman Papers* appear on pp. 2337–403. The Whearty quote appears in *Hearings*, p. 2348.

[56]For Kaufman's secret contacts with Cohn, Saypol, *et al.*, see Memo, Ladd to Hoover, April 3, 1951 [K]. Also in *Hearings*, p. 2349. See also memo Roy J. Barloga to file, JR NY 1579, April 3, 1951. See also letter Saypol to Kelley, JR HQ 2498, March 13, 1975 [K]. Also in *Hearings*, p. 2391f.

[57]Record, p. 1614.

[58]See, for example, Schneir, p. 38.

[59]Their statements were reported in the *New York Times* of September 24, 1949, p. 1 (Truman) and 2 (Eisenhower).

[60]See Schneir, p. 53.

[61]Record, p. 1615.

the North.[62] *Most observers believe the North Korean decision caught the Soviets by surprise. Calling the actions for which they were convicted "treason" is a distortion of mammoth proportions for a judge. Treason is a crime described in the Constitution as requiring proof through the testimony of disinterested witnesses (in other words, the testimony of the Greenglasses, alleged co-conspirators, would not have been permissible) that one has "made war upon the United States." This error continued to creep into judicial pronouncements. When Robby and I sued Louis Nizer for appropriating some of the published prison correspondence in his book without obtaining permission, the first judge described our parents as having been convicted of treason.*[63]

Finally, just before he pronounced sentence, he gratuitously accused our parents of willfully sacrificing Robby and me. "Love for their cause dominated their lives—it was even greater than their love for their children."[64] *During the period of the trial, as one can see from the following letter, our parents did not write to us.*

April 9, 1951

Dearest Michael and Robby,

I know that it has been some time since you have heard from me and that by now you must be getting impatient with your Mommy.

As you must have heard, darlings, Daddy and I went through a long trial and were using all our time and energies to convince the jury to send us back to you where we belong. I am terribly sorry to have to tell you that we didn't succeed, but I am very happy to say that we are going to keep right on trying until we do succeed.

There are a few things I'd like you to keep in mind and try to remember when you are feeling lonesome for us. It's a funny thing; but sometimes a jury brings in a verdict of guilty even though the people involved (in this case your own Mommy & Daddy) are innocent. My dear children, never forget, no matter what anyone else may say to the contrary, we have done no wrong and we are not guilty. And never forget, either, that we love you even more than we did before we were taken from you, and we can hardly wait until we are allowed to see you again.

When a visit between us is finally arranged, Daddy and I will answer all those questions which we know are troubling you and help you to

---

[62]For a good instant analysis of some of the unsettling questions about the origins of the Korean War, see I.F. Stone, *The Hidden History of the Korean War* (NY: Monthly Review Press, 1953).

[63]See *Meeropol vs. Nizer*, Civ. 2720.

[64]Record, p. 1616.

understand just what this is all about. In the meantime, trust us to go on loving you no matter how long it takes for us all to be together again for good. I must hug and kiss you good-bye now.

xxxxxx Mommy

Julius to Ethel

April 10, 1951

{Please rush this letter} JR

Dearest Sweetest Honey Boy Michael,

I am writting [*sic*] you my son because I believe you will be able to understand and somehow tell your brother so he too might know. At first I want you to know that Mommy and I always loved you fellows with all our hearts and we will always continue to love you, care for you and do all we can to help you and be with you. Darling you wrote a most wonderful letter. Your handwritting [*sic*] is very good and I am happy to see you are learning quickly and improving yourself. The things you tell me about in your letter make me feel great and I am certainly proud to be the father of such a wonderful boy. We want to see you boys and we are trying to get permission for you to visit us. You asked a number of questions in your letter and I will answer each and every one of them.

You want to know why I didn't write and also what is the matter. For the last few months your mother, I and our lawyers were busy preparing our case for court and then we were on trial. I was, therefore, very busy, I did not have much time to write you and I also wanted to wait in order to be able to tell you the results of the trial. You, Michael, have read and heard stories how men and women are brought into court and are tried. Some people are freed and some are found guilty. Those people who are found guilty have the right, as is the law of our country, to appeal their cases to the higher courts in order to be freed. This takes a lot of time. In some cases a year or perhaps even more. Your mother and father were found guilty. Just as you said we never did anything wrong and we always taught you our children never to do anything wrong. You our children mean more than anything else in the world to us and we want to repeat even though I am sure you already know that we your parents are innocent of the charges. Everything possible within our power is being done to win our freedom and be together with you boys again.

You ask what you can do for me. All you can do my loved ones is know that we love you and you must believe as we your mother and father believe that there will come a time when we will be set free and once again live together as one happy family. I will wait until I see you and then I will explain all about our case. Remember we want to see you and be with you but it is not up to us, as the court is the only one that can let us see each other.

I have heard such excellent reports about you from Bubbie Sophie, Aunt Ethel and Aunt Lena. They all love you and are so proud of you. I am well, feeling fine and thinking about you darlings all the time. I want you to tell me more about what you are doing at the home, at school and at play. I like your questions. Ask all you can think of. I will try to answer them so you will be able to understand. Now that I have more time I will write to you more often. In this way we will be able to be closer together. I am going to have your lovely mommy read your letter as I am sure she will get a lot of pleasure from it. Never for one moment doubt or have fears as everything will turn out all right. With all my heart and all my love to my boys Michael and Robert.

Your very own Daddy
Julius

Kisses xxxxxx [filled the line with x's]
Hugs xxxxxx [filled the line with x's]
LOVE xxxxxx [filled the line with x's]

April 10, 1951

Precious Woman
Ethel my darling you are truly a great, dignified and sweet person. Tears fill my eyes as I try to put my sentiments on paper. I can only say that life has been worth while because you have been besides me. I firmly believe that we are better people because we stood up with courage, character and confidence through a very grueling trial and a most brutal sentence. All because we are innocent. It's very difficult for people who are uninformed and who have no feelings to understand our stamina. Our upbringing, the full meaning of our lives, based on a true amalgamation of our American and Jewish Heritage which to us ["is" CO] means freedom[,] culture and character, ["and this" CO] has made us the people we are. All the filth, lies and slanders of this grotesque political frameup, in a background of world hysteria, will not in anyway deter us but [NWI] rather spur us on until we are completely vindicated. We didn't ask for this we only wanted to be left alone but the gauntlet was laid down to us and with every ounce of life in our bodies we will fight till we are free.

Honey I think of you constantly, I hunger for you, I want to be with you. It is so painful that such a great hurt can only mean that I love you with every fibre of my being. I can only repeat over and over again that the thought of you more than compensates for this pain because of all the happiness you have brought me as my wife. Sweetheart I can't let go of you; ["as" CO] you are so dear to me. If you are able to get just part of the sustenance you engender in me I am sure you will have the strength to withstand the hardships that face us.

Now I'd like to talk about our greatest possession our two dears. I got a wonderful letter from Michael and it moved me very deeply. I promptly wrote, reassuring him of our love and answering his two questions on a level he could comprehend. I told him we were found guilty and I also explained about the appeal to the higher courts and let him know everything will finally come out all right. That we want very much to see him and we are making every effort to get permission from the court for us to have a visit with the children. On the whole I think Michael will be able to understand. I did not tell him of our sentence. I said we will tell him all about our case when we see him. It is cruel to be separated from our children but it is good to know they are well and growing up. Something very big is missing. It all seems so unreal but yet the cold reality of the steel bars are all around me. I eat, sleep, read and walk four paces back and forth in my cell. I do a bit of thinking about you and the children & I intend to write at least once a week to each of you. My family is 100% behind us and it encourages me. I know as time goes on more and more people [N2WI] will come to our defense and help set us free of this nightmare. I caress you tenderly and send all my love. Your own

Julius

Our mother did not receive this letter until after she was transferred to Sing Sing prison in Ossining, N.Y. where federal Death Row prisoners were housed pending execution. The transfer occurred on April 11 and the letter was stamped by the prison censor at our father's prison that same day, April 11.

Emanuel H. Bloch
270 Broadway
New York New York

April 16, 1951

Dear Manny,

Even though you may get to see me before this letter reaches you, I feel compelled to discuss a number of things which were of necessity neglected on Saturday [April 14]. Incidentally your visit was a shot in the arm and even though I was inclined to be a bit tearful after you had gone, I was also greatly encouraged. Perhaps in time I shall truly become one of those people whom you once characterized as having "that kind of spirit that can never be extinguished!" I'm certainly going to try hard enough!

1) I forgot to tell you that you are permitted to send me newspaper clippings via the mail. First of all, I am just conceited enough to want to see the latest pictures and publicity concerning my removal here. But seriously, I feel the adoption of such a regular procedure to help keep me in touch with things between your visits will serve an excellent morale purpose. Kindly implement said obviously agreeable purpose at once!

2) The more I think of it, the more I am inclined to believe that it would be extremely valuable for me to see Mrs. Epstein before my contemplated visit with the children. I know there may be complications involved but it might be worthwhile to broach the question to her supervisor on the basis that I have not seen Mrs. Epstein in months and since I am therefore very much behind on matters concerning the kids, I will be at a distinct disadvantage when I see them and may pull some unnecessary boners.

If for any reason, however, she can't make it, I feel it absolutely imperative for her to write me in detail what kind of questions they have been asking, what answers people have been giving them, on what level they have generally been discussing us & the case & any other information concerning their development up to this point she things it might be helpful for me to know. In any case, there is no reason she cannot at least see Julie & give him such a picture as I have outlined. Personally, I would urge every effort on the agency's part to see me directly. There are so many questions bumbling about in my head regarding the kids and I feel so strongly about making their initial visits both to me & Julie as positive an experience for us all as I can, that I am most anxious to see her.

Now in connection with the matter of visiting more naturally with them than the present set-up permits, perhaps if the child doctor at the Jewish Child Care could phone the warden directly and explain the situation from the point of view of a possible traumatic reaction involved in such an experience,[65] or write him stressing Michael's anxiety neurosis & the treatment he has been undergoing and Robby's sharp disturbance since our separation, we might get the proper kind of response. What do you think? Please do try to get Mrs. Epstein down here so she can see the set-up for herself.

---

[65]In an interview in 1974, Gloria Agrin, Emanuel Bloch's assistant, claimed that they had consulted Dr. Frederic Wertham about a number of issues—see *Sons*, pp. 59, 253—including the effect of a prison visit on us. He had advised against our seeing them in prison through bars. When the visits were finally arranged, they took place in the counsel room in the presence of Emanuel Bloch.

3) Please encourage my friends to write! I should dearly love to hear from them because even though I know I'm not forgotten, my all too human feelings demand some tangible proof, some concrete evidence. (Help! Listen to the up-and-coming advocate!)

Speaking of advocates, how is my "Pop"?[66] And Mr Phillips and Mr. Kuntz? [Morton Sobell's lawyers] Please send them all my best, and assure them I am still alive and kicking like a team [of] mules.

And for heaven's sake, read this letter to Julie and tell him to be patient just a little while longer and he will get a nice big, juicy book from his silly wife who perversely (it might seem to him) writes her lawyer before she gets around to writing him! I am still trying to kind of catch my breath and so far I think I've made progress. Only it shouldn't happen to two dogs!

One more technical item. I have just been informed that unless a pass for a visitor is filled out here by me by Tuesday, said visitor will not be allowed in for a Sunday visit. In other words, it may be better for my in-laws to try to get here sometime during the week (at least for this week) because I can't very well fill in such a form when I don't know who intends to come [N4WI] here Sunday, if anyone. After a while things will regularize and we'll all get into the swing of things; it is irksome and frustrating however in the meantime. I've written to you rather than Julie and his folks first to save time and to try to avoid unnecessary repetition and confusion.

Affectionately,
Ethel

April 17, 1951

My very own dearest husband,

I don't know when I've had such a time bringing myself to write you. My brain seems to have slowed to all but a complete halt under the weight of the myriad impressions that have been stamping themselves upon it minute upon minute, hour upon hour, since my removal here. I feel, on the one hand, a sharp need to share all that burdens my mind and heart and so bring to naught, make invalid the bitter physical reality of our separation, yet am stabbed by the implacable & desolate knowledge that the swift spinning of time presents a never to be solved enigma.

Be that as it may, (and you know my perfectionist's passion for chronological sequence and detail) I shall seek to console myself by recounting for you all that it is humanly possible for me to do, at one writing or another,

---

[66]Emanuel Bloch's father Alexander was a co-counsel at the trial, officially listed as the lawyer for our mother, even though his son headed the defense effort. His nickname was "Pop" Bloch.

though the incident described, the thought circumvented, the emotion captured be not of that exact moment's making.

Darling, do I sound a bit cracked? Actually I am serious about it and find that I must at least express my deep-seated frustration so that you will comprehend all I must endure in order to "wrest from my locked spirit my soul's language". That's from Thomas Wolfe's "You Can't Go Home Again," from which inspired writing I am draining deep emotional and intellectual gratification.

As you see, sweetheart, I have already embarked on the next lap of our history making journey. Already there appear the signs of my growing maturity. The bars of my large, comfortable cell held several books, the lovely colorful cards (including your exquisite birthday greeting to me) that I accumulated at the House of Detention line the top ledge of my writing table to pleasure the eye and brighten the spirit, the children's snapshots are taped onto a "picture frame" made of cardboard and smile sweetly upon me whenever I so desire, and within me there begins to develop the profoundest kind of belief that somehow, somewhere, I shall find that "courage, confidence and perspective" I shall need to see me through days and nights of bottomless horror, of tortured screams I may not utter, of frenzied longings I must deny! Julie dearest, how I wait upon the journey's end and our triumphant return to that precious life from which the foul monsters of our time have sought to drag us!

Bunny, I'll have to write you a second letter after this one goes out as I don't want to keep you waiting a minute longer for word from me. Darling, I love you.

Ethel

The following letter is perhaps the first indication of our parents' self-consciousness about their writing. Here, we see our father editing a first draft of a letter to our mother. The letter printed here is that first draft, with all of the editorial changes that could be deciphered included. The final draft was then copied by him and sent out by regular prison mail.

April 18, 1951

Dearest Ethel,

I received your wonderful letter this afternoon. Frankly I've been impatiently awaiting news from you. Whenever Manny comes to see me he tells me all he knows about you. He described in great detail how you live (that is as much as he is aware of) and how Sing Sing affects one as sensitive as you. Before I forget I hope you received the letter I sent you last week. Darling, just as you said in the statement our lawyer released to the press at the time of your removal to this new mental horror house[67] it [in the final version "it" was replaced by "that this"] is a cruel and vindictive action however [in the final draft the previous word was omitted, and a new sentence begun at this point] I am sure I express both our feelings when I state the gentlemen of the "Justice" dept and their lackeys will not succeed in their campaign to physically and emotionally pressure us to let ourselves be used as pawns in their political game of chess.

Your letter is so terriffic [*sic*] that I took time out to analyze it. The first impression I got is that the situation as it confronted you was both overwhelming and to some degree ["started you off" CO, N4WI] you ["was a" CO] were a bit emotionally shocked. This is no doubt the effect one expects. However [comma added in final draft] in spite of this initial observation more important [changed to "and most important" in the final version] I notice a marked clarity ["in this turbulence" CO] & [changed to "and" in the final version] steadfastness in all this turbulence. It is certainly remarkable to see that at this early date ["the" CO, NWI] your pendulum of emotions still hover about a stable core and already you have begun to organize yourself. Your perfectionist['] passion for detail will do you stead. Now that you have made yourself as physically comfortable as possible I advise you to regiment yourself to a very strict scheduale [*sic*] of reading, writting [*sic*] and also embarking on a course of self study whether it be music, physchiatry [*sic*] or both. This darling is the only way to overcome ["and" CO] these hardships and at the same time maintain ones [*sic*] own equilibrium. Of course, every effort will be made to see that the lawyers and my family visit you as often as is humanely [*sic*] possible. If our lawyers do not succeed in bringing you back to the Women Det. Home at 10th St in New York I will move heaven and earth to be sent to Sing Sing to be near you and to be able to see you whenever it is possible. I beg you not to try to sway me from this decision as this is what I must do. [Four illegible words CO, the next word in the text looks like "This" superimposed over "Your," the final version reads as follows] This single document is indelible proof that not only are you a tremendous person but you have the courage, confidence and enlightened perspective to ["have" CO] come through all this [NWI] hell and ["more if necessary" CO, N2WI] then some in flying colors. My wife, I stand ["proud and" CO] humble ["besides you, instilled," CO, next two words written above] beside you, proud of you and inspired by such a woman.

Manny if [changed to "is" in the final version] truly a Jewel. He is doing a lot of running around but contrary to the proverbial expression like

---

[67]Emanuel Bloch filed a writ of *habeas corpus* to have our mother returned to New York. Part of her affidavit is reprinted in *Sons*, p. 40.

a chicken without a head such brains can only fit in two heads and the unfortunate thing is only one body so he can't be in two places at once. All power to him as he is doing a magnificent job. Certain things I will not put in letters but leave for our attorneys to convey to you by word of mouth. You understand the American Gestapo is all [next three words in quotes in the final version] eyes and ears ["to help them" CO] in their drive to establish thought control over the people. [illegible word CO] The [illegible word CO] undemocratic "Loyalty" oaths, political frameup trials through which they parade perjured stool pigeons and professional witnessses,[68] all ["of which" CO] these are links in their witch hunt to shackle the minds or ["hands" CO] bodies of the Great [*sic*] freedom loving American nation [all the last five words capitalized in the final version]. As surely as they will ["not succeed in this effort" CO] fail in this effort so to ["too" in the final version] we will succeed in winning our freedom with the help of these same forward looking people. It is impossible to keep the truth and fact of our case hidden from the public. Sooner or later the true picture will become known to all. Many people have already expressed to ["my" CO] our lawyers & my family their sentiments and desire to help us. Take heart and know that we are not alone and ["that as time goes on yes there" CO] that the monstrous sentence passed on us [NWI] which at first stunned the people [NWI] will ["but" CO] as time goes on ["become" CO, NWI] result [next word superimposed upon the word "an"] in [NWI] an avalanche of protest and this great movement coupled to our legal fight will set us free.

["Darling" CO] Sweetheart I am not trying to minimize all the difficulties you face ["nor do I in the least bit" CO] believe me I am fully aware of the nightmares the pain and hurt you feel my heart crys [*sic*] out for you and I want so to shield ["and" CO] protect you and be with you in this time of need & to hold you in my arms. Yet I feel so sure of you that I just know you'll always be there and ["in" CO] that is the assurance that we will some day find [illegible word CO] each other again and ["on a higher plain"

---

[68]This is obviously a reference to Elizabeth Bentley, the "blonde spy queen." Bentley had joined the Communist Party in the 1930s and left in 1945 to become an FBI informant. Her long, detailed "confession" and the information she provided to the FBI led to accusations against countless Americans for involvement in espionage. She testified at length before Grand Juries and Congressional Committees, but only testified at two trials, our parents' and the Brothman-Moskowitz case. For Bentley's trial testimony, see Record pp. 973–80, 986–96. Her first FBI statement is EB NY 264, December 5, 1945. For a full discussion of the Bentley issues in the case, see Walter and Miriam Schneir, "The Story the 'Red Spy Queen' Didn't Tell," *The Nation*, June 25, 1983, pp. 790–94. For a discussion beyond the case, see Schneir, *Invitation to an Inquest,* pp. 92–95, 309–22. For a refutation of Radosh and Milton's (*The Rosenberg File*, Ch. 14) attempt to rehabilitate Bentley's testimony, see *Sons*, pp. 420–22.

CO] go back ["to our" CO] as you say to our previous life and wonderful family.

Constantly you are in my thoughts at times I close my eyes and see you so clearly, your sweet pretty face, wide awake eyes, a [word repeated as he started a new page, only appears once in the final version, with the word "warm" inserted here] pleasant smile, you are ever beckoning to me and I very willingly pursue you but you seem elusive and the reality of our separation jolts me back to consciousness. I am positive it would take me many hours to tell you of my profoundest feeling of my deep love for you but I am sure I cannot convey ["my" CO] all this to you in writting [*sic*]. Ethel your [*sic*] just my girl and nothing on this earth can change that.

In a couple of days the Passover holiday of our peoples [*sic*] search for freedom will be here. This cultural heritage has added meaning to us who are locked away from each other and our loved ones by this modern Pharaoh. It has such meaning to us and our children. Yes we are missing a lot but this too shall pass and we will have cause for a greater celebration. Since we are unable to do much but talk about the children [changed to "our sons" in the final version] do no [*sic*, changed to "not" in the final version] worry as everything ["that is" CO] possible is being done for them. See if you could do a great deal of writting [*sic*] I want so to be closer to you and ["then, too," inserted in the final draft] your letters are so ["gratif" CO, probably was going to write "gratifying"] satisfying. Try to ["make some time" CO] drop a few words to ["your" CO] our two dears. Let me know when you receive this letter.

[In the final version the next paragraph was added] It is almost 10:00 P.M. now and I will be with you tonight as usual. Let me kiss you to sleep as I hold you in my arms.

Always your very own
Julius

[The next letter is available in two copies, one retained by our father as a carbon of the one actually sent.]

April 19, 1951

Sweetheart of My Life,

Good morning! It's 8:15 A.M. Friday. At 6:30 A.M. they play a record over the loud speaker system and with a defeaning [*sic*] roar it blares forth bugle taps "You got to get up in the morning" and believe me the tone is plenty clear. I usually remain in bed until 7:45 A.M. sometimes just out of sheer laziness and I recheck the image, that by now is firmly imprinted on my mind, of my prison cell.

The room is a rectangle, three paces wide by four paces long and seven feet high. A fine wire mesh acts as the ceiling. An electric bulb struggles in vain to send it's [*sic*] much needed light through the accumulated dust that has settled on the thick paint that covers the mesh and the net result is a dull dreary atmosphere and because of it my eyes are physically incapable of more than one hour of steady reading. Two sides are of solid steel plates, the back has some of the same wire mesh covering steel bars and the front has a series of parralell [*sic*] steel bars four inches apart perpendicularly intersecting at ten inch intervals flat steel reinforcing bars. What do you know I can actually put my hands through, clear past my elbows, and also take in all that transpires in the receiving room. A flat solid steel plate hangs between two triangular steel gusset plates that are welded to the right side wall. There are two of these beds hanging in cantilever fashion one above the other. On the top one I keep my books, commissary and personal belongings. On the bottom one there are blankets, mattress[,] pillow and bed linens, that make [NWI] up my hard uncomfortable bed. Nevertheless, I somehow manage to get my share of sleeping but not for long continuous stretches. Towards the left side of the rear wall a small sink hangs from which I get cold water to wash and drink. Alongside of this and in the corner is a flushometer partitioned off by steel plates four feet high rising vertically from the floor. In the front left hand corner is a steel table four feet long, two feet wide standing two and half feet off the ground and on both sides of it are steel benches all three items are fixed in place by being permanently welded into the ground. There is a slot opening above the top of the table with just enough room for a metal food tray to fit. {Excuse me time out for the New York Times} This is a very fitting place to continue as we now come to the most important part of my cell the means of exit and this is a bulky door of steel bars that makes a lot of noise as it slides and shuts with a loud positive clang. All the metal surfaces in the room is painted an egg shell enamel that has darkened with age and has been applied so unevenly with lumps and streaks looking like it were slopped on carelessly. This my love is your husbands [*sic*] home twenty-four hours a day. My solitary confinement is pleasantly interrupted, on occassion [*sic*], by a visit from the attorney, my family or a bath.

My quarters are situated along the right hand side of the spacious receiving room. To the right is a large bull pen for men in transit to and from the Detention House and besides it is a small chaplain's room. Over on the other side are a long series of desks behind which the receiving room officer and the lieutenant in charge of the watch work. Next is the Captain's office, the clothing room and the record office. Directly in front of my cell is a clearing 30 feet long by twenty feet wide and in front of that passes the main traffic lane of the institution and it's the busiest spot in the place. So you see, I am constantly under surveillance and caged in full view of all passing inmates.

Even though, they are not permitted to come over to me, each and every inmate almost to a man, as he passes the receiving room waves, shouts a greeting, smiles warmly. Their support and encouragement is further transmitted to me by the understanding portrayed on their faces and this gives me no end of satisfaction. In many ways both open and surreptitious, their true feelings are made known to me. They respect us for the people we are, admire our courage, wish us luck. [*sic*] and state "Keep Your Chin Up" as we and many other people are behind you in your fight to win your freedom. Darling, I am reporting this to you objectively and I am sure you have had similar experiences with the women inmates at 10th Street New York City. If this is the kind of reception we get from people who have had physical contact with us in jail and to whom we are known as a man and a woman of character, dignity and principal. Mind you, this is without them being aware of the facts in our case. How much more support will we get when the true facts of our complete innocence becomes evident to them and the nakedness of this political frameup lies bare for all people to plainly see. When the public becomes convinced and transmits their feelings into concrete action then my dear our ultimate victory is assured. The Zombie existance [*sic*] forced upon us has only physically imprisioned [*sic*] us, but our hearts and minds that can never except in death be shackled will continue vigorously to struggle, as we have in the past and we hope in the future in a better environment, for a people's peace, freedom and true justice in the American tradition of liberty and fair play.

To continue my day. {like Eleanor Roosevelt only slightly different} At 7:45 AM an ambulatory food cart that delivers the special diets to the hospital brings me my meals. Breakfast rice crispy's [*sic*] powdered milk and coffee. Note the lack of exercise is not conducive to a hearty appetite and therefore I eat sparingly, but of sufficient amount to keep body and soul alive and kicking. I make my bed, tidy up the room, smoke a couple of cigarettes and pace back and forth for about half an hour. Incidentally, your husband has taken to cigarettes with a vengence [*sic*]. Imagine more than a pack a day. Two of the fingers on my right hand are nicotine stained and I have developed an uncanny knack of accurately flipping the finished butts into the toilet bowl. Ethel, I'm afraid that your man is going to the dogs and is developing a vice. With no drinking and no women anything can happen. 10:00 A.M New York Times. 11:00 A.M. lunch fried filet of flounder, potatoes, tea and lemon merangue [*sic*] pie. The fish was good and was all I ate. You see I am trying to preserve my appetite for tonights [*sic*] passover [*sic*] seder a big feast with all the trimmings, that is being ordered by the Bureau of Prisons from a private caterer Segal's Restaurant. Gefilty [*sic*, correct spelling is "gefilte"] fish, knadels, chicken and the rest of the works.—A couple of hours are spent napping, an hour for reading and some more walking. It looks like I'm practicing picketing. Then at 4: P.M[.] I am served supper, a little foot exercise, a couple of cigarettes while I muse reclining on my bed and follow it with another hour of reading.

The warden has given one of the inmates, a trusty, who is due to go home soon, permission to enter my cell, talk to me and play cards and chess with me.[69] This takes place from 6:30 to 8:30 P.M and it serves as a recreation period for me. It is a relaxing pleasant interlude and I make the most of it. It looks like I'm fast becoming a gin rummy and chess expert. You must keep in mind that these are jailhouse accomplishments. For about one hour beginning at about 9:00 P.M[.] I walk and sing songs mostly folk music, workers [*sic*] songs, peoples [*sic*] songs, popular tunes also excerpts from operas and symphonies. Some of my favorite tunes are Peat Bog Soldiers,[70] Kevin Barry, United Nations, Tennessee Waltz, Irene, Down in the Valley, Beethovens' [*sic*] 9th Choral Symphony and as many of the childrens [*sic*] records as I can remember. I find this mentally stimulating and emotionally satisfying. In all frankness I feel good and strong while I sing as I am expressing something no one can stifle. The balance of the time I read until I get sleepy and then to bed.

Oh Yes! I am presently reading Nathan Ausubel's A Treasury of Jewish Folklore. It contains stories, traditions, legends, humor, wisdom and folk songs of the Jewish people and it is a very worthwhile book and quite entertaining. I must not forget my daily diversion which is very interesting. Game hunting. That is the time I massacre cockroaches.

Yesterday afternoon Manny was over to see me[.] He read me the letter you sent him as you instructed him. Darling your [*sic*] a wonderful girl and I love you, [*sic*] Such ability to put on paper your innermost thoughts and feelings, so that they clearly present to the reader your intention and meaning. I, too, am concerned about the children and their visit and I am sure that when it does occur we will each of us be able to handle the situation appropriately without any emotional harm to our two dears. My wife, I share your pain as I know how you suffer being cheated of your prerogative the motherly love and care you have for our children. Try to get

---

[69]This man was Jerome Eugene Tartakow, a jailhouse informer who had been talking to the FBI about our father's alleged confessions since December. For how Tartakow has come to be used as proof positive of my father's guilt, see Radosh and Milton's *The Rosenberg File*, Ch. 20. For our rebuttal, see *Sons*, Ch. 15, passim, but especially pages 392–93, 404–7, 408–19.

[70]"Peat Bog Soldiers" was a song of labor camp workers under the Nazis during World War II; "Kevin Barry" was about an Irish Republican revolutionary hanged by the British.

some comfort by converting as much of this intense desire as possible into a steadfast determination to maintain your equilibrium in these most crucial hours of your life. The only way I know how to help you is conduct myself as the man you know and married and I promise you to strive with every ounce of energy to live up to the standard you set by your fine example.

Ethel there is something that ties me very closely to Manny. He is truely [*sic*] a prince of a fellow, unassuming, intelligent, deep thinker, man of action and a sweet person. There is an emotional and social bond of brotherhood and comradeship that has grown up between us and I feel so proud to have him on my team. Our own Jewish expression is best suited to summarize my feelings for him. "Ich shep nachass ind quell far imh."[71] As for Alexander Bloch I have adopted him as my father. I love and respect him as he's a warm person and a good guy. When it comes to legal men they have no peers. So you see I think we've got the best and that's how it should be as in all modesty we're not so bad ourselves.

My sister, Lena, was over and sends her best holiday wishes and hopes that when they open the door tonight during the passover [*sic*] seder for the prophet Elijah you and I will enter the room and take our rightful seats besides [*sic*] our dear mother. When I sing the traditional songs of celebration of freedom from bondage of our people I will think of you my love and our own redemption from death and imprisionment [*sic*] to a better life.

Be what you are for I love you that way. Always your own. I send you all my heart.

Love—Julius

Mrs. Lena Cohen
140 Baruch Place
New York New York

April 19, 1951

Dearest Lee,

I have just finished putting fresh linen on my nice, comfortable bed, Groucho Marx is on the radio and I'm eating an apple for a change. Before that, I had spent two hours in my very own exclusive, sunny yard, had splashed around in my substantial stall shower (I wear a pretty lilac-colored plastic cap and wrap into a warm terry robe when I'm through bathing), and then had stowed away a sardine and onion sandwich, canned peaches and milk. I was so tired from all these exertions that I then proceeded to enjoy a two hour nap. Since I started this letter, I have managed to eat (besides the

---

[71]Loose translation: I experience great pride and pleasure from him.

apple) most of a large bar of bitter sweet Swiss style chocolate sent me by "The New York Board of Rabbis".

By now I hope it has grown clear to you that I'm not in the worst place in the world; on the contrary everyone has been most pleasant and cooperative, thus far, and I don't see any reason this encouraging state of affairs shouldn't continue. Even in the short time I've been here, they must already have realized that I'm an intelligent, well-balanced person who intends to put my energies to good use here. I'm already halfway through one excellent book and expect to really catch up on my reading now that there is no longer a trial to concern myself with.

Manny Bloch was here Saturday and his Dad turned up today. Bless them both, each is equally wonderful in his own way; how can we fail with two such precious, dignified human beings in our corner! I beg you to believe me, Lee, that although I don't kid myself that I can really be happy under the circumstances, and although the picture is actually not the rosy one it might seem from all the cheerful things I have said,—I still beg you to believe me that I am already recovering from the initial dismay of my removal, and have begun to dig in & come to grips with the situation.

So take heart, all my dear family; I wish there were some way to truly convey to you the tremendous confidence, the unwavering faith I have, that decency and justice must triumph. How is my dear mother bearing up under [NWI] all this inhumanity? (You don't mind sharing her with me, do you) Tell her to have a most enjoyable Passover for Julie and me. Incidentally, I also received a large box of matzohs, a tin of cocoanut [*sic*] macaroons and a jar of gefuelte [*sic*] fish! Please send my best to everybody, especially my [N2WI] dear Julie. As soon as you send me Ethel's [Julius's sister, Ethel] address, I will be glad to answer her swell letter. All my love—
    Ethel

P.S. Phone Mr. Bloch about the family's intended visit on Sunday—He may have to phone here & get permission since I did not know in time who was planning to come, I did not fill out the necessary forms—

Lena Cohen
140 Baruch Place
New York, New York

                                                    April 20, 1951
Dearest Lee,
    I am so delighted to receive word from you that even though I have already sent out my letter to you, I am anxious that all your questions

should be answered with as little delay on my part as possible. I realize that until you actually do see me, you are bound to be concerned about my welfare.

I know, dear, it must have hit you like a ton of bricks when you received my things, and yet I was unable to prepare you for it, because I was in too numb a state myself for some time after my arrival here to attempt to comfort anyone else. By now, however, I've got my bearings once more and can assure you that I'm doing O.K.

Yes, I had begun to knit a slip-over for Michael and was planning a duplicate for Robby, but since I am not permitted to have needles, I must forgo this pleasure. It is entirely up to you whether you think such a pair of sweaters ought to be completed. I know how very busy you and Ethel are, particularly at this time of year, so I shall be not the slightest offended if you tell me frankly you'd rather not undertake the job, at least for the present. If, however, you think you'd like a go at it, perhaps Ethel could knit Robby's and you, Michael's. I'd like the same color "Harding Blue" and style for both. The front should be an attractive but simple pattern, boyish and good-looking. But if you can't manage it, just let it ride and don't worry yourself about it.

Now about visits, don't feel badly if you don't work it out for this Sunday. I am pleased as punch that Ethel is due to take the kids out and by all means you do as you had planned and see Julie. Of course I understand the difficulties involved in getting here, particularly for Mama [Julius' mother, Sophie], and I have nothing but the utmost contempt and loathing for those who are responsible for my transfer from the city. My lawyers will do all they can to have me brought back; however, I am under no illusions about this business. The foul beasts who have so unjustly and cruelly condemned us have no scruples about crucifying us further, so I have made up my mind to remain where I am, if I must, and make the best of a bad bargain. It will be up to the family to work out some schedule for bringing Mama up here as often as it is humanly possible. Need I add that frequent visits will go a long way towards keeping me strong and steadfast?

Thanks again for your sweet letter. Your love is a precious thing to me, as is my dear Julie's. It is just like him to think of me first. My heart weeps for him and the children. Affectionately, Ethel.

Ethel to Julius

April 20, 1951[72]

Dearest Julie,

My most heartfelt greetings to you, darling, on this, the evening of the first Passover Seder. How bitter it is to be spending it away from all my loved ones! I sit behind the indifferent gray bars and listen to the ticking of the indifferent clock, and know the full agony of the heart's deep yearning.

But enough of this. I have lots to tell you about myself and my doings here, that I know you are anxious to hear. By dint of patient but persistant [*sic*] prodding I have now become an established and respected (although) female member of the Sing Sing community, and have set up jail-keeping in earnest! On my sink there reposes a giant size tube of Colgate's tooth paste inside an imposing red box, on top of which my long black comb lies [N2WI] stretched out ready, willing & able to obey my slightest command. A sturdy, red toothbrush stands stiffly in its holder in the middle of the basin and two cakes of soap, (the coarse white for laundering purposes and the gentle green for the gentlewoman) sit quietly at its side. The toilet plunger is gaily camouflaged by my bright salmon colored wash cloth while the white toilet paper directly below it presents a sharp and unashamed contrast. My book-case (prison style of necessity, and therefore fashioned of vertical round bars and horizontal flat metal strips across them), is a handy catch-all for stationary [*sic*], newspapers[,] dust cloths and Sapolio,[73] as well as a good supply of books. A paper carton for old letters and clippings stands beneath my writing table which displays among other things (for example, the children's snapshots, greeting cards & blue plastic glass) my latest and highly prized acquisition, a small desk calendar! And a smaller box for current mail, literary notes, commissary bills, money receipts and all the other paraphernalia that [N2WI] so eloquently bespeaks the rich and varied life that may be led within these walls if one works assiduously at it (and knocks one's brains out doing it)—this box completes the picture. Ah, yes, the bed—clean and comfortable, with the necessary supplies of sheets and blankets and face towels [NWI] hanging on the white metal head post; the bed, cold and chaste and uncaring of its lone and lonely occupant!

Seven A.M. finds me reluctantly crawling out from under its covers and after a leisurely breakfast of toast and coffee, eaten in my terry robe, I don my prison finery and sally forth onto my own private little Riviera, where I bang a ball around the four towering brick walls and run like mad as I

---

[72]The second page of this letter was dated April 22, the third page, April 23, so she wrote it over those four days.

[73]This word is clearly written but meaning is unknown. Perhaps it is a brand name.

dribble it along the concrete floor. I am now the proud possessor of 1) a pair of comfortable, low-heeled ugly black oxfords, 2) a pair of thick seamless, brown cotton stockings 3) a pair of long heavy drawers which by tacit consent are known as my "ski pants" and which have a way of sliding down [NWI] past my derriere and over my knees and coming perilously close to slipping off altogether as I dash about the yard, 4) two surprisingly pretty printed cotton dresses, not too ill-fitting, either 5) a really nice looking, soft, well-made, navy blue, wool cardigan 6) a pair of roomy brown leather bedroom slippers 7) a fairly good-looking double breasted mannish sport coat in a rough-textured, greyish black flannel material with which the tailor proudly presented me. After looking like a scarecrow [N3WI] for a week in an over-sized, heavy, itchy, clumsy one, with tremendous pockets that reached to my knees, (I'd put it on like a cape and say I was George Washington about to cross the Delaware), one of the four matrons who look after my needs and I successfully grappled with a tape measure and I am now a thoroughly presentable inmate. 8) A number of other lesser items of clothing which the guards have delicately referred to as "unmentionables" and so I shan't offend against their good taste by giving details. (It's enough that I described my "ski pants," the likes of which have [NWI] not been seen, I am certain, since Hector was a pup, and which I will happily discard just as soon as the weather permits.)

And now with the purchase of cold cream, deodorant, powder, lipstick and side combs to help me look neat at all times, an accomplished fact, I am "at home" and ready to receive all comers. Pop had openly complained at seeing my pale, wan map and unruly locks, and Manny's first remark [N4WI] by way of greeting on the occasion of his second visit was "Where'd you get the lipstick?" 'S a funny thing, though this ungracious ungrate-fulness on my part. It's like the kid who goes to camp for the first time in his life and writes [N2WI] his parents of all the wonders and glories of it and then concludes his letter by mournfully wailing, "I wanna go home!"

To speak now in more serious vein, your letter (with Michael's pathetic, touching one enclosed) finally arrived after landing first at the House of Detention. Sweetheart, how eloquently you expressed to me the quality of the love that is mine. How humble I am before you and yet how proud and happy that I should be the one capable of inspiring such noble thoughts in another human being. Where shall I find answering words to match the fine integrity of your own? Dearly do I love you, my sweet, and dearly do I desire you to understand what warm comfort your writing brought with it [NWI] and what warm response it evoked in my own heart. I look forward with eager anticipation to our continued correspondence and grow ever more certain of our eventual release. Let the jackals bray while they still may, for the winds of time are fashioning a sound and a song that must finally, and inexorably drown out their ugly voices!

Darling I had meant to discuss also the subject of the children, every thought of whom brings [NWI] such stabbing anguish and pain, as I cannot describe, but the mail is going out right away and I want this letter to go with it.

Until I write again, then, and it will be soon, I promise, I embrace you in all love and tenderness and reluctantly say good-bye.

As ever,
Ethel

From Julius Rosenberg   April 24, 1951

To Mr. Emanuel Bloch
270 Broadway, New York City

Dear Manny,

I've decided to preserve the letters Ethel and I are sending to each other. Since I don't have the necessary means to effectively do this, I am sending you copies as soon as they become available to me, for you to store in an album for us. I consider my wife's writting [*sic*] a personal treasure and I know no one else who will take better care of it than you. Send my deepest devotion to Pop. Keep on punching we're always with you[.]
Julius

P.S. I am enclosing 4 pages I sent Ethel on April 19, 1951.

[The next letter exists in the original handwriting and on a carbon.]

Julius to Ethel

                                                            April 24, 1951
Hello Honey Wife,

Tuesday night Bob Hope is on the loud speaker system and it's hard for me to concentrate but I'm a persistent fellow, so here goes. I've been hearing glowing reports about you. I read the two letters you sent Lena and Manny related all the details of his last visit. It all adds up to this. You are your old self again, full of spirit, spunk and in the groove.

Darling, I'm a little jealous. Everybody is being buoyed up by you. You're a fountain of encouragement to my family. The lawyers are confident you'll stand up and I'd like to be able to lean on your shoulders and get a little special comfort from you, too. You know the real stuff. Just a little warmth and love. How I miss it. But enough of that as jailbirds our lot is supposed to be a mechanical one devoid of many physiological needs. Present day penology is said to be rehabilitative and constructive. Sufficient for me to say I could write a book on it's [sic] present evils and another on recommendations I would make to humanize and modernize it.

April 25, 1951

I wasn't able to complete your letter but I'm glad I waited for I received one of your famous megillahs[74] dated the 20th, 22nd and 23rd.

Ethel, your [sic] a lovely ninny, sweet and wonderful. Of course I'm quvelling[75] from you {some Yiddish English}. The glowing description you give of Sing Sing is both encouraging and inviting and since I expect to be there anyway soon I am looking forward to experiencing for myself the wonders of Ossining Manor. However, since I know you well, the physical setup is the least important but the emotional security and mental stimulii [sic] are the paramount things. My witty one your letter is conclusive. As the popular prision [sic] expression goes "You've got it made." What you wrote was so refreshing that I took the liberty of sharing your wonderful gift with my chess opponent. He remarked "A terrific letter. She's in better shape than you."[76] Last Monday after the regular roof period they finally let me have a half hour of fresh air. Even though I was alone except for a guard who accompanied me and another one who watched us from a tower I enjoyed every minute of it very much. The cool breeze and sunshine were envigorating [sic]. I am trying to have this established as a regular exercise period as it is essential for continued good health and it serves as a break in the monotony and closeness of my cell.

I am presently engaged in reading "Science and Politics in the Ancient World" by Benjamin Farrington an English Professor of Classics and an eminent student of ancient history and sience [sic]. This masterful treatise deals with the obstacles to the growth of science and the integrated relationship between it and politics. The author quotes from the recognized authorities that lived during the period covered 600 BC through 600 A.D. {Greek civilization and early Christianity} He gives substantial

---

[74]The Megillah is the story of the Jewish holiday Purim. It is a long story and often an expression "the whole megillah" is a way of identifying a long drawn out story.

[75]A Yiddish word, meaning "deriving pleasure."

[76]This chess opponent, as mentioned above (see footnote 69) was FBI informer Jerome Eugene Tartakow, who no doubt shared the content of the letter and its impact on our father with the FBI at the earliest possible convenience.

corroborative documentary proof that the enemy of scientific growth was not popular superstition by the people, but supestitution [*sic*] imposed on the people by the nobles of the state and the heads of the church for the purpose of maintaining the status quo and their preferred class position. The thing that they set up as the greatest crime or heresy was the dissemination of scientific knowledge to the mass of the people. This is so true today and, even in our own case, when the government is trying to sell the people on the myth of atomic secrecy and is trying to prevent the dissemination of scientific [illegible—could be "articles"] to the people. This book is very informative and I recommend it.

It is easy for me to gather from your letters and my own personal experiences and feelings that we're both trying very hard and we'll do the best under the circumstances and we miss each other very much. There is no substitute for our being together. I feel like screaming from the roof tops. Hark! People a tragedy has been perpertrated [*sic*]. The gruesome reality is that our case is being used as a camouflage to establish a fear paralysis among the outspoken progressives and to stifle criticism or opposition to the mad drive to atomic war.[77] The public must be made aware of this political trick especially for us since our personal fight is thereby linked to this general movement for peace. We see it and somewhere, somehow, as soon as possible, everyone must be made aware of it.

I read in the newspapers that two of the new crop [I believe I misspelled it] of government informers the stool pigeons David and Ruth Greenglass have sold their story to a Sunday magazine {Colliers?} Note: a la Budenz & Bentley fashion.[78] History records that David Greenglass stands without parallel and ahead of even Judas Iscariot in infamy.

---

[77] In a speech by Emmanuel Bloch made in late 1953 after the execution, he described our father's first response to being sentenced to death. He told the group our father had said, "This death sentence is not surprising. It had to be. There had to be a Rosenberg Case. There had to be a Rosenberg Case because there had to be an intensification of the hysteria in America to make the Korean War acceptable to the American people. There had to be a hysteria and a fear sent through America in order to get increased war budgets. And there had to be a dagger thrust in the heart of the left to tell them that you are no longer gonna get five years for a Smith Act prosecution or one year for contempt of Court, but we're gonna kill ya!" (*Sons*, first ed., p. 352) The Smith Act was a law that outlawed organizations which taught and advocated the overthrow of the government by force. The Communist Party was convicted under the Smith Act in 1951.

[78] Louis Budenz was one of a number of ex-Communist witnesses who provided "expert" testimony against his former comrades in helping the government convict the Communist Party under the Smith Act. Re Elizabeth Bentley, see

Michael scribbled a couple of words in a letter Ethel [Julius' sister] sent me. He is a peach and so sweet. How I long for our boys. The kids are doing fine so don't be concerned. It is hard to leave but I must go to bed now. Gosh how sad without you. All my love. Your own—Julius

I am enclosing two newspaper clippings.

April 25, 1951

Dear Manny,

I have been swamped with so many things this week, I have only just awakened to the fact that I neglected to turn in my request for a Sunday visit. What gets me is that I had it all filled out and somehow it got lost in the rush. To-night I discovered it still among my papers.

I notice also on the back of the form that after it has been stamped approved, passes must be mailed to the persons who will be visiting. Since to-morrow is already Thursday, perhaps it might be wiser to notify Julie's folks to let it ride for this week. On second thought, though, maybe you could phone the warden direct and request that they be permitted to get these passes when they arrive at the prison, just this once so that they don't suffer the disappointment of still another week's delay. What do you think?

Also, it might be wise to check as to when Dr. Miller is planning to come. Since he did not see me last Sunday, I am assuming he intends to come this Sunday, & it would be foolish for everyone to arrive during the period of time he expects to spend with me.

I am making progress here at a fairly rapid pace, I should say. Already the outlines of my routine begin to take shape and I feel somewhat like a runner, breathing deeply with [NWI] each slow, deliberate, relaxed intake of air, yet tensing in anticipation of the challenge. Indeed, there is even an eagerness for the race a quiet calm acceptance, and a genuine humility in the realization that it should have been given to two ordinary people like the Rosenbergs to stand up and be counted. Whatever may come to pass, it will never be said that we ever permitted ourselves to be counted as anything but decent [emphasis in original] people!

To come down from my exalted heights, for a minute, I confess I am worried sick about the children. I implore you to concentrate most of your efforts on the solution of this pressing problem, as I simply won't rest until

---

footnote 68 above. Budenz and Bentley published their stories and made money giving speeches.

they are in the family's hands.[79] Please don't think me an ingrate, however. I am fully aware, believe me, that you are leaving no stone unturned in your concern for them and us.

The truth of the matter is, Manny dear (and the devil take the censor) that I love you! Can I be any plainer than that? Give my best as per usual to your Pop and my old sweetie pie!

Salud and No Pasaran![80]   Ethel—

April 25, 1951

Dear Manny,

I am sending for your safekeeping a gem of a letter from Ethel and one I sent her in return. Thanks for all[.]

Julius

This note probably covered the enclosure of the April 24–25 letter from our father to our mother and the letter he was answering, the April 20–23 one from our mother. The next letter obviously answers the letter of April 18.

Ethel to Julius

April 25, 1951

My dearest, sweetest, most precious idiot,

Whatever in the world am I going to do with you? And since when does this wife obey this husband without question? At this late date, sweetheart, it is folly on your part to [N2WI] attempt to make a decision that concerns me so vitally without permitting me that kind of voice in the matter which I have rightly come to expect, after nearly twelve richly creative years with you. Beg me as you may, then, I can brook no such arbitrary abrogation of

---

[79]This reference to the family means that they had abandoned thoughts of placement in a foster home.

[80]"No Pasaran," Spanish for "they shall not pass," was the slogan of the Spanish Republican defenders of Madrid during the Spanish Civil War of 1936–1939. Leftists all over the world made the defense of Republican Spain (with Communists as part of the coalition) a high priority when the right-wing Generals under Francisco Franco revolted and plunged that nation into Civil War. The German Nazis and Italian fascists aided Franco while the Soviets aided the Republic and the west hid behind "non-intervention" which actually helped the Franco forces, given the amount of material aid they received from the Axis powers. At the trial (Record, pp. 1176–78) Prosecutor Saypol made much of our parents' support for the Spanish Republic. Such activities were considered evidence of communist leanings during the McCarthy era.

my wifely rights in the matter as you intend I should, and on the contrary, my dear lord and master, for all that I do truly adore you, I must insist that you hear me out, or it giffs murder!

Let's be really honest about this thing and examine the dynamics involved. Isn't it the fact that when the authorities decreed the harsh punishment of incarceration at Sing Sing for me, they also dealt your manhood a severe blow? Every last ounce of prideful masculinity in you (and mind you I bear you nothing but the deepest [N3WI] kind of respect for the tender protectiveness and strength said masculinity actually constitutes) stands outraged at a fate that perversely persists in forcing me [emphasis in original] to bear the full brunt of its fury.

It is only thru [sic] the full recognition of this basic factor and all the ramifications thereof, that we can hope [NWI] to come to an understanding that is compatible with reality in this situation.

Mail going out, darling—will continue this discourse further—Love you, dearest—

Ethel

The following letter does not exist in its original form. It was copied by our mother and sent to Emanuel Bloch on April 28–29, 1951 and that is how we know of its existence.

Emanuel H. Bloch
7 W. 16th Street
New York New York

April 28, 1951
Letter I

Dear Manny,

The following is copy of the letter I promised you written by me to Julie while I was at the House of Detention—

Oct. 11, 1950 [underlining in original]

"Dearest Julie,

My heart is so full of love for you that I could burst with the need to express it. Such a tiny bit of time with you, such a suppression of our deepest feelings for each other, such hunger and thirst unassuaged! And yet, this last meeting freed me of so many burdens, sent my spirits soaring so high, I'm happier than I've been since I came here.

Yesterday your mother paid me a visit, bringing me some necessary items of clothing. Darling, with all her limitations, she is a truly fine, sweet woman and I love her more and more all the time. I do fear for her health, however, and it hurts my heart to know how she must be suffering. It was gratifying to me therefore that she seemed a lot more confident and less fearful about our situation; and I assured her that it would be to her house that I should go first upon my release. She laughed happily at my words and kissed her hand to me.

The rest of the day went most pleasantly in the company of my special buddies. It is a source of never ending delight to me to know the love of which I am ever increasingly capable of giving and receiving right here in the arid wasteland that is jail. Those relationships which I have sought and of which I have come to be an accepted and integral part, give me the keenest kind of pleasure & satisfaction. It would appear strange, at first glance, that in this confining existence where irritation and annoyance are our daily portion and are exaggerated out of all proportion to a more normal way of life,—where the human being wallows in depths of despair and torment that have no bottom,—it would seem strange, I say, that the flowers of friendship, understanding and love bloom so brightly and drench the fetid air of hate & blind resentment with such life-giving, fresh fragrance. And yet, it's not so strange. The very pain and anguish that gives rise to the most brutal qualities, needs must arouse in those of us with intelligence & conscience & good-will, an even fiercer kind of striving for their expression than would be impingent upon us to express outside these walls. So it is that each friend jealously guards the well being of her sister, nor will she relinquish the sacred trust, that trust which is in truth her very own security. To which the "jitterbug jailbirds" who have so kindly undertaken to educate your ignorant wife would respond in the best jitterbug tradition, "Dig her!"

Honey, another positive factor that I can lean upon is my growing trust in and affection for the two swell guys who are our lawyers. They are warm, gracious, understanding individuals to whom I am finding myself gradually better able to relate. On a phone call I had requested Lee to make for me, Manny Bloch came down to see me yesterday & I had a good half hour in which to straighten out with him a number of items that had been bumbling about in my head since Monday. By the time he left I was a lot more serene."

Manny, I'll have to stop here and go on, on another page. There are a few things, besides, that I want to take up with you anyway.

As ever, Ethel—

Emanuel H. Bloch
7 W. 16th Street
New York New York

April 28, 1951
Letter II

P.S. Please be sure to read the letter I sent you last week to Julie—

Dear Manny,

Following is a continuation of the letter, of which I am sending you a copy.

Oct. 12, 1950

This has been a peculiar day indeed. First rain, then a gradual clearing with a promise of a lovely, sunny day, then a wind and rain storm almost like a hurricane, and now the downpour has stopped and the sun is beginning to tease us again. In the meantime, I am impatiently awaiting the last letter you wrote which you mentioned to me on Monday.

Oh yes, I received a letter from Miss Bodek of the Children's Day & Night Shelter informing me, "that there is a mild epidemic of an infectious disorder" and all admissions of new children have had to be halted until further notice. Dearest how I long to see my sweeties and how well I know your own cheated father's feelings. How you glow when I speak of them to you, my poor dear. Incidentally, I wrote Mike a letter addressing it to the shelter so that it would greet him upon his expected arrival there. I'll have to drop a line to Miss Bodek, asking her to see to it that it is forwarded to him at once.

Ah, words, words, when I want to be held in the old familiar thrilling embrace! Sweetheart, I love you and miss you terribly. (The girls promptly nicknamed me their "love-sick calf" after I had confessed to "spring fever"!) Your silly but always loving wife—
xxxxxxxxxxxxxxxxxxxxxxxxxxxxxxx

Incidentally, this letter is the one that Julie brought down to Foley Square with the intention of having both your Dad and you read it. You never got around to it (we were too busy that day) but he managed to do so before you arrived for the consultation and was very much impressed. As a matter of fact, his belief in my writing ability (and his subsequent insistence that I write "my story") stems from his admiration of this letter, so use it for whatever it is worth to you.[81]

I forgot to mention that I wrote my sister-in-law Lena two letters which Julie feels ought to be in your hands, too. And Mrs. Phillips turned over the letters I wrote her to Dr. Miller, one of which she referred to as being particularly moving. I'll make a note reminding me to request him to mail these to you, if and when I see him tomorrow, so you'll know what they are when you receive them.

I should have told you what was bothering me during your visit, especially in view of the fact that you were planning to go back to the Warden before leaving the premises [N4WI] but somehow I couldn't.—I should like to be clear in my own mind (subject of course to whatever ruling there may be concerning the matter) as to whether or not I am under any obligation to receive chaplains other than [NWI] those of my own [N9WI] (or for that matter even of my own faith) faith. At first I was certain it was understood that this was a purely personal matter that had nothing to do with any rule, but lately (for reasons I will explain to you another time) I have been getting the impression [N4WI] (whether rightly or wrongly) that it's part of their job [N4WI] (I mean the chaplains) to kind of check on how the inmates are getting along. Mind you, you are to [illegible word CO, NWI] speak to the Warden [NWI] only in very general terms. So far as you know, your client is lodging no [NWI] specific complaint. I just want to know if it is [word "expected" CO, NWI] required of me to see any such person (even though no religious matters are discussed) for any reason (religious or otherwise), so that I will then be able to handle a certain matter that has arisen, to my own satisfaction. I believe I know how to handle same; what concerns me is whether or not I have the right to so handle it. ["our" CO] When, after you have seen the warden (next Saturday before you see me, please) I can tell you what goes & you can help me work it out. Don't worry about it meanwhile—It's not that world-shaking!

Love, Ethel

---

[81]This appears to be the first explicit reference in the letters that survive to the possibility of using the letters. With no campaign, no publicity, it is doubtful if this idea included actually publishing the letters. The first publications appear to have been in the *National Guardian* in October of 1951. Perhaps the reference was to Emanuel Bloch using the letters when making personal appeals for assistance from individuals.

Ethel to Julius

April 29, 1951

Dearest sweetheart,

To continue with the dissertation I was forced to cut short Friday, I admit to having unconscious personal feelings about the matter of your trying to be transferred here that need to be as thoroughly examined as your own. The difference lies however, in the fact that my feelings do not in effect militate against the political aspects involved in a decision of this kind, whereas yours do!

To elaborate a bit on this theme, I grant you that Sing Sing presents a challenge in personal terms of which I am not exactly unaware, and one for which I am coming more and more to understand, all my previous emotional experiences have been conditioning me. I further grant you that it is [NWI] therefore, a challenge I am loath to share. But the task which the sum total of an intricate set of factors has inexorably fashioned and delivered into my special keeping for its proper resolution, demands also (and indeed for that very resolution) full understanding on your part as to what your own role constitutes, never mind the personal feelings.

In other words, does "moving heaven and earth to be with me" (bless you, dearest, I love you for it) really help me as much as refusing to permit yourself to fall into the very trap the authorities have so craftily laid for you and ["sticking to" CO, N2WI] standing by your guns at West Street while I ["stick to" CO, N2WI] stand by mine at Sing Sing! For one thing, you have the incalculably valuable opportunity of associating with your fellows, (and they are people who regard you with the utmost kind of liking and respect); for another, you are easily accessible to Manny and your folks and you can therefore actually participate in the development of the campaign for our release.

Of course [N2WI] even though I don't deny that I could certainly do with some of the emotional gratification my being able to see you would promote, it won't constitute a major disaster if you remain in the city. Darling, I know how much like rejection this must sound to you and what hurt I may be therefore be inflicting upon you. I know, too, however, how deep your understanding of our situation goes and in what a true light that understanding must [word "picture" CO, N2WI] help to frame my [N2WI] seemingly harsh words. In all humility I tell you, it is your love [N2WI] for me and mine for you (even though the expression of it must of necessity, now be dammed up) that is enabling me to strive every more ["bravely" CO, NWI] consciously to ["rise to" CO, NWI] reach that [illegible word CO] height for which I seem somehow to have been singled out. In view of all that has transpired, I can come to but that one conclusion.

No, stay where you are, my dear love, if so you can do, and be my voice for me, since mine ["is" CO] dissipates [NWI] itself upon the Ossining air ["and" CO, NWI] even while I raise it. So you to your job and I to mine and to-gether we will make the victory!

In the spirit of the unquenchable Spanish people, beloved, and with my [NWI] warmest most ardent kisses, I say,
"Salud and No Pasaran"
As ever, Ethel

Julius Rosenberg [pencil]

                                                                May 2nd 1951

Mr. Emanuel H. Bloch
270 Broadway, New York City

Dear Manny,

I am enclosing two letters from Ethel and a reply from me for your safekeeping. I would like to ask you to get me a couple of beautiful and sincere Mothers Day Cards. One for my mother and the other for Ethel. One more request May 14th is Roberts [*sic*] birthday[.] get [*sic*] a card for him and one for Michael ["and" CO]. Ethel and I will sign all the cards including the one to my mother. Try to get me something special for my wife as she is so appreciative. Thanks for all the trouble.

Spring is here and a young mans [*sic*] fancy turns to love. As for me I want to go home. All our wishes are with you keep healthy and strong so that you may continue doing all you can for us.

Always confident,
Julius

P.S.
Regards to all our friends and especially to Pop.

[The following letter exists both in the original and in a carbon.]

Julius to Ethel

                                                                May 2nd, 1951
Dearest Ethel,

There are three main springs of my life at West St. First and foremost are your letters, second consultations with Manny and third visits from my family. Your letters have become part of my being. Habit forming to the extent that they are emotionally envigorating [*sic*], mentally stimulating and above all reinforcing my strength. The two you sent me dated the 25th and 29th were such excellent injection.

Your choice of language is such that it sounds like music. It is poetry in it's [*sic*] form and presentation. The content shows thoroughness of analysis, depth of understanding and it's [*sic*] logic is devastating. It may seem that after all I am a bit prejudiced but in all earnestness I feel that this is a truely [*sic*] objective observation because you are a writer of high calibre. This is enhanced because your personality and character has been so completely transferred to the written word. You are really wonderful sweetheart and such a great talent should be exploited. Therefore, I'd like to ask you to write me daily that I may continue to enjoy this pleasure and obtain profound nourishments. When in spite of difficulties and great hardships you are able to improve yourself and reach new heights of human stature then ones [*sic*] latent potentialities are released and come to the fore and know no limits and as an individual you are able to make your maximum personal creative contribution and to me this is integrated living the epitomy [*sic*] of life itself.

These qualities won my heart in the winter of 1936 and was [*sic*] the basis of my love for you that since then has continually grown and matured to it's [*sic*] all encompassing summit. I am a better person, a happy man to be your husband and so much at one with you. There is no doubt that together we make an impregnable team because each of us knows and does his own job. You put it correctly when you said collectively we'll make the victory.

Our swell counselor was over to see me yesterday and his vivid report on your progress and well being was inspirational to say the least. He says that your conduct and demeanor is remarkable. I expect it as I am fully aware of the jewel I possess as my mate. Since his visit to you and your receipt of my last letter, which arrived after your dissertation was mailed to me, you are now informed of the additional facts that sheds light on the justice of my position.[82] Besides which the solution of this matter is not fully in our hands, much as we might strive to effect it's [*sic*] ultimate outcome, but for the present moment we are at the mercy of the authorities who may continue or even intensify the fury and vengence [*sic*] of their harsh pressures on us. We live under no illusions and we are fully cognizant of all that is going on. Knowing how to meet this situation and being able to face it success is assured.

---

[82]This probably refers to his virtual solitary confinement in the Men's House of Detention.

My family is impatiently awaiting [NWI] the approval of the authorities for permission to see you and again we have to fight in order to effectuate such a simple, decent and humane right. You concluded your letter with the Spanish cry "Salud and No Pasaran"[.] I would like to add [N2WI] to it the heritage of the Maccabeans & the great history of the American people's fight for freedom and justice. With these as our standards and in their spirit we must win our complete freedom.

All my love—Your own—
Julius

Ethel to Julius

May 4, 1951

My dearest Sweetheart,
Probably Manny has already told you that I received your letter of the 19th the same day as the one written by you on the 24th. Under the circumstances, of course, I had no way of knowing just what kind of an inexcusably harsh, severe, physically and mentally debilitating regimen had been foisted upon you; you may well imagine, then, how appalled I was to read of the shocking circumstances of your present mode of life.
Oh, my poor darling, how I ached for you and how ashamed I felt to have [NWI] had to scold you for wanting to come here! Small wonder, I thought scornfully, that I was able to set such an example and send such encouraging letters to the folks.
Upon closer examination of your situation however, and a more honest appraisal thereof, (laying aside, of course, my needlessly guilty feelings about the bright spots of my [NWI] own existence) you actually have the edge over me in that you are still associating [NWI] (even if to a much lessened degree) with the other inmates, and visiting presents no difficulties. Still, I am filled with indignation that you have had to convince [NWI] them about such [NWI] an elementary and easily supplied need like outdoor exercise! For heaven's sake, bunny, it is imperative for you to maintain a certain minimum standard of health and somehow I get the impression that you are inclined to take the matter of your physical comforts a little too lightly. I don't "appreciate"* such a state of affairs one tiny bit and strongly suggest you begin to "perform"* accordingly, until you succeed in instituting some vitally important & long-overdue changes. (*Jitterbug language by the courtesy of the late lamented but still fondly remembered House of Detention)!
And now, my love, may I properly congratulate you on your rapidly growing literary ability. The description of your cell is a masterpiece of

graphic detail to say nothing of the clear-cut quality of your refreshingly sharp, perceptive comments on the books you are reading, the enormity of the political frame-up that has been perpetrated against us & the monstrous immorality of the Greenglass' [*sic*]. Incidentally I am already reading and enjoying "A Treasury of Jewish Humor" and look forward to tackling "Main Currents in American Thought" by Parrington, in the very near future. Every day now I regale the matron with my own inimitable renderings[83] of the "Fireside Folk Songs" and you may be sure that as I sing, you are never absent from my heart. Dearest tell me, find me a way, to express love with [N2WI] something more than these poor, pale words! Hold me close to you, always closer when you go to sleep; I miss you so terribly!— Your own loving
[no signature]

Ethel to Julius

May 5, 1951

Dearest darling,

It wasn't until the mail was collected (daily except Saturday at 8:00 A.M.) and my letter of the 4th on its way to you that I realized I had used the word "renderings" instead of "renditions" to describe my warbling at "Sing Song" (Haw, a joke!) I at once seized upon this item as another excuse to send my matron into hysterics by pointing out to her that you might think I was busily engaged [N5WI] in the delicate art of rendering chicken fat on the premises! In view of the fact, however, that I had already caused her to go home the day before in a state of near collapse induced by my highly expressive readings from "Treasury of Jewish Humor," all she would do was to giggle convulsively and then give me a dirty look, which very effectively squelched me for all of one minute!

Believe me, this dear lady and I are a proper pair of lunatics; indeed, we are both thoroughly convinced that we simply didn't meet each other soon enough! The hilarious shrieks that issue forth from the women's wing (the No-Man's Land in which I am spending my summer vacation, a zuch in weh)[84] would certainly incline any listener to believe he had landed at Luna Park, not the death house! Ooh, I just got a brilliant idea; to-morrow when she arrives at 6:30 A.M. I am going to panic her (by way of greeting) with a gay little ditty entitled, "Who's Afraid of the Big Electric Chair, They Can

---

[83] See the next letter for a comment on this word choice.

[84] A basically untranslatable Yiddish idiom of which the closest approximation is "woe is me" though the connotation is somewhat humorous and self-mocking.

Shove It Up Their "Spine" For all I Care" (Variation: "They Can Dump It In the Hudson For All I Care")!

Be sure of it, begorra, it is stir-crazy she'll be goin', long before me; and don't think, m' pretty one, it isn't worried she is abaht it; already she's admittin' to hearin' bells when they don't ring! (You ought to hear the magnificent Irish brogue I've developed; it tickles the Irish in <u>her</u> [underlining in original] no end!)

But she isn't the only zany in these parts. There's still another [NWI] one who rounds out this delightfully cozy little family circle, a willing vessel for my increasingly perverted sense of humor, whom I am fast converting from a "square" into a "hep-cat," House of Detention style. You just never appreciated just what [NWI] kind of a little ray of sunshine you possessed! And why not? To be a Condemned-nik, I'm absolutely refusing—If you'll be so kindly, I'll already better [*sic*] taking "paskudnik"! (My God, that book's got me coming and going!)

<u>May 6, 1951</u> [underlining in original]

Pussy-cat, I'm lonesome. Last night I went to sleep with streaming eyes and full heart. The reason? Manny's usual Saturday visit which evoked a tremendous intellectual and emotional response from me and [NWI] which for that very reason, hurts all the worse when it's over and he's departed for that bright world I shan't be knowing for many months & possibly many years to come.[85] Yet never fear, beloved—I stand steadfast though my eyes weep and my heart breaks. Your always loving wife—

May 5, 1951

Master Michael Rosenberg
c/o Hebrew Childrens Home
1682 Monroe Ave. Bronx N.Y.

Dearest Michael and Robert,

Your aunt Ethel sent me a letter and I was very pleased to read what you wrote Michael. She also told me of the one you sent to Mommy. They were both very good letters and I am sure from what you said that you had a wonderful time with the Goldbergs. She related to me how you and Robert were sitting on the wishing stone at the childrens [*sic*] Zoo at Bronx Park and your cousin Seymour asked you what was your wish. Then you replied,

---

[85]In an interview, the psychiatrist reported that she expected "a long incarceration." See *Sons*, p. 148.

"What do you think? I want to be with my mother and father." You are certainly very sweet. I am positive that as long as you keep hoping surely we your parents who love you our boys with all our hearts will be together with you again in our own house just as we were in the past.

Since you are doing so well in writting [*sic*], why don't you write to me more often. Tell me what you are studying at school and about your new reader. The weather being nice gives you an opportunity to be outdoors more often. Let me hear about the games you play, the friends you have and what your brother does. I think if you write to me not only will I get the pleasure of hearing from you but I will be able to see your improvement and you will also get some good practice in penmanship. You haven't as yet told me if you received my last letter. Please tell Mr. Witover to keep all the letters that your sweet Mommy and I have sent you. Better still ask him to send them to Mr. Emanuel Bloch our attorney after you have read them.

Before I went to bed last night I stayed awake thinking about my two sweet fellows. I remember the swell times we had together especially on Saturdays and Sundays. We used to walk to the bus and from there take a subway ride to a City Park. We played some baseball and after a while a nice refreshing lunch. Then a rowboat on the lake, some peanuts and popcorn. Sometimes we took a trolley car or else a Third Ave Elevated train. It was always fun, moving around all the time, seeing things and enjoying ourselves. Of course, then home and some play with the Erector set, blocks, trains and trucks or card games. I always liked our reading books and listening to records. My darlings you boys know how to live and be happy and it is very necessary that you continue to play, have fun and grow up as healthy children because in time we will all be together and we'll be living again where we left off. Do not worry my precious ones as everything will turn out just right. With many hugs, kisses and all my love. I say goodbye for now.

Your Daddy—Julius

Ethel to Julius

                                                          May 7, 1951
Hello, honey dear,

Thank you so much for your most beautiful letter of May 2nd which arrived on Saturday. It came as a fitting climax to a day already marked by excitement in the form of Mssrs. Bloch & Miller, an amazing pair of guys if ever I saw any, and wonderfully satisfying company to boot.[86]

Darling, your letter brought you right into a cell grown suddenly quiet as a tomb, much as though you, too, were visiting me, moving me profoundly and stirring me to the depths. Look, tootsie-roll, what are you trying to do; ursurp [*sic*] my hitherto undisputed position as the literary genius in the family? Apparently, it isn't enough for you that you are an atomic Svengali, a shnookle and an octopus, now you have also got to be a plain, ordinary no-goodnick and steal your wife's (highly doubtful) superiority as a writer! Sweetheart, more power to you. The unutterably sweet expressions of love and devotion contained in this last epistle filled me with such a deep and abiding happiness and brought you so close, I could almost (but not quite) reach out and touch you.

Indeed, after a listless game of handball (played solo, of course), a shower, dinner and an evening of enchanting music, during which you made passionate love to me, I could no longer withstand the disquieting sense of dismay that had been steadily gnawing at my vitals, and finally succumbed to homesick tears. It is a luxury I rarely permit myself, however, and you will be happy, I know, to hear that I am your own good girl once more!

Oh, darling, how greedy I am for life and living. All at once I want to see and hear all there is to see and hear, know and be all there is to know and be! I've never been quite so conscious of all the glowing beauty that bears within me, felt quite such an aching desire to share it, nor been so aware of my own powers as an individual. My voice wells up from way down deep inside me somewhere and my heart bursts with the burden of my song! And of what do I sing? Of noble Man & Woman, of noble Freedom! Were there ever any more precious words? For of what value be the love and joy of Man and Woman, without the right also of its truest and most untrammelled expression? Bunny, I'm beginning to sound like a real old gray-beard, am I not.

Oh, mail call—

Goodbye, My dearest love—

Ethel—

---

[86]It is unclear if this is the first visit Dr. Miller made to Sing Sing. He had not been able to see her between the time of her arrest and her transfer to Sing Sing. See *Sons*, p. 71.

Julius to Ethel

May 8, 1951

My Dearest Wife,

Upon reading your message of May 4th I want you to calm your fears as to my physical surroundings and more important I am surprised to hear you admonished yourself because you had wrongly felt your situation was worse than mine. Truthfully, you are suffering a harder incarceration than I. Darling, neither of us is exactly living in comfort or enjoying a life of milk and honey. You are to be congratulated for your stamina and excellent adjustment to such a horrible and barbaric confinement. Your conduct is admirable and your bearing is praiseworthy. I am both proud and happy that you are doing so well. Keep up the good work honey.

There has been a slight improvement in my routine in so far as I am presently allowed one half hour on the roof almost every day of the week. Since I am not permitted to have a belt or shoe laces[87] my [NWI] handball performance is not exactly professional. Falling pants or a shoe slipping off my foot hinders my speed and gives me a handy alibi for the fearful trouncings administered to me.[88] However, I try very hard and I find my game is improving. As the weather gets warmer my quarters are getting more stifling daily and I hope something can be done to alleviate this uncomfortable situation. Again, I repeat I do not wish to worry you with my complaints but what are you my wife for anyway if not to listen to my cranky moanings. After all I can't exercise any other priviledge [*sic*] as your husband. Of course, you can be certain that I am making the best of these hardships.

May 9th 1951

It wasn't necessary for me to be coaxed but an invitation such as you presented I could not pass up so I therefore took me to bed early and tried to do right by my misses [*sic*].[89] It's no use no satisfaction and up most of the night. This entire morning was spent snoozing and I was pleasantly surprised to receive two more letters from you dated the 5th and 7th. They were so refreshing. My heart was glad. My spirit was bright and it felt good to be awake. Since my lunch was due any moment I decided to read the morning Times before I continue this letter.

---

[87] A rule designed to reduce the danger of suicide.

[88] From the FBI documents, it is clear that his handball partner was the FBI informer, Jerome Eugene Tartakow.

[89] Obviously a reference to the last lines of my mother's May 4 letter.

Ethel I was terribly shocked to read that Willie McGee was executed.[90]
You know how I am affected by these things. First my stomach felt sick
and even though we had the lunch I like best sunnyside eggs I found it
difficult to swallow and I had no appetite for the cream puff. My heart is sad
my eyes are filled with tears. [The words "I must yell!" CO] Shame,
America!! Shame on those who perpretrated [*sic*] this heinous act!! Greater
Shame on those who did not lift their voices and hands to stop the the [*sic*]
Mississippi executioner. It seems to me that the Federal Courts have
adopted the abominable medieval practice of the Southern Bourbons, legal
lynching of Negros [*sic*] and is now attempting, as in our case, to apply this
to political prisioners [*sic*]. Mark my words, dearest, the harsh sentence
passed on us is part of the atomic hysteria designed to brutalize the minds of
the people in order to make it easier for them to accept as a commonplace
thing long prison [*sic*] terms and even death sentences for political
prisioners [*sic*]. It serves the added nefarious purpose of establishing a fear
paralysis among progressive Americans. Before it is too late our countrymen must be awakened to the hideous plans of the war makers who are
utilizing these fascistic acts to pave the way for ["the" CO] spilling rivers of
human blood in a modern, efficient and scientific way. Now! Today! People
must stand firm on these issues as life itself depends on it. The most
important thing is that the camouflage has to be ripped away, the loud
braying of the jackals of hate has to be answered with reason and fact and
only positive organization of free people and their ensuing direct action can
successfully save the peace and assure freedom in our country. That is why I
am positive growing numbers of people will come to understand our fight
and join with us to win so just a cause. McGee's death spurs me on with
added determination. I am impatiently awaiting news of the beginning of a
great campaign to save us.[91] Right is on our side and we must be
successful.

Mrs. Epstein was over to see me yesterday and we had a lengthy discussion on the welfare of our two dears. By the time the jury pronounced us
guilty, Michael had already had a great deal of the comments on our trial
from the radio, television and the Greenglasses all great purveyors of the
"truth." When he saw the social worker he asked what was the sentence and
in all truthfulness she answered she did not know. Whereupon, he replied

---

[90]Willie McGee, a black World War II veteran who had slept with a white woman,
was charged, convicted, and executed for "rape." See Cedric Belfrage, *The
American Inquisition* (NY: Bobbs-Merrill, 1973), pp. 141f.
[91]At this point there was no organized defense committee and no publication
anywhere on the political spectrum had questioned the justice of the conviction.
There had been a few editorials questioning the death penalty in mid-April but
there had been no follow-up.

my Mommy and Daddy could not get the death penalty as they didn't kill anybody and many people would have to be killed for them to deserve that. He was aware that the Greenglasses were witnesses against us and he wanted to know who lied and more about the case. He asked many questions and Mrs. Epstein told him there is good and bad in all people even in herself and Mr. Witover. After exhausting his questions he lay his head on her lap, began whimpering and sucking his thumb. The boy told her he would not be able to get up. She comforted and soothed him and after fifteen minutes he was himself again. He knows we are in prision [sic] kept behind bars and we are not allowed to leave. Do you know that he said it's like the North Koreans and Americans. They both say they are right and maybe both are. Can you beat such a mature statement from our eight year old. He has progressed to the point when at times he tells her to come next week as he is too busy to interrupt his playing by talking to her. There is definite improvement emotionally and in his eating habits. He looks well and is healthy. As for Robert she can also report advances. He has learned to play with other children and is developing normally. The baby still trys [sic] to latch on to a grownup for support. With the proper guidance and supervision both boys will continue to grow mentally and physically well. They need us so and to say the least we need them too. She will try to see you to give you a personal briefing on your sweet boys.

Relax sweetheart, you still reign supreme as the pen laureate of our family. My meager pencil can't even hold a scribble to your mighty script. You are able to put in words exactly what I feel and in a manner that is delightful to read, intellectually satisfying and mentally stimulating. To me it has an additional stimulus but I'll have to wait till I see you in order to convey it to you.

This Sunday being Mother's Day is a particular difficult occassion [sic] for you the mother of our children. I can only imagine the deep pain and suffering you undergo being separated from your darlings and not being able to exercise your motherly prerogatives. It is that tremendous power of motherhood and deep understanding that you so ably [sic] have utilized to buttress yourself and stand up a great woman. Your children will always be proud of their mother. As for me I send you my warmest greetings and love. The two things I posses [sic], my mind and body someway, somehow through space and time I send to you. Such capabilities of pain and tears signifies deep understanding creative ability and great possibilities and promise for a happy future.

Your very own
—Julius—
Enclosing some newspaper clippings

Julius Rosenberg   May 9th 1951
Mr. Emanuel H. Bloch
270 Broadway, New York City

Dear Manny,
    I am enclosing three letters from Ethel and my answer to her for your safekeeping. With deep interest I am following your activities in the courts on our behalf. The scant news tells a great story to me.[92] You are doing fine keep it up. I can't wait to see you and talk to you. Always proud to have you as my attorney advisor and friend. Send my best regards to Pop.
—Julius—

Julius Rosenberg   May 9, 1951

Master Robert Harry Rosenberg
c/o Hebrew Childrens Shelter
1682 Monroe Ave Bronx, N.Y.

Hello Robbie,
    How is daddy's big fellow. Imagine four years old on May 14th. Happy Birthday sweetheart. I send you lots of love, kisses and hugs. I am also going to make some drawings you like.
    Darling I hope you like these. All my love. Your own Daddy
Julius

Mrs. Ethel Goldberg
5347–65th Place
Maspeth Long Island
                                                      May 10, 1951

    Wherever did you find such a heavenly beautiful card? When I opened it and saw the exquisitely dainty handkerchief peeping out from among the softly colored flowers, I was enchanted. The words on the other side were also well-chosen, so much so that I could not contain myself and permitted myself the luxury of a few tears; just a very few, I hasten to add. Nevertheless, I was too moved to control myself, you understand!

---

[92]In addition to preparing the appeal, attorney Bloch was involved in an effort to have our mother brought back to New York City. See *Sons*, pp. 40–1, 58–59.

And now may I take this opportunity to thank you lovingly not only for this sweet expression (it was your's [*sic*] too, you know, as well as Julie's) but for all those many others you managed to continue to keep flowing to me throughout those nine heart-rending months leading up to and including the trial. Whether I told you or not, it gave me a wonderful feeling to know that just when I needed something to pick me up, those precious few lines would arrive from you, telling me about the children and strengthening my faith in myself and in my husband. And now, when I face an ordeal even more painful than the first, I feel an ever deepening bond with you, of which the warm, encouraging letters I have been receiving are an integral part. In a word, "keep 'em coming"! They help to fill the emptiness and nourish the need for that emotional gratification which normal human associations promote and of which I am now so sorely deprived.

Right now, I am re-reading the account of your trip with the children to the Bronx Zoo. I don't suppose I could ever really tell you how safe and secure I feel to know without question that you and yours will never turn a deaf ear on my two precious ones and their overwhelming need to be loved [N3WI] and cared for in our absence. The wound of my separation from them is brutal, as you may well imagine, but at least I rest easy in the knowledge that, come what may, their darling Daddy's family will never desert them!

As for myself, I have made myself right to home here in "Ossining Manor" (as your whacky brother and my honey bunny chooses to label it), and am making excellent use of my time. Already I have routinized myself to such a degree that I manage to accomplish a certain amount of reading, writing, singing and handball practise [*sic*] daily. After knocking myself out in the yard, I head for the shower and then put away a fairly decent meal. Before I go to bed I generally have a light snack (I buy crackers, cheese, fruit, canned goods, mayonnaise, mustard, & salami from Commissary) and plenty of fresh milk.

Please read this letter to the others. And since Julie will [NWI] probably not receive his from me in time to greet him on his birthday, please give him wifely wishes for his continued well being, for me. My very best regards, too, to Oscar and your own brood. They must make you feel proud! And why not!
Love, Ethel—

Emanuel H. Bloch
7 W. 16th Street
New York New York

May 16, 1951
Letter #1

Dear Manny,

When you left on Saturday, I was beside myself with all that time had not permitted me to say. Actually, I had only just about warmed to my subject and although further discussion would simply have rounded out my original thesis and might thereby easily have run the risk of being considered relatively unimportant, there were some very interesting ramifications involved that might certainly have better been propounded to you than left unsaid judging from my disturbance. So I'll say them now, and forever after hold my peace. (Ho, ho, that'll sure be the day!)

At any rate, there are a few things with which you should be acquainted in order to properly participate in the conversation in which you expect to engage prior to seeing me again. You see, the problem child [NWI] we discussed may very well raise the issue of hue and cry havoc![93] Now in view of what you already know about said problem child, I think you should be able to put two and two together and realize that it would be just such a problem child that would exploit the very valid complaints of others of similar pigmentation to jockey for personal position and sympathy, meanwhile looking down upon them with contempt, and licking more suitable persons' posteriors (suitable [NWI] because their's [*sic*] is a more conventional, more acceptable hue) [N3WI] with the proper degree of ardor.

Personally, I'm all for deflating the ego of just this type of problem child, although I have a sneaking [*sic*] suspicion I am now meeting resistance on your part. In which case, I must entreat you to trust my political judgment. For although no one makes any less claim than I to be an expert in [N2WI] the field of politics, or any other field, [N3WI] for that matter, yet I think it fair to say that my feelings about matters of this kind have, in the main, proven valid. Perhaps I sound a bit ambiguous but a careful analysis of the foregoing ought to make it clear enough.

I had planned, when I first began writing this treatise, (ahem) to give you the details of another incident or two, but I'm not going to; what I told you originally is quite damning enough in the light of past recorded dastardliness [NWI] (about which of course I must acknowledge to know [N2WI] very little factually but [NWI] about which I nevertheless strongly suspect [N2WI] there is palpable evidence). Besides, I am more concerned

---

[93]We have no independent information as to who this "problem child" was and what the issues were, but one can get a fairly good idea from context.

that you should realize my purpose in bringing the matter to the proper person as you had suggested and as I promptly did. At the moment, there is a lull in the hostilities; not that I want this to signify to you a weakening on my part in pressing the matter. On the contrary, if anything, this fact only bolsters my contention that we are dealing with a most wily snake. (Continued in Letter # 2)—Love, Ethel

Emanuel H. Bloch
7 W. 16th Street
New York New York

May 16, 1951
Letter #2

Dear Manny,

To continue right along from Letter # 1.

No, I simply want you to get it over to the one whom it should concern that should other difficulties arise about which we shall see fit to raise our voices, that they will be viewed in relation to what we had previously represented. Based on a picture drawn with due regard to context and continuity his concept of the relationship involved cannot then be other than the true one and will thereby constitute some form of protection and redress for me.

Too, I don't think it will hurt anything to let it be known that there is much more to this business than I had a chance to describe and that you would appreciate the opportunity for a more thorough presentation of it to him at a later date. It should also be requested that the problem child be not raked over the coals just yet; you see, I've got my own ideas on the subject which I want very much to carefully examine with you and spilling the beans at this moment may tend to militate against what I hope we will be able to eventually work out. So try to persuade him not to give the problem child any occasion for self-expression yet, but subtly of course. I should not appreciate any confrontation, on this score, either for that matter, unless he wants to speak with me, alone.

Enough of this troublesome topic. It gets to be positively torturous. Oh, yes, before we do actually leave it, I am hoping you have communicated all that transpired here between us on Saturday to Dr. Miller since I was only able to mention in a letter [N2WI] to him that I had been unable to discuss a particular problem with him during our initial visit that I was most anxious for him to know about. In any case, I feel it is imperative that each [N3WI] of you should be in constant touch with the other concerning me. More about that however when I see you.

Now I have a special request to make of you. Please, [N2WI] when you see the Warden next, won't you plead with him to allow me to have Michael's plant outside the cell where I can see it but not touch it? At the very least, couldn't I see it just once so that I can truthfully tell Michael what it looks like. Do you really think that it won't occur to a sensitive, perceptive child like Mike that my silence about it is due to the fact that I was not permitted to receive it? My God, what harm can there possibly be, what crime committed if I am allowed to this one token of love from my darling children whom I have not seen for close to a year now! Beg him to let me have it, won't you, Manny? By the way, I certainly cannot use this regular letter paper either, if I wanted to write the children, you understand—

Mail call now— Love, Ethel

Our father was transferred to Sing Sing that very day.

Julius to Ethel

May 17, 1951

Hello My Love,

You are so close at hand and yet you being in a different corridor separated by so much steel, locked away from my sight and beyond my hearing range the frustration is terriffic [*sic*]. Tonight I was able to hear your voice when a few of the high notes of one of your arias was faintly audible. To insure a daily contact I will try to write you a note each day and I hope you can manage to do the same. Yesterday even though it was wonderful was to some extent overwhelming due to the excitement of seeing you and Manny at the same time. While I was with you two lovely human beings it was great. I felt so good and confident talking over our defense and personal problems but when it was over there was a terrible letdown. Darling, I miss you so much and I am so concerned for your welfare and peace of mind. All during the lawyer consultation I couldn't take my eyes of [*sic*] you nor could I get myself to express the tender and deep love I feel for you my precious. Something prevented me from telling you my innermost thoughts and I guess I'll get around to them after I am more relaxed. Only one who experiences this nightmare is capable of comprehending the tremendous emotional pressure of this type of incarceration. Ethel please keep on holding your chin up as it does so much for our confidence. The other men here are swell. The're [*sic*] helping me with commissary until I am able to buy my own. Incidentally, I was told to inform you that it is possible to purchase tomatoes even though they are not on the commissary list. There are two yard periods one in the morning and one in the afternoon. Physically, I am fairly comfortable and already in the routine of things. The food is much better than West St. and so far I manage very nicely in the eating department. As for recreation besides the sunshine and exercise in the yard, and incidentally a keeper plays handball with me in the afternoon, I read about six newspapers a day, I play chess in a numbered board by remote control with another inmate and I am reading "The Old Country" by Sholom Aleichem. Most important the other men here are nice, intelligent and we manage to have interesting conversations and kid around quite a bit and the time passes pleasantly. I'll make a copy of my letter to you and send it ["to" probably omitted here] Manny and you do the same for yours to me. I'm sure we'll make it darling. With decency and justice we'll be delivered from this darkness to beautiful life and freedom.

    Goodnight my wife
    Your own Julius
    #110649

The following letter was sent to Robby at the Hebrew Children's Home. Our mother was afraid to let us know she was in Sing Sing so she asked the head of the shelter (Mr. Witover) to take steps so that Robby would not see the return address. She drew a line in pencil under the two addresses and wrote:

Mr. Witover—Please cut off top [next two words written under] [penciled line] up to the date until such time as we can tell the kids about our removal to Sing Sing so there'll be no questions in the meantime. Thanks loads— ER.

Robert Rosenberg c/o Children's Hebrew Home
1682 Monroe Avenue
Bronx New York

                                       May 17, 1951
Dearest Robby,
    Do you know what I am looking at? The beautiful Mother's Day card you and Michael sent me, with the pretty red carnation flowers and the cute little pussy cats. I like the one with the green eyes especially, because they shine even in the dark. And when I see them shining, I say "That's my own sweet little boy telling me he loves me," just like the words he wrote on the back of the card.
    I am so sorry we could not see you and wish you a happy birthday, but I hope you liked the card Daddy and Mommy sent our darling four year old

boy-le.[94] And although we aren't with you, we never stop thinking of you and loving you the way we always used to, and always will.

I am feeling fine darling, except that I miss you and Mike. Bubby Sophie and Aunt Lee and Aunt Ethel tell me all about you children of course and I am very glad that you are both getting along so well. Robby dear, tell Bubby to get you a hand spray so that you can really enjoy your shower.

Michael dear, thank you too for the card ["and" CO] I mentioned above and also for the two to which you signed yours and Robby's names, when Mrs. Bloch brought them to you. She told everybody how much she liked you.

I want you to know also that it was a perfectly wonderful [NWI] idea on your part to send me your class picture. Tell me, pretty, are your eyes as blue as ever? You are growing into such a good-looking fellow; I am delighted to see you among the other children standing there so tall and straight and smiling so sweetly. I guess I couldn't ever say how very dear my Robert and Michael are to me. Won't we make up for [illegible letter CO] lost time when we are all to-gether again, won't we though? Just wait & see!

They are ready to collect the mail—Good-bye, darlings—I'll write again soon—

Your loving Mommy—

xxxxxx

Mr. Emanuel Bloch
299 Broadway
New York N. Y.

May 17th, 1951

Dear Manny,

Please hold up on sending me the New York Times. I'll discuss it with you later. I've got a few minutes to dash off a copy of a letter to Ethel—Copy

---

[94]See footnote 46.

Here begins a re-write of the letter of May 17 above.

May 18, 1951

My Dearest Sweetheart,

I can now report to my better half that I am acclimating myself to my new home and I see that I am able to find enough things to occupy my time. The food situation is particularly gratifying because the other inmates contributed commissary that helps fill out the meals just right. A good example of this was to-days [*sic*] lunch of two eggs. The fellows gave me a tomatoe [*sic*], fried spam, mayonnaise and catsup. Yesterday they gave me lemon meringue pie and a box of tea bags for eight P.M. tea time.

The yard periods are arranged as follows. The four hours in the morning are equally divided among the six men here and the same procedure is followed with the five hours in the afternoon. I take ten minutes out of my afternoon recreation period for a shower. I spend the time playing ball, walking in the sun and singing songs. I intend to continue playing handball at an increasing rate so I can improve my game and at the same time better condition myself. Tuesday and Saturdays are the days set aside for the barber to give us our free shaves. These are the parts of my routine that until now you the female inhabitant of our "cozy palace", were not familiar with. The chess competition here is quite keen and I enjoy the games very much.

Ethel honey I'm impatient for our next meeting. I want to see you, be with you and talk to you. There is so much to say and I feel we ought to discuss the legal aspects of our case in greater detail, with our attorneys. I read in today's Post that Judge Knox was taken to the hospital. There have been so many delays in reaching a conclusion on your writ[95] and on its ramifications.

It's no use my wife I'm terribly lonesome and I want to send you all my love even though it is a poor substitute for its proper expression. So long for now till tomorrow—Always your own—Julius—
#110649

---

[95]This is the writ of *habeas corpus* filed in an attempt to get our mother removed from Sing Sing. Judge Knox was obviously the judge before whom the writ was filed.

Mr. Emanuel Bloch
299 Broadway
New York N.Y.

May 18, 1951

Dear Manny,

I would like you to let my folks read my letters to Ethel as I'll not be able to find too much time to write them often. Please ask them to write me as I look forward to get news from home.—

What follows is the text of the May 18, 1951 letter above.

Manny—I haven't as yet received my mail, books or pictures that Warden Thompson said he would send up to Sing Sing for me. Let me know what's cooking. Send my regards to all my friends.

   Julius

Ethel to Julius

May 19, 1951

My own dear sweetheart,

How loath was I to leave your fond embrace,[96] how loath & how reluctant my step as I approached my cell. It was there waiting for me, silent, inexorable, disdainful, seemingly unaware of its occupant's departures but smug in the knowledge of her eventual return.

It's only three days ago that my lips clung in desperate hunger to yours and my glance kindled to behold the long-loved, oddly familiar, oddly strange being, close to whom I had lain and sweetly slumbered through how many nights—only three days by the calendar, yet am I certain that eons have elapsed and that I dreamed our meeting, in any case. Darling, you state it for me, too, when you say you were overwhelmed. The staircase I had just climbed, the sight of you as I entered, Manny's voice that I heard only dimly, the room itself—all rushed upon my consciousness with such a mad pounding I was unable to give response to the very tumult of my response.

---

[96]At their first joint meeting with their attorney, the first time they had been together since they had been sentenced to death, they greeted one another with an embrace. This caused the Warden to order them never to touch again. Louis Nizer, in his book *The Implosion Conspiracy,* turned that embrace into a virtual sex scene from an R-rated movie and claimed that whenever they met together with counsel after that, they were in handcuffs, even at joint visits with us! (See Nizer, pp. 395–96, 433–34.) It was such total fabrications that led us to sue Nizer for both copyright infringement, invasion of privacy and libel, a suit that was settled out of court.

And then before I could fully savor the painful taste of our physical salutation, while yet keenly aware of an even greater thirst as I drank, we were
apart and the table stood immovable between us!

How my heart smote me for your pale, drawn face for your eloquently
pleading eyes, for your slender, boyish frame your evident suffering. My
dearest husband, what heaven and what hell to welcome you to monotonous
days and joyless nights, to endless desire and endless denial. And yet here
shall we plight our troth anew, here held fast by brick and concrete and steel,
shall our love put forth gripping root and tender blossom here shall we soar
defiance and give battle; yes, and here shall we expose the predatory plans of
our madmen to institute thought control and drag our people to slaughter!

Sweetheart, I know how impatiently we [NWI] both sat watching the
clock yesterday, longing for one of the Blochs to turn up and bring us
together. Doubtless they were engaged elsewhere on some other sector of the
fighting front, on our behalf, so we must swallow our disappointment,
bitter though it surely is and bide our time. Pussy cat, of course you
couldn't give free tongue to all the crowding thoughts and sensitive feelings,
nor could I. Did you expect that it would be easy to open our hearts to each
other under those cold, forbidding circumstances? And yet I confess I had
myself anticipated a tremendous release, an end to anguish. And when such
surcease was not forthcoming and there remained instead a vague sense of
loss and anti-climax, I was like you, quite overcome with frustration.
Indeed, until your letter arrived (for which many kisses) I couldn't even
begin to express it on paper. So glad for you, my dearest that you are
handling the situation with your usual elan! Ah, Monsieur, je t'aime, je
t'adore! Your lonely wife.

P.S. I wrote the kids following our visit. Lets of things to tell you next
time. Ethel's address is 5347—65th Pl. Maspeth, L.I.

Emanuel H. Bloch
7 W. 16th Street
New York New York

                                                    May 20, 1951

Dear Manny,

Following is a copy of my 1st letter to Julie since his arrival here:[97]

---

[97]The May 19 letter is then written verbatim with the omission of the PS. The
Warden attached a letter to attorney Bloch which stated: "From the enclosed
letter which is being sent to you by Mrs. Ethel Rosenberg, it is noted that she

Ethel to Julius

May 20, 1951

Dearest Julie,

Today I am at such loose ends I don't know where to turn for comfort. There has been a fine intermittent rain all afternoon and I have sat in my chair at the entrance of the yard, drinking in the fragrance of flowers growing somewhere unbeknownst to me, and watching the bedraggled sparrows picking dispassionately at the bread I had scattered earlier for them. Every once in so often, the rain lets up and then I stalk disconsolately about inspecting the few green things [N2WI] I possess miraculously pushing their way up through the [NWI] apparently unyielding concrete; here growing between the brick wall and the stone walk are sprigs of crisply curling, bright green parsley, and there along another wall, the shapely leaves of a wild violet plant luxuriously unfold while [N2WI] under them two buds cosily nestle, only vaguely aware as yet of the world outside. Now I kneel down and glumly scrutinize a crevice in the concrete, filled with earth painstakingly accumulated from the underpart of moss, small, velvety clumps of which cling to the damp cool parts of the yard where the rays of the sun seldom penetrate. In this earth, an apple seed which I [NWI] had carefully planted some ten days before and which I had ever since been patiently watering is bravely sprouting, but I sigh and turn away from the all but visible bit of green.

May 21, 1951

So glad Sunday is over and with it the tears I [NWI] had shed over you and the children and my own loneliness before bed-time.[98] The morning dragged by but in the afternoon arrived three letters from you, Lena and Dr. Miller, and my spirits are soaring once more.

---

states that she was 'longing for one of the Blochs to turn up and bring us together'. It is not desired to establish a practice for you to visit them here for the express purpose of bring [*sic*] them together. Your visits with your clients should be confined strictly to legal matters. Arrangements for personal visits between themselves will be arranged here. In the event that it is found that your visits are made just for the purpose of their conducting a social visit together, it will become necessary for me to have you see your clients one at a time."

[98]That Sunday was no doubt Mother's Day.

May 24, 1951

Dear one, I feel terribly remiss. This should have gone to you yesterday at the latest so all that I want to say about Manny's visit will have to wait till to-morrow morning's mail is collected. I am hoping that in the meantime you will receive the letter that landed [NWI] up at West Street.

All my love, darling sweetheart—

Your own Ethel

Julius to Ethel

May 21, 1951

My Sweetest Darling,

When I finished writing you Friday evening I was told mail is not pick [*sic*] up until Monday morning so I lapsed into a lazy existence of eating, sleeping, some reading and day dreaming about you. I spent quite a bit of time on my bed absorbing as much as possible of the full reality of my being here as possible. What you wrote Ethel so eloquently expresses our profoundest frustrations, our understanding and deep love for each other. The hemmed in solitude that surrounds us, and the oppressive nature of this sombre tomb must not succeed in removing our strong ties to the vibrating and pulsating outside world. We caged here can only protest our innocence and stand up firmly but it is the task of the American people to stay the executioners [*sic*] hand and see that justice is done. I gaze at the walls of my cell and contemplate the great sufferings of my wife and children and I am helpless to aid them. My heart aches as I tell myself yours is to stay strong so that you can clear your name and in that way bring the greatest comfort to your loved ones. The most difficult thing for me to take is that you my heart are also in this gehenna[99] and only your splendid steadfastness has made it possible for me to stand up. I ask myself over and over again why it is necessary for them to keep us apart and I find no satisfactory answer.

Strength comes from knowledge and we are thoroughly familiar with all that is going on and we are therefore well prepared to meet the tribulations of the coming period. The cards were stacked against us and we lost the first round. As realists we know that we face a long tough uphill fight and we need very much support from many good decent people. I am sure we are confident and I hope that the people don't disappoint us. Your letter of the 19th arrived across the corridor this morning and you can tell it had a very stimulating effect. My sister Lena wrote and said she'd try to visit the early

---

[99]Yiddish for "Hell."

part of this week. She wants to hear from me and I expect to get around to writting [*sic*] all the folks after I settle down.

Do not be concerned about my looks as I feel healthy and can take care of myself. Sunday afternoon I heard you telling the guard that you wanted to have some of your commissary cream cheese with your supper. I was thrilled to hear your voice you are so sweet. This occured [*sic*] while I was resting on the yard steps and I believe the door to your corridor was slightly ajar. Honey we have a license and we should be allowed to set up house-keeping here. In all earnestness only our complete freedom will satisfy me. All my love—your own Julius—

Always impatient to see you and be near you until we meet I send my kisses.

Emanuel H. Bloch
7 W. 16th Street
New York New York

May 26, 1951

Dear Manny,

As you must have understood from my abrupt ending, I was forced to cut my last letter short before I was really through talking to you.

You recall that I was discussing the unwitting boner I had pulled in attempting to correspond with your wife. I trust that you will be able to make the Warden understand how it happened and the purpose of my writing her. I hope, too that he will permit you to have the letter, for beyond this one communication to her I had not intended to go in any event, and now [N2WI] of course that I have been expressly forbidden to do so, I certainly propose to abide by that rule. So much for that.

Did you phone Dr. Miller? You see, I wrote him a couple of days ago asking him to get in touch with you concerning the particular problem I've been pestering you with. Even if he has already done so, I wish you would call him anyway to get his thoughts on 1) the advisability of the children's visit on these premises and 2) the handling of their expected questions concerning Sing Sing and the [NWI] death penalty. Naturally, if you people have already discussed same (including while you're at it—the question of the plant) it's all to the good. If not, I wish you'd speak with him before he leaves the city Saturday to come up here, so we'll waste less time during our visit and cover as much ground as possible.

Another little chore. I'd greatly appreciate someone phoning my sister-in-law Lena & asking her to notify her sister Ethel that her address is desired on the letters themselves, or on the outside of the envelopes, by the Correspondence Dept. here; this goes for all correspondents.

Last item now coming up. If you plan to get up here either Saturday or sometime during the following week, perhaps you could manage to make it an afternoon visit for a change. If you arrived somewhere between 1:00 and 2:00 P.M. we'd be able to visit until 3:30 P.M. and I'd be able to get a few very important things off my chest, with a fair degree of privacy—Savvy?

I'd like to drop your Dad a few lines but since I don't know if it would be permissible, I'd better just send my love through you. How is my adopted "pop" anyway? Tell him his adopted "daughter" is as rebellious as ever; let him just come and see me and I'll give him a sample of the old lung power! Gosh, how I used to bawl him out during our consultations and how he'd plead with you to make me "Stop yelling" at him![100] How far away it all seems; I can see him this minute, after the verdict sitting there heart-broken overcome, sick to the soul of him at all the rotten hypocrisy of the impartial judge and the impartial jury. His old eyes have beheld so many slimy things, I'm hoping it's in the cards for him to behold our eventual victory! Love you all.

Ethel

Julius to Ethel

May 24, 1951

My Dearest Sweetheart,

I'm slowly relaxing into a humdrum routine thats [*sic*] setting the pattern in this period of my life that is marking time. Much time is spent reviewing as much of the past events in our lives as I can recollect. Not that I want to live in the past but I want to be able to draw sustenance and additional strength to sustain me through this zombie existance [*sic*]. How

---

[100]There is absolutely no information from any of the written or oral testimony left behind to indicate if this is purely humorous fiction or if there were serious disagreements about defense strategy that produced "yelling" during the consultations. The one disagreement alluded to in Virginia Gardner's *The Rosenberg Story* was over whether or not to take the Fifth Amendment when asked about Communist Party affiliations and membership. According to Gardner, it was Alexander Bloch who suggested the strategy of admitting Communist Party membership. Gloria Agrin, interviewed by Ted Morgan for *Esquire* in 1975, stated that such an admission would leave my father open for a perjury prosecution because he had stated under oath in 1945 that he was not a Communist. (See Record, pp. 1152–57, 1191–92; Radosh and Milton, pp. 54–56.) Cedric Belfrage in *The American Inquisition* insisted that Emanuel Bloch never doubted the strategy of taking the Fifth Amendment at the trial (Belfrage, p. 144).

wonderful and glorious youth is. Plein de joi de vivre, creative and wholesome. Starting with my high school days I was always seeking solutions of
issues of religious, social and political context and constantly I participated
in activities that not only made me an integral citizen of the community but
also gave me solid roots in the life stream of progressive America.[101] Born
of orthodox parents and raised in the slum tenements of the lower East Side
my childhood memories are full of the struggles of my parents to feed and
clothe five children. There was a time when my father was engaged in a long
strike of the clothing workers to eliminate the evils of the sweat shops and
many times the family went hungry and fell into deep debt. Because he was
a shop chairman and active my father was blacklisted and had to seek
employment in the dress industry and found it quite a pull to make ends
meet. The constant battle against rats and vermin is still vivid in my mind.
At Hebrew school I studied diligently and I made the class valedictory speech
upon graduation. I hungrily absorbed the culture of my people and treasured
the great heritage of it's [*sic*] fight for freedom from slavery in Egypt and
from the Hamens.[102] I found the same great traditions in American history
and as an American Jew with this background and my early youth experiences it was natural that I should follow in their footsteps and be in favor
of bettering the lot of the common man. I met you my darling in 1936 and
you already knew me as an outspoken anti-Nazi and anti-fascist.

I found in you a profound understand [*sic*], an excellent character and a
sweet person. You were for me. Together our perspective was clearer and life
was fuller.

I want this letter to go out tonight so I'll continue my discourse tomorrow. I received your letter and it's always a breath of fresh air to hear from
you[.] Until tomorrow I send you my love and heart—Your own—
Julius

*In this letter one can see evidence that our father knew that someday people
other than our mother would read this letter. The reiteration of some of his
early experiences and political roots were not necessary for our mother, she*

---

[101]The word "progressive" was used in the late 1940s and 1950s as a code word
for "left-wing," "radical," or even Communist. Though there were plenty of non-
Communists involved in, for example, the Progressive Party which ran Henry
Wallace for President in 1948, the policies they advocated were exactly the same
as the policies advocated by the Communist Party. Thus, it is a fair statement to
say that Communists and other leftists with similar views used the word
"progressive" to indicate their politics without coming right out and admitting
it.
[102]The oppressive Greek ruler against whom the Jews resisted, as told in the
story of Purim.

*knew them. Nevertheless, given the non-existence of any organized move-
ment to protest the convictions and the sentences, it is hard to imagine that
he only wrote this with publication in mind.*

Julius to Ethel

May 25, 1951

My Precious Woman,
    Ah it was so good to see you this afternoon and the hour seemed to
evaporate so quickly. Honey I sat so reserved and pent up looking at you
through the screen[103] and all the time I wanted to take you in my arms,
smother you with kisses and convey to you in more than words my consuming love for you. Darling I hope we are allowed to visit on a regular
basis. Your company even with the limitations and for so short a time lifted
me out of the gloom of our despair and filled me with the warmth of your
lovely person. How I want to tell you that this too shall pass quickly and
we can once more take up our joyous happy family life. Our continued
stamina, our lawyers [*sic*] thorough legal job and above all an informed
public coming to our aid will guarantee our complete freedom. Therefore let
us continue and live up to our motto courage, confidence and perspective.
    I received another letter from Lee and it looks like she didn't as yet
receive the last letter I sent her and she is concerned about my welfare. I'll
tell Manny to calm her fears and make sure that my family is kept informed
on how we're getting along.

May 27, 1951

Yesterday my package of letters and pictures finally arrived from West St. I
checked them through, reminised [*sic*] a bit and promptly obtained a cardboard (the back of a large paper pad) and mounted the six pictures I have of
our little bunnies. One of the guards cut diagonal slots in each of the four
corners of a penciled layout of the outline of the photos and by inserting the
corners of the pictures [N3WI] in the slots they were neatly set up. Their
bright smiling faces dominate the top of my table crowded with books,
commissary, toilet articles and give me great comfort and promise for the
future. How my heart aches for our dears. Their's [*sic*] is such a hard lot,
bewildered by events, no parents near them to understand & love them and
help guide them. Much as ["it" CO, N2WI] all this is painful, for their sake

---

[103]"Social visits" between our parents were arranged weekly during which a wire
mesh screen was placed in front of our mother's cell in women's wing and our
father was allowed into that wing to visit with her through this double barrier.

we must be strong darling so that we will be able once more to take over our rightful place as mother and father and brighten the lives of our boys. I promised to continue writting [*sic*] about my past but somehow I can't get myself attuned to continue at present[104] as my mind is constantly thinking about you and the children. During the week and on Sunday the Daily News and also the Sunday Daily Mirror carried short articles about us. Since you don't see these papers remind me to tell you about these items the next time we meet. It is true that hope springs eternal but in our case we have very substantial basis to maintain our spirits. Through the hundred feet of matter and space that separates us I send my all—Love your very own

    Julius
    #110649

Mrs. Ethel Goldberg
5347-65th Place
Maspeth, Long Island

                              May 26, 1951

[Boxed under the date is the following] P.S. Will you do me a big favor & recopy this letter for Manny Bloch

Dearest Ethel,
    You mustn't mind when I don't answer your letters as promptly as I might. My seeming neglect of you and Lena so far as correspondence goes is not due to lack of interest on my part, believe me. Actually I am so busy trying to build up some semblance of normal living inside the fortress of concrete and steel which houses me that I find myself constantly behind schedule on the matter of letters. Don't, however, take this as a signal to slow down your own mail; on the contrary, write just as often as you please, whenever time & energy permit, that is.
    Much of my day is spent outdoors in a good-sized yard with stone walk and brick walls. There are a few green things bravely struggling to live and grow (the same as the inmate) which I delight in watering daily. I practice hand-ball with an [NWI] almost religious regularity and sometimes I play a game of catch with a matron. Often I sit quietly in the sun and read an absorbing book. Indoors I spend time singing, listening to the radio, reading

---

[104]Perhaps Emanuel Bloch had suggested that a letter or some letters about their background would be useful in his efforts to garner political support. This is strong indication that the material in the letter of May 24 was purposely written with a larger audience in mind.

and writing—I have a most wonderful collection of folk songs known as "The Fireside Book of Folk Songs" (largely secured, along with other interesting selections, through the efforts of my lawyer) which makes for many pleasant hours.

Darling, thanks so much for quoting [NWI] me Michael's letter to his father. What was his and Robby's reaction to the one I wrote them, thanking them for their Mother's Day cards? Oh, Ethel, how indescribably bitter it is to be separated from one's children. Can the heart-ache ever really be measured? I am a vessel filled to overflowing with so much sorrow, so much pain, it seems as though I shall never be quite free of these feelings again. My desire to see my two pussy cats grows steadily with each passing hour, yet must I curb my longing, & bid myself to be patient yet a while more. The thought of my sweet husband ever comforts and sustains me. I simply must not be found wanting in his hour of need!

The most wonderful thing happened on Friday right after lunch. My sweetheart was allowed in to the Women's Wing and under [NWI] the double surveillance of a matron and a guard, of course, visited "his Monkey in the cage," as I gaily characterized myself to him when he walked in. We spent a most enjoyable hour, as you may well imagine, exchanging notes as to our respective doings and expressing our love for each other thru the all too inadequate means permitted us. A thick screen separated us, through which he managed, nevertheless to pick out his son standing proud & tall among the other children of his class; I am referring to the picture Michael had seen fit to yank off the wall at the House and turn over to Mrs. Bloch as a gift for me, bless his sweet thoughtfulness! Give everybody my love—As ever, Ethel

P.S. Just to reassure you—I am very much alive and kicking "like a team ["of" omitted] mules"—and always will be, never fear!

Ethel to Julius

May 27, 1951

[Underneath the date is written the following]: P.S.—Honey, no time to recopy this letter for Manny—Do it for me, please. [Then, an arrow from the P.S. is drawn to the left to a box in which is written]: Same goes for the one I wrote to you about plants.

Dearest darling one,

Of course, you experienced the same pangs of unfulfilled hunger at the termination of our visit as I did; and yet what swell gratification there was for us in the simple fact of our being together. Do you know how madly in love with you I am? And how utterly shameless were my thoughts as I gazed at your glowing face through the double barrier of screen and bar! Bunny dear, I wanted you so much, and all I could do was to kiss my hand at you! Now I am looking forward impatiently to Manny's coming so that we can [N2WI] more fully discuss all those matters which we touched on only briefly and which are still hanging fire. There are several personal items that I am anxious to thrash out with both of you for my own peace of mind and well-being.

My sweet, I loved your letter. Can we ever forget the turbulence and struggle, the joy and beauty of the early years of our relationship when you courted me and I accepted you as my heart's dearest. Together we hunted down the answers to [NWI] all the seemingly insoluble riddles a complex and withal callous society presented. Those answers[105] have stood the test of time [N2WI] & change and still stand for all those who are not afraid to look and see and examine as we did in that long ago and far away. Indeed, it is because we didn't hesitate to blazon forth those very answers, it is because we were relentless, uncompromising, implacable, in implementing our beliefs with action, that we sit [NWI] today within the gray walls of Sing Sing and await we know not what further pain and sorrow and emptiness.[106] And yet for the sake of these answers for the sake of American democracy, justice and brotherhood, for the sake of peace and bread and roses, and the innocent laughter of little children, shall we continue to sit here in dignity and in pride and in the deep abiding knowledge of our innocence before God and man, until the truth becomes a clarion call to all decent humanity and the doors of this slaughter house are flung wide!

There was once a wise man, I forget his name, who marvelled about the "indestructibility of human character." Beloved, we shall prove him right, upon my soul we shall prove him right; perhaps then will other human beings believe in their indestructibility, too, and rally in ever increasing numbers to our defense and their own. For they who have the courage and the foresight [N3WI] & the decency to aid the Rosenbergs' fight for freedom, ensure their own eventual release.

---

[105]Clearly a veiled reference to their acceptance of socialism as the solution to America's problems, and perhaps even to their joining the Communist Party, though the date of their joining is unknown. The way this is written communicates to anyone knowing their specific affiliation that they (or at least our mother) still believed in their previous politics without directly admitting it, something that Communists in those days almost never did.

[106]Note, this supports her psychiatrist's recollection that she did not expect the death sentence to be carried out. (See *Sons*, p. 148 where he refers to her expecting "a long incarceration.")

My sweet husband, your miserable wretch of a woman salutes you but why must you sleep in one bed and I in another? Tch, tch, the state is awfully wasteful—Shame on them!—Your own girl—

Mr. Emanuel Bloch
299 Broadway
New York N.Y.

May 28, 1951

Dear Manny—Here is the second letter I promised you— [What follows is an exact rewrite of the previous letter from Ethel to Julius.]
See I told you the best there is.   —Julius

Mrs. Lena Cohen
140 Baruch Place
New York New York

May 28, 1951

Dearest Lee,
    It is a most heart-rending thing indeed for me to have to contemplate the extra sorrow and hurt Julie's transfer here have [sic] added to the family's already bitter lot. It is no simple matter to accept the fact that one's son and brother is in the death house. I, too, was horrified at first, even though I am also an inmate here and expected his arrival momentarily. So it is not difficult for me to picture what an effect the news must have had upon all of you. Furthermore, I am incensed at the shock Mama must have sustained through the heartless indifference or stupid blunder (whichever it was, it was an unpardonable action) which caused her to drop everything and run to West Street only to find Julie gone. Suppose she had collapsed up there, what should they have done then. As it is, if I know Mama, she must have come close enough to it to cause me to shudder! I trust that she has since recovered somewhat and has adjusted herself to this new blow, to some small degree.
    Actually, there is a brighter side to the situation. Food is much better, there is fresh air and exercise morning and afternoon, the cells are a lot more comfortable, and treatment is generally decent and fair. For instance, they have taken the fact of our relationship into proper consideration and have already allowed us one visit over in the women's wing, the No Man's Land where I reside. Of course, a heavy screen separated us, and we were by no means left to ourselves, but the sight and sound of each other held such mutually shared pleasure that it created the effect of a tonic. How regularly

we will be permitted to visit in this manner we do not, as yet, know; it is certainly safe to assume, however, that the warden intends to do right by us and accord us all the courtesy that a decent, well-behaved married pair of people deserves.

So take heart, dear folks, actually we have gained ground rather than lost, even though visiting for you all now constitutes a fresh problem. I have the utmost confidence, [NWI] however, that such a problem can eventually be hacked down to its proper size. It will require some amount of organization and effort, but you will have help from Manny Bloch and his friends, be of good cheer in that respect.

No, dear, Julie and I take our recreation in separate yards and have no access to each other whatever except through officially approved visits. Was surprised to hear that my winter coat had only just arrived home. The institution made me a simple, dark, nicely fitted coat soon after I settled down here, and also supplied me with other necessary items of clothing, so do not be concerned. We are both well and eager to see our dear ones. My best to Mamma [N3WI] & the kids—May she have only my blouses and sweaters to [NWI] ever worry about, bless her sweet soul.   Love you all—Ethel

Emanuel H. Bloch
7 W. 16th Street
New York New York

                                                            May 28, 1951

Dear Manny,

Following is a copy of a letter I sent to Lena Cohen—

[Then follows a verbatim copy of the letter above.]

Mr. Emanuel Bloch
299 Broadway
New York N.Y.

                                                            May 29, 1951

Dear Manny,

It has been very gratifying to me that we have been able to go over every step in our legal defense on a current basis. You must realize that because so much is at stake for us I keep on hammering away at every legal and extra legal matter that should be used in our defense. Please bear with me and understand I have utmost confidence in you and I've placed everything in your competent hands. However, it is necessary for me to be part of

..is fight in order to lighten the burden of this nightmare imprisonment. The little woman didn't find the time to copy her last two letters so here goes.

[Then follows a copy of the letter of May 20-21-24 above.]

Manny—
    I've got a jewel of a wife and I want us to do all we can to make things easier for her as she is under such pressure. If it's possible try to let my folks read some of our letters as it isn't possible to do all this writting [*sic*] and keep up with my reading. So long till next time[.]
    —Julius—

Ethel to Julius

                                                                    May 29, 1951
My dearest loved one,
    By now you have my letter describing my reaction to our first visit, much the same as those you experienced yourself and so poignantly expressed in your own [NWI] latest writing [N2WI] to me. Sweetheart, I love you so very much; every day that I spend apart from you endears you all the more to me. And I dream of the time when our separation shall be but a dimly remembered ghost of the past and our children shall be brothers to suffering no longer.
    Speaking of the children reminds me of your birthday card. When you write me next, darling, will you remember to send me the lines of the verse and those that Michael composed himself for your special edification. I don't know when I have been so thrilled by anything as this sweet expression of a child's love. Truly we have two treasures, than which there is nothing more precious in the whole wide world!
    Bunny dear, you tell me that you [NWI] have finally received your belongings from West Street but you do not mention the last letter I sent to that address which must have arrived as you left for Sing Sing. What I said in part was so complimentary to Manny that I want to make certain a copy of it gets into his hands. Anyway, it happens to be a favorite with me and I hope it meets with your approval, too.
    My darling, what dear solace to hear your voice during the Jewish Services.[107] And the contribution you made to the general discussion

---

[107]"Every week the prison's Jewish chaplain, . . . conducted services in the men's wing of the Condemned Cells. My mother, the only woman in the Condemned Cells, was allowed to attend services. She could not see the male

following the sermon was certainly very much apropos. Did you agree with my comments, incidentally? I think the Rabbi is a very fine, intelligent, sincere and decent young man and what he has to present always gives me food for thought. What was the reaction among the other men? I sense a warmth and spirit of good-will toward him and toward me, for that matter, which is most gratifying. Today I felt this friendliness reaching out to encircle you [NWI] too; in sooth, I have an idea, my one and only, that you have very definitely ["have" CO] arrived and are now a veritable pillar of "CC" society. Am I correct?

My thoughts turn now to those newspaper articles you recounted for me, insinuating that we don't want our folks to visit us and are not interested in requesting visits for ourselves. What vile, disgusting lice crawl forth their petty days upon this wondrous earth of ours, spewing forth this filth upon people who wouldn't lower themselves to spit at them! I have nothing but the most profound contempt and loathing for this kind of worm; lo, when the Judgment Day comes they will be ground into the dust where they belong!

Dear one, it is torture to be without you! All my love and the intense longings of my body and soul do I send you   —Ethel

Emanuel H. Bloch
7 W. 16th Street
New York New York

May 29, 1951

Dear Manny,

There was so much ground to cover yesterday, and you came so late and left in such haste, that I neglected to broach a number of problems that I had intended for your consumption before you saw the individuals you mentioned as expected in court today and possibly Thursday.

Be that as it may and figuring that you probably still won't be able to make it up here before Friday or Saturday, you will still be able to get in touch with him by phone before too much more time elapses, after your courtroom business is finished—and despite the fact that it may be finished for him, too—

---

prisoners, nor they her. These services provided human contact for the prisoners. Some regarded them as a break in the boredom of prison existence, others as a sincere religious experience. The rabbi could not determine the priority for my parents, 'but if they came only for an opportunity to hear each other, it would be understandable.'" (*Sons*, p. 68.)

In other words, although I know you have a tough week ahead, I am wondering whether you cannot relegate some of your doings (other than purely legal, of course) to someone else and try to be here by Friday or Saturday afternoon. You yourself touched on these matters yesterday but you remember that we left them in abeyance for the end of our visit and then you have to leave before we could really discuss them. I feel that they are much too pressing to let them ride any longer than is absolutely necessary so I am urging you to do your best to come the very first afternoon you can.

I'll understand, naturally, if you can't work it in, but I had to let you know that I am most anxious for you to try to do this for me, if you possibly can.

Thanks loads—Best regards—
Ethel—

What this issue they were discussing was, or who the "he" is in the letter, is unclear from the context or from any other information available at this time.

Emanuel H. Bloch
7 W. 16th Street
New York New York

                                                    May 30, 1951
Dear Manny,

Am already feeling remiss because I gave way to an impulse to urge your coming at the cost of your precious time and energy. Now that I have thought things over, really, it isn't necessary for you to come until next week, at your own convenience. Whatever ideas I had in mind won't [NWI] exactly run away, so please don't break your neck. Honest Injun, unless it is fairly easy for you to manage to get here Friday afternoon it will be a foolish expenditure to get here Saturday since that day is so close to the beginning of a new week that it would be far wiser to do what you need to over the week-end (& get some badly needed rest, while you're at it) and see us Monday or Tuesday afternoon, instead.

Sorry if I upset any plans. It seemed like a bright idea when I dashed off the letter.

Best of luck—Thursday in Court[108]—think you're [NWI] doing swell—and don't be angry with me for making you. One impatient character ought

---

[108]If the court action related to the case, it could only have been argument over the request for a writ of *habeas corpus* to compel the government to return our

to understand another—anyway, this one is crazy about you!—In all sincerity, Ethel

Julius to Ethel

May 31, 1951

My Dearest Wife,

By now Manny has received copies of the two letters you sent me and they have been made part of my treasured archives. It is true that I got my mail from West St. but the last letter you sent me was not included. I'll ask our attorney to check with Warden Thompson about this letter. The books I had that were sent me while I was at the Fed. Det. House were denied me and I've already reserved the "Rise of American Civilization" by Charles and Mary Beard. I believe our illustrious counselor sent it. Between that book and Thomas Wolfe's "You Can't Go Home" [*sic*] I have enough reading material for the present. One choice bit of news. The P.K.[109] informed me that Friday from 1 to 2PM we will have our weekly visit period.

As for our budding poet Michael. His birthday card to me had a picture of a sailboat on a lake and the printed verse said,

On the tides of deep affection, Dad
This thought sails on its way
To hope you'll have more Birthday Joy
Than Words can ever say!
He added in his own precious hand these beautiful thoughts
The Merry Wind is blowing
My lovely words are flowing   —Michael.
This my dearest is our pride and joy eight year old.

The Jewish services were rather novel and impressive. Without a doubt the Rabbi is a sincere, intelligent and learned man and the method he uses to integrate prayer and present circumstances and obtain uniform participation is very effective. Naturally, light of my life, your contribution hit the core of the topic under discussion by going to the principle of the argument. The men here have deep respect for you and keep you in high regard. You impress them as a "balla busta"[110] and one who knows how to handle herself. This is not me speaking. I just shep nachass.[111]

---

mother to New York. See *Sons*, pp. 40–41 for an excerpt from her affidavit. Needless to say, the request was denied.

[109]Principal Keeper

[110]Yiddish term for "strong, independent woman."

[111]Another Yiddish term meaning "experience great pride."

Lena set me a letter and told me how they repaired your old ironing board, like new, washed my shirts and socks and put all our clothes in order. You see our loved ones are all prepared for our eventual homecoming.

Shut away from the world by layers of massive steel, concrete and numerous locks, reading blasphemous lies about ourselves in [NWI] newspapers that are poisin [sic] spread by pen prostitutes and, finding myself and my wife condemned to [NWI] an early doom it takes every ounce of my strength and my all my [sic] understanding to stand up to all this. However, seeing you, hearing your voice and receiving such letters give me terrific stimuli and it seems easy to take all this in my stride. Your words are so expressive, and full of meaning and I adore you for every bit of the person you are. To me love is all inclusive, the culmination and the ultimate creative expression of life itself. If I am not expressing [N2WI] some of my innermost thoughts it's because I want to keep these private for the two of us and most important just knowing that you're always there is sufficient comfort for me. Through all of this you stand out in dignity and character as a woman. I am proud of you my lovely wife. I too miss you very much but this is our unfortunate lot.

We are not afraid as right is on our side and I know we will hold up well. All the ingredients of victory are present in spite of a long and tedious road. My sweetheart I send all my love—Your own Julius

Mrs. Ethel Goldberg
53 47—65th Place
Maspeth Long Island

Saturday
June 2, 1951

Dear Ethel,

By now you must know that Mama and Lena were up here on Friday and through Manny Bloch's thoughtful action the night before in getting the court order to them, were successful in their efforts to see me as well as Julie. I had a perfectly wonderful hour with them except that it fairly flew by and was over just about as we were getting warmed up. However, the important thing was for them to reassure themselves that I was my usual healthy, well-balanced self and as long as they departed somewhat more serene than they had arrived, I felt satisfied.

To add to our happiness, Julie and I were permitted our weekly visit today, despite the fact that our first meeting took place on a Friday. Believe me, he's looking very well. There's color in his face, he's gained weight (although he can [NWI] do with some more) and he appears very much more at ease. During the visit, we discussed the children, visits, legal matters and our own personal feelings. Of course, it is not easy to look upon your [NWI] most loved one through the double barrier of bars and screen, (Lena will describe same to you more fully, so if you do by some lucky chance manage to get here [N3WI] by the 15th you will not be unprepared)—but it's so unbelieveably [*sic*] sweet to see him at all after I had been deprived of this privilege for some eight weeks, that I'm ready to shout "Hallelujah"!

Darling, the lies of the untrustworthy press fill me with the deepest contempt and loathing. The purveyors of this kind of sensation seeking filth aren't fit to kiss our feet. Let me assure you that Julie and I cannot be corrupted by such vile mud-slinging and properly relegate same to the dung heap where it belongs![112]

To speak of your brother a bit, you express my own deep respect and love for him where you characterize him as you do. The longer I know him, the more am I impressed with his warm-hearted sincerity, his dignity and integrity as an individual, and the gentleness of his feelings toward other human beings. If we live without these precious gifts, what are we but "dwellers in the dust" who know not, who sing not, who care not—and who can inspire no other to know or to sing or to care!

Ethel dear, I could not possibly be [NWI] really depressed, when I [NWI] still possess the three pearls which have always made my life bright, (no matter the hardships which were also my lot) and to whom I shall fight tooth and nail to return. Forgive me then if I must be human, also, and yearn for this reunion to be nearer at hand instead of so far off—Please give my best to Oscar and the children—And kiss the Sharon kitten for me—I still remember how she kissed her little hand to me at the House of Detention!—

Love, Ethel

Mrs. Ethel Goldberg
53-47 65th Place
Maspeth, Long Island N. Y.

June 3rd 1951

Dear Ethel,

It never was my intention to forget to communicate with you my sweet sister as I had hoped you will keep in close touch with Mamma and the lawyer to get the latest news from us. However I'll try to keep some kind of word contact with you as letters from my dear ones mean so much to me

---

[112]Among the comments in the press were statements that they had refused to see relatives and had refused to participate in religious activities. See, for example, the comments of Irving Koslowe, the Jewish Chaplain at Sing Sing, in *Sons*, p. 70.

and I realize that my letters have the same effect on my family. From what you have already heard about this "Ossining Hotel" you have a general idea of the life here. As for me I've already become an established tennent [*sic*]. Comparing it to my last place of confinement in every respect it is far superior. The quarters are larger, more modern, cleaner [N3WI] than West St. and comfortable. Food supplemented by commissary is ["will" CO] generally good and the diet is a balanced one. Sunshine and morning and afternoon yard recreation periods are by far the greatest improvement over the Federal Detention House. Considering the extenuating circumstances my physical set up is adequate. My darling wife says I've already put on some weight and look much better. Being isolated from the world especially [NWI] from my loved ones ["and" erased], having a fearful sentence hanging over the head of the mother of my children and myself facing the same fate to say the least our situation is a very difficult one. However the splendid stamina and love of my sweetheart Ethel, the devoted loyalty and ardent support of my family, the expert help of my lawyer and a firm conviction in our innocence gives me the strength to face all this and keep going. I read newspapers, periodicals, books and play chess with the other inmates, carry on social commentaries with the fellows here and manage to occuppy [*sic*] my time. Don't let me create the impression that all is rosy and as the expressing [*sic*] goes like water off a ducks [*sic*] back for on the contrary I am sure you understand that loneliness and frustrations are also part of my caged existance [*sic*]. It is not possible for me to convey to you the magnitude of the emotional strain we are subject to but rest assured that both of us are holding our own and are convinced that we will win the final fight and be set free.

Ethel I want you to know that it has been a great satisfaction to me that my flesh and blood has so nobly stepped into the breach with moral & financial help and above all contributed love and understanding to our children.[113] When a person is a social being and lives as a principled individual it is very gratifying for him to see others of their own free volition act in the same manner as he would. Naturally I would like to keep in touch with you and therefore I ask that you be indulgent enough to write me as regularly as possible even though I may not answer you promptly or [NWI] send letter for letter. We have been granted permission to have a weekly visit and I see my wife through a wire screen for one hour during the week. My lawyer manages to get up here once a week for a legal consultation and now that my family has begun to visit the week is nicely broken up. Send all my love to your wonderful family.

Love—Julius

---

[113]See *Sons*, p. 25 and 31 for our recollections on this point.

Julius to Ethel

June 3, 1951

My Dearest and Most Precious Woman,

Looking at your sweet youthful face, your beautiful twinkling eyes, your captivating smile conveyed to me more than words what you couldn't express when we sat facing each other. The manner in which both of us couldn't find words but were able to through our other visible senses and radiant faces communicate our deep love for each other. Yes darling seeing you acts as a terrific emotional tonic and at once washes away the horror of our predicament. Dr. Franz Blau the psychiatrist in a recent article said the expression of true love is tenderness and sensuousness and I believe we have because of our circumstances found an additional way, one of mutual understanding. Because we are able to exude such warmth and oneness our resulting frustration is all the more difficult. Since we are people whose lives are fairly well integrated our character, knowledge and love fortify us against this adverse situation. Again darling we take heart and strenght [*sic*] in each other to withstand the rigors of our caged separation. My wonderful wife, I adore and love you more than my written words can express and your very being makes my life fuller and more beautiful. It is not necessary for me to attempt to describe our life free from this horror it is sufficient to observe that it will be on a much higher plain [*sic*] than we have hithertofar [*sic*] experienced. Never have I lost faith in the people because there is such inherent good in them and I am sure that [N2WI] my faith will be justified and we will once more take our rightful place among our fellow men.

At long last I sent my sister Ethel a letter. I find it difficult to write as I know these are not private communications. However, since I understand that letters are as important to my families [*sic*] moral [*sic*] as it is to mine I'll continue to try hard. To some extent I'm relying on you as the writter [*sic*] in our family to talk [*sic*, should be "take] care of all this family correspondence as I would like to concentrate my meager efforts on sending you my letters. Because I feel my words so inadequate I cannot get myself to write too often. I sent the P.K. a note, just as you agreed and asked that Thursday 3:45–4:45 be our regular visit time. Naturally the high point of the week will always be the time we're together. Oh, Honey how I long to hold you in my arms, kiss you and express my love as Dr. Franz Blau puts it. Well, my woman I'm eating well and putting on weight and believe me I'm expanding around [NWI] the waist line. Read all the Sunday papers and funnies, played handball, ate well and now I'm going to have me some eight P.M. tea with some doughnuts. Goodbye for now love of my heart Your own—Julius

Ethel to Julius

June 4, 1951

Dearest loved one,

Your much anticipated letter informing me concerning certain specific matters I had broached arrived soon after our visit ended on Saturday. And what a letter; indeed a veritable emotional and intellectual feast! All your dear expressions of pride and love are as balm to my wounded soul, my aching heart, my thwarted feelings. The tenderness of you reaches out to me through them, the very words are a caress that soothes away sorrow and brings me some respite from the desolation that hems me in so mercilessly.

Beloved, as I gaze upon you, my dumb lips cry out all the need and hunger that a wife is capable of feeling for the husband with whom she has shared so many enriching experiences, often sad, sometimes glad, but always made wonderful by dint of the love that transfigures all of living! I am never through dreaming of that happy day when we shall [NWI] claim each other and our wholesome lives once more.

Bunny, I think I begin to understand what you were driving at when you cautioned me about our correspondence. Were you by any chance trying to convince your wench of a woman to be a little less lusty in her appetites, or at least to curb the expression of them on paper a bit? But, darling, you said yourself that you wished they'd see the light and let us set up house-keeping here and in line with that, I innocently (!) scolded them for their extravagance in giving us two beds instead of one, nothing more. Don't look so embarrassed, sweetheart, the [N3WI] folks in the Correspondence Dept. know all about the facts of life and if they don't or they choose to pre-tend otherwise, the more shame on them, not us. As far as I'm concerned, (and here I can do with a little pretending myself), my heart reveals itself only to you. Down with all Censors!

Julie dear, I don't feel nearly as chipper as I sound; I just plod through every day, stubbornly filling the time with one thing and another, until I see you again. I wrote letters to Ethel and Lee, so now I am all caught up on my correspondence. I meant to quote you a few lines from Ethel's, but there's no space left; I shall do so next time, promise.

Crazy about you—darling—
Your dopey girl
Ethel—

Julius to Ethel

June 5, 1951

My Sweetest Darling,

When I'm with you and Manny time just evaporates and we never seem to have enough to finish our pressing business. Believe me dearest I am fully aware of your deep torture and horrible mental torment and in all sincerity the major portion of the solution, because of circumstances rests with you. Our next visit will be spent by us discussing in as sober a fashion as we can this perplexing problem. Ethel how I wish to comfort you and ease your pain. You can count on me to give my all to help you over this hurdle.[114] Honey you looked so sweet and nice but I was so busy going over the legal points I listed that I didn't have much time to enjoy my prize. I promise to let you have first choice next time the lawyer comes so you can have your say.

After the consultation I felt pretty bad seeing you in such an agitated state and when your letter arrived I was back in the groove again. What a luscious tid-bit. Perish the thought woman I'm not admonishing you for being a lusty girl with healthy appetites. However, I would say that concentration on such thoughts and expressions is not for a jailbird and certainly makes one all the more frustrated. So be good now & try a little sublimation.[115] Yes dear this shouldn't happen to two dogs.

More and more, sweetheart, my past and present contact with you are the mainstay of my continued inspiration. Your ability to analyze and put things in there [*sic*] proper places will do you stead in arriving at a satisfactory answer to this present dilemma. Keep in mind that a thing must be thoroughly searched and all aspects must be known before a correct result is obtained. I caught a few notes coming from your corridor and it was gratifying to hear you singing. For several moments I drifted off into memories of your long and tedious strivings to master voice and music. If you can patiently take up [N4WI] where you left off and perfect your voice you will have accomplished one of my greatest desires. It has always been my wish for you to continue studying so that we can thrive on such beautiful creative expression. In spite of so harsh an incarceration you have such wonderful talent to put to constructive use and I am sure that the pleasure derived will pay off many dividends. Let us continue to improve ourselves culturally and personally and we will be better people for all this horror. Our strongest assets are the two of us and we must continue to be strong. Our

---

[114]It is unclear what specific problem this refers to; it might involve conflict with one of the matrons.

[115]See *Sons*, p. 71 for the views of the rabbi and psychiatrist.

mutual love and regard for each other assures our steadfastness. In every way and all the words. I love you my sugar bun

Your own—Julius—

Ethel to Julius

June 6, 1951

My dearest sweetheart,

I must confess I didn't feel [NWI] any too good myself after our last lawyer consultation; I was genuinely concerned with what I was convinced would be a reaction of anxiety on your part, yet I was just as convinced of the justice of my position. Certainly I could not share your feelings at the expense of my own, much as I should have welcomed such an opportunity. But, oh, my sweetest, most precious darling, it was so painful to realize how you must be aching for my ache, that when evening came and I was locked in for the night I could no longer contain my feelings and wept bitterly. After I had thus relieved myself, I dropped a few lines to Dr. Miller urgently requesting a visit from him at the earliest opportunity. I shall get to the bottom of this business, all right, and I shall make myself unmistakably clear to all you guys, of that you may be sure.[116] Nevertheless, I was delighted to learn that my letter put you in such fine good humor; honey, I'm so happy when you're happy, I just hate to have you unhappy on my account. Hub, maybe you think that just because I am a jailbird my blood has turned to water. Let Saypol and Kaufman try sublimation and see how they like it; me, I'll take the McCoy, every time!

Julie dear, I can't wait to see you Friday, whatever the hour, for more than the usual reasons. You see, bunny, today I received two wonderful snapshots of the children in a letter from my brother Bernie that I want very badly to share with you. The glow that must suffuse your [NWI] manly face as you gaze at their childish ones will serve to make me love you all the more, sweet father of my sweet sons. And yet the sight of their amazingly mature features will be hurtful, too; with what pangs of regret I realize that their growth is taking place without benefit of our physical presence and guidance. And the horrible idea, of which I am never completely rid, that we may never be with them ever again, drives relentlessly through me, chilling my ["very" CO] blood and contracting my heart. My eyes fill and the very soul of me groans in agony!

Sweetie, I'm afraid I'm not being exactly cheerful. Oh, yes, before I close, want to say I received letters from both Lee and Ethel today. Lee had phoned Mrs. Epstein about the expected change of stories, but she had been

---

[116]Again, there is no evidence as to what this important issue was.

out, so we still don't know anything about the kids and of our mother—Oh, if only there are no hitches in this one matter, perhaps I'll be able to develop a little peace of mind.[117]

—Always loving you.

Ethel—

Emanuel H. Bloch
7 W. 16th Street
New York New York

June 7, 1951

Dear Manny,

You may well ask me why I am writing; I really don't know myself, except perhaps that I am in such a state of turmoil that using my pencil may help to calm me down some. Actually, I want very badly to continue discussing the problem I raised at our last consultation and am frustrated because I can't do so until I see you again. So I have to write to at least inform you I am still hot on its trail and have to exert terrific pressure on myself to keep in control until you do arrive.

All I ask is that you shall lay aside all those bromides with which both you and Julie saw fit to ply me until I was nearly driven to distraction, and let me give you the details to my complete satisfaction. Because, my good friend, believe me, if I cannot depend on redress from you, if I begin to despair of success in making myself understood to you on any score (this one in particular, of course, claims my [NWI] full attention at the moment) it will be most discouraging to say the least.

Manny, if you have any choice in the matter, please try to come Monday or Wednesday rather than Tuesday—Although you are most welcome any time you can manage to see us, we do greatly enjoy the Tuesday Jewish Services of which we were unfortunately deprived because we were engaged with you this past Tuesday.

Am on pins and needles on account of the children—As soon as there is any further word regarding their status, could you let us know quick? Received two beautiful snapshots of them from Bernie; am terribly torn between pride and heartbreak!

Don't be displeased with me—I couldn't bear it—

---

[117]This is the first reference to what was undoubtedly the plan to have us leave the Shelter and live with our paternal grandmother. Such a plan had to be approved by the New York City Department of Welfare. We were "discharged" from their custody later on in that month. See *Sons*, pp. 75–76, 246–47.

Never did get to thank you on Tuesday for getting that Court Order to Julie's folks [NWI] late last Thursday night so that they were able to see me, too—It was a very sweet thing to do, you know—

Best to your wife and Dad—and our other good friends—but urge them—please, please, to shake a leg—Can't seem to shake off the doldrums—hang it!

Love, Ethel—

Mrs. Ethel Goldberg
53-47 65th Place
Maspeth, Long Island N. Y.

June 9, 1951

My Dearest Sister,

Although it's a little late nevertheless I'm keeping in touch with all my loved ones and I'm sure you'll understand. This twilight of my existence allows me much time for thought and I try to fathom the whys of our predicament. It is important to note that social relationships are not governed by a mathematical formula but one can take the scientific method of investigation and with all the factors in a given situation arrive at the correct solution. It is obvious to all that a very tense and hysterical political climate exists in our country and there are forces at work that use the present emergency to establish a new order of life. Ergo everything now depends on a persons [sic] view particularly if he dares say anything that the powers that be do not politically espouse. When I was arrested and subsequently when I went to trial I told our lawyers it is very difficult to beat a case like this in an atmosphere fraught with war talk, witch hunts and frenzied super patriotic mouthings of 200 + % "Americans". In plain English the facts and laws of the land were thrown out the window and prejudice and emotion ruled. It is now our only salvation to fight all this and force the truth out [NWI] and couple it with an expert legal defense. We are positive of the one fact that we are not part of this conspiracy but only were victims of a political frame-up. Ours is a lot full of frustration and emotional torture [period omitted, "We" omitted] need all the help we can get to free us as quickly as possible from this terrible tomb. Your steadfast support and devotion has bolstered us a great deal particularly your kindness and love for our children. Know that in spite of our great hardships Ethel and I are strong and we'll continue to hold our heads high but to all of our family and friends I repeat please hurry and help us.

I hope I didn't give you the impression that I sit and mope all day for on the contrary I read books and newspapers, exercise in the yard, play chess and shoot the bull with the other inmates. Of course the high point of my week is the one hour visit with my lovely sweet wife. Then there is the weekly legal consultations [*sic*] with our attorney and also a possible visit from my family. Contact with the wonderful world we know is what we hunger for most. Since I read most of the newspapers I send the clippings to my wife. My boys have been made victims of this situation and only my family's efforts has eased some of the cruel pain inflicted on them. We are counting on you and you can count on us—All my love—Julius

Julius to Ethel

Saturday
June 9, 1951

My Dearest Ethel,

I've been impatiently awaiting your letter of the 6th and it finally arrived after my noon exercise period. Darling it is necessary for both our peace of minds that you tell me as frankly, as only you are capable of your innermost feelings, as in almost all cases they are the same that are torturing me and you by expressing them so plainly give me relief from my agony. Perhaps because of my makeup I don't show my emotions as readily as you do but I too run the gamut of joy and then frustration and heartache. Yes, you noticed my emotions when I saw the pictures of our two little treasures and you described my reaction to the "T" before it even took place. What do you say I have a clairvoyant wife besides all her other abilities. All kidding aside the fact remains we have grown together, know each other well and are able to fully understand each other. It is therefore incumbent on any part of our wonderful partnership to share with the other for better or worse. Since we are at the present low level we can look forward to better and promising things.

Our last visit was very satisfying to me as I got the feeling that I was able to get closer to you. I believe we made a lot of progress as you were able to bring me up to date on a most pressing problem and at least we can see eye to eye and eliminate this hardship as soon as possible. We don't ask much only to be treated as human beings and most of all we wish to be let alone. How lucky I am to have you as my wife as I sit across from you and realize that you [NWI] possess integrity of character, sensitivity of feeling, warmth of personality and sweetness of womanhood. If it is possible for one to get such nourishment being apart from you how much more fruitful will life be when we are together again. There is much in the future for us, our two dear children, ourselves and our wonderful way of life. We do have hope and we are confident and there can be only one answer our final freedom from this nightmare.

I go through the motions of living, eat, sleep, exercise and read a bit and I mark time until I see you again. Such powerful feelings, profound desires and deep thought all with the same thing in mind the big Why! of this frameup and the question when will it all be over. You my love are my strength and my understanding is the sobering force. Happy in our love, courage in the justice of our position we are confident of the ultimate future. Sweet, tender love to you my heart—Julius

P.S. Sent my sister Ethel a letter. Sunday a dull dreary day, lonesome and full of longing for you, think of you and keep on dreaming to keep my spirits up. I'm positive our thoughts are mutual on the subject. You're with me as often as I can pretend it. Impatient for our next visit—J

Ethel to Julius

Sunday
June 10, 1951

Julie dearest,

Another rainy Sunday—I have been buried away in my own drear thoughts for too long; so now let me seek solace in my always precious love. Sweetheart of mine, it's such a sweet comfort to me to know you are just across the hall; somehow it's easier to pretend I'm falling asleep in your arms with my head in its old familiar resting place on your shoulder.

All week I had been assaulted by such feelings of frustration and self-doubt as to render me virtually helpless in their grip. My mood of depression deepened as Dr. Miller's usual visiting hour came and went without his expected appearance. I had completely resigned myself to disappointment when word came that he had just arrived. At 3:18 P.M. he rushed in, all apologies, and at 3:30 P.M. he regretfully said good-bye. What a peach he is! When I expressed concern for his wasted time, he assured [NWI] me in the most whole-hearted way that he didn't mind in the least; you see, thus far he's only been able to make it every 2nd Saturday and since he realized if he missed seeing me this time I should be deprived of his company for rather a long while, and in the face of an unavoidable delay, he took his chances on a ridiculously short visit and possibly none at all, simply to demonstrate his continuing interest and affection. Indeed it made me feel wonderful to know such friendship was in my possession, but it also heightened the cloud of despondency that had been hanging over me. When should I ever have the opportunity to submit a complete report of my findings in an uninterrupted fashion—and begin to make some headway in ridding myself of the burden [NWI] with which I was saddled!—

Monday June 11, 1951

Woke up with a heavy head this morning after a night of battling several
very persistent mosquitoes. Still marking time until Manny's next visit;
have so much to tell him. Am feeling far less dejected, however, because
somehow I am confident things will work out. Darling boy, your letter
wasn't exactly hard to take either. My dearest dear, how much I wish to be
worthy of that woman you are always praising to the skies—Do you recall
what I said to your sister concerning her brother? Believe me, sweetie, I
meant every last word of it; all those qualities you ascribe to me you have
in full measure yourself. I long for the beautiful life we can make together
for ourselves and for our two bunnies; there are times my heart must surely
break with my tortured yearning for them. Yes, children, some day you will
learn [N2WI] in full on whose wicked, yet uneasy heads rests the responsibility for the outrage that was once perpetrated against your innocent
parents—Love you,
      My soul—
      Ethel

Julius to Ethel

                                                                    Tuesday
                                                              June 12, 1951
Hello Sweetheart

      Heard your sweet voice and intellegent [*sic*] offering at services today
and also received a lovely message from you. Of course you say those nice
things about me because there [*sic*] true. Ouch I hurt my hand patting
myself on the back. I don't want to urge you but it sure is nice to hear you
say all those wonderful things about your husband. In all sincerity we're
alright people, who practice what we believe and that is as the Rabbi put it
"Do unto others as you want them to do unto you"[.] Many people can have
different interpretations but to my way of looking at it it is not a theoretical
things [*sic*] but a living, dynamic and practical philosphy [*sic*] that when
put into effect signifies real brotherhood of man and human dignity. It is
amazing to me how intellectually stimulating Jewish services can be and
how worthwhile especially to us so incarcerated. Discussion and advocacy of
ideas is the mainstay of American life and of modern democratic principles.
This religious service set me thinking about the recent supreme court
decision and I can't help thinking what a blow to constitutional, political
and yes religious freedom this is because for all intents and purposes it

emasculates an inalienable right of freedom of speech.[118] Since our last visit I've come to realize more fully your problem and I feel that you should write Dr. Miller as much as you think you can put in a letter. Naturally some of the discussion must be had on a personal basis. This week Manny and I will discuss with you so that we can better be able to face the tribulations of the coming period. I'm anxious for an early conclusion of the pending court action so that we can know where we stand on visits from my family. Once they receive court permission we can get passes for periodic Sunday visits as that seems to be the most convient [sic]time.

The pictures of our two darlings keeps [sic] on flashing through my mind and it is apparant [sic] that not only are they innocent victims of this madness but we two are being deprived of our parental prerogatives of growing with our loved ones. Denial of family and freedom is tantamount to a living death and it is incumbent on us to continue striving to maintain our equilibrium in face of all this emotional pressure.

Without a doubt my sweet nightingale when I go to bed you're in my arms and we lock out the bars & the nightmares and find peace in each [N2WI] other & sleep. Only the morning rays of sunshine that rudely awaking [sic] me and announce my forced separation from the love of my life. Sweet beautiful girl I send you kisses and tenderly embrace you my precious. The storage bin of feeling for you is overflowing and only awaits you dear person. Take heart the future is wonderful—Love—Julius
P.S. That Dr. Miller is such a sweet guy I'm sorry I can't tell him so myself but he is what I call "Dignity of the individual"—Some more Hugs sugar—

Julius to Ethel

June 13, 1951
My Lovely and Most Precious Woman,
    At first I wanted to continue our discussion of the problem you raised but I think it best to put it off for our next private meeting. After long consideration I believe we can accomplish together a definite emotional advance if we thoroughly exhaust this matter and draw all the necessary lessons from this situation. It is my feeling that far from belaboring this point as principled forward looking people we must turn this temporary difficulty into an

---

[118]On June 4, 1951, the Supreme Court upheld the constitutionality of the Smith Act and thus the convictions of the top Communist party leaders. They had been charged with running an organization that advocated and/or taught the overthrow of the United States by force and violence. See Jay Walz, "High Court Upholds Guilt of 11 Top U.S. Communists; Other Prosecutions Are Set," *New York Times* (June 5, 1951): 1, 27.

advantage. Since we are limited in the time we have at our visits we should each of us come prepared with notes and ideas in order to better utilize the alloted [*sic*] time. A lot of ground was covered at our lst meeting and somehow there never is enough time. Incidentally I want to thank you for recommending Thomas Wolfe's book "You Can't Go Home" [*sic*] as it is very enjoyable reading. Methinks my darling that some extra avoirdupois is showing. So beware and take the necessary precautions as you still belong to me and I like you as you are. Perhaps I shouldn't be the one to talk the way I'm packing in ice cream, candy and cake and in spite of strenuous handball play my waistline is increasing. To me dearest you look wonderful. Good enough to pinch, squeeze, hug and of course love. You are pleasant to look at, sweet as sugar, marvelous to think about and the ultimate when we're together. It looks like you got me hooked cookie and I don't mind a bit. Sometimes I feel like singing, doing something creative as a warm glow overcomes me as my mind enumerates your charming virtues. It's wonderful to have such a jewel and the harder the frustration and pain the more glorious the joy and final reunion. Already, just a few points and a brief outline of our Circuit Court Appeal gives me new courage. Our principled integrated approach is the most important factor in our favor. There is no doubt about it that it is a tribute to us that we have stood up in such a mature and dignified way. Honey if one is able to withstand this terrible ordeal and then on top of it improve his character, then that person has accomplished the maximum under these circumstances. When I look at our childrens [*sic*] pictures I tell them they can be proud of their parents and when they can understand I am sure the'll [*sic*] hold their heads up high. Our spirit is good and our hopes for a successful termination of the appeal are based on solid ground. Our lives and the future of our family depends on this outcome and given an even chance under the laws of our land we must win. Adorable wife we're pulling hard but the reward is great. Keep it up—Your own Julius

Julius to Ethel

                                                                    June 17, 1951
Dearest Bunny Girl,

   Friday! It was glorious. Seeing my lovely woman and hanging on to every word of wisdom that uttered from her sweet lips. Sparkling, twinkling meaningful eyes that seemed to devour all they could encompass and lend color to your youthful pretty face. Agile mind always probing, deep in thought, precise in analysis and exacting in detail and no hasty decision and an outside observer who knows you can bank on your studied conclusions. Is it possible that such treasure can hide endless pain, profound emotional torture and deep agony? Through it all you convey to me a warm, glowing and tender love. How I hoped I could have been with you the moment my sister told you the splendid news about the children.[119] I heard your joyfull [sic] shout and it was sweet music to my ears. Honey we have passed another milestone and I'm positive this will ease that ache in your heart and soothe some of the pain of your motherhood. Over and over again my Mama wanted to see you and tell you all she will do to give our children all the love comfort and understanding and she is constantly hoping and praying for us to come home soon and take our rightful places as the parents. When I see you I'll try to recall all the details as she told them to me. She sends you a warm embrace and best wishes for a speedy homecoming.

Today is Fathers [sic] Day and I received quite a few cards from everybody and I'll bring them along to show you on Wednesday. Of course, let me take this opportunity my precious woman and congratulate you on our 12th wedding anniversary.[120] So vividly do I remember that lovely Sunday in June when you became my Mrs. Every minute of it through all situations we worked hard improved ourselves always building and we were happy. Is it not obvious love of my heart that life together has been very fruitful and in spite of even this miserable catastrophe hanging over our heads. We have the strength just because of our past and present relationship. Our living has always championed the dignity of the human being surrounded in culture and the security of family. This is another facet of our stamina and our two little dears help to further buttress our pleasure. Made of the kind of stuff that will not be stifled, built on a solid foundation and possessing character and forward looking ideas we are equipped to better stand up. You my dear have held the key to our growth and advancement and continue to be our bulwark. To you my wife, friend and fellow victim on this day of ours I send you my total love. We have practiced our way of life and we found it good and all that we've been through is our guarantee for a better future. No it must not and it will not come to pass. Truth and love must conquer—Yours—Julius

---

[119]This was the move from the Hebrew Children's Home to Sophie Rosenberg's new apartment.
[120]June 18

Ethel to Julius

June 18, 1951

My very dearest darling sweetheart,

Please forgive me for not having written you this week-end; your bad girl was too busy batting her brains out and wallowing in tears of self pity. And now I sit here feeling like a perfect hog and weeping all over again as I read your treasured words and know that there are none from me to comfort you for our separation on this the 12th anniversary of our first joyous coming to-gether. My sweetest husband, I was never so much in love with you as I am today, thrilling though it was to be embracing the duties and privileges (ahem) of wifehood at the comparatively tender age of 23, that lovely June day. Young and eager for life and love, we faced we knew not what turbulent future, confident, unafraid, serene.

It is incredible to me that after twelve years of the kind of principled, constructive, wholesome living to-gether that we did, that I should sit in a cell at Sing Sing awaiting my own legal murder, my heart crying out to you in bitter anguish by way of greeting you on what would have been a joyous celebration of two memorable days. Incredible to me, too, that you shall receive this message of felicitous congratulations as husband and father in another such cell, similarly carefully and grimly barred, in which you sit in anticipation of a similar doom! Bless you my own precious love, for that indomitable spirit that beats within you and gives me renewed courage and strength. Truly it is a godly spirit, forever thirsting for the knowledge that will set men free, forever reaching for the stars of truth and love, indestructible, invincible, unconquerable!

Darling, are you telling me your mother was here [NWI] too that day Ethel visited me; because she never mentioned it to me at all.

Honey, I am forced to cut this short. Mail is being collected and I want to lessen the disappointment you must surely have felt yesterday when no word arrived from me.

I love you with all my being and want desperately to be worthy of my sweet dear Julie—Always and forever—

Your own Ethel—

Julius to Ethel

June 20, 1951

My Sweet Lady Fair,

By the time you receive this letter, officially spring will be over. As all the poets put it the season of the year when a young man's fancy turns to love and as far as this old married man is concerned it only served to add fuel to my dammed up passion. This is all the more so because I have such a wonderful person [N2WI] as you as the object of my affections. My dearest one how I treasure the memories of many wonderful summers we spent together. Spring Glen 1939 it was glorious. Youth, vibrant romance, full of energy and flowing over with joy of life. We were able to capture the spirit of that part of our lives in the photos we saved from our honeymoon. You were pretty and sweet then and in many ways with added maturity you are prettier and lovlier than ever now. In spite of your temporary burial in this [NWI] tomb, it is impossible to hide your sparkle my jewel and you are more precious to me than ever before. Darling since I saw you this morning I've been feeling inspired intellectually and emotionally. You conveyed to me beyond any words by your actions and looks what deep feelings you felt for me and I hope I was able to in some small way get across to you my innermost emotions. Of course never can all this satisfy our real unity as man and wife except only when we are together again and far away from this mad situation. How much you have enhanced my life by presenting me with two dear boys and helping guide their young lives with understanding, motherly love and devoted care? Sometimes I feel tremendous power to just blow the mask of this nightmare away from our lives but I'm not under any illusions as I know we have to be as strong as iron to withstand an existance [*sic*] empty of all the beauties and freedom of civilized living. Tilt windmills, shout in the wind we don't have to do any of these things as the truth and justice is as powerful as natures [*sic*] bolt of lightning. Sooner or later it has to be known that we through our background and way of life to this day and especially since we are totally innocent of this ghastly political frameup.[121] Knowledge in the truth of our position, courage in ourselves, confident in the people helping us I am sure we can maintain our equilibrium. With our belief in the dignity of man and having a proven perspective we will never bend our knees to the usurpers of decency and democracy. Sweetheart we continue to fight & continue to be optimistic about the ultimate outcome.

All my love—your own Julius—Always worshipping you.

Ethel to Julius

June 21, 1951

My beloved husband,

I am so heart-sick, so grieved, so profoundly shocked and horrified by the unwarranted attack upon a legally constituted American political party that I must express my sense of loss and shame in some measure. Your head is bowed, my fair, bright land, the sun of liberty is blacked-out and your

---

[121]This sentence is as it appears in the original.

people are in mourning! The shadow of Fascism looms large and ominous, the Concentration Camps are being readied!! Oh, my brothers and sisters, how many of you will realize in what terrible danger you must now live your lives, how many of you will cry out in fear, "We are undone!", how many of you will rise in your collective wrath and right the wrong![122]

June 22, 1951 (a historic date!)[123]

Dearest, good morning. It was so sweet to see you Wednesday, so good to open my aching heart to you somewhat, my darling. Only, it's miserable to set there cozily talking and yet not to touch your hand or tenderly caress your face as I want to so much. What a second honeymoon we'll have, sweetheart, when this nightmare of an enforced separation is over. My own dear person, how I love you!

Lena will probably be too busy to write you about it and I don't know that Ethel has already done so or not; in any case, you will be overjoyed, as I was, to hear that she and your mother are moving ahead with dispatch and may, at this very writing already be settled in the new apartment. The beds were expected yesterday and they are packing feverishly. I am beside myself with expectancy; I can just imagine what a pile of things Manny must be struggling to get out from under!

Lover bunny, am forced to cut this short or you won't have it for the week-end. I'm afraid your bulwark (as you so fondly call me) is leaning far too heavily upon you, these days. You must remember that my personal problems make an already difficult situation a veritable hell for me; my skin just gets too tight for comfort. Be that as it may, we will yet win through

---

[122]This is in response to the arrest by the FBI of seventeen "second string" Communist Party leaders on June 20, two weeks after the Supreme Court had upheld the conviction of the top Communist Party leaders at the Smith Act trial in 1949. See David Caute, *The Great Fear* (New York: Simon and Schuster, 1978), pp. 187–95. Note the unwillingness to explicitly state that the Communist Party is the "legally constituted American political party" being mentioned. Note also, that the fear of concentration camps was not fanciful. The Internal Security Act of 1950 had incorporated a section which provided "for camps in times of national emergency, invasion or insurrection to detain without trial anyone who had been a member of the Communist Party since January 1, 1949." (Caute, p. 39). Indicative of the fear that this albeit oblique support for Communists' rights might have on the defense efforts is the fact that this section of this letter was omitted from the first edition of *Death House Letters* (see p. 45). After their deaths, the new 1954 edition did include the above passage. See *The Testament of Ethel and Julius Rosenberg* (New York, 1954), p. 38.
[123]The Nazi invasion of the Soviet Union, ten years earlier.

and return to our loved ones; our task is to find the strength to endure our suffering until that joyous day is at hand.

    I kiss you with all my heart and soul!

    Your loving wife—Ethel

Julius to Ethel

June 22, 1951[124]

My Dearest Ethel,

    Yes as all lovers of democracy I too, just as you, am aroused and incensed at the outrageous fascistic trend [N3WI] that is evident by the actions of the Justice Department. Since our arrest we have witnessed a pattern that parallels the history of the coming to power of Hitler and Mussolini. Isn't it now abundantly [NWI] clear that our own case was used by these demagogues to instill in the minds of the people [N2WI] the idea that members of a certain political philosophy indulge in spying. The constant and increasing stream of arrests, high bail, long prision [*sic*] terms and even death sentences are used to attune the American people to this state of affairs so that it should seem that these are "normal occurences." [*sic*] Besides this is utilizing a Nazi trick to brutilize [*sic*] the minds of the public. The Constitution of our country is the standard of Law that can not be changed except as provided by law. Only in this way can the citizens of our land be protected from autocratic acts of the politicians who rule the country. This tragedy of America is even a greater tragedy for us because we are at the mercy of the Justice Department, as the appeal to save our lives goes before the very Judges who have seen fit for political purposes to talk out of both sides of their faces at the same time, and find excuses to obliterate the first Ammendment [*sic*] of our Constitution. Let us hope that they don't succeed in establishing a fear paralysis and subsequent thought control over the people. If our appeal gets a fair and just hearing and is judged according to the Law we will get a reversal and in spite of the present indication and trend I continue to be confident and full of fight. In the tradition of the forefathers of these United States we are defending ourselves in a principled way in the manner we are answering the charges and [NWI] therefore take our place with our fellow men to stop this mad dash to do away with opposition, free speech and press. I have confidence that free men and women will rise up and answer this legal attack against their fundamental rights and restore the 1st Ammendament [*sic*] as the cardinal principle of our Law. As I said at our trial I am whole heartedly in favor of

---

[124]This letter was omitted from *Death House Letters* but included in the post-execution version, *The Testament* . . . See pp. 38–39.

Anglo Saxon Juris Prudence[125] and I hope that the Circuit Court is not swayed by the hysterical climate in our country and practices the law in the great tradition that has earned it the respect and admiration of civilized man. I have faith and our freedom will reaffirm this.

Love—Julius

Master Michael Allen Rosenberg
24-36 Laurel Hill Terrace
New York City N. Y.

June 24, 1951

My Dearest Darling Boy Michael,

Welcome to your own home son. Your mother and I told you not to worry as we'd do all in our power to see that you were well, comfortable and happy. Now that all arrangements have been completed you and Robert will have a nice big room, your own beds, all your old toys and of course your sweet Bubbie Sophie and a nice lady to help take care of you.[126] We your parents still can't come home as our appeal to the higher courts has not as yet been heard. Be patient honey as every thing will turn out alright and we'll come home too, when all this is over. I see your mommy regularly and we talk about you two fellows. We look at your pictures and hug and kiss you with all our hearts. You are very dear and precious to us and I send you all my love. We'd like to hear from you as to all the things you do, see and hear. You write so well and it gives us so much pleasure to hear from you. Oh by the way thank you for the lovely Fathers [*sic*] Day and Anniversary cards you sent me. Imagine you are becoming a poet taking after your wonderful mother. Well there is the erector set and many things you can build. I remember the fun we had with the cranes and boom derricks and how we used it with the tracks, trains and blocks. It's fun to play and build so lets hear about it. How is my baseball champ getting on? Did you have a chance to go swimming? Summer is here and you'll have a chance to go places on trips and see many new things and I've been told you'll always have people near you who understand and love you and I'm positive you are going to make new friends and have many good times.

Hello Robbie boy. I've already been told by my lawyer that both you fellows were very happy when you heard the good news. From your picture I can tell you're growing up to be a big fellow like your brother. Yes sweetheart play, enjoy yourself and have fun. Your mother and I are always looking out for you and we send all our love to you.

---

[125]See Record, p. 1078–79.

[126]For a description of the apartment see *Sons*, p. 77.

By the way Mike send our love and best wishes to your Grandma
Sophie and the nice lady and tell them I'm sure that everything will work
out alright because we are all working together, from the heart and we are
doing a wonderful thing for all of us.

We are well and glad to hear such good news about you. We will be home
you can bet on that—   Your own Daddy Julius

Julius to Ethel

June 24, 1951

Sweetheart

In your presence my love I was so relaxed and calm. See we are making
terriffic [*sic*] progress against pressing problems. Both of us understand and
know that the important thing is that you should be thoroughly understood
and give complete support for your just needs. It would help immensely if
circumstances work for your benefit for a change. Your comfort and well
being is paramount and these have to take precedence over other considerations in view of this miserable regimentation. You are a peacheroo and I
adore you.

Somehow I get this feeling that all will work out well with my mother
and I am not too concerned about the situation. The thing that sticks in my
mind is that she said that the lady is a very nice, warm and good women
[*sic*] and that she likes her and is sure that they'll get along nicely. I'm
actually thrilled about all this and I can't wait to hear how the kids have
begun to take to their own home. This will give us our opportunity to have
a hand in the upbringing of our two dears. I hope I'll be able to establish a
running correspondence with Michael so that we'll be able even though in a
remote way, to live through some of their joys. Oh my poor darlings how
you need your parents who are heartbroken over your innocent plight. At the
same time that ours [*sic*] hearts beat in mutual pain I am sure that wonderful
help we are getting gives us a great deal of strength.

Honey, you know that our consultations and the manner in which we
take up our problems and appeal reminds me of the way you and I used to
discuss our plans and that was the time we found such comfort and satisfaction in working things out. It is true that the present situation deals with
our very lives and the successes we've had in the past have prepared us for
this supreme test. Our background and experiences have given us an opportunity to evaluate ourselves and what we've seen and know we have confidence in each other and the American people. We have shown we have the
courage to face all that is before us. Based on these facts we have the perspective of a successful end to this frame up and a fuller richer life on a
higher plane. Just keep telling me with your pencil, your eyes, your smile

and your voice what you have in the past and our team must win. Of course I'm head over heals [*sic*] in love with you and for the time being I can only smile and convey my heart to you in this manner. I embrace you my sweet girl love.
     Julius
P.S. Sent the dears a letter. Welcome, love and reassurance. Love JR.

Ethel to Julius
                                                  June 24, 1951
Dearest darling,
     How is it, my sweet, you always share my own deep feelings; but what a foolish question when the answer is so obvious. There isn't a sufficient quantity of concrete and brick and steel in the entire world to bury our love or prevent its always increasingly noble development and growth. I could have whooped with delight after our last attorney consultation for the very reason you set forth with such gratifying clarity in your latest writing. My loved one, my heart is filled with a glad peace and an exultant pride in the kind of insight & understanding you continue to display, where I am concerned.
     Elated as I was however that I had been able to accomplish something on my own toward a solution of a pressing problem, and gratifying as it had been to share my experience with you and Manny so fully, the entire incident weighed heavily upon me. As a matter of fact, I went to bed feeling ill and awoke Sunday morning with a miserable headache and a sick stomach. As the day wore on and the pain and nausea grew worse I finally summoned the courage to force myself to vomit, after which I was able to fall asleep for an hour and feel a little more like myself again. The evening meal found me ravenous, (Terry had been kind enough to save my steak dinner for me, upon my request) and by Monday my digestive tract was functioning as per usual and I was in a generally calmer state.
     What then was my surprise to learn that Bernie was on his way down to see me right after lunch. The butterflies began fluttering again but they didn't get out of hand, this time, and the visit went off without a hitch. As you may well imagine, I shall have plenty to relate to you Wednesday morning. Oh, my heart, how terribly I miss the untold sweetness of the physical relationship that was ours; how [NWI] painfully I long for the release and forgetfulness of your arms about me and your dear body embracing my own. I love you, darling, and will need your [NWI] constant encouragement and support as time goes on and I [N6WI] continue to be called upon to wrestle with all kinds of personal difficulties. You'll be with me,

won't you, Sweetheart? Oh, heck, my eyes are filling again for a change, but I can't help it, I'm so lonely and blue.

Honey, I shall never get over marvelling at Manny. It is to him we owe our thanks for the accomplished fact of the children's new lease on life. He is the dearest person and I love him with all my heart—

As I do you, dear—   Kisses—Ethel

Mrs. Ethel Goldberg
5347—65th Place
Maspeth Long Island

June 26, 1951

Dearest Ethel,

At last I am getting around to answering the delightful letter I last received from you clearing up the mystery of the "Fingerprinting and the Matron" (to give it a proper title), relating your experience with the friendly old codger, (about whom, incidentally, Lena never had the chance to tell me) and giving Michael an opportunity to drop me a few lines on his own. It was all most enjoyable, including his spelling of "Mutiner on the Bounty"—Don't you dare correct him for it either; I loved it just as it was! You understand!

You silly girl, of course there was no way of my knowing that Mama had gone along with you and was outside visiting with Julie. I was of course pleased as punch to hear from him to that effect. It was comical, though, while it was happening; neither of us knew what the other was bothering about! Kindly disregard what I was trying without success to get across to you. It was really comparatively unimportant and something that has already straightened itself out.

On Saturday, Manny Bloch arrived with the glad news concerning the children. Yesterday a letter came from Mrs. Epstein describing their preparatory visit to the apartment and notifying me that they would be released early this week; and today I have Lena's word that their release is an accomplished fact and they are now residing in their own home! I wish with all my heart that their parents could say the same; until that anxiously awaited day, however, my everlastingly grateful thanks to all of you who have had a share in causing this wonderful event to finally take place; I am humble before your steadfast loyalty and unchanging loving devotion! Life seems so strange, so unfathomable sometimes. Certainly we all needed this fearsome experience like a hole in the head. and [sic] yet, for all that we have lost—in terms of compassion, growth and understanding, we have all gained immeasurably. There isn't a one of us who has become involved in this phantastic [sic] nightmare, through one means or another, who has not been lifted out of his own small self and been found equal to the terrible test. There isn't a one of us whose actions have not proven that the divine spark which sets the human creature apart from all the other beasts, can never [NWI] really be extinguished!

Thus it is that I look out upon the future with serene eyes, firm in the belief that our cause is a just one and secure in the knowledge that all decent humanity must eventually rise to our defense—Love you all—Am feeling great! Ethel

Emanuel H. Bloch
7 W. 16th Street
New York New York

June 27, 1951

Dearest Manny,

Affectionate little thing, aren't I! Well, you said yourself that I had progressed by leaps and bounds, so I can't very well make a liar out of you, now can I! Because whether you realize it or not, that salutation, which is only a symbol of the actual relationship that exists between us, is an good an indication as any I know, of said progress. Just a short year ago, I should as soon have thought of taking it for granted that anyone like you would welcome or even merely entertain such an expression, as I should have thought of attempting a trip to the moon. It would have seemed just as daring and [NWI] as unattainable!

The step I took toward a solution of the problem I had been discussing with you week in, week out, appears [NWI] even at this early moment, to have been a correct one; that I shall prove capable of consolidating the victory, of course, still remains to be seen. Yet am I certain of one thing and it is something that will gratify you every bit as much as it does me; I am a generous victor. Would that every vanquished nation could say the same for its occupying armies! Obviously the tension has lessened, but it does take two to make a bargain and I'm under no illusions that every thing will automatically be smooth sailing from here on in.

Oh, incidentally, the warden and I had a most satisfactory chat early Tuesday morning. I was very favorably impressed with his evident warmth, geniality, and sincere desire to understand the situation; I am hoping he was as cognizant of my own good intentions.

Manny, will you do me a favor and telephone Dr. Miller and Lena Cohen, concerning this Saturday's possible visit of one or both of them. You see, Dr. Miller did not get here last Saturday and may possibly be planning to do so June 30 instead of July 7, as per his usual arrangement with me for every other Saturday. Into this bargain, Lee has written both

Julie and me, expressing the hope of seeing us this Saturday. I should hate
for either of them to be denied their proper time [N2WI] with me. So do not
fail to check with both of them as to their final plans. If Dr. Miller can
manage it as easily for July 7th, (I have already written him to that effect
but still do not know what's what, as I've had no word, yet) I'll be glad to
see Lee instead of him on June 30th. However, his convenience has to take
precedence; am counting on you to give out with that famous Bloch pen-
chant for charm and tact, if you find it necessary.

It's no use; your wife will simply have to understand that I'm badly
smitten and share you with me for the duration! Best to everybody, especially that other charmer—your Pop—   Ethel

Ethel to Julius

                                                          June 27, 1951
My own dearest, darlingest one,

How much I've missed you since you came to see your monkey in the
cage on Wednesday. My sweetheart, I am simply beside myself, after you go
home, with the mixed emotions the sweetly disturbing immensely attractive
presence of you invariably arouses in me, and which must of necessity be
denied their most exquisitely consummate expression. Every last nerve sets
up a piteous clamor in its imperative need to make itself heard, the blood
sings with a tumultous [*sic*] pounding along my veins, and I am helpless
before the onslaught of a fierce and imperious hunger.

Darling, this last visit was particularly distressing due to the [NWI]
mutual agitation engendered by the painful subject we were forced to [N2WI]
attempt to analyze. I am so terribly so achingly regretful for the wound you
are suffering through my seeming inability to render the sting of a certain
group of poisonous snakes of my sorry acquaintance powerless against
me.[127] Love of my heart, in [NWI] all humility, I ask your forgiveness;
["and" CO] I solemnly promise you that I shall take the necessary steps to

---

[127]An obvious reference to the Greenglass family. In an interview in 1974, her
psychiatrist asserted that ". . . the root of the problem was her relationship with
her immediate family. She felt she was 'Looked down upon' by her mother and
brothers. Her mother had always dominated the family and treated her brothers as
the consequential human beings. [She] never felt her own mother really loved
her." (*Sons*, p. 38) With the total support of the Greenglass family for David and
Ruth before and during the trial (see the letter above from Sam Greenglass, her
oldest brother), one can imagine that the long-standing problem identified by
the psychiatrist was compounded in a most extreme way. Only her brother
Bernard continued to visit her regularly, and the most recent visit must have
caused the need to discuss "the painful subject" mentioned in the letter.

break loose [N3WI] once for all from the emotional trap that has held me a
prisoner, far more than the bars behind which I have been living some
eleven months [NWI] now ever bars!

Bunny, your letters continue to be a source of tremendous inspiration
and comfort to me; and although you are not there to see my reaction, I
want with all my heart and soul for you to know that your words are your
tender arms about me and your tender lips on mine—

Sorry—Mail call—

Love, Ethel—

Mrs. Ethel Goldberg
53-47 65th Place
Maspeth L.I. N. Y.

June 28, 1951

My Dear Sweet Sister Ethel,

Today I arose unusually early and dashed off a letter to my wonderful
wife before breakfast. Thursday is my special cleaning day. After my
morning yard period I get me a bucket of hot soapy water and a scrubbing
brush. My books and wordly [*sic*] possessions are stacked on my bed and
my weekly ritual begins. First my table is scoured clean, then the bars and
my sink are washed and I get down on hands and knees and scrub the floor
drying and finishing it with hand rags. The soapy water is dumped in the
flushometer and I thoroughly clean the bowl. Not only is cleanliness a
physical necessity but it gives one satisfaction and a sense of well being.
The only other work I do is wash my personal laundry. These activities
consume very little time. One hour each day is spent in the yard about one
and half hours are taken eating and the rest of the time is free. I do a lot of
reading resting and some writting [*sic*]. Many of the books I read at Junior
and High School I'm rereading and finding additional spiritual and emotional
stimulation. Sometimes I go at it hammer and tongs and complete a book
in a day or on other occasions it takes me the better part of a week to finish
one. Two hours each afternoon I spent [*sic*] reading newspapers. The only
time I am removed, at least mentally from this drab existence is when I have
a visit. This is my routine and it affords me a great deal of time to examine
my life and principles to the present. When one is facing death as is my
situation all issues become clear and things resolve to their fundamental.

As early as I can remember I was always studying, seeking and striving
to find the answers. The unit of the whole is man and his relation to fellow
men and his contribution and creativeness is an expression of his growth,
maturity, joy and happiness. This search/struggle against forces of nature
and man not only is creative in itself but affords one the true dignity of the

individual and allows him the opportunity to progress to higher levels. At the present stage of world development mankind possess [*sic*] the means scientific, philosophic for a better richer and freer life and only social and political forces have to be orientated to attain this precious goal. In my wife I have found all these wonderful elements of character, understanding and warmth and together with her in our mutual strivings we have grown culturally & emotionally and find this is the key to our happiness. We hold our heads up and are confident of ourselves. Our faith in the people shall not be denied. We want to get back in the life stream of our world and get the necessary sustenance to continue growing. Believe me I can go on and on but enough for now. I'll send Lee a letter today exchange [*sic*] letters with her. Send my regards to all your family. loads of love—Julius

Ethel to Julius

June 30, 1951

Dearest love of mine, sweetheart, darling,

The intolerable loneliness of this place seems to [NWI] have filtered into my very bones today; the abundant gloom and rain with which the elements have seen fit to further afflict us have contrived to drag out the already interminable hours unmercifully, making them well nigh unendurable. And yet, lest I appear discouraged, my confidence shaken, let those who would destroy me and mine disabuse their gross stupidity, their undiscerning minds; endure it I shall, heart and head held high, spirit unimpaired and still seeking, still soaring. For I am made of the stuff of the early pioneers and in my veins beats the blood of the Macabees! [*sic*] And this incalculably rich heritage that is my [NWI] dearly cherished possession shall at long [NWI] last beat you to your knees. Submit I shall not, for I am an American, & thereby am I proud as proud as [NWI] that flag of mine which you have defiled and dragged in the dust, to the everlasting shame of my Native land! With all the power that lies within me to love liberty and hate oppression, I shall defy the amalgam of evil which you represent and with my last breath cry,

"Down with all tyrants! Hail Freedom!"

There, now I feel better! No Pasaran!

Honey dear, I adore you for the extravagant beauty of the feelings which animate you and give rise to such compelling verbal love-making. How I wish I might shower upon you all that wealth of emotion that stirs to [NWI] such glowing life within me as I read. With what womanly fire and tenderness I should caress you and give you delight, and we should share once again the frenzied ecstacy [*sic*] and joy of marital love. (Darling, tell me, are you still concerned about my [The next word ends in "eak" but the first letter is unclear.]). [Paragraph sign inserted here] If anything, I am now capable of a far deeper understanding and maturity of feeling than I have hitherto possessed; as you have yourself so masterfully interpreted our relationship and our tremendous potentialities for growth and development, the realization of which we are each [NWI] miraculously bringing to pass even under these perilous and abnormal circumstances, I am impatient of all delay and eager to participate in the far richer opportunities that await us for fine, untrammeled living. Sweetheart, [NWI] when will you marry me and release me from this dungeon? This engagement is lasting [NWI] far too long for my tastes!

Dearest, Daddy, your son Michael sent me a most precious letter, informing me that both he and Robby are expected to attend Day Camp beginning to-morrow and describing a visit to the apartment by Ethel, Seymour and Sharon. I am so thrilled by the apparent progress that is being made, I could weep with thanksgiving. At the same time, my appetite is being whetted to such a degree that I could also scream with frustration—Love you my very dearest

Ever yours, Ethel—

Julius to Ethel

July 1, 1951

My Sweetest Wife,

Before I go any further I want one thing understood[.] You are not to admonish yourself or have any guilt feelings because you act and react emotionally as your person dictates. You should know by this time that it is most important that you dont [*sic*] negate your innermost feelings and this is especially so because you have just cause and it is a necessary process for you. I kept kicking myself and feeling bad that I did not take an objective approach to this problem and let my passions run away with me. Believe me you have done exceeding [*sic*] well and I am more than satisfied at the pace you're going[.] I'll be patient I promise until you can honestly and sincerely arrive at the point that there is a complete unity between your conscience and your emotional makeup and then you will really be master of yourself. It is because I too have experienced similar contradictions that I can comprehend the true status of your entire psychological makeup. By this I mean not all it's [*sic*] detailed ramifications but the scope of it, so that each part can be judge [*sic*] in it's [*sic*] proper perspective. What do you think! I'm begining [*sic*] to sound like an analyst tch! tch!

Listen adorable monkey this ape of yours is dying to get a strangle hold on his woman because as you can guess he's nuts about her. I've been hoping we'd see our lawyer this week or at the least get a visit and I'm a little disappointed. Michael sent me an adorable letter I can't wait to let you see it. My sister Ethel sent me a meghilla [*sic*] and I'll read it to you at our next visit. My wonderful honey bun when I read your tender words I can't wait to be near you and look in your lovely face and tell you to your understanding eyes how much you mean to me and here and now I resolve we spend more time at our Wednesday tete a tete on more pleasant things. Although your words are always an inspiration to me and they move me deeply I also like to hear and see from you through these additional senses our boundless love. Let us, love of my life use the limited means [N2WI] we possess to convey to each other our unity. The news of the possibilities of peace are of tremendous import.[128] We together with the world's millions have a great stake in there [*sic*] successful outcome. Hope springs eternal and I am very confident of the future. I do feel so lonely without you but the thought of you dispells [*sic*] even that. Precious woman accept my embrace and kisses—   Forever your own—Julius

Ethel to Julius

                                                         July 2, 1951
Dearest Julie,
   How black my world has gone. Tears blind me as I write, nor have I been able to staunch their flow, ever since I learned of the untimely passing of the dearest friend I owned inside these walls. At six o'clock this evening the news came that Mrs. Bessie Irving had died suddenly of a cerebral hemorrhage. Darling I am so overwhelmed with shock and grief, that my personal problems, my sentence, everything, has paled into complete insignificance. My dearest, sweetest lady, how shall I ever go on without you!
   Oh, but this is a bitter blow, how bitter I shall only [NWI] begin to understand as I go on living through the torturous days which stretch endlessly ahead of me, without her. She it was with whom I shared my every joy, my every sorrow; the sheer goodness of her shone like a beacon through my darkness, and her love kept me warm and safe from harm. Indeed, she had an incomparable talent for loving, than which there is no greater in this world, and all those who were fortunate enough to come within the circle of her influence were immeasurably richer for it.
   Last night she smiled that lovely, unassuming gracious smile of hers for me, as we said our affectionate good-nights; with what happiness I looked forward to seeing her again! Now it's all over, all over except for the

---

[128]Reference to the Korean War peace talks set to begin July 10 in Panmunjom on the border between North and South Korea.

anguish of my bereavement. Honey, I'm so terribly in need of comfort, I don't know what to do with myself, nor where to turn.

I will have to wait until Wednesday morning to take up things that got left unsaid when Manny and his Dad were here. Right now, the sun has set and I am frightened and alone and lost in a world that is bleak and empty and strange! Warm-hearted mother & loyal friend, I loved you so very much!

It's no use—I can't say a word about anything or anyone else—Am absolutely heart-broken—   Ethel

Mr Emanuel Bloch
297 Broadway
New York N. Y.

July 4, 1951

Dear Manny,

I would appreciate it very much if you would make your regular visit this coming Monday July 9th as I have some important matters I'd like to talk to you about.

At my last meeting with Ethel she was feeling kind of low because one of her matrons passed away and she feels the loss very deeply. They had established a harmonious relation of mutual trust and understanding and what more can one treasure than real decency, humane feeling and true dignity in human relationships[.]

My sister Lena was up to see me and had quite a bit of trouble getting in to visit us as she came on a holiday without a pass. Try to see to it that my folks establish, on a regular basis, periodic visits to us. It is preferable that they come one at a time because if two come at once they are not allowed to separate but have to see each of us to-gether. If you are able to standardize your visits to us on one particular day we would then expect you and prepare our notes accordingly. I realize your [*sic*] busy preparing the appeal but we need so to be part of our defense for in this way we satisfy our personal social need. From all that I can gather about my children they are in need of a great deal of help and I ask that you see to it that trained professional people are available.

I've been thinking about the need to have some degree of privacy during our consultations as is granted us by law. Perhaps you can come up with some suggestion on this matter.[129]

---

[129]In fact, the FBI regularly received reports detailing what went on during family visits and visits with counsel. It is unclear whether this was from electronic surveillance or merely as a result of guards overhearing conversations

It is almost a year now that the Justice department began forging the phony spy frameup as a major link in the reactionary drive against the constitutional and democratic rights of the American people. To a great degree they have succeeded to frighten outspoken liberals and progressives. We saw this coming and recognized it as an organized campaign of hysteria and we have faith in the American people that they will not allow these attacks on their inalienable rights to go unanswered. This faith in the people coupled with the knowledge of the correctness of our position gives us confidence and strength to stand up proud against all this horrible pressure. Above all else a progressive perspective for a better and fuller life has been the source of our stamina. We have just cause to feel optimistic but only redoubling of efforts on all our parts will assure us our independence. July 4th is a good day to reaffirm in every way the glories of independence. Send my best to your father and wife.

Yours Julius

Julius to Ethel

July 4, 1951

My Sweetest Precious Girl,

Fortified by Ossining Manors [*sic*] delicious ice cream on the occasion of Independence [NWI] Day my thoughts naturally go to this memorable holiday of freedom in our country. I clipped out a copy of of [*sic*] the Delaration [*sic*] of Independence that appeared in the New York Times. It should be read and studied especially the history surrounding it. The greatness of our country is the heritage of liberty derived from the sacred words of free speech, press and religion. These rights that the forefathers and patriots of our country have fought, bled and died for cannot even by Congress or the courts be taken away from the people. It is a source of encouragement to me that in this spirit and the justice of our position we are fighting for our freedom. Certain politicians have used our case as a wedge to scare liberal and progressive people but we'll continue to expose this black frameup and in this effort we arc not alone. At present this is a fight for our very lives but it is also part of the fight for justice and free thought.

I sent Manny a letter asking him to be here this coming Monday as I want to take up some important matters with him. Concerning the visits I asked him to try to arrange a periodic visit for our family and recommended individual visits as two people will not be allowed to split and visit us separately and then shift. Perhaps we ought to have Manny take this up

---

and reporting them. See *Sons,* pp. 419 and 424 for two examples quoting FBI reports JR HQ 1258, February 29, 1952 and JR HQ 1185, November 19, 1951.

with the Warden, although it would be better for us to get these additional visits.

Of course, I was delighted and pleasantly surprised to see Lee. She is such a honey and I'm happy she was very frank when she told me about the kids. Darling I asked our good friend and lawyer to see to it that professional people are available to help our dears. They are terribly disturbed. I have no doubt that in a little time the loving care of my mother and the warm attention of our family and good friends, will go a long way to alleviate their tensions but I still want to make certain that a conscious and determined watch is kept on their emotional well being. Let us get in the swing of things and lend a hand to straighten out our sweet children. They have been terribly shocked and wronged and they need us. We've got to have the strength and do our best more so for their sake. How I miss and love them with all my heart.

Your letter was from the heart. Such sorrow can only mean the relationship you had was fruitful and creative. You can take solace in the fact that you had her confidence and best wishes. Where truth and decency rule true self satisfaction is possible. Ah my darling! we must continue to strive hope and fight for what is ours—All my love—Julius

Ethel to Julius

July 5, 1951

My heart's sweetest dear,

How impatiently I awaited your arrival yesterday; by the time you actually entered and seated yourself opposite me, I could scarcely contain the anguish that had been stabbing through me since I had first learned of Bessie Irving's death on Monday. Through the opportunity that our visit presented, I was enabled to give vent to some of my grief, so that by the time you took your leave I was inclined to be somewhat calmer, somewhat consoled.

Seeing Lee, however, while I was overjoyed at the unexpected piece of good fortune her visit constituted, gave me renewed cause for pain. Darling, I am so pleased with your reaction as you describe it in your [N4WI] letter of the 4th, concerning the emotional well-being of the children, that I am greatly heartened. As you must by now have realized, it was the picture that Lena painted of them that so distressed and alarmed me. At least we are absolutely in accord about our poor dears; oh, sweetheart, I lay on my bed later weeping bitterly for their despoiled young lives and wanting desperately to be home with them and you!

6:30 A.M. July 6, 1951.

Good morning, bunny dear; am up early so that my dearest sweetheart will not be deprived of the usual scribble from his best girl.

To continue with the story of my July 4 celebration, evening found me struggling for some kind of emotional balance. I was drinking deeply from the Cup of Sorrow when the State ice-cream arrived and I dug into it with a vengeance. Occasionally I choked up thinking of the ice-cream orgies we used to enjoy with the kids (I recalled "Cherry-Oonilla" [N2WI] to begin incidentally, when I wrote Robby), but I managed to plough through most of it. Next I forced myself to begin a letter to Dr. Miller; in a while, the burden lightened and some of the panic that had been gripping me eased. It needed only the finishing touch of a [NWI] radio program entitled "Ballad for Americans," during which [N2WI] I heard the [NWI] recorded rendition of this immortal masterpiece by Bing Crosby[130] and also Frank Sinatra's recording of "House I Live In"[131] to inspire a tremendous response of "courage, confidence and perspective"! No, we Americans just don't scare easy!

Julie dear, I have such utter respect and regard for you; how well you know the score and what a wonderful example you set me! My beloved husband, hold me close to you and impart to me some of your own noble spirit! Many kisses—

Always lovingly, Ethel—

---

[130]The first recording of the cantata *Ballad for Americans* which was written by Earl Robinson and John La Touche (both later to be blacklisted) was made by Paul Robeson in the 1930s. By the early 1950s, Paul Robeson had been so completely blacklisted that even the records of his previous artistic achievements were being eliminated. See Martin Bauml Duberman, *Paul Robeson* (NY: Alfred A. Knopf, 1989), pp. 381–428. Our mother surely knew of the politics of the writers of the cantata as well as Robeson's role in recording it. Thus, the joy of hearing the program must have been tempered by the knowledge that she could not have heard Robeson's version over the radio in 1951.

[131]Earl Robinson collaborated on "The House I Live In" with Lewis Allan, whose non-professional name was Abel Meeropol, later to become our adoptive father. Since Abel had also written "Strange Fruit," the very strong anti-lynching song, I believe my mother also knew that "progressives" had written "The House I Live In." It is rather ironic that at the height of the Cold War, with war raging in Korea, the cultural products of American leftists were still being utilized for their positive contributions to what was (and still is) good in America even while the individuals who had produced such works were being blacklisted and/or harassed by investigative committees.

Julius to Ethel

July 8, 1951

My Dearest Sweetest Honey,

All week long I've been procrastinating and lazying around and now it's Sunday morning and there is lots of writting [*sic*] to do to my charming wife, her lovely children and if my pencil arm holds out to my family. With the increasing heat, the mosquitos and especially a terrible lonesomeness my sleeping has been intermitent, [*sic*] tiresome and tortuous. How difficult it is to be forcefully separated from the wonderfull [*sic*] company of an adorable loving woman who is so stimulating emotionally, mentally and physically? My mind goes back to the leisure [*sic*] Sunday mornings we spent together with our children. By now it seems so far away but the beauty of it all lingers. Life has such deep meaning when we can see in retrospect how relaxed and natural our family lived and yet it probed deeper all the time into newer and richer experiences always striving and developing character and person. What joy to analize [*sic*] a problem, such as some that we faced in the growth of our two dears, plan it's [*sic*] solution and participate in it's [*sic*] fruition. The creative urge must be mutual and fed like a new born babe so that it can burst forth regardless of the many hurdles of every day living it must overcome. That is the reason we need so to be with our kids because we understand the fragile nature of their emotional security and we know we can help them and allow them to release the tremendous latent potentialities that they have. The foundation of all life is the family and the basis laid in this relationship serves as the governing factor in the individual and his position in society. It has always been my contention that solving the three basic needs of man food, clothing and shelter and [NWI] being part of a social society politically organized for the physical and emotional security of its members man's accomplishments scientifically, medically and intellectually know no bounds because his creative ability is as limitless as the depths of the universe he lives in. Philosophizing this way removes me at once from the confines of this wickedness and out of the reach of those puny self seekers who would doom me and my kind. Far from being an escapist I am alive to the reality of the world and the trap I'm in. Yes I suffer, pain, hunger, agony and frustrations to the same degree that I can love and drink in the fruits of happiness. Just because of our background we have the courage the confidence and the perspective. No matter how many times I repeat this to us it has special meaning. Our unity is the strength. Together we will reach higher planes and derive greater satisfaction—I am always discovering new things and more and more I love you with all my heart—Your own Julius.

Emanuel H. Bloch
7 W. 16th Street
New York New York

July 9, 1951

Dear Manny,

As per usual, there were a few things I might have discussed with you today that I didn't, to wit: (You aren't kidding; I'll be a lawyer, yet, before this is over!)

1) Re Dr. Miller's still undetermined interview with the children, he may not think it advisable from the point of view of me, his patient, to visit the children in their present surroundings unless you both decide on some feasible method of his introduction to them and my mother-in-law, I believe he'll understand what I'm driving at. For that matter, he may feel it a less personal and [NWI] therefore more desirable way of visiting with them either in his own office or at the office of the Jewish Board of Guardians. Anyway he thinks it should be done, if he feels contact with the [letter CO] children is necessary to begin with, is OK. with me. My own preference [NWI] however, is [N4WI] 1. for an interview Somewhere [*sic*] away from [NWI] the apt.

2) Tell him, also, I was too self-conscious [inserted word erased] to explain [N3WI] to you, myself what is at the bottom of my reluctance to see the children just yet, but that I should be most happy to have him give you the details.

3) Just to remind you to phone Miss Schidell[132] at the JBG to request her making contact ["with" CO] and establishing a regular rapport with Dr. Miller about the kids—

4) Re Robby's attendance at day camp—You may encounter difficulty unless they let the woman stay with Robby the first couple of days, at least, during the lunch hour, too. Perhaps suggesting that the woman is there to help out with the servicing [*sic*] (or some similar small duty that she won't mind, of course) will help Robby get used ["to" omitted] an entirely new group of children other than the one he had been accustomed to eating with [NWI] for so long [N4WI] at the Hebrew House—Even if it means a week [N4WI, followed by a CO letter or two] or even 10 days of patient encouragement and gentle, gradual diminishing of the amount of time she remains with him, it will pay off so well in the long run that I feel every possible effort should be made to [word CO] bring about the child's adjustment and subsequent regular attendance

[Between this paragraph and the next, there is a line full of dashes.]

---

[132] A social worker I began seeing while living with my grandmother but with whom I had also had contact while seeing Mrs. Phillips.

Manny dear, I don't think we ever thank you enough for every thing—
so my [NWI] heartfelt thanks (& Julie's too, I'm sure) to you now! Looks
like I'm beginning to function again, hey?
            Love you—
            Ethel

Ethel to Julius

                                                              July 11, 1951
My dearest, sweetest, most wonderful husband,
    Your charming wife, as you so generously describe her, simply has to
take time out from the difficult writing chore she has set herself for the good
of her soul, to tell you how delighted she was to receive your most precious
letter. It served to further enhance a day already made bright and happy by
your dear presence in the morning. I was never more deeply in love with
you nor more [NWI] truly cognizant of your increasingly high level of
maturity and understanding! Sweet-heart, aren't you ever going to ask me to
marry you?
    How often I find myself pretending that freedom is ours, at least until a
new trial date is set, and that we are once again a going concern, putting
into daily practice all of those beliefs and feelings about which we are for
the present, only permitted to theorize! Darling, never forget that no matter
how discouraged I may appear, on occasion, the flame of truth that burns so
steadfastly within me can never really be extinguished; nor can either of us
ever disavow all the wondrous beauties our richly creative, socially conscious lives [NWI] have revealed to us. Darling, your writing is so satis-
fyingly conclusive on this very score, that I am lifted out of my own small
self and given inspiration and incentive. Dearest one, it certainly redounds to
the credit of our relationship and is, indeed, a true measure of its intrinsic
worth, that we continue to speak the same fair language we always did, and
that the development of our respective personalities proceeds unaborted,
serving to increase the enjoyment of each of us, as in the same instant both
personalities blend to promote that limitless mutual joy and harmony that is
the epitome of a sound marriage. It is this whole-hearted sharing that
enables us to successfully come to grips with the problems that confront us
today; by the same token, our separation is all the more heart-breakingly
painful!
    Bunny dear, I feel somewhat disturbed over some altercation or other
you mentioned in passing but which I am afraid your terrible chatterbox
never gave you an opportunity to enlarge upon. You didn't seem unduly
concerned about it, though, so I hope I am not in error if I refuse to permit
myself to worry unnecessarily. That doesn't mean [N2WI] however that I am

not consumed with curiosity, or that I am not inclined to be a little anxious about the treatment that is being accorded you. They'll have me to contend with if they dare to misuse my honey!

Dispatched the most humorous letter yet to Manny, this morning; he'll probably split his sides laughing over it![133] Now I'm going to concentrate on the kids. You know [NWI] somehow I have every confidence we will come through this intended visit with flying colors!—Here is to our everlasting faith in human decency, and honor, which must at long last triumph over evil!

All Love, Your girl
Ethel

Julius to Ethel

July 11th 1951

Dearest Most Precious Darling,

You made my day wonderful. I saw you a beautiful flower, charming, pleasantly plump and good to look at. Most important for me is what I find beneath the surface understanding and warmth. It is always refreshing and intellectually stimulating to talk to you and the emotional satisfaction derived from our tete a tete was most gratifying. Honey girl I held you in my arms, hugged you and I couldn't let you go. Believe me my eyes devoured you. What a treasure, together in misery so close by and yet torn from it's [*sic*] rightful place by a great wrong and brutally entombed by steel and concrete. Yet through it all your glowing personality and wonderful being is always with me. This misery is too deep [NWI] therefore and [NWI] must be the forerunner of happier days for us, and an end to this.[134] We packed so much jawing in one hour that it kept me going all day but now I miss you so much and the only thing I can do is close my eyes and see the beautiful future. Our visits are mutually beneficial and it does me a world of

---

[133]That letter has not survived.

[134]Here the next five words are crossed out so as to totally obliterate the words. The crossing out appears to be the work of the prison censor as it is in ink. Over the years, the original pencil has come through the ink far enough to reveal the word "gehenna" ending the sentence. The next sentence is enclosed in brackets and as far as I and my Yiddish translations consultant Rabbi Jerome Gurland could make out the four words are "Lummen mir debatten (in more normal transliteration it would be "debetten") stendig" which literally translates "Let's keep asking (or praying) always" but which can be idiomatically rendered as "Let's keep hoping." I surmise that the censor didn't recognize them as Yiddish words and censored them to avoid possible illegal communication! On the other side of the letter, two Yiddish words are also crossed out in the same manner.

good that we are able to accomplish concrete results. I guess I'm making my wife a better woman to live with. As for me I can tell you I've learned and improved to a great degree and my perspective is much clearer. Well menschen[135] we're willing and able what the heck are we waiting for.

Sweetheart your spouse shoveled in the following supper. A bowl full of bean soup and oysterette crackers, lettuce and tomatoe sandwich loaded with mayonaise [sic], a half of cantelope [sic], a bowl of stewed figs and prunes, a piece of coconut custard pie, three ginger cookies and a cup of tea. I plop into bed but my sweet tooth got me, so nasher[136] ate two chocolate nestles. Honey do you think your boy is being starved? You know its terrible after I finished [NWI] eating I lost my appetite. They say [next word CO, again in the manner of the censor above but can be read] efshe[137] I'm gaining a little weight. Perhaps on me [again the same kind of cross out but can be read] tzuris[138] grows avoir dupois.[139] Oh! Gevalt![140] let me away from this misshigos.[141] I just wanna go home. Don't worry my love your man is only a little nuts. It must be the heat that got me. To tell you the truth I'm just lazy and I don't feel like writting [sic] letters although I know I should send some to my sisters. They have been awfully nice and news from the family is like a transfusion and I don't want them to stop sending those letters. How about us asking for more pictures of the kids. I think Oscar has a camera maybe he'll take some nice ones of the boys. Ethel words and words and all the time I need you. All my heart my lovely woman—your own fellow—Julius

---

[135]Yiddish for "people" with the connotation of good people.

[136]Probably meant "nosher," Yiddish for "one who eats snacks."

[137]"Maybe"

[138]Trouble, difficulty

[139]To a Yiddish speaker or someone familiar with Jewish humor, this sentence would be read with a special kind of intonation. The joke of course is that usually troubles or worries make one lose weight. But on him, it makes him fat! In fact there is a Yiddish idiom which translates into English as "I get heavy from tzuris."

[140]Yiddish literally meaning "Give me strength!" or "God, give me strength!" From context there is a lightness about this expression, but in fact, "Gevalt," which is usually spoken in Yiddish as "Oi, Gevalt" instead of being combined with the English "Oh," is a much more serious and strong statement than appears in this context.

[141]Another garbled transliteration of a Yiddish word. In this case, the word is "meshigas" meaning "craziness."

Julius to Ethel

July 12, 1951

My Dearest Sweetest Vibelle,[142]
It is indeed a pleasure to know that the fairest flower at Ossining Manor is my lovely wife. Wherever you are you enhance with your charm and presence the entire place. I am sure we would gladly let these pleasures to others for our own quiet satisfying relationship. You know I'm crazy about you.

You recall I wrote the Warden about the news item in Walter Winchell's column[143] and I received a very satisfactory answer. To wit I quote:—I wish to advise that this office or to my knowledge have any guards given this information to any newspaper men and cannot find where you made any such statement [*sic*].—Of course this is all he could do within the limits of the regulations of this institution. The rest is up to Manny.

My sister Ethel sent me a newsy letter. She was over to see Mama this Tuesday. Robbie is fine and Michael likes the day camp very much. Mama's window is overlooking the river and also the railroad track, it is a beautiful sight and naturally the view is just the right thing for Robby. He is constantly watching the boats and trains passing by. I'll bring the letter to our next meeting for you to see and I didn't want to let you wait too long to hear some of the choice bits. She said that my brother expects to see us Friday and she will be down next week for a visit.

I finished the book the Rabbi lent me Birth of Israel by Don Grandos [*sic*] and I recommend it highly. Honey girl I'm thinking about you a lot these days and I miss you so much. I can't wait for our next meeting because I look forward to seeing you. Before my eyes is a vivid picture [N2WI] of you and the firmer it's implanted on my mind by frequent visits the easier it is to pass the lonesome moments away from you. Be with me always my courageous woman. Your dignity of person and wholesomeness of character inspires me. Because of this treasure I possess your love is my bulwark. We can hold our heads high and walk with confidence as principled forward looking people. With all the power of every fibre of our being we must continue to strive forward in every way as this is the only guarantee of our freedom and happier existence. Yes it is necessary to have hope and all we

---

[142]Yiddish for "wife."

[143]Walter Winchell had written that Julius Rosenberg had "reportedly" told guards that if he could hold out for three years he would be rescued by Soviet airmen! This actually is a variation of a story that Jerome Eugene Tartakow, the jailhouse informer at the Men's House of Detention between December of 1950 and the time of our father's transfer to Sing Sing, told the FBI. Tartakow said that our father had told him he would not have to serve more than five years in jail because by then we would have a "Sovietized America" (JR HQ 639, p. 4).

ask is a fair and just judgement of the issues. We must continue to find strength in the kind of people we are and in our love for each other—always yours

Julius

Ethel to Julius

July 14, 1951

Dearest sweetheart,

First, thank you for your most heart-warming letter. The words, "beautiful" "charming," and "good to look at," would flatter any woman's ego, but where do you get this "pleasantly plump" stuff? Aren't you kind of getting things slightly confused? After that seven course dinner you took such pains to describe to me in all its caloric glory, it might be you were forsooth, referring to yourself might it not? Listen, brother, it had better be, or I'll call you "fatso" the next time you come over to my yard to play, and then you'll be sorry, you'll see. As you notice, the brand of lunacy to which you seem to be steadily becoming addicted is a highly communicable disease!

Darling, to come back to reality, and it's an inconceivably bitter reality for us, I grant you, I, too, feel immeasurably strengthened and refreshed after our eagerly anticipated weekly hour together. The glow of our interchange remains with me long after you've gone; it gives me a chance to kind of catch my breath and psychologically set my teeth for another period of loneliness and hunger.

Dearest, your brother was terribly disappointed upon his return here, after lunch, to learn he would not be permitted to see you again after spending the alloted [*sic*] time with me, and urged me to impress upon you that the situation was not of his making. He was visibly shaken by his experience and came perilously close to crying every time he spoke of you. Bunny, whatever his weaknesses and faults may be, he loves you sincerely and wants nothing so much as to command your respect and approval. Actually, it requires a much more thorough verbal discussion. Yes?

I take up a problem that affects me more directly, the matron situation is still up in the air, and I with it! In view of the misery suffered until I convinced one lady here I was under no obligation to be "palsy walsy" with her (& it is only my own continued efforts to keep her at a comfortable distance that is causing her to reluctantly curb her actual feelings on this score), and the misery I am now suffering through the loss of my unforgettable "Mother Bessy," it is certainly to be expected that I should be apprenhensive [*sic*] about a newcomer. I had even been debating the desirability of writing the Warden about it, but apart from a feeling of self-consciousness about making a suggestion that might involve policy, (I realize full well it's his jail, not mine), if my intelligence served me correctly when I last saw him, I would hazard a guess that he is a pretty shrewd observer of people, and that, by and large, I ought to be able to trust his judgment. However, I can't help hoping that he will further exercise the good taste I believe he has & not engender an embarrassing situation for me by "breaking in" the new matron during those hours when the offending one is on duty. She is such a confirmed exhibitionist that such a procedure will only serve to further inflate her already over-inflated ego and present her with a real opportunity to throw her weight around, thus undoing the good I've been able to accomplish & starting me off with the new lady under a handicap at the outset. I trust that at least this minimum consideration of my feelings in the matter will be forthcoming.

Love, Ethel

The previous letter was obviously not only for Julius' eyes but for the Warden's as well, since everything passed through prison censorship.

Julius to Ethel

July 15, 1951

My Darling Sweetheart,

Here it is Sunday evening 6:00 P.M. and cabaret night stats [*sic*] in the C-C's.[144] To wit we have the radio on for a couple of selected musical programs. I've read the comics and newspapers, played ball in the yard and took my daily shower and I'm writting [*sic*] to my jewels my wife and children. Lately I've been doing quite a bit of reading. One interesting and novel book is Ullman's—Great White Tower portraying the lives of six people who together try to climb a mountain while around them in neighboring ["local" erased] countries wages [*sic*] World War II. Put in a request for it I'm sure you'll find it entertaining. At present I'm reading Good Night Sweet Prince by Gene Fowler a biography of John Barrymore and I'm positive you'll like this one. The only relaxation that is open to me is reading books and I'm really struggling to fill in the endless hours. This week I managed to squeeze in a couple of chess games. Somehow it seems so long ago that I saw you and everything is strange and distant. An empty feeling grips me and by the time you read this letter it will be one year that I have for all intents and purposes stopped living. Yes I understand all the ramifications of our case, I'm not defeatist. My courage and strength is all there but nevertheless life without you, the kids and freedom is pretty empty.

---

[144]Condemned Cells, the official name for the Death House.

Therefore as a realist I know that I'm marking time until this zombie existence [*sic*] is terminated. Lest I give you a wrong impression let me assure you that when I'm with you, when I read your letters and when I'm busy reading I am completely removed from the depths of despair and emotional barreness [*sic*] that entombs me here. The contrast between this Gehenna[145] and our beautiful life is so great that it seems I am grabbing at a straw to prevent me from drowning. Honey I want the time to fly quickly so that we can once more take up our fruitful life and together drink happiness. The time that we've been apart seems ages and I believe I'm courting you all over again. It's exciting and fascinating more so because I'm sure of the excellent merchandise and positive that it is mine. We will need a little time to get "reacquainted" and have the luxury of a second honeymoon. Ethel my precious faithful woman and loving wife there must be an end to this misery of ours and we must be vindicated from this frameup. Many times during the day I ask myself over and over why and I have to put it out of my mind because it doesn't make sense. I can't help it I'm day dreaming quite a lot and you my heart are the center of my thoughts. When we are home together I will try to convey to you what you mean to me. With all my heart my precious I love you[.] Your own—Julius

Julius to Ethel

July 17, 1951

My Most Wonderful Wonderful Swiney[146] Darling,

Joy of joy two letters one yesterday and a terrific one today. When I read your letter I got a sense of well being and inner satisfaction. What happiness to hear ones own sweet partner put in words so clearly our manner of living. Previous to this catastrophe that has befallen us we went about our daily activities in a natural way and approached our problems as they came along in an analytical fashion. We never stopped to put in any sort of organized way our complete conception of our basic philosophy and the practical carrying out in all its details, fruitful social and family life. Even though it is only in the degree of our maturity in mutually working out ["our" erased] daily problems and plans, this has been so advanced that there seems to be a qualitative change. It seems to be second nature the way we grasp so quickly what is happening to us as individuals and the world we live in. In all candor we know ourselves well, both our good and weak points, and we are

---

[145]Note the word wasn't censored this time. Perhaps after our mother received the previously censored letter, the prison censor had been informed of the meaning of these Yiddish words and began to pass them.

[146]Perhaps a reference to their weight gain problems!

able to work with what we have to achieve emotional, mental and physical satisfaction in our constructive accomplishments. That is the reason we continue to strive in a creative way to better ourselves and make our contribution to ourselves, our family and as such to man. To be able to objectively judge oneself in his own small family group gives him the proper perspective to understand his fellow men and to see clearly the social need for a progressive perspective. Therefore to me a forward looking person is the one [NWI] who sees and talks democracy and really practices it every day at home with his wife and children so that it becomes part of his dealings with his fellow men. When in practice tolerence [sic] and fair play are the byword then each person can enjoy the full benefits of ["the" erased] human dignity in higher and higher levels. I didn't intend to wax philosophical but you inspired me. Your words are an excellent tonic to me and I love you and adore you for all that you are. I find it easier ["for me" erased] to discuss our personal problems at our Wednesday visits. This Tuesday when I was exercising in the yard at the time the afternoon shift changed I noticed a gray haired lady in street clothes go to your door. I guess she's the new matron. Rather than cover some questions inadequately I'll talk to you about them. Thank Goodness tomorrow morning I'll be regaled by my lady woman. The thought of it is sufficient to bolster my spirits and as the time approaches my impatience increases. Dearest Honey our letters alone are the proof of our wholesome and complete marriage. This transient nightmare cannot harm our person or our solid relationships[.]

All my love—Julius

Julius to Ethel

July 19, 1951

Dearest Bunny Wife,

It's 8:30 P.M. now. Day was spent reading Thomas Wolfe, Look Homeward Angel. Thoroughly absorbing beautiful prose, an excellent book something you must read. I managed to squeeze in a good game of handball before the deluge drenched the court. Did you ever notice the comfortable feeling one gets reading and listening to nature's violent growls, react with lightning and pour it's [sic] water earth-ward? as I contemplated the elements acting in all their splendor I thought, gosh what a wonderful world we live in and how much man can do with full utilization of his creative ability.

The afternoon was spent reading the days newspapers and I was shocked to read that our government was moving to make a deal with Spain. Fascist Hangman bloody butcher Franco is going to help defend "Democracy." Perhaps, gentlemen of reaction it is you who want to bolster him finan-cially and militarily against the rising wrath of the freedom loving Spanish people. This will only expose the phoney [*sic*] game of war makers. It must be strange to people the [*sic*—obviously meant "that"] all the time it seems necessary to ally with the most reactionary, feudal and fascistic elements to defend democracy. Something is very rotten in Denmark. Thank Goodness there are enough people of vision and courage to make their wishes heard. The duty of an American citizen is to make his views known to his government and take an active part in making his free land a reality.

The last hour I spent in a hotly contested game of chess and I won this one. Concentrating on these activities temporarily dissolves the bars the concrete and the loneliness. Now as I write about it I know I'm not escaping from the reality of my incarceration. As I sit at my desk and look at the smiling faces of my two dearest sons a terrible pain grows at my heart. They need us. This unearthly madness and brutality has no right to hit at such defenseless sweet children. We must not let this loneliness make a permanent mark on our kids. Look Julius it's been more than a year and your [*sic*] away from your Ethel. You love her more than anything in the world and because it is an all encompassing relationship you have been able to stand with dignity this horrible separation and even the possibility of death. Yes, facts, truth and right is [*sic*] on our side and we must triumph in this appeal. I am sure our lawyers will do everything possible to prevent another political verdict instead of one [NWI] based on the judicial merits of the case. You remain my hope and with you life is real happiness. Always proud to be your husband—your—Julius

Ethel to Julius

                                                                July 19, 1951
My dearest sweetheart,

I have arisen early in order to insure your receipt of a letter from me for the week-end; as you [NWI] may recall I explained to you on Wednesday, I was in the throes of strenuous creative effort and had hope to see the end of ["this" CO, NWI] a particular writing stint by this morning. Since this is not to be and I have the benefit of the week-end before I can mail the rest of my "brain-child" Monday morning, I am taking a breather, so to speak, and addressing myself to my own sweet dear. I hope you have not been feeling left out darling; personally, I have been deriving much comfort and satisfaction in the knowledge that whatever my feelings may lead me to say, my expression will be received with that complete acceptance and sympathy which have sustained me in the past, and which, by now, I have come to expect as my due.

Honeybunny, yesterday there arrived another letter from our big pussy cat, in which he proudly informs me he is a "B" swimmer and therefore a "high" swimmer![147] Obviously he is making progress and my mother's heart swells with pride and with pain. Julie dear, there are times when I am rife with such terrible longing for my rightful return to you and them that I find myself wondering how [N3WI] it is that my mind and body continue to operate as well as they do. By what miracle, I ask myself am I accomplishing even those fitfully ["few" CO, NWI] small tasks I have undertaken thus far!

Beloved, my breakfast is getting cold and they'll be coming to pick up the tray and this letter in a very few minutes. I regret that we did not spend more time on Wednesday, discussing the emotional problems of the children. For instance Ethel told me that even with the woman's ["well" CO] expressed willingness to stay with Robby at the day camp all day, the child turned the idea down right with flat finality and even bitterness.[148] I can't help feeling that something very definite in the way of therapy should be sought for Robby, just as earnestly as for Michael.

Really must close now. Your letter was typical of the wonderful guy with whom I am so madly in love! I want you, sweetest! Many, many kisses, my love.

Ethel

Master Michael Allen Rosenberg
24-36 Laurel Hill Terrace
New York N. Y.

July 22, 1951

My Dearest Honey Boy,

When I saw your sweet mommy this week she was smiling and oh so happy. Of course, it was a splendid letter from her wonderful son Michael. Naturally the first thing I did was read the news you wrote in nice round penmanship on ruled lines. Yes we were both justly proud of you as you had progressed to the high swimming group "B". This is only one example of the pleasure you can get from trying, learning new things and accomplishing something concrete. Such is life for all people to advance themselves and create new joys in living. At this point play is very important to you as you find out how to get along with others. You see your own worth that you [NWI] too can achieve things and improve yourself. How I'd like to be with you and talk to you and together we can grow and derive so much fun. But I am forcefully kept from you and we have to be patient until the time I am free to once again live with my own family. However until

[147]See *Sons*, p. 79.
[148]*Ibid.*

that time all of us in our own jobs and ways will continue to work hard to improve ourselves in order for us to better be able to live a healthy happy life. From your letter and all that your Aunt Ethel told me this week I know you are more than holding your own. You like Day Camp and it is helping you find more relaxation and comfort. The care and love of Bubbie Sophie, the help and warm understanding of the other lady Sophie and the fact that you have your own things and home makes it a lot easier to get along. Know that no matter what the situation your mother and I with the help of many devoted people, both family and friends, think of you, plan to do all we can to help you and we are moving heaven and earth to win our appeal and go home to our dear children. You boys are our greatest pleasure and joy in life and we love you more than anything else in the world. Do not worry conditions will change and all will be well again. Robbie fellow you too are beginning to learn that things are improving for you and it's wonderful to be home again and with people who know, understand and above all love you. The news we hear from letters and the people who see us confirms that you are much happier and are adjusting nicely in your new home. Let me take you in my arms my sons, hug you tightly, smother you with kisses and be consummed [*sic*] with the happiness of my love because we are together. Have a good time and be happy boys. Send my love and best wishes to two wonderful, sweet and lovely Sophie's [*sic*]. Your own Daddy—Julius—

#110649

Julius to Ethel

July 22, 1951

Hello My Sweet,

10:00 AM a dull, dreary sticky and rotten Sunday morning and sad to say in tune with the summer doings I'm in the dumps. After $1^1/_2$ hours of twisting, turning and day dreaming I forced my lazy limbs out of bed and sent our off-springs a cheerful letter. Naturally it was the thought of them and their apparent rapid progress that brightened my words and spirits. Sometimes the hunger and loneliness for them and you dominates my mental state and leaves me emotionally debilitated as if the gnawing pain had eaten away my last will to rise above my misery. Yet, even though these temporary lapses take their toll, I am able to understand as I sense these extremes of emotions the true state of affairs and put each of these in their proper places. This note to you was interrupted at 10:30 for a yard period. Banged the ball around for ten minutes, until I hit it over the wall. After all I have to use up my energy somehow. The rest of the exercise time, I spent trooping around singing. Mario Lanza's favorite one "Be My Love" and some snatches from the classics. Then read the Sunday Times, lunch, an hours [*sic*] nap, more papers. Then $^3/_4$ of an hour of a hectic handball game. I managed to get all of six points and a good sweat. Shower, read the funnies, had supper, half hour rest and now back to a most pleasant pastime. This past week I've been bothered by sinous [*sic*] headaches but thank goodness I feel much better now. Sweetheart this is the way I mark time. It's been a long week and I'm going to prepare a detailed outline for my discussion with Manny after I finish this epistle.

Let me try my sweetheart to explain to you what you mean to me especially now in our hour of need. Fourteen and a half years of fruitful living where each of us in our own right has contributed to our mutual effort advancing ourselves culturally, mentally and socially. We have reached a smooth harmony of creative happy endeavor. You have constantly encouraged me, understood me. Your analytical mind and intense search for truth has aided me and shown me your great depth and warmth. Your dignity, decency and wholesome character has set me an example to emulate. How else could it be? As a sweet woman, a loving mother that you should be socially conscious, progressive & wide awake to the needs of your family and fellow men[.] I don't place you on a pedestal as your [*sic*] not excellent[149] but for me your [*sic*] tops and I'm the happiest person to share with you, to strive with you and to love you. My sweet person & precious wife—Always your own—Julius

Ethel to Julius

July 23, 1951

Dearest darling husband,

I had been delving so deeply into my own thoughts and feelings since our last personal visit, replete with [NWI] the usual mixture of joy and pain, that I feel as though I have only just closed my eyes upon a world of images my brain had created for my lone bedazzlement, and opened them [N3WI] all the more refreshed and clear-sighted for their earnest seeking. Do not, however, my sweet love, be led astray; the word "bedazzlement" does not [N4WI] as you might imagine necessarily indicate a state of pleasure and ecstacy [*sic*] beyond compare. Your woman labored most painstakingly to bring forth a pattern of some shape and color from out of the chaotic disorder that had taken such determined possession of her. As I plodded stubbornly ahead with my scribbling, often, as it seemed to me, at a snail's pace, the lines of it gradually grew more discernible; when Sunday brought with it my dear

---

[149]From context it appears he meant to say "perfect."

anxieties let up miraculously. Somehow, with his [NWI] continued support and guidance, I shall win through to a far greater degree of emotional security than I have yet been able to achieve. That there will be suffering in the interim I have no doubt but there will also be comfort and assurance in the knowledge that my feet are set upon the right path.

To refer [NWI] now to our wonderfully conscientious, brilliant legal adviser, there is an example of still another jewel in human form. Our visit with him was, I felt, most fruitful and encouraging; the way in which he ended it for his always affectionate client lent such a sweet, heart-warming touch to the [NWI] practical proceedings that had gone before, that I was moved beyond measure. Oh, but it's great to be alive and to know yourself as one with others who possess that divine spark of humanity in such extravagant abundance.

Darling, I am on fire with impatience for Wednesday morning; there is so much I want to discuss with you, I want it to come fast, fast! As you may well imagine, it will be difficult until I see them, to think of much else than the children![150]

Bunny dear, I love you and miss you so desperately. Did you guess all the sweet words I wanted to say yesterday? You must have because I heard the ones you would have liked to say to me! My dear love, I embrace you, with all my woman's tenderness and passion!

As always, your loving Ethel—

Julius to Ethel

July 25, 1951

Hello My Pretty,

Finished winning my chess at 9:15 PM and it was a long battle right down to the finish and I have to hustle to get this note off to you my sweet. Oh that wonderful one hour this morning. I didn't have an opportunity to tell you how beautiful you are. Lovely face, luscious skin, sparkling eyes and so attractive. Darling I'm so lucky to have such a flower [the next three words are written over other words but you can see what he wanted to say]

---

[150]This is the first indication that after a year of separation a visit by us to them in prison was actually being planned. When we wrote *We Are Your Sons* we were told that a psychologist advised against us seeing them before their trial because the sight of them behind bars might be too traumatic. The length of time it took to set up the first visit after our father's transfer to Sing Sing is unexplained as far as I know. The Phillipson biography (see Preface for our general comments) asserts that our mother "refused" to see us, perhaps out of guilt at being a "bad" mother. Mrs. Phillips remembers that from the moment she began seeing our mother in prison she was "wild" to see us.

words are written over other words but you can see what he wanted to say] in full bloom as my wife, and all I can do is worship it from afar. The frustration is terriffic! [*sic*] How I long to hold you close and drink the joy of our love. Because there is a great deal of depth in our relationship the pain and suffering is extreme. Tell me my woman do you see what's in my eyes and all that they wish to convey to you? Can you get from the expression on my face, the consumming [*sic*] desires of my heart? I am sure you can feel, all that my presence strives to transmit to you. [NWI] Even If [*sic*] I have to repeat countless times it nevertheless is true that you mean everything to me. It is amazing how much strenght [*sic*] it takes to continue about my routine and tear myself away from thoughts of you. It certainly is a revelation to me the heights our relationship can reach even in such negative surroundings [N2WI] because of ["from" CO] our combined and mutual sharing, trust, understanding and of course it all adds up to love. Time doesn't stand still, things are happening and concerted efforts are being made on our behalf. Right now I'm looking forward to seeing my own sweet sons after more than a year of forced separation. Even though it's an entire week off the tension is mounting and I'm going to have to exercise a maximum of control to keep my anxiety down. I want so for this to be a real positive experience for the boys. I am glad you are going to break the ice with them because I am certain you will come through with flying colors and set the stage for my visit.[151] You know I just got a wonderful idea. The children will get a kick out of it. I'll make pages of pictures of trains, boats and buses and I'm positive Michael and especially Robbie will like them. What do you think of this idea?

Honey the man is asked for the pencil. Tonight my love you'll be in my arms again more vividly than before and you can sleep peacefully. ["as" CO, next word has a capital letter superimposed on the lower case] Progress is being made. Only a short distance separates us but we are at one, [*sic*] For the time being only mentally. But we are confident of a glorious future together with our children. I am happy in my great treasures. My adorable wife and two boys. The desire, the will, the right is there and I'm sure we've got to win through. Bunny sugar all my heart to you—

Your Julius.

---

[151]Most of the prison visits occurred with them separately, one after the other. See *Sons*, pp. 85–87.

Ethel to Julius

July 25, 1951

My darling Sweetheart,

There was such emphasis on l'amour (!) this morning or rather the lack of it and the implacable hunger for it, that I was far too agitated to actually discuss the answer to some of the questions with which we may have to cope during our children's visit. Just as soon as you left, however, my brain began hitting on all cylinders; see what a disturbing influence you are! (Go right on disturbing me, dearest, I love it; if you could only practise [*sic*] what you so ably preach!)

To begin with, I view it as a healthy sign that I did not become bogged down with anxiety over our seeming indifference; after an initial stab of regret and feeling of panic, I recognize that this apparent lack of concern over the long-awaited day was more likely a solid confidence in our ability to handle whatever might arise. It is for the [NWI] sole purpose of firmly anchoring this confidence and using it to the best possible advantage, therefore, that I present some of my thoughts and ideas for your careful consideration.

The most important thing to remember is that Rome wasn't built in a day; better to take the attitude that we won't be able to answer every question with all-inclusive finality and that this visit is simply the opening gun in a campaign that will of necessity have to continue over an extended period of time. If we can manage to also give them the impression that we are not unduly upset because we may have to say something to that effect we will be setting the stage for the proper reaction. The following is a verbal picturization of the kind of thing I have [NWI] been dreaming up as a sample [N2WI] of the conversation that may take place, only for the sake of brevity [NWI] here I'm putting it in the form of a monologue to wit:

"Of course it's not easy to know about the death penalty and not worry about it sometimes, but let's look at it this way. We know that a car could strike us and kill us, but that doesn't dispose us to spend every minute being fearful about cars. You see, we are the very same people we ever were, except that our physical selves are housed [NWI] under a different roof from yours. Of course, we feel badly that we are separated from you but we also know that we are not guilty and that an injustice has been done to us by people who solved their own problems by lying about us. It's all right to feel anyway you like about them,[152] so long as your feelings don't give you pain and make you unhappy. What they have done because they are sick, unhappy people who have tried to solve their problems through hurting others is something for them to concern themselves with; that's why we

---

[152] The Greenglasses

have had you removed out of the reach of their influence because it isn't right that they should be given the opportunity to continue to hurt you."

This isn't the end of it, but it is the end of the page. Also I sense a certain self-consciousness growing inside me as I write. Naturally, the words are probably not quite what I shall use actually, in speaking with them. But my heart beats even with yours, darling, and I just had to share my thoughts with you [N2WI] even if imperfectly—Will write more about this—Love you—Ethel

Ethel to Julius

July 29, 1951

Hello, darling,

I scarcely know how to begin, my mind is in such a turmoil. Fortunately, my scribbling kept me so well-occupied this week-end that it passed much more quickly than I had hoped. Lee's visit, too, was tremendously helpful along these lines; the picture she drew of the children's reactions, however, pleased me none too well, and served to dramatize their very real need for proper emotional re-orientation.

All the same, dearest, there is a most gratifying upsurge of parental feeling and eagerness to see them which should do a good deal to promote the kind of atmosphere in the counsel room which we so fervently desire. Sweetheart, I shall do all that is within my power to set them at ease and prepare them for your coming; do try to lay aside some of your anxiety, meanwhile. Believe me, I am trying to convince myself, at the same time!

Hah! You can't make me jealous with your boats and trains; I have an envelope full of rare specimens collected with painstaking care by that intrepid hunter of wild insects, namely your wife! Dearest daddy, how sweet and thoughtful of you to have hit on such a splendid plan! It's just the thing, particularly for Robby, who methinks may be a little shy and strange with us.

Continuing the monologue I was in the process of developing for you in my last letter:

"Yes, I know, you wish that you could kill those who are responsible for the crime that has been committed against [NWI] us and it's perfectly natural to feel that way as long as we don't make ourselves unhappy [NWI] worrying about problems that are really their responsibility, not ours. Our responsibility lies in continuing to learn and grow and become close to the decent people around us; there are many such people upon whom you will always be able to depend for love and understanding and who will never permit wrong to be done you in our absence."

There is a great deal more that will come to me later in the day as I walk slowly about the yard and ruminate, that I'll be simply aching to share with you. Oh, yes, if he[153] neglects to question me as to the form of the death penalty, this lovely job will fall to you, in which case answer him briefly but unequivocally that it is painless electrocution, which we feel, of course, will never come to pass. You can explain it in terms of a highly magnified electric shock that anybody might sustain through contact. Believe me, my loved one, children are what their parents truly expect them to be. If we can face the thought of our intended execution without terror, so then will they. Certainly, neither of us will seek to dwell on these matters unduly, but let's not be afraid and they won't either. I am utterly convinced [NWI] that that's all there is to it!
All my love, darling—Ethel

P.S. Remember there is danger in being too flip and casual but the light touch is always in order and can be of real in getting over a tough spot. I have complete faith in us both—
       Many kisses—
       Your loving wife

Julius to Ethel

                                              July 29, 1951
My Most Dearest Wife,
       A couple of letters were just finished. One to my mother and the other one to our dears. Ever since our last meeting I've missed you terribly. What you say and the words you use in expressing it are so excellent that I can state it best in the famous Jewish saying "From your mouth to God's ear." I hunger for you. I need you my love and because of this and in spite of the great pain I manage to come through all this suffering with confidence. Your suggestions on the meeting with the children are quite good and your observation on the need to understand that we've got to take things slowly so as not to overwhelm the boys is well taken. It is definitely a sign of growing maturity on our part that we are not so terribly anxious about our ability to properly handle the situation as it arise [*sic*] during the visit. Note that I, too, feel a great improvement in my own emotional stability on this matter. Do not for one moment think that I was not concerned about my reactions and the effect on the kids. The common sharing of these problems is a great equalizer and pays such great dividends in mental well being.

---

[153]Michael

Darling I have you to thank for the pioneering ground-work and tireless efforts all the past years for our mutual progress in this important matter.

Wednesday will be the fifth anniversary of my Father's death. The passing of this fine, intelligent, sensitive loving father dear friend and counselor was a great loss to us Ethel. I'll ask the Rabbi to burn a candle in his memory and I'll say Kaddish[154] at Jewish Services.

I keep thinking how much easier it would be if we could spend this time together. Such a dream. Yet it is so cruel to be separated from you and the children. Sometimes I muse and say perhaps there is a method, mathematical in its exactness of course, where the facts can be fed in and the answer is a result of a scientific accurate appraisal. Coming back to reality I still keep my hopes high and I know we'll get that fair chance and win true justice. We've got to spend more time and go over all the details about the school, social life and emotional needs of our boys. Not only should we take part in the planning but we must list all these things and check on the periodic progress. It is not necessary to only burden Manny although the initial start has to be made through him. Many things have to be set in motion before the summer vacation is over.

Lovely woman of my heart, you are in my arms that's as it should be and I'm at peace. The devotion and loyalty of my family has been comforting. It sure is swell the way they visit and try to help. We're lucky to have them. They know us for our worth and are behind us 100%. Keep your beautiful face glowing. Your lover—Julius

Ethel to Julius

August 1, 1951

My dearest love,

My heart is leaden within me; I'm afraid I was anything but calm, although Manny probably indicated to you that I was wonderful. And to judge by outward appearances, I guess that I was. But as I smiled and kissed the children, I was experiencing such a bewildering assortment of emotions, that I don't think I was enough in control of myself to [NWI] have accomplished anything very far-reaching. Actually, I doubt anyone else could have [NWI] either; after all, a first visit after a year's separation, can hardly be expected to [N4WI] do much more than "break the ice." Nevertheless, I am unable to set aside my sense of let-down and frustration; nor can I, needless to say, escape the terrible ache and longing that relentlessly pursues me now that the [NWI] sweet sound of them is no more.

---

[154]Jewish prayer for the dead.

And yet I am also so full of pride and joy—Mail call—See you Friday—
Love. Ethel

Julius to Ethel

August 1, 1951

Dearest Love of my life,
   Just a brief resume of todays [*sic*] occurences [*sic*]. This morning found me restless tense and very anxious. All different thoughts went through my mind and now in retrospect I can frankly say that they were products of a terrific [*sic*] desire to do right by the kids. When the sound of your voices singing drifted down to the cell block my tensions began to vanish. Roberts [*sic*] shrieking was music to my ears. After lunch I went into the counsel room and the kids were hiding behind the door. When I hugged them they seemed so small and far away. I was a bit dazed. I choked up and my eyes teared and Michael kept repeating, Daddy your voice has changed. After a couple of minutes I was back on an even keel. A round of kissing and hugging and then Robbie sat on my lap. His peaked thin face, ringed eyes, looked up at me and he said "Daddy why you no come home". I carefully explained. He replied "Why did you not visit us Sundays at the Shelter.["] Again I explained. Naturally the baby could not comprehend. He dashed around the room and played with the chairs. I gave the boys a bag of hard candies and showed them the drawing of trains buses and cars. Michael spent most of his time drawing tracks with a pencil.[155] Constantly I kept drawing him out. The big fellow was reserved and shy. He hardly looked at me. Using your suggestions I asked what you discussed. He finally said a few things about Dave, Tessie and Ruth.[156] The only time we really got warm was after explanations about your family. Then he popped out, was there an amicus curia in your trial.[157] Who besides Mr. Bloch was a witness for you? The fact is both children are disturbed. One thing he said stands out and that is that it would be better if he were here and not I. Of course, I could not develope [*sic*] very manny [*sic*] things in this first visit. Some songs and a talk on the play school loosened the kids up. Again I must state that

---

[155]See *Sons*, pp. 19–20
[156]The Greenglasses
[157]An *amicus curiae* is a "friend of the Court" who intervenes in a legal proceeding to bring to the attention of the Court information that might not be contained in the papers filed by the contending parties. There was a radio show called "Amicus Curiae." See Schneir, p. 178n for a discussion of the Supreme Court's 1952 refusal to accept an *amicus* brief from W.E.B. DuBois and others urging them to review the case.

you set a good tone for the visit and it went off better than I had expected. Do you know that your boys insisted that the guards frisk them also. The children said that you look smaller. I showed the boys I am sans mustache and the little one asked, where did it go? It is evident to me from their answers that they don't play with their blocks, tracks, clay, erector set and other materials. It may be that either things are lost or just not available for their use. We'll have to go into this in detail. Darling the children need us and I hope it is not much longer that we will suffer such anguish being separated from them. Michael told me about our room being ready and about Bubbie shifting to the living room showing that he is all set[.] I hope you see this before our visit so we can use it as a basis of discussion. After I left them I felt I tore out a piece of heart. [next parenthetic statement written under these words] (rare Jewish idiom).—Love—Julius

Ethel to Julius

August 2, 1951

My own dearest, darling husband,

Your very vivid description of the by now famous Wednesday as it was given to you to spend it, moved me deeply, giving my aching heart some surcease, but making me yearn all the more desperately for the passage of time and the opportunity to give way to my pent up feelings in your dear presence. Oh, sweetheart, I love them so much, how shall I ever go on enduring without them. Dearest, I need to weep on your shoulder; I need to feel your arms about me.

The picture of my bewildered, sad-faced baby with the haunted eyes and serious mien is a sight I cannot put out of my mind; and Michael, with his deceptively cheerful demeanor and flippant chatter, doesn't exactly allay my anxiety, either. They need help urgently, make no mistake about it; and there are a number of concrete suggestions I have to make toward this end that I am impatiently waiting to share with you. In order to save time, I have already jotted down some of my criticisms and will add anything else that may hit me right up to your scheduled arrival in No Man's Land!

Just in case we don't get around to it, [N5WI] let me tell you now I had just received your letter of the 29th and was weeping over your reverent remarks concerning your father and his tragic loss five years ago, when Jewish Services were announced. My sweetest dear, what can I say other than to echo those sentiments you have yourself [NWI] already expressed. I think frequently of those happy days we were privileged to spend in his house; shall I ever forget his dignity, his love of wife and children, his enjoyment of good music, his devotion to conscience and decency![158] How bitterly deprived are we now of his tenderness and sincerity! And how proud am I to be the wife of this gracious man's son, how proud your children of their gentle father!

I think I had better go to sleep; the tears have begun to flow again! Darling, I need you, I love you—oh, my God, where is there an end to this wretched misery, this horrible torment!

Good-night, Julie dear—

August 3, 1951—6:15 A.M.

Just woke up. Still hopelessly depressed. Want to see Manny as soon as possible—I'm hoping that [NWI] seeing you will help to calm me and dispel some of the gloom in which I've been unhappily moving these last days. My warmest love, my dearest one; I am heart-broken with longing & loneliness

As ever, Your own Ethel

Mrs. Ethel Goldberg
5347—65th Place
Maspeth Long Island

August 3, 1951

Dearest Ethel,

It was only when Lena visited me on Saturday that I learned of your own little bit of trouble. Thanks so much for letting me know that all's well that ends well. I'm not going to pretend I was exactly unconcerned for my dear Oscar's welfare. Quite the contrary, I awaited word of his condition with impatience. Please give him my very best wishes for a speedy recovery; I am truly sorry that he had to suffer so much pain until coming to the decision to undergo the operation. Keep me posted, won't you, as to his progress and don't worry about how soon you will be able to get to see me; he's your first responsibility until he is on his feet again!

Probably the children have already regaled you with a telling account of their trip to our delightful abode. For my own part let me say it was an occasion for joy and sorrow both; my heart rejoiced as I held each precious little boy close, but once the good-byes were said, such a terrible longing to take up my life with them again, overcame me that I was quite desolated for days after. I have since regained my usual cheerfulness and look forward to their next visit with impatience.

[158]For information about Harry Rosenberg, see Gardner, pp. 35–37, 39.

I am so delighted with the progress that has already been made and am certain that we shall be able to solve whatever other problems may arise from time to time.

Yes, I was a bit disturbed about Mama's foot; a doctor should have been called the following morning, as [NWI] an infection can be a very dangerous business. I trust that she is not being foolish and is taking all the necessary precautions.

I don't want to delay this letter any longer. If I go on writing I may miss mail call. So all my love and best to everyone—I am in good spirits, never fear and sleep the quite peaceful sleep of the innocent. Again, take [NWI] good care of Oscar and admonish Mama to look out for herself. I love her with all my heart as I do the other members of my wonderful family!

As ever, Ethel

P.S.—I see my Sweetheart to-morrow morning, Wednesday! And to-day is Jewish Services—Yippie!

Julius to Ethel

August 5th 1951

Adorable Honey Girl,

Misery and grief, we have plenty of and I fully understand and share your terrible anguish but we are very well qualified to organize the proper program of rehabilitation for our children and only by persistent concentration can we aid our boys and salve some of our own wounds. Now that a number of days have passed since the visit with our dears it can be objectively stated that for me the meeting served to place me in a position to see the cold reality of our situation. Particularly from a family point of view we must never for one minute become lax in the guarding of our sweet boys [*sic*] emotional security. At our last tete a tete we discussed in general terms some of the concrete plans and from here on in I suggest you make an outline step by step and we'll discuss with Manny and members of my family and give them in writting [*sic*] our recommendations. The entire home play and play materials situation needs a radical change. A trained specialist, if possible the one who has already been recommended should begin to see the kids. During my family visits we must bring this problem to their attention and at least make them aware of the direction needed to bring relief. It is my further suggestion that every effort be made to get Mike in the private school and to try to get the baby to attend it's [*sic*] nursery. Mind you I'm not alarmed over the situation as I feel that the necessary conditions exist to do a good job. Darling I've gone through all kinds of hell since last Wednesday and I can say I've finally reached the usual state of suspended equilibrium. How my heart aches for you my

wonderful wife and dearest mother of my children. Try to get some comfort
from my profound love for you. Yes, if we were together and I could hold
you close, your pain would be easier to take. In all future plans for the
children I'm counting on your analytical mind and perfectionist detail to
[NWI] help carry the ball for us. It was good to read that the Circuit Court
granted Manny two more months for the filing of the brief and I think this
also includes approval of the additional papers. Now our counselor will have
sufficient time to perfect his legal efforts. Sweetheart we're set for a long
haul and with confidence in our lawyers, ourselves and the American people
we can go forward with adequate courage to face the coming tribulations of
our case. Of course, the promise of the future is the necessary key to our
strength. For our childrens [*sic*] sake we must come through in flying
colors. I know you my precious, wonderful woman and I'm sure you'll
continue as in the past to make me proud to be your husband by carrying
yourself with dignity, stature and noble character. I'm madly in love with
you. When are you coming home with me? Always your own—Julius.—
I'm going to write the boys a letter now.

Ethel to Julius

August 7, 1951

Dearest Sweetheart,

I was so busy this week-end thinking through and working out a certain
problem, that I neglected my correspondence completely; so you, my poor
honey, got nary a word from your bad girl. Please do forgive me, darling; it
also happens I awoke Saturday morning with a dull throbbing in the head
and a sick feeling in the stomach, the understandable aftermath of a week of
emotional stress and storm.

I'm fit as a fiddle once more, however, so don't be unduly concerned.
Too bad the Rabbi was unable to hold services today, but as though to make
up for this deprivation, I received three letters; yours, Michael's and
Davy's.[159] Quite a haul, eh wot? I'll show them all to you to-morrow
morning.

You know, I wrote Manny requesting him to come on Friday but since
your brother intends to visit us then himself, I'll notify Lee to phone Davy
to plan to get here in the afternoon. If Manny puts in an appearance tomorrow, however, it will settle the entire question to everyone's satisfaction.

You are absolutely right, dear, about the children and the imperative
need for us to play our rightful role as their parents. The most important

159Julius' brother

thing right now as I see it is the establishment of a relationship between them and this trained person we have in mind. The play situation plus [NWI] their proper handling in all other areas of living will then be given the necessary stimulus; I am now thinking [NWI] also in terms of a rapport between the specialist and the two adults that are [NWI] more closely involved in the children's guidance. And by all means let's have a really thorough discussion about and lay definite plans for school with Manny.

My sweet, I love you for your tenderness and devotion and courage, and its [*sic*] hurts my heart to know how you suffer for your wife and children. I ask of myself only that my character shall match your own; it's your [NWI] continued appreciation of my problems and belief in my ability to seek them that sees me through each bitter day.

Your always loving
Ethel

Julius to Ethel

August 9th 1951

My dearest Sweetest Ethel,

Honey we can be proud of ourselves for the fruitful results of our Wednesday visit and the subsequent legal consultation. Isn't it clear that we have come a long way and I mean all three of us in clearly analyzing in give and take fashion and mutually arriving at the correct necessary steps. You my sweetheart deserve the greatest share of credit because it was your persistence and thoroughness that won me over a long time ago and from the earliest days of our relationship I have respected you and your opinions and wishes as a separate human being[.] More and more through the years of our married life your stature as a fine person with dignity of character has continually grown. Not only has this spurred me on to emulate such high standards but it has in itself helped me develope [*sic*] my own potentialities. Perhaps you may think I am prejudiced but let me state that even Manny who at times is brutally frank and who observed you way down deep where the net result is the true character and personality of the individual has learned your fundamental worth and admires you. Darling it is not only what is said but how he acts and above all how he feels. Of course, it's almost impossible to be objective about oneself but please don't underestimate your abilities and above all don't sell yourself short. The positive effects of these splendid visits presented the usual letdown. I have been at a high emotional and mental pitch and naturally I miss you all the more. The lack of social and physical contact with you is horribly frustrating. Clearly your constant support and being the kind of woman you are has given me the strength to stand erect and keep on an even keel. My heart overflows with love for you, my mind sings with joy knowing that you are my own sweet wife. How cruel to be apart and yet how proud I am that we can stand so firm and fling back the challenge at our accusers and in spite of the great hardships we as man and woman are growing. Rest assured that our children are in excellent hands and all that is necessary will be done to help them. Our dears will have just cause to be proud of their parents and we will be the ones to once again assume our rightful place at the helm of our own home. We have made a very good start and we must continue to guard the welfare of our boys. As we discuss in detail our legal efforts I am becoming more confident of the successful outcome of our appeal. Let us keep our courage up the horizon is not too far away. For us life has so much in store. I think of the future and it looks good—Always your boy—Julius

Ethel to Julius

August 9, 1951

My own darling Julie,

Did ever a girl have a husband such as you? (I mean, another one of course, not me, because this girl certainly does know what kind of a husband she's got! The only thing this girl doesn't know is how to properly impress him with his own worth). No, sweetheart, no other girl ever did! And what has brought on this affectionate outburst, do you think? Well, while rummaging around "among my souvenirs" today, I could not help looking [N2WI] once more at your exquisitely lovely Mother's Day card with its genuinely touching, unusually expressive tribute and remembering how simply floored I was to receive it. And even though you were not there to deliver it personally (along, with the appropriate embraces, of course,— and lots of them) I can't think of anyone more eminently fitted to be your emissary than Manny Bloch was that day. This self styled "cynic" simply glowed to see my tremulous response but it was when, with prideful flourish, he produced the piece de resistance, Michael's class picture, that the man's rich, deep-flowing humanity manifested itself in all its blazing splendor. What warm, sweet feeling was then shared between us as I gazed on the inspiring sight of the child. How merry and bright are the eyes in the softly rounded, tender face of him and his teeth are coming along nicely, in so far as I could determine from the crooked smile of him. And he is standing at the end of the back row with such an air of belonging and mature cheeriness, that I am positively thrilled.

I also experience such a stab of mother longing that I could howl like a she-animal who has had its young forcibly torn from her! How dare they, how dared they, the low, vile creatures lay unclean hands upon our sacred family? And tell me, oh, my sister Americans, how long shall any of your own husbands and children be safe if you permit by your silence, your inertia this foul deed to go unchallenged! Shall you sit, too, in a soundless horror, entombed, buried alive, ears forever strained for the voice of a friend, eyes forever filled with nightmare terror, upon your brain forever stamped as thousand shocking imprints, heart forever fraught with mute, abysmal anguish! Shall you? [she then filled the line with dashes]

Dearest, already Wednesday's visit is dim and distant; still does my mind's eye delight in its picture of you, nose pressed determinedly against that outrageous yet ludicrously funny wired barrier that separates us, eyes brimming over with mischievous devilment, face now bright and alive with intelligence, now soft and sweet with tenderness for me! As you have no doubt gathered by now, you are [NWI] my dearest love and I can't wait for that glad day when I may once more properly [NWI] demonstrate my wifely feelings—I kiss you good-night darling, with all my heart—

Lovingly, Ethel—

Julius to Ethel

August 12, 1951

My Dearest Ethel,

Flower of my life, nightingale of my heart. How wonderful to have such a sweet lovely wife! As you will note I intended to write you on the 12th and it's now Monday morning and I have only a few minutes to drop you a few lines[.] I was up all Saturday night with a sick stomach and it continued until this morning. After receiving such an excellent thought provoking letter and especially since yesterday had certain significance I'll try to convey some of my sentiments.

One solid year of free untrammeled development has been taken away from you. For 365 days you have been robbed of your rightful motherly duties. Endless minutes of worry for the safety of your children, for their welfare and every single need and for 12 months untold agony of frustrated mother love. Always denied the comfort and love of your family and prevented from giving expression to innermost feelings and needs. An ominous horrible sentence hanging over your head. Caged and oppressed like an animal and constantly faced with myriads of tortures of the mind. This has been your sorry lot my sweetheart. It is all so unjust and unfair that they can perpretrate [*sic*] in this modern civilized era so foul a frameup that only silence and camouflage can hide the truth for all to see. To yourself and to all who see and know you this year ["has" probably omitted] shown your mettle and has proven your worth. You are a finer, greater, nobler, person my love.

This situation was not of our making. It was not our wish to go through this kind of test. Now that we have already ["hit" CO] passed through a year we can clearly see ourselves. When stripped bare the mirror of life is all revealing. I am well satisfied with what I find. We have built on solid foundations and are reaching newer heights. Because of all we are and what we have experienced I can unequivocally state we'll take all they throw at us and then some. As long as we can depend on our individual resources and maintain our principles of life we must win.

We have faith in the people. From the begining [*sic*] we have known this to be an uphill fight all the way and we are well prepared for it. As long as our position remains firm as time passes the public will get to discover the truth and then we'll not be alone.

Continue to stand fast my heart so that I too can with head high proudly stand with you in our way of life and support our just cause. As always with courage, confidence and perspective to a better future.

Your own Julius

Ethel to Julius

August 13, 1951

My dearest Julie darling,

What do you think you're doing with a sick stomach? Only your wife is allowed such a luxury! Sweetheart, please do stop stuffing that gut of yours with all that junk you've been boasting about; enough is enough by cracky! After all by now the lean days at Federal Detention should be but an ill-[NWI] remembered memory; you have now gained back enough of the weight you lost [NWI] there to warrant a slow-down in gastronomical activity. After all, if I didn't boss you and nag you, I shouldn't be your own precious girl now, would I? Honey, I'm not fooling, please do be a little more careful; I hate to think of you sick enough to be awake with indigestion all night and the next day, too!

What shall I tell you now, my dear one; already my mind is leaping ahead to Wednesday morning. It is when you cross the distance that separates us and call out your cheery greeting that I come alive once more and know that I am still my own self and not some fantastic being from another realm. Still, I think I have progressed to a point where I am more capable of accepting the prospect of many more dreary months here without undue agitation. I am kind of begining to dig in and want desperately for this philosophical mood to remain with me.

Actually, I have begun to feel I am merely waiting out the time before I am sent home to you and my darlings; in all decency, in all justice, there can be no other end to this horror. So say I, let's be gay about it; at least, I needs must draw such a conclusion, else why have I been singing these ["the" CO] last two days?

The children's visit [N2WI] I believe, is at the bottom of my rising optimism and they are, indeed, cause for singing, in anybody's book. Manny's last visit too, was most encouraging; certainly, it grows clearer a reversal is in proper legal order.

My sweetheart, how I do miss you and long for you. Unfortunately, my personal problems have a way of unpredictably inundating me so that I am more often than not saturated with anxieties that I [NWI] really ought not have to cope with in an already danger-laden atmosphere.

Love, I hear keys; mail is being collected, and my tray has not even been touched. Perhaps I shall feel free to share some ["the" CO, N2WI] of the problems that ["are" CO, N2WI] have been causing me unhappiness, on Wednesday. I feel it most important that we [NWI] should use our personal visit to more [NWI] direct personal advantage than we have yet done.

I send my loving heart, my sweetest dear. I love you, darling—

Ever, Your Ethel—

Master Michael Allen Rosenberg
24-36 Laurel Hill Terrace
New York N. Y.

                                                            Aug 16th 1951
My Dearest Son Michael,

It is indeed very gratifying to hear from those who come to visit me and read from the letters I receive that you enjoyed the visit very much and you want to see us as soon as possible. Your mommy and I discussed this matter and we're trying to make arrangements for another visit sometimes next month. Now that a beginning has been made we'll have a better chance to get reacquainted. This time it will be easier for both of us to discuss all the things you have on your mind. That includes questions about our case and your future. By now you have no doubt begun to appreciate the fact that it takes time to accomplish things and even to discuss and talk matters over. For me your visit was wonderful. It made me happy to hold you in my arms and kiss you. You have grown my darling and even though at times it has been very hard for you, it is easy to see that many improvements have been made. We will continue to strive to see that you are happy and all possible is done to help you and care for you. Again I want to tell you that I am confident in the end we will be set free because Mommy and I are innocent and we will fight in every possible way & through the courts to win our freedom as soon as possible. In the meantime I want you my love to be healthy and happy and know that your parents will be home with you when this case is over. I think about you and love you with all my heart and I'm anxious to see you soon again.

My dearest boy Robert—I am happy that you liked the trip on the train and you enjoyed the visit. It was fun picking you up and throwing you into the air, giving you a horsie ride on my back and playing games. When I see you again we'll be able to play some more. If you like let me know and I will make more pictures of trains, buses, cars and boats. It's good to see that you fellows get along so well with Mr. Bloch as he is a wonderful man, likes you boys and is working very hard to win our case. The thing that is giving me a great deal of satisfaction is that you are so happy with the lovely Bubbie Sophie and the lady Sophie. Word from you and views about you is always welcome. I send you my children, kisses, hugs and all my love. Let me hear from you. Your own Daddy—Julius

Sweet Mama—please take care of your health as we're depending on you and I'm sure you understand that the children are growing boys and they should be given a great deal of leeway in play and you should take it easy and be calm[.] I know you are terribly upset but for my sake please try[.] All my love Your son Julius—Regards to Sophie

Julius to Ethel

Aug. 16, 1951

My Most Precious Darling Ethel,

Overwhelming longings have taken hold of me and I desire so to hold you in my arms. It is not enough to see you and talk to you. My love for you is overflowing and it crys [*sic*] out for more adequate expression. After all the highest emotional and mental feeling [*sic*] are culminated in the physical sense. Because of these thoughts of you I have driven myself to higher efforts. My eating habits are improving to the extent of lowering my food intake. Setting up exercises to keep me in better physical shape has been started and I hope to be able to continue this effort. To our two dears I sent a lovely letter. Honey you may not think so but you are the determing [*sic*] influence in my stability. Of your beauty I can sing. Your loveliness is so satisfying to my eyes and your sweetness warms my heart. The time I am with you I am completely removed from this tomb of steel and concrete and filled with sufficient inspiration, emotional uplift and mental stimulation to make me strong to stand erect in facing the daily hardships. My words are not able to express completely how tremendous an effect you have on me. If only we could spend the time together the torture and hurt would not be so great. However reason and humane treatment is not the criteria here. It is so hard to take and conceive particularly because we are so completely innocent of this charge and are only victims of a hedious [*sic*]

political frameup. How the pattern keeps on unfolding, more politial [*sic*] arrests, arrogant disregard for the rights of people or the Constitution of our land and a greater hysteria spreads through the country. Now is the time for the people to stand up and defend their rights. We see so clearly the similarity [N3WI] with all this of our own case the complete identity of our position with that of the American peoples [*sic*] fight for Democracy and peace. It is essential that the truth and the facts be made known to all. Lee sent me a letter and among other news told me of Michael's sleeping problem that he wants to sleep with Mama. She said she'll discuss the problem when she sees us this Saturday. We know this problem and I am sure you will be able to recommend the correct remedy. Just like his Mother and Father he thinks all the time and finds it difficult to fall asleep. He wants us his parents to kiss him good night and put him to sleep. This kind of stuff tears my heart out. So much strength is needed to withstand such heartaches. Only our complete freedom and an early reunion with our family can serve to heal the harm done to us. No matter what I'll continue to fight for our vindication[.] All my love
    Julius

Ethel to Julius

                                                        August 16, 1951

My very dearest sweetheart,
    I expend so much energy feasting my eyes upon the tempting maleness of you, basking in your boldly appreciative smile, listening to your most delightfully welcome verbal love-making, and whispering sweet nothing's of my own to you in reciprocation, that it takes me the rest of the day to come out of my happily dizzy state. Then it is that there appear to me many things that I feel I could [NWI] seriously discuss with [NWI] you and clarify to our mutual gratification if the opportunity were [NWI] made available. Since it is not, however, I am hoping to press this letter into our service as a substitute of a kind, comparatively poor though it admittedly is.
    I believe I attempted to describe somewhat, the last time I wrote, the latest frame of mind toward which I seem to be gradually progressing. Actually, it is a very difficult mood to capture on paper, since there are quite a few apparently unrelated facets that comprise its [*sic*] format, that yet are all one and the same thing. For example, I have the curious feeling of living in a world beyond whose walls no other exists; in jail terminology, I've "made it", I've "arrived," because the "Street" no longer constitutes[160] the

---

[160]This word is written rather illegibly. From context this is the best option given the letters that are certain.

magnet, the painfully plaguing goal, it once did. The carefully restricted demarcations of the area in which I am permitted, have dissolved because there is no longer any other area. I am conscious of a need to remain immersed in my own being that amounts to an actual resistance to showing my thoughts and feelings. Oh, I make plans about the children, Manny, and Dr. Miller, but it's all so mechanical, it's as though I don't really believe that events will actually transpire; they are dreams I have yet to dream. I am withdrawn into myself and a lethargic lassitude envelopes me, yet there is awareness of a stronger bond with you and all those others, if anything, just because I don't feel so driven to overtake you and them. In other words, this outside world which I have to all intents and purposes renounced, is more sharply with me than ever, by dint of the fact that the situation of which I am presently a part, holds so much less strangeness and terror for me than it did.

I know it's all very paradoxical and maybe my brain is so worn with poking and pulling that it cannot function keenly enough to properly expound the particular ideas that have been streaming back and forth across it, of late. So take them for what they are worth to you, and perhaps I'll try my luck another time, along these lines.

There are of course any number of items concerning the childrens' [*sic*] future visits and their upbringing generally that I didn't even get to mention; I guess it will have to keep awhile. My eyes are begging for slumber. My dearest, my arms tenderly enfold you, my mouth presses yours in a fervent caress—with deepest, most reverent feeling, I love you—Ethel—

Julius to Ethel

Aug. 19, 1951

My own wonderous [*sic*] love,

Such a beautiful letter sweetheart. Glorious to read and mentally very provoking. It was very profound and I reread it a number of times. In the first place I too find myself in a happy state walking on air after each of our visits. The fact that we verbally coo and mentally exchange our love is a good sign in itself as we show our confidence. Now as a first observation I would say that your reactions prove that you are reaching a state of equilibrium so that you can put each [NWI] thing in it's [*sic*] proper place. Of course there will continue to be oscillations about this mean but it will be of lesser and lesser magnitude and not reflect in to violent emotional [an erased word follows] gyrations. How funny it feels to read you describe a situation that I too have experienced. To me this is a natural state of dervelopement [*sic*] as we feel secure in the future and we also know what this place holds in store for us. I am only referring to the physical set up and our own adjustments here. Then, too, a great deal of progress has been made with getting the children set and we're sure all possible will be done to help them. Since we know we're innocent and we've familiarized ourselves with the legal efforts of our attorneys we feel more confident. Note the fact the [from context should be "that"] you can take for granted in a sort of matter of fact way by making plans for the children, Manny and Dr. Miller "mechanically" it proves what I have said. Most important for both of us is that at this point you are finally getting to know your own worth and seeing yourself in a more objective light. My darling it is obvious to me that you are a woman of great courage and depth and you have passed the great hurdles with flying colors. This holds great promise for our continued ability to grow and develope [sic] further and will enable us to surmount the tribulations that still face us. You are correct my dear it is too difficult a task to try to discuss this question through our letters as I don't want you to get the wrong impression. Therefore I'll take this matter up with you in greater detail at our next visual amour session.

Oh my precious heart visual, oral & mental love are not enough I must have you in my arms to fully be at one with you. I have such a great treasure and it is kept from me. On top of this frameup we are subjected to this horrible frustration. Flower of my life keep shining to give me strength to hold myself up besides you in our common effort. With every fibre [sic] of my body I love you. Your own fellow—Julius

Ethel to Julius

August 20, 1951

My very own darling,

Ever since Lena's visit on Saturday and her disclosure of the widening rift that threatens the very foundation of the relationship we had hoped to build, a hundred different thoughts and feelings have been hammering heavily at my brain and heart. It was all the more frustrating then to learn that we should have to postpone a really thorough-going discussion of the problems involved until Manny returned next week.

Indeed, I had such a sense of haste and hurry that I forgot altogether to impress upon you the need to exercise the greatest [NWI] possible restraint and tact in speaking with your mother on Wednesday. Whether rightly or wrongly, I know she must be suffering deep hurt and I, for one, don't propose to wound her further. On the contrary, I'm sure you will agree, that every sympathy and kindness must be shown her; it is on this basis, alone, that we shall finally win through to the necessary solution.

In the meantime, my heart aches for my sweet pussies; with what joyful eagerness I should set about re-establishing their emotional balance and security. Whatever difficulties their lives might present, the simple fact of our strong desire to understand and guide them would serve to promote their needs and bring about their eventual well-being. Oh, darling, what manner of monster are the so-called humans, who with cold deliberation, brought us to this pass and can now witness our collective distress with no single sign of remorse, no twinge of conscience, no cry of shame!

Tuesday, August 21, 1951

Sweetheart, another night has winged its black-bowed way beyond all returning! (Influence of Thomas Wolfe, but courtesy of your poetic wife, honest Injun!) My God, that man can write; whatever his faults, and I find very definite fault with an over-emphasized, too facile racialism, he is a master of imagery, a painter of powerful dimensions, indeed! Is it possible to ever forget Ben's death scene? I have read it over three times, already, and each time I have found myself, through the indescribable magic of his word-weaving, standing at that grim bed-side with Eugene, and sharing his terrible anguish![161]

My dear love, when is there an end to our intolerable longings; when shall I draw near to me the precious flesh and bone and blood of you, not merely my elusive thought of you!

My lips kiss you and say "I love you"—

Your Ethel

Emanuel H. Bloch
7 W. 16th Street
New York New York

August 22, 1951

Dear Manny,

I'm hoping you can get here as early next week as you can; after to-day's visit with Ethel and my mother-in-law, I feel that it is imperative to begin straightening out an increasingly negative situation, as soon as humanly possible.

Even if you have to get here Wednesday (the day of my visit with Julie) I should prefer that to having to wait for you until Friday. Of course, if you can make it Monday or Tuesday, it would be so much the better.

In the meantime I have a practical suggestion for one particular problem my sister-in-law mentioned. She claims there is annoyance over the fact that

---

[161] See Thomas Wolfe, *Look Homeward Angel* (New York: Charles Scribner's Sons, 1929), Ch. 35.

the children rough it up rather noisily to-gether in the early morning before the adults are ready to rise and supervise their dressing and breakfasting. I used to prepare them, by a proper suggestion the night before, for them to use certain play materials, specifically laid out for their use [N3WI] (within easy reach) for quiet early morning play—to wit, materials like plasticene, a couple of particularly attractive books, (Something large and colorful which they don't get to see as often as [NWI] their other books—) a magic slate for each of them to scribble on, and nice, large, inviting pads of unlined drawing paper with a box of good crayons for each. —You might even say that their Mommy had made the suggestion for them to so behave in the morning and would be happy if they would [N2WI] try to remember to undertake this kind of play—just the same way they used to when Mommy and Daddy were still asleep at home. The adults have to be patient, however and realize they need [NWI] constant encouragement, and do their part also by making the necessary materials accessible. A new comic book, for instance, is a fine thing to ["get" CO, NWI above cross-out] start the ball rolling for Michael—and a couple of new rubber cars (for their noise-lessness) would be fine to get Robby started along those lines.—

No more now—So much to discuss with you early next week—Love
Ethel

P.S. The plasticene is molding clay with an oil base—["a new box for each" CO] (you ask for it as "plasticene" & you could tell my sister-in-law Lena to buy a few pounds of it [N3WI] in various colors at Hershey's before she comes to see them on Sunday)—a new portion for each child with a set of plastic, colored cookie cutters for each will keep them happy for a long time—

Emanuel H. Bloch
7 W. 16th Street
New York New York

August 22, 1951

Dear Manny,

It is only because I am terribly worried about my mother's health that I am forced to ask you to do something about this situation at a time when you are deep in work on our appeal. When my mother visited me today I noticed that she had lost a considerable amount of weight and that she had a sickly [N3WI] look about her. In the past she has been under constant medical care for her high blood pressure. For the last three months she hasn't seen a doctor. It is imperative that she see a neighborhood doctor at once as she might have a stroke if her pressure goes too high. Besides this, it is obvious that relations at home are are [*sic*] not good. It is necessary that Sophie and my mother individually discuss this problem with you and they be made to understand the necessity of accepting each other as a grown individual. There must be an early resolution of this difficulty. A complete listing of duties and responsibilities might help. Please understand that I feel that my mothers [*sic*] health is much worse and she needs medical attention.

The radio just announced the Circuit Court reversal of the Remington conviction and from what was said I can gather it will have far reaching effect and may be of use in our appeal.[162] This is certainly a blow against the high handed tactics of Saypol and the Justice Dept. This together with the splendid news you brought us[163] has bolstered our courage. We have never lost heart but it feels good to know things are happening.

Ethel showed me her subscription for parents magazine [*sic*] this morning and I received Amos Landman [*sic*] new book today. Tell Jerry his sincere efforts are boosting our moral [*sic*].[164] [N2WI] It is especially [NWI] good to know that we have a new and devoted friend. I always had faith in the people and I am sure this is only the beginning. Let all our friends know we're confident and we're counting on them to unmask this political frameup and help set us free. Our cause is just and right is on our side and it is only a matter of time, as soon as the facts are made known to them, that increasing numbers of my fellow Americans will raise their voices to rectify this injustic [*sic*]. I feel pretty good keep up the good work let me hear the positive results. Send all my best regards. Remember me to Pop. I am impatiently awaiting our next consultation.

With courage, confidence and perspective—Julius

---

[162]For the Remington case, see Caute, pp. 287–89.

[163]This must be a reference to the decision of the leftist but non-Communist *National Guardian* newspaper to do a series on the case. This seven-part series written by William A. Reuben began on August 15, 1951 with an article entitled, "The Rosenberg Conviction: Is This the Dreyfus Case of Cold-War America?" When this series was finished, enough interest had been generated to lead to the formation in October of the National Committee to Secure Justice in the Rosenberg Case. See James Aronson, *The Press and the Cold War* (NY: Monthly Review Press, 1990), pp. 58–60. See also Aronson and Cedric Belfrage, *Something to Guard: The Stormy Life of the National Guardian: 1948-1967* (NY: Columbia University Press, 1978), pp. 169–71.

[164]This "Jerry" is undoubtedly Jerome Eugene Tartakow. For a pro-Tartakow discussion see Radosh and Milton, *The Rosenberg File,* pp. 291-318. For a rebuttal, see *Sons,* pp. 392–93, 404–7, 408–19. See especially my discussion of Tartakow's alleged "infiltration" of the defense camp, pp. 418–19.

Ethel to Julius

August 23, 1951

My dearest Sweetheart,

The sweet serenity of this blue and golden day has laid a balm upon my sore and troubled spirit. I drink deeply of the heady wine of bright sun and jewelled air and know myself intoxicatingly alive and strong!

Which brings me right to the point; darling, your mother's life and strength are being sapped so appallingly that I am heartsick to think on her appearance. I wrote Manny at once urgently requesting an audience with him early next week for the purpose of working out a proper solution as soon as is humanly possible. In the meantime, I also went into some detail concerning certain materials that need to be made available for the children's unsupervised use in the early morning before the adults are ready to rise, since their noisy romping [N3WI] at this hour is a source of irritation. I suggested that he notify Lena to purchase plasticene [N3WI] and cookie cutters and magic slates and rubber cars at Hershey's before visiting the children on Sunday, for the period in question.

Something tells me, however, dear, that the situation involves not so much the matter of "way" so much as "will"—the crux of the matter [N2WI] to me lies in ascertaining just how much more desire the individual has to accept the hardships of the job[165] than the freedom to do as she pleases. More and more I get the feeling that whereas she was enamored at first of the idea of such a worthwhile undertaking, the actual daily requirements of it in terms of a sustained [NWI] highly personal giving and her possible negative reaction to same, she could not foresee. And now that the undertaking has turned into an onerous duty that binds and fetters, and in effect prevents her from living as she really is longing to live (and hasn't the courage to admit)—Mail call—

Love, Ethel
Continue next letter.

Julius to Ethel

Aug. 23rd, 1951

My Dearest Sweetest Wife,

Wednesday was quite wonderful. Seeing you my sister and mother all in one day. We had a two hour visit and it was very pleasant. Nevertheless I was terribly shocked to see my mother's sickly appearance. I, therefore, sent Manny a letter telling him to get my mother under a doctor's care at once and also asking him to clear up the difficult situation at home. Yesterday I

---

[165]"The other Sophie."

received the Amos Landman book and I ask our illustrious counselor to thank Jerry for the Parents magazine and the book and his sincere efforts on our behalf. Darling I hope you read the Circuit Court reversal of the Remington Conviction as it was a noteworthy one. I call your attention to the courts [*sic*] admonishment of the practices of Saypol and the errors of the Judge. If the court gives our case a fair review I feel confident it will reverse the conviction.

Daily in the New York Post there appears a word puzzle and it usually is a ten letter word and one has to try to form as many five letter words as possible. This has been added to my evening recreation. I got me a small brown butterfly and a nice white moth which I pressed between the pages of a book. Of course I'm following your lead and am already looking forward to the next time the children come to visit us. Darling please make notes so that we can go into the coming visit of our dears at our next Wednesday tete a tete. It will be necessary for us to see that Manny takes care of the technical details in advance of the visit.

Oh Honey, how I miss you. More and more I lie awake recounting our life together how wonderful it was. This horrible separation and terrible danger that we face has given me an opportunity to learn your true worth. Dearest you symbolize all that is good in life to me and I can only look forward to time of the triumphant return to our home. I imagine all the details of greeting the children and my mother and then being together with you. It cannot be otherwise as the issues are so clear and morally and legally we are not guilty of anything. So much suffering and heartache but the joy will be greater when we finally win. Can you see in my eyes my sweet what I want you to know? Does the smile that you've put on my face mean anything to you? Can you sense the feeling in my heart for you? You my love have a powerful pencil please put it in words for me. To you my life I give my very being. The passing of time raises my hope and increases my longing for you. My heart is bursting with love for you. Impatiently awaiting our next meeting—Always your fellow—Julius

Julius to Ethel

Aug. 26, 1951

My Most Dearest Ethel,

The last few days passed nicely as I was able to fill in the spare time reading a couple of light novels. Unfortunately my chess games have stopped because the fellows I play with have received copies of the printed record of their cases and are busy at work. As long as I'm able to keep occuppied [*sic*] I manage alright. To my collection of insects I've added a ɔcust and a dragon fly and I hope to have quite a few by the time of the ɔhildrens [*sic*] next visit.

Lena sent me a letter and told me that Michael had made friends with one of the boys at the day camp who lives in the neighborhood. He has already been at the boys' home, eaten there and a mutual arrangement has been made to exchange visits at each others['] house. If we can get a trained person to supervise our boys I'm certain their tensions will be eased. I am impatiently awaiting Manny's next visit. In the first place I am most concerned about my mother's health and the situation with Sophie at home. Then, of course, I want to hear more of the same kind of good news we heard last week. This has been the real bright spot and for us it holds great promise. However I still feel that things are moving too slowly both [N2WI] as to the passing of time and the progress of favorable developments. I hope, now that a good beginning [*sic*] has been made and the crucial period approaches, the tempo of events will increase.

As I sit and smoke my cigarette I think of the evenings we spent at home listening to records. It was so satisfying to relax together with you and enjoy the music and each others [*sic*] company while our sweets slept peacefully in their own room. All the little things we did together take on new and greater meaning and tell me I didn't know how lucky I was to have you and the children. I have learned the true worth of all this and I am a happier man for it. We didn't lose faith and now our position is going to be clarified and shown to greater and greater numbers of people and I am confident that this coupled to our expert legal defense will free us and prove our innocence. It cannot happen too soon for me and I'll make up to you and the boys for this lost time and all the horrible torture we suffered. Darling sweetheart continue to be my shining star and give me inspiration and strength[.] I need you more than ever. I love you my wife. Yours always—Julius
P.S. My warmest embrace and kisses will put you to sleep.

Ethel to Julius

August 27, 1951

My dearest darling love,

It was so frustrating to have to cut short my thoughts concerning the family situation on Friday; the only thing that prevented me from continuing to express myself over the week-end was the understanding that Manny might turn up this morning and so obviate the need to state my ideas in writing. Since he probably won't get here until Wednesday, however, and since I want both of us to be entirely capable of clarifying our position concerning the children, your mother and Sophie, I wish at this time to put

forth for your much desired consideration, certain conclusions which I hav̶
whether rightfully or wrongfully, nevertheless inevitably reached in the
interim of your folks' last two visits. You see, dear, I am convinced that
unless there is a radical and deep-going change of heart on the part of a far
too snobbish & self-seeking person, not only may we not expect a lessening of tensions but an intensification of the difficulties.[166]

Before I develop my theme more fully, darling, let me first tell you that
for some reason I cannot fathom, both your letters (of the 23rd and the 26th)
arrived to-gether this afternoon so I am wondering if mine, dated the 24th
was also held up until today.[167] From your lack of [NWI] any reference to
it, I gather as much. It must have given you quite a thrill, then, to have
[NWI] observed how closely my thoughts and feelings have been matching
your own on the all-important subject of your mother's distress and ill-
health, with no prompting whatever on your part, since I had not [NWI] as
yet [NWI] been in receipt of any word from you regarding your own reaction.
Darling, how could it be otherwise when we have possessed each other,
body and soul, in such richly satisfying, sweet mutuality, over such a
sizeable [*sic*] period of time!

Sweetheart, I appreciate what a labor of love your letters represent (as
indeed do my own to you); thereby was I the more delighted to behold not
one, but two such precious expressions. My heart swelled painfully and the
quick tears welled into my eyes; how touching was your tribute to me, how
beautiful your devotion! I want nothing so much as the strength and courage
to be true to myself and you!

Re the children, Manny must be made to realize that whatever your
mother's shortcomings, it does not add up to a row of pins compared to the
really excellent job she has been doing; as far as I have been able to see, it
is she who has been contributing the major share of the undertaking as
compared to the outrageously high-handed and childishly sullen behavior of
Sophie. [N6WI] There's no two ways about it. Your mother must be
accorded the same respect and consideration that she accords, or a proper
relationship cannot be maintained. Furthermore, it must be determined
whether she[168] wants the freedom to do as she pleases with her time more
than she wants to meet the demands [N2WI] of a (perhaps by now) onerous
job. Children don't grow right, you know, when they have to be over-
concerned with a touchy adult's feelings; it is not enough to know child
psychology if one is not [NWI] oneself emotionally disposed to put same

---

[166]See *Sons*, pp. 98, 108 for a contrary view of the problem.
[167]She must be referring to the one dated the 23rd above.
[168]From context, clearly referring to Sophie.

.to practice in a day to day giving. Have some practical suggestions, which will discuss with you on Wed—Love you, dearest Your Ethel

Julius to Ethel

Aug. 30th, 1951

To My Fair Flower of Ossining Manor,

Sweetheart your lover can report that since seeing you and Manny my morale is excellent and I'm in very good spirits. You do wonders to me darling and because of this great satisfaction I miss you all the more. Who ever invented celibacy deserves to be shot. It's not for me. The news our counselor brings us continues to raise my hopes and it's better to know exactly how long these legal matters will take and what we can expect. Yes my dear we're getting the best legal service there is. But more important to us is that the facts in the trial record be made public to prove our complete innocence. I am sure that you as well as I derived a great deal of satisfaction to know many people including strangers are taking a personal interest in our case. I wrote Michael a letter yesterday and told him of my insect collection. By the way I added four more speimans [*sic*] to-day. It makes me happy to know that Michael and Robert are going to go on outings and have a lot of fun with warm hearted people like Manny. I'm already looking forward to their next visit and I know it's going ["to" omitted] be a positive experience for them.

Even though Manny is cognizant of the home problem and my mothes [*sic*] deteriorating health I'll be concerned until I hear an adequate solution of this matter. However the fact that they are going about it in a proper way and are seeking expert advice I feel secure they'll work it out.

By the way honey I was elated to hear how well you handled Bernie and now that I've heard the details I'm convinced that your approach is the best and besides you're able to go at your own pace. I have to give you credit for trying to help others when you yourself are in such difficult circumstances. I know what a jewel you are and I can appreciate it but it hurts to see how even at this time your family still trys [*sic*] to get at you. How cruel this is and good for you that you saw through it and ["didn't let it" CO] acted correctly and didn't let it faze you. Your [*sic*] so wonderful sweetheart and growing mentally and emotionally all the time. Keep it up as you set a good example for me and spur me on to emulate you. Considering the situation and the separation from you, I'm feeling pretty good on the whole. Ethel I miss you very much but it will hold as I'm certain we will beat this frameup and make up for all this lost time. Let us continue my love in the spirit of courage, confidence and perspective.—So long for now—Your man—Julius [Words "growing up" written in parenthesis under the word "Your man"]

Ethel to Julius

August 30, 1951

My dearest, sweetest Julie bunny,

Ever since our immensely satisfying legal visit on Wednesday (to say nothing of our own sweet personal exchange directly preceding it) I have been mulling over the matters in question to such sound advantage, that I am now in process of composing one of my famous (!) expositions, intended to properly re-evaluate the entire situation and orientate Manny's thinking along certain definite lines with a view to the best possible solution. I'll go into [NWI] specific detail at the first opportunity; the intended trip [N2WI] up here of the children will also [N2WI] of course come in for serious attention from us.

It is amazing to me on what a comparatively high level of endeavor I am operating. Darling how much your love encourages and sustains me! The thought of you, my husband, my dear, sets up such a deep, warm response, it seems as though I must perish of tender longing. The thought, too, of the children, renders me helpless with fear and anguish!

Speaking of the children reminds me that I neglected to tell you that Bernie had left a number of snapshots upon leaving; unfortunately, they arrived Wednesday afternoon, making it impossible for you to see them. They are so good (you will simply go overboard for one in particular, I know) that you will be as thrilled as I was to have them.

Mail Call—

Love, Ethel

Emanuel H. Bloch
7 W. 16th Street
New York New York

August 31, 1951
Letter # 1

Dearest Manny,

I feel I must write to tell you how highly gratifying your visit was; for us to have been able to exchange views in which each of us is emotionally involved in one way or another, on the intellectually honest level that was maintained throughout not only is most commendable in itself but augurs well for an eventual solution. At the same time, I am not exactly unaware of the difficulties the situation poses.

However, due to the [NWI] particular facts around which our talk revolved and the light it served to throw upon the existant [*sic*] negative relationship, a certain picture that [*sic*] has begun to take shape in my mind that I should like to share with you. The fact that stands out most sharply from among the welter of detail and seems to me to deserve the most serious attention, is the imperative need, in that household, for a single authority, which must operate despite the fact that there will of necessity have to be two sets of people (Julie's folks on the one hand, and the stranger, or pair of strangers, on the other), that will be guided by that authority. Obviously, in the present set-up, the representatives of each of the two sides are very self-assertive; Sophie very vocally and demandingly so, Julie's mother, benevolently and apparently undemandingly, but nonetheless so. Now, since we agreed for various [NWI] substantial reasons that my mother-in-law stays, no matter who does not, it behooves us to try to determine just what kind of person or persons would hit it off best with her and yet be capable of holding the reins firmly and enforcing the single authority that is so vital for the provision of the common good.

You see Manny, there is one glaring error in Sophie's calculations, [N3WI] the recognition & the rooting out of which might have spelled the difference between the gentle yet intelligent authority so desperately needed, & the tense, chaotic state of conflict that does [N2WI] in fact exist. The fact remains that no matter how important it may be to properly guide the intellectual and emotional development of children, these do not proceed counter to and apart from what Sophie (and you, too, to a lesser degree) has chosen to contemptuously designate & push aside as "mechanics", unfortunately, one cannot behave inconsistently with children, gaining their confidence and respect in one area, and exposing our lack of will and love (& perhaps even, incidentally, jealousy of the people who do have those very abilities we pretend to scorn), on other fronts. The good mother (or mother-substitute) wisely recognizes that "integration" is the key to proper childrearing. Furthermore, it has been proven time and again that the worker in the shop who commands the respect and admiration of other workers is not necessarily the one who can spout political quotations at will and at the same [here the letter breaks off at the end of the page]

Emanuel H. Bloch
7 W. 16th St
NY NY

Letter # 2

Dear Manny,
        C't'd from Letter # 1
—time performs his duties with a grumbling and sloppy indifference; no, rather is it the best worker of the job to whom the others will listen and by whom they will be happy to let themselves be guided. Translating this in terms of our own problem, it seems to me only correct to assume that no matter how sympathetic and understanding we may be about the peculiar difficulties involved on this particular job (Julie's mother, the children's needs, etc), and no matter how valid these reasons may have been,—I say it would be dodging our responsibilities if we did not unequivocally recognize that Sophie was not able to rise above the feelings of personal discomfiture that the job (with all its attendant headaches) engendered, and thereby lost a splendid opportunity to command respect through sheer performance. Not only did she fail to take the lead, not only did she complain about the miseries of her lot, but at the same time, she secretly resented the top grade performance of an individual who was clearly inferior to her in many other respects.

        Believe me, the foregoing emphasis on Sophie's lacks, does not by any means set aside my genuine understanding (expressed to you during our visit) that my mother-in-law was herself harboring a similar resentment & jealousy; however, it is nevertheless my contention that despite such a natural inclination on her part & despite her other faults, these would have [unreadable word crossed out here] taken a back seat in the face of proper appreciation of her very real abilities & virtues combined with an authority bolstered by the type of initiative & performance as I have already indicated. In other words, the complaint was lodged that Julie's mom was not permitting Sophie to take the initiative with the kids but there is no getting around it that Sophie was emotionally incapable of taking that initiative when she might have—
        No more now. Mail call

Love, Ethel

        Will continue—

Julius to Ethel

Sept. 2nd, 1951

My Dearest Sweetheart Ethel,

Your splendid demeanor at our last meeting and the bright tone of your last letter tells me that you are confident and you are vigorously applying yourself to help solve the problems at home and of the children. It sets me at ease to know that in spite of all the great pain that your motherhood has been suffering and not withstanding endless longing and mental pressure and emotional anguish you can find the strenghth [*sic*] to bear up under it and also be able to participate in planning our legal defense and the future of our family. By your example you have encouraged me and especially so since Wednesday. I've been quite relaxed, reading a couple light novels, solving word puzzles, playing ball, reading newspapers and generally taking it easy. Since my days are pretty well occuppied [*sic*] I've spared myself from long periods of musing on our predicament. That is not to imply that I don't have my bad moments of being fed up with this separation from you, the children and the knowledge of the Damoclean sword that hangs over our heads. But I feel we have found within ourselves the stamina and strength to carry on. How could it be otherwise when in truth we are mere victims of a hideous political frameup that is [N4WI] being used in order to add to the mounting hysteria of the cold war. Oh my darling what great wrong has been perpetrated and what terrible harm has [NWI] been heaped on our family. I can thank you for the wonderful years and experiences we have had together that is doing us stead in this hour of our great need. Our complete unity, mutual sharing and understanding is the bulwark of our character and the foundation of our confidence. Naturally because I'm fully cognizant of your virtues do I find the pain in my heart so overwhelming. Only because I am sure of the future and the victory it has in store for us can I satisfy myself with the slow progress being made in our case and with the personal family difficulties. When I first met you I was captivated by your personality and charm and even after you became [N2WI] my wife and our relationship grew and matured I could not conceive that it could possibly reach such a high level of human dignity and stature as it now has. It has always been my contention that [N4WI] under the proper conditions there are no limits to the heights people can reach, scientifically, mentally, socially and personally. I'll always be grateful for the full life we've enjoyed together the years of our marriage and I look forward in great anticipation of a happier and fuller life with you and the children. You guessed it I'm in love with you and therefore happy—Your Julius

[Letter continued on top of second side] Lots to talk to you about Wednesday—I hold you close to my heart—J

Order your candy for the kids

Emanuel H. Bloch
7 W. 16th Street
New York New York

September 3, 1951
Letter # 3

Dear Manny,

To continue directly from Letter # 2

One of the best examples of this inability on her part (there were a number of similar examples which got lost in the shuffle when you were last here), was her attitude toward bathing the children. Personally, I'm all for cutting corners myself & found nothing to decry in the fact that Mike was showered, even though after months of showering at the Shelter, he certainly could have stood to gain by the luxury of frequent baths in the heat of summer. However, in the case of Robby, whom she saw fit to stand up in a small, slippery wash bowl (with the attendant danger of protruding faucets), even after the well-taken suggestion was made that she seat herself near the tub on the ladder stool so as to avoid straining her back (which she had originally given as her reason for not properly bathing him)—I say, this is an example of the kind of thing which forced my mother-in-law to take the initiative, willy nilly, you see, by taking a self-willed and childishly offended attitude when she did not meet the requirements of the job & when they then, of necessity, had to be pointed out to her, she actually reinforced my mother-in-law's hand, rather than her own.

Let's take a look for a minute at her attitude concerning the children's romping in the early morning prior to the time of her own rising. During one of my sister-in-law Ethel's visits to the house, she very pleasantly suggested a possible course of action for the temporary separation of the kids, Robby to stay with her, until the household was ready to begin the day, and asked for her own ideas if any, on the subject. The only response was a sullen silence; now while it is understandable that Sophie was perhaps not inclined to embrace a suggestion which involved the further taxing of her patience just when she wanted most to rest, it is patently clear that her reaction represented not so much an interest in solving the problem her own way as opposed to Ethel's, as a resentment that there should be such a problem to begin with and a resistance to coping with same at all.

Incidentally, [N3WI] let me state for the record, that I was mistaken when I said my mother-in-law had not told me of her [NWI] sudden exit from the house, when Sophie without a word of warning silently prepared to leave. She very definitely did [N4WI] tell me of it and although I reprimanded her for her own lack of consideration, I could not help but feel that she was simply giving her a dose of the kind of unpleasant medicine she had been dishing out herself. After all, it was for Sophie to explain her need to go out & to assure her she would be back at a reasonable hour.

Perhaps it will seem to you that I am needlessly belaboring the point & thereby, also unmercifully flaying Sophie; however there are some very vital lessons

c't'd Letter # 4 Yours, Ethel

Emanuel H. Bloch
7 W. 16th St
New York New York

September 4, 1951[169]
Letter # 4

Dear Manny,—c't'd from Letter #3
to be learned from such a thorough-going analysis which we would do well to heed; that is my sole purpose for making it along the lines I have. As I said before, (and I have not changed my mind) there is a crying need for a single authority, one comprising Sara,[170] your wife, a really good child psychologist, Dr. Miller, Julie and myself, who will be responsible to do the following:

1) Make recommendations concerning the setting up of the proper routines and schedules for the children, taking into account attendance at school and extra-curricular activities outside & inside the home.

2) Act as an Advisory Committee to whom those who will be handling the children may turn for general guidance, the solution of specific problems and the redress of any grievances that may arise.

3) Screen prospective candidates for the position that Sophie proposes to vacate, in terms of their own emotional balance, [NWI] their knowledge & experience in the field of child psychology, and their sympathy for us.

This last brings us back to the business of the kind of relationship we should seek to establish between the adults who will have the daily responsibility of the children. As I said before, it is largely a question of determining what kind of person would hit it off best with my mother-in-law. I think the selection narrows down to one of two main categories; either the person (or persons) must be 1) less assertive than my mother in-law and happy to follow her lead, or 2) more assertive than her, but knowing what she's about in terms of child care & accustomed to actual

---

[169]Because of the contents of a letter written to Julius on September 3, continued on the morning of September 4, I believe this is misdated and was actually written on September 3. This is true for the letters numbered 5 and 6 also.

[170]The identity of this woman is not known.

physical contact with them, having a genuine desire and ability to understand and appreciate their needs, and to derive satisfaction from working out
solutions in unison with my mother-in-law (where necessary) & in serving
these needs. Personally, I should prefer the 2nd style for she would be far
more capable of implementing the recommendations of the Advisory
Committee & keeping my mother-in-law under control, than the 1st.
Actually, however, it doesn't much matter which style is chosen for I intend
this Committee to play a major role & be the over-all authority to which
both parties must give their undivided support and to whom they must
consider themselves responsible.

The one thing that does matter is an ability to be realistic about the
requirements of the job, and a sincere desire on an unconscious as well as a
conscious level to undertake it. Of course, I can hear you saying impatiently, "But we went over all this, so why the re-hash?" That is true only
in the sense that some of these ideas have been voiced. I am taking our
discussion a step further by specifically aligning our thinking along those
lines that will begin to make for a practical application. Our talk while
vastly
c't'd Letter # 5 Yours, Ethel—

Emanuel H. Bloch
7 W. 16th Street
New York New York

September 4, 1951
Letter # 5

Dear Manny,
        C't'd from Letter #4
stimulating and fruitful, left matters far too vague and nebulous for my
comfort; hence the foregoing attempts to draw a more clearly defined picture.

To elucidate now a bit about the composition of the Committee; you
may have been surprised to note the proposed inclusion of your wife and Dr.
Miller. Nevertheless, they are both absolutely vital to the proper functioning of the Committee. First of all, your wife has already established an
excellent rapport with my mother-in-law, the need for which is implicit; and
will make it her business (because she has already clearly shown she wants
to) to see both parties more frequently than Sara and the psychologist will
perforce be able to manage. Now, why Dr. Miller, when it is planned to
have a child psychologist, anyway? Well, to begin with, Dr. Miller is the
only person in the group (apart from Julie & me) who knows Michael's
previous history in its entirety and is in a position to obtain from the JBG
[Jewish Board of Guardians] all the records that are available up to the

resent moment; for this reason, and others involving my own rapport with him, he is a natural for the task of keeping me (& thru me, Julie) informed as to the development of the children & their continuing needs. With Dr. Miller, one trained person, bringing me the observations of the trained person who will be working directly with the kids, Julie and I will be able to evaluate their needs on a far more solidly scientific basis than we have hitherto been able to do on the basis of the necessarily haphazard, oft-times half-baked and scientifically unsound opinions & feelings of Julie's sisters, Sophie (thru your wife & you) and yourself. And through him, by the same token, Julie & I, the parents, will be able to make our wishes about the kids understood to the trained people on the Committee at the same time, freeing you from a responsibility that forces you to continually divert your energies and concentration. I know it sounds complicated but then no apparatus looks like there's a ghost of a chance that it will ever operate while it's still on paper. Once we know what we want from an apparatus & we then set it in motion, it's amazing how simply and easily it begins to produce.

Whew, I'm glad that's off my chest. Now, Manny dear, I'd like you to start the ball rolling by contacting Dr. Miller, if possible before coming here on Friday, and giving him a detailed report of the present precarious situation, so that whatever I may see fit to suggest to him when I write him will add up to sense.

c't'd—Letter # 6—Yours, Ethel

Emanuel H. Bloch
7 W. 16th Street
New York New York

September 4, 1951
Letter #6

Dear Manny,
     C't'd from Letter #5
     I want to caution you in closing to give yourself enough of a head-start from the city on Friday to cover any unexpected delays and still enable you to get here at 12:30 as planned. Make sure in advance that Jerry[171] knows

---

[171]This is the only documented time that Jerome Eugene Tartakow drove Robby, Manny and me to Sing Sing to see our parents. Radosh and Milton write, "Bloch was not at home behind the wheel of a car, and the problem of getting two nervous and overexcited children to the Hudson Valley hamlet of Ossining, . . . suddenly created a job for a willing volunteer. And so it happened that, beginning in October, Jerry Tartakow took over the task of chauffeuring Manny Bloch and the children on their trips to Ossining." (p. 316) According to Tartakow's own reports to the FBI he only drove us to Sing Sing once not

exactly how to get here, so that there shall be no slip-ups and consequen. loss of time. You might also take the precaution of bringing a bit of food along from home and then just in case there is inadequate time to stop for lunch, you can feed them just before you hit Ossining, & they can eat more substantially, if it is required, after the visits are over.

I know you're probably sore as bats because I'm instructing you as though you were a simpleton; be that as it may I shall beat your brains out (& Jerry's, too) if you frustrate me by coming late. Remember, you once told me you wouldn't mind being my whipping boy? Well, this is it!

Seriously though, the thought that has gone into all these letters stems from a torment of anxiety about the future of the children. You can understand that, can't you?

Love, Ethel

Ethel to Julius

September 3, 1951

Dearest darling sweetheart,

What a dull dreary, gloom-laden week-end this has been; I feel like some disembodied wraith moving apathetically through the gray mist of my tomb, watching a strange creature who, by permission of some weird trick of the imagination, still fancies itself alive and affects some feeble, mechanical gestures to support its futile claim!

And yet does my shining spirit still flaunt its gold-bright banner upon wind and rain; to-morrow it [NWI] will match the sun's own blaze for Man is a Sun unto himself, strive he but for his own nobility! [here she filled a line across the page with dashes]

After that little flight of fancy, you deserve to be informed that I have completed the detailed analysis intended for Manny's special delectation (he'll probably want to murder me for my trouble); actually, I have made a number of serious suggestions which I am certain will receive his serious attention. But you know how I must always be belittling my perfectly valid & worthy efforts! Please, darling, marry me soon and take me home to the children; I am in a torment of anxiety for their future!

---

monthly [see JR NY 1841, October 25, 1951] and according to this letter it was in September not October. Meanwhile, we had already had our first visit and had gone by train.

7:00 A.M.—September 4, 1951

Dearest, last night I gorged myself on Labor Day ice-cream, thinking of you as I ate, doing likewise, all by your lonesome, except of course that yours was made a shade more palatable by the [NWI] brilliant repartee of the "CC Cynics." I became slightly hysterical, myself, when, upon tuning in on "Suspense," we were regaled by a thrilling account of a jail-break. Fitting fare, indeed, eh wot, for a cozy evening at Ossining Manor? Fortunately, there were some very fine musical programs which I enjoyed immensely.

Dearest, I'd like you to make a list of the kind of questions that are likely to arise on Friday, guiding yourself by the style of thing that came out during the children's first visit. On Wednesday, we might manage [N2WI] between us to nail down a bit more concretely what ought to be our goals in order to promote the most positive kinds of contact with them until we are once more a part of their daily lives.

Sweetheart, I can't write any more; my heart is too full of sorrow! Dear love, I need you so desperately. Summer is over and I can't help feeling depressed! The sight of you will, I know, gladden me back to happiness; I love you, dear sweet husband!

Always, Your own girl, Ethel.

P.S.—Honey bun, am ordering a box of Schraffts candy for the kids, as a joint offering, but if you still wish to get them some hard candy or chocolate bars by all means do so—Kisses—Ethel

Ethel to Julius

Sept. 5, 1951

My very own dear, precious boy,

The sweet light that shone softly in your eyes as they rested tenderly upon me opened [NWI] wide the flood-gates of my deepest love feelings, washing away all my heart's bitter ache and suffusing me with its warmth. Only now, my beloved, by contrast, nothing has any power to charm me, and my longings will not relent. Sweetest darling, shall that bright day ever dawn when we shall be in each other's arms again!

Bunny dear, since our visit, I have been feverishly pacing about indoors and out, thinking of the children's coming visit and jotting down possible answers to possible questions. The following will give you some clue as to my mental ramblings, supplementing the suggestions I made earlier to you with regard to our status here as inmates awaiting outcome of appeal.

"The reason I play ball alone except for the Matrons is that I am the only lady inmate in a men's prison; you see since Daddy and I stood trial together, it was decided that we should not be separated pending our appeal. Of course, it makes us very happy that we are in the same prison; first of all, we [N3WI] are able to see each other once a week and [NWI] secondly, it makes it easier for everybody else to see us. Naturally, we wish we could live to-gether while we are here, but there are certain rules and regulations that must be enforced when there are so many people to be guarded, and although to you it seems mean that we should be kept apart, the authorities have to treat us the same as everybody else. Besides, Daddy couldn't have matrons looking after him any more than I could have guards looking after me. [There is a "^" here with a line running down nine lines to five lines that she obviously wished to insert here. The text as follows is the way she first wrote it. The insertion will be identified as such when we reach it.] Living alone, makes it hard for us but lots easier for the authorities to do their job, which is to keep us well and safe and sound so that when the reversal we are working for so hard comes through, they can produce us in court. Of course, knowing your Daddy and Mommy as you do, you are sure we would never do any foolish thing like trying to escape or doing ourselves or someone else harm. But there are prisoners who do attempt such acts, so they are simply not taking any chances with us."

[Here the "^" sign begins a new line] "Question of privacy involved in men taking care of men and women of women. Only when there is an intimate relation into which the man and woman have entered through deliberate choice is their [*sic*] not need for such privacy."

I don't know what, if any good, the foregoing will do you; I am laboring with an increasing sense of self-consciousness and lack of confidence in my ability to do right by them. I have determined to let Mike help me by first asking him what he figure's [*sic*] an answer might be, before I attempt to give an opinion. Probably it will be a lot easier when I have got them in my arms, at last and can [NWI] really demonstrate how much I love them—Julie dearest, I miss you and them and the [NWI] beautiful life we lead as dreadfully, I am suffocating—I love you, my sweetheart—Yours always, Ethel

Mrs. Ethel Goldberg
5347–65th Place
Maspeth Long Island

Sept. 6, 1951

Dearest Ethel,

It was so very thoughtful of you to supply the children with a radio pending acquisition of the one you mentioned in your letter to me; Julie and I are most appreciative, believe me.

I saw him on Wednesday, as usual, and enjoyed hearing what you had written him. You addressed him, I clearly remember, as "Precious Brother"; he is that, indeed, you may be sure, we gazed at each other longingly through "The Thing" (yep, we've finally solved the mystery) and fought back the tears. And yet, bitter though such a visit cannot help but be, we are so happy in each other's company and have so much to talk about, that the hour is full to the brim with love and laughter.

I have just finished reading a book called "The Birth of Israel" by Garcia Granadas [*sic*]. During a description of the ramming of a Jewish D. P.[172] ship headed for Palestine by a British destroyer, an old man is calmly heard to remark, "I have lived through the Tsarist hell, the Polish hell, and the Nazi hell, and something tells me that I'll live through the British hell, too!"

We, too, are calm in the face of danger for our cause, too, is a just one! It cannot be otherwise but that right must prevail! That we are human and that we therefore suffer, goes without saying, but we are proud in our innocence and firm in our belief that the victory will but be the sweeter for all the fearful torment of the time we now spend apart!

At this moment, I am surprised that I am able to formulate a [NWI] single coherent sentence; as you may well imagine, I am tense with expectancy over the children's intended visit to-morrow.

Speaking of the children reminds me of the turbulent situation at home. Of course, I am delighted at whatever progress has already been made; your comment about the change of attitude on Sophie's part toward you would indicate as much. I wrote Manny making a number of practical suggestions and I am hopeful that eventually a real solution will be worked out. In the meantime, I know that it's tough going all around.

Send Oscar my best wishes for fully recovered health and strength; tell him for me that it's a wise man who makes haste slowly! Please telephone Lena and tell her I am waiting to write her until after her visit; according to what you wrote Julie I take it she'll be here on Saturday. In any case, I'll correspond with her next week. My very best regards to all my loved ones.—Ethel P.S.—I'd appreciate very much if you would bring with you [N4WI] on your next visit a sample of Deanna's[173] work; I am full of curiosity and pride—Love you all, Ethel

---

[172]Displaced Persons, a term used to describe the many people made refugees by World War II.
[173]Ethel's daughter, a high school graduate.

Julius to Ethel

Sept. 6, 1951

My Dearest Love Ethel,

Your letters are awaited with great expectation and the reward [N2WI] for one is very gratifying as it soothes the ache in my heart. I am deeply honored and thrilled to get such glowing bouquets from my better half. When I hear from you my moral [*sic*] reaches a high point but never the high peak of our weekly visit. It is only natural that everything else in comparison is on a much lower level and therefore is a great letdown. The day getting shorter and the approach of winter has it's [*sic*] dimming effect on us who are isolated from the world we love. But I am sure we are well fortified to overcome all these temporary moments of gloom. To me it is remarkable that the mind and body is able to withstand such punishment. Only I who share this misery with you can know fully the endless torment and anguish the rivers of tears and the bushels of pain. Many times it seems the mortal individual cannot withstand the pressure that only steel is designed to resist. If I may make use of our Tuesday discussion I can put my faith in the one word, that we in the past and today are truely [*sic*] honest [emphasis in original]. Explanations are not needed as you and I understand each other and know the solid foundations on which it's built. This is our strenght [*sic*] and our perspective gives us the hope and courage. It cannot be otherwise as we must be set free to return to each other and our children as that is the only justice in our case.

I had hoped that you would receive this letter before you visit the children but I'm confident that you'll come through with flying colors as usual. Before any new experience I too am apprehensive lest I do not measure up as in the case of our childrens [*sic*] visit. Because of your great love for them and your anxiety over their emotional security you are concerned as any mother in like situation would be. Don't go back to belittling yourself but now that the visit is over take credit for a job well done. My talks with you and your letters of advice has [*sic*] prepared me to play a more constructive role and it is you who deserve the praise for all the groundwork in this matter. Now that you are able to review your past handling of the children in all objectivity you can be proud of your accomplishment. Of one thing I am sure both of us will be better able to help our two dears and guide their emotional, mental and physical lives. I too join you in the plea, how long must we suffer for we are innocent. I can only take comfort in my love for you and I hope that as time passes my faith in the people and American Justice will be reaffirmed by our final victory and freedom from this black despair. Only you can keep me going with your love and support. Your own fellow—Julius

Sept. 9, 1951

My Dearest Sweetheart,

The childrens [*sic*] visit turned out just perfect. They were in excellent spirits from the time I entered the room and enjoyed it so much that they were disappointed when it was over and Michael said he wants more. Because of the good effect you had on them the atmosphere was like a warm family get together. The boys were hidding [*sic*] under the desk and Robbie [*sic*] childlike giggles gave them away. They rushed to me and we embraced. "Oh Goodie"! said Michael [the words "I gave him" probably belong here] a pencil and pad and he began to draw. I showed them my collection of insects and put a couple of bananas and two hershey bars on the table. The big fellow said Daddy Please don't stuff us. Robbie however proceeded to down both hersheys and a banana and romped around screeching and acting mischievous. I held him close kissed him and carried him around so I could talk to Michael. Most of the hour was spent in discussion. It started with a discussion of the death sentence which he said he read about in the paper. I told him we were not concerned about that we were innocent and we had many avenues of appeal and that it was not his job to be concerned about it but to grow up and be well. He asked me how you die and I told him and he asked if there is an electric chair here and I said yes. He kept on asking about the appeals and what if finally we might lose then death faced us. I kept on assuring him but I could see he was terribly upset over it. He then looked at the Sgt. and said you'd better watch me for I don't want my mother and father to die for if they do I'll kill Dave. His determination, sincerity and youthful grave look moved me so. Another time he said Daddy the man in the Guardian says you are innocent too and I'd like to give him the four dollars I saved in my piggy bank because he's for you. He asked many questions of what he read about money, fingerprints[,] the actions of the F.B.I. and the jury. I explained as well as I could and Manny helped and told him on the ride back home he'll go into more detail. The boy said Daddy maybe I'll study to be a lawyer and help you in your case and I said we wont [*sic*] wait that long as we want to be with him and grow up together. He wants so to help us, to do something and be assured that all will be well, with us. Oh Darling he is burdened with all these grownup problems and he feels them deeply. I asked him how his Bubbie Sophie was and he said not so good because he gives her trouble. You understand he makes noise and the neighbors complain and he has guilt feelings that they'll make them move because of it. A little incident took place that revealed something of Robbie's problem. In his exuberance he spun the tray with the glasses around and one of them fell off and broke and immediately he skooted [*sic*] around Manny to hide and Mike said look what you done. But I pooh poohed it and reassured him. The baby and Michael are both frightened and only our early return to them will quickly heal all the harm done. When I see you I'll have lots more to tell you. I'm sorry if I rambled. I miss you terribly. All my love my sweetest darling

Julius

Ethel to Julius

Sept. 9, 1951

My dearest one,

This afternoon I basked in the sun, mind and body blessedly at rest, face uplifted to its pleasant warmth. I closed my eyes and floated in happy forgetfulness, grateful for the kindness of a sparkling breeze that occasionally wafted its playful way across my deliciously relaxed being. It was a forgetfulness I sought out deliberately, knowing full well its temporary nature, its short-lived enjoyment, yet desperate to escape my tormentingly vivid recollections of the children's visit on Friday.

At first, each joyous moment [N2WI] of it that memory served to recapture so charmingly for me brought only glad delight but last night Michael's mischievously smiling face twisted with grief before my horrified eyes and Robby's sweetly appealing mien grew sad and bewildered. Make no mistake about it; my mother's heart is being methodically and mercilessly broken for me and the pain is simply not to be imagined! My only hope for the attainment of some kind of mental peace for myself lies in my continuing concern with their guidance and active involvement in problems relating to same; and the establishment of a more far-reaching continuity between visits than has yet been achieved. By the same token, however, this kind of activity by its very nature will open me up to further pain and sorrow; yet must the anguish of the mold into which my parenthood has ruthlessly been poured by a hideous wolf-pack which still dares to consider itself human, somehow also be my job and my triumph!

Sept. 10, 1951

And how fare you today, my love, in this glorified slaughter-house? Your dear wife is presently thrilling [N2WI] to the masterful artistry of Ezio Pinza and the brilliant rendition of Brahm's Hungarian Dance #4 by the Don Voorhees Orchestra. Music never fails to weave its magical enchantment for me, gently exhorting me to lay aside the day's onerous burden and succumb to its blandishments.

7:15 A.M. Sept. 11, 1951

Good morning, sweetest—I just et!

Darling, I am quite distressed at some of the mistaken attitudes that seem to be for the most part prevalent at the house, as expressed by Lena during her visit. I am afraid I was a bit too vehement in my anxious desire to make her understand. It is imperative that trained people begin to make themselves felt or both kids will become more nervous counterparts of the adults now handling them. Sweetheart, you must try to remember every last precious thing our two darling pussy cats said and did while they were with you; I shall be on tenterhooks until you "come on a my house"[174] tomorrow. Incidentally, I wrote Miller urging him to do just that at his earliest convenience. He's bound to phone Manny and get the complete lowdown; then when the women we need return to the city, all of us can begin to really hammer out a solution—

All my heart—dearest—Ethel

Ethel to Julius

Sept. 12, 1951

My dearest darling Julie,

Miraculously, a stone has rolled off my heart; the precious sight and sound of you put an entirely different complexion upon the day. And from the depths of me there wells such a paen [*sic*] of proud thanksgiving; they are sorry swine indeed, who think they can beat people of our integrity to our knees!

At this point, I want to commend most strongly to your attention Dr. Alfred Blazer's column in Friday's "Compass";[175] I am sure you will agree that it is "must" reading for anyone who professes to be enlightened. Its interest is further enhanced for us as forward-looking socially conscious parents who are genuinely concerned with giving our children that kind of emotional security that will enable them to face with confidence the special problems that the horror of our situation has imposed upon them. Oddly enough, a point that I raised [NWI] very specifically during our visit is the very one that is so intelligently discussed in the column; the following paragraph beautifully expresses exactly what I myself was struggling rather ineffectively to explain.

---

[174]The words of a popular song meaning "come over to my house" but sung with what passed for an Italian accent among non-Italians.
[175]The *New York Compass* was a left-liberal newspaper which published in the late 1940s and into the early 1950s.

"Even if the rational, intellectual approach of your letter were translated into the language of children, it would be ineffective. Children have no "frame of reference" to begin with. Each one develops his own, beginning like soft sculptor's clay and molded by the environment around him."

Darling, that hour is so pitifully little; no matter how quickly we dispose of the various items under advisement, we are still talking fast and furious when it comes time for you to leave. I wanted so badly to take up Lena's visit in detail, but we were able to only just touch upon it. Did she mention an incident involving a phone call that Michael asked permission to put through to a kid residing at Knickerbocker Village? Your mother refused to let him do so on the ground, as Lena explained it to me, that it was raking up old fires which were better left to burn out. Also, Lee told me she had advised Michael to tell anyone who asked that we were away on a trip; I suggested it might be wiser [N3WI] for the child to avoid having to give any kind of answer by simply saying he didn't care to discuss a personal matter. Now it comes to me that curious adults ought to be referred [NWI] directly to the adults in the house but that curious children are a matter for Michael's own judgment right on the spot. Of course, the problem requires a great deal more thought and effort; the longer I live the more I realize there are no facile answers, arrived at over-night! Kind of mull over all that I have written; it is by no means my last word on the subject, either.

I love you, sweetheart. Ethel

Julius to Ethel

September 13, 1951

My Dearest Honey Wife,

You told me of the letter you sent me Tuesday morning and even though I've already received the one you sent dated the 12th I didn't as yet receive the one of the 10th. I sent the P.K. [principal keeper] a note asking him to look into the matter. Speaking of letters your last one was good reading and I'm glad to see that your [sic] back on an even keel. The incident you mentioned concerning Michael is new to my ears and I'm glad you gave me all the details because it is important that we take cognizance of the existance [sic] of these problems and recommend our ideas on this subject to my people. As for Blazers [sic] column I agree with you it is very edifying [NWI] particularly on this matter we are now thinking about and in passing I'd like to say that the entire paper should be read very carefully as it fills in a void that is left because of our isolation from the street. Outside of our visits and mail this is the closest contact we have with people and the world we know and love. Coming back to our big fellow my first impression is

that it is wrong to burden him with growup [*sic*] problems such as having
to answer as to where we are to adults. I am in accord with your idea that he
say he refuses to discuss this matter with them. Then, too, it is good not to
put too many restrictions on what he should answer and let him say what he
wishes. The thing that is most important is that he feel secure and not be
disturbed about our predicament and that he know as much as he can
understand of our trial, our appeal, our chances and how we feel. This
knowledge coupled with ["to" CO] a happier home and play life will set the
basis for him being able in his stride to face the questions his playmates
might ask about his parents. To me this is a necessary must so that he will
not be disturbed about what he has to answer to whomever he meets. Of
course, it is essential that my mother and family see eye to eye with us on
this matter and when similar circumstances arise in the future they will be
prepared to properly direct his course. In a way I'm glad this came up now
and I look to you to prepare an outline for our next Wednesday meeting to
concentrate on this subject and thereby anticipate possible situations. I,
further, believe it is a healthy sign that he should make efforts to find links
to his happy past and he should be encouraged in a constructive manner to
continue in this way in order for him to regain his confidence and emotional
security. We must not fail to talk to Manny about this and you ought to
talk to Dr. Miller about it. Let me hear more about this matter before our
next visit —Sweetheart adorable darling I send you all my love—Julius

Ethel to Julius

Sept. 13, 1951

Dearest sweetheart of mine,

In contrast to the mental state I last described to you, I have since
developed a case of the "CC Conundrums". This is a malady compounded
chiefly of monotony, generously sprinkled with lassitude and garnished with
a plenitude of loneliness and boredom. Last night I was fired with the determination to shake some of the problems that had gone unheard at our
weekly meeting; this morning the frustration of this dreary, endless scribbling, made a quick end of my enthusiasm. The day has [NWI] since wended
its weary way onward, and as I indifferently await my cheese and tomato
dinner, I come to the inescapable conclusion that your wife is lazy, looney
and lousy! Also lackadaisical!

Honey bun, why must I be subject to these dismally discouraging
periods of inertia, when I'm so much happier hitting on all cylinders! But I

suppose I had better resign myself to a certain amount of depression and let-down as part payment for my "priceless" experience of Sing Sing![176]
    I am looking forward more eagerly than is customary even for me, to your sister's visit on Saturday; I am taking same for granted, in view [NWI] of your mother's absence on Wednesday. If you see her first, don't fail to raise the entire matter of the establishment of solid relationships with new people (both children and adults) in a new neighborhood; I am very anxious to hear your opinions about same and would welcome any suggestions that you might care to make for the benefit of my own subsequent thinking through to some more specific understanding than I have as yet been able to attain.
    I wonder if you know just how much I love you, my sweet dear; there is the most profound joy for me in the knowledge that I am your wife and the mother of your children. Darling husband, how happy we shall all be one day when we shall once more gaze upon the peaceful faces of our sleeping children and exchange our own "good nights" in each other's fond embrace.
    For the present, I must, unhappily, still write my good night, still use pencil and paper instead of arms and lips; dearest love, how I long for the touch of you, close and warm beside me. I miss you so terribly, it's an effort to push through the killing futility of each long, meaningless day, each long, unshared night!
    My heart is yours, my dear one—

Your loving wife
Ethel

Julius to Ethel

Sept. 15, 1951

My Dearest Most Wonderful Wife,
    I've simply been deluged with not one but three glowing epistles from your pungent pencil. They are a source of never ending pleasure as I reread them many times and because they are so meaty it is a constant source of emotional and intellectual stimulation. Your words are so well chosen and descriptive that it is easy for me to capture your mood and I must say that I too have found myself in similar states of suspended zombie existence [*sic*].
    Ethel it is only natural that there be nodal periods during the entire time when the pendulum, which is the sum total of our character, swings back to a higher plane of oscillation. How else would it be possible for use [*sic*] to

---

[176]Probably a reference to a *Time* magazine article which detailed how much it was costing the government to house her in Sing Sing.

have the necessary resilience to rebound from our mental stresses and is this not also a means of catching our breath and pausing to collect our strenght [sic] to once more pitch in with both hands into constructive cerrabrations [sic]. Sometimes I feel that I allow myself too many and also too often periods of just plain marking time. The important thing is that we do not feel guilty about this and begin to admonish ourselves and if I may choose one of your quaint expressions "hitting on all cylinders". Both of us will be better off if we take our moods as they come and just keep trying to raise ourselves to the point where we can keep before us the proper perspective.

When my brother was here I began to discuss a number of problems with him about the children. But as he sees it the paramount problem is that Mama is too nervous and high strung and that state filters down to the children. He says he spends most of his visits to our home telling Mama to give the kids more freedom and to take it a lot easier. It becomes more and more clear to me that somehow a higher authority especially one to direct the activities of the children be set up over our boys. If this person is a trained individual he will be able to obtain a maximum of cooperation from my mother. This in turn will also serve to heal the friction that exists in the house.

Time is so burdensome except for the short periods I'm with you. How I miss you and the children. Their mischiev [sic] doings, the happy laughter and the youthful noise while playing with their toys I hunger for all of this. My heart aches when I think of the security we can comfort them with when we are home. We know we must someday go home to each other and let us keep our spirits high for the future is much brighter—Holding you close all the time—All my love—Julius

Julius to Ethel

Sept. 16, 1951

My Most Precious Sweetheart,

There is one incident that I forgot to relate to you that ocurred [sic] during the childrens [sic] last visit here. While we were discussing the article in the Guardian Mike suddenly looked at me in a quizzical way and anxiously asked "Daddy I never saw you and Mommy kiss." I guess he saw a picture of us kissing in the van that appeared in the newspaper. The way he said it, the hunger I saw in his eyes and the terrific [sic] need for parental affection was all too obvious. He seemed to cry out I need my mother and father. There [sic] love, security and comfort has been taken away from me. I guess because he misses it so keenly now especially the last year that he has forgotten how openly affectionate we've been to each other. This great hurt to our children is the thing that plagues me most. Not only this but as you put it he cannot conceive, as we as adults do, the exact nature of our case, the issues at stake, our legal efforts and the support we are now receiving and the fact that as time passes we will have many more people in our corner. Because he could not understand & because he is insecure he feels he must do something to help us. Perhaps he feels guilty that he may be inadequate. Of course, it is natural for him to want to help us and to have us home with him. I have no doubts that with the good beginning that has been made and the anticipated help of a trained person we'll be able to restore his confidence in himself. The next time we see each other I'll discuss what I think [NWI] are the implications in this incident.

About three months ago one of the fellows here planted an orange pit in the dirt in a crack in the cement. As all of us are interested in living things in this bleak place we watered it, nursed it along and behold in [*sic*—should be "it"] took firmly in the soil and began to flourish. By now it grew to eight inches off the ground, bloomed, flowered and now we see small oranges on the branches. Can you imagine the contrast? Bars, concrete, walls and an orange tree growing in a crack. Mother nature defying the elements and [the first letters of the next word are written over other letters—the letters covered appear to be "th"] bringing [*sic*] freshness, beauty and life in this still, grey somber tomb. We, too, have the where with all [*sic*], the background, and justice on our side and we are and will continue to grow in this negative atmosphere. No courage is greater than that derived from confidence and when it is based on right there is no greater strenght [*sic*]. My most wonderous [*sic*] woman keep on flowering as it builds my moral [*sic*] and keeps my courage high. I think only of the time when you will be in my arms again and we'll enjoy the comforts of our home and the sweetness of our children. All my heart I sent to you
    —Julius
[letter continued on top of second side]
Please write the kids darling—Love JR

Ethel to Julius

Sept. 17, 1951
My darling Julie,

    It is so many years since I've seen you; Manny's long absence further enhances the illusion and Dr. Miller's entirely unheralded appearance on Saturday, while most gratifying, nevertheless serves to point up all those Saturdays that he was away and by contrast exaggerates the span of time they actually consumed. During some seventy minutes of conversation, I managed to give him a fairly decent but necessarily sketchy picture of the children's present home situation and their relationship to us but since I had neglected to discuss certain aspects of the existant [sic] problems, I sent him a more detailed description this morning and expect to write him again this week in order to bring him [NWI] even more fully up to date. He was his usual kind, sympathetic, attentive self and assured me he would get in touch with Manny at once. At least I know that here is one person upon whom we may definitely rely for the most whole-hearted kind of cooperation; I shall never be done singing his praises!

Sweetie, since your brother remained with me for less than a half-hour on Friday, the letter that arrived that afternoon from you was most welcome, and the ideas expressed [NWI] therein concerning the children, exceptionally good. Your analysis is [NWI] so remarkably accurate, demonstrating as it does such genuine insight into the needs of the children and finding such favor with me that I am simply delighted with my intellectual husband. Delighted, too, was I to find two pencilled pages instead of one in the envelope today. My sweetest dear, I adore you for the precious love you give me so unstintingly; in fond memory I twine my arms seductively about your neck and lift my willing lips to yours! M-m-m, sounds delicious doesn't it; gosh, I'd better cut it out, I'm beginning to drool!

Speaking of kisses (and I am building up a voracious appetite for same, my man) it was a most interesting comment indeed that Michael made; I can't wait to see a program for their proper guidance get under way. Nor can I wait to see you, dearest darling that I love with all my soul!

More power to your orange tree; did you know that I eat parsley whenever the urge seizes me? I simply help myself from the "garden". You know, bunny dear, this kind of material would make happy reading for Mike and Robby. Daddy, I hate to confess it but bad Mommy that I am, I have not as yet communicated with them. You see I am so full of things I'm bursting [NWI] to say, I don't trust myself yet; I want so desperately to be a source of courage and inspiration that I must wait for my feelings to crystallize into the beautiful words they deserve. Good-night my lover— May we find that sweet bliss we used to share in that reality of long ago, once more in our dreams—

All my love—your own girl
Ethel

The next letter is one of many for which the originals do not survive. We are unaware of what happened to them, except to know that at least one original was sold for fund-raising after our parents' death. We learned this during our re-opening campaign when one person who had bought an original approached us in 1975 and told us she still had it. It was returned to us. We have no idea if any other originals survive. We will just have to work under the assumption that the original typed copy (which bears the editing marks of the person who prepared them for publication in Death House Letters*) is an accurate representation of the original. The headings are omitted from the typed copy, so we will note the sender and receiver at the top of each such letter. All letters for which originals were not used will be headed [typed copy].*

Ethel to Julius

September 20, 1951

Dearest love,

It seems that I have "fallen upon evil days", even the ardor of your weekly wooing, fetchingly spiked with those quaint pet names you so inevitably and endearingly call me, fails to dissipate the gloom that hangs like a pall over me not to dispel the sense of doom and foreboding which dogs my footsteps as I drag myself unwillingly about the quiet desolation of the yard. In desperation, I forcibly turn my thoughts to the anticipated gratification of a thorough legal discussion with our brilliant attorney, only to realize with dismay that his visit will be an all too temporary respite from the cold, bitter, inhuman loneliness of that camouflaged vault politely known as the "Women's Wing' to which I shall subsequently have to return. And then the grim warfare that I must constantly wage goes forward relentlessly. Oh, the barbaric horror of my living internment must surely engulf me! All hail to the CC's, venerable College of Cycles; the wheels of chance spin round and round with never a resolution. One leaves the familiar setting for a short space in order to come back to it, in order to leave it again, in order yet once more to return. Good God, is there only this one groove upon which the wheel of my life must forever spin in endless torment!

And you my sweetest dear, my darling one, for you, too there is a groove and a wheel! Dearest, I want our lives to move along paths of our own sweet choosing, the paths of decency and beauty and honor! With what happy pride and courage we once traversed these paths; never doubt, my heart's treasure, we shall seek them out yet again even as the world's oppressed millions irresistably [*sic*] seek and may not be swerved from their search! Already the sound of their footsteps reverberates around the globe, swelling into a mighty roar and striking terror into the hearts of the tyrants! History demands human progress, Chiang-Kai-Shek, Franco, Syngman Rhee and Saypol to the contrary, notwithstanding!

Oh, to be with you this minute such impassioned sentiment and no opportunity to translate it into the language of love! Only I don't think we'd spend much time talking! Sweetheart, I am devastated with longing for you but my bed will remain as cold and lonely as it always is!

I kiss and caress you tenderly, dear husband—

Always lovingly,
Ethel

Julius to Ethel [typed copy]

September 21, 1951

My Sweetest Wife,

It's 7:00 AM and I'll have to hurry to dash off this note to you. I meant to get this off last night but somehow I just plain forgot. What with reading 6 newspapers, yard exercise, playing a ten game series of pinnochile [*sic*] with my left hand neighbor, by the time I remembered my pencil and glasses were collected for the night. You understand people are so solicitous of my welfare.

My sister Ethel sent me a short letter and said she is enclosing an article and two clippings from the [Here there is an inexplicable blank in the typed copy. Perhaps it is a newspaper title which the typist omitted.]—will of the people. Since you spoke about newspaper clippings at our last meeting this is to inform you that they are out as the warden typed a note that no newspaper clippings or such material is permitted. Newspapers, if sent in, must come direct from the publishers. He also informed my sister about this. I suppose by the time you read this letter we'll already have our visit with Manny and ask him to have the publishers send us the Guardian regularly. I believe he'll be here today as he's overdue and my sister didn't mention anything about my mother's next visit so I surmise she'll make her pre-holiday visit next Wednesday.

Your letters are so wonderful that I can't stop thanking you for them and letting you know how good they make me feel. Beside the positive personal satisfaction I obtain from them they make me so proud that you my wife are such an accomplished pen artist.

At this moment I am full of spirit in anticipation of our next gabfest particularly so since there has been such a long interval between the last legal consultation we held and this coming one. There are a great deal of problems to cover and already I'm concerned that we will not have the time to cover most of the important ones. I want so to carefully cover the appeal brief and discuss it thoroughly amongst us in order for me not to feel guilty later on that I didn't do everything possible to get the best final result.

Honey, I liked our last Wednesday tete a tete because we covered a lot of ground. Since I was so intense I came away with a splitting headache. Darling you no doubt can guess that I'm madly in love with you, hungry for each fleeting moment we spend together, bolstered up by every sweet word you tell me and strong in your support and confidence in me. Whenever I think of you and all that you mean to me I feel so happy and satisfied with my great treasure. Only I want so to be close to you all the time—

All my heart,
Julius

Julius to Ethel

September 21, 1951

Hello Proud Mommie,

You certainly have just cause to be proud because of what you are ["but" CO; NWI] and also ["look at" CO; NWI] for the two swell children you have. It is obvious to me that there is very definite improvement in the boys and their behavior runs proof of it. I was well pleased with the visit and we'll have a great deal to talk about when I see you this week.

As we had decided I am [NWI over an erasure] sending Manny your letters and I also wrote him a letter. I suppose you too are sending my letters to him.[177] Since I received the trial record I've been busy going through the testimony. It certainly is a tedious job reading the small print. My suggestion to you is to concentrate your attention on Dave and Ruth's testimony if you don't have the time to read it all through. Anyhow this is the important part of the record and I'm sure you'll want to refresh your memory on the facts in the record.

I received New Years cards[178] from the Almans,[179] Peggie & Eugene Siegel, Cecile & Charles Ryweek. I hope you know some of these people. It really is good to be remembered by people even though we are locked away from them. It gave me a wonderful feeling to hear the report Manny gave as to ["how" CO] high [N3WI, followed by "by" also inserted and CO] regard for you the people at the Women's House of Detention had as told to him by a friend of yours. If you can instill such fine feelings among others you are really a very worthwhile person. In such a short time you have impressed them with the calibre of your character and the decency of your person. It gives me a good feeling to see you carry yourself with humble

---

[177]When the *National Guardian* series on the case ended, some of the prison letters were published there. This makes it clear that such publication was agreed upon at some meeting with attorney Bloch.

[178]Rosh Hashanah, the Jewish New Year

[179]Emily and Dave Alman lived in Knickerbocker Village and later were the leaders of the National Committee to Secure Justice in the Rosenberg Case.

dignity in the best tradition of womanhood. No matter how heavy your burden or foul the deeds of those who ["would" CO; N3WI] are trying to legally murder us you will rise above all this because your [sic] made of pure goodness. We look beneath the surface for the real you and that is what basically matters, not the transient faults that all of us possess. For you my dearest I am very happy and I can only think of the day you will be spared of all this pain and heartaches and will again take [next three words inserted] your place as mother of our precious children and partner in our sweet relationship. With the treasure I possess in you and the boys I am able to be completely satisfied and [N3WI] have strength to right with every fibre of my whole being to win our freedom. May this New Year bring you the joy and happiness that you deserve. I love you very much my sweet wife and I believe we'll be able to share our love again together in our own home surrounded by our family.

I am not at all pleased with the gyrations of some liberals when it comes to important political matters. How many terrible blows must democracy receive before they act correctly? I'm satisfied with our principled position and I hope that many will see the light and come to our aid before it is too late— All my love—Julie

Julius to Ethel [typed copy]

Sept. 23, 1951

Dearest Sweetheart,

In spite of the gloom and terrible lament, which I share with you, your powerful words exude courage and understanding. This is all the more admirable because at the time when the cold endless torment of this incarceration engulfs you, you take heart and see clearly as a socially conscious person, that our fight is part and parcel of mankinds [sic] seeking and striving against the tyrants. Even though I take heart from your encouraging words my heart aches for you, my love. Your lot is such a difficult one and I can only send you by way of this paper some little comfort. If I could only be with you, it would be so much easier for us to pass the coming hurdles together. Keep in mind that there will be a happy ending to our present predicament and together we will once more move along paths of decency, honor and love.

Our legal consultation was excellent but all too short. The manner in which Manny presented this one point for our appeal, its thoroughness both morally and legally proves once again that he's tops as a lawyer. I have all the confidence in the world that the appeal brief will be a masterpiece. It is gratifying to me to see that he has his whole heart in it. The Guardian articles are swell but are only a small beginning as I feel that a greater effort is needed and more means have to be found to make public the facts in our case to counteract the adverse distortions that have been foisted on the public. I hope to hear that within a month's time some definite organizational steps will have be [*sic*] made to coordinate this campaign and start the avalanche of truth. Believe me honey I feel a lot better with every bit of progress and every positive step made in our behalf. We must keep in mind that a tremendous and long drawn out effort is necessary as the despoilers of truth are well entrenched and their political motives blindly drives [*sic*] them to perpetuate this frameup. I have faith in the people and their will will force the justice department to honor the law of the land and set us free.

It is true that not enough discussion was had on the crucial situation at home but it is my opinion that the next few weeks will bring some positive results on this problem also. We'll have to ease up on pressing Manny at least until his appeal brief is completed. My glorious woman we were so busy I could only look at you for but moments when all the time I wanted to look at you and to devour you with my eyes. I join you in our eternal longing and vigil always wanting to be in your arms. My lovely one I send you all my heart—

Your Julius

Ethel to Julius [typed copy]

Sept. 24, 1951

My darling Julie,

The words well up spontaneously from somewhere deep inside me and rise impulsively to my lips at the dear thought of you. How sweet you are, dearest and how handsome, and how winsome your ways! I, too, wished to gaze long and fondly upon my lover's face; instead I had to content myself with brief, incidental glances! Just one more day and then I'll have the opportunity to look my fill,—for all of one hour!

Sweetheart, there is no question about it, we have a legal expert to be reckoned with; what's just as important is that we have a friend in whom we ["have" CO; we have no way of knowing if that was a typographical error or an accurate rendition of the original] may place complete confidence and trust not to fail us whatever our need. It is, however, when I watch him handling our children with his firm but kind, loving hand, that my love for him grows even more boundless than it already is.

Dearest husband, I am desperately in need of you; for the children haunt me day and night. After our most heartening consultation with Manny (incidentally I heartily concur that the campaign which has had a most auspicious start, should now begin to accelerate). I wrote to Dr. Miller explaining the woman's change of heart[180] and enlisting the cooperation that Manny will be shortly asking of him. I have yet to make fully known to him, however, my misgivings and anxieties, even in the face of the progress toward a solution that appears to have been already stimulated. Nevertheless, I did manage to describe "Pop's" "Mediation", about which unhappily, I find I have mixed feelings. Quite frankly, dear, I am getting fed to the teeth with the ignorance and backwardness on the part of people who pride themselves on being regular "child psychologists", no kidding! Oh, and dieticians, [*sic*] too, let's not forget that important item, let's give them full credit!

You are absolutely right, though, to feel that Manny should not be pressed about the situation until his brief is in. I was delighted to hear him at long last express a desire for Dr. Miller's counsel; at least he has begun to realize that the children require a great deal more skillful attention than they have yet received.

I'll have much more to say on this score on Wednesday; in the meantime, all my heart's love, my dear one!

Always your own girl—
Ethel

P.S. I'll want to hear all that Ethel had to say to you, honey. I love you, sweetest; seeing the children has opened wide a floodgate of mingled joy and grief. I am one vast vessel of pain; it feels as though every last inch of me beats with hurt—

Lovingly, E.

Julius to Ethel [typed copy]

Sept. 26, 1951

My Sweetest Darling,

More than a decade ago Christmas time 1937 I met me my special young lady fair, sweet, charming, unassuming, ebullient, tremendous latent potential and also some deterring emotional difficulties, and always a prodigious striver to release these positive creative talents, and with its gratifying accomplishments building a fine, solid, dignified character. This is the Ethel I married and it's the best thing that ever happened to me and you are my greatest asset.

Twelve glorious years we've spent together. Always sharing, seeking together life's joy, satiating ourselves fully from the cup of love and as honest decent socially conscious citizens participating in mankind's progres-

---

[180]Perhaps this is a reference to Sophie leaving.

sive efforts. Because we practiced democracy as well as believing it we enjoyed our efforts and learned the true meaning of freedom. All was not milk and honey but as man and wife we courageously and unhesitatingly assaulted life's hurdles as a unit and managed to come through in flying colors. We drank the fruits of culture, of mental stimulation and were happy in our homelife. We liked our work and our two lovely boys were products of our complete union. Without doubt we have lived, been happy, learned and continued to grow, particularly in stature.

From our experience, background and personal character, at the time this dark cataclysm suddenly descended on us in July 1950 we had attained a solid stable foundation in our complete relationship and our individual personalities. We have weathered the storms of the unwarranted aggression against us by the blackguard politicians who are stomping freedom into the ground and are using our political frameup as one of their wedges. All that is happening we see clearly and we will never bend a knee to this tyrranny [*sic*]. Our courage is derived not only from the fact of our innocence but the knowledge that the people will support our fight to be set free. In the relationship to the whole picture we have a clear perspective and the future for us is bright.

To me it's remarkable that we have stood up so well against physical discomfort, mental agony, emotional stress, complete isolation and always in the shadow of death. In spite of this gloom and despair we are holding our heads high and are completely confident of our final victory and its fruits—going home with you to our children.

My one true love I've recapitulated for us some of the treasure I've possessed in you and how complete you've made my life. I hope on this birthday of yours you can get some sustenance in your bleak tomb from my mind and heart on paper.

Always adoring you my guiding light—your own man—Julius

Ethel to Julius [typed copy]

Sept. 26, 1961

My very dearest darling husband;

Is it in your heart to forgive me for having been so foolishly unhappy this morning? Please write me a letter at once, sweetheart, assuring me you understand and bear with me in my struggle to attain maturity; plaster it with declarations of love and don't spare the extravagant language. Myself, I love you so deeply, I am bereft of words that will truly convey my soul's need to give you joy and tenderness and devotion. I can only sit here and weep bitterly for you and the children and our devastated lives.

Honey, if I don't manage to get another letter off to you by Friday morning, I hope you won't mind. There is no day, indeed no hour, that you are totally banished from my consciousness. The image of you is stamped upon my brain and the vibrant emotion that touched both our lives with magic abides with me at all times. However, due to what circumstances you might well imagine, I am apt to be so involved with my own thoughts in preparation for Dr. Miller's expected Saturday visit, that I may not meet the deadline.

My dear one, have faith in me; your faith alone builds my confidence, restores me to my rightful place in my own eyes, and defends me against the cold, barren emptiness of my miserable existence here.

All in all, the day might have turned out far worse; you see, mistakes are often very enlightening, painfully so, all too frequently and yet an unavoidable evil that can add up to highly profitable experience. I think it is significant that I am able to bring myself to look upon the situation in such a philosophical light and that I have succeeded in keeping the usual reactions of anxiety and dread down to a minimum.

I guess your Mommy simply couldn't make it; she's bound to turn up very shortly, however, so be of good cheer, my loved one.

Julie dear, I continue to be seriously concerned about the children and may therefore see fit to drop Manny a few lines before the weekend.

Do you remember how hard I tried to recall some matter I had intended discussing with you during our session? I'd appreciate it, sweetie, if you would give the question of the Jewish holidays and their special significance for us as part of a prison congregation, your serious consideration, between now and our next talk.

And now, dearest, goodnight. Whatever the morrow may bring, I lay aside the burdens of the day with the clear conscience that is given only to the pure in heart to possess. I hold your dear face between my hands as I used to so long ago and kiss you with all my heart.

Lovingly,
Ethel.

Julius to Ethel [typed copy]

Sept. 27, 1951

Hello My Birthday Girl:

Happy Birthday sweetheart. In the card that I send you and the letter of the 28th that I put so much effort in I pencil my birthday present to you with all the love of every fibre of my body.

Before your letter of the 20th arrived I had carefully planned all this and I have been giving deep thought to our last Wednesday visit. In the first place did you notice even at the time of the small incident that occurred I was hesitant about what I should say because even then I wanted to agree with you and take your side after I thought it through I felt I should have sided with you because you are completely hemmed in at the mercy of these outrageous emotional barbs and the butt of terrific mental tension. Because your outburst even though softly said and politely stated is the result of a boiling cauldron that has been long seething because of many just grievances and when the volcano finally does overflow it hits out blindly at friend and foe. What grieves me is that it takes a terrible toll of you and you suffer unjustly endless pain.

Oh darling I'm glad you stood up and sounded off but please don't spoil the good points by tearing yourself down and belittling. The only important thing is that you don't let this effect [*sic*] you so.

Honey you're making progress even now and I'm sorry I can't be more helpful but rest assured I'm in your corner 100% of the time. Your [*sic*] swell, wonderful, sweet but too soft hearted. Please don't make my precious jewel seem less valuable or you'll have me to contend with.

How unfair, terrible and unwarranted your tears and heartaches are. You're sweet and a good and really great person, noble in every respect, full of compassion, warmth, understanding and always charitable. My dear let us link hands and mind (even though we can't as yet link bodies) and resolutely march with heads high in our battle for truth and honesty. I'm proud of you my dear and I love you more than anything else in the world even life itself.

I hope we may be able to spend my birthday and our anniversary together in our home. Perhaps I'm a bit optomistic [*sic*] but our kind of people always are.

I clasp you in my arms and shower you with kisses and I repeat over and over again I love you for the fine person you are my wife.

Happy Birthday,
Your Julius

Ethel to Julius

Sept. 30, 1951

My sweetest darling,

So now I am thirty-six years old; my 2nd birthday behind bars was marked by a fairly equal mixture of smiles and tears, chiefly engendered by a variety of lovely cards, sent me in loving remembrance by my dear husband's family, his precious children and his own wonderful self. Sweetheart, the roses, the musical score, and the verbal sentiment were all in such perfect taste; but it was your personal tribute that touched me most. Dearest, may I continue to be in the future the kind of woman that is today capable of commanding "the love and respect" you so sincerely proferred [*sic*] in honor of my special day. Perhaps we shall be fortunate enough to celebrate your next birthday in the warmth and privacy of our own home and with the active participation of all our loved ones! Amen!

I am thinking now of the darkened streets of the Lower East Side[181] early tomorrow morning, throngs of people will be hurrying to the synagogues to pray. I earnestly hope their prayers are answered, yet life has taught me that theory without practice can be a pretty empty, meaningless gesture—lip service simply does not bring about the peace and good-will and security all decent humanity so bitterly craves; we must not use prayer to an Omnipotent Being as a pretext for evading our responsibility to our fellow-beings in the daily struggles for the establishment of social justice. Jew and Gentile, black and white, all must stand together in their might, to win the right!

My dear one, winter seems to have descended upon us without preliminary; today's lowering sky was much more typical of January and it ain't fair. Grimly I paced the concrete, lost in thought and unmindful of the wind's sharp sting! The Dodgers victory over the Phillies, however, speedily restored me to my usual cheerfulness and I am looking forward with eager anticipation to their game with the Giants tomorrow.

And so the day that is always the dullest for me to muddle through is drawing to a close. I greet Monday with renewed vigor and determination; after all, if Monday comes, can Wednesday be far behind? How wonderful it would be to have a week chock full of Wednesdays; maybe I should work on it, huh?

I adore you, heart of mine, and am desperate for a glimpse of your fair countenance and the oft-longed for sound of your voice. How wisely you counselled me last week; your rebel had subsided considerably but begs to inform you that the lesson had a telling effect! Think I'll become a preacher; I certainly know how to thunder like one, on occasion! If only you were here to kiss the thunder out of me, I shouldn't mind at all!

Love you darling—Your old lady,

Ethel

---

[181]The poor Jewish neighborhood in lower Manhattan where our parents both grew up and lived.

Julius to Ethel [typed copy]

Sept. 30, 1951

My Charming Wife:

I'm sitting at my desk looking at your sweet face that adorns a large picture of you, which I have pasted on the wall besides the childrens [*sic*] pictures. I communicate with you quite often and I love you so much. On the occassion [*sic*] of the Jewish New Year I want to wish you a happier and fruitful life and I want you to continue being the same fine good person you are. Speaking of New Years my sister Ethel sent me an exquisite card in such good taste concerning the usual warm wishes from her and her lovely family. I believe it comes from Palestine. Perhaps you've too received one.

Lena's visit was a good one as we had plenty of time to discuss family matters. My sisters are swell and they're for us 100%. I love them and feel so proud to be their brother. She asked me to tell you that Manny's wife sent Mike two cowboy guns and a holster and Robbie a ferris wheel that goes around and rings a bell. Of course there [*sic*] nice things for the lads but my sweet Momie [*sic*] says "so many toys and it gregers me in the head".[182]

Ever since I received the Guardian articles I've been reading and re-reading them. You too must have the same gratifying feeling that I'm experiencing to know that the truth is finally being made public and good decent people are beginning to come to our aid in increasing numbers. The fine letters to the editor are particularly heart warming. The paper is a swell paper and it's a fighting progressive one and it doesn't pull any punches. Many more like it are needed in our hysteria filled land to bring some light at the time of the twilight of the democratic Rights of the American People.

Today I spent most of the afternoon keeping my ear glued to the radio tensely listening to the splendid game which the Dodgers finally won. The remarkable playing of the heart of the game Jackie Robinson gave it a thrilling finish with a home run. Now I hope they beat the Giants in the playoff and go on to win the World Series from the Yankees.

Oh my darling how beautiful you look at it's so good to see you always in front of my eyes. I can't wait to see you again I want to tell you to your face all you mean to me and see your shining eyes and hear your sweet voice. My wonderful sweetheart only the thought of having you in my arms in our own home keeps me strong and steadfast. All my heart I send you—Your Julius

---

[182]Gregers are noisemakers used as part of the "sound effects" for the telling of the Purim story. Every time the name of the villain, Haamen, is mentioned, the audience whirls the "gregers" around making a loud scraping sound. My grandmother turned the noun into a verb.

Ethel to Julius [typed copy]

Oct. 1, 1951

My heart's dearest, my darling husband,
    The week-end came and went with nary a word from you; of course, I
correctly laid it to "institutional delay"[183] and consoled myself with your
beautiful card, when lo and behold this afternoon brought a regular windfall
of affectionate salutations and greetings. Sweetheart, have you any idea with
what sheer, glowing pleasure your ardent lover's expressions fill me? Oh,
my sweetest dear, I do truly love and cherish and respect you; for all my
emotional turbulence and the cruelty of our separation, there is profound
happiness in the certainty of your tenderness and compassion. Each morning
I arise with the thought of you warm and unspeakably sweet within me and
each night I give myself into your keeping yet once more; and all day my
heart sings its joyful refrain, "I am loved, I am loved!" At long last we shall
come together in an embrace we shall not have to merely imagine; by all
the laws of common human decency, we must be brought from darkness
into light!

Oct. 2, 1951

    Honey, the National Guardian articles are excellent; I don't know when
I have felt so confident of our eventual release. As you point out, however,
there must soon begin to take definite shape a strong, fighting campaign.
Incidentally, I have since recalled the young couple who have proffered their
services to Manny on our behalf, as active members of the K.V. [Knicker-
bocker Village] Parent Teachers Association.[184] I'll have more to say about
them on Wednesday, if you remind me, that is; I am so loath to say anything other than love words, so delighted to be silent and to look my fill of
you!
    Concerning the Dodgers, I must confess that I have bitten off every last
confounded nail; 10-0 what a trouncing! It's that indomitable spirit, that
inability to say "Die" that has endeared them to so many thousands of
human beings. But it is chiefly in their outstanding contribution to the eradication of racial prejudice that they have covered themselves with glory;[185]
by their simple demonstration of victorious team-work have they flung back

---

[183]This is probably a euphemism for the need for all correspondence to go
through prison censorship.
[184]This probably refers to Dave and Emily Alman.
[185]A reference to the role of Dodger owner Branch Rickey in bringing Jackie
Robinson into the Dodger organization in 1946 and into the major leagues in
1947, thereby breaking the color bar in "the national pastime."

the lie into the teeth of the Fascists [*sic*], and the American people owe them a very real debt of gratitude!

And now, with the close of Rosh Hoshanah, may I wish for us and for our children, an end to our horror and our torment. I was unutterably moved to hear the Shofar, sounding amid the grim stark grayness of our surroundings during Jewish Services today; truly am I proud of the inheritance of an ancient people who have made an eternal contribution to the civilization of mankind and with whom I shall ever be privileged to be identified!

My dear one, good night; in your arms all my dreams will come true! Love you, darling—Your own girl—

                                                                    Ethel

Julius to Ethel [typed copy]

                                                            Oct. 4, 1951
My Most Precious Darling:

Of late our correspondence has been a little delayed as witness I just got your letter of the 2nd this afternoon. Don't be worried when you don't get any mail from me as it's probably due to "institutional delay."

Your letters are so beautifully written and are full of sweetness, warmth and tenderness. I am deeply moved by them. When I read your glowing epistles there wells up inside of me a fountain of love for you and a tremendous pride in the wonderful wife I have.

Since our last hour together I too have felt blue and I missed you terribly and the only way I could shake off the endless agony gnawing at my heart was to take out the Guardian articles once more and reread them. For your suffering and the childrens [*sic*] plight I go through endless torture[.] I want so to exercise my fatherly prerogative and protect and care for my beloved family. Somewhere, somehow this nightmare must pass over quickly so that we can together see the light again.

Incidently [*sic*] I hope we continue to get the articles[.] I'm a bit aprehensive [*sic*] as we haven't as yet received this weeks [*sic*] issue. Perhaps it will come in with tomorrows [*sic*] mail. I'm looking forward to it and I hope I'm not disappointed. If our illustrious counselor Manny puts in an appearance tomorrow I'll make sure to tell him to see that we get subscriptions.

Gloom of glooms the dear Dodgers lost the penant [*sic*] and now I'm rooting for the Giants to lick the Yankees. When will the N. Y. Yankees become part of modern American baseball and lift the discriminately [*sic*] ban on Negro baseball stars. The superb performance of the Negro stars on both the Dodgers and the Giants has blasted the theory of the race supremacists.

I too share your sentiments about the Rosh Hashannah holidays and to us it has a special significance because the great history and culture of the Jewish People is one based on justice freedom and peace among all peoples. I am proud of this heritage and the contribution to world culture, literature, science and social enlightment [*sic*] my fellow co-religionists have made. When it's possible for us as people to see the decent role we play then we can have the courage to face all this hardship. As the children of Israel were freed from bondage so too will progressive Americans help us win our freedom. Sweetheart, honey wife I take you in my arms and hold you close—All my love

—Your man Julius

Ethel to Julius

Oct. 4, 1951

Dearest Sweetheart:

Since my last letter to the children in which I described the activities of the trash I have been observing I find it increasingly difficult to sort out my thoughts and feelings concerning them, and to communicate there with some degree of clarity to myself, let alone to attempt to establish an unbroken line of correspondence with them. There is a commingling of resistance and guilt which is most disconcerting indeed. Perhaps I need the stimulus of a visit from Manny and for [*sic*] Dr. Miller, bringing me news of them and the home situation generally to arouse me out of the stupor into which I seem to have sunk. I am most desirous of seeing one of them at least this week end.

My darling, I had never dreamed I could experience such intense hunger such bitter longing; I glow with aliveness the better to savor the ashes of death. Yes [perhaps this should be "yet" which fits better in the context] can the acrid taste accomplish aught but a fanning of the flame, a fiercer burning, a renewed striving to triumph and to live.

Sweetheart, I find myself regretting that we were unable to "exchange" our individual visits with Lee. Neither of us got around to sharing information the other had received about the kids. For example did she recount for you a certain phone call during which Robby assured her he always gave Michael her regards "but what's the use, he never pays any attention to what I say anyway!" She also mentioned that "Pop" had urged her not to forget to tell Ethel that I am fast becoming acquainted with them and they are very bright children! Incidentally Robby, with that refreshing lack of inhibition common to our emotionally healthy normal child, complained to "POP" about the size of the Hershey bar he had brough [*sic*] him compared it in favorable [*sic*] (and out loud) ["terms" may be omitted here] to the kind his Uncle Dave usually buys!

Oh, darling, what a wave of wanting washes over me for them and for you; it grows more and more difficult for me to put off my natural human desires, to warn myself of the searing destruction of our hopes that may yet be ours to contend with!

Only love me, my dear husband, only love me; I am your wife with all of myself!

Your loving Ethel

Julius to Ethel [typed copy]

Oct. 7, 1951

My wonderful Sweetheart:

The monotony grinds slowly forward and in its wake time seems to crawl and I find it harder and harder to busy myself in reading or card playing to ease the great longing in my heart. Only as I write to you and look at your sweet face on the wall, say "hello you beautie.", and throw you a big fat kiss can I feel relieved and also I know that in a few days our one hour Wednesday [here the typist left a space, perhaps because the word was illegible] will arrive. It is amazing that I can close my eyes and remember your smiling face as it looked out at me from behind the bars of your cell. Honey my precious darling I miss you so much I wait with all my being to hold you close to me and love you.

Not having a visit from our family and the eminent lawyer friend of ours was a great disappointment. This was especially true when I did not receive the weekly copy of the Guardian. I've reread the complete issues a number of times and I get a great deal of solace from reading them. Perhaps you know of some good magazine or weekly publication that we can subscribe to I'm referring to one of current events that has a progressive slant. My dearest you understand that I'm entitled to my gripes but by the time I'll see you I'll feel good again.

Another reason for my blue feeling is I haven't as yet written our two dears and I don't seem to know just what to write to them. Lord knows I love them with all my heart and I want to hear about Mikes [*sic*] school, the house and how things are progressing.

It's no use Ethel I keep thinking about our former life together and all the things we did together and I want it so. We are fully aware of all those who participated in this brutal frameup and we will do all in our power to see that the public becomes famaliar [*sic*] with their fowl [*sic*] deeds. I read an item in the Sunday News column of the New York reporter and he said that the New York Bar Association will soon come out with a blast against the conduct of a certain bipartisan candidate for a N.Y. Judgeship because of his conduct at a recent famous trial. Of course they are speaking about the low life Saypol and I believe they're referring to our case. If I figure correctly this will be the first positive results of the newspaper based on the trial record. Yes my love I feel better already. This is the kind of medicine I need. My thought as always on the future for there lies our salvation. I kiss you with all of me. Your Julius

Ethel to Julius [typed copy]

October 7, 1951
7 P.M.

My own dear love,

All day I have vainly sought to accomplish a certain minimum of reading and writing; evening finds me still struggling for some semblance of control over my concentrative powers. But they have lit out and left me stranded and helpless before the raging storm of emotion that has been buffeting my spirit about this way and that. Outside a torrential rain is sweeping down sharply; my thoughts whip and last about me with much the same violence. My dear husband, my sweet children, there is no light, no joy, no life without you!

Monday Morning

Darling, left word that I be aroused at 6:00 o'clock; it was done but I never budged until 7:00. I guess I just didn't want to face another day here. But now I am talking to you and it is already bright outdoors; the birds are busying themselves with the bread I had made certain to scatter for them before coming in for the night and their merry sound awakens an answering song within me.

I managed to begin a letter to the children that will doubtless leave my hands by tomorrow. The rain prompted me to recall the beautiful lines by Robert Louis Stevenson which I thought they might enjoy. I then suggested to Michael that the library could supply him with a book of poems by this most gifted writer, if he so desired.

After a week of loneliness and tense expectation, (sans Manny, sans family, sans anybody), Dr. Miller walked calmly in at 3:05 P.M. Saturday. He said he was surprised he had actually managed to get there in time but that since the pressure of his work would intensify even more during the next weeks, he had taken a chance on driving up. Twenty-five minutes was pitifully little, but I was able to get across my anxiety about the home picture and also to receive the assurance that he stands ready to cooperate whenever Manny calls on him. He even has an excellent woman therapist in mind who used to work at J.B.G. and knows of Michael's difficulties (although she never saw the child herself) just in case Manny's prospect doesn't come through. Of course there is no guarantee since he does not know, at this point, whether or not this individual is inclined to take on such an assignment. However I am confident that sooner or later we'll connect. He noted with interest that I was reading "Listening with the Third Ear" and expressed admiration for Dr. Theodor Reik as a very astute man. There was a fly in the ointment, however, in the form of a certain obnoxious individual (about whose conduct during the Jewish Services you saw fit to comment unfavorably yourself)[186] who served to make me most uncomfortable.

Can't wait to see you, my dearest dear.

Love you,
Ethel

Julius to Ethel [typed copy]

Oct. 11, 1951

My Wonderful Woman:

How I adore you my sweetheart. My heart flows out to you in tender love. During our excellent legal session I couldn't help looking at you and seeing all the sweetness and warmth glowing in your face. I felt such a closeness and oneness with you and I can best sum it up by saying I bit my nails besides you biting yours. Honey yesterday was overwhelming for me. Naturally when I see you there is a heightening of tension and a quickening of pulse. I become very intense and heped [*sic*] up. Since I didn't eat all day and then was subjected to the splendid brief of our beloved legal impresario, to which I devoted my fullest concentration (except for stealing an occassional [*sic*] glimpse of my hearts treasure) I developed a nervioous [*sic*] stomach a wracking headache and a terribly sick feeling. As soon as I came down from the consultation room I took two emperin pills and went to bed. Had a cream cheese sandwich for supper and two more empirin pills and suffered through all evening and finally I slept through the night. Thank goodness I'm feeling much better now except for a little weakness in the knees and greaseness [*sic*—perhaps he wrote "queasiness" and the typist misread it] in the stomach. Don't worry about your spouse since I don't

---

[186]This almost certainly does not refer to the Jewish Chaplain, Rabbi Irving Koslowe, whose relationship with my parents was extremely positive. See *Sons,* p. 70 for an example of the Rabbi's recollections.

have my dearest to properly nurse me back to normal there's no fun in being ill.

Oh darling it was so wonderful to hear that many good people are rallying to our aid and showing there [*sic*] support in many little ways. It is indeed gratifying to witness the mushrooming of a committee and this will really start the ball rolling at a steady pace. My most precious wife take heart time will pass quickly as constructive steps are taken in the march for our freedom. I too throb with impatient [*sic*] to be home with you and our two dear boys.

Since we are realists we must keep our feet on the ground and know that we face evil forces with much power in their hands who are riding high and roughshod over the legal rights of the American People and a strong heart and active campaign is needed to assure victory. We were always confident because of our innocence. We have the courage because of our convictions. Above all we have the perspective of a bright future. If we keep this before us we'll come through with flying colors. Again I can't wait to see you and talk to you about all these new developments.

Always your boy—Julius

Ethel to Julius [typed copy]

Oct. 11, 1951

Dearest Sweetest Julie:

I confess that I am at a loss for words; since yesterday's exceptionally gratifying visits with you and Manny, I just can't seem to calm down and get back to normal. Darling, I trust you are over your sick headache; the truth is I had one myself and spent the rest of the day relaxing and reliving the precious moments that were over.

Disappointing as it was to learn once and for all that acquittal cannot be ours except by verdict of a jury,[187] I have already re-oriented my thinking along more realistic lines; since I have not, however, as yet been able to completely accept this fact emotionally, I am still not "with it" and foolishly cling to my pipe dreams. My heart is simply bursting with the desire to cross the threshold arm in arm with you and to hear the children shout for joy at the sight of us. Somehow, by some extraordinary exertion of will, I must tear myself from this tantalizing picture, and face the far more probable one of further incarceration until the political frameup of which we are helpless victims is ripped to shreds and at long last exposed for what it is; and thus far "the spirit is willing but the flesh is weak!"

---

[187]In other words, she had been hoping that the Appeals Court reversal of the convictions would set them free instead of requiring a new trial.

Sweetheart, we may truly congratulate ourselves upon our choice of Manny Bloch as legal counsel. The guy is remarkably keen and a master of the English language. I am convinced that the brief is as brilliant a piece of writing as any produced by any professional author. To the bargain it would be difficult to match him for integrity, wholesomeness and sheer human calibre. I love him for the brother he is to me that I never really had!

If I don't stop now, I shan't make the mail. Visits from the family are due to-day and for tomorrow, however, and perhaps these will serve to tied [*sic*] us over somewhat until our next meeting.

Darling, I love you—and send all my kisses—"Patience and fortitude" as Butch La Guardia was wont to say, but oh, what misery surrounds us— my heart, all my love to you—

Your girl Ethel

Julius to Ethel

Oct. 14, 1951

My Dearest Sweetheart:

I'm in the pink of condition again and I'm feeling pretty good. It was indeed a pleasure to have a nice long visit with my sister Ethel. By the way I think it outrageous that she came before 10 AM this Saturday had to wait more than $1/_2$ Hr. at the administration building before she got to the "CC" and had to wait here until 11:15 till a sergaent [*sic*] finally came and that left you only a short visit. Perhaps we ought to discuss this matter with the P.K. there is no reason on earth why you should be deprived of any time on a visit. The most heartening news is that things at home have been straightened out and there is much more harmony, consideration and pitching in by Sophie. The fact that people know the whole story and see other people helping they too take heart and begin to do their share. I am particularly glad because my mother is happier and feels better about Sophie and the house and people are coming around and showing an interest. We'll probably get a visit from my sweet mother this Wednesday but don't be disappointed if she can't make it. It is my opinion that the kids should come here on a Saturday and I'm leaving it to you to tell Manny all the details and when you think the time will be best for all concerned.

I don't know if Ethel told you of a disagreeable incident that happened to Michael. He had gone to the house of a boy he met and told this kids [*sic*] mother about us and she chased him out of the house and made him feel terrible.[188] When he got home he cried but Sophie explained that some people are ignorant and prejudiced and reassured him after a while he got

---

[188]See *Sons*, p. 112 for my description.

over it and was himself again. From all indications he's getting along nicely at school. He likes his teacher and the work. Now that friends are taking an interest I'm sure they'll see to it that he is surrounded with enough decent people to offset the bad effect of low lifes [*sic*]. How I miss the children and long to share the sweetness of our own family life. Now that a committee is being formed I'm sure we'll be able to have them look after our boys['] welfare. Incidentally the P.K. told me that it's against regulations for you to transfer money so I told my sister to see about this matter.

I can't wait to see this weeks [*sic*] issue of the Guardian and read about the proposed committee. Naturally after the week end [*sic*] comes our Wed. morning visit until then I'll count the minutes. I love you so much my sweet that it hurts. Thank goodness time is passing and progress is being made. It's been $1/2$ year for you at the "CC". The next half will bring better times. All my love—

Your own Julius

Ethel to Julius [typed copy]

Oct. 14, 1951

My wonderful sweetheart,

Although I enjoyed my hour with your sister Ethel immensely, it was your beautiful letter that constituted the high spot of the day for me. Darling, for such an old married couple as we, it ought to be an old story by now; yet each time you write, avowing your love I experience afresh, a thrill of pride in my wifehood and the most genuine kind of guileless pleasure in my priceless possession. It is indeed a rare gift which you proffer, of my husband, and the source of my will to hope and to life!

I know you were ill, honey, and fretted a bit until I had the assurance that you had fully recovered. Nervous tension can certainly play havoc with one's physical state, and while I realize from sad personal experience how difficult it is to control this demon, we should each make a more concerted effort to fight its corroding effects. Certainly, we might at least avoid some of the grief by taking preventative measures wherever possible. For instance, I have this morning notified both Manny and your sister Lee that I shall look for the children on Monday, Oct. 22 and gave strict orders for our immediate notification thereof, under threat of the unnecessary anxiety that was sure to be caused us through their neglect to confirm the date in advance. Ain't I a good girl? Yes, but I could have saved myself the rush and bother if I were also a girl with a head screwed on tight instead of loose; it would have been a simple matter to have requested Ethel to phone Mrs. Bloch directly about it, and drop us a line at once! It's no use, your wife is still the world's most "absent-minded Professor", never mind Albert Einstein!

Oct. 15, 1951

My sweet, I am sick at heart for our dear innocent Michael; oh, the savage cruelty with which he must perforce become acquainted so soon, so soon. There will be enough rebuffs of the same sort which will warrant the most clear-sighted efforts on the part of our well-wishers to insure the kind of self-esteem that will enable the child to withstand the emotional shocks involved. You see, it isn't enough to make certain that he has positive human relationships (imperative as these are). There must also begin to be recognized Michael's inner needs which tend to drive him to unconsciously "set up" situations which will eventually end by inflicting suffering upon him. When his internal problems begin to receive careful, sympathetic consideration, he will have the necessary confidence to take rejection in his stride. In the meantime, I weep bitterly and reflect sadly upon the sort of inhumanity that can bring itself to so brutally punish an unprotected little boy who has never done any harm to anyone. Small wonder, however, when you consider the steadily mounting and alarming tide of callous disregard for elemental human rights that is innundating [*sic*] our country today!

Love you,
Ethel

Julius to Ethel [typed copy]

Oct. 18, 1951

My Most Sweetest Darling,

Your man is crazy about you and can't stop loving you. It is a source of rare pride to me to have such a wonderful person as you for my wife. I just feel great when I see you and think of you and my week passes quickly. My thoughts and all my concentration are already concerned with the coming visit of our two dears. To be sure I am anxious to see them so I can hear from their sweet lips how things are progressing at home and how they are getting along. I can't wait to hear what Michael will have to say about our case and his new found friends.[189] This time although I will go up to see them empty handed I'll be ready with many topics of discussion which will make the visit a fruitful one. The thought just occurred to me that since our lawyer is present it would be so much better especially for the boys if we were able to see them together. Perhaps this should wait until we can talk it over and then approach the Warden on this matter. Sweetheart he's

---

[189]This might very well refer to the Minor family. See *Sons*, pp. 111, 116–18.

been awfully nice and I'm sure he'll understand. Then, too, after the visit we'll be able to look forward to the next issue of the Guardian. Again I'm impatient for more concrete results on the committee and the campaign to disseminate the facts in our case to ever large numbers of people. I hope the paper continues to print letters from the readers as this kind of stuff gives me great satisfaction. What we both said before our trial, during and after it, is coming to pass and it cannot be otherwise. After all the real final court and judge is the American people. They are the guardians of our rights, liberty and yes our lives. The tyrants and their jackal lackeys will not get away with this hideous political frameup and truth must conquer and win for us complete vindication and freedom.

Dearest we didn't seek this fight but when justice is on our side and yes the very fundamental law of Nature is in our favor then we take heart. We're confident that we're not alone and convinced in the triumph of our cause. With great hope I see the wonderful future and the complete happiness of being with you and the children. This thought keeps my spirit high and my courage strong. If it's possible I'm happy even now because we have not faltered and measured up to our own expectations. Again my love take heart we're made of solid stuff and we can hold our heads up high and be proud of ourselves as man and woman. All my love—Your Julius

Ethel to Julius [typed copy]

October 18, 1951

Hello dearest,

Just two days ago, I looked out through the cold gray bars and hungrily filled my eyes with the warm, bright sight of you. I felt a stab of tenderness to see the sweetly smiling mouth that has in times past so greedily devoured my own and the touseled [*sic*] hair with the part meandering every which way, that I so gently caressed that memorable evening while the jury deliberated our fate and we steadfastly refused to give up hope! Sweetheart, what a long, tortorous [*sic*] road we have since travelled; and yet somehow, for all the pain and torment, nothing shakes my conviction that only the proud and the noble are to be found upon this thorny trail, and that the shining abode which awaits at the end of our heartbreaking trek is truly the Kingdom of Heaven on earth!

October 19, 1951

I'm hoping your brother visits with us today. Since I have as yet received no word from home regarding the children's coming on Monday, and he might know one way or another. Somehow I am not as tense in anticipation as I am wont to be ordinarily; perhaps it is just as well, although every once in so often I am inclined to berate myself for not trying to do some "figuring" in advance. It is as though there are periods of dull suspension smack between varying moods of hilarity and depression. Actually, it is really a kind of resigned, weary despair, that causes me to more or less mark time; I'm as heavy as lead and at such moments won't budge for anything, and simpley [sic] do not "produce". Soon I head for a sharper, more anguished despondency that makes itself so keenly felt, I ask [sic—perhaps this was "gasp" and the typist misread it] for breath and struggle for equilibrium. Finally, I "make" it and once more head for battle!

Darling, I have been re-reading the Guardian articles. I get so hopeful. I also get scared and yet I just can't bring myself to think in terms other than victory and our eventual release; why should I thus punish myself when there is so much punishment already? Honey, did you notice the "ad" under the heading of "Calendar" in the last issue we received? If you don't recall it, hunt it up at once, you are due for a terrific thrill when you find it!

Tell me, have you been enjoying the Jewish Services as much as I have? What a lucky break for us that our own rabbi could secure the attention of such a fine substitute in his absence.—Mail call.

Love you,
Ethel

The next letter indicates that the National Guardian *had begun to publish some of their prison correspondence.*

Julius to Ethel [typed copy]

October 21, 1951

My Most Wonderful Woman,

Now many people know who you are and how much I think of you. It seems to me that there are now many people who know what a swell person you are (reading my letters and yours). To be sure I'm pretty proud of you, my wife. Speaking of how well you write and express your true feelings some day when this misery is past history, I hope you'll find it in yourself to write a book so that large number of readers can get mental nourishment from your creative talent. Were I to enumerate the wonderful virtues you possess, I'd run out of glowing adjectives, however, besides being an excellent writer and singer, you're a good sweet, warm, socially-conscious human being, humble understanding and have a lovely personality and above all, you're my girl. I am very glad its [sic] understood that you're all mine because I'm extremely jealous of such a great prize. Oh how glorious it would be to enjoy the sweetness of being with you in the comforts of our own home. Sweetheart, I'm madly in love with you.

Thank goodness, tomorrow is Monday and we'll be seeing the two prides of our union. I suppose Lena filled in the messy details of the incident with Mike as they were even worse than I had feared. I hope to be able to speak to Manny about the situation with Mike and the social worker. I'm sure this visit will be as fruitful as those in the past. Did my sister tell you about how Robbie enumerated all the people he loves and left us out? When he was asked about Mommy and Daddy he replied, but why they no come home? Naturally he was happy to know he's going to visit us and asked Lena to bring us home with her. It isn't necessary for me to tell you of the ache in my heart for the pain our boys suffer. As their mother I know you're besides yourself in torment. Oh my darling even though I'm confident and know we'll eventually be set free, for the sake of our children and our innocence I hope our going home happens fast. Also, because of what I know of you and how I feel about you, I go through all kinds of hell thinking of how you're suffering. Please good people do right by yourselves and us and make an end to this brutal frame-up. I'm keeping my eyes peeled for letters from people and activity in our behalf. Saypol didn't know what he started and his name will be mud for the miscarriage of justice he helped perpetrate.

Of course I'm looking forward to our Wednesday hour. It is always the brightest hour of the week. Honey Bunny things are picking up and it is a good omen for us.

Your own lover,
Julius

Ethel to Julius [typed copy]

Oct. 22, 1951

My dearest darling,

I have done all the crying tonight, I hope, that I'm going to; my end of the visit with the children was all but a complete fiasco! And I am in the most wretchedly unhappy state I have yet been.

First of all, Lee brought me a piece of information on Saturday which had me frantically casting about hours after her visit for some way of avoiding a meeting between Michael and my mother. Realizing that I might not have the opportunity to discuss it with any degree of privacy on Monday, I finally decided to write Dr. Miller, expressing my anxiety and disapproval and instructing him to phone Manny first and to and then, if necessary, to get in touch with the J.B.G.

Bernie's coming was another disturbing factor;[190] both of us labored under terrible tension and were mutually relieved when the bus arrived. I am hoping that Lena gave him the earful that I, for some strange reason, contained within me for a solid hour!

So it was in a kind of resigned stupor that I awaited the children's arrival; and now, no matter how sensibly I try to reason with myself that Robby's truculence and Michael's anxiety were the necessarily logical outcome of a set of circumstances over which I had no control, I am rife with a sense of personal failure.

Darling, I shall have no peace until I have poured out my anguish and chagrin to you on Wednesday. I trust that the description you give of the hour you spent, will serve to somewhat allay my own suffering.

Sweetheart, I love you, tummy and all!

Your mis'able wretch of a wife—

Ethel to Julius [typed copy]

Oct. 24, 1951

Dearest Julie:

The sound of the torrential down pour blends with Dr. Bringles singing as I struggle to collect my incoherent thoughts and watch with dismay my slowly but surely disappearing fingernails. Darling, I feel utterly neglected; there was no chance left at all this morning for verbal smooching and I am understandably bitter about it.

Unfortunately, too, I had some pertinent suggestions concerning the future visits of the children which time, or rather the lack of it, prevented me from broaching; since letter writing can be most frustrating however I refuse to tantalize myself at the moment and would far sooner wait until I can have the pleasure of discussing the matter with you more directly, and receiving your on-the-spot response.

The more I think about it, the more am I incensed over the gross stupidity that has been displayed in the handling of the children. Oh, sweetheart, it's about time we make our feelings unmistakably plain. I am sick and tired of people who are themselves emotionally trapped trying to persuade us to swallow the same vicious trapping for them.

Darling it's no use; I am so choked up with all that I know and they don't know that will have to be revealed to them if we want those boys of

---

[190]Bernard Greenglass continued attempting to keep in contact with both of his siblings. Later in 1953, he signed an affidavit that called into question David Greenglass' veracity at the trial about the theft of uranium from Los Alamos. See Schneir, p. 211.

ours to grow strong and interested and healthy in mind and soul that I simply can't tear it out of me and get it down in words.

Perhaps I'll be able to get some things across to Ethel, if she turns up on Saturday—

In the meantime, honey, bear with me; I miss you and need you so desperately—Oh, my God, I'm so unhappy, so agonized!

Love you—Ethel

Mail call—Sorry

Julius to Ethel [typed copy]

Oct. 25, 1951

My dearest Sweetest Wife:

I'm on pins and needles until I hear from you. I want to be reassured that you are feeling much better and are able to withstand the horrible tortorous [*sic*] thoughts that your two innocent darling [*sic*] are facing such cruel hardships, frustrations and emotional torments. How your mother's heart is crying for them! As for me, their father, I feel so helpless that I can't help my family. Therefore, honey, let us resolve here and now to tell Manny we are very troubled and unhappy about the children's personal situation. The joint plans we've agreed upon must be put in execution at once. There is no reason for any more delay and they must have the help of a professionally trained social worker to look after their needs. In this way not only their personal emotional lives will be aided, but the situation at home will improve with a healthier understanding of how to handle their problems and give careful consideration to both boys' emotional status. Oh, Ethel, I can't wait for Manny to show himself so that we can finally have a thorough discussion on this most pressing matter. Our road through hell is beset with numerous pitfalls and heartaches and my thoughts and hopes go out to you, my wife, and I want you to get some solace from my deep seated love and devotion for you. Many will be the obstacles that we will have to face until that glorious homecomeing [*sic*]. For the sake of our children, may it come quickly.

Perhaps by the time you get this letter we will already have received the legal brief from our Circuit Court Appeal. My suggestion to you is that you read it thoroughly and carefully and prepare notes for we might come up with some suggestions that could be used in our oral argument or possible [*sic*] in the rebuttal brief. It would certainly bolster up my spirits to read some good news in the Guardian of activity in our behalf. Yes, my woman, you put it correctly when you state the monsters of our time have perpetrated a heinous crime in railroading us to this tomb. If it will ease the pain, take heart in the knowledge that already large numbers of people know the true facts in our case and are coming to our aid. Of course, it isn't easy for innocent people to sit in the shadow of death and not go to pieces but sweetheart we are here because we wouldn't knuckle under the heels of the modern tyrants and we stand our ground with all progressives for decency, freedom, peace and real justice.

Remember our motto, my loved one—Courage, confidence and perspective. The fact that we've weathered many storms and came through with flying colors is the guarantee of our success. Always confident in victory.

Your loyal and loving husband,
Julius

Ethel to Julius

Oct. 25, 1951

Hello, sweetheart darling,

I hereby ask your full support for the insurance of more regular legal visits from here on in; I sincerely contend that a good deal of the lassitude and inertia to which I have periodically fallen a victim in the last two months, must be traced to the increasing infrequency of our consultations with Manny. Obviously, there has been valid reason heretofore but starting as of next week, we must raise very sharply the question of a return to normalcy! ('ear, 'ear, sounds like an election speech!)

Honey, whatever in thunderation shall I do until next Wednesday; there simply isn't another bit of nail left to bite! Of course, I could go to work on a few candy bars, but they won't take long to polish off! Besides, that kind of activity is not exactly conducive to the preservation of youthful slenderness, as you must by this time have realized, my good man (very sternly); don't look now but I think your posterior, to say nothing of your fronterior, is beginning to show!

Hooray, tomorrow is Friday or to be more specific, "National Guardian Day". I let out a whoop of pure joy when the last issue was handed me. My happiness was short-lived, of course, for reasons I have already divulged to you; and I am hoping against hope that I have a less difficult time of it this week-end. As a matter of fact, I am eagerly looking forward to a possible visit from your brother Dave and for [*sic*] your sister Ethel.

My sweet, I'm so sorry I was impatient during our last meeting, but I was fresh from several days of horrible mental anguish and my brains felt like so many scrambled eggs. I'm afraid you must be getting rather fed up with all the moaning I am doing via the mail of late. Dearest I entreat you to show me forbearance. I am half out of my head with anxiety, and with the determination to secure for the children their day in court. (I shall end up as an advocate, yet (my words; this legal stuff is getting into my very bones!)

Which reminds me that copies of the brief ought to be forthcoming any day now; I know it will have a tonic effect upon us both.

Friday A.M.—Oct. 26, 1951

Just before I turned in last night I heard Jack Benny in a play sponsored by the United Jewish Appeal, "The Incredible Village", which tells the story of former blind beggars in Israel who undertook the building of a village for themselves and established families for the first time in their lives. The painful evolution of this modern miracle which at last wiped out the darkness of their previous way of life was simply but most heart-warmingly narrated and dramatized by Benny and a most excellent supporting cast including John Hodiak and Mercedes McCambridge of Hollywood.

All my love and my aching heart,

As always, your Ethel

[From the following letter through that of December 14, 1951, the letters are typed copies unless otherwise noted.]

Julius to Ethel

Oct. 28, 1951

My Most Precious Bunny:

The fact that you keep sending me such beautiful love epistles makes it easier to take this cruel separation. I join you in a vehement demand to our beloved friend Manny that he come once a week for legal consultations. We have indulged in self denial long enough and now that the bulk of his work on our behalf is done we should insist that he give us the time even though it may have to be on a Sat. or Sun. and I'm sure we'll be able to contribute quite a bit to our legal campaign and to the efforts of the committee to attain justice for us. There is a lot of ground we have to cover and we must convince our lawyer of the urgent necessity for him to make the time available to us.

Darling, it seems to be an eternity since I last saw you. Oh I miss you so much I want to be with you, to talk to you, see your sweet smile and hear from your lovely lips that all's well with you. As for me all my thoughts are of you and the children and I'm plagued with thoughts of how you and the boys are suffering. If only time would pass quickly and we were already on the eve of our homegoing then I would be much calmer. Constantly, I busy myself with trifles to shut out the stark reality of our horrible incarceration but it only gives temporary relief and the most welcome feeling is always sleep because I can dream of the good life we've had together and the beautiful future we face together. My love I love you so much it hurts. My sweet girl please tell me that you get comfort and ease from my complete devotion to you because it will make me happy to know I'm able to be of some help. More and more as time passes the only thing that counts is the one solitary hour we spend together every Wednesday. It is a source of great satisfaction to me that we are able to cover a great deal of ground in so little time. Many are the thoughts that I've not been able to discuss with you because we've been pressed by the most current problem facing us and if we could at least have another hour each week it would go a long way to bring us up to date on our personal matters. Do you think ["it" probably omitted here] is possible for us to get just a little consideration and have the luck to have a few nice things happen to us? I don't know somehow everything comes hard for us. Anyhow why worry only two more days and I see my hearts desire.

I kiss you tenderly till I see you— Your own Julius

Ethel to Julius

October 29, 1951

Dearest, darling, sweetheart,

Your last two letters, dated October 25th and 28th, were just right for what ailed me. My dear one, your love is a thing of surpassing beauty that commits me to unremitting battle for the coming of age of my own sacred spirit and, by some miracle of tenderness, becalms the turbulent waves of fear and despair that pound upon the shores of my heart and inexorably demand admittance. Thought of you brings emotional peace to the swelling-place [*sic*—probably a typographical error; meant to be "dwelling place"] of my soul and evokes the deepest kind of contentment within me. And now, sweetest, do you still ask what you mean to me? If only I might once again have that dear opportunity to lavish upon you all the affection that is yours; then would even my silence speak more eloquently than all these pitiful words!

Honey, things seem to be looking up all around for our side. First of all, your brother's visit was a most pleasurable one for me, lasting as it did for a whole ["hour" probably omitted here] and a half and covering a wide range of topics. Saturday afternoon brought Dr. Miller for a tantalizing short but very fruitful twenty-five minutes; and when he left, I received the latest issue of the Guardian.

On the basis of my conversation with Dr. Miller, I was able to write another of my very "instructive" letters to Manny; incidentally, they are finally getting together some time this week, so I requested Manny to see us on Friday, rather than Wednesday, or for that matter, Saturday, (As Ethel may be planning to come then). Perhaps, also, in the interim, we shall have had the opportunity to peruse our long-awaited legal brief and so be the better prepared to carry on an intelligent discussion when he does get here.

I am hoping to hear when I see you tomorrow, that you received this letter this afternoon; when you receive it Wednesday afternoon instead, some of the items are bound to be a re-hash of our talk that very morning. Please, Correspondence Dept., pretty please, just this once!

Dear, it's too late for anything but love and kisses. And that with all my heart, my very dearest.

Your loving
Ethel

Julius to Ethel

November 1, 1951

My Dearest Darling:

How could I help loving you so much!! You're so sweet and beautiful. It is with deep satisfaction that I look at you and swell with pride. I can't get the thought of you out of my mind. I hunger and long for you constantly. Oh my precious sweetheart how cruel our separation, how horrible the enforced loneliness, unspeakable mental anguish grips me as I think of the sufferings of my wonderful lovely family. Ethel my sweetheart it was such a pleasure to see you in good spirits and looking so well. When I see you as I've just said I feel strong and elated and I'm able to plow through another week until our hour. An eternity of time is crawling along and it seems that we are marking time in a bottomless pit with no connection to reality. Only contact with you, Manny and the children continues to be the stabilizing force and the magnet that drags me back to life. Both of us keep hoping for a speedy victory and an early return to the comfort of our own home and our two darlings. There is no doubt we will reach new heights of happiness when we are together again.

I don't know what's holding up the brief. Maybe our counsel intends to bring them up with him on his next visit? Before I forget I want to tell you how much I appreciate the fact that you prepared the material for our tete a tete and we were able to cover so much ground. If we can hear concrete results on the solution of the home problem and a start on helping our boys I'll be more than pleased. Then too if we can get some good news from the committee as to what they've accomplished and some of their plans we'll feel a whole lot better. It is important that we become part of a living thing that is presenting the true facts about our case. I propose we have Manny and our family give us regular reports on what's happening and this should become second nature to them that they acquaint themselves with as much detail as possible before they come to visit. Another day, week, month— soon soon—this can't go on forever. There must be an end to this and above all we will win our freedom. I have no doubt regardless of how long it will take that we, my wife will be completely vindicated. I think of, I dream of, yes I can clearly see myself taking you home and possessing you completely. There is no greater thing than good decent wholesome life with dignity. All my love honey. We'll see the day— Your own Julius

Ethel to Julius

November 1, 1951

Hello Julie dearest,

Since Wednesday morning and all the good, sweet words that passed between us, I have been walking on air; was there foul weather or fair, I followed the unhurried progress of the clock, undismayed. And whatever the hour brought of loneliness and distaste, could not overthrow the shining monument that is our union. My dear one, rest easy; I am ever fortified in your love.

Also am I fortified in the support of decent people everywhere which is so heart-warmingly and so selflessly increasingly forthcoming. Darling, what a treat it is to be reading this week's issue of the Guardian, today of all gloomy rainy days; all of a sudden the drab gray of my wretched surrounding is touched with magical radiance and color. How unutterably thrilling are the expressions of sympathy and devotion from other precious human beings; I am overwhelmed with an answering love and gratified and the profound desire to be worthy of the beautiful tribute with which they have honored us![191] In all humility, I pledge my self [*sic*] anew, to the unceasing war against man's inhumanity to man, in whatever shape, manner or form it may rear its ugly brute's head. Nor shall I ever sell short the priceless trust and faith they have reposed in me for a questionable reward of a "mess of pottage"; else shall I have lived my life for naught!

Sweetheart dear, how very much I love you and want you at my side; and with how much longing do I recall the happy life we led and all the problems of parenthood we were so eagerly in process of solving! The healthy growth and development of the children often gave us cause for grave concern, but they were also a source of so much genuine enjoyment

---

[191]The way this sentence reads indicates that the typist must have missed something from the original, but it is impossible to figure out what is missing.

and pleasure, that no difficulty was too great to dampen our enthusiasm and pride in them.

I am hoping to compose myself enough this week-end to drop them a few lines[.] honey [*sic*] I am reminded of the many kind offers of assistance the Guardian has received with regard to the bunnies. There are no words that will adequately describe the sense of bond and tenderness these "strangers" woke. I am simply speechless with admiration for my new-found brothers and sisters!

Mail call—dearest.

I love you—Ethel

Julius to Ethel

November 4, 1951

Love of my life: How thrilled I was to hear such splendid news from Manny's lips. I was moved to tears to hear such tender and compassionate letters from good people with humane feelings. The lawyer consultation was a stirring and emotionally satisfying experience. Of course, when I'm so happy and seeing you in such good spirits I feel like I'm floating on air. I feel so close to you and I loved you with all my senses. Darling it is indeed inspiring in this hour of our greatest need to see the visible evidence of concrete support from many ordinary people. We are truly not alone. There is a tremendous resevoir [*sic*] of good people in our land and they will see to it that the facts are made known and that we will get the justice we're entitled to. There are so many mixed feelings I have and most of all I want to be able to share them with you. How my arms ached to hold you! How my lips wanted to taste the sweetness of yours! I repeated over and over again how lucky I am to have such a wonderful precious woman as you for my wife. I am proud of you and for your sake I want us to be home with our children. The difficulties we face are many and the torment great but the successful termination of this mess we're in looks more promising as time passes.

I read the brief and I wrote Manny telling him what a stupendous job he did and how everlastingly grateful we are for his tireless efforts for us both his legal work and the humane acts of devoted friendship he has performed for us and our boys. He's swell, I just love the guy. Darling the brief is a legal masterpiece and in addition is a literary gem. Although I don't have the background to really pass on the legal fine points I can attest to its excellent organization, its meticulousness in presenting in a fair light our case, the devastating logic of his points and the tremendous assiduous effort Manny exerted in preparing this document. Believe me it's a priceless piece of work from a great man. How proud we are to be considered his friends. I intend to reread it a number of times so I'll be able to better understand some of the legal points raised.

My dear sister's visit was very pleasant and we enjoyed ourselves immensely. She sure loves and admires you. It is a source of great satisfaction that my family has taken you to their hearts. They love you for yourself and the swell woman you are.

More—so do I.
Julius

Ethel to Julius

November 6, 1951

My dearest darling husband:

How I have been neglecting you; not a word from me since Friday or Saturday, depending on which day my last letter reached you.

As usual, when Manny's visit to us was terminated, I was dissatisfied about several omissions on my part. I sought to remedy this state of affairs by writing him but all I could manage to do was to repeat how deeply all those messages of support printed by the "Guardian" had moved me and to beg him to make known our desire to contribute financially on behalf of this "Voice of America's Conscience" as I characterize it. I also requested that his wife purchase a new record album, Prokofieff's "Cinderella", as a special Chanukah piece from us to the children. If it is anywhere near as good as "Peter and the Wolf" it will be a most worthwhile addition to their record library.

November 7, 1951

Honey, how much I enjoyed seeing you this morning; how sweet it was for me as a wife to lean upon my husband's strength and to savor in full the tender solicitousness of his concern for my well-being. I love you so very dearly, my heart; how I ache for the joy and peace I once knew within your arms! I am a woman bereft of all the loveliest privileges life has to offer and yet do I hold myself blessed among women for have I not found favor in your eyes and am I not truly beloved of you?

Dearest, I slept very well last night and look forward to a pleasant, relaxed day; I know how happy said statement must make you feel. I shall do my utmost to sort out my entangled thoughts and communicate with the children.

Sweetheart, good-bye for now. I hope to write you once more before the week-end but should I be unable to for one reason or another do not be anxious as I am confident I can keep things under control[.]

All my heart and soul's love—and a longing kiss,

Your adoring wife
Ethel

Julius to Ethel

November 8, 1951

My dearest Ethel: My! my! do I have a spunky wife. It was indeed a pleasure to hear, in detail, how you are able to defend your interests. I'm not stating this just to glad hand you but in view of past history and the terrible emotional burden you face you are doing splendidly. You must keep in mind that as long as our hour each week is so productive and mutually satisfying it fills in a great void and acts as a mental stimulus. Darling no matter how many times I repeat it, the fact still remains that your position is the more difficult one and only when the myriad of tortures are but a memory can I begin to unravel the nightmareish [*sic*] picture that you my love face. In all my contemplations I keep repeating back in my mind, can we be living through so terrible a situation. The reality strikes me that there are forces, evil creatures who stoop to lie, besmirch, distort, defame and ever perpetrate brutal frameups for their own partisn [*sic*] political purposes. These foul deeds of theirs attest to the fear they hold of the truth and justice. That is why I have such faith in the people and I am sure they will act when the facts and issues of our case are put before them. As long as there are decent people in our land who think with their mind and feel with their hearts and continue to be charitable to their fellow men then there is hope in America. The real hope and shining example is the Guardian and thank goodness for its fearless and steadfast policy. Please dearest when you write the children next put in some words for me. Tell my boys how much I love them. After all as the scriviner [*sic*] of our family (note the language of the brief) you do the honors. I'm expecting Lee this weekend with some welcome news and with the latest Guardian that will have to do me stead until I feast my eyes on your beaming beautiful face and I can drink in all your glowing splendor. Woman of my heart I adore you and I admire you for the swell wonderful person you are. The greatest privilege I have is to be considered so highly by you my mate. It makes me strong and more determined to live up to the high standards you set and I am constantly striving to attain the calibre of character you have. As wife, friend, human being and a mother you make me happy to share life with you. When I talk in this vein I want so to share my thoughts feelings with you. Consider yourself crushed in my arms, smothered with kisses and the object of my total love. Imagine such stuff from an old married man. For me I'm still courting my girl. Always your Julius.

Julius to Ethel

November 11, 1951

My Dearest Ethel: Today is Armistice Day. ["The" probably omitted here] time to cogitate about those who lost their lives in wartime. This is the hour when each human being should analize [*sic*] the significance of those who died, better to be able to learn the lesson for the need of world peace. Every life has feeling, mind, body, family, hopes, wishes and desires. Mankind cannot be callous to decency and his own salvation and the future of his children make it imperative that the solution to war be found at this late hour when civilization is at a crossroads. I speak of these things realizing that we two are in a little sideshow in the martial game of world chess and factors beyond our own control will decide our fate. But as vigorous, conscious citizens it is our duty to add our voices in this supreme issue of our time. It is to our benefit that the campaign to secure justice and right in our case is part of the main stream of peace[192] Americans and this is further guarantee that we will have the opportunity to fully vindicate ourselves. As I read this weeks [*sic*] issue of the Guardian I saw your beautiful face before me, beaming. I know the pride and confidence it exuded when the visible evidence of human decency and love of our fellow men for us meet your eyes. Far from belittling the personal motive which is ever present, the superlatives used in the warm letters that were sent to the Guardian make me feel humble. This is particularly so because this predicament happens to strike at our family out of the blue and bewildered as we were we carried ourselves in dignity with our heads held high. To me the beauty of our personal lives is in sharing completely the everyday problems and meeting every issue squarely and participating physically and mentally as social human beings. I think the thing that stands out is that we are just ordinary people similar in many ways to thousands of our fellow citizens and in our case and our cause they see part of themselves and the thought strikes them that they too are threatened with similar catastrophe. The fact that a 16 page pamphlet is being printed is the first real beginning and we can expect a mounting tide of support and a rising clamor for seeing that justice tri-

---

[192]Here the typist wrote "deserving" while another reader wrote in pencil "seeking" with a question mark. Obviously the handwriting was not clear.

umphs. Of course, darling I feel stronger and more hopeful but it doesn't diminish my longing for you and the children. It just increases my determination to come through all this mess in flying colors. Love of my life, woman of my heart, sweet dear person my heart goes out for you. Honey only a few more days and Wednesday again. How hard it is to wait. Always your own— Julius

P. S. Monday night now, one day closer to my sweetest. Adoring you more and more — someday we'll get married. Yes!

Ethel to Julius

November 12, 1951

Hello, my own sweet darling: Since your last visit to me and my subsequent readjustment to a particular situation, I have been operating with a steadily developing sense of self-confidence and aplomb. Indeed, with the appearance of the Guardian on Saturday and two swell visits [What follows is an open parenthesis with a blank space in which the typist has written a question mark] and Dr. Miller) [There is another blank space here in which the typist has written a question mark] even the prospect of Sunday with its expected funereal atmosphere and disquieting silence, failed to dampen my spirits. As it happened, even the weather seemed disposed to favor me; the sun shone warmly upon my soft, freshly shampooed hair and a mood of genuine serenity stole gently over me.

Darling, I grow ever stronger in the belief that the conspiracy against us, and with us, every right-thinking man, woman and child in this great land of ours, cannot stand. Thus was it ever since time began there is no evil that is powerful enough to destroy the essential good that beats in the human heart. And so we must surely "go home again"! In the meantime, one occupies oneself as well as one knows how and seeks to stifle the bitterness of one's overwhelming hungers! My sweet husband, I love you so very dearly. And there will be so much heart-warming news to share Wednesday morning!

November 13, 1951

Good morning, sweetheart, I just had a pleasant breakfast, it is only 7.30 A.M. but already our merry laughter ripples through the wing. It is so wonderful to wake up and find a sweet little lady on hand, with whom one is able to be entirely relaxed and natural and enjoy a humorous exchange. There is only one other such gal here and I am truly grateful for them both, especially in view of the death of Bessie Irving, whose selfless devotion in the service of others, the passage of time and tide can never efface.

Honey dear, your letter of the 4th arrived many days after the one dated the 8th— nevertheless I thoroughly relished every last word of it. Sweetheart, mail call— Love you— Ethel

Julius to Ethel

November 15, 1951

My wonderful woman: Today it is six months that I have spent in this tomb. I look at this place as a cold storage filing cabinet with human beings kept in constant terror awaiting the executioner. But I must put away these morbid thoughts because in the last half year things are looking up for us. As we had hoped the facts of our case are being brought before ever larger sections of the people and an excellent brief has been submitted on our behalf. We have to be patient my sweet because this stuff takes a lot of time and moves slowly. It will be some time till the cumulative effect in quantity shows a marked qualitative difference in the atmosphere around our case. I'll probably have seen you before you get this letter so I will not burden you with matters that we'll be able to discuss at our legal consultation. Just one point, it certainly is remarkable that both of us took last weekend as the time to write our two diamonds. There are many times that our minds' thoughts and actions run in parallel paths, even though we are not in physical contact with each other. Darling it must be because we are so much at one with each other that we act as an unit.

First of all sweetheart I want to repeat again since our real happiness depends on sharing completely each other's problems I hope you'll keep that in mind and not feel bad about our taking time to discuss these matters. Please for my sake don't concern yourself again about this and above all try as hard as possible not to let those lowdown barbs that are thrown at you affect you so much. Believe me, I fully understand and suffer with you the mental torment you face because of your incarceration in the "C-C". Ethel as soon as you feel better after our visit let me hear the good news even if you only write a few lines. Oh my wife how I love you and long to touch you and to feel your body pressed close to mine and to kiss you with all my heart. It seems so long since we've been in each others [sic] arms. The comfort and feeling of well being that was always part of our relationship is so sorely needed now. Only the knowledge of your love and devotion makes me strong to withstand this endless torture. Hold your hopes high my wife we are near the final victory and we have truly earned the fruits of happier days. I keep my mind flooded with the glorious memories of our married life together and it gives me sustenance till we see each other. I can just picture the image of you and I in our own home surrounded by Michael and Robbie. Always loving you with all my heart and having complete confidence and faith in you—

Your adoring fellow— Julius

Ethel to Julius

November 15, 1951

My sweet soul, my dearest love

Since my last precious glimpse of you, as you waved good-bye at the door, I have run the gamut of emotions. At the moment I am as comfortable, relaxed and contented as a student in good standing of the College of Civil (CC's to you) possibly can be, except that I feel like I've been put through a wringer. At first I was so unhappy, I collapsed and sobbed uncontrollably, after which I spent a miserable afternoon and evening, alternately tense with apprehension and calm with the determination to stand my ground. My head ached and my stomach knotted but I made it; for a change, I spent a fairly decent night and awoke close to 9.00 A.M., elated to realize that by dint of sheer will and intelligence, I had turned the tables once more. Indeed, I experienced such a sense of profound relief, I became almost hysterical with delight and whooped it up all morning, laughing and singing gaily. At 2.30 P.M. of course, the curtain of silence was lowered as per usual, but then I was no longer interested in conversation anyway![193]

Sweetheart, I am so grateful to you for being all that you are to me. We are apart, it is true, and yet I feel myself growing always closer to and more at one with you. The love and understanding you pour out of [*sic*] me is a fountain of refreshment upon which I may draw unceasingly. My dearest, I am more and more in love with you, as time inches its dreary way onward!

Friday, November 16, 1951

I wrote Manny, requesting a visit from him either today, Saturday or Monday at the very latest, depending on who else is intending to come when. I hope to have drawn up a list of gift items for the children, culled from the pages of Parents Magazine, the Compass and the Guardian.

Mail call, honey
Love, Ethel

---

[193]A reference to the fact that one of her matrons refused to speak to her.

Julius to Ethel

November 18, 1951

My sweetest bunny: It makes me feel so good when I get one of your letters. Each and every one of them are different and exude freshness and warmth. Surely they are the products of a brilliant and agile mind, creating beauty out of the simplicity of expression and picturesqueness of well chosen words. To me who has lived with you, I am able to fully appreciate it because it is so much like you. As meticulous as is your analytical mind so devastating is your written word. Oh my darling how proud I am of your ability and achievements and I have so many plans in the offing that will find their fruition after that happy day we go home together. Never before my love have you faced such hardships and so many difficult obstacles and yet in this gloom so much of your beauty has begun to shine forth. Of course, I am referring to the great potential, that I was always sure you had stored in you. You are a great person. There is no question that when one is weighed down with tremendous problems there will no doubt be some weaknesses but in the overall picture your fine qualities, good character and wholesomeness overshadows to nothing these negative aspects. When I stop to consider what it will be like once we are home again, I'm sure that now that this latent creativeness has begun to come forth life will be much fuller and hold more meaning. This marvellous [*sic*] occurrence is in itself additional testimony to the kind of person you basically are and to the fact that only the innocent can be so strong at the most threatening hour of their life. For me I am happy to see my most precious wife as such a wonderful, beautiful human being.

Ethel sometimes I get to think about all the small and picayune hurts that beset us, and at the moment they are like salt in an open wound, but in retrospect as part of the entire picture it is a mere trifle that will pass and as all dust settle with time. It seems an age since I last laid my eyes on you and was treated with the musical sound of your voice. As yet I haven't read the latest issue of the Guardian and I guess we'll have all good things come at once, Manny, the paper and news of home. Soon the Thanksgiving holiday will be here and at such times I feel most the wretched separation from you and our children. Another week has gone by and we are close to our day my sweetheart my love, all my heart and tenderness I send you. I adore you and kiss you with all my love — Your Julius

Ethel to Julius

November 18, 1951

My dearest darling Julie: Talk of your blue Mondays; in here it is blue Sundays! A wintry sky and a sharp wind sent me briskly stamping about the yard, as though by so doing I might stamp out the rising panic, the threatened assault upon my decent human courage. Darling, the unyielding loneliness which engages me in a grim and continuous battle, took possession unopposed today; it sank its fangs so deep, I wept helplessly. Oh, when shall I know again the sweetness of sharing all the[194] the precious, that are within the grasp of a man and a woman!

I have been re-reading "Gentlemen's Agreement",[195] a solid, exciting piece of writing, indeed. It was emotional food upon which I fell hungrily and which made me realize only too clearly how starved I was for intellectual exchange, for stimulating talk, for warm bond with other human beings, who could truly appreciate and understand. There is such a bare minimum of anything remotely resembling such vigorous, creative sociality, in any case, that these last two days, without even that minimum, have been horribly punishing. To the bargain, the descriptions of pain, of loss, of anguished longing through which the two principal characters must make their way before all misunderstanding and all parting may be over for them, at last, brought such painful awareness of our own separation that my heart was wrenched out of me. Oh, to put this intolerable time behind us in one fell swoop—dearest how I have been missing you.

There are any number of matters which I have carefully noted and which only await Manny's coming for thorough discussion and analysis. I must confess I'll be keenly disappointed if he doesn't turn up today. It is Monday morning, my love, and the tedium of Sunday is lifted. I am in a constant fever to be ever hastening elsewhere, all of the tremendous distance that lies between one day and the next. Big deal!

In my letter to Michael, I encouraged him about his handwriting and stressed easy, related effort, (no matter how far short of perfect the end result might be) and a realization on his part that he can only go just so fast, no matter what any mutton-headed grown-up had to say about it. (I was of course slightly less outspoken in my explanation to him, you understand, but maybe somebody will sit up and take notice on similar scores.)

---

[194]Here the typist wrote in a word that is illegible because it was crossed out by the editor. The word might be "innermost" or "warmest."

[195]A best selling novel by Laura Z. Hobson (later made into a movie) about a writer who writes about anti-semitism by assuming a Jewish identity.

Please, sweetheart, where's that magic formula that will insure our happy ending?

Aren't you ever going to propose to me, my reluctant love? love you and kiss you with all my soul! Ethel

Julius to Ethel

November 22, 1951

My wonderful sweet wife: After a long wait Manny showed up and we had an excellent consultation. In reviewing all that we covered it is indeed remarkable how completely satisfying and emotionally stimulating these sessions are. With all due modesty your guy is getting to be a legal light. What do you think? Eh what? There is nothing else, short of going home, that we could ask for, in view of the splendid news from the activities on our behalf and also the heartening sign that things are under control at home. How hungry we are for contact with the life we know and want and looking at you thriving from participation [*sic*] heart and soul in discussion on our problems, I was sure you felt as I, completely removed from these miserable surroundings and once again part of worthwhile living. But oh darling when the flush of stimulus from Manny's visit and his component good news has been absorbed the letdown is terrific. At this time of happiness it is so important to share with you, to exchange views, to smell the fragrance of your hair, to touch your smooth skin, to feel your warm body against mine and hold you close to my heart. There is no real understanding and joy without you. When I consider the great deal of suffering you've been through, and the long uphill fight we still face my heart aches for you my love.

Oh yes, my dearest I can't forget today is Thanksgiving day, after all I have a very substantial chicken dinner under my belt to remind me of this fact. At this time my thoughts go to my family, to you and to our beloved children. As for me, food can never be any consolation for the deep pain and hurt of our separation from our dears who need us so much and in the holiday season they are most sharply aware of their parents not being home. We can be thankful that we are still able to participate in fighting for justice, peace and a better life for all. The encouraging signs of support and the bettering political picture gives [*sic*] us added hope for improved public opinion and an indication that we can expect a fair judicial weighing of our appeal and a reversal of our conviction. Honey I'm only a layman and aside from the fact that we're innocent an impartial reading of the brief based on our trial record can give no other answer but a complete vindication for us. Ethel, sweetheart, we need so much strength to continue to withstand all this heavy pressure and be able to come through this torture quickly and with credit to our honor and in the kind of dignity to which we aspire. Precious woman my will and love for you are stronger than these bars don't [*sic*] worry you're always mine and only death can change that—your own— Julius

Ethel to Julius

November 25, 1951

My dearest loved one: Saturday came and went for you with nary a word from your old woman, who worked herself into a headache Thursday night and woke up the next day with an even worse tummy ache. Your brother came in to find his usually spirited sister-in-law rather green in the face; I had caused myself to vomit a few minutes before and was still feeling rotten. We spent a pleasant half-hour, however, and he left with my assurance that I would dose myself with aspirin, at once. Within an hour, my headache had subsided enough to permit me to continue reading "The Cruel Sea"; to descend to something in the nature of a pun, I was "ship-shape" again!

Somehow, I had also managed to get a letter out to Manny by Friday morning; hence your own deprivation. Am I forgiven, darling? So long, so dreadfully long since I've seen you my sweet; I have been weeping the usual bucket of week-end tears and wrestling with my own private devils. Of course, Dr. Miller stirs these up every time he appears but from past experience I know that the insight and strength with which I am subsequently rewarded for my pains, will be forthcoming now, too, as it has in the times past. Still, the anguish does not lessen thereby; it has to be reckoned with before there may be comfort within me once again. With Manny I took up in a bit more detail the idea of paid relief for Sophie. You see, I had modified the original plan in my own mind after our consultation. As it stands now, I believe four evenings (from 8 PM on) and nights, might prove more feasible all around. Obviously, it will be easier to find someone on such a basis, and at the same time it will head off any inclination of Sophie's part to feel rather shooed aside. Incidentally, in view of her perfectly natural desire for a bit more tangible proof of appreciation, I also directed Manny to purchase one of those prettily papered, small plywood (or cardboard) chests for her personally to be presented to her as a Christmas present from us both. You, honey, may be getting to be a "legal light" but I am learning the gentle art of "skinning a cat" the easiest way! All kidding aside, though I have long felt the lack of personal contact with the woman and want most sincerely for her to realize how genuinely grateful we are. Yippee, tomorrow

is Monday! Comes Wednesday, I shall probably blubber away most of our
precious hour. Sweetheart, your girl is desperately in need of you; I didn't
know such unhappiness could exist in one person's being. How sweet it
used to be to nestle close to you, murmuring the last good nights and
exchanging the last kisses! How wretched it is now and how brutal to be
spending the same once rapturous hours apart. Your loving wife.

Julius to Ethel

November 25, 1951

My dearest Wife: This morning I finished a letter to Manny concerning the
necessity of our receiving the Guardian and for him to see to it that we get
the two issues we've missed. I told him of how difficult things are during
the time between our regular consultations and that he should try to send us
some good material to read and also any pertinent written matter on our
case. Sweetheart I can just imagine how you feel as for myself I miss you
terribly. The days just seem to drag. I manage to keep reading part of the
time but generally the contents are mediocre and the books aren't very
appealing. It is so essential that we receive regular reports on the activities
of the committee on our behalf. Only the knowledge of progress in our case
can continue to furnish the necessary stimulant to fill some of the void.
Incidentally I talked to the P.K. last week about our visit and we should get
some clarification soon on the questions I raised. At our last meeting with
our lawyer we didn't get to talk about the boys [*sic*] next visit. It is my
suggestion you write our counselor telling him the day and what time they
should arrive. In connection with the children I think we should ask the
Rabbi to get us Chanukah cards for the boys so that we can send the cards to
be included in our gifts to them for the holiday. Since it has always been
our custom to give my mother a present this time of the year what do you
think about Manny getting one for her in our name. Talking about gifts I'd
like one for us. To be home with our loved ones. The holiday season to me
means that we are coming close to the time when we will be coming home
together. It must be this way, we have already suffered so much needlessly
and justice demands that we[196] by right to be completely vindicated. Oh my
darling so many long lonely nights are in store for us and all I could do is
dream of you lying in my arms. Know my woman that the high esteem you
hold me in and the love you show me continues to be a source of endless

---

[196]The next two words are handwritten into a blank space indicating that the
typist could not make out the original. The ungrammatical writing casts doubt on
the typist's guess.

courage for me and is a guarantee that we will find in each other the strength to together conquer this bottomless pit of despair. There are times my heart when I too feel simply desolate and tortured with thoughts of your hardships and the difficulties of our children and my heart cries out for an end to all this misery. I can't wait to see you and I'm sure that this Wednesday will again raise up my sagging spirits. All this would be so much easier to take if I were able to be with you. We can, nevertheless rest assured that this too will come to pass and our reunion will be all the sweeter. I press you close to my heart. All my love— your Julius

[The next letter is an original.]

Mrs. Lena Cohen
140 Baruch Place
New York, New York

Nov. 28, 1951

Dearest Lee,

I received a card from Ethel in Mama's name, yesterday, expressing alarm over my having been sick during Davy's last visit. I could have written her directly but for the fact that there was no time left to really compose a nice letter to the kids. Until I do so, I want Mama to know I was perfectly well two hours after he left and have been in excellent health since. Please phone her at once. After all, it was just a slight stomach upset and headache due chiefly to nerves and I am surprised that he should have mentioned it at all, especially in view of my admonition to him not to say anything.

Sorry I didn't write you before as I had promised; one of these days you'll get a long and (I hope) interesting letter from me—

Best regards to everybody—& please phone Mama

Love— Ethel

Julius to Ethel

November 29, 1951

My Dearest Ethel: Already, it seems that somewhere in the distant past I spent a few fleeting moments talking to you and now there exists an eternity of time till we can exchange some sweet sharing. The fact that I'm busying myself reading the newspapers, magazines, and the latest book "Cheaper by the Dozen" helps the time pass but the most refreshing pastime is a good session of chess. Yesterday Cal played me to a 3 hour draw. It was a fascinating game right down to the last move. Somehow tonight I managed to beat him two quick ones. On the whole we're evenly matched and I enjoy myself very much but soon he'll be getting some more legal papers and again even this little bit is denied. Darling I don't know but I believe that even though it might be construed as escapist I still feel anything that will help make it easier for us is very important for our morale. Today I finally received the Nov. 14 issue of the Guardian and we can now expect to be brought up to date on our subscription. I hope to be seeing a copy of the booklet they've printed on our case. In the past we didn't manage to discuss any of our ideas with Manny about the campaign and I think it's time that we make some definite proposals. On this point I want you to concentrate and bring forth some concrete suggestions. Things such as newspaper advertisements and other ways to inform the public about the facts in our case. Even though such an operation requires time, planning ahead is vital. Honey so much is at stake for us and all justice in our land, and a tremendous effort is needed to raise funds to carry the message to the people. Sweetheart are you aware of the fact that many times during the day I sit at my table and look at your picture on the wall and talk to you. You're so sweet my wife I can't help loving you. In a couple of days we'll be in the month of December and we're crawling at a snail's pace close to the day when all this existence will be just a horrible memory. In the meantime let us continue to seek sustenance in each other, in our love and from the experience of the life we've lived we can be assured how much more beautiful our life together will be on our victorious homecoming. Yes my dear I worry too and do have some doubts but only for moments because it cannot be otherwise our innocence is our strongest weapon. With all my confidence I miss you so terribly and I have to think of our next meeting and the future to dispel all my mental agony. I'll be holding you in my arms tonight and closest to my heart and you will fill all my dreams. With all my being I love you — Julius

Ethel to Julius

November 29, 1951

My very own dear love:

After your dear presence could no longer make itself felt, the loneliness closed around me. By evening, there swept over me an impotent rage a violent urge to shriek forth my soul's unspeakable anguish; my brain stood aghast while grotesque and fearsome images began to take shape around me. And yet my will persisted and refused to acknowledge defeat! Only the question beat dully within me. How much agony could the human heart contain without bursting asunder, how much cruel blocking could the natural instincts countenance without release, and where was the release to be obtained? Thought of you and the children was a live torture, intruding itself upon my desperate mental concentration; at long last my soundless weeping abated; the distasteful surroundings blurred and the book I had been gazing at with unseeing eyes claimed my complete attention. Sweet, tonight the storm is spent and I am at peace. I have the surest, calmest, conviction that such will be the fate of all those still to be conquered. Oh, darling keep me ever within your heart and bid me welcome. The day must inevitably arrive that will herald our closer, our deeper, our more divinely joyous reunion. I love you, dearest, and wish I didn't have to pretend you were embracing me ardently, and I was matching your passion with my own! (I strongly suspect that you consider me a shameless hussy; you're right, too!)

7:15 a.m. Friday Nov. 30, 1951

Dear, now I ought to reassure you that all is well with me physically and armed with snuggies wool socks and rubbers, I am all set to withstand the rigors of the Ossining winter. The longer I remain here, the more firmly I am convinced that not only does it require a difficult course of diligent study to become a successful inmate but it also demands a hefty purse. Speak of your "keeping up with the Jones" [sic] one can't live onself [sic] [From context this appears to have been a misreading by the typist] avoid this noble concept even in the Sing Sing death house![197] Well, well, and where is the sponge cake and the latkes?[198] After all, it's my confirmation, belated though it may be; how do you like my taste in hotels, at least as good as the Astor: [sic]

Sweetheart, how happy I am when I talk with you, only why do I need this miserable pencil and paper when you're just across the hall from me! A joke, why don't you laugh! I'm looking forward to Ethel's visit on Saturday; honey do your best to explain to her the need for forbearance on your mother's part. Obviously Sophie has made the necessary adjustment and needs some little sign of appreciation and acceptance. Mail call, my darling love you dearly— Ethel

---

[197]This sentence appears to have been misread by the typist.
[198]Potato pancakes, served traditionally at Chanukah.

Julius to Ethel

December 2, 1951

My Dearest Sweetheart: It's wonderful to get such newsy letters from you but I'm sorry to see that you have to go through a tortuous cycle in running the gamut of emotions. Tsh! Tsh! such ardent love but honey it's only words. Do you want to burn up the paper? Save it. I'd like to hear such personal tid-bits from your own sweet lips. Certainly from what you write it is easy to see that you still have a good resiliency and you come back stronger and more firmly confident. A true measure of your ability is the hilarious repartee of your coming out party (winter style). No my love I do not lose sight of the fact that conditions are difficult and we still have endless mental and emotional agony to wade through. If there were only some way I could ease your pain and give you some measure of relief I would be so happy. Know my wonderful person you are the mainstay of my life. Always uppermost in my heart and in my mind, you symbolize for me everything noble, decent and good in life and epitomize the best in a human being. Naturally, in the present environment and all the hardships of a confinement while awaiting doom especially since we are innocent it requires tremendous courage and strength to prevent one from breaking down and losing one's mind. The last month of the year is at hand and we can look forward to a better year for us. We will have to look to the passing of time and good news reports on our case to maintain our high morale. My sister and I had a pleasant visit and on the whole the conditions at home are good at the same time I feel we should ask Manny to look into the situation that has developed at school with Mike. I am interested in any steps that might be taken to reassure our boy of our support and encourage him to have more self-confidence and I'm not concerned with his negativeness and his asserting his independence. This may be indicative of some difficulty but I'm glad to see that as yet he hasn't knuckled under and I want him to be strengthened constructively before any damage is done to him. In order for me not to be misunderstood I'll discuss this matter with you in detail when I see you. Now that I've talked to my sister I'm enthusiastic about your suggestion of rings for the childrens' [*sic*] presents and you will make the show of presenting the rings (or if possible it will be done in your presence) and then I'll be able to see the boys wearing our tokens of love. My lovely wife how thoughtful you are for your boys and my mother and other people and all the time it's you who need the gifts and presents as just rewards for the swell woman that you are. I'll save up my gift to you until the day we go home together and then we both can live again. Nothing I say or do can bring our joyous moment close but my confidence is solid and my hopes and convictions are very optimistic. Always your own — Julius

Ethel to Julius

December 3, 1951

My dearest bunny: Bless you for that delightful letter; it satisfied in every way, whether you were mischievously chiding me for my shameless expressions of desire, poking fun at my "coming-out party", or seriously discussing Michael's problems. Sir, you are an unmitigated and altogether charming rascal and I love you passionately (spoken in a husky tone, a la Tallulah!)

But concerning Michael, wouldn't you just know that I had already begun to mull over in my own mind the almost identical thoughts you saw fit to set down on paper! As a matter of fact, I have already notified Manny to obtain, through Dr. Miller's good offices, an up-to-date report from Miss _____ [199] concerning the school situation and Michael's development generally, so that we may be the better prepared for our next visit with the child. I also urged him to be here on Friday, so that we might discuss plans for the most enjoyable holiday week for the children that can possibly be organized in terms of gifts, entertainment events and our own family with them. I have a number of interesting ideas about same which I am simply on tenterhooks to share with you Wednesday morning!

Ethel's visit was so conducive to fruitful reflection concerning our bunnies and the weather was so marvellously [*sic*] mild and pleasant, that the weekend was marked by very little of the emotional upheaval that is usually my lot. No appraisal of this almost miraculous peace of mind would be completely fair, however, if it did not include some word about Ruth Chatterton's most unusual first book, "Homeward Borne." Here is a theme of the utmost importance and of the most far reaching implications, woven simply and sincerely into a story at once heart-wrenching and heart-warming. Furthermore, it is a theme that must have taken a good deal of personal courage and integrity to tackle, and congratulations to the author on this score alone are very definitely in order. Not that it purports to be anything world shaking, because it isn't; but there is a straightforward quality to the writing, a clarity of purpose and an ability to hold and grip the reader, and touch his innermost emotions, that make this unpretentious, sometimes faulty book, entirely worth the reading.

And so to bed, my sweet, but not with you, more's the pity, alack and alas. Oh darling! but my longing grows intolerable especially when you describe me as your "wonderful person" and "your lovely wife"—dear

---

[199]Here I have blanked out the name of my social worker from those years, following the decision I made in *We Are Your Sons* to respect her privacy. See *Sons*, p. xxv.

husband, please know in return that I feel myself wholly encompassed by your love and greatly heartened by your confidence. Gently I kiss you goodnight; sleep sweetly my love, until we next rest in each other's arms once more— Your loving Ethel

Julius to Ethel

December 6, 1951

My lovely Person: At present I'm relaxed and feeling pretty good. The rice dinner, which I'm quite fond of, is in tune with a good book I'm now reading, Pearl Buck's latest novel "Gods [*sic*] Men". I've already completed my quota of todays [*sic*] newspapers and I'll be able really to dig into this book. However, as I write I can't help recalling the splendid visit we had this week. You looked so beautiful, full of joie de vivre, overflowing with sweetness and vitality. That is why I spent so much time pausing to fully partake of all your charms. Indeed it is certainly my greatest pleasure to have such a wonderful woman as you for my wife. Because of what you are and all that you mean to me it is beyond all reason and sanity that you my darling should find yourself in such a terrible predicament. No matter how many times I try to objectively and calmly try to fathom all the intricacies of our case I can only conclude that I'll be able to understand it fully in retrospect only when all this black period in our lives is only a distant memory. It is true that there are many decent and sincere people in our land and some of them are even now playing an active role in the work of the committee to secure justice for us. Recognizing this fact I still want them to know exactly how we feel and also all the myriad of mental and emotional tortures we constantly face. There is a tremendous task ahead for the committee but our lives and yes greater issues for all the American people are at stake here. Each and every citizen must be made aware that it is his own security and liberty and peace in the world which will directly affect him and his family. Many are the difficulties, long is the sorrow but we've made very good progress to date and we are getting close to a solution of our case. Regardless of the length of time we are confident of the inevitable conclusion in our favor. That is how it should be for we are completely innocent and were victims of a political frameup. Besides, Ethel for all our suffering we are entitled to a decent chance to have our case judged on its legal merits and not on extraneous matters. I find that I am completely optimistic and I hope that we will not have too much longer to wait until our happy reunion with our dearest boys in our own home. Somehow by this weekend I expect to hear some good news and it will help the time pass quickly until our next meeting.

You must know that I've missed you so much my darling all that is mine is to dream of you and every moment I want to hold you tightly in my arms pressed to my heart. I kiss you my love with all my heart and tell you that you make life full and worthwhile. Continue to be my shining star and nothing will be able to get me down. Let's keep it up dearest and we'll lick this yet. Always loving you, Julius

Ethel to Julius

December 6, 1951

Dearest sweetheart: "Tomorrow and tomorrow and tomorrow creeps in this petty pace from day to day"—William Shakespeare may not have known it when he wrote those significant lines, but he certainly must have had our murderously monotonous existence on his brain! All sweetness and sparkle depart with you, darling, and my spirits make with the nose-dive! How to at long last satisfy this insatiable maw within whose fearsome shadow we dwell, that's the question! A shot in the arm, in the form of a legal consultation, would not be at all amiss, I'm sure you will agree.

Friday 7:30 AM December 7, 1951

It was a Sunday when it happened in 1941, and I was enjoying my first holiday without the usual responsibility for the completion of some piece of Civilian Defense work or other in months; as the heart-stopping news leaped across the air-waves, shattering the calm and leaving consternation in its wake, I put away my book, dressed quickly and headed for the office. Other volunteers followed suit, the resultant hubbub and excitement turning the place into a beehive of activity in short order. On the 10th anniversary of Pearl Harbor, an apathy and cynicism that are shamefully violative of everything our country is supposed to represent, pervades the American scene. And this volunteer who proudly and with tireless energy upheld her government and espoused its cause, has been robbed of her sacred right to discharge her duties as a citizen and condemned to die in the interests of our political blackguards! The plot will fail dismally; already other citizens roused to action on our behalf, already the handwriting begins to appear on the wall! The very words and acts which were to have been the instruments for our destruction, are turning into an avenging force that will in time bring about their own downfall!

Dec. 9, 1951

Darling, I trust your visit with Lee was as wonderfully satisfying as mine. I look forward with delight to a most excellent hunk of time with Manny; even from the sparse bits of information your sister mentioned, I gather that the campaign is gaining notably in momentum and I know that Manny will be filling in the blank spaces. Hence my impatience at the delay. Nevertheless, I've been so much easier because of the good news from home, that I have permitted myself to revel in the most wildly pleasant dreams. My sweet dear, I am so happy in the thought of you and the children; only I wish I might tell my love with my lips on your own, only I wish I might gaze upon their softly sleeping faces, with your arms close about me— Good-night my dear one— Your loving Ethel

Julius to Ethel

December 9, 1951

My Sweetest Darling: You must know that I fully understand and do not expect more than one letter a week from you. When more than that arrive I am pleasantly surprised. I don't mean to give the impression that word from you is any less precious to me. Lena's visit was swell and it is always good to hear that you are in good spirits and keeping busy. A sure sign that you're able to keep your morale high. Sweetheart, when the members of my family praise us so highly for the kind of people we are and for our steadfast courage I can't help feeling shy and at the same time humble but believe me I'm deeply proud of us. Although she did not directly state that conditions at home were improving for all the news she related, the atmosphere is more friendly and cooperative. The most gratifying news is that neighborhood people have begun to show their friendship and my mother and [Here the typist left a blank, perhaps the name "Sophie" was written here and indecipherable.] begin to feel the delight of the support of decent people that is an ever present example that they are not alone.[200] I was very glad to know that many plans have already been made for a nice holiday for our two dears and that already new people have come forth and are taking the kids to outings and to their homes and the fact that Michael has begun to take his piano lessons again[201] and that this also gives him an opportunity to make new friends among his contemporaries of his own age that he meets in connection with this new activity of his. The "piece de resistance" of course

---

[200]This might be a reference to the Minor family. See *Sons*, p. 111.
[201]See *Sons*, p. 116.

is the splendid news of the progress the committee is making. I hope that when you read this letter our sweet Manny will have already graced us with his noble presence and filled our ears with lots more good news. Whenever Sunday evening rolls around I begin to feel that another week has finally passed and only so much more time before the next step in our case. Then, too, I'll be seeing you and spending a delightful hour listening, talking and above all, loving. My wonderful woman the good news that I hear about you has such a refreshing effect on me and it helps buoy my spirits and brighten my mood and lately I've been feeling pretty good because of it. It's too terribly long since I've held you in my arms and tasted the sweetness of your lips and the comfort of your love. I glance over at your picture and say: "Hello sweet person don't you realize this guy of yours is nuts about you and can't continue to live without you. Don't you think it's about time you let me come to your house." Oh love of my life only because you mean so much to me can I find the strength to withstand the morass of horror that has surrounded us. But as all things in the proper perspective this too will pass and the future is much more permanent and holds a great deal of beautiful life in store for us. To the approaching promising day.

Your own—Julius

Julius to Ethel

December 13, 1951

My sweet wife: It is now 7 PM. I was relaxing on my bed as I listened to the 6:30 news broadcast and after it was finished I began to muse. Somehow it seemed like you were in the kitchen and the kids were in the bedroom playing with their toys and I didn't want to call or reach out for you because I didn't want the spell to be broken. We were always so happy together and we never can forget. There is only one answer and it will come to pass. Oh my darling I love you so much it hurts. How true the immortal words of Shakespeare you quoted but we must keep uppermost in our mind that even though slowly we are nevertheless approaching the final solution of our case. From here it looks pretty good and I'm optimistic. We'll have it yet my dearest and we will enjoy our mutual love and our children on a much higher plane. Incidentally before I forget the P.K. has consented to us changing our regular visit next Wednesday to Friday so that it won't interfere with the childrens' [sic] visit. A letter went out to our counselor Wednesday and in a nice way I stressed the need for prompt action for a trained social worker for our boys and recommended he look into the person Dr. Miller has suggested. I pointed out to him the need to get results now as he'll soon be tied up in additional legal work for us and that you and I will rest easier if we get some news at the childrens' [*sic*] visit that things are happening. It is a long way off till I see you next Friday but I'm sure we'll have lots to share at our big hour. Honey I recommend you plan in your own mind how to keep Robbie in hand so you can get to have some kind of a visit with Michael. If it should come to pass that he demands most of the attention give it to him as he no doubt needs it and I'll adequately make up for it with Mike. I'll be able to get the gist of the picture from Manny in a couple of moments and I'll complement your efforts. Remember Ethel it is such a short time so don't set your sights too high. What I'm trying to say is don't allow yourself to be set up for a great disappointment. Yes my love the children mean everything to us and it is our duty at this point to reassure them of our love, of our complete devotion and the fact that we are here against our will. We must also stress that this terrible situation is only temporary and we will be coming home in due time when this is over. Do you think you can suggest to Mike the idea of him making pictures, drawings, paintings and crayon sketches at home and sending us some of his accomplishments? In general see if you can get him to agree to write us as he did in the past. Naturally I don't want to burden him but I want in some manner to establish some rapport between us. I'd prefer that he do all his writing to you. Let me hear from you on this topic and if you have any suggestions for me on my visit with our two dears, let's have it. Sweetheart you saw the way I looked at you at our last tete a tete and I know you are aware of all that it means. You're always in my arms my heart and I love you with all my soul. Your own Julius

Ethel to Julius

December 14, 1951

Sweetheart: I'm afraid this will have to be a rather perfunctory few lines but I do want you to know what I accomplished since our talk Wednesday morning.

First, I sent a letter to Manny informing him we were expecting him to bring the kids on the 19th, instructing him also about how to minimize wear and tear all around in making early train connections (he's to go to the house in a cab which is also to serve to take everybody to the train and he's to give the kids bread and butter and fruit en route, rather than bother rushing them thru a full breakfast at home.) I reminded him to buy their milk in Ossining, too, before arriving here.

I mentioned the demolition of the shop[202] and also asked that some of the toy money go toward such materials (records, books, etc.) as will further dramatize Chanukah for the children.

Yesterday, when I was notified the switch to Friday had been permitted, I again wrote Manny, urging a response to the effect that he was planning to follow my instructions, so by Monday or Tuesday we should receive some word. I have no doubt that he'll be here the 19th as planned.

All the cards are addressed to him and I explained this matter too.

Mail call,
Love— Ethel

[Beginning with the next letter, all that follow, though the end of 1951, are from originals in pencil.]

Julius to Ethel

Dec. 16, 1951

Fairest Flower of My Heart,

At the time when the snow is on the ground and the weather outside chills the marrow of the bone I look to you my sweetheart to continue to inspire and warm my spirit. After all as my own sweet wife it is not only your duty but your responsibility to negative [*sic*] the cold. Of course, I'm not exactly averse to the wonderful pleasures that go hand in hand with such a prerogative of married life. Ethel darling it's cold. How about taking me to your heart? Oh my dearest I miss you terribly and want the remaining time to pass quickly. I'm sending out my Christmas cards today but I haven't as yet sent out the Chanukah cards. Write me at once and tell me which card goes to whom I'm a bit mixed up on the plans we made at our last visit. You see your guy makes mistakes too. But note, very few. Some conceited man you have. Eh what!

Well I'm looking forward to our childrens [*sic*] visit. The holiday season of the year is always dedicated to family when man in all his humilty [*sic*] can expess [*sic*] his good will to his fellow men and take pride in the love of his children and the warmth of his family. More than ever do I [NWI] often-time feel the great frustration of not being able to give comfort, care and support to my own children and my wife. This terrible hurt that has been visited upon them, by those who would send their innocent parents ["to their" erased behind the next word] to death, is the greatest tragedy of our predicament and I know that it will always be our prime objective to do

---

[202]A reference to the site of the business, see above, footnote 5.

our best by our dears. Honey, one consolation we can have is that good decent people will try in every way to make this a positive holiday week for Mike and Robbie. The childrens [*sic*] visit will be a very good present for us as a prelude to the end of the year. This and my coming visit with you will help this week pass quickly and pleasantly. I might get to write you again before our visit possibly on Wednesday. However if I don't we should scheduale [*sic*] most of the time to discuss the children and I ask for a [*sic*] least 5 minutes to verbally smooch. From here on in I look forward to more and better presents in the form of good news on our case. In spite of the difficulties and dangers we face we've come a long way these last 9 months (I'm sure this is much tougher and not as pleasant as having a baby. Bad joke) and in every respect there are many promising signs. These must become a reality and time will hold the answer for us.

The other night I had a most wonderful dream. We had just come home from a wedding and you were wearing a lovely evening gown a strapless one and you looked ravishingly beautiful in it and I adored you and our love tasted so sweet. You were so real I could touch you and it's too bad I awakened and saw the darkness & gloom of my cell with the long shadows of the bars on the wall as the faint rays of the night lamp outlined them. Such powerful feelings coupled to right must guarantee our ultimate home-coming. Next time it will be the real stuff. All my love—Your

Julius

Ethel to Julius

Dec. 16, 1951

My very dearest love,

During the week, it seemed to me my feelings had congealed like the very ice out in the yard; your warmly expressive words had such a thawing effect I am only just now realizing what kind of a hard crust had formed across my heart. Of course, while I wrote you, [N3WI] on Friday morning I felt a stirring within me and if there had been a little extra time before the pick-up of mail, I think I might have loosened up considerably more. As it turned out, it feel to your last letter to me to break through the deep freeze into which I seemed to have settled.

Darling, I am looking at my writing through a blur of tears. I miss you so badly! It is indeed fortunate that this lonely [NWI] visitless week-end was bright with sun instead of [N2WI] dark with the gloom that might [N2WI] so easily have prevailed after such a snow storm. All togged out in my "CC" finery, and looking like a small, roly poly cop in my visor hat and military coat, I trudged determinedly through the snow (by now there is very little left that doesn't bear my foot-print). Come what may, be it fair weather or foul, my feathered friends must be fed!

I am apprehensive about the weather, however, insofar as the children's travelling here is concerned, and am hoping they can be brought here with a minimum of difficulty. Sweetheart, I am so delighted whenever your thoughts coincide with my own. How did you know that I had been planning to let Robby more or less set the pace and give him as much of the attention he needs as I possibly can without depriving Michael altogether; [N2WI] & that in the event that such did happen it had already occurred to me that you should have to make it up to him.

You are absolutely right; if I could learn to set less store by what does or does not get accomplished in the short time that is allotted to us, I should gain tremendously thereby and certainly the children wouldn't suffer and [NWI] more because of it. It is easier said than done, however, my friend, and tension is bound to build up in me until I actually lay eyes on them. I'm sure your own nail-biting activities have not exactly let up and you have all my sympathy, dearest, believe me—

Mail Call, honey—

Love you—Ethel

Julius to Ethel

Dec 20, 1951

Most Precious Dear,

You'll get this letter after our visit so I'll not discuss things that will be repetitious. However I must let you know again that the childrens [*sic*] visit was most excellent and all of us enjoyed it to the utmost. Oh Dearest you have given us two wonderful children to brighten our lives and make living so worth while. Remarkable improvement must be noted in our children. I sent Manny a letter on our Compass subscriptions. It may be necessary for you to inform him of your renewal number. Since I didn't receive your letter yet I sent out my Chanukah and Christmas cards to our entire family.

The Chanukah services last Tuesday brought back many pleasant memories. Vividly do I recall two years ago when we celebrated the festival of lights in our own home with our two boys. Little Robbie would not let matters proceed until he had his own kepal[203] on his head. Then Michael sang the benediction in his shrill high pitched soprano and the kids tromped around singing. As at our services we played the same records at home and we certainly made it a memorable occassion [*sic*] for our youngsters. At this time I particularly recall your preparations for the occassion [*sic*] by

---

[203]A more colloquial Yiddish word for yarmulke, the skull cap worn by males to cover their heads while at prayer.

thoroughly informing yourself on the full meaning of every day and the careful selections of toys and gifts to mark the holiday in its true spirit. To us this holiday signifying the victory of our forefathers for freedom from oppression and tyranny is a firm part of our heritage and solidifyies [sic] our determination to win our own freedom. How paradoxical it is that at the same time that I feel such a sense of satisfaction at the full life we've lived can I at the same time feel the terrible pangs of pain, illimitable sorrow and furious loneliness. Soon, soon my sweetheart we'll be in the New Year and I am optimistic [sic] that 1952 will be much better for us. I know I'll not have enough time to tell you how much I love you this Friday morning. Honey wife I need you so and all the love locked in my soul needs it's [sic] most natural outlet of sharing with you the sweetness of life. We cannot be denied this and I'm sure we will find our way in each others arms and know the job of our union. I'm finding it difficult to concentrate because my mind is so preoccuppid [sic] with thoughts of you. I'll continue to try to loose [sic] myself in the 2,000 pages of Thomas Wolfes [sic] potent prose. Oh my hearts [sic] desire only when your [sic] with me can I satisfy some of my yearnings. Love of my life this has to end sometime. I'm confident of the results. Hurry, Hurry let it happen soon.

Your own—Julius—

Julius to Ethel

Dec. 23, 1951

My Beloved Wife,

What a pleasant surprise to receive such a beautiful card for Christmas from you. The verse is so meaningful and the decorations so colorful and it will therefore take a permanent place adorning the cell wall alongside the pictures of my precious family. At once I am filled with a great deal of joy and it makes me happy because I am aware of all the sentiment and deep feeling that is behind your gift. Usually, I don't give matters such as this much thought but somehow in the enigma of the cataclysmic events that have led to our entombment here and [N2WI] that therefore has funnelled into the narrow confines of our solitary cells endless emotional torment commingled with acute mental agony, ["and yet" CO] this single act of your stands out and symbolizes the full meaning of our relationship. Darling the unity of our lives, the complete sharing which is an integral part of our love has enhanced our individual stature and given us the strength of our collective stamina, that affords us the opportunity to withstand the avalanche of difficulties that have engulfed us. Because we are innocent and our cause is just we are able to maintain our dignity and continue in our determination to win complete vindication. Sweetheart when I stop and evaluate all that life has given me, I see so clearly the tremendous effect you have had on me and I am constantly aware of the great treasure I possess in you. I have such a terriffic [*sic*] desire to be with you and share the sweetness of our love. Thank you again for your special efforts of being so thoughtful to bring me this cheer.

Although Daves [*sic*][204] visit was short it was most welcome. I concentrated my part of the discussion explaining in detail the important observations that we've made concerning Mike & Robbie. He understood full well and explained how difficult it is for Mama to comprehend the situation and too much talk only leads to heartache and tears. We will only see results on this problem when Manny begins to move on obtaining the services of a trained social worker to oversee the play and emotional upbringing of our boys. It is true that your pointing this matter out to me prevented me from falling back on the convenient idea that only when we are out can we solve this problem. Yes, on examining the question thoroughly I have to gree [*sic*] with your view that we must not be satisfied with second best. If you do get a chance to write our dear counselor please ask him to make available a substantial [N3WI] amount of his time for our next consultation. I will again put the welfare of our children first on the agenda. The knowledge that decent people are helping our boys celebrate the holiday season eases the pain of my separation from my family. To you my wonderful [NWI] woman on this second holiday season behind bars I send my best wishes with the thought that we've already traversed the depths of despair and are tediously making the ascent to our ultimate freedom. Although there are still many pithfalls [*sic*] in our way we can look ahead with optimism. All intelligence, reason and sanity yells one answer and that is a complete victory for us over this terrible, shameful frameup. I'm confident even though I'm impatient

all my love—Your own—Julius

Ethel to Julius

Dec. 27, 1951

My dearest one,

Of course I know how your heart beat with mine and our thoughts hurtled across the space that separated us as the Chanukah Candles burned and the music played! Oh, sweetheart, the dramatic intensity and beauty of the songs we heard so richly expressive of the [NWI] tremendous creative powers [N7WI] of the people of Israel & their capacity to struggle for the freedom which held forth the promise of the noble, joyous life to come,

---

[204]His brother David.

filled me with an overwhelming pride and gladness. And although the tears spilled over once I gained the solitude of my cell and saw the greeting cards that had arrived from Lena and Ethel and their respective families, I felt myself thrilled and inspired beyond measure.

Darling, I'm dreadfully sorry I have to cut this short, when I have such a strong need to share with you. Of course I shall continue writing you over the week-end, but I just had to let you hear from me after such a moving session. The sermon was exceptionally fine, don't you agree?

I love you, sweetheart—Yours always, Ethel

Julius to Ethel

Dec. 27, 1951

Dearest Sweetheart,

It was a very relaxing visit. Right! At the time I'm with you every fibre of my body is tunned [*sic*] and my mind is pulsing on all cylinders and a glorious feeling takes hold of me. Even though, it's so short a period it nevertheless is amazing that I can actually feel so close a bond between us and at the same time, that we are completely removed from here. I tell you all this because at our Jewish Chanukah Services when we listened to Jan Pierce [*sic*] singing I closed my eyes and once more I was lifted from my cell and found myself at home listening to stimulating music and in surroundings familiar, and conducive to mental satisfaction. Verily, if we have more of such nourishments, time will pass much more pleasantly and quickly. Music, especially folk music, [N2WI] which was born in the life and death struggle of the people of Israel is both beautiful and soul stirring. This was truely [*sic*] a worthwhile and meaningful session in keeping with the "festival of lights" holiday. A complete study of the history of the events leading up to the victory of Israel's freedom 2100 years ago, will point out the salient lesson of the complete integration and interrelation of economic, moral, social, political and philosophical forces on history. As Jews we have a wonderful heritage and we can justly be proud of it. The most important thing is that the individual understand it fully and make proper use of it's [*sic*] lessons. This foundation is similar to the historic principles of our own country for freedom, decency and justice. Since we have absorbed both of these heritages and acted in faith with them in our daily lives we are better and happier people for it. I believe that this back-ground is the firm foundation that allows us to maintain our dignity and decency in the face of such terrible, nightmarish hardships. Darling, the more I taste just little snatches of creativeness and real life the more I long for a quick and speedy return to our former beautiful life. There is so much more that we have to live for and both of us are aware of the great promise that the future has for us as a family and as individuals. Soon we will see the New Year and this will bring us closer to our final return home to our loved ones.

My two sisters sent me holiday greeting cards and they send the warmest love and one wish and one hope for our return to our rightful place to our boys. Honey girl I'm so horribly lonesome for you and the children. I need you and them more than I need life itself because my precious family is the full meaning of my life. Hurry, hurry, good news. This misery cannot last forever it has to end soon and it will end with our complete vindication. Love you with all my heart Ethel and I'm confident we [NWI] will go home arm in arm— Your own Julius

Julius to Ethel

Dec. 30, 1951

My Most Adorable Wife,

By the time you get this letter a very dark year for us will have become history. We have seen ourselves put to sever [*sic*] tests and learned many lessons. Without a doubt we can be proud of the kind of people we are and the manner in which we conduct ourselves. Compared to last year a great deal of progress has been made in organizing a campaign to secure justice for us but it still is to [*sic*] little and to [*sic*] slow. Being a realist I am fully aware of all the difficulties we face and the great effort that is needed to overcome the paralyzing inertia that the Justice Dept has instilled in the American People. However there is still a great reservoir of good decent men and women in our country who when they know the facts will fight for justice and fair play. That is the reason I'm certain that the pamphets [*sic*] summarising the facts as they appear in the trial records will be the stimulus to Public Opinion in our behalf[.] I am optomistic [*sic*] and confident and I am hopefully looking forward to the New Year being the time of the reunion with my precious family. With courage, added confidence and perspective a Happy and most promising New Year to you my love.

Just a few items of reminder to you. There is a possibility that we may be able to buy Jewish Salami soon and since it will be in great demand I urge you to stock up on it the first commissary day it's available as it won't last long. Yum! Yum! My sister asked me to please wish you a Happy New Year for her and her family. Also Mama as yet hasn't received a present from us for Chanukah although I asked Manny to take care of this. Ethel told me that my mother likes the bag that Sophie got as a present from us and I feel we should ask our counselor to get this same gift for her.

Of course my sister's visit was very satisfying. We had a chance to go [NWI] over all the activities our boys were involved in and it was most heart warming to hear how complete their holiday has been filled with, interesting

visits, company of warm people, plenty of thoughtful gifts and love. I'm so happy for the children and for us, that many friends are coming forward and volunteering aid with a full heart. Not only our boys but [NWI] also my mother is benefiting from the new developments. It is apparent to me that a great deal of work in [*sic*] being put in to help our children and this is a good sign that our concern about the kids [*sic*] welfare will get close attention from a trained social worker. Although my heart aches for them I'm glad to know their [*sic*] in such good hands. Sweetheart, we will make up to our two dears for all that they've been denied and it is my primary wish that it will happen soon. I may see you before this letter reaches you and I repeat over again that I look to you in the coming year to continue to be my rock, my inspiration and all that is beautiful in life to me. Honey things are bound to be better. All my best—Your own—Julius
[The next line is printed across the bottom of the page]

–1952–BEST WISHES–LOVE–HAPPINESS–FREEDOM–PEACE

1952

Ethel to Julius

January 3, 1952

My dearest love,

I simply have to try [NWI] to convey to you how much pleasure your last letter afforded me. You notice I say "try", because more and more I despair of [NWI] ever telling you to my complete satisfaction how very much I love you!

Our visit, of course, was most gratifying; however, I plumb forgot to discuss certain items which were somewhat disturbing to me that your sister Ethel raised and to which I reacted rather sharply. Naturally they concern the children, particularly Michael, so please remind me on Wednesday, when we meet again, just in case I neglect to do so, initially.

Incidentally, I received a most encouraging letter from Ethel, in which she stated she was also writing you to like effect. So I am taking it for granted you know all that she informed me of.

My sweet, your wife is a stinker; if she had begun writing to you at an earlier hour, she would no doubt have filled both sides with very little difficulty. Instead, she spent far too much time contemplating on her lot and all the deadly dreariness it entails—

Darling, the inexorable mail call—

All my love—Ethel

283

Julius to Ethel

January 3rd, 1951[205]

My Dearest Ethel,

It was a wonderful thing getting such a newsy letter from my sister and I'm very glad that she also sent you one. If it were possible to receive one such letter the early part of each week from one of the family filling in on details of whats [sic] what with the kids and the committee I would be elated. I intend to make this modest request of Lena when she comes this weekend. By the way none of the Christmas presents (books) have as yet been received here and I'll also tell my sister to check with Manny on this. Just a reminder to check Thursday's Compass for an interesting item on page 2 concerning the committee. Incidently [sic] I ordered the N.Y. Post for a month so that I'll be able to follow any articles that appear dealing with our case. In the immediate period we will probably read quite a bit concerning our case since the D.A. will be submitting his brief on Jan 7, then there will come our reply brief and finally the oral argument. This will, of course, be the parting shot at the Circuit Court of Appeals and then our fate will rest in the hand of three men. I hope they are in a good frame of mind and receive our appeal in a calm and judicial attitude and a fair judgement can only bring a reversal. I am hoping for a strong opinion in our favor to help beat this case hands down if we do have to go on trial again. From here on in I'll keep my fingers crossed. Darling we've got the fact and law on our side what we need now is public opinion and mazol.[206] Again I repeat I'm optimistic [sic] and I have high hopes.

Lately because of the sedantary [sic] existence I follow and the fact that my normal intake of food is more than that which is required by my body for energy I'm beginning to get a rubber tire about my midsection. Since I'm beginning to feel sluggish and uncomfortable I resolved to control the amount of food I eat and I'm going on a limited diet. As yet I'm not exercising but I believe I'll have to apply myself as I've got to consider my better half and I don't want your man getting so out of shape. Now after such thoughtfullness [sic] on my part don't you think it is about time that you invited me to your house. Oh my sweetheart I miss you terribly and it's ages ago that I've held you in my arms and enjoyed the sweetness of your lips and was warmed by your love. The agony, endless emotional strains, fearful torment cannot be equated but for us it represents untold misery and only the exultant joy of our reunion at home will be able to salve the wounds and do away with this nightmare. Let us find in each other the

---

[205]This is misdated, it was 1952.
[206]Yiddish for "luck."

additional strenght [*sic*] to overcome the approaching crisis of this next hurdle. Be strong my wife so that I may get some sustenance from you.

—Confidently—Love—Julius

Julius to Ethel

January 6, 1952

My Darling Ethel,

How happy I am to have two such wonderful sisters who are completely devoted to us, are constantly working in our behalf and by their tireless efforts have shown us warm sisterly love. Lena was brimming over with news. That you are fine and feeling good and that the committee has accentuated it's [*sic*] work and that the office is a beehive of activity on our behalf. Support is pouring in from all over the world and in increasing volume. We, too, have been able to see the visible evidence of the campaign to win public opinion to the truth in our case by the advertisement in the newspaper. This comes at a time when the oral argument will be heard and according to a news item in Sundays [*sic*] Daily News the District Attorney filed his 82-page [*sic*] in court. (It doesn't say [NWI] when but it was probably on Saturday). The article states that since the Appeals Court calendar was so heavy that a protracted delay may be necessary even though we are listed on the Jan. 7 calender [*sic*]. My guess is that the oral argument will take place within the next two weeks. We can expect that the next time Manny will be up to see us and I believe it will be the week of the 21 Jan. we will have lots of legal stuff to cover. There is a very good possibility that even the reply brief will be in by the time of our next consultation. As far as this court is concerned this is it. Because we have many telling points and sound legal reasoning in our brief I am optomistic and hopeful but I still keep my feet firmly planted in reality since anything is possible because of the nature of our case.

Coming back to the excellent visit I had with Lena I have a great deal to go over with you on the report she gave me of Michael's and Robbie's behavior in the last month. Without going into too much detail it is sufficient to say there is a noticeable improvement in their emotional security as evidenced by their actions. Remind me to discuss this with you on Wednesday particularly the childrens [*sic*] reactions when they come home from a visit to us. She told me of all the nice presents they've gotten and how well they play with the new toys. Yes my darling because they took your suggestion and planned the holiday week for our boys it was [word erased here] overwhelmingly successful. It is also encourageing [*sic*] to hear my mother is much happier because she has found new friends and she feels the strenght [*sic*] and goodwill of many decent people that have surrounded her with warm understanding and kindness. Honey from all indication progress is being made and now the fact should begin to become public knowledge. This is only the beginning but it is on solid foundation and has much promise to be really effective. Sweetheart the important thing is that I love you more than ever and there is so little time to talk to you about that because we only have an hour. Can't wait to see you Love you with all my being—Your man—Julius

Mrs. Sophie Rosenberg
24-36 Laurel Hill Terrace
New York, N. Y.

[This letter is undated but from context it is clear it was written about this time.]

My Sweet Mother,
    I am enclosing a pass for this Sunday Jan. 13 which is good from 1 to 3:30 P.M. Since I didn't know exactly what your plans are & if I don't hear anything from you or if you are not able to make it this week I'll get another pass for the following week. If my brother Dave can make it for January 20 let us know in advance as we can have as many as three people [N3WI] at a time. However, I would suggest that you and only one other person come together as we want to make certain that we will have a visit the following week from [N2WI] one of the family. Should you be able to only spend a Sunday morning or an afternoon you must let me know at least one week in advance so that Ethel and I can put in passes covering the same time and you will be able to split your visit between us. Much as we would love to see you please don't make this arduous trip alone and if it cannot be worked out otherwise perhaps one of my dear sisters will come with you on a Wednesday.
    As for us we've been more than holding our own and no small measure of the credit belongs to you my beloved mother because you have taken a great burden of worry off our minds by taking care of our children and giving them the care, comfort and love that only a devoted Grandma can give her own family. The visible evidence of the physical and emotional well being [N3WI] of the boys was so apparent to us at their last visit. To me your son, who is proud of his understanding mother, it is a great personal satisfaction that in spite of all the physical and mental difficulties you [NWI] nevertheless are selflessly and tirelessly giving your all for our children and for us.

Mama I know you find some happiness in once again seeing the smiles on Michael and Robert [*sic*] faces and knowing that they feel secure with you and we too have had our moral [*sic*] lifted and [N2WI] have been encouraged to keep our chin up. Just take care of yourself we are counting on you and depend on the strength of your mother love. Since we know exactly how you feel it isn't necessary for you to strain yourself too much to visit us.

We have seen so many heartening signs. Conditions at home have measurably improved. Many good decent people are working on our behalf and making the facts of our case public knowledge. This will make known to all the nature of our case and the fact that we are victims of a political frameup and [NWI] that we are completely innocent. We can also be thankful that we have excellent [some words erased here] legal counsel. No matter how long it takes we will never lose faith. We are confident of our final vindication and happy reunion at home with you and the children.

All my love —Your son—Julius

Mrs. Sophie Rosenberg
24-36 Laurel Hill Terrace
New York New York

                                                                January 8, 1952

Dear Ma,

Enclosed please find a slip permitting you to visit me Sunday morning, January 13th. If you are able to make it, all well and good. If not, you are under no obligation to use same, and I will send you another such slip for the Sunday that you do plan to come. If you do manage to get here, on the 13th, [NWI] however, be sure to bring the slip with you.

How are my darling children? Tell them I love them very much and will write them specially soon— In the meantime, many thanks to Michael for his lovely present, and many regards to Robby's rocking horse! Happy bouncing!

My best wishes for a happy New Year to Sophie—I trust that she is well and that the same is true of you—

The mail is about due to go so this has to be a hurried note—Besides, I have to get ready for Jewish Services; the Rabbi will be here any minute. Am feeling fine—

All my love to you and the children—

                                                                As always, Ethel

Julius to Ethel

Jan. 10, 1952

My Lovely Bunny,

First, a bit of news that I got from Thursdays [*sic*] Law Journal. As of that day's calendar before the 2nd Circuit Court of Appeals our case was listed as the third one to be heard. Therefore, in all likelihood the oral argument will take place Friday January 11th. I don't know but there is a possibility that it may finally windup on Monday. Probably by next week the Rebuttal brief will be submitted and this will be the end of the first round. Dearest, for us we've got to grit our teeth and bear up under the new strains while the three judges deliberate on the appeal. Darling what we need now is a fair shake and that requires a little mazol. Above all we must be prepared for a negative decision because there is no guarantee in a case of this nature that only law, facts and fair play will be the deciding factors. In spite of this I am still confident and optimistic that we'll get a reversal.

There is a pleasant aroma in my cell and it is due to four salamis hanging from the juncture of my flyleaf table. A one such remanent [*sic*] of the first proud delicacy that I devoured is beckoning me to complete my gluttonous feasting. I must admit I've put aside my diet to do justice to my appetite. But I assure you I eat no more than half of one a day. Say wouldn't it be swell if we could get some pastrami. Better still how I'd like to eat it a [*sic*] Katz's.[207] If all goes well it won't be long now. I'll take you there.

How I'd like to be pleasantly surprised by a visit from Mama this Sunday? [*sic*] Don't count on it sweetie because it may be difficult for them to make arrangements and the weather might not warrant it. Anyhow I hope we get some news from home at least by way of a letter telling us the latest developments. I plan to send off a letter to Michael tomorrow and include some words for little Robbie.

Now let me take you to task. I don't like anybody riding down my ideal and better half least of all you. Again let me say that I am well aware of what's going on and if you don't manage to write me I understand and I want you to know it doesn't matter to me. Right now particularly I [NWI] am pretty busy with Thomas Wolfe and find myself pleasantly occupied [*sic*]. Then, too, you must realize that because you have given the matters for our discussion careful consideration and prepare notes on it we are able to cover a great deal of ground. It is most important to my moral [*sic*] that you continue to lead the way in solving the problems pertaining to our childrens' welfare. Besides darling it is so heartening to see you happy, smiling and bubbling over with enthusiasm, mind working actively and emotionally stimulated. Know my heart you are the fountain of my strenght

---

[207]A well-known delicatessen in lower Manhattan.

[*sic*], hope and happiness. I press you close to me —All my love— Your Julius

Ethel to Julius

January 10, 1952

My dearest Julie,
    Time continues to beat out its merciless measure composing a savage theme that winds through my life seemingly without end. Oh, the unspeakably horrible, monotonous, senseless waste of it; as you will doubtless be able to imagine, only too well, I am fed to the teeth with it!

January 11, 1952

My Sweet, your letters are so inspiring and speak with such remarkable effectiveness to my heart, that I must confess myself hopelessly enamored of you. Oh, darling, all kidding aside, I do love you so very much and miss you so terribly, I am quite beside myself with need!
    Honey, I laughed fit to kill myself at your screamingly funny account of "Life with Salami." The idea of 21 of these delectable delights mingling their collective essences and subtly enhancing the hitherto prosaic atmosphere is simply devastating. Never mind the "lilies of the field"; consider the lowly salamis! They don't have to "spin," they don't have to "toil," they just have to contain plenty of garlic! To permit a serious note to creep in, however, I can see that they are not long for this world, if you don't cut down on your rate of consumption, that is. As for your diet, [N3WI] needless to add that's already out of this world, alack and a day! Diet, shmiet, I deem myself most fortunate in having been able to enlarge my own supply (by two) of these "Agents of Heavenly Heartburn." (ugh, how corny!)

January 13, 1952

By now, I know you have no nails left to bite, as is the case with me, the increase in this kind of oral activity traceable, of course, to certain newspaper items concerning the latest developments in our case. I expect we'll both be jumpy until Manny puts in an appearance, so I'm dropping Ethel a line (because I want to thank her, incidentally, for writing me), requesting his presence on Friday. For all we know, he may turn up without notice before then; I should think that would depend on how early in the week he's due to file his rebuttal brief. Thank goodness we have reached this stage of the game, at least.

Incidentally Ethel sent me a second letter, the contents of which you may not have been informed of by her, to wit: Since the committee was planning to meet on Monday, Lee and she were seeing Mrs. Allman[208] [*sic*] at her house on Monday, after which meeting Ethel was to [NWI] have communicated with us again. Perhaps we'll get some word from her to-morrow afternoon. She and one of her cousins are also undertaking to spread the facts to their Family Circle, whose membership comprises residents of "New Jersey, Bronx, Bklyn, Man., Rockaway and Astoria." Her letter ends, "Be well, sweets, and our deepest and most devoted love to you & Julius"!

Darling, it's a rainy Monday morning, but Wednesday's coming and I'm breathing a sigh of relief —Love you, dearest —Ethel

Julius to Ethel

Jan. 13, 1952

My Sweetest Wife,

I miss you terribly and I'm lonesome. Of course, it is also due to the fact that I'm impatiently awaiting Manny's next visit so we can get the accurate details of what took place at the oral argument and hear the D.A. brief and our rebuttal to it. Then, too, not getting a visit from home this week and no letters telling us all thats [*sic*] happening leaves me famished for news. It is at times like this that, more than ever, I feel the need of your assuring voice, your sympathetic mind and your comforting heart. Darling, now that a crucial period of waiting is here, time seems to crawl and I find it difficult to concentrate one reading for too long a stretch. However I managed to finally complete Thomas Wolfe "Of Time and the River" and passed it on to one of the other fellows. Although it has over nine hundred pages it is a [NWI] continual treat to read such beautiful prose that is very picturesque and expressive. I know I don't have to recommend it to you because you are a "Wolfe" fan by now but allow me to say that he writes powerfully and realistically. I've started "The Web and the Rock" which is reputed to be his best book[.] I know I have a great treat in store for myself. Yet it may seem to you that I am doing nicely with my time and I've got to say that it isn't so. At moments of real spiritual emotional and mental joy I find I must share them with you to really get the full benefit of my feelings. Yes one can get some satisfaction out of his own resources by himself but to me life is barren without social intercourse especially if one has tasted the

[208]Emily Alman, who together with her husband David was an extremely active member of the Committee to Secure Justice in the Rosenberg Case. The personal papers of David and Emily Alman are archived at Boston University.

beauty of so complete a relationship as I have had with you my wife. My innermost thoughts, hopes cry out with ever powerful fury for an outlet, for relief and all the strength of my body and mind keep fighting back this upsurge, soothing with reason, logic and all the will at my command and in spite of this I must go to you as I need you so desperately. How much can one endure? How horribly long is the deep dark journey? Can there be any more powerful accumulation of personal desires, confidences, and hopes? Do not for one moment think that I am weakening, that I have lost courage. On the contrary, I feel stronger than ever and that is why I seek further sustenance from the woman I adore and look up to. Now more than ever we must find in each other the superhuman strength to withstand the many difficult and trying vicissitudes of the period ahead. If past performance is indicative I'm sure we'll come through with flying colors besides I know us my dearest and I have no doubts how we'll react to the situation.

But only please the correct decision and quickly too. I'm still optomistic [*sic*] and hopefully awaiting the rectification of this miscarriage of justice. I keep before me the vision of our going home together

—All my love—Julius

See you soon sweets

Mr. David Rosenberg [ink]
430 E. 63rd St.
New York NY

Jan. 14, 1952

Dearest Brother,

You'll find enclosed a pass for this Sunday morning 10-11 AM please come loaded down with all the latest news.

I want to take this opportunity to express to you, my sisters and my mother my everlasting gratitude and profoundest love for you and [N2WI] for your consistent relentless devotion to me and my family and for your tireless efforts in working on our behalf. It is above and beyond what one can expect and it comes of a firm realization and conviction that we are innocent and you who know us best, who've read the facts and experienced shocking [next word illegible] in your dealings with the authorities understand the full enormity of this miscarriage of justice. The body politic [N3WI] in our land is sick[.] Dave [*sic*] and our case is one of the boils that have come forth as a warning that the infection might spread and become fatal. That is why the good men and women in all walks of life and in every corner of the globe are rallying to our support. Before it is to [*sic*] late and leads to greater madness this political plot must be exposed, fought against and it must be stopped. ["by" CO] The first step is to save our lives. Truth is we are winning wider and greater support daily and we are confident that the conscience of the world is with us and we have high hopes that we will live to prove our complete innocence.

But there are very dangerous signs. To one who has read the record & [NWI] knows the facts the monotonious [*sic*] press campaign of lies and distortions in ["the entire" CO, N3WI] almost all the metropolitan ["press" CO] newspapers will have no effect. However, large numbers of people are misinformed and thousands of others are frightened into inaction. The danger always exists that evil men in [NWI] their desperation may pull the switch on us. Therefore, there must be no letup in putting the truth before the public. Every effort must be exerted to get the newspapers to print our side, advertisements and letters to the editors. Do not despair because the kept press does not represent American sentiment and above all it is printing a pack of lies. ["that" CO] Given the opportunity we can easily expose and demolish them. Again, I urge steady and increasing work on our behalf this is the only way we can win this fight for life.

No matter what the situation is or what happens we must not give up because I sincerely believe we will succeed in [NWI] our struggle for this worthy cause. When you pause take stock of the great deal of progress we've made in this campaign and you'll notice that it is picking up momentum. Naturally, the enemy will use every conceivable means to discredit us and all those who come to our support but hard facts and the truth can ["withstand" CO, NWI] overwhelm vicious slander and distortions. It should be obvious to all now that we were correct in our estimations of the nature of this case as a political frameup and in due time the entire world will be aware of this truth.

The crisis is approaching right decency and love will win out if we fight hard enough for it. We and you my beloved family are doing our all. We have won a partial victory let us go on to win the battle for truth, justice and principles. This is [N2WI] in the interest and welfare of all mankind and particularly [N3WI] in this time for our country—As ever—
Julie

Mrs. Sophie Rosenberg [pencil]
24-36 Laurel Hill Terrace
New York N.Y.

January 15, 1952

Dearest Ma,

Since you cannot get here on Sunday morning, we have made arrangements for an afternoon visit. The enclosed request slip for Sunday, Jan. 20, is marked "afternoon," for this reason, and permits you to see me from

1:00–2:00 P.M. and Julie from 2:00–3:30 P.M. So be sure to request to be taken to visit me first; you will thus be insured of seeing Julie right till closing time.

Tell the children their Daddy and Mommy are fine and never stop thinking of them and loving them. Mike dear, that was a wonderful Chanukah card! How about you, Robby, sending me any picture you feel like drawing on a piece of paper. Whatever you make will be very welcome, darling, and Sophie can help you write your name at the bottom. Otherwise, no help, unless he asks you for it, O.K. Sophie, so it will be his very own precious present, if he feels like doing it, that is. A little judicious encouragement, you understand, but no direct pressure, thank you, Sophie.

Are my dear boys wearing their rings, or haven't the guards for them been made, as yet? I enjoyed presenting these tokens of our love to them so much; every time I remember their last visit here, I am happy as I can be, and look forward eagerly to seeing them again.

Please phone Lena and thank her for her letters, notifying me you were planning to visit us Sunday afternoon. I can't wait for the days to pass. when you speak with Lena don't forget to tell her to phone Manny to make the necessary arrangements, in order for the children to have a pleasant day while you are here. It is better for them not to go along with you; Lena and Ethel and Manny know our feelings about this already and will understand what to do about it.

I was so pleased to hear about your new friends and the interest they are taking in your welfare. I know how hard it is to go on being patient, month in month out, but there is so much to be hopeful about lately that we've simply got to see it through the best way we know how. Julie and I are in pretty good spirits, considering how much we miss the children, and will do all we can to make the time you spend with us this Sunday, something to remember pleasantly.

In the meantime, my love to my bunnies and to all our fine friends— and of course to my dear Bubbie Sophie— Ethel—

Julius to Ethel

Jan. 17, 1952

My Sweetest Wife,

At this moment I feel quite disturbed because we didn't have enough time to finish our discussion at our legal consultation and I believe because of it I left you with the wrong impression and also did not have sufficient time to make amends for my brusque conduct. First of all, darling, I was terribly keyed up until our counselor put in his appearance and I was so completely set on hearing as much as possible about the legal argument and the briefs in the alotted [*sic*] time that I was a bit hasty and impatient. Then, too, I feel so strongly that we must discuss these two matters you brought up privately and I intend to dwell in detail on this point at our next visit. Please sweetheart [NWI] understand me. I know you must feel that I didn't give you enough consideration when you were presenting your viewpoint and to an extent you are right but if we were able to trash [*sic*] this out I wouldn't feel so bad about it. Drop me a note as soon as you can and tell me all is forgiven. I love you very much and I don't want to infringe on your rights or cause you any unnecessary pain. I promise to continue to strive to be alert and check my actions. Of course you realize that this guy is madly in love with you and wants to do right by his better half.

As for sweet Manny's legal efforts on our behalf it can be summed up by giving him 100 A-plus for his superb performance. I am well satisfied with the way the oral argument was conducted and with his presentation of our case. We can now truthfully say we have had the best possible legal defense. It is only an academic interest on my part that I am looking forward to read the district attorneys [*sic*] brief and our rebuttal brief. Even more so than the legal phase I am elated with the news that many people are flocking to our support and that a much large [*sic*] section of public opinion will receive literature with the facts of our case. What is very heartening is that all who read the pamphlet immediately see the nature of our case and want to do something to help. This is the real guarantee that we are not alone and that our chances of securing justice are much better.

[erasure here] Incidentally my wonderful woman I hope I am able to be of some incentive to you in the effort to complete your writting [*sic*]. I am so confident that you can and I am sure you will do a very good job. Can I help being so proud? I have you as my wife. Never for one moment doubt the high esteem I hold for you. For after all I am only a man and I have my weaknesses too and I make my share of mistakes. On the whole I feel in high spirit [*sic*] and am very confident.

I love you with all my heart
Your own Julius

Ethel to Julius

January 17, 1952

My sweetest dear,

I have been in such an emotional dither since Manny left, especially since there were so many things my heart longed to say to you, darling, as we parted. Julie, dearest, of course I'm not angry! Yes, I am at that; I'm angry to a point of boiling fury for our helplessness in the face of our enforced separation. The injustice of the misery we have had to endure fills me with a righteous indignation that will not be denied.

Sweetheart, expect me to pull a couple of boners now and then; perhaps I pull them merely to test your attitude toward them and me. Not that your temporarily sharp reaction exactly cramped my style outwardly or [NWI] even caused me to lose any sleep over it; still it does make me feel I haven't genuinely, your acceptance of my right to, yes, make an ass of myself, if you will—

Whatever might be involved, I love you, dear one, as I love my very own life. And speaking of life, what an appetite [N2WI] for living our Manny arouses with his thrilling account of the activity on our behalf. All honor, say I, to the people—and to the People's Advocate!

All my love—Your Ethel

Julius to Ethel

Jan. 20, 1952

My Sweetest Dear,

Now perhaps you can understand why I'm so nuts about you. I am so very fortunate to have a woman who instinctively knows and grasps the situation and is at one with her man. Yes your letter was just what I needed and I am grateful to you for expressing my own wishes. It is also good that you are vigilant on these matters and I too am developing a sensitivity ["on" CO] to your prerogatives. My darling I am completely and thoroughly enamored of you.

Ever since Manny's visit I've been operating at a very high level of moral [*sic*]. Our counselor is every inch a wonderful human being, devoted to decency, completely sincere and impecably [*sic*] ethical as a lawyer. He is indeed a dear friend and rightfully beloved by us. It is a satisfying feeling to know his efforts on our behalf are tireless and we are in very good hands. Since then there has been a continual chain of contact with the world outside. First the news of all the stepped up activities on our behalf. Then a splendid issue of that swell crusading paper the Guardian and a very informative add [*sic*] on the accomplishments of the committee. A short but a delightful visit with my brother. Of course, your very welcome letter and it's [*sic*] envigorating [*sic*] sustenance. Finally, my sweet mother spend [*sic*] a very wonderful hour and a half with me.

Well Ethel, we've got lots to talk about at our next visit. I know you'll have quite a bit of news for me and we'll be able to discuss my mother's and brother's visits when I see you on Wednesday. Naturally I'm very impatient but I guess good things will hold till then.

From all sides we hear of new support. The ball is really rolling now. More and more people are joining the Committee, contributing funds, writting [*sic*] letters and increasing thousands of people are being made aware of the facts in our case and it's [*sic*] nature. Whoever reads the booklet invariably takes our side. This only proves further that there is a tremendous wealth of good people who will campaign for right and justice when they are aware of the truth. We can [erasure here] feel proud that our faith in the American people has born [*sic*] fruit so soon and this is the guarantee of our eventual freedom and complete vindication.

But, oh my wife, how cruel it is to ["be" probably omitted here] apart from you and suffer in isolation when we are innocent. We must continue to stoically withstand the constant agony of our unjust imprisonment and brutal sentence. Mankind for your dignity you must rectify this travesty on [*sic*] justice and obliterate this shameful political frameup. Our victory will have this added meaning and our personal reunion will be all the more beautiful because of it. My soul cries out for you. All my love

Till I see you again— Your Julius

Ethel to Julius

January 20, 1952

Hello, Sweetest,

There are any number of matters I shall be holding in abeyance until Wednesday, but I simply must write you in the interim, anyway.

What a perfectly marvellous [*sic*] week this has been. Although it was unfortunate your brother had so little time to "lavish" upon either one of us, I'm sure you were as gratified as I to have [NWI] had even so short a visit. He came in to find me [NWI] still wildly flinging the bed-clothes into place; until I finally heeded his advice to sit down, I was somewhat out of breath. Actually it took me perhaps three minutes to get settled, but we both thoroughly enjoyed it. As a matter of fact, I'm afraid I rather hogged the show and ran over into your allotted half hour! I had close to 45 minutes; shall I go stand in the corner, darling?

Saturday afternoon brought Dr. Miller; it was one of the most provocative sessions of all and I gained considerably in terms of deepened understanding and self-confidence. There was also a good deal of valuable information regarding the conference at the JBG [Jewish Board of Guardians], about which I'm sure you must be anxious to learn.

January 21, 1952

Sweetheart, how beautifully you expressed your sentiments toward Manny, the Committee and your scintillating wife! At the moment, I am feeling slightly less than bright, let alone scintillating; I don't mean I'm unhappy, dearest, please don't misunderstand. Quite the contrary, my trouble lies [NWI] rather in the direction of an over abundance of merriment, bordering on the hysterical, with the result that I am [NWI] far too stimulated to permit of the maximum amount of peaceful slumber; hence Ethel the Enervated! (Wow, how dull can you get!)

Your mommy's visit was painful to me in ways that I shall discuss with you at length, even while it was pleasant. Whatever else she may have seen fit to raise with you that she could not bring herself to reveal to me I feel secure that my words brought [NWI] her comfort and encouragement. I am preparing myself properly [N4WI] you may be sure for a very thorough-going analysis of the entire home situation, on Wednesday, and trust this letter reaches you before then.

Daddy dear, did you receive a coloring signed by the artist himself, your precious Robby? And do you have any inkling of the thrill of gratification with which I am filled to realize that a chance idea of mine casually broached in a letter has furthered [N2WI] the establishment of the [NWI] very rapport with our younger child, for which we had both been longing over a rather extended period ["to establish" CO, N2WI] of time? It is joy beyond imagining to exercise our power as parents for our children's well-being and to receive such whole-hearted reciprocation of our love. Good-night, my darling husband—I kiss you fondly, my own — your affectionate Ethel

Julius to Ethel

Jan. 24, 1952

My Dearest Bunny,

Truly, our last tete a tete was most productive. But as you said when we started our discussion it hurts to know the truth of the situation. Darling the fact that they are closely in touch with the home relations of our boys and are keeping well abrest [*sic*] of all that is taking place assures us that the children's welfare is in good hands. I don't find letters a good medium for [N2WI] use in interchanging our ideas concerning this problem and I believe we should devote a good portion of each of our visits to mull over this matter. Incidentally before I forget, Thursday, February 7th is alright for Manny's visit. We'll have an opportunity to go over this matter in greater detail. In the meantime it is my opinion that when we talk to my sisters we try to have them help arrange activities for the boys, particularly for Mike, away from home. If you have any suggestions I'd like to hear your ideas. Ethel we really could use more time together to discuss our mutual problems. If we continue to make notes and come prepared for our visits we'll be able to get the maximum results out of our limited time.

I'm looking forward to a newsy visit from my sister this Saturday. Until then I continue to plod through "The Web and The Rock". Although I'm enjoying every page of this literary gem I feel bad that I am nearing the end of this book and I do not have any other of like calibre to look forward to. Oh my sweetheart, how I miss you. Is it possible for one to fully enjoy books even when they are mentally stimulating, when the mind cries out to share with his loved one. Where is the outlet for emotional satisfaction? What can be the significance of joy? Once I have known the sweetness of our life and the exultancy of our happiness then is our present separation all the harder. The horrible feeling of impotency, the sheer frustration of not being able to give comfort and love to my family fills me with great pain. In spite of this agony and because of the treasures I posses [*sic*] in my family I find in them the sustenance to keep on going. Before me at all times is the knowledge of what the future holds in store for us and I am more confident than ever that we will meet it and do magnificently. The only question that has to be resolved is our speedy vindication from this nightmare. At present that is in the hands of the "Gods". It is my greatest hope that decency and justice will triumph and we will go home together arm in arm. Then with you besides me life will be so beautiful. Our faith in the people will be sustained and no matter how long it takes we shall have the final victory. Love you my glorious precious woman—Your—

Julius

Ethel to Julius

January 24, 1952

My dearest,

I've spent rather a tense couple of days since your visit, but this morning I accomplished the highly unpleasant task I had set for myself and although I've had a fearful headache all evening, emotionally I am very much at ease.

Sweetie, I wrote Manny as per your request emphasizing our need to see him by Friday, Feb. 1st, and have a feeling he will heed our wishes. In the meantime, I'm looking forward impatiently to the next issue of the Guardian.

What a severe blow the American people have sustained with the death of Carol King![209] Shall I ever forget the remarkable expose of the Harry Bridges deportation frameup which I read some ten or twelve years ago![210] She was a public servant in the true sense of the word and by her unquestioned integrity and devotion to the cause of civil liberties in this country, puts to shame all the leeches and parasites and predatory frauds, the duly elected officials, feasting on the fat of the land and fattening on our blood!—

Honey, mail call— this week-end, I believe, will see an end to the stalemate—

Love—Ethel

Julius to Ethel

Jan. 27, 1952

My Sweetest Wife,

I had a most gratifying visit with my sister this Saturday. Isn't it remarkable how people can grow and rise to the occassion [*sic*]? There has been a tremendous development on the part of my sisters. I am sure they even amaze themselves by the effectiveness of their actions and the fact that they have such latent potentials. Of course the reason is obvious since they are good decent women and the cause is just and it is tied to home by flesh and blood. Yes my dearest the actions of these two can make your womanly breast swell with pride for your sex and also more than compensate for the shameful behavior of your own family. We can take a little bit of the credit for this because we have been able to inspire them and they themselves derive new found strenght [*sic*] and satisfaction from their efforts. A great deal of confidence is obtained by participating in campaigns to better human welfare as in our own case and this becomes a good character builder and stabilizing force in the home and community. My sisters are certainly better people in spite of the emotional pains they are suffering. I'll discuss her visit with you in detail this Wednesday.

Well I finally finished the last of Thomas Wolfe and I'll have to be satisfied with some light reading until some better material comes along. I'm anxiously awaiting Manny's next visit, which will probably be

---

[209]For information on this radical civil liberties lawyer, see Carol Hurd Green and Barbara Sicherman, eds., *Notable American Women: The Modern Period* (Cambridge, MA: Belknap-Harvard University Press), pp. 397–98.

[210]Harry Bridges was an Australian-born leader of the International Longshoremen's and Warehousemen's Union (ILWU), a radical West Coast union, whom the government attempted to deport in 1938 for alleged membership in the Communist party. Carol King was his lawyer and eventually won the fight against his deportation.

sometime thise [*sic*] week, so that I can hear the latest on the children and what the committee is doing. By the way I hope you can complete at least one of the letters you are working on by time he next puts in an appearance. Although I'm wrapped up in our troubles I still want to spend some time discussing world events with you. The world is in very great flux and in mounting turmoil and at the same time there is growing support for peace and compromise between east and west. Always I keep thinking of what Manny said, "You are two straws buffetted [*sic*] about by the political winds" and I keep hoping that public opinion will be sufficiently neutralized, that the judges will be able to render a decision based strictly on the legal merits of the trial and not on extraneous issues that stem from the hysterical atmosphere in our land.

Darling Ethel I'm so terribly lonesome. Would that I were able to hold you in my arms pressed close to my body, kiss your sweet lips and love you with all my heart. My soul cries out for you my precious. It has been so long since we knew the exultant joy of our relationship and yet the eons of time seem to crawl endlessly onward. When? How Soon? How much more can body and mind take? The only consolation is that we are coming closer to our final homecoming. I need your strenght [*sic*] my woman— Love you more than life itself— Julius

Julius to Ethel

Jan. 31, 1952

Hello My Sweetie,

In the past few days, I've been in a state of suspended animation awaiting [NWI] both the pleasant prospects of a stirring consultation with the eminent people's advocate, Manny, and the ever satisfying visit of my sister Lena. In the meantime I've had an opportunity to do some musing and I've been thinking about how I would summarize my concept of what is important in life based on my personal experiences and I find it quite difficult to put my views in writting [*sic*] but I'll try to give you the gist of my ideas.

First of all we must be aware of the society we live in and using the examples we learn from our own family units [*sic*] experiences we are equipped to judge what part we as individuals can play to develope [*sic*] our physical, mental and social character to obtain a maximum amount of security & satisfaction which is the basis of happiness. In the normal course of our daily activities we find more and more a social relationship exists between the people in our country not only on the job but in entertainment, recreation and activities of good citizenship. A person obtains the greatest amount of inner gratification in his creative endeavors and a great deal of this is derived in his common efforts to improve the welfare of all the people and in that category we have civil rights, justice, eradication of discrimination & establishing economic security [three letters CO, an arrow is drawn from this point to the top margin where "advance" is CO and the next six words are written] & advancement of science and culture and these can only be worked for [N2WI] & developed in time of peace. Therefore the major effort of all decent citizens of the community is to work for peace in the world. It is the duty of all Americans of character to speak their minds and contribute their wills, efforts and activities in the problems that confront our country[.] Only then can each of us maintain our dignity and honor. Then we are able to be at peace with ourselves and proud of our heritage as human beings. We and our children can develope [sic] normally and with confidence in the future and [NWI] then there is no limit to the individuals [sic] achievements and the exultant joy that one can know. It is important to note that only constant participation and experiences make living worth-while and although all is not milk and honey the ever constant striving to better the general welfare benefits each of us. This kind of relationships with our fellow men give [sic] us a wholesome and good character sharpens the clarity of our judgement, raises our moral [sic] and equips us to meet lifes [sic] challenges. This is no easy task for man as the pressures of society are tremendous and each retreat from his way of life is the [NWI] opening wedge that completely destroys his dignity as an individual and his principles and his pride as a man.

Sweetheart I know I rambled a bit but if I had more time I'd like to go on and discuss this topic with you at our next session. I believe the idea I make is that in applying this precept of one of natures [sic] laws (social) we can find real happiness— All my love Your Julius (Philospher?) [sic]

Julius to Ethel

Feb. 3, 1952

My Dearest Bunny,

We had a very thorough session with Manny and we scarcely managed to exchange a few pleasantries. Darling I am well aware of how your motherly heart pines for your boys and know that the full realization of the environment and it's [sic] detrimental effects on the children gives you additional cause for pain because you cannot directly help your dears. How-ever, sweetheart, perhaps the fact that your consistent efforts were respons-ible for a thorough and conclusive investigation and has already borne fruit in the initial corrective steps that have been taken is the guarantee that this matter will get the maximum amount of professional attention and no stone will be left unturned to rectify this situation. Sweet Mommie you have made both Manny and me, very sensitive [N3WI] when it comes to the childrens [*sic*] welfare and our vigilance will pay off. Now that everything is out in the open we will be able to proceed with our plans rapidly.

In this connection Lena's visit was a very fruitful one. Although she mentioned you discussing this subject with her I waited until she told me all the news she had for me and then I launched into the current problem. I told her of my wishes based on the reports of experts in this field and after thoroughly covering all the ramifications we both saw eye to eye. Of course, there are some reservations but considering the circumstances they are understandable and we will have her cooperation. Dr. Miller met her on the bus coming into the "C-C" and imparted to her the need for a quick change in the home situation. As soon as I've had an opportunity to talk to Ethel an immediate conference of my family and all interested parties [NWI] should be held to plan the actual steps necessary. If the matter should become urgent they might even hold the conference sooner as I've imparted our decision as parents and Lena will convey my wishes to the others. I'll save all of the details for our Wednesday briefing.

The more I talk to my two sisters the prouder I feel to know that we've inspired them to the point that they are able to rise to greater heights of human stature. Ethel their love for us has increased and most important so has their understanding of us and life itself. It is heartening to hear that there is a great upsurge of activity on our behalf and on all sides we can see the sympathy and support we are getting from many diligent decent and compassionate people and I believe that these actions will help us secure justice. Even though I'm confident of our eventual vindication, I'm in great agony because I can't help my boys when they need their parents most. Although I'm a realist I still hope we may have the mazol to be home in short order and take our rightful place with our two dears. Glory be I'll be seeing ["you" probably omitted here] in a couple of days I love you with all my heart my wife. Your man—Julius—
Keep your chin up the sun has to shine again.

Ethel to Julius

February 6, 1952

My most precious love, my darling husband,

I must caution you to sit tight until next Wednesday, when we shall have the opportunity to discuss more thoroughly the attitude and line of action based upon it that it would be most advisable [N2WI] for us to adopt. I am of course referring to the altogether un-called for, execrable, boorishness of a certain crude individual with whom we must occasionally, and most unfortunately, come into contact. You see, dear, our objection is predicated upon the unacceptable behavior pattern so abundantly evidenced, not upon the regulation involved. I should therefore refrain, if I were you, for the present, in any case, from forging a possible boomerang for ourselves; however, there are other, more [next word appears to be "sweetning" which doesn't make much sense in context] ramifications which I should very much like to explore with you next week.

As a last word for the moment at least, what an assinine [*sic*] tin-horn of this contemptible type needs is nothing so much as a prolonged and refreshing immersion in the soothing depths of the Hudson.—I'm told cold water is [NWI] very good for the nerves!

In the final analysis one has to learn to take things from whom they come. In the main, I am most happy to admit that most people around these parts are basically fine, decent human beings—

My love, my soul, I adore you—My heart is yours—my sweetest, dearest husband— Your always loving wife

Ethel—

P.S.—Sweetheart, if you have already mentioned anything to anyone, please don't concern yourself—I know I can rely upon your judgment, in any case—

Am kissing you madly, my sweet

E—

Julius to Ethel

Feb. 7, 1952

My Wonderful Girl,

Your letter was swell, delightful to read and it echoes my sentiments. I had been debating with myself to write you yesterday to make sure that we recognize that this little incident is picayune in relation to our main problems and we can shed it like a duck sheds water off its back. The description and language was beautiful and I consider your presentation very appropriate. Well we'll make up for it in many other ways. Besides sweet-heart I love you with all my heart and think the world of you. I'm so proud of you my wife and I derive such great satisfaction at seeing the great stature of a person you are. We have lots of work to do to straighten ourselves out and knuckle down and begin to exert all our energies on the main objective. I am positive that in due time you will reach the point where with ease you'll be able to produce for our team the high calibre of creative work that will help us. My suggestion is for us to concentrate on keeping ourselves busy and indulge in as many activities as possible that will help make our stay here easier.

The books and papers we got are just what is needed and I know that we will make proper use of them. I've been quite busy these days reading, playing chess and kidding around with the boys that I've only got 15 more minutes before my jewelry (pencil, pen & glasses) gets collected.

Let me know what your plans are for the children's next visit. It looks like it will take at least a month [erasure here] before we will have our next legal consultation & it is my fondest wish that by that time both of us we'll be able to report some progress and we will hear a lot more good news about [NWI] the home [NWI] situation and about the work of the committee. Time is passing slowly but every day brings us closer to the final decision. Naturally all our thoughts, hopes and actions are directed to this fateful day and I am confident that we will win complete vindication from this miscarriage of justice. My daily thoughts and concentrations of the world around us and all that is taking place &, of course, in the background is our own terrible catastrophe, shows me very clearly the issues involved in our cases [*sic*] and the knowledge of all its ramification [*sic*] indicates that our steadfast stand must succeed because it is based on truth and fact.

Ethel Honey it is so true just to look at you is enough for me. Then to hear you is very stimulating. Above all to know the great treasure I posses [*sic*] in you is what makes me happy. I kiss you my dearest—Your Julius P.S. Excuse this one was in such hurry—Better next time—my heart.

Julius to Ethel

Feb. 10, 1952

My Dearest Wife,

Putting down todays [*sic*] date brings to mind that next month this day is the birthday of our big fellow, Michael. Nine years ago when you presented us with our first born son we had come to a new stage of our growing relationship. We have had our share of difficulties, sorrows and joys and all the time we kept on striving to improve our knowledge and experience in order to better be able to enjoy the fruits of creative, wholesome living. Indeed an important component of our life is the integration and sharing with each other and our children and our greatest grief at this time is that we have been removed from our important role as parents, as the main source of security, comfort, understanding and love for our two dears. At best we can hope that the present efforts will be able to be the temporary stop gap until we can assume our rightful place with our beloved children. At the time of our childrens [*sic*] birthdays [N2WI] especially now I use the occassion [*sic*] to reassert to you my precious my deepest love and devotion for those beautiful products of our unity that you have brought forth for us. As a mother, wife and companion you have more than filled the bill. I'll try to get some cards to send Mike to help him celebrate the event and I'd like us to ask Manny and our family to make this day a happy one for our boy.

In this Sunday's paper I found a notice that one of the "Compass Clubs"[211] in Manhattan Beach is holding a meeting on the "Rosenberg Case" and, of course, you are already aware of the series of meetings in Chicago. By this coming weekend we'll hear of much more of the same type of activity which is spreading the facts in our case and is clarifying the issues at stake. These are the most effect [sic] answer to the political frame-up that has been perpretrated [sic] and is the guarantee that this miscarriage of justice will be rectified. We've always had faith and these occurences [sic] bolster our confidence.

I just came in from my afternoon yard period. The air has a crisp freshness to it, salty with a fishy odor of the open sea that gives one a glorious feeling of the vigor, magnitude and ever moving strenght [sic] of the river and also it brings with it a certainty of life and a promise of new and greater things. The warming rays of sunshine tells me that spring is close by and there is a great expectancy in the air and for us the dawn of a new day is approaching. As I walk briskly around the yard, eyes focused on the bright clear sky, picking out, patches of cirrus clouds, a droning airplane in the distance, gliding seagulls, gyrating sparrows ["and" CO, NWI] and mind outlines a picture of you walking with me arm in arm. Now I am filled with exultant happiness and every fibre of me is tense and throbbing with the joy of living because I have you. Sweetheart you are mine.

Always your Julie
P.S. Note Feb 12 & 22 are ordinary visiting days. No special passes needed—See you Wednesday Bunny

Emanuel H. Bloch
7 W. 16th Street
New York New York

Feb. 11, 1952

Dear Manny,

Am forced to drop you a short note to tide me over until I have finished rather lengthy discourse to you on some vitally important personal matters.

I have changed my mind about having the children just yet. In view of my present emotional turmoil, I should prefer to see them somewhere in the vicinity of Michael's birthday*, either slightly before or soon thereafter—

My subsequent letter to you will properly explain; in the meantime, I must ask you to lend me your kind indulgence.

I must also ask you to see us once more before the children's visit; my letter will throw ample light upon this request, also. Would appreciate your making it here either Monday, Feb. 18th or Friday, Feb. 22. Of course, if you could manage to get here this Friday, Feb. 15th or any day of the week of the 18th (other than dates mentioned) I would be most grateful. The sooner the better, I want to talk to you very badly— Regards— Love, Ethel—

*Forgot to mention—Mike's birthday is March 10[.] Please don't bring them until you have seen us first & we have properly discussed same, among a number of other items—Thanks (over)
P.S.—Will you be my Valentine?— Say "yes"—or it giffs murder!

Julius to Ethel

Feb. 14, 1952

My Wonderful Darling

This day and every day you are always my sweet "Valentine." My sister Ethel sent me a very lovely card for this occassion [*sic*] that in it's [*sic*] simplicity and sincerity was very heart warming. Precious one why does it have to be that particularly at this time of our greatest trouble I have developed to the point that I can more fully appreciate and understand you and we can build a more beautiful life together? As I sat opposite you and we shared our precious hour I too felt such deep satisfaction to see the splendid progress you are making and it is truely [*sic*] praiseworthy to see the visible evidence of improvement in the face of the most adverse circumstances. Only I ask that you take stock of yourself periodically and measure as objectively, as the situation allows, the sum total of the person you are so that even in your own eyes you don't for one minute lose sight of the entire picture and indulge in self deprecation. Many is the time that I visualize us being home with our two dears and working out all the little problems together. Oh how gloriously thrilling it is to know how stimulating and gratifying our common sharing will be when we are back home again. This knowledge serves as an endless source of revitalizing stength [*sic*] so I can continue to fight with increasing vigor for our complete vindication. Your strength sustains me. Good news from home and the committee encourages me. Public opinion becoming increasing [*sic*] aware of the facts and coming to our aid is the surest sign that will will [*sic*] win our complete freedom. It also helps when I mark off the days on the calender [*sic*] and know that we are coming closer to the time when we will be able to secure the justice we deserve under the laws of our land. I am very confident but I am prepared for any eventuality and my optimism is derived from a deep conviction that ultimately our cause will triumph.

Sweetheart your poetry had the desired effect and it is our suggestion that you devote more of your leisure time to amuse us with your scintillating lyrics of rhythmic verse. You have captured the crux of the "C-C" atmosphere and embarked on a noble crusade to satirize in true Shakespearian style the great evil. As a reward you have now become the poetess laureate of "Sing-Sing manor." Enough of levity while I take time out to chew my cud with the piece of [the next word looks like "buxer." If it is meant to be "butter" it is written with only one "t."]. Dry and barren as it appears it is nevertheless tasty and sweet and like all things we must look for the good wherever it may be hidden. Even though I'm going through the Lamont book[212] at a very slow pace I am enjoying every page of it and find it a very stimulating and thought provoking work. You too will find this book very worthwhile reading. There is a big backlog of books on my bars awaiting to offer me the pleasure of many edifying hours but it takes quite a bit of doing to overcome my mental inertia and drive away my worries and apply myself to this diversion. Bunny girl I press you close and kiss you tenderly—All my heart is full of love for you— Julius

Julius to Ethel [ink]

Feb. 15, 1952

Most Precious Heart of Mine,

With the turmoil and excitement of the childrens [*sic*] visit and the rushing developments of events in our case[213] I didn't have time to tell you that your face was beaming that you looked very lovely and that I love you very much. Considering the circumstances we managed beautifully and accomplished a great deal. The contribution we made to the cause of our fight was considerable and it continues to be a source of personal satisfaction.

Oh dearest, it was wonderful, despite the anxious atmosphere, to live together again as one happy family and ["for" CO] this [N2WI] is worth any sacrifice ["is worth" CO] for it is true love of family and the real dignity of human life. The boys are making progress. Michael is doing much better and I am convinced our little baby needs a great deal of help. Also they are both physically run down and I get the feeling there is to [*sic*] much of a

---

[212]Corliss Lamont was a well known supporter of left-wing causes in the 1950s, 60s and 70s.
[213]The Court of Appeals decision was due any week.

burden on their minds. The sweet memory of the smile, the kiss, the gay laughter and the young voices still pleasures the hours of my loneliness. Can people really understand that our hearts, sinerity [*sic*] and conscience goes into what we write say or do and to those who see the truth it is good and right and to those who hate it is defiant and arrogant. We have experienced unbelievable rotteness [*sic*] because of this case but in our wildest dreams we never could comprehend such base knavery. All the world knows that the perpetrators of this latest fraud are monsters and I am confident they will come to know the entire story of this ["grave" CO, NWI] terrible miscarriage of justice. It's a very rough fight and a most difficult one but I still feel confident I'll just never give up to lies, to indecency and unjustness. And if I repeat to [*sic*] often, it is because I have to express ["it" co] my feeling or I'll bust for I adore you sweetheart. ["and" CO, NWI] I admire you for all that you are Ethel and my love for you is undying. As long as we do the right thing by our children and by the good people of the world nothing else matters. We will have to call on the great strength of the solid union of our hearts and souls to find the [illegible word CO] stamina to face what is in store for us with courage and dignity. If I may say so myself I think we might to [*sic*] be proud that we didn't weaken to any blandishments that would have compromised any of our principles. Fears ["and" CO] cajoling & threats don't bother me but we must be very careful of the coming tricks of vicious madmen.

I've been quite busy reading and writing and I haven't had much time to think about putting necessary things on paper that will have to be attended to without to [*sic*] much delay. Soon as I catch up on my writing I'll tackle the job. See you soon my dearest and [N4WI] I want you to know that you are always in my heart and mind and the [NWI] mere thought of you is solace enough for my aching heart and builds up my morale. Always devoted to you Your Julie

The letter continues on the top of the second side. On the far left of the top margin are two overlapping hearts with an arrow going through both. The words "With love" are to the left of the hearts and squeezed onto four lines. To the right of the hearts is the following:

A Valentine to Ethel my wife my lady fair
In pain, in suffering in deep hurt but not in despair
Look at yourself my woman you'll clearly see
A sweet fine person of great worth and human nobility JR

Julius to Ethel [pencil]

Feb. 17, 1952

My Sweetest Bunny,

It is almost 9:00 P.M. now. I started to play a game of chess at 4:45 after supper with a half hour time out for a news broadcast and we played one to a draw and the second one I finally won. I had intended to leave enough time to concentrate on your letter but I'll have to be satisfied with a quick job. As you can guess I'm pretty well occupied nevertheless I always look forward to writting [*sic*] my sweetheart.

As usual my sisters [*sic*] visit was quite good and there is a great deal I'll have to talk to you about based on what we discussed. To some degree I was a bit disappointed because she was unable to bring us enough news of the committees [*sic*] activities so I guess we'll have to wait for our dear Manny to tell us the latest. This weeks [*sic*] "Guardian" is a bit late but I'm sure it'll be here on Monday. For me I'm marking time by reading and playing chess and as the days go by I'm getting anxious. Even though it's natural, I keep mulling over in mind all the possibilities and I repeat to myself that I should expect any eventuality and be prepared to meet it emotionally and mentally. Ethel darling now more than ever we've got to keep our collective chins up so that we don't lose our perspective. It is most gratifying for me to know that in this hour of our greatest need you are not only holding up but improving yourself to be able to live a most wholesome life. There are many hardships in store for us my wife and your strength is a most important part of our continued courage and confidence. Again I wish to reiterate that under this supreme test the high calibre of your [the next eleven words are written over an erasure] noble character your stature as a fine person and your proud dignity as a human being become evident. These are the attributes that are important in a person and besides you are my own sweet Ethel. I find that my greatest asset is being loved by you and the fact that we each as individuals accept and build our common relationship on such a solid foundation gives us the ability to live as proud decent principled people.

The fact that I can love you and the children more than my own self proves to me that I really love life and I have found happiness in sharing this kind of existence with you. I have no doubt we'll measure up and do our part and I'm hoping that the American people will rise to this occassion [*sic*] and make known their views on this foul injustice.

My love I'm holding you close to my heart and your sweet presence has a quiet but profound effect. At once I am filled with exultant joy, my body feels strong and in my mind all is serene for there is no greater beauty than complete mutual sharing. Have courage we are coming closer to our final home going. As ever—Julius

Julius to Ethel [ink]

Feb. 19, 1952

Hello Bunny,

Kind of miss you sweetheart. Since we've got a little more time I think now we should go ahead with your plans for the children, [NWI] but at once. You understand the decision was expected mometarily [*sic*] and everyone was keyed up to concentrate on the most pressing immediate objective, the question of life or death. But as you say we must go on planning and living and I'll help you in urging that this matter be given prompt and serious attention.

Again I believe we ought to carefully think through the Greenglass testimony and see what items might be gone into in order to find additional grounds to prove perjury. This we must do in a conscious way because regardless of the posture of the case at this very moment we will need this information in the very near future. At the same time it is my belief that we each should continue on our personal projects of writing and if possible coordinate the results for I feel we can accomplish many good things at the same time. Not only will this be useful in aiding our defense but it will pay great dividend in personal gratification. In my suggestion I am not precluding the fact that if we need to we should take care of our personal emotional needs.

The problem of the children and their future must receive close ["and more" CO] scrutiny and result in concrete plans concerning health (all phases), schooling, environment, etc. I am sure if we have some positive plans in motion we'll feel a lot more secure and relieved of a great amount of anxiety. Especially went [*sic*—probably meant "when"] decision time comes around.

As for us, the problem of our visits takes on a great deal of importance ["at" CO] from now on. We realize that in the immediate future a normal life for our children will continue to be a problem and also we are beset with the big question of our legal fight and our personal needs. It seems to me that since other co-defendants are always next to each other and can discuss their case regularly they can help themselves. Because you are my wife and a woman we can only see each other for 2 hours per week. Every other person here is entitled to 2 regular visits a week from 10–12 & [the next number is written over. It looks like "1130" but should be 1:30]–330 which is about 8 hours per week and 2–2 hour Sunday visits a month. Yes I understand the technical difficulties involved but the need is so great in all seriousness they ought to put me into the women's wing altogether. That would be just swell. Anyhow the Warden has been real nice to us and I'm sure he'll try to do the best by us.

You know honey the fact we are here still seems so unreal to me. Somewhere in the long ago I had a normal life with a sweet wife and two fine children and now all is gone and we're facing death. Yet the yearning for a wife's sweet kiss and a sons [*sic*] warm hug hold the promise of a return to the beautiful life I know & then ["that" CO, NWI] we will be so much happier when we're reunited. It is this human force and the support of good decent people everywhere that makes me fight so hard for this [illegible word, looks like "kind"] of victory— Your husband

                                                                                    Julie

Julius to Ethel [pencil]

                                                                          Feb. 23 1952

My Darling Bunny,

        You looked very beautiful and I particularly liked your appearance in the dress you wore at the legal consultation. Although there was no time to tell you of your charms they nevertheless made a lasting impression on my mind I just fell in love with you again.

        Ever since last Friday's discussion I've been thinking over all that was said and I feel compelled to begin a detailed exchange with you on this matter by letter as we never have enough time to cover this subject thoroughly in our brief visits. In the first [NWI] place I plead with you not to misunderstand what I say as I'm putting down on paper my ideas in a manner of thinking out loud and in analysing the question in it's [*sic*] entirety my thoughts will jell and my opinions may change.

        Frankly, I was very troubled and initially it was due to knowing you were in such terribly [*sic*] mental agony and also our own dear children where [*sic*] suffering untold harm and I felt that here I was unable to in an [*sic*] measurable degree be of assisstance [*sic*] to my precious family and aid them and so perform my elementary fatherly duty. But besides this I felt there was something wrong with our discussion, that rankled in me and I felt that that [*sic*] it was not correct for us to go into this matter on this plane. Of course, I may be wrong but I'd like to give you my views.

        Each of us, hase [*sic*—the word "have" is overwritten to change to "has" but the "e" was not erased] learned to appreciate the fact that we can respect an individual for his opinions but we go to the trained expert in his field to answer problems on his own subjct [*sic*]. This I believe is the basic mistake both you and Manny made first by talking and looking for the underlining causes and suggesting cures. When you go out of your fields you cannot fully appreciate all the ramifications you cannot fully understand and therefore the net result is some in between unsatisfactory [NWI] result and at best a hodge-podge. Believe me sweetheart I know the terrible drive to be understood and especially to have those close to see eye to eye on this matter but I insist that it is impossible to expect complete understanding from anybody when he is out of his element. Speciffically [*sic*] I am referring to our own Manny. It is sufficient that he is fully aware that a deep problem exists and is able to [erasure under the next six words] have a sympathetic attitude and in this way is helpful. This in no manner detracts from the fact that our lawyer is a sincere and devoted friend and is interested in us more than just as clients. It seems to me that I've rambled on this point and may not be too clear but I hope what I've put down is enough as a start for us to really go into a thorough analysis on this point next Wednesday. This I feel is not the major point I wish to make see letter of Feb 24th for continuation —Love Julius

Julius to Ethel

Feb. 24, 1952

My Dearest Ethel,

The most important thing to my way of thinking and I believe it was also the major purpose behind what our counsel was saying is that it's necessary for there to be established a working relationship between theoretical understanding, and action derived therefrom. Subsequently that action leads to clear and better understanding. [next six words written over an erasure] You too have shown the keenest integration of this kind of solution of problems many times in the past in your own life. I want to assure you that I understand there are very great difficulties in putting into effect certain solutions especially in this case. The gist of what I'm trying to say is that it is essential for you to seek release, even though at times only temporary, in some mentally & emotionally satisfying pursuits so that with renewed vigor and greater chance of success you can return to take up the battle. However I don't feel any amount of saying will be of any use because you yourself know of it and I am sure you're making efforts in this direction. Somehow and at certain stages it is essential to stop self punishment and seek some surcease. It is my fervent hope that I've made myself clear and that I not be misunderstood by you. Perhaps I too in my haste have fallen into the same trap I am accussing [*sic*] you and Manny of falling into. It may be that we are overemphasizing the magnitude of this dilemma and possibly because of our emotional proximity can't see the forest because of the trees. Again I want you to make notes on what I've said so we can hammer this thing back & forth this Wednesday.

On one score I feel positive that at best, under the present environment, we can only wish for some temporary relief on this vital problem. My sweets there is a picture in my mind of how you looked last Friday and

I must say to me it was very provocative. Well that's the way it should be my wife. You haven't lost any of your charms and it makes me feel good to see you looking so well.

Honey how I look forward to the day when we will be able to spend all the time we want talking over our problems and we will be so happy to share more of life together. In spite of our horrible experience here we will come out of it better people and I'll make up to you in every possible way to make life more beautiful and enjoyable.

I composed a letter to Manny but I want to read it to you before I send it off. Oh my honey bun if I could only hold you in my arms I would be so happy I hold you in the highest esteem and I am proud of you [NWI] for the swell person you are but it's about time I had you home so I can love you in the manner that a good wife rightfully deserves.—Your own Julius

P.S. It looks like I'm nuts about you but very happy because of it.

Ethel to Julius

February 25, 1952

My Sweetest dear,

Deeply involved as I am with introspective "soul-searching," I simply have to take time out to thank you for your most sincere and thoughtful presentation. How could I possibly misunderstand an expression so patently laden with loving concern and husbandly devotion! Darling, don't you know yet how solid this combine really is? Our team is re—d hot! Remember!

7:30 A.M. Feb. 26

My dear one, last night at 10:00 o'clock, I heard the shocking news;[214] at the present moment with little or no detail to hand, it is difficult for me to make any comment, beyond an expression of horror at the shameless haste with which the government [NWI] appears to be pressing for our liquidation. Certainly, it proves that all our [next word illegible, could be "conviction" or "conclusions"] [N3WI] in the past, regarding the political nature of our case, have been amazingly correct.

My heart aches for the children; unfortunately, they are old enough to have heard for themselves, and no matter what amount of control I am able to exercise, my brain reels picturing their terror. It is for them I am most

---

[214]The Court of Appeals, in a unanimous decision written by the well-respected liberal Judge Jerome Frank, had affirmed the conviction. See Record, pp. 1644–82.

concerned and it is of their reaction I am anxiously awaiting some word. Of course, Manny will get here just as soon as he puts in motion proper legal procedures for our continued defense, but meanwhile, my emotions are in storm, as your own must be—

Sweetheart, if only I could truly comfort you, I love you so very dearly—

Mail call—Courage, darling, there's much to be done—

Your devoted wife
Ethel

Julius to Ethel

Feb 28, 1952

My Loveliest One,

I started this letter earlier but found myself tied up in a chess game therefore I have only a short time to scribble a few lines to my most adorable, sweetest, dearest, honey of a woman. Believe me I'm still terribly shocked by the horrible and shameless affirmation of our conviction in such apparent haste. The more I think of it the more an idea jells in my mind and to [NWI] help effectuate my purpose I hope the clerk of the court sends me a copy of Judge Franks [sic] "opinion." Ethel I intend to carefully go over all he said and pick out all his distortions, omissions, placing of facts in the record that are not there, building up straw men and knocking them down, presenting his personal views of what took place at our trial in short exposing his legal chicanery [sic]. Your husband intends to write an opinion of this "distinguished" jurist's propaganda treatise. It is impossible for me to conceive the far reaching effect their decision will have on furthering the judicial attack on the American people but I can't help but see the crass deceit and sophistry used by a so called "liberal" and honorable man to continue this political frameup and use all sorts of rhetoric to camoflage [sic] the fact that our lives are being sacrificed in the interest of keeping nonconformists in line.[215] Honey now more than ever is it necessary for us

---

[215]This is clearly a reference to the dismissal of the prejudicial introduction of my parents' "Communist preferences" into the trial. My parents had argued that this emphasis, engaged in by both prosecution and trial judge, prejudiced the jury and should not have been allowed. Judge Jerome Frank's opinion denied reversal, because the trial judge had cautioned the jury that such information was not to be used as proof of guilt. He then mused, "It may be that such warnings are no more than an empty ritual without any practical effect on the jurors." [Record, p. 1656] What my parents could not know is that Frank and other appeals court judges had been inundated with anti-semitic hate mail threatening any "Jew Judge" who might let the "Jew-Commie Rosenbergs" off. [See Daniel H. Yergin

to exert all our efforts in the only manner we have left to us and that is to write what we know and feel about this star chamber proceeding & expose it. Sweetheart I am sure that your wonderful talents will help put our side across to our fellow citizens. Yes my love we got the stuff and we ["are" probably omitted here] going to town to win our cause. I'm not worried we can be strong because we are perfectly in the right and we must suceed [sic] regardless of the length of time it takes.

Of course I could keep on in this vane [sic] but I want to tell you what you symbolize to me. Because we are coming closer to the final decision and at the present rate we are also closer to our death I see more clearly than ever that you mean more to me than anything else in life including my own flesh and blood. You inspire me, set them [this word is written over, it might be the word "an" instead which would make more sense] example of a profound understanding woman of dignity and of very noble character. Indeed you are a most worthwhile person to know let alone be associated with so ["a most" CO] respected an individual and so devoted a mate. There wells up in one a great desire to write of your tremendous stature but alas I do [NWI] not possess the pen of an author or the prose of a poet but my heart sings joyously of your virtues and my mind paints beautiful pictures of my wholesome, warm & charming wife. Love, because of you I've lived a fruitful life and nothing can detract or change it. The future can only enhance my happiness— Always your

Julius

P.S. Saturday morning miss you very much I want to be in your arms always. You are always in my heart & mind and I need you in my arms also. Keep your spirit high. You are in my tender embrace & I kiss you goodbye till next time[.]

"Victims of a Desperate Age," *New Times Magazine*, May, 1975.] According to one of Frank's former students the judge had purposely written his affirming decision calling attention to the Supreme Court by putting arrows as it were to certain issues raised on appeal which he felt only the Supreme Court had the prestige and independence to use as a basis for overturning the conviction or at least the sentence. In the end, Judge Frank's personal timidity both then and in 1953 cost my parents their lives. See *Sons*, pp. 232, 234. See also Arthur Kinoy, *Rights on Trial* (Boston: Harvard University Press, 1983), pp. 115–27.

Ethel to Julius

Feb. 29, 1952

Dearest darling,

My bewilderment defies description, and of course it is what one must expect, but I think I should be feeling somewhat less anxious if we had had the opportunity to discuss at greater length all that was on our respective minds on Wednesday.

For example, although I don't imagine any one will exactly feel in the mood for a birthday celebration, it is important that the children's lives be as little affected by it as possible. Certainly I myself should not desire a large gathering where everyone strains for a gaiety that is non-existent, but Mike should have the happy privilege of inviting a couple of kids in to share a birthday cake [N4WI] with him & Robby and have some fun, and both children should be taken out for a special treat. I plan to talk to Lena on this score, stressing particularly the need to maintain a genuine cheerfulness about the house, as nothing is so destructive to the emotional well-being of a child as an atmosphere of [NWI] continual gloom and despair.

My sweet, I love you with all my heart. I intended starting this letter last night, but instead succumbed to an all-too human need for respite and escape [NWI] by [second syllable of next word inserted] shutting out all thought [N3WI] for the evening and listening to the radio. [N4WI] Hence this brief note—I paid for my dereliction, however, by wrestling with my problems all night and sleeping rather poorly. Once I have begun to implement a few ideas with action, however, I know I'll adjust to the new and loathsome idea that the powers that be have been able to secure a renewal of my lease here, after all. I have a feeling these "renting agents" may have cause to regret their rash act before the American people are through with them!

In the meantime, I am lashed by the most tormented kind of longing— Dearest, if only we could be together, I love you so much—

Your devoted Ethel

Julius to Ethel

March 2nd, 1952

Dearest Wife,

Even as you, I too cannot feel the same after this terribly [*sic*] blow from the "renting agents" (pardon I mean gentlemen of the Circuit Court of Appeals) of the death house. This shock is all the more severe because any illusions we may have had that even a fifty-fifty chance existed that judges of the higher courts are above hysteria and politics, are completely destroyed and we must soberly realize in spite of the stark terror of the impending death sentence that our only hope rests with the people and that they be aroused to stop this legal lynching. Since the interpretation of the law as set forth by Franks [*sic*] puts in grave danger all progressives and noncomformists [*sic*] I am positive that our fellow citizens will exert every effort to nullify and reverse this action and fight to maintain the basic rights guaranteed us all under the constitution of our land. I expect that at this late hour the campaign to bring our case before the public will gather momentum and from this mass rally on we'll begin to make headway. We are presented with the opportunity of telling our American brothers and sisters of our feelings, of the impact on our little children and of the importance of this case to every family in our country. We owe it to them that they be fully informed of the drama of the situation and [N4WI] be made aware of the [word "probability" crossed out above the next word] tragedy of such a catastrophy [*sic*] befalling any ordinary family like ours.

I am sure we'll do our part and that is why I'm looking forward to getting a copy of the opinion and going to work on it. I have a feeling that if I had the record of our trial and I had the opportunity to study it I would come up with ideas for investigations which would help exculpate us.[216] The next time I talk to Manny I'm going to suggest that each of us get a copy when the records are printed for certiorari[217] and then we will be able to look into the matter. Remind me to discuss with you next Wednesday certain thoughts I have concerning <u>letters</u> and also about <u>Bernie</u> [the two underlined words were underlined twice in the original] perhaps these can be of some help to us.[218] Independently, I talked to Lena about ["the" CO] Mike's birthday and I got the impression that they will do something but on a very limited scale. The point you made in your letter about the need for a normal and cheerful atmosphere at home and not one of mourning [N3WI] is very important. Honey, I suggest you write a letter to one of my sisters or Manny stressing this point and giving your suggestions for the birthday occassion [*sic*] for our big fellow. Your plans for combining the children's

---

[216]They still had not been allowed access to a complete transcript of the trial.

[217]In appealing to the Supreme Court, one must present a writ of *certiorari* to convince the Court to accept the appeal. There is no automatic acceptance by the Supreme Court of appeals from an Appeals Court ruling.

[218]My mother's brother Bernard ultimately did provide an affidavit which proved David Greenglass lied at the trial when he denied stealing anything from Los Alamos. He had, in fact, admitted to his brother, Bernard, that he had taken a sample of uranium from Los Alamos. This corroborated my father's testimony that David had stolen something from Los Alamos. Perhaps this affidavit was the kind of help our father was hoping to get. It is unclear what he means by reference to "letters" unless it is the beginning of thoughts that their prison correspondence might be published.

visit with a consultation are excellent, I approve, but it will depend on our counselors [*sic*] ability to spare us the time. Concerning next weeks [*sic*] visits I suggested that my sister Ethel come on Saturday & in the meantime I'll write Dave telling him the procedure we have to follow for Sunday visits and that we must know (both of us) at least one week in advance the day & time he will appear. Don't fail to read all of this Sunday's Compass particularly the swell ad. by the Committee. See you Wednesday my sugar bun. Until then [N2WI] I am continually hugging & kissing you. Can you imagine I wont [*sic*] let you go. Your lover Julius

Keep singing and punching my wonderful girl the future holds many good possibilities. You know courage, confidence & perspective.

Michael & Robert Rosenberg
24-36 Laurel Hill Terrace
New York New York

March 4, 1952

Dearest children,

Did Aunt Lee tell you of her visit to me and of my messages of love to you both? Darlings, I am so sorry you had to be disappointed; I am just as unhappy about it all as you are. However, if you think we're licked, you just don't know your Mommy and your Daddy! So do the best you can to get used to waiting all over again, but give yourself time because it's very hard not to mind. Daddy and I understand only too well just how hard it is and we're slightly bigger and stronger than you are. Nevertheless, let's not forget the old team cheer: "The Rosenbergs are re-e-a-l hot!" And more and more wonderful people are beginning to realize this and are pitching in to help send us home to you where we belong.

The snow is whirling outside my window as I sit at my writing table and wonder what my pussies might be doing at this moment. The other day when I was outside in the yard, the snow that had fallen the night before looked so much like the icing on a birthday cake, that I couldn't resist "printing" letters in it with my right foot. By the time I was through, all our initials were outlined clearly, M.R., R.R., E.R., and J.R. Do you remember how we used to tease Daddy by calling him, "J.R. the Wonder Dog?"

Speaking of birthday cake reminds me of a certain date, (March 10) when my dear Michael will be nine years old. I wish I could really tell you how happy I should be to celebrate the day with you and Robby in person. But since this is not possible I can only say that I shall [NWI] be thinking of you both and loving you with all my heart.

Mike dear, what a perfectly wonderful picture of you I received; you know, the one that was taken in school. Since Robby doesn't attend school yet, I told Aunt Lee to make arrangements to have a good picture done of him outside, so that I can see my boys just as they are right now whenever I get hungry for a glimpse of them.

Robby dear, how do you like the drawings Daddy made for you? I didn't see them but I bet they must be swell. I am hoping you have fun on Mike's birthday; when you are five on May 14th, he will enjoy yours, too.

Again, all my love, my very dearest children,

Mommy—

Julius to Ethel

March 6th, 1952

My Sweetest Wife,

Wednesday afternoon I got Michaels [*sic*] picture. Darling it's beautiful just like our boy and on his face you could see character and intelligence and so much charm. There is something about this picture with it's [*sic*] slight smile that reminds me of you and I must say I just love you for giving us such a sweet boy. On the birthday card I am sending out tonight I wrote a page on how happy it makes me to have this gift of his and that he is my son and my sunshine. These words I printed on the wall above his picture. The letter to Robbie also went out and I am sure the kids will get a kick out of my efforts. Do you think Mommy your boy is getting to look handsome? Like his father!!! (Ho-hum such ego) (perhaps the question mark belongs after father)

Ethel last Wednesday [*sic*] tete a tete was a pretty good one and if we are able to continue to concentrate on our personal and legal problems we will be able to keep our feet firmly planted on solid ground and work on the important matters that will help us. Believe me it is only in this sense that I am interested in having the appeals court decision and the trial record. We are [N2WI] the ones best suited to suggest possible discrepancies in the testimony of those witnesses who helped frame us. I feel it is also an important part of our moral [*sic*] to participate actively in this fight for our lives that at the same time [NWI] also has such great significance for the American people. The newspapers are being examined by me carefully and I hope to see certain articles written that expose this decision and [NWI] present the facts in our case. There is a good chance that we'll get two visits this weekend one by Ethel & one by Dave and I do wish this will come to pass because I could use theses [*sic*] visits for good purpose.

Honey I'm pretty lonely and I know you too are going through all kinds of hell. My heart cries out for you my love and all my thoughts are concentrated on your welfare. All I could do is think about ways of comforting you and making your temporary stay here as easy as possible. When I think of all this I feel sure that you are basically strong because you fully understand the issues in our case and are a determined battler for decency, right and justice. We can best derive satisfaction from adequate accomplishments in this difficult task we have set for ourselves. We never were wallflowers and we intend to actively make our weight felt this time also. I hope you can get as much strenght [sic] from my love for you as your love [erasure here] has given me. Keep trying sweetheart & I know you'll come through with flying colors.

Always your devoted—Julius

Julius to Ethel

March 9th, 1952

Hello Mommy,

Congratulations are in order to you on the 9th Anniversary of your giving to us our first born. I look at Mike's picture and I can say it is indeed a tribute to you to know the great treasure we possess due [NWI] to the kind of child our boy is. To me, what is so evident is the effect your patient and tireless efforts have had in helping make him a happier and better person. This is obvious to me because this evening I have recalled the years of his birth and childhood and all that has transpired. Parenthood in all it's hardship work and pain also brings with it the greatest joy husband and wife can experience. Consider yourself hugged, kissed, loved showered with presents by your devoted spouse. Sincerely you deserve this and even more and it is my fervent wish that for one moment you don't become despondent and keep high your faith that we will be completely vindicated and in time go home to our two dears. Things do look bad and the going is rough but our understanding tells us the reasons for all of this and only the principled fight we are waging on the issues in our case can bring the victory we are so urgently seeking.

That brings me to my brothers [sic] visit. Short as it was nevertheless it was one of the most fruitful we've ever had. We got down to fundamentals and I believe something will come of it. Of his feelings I have no doubt and we were concerned with the practical efforts he could make on our behalf. Incidentally I'll discuss with you in detail at our next Wednesday session all that we talked about.

Darling somehow I have a feeling of frustration in connection with our legal consultation because there are so many matters I must take up with Manny and there never is enough time and if I want to take more time I think I'm selfish by depriving you of the opportunity to un-burden yourself.

Then too, I don't want to interfere with his legal efforts on our behalf but it is precisely legal matters that I must take up with him. Perhaps you dearest can appeal to him to make available to us sufficient time to do justice to these pressing problems. I have a complete outline prepared and I have hopes we will cover it at an early date.

I am itching for news of substantial accomplishments by our committee and I want to hear that the campaign is beginning to roll in high gear. Oh Ethel I miss you so much I need you in my arms pressed close to me and then I can be happy. Sweetheart It's terribly hard but the bright future is well worth it. I'm still very confident. I haven't lost my courage and my perspective is very clear and above all we are right. See you Wednesday when we can kiss and coo—verbally (aw shucks)

Love—Your devoted mate—Julius

Julius to Ethel

March 13, 1952

Sweetest Flower of My Life,

Ever since I saw you last I've been mulling over in my mind all that we talked about and I want you to know that it is precisely because I respect you so much that ["I" probably omitted here] tell you my thoughts on the matter. It is because I know you want me to be completely truthful on this subject that I discard any other approach even though it may salve your feelings and give you temporary respite by automatically agreeing to what you say even though I believe that there is a possibility you may have the wrong approach. Therefore, it is my fervent hope that you will understand that in no way do I close my eyes to a problem that exists or deny reality but it is my view that you should reevaluate the goal you set yourself and limit the scope of planned relief to bring it into the realm of feasible accomplishment considering circumstances and environment. This is just the views [*sic*] of a very interested layman your devoted husband. I think this covers my idea at least the one which I had hoped to convey to you last Wednesday.

Before I discuss anything else I want us to be sure to emphasize that we only require sufficient time from Manny to cover our own participation in [word CO here] the legal practical and family problems that effect [*sic*] us keeping in mind that we are aware that he has a very difficult task ahead [N2WI] and one that is very time consumming [*sic*].

As usual we didn't have enough time. I had planned to talk to you in greater detail about the latest Supreme Court rulings and the trend that is indicated. I feel it's very important for us to keep abreast of current events which will help clarify the atmosphere that effects [*sic*] the political thinking of the judiciary. Darling we've got to be strong because there is a storm of fear sweeping our land & only a powerful public opinion counterattack demanding justice for us will make the genttlemen [*sic*] of the judiciary amenable to reviewing our case on it's [*sic*] legal merits. If this happens, we have no doubts our conviction will be reversed. Our only course is to fight for this and keep confident that the people will act.

Of course, I never have an opportunity to talk about us. At least if we can't make love, we should be able to verbally coo and make eyes at each other. Oh Sweetheart I love you and need you. But this we can be certain of that all this will pass and with every passing day we are closer to the final decision and because I am optimistic I am able to continue to contain myself. The agony and horror we are suffering can never be fully erased, especially since there is no basis for our being here. We will always remember and I am sure make good use of this knowledge to live a happier and better life with our children. Accept my heart my love as completely as I accept you—

Always Your own—Julius

Ethel to Julius

March 13, 1952

My Sweetest darling,

I wonder if you know how extraordinarily precious you are? It's an altogether astonishing idea [N2WI] to me that seeing you and hearing [NWI] you for [NWI] such a comparatively insignificant length of time should do me so much good!

Into the bargain, Wednesday afternoon brought a letter from Ethel, with a few lines from Michael, to wit: "Dear Mommy I had my birthday party on March 9, 1952. I had a wonderful time. Aunt Ethel and her family, Aunt Lena and her family, and Adele came. (I believe this must be Bill's girl friend, whom Ethel mentions as having taken Mike out one Saturday). Ethel brought the birthday cake and candy. We played musical chairs, and I played the piano. Thanks for the cards. Love from Michael and Robert." Of course, you will have to wait until next week for the pleasure of seeing the kid's beautiful handwriting and precious misspelling, although I really must say that in the main he does amazingly well.

Ethel's writing has to do chiefly with the party; she and Lena went to town with "cake, candy, candles, napkins, chocolates, party hats and ice-cream". They also bought him long-sleeved white shirts, sport shirts and slacks. Mike's friend gave him some kind of stencil and lacquer set and Robby a weaving set, which he enjoyed with the help of the boy's mother.

She never so much as mentions Sophie; obviously there are guilt feelings about the entire episode. I'm awaiting our next legal consultation with baited [*sic*] breath, as you may well imagine! Do you remember what you told me on Wednesday re these consultations? Well, I think you ought to raise this item at the very outset, so that it doesn't get lost in the rush; and for heaven's sake let's not be so confoundedly apologetic. Up to now, this fault was largely my own and with my personal timidity, I unwittingly pressurized you into feeling the same way. Neither of us, however, should allow such lackadaisical behavior to continue; as for Manny, he is so utterly trustworthy, so truly and sincerely our friend, that he's bound to take it in the spirit that it is given. There isn't anyone who commands any deeper regard and affection than he does.

Darling, just go on loving me; I need your support and approval so badly. The loneliness is ghastly when you're not with me—

All my love—Ethel—

Julius to Ethel

March 16, 1952

My Wonderful Woman,

It is always with great anticipation I await my sweet sisters [*sic*] visits and they never fail us. Their complete devotion to us and our cause is very heartening and the splendid news they bring of the meeting and the activities on our behalf surpasses even my objective estimate on the success that has been obtained to date. That proves most conclusively that the inherent goodness and decency is latent in the American People and it is only necessary to acquaint them with the issues and they will fight for a just cause. The hour is late the need is great and the opposition is formidable but right is on our side and we must win through. Now it is necessary to strain every effort to involve non-partisan liberal and conservative elements to enter the lists on our behalf. Particularly because at stake here is the rights, security and very lives of all the people. No small factor is the need to combat the anti-semitism that surrounds the case and I have reference to the fact that since we are innocent they seize on the conviction, although it is illegal, and say "look it is the Jews who are responsible." I am still very confident but without any illusions as to all the difficulties we face. Our family is doing a good job and they are right on the ball and I look forward to great accomplishments from their sincere efforts.

The news from home isn't to my liking but from talking to my sister I got the idea that perhaps they should try to obtain a mother-helper from the Jewish Family Service as a temporary stop gap. If you think it is of some use write all the details and recommendations on this score to Lena and let them get to work on it at once. Of course, now is the time to push for rapid realization of our plan to have a complete change of the personnel and the environment of our two dears.[219] This is all the more urgent because my mother is ailing under the additional burden that has been placed on her.

Darling I think of you constantly and I feel the terrific loss of not being with you. Each of us could lend the other comfort, tenderness and devoted love. How hard it is!! and it's being [*sic*—probably meant "been"] so long that I've held you in my arms. There is lots to talk to you about and since the possibility exists that we might have a legal consultation this Monday I will not take the time to repeat any items we will have a chance to discuss in person. I am looking forward to positive accomplishments in the campaign to secure justice for us and only this will be able to keep my spirits high. This is said not in the way of any defeatism but with the firm conviction that the need is great and the situations [*sic*] demands it. I am not worried our friends and the good people will not let us down.

Only to be with you my sweetheart in our own home with our boys that is my constant hope. Ethel we've just begun to fight and our team has a great deal of strength. Keep your sights on the future. Always your devoted fellow—Julius

Julius to Ethel

March 20, 1952

My Most Precious Human Being,

You can tell from the way I look at you that I'm madly in love with you and I fully appreciate all your wonderful virtues. It is because of what you are, faults included and the very great store of potentials you possess that you measure up to being such a swell person. Difficult as it is I hope you can keep this in mind so that in retrospect you can take some comfort in the basic positive characteristics you have. I know you had a hard time yesterday but I have confidence that you will pass these periodic cycles and still keep on an even keel. Be that as it may I still am concerned for your welfare and peace of mind[.] Always be ready to tell me in case there is anyway that I may ease the terrible burden that you carry. I am sure that you take some courage from the fact that I am completely devoted to you, accept you for the fine woman you are and hold you in the highest esteem as an individual. Naturally the only real avenue [*sic*] of relief are available to us in our own visit and those near and dear to us because this is the link to the life we know and love. For both of us are able to seek great satisfaction

---

[219]This is the first clear indication that plans were afoot to move us out of our grandmother's house. See *Sons*, p. 136.

from the splendid news we are receiving from the Committee that is working on our behalf. I sent our sweet Manny the letter I spoke to you about concerning our ideas on the New York Post. It is my sincere hope that William Reuben[220] will do a bangup job on this matter. Anyhow I'm impatiently awaiting this weeks [*sic*] National Guardian and I hope they give the meeting good coverage. Of course, my darling sister Lena will fill in on many details to bring us up to date.

I'm still very anxious, keeping my fingers crossed and hoping to hear the good news we talk about. We are entitled to this small amount of good fortune but I'll be satisfied when I hear it. Perhaps my sister will bring us word on when the children will put in their next appearance. I'm looking forward to a very positive experience for the boys and I know we'll both do our part to make it a success for our two dears. By the way I've been think-ing about the part of the letter you read me and I must say I was very measurable [*sic*] impressed with the simplicity and sincerity it exuded. This will truly be a heart warming document. Sweetheart make sure you direct it particularly to women and mothers. It seems to me that it will have a very good appeal. Keep trying it just needs a little more to finish it up. Bunny dearest such an accomplishment will pay great dividends especially in emotional gratification. Ethel the going from here on in will increase in intensity and fury so keep your chin up and keep your feet as firmly on the ground as possible. It will be enough if we can hold our own and it will be better still if we can contribute to our own campaign. Still very confident— Your lover boy—Julius

Julius to Ethel

March 23rd, 1952

Hello Beautiful,

Long time no see and as I can't set my eyes on you and talk to you but once a week the overwhelming longing I have for you must be spilled out on paper. It is apparent to me that you've had a difficult week of it and my sister Lena was so concerned that she left you in a bad frame of mind that she begged me to tell you how sorrow [*sic*—obviously meant "sorry"] she was that you couldn't have a pleasanter visit and since she wasn't able to tell you all her news I'll do the honors. By this time I'm sure the P.K. has told you the excellent news and it comes at the right moment because I have a great deal to discuss with you. Since this letter will not be a good means of telling you all about my sister's visit I'll just give you an idea of what

---

[220]The man who wrote the original series in the *National Guardian* about the case. See above, footnote 163.

we covered. First, we discussed the home situation & for $^1/_2$ hour we got no where but excited & as she put it "the same results and talk she had with you." However we got the subject back to the rally and the committee and talked over all details. As for my brother he is going to accompany the girls on their visits. Then in an hour I went to town on the home situation and included the need for them to be prepared to move when the situation is ready. I must say she will not understand and there are two reasons [N2WI] for this. One she cannot and two other factors make it difficult for her to agree to the correct approach. However she says that she wants to see the trained people and go over the entire picture with them. Lucky for us Dr. Miller put in an appearance and she stayed with me so that she would be able to get a ride into the city and also to talk to him about the children. The important thing is that a sincere effort be made to acquaint them fully with the facts about the environment. A contributing factor is the idea that Manny has hurt their feelings because of the difficulties that took place at home. However we know what the underlying cause is and how it affects their view on our plan for the children. Well [*sic*] talk about this when I see you.

Reading the Guardian report on the rally convinces me that the letter you began to write is on the right track and I want to stress that it must continue to have that personal warm touch. After all it's right from the heart and that hits home. Daily my thoughts revert to being with you and although the present set up here does not allow us to be together I still think about it and somehow I'm sure we will be together again. Perhaps I'm a dreamer but so help me I can actually feel you in my arms and as I wispher [*sic*] sweet things in your ear and as my lips meet yours I know how much I love you. Be strong my sweet don't let minor things get you down. Remember when you handle dirt you are bound to get some on yourself. Keep the entire picture before you always and your perspective will be clear.

Your devoted man—Julius

Julius to Ethel

March 27, 1952

My Sweetheart

Light of my life, rose of my heart, you my treasure that is being kept apart from me is [*sic*] the sweetest and most precious thing I hold dear. I am sure you feel as I do when I look in your eyes and see your beautiful expressive face and I sense at once that we are at one with each other. In retrospect thinking about our last wonderful tete a tete I can't help but notice how paralell [*sic*] our minds run and the rapid manner we harmonize our thoughts. It seems to me that our understanding of each other has been vastly enhanced and we are able to give our partner his due. I for one marvel at the growth of our relationship in spite of our adverse surroundings and I can't begin to picture the high level it would have reached had this miserable catastrophe not befallen us. I am firmly convinced that pure physical separation shall not deny us our love and our complete union. Although we must for the time being, each in his own little horror chamber, suffer through till we cannot further be denied that which is rightfully ours. Since you have become an organic part of me I am not completely separated from you but your physical presence in my arms will signify our complete triumph.

I had meant to ask you if Dr. Miller spoke to you about the meeting he had with Manny that was schedualed [*sic*] for last Friday to discuss the home situation. Keep this subject in mind for our next visit. Within the next few days you'll probably see our two dears and I know you'll acquit your motherly obligations to them [NWI] nobly and make this a real positive experience for them. Lucky me I, of course, will benefit from your preparatory efforts and I'll have the satisfaction of seeing them after you've warmed them up. For their future and their sake we must do the best possible job to maintain our dignity and integrity, no matter what the odds, and then, we will be in a position to be most effective in our own behalf. Darling, it's a long, long, hard road and I know ["we" probably omitted here] will not be found wanting. Keep your sights on the future because the principled fight we are carrying on for justice must end in our victory and complete vindication. As always regardless of the reading I do and all the little ways I try to busy myself I still think of you often and I must say I miss you so much. Ethel reading the book on Negro History gives me a great deal of emotional satisfaction besides the mental stimulus such a profound work has on a reader. Now more than ever can one derive real insight from reading these historic documents of mans [*sic*] striving for dignity freedom and justice. Right now I'm awaiting some good news, hopeful signs of progress and marking time until I see you my sweet. Just keep on being my Ethel. I want you the way you are—Your devoted husband—Julius

Mrs. Lena Cohen
140 Baruch Place
New York New York

                                              March 27, 1952
Dearest Lee,

      Can't possibly imagine why no word as yet from home as to the children's visit—I trust Manny is planning to get them here by Saturday as we are on pins and needles to see them without fail by the end of this week, no later!

Lee, dear, Julie tells me you were concerned over my alleged anxiety on Saturday due to what was discussed between us—Believe me, you are a very foolish girl; please stop worrying about it. The important thing is to heed what both of us said regarding the welfare of the children, as our personal feelings count for much less than their future happiness.

If Manny is planning to bring them later than the day you receive this letter, please phone him at once & urge him on my behalf to phone Sing Sing & leave a message for us—Be sure to stress to him that we want them here sometime this week, not next—OK? Of course, they may arrive this morning or to-morrow for all we know—but I just had to write anyway.

Love—Must rush because of Mail Call—Am fine—So is Julie—We had a wonderful visit yesterday—Best—Ethel

Julius to Ethel

March 30, 1952

My Sweetest Wife,

Thank goodness for my sisters' [*sic*] letter relieving us of the anxiety of the children's visit. I suppose by the time you receive this letter you will have already written Manny as to what day you prefer the boys' visit. What does concern me is the health of our esteemed counselor. It is so important that he be well both for his own sake and for our best welfare. Heaven knows we need him like we need our right arms. I hope my sister got our lawyer's message right as to the result of his trip to Washington. Somehow, I believe she got a garbled account of it and that accounts for the news on the Supreme Court. Anyhow it seems premature for them to know whether certiorari will be granted. This weeks [*sic*] editorial in the Guardian pleased me very much as it covered very well the points I had protested in the Post editorial in a letter to our Manny. At this late date I am surprised that the Compass has as yet taken no stand on our case or even written any substantial articles about it. How could a sincere and decent newspaper deliberately avoid to take a position and ["at the same time" CO, N3WI] in so doing help the conspiracy of silence that surrounds the facts and issues in our case. Yes dearest so very much more work and results are necessary. It is my fondest hope that the visit with our two dears will bring us some heartening news of positive accomplishments on our behalf. I am happy to see that my sisters and brother are keeping busy always working on our behalf. This is the sign that they too will mature to a better understanding of the issues involved and already their self respect and confidence is improving. The best character builder is activity based on sound reasoning and judgement that has a social and useful purpose. Especially when one is fighting for fundamental principles of justice and right that effects all Americans. Now that the campaign for the presidency of our country gets underway in earnest there will be a lot of tall talk filling the airways and it is a good time to bring clarity to the public by showing them facts and not empty phrases on the dangers that confront their lives, their civil liberties and [NWI] their security. You know Ethel one thing our trial proved to us that talk is cheap and empty unless backed up with evidence. No matter what, the truth will out and the people will act to rectify this the political frameup. Hold on to your chair dear the mud will begin to fly now.

Honey Wednesday is just a couple of more lonely nights and I'll be with my sweetheart, my wonderful precious darling, for this is what really counts in this torture chamber—Always strong because of you. Your devoted husband—Julius

Ethel to Julius

March 31, 1952

Dearest,   Thursday, March 27, 1952 [dates *sic*]

To-night I am oddly restive; a soft languor drifts like a fragrance upon the breeze, assailing the senses and stirring to uneasy life a multitude of longings. I am lonely, I am melancholy, I am unhappy; the gloom of the sad, slowly descending dusk fills my entire being with an ache that in as sharp and uncompromising as any physical pain! What to do!

Monday, March 31, 1952

Sweetheart, Ethel's letter relating the news of Manny's unfortunate indisposition just about knocked me for a loop; much as I tried to be sensible, anxiety for him, for the children and for ourselves, rode me mercilessly. Now that I've composed a letter to him, however, warning him to take it easy for as long as necessary and assuring him of my willingness to postpone the children's visit for a few weeks, I feel a good deal better. Besides now that Monday is here, can Wednesday be far behind? Darling, I love you with all my heart; how you do go on about me in your letters, it's so immensely satisfying to my female ego!

Can't think coherently any more, too close to mail call. Anyway, I want desperately to see you and talk to you, not to a hunk of paper!—

All my heart's deepest love—Sweetest—Ethel

Ethel to Julius

April 2, 1952

My dear one,

How happy I am when I am with you; the very air changes and the heaviness lifts, and will to live and work and fight is mine again!

April 4, 1952

Darling, this morning a letter is going out to the children, reassuring them of our love and continued desire to see them and explaining the delay. Incidentally, on Wednesday afternoon I received a lovely Easter card from them; it is a riot of purple lilacs on a pale blue background, but you'll have to see it for yourself to really appreciate it.

There was also a letter from Ethel, a copy of which, she stated, would go to you. I am wondering however if she wrote you the following: "Thank goodness the children are fine now, but whenever Michael goes to the toilet at night he arouses Mama to tell her. A small light is [NWI] on in the foyer between the bedrooms and bathroom, and it burns all night. Perhaps you can tell Michael that once he arouses Bubbie, it is hard for her to fall asleep again." You will no doubt understand from this passage that people are still unduly concerned with externals, to the detriment of any real progress.

Please, dearest, be as calm and as clear and as firm as you possibly know how to be when you see Ethel or Davy (or both) this week-end. I am simply at my wit's ends as to just how to place the most effective emphasis on what!

Mail call —Love—Ethel

Julius to Ethel

April 3rd, 1952

Dearest Bunny,

They say that a young man's fancy turns to love in spring. What can I describe my feelings when all along I've been head over heels in love with my maiden fair even though we are forcibly kept entombed separated from each other awaiting a horrible end. Yes it's true I'm madly in love with you. Wednesday visits are a great boost to my moral [*sic*] but I'm sure that you even as I feel a terrible let down after we go back to our respective cells. The wish uppermost in my mind is that you receive some respite from your horrible confinement and I always look forward to hear that in spite of all the hardship you face that you've accomplished something and are able to benefit by emotional and personal gratification. Darling my sisters [*sic*] letter, and I heard from her again, the news item I read in todays [*sic*]

Compass causes me to be impatient until I see Manny again. I want to hear what's new direct from the oracle himself. One thing is definite from the tone of Ethel's letter Manny is recovering quickly. I do hope he heeds your warning and takes care of his health. He's too valuable a guy to be out of circulation even for a little while. Of course I'm looking forward to seeing our two dears but I do hope we can see Manny soon because there are many things that only he can clarify to me. I suppose because of the kind of people we are we will always hunger for the company and wisdom of such a fine mind as our swell counselor has.

As I read the letter concerning the kids [*sic*] recent sickness I can't help feeling bad that we their parents were not able to be present to comfort them, take care of them and nurse them back to health. Dearest we who experience the terrific pangs of pain that goes with this type of separation from our family feel robbed of our birth right, our prerogative as father and mother. More so does our heart ache for the lose [*sic*] our children feel. Can this torture be sensible? is this justice? Honey it outrages the common decency of man and it makes every fibre of me feel wretched. No wife I am not weakening but I must put my innermost thoughts down and I resolve to fight the harder to hasten the day when this nightmare will be over and we can do right by our misfortunate [*sic*] children. Know my wondrous woman that the thought of you gives me courage, the sight of you gives me strenght [*sic*] and being at one with you satisfies my most pressing need and permits me to maintain my stability. Because of you life is good to me and with you I am sure we will live more beautifully. I am not dismayed basically we got the stuff and right is on our side. The end, no matter how long it will take, must lead to our victory—Your devoted husband—Julius

Julius to Ethel

April 6, 1952

Hello Bunny Dear,

Sunday night and a couple of visits under your belt with the propects [*sic*] of seeing the children, Manny and my sister this week. Write Manny of your wishes as to when the boys should come to see us because he may just up and come without any notice. Of course I'm looking forward to our tete a tete and I hope that if our two dears do come it will be before Wednesday so we can discuss their visit. I was very glad to see my brother and I was particularly gratified with his understanding of the home situation and I am sure he was sufficiently impressed with our views and the correctness of our position and we can count on his support on the need to change the boys [*sic*] environment. Honey dearest I miss our beloved offspring and feel such a terrible lack because I cannot share life with them. More so does my heart ache that you too my wonderful wife must suffer all the same privations and even more hardship than I. As for me I can only find relief in thoughts of you and the children and the many decent people who are working on our behalf. We can look forward to our ultimate victory and with each passing day we come nearer to being together again. Time hangs heavy but in [N2WI] spite of its creeping agony we can find surcease in each other and in the principled manner in which we conduct ourselves. If we can keep before us the knowledge of the issues involved in our case and the effect of it's [*sic*] outcome on many other people we will continue to take courage and see the perspective clearly. Oh my sweet woman how lonely it is without you and ever so often I imagine you next to me and I talk to you and share with you and I am so happy just thinking about you. Yes Ethel this too must come to an end and we are coming closer and closer to the final decision. I am not afraid because we are fighting a just cause and I just know we've got to win. Let's keep our heads high darling and wherever possible contribute our share to the campaign.

As you put it so well I am sick and tired of putting things on paper I want to be near you always, to see you, talk to you and hold you in my arms. I'll go back to marking time. Trying in every possible way to help the hours pass quickly. Not reading much but newspapers and playing pinochle. Oh how I await news of positive accomplishments on our behalf. If it were possible to have our good counselor come up once a week it would make things easier. Anyhow Wednesday is just a couple of days off and I live for our time together. I love you with every fibre of my being. Your devoted husband

Julius

Julius to Ethel

April 9, 1952

Hello Sweetheart,

Here is what appeared in April 9th N.Y. Times. "Judge Frank wrote that there were <u>debatable questions of law</u> involving the death sentence and <u>urged</u> the Supreme Court to decide these issues. The jurist noted that in the Rosenbergs' petition for a rehearing, for the first time, they urged as pertinent an article of the Constitution as follows:

"Treason against the United States shall consist only in levying war against them, or in adhering to their enemies, giving them aid and comfort. No person shall be convicted of treason unless on the testimony of two witnesses to the same overt act, or on confession in open court."

Judge Frank further noted that the Rosenbergs rested two arguments on the provision.

1. Had the defendents [*sic*] been indicated [*sic*—obviously means "indicted"] and tried for giving aid to an "enemy" the crime charge would have been treason and they could not have been convicted unless the trial judge instructed the jury as to the two witness rule and told the jury specifically the ovet [*sic*] act or acts that a jury must find to justify a verdict of guilty.
2. Traditionally, and in this country by statue [*sic*—obviously means "statute"], the courts have been authorized to impose the death penalty for treason. To authorize such a sentence for a similar but less grave offense, in trial of which are omitted the guaranteed safeguards of a treason trial, is to permit "cruel and unusual" punishment in violation of the Constitution.

Judge Frank added that the Rosenbergs argued that the part of the Espionage Act authorizing the death sentence "is therefore unconstitutional; and accordingly, the trial judge should be directed to reduce the sentence."

"This argument we think" Judge Frank says "involves an unfounded assumption, i.e. that Congress will always authorize the death sentence for treason. Without that assumption the argument would compell [*sic*] the strange conclusion that, if Congress, in its discretion, authorized a maximum 20 yr. penalty for treason no greater punishment could be given for Espionage sedition or similar crimes without its becoming "cruel and unusual."

As to the first argument propounded by the defense, Judge Fank [*sic*] said the Court was bound by the law as interpretated [*sic*] by the Supreme Court on the case of the Nazi saboteurs who were landed on Long Island in World War II captured and later executed after trial. The Judge added

"This ruling has been criticized. But this ruling binds inferior courts such as ours. In the Rosenberg case an essential element of treason, giving aid to the "enemy" is irrelevant to the espionage offense!"

When Manny comes will hear more on this. Love you it's late now. Good night my heart— Julius

Julius to Ethel

April 10th, 1952

My Wonderful Woman,

I sent you yesterdays [*sic*] letter because I wanted you to be acquainted with the latest opinion handed down by the Circuit court of Appeals. It seems to me that the language Judge Frank uses clearly proves we will positively get certiorari. The thing that is most interesting besides his concession that there are debatable questions of law is that his answer on our two points instead of destroying them actually makes them stronger. This looks to me like our first opening wedge in the courts. Since our lawyer has to be in Court on Monday at the hearing of delaying the courts mandate until the Supreme Court gets our case, he will not be free to see us. From Ethel's letter it looks like he may be tied up Friday and he may not be able to be here this weekend. From the newspaper I gather he will have to have his brief for certiorari filed within thirty days. Anyhow I've got many things to talk to him about and I hope we don't have to wait too long before we have a legal consultation. Manny has a great deal of work cut out for him in the next few weeks. Saturday my sister will visit us and bring us up to date on all the latest doings on our behalf.

Sweetheart I've been very lonely lately and I miss your company very much. It is true that the good reading I've been doing is very satisfying but it also sharpens my hunger for you. Oh darling I need you so much, even as you too I suffer the pain of our separation and my only relief is to think of how beautiful our life was together. Sometimes I just feel sick to the stomach with all this barren, senseless and cruel terror filled waiting for execution. How true are the thoughts expressed about our situation that appear in the articles of Jewish Life.[221] It is good to know that even without the facts the entire Jewish press were aghast at the brutal sentence and condemned it. Now that the facts are being spread to ever wider groups of people they will come to our support and be the lever that will see to it that the Supreme Court grants us the justice we deserve. It's tough, hard and oh so long but it is the only road we can travel to win our complete vindication and still maintain our dignity, self respect and human stature. If truth prevails there can be only one conclusion and we will be home once again with our beloved family. Dearest you are with me all the time even though steel and concrete separate us and as long as I can be sure of you nothing else really matters. I'll manage to find the strength and sustain it with thougths [*sic*] of our relationship. Love you more than anything else in the world. Keep on being as you are and you will always inspire me.—Always devoted to my sweet wife—Julius

Julius to Ethel

April 13th, 1952

Darling Woman,

You know it's just wonderful to look at you and see you feeling good. While you were busy sopping up all the good news our dear Manny was telling us I had the pleasure to view your profound enjoyment and see the visible evidence of gratification you showed and your sweet face beamed beautifully. I too soared to new heights of emotional satisfaction at the

---

[221]A left-wing Jewish weekly which changed its name to *Jewish Currents* in the 1960s and still publishes today.

splendid work that is being done on our behalf by our lawyer, the committee and the many decent human beings who are supporting our fight for justice. Truely [sic] the news was very good and I am looking forward to hear continuous positive accomplishments by the committee on rallying the people to our cause. The news about our visit with the children was also very heartening and I am glad that after 1 year of your entombment in this slaughter house things are beginning to look a little better for us. Dearest many are the pitfalls that face us and the enemies we have are very powerful but we are right and are conducting a principled fight and that is the guarantee that we will win. The possibility of peace in Korea and a lessening of world tension will contribute materially to us obtaining a review of our case in the Supreme Court on it's [sic] legal merits and our chances for a reversal will be enhanced. Sweetheart I'm more confident than ever as we enter the last major round to reverse this travesty on justice that has been perpetrated against all Americans in our case. Yes my love hold on to your seat we're in for some rough times. However we know the score. We've got the courage of our convictions. We're confident the people will not let us down and we've got our perspective on [NWI] our complete vindication. Keep your chin up Ethel if we must suffer through this nightmare then in the manner we conduct ourselves we will contribute to the general welfare of the people by serving notice on the tyrants that they can't get away with political frameups such as ours. The common men [two words erased here] in our country when they know the facts [one word erased here] will fight for a just cause. It takes a lot of time and hard work to get them to overcome their inertia but now that grass root sentiments are aroused public opinion will have its effect. I had a nice long visit with my sweet sister and I'll save all of what we talked about for our Wednesday get together. Well in a couple of more days I'll be able to look into your sparkling eyes and see your winsome smile and adorable face and convey to you with my voice, eyes and demeanor my profound love for you my precious wife. We've left a big chunk of suffering behind us these last two years and we are coming closer to our emancipation from all this torture. All my heart I send you—Always devoted to you—Julius

Julius to Ethel

April 17, 1952

My Lovely Sweetheart,

It is now 6:30 P.M and dusk is settling rapidly into night and a couple of late birds, chipping [sic—probably meant "chirping"] sparrows, are still noisily flitting [N3WI] back & forth in front of the window facing my cell. Yes my love summer is approaching rapidly and the half hour the sun warmed my body gave me new desire to be free because basically I am a lover of nature and natural laws. The enemy of life is not nature but the tyranny of man and his inhumanity to his fellow man. Poets write about it, painters put it on canvas and singers give voice to it but the great people are the ones who practice brotherhood understanding and decency in their daily lives. The more I read the newspapers the more I become convinced that their [*sic*] are many powerful forces that are making our society sick and the tragedy is that there are too few people ready and wiling [*sic*] to take up the cudgels for right because they are afraid of being labeled as unorthodox in these days of conformism. This darling is the toughest part of our fight because a tremendous amount of work is necessary to overcome the inertia of the masses and to offset the opposition of the entrenched leaders, in the so-called "liberal" organizations representing the peoples [*sic*] interest, from preventing the people to rally to our support. To fully comprehend the difficulties we face is to know that even on the question of peace many of this [*sic*] "leaders" have refused to speak up. In spite of them and the reactionary forces, the interests of the people for peace and justice will move mankind to act in their own behalf. One thing we can be sure of is that in the teeth of these hardships steady progress is being made in getting the facts in our case to the citizens in our land and they are beginning to seriously discuss the issues that effect [*sic*] the lives of all of us. Since every day seems to take eons of time, I hunger to hear news of further progress on our behalf and I am glad that this Saturday my sister will bring [NWI] us the latest developements [*sic*] of what is taking place. Of course, as the weather gets warmer and the days are longer I miss you more and more but life has been good to me to give me such a wonderful wife and two precious boys and all I could ask for is to be free to build my life with my beautiful family. Just got a thought I want you to know that I wholeheartedly support you in your efforts as to ["what" CO] your plans ["are" CO] with Dr. Miller[.] I do hope the children will come this Monday I'm looking to a swell visit with them. Sweet Mommie take it easy and don't worry your beloved children look up to their mother and are proud of her and you always manage to come through with flying colors. Your devoted husband—Julius

Julius to Ethel

April 19th, 1952

My Sweet Bunny,

From the newspapers and from all that my dear sister Lena told me it is evident that the committee is having a great deal of success in reaching people and the responses that are pouring in are most heartening. When I see you I [NWI] will read to you from a newspaper clipping that will give you visible proof of the effectiveness of the campaign. We can be very gratified because the facts are beginning to reach the public and they are discussing the issues involved in our case. The attendances [*sic*] at rallies, the contributions and petitions coming into the office of the committee are bearing out our faith that the American people will fight for a just cause. Because of the results we are obtaining the jackals of hate and tyranny are spewing their filth and howling red to frighten and scare those decent people who have come to our support. But these monsters have helped sow the seeds of this monstrous frameup against the interest and lives of every citizen and they can not stop the storm of protest now that their nefarious game is exposed. I expect to see their campaign of vilification grow in volume and all the pen prostitutes of the yellow press will have a field day but the truth is out and they haven't heard anything yet. It feels good to know that we are fighting back on the important front of public opinion. This is notice to the usurpers of the constitutional rights of the American people that they cannot get away with it. Take courage sweetheart there are many thousands of good people behind us and daily more are flocking to our support. But as always because I feel good that progress is being made, I miss sharing the joy of the moment with you my dove and I have to be satisfied that the process of our freedom will be a slow tortuous grind but the victory will be all the sweeter. It isn't easy to carry on a principled fight when your beloved wife's life and your own hangs precariously in the balance. But for us there can be no other way for we are innocent and we are forward looking individuals who walk in dignity proudly holding our heads erect because we are at one with all decent human beings. We are conscious of our social duty to our fellow man and we will not let them down because the future happiness of children men and women are at stake in justice and peace. We did not create these issues they exist and we take our stand with the people fighting for peace and right.

Honey I'm going to write to my family on our behalf asking them to contribute funds to help defray our legal expenses. I'm sure they'll not let us down. Oh goody, goody. Wednesday is almost here and I'm happy when I'm with you. I hope we'll be able to talk about the childrens [*sic*] visit by then. Love you my precious woman—Your devoted husband Juluis [*sic*]

Mrs. Lena Cohen
140 Baruch Place
New York New York

April 24, 1952

Dearest Lee,

Today I received a letter from Ethel informing me that Manny was due here with the kids on Sunday. She said she thought you had mentioned they would arrive in the morning.

I would greatly appreciate your phoning Dr. Miller to this effect (that is, if Ethel heard you correctly) so that he'll know the afternoon is open for his usual visit. I wrote him asking him to check with Manny but since he may find it difficult to connect with that busy lawyer of mine, it would save time and energy if you undertook to get in touch with him yourself and advised him he will be able to see me Saturday, if he so desires. Full name is Saul D. Miller—400 West End Avenue, N.Y.C. If he's not in when you phone, leave following message—"Saturday afternoon visit for Ethel Rosenberg O.K., as usual"—That is all you need to say. If, however, Ethel was mistaken & Manny is due in the afternoon, say "Saturday afternoon not open for visit to Ethel Rosenberg"—

It might perhaps be a better idea to simply leave your name and phone number and have him call you back in the evening, if he's not available when you phone him; then you can speak with him directly, and make yourself perfectly clear. I really think it is better to do it that way; he's sure to call you back as you specify and there can then be no misunderstanding—

Will you do me this favor, Lee, just as soon as this letter is to hand? There's very little time left until Saturday and I'm hoping it goes right out—Thanks loads—

Want to drop Julie a few lines—Good-bye for now—and best to all—

Love, Ethel

Ethel to Julius

April 24, 1952

Dearest Julie,

Of course, we never even attempted to discuss what might possibly arise in the course of our conversation with the children. Personally, I feel that for this particular visit, we should simply guide our selves by the children's reactions as they reveal themselves to us and concern ourselves with nothing so much as just being natural and showing them the utmost approval and affection.

However there is one item that it might be well for you to be informed of. Perhaps Lee told you, as she told me, that Mike has expressed himself in no uncertain terms on the subject of camp; very simply, he's agin it! If he happens to broach the matter at all, will you permit me to sort of throw out the first ball and then, if it is opportune you might follow my lead and back me up tactfully. It is most important that we employ the light touch throughout, in any case, light but firm and self-confident. Oh, darling, it will be hard to wait but I feel [NWI] absolutely secure that we'll do right by them and ourselves!

Sweetheart, forgive me for being so stingy of late; I have an idea that I am [NWI] quickly approaching the end of the impasse! In the meantime, dearest, take all my love and all my heart—

Your always devoted
Ethel—

P.S.—Wrote Lena requesting she inform Dr. Miller about Saturday—E.R.

Julius to Ethel

April 24, 1952

My Sweet Mommie,

This guy here is nuts about you and wants you to know even when I'm not with you the thought of you is enough to make me feel good. Generally speaking I'm in a fine frame of mind and I'm looking forward to a wonderful visit with my boys this Saturday morning. Incidentally, I sent the letter we discussed to my family and I hope it will have the desired effect because we sure need the money to help defray legal expenses. I was elated to get my sisters [*sic*] letter and the snap shot the budding photographer Mike took of his little brother and his Bubbie. At our next visit I'll see those that your big fellow sent to his sweet mother. It moved me so to see our little fellow dressed, like a little man, with a nice new haircut, a colorful tie and standing next to his Grandma in his own home. How I long for our boys. It makes me nostalgic for the warmth and family atmosphere of our own home. Yet I am happy to know that they are healthy and for the time being getting affection and love. Of course, I'll be even happier when the home environment is the best possible available considering the fact that we are still incarcerated. I suppose we'll have to sign certain legal papers for our attorney in reference to our Supreme Court Appeal. For the present I've ["all my" CO, NWI] been concentrating on our beloved childrens [*sic*] visit and I'm sure we'll make it a very positive experience for the boys. Too bad they had to wait so long but I'd like to say now that if plans are made for them to go to camp I'd like to see them before they go away for the summer vacation. Since we do have to spend quite a bit more time at this Ossining Manor vacation resort we ought to plan to see our two dears on a more regular basis. This [partial word "nat" CO] naturally, depends on Manny's time. Oh sweet wife I can picture us going home to our two fellows and doing so many things with them. We must have the good fortune to have our appeal received properly and a just decision must reverse this brutal sentence. If all goes well by next time this year we may be planning the childrens [*sic*] vacation with them. I'll just have to stop writting [*sic*] in this vein. We'll have to go step by step torturously slow until we reach the first goal the reversal of the verdict of the district court. I'm going to talk to Manny about getting permission for the girls to come once in two weeks instead of every three weeks. I hunger for news from the Committee. I guess I'll get the National Guardian this weekend and seek some emotional relief there. Remember precious I love you with all my heart—Your devoted husband—Julius

Julius to Ethel

April 27, 1952

Hello Sweet Mommie,

Don't forget to send my brother a pass for this Sunday morning May 4th. I've just finished a chore. Four copies of the letter we composed to my family to help raise funds. After our visit I got a letter from my sister requesting me to write her copies of the last letter so all the family can get to see it. They were at a meeting last week and heard Mrs. Sobell speak[222] and they say that lots of meetings are being held. Anyway they want to do their bit for us. She sends you her best and hopes you are holding up under the tremendous pressure that is upon you.

Words cannot express as eloquently as your beaming face portrayed the effect of the childrens [*sic*] visit. It was such a grand feeling to even in a small way to capture some of the family atmosphere that two little dears create in just being children.[223] We will have many details to exchange at our next visit because each of us obtained individual gems from our boys.

---

[222]Helen Sobell, the wife of co-defendant Morton Sobell, became very active with the Committee to Secure Justice in the Rosenberg Case. After the execution of my parents, she continued the fight to free her husband which lasted until his release in 1969. For more on her role, see Morton Sobell, *On Doing Time*.

[223]Note that this indicates the visits were no longer separate. Louis Nizer's book *The Implosion Conspiracy* erroneously asserts that until the final visit we were not allowed to see them together (see pp. 395–96 and 433). This is based on a story created by Nizer that at a previous legal conference (allegedly occurring sometime in 1952, many months after their first joint meeting with Manny in Sing Sing) they had embraced so passionately that the Warden had ordered they be handcuffed and at the opposite ends of a table whenever they were in the same room together. Both of Nizer's stories are false—in fact, maliciously so.

We'll help each other recall the visit and in that way relive the delightful experience all over again. Ethel honey it was just wonderful and I knew we would make it a positive experience for the boys. The best commentary on the effect of the visit was the happy frame of mind we left the children in and they really enjoyed it and hated to see it over. We must repeat this again as soon as it's practical. Mike and Robbie have grown so and I like the rapporte [*sic*] that exists between them. I want us to emphasize in our letters to our family to make the little ones [*sic*] birthday a special occassion [*sic*]. If you have any idea on the matter write them as to the present they should get him in our name. In my letter to my sisters I stressed that they should make sure my brother is well briefed on all the latest news before he comes to see us next weekend.

Sweetheart I just love Mike and Robbie's mother and I was so glad to see you looking so well and happy. This is only a taste of what is in store for us when we do go home again. We must always keep the bright future in mind so that it will make our present hardship easier to take. The fact that so many good people are looking after our children and working for our freedom gives us added hope and courage to face the difficulties ahead. It is already Sunday night and Wednesday is not too far removed and of course the only time in the week that really counts ["is" probably omitted here] when I'm with you. Daylight savings time is here and we have two more hours of yard time and with one fellow going out of this place we'll each have more time in the yard. I'm still marking time and waiting for good news. I can be happy that I have such a wonderful wife and two precious boys to enlighten my life. We have all we need to live beautifully and and [*sic*] our freedom will give us the opportunity to fullfil [*sic*] our fondest hopes. You are always in my heart and mind. I love you so much my dearest. Your devoted husband—Julius

Ethel to Julius

April 29, 1952

Dearest Daddy,

You were so very sweet to watch on Saturday; so, for that matter were your sons. Am I ever in a state of gloom since; when will there be an end to all these partings.

It is so very difficult for me to sit still and to make some order out of all my jumbled thoughts, (especially when the mail is due to be collected any minute!); your silly girl procrastinates and indulges all her most unrealistic phantasies these evenings, when she should be writing her darling.

So I just had to get [N2WI] at least these few lines off before Wednesday, if only to let you receive some tangible evidence of the deep love and yearning the sight of my beautiful family has awakened afresh.

I love you, dear husband and dear daddy—and await your coming impatiently—

Yours, as ever,
Ethel

P.S.—Am sending out necessary request slip for your brother's visit on Sunday—

Julius to Ethel

May 1st, 1952

Hello Sweetheart,

It is now the month of May and naturally all my thoughts are of the fairest flower of my heart my sweet, adorable, beautiful wife. This has always been our month what we [*sic*—probably meant "with"] mothers [*sic*] day, Robbies [*sic*] and my birthdays and the blossoming spring, it has always been a time we enjoyed together. I hearken back to the hikes and outings we went on together and see the beautiful mental pictures of the many memorable moments we spent surrounded by natures [*sic*] own decorations of greens and flowers. We were so happy and youthful then and somehow even though time is passing in mind and spirit, I still have the same drive and zest as we experienced at that time. It isn't too difficult for me to readily understand this because a progressive active individual keeps the mind agile the emotions satisfied and makes for general well being. It is indeed remarkable the tremendous possibilities the human being has and the unlimited heights he can reach if the physical and social fetters that hold man back can be done away with. Above all this requires an understanding of people and conditions and with knowledge and perspective this can be a better place to live in. Many are the times, particularly after I read about some new scientific discoveries or medical advances that I think of how all people will benefit from these improvements and my thoughts go to our children and [N2WI] of all little ones in general and I know it is the primary task of all men and women of good will to make this a better world. That is why it is impossible to conceive of the horrible drift towards war and I am happy to know that many are the voices that are raised for peace and that the major part of the worlds [*sic*] population in all lands and among all people are fighting to win the peace. As in our case the facts and truth of the situation can not be hidden from the public and as time goes on the reports in the newspapers, even though many of them are slanted against us, proves that the Committee is becoming very effective and that these [N2WI] articles are only due to the fact that our enemies wish to counteract the good work done on our behalf. I am sure my brother will have lots of news to tell us and you no doubt have already read of the fact that Associate Judge [*sic*—should be "Justice"] Jackson of the Supreme Court has granted us until June 7th to get in our petition and briefs for certiorari. This will give our eminent counselor the much needed time he requires to dig the law and hammer out a good brief for our appeal. I'm confident that we'll get the writ granted to us and the important decision will come when our Supreme Court appeal is heard. Much as I hope extraneous issues will not effect [*sic*] the judges [*sic*] opinions I must be realistic and know that by past performances political considerations are most important factors in swaying their minds. Since our decision depends on many different things no one can guess what the outcome will be. However we must make sure that the best fight is made on our behalf. I am confident that we will not be disappointed by the American people.—All my love your devoted fellow—Julius

Julius to Ethel

                                                        May 4th, 1952

My Sweetest Darling,

I'll have to admit my sunshine that I have spring fever. How could it be otherwise when I have such a wonderful jewel for my wife and two precious dears for children and I have to be separated from them. The days are getting longer and even though we do get an extra ten minutes in the yard, the glory of living that the warm sunshine engenders is terribly marred by the agonizing loneliness of our incarceration. The brutal sentence that hangs over our heads doesn't make it any easier to wait out the time for our decision. One thing is absolutely certain and that is that a great deal of very effective work is being done by the Committee and they are reaching many people daily with the facts in our case and [N2WI] the people ["they" CO] are becoming acquainted with the issues involved and the ensuing discussion and thoughts are leading to positive action. I have high hopes that we will be granted the writ of certiorari and I am optimistic that the Supreme court will give us a fair shake and judge the case on it's [*sic*] legal merits which in turn must result in a reversal of the district courts [*sic*] verdict. The fact that the public is becoming aware of the truth will help nullify the mud slinging that the pen prostitutes are indulging in to prejudice our case. It is only possible for me to seek sustenance from my sweet family and [NWI] from news of progress in our behalf. It seems like eons of time are trickling by and endless torment, barrels of mental anguish constant emotional stress has been our lot and again we can tell the loss of time. Little Robbies [*sic*] birthday is near again, my birthday, mother's day and our anniversary. Incidentally try to get from the Rabbi a birthday card for the baby and write his big brother a note for the occassion [*sic*]. I'll do the same. If possible send my mother a card on mothers [*sic*] day. I can only be grateful that so much of our difficulties are already behind us and I have high hopes that the future will in a short period of time be much brighter for us. I am glad to report that my letter has had good results with our relatives and they are beginning to contribute financial help for us. My brothers [*sic*] visit although it was short was very fruitful. I'll have to write my family on a more regular basis because our letters are passed around and they are galvanizing people into action on our behalf. Well Wednesday isn't too far off and we'll be able to chew the fat together. When I'm with you I'm in heaven and all the horror that surrounds us ceases to exist when we are together. Oh my honey how I long for you and force myself to think of how beautiful our future will be. For otherwise it is so very difficult to be separated from you. Accept the love of all my heart—Your devoted husband

Julius

Ethel to Julius

May 6, 1952

My very dearest Julie,

Your last letter gave me so much pleasure, I simply have to attempt to drop you a few lines in kind.

First, belated May Day greetings! The time flew by so quickly last Wednesday, 11:00 P.M. was at hand before I could voice my sentiments. Please be sure, darling, to come prepared to-morrow to give me all the newspaper comment concerning this inspiring holiday, which [NWI] commemorates a far more genuine demonstration of Americanism than say, for example, the annual (?) world-shaking conference of U.S. Steel Stockholders![224]

Bunny dear, I miss you and my honies! [*sic*] Yesterday I looked at my precious photo of Mike, with his hair falling down over his forehead and his tie awry, and thought I should burst with longing! How I should love to

---

[224]May Day originated in the United States as a massive demonstration on May 1, 1886 demanding an eight hour work day. A few days later a violent clash between police and demonstrators led to the "Haymarket Affair." In 1889 the Socialist International designated May 1 as an eight-hour holiday for workers and it remained an official holiday of the socialist and communist movements. In the U.S., by the 1950s public activities had declined and anti-Communists attacked May Day as a holiday only for subversives. Anyone who marched in a May Day parade in the 1950s was a member of a small, vilified minority in the U.S. (See *Encyclopedia of the American Left* [NY: Garland, 1990], pp. 455f.)

have a similar photo of my Robby instead of merely a snap; I'll make a note to remind Ethel of a request for same that I made to Lee many weeks ago, that somehow got lost in the rush.

On May 14, my sweet [NWI] as the State of Israel ["will" CO] cele-brates its 4th birthday, ["while" CO] our Robby will [NWI] be celebrating his 5th; did you realize that this is so? [In the left margin alongside these three lines, the next four words are written vertically from bottom to top.] More power to them both!

Lover, good-bye for now; many kisses until I'm looking across at you from out of my cage [NWI] again!—Love you ever so much

—Ethel

Julius to Ethel

May 8, 1952

My Sweetest Wife,

It fills me with great pride to know that my letters can evoke such good feeling on your part. As for me I want you to know that your letters are just like "manna from heaven" and when I read them it is as if I am looking at a mirror and seeing the thoughts of my own mind before me. It is indeed uncanny that on such a great deal of topics our respective minds run in a paralell [*sic*] course. Therefore you too should not be surprised when your spouse is capable of thoroughly understanding the basic problems of our children and can express himself properly on the matter and suggest some remedies. However I must admit that it has been through your patient efforts that I have acquired a natural sensitivity and sound basis of relationship where our two dears are concerned. I know that when we do have the opportunity to live again as one happy family our boys will be able to reap the benefits of our better understanding. We who [number of words erased here] know how great the childrens [*sic*] need is especial [*sic*] is this true when they depend on their parents for the solid security that is needed in their formative years. Yes, sweet mother of our sons, I don't have to tell you as I am aware of your broken heart and endless torment for the health and welfare of your precious ones. You can get some solace from the fact that many good people are looking after them and we've acquired a great deal of support for our cause. More so can we take heart because of the principled fight we are waging to expose this miserable political frameup and in so doing stop this dangerous march of injustice. In spite of all the power of the press and radio the hollow high sounding phrases are not convincing and people are opposing the attacks against their liberties and are working for world peace. It doesn't take much to see that the foreign and domestic policies of our government are related to each other and they both are either progressive or reactionary. It is true that at times depending on situations and public opinion the politicians are forced to bow to the will of people. This is precisely why we can succeed even though the Justice Department is embarked on a repressive drive against the liberties and rights of the American people. Well this weekend should bring us a great deal of news and I hope it's good. I'll talk to my sister about the home situation and Robert's birthday and our present for him. I think you should take these items up with her too. Perhaps she will be able to tell us when our Manny will be able to see us. He does have a lot of legal work to do but I would like to hear some of ["the" probably omitted here] brief before he submits it. Anyhow he'll have to have our signatures on the petition so we can read it then. I've already received a birthday card from Lena & family. How sweet. All my love—your devoted Julius

Ethel to Julius

                                                                    May 8, 1952
My sweetest dear,

This afternoon there arrived an altogether captivating Mother's Day card from Lee. It has a cardboard base on which is mounted a huge cat over whose shoulders is slung a bag from which a kitten waves a paw. Each pussy is adorably fuzzy, and the big one is wearing an outlandish costume consisting of blue and white striped trousers, red jacket and cap to match sitting jauntily between two perky ears and shiny black shoes. I guess they are intended to represent Michael and Robby; in any case, it's an awfully cute affair which you will enjoy more fully when you can see it for yourself on Wednesday.

Darling, at this moment I am listening to a record of Rise Stevens singing Brahm's "Lullaby," eyes streaming, and the hurt and longing are so fearsome, I cannot contain my sobs. Please, sweetheart, we must urge Manny to do his utmost to get action as soon as it is humanly possible, on the children's needs. I have a feeling he will most likely choose to come on Monday, the 12th.

Which brings me right straight to my real reason for writing you, today. Julie dear, whatever greeting you [NWI] may receive in my name, will not possibly express the deep regard and love that fills me to over-flowing. I weep bitterly for the birthday joy that was once ours to share and am inconsolable—

Mail call— Love—Ethel—

Julius to Ethel

May 11, 1952

My One True Love,

Maytime has always been our month and it is replete with days that have special significance for us and is a constant reminder to me of the wonderful person I have for a wife.

In the first place the beginning of this month is a labor holiday born in the campaign of American Workers for the eight hour day begun in 1886. For us progressive people it has the added meaning of working for a peaceful happier and better world that all people need in order to more fully enjoy the fruits of our planet both physically and mentally. Since we clearly understand that the general welfare of all will benefit us as individuals and in the common effort lies the real chance of success.

Mothers [*sic*] day to us is not a sentimental occassion [*sic*] or one that has been thoroughly commercialized by business interest but is the time to reevaluate the mores that are based on motherhood. I refer particularly to the strong blood ties that welds [*sic*] the family together and the mother who bears the young has by natural instinct the inherent strenght [*sic*], love and drive to give security to her offspring. Naturally the father participates but the woman physiologically plays the greater part. I am not expanding any new theory or stressing the matriarchal nature of our present society but I am stressing the great reservoir of potential that when properly released not only serves to build a secure and stable homelife for the family but is also a tremendous force for peace and goodwill in the community. So my sweetheart on this occassion [*sic*] I salute you the mother of our sons because you have in the past and more so in the present continued to firmly protect the best interests of your family by standing in true dignity as a woman of principle and stature. Your children will always derive strenght [*sic*] and satisfaction from their mother. I know we are all proud of you. If we cannot share this day together we can [NWI] still be happy that you are a devoted sincere woman maintaining the best principles of Mothers [*sic*] Day.

It is difficult for me to tell you how moved I was to receive [N3WI] your letter with such a wonderful expression of love from you on the occassion [*sic*] of my birthday. Again I can say that the relationship we have been able to maintain in this death house, and in spite of all the horror and torment we've suffered, has still been of such a nature that it has inspired me to new strenght [*sic*] and courage and helped me see things with greater clarity. Thank you agan my dearest and I will continue to strive to make myself worthy of your love and high regard.

Wednesday is little Robbies [*sic*] birthday and our children are not only an expression of our union but [NWI] also our pride and joy. It is difficult to celebrate this day being separated from your precious dears but take solace in the knowledge that many decent friends are looking out for their welfare.

Ethel my sweet adorable person I love you with all my heart

You devoted husband— Julius

Michael Rosenberg
24-36 Laurel Hill Terrace
New York New York

May 13, 1952

My dearest Michael,

This letter is by way of special greeting to you on the occasion of Robby's 5th birthday and I am hoping you will enjoy celebrating it with him as much as he enjoyed yours.

Speaking of enjoyment, darling, I wonder if you can guess how much pleasure your visit provided for Daddy and me. Many times since I have thought of how you looked and what you said and how those precious blue eyes danced. Many times, since I have missed you and always do I love you.

Honey, this will have to do for now as they will be collecting the mail any minute. I am planning to write you a longer letter soon. In the meantime, however, I wanted you to know that all the miles in this world couldn't really separate us from one another and that we, too, Daddy and I, are sharing the birthday joy!

Now I am hugging you both [NWI] hard and smothering you with kisses. xxxxxxxxx

Lovingly, Mommy

P.S. My best to Bubbie.

Mrs. Ethel Goldberg
5347-65th Place
Maspeth, L.I. New York

May 14, 1952

Dearest Ethel,

The cards were simply exquisite, the rich roses of yours presenting a vivid contrast to the delicately soft coloring of your children's. It was their simple yet deeply sincere expression of concern for my health that wrung the unwilling tears from my heart. I wept then unashamedly for our collective pain and bitterly assailed the fate that had befallen your innocent brother through the unspeakably facile lies of my guilty one. For myself, I have disclaimed from the beginning of this fantastic frame-up, and shall continue to disclaim, any knowledge of or share in espionage activities of any kind whatever. Indeed, though I wish dearly to live, disclaim it I shall with the last tortured breath I draw!

But now lest I cast a cloud upon the richly deserved brightness of your own Mother's Day, I shan't delay a minute longer to share with you the many other "bouquets" I received from all over our beloved land! Artificial though they had to be, they transformed the plain dull, white of my bed into a lush blanket of breath-taking loveliness. I sat in the center of this gorgeous "garden," revelling [sic] in a veritable profusion of beautiful flowers. No color lines here! Violets, pansies, roses and daffodils, brown-eyed susans, tulips, daisies and orchids, Queen Anne's lace, buttercups, carnations and dogwood—all displayed their varied charms with a refreshing lack of concern for the proprieties. No less thrilling were the accompanying verbal messages, all expressive, that I am quite overcome with emotion.

How I should love to personally thank the "two expectant parents who fight for a better world for all children; the "unknown friend" who assured me that "we are many who believe in you"; the sister who admired "your courageous stand"; the couple who pledged, "to make the bravest mother in America the happiest"; and the individual who penned the stark but tremendously inspiring works, "we struggle on"! This does not omit of course all those others who expressed a heart-warming wish to see me re-united at last with my husband and children, and offered their [NWI] enduring love. Greetings to you all, good brothers and sisters, I am humble before your cherished gifts!

While I must spend my hours among the shadows, I am unyielding in my belief that the American people will not tolerate our legal murder and will find the means to bring the real conspirators against the peace and progress of us all to justice! Verily, the prophets of old spoke truly when they said, "Resistance to tyranny is obedience to God!"

Always lovingly,
Ethel—

P.S.—Please phone Manny immediately upon receipt of this letter—He is waiting for your call. Tell him [N2WI] also that I shall mail some stuff directly to him early next week. The foregoing letter is to be used for Academy rally—or [N4WI] for East Side rally—

Julius to Ethel

May 15, 1952

My Noble Darling,

I cannot begin to tell you how moved and touched I was after seeing with my own eyes the visible evidence of the expressions of support from many of our new found brothers and sisters. There can be no doubt that there is a tremendous grass root sentiment in our land that will fight for justice and right. This is also proof that the committee has been reaching large sections of the population with the facts and issues in our case. What is more important is that once the people are acquainted with the truth they are moved to action. This will go along way to neutralize the propaganda against us and in turn arouse public opinion to the point that will guarantee that our case will be judged on it's [*sic*] legal merits. Now that this political frameup is exposed our chances of getting a fair shake are greatly enhanced. Oh love of my life let us take heart for we are not alone and many decent men and women of all walks of life are working to help set us free. I would like to add this tribute to you my wife that your conduct [word erased here] principled stand and humble human dignity is in the best traditions of motherhood and you are a fine example of the courageous leadership of American womenhood fighting for the traditional [NWI] heritage of freedom and justice for all. Your [*sic*] just wonderful sweetheart and I want you to know I love you with all my heart.

When I'm with you everything is wonderful but once I leave you all seems empty but I carry along with me thoughts of you and I manage to make it. I'm looking forward to a real good session with our esteemed and distinguished counselor. Then the weekend visit of my sister Lena and additional news. Of course, I always appreciate reading the National Guardian and I expect to hear a report on the progress of the committee's work around the country. Oh Ethel darling I miss you so much and I'm concentrating my thoughts on the future and how beautiful it will be to set up house with you and the children again. Remember sweetheart things look a bit better than a year ago when I first came to this private manor at Ossining. Still I'm not under any illusions. I am well aware that we face many long days and difficult obstacles have to be overcome before we can really see victory but I'm still confident that we'll win our freedom. In the meantime I'll keep busy untill [*sic*] we see each other. I started reading William O. Douglas' "Strange Lands and Friendly People" and it promises to be a wonderful book. Take it easy my dearest I'll probably see you before you read this letter.

Always holding you close to my heart and in my mind. Your devoted husband— Julius

Julius to Ethel

May 18, 1952

My Wonderful Woman,

   I had contemplated writing this letter at 6:00 P.M. today but I got lazy and took a little siesta after supper. Then I awoke to have my eight o'clock coffee with the pie I left over from my lunch. Finally I got involved in a pinochle game and I had to interrupt my game because it is one half hour to jewelry collection time. You understand after reading one hundred pounds of newspapers a man gets tired and since it was a sleepy day in general with the weather uncertain I've been sort of lackadaisical all day. This weeks [*sic*] National Guardian brought lots of good news on the committees [*sic*] progress and my sister Lena filled me in on many other details. When we get together we'll be able to talk about it. Our good counselor is quite busy but we can expect him this coming weekend. By that time we will hear something of his brief because he may have a rough draft ready. I'll prepare an agenda for this session because we have a great deal to discuss with him. I forgot to tell my sister to call him and stress the fact that he should come prepared to give us enough time to adequately cover all that is uppermost in our minds. I refer particularly to the home situation. Of all my family Lena seems to understand it least and I think it is necessary for them to have an immediate conference with _____ & Dr. Freund[225] on the urgency of the situation because when they become fully convinced it will be easier to make the arrangements for my mother. I hope we'll be able to hear definitely that plans are afoot for the summer vacation. One thing is certain that our children's welfare is being looked after by my good people.

   Darling I'm lonesome and I miss you my sweetheart but I'll make it and I hope that you'll be able to find the going a bit easier while we're waiting for the courts to give the decision. I manage to pass the time reading, day dreaming, sleeping and of course eating. Then I wait from Wednesday to Wednesday when I can look into your beautiful face and see your sparkling eyes and take in all that you say. You must realize that our visit is very stimulating to me and the emotional satisfaction I derive from our talk keeps me in a bouyant [*sic*] spirit all day. As the new week approaches in anticipation of our tete a tete I begin feeling good and have something to look forward to. Naturally we're not in the best environment nor free of mental torment but I think it is to our credit that we have held up as well as we have. How could it be otherwise when we are innocent and are determined to fight this case on a principled basis and expose the threat that this type of political frameup holds for all Americans not only progressives. I

---

[225]The social worker that I saw regularly during this period. Dr. Freund had not had direct contact with us.

am pleased with the good progress that has been made to date[.] I expect nothing short of complete freedom short of complete freedom— Love your devoted husband— Julius

P.S. If you get the chance to write Manny tell him to give us enough time for our consultation. Love you Ethel

Julius to Ethel

                                                              May 22, 1952
My Sweetheart,
     No matter how many times I repeat the fact whenever I have the opportunity I must reiterate over and over that I love you with all my heart. You can understand it best by the fact that our side is strengthened because of the wonderful person you are and the wealth of abilities you possess. That is the reason that I am certain that your letters will mean so much to my family and I am sure the whoever will read them will be moved even as I your own husband am visibly affected by the power of your pen and the profound expressions of your analytical mind. At this time it is necessary for us to steel ourselves because as we approach closer to the critical stages of our lives' battle we must seek sustenance from our own strength and from each other and must at all times keep our heads clear and our feet firmly planted on the ground. We are not children and we fully realize the cruel foes we have and we must be on our guard for all sorts of obstacles and hardships. I have no doubt that we'll make the grade but nevertheless I want you my dearest to know that I have complete faith in you and your ability to stand up. As the weekend approaches my anxiety over our counselors [*sic*] visit increases and I've already made extensive notes to aid in our discussions. I do hope he is able to give us enough time to cover all the points that are uppermost in my mind. Ethel honey there are many occassions [*sic*] during the day that I think about our trial and if I could discuss these situations on the spot with you I am positive we would come up with pertinent material for our lawyer to work on. The greatest loss that I feel is the inability to share with you my jobs, thoughts and my love. For letters and a short period of visiting through a wire mesh does not adequately satisfy. If you do have the opportunity I would suggest that you too make copious notes to aid you in presenting a clear picture of what we need answers on. I want to take this opportunity to repeat to you that I think the letters you are writting [*sic*] are excellent, that is, as far as they go, and it is important that they go out as soon as possible in order to be really

effective.[226] I'm still eating, sleeping reading and just moping around and I'll keep on marking time till I see you my precious darling. Let us repeat our motto for we understand all the significance it holds for us. Courage, confidence and perspective. I'd like you to put on your agenda a letter to Michael that should go out by next weekend. Don't forget to remember me to the boys. All my love—your devoted husband—Julius

Julius to Ethel

May 25, 1952

Hello Sweetheart,

All of my concentration was on our consultation and I was straining to get as much as possible into the short time alotted [*sic*] us that I could scarcely look at you or talk to you. One thing you can count on is that all three of us will gladly give you preference at our next lawyer session and let you carry the ball until ["you" CO, N2WI] you are satisfied that the points you raise will be adequately covered. It was only natural that we should feel some frustration because in the rush we could not do justice to all the pressing problems that are crowding our minds. I am very gratified that we managed to get the ball rolling on a plan for the summer vacation for our boys. If you feel that it needs a more detailed explanation don't fail to write Manny a letter and give him a complete outline including the proposed alternatives. From now on we must work step by step on this matter and see that a proper solution is had to the house situation before the end of the summer. We'll talk about this in detail Wednesday so we'll be in a better position to brief our family & Dr. Miller on our views. Incidentally don't forget to put in for a Sunday morning pass for Dave.

We can well be happy and feel secure to have such a wonderful person as Manny handling our legal defense. He is worth his weight in gold and I am positive we'll get the best possible brief and petition prepared by him on our behalf. In a couple of weeks we'll be able to read his contribution. Honey I have no qualms or fears on the competance [*sic*] of our counselor on the contrary I think he's tops. I could tell by your exclamation that you too were very pleased with all the excellent news he brought us. I am sure this is only the beginning and we're bound to hear a great deal more good news of progress in the campaign to win our freedom.

It is amazing to read of the danger signs in international affairs and of the deterioration of the rights and freedoms of our American people on the

---

[226]From our mother's letter to Ethel Goldberg and her as well, it is clear that they had decided that at least some of the letters should be used in the struggle to save them, and thus they were obviously written with a larger audience in mind.

home front. Many very vital issues that effect the lives and interests of the people of the world are rushing to a decisive stage of decision and I am glad to see that the war makers and reactionaries are not having an easy time of it. Honey we have always been consistent and we will continue to be on the side of peace, justice and freedom and we will, as usual participate actively in this fight. This is the only way we can be true to our principles and know that we are working for a peaceful better world for our children to live in. I am therefore confident that with justice on our side, the truth will out and our complete vindication must follow. Love you with all my heart. Your devoted husband

Julius

David Rosenberg
430 E. 63rd St.
New York N.Y.

May 27, 1952

My Dear Brother,

I am enclosing a Sunday morning pass for June 1st. Please follow the usual procedure and visit me first. Your visits are all to [*sic*] infrequent and very short and I would appreciate it if you could work out something to give us a little more time. You no doubt realize that our only direct contact with the world we know and love is through our lawyer and family and visits are a very important part of our steady morale. We are very pleased with the great deal of progress the committee has made to date and don't fail to bring us a current roundup of all the late developments in our behalf.

Most of my day is still taken up with reading newspapers, periodicals and books. Of course for obvious personal interests I'm deeply concerned with our case but I'm also aware of its ramifications and direct linkup with the fundamental rights and interests of all the people. What is so terribly disturbing is the dangerous drive by vested interests that are pushing policies of massive armaments and situations of international friction that can only result in war. The daily press is so full of this news and it is easy to see through the high sounding empty verbiage of military men and servants of reaction whose basic interest leads them to the abyss of this madness that can only end in a great blood bath. I am entombed here awaiting my death at the hands of the same people who are backing this campaign that can result in mass death and this is ["what is" CO] the most crucial problem facing our people. Ethel and I have always been on the side of those working for peace and a better world for our children and for all children to live in. I have faith that the American people will rise to the occassion [*sic*] and save the peace. Brother you must understand that we are part of progressive mankind and as

long as we have life we will continue to stand by our principles. That is why we receive new strength and vigor when we hear that the peace movement is growing and that progress is being made in the fight for decency & justice so that all men can walk in human dignity. This is the reason for me and my wife sitting in the death house today and now that the frameup is being exposed our ultimate freedom is assured and our victory will be all the sweeter. I am confident and I want my family and friends to redouble their efforts because our cause is just and we must not fail. Send my love to Mama and the kids. Best regards to my sweet sisters and their families. Love—Your devoted brother—Julius
P.S. Show this letter to the girls.

Julius to Ethel

May 29, 1952

My Sweetheart Ethel,
    As I was playing my evening game of cards with my neighbor I glanced up and saw the bright sun reappear in the sky after the thunder shower. At once I got a nostalgic feeling to be with my family. I missed our sons so much and I felt so lonely. It was only for a few moments that I sunk into the depths of despair but I quickly snapped out of it. My darling our last visit was wonderful and I'm still under the wonderful effects of all your charms. I'm also looking forward to a great deal of news from my loving brother. Our lawyer is to [*sic*] involved in the legal preparations for our Supreme Court fight and he has not been in touch with all new developments and then too we haven't had a visit for two weeks therefore I expect we'll hit the jackpot. Good news is just what the doctor ordered. In another week our petition and it's [*sic*] supporting brief for certiorari will be filed and we'll have taken another step in our uphill fight to win complete vindication. In a couple of months it will be two complete years that the hysterical tidal wave of political prosecutions has engulfed us and made us into a case. But the catastrophe and hardship that has befallen us and our family did not succeed in its purpose to frighten the progressive movement and hide the nature of the political frameup. Besides our innocence I attribute our own stamina to our thorough understanding of the issues at stake and our standing firm on the principles of human dignity, justice and freedom that we have always espoused. We have always been clear, forthright and outspoken because we have nothing to hide but it is our accusers and prosecutors who are in mortal fear of the truth. This can be the only explanation of the lies and smears they have printed against us and the organized campaign to discredit us by preventing the people from examining the facts in the case. The fact that the hyenas of yellow journalism are braying so

loudly attests to the effectiveness of the committee in bringing the message to the public. The opposition is very strong and powerful and is still able to introduce some confusion but I feel certain that in the not to [*sic*] distant future our supporters will really break through and confound them with the growing tide of their positive actions on our behalf. I am confident we will win this fight to secure the justice we rightfully deserve. Daily I scan the newspapers for signs that peace is nearer and I am sure that most of the world feels as I do that this is what we all need. The hope of mankind this Memorial Day will be on peace in the world. For this all decent people must continue to work for. Remember my wife this here guy is madly in love with you—Your Julie

Julius to Ethel

June 2, 1952

My Adorable Darling,

I had intended for you to receive my last letter before my brothers [*sic*] visit but I forgot about the Memorial Day holiday stopping the mail. The net result is you'll read two at one time. Rain! Rain and more rain and after reading newspapers all day I fell into a drugged sleep. It has been my experience that after a visit with Manny, the family or you I reach such an emotional peak that when I lie down on my bed to rest for a few minutes I doze off. The funny thing about it is that after I wake up I feel so tired as if I've done a hard days [*sic*] work with a pick and shovel. Since I am so emotionally starved when I do get my satisfaction it is at such a rapid rate that I feel completed [*sic*] drained it's over. Anyhow I'm awake now and feeling good that in a couple of days I'll be seeing your beautiful face again. Remember dearest short as my brother's visit was it was packed full of good news and I was delighted to hear of the excellent progress being made by the committee in our campaign. I managed to squeeze in the couple of things we planned to tell him and I was well satisfied with the visit. We'll get to talk about it when I see you as I've made extensive notes. Keep your hat on my sweet in ten days our swell counselor we'll [*sic*] be here with the petition and brief and we'll have plenty of time to discuss things and plan the next period ahead. We've got a long stretch ahead of us my love so renew your lease and plan for a couple of seasons of Ossining housekeeping. In the next period ahead I'd like to see us do a little letter writting [*sic*] and I'm looking forward to a pleasant summer replete with good news on our behalf. Honey prepare an agenda for our next Wednesday tete a tete so we'll be able to cover a great deal of ground.

Sweetheart I looked up at the picture of our little Robbie standing in front of his sweet Grandma. Ethel what I saw moved me so. There was my beloved Yiddish Mother full of compassion, aged with experience pain and hardships and yet a symbol of courage and strength. We have so much to look forward to and it is so important for our loved ones and all Americans that we win a decisive victory in our case. I'm optimistic and with each passing day I feel more certain that we'll get the justice that is rightfully ours because many people are rallying to our support. It is gratifying to see how enthusiastic my brother and sister become as they become aware of the great extent of help the public is giving us. The positive results [*sic*] is in itself the precursor of more and greater progress in the campaign to win a new trial and eventual freedom. We must take new courage from our new found friends because they have made the issues clear to the public and the frameup is exposed and an aroused people will fight for decency and right— All my love your Julie

Julius to Ethel

June 5, 1952

My Sweet Woman,

It is June and spring and a young man's fancy naturally turns to love. For one who has been caged for so long, denied all means of fundamental satisfactions and having a wonderful person such as you for my girl I find the forces that effect [*sic*] me are of tremendous weight. That is the reason why I am completely captured by your charms and I am drawn like a magnet to you. My sweetheart I am [N4WI] at the same time both pained by our separation and miserable predicament and also proud to be married to such a fine and noble human being. Our visit and ensuing conversation brought back memories of our home life and I long to spend the hours talking to you of our own problems and of the world we live in. This period we live in is marked by many grave political struggles going on both at home and abroad. The crux of the entire situation is world peace and everything else is colored by the outcome of the great fight for peace. The national elections in our country through [*sic*—meant "throw"] into sharper focus these issues and it's the extent that the American People can discuss them and the manner in which they can express their choice that will have an important effect [*sic*] on the future outcome. We who understand must not be fatalistic but continue to work for our fundamental principles because no matter how rough the going may be the effects for peace and justice are never wasted but serve to strengthen the campaign to win a better world. For nobody who sees the issues is willing to surrender to death. Enough said about this for I'm sure you read the newspapers and are able to decipher truth from the pile of propaganda that is foisted on the reading public. That is the reason I look forward to my sisters [*sic*] visits so that I can hear our side of what is taken place [N2WI] and all that the press is trying to hide from the people. Again I will bring up the home situation, cover the vacation period and what we propose for our boys. My suggestion is that you tell my sister when you would like our counselor to put in his next appearance. It is my opinion the sooner the better and I hope we have plenty of time because a great deal of questions have been accumulating and I want us to discuss them and I'd like to get some answers from our sweet Manny. Dearest Ethel I want to congratulate you on the beautiful letter you've written to our two darlings and I hope you don't tarry any more in sending it out. Now is the time to get off some of your gems & they mean a great deal to us. You know honey that it means so much to me to hear your beautiful expressions and if I feel that way I'm certain others too will be moved by them. It is still June and I want you in my arms held close to my body and I'm confident this is the way it will come to pass—Your devoted fellow —Julie

Julius to Ethel

June 8, 1952

My Sweetest Honey,

Just a couple of reminders. Since my brother is due to go on vacation and the next week the committee will be very busy with last minute preparation for a number of New York rallies, my sister and I have tentatively agreed that Lena should skip this Saturday and come next week. Then, too, we are expecting our lawyer sometime this coming week. We leave the matter to your wishes. If you want my sister to come this weekend write her at once and she will come. Another thing you must keep in mind is that your letters must go out as soon as possible or they will not arrive in time to be most effective. So much for the present and now I can keep my mind on our coming visit and look forward to see my sweetheart again. We'll talk about my sisters [*sic*] visit this Wednesday but I want you to know that I discussed the summer situation for the children with her and she said she'll take it up with the others. I hope Manny puts in an early appearance so we can talk it over thoroughly and make our final plans. It is now 8:00 P.M. and I'll have to interrupt for my coffee interlude. I topped it off with a couple of cookies and they hit the spot. Outside of my reading and the boys making a bit of merry, time just drags and only the passing days and hope for a better future offsets the depressed feelings I am able to measure the effectiveness of the committees [*sic*] work by the loudness of the jackals of the prostitute press. It takes a great deal of strength to withstand the merciless lies and hysterical atmosphere and still maintain ones equilibrium. People who are politically immature can be stampeded into a fear paralysis but an awakened and alert public with full knowledge of the facts can act independently and fight for right and justice in order to maintain their own decency and dignity and protect their interests. I hope we'll be able to hear of many positive accomplishments on our behalf from our dear friend and counselor Manny. Make an outline dear so we can be ready to cover a maximum of ground during the time we spend at our consultation. At the moment I'm very lonely for you my sweet and I want so to have you in my arms and hug and kiss you with all my heart. It is me [*sic*] belief that in due time this too will come to pass and we'll both be very happy. Incidentally we should tell our lawyer at our next meeting just when the children should put in their next appearance before they leave for the summer vacation. Perhaps this time we can arrange for an entire morning visit. I miss them so much and am constantly concerned over their welfare. For their sake and for the good of all of us we must win this case. I am still very optimistic and I'm confident of our position and the justice of our cause and I have high hopes that we'll win a decisive victory. The nature of the case does not leave very much room for the Supreme Court to duck the issues and if they rule on them we must win complete vindication—All my love—Your Julie

Mrs. Lena Cohen
140 Baruch Place
New York New York

June 10, 1952

Dearest Lee,

Julie has written me concerning the intended switch of this Saturday's visit from you, to the following week, that is the 21st. I am simply letting you know that I think it is a fine idea in view of Davy's absence and Manny's expected appearance by the week-end—At least, I'm hoping he won't be disappointing us and postponing his next legal consultation until next week. Please, just to make sure, will you phone him and say we'll be looking for him by Thursday or Friday at the latest, Thursday preferably—If he has to delay coming until Saturday, please don't forget to tell him to come early morning as Dr. Miller is due Saturday P.M. You won't neglect to phone him will you, huh?

Everything is fine except that we miss the kids dreadfully and ages seem to elapse until we see one or another of our loved ones—and of course that includes our dear Manny—

Good-night—tomorrow's another day—and then it will be Wednesday and your brother and I can make eyes at each other through the screen! Until I see you Saturday, the 21st—all my love to every body, dear! Ethel

Julius to Ethel

June 14, 1952

Flower of My Heart,

It is a beautiful day, and I've just finished my Sunday dinner and I'm in a good mood to accomplish a pleasant task of writting [*sic*] to my sweet sunshine. Honey, I've actually been conscious [*sic*] stricken as I had planned to write you this Thursday especially so since I knew we would not receive the usual visit from my sister this weekend. Because I was so taken up with sending our dear Manny the first of two letters I had promised him and it was not until Friday afternoon while I was in the midst of hammering the second one that I remembered that I had neglected to communicate to you my deep love and high regard for you. I felt pretty bad as if I had lost an opportunity to be with you. For after all I do get so much pleasure in being able to share with you even though it is through the medium of pencil and paper. Enough said I've promised myself to be most vigilant to do right by my hearts [*sic*] desire.

From the little I could gather while our counselor read us portions of the petition for certiorari I can see we are very well represented in our brief to the Court and he has indeed submitted a [NWI] great legal piece of work. We'll have a chance to really appreciate it after we've received copies of it and can study it more carefully. I'm sure that as far as the legal end of our situation is concerned we're in very good hands and I am satisfied that we are very well represented.

Concerning the committees [*sic*] work from every indication they are doing a bangup job and we too are able to see the visible evidence of the positive accomplishments on our behalf. The news of the rallies, pamphlets and other activities will be anxiously awaited by both of us and I'm expecting good results. Anyhow when I see you this Wednesday we'll have a great deal to talk about concerning this end of our case.

I must say I was more than pleased with the progress to date on the summer vaction [*sic*] and more so on the ["the" CO, N3WI] solution to the longer term problem the general home situation. This is the news I'm most anxiously awaiting and it may be some time before we are able to get a comprehensive report from Manny about the latest developments. It is indeed heart warming to hear of the whole hearted support and concern strangers are showing for our boys. One begins to feel good that their [*sic*] is so much inherent goodness compassion and decency in people. True situations like this bring out the true colors in people and what I've been able to gather I am happy that my faith in people is more than well justified. After all is said and done this is the important asset on the side of peace and good will to man. Since we did become a "case"—although not of our own choosing, I am proud of the manner [N2WI] in which we have been able to maintain our dignity and self respect in the face of such hardship. Take new courage my love the future brings with it complete freedom and a [illegible word in parenthesis below] return to the life we know so well and cherish. Our day of happiness will surely come— Your devoted fellow— Julie

Julius to Ethel

June 15, 1952

My Charming Girl,

It is almost coffee time and I'm sitting opposite an open window catching the occassional [*sic*] breeze that wafts across my body that is only clad in shorts, in season with the summer heat. I look up at the calender [*sic*] and June 18th catches my eye. Immediately I think back to our preparations thirteen years ago in anxious anticipation of our coming marriage. We were so full of joie de vivre, so happy and so much in love. All through these years our union has been firmly built on a foundation of complete sharing and understanding and has continued to grow as we matured together. Is it any wonder that as soon as I begin to reminise [*sic*] of how beautiful our relationship has been I feel such a terrible loss and hunger for you. The little things we did together sitting down talking problems over, engaging in discussing [*sic*] that were mentally and emotionally stimulating and of course being able to make love to my adorable wife. Our accomplishments and personal developments, the fine family life we had, the growth and advancement of our children and best of all is the high regard, that people who knew us, held us in[.]

Ethel, wonderful woman, precious dear, life has been so good to me because of you and all that you have been to me in the past my courage and my strength is based on it. The splendid example you set for me of humble self-respect in demeanor and unassuming dignity of person fortifies my determination to strive to follow such noble characteristics. Because I know you are all these in spite of all difficulties that you face it is easier for me to withstand the vicissitudes of the coming period. I am humble before you my sweet and proud to ["be" probably omitted here] associated in life with so fine a person as you. Perhaps I can't put it on paper [word CO here] much of [N2WI] all that I feel inside of me for it would be easier to explain and tell you [NWI] personally all that you mean to me. I am using this letter as a prelude to our Anniversary visit this coming Wednesday and that will be our gift to each other. Accept my dearest all my heart felt wishes and the profound love of every fibre of my body. I am sure that by maintain [*sic*] the high standards you have set forth and by sticking to our principles of decency; [*sic*] dignity and right I am giving you the best present for this occassion [*sic*]. Fear not my wife all this misery must eventually pass and we will surely be restored to our beloved children and then we will begin to live again. Until I see you again I will fill every spare moment with thoughts of you. Remember my dearest if the past was good it is only a small percentage of what the future will mean to us. Let us take new courage from each other reaffirm our confidence and keep a clear perspective—Your devoted husband —Julie

Ethel to Julius

June 16, 1952

My dearest sweetheart,

All day I have been hankering to talk to you! Try to convince this silly heart, just try, that conversation between us takes place on Wednesdays only. It pays me exactly no attention and goes on longing for you. I am fully and painfully aware, of course, that your own heart is every bit as captious as mine!

Darling daddy, your special day came and went with nary a kiss from your wife or hug from your children. It came and it went much the same as every day comes and goes in here. How strange it is that some men should have the power to strip other men like themselves of their manhood, and force them to pattern their lives after the caged beasts all of us have gaped at, open-mouthed, at one time or another! Only how much more heart-rending it is for the beast in human form, whose brain persists in reminding him he is a man, not an animal!

I know you are on fire to know what, if any progress, I have made with my writing. Be duly informed, therefore, my love, your would-be literary aspirant finally sweated out one letter to your sister Ethel which took off from here on Friday. I am presently in the throes of two more, one of which, at least, I believe will go out by Tuesday morning. I have set Thursday as the final deadline for all my work, and feel confident I'll make it—

Dear, I am looking forward with pleasure to an exceptionally thorough confab with you on Wednesday. I'll want to take up, among other things, the question of the children's next visit and the gist of my conversation with Dr. Miller on Friday. He breezed in here like the breath of fresh air that he is and breezed out again just about 35 minutes later, but he managed to accomplish a fair amount of stuff—I'm so anxious to know the outcome of the plans that were in work for the children's week-end, that I'm hoping someone will be thoughtful enough to drop us a few lines concerning same, very soon—

All in all, it will be a difficult week to plod through until Lee arrives on Saturday. Forgive me, [NWI] then, dearest, if I grow impatient this very minute and throw down my pencil—Wednesday—and you, my darling,—can't get here soon enough to suit me—Be sure you come prepared to share your literary efforts with me; somehow I am not [NWI] too happy about my own—But, who knows, perhaps you won't agree with me and [NWI] will encourage me to keep trying—

Love you so very dearly, my sweet—and miss you worse all the time—Kiss me good-night, the way you used to, my dear husband—Your wife and children adore their wonderful Daddy— Your loving Ethel—

Mrs. Lena Cohen
140 Baruch Place
New York New York

                                                        June 18, 1952
Dearest Lee,
Thought I'd just remind you to come prepared to tell us all about the children's week-end, if it came off as planned, that is—Also, I understand Mrs. Allman had been due to go to New Jersey to size up the prospective summer vacation and report back on same, we'll want to hear all about that, too!

You might also let Manny know as soon as you receive this letter that we are not figuring to see the children until after the coming rallies—Perhaps by the time you get here Saturday, I'll be able to give you a fairly definite date—But he is not to come until further notice from us. You see, Julie and I are all tensed up over what has been happening and we are at present very taken up with a number of important written comments for Manny—So we feel it would be wiser to postpone our next visit with the children for at least another week—

We are both extremely anxious to see you, of course, especially since we have as yet seen nothing in the Compass concerning the meeting at the Biltmore—To-morrow's edition, [NWI] however may carry a news item—

Did you remember that to-day [next two words written under previous word] (June 18) marked our 13th wedding anniversary? We are not exactly delighted to be celebrating it behind bars, you understand, but we hold our heads up proudly, nevertheless, and are happy in the knowledge that we have led a decent, constructive life together and have built a fine family—One day we shall return to all that is sweet and bright, never doubt that we shall!

Give our love and best regards to all our well-wishers—Good-night, Lee, dear—

                                                        Affectionately,
                                                        Ethel

Ethel to Julius

June 18, 1952

My dearest darling husband,

How could I forget our biggest day; ashamed as I am to admit it, I must own up to this truly reprehensible omission on my part and beg your indulgence. I have only the [NWI] one thing to say in my behalf; I live with such a nagging, blinding misery, that I grow dully indifferent to the passage of time, even to messing up on a day with as much significance as June 18! The joy and beauty of our wedding day, my sweet, lights the dreary gloom for me, [NWI] however, on whichever date I desire; that I am also saddened to think on all that has been forcely [*sic*—could be a poorly written "forcibly"] wrenched from us, does not in any way dim its radiance. On the contrary, there is a deep and quiet exultation for what we have, with so much loving pride, shaped and molded, over the endlessly rich and varied thirteen years we have spent together. How very dear you have grown, my loved one; the future holds nothing more attractive [N2WI] for me than you and our blessed children!

Thursday, June 19, 1952

Bunny, I dropped your sister Lee a few lines reminding her to come prepared with a full report concerning the children's week-end, vacation plans, etc. I also requested her to phone Manny advising him to delay bringing them here for the time being. When I see her on Saturday, I'll have the date definitely set so she can pass it along to you.

Honey, next Wednesday we must discuss along more personal lines, you see, even though I thoroughly enjoyed the highly intellectual exchange that took place during our last visit, I felt cheated of a badly needed opportunity to let my emotional hair down. Besides, there are a number of urgent points with regard to the kids that require proper investigation. What can I do, your wife is a worry wart—She is, however, trying desperately to become a fairly presentable woman; to date, unfortunately, my efforts have availed me nothing but three shapeless, formless garments that will very definitely stand to gain by drastic alteration, [next words inserted] concerning which I am hopeful the authorities will lend a hand. Already, a desire to cooperate and give my [NWI] latest clothing needs the necessary attention, has been ["most" CO] admirably demonstrated and I am most appreciative, indeed!

I wish I could tell you that the work has been proceeding at a brisk pace, but the fact is, it has been dragging. Don't think that I am discouraged, sweetheart; I feel perfectly sure I'll make the grade!

Have you been kissing me good-night of late? Because I never fail to kiss you!—oh, darling, what a ghastly farce we are compelled to endure.—Is there no bottom to this pit of horror! So impossibly lonely and blue— Your loving Ethel—

Julius to Ethel

June 19, 1952

My Lovely Darling,

Ever since reading about the events leading up to the cancellation of the meeting I've been searching in vain through all newspapers and nary an inkling of what happened. Of course no one but the Compass protested this undemocratic act but how come they didn't follow it up and report on the meeting. Anyhow we'll know this Saturday when my sister gets here. I managed to get off a three page letter to our sweet Manny about this situation and I told him that we had both decided to write him on this matter and we would like him to fashion one coherent document out of it and use it to our advantage. Honey I'm sorry I monopolized so much of our short visit together and I'm sure you feel a bit disappointed because we were not able to discuss all the things you had planned for this tete a tete. Rest assured that next time I'll more than make it up to you as we don't often run into a situation like this. My thoughts begin to wander and I recall how wonderful it used to be when we were both home together. Each of us working and how much fun it was to help each other and share our work, problems, fun and love. It's just so good to know how it was and that when we win it will be heavenly.

My love I'm so proud of you. Believe me you wrote such a stirring letter it grips at the heart, emotionally moves to tears and is devastatingly effective. Truly my women [*sic*] you are a gifted writer and what is even more remarkable that you have such honest feelings and are capable of putting them in writting [*sic*] and I can recognize you by it. It's sincere, warm, nobel [*sic*] and yet it has a humble dignity to it. Such beauty my darling languishing in brutal isolation, overwhelmed by emotional tortures with death hanging over you and yet able to collect your resources and out of your person create this clarion call for justice and so re-echo the powerful drive to live and uphold your self-respect. Your principled conduct is a glorious example of the finest qualities of womanhood. Sweetheart I'm elated and honored to be married to such a fine person. Ethel you must understand it is not easy to put things in writting [*sic*] I would much prefer telling it to you directly. We'll have to wait till next visit and spend a little more of our time pitching verbal woo. You can guess it by now my dearest I'm crazy about you and madly in love. Do you suppose your guy is to [*sic*] old a married man for such youthful talk? Tell me when I see you what you think. Incidentally I told Manny that you would let him know when you want the children to visit us and that you'll probably postpone it for a week to someday around June 30th [the words "or thereabouts" CO here]. I am hoping that Manny sends along copies of the certiorari petition with my sister this weekend for I'd like to study it before he puts in his next appearance. Bunny girl this fellow if [*sic*—probably meant "is"] awfully lonesome and I miss you terrible. Thank goodness this misery too must pass and I'll just have to keep my sights on the future—Love you always devoted—Julie

Mr. Emanuel Bloch
7 W. 16th St.
New York N.Y.

                                                                June 21, 1952
Dear Friend,
     Today is the first day of summer and the only way I can take notice of it is to mention the occassion [*sic*] in this letter but the fight must go on and I'd like to bring a few things to your attention.
     On June 20th in the New York Times there appeared an item under heading "Epionage [*sic*] Bill Snagged" subheading "House Group Rejects Senate's Death Penalty Provision.["] The reason given that members said the bill's language was so broad that officials who supplied defense information to Britain or any other friendly power could be found guilty of espionage. Comparing the language of this bill as presented in this article and that of Sect 32 & 34 of the espionage [NWI] act we were tried under I find the identical language in both. The reason given above is the same as the one you gave in your brief to the circuit court and even uses the exact phrases. Perhaps it might be to our advantage if we secured a copy of the minutes of the committee and it is possible we would find that the tenor of the legislative ["action" CO, N6WI] as brought out in the debate supports our position. In all probability you have already taken care of this but I'm sure you don't mind my suggestion.
     I read Max Lerner's column appearing in the July 19[227] issue of the New York Post.[228] I will not dignify this demagogic disgusting [NWI] vicious baseless attack by entering into any polemics with this so called

---

[227]Since he was writing this in June, the date he meant to write was probably June 19.

[228]This column was an attack on a Rosenberg Committee meeting that Lerner attended run by, in his words, "pint-sized commissars" who had a real "catch," an orthodox rabbi. "How could he let himself be used?" Lerner wondered.

"liberal" apologist and hireling of the American Judenrat.[229] However I'll just make a few pertinent observations. The basis for Nazism was laid by the Goebells [sic] technique of propaganda. Attack the Communist and Jew and [NWI] then everything goes lies, brutality genocide and destruction of all opposition, socialist, labor, unions catholics free-mason and democrats. Today in our country this trend is yet at the ["first" CO, NWI] early stages and the hysteria is raised and created with the persecution of communist and all those accused of communism. This "eminent" columnist is guilty of the very things he accuses the Committee to Secure Justice in our case. [word CO, NWI] He presents no facts but he shouts red. No mention is made of the undemocratic act of denying the Academy of Music for a Public meeting, ["of" CO, N3WI] nor does he answer [the suffix "ing" crossed out from the previous word] all the questions the [N3WI] lack of a fair and impartial trial, the lack of even one shred of evidence to substantiate any charge against us only the obvious motives of the self confessed spies for doing the bidding of the prosecution as their part in a deal to frame us. The gentlemen asks us to prove we are not guilty neglecting to state this is not the way our system of justice operates for it is the duty of the district attorney to prove beyond a reasonable doubt by use of hard facts that we are guilty. Remember dear sir only recently you were denied the right to speak at a university because it was alleged you were a red. You cannot buy immunity by joining the conformists in their political pogroms against the left and the progressive. You howled because you saw the visible evidence ["of" CO, NWI] that the American people, the Jews of Flatbush [N7WI, "and" CO between sixth and seventh word] who learned the lessons of Hitlerism are rallying to support the Committee in its fight to rectify this miscarriage of justice and are rejecting your poisonous propaganda. Today my wife and I are [NWI] innocent victims of the political climate beware Mr. Lerner the Justice Dept has concentration [NWI] camps all ready[230] [NWI] tomorrow you too may be one of the many victims of growing neo-facism [sic]. Tell the Committee to keep punching the're [sic] getting results—Let me hear all that's taking place I'm feeling fine and very confident [letter continued on top of second side] Regards to all—As ever—Julius—

---

[229]The Judenrat were the Jewish authorities hired by the Nazis to keep order in the various ghettos. They often facilitated "orderly transportation" which inadvertently helped the Nazi killing machine.

[230]There was a section of the Internal Security Act of 1950 that provided for "preventive detention" of all individuals on a security index should the President declare a national emergency. See Belfrage, p. 137.

Julius to Ethel

June 22, 1952

Hello My Darling,

We wouldn't know it by the weather but the calendar tells us it is the second day of summer. It was the type of Sunday one likes to spend in bed but where's the inducement. Oh gosh! I do love you so much. Just the thought of you in my arms gives me a glorious feeling. I received and thoroughly enjoyed your last letter and we will definitely spend more time on personal things. One of the plans that was being [NWI] worked on for a change of home environment for our boys with the doctor in Jersey fell through.[231] I do not know any of the details perhaps you'll be able to get them from Dr. Miller if he is aware of the situation. I would suggest you write him or Manny that he be thoroughly acquainted with the facts so that he will be able to tell you and in turn I'll hear it at our subsequent Wednesday visit. It's too bad but we'll have to make sure that everything possible is done this summer to prepare for a change by fall for our children.

Lena's visit and the splendid news she brought was most gratifying. Honey the results the committee is getting on a grass roots level is most promising and they have begun to prove to me that they can really make this campaign the kind of one we had both hoped for. See dearest our faith in the goodness of the American People is well justified and this is the best sign that they will be effective in assuring us the justice we rightfully deserve. I've prepared a number of interesting items to tell you about when I see you at our weekly session of jawing. I am anxiously awaiting the coming issue of the Guardian to read about the rally. Anyhow my sweet sister Ethel will be able to fill in more of the details next Saturday. Remember darling we expected to measure the effectiveness of the committee work by the loud braying of the pen prostitutes and we are reading about that now. I am very elated to hear that you have been able to finish some of the writting [*sic*] you were working on but I want you to know that whatever you do or don't do it is all right with me. I'd like to get some copies of the material the committee is issuing. I'll talk to my sister about it and see if Manny can arrange it. Right now Ethel I feel cold lonely and a little bit fed up but I guess I'm entitled to my share of griping. Well I'll just think about you and I'm already [N2WI] beginning to feel better. This Wednesday I intend to pitch a little verbal woo. Aftert all we're certainly entitled to that little. I suppose I rambled in this letter because I didn't want to take up Any [*sic*] of the matters we can discuss face to face. Many times today I thought of the children and I realized how your motherly heart aches for your two dears. It is my fervent hope and wish that this suffering should come to a

---

[231]See *Sons*, p. 136 for a brief reference.

happy end as soon as possible. We'll talk about the boys when I see you— Precious woman accept all my love my heart goes out to you—Your Julie

Julius to Ethel

June 26, 1952

Hello Sweetheart,

It's almost coffee time and I just remembered that it's time to send you a letter. Today was moving day for five of us and I'm now closer to you residing in #1 cell in the west wing. What a day to move and I spent a couple of hours washing bars, sink, bowl and floor. For most of the day I was bathed in sweat but I feel pretty good now as the cell is very clean and has been recently painted. The piece de resistance is a new and fluffy mattress and outside of missing the pleasant company of people I've lived with for more than a year, I'll get along. Dearest I can tell by the loud braying Howard Rushmore is doing in the Journal American and trying his darndest to present public rallies on our case that the committee is having a great deal of effect in order to provoke such a barrage of lies, distortion and vicious statements by the pen prostitutes, the propagandists of reaction. I am positive my sister will have a great deal of news about the rallies and the committee's work and we'll get briefed on all the latest happenings. Incidentally if Dr. Miller has any significant news on the children tell my sister to pass it on to me at our visit Saturday afternoon.

Honey I am greatly inspired by the letter you wrote and it's [sic] sincerity and basic humaness [sic] is evident for all to see and it will have a good effect on the reader because he will see us as the people we really are. You see Ethel when we are both prepared for our weekly visit it is a most fruitful one and we cover a great deal of ground. Darling keep on trying we're doing alright and I can see by your accomplishments to date that you too derive the personal gratification from a good job well done especially when one considers all the adverse conditions you are living under. This fellow of yours is just nuts about you and I know he has the best girl in the world for a wife. I am beginning to get a little anxious over the coming visit of our two dears but it's only natural as the time draws closer when their precious presence makes itself felt on our hearts and minds. Without a doubt we'll come through with flying colors as usual and from past performances each succeeding visit with our boys is better than the last one. I hope they'll be leaving for the country soon for this weather is oppressive and I'm sure the're [sic] going to thrive [NWI] what with good company, good play and good fun. We'll have to tell my sister to make arrangements for us to hear from the boys and all about their progress at regular intervals. Perhaps they can write us directly, anyhow let us suggest it to her. Also I'll talk to my family about my mother visiting us. You understand I'm worried about her traveling alone and in this hot weather I'd feel more secure if some arrangements could be made for her to get a ride to and from Ossining. Try to keep cool and collected my love. This here husband of yours is still carrying the torch for you in spite of the great heat wave. All my love—Julie

Julius to Ethel

6/28/52

Dearest Sweetest Wife,

Look at me I have fifteen minutes before breakfast so here is a short note. Honey we were so busy talking I clean forgot to tell you about the wonderful letter you sent me. It is always a source of hidden pleasure and joy for me to read and reread your flowing epistles. Darling I too long for you and thrill at the fact that you echo my sentiments with your written word. With us there is no diluted method or half way measure our relationship has grown and sustained itself to the point that our complete unity found it's [*sic*] expression mentally and physically very satisfying. In these days of our forced separation a painful void exists in our loneliness from each other, our family and from our cherished freedom. However, it seems to me that we have been able ["able" CO] to find in ourselves and the thought of each other that emotional and mental stimulas [*sic*] to not only withstand this miserable existence but to continue living in dignity and strive to enhance our character. Locked up in the "C-Cs" life is seen in sharp relief and we can observe our fundamental character as it is stripped bare. We see it clearly, shortcomings and good points and we are proud. For that's the way it should be. The basic stuff is there and we are building upon it and developing ourselves to better absorb the fruits of life. ["in this" CO] It is because we are at this point in our development that we discussed at the last visit our mutual personal problems. Yet I didn't feel comfortable because we had to share with outside parties what is our own and I don't want to share these with people even though they might understand. I just don't want to be bothered that they might not be able to see the justice of our position and somehow I was on the verge of telling them now go away. Why do we have to be the butt of other people's mistakes? Always we have to give and heaven knows we have leaned over backwards swallowing our pride and pains. I hope we'll have the strength to throw off these shackles and feel free to objectively react to these circumstances. We must continue to search these problems out and lay them bare so we can put them in there [*sic*] proper places. My love, my heart you suffer so have courage the joys and beauties beyond each obstacle are greater and better. We have tasted some of the fruits ɔf life and as our horizon increases we must have more. All my love your own—Julius.

Julius to Ethel

June 29, 1952

Hello Darling,

I am so completely enamored of Manny's petition for certiorari ["that" CO, NWI] and with every additional reading I am further impressed. It is without doubt a stupendous legal document concisely and poingnantly [*sic*] hitting at the core of our defense displaying a beautiful integration of language legal argument and devastating logic. This is a splendid piece of work and if it gets the attention it is supposed to receive ["in" overwritten by next word] I have very high hopes we will be granted certiorari. I would like to see that copies of the petition and the appendix are circulated as widely as possible to clearly show the nature of our case to all those who care to learn the truth. By the time you read this you will already be acquainted with my personal congratulations to our illustrious counselor. His superb performance is the best possible we could expect. He has earned our everlasting respect and gratitude for this job alone not counting his firm and constant devotion as a friend and for all the support & help he has given to our children. Our relationship with him is the high point of two miserable years we have spent since our arrest and helps us to maintain faith in the goodness, dignity and virtue of mankind. Manny is a jewel and a prince of a man. I am proud to be represented by a person of such ["calibre" CO, NWI] nobel [*sic*] character.

My sister and I had a wonderful visit. She was able to stay till the end of the visiting period because one of the other people would give her a ["lift by car" CO, N2WI] car ride into the city. I was elated over the good news she brought of the successful rallies and I was pleased to hear that H. Rushmore lied when he reported in his column that Rabbi Sharff would not appear anymore at our rallies because it was charged that they were "communist controlled." When I see you this Wednesday we'll have a great deal to talk about. Because I'm positive our visit with our precious boys will come off with flying colors I want to congratulate you on you [*sic*] beautiful handling of the situation. I just love the mother of my boys and I see in them the great deep part you play in my life. To tell you the truth dearest I am a little anxious in anticipation of tomorrows [*sic*] visit with our sweet family and I want it to be a very positive experience for our boys to take along with them on their summer vacation. I spoke to my sister about arrangements to keep directly in touch with the boys and plans for my mother visiting us once in three weeks.

Say darling I'm only thirty feet away from you and yet I'm so terribly lonesome for the steel doors and concrete that separate us are equivilent [*sic*] to endless ["space" CO, NWI] distances and impenetrable barriers. The petition & the splendid news of the committees [*sic*] work gives one new courage and stamina to withstand the trials & tribulations of all that still falls [*sic*—perhaps meant "follows" or "falls to"] us. We are getting closer to our final decision and I'm optimistic that we'll win our freedom. Love you with all my heart—Your devoted— Julie

Julius to Ethel
                                                              July 2nd, 1952
My Sweetest Girl,
     It makes me so happy to look into your sparkling eyes and hear your sweet voice talking about things we are glad to share. Fortunately I became aware that Friday is a holiday and therefore no mail and I must avail myself of this opportunity to write you. We have had two splendid visits this week and our personal satisfaction is enhanced by our own contributions and our steadfast maintance [*sic*] of self-respect and human dignity. You know sweetheart our team is pretty good and I'm proud of us. Let's try to pass this summer by continuing to do our utmost to help our children and our case. Now that we're making progress [N2WI] let's keep a steady pace ["within" CO, N3WI] in spite of physical [N2WI] & mental limitations will go a long way to keep our spirits high. Decorating most of ["the" probably omitted here] wall above my desk is a full page of the July 4th issue of last years New York Times on which appeared the Declaration of Independence. By now it's turning yellow with age and in one corner alongside the other signers appears my name. Since I don't take second place to any other American in my loyalty to my country, it's great principles and glorious traditions and I have always held this Declaration of Independence as the cardinal cornerstone of our republic I too with many other of my fellow citizens celebrate this occassion [*sic*] in keeping with this nobel [*sic*] heritage. And by our conduct in this case, where our life is at stake, is in keeping with these fundamental tenets of our democracy. Advocacy of better conditions, social improvements, civil liberties and world peace are in the best traditions of the forefathers of our country. It is not necessary to conform with the political hacks who are in the saddle to-day to be a real patriot. No amount of distortions and deliberate rewritting [*sic*] of history can hide the real lessons of the progressive drive of the modern minute-men and women for life, liberty and the pursuit of happiness. To me I can best use this occassion [*sic*] to read Charles & Mary Beard's history of America and study the meaning of all that is happening today. The new tyrants are

usurping our rights, emasculating our constitutional safeguards and threatening the peoples [*sic*] liberties and lives. We are right and we must win. The knowledge that our foundation is sound, confident that our cause is just with courage in our determination to vindicate our names we face the future with optimism. Our perspective is clear and although we suffer through endless hunger, longing and torment we are positive that the final victory will bring us our freedom. This is the thought that is uppermost in my mind tonight and I take you in my arms and hold you close as I kiss you tendely [*sic*]. Without doubt ours [*sic*] is a beautiful relationship and this is what makes us strong. I'll write to you again this weekend—Your [*sic*] always in my heart and mind—Your devoted fellow—Julie

Julius to Ethel

July 6, 1952

Hello Sweets,

I'm sitting in my cell dressed in shorts and I'm sweating, but the weather doesn't bother me now for I'm taking myself to a pleasant pastime writting [*sic*] dearest a letter. The long holiday weekend, no mail and no family visits makes it seem so long ago that I've been in touch with the world I love. Thank goodness Wednesday is drawing near and I'll have the pleasure of your wonderful company. Incidentally through some slip up I didn't receive a copy of this last Friday's Compass. If anything of interest appeared in that issue tell me about it when we meet. I am impatient for our next legal consultation and I hope you will make arrangements with Manny to put in an early appearance and to be sure to let us have enough time to discuss all pressing problems. By the time I see you I hope one of us has received word about the boys. In all probability my sister will send us a letter and tell us about our two dears and when my mother is coming to see us. Darling it must be the climate that seems to slow everything up and time hangs so heavy but we're in July now and before we know it the second anniversary of our incarceration will have passed. Slowly but steadily we are moving closer to the ultimate decision in our case. I've reread our petition to the Supreme Court a number of times and with each succeeding reading I come away more convinced than ever that we must be granted certiorari and have our conviction reversed. The analysis leaves no doubt that there can be no argument against the facts and the legal logic. Again I must repeat it is a stupendous piece of work and I'm totally enamored of it. I suppose in a little while Manny will receive the reply brief and we'll hear the opposition's case and I believe it will be a repetition of the prosecutors [*sic*] tactics at our trial and at the Circuit Court of Appeals. I have high hopes that here it will not work and the case will be decided on it's [*sic*] merits only. Honey girl I look at your picture and I sigh. Heck! I'm so lonely I miss your precious presence near me, the tender warmth and good heart and fine mind. So near and yet so terribly far away. My wife, my heartache increases my determination to fight all the harder for our speedy victory and with renewed vigor I prepare myself for the difficulties that face us. I've been digging into the "Fight against Fears" and I've only seventy full pages left to go. It is truly a remarkable book because of the insight one gets from the problem analyzed but I must caution that the lessons one learns must take into account the specific and not try to generalize. For that must be left to the professional who is better equipped to handle such matters. If we have the opportunity we might spend some time discussing this book. Sweetheart I kiss you tenderly every night as I hold you in my arms. Your [*sic*] always in my mind and in my heart—Your devoted husband

Julie

Julius to Ethel

July 10, 1952

Hello Darling,

When I left you yesterday I went away with many mixed feelings and at first I was going to get it off my chest and write you at once but I decided instead to prepare myself for Daves [*sic*] visit. In the meantime my thoughts Jelled [*sic*] and I must confess that I let my emotions dominate my better judgement and the net effect way [*sic*—probably meant "was"] a disturbed visit and I was not able to be objective about the situation, I ask that you understand my own short-comings and I will try harder to give you your due. Instead of building your own self confidence I erred. This is the main point that our objective must be confidence between us and among our friends and in this spirit we can accomplish what has to be done. Dearest you looked so beautiful in your new dress and were in such good spirits that I just feel terrible[.] I hope when you receive this note you will be in a better frame of mind. At our next get together we'll discuss the lessons this should teach us {better still just me}. Besides the matter we decided I should talk to my brother about I'll discuss the situation concerning my mother with him. By the way I don't know if you received a typewritten letter from your big boy Michael like I got. He says the're [*sic*] both fine, enjoying themselves, swimming and having fun. I'll try to get a letter off to him sometime tonight. It sounds just like him and I'm sure he typed it. I have high hopes that this summer vacation will be a most positive experience for our children and that they will be able to broaden their experience through contact with other children and good wholesome outdoors play. I'm sure they will not be lacking in love, affection companionship and a feeling of security that they are being accepted for what they are, [NWI] just children.

Sweetheart we have so little time to discuss what we feel ["need" CO, N2WI] we ought to and I again suggest that we prepare an outline to guide each of us in presenting in concise form all that we wish to cover. Many things were left unsaid this last time and I want to make sure that at our next visit we don't part with any frustrated feelings. Again honey accept my sincere regret for helping mess up our precious visit and I'll try hard to be on the ball from now on. I want so to prove my love to you by my exemplary conduct in our relations. Because without a doubt I was at fault this time and I created, by my demeanor unnecessary tensions on your part. Say alls' [*sic*] forgiven Ethel. I've been holding you in my arms and kissing you sweetly and whispering love to you sweet wife and I hope that [word "it" CO] I was able to salve some of your pain. Keep your chin up and continue to brighten my eyes with your lovely smiling face for you set the pattern for my morale. I guess I'm in the mood now to write to our sweet fellows. Have a good visit with my brother this Sunday. I'll write you again this weekend— All my love— Your devoted fellow— Julie

Master Michael Rosenberg c/o B. Bach
R.D. 2 Box 148M
Toms River N. J.
                    [No date, but the envelope was postmarked July 11, 1952]
My Dearest Sons,

I was very much pleased by the nice letter I received from Michael. It warms my heart to know that you are having fun and getting along nicely. Just as your mother and I told you at our last visit and which you yourselves know we have many dear friends and there are lots of good people who are decent and are doing all they can to help us. Now my boys you are experiencing the understanding, affection and love of two fine people Ben and Sonia who are strangers.[232] Therefore you should feel free to ask them for answers to any questions that are troubling you and I am sure you will get the right kind of response.

Since you are going to be busy having a good time, going places and doing things and you may not find enough time to write to both Mommie and me I suggest you write to your mother and Wednesday when I visit her she will be able to read me all the news you send her. Of course I want you

---

[232]From context he appears to have left out the word "not" before the word "strangers." Ben and Sonia were definitely not strangers to the family. See *Sons,* p. 136.

to know I am most interested in hearing about the day camp, the swimming and all the activities [NWI] that you and Robbie are indulging in. I'd like very much to be with you boys and your mother on vacation but that will have to wait until we win this case. In the meantime I want to assure [NWI] you my children that I miss you very much and I love you with all my heart and we your parents will keep in touch to make certain that you are doing alright. Bubbie Sophie was up to see us and told us how you managed at home and I am very confident that you will have a wonderful summer vacation.

Don't forget to send my regards to Ben, Sonia, Leo and Maxine[233] and all our other unknown friends. Remember sweethearts your job is to play, be happy and have fun and we your parents, Manny and other grownups will continue to work on our case to win our freedom. You have seen how confident we are so don't worry because many people are learning the facts of our innocence and are coming to our support. Before I forget I want you to know that we enjoyed our last visit very much and the next time I see my two dears we'll both have many good things to talk about. So let's hear good reports of your progress. As for me I'll keep on reading, writting [*sic*] and working on our case and I am very confident that in time we will be reunited as one happy family as we have lived in the past. I'll talk to your mother and arrange with her for us to take turns writting [*sic*] you. Have fun kids the country is a wonderful place to be in the summertime. Perhaps it will be hard to recognize you what with all that sun, good food and nice people. So long for now—Daddy—Julie
110649

Julius to Ethel

July 13, 1952

My Precious Woman Ethel,

I hope this letter finds you in a pleasant frame of mind. As for myself I am in very good spirits. Dave brought very good news about our children and the work of the committee. Also we talked about all that you and I discussed and I am well satisfied that he will do his best to help us in carrying out his part of working with our lawyer. Since Manny went to see the kids we'll get a first hand account of how they are getting along. Dave spoke to my mother but it is quite hard for her to understand but we can rest assured that he sees eye to eye with us on the need for a proper solution this summer to the home situation. Of course I was terribly upset about the

---

[233]Ben and Sonia's children. Maxine was a college student living away from home, Leo was four.

trouble my mother is having with her eyes and we'll talk to Manny about getting her a specialist ["and" CO, NWI] to look [suffix "ing" crossed out from previous word] into the matter before it gets any worse. It was a very good idea that you had in writting [*sic*] my sister not to come because she had planned to be here last Saturday. Our counselor would make me happy if he puts in an early appearance so that we can settle a number of important questions in my mind. I particularly hope we can complete this consultation before our Wednesday visit. Before I forget there was something I read in the Herald Tribune that corroborated what my brother told me that the Committee to Secure Justice is forming many committees all over the country. They are getting very good results and I am very pleased with the progress. Our distinguished counselor and dear friend Manny will give us all the latest developments in our case.

Sweetheart I am pining for you and I wont [*sic*] feel better untill [*sic*] I see your beautiful face and lovely smile again. Then your voice will be sweet music to my ears and my heart and mind will be gratified with our mutual sharing. This week will be two years that we have been torn from each others arms and [NWI] away from the warmth of our love. But the physical separation combined with the many difficulties we face has not been able to change our individuality nor our wonderful relationship and as man and wife we have stood up well under this ordeal. A great deal of heartache is behind us and I guess there is still more ahead of us but I am certain we will make it and above all we will win our principled fight for justice. Time is passing although very slowly and we are getting to the most crucial part of our fight. Keep your spirits high and your chin up for we will win our freedom. Darling the beautiful part of it is that we will win in more ways than one and I am ["discounting" CO, word "not" inserted and CO, N2WI] talking about our own personal makeup as human beings in this consideration. To the world and also for our future peace has a most important effect on our situation. For if extraneous things don't enter our case we'll get a reversal. Honey girl accept all the love of my heart. Your devoted husband —Julie

Julius to Ethel

July 17, 1952

Hello Sweets,

After such a wonderful visit with you I am in an excellent state of morale. Why do you know that some of the people here say that when I come out from the womens [*sic*] wing my face is all lit up and my eyes seem to sparkle? Do you know that it is exactly how I feel? It is so refreshing and just plain beautiful to be with you for this period of time. Of course, we accomplished a great deal and I am positive we're getting into a routine that will continue to give us very fruitful sessions. Sweetheart it is already two years that we've been plagued with this unbelievable nightmare. Can we ever measure it in tears, heartache and endless mental anguish? Who can tell the permanent marks this will leave on our beloved childrens [*sic*] lives? We are optomistic [*sic*] about the ultimate outcome and we fully understand the importance that our case holds to our fellow citizens. The past has been difficult but I go into the third year with renewed confidence in our chances to win a square shake and have our conviction reversed. No matter what confronts us [N2WI] I'm sure we'll continue trying to win our complete vindication.

It is hot and uncomfortable and here am I only a short distance away from the one I adore and all my thoughts revolve about how much longer must we endure this cruel separation. Quick, quick time bring us at once to our future happiness—at home with our two boys. This too must surely come to pass and in the meantime we hope to meet it in the best possible emotional mental and physical state. More than anything this trouble has given us an opportunity to look at ourselves and what I found pleases me very much. We've got the stuff honey and we'll make it with flying colors. Another three months and we'll know where we stand on certiorari so keep smiling and keep that lovely chin of yours high. Remember darling your three boys are rooting for you and we count on you keeping your spirits high. That in turn puts us in the proper frame of mind. As I look at you and your sons [three words CO: first: "on," third "hanging", second unreadable— "your" inserted above and CO, N3WI] in the pictures on my wall they give [NWI] me such courage and guarantee me that I will have the strength to withstand all that faces us. For although all I possess is my family it is a most precious treasure and it insures us a happy life when we are free again. I take pride in you and the boys and I try my utmost to enhance our common worth with my humble contributions to our relationship. Wife of mine better days are bound to come and righteousness must conquer [NWI] over evil and in spite of all obstacles our innocence will become known to all. Words, words when what I need is you in my arms and I can hear your comforting voice —All my love—Julie

Julius to Ethel

July 20, 1952

My Precious Darling,

You looked lovely as usual last Friday and although you didn't know it from my demeanor or from what I said I was so pleased with the clarity of your understand [*sic*] particularly when it comes to our case. You must

believe me when I tell you that this fact plays a very important part in my own confidence and gives me a secure feeling because we're on the ball. We can be thankful that this summer will be one of a very fruitful nature for our boys and will result in very definite and positive benefits for them. We are on the right track if we continue to work for an uninterrupted line of progress in their home relationship. Of course we are not going to neglect the other considerations but first steps first. As we had previously discussed Lenas [*sic*] main objection stemmed from self-interest and although she denies this vehemently she stated that her husband put his foot down and all suggest my mother have her own home and that this is the key to the situation. I assured her that this was a minor problem compared to the solution of the main issue. Anyhow I believe everything possible is being done about this matter and we can expect some degree of success before the summer is over. In passing I'd like to congratulate you on your stubborn prodding on this point because I believe it contributed considerably to Manny and our friends following the correct procedure in arriving at the best possible answer. I'll clarify what I mean at our next Wednesday session. Dearest as a gesture of our high regard for our most esteemed friend and counselor Manny would you please on our behalf send him and his wife a letter wishing them a very happy vacation. Also [N3WI] when he returns we want to see by his appearance that he really benefited from it. Not that we're selfish about it but a healthy, vigorous guy having his excellent qualities is a great asset to us. He's a swell guy and we can't help loving him. By the way I'm greatly relieved [*sic*] over what my sister reported on my mothers [*sic*] eye [NWI] condition but I'll keeping [*sic*] asking about her health to see that it is not neglected. I hope you are feeling much better by now because at our last consultation you were under the weather. Sing Sing Manor is not always conducive to good health. If you find the time drop Mike and Robbie a line[.] I sent the boys a letter last week and if between the two of us we can write them at least once a week I'm sure they will ["be" probably omitted] pleased to hear from us. I suppose my sister Ethel will have lots of things to talk to us about and perhaps she will be able to bring us some late news from our fellows. I've been day dreaming darling and imagining myself with you & the boys on vacation and it sure is a wonderful feeling to be with one's family for then we'll be really living. Keep that lovely face of yours smiling beautiful and our spirits will remain high— All my love—
Julie

Mrs. Lena Cohen
140 Baruch Place
New York New York

July 21, 1952

Dearest Lee,

As per my promise during our last visit am herewith giving you the required measurements:

Waist—36"
Hips—42"

That ought to help you to make the proper selection—and many thanks—

Many thanks, too, for a wonderful visit. Now I am looking forward to seeing my darling husband on Wednesday, so we may exchange notes and feel as though you are with us all over again! I am really in the most marvellous [*sic*] spirits, of late! Soon the summer will be gone and then it won't be quite so long to wait for the decision on certiorari. I am confident of the outcome, so take heart!

My best to all—!

Love,
Ethel

Ethel to Julius

July 22, 1952

My Sweetest dear,

I simply must take time out from my reading to share a most wonderful piece of news with you. Along with your letter this afternoon, I received another from the children, in answer evidently, to the one you [NWI] had sent them last week. Of course, I shall read it to you on Wednesday, but I couldn't contain myself until then without at least attempting to get word to you that I had received it.

You can't possibly know how eagerly I look forward to seeing you each Wednesday my darling; your tender words so faithfully communicated week in, week out, are so sweet and comforting to me. They evoke memories of a communication of quite another sort, however, that leave me quite limp with longing. Sweetheart, I love you with all my being!

And what might I have been doing with myself since last you saw me? Very little, dear—This horrible heat has successfully dampened my ardor for handball, writing or anything at all even remotely connected with strenuous effort, either physical or mental. So I have been indulging myself with a book of plays that does not require too great a degree of concentration.

Love, I grow impatient; I want you so desperately and all I may do is importune with a confounded pencil on a confounded piece of paper! How much dearer you are to me than you have ever been!

Until we meet once more at our favorite screen, darling, I send you my heart's love.

Your lonely one—

Julius to Ethel

July 24, 1952

My Most Charming Wife,

Would you believe it this husband of yours has been walking on a cloud ever since our last visit? I guess it's the seasonal love fever but it sure has hit me hard. A good session of jawing with you is just what I need to keep my spirits very high. Then, too, you look so lovely in your new clothes and they lend an air of freshness and a promise of better and happier surroundings for you my dearest. I am hopelessly in love with you my darling and each time I see you I feel so good about you. Much as my sincere feelings for you are very good for my morale it nevertheless takes a terrible toll [N2WI] of me because of my concern for you and horrible separation we have to endure.

My sister Ethel sent me a letter telling me that my mother wanted her to send me a telegram to observe the yearly rememberence [*sic*] for my beloved and departed father but she decided the letter would have to do. Paul[234] spoke to our boys and they are getting along nicely and are constantly occuppied [*sic*]. They have acquired many new friends and are really enjoying every minute of the day camp & their stay at Sonia and Ben's. Arrangements are being made for the boys to call my mother every Monday evening and reverse the [NWI] phone charges so she can have the pleasure of talking to them once a week. Ethel will see us Saturday and fill in on all the details. By the way you didn't tell me whether you would write the children a letter this week. Tell my sister if you plan to do so, in order for her to let me know. Sweetheart I was very pleased to hear the splendid news Mike wrote us in his letter and by all indications a great deal of the questions perplexing him concerning our case will receive adequate answers and his contact with warm and friendly people will result in positive experiences for him. Both of our two dears will definitely benefit from this summer vacation. I'm so glad one of our plans is working so well.

Oh honey girl the days are so long and time just crawls along and all this time I should be near you holding you pressed to my heart. Such an

---

[234]We are unable to identify this person.

unbelievable nightmare but when will we wake up to find it a thing of the past, a horrible experience that has already been rectified and can ["all" CO] be pushed into memory by the joy of our reunion at home with our family. The happiness of our future relationship will obscure our present sufferings and allow our wounds to heal. The Great William Shakespeare—beats in this petty pace from day to day to the last syllable of recorded time—put it in descriptive language for we are living through it. However in spite of it all we know the score and we are confident of the justice of our cause and our ultimate victory in this case—All my hearts [*sic*] love I send you —Julie

P.S. I hope you don't mind the jumble this time.

Mrs. Lena Cohen
140 Baruch Place
New York New York

July 25, 1952

Dearest Lee,

I'm ever so grateful to you for all the trouble you have been going to, in order to make the most suitable selection. By all means don't expend any more time and energy in this horrible heat. I should say your best bet is to place an order with Lord and Taylor for "large"; I don't need it until Fall anyway—Now, as soon as it gets cooler and you feel up to it, try to find something comparable in "extra large." Even if it's [NWI] only a nylon panty with garters, if it's "extra large" it will do as well as a "large" Wolverine Cuddle Pants. In other words, if you find the type of thing I want in "extra large," before Lord and Taylor re-stocks on "Wolverine," send two of those, and if they are O.K., the "Wolverine" order can be cancelled. If, on the other hand, you aren't successful in securing anything within the next few weeks, [N3WI] in "extra large" Wolverine "large" from Lord and Taylor, when they get them that is, will come handy.—Do you savvy?

Now, as for the one I have home, it won't be permitted, so please do not send it; besides, it isn't urgent for me to have this item before September—OK? Again, many many thanks, darling, you're a peach; you don't know how I'm looking forward to the day, when I can reciprocate in some small measure, for all the love my husband's people shower upon me—And you don't know how I abhor the fact that they were people who belonged to me that did your brother and all those dear to him such a horrible wrong—Believe me, dear, I forgive you all your anger; they are deserving of every last bit of it!

I just thought of it—"Gaswith's" might have an "extra large" panty with garters and it would save you further running around to department stores. I trust you are using the measurements I sent you, since certain garments might be marked only "large" and still be big enough to correspond to these measurements. I'm sure you'll do fine—

Received a wonderful letter from the kids which I'll read to Ethel on Saturday—If there's anything else I think might be helpful to you I'll tell her about it—In the meantime, rest assured that I am fine. At the moment, I am cool and comfortable in a fresh cotton gown; into the bargain, my cell is nice and clean (every Thursday, a hard-working inmate mops the entire woman's wing), and there is a wonderful breeze blowing in on me as I sit and write and listen to the rich music of WQXR—Don't worry, honey, we'll make it—My very best to all—

Ethel—

Master Michael Rosenberg
c/o B. Bach
RD 2 Box 148M
Toms River N.Y.

July 27, 1952

To Our Most Precious Sons Michael & Robert,

Your mother and I were very happy to receive such a nice letter from our sweet boys. After Mr. Bloch and his wife visited you he came up here and spent a couple of hours with us. Most of the time was used in discussing his report on your living with Sonia and Ben and on the day camp. From all that he said we know that you like it and are really enjoying every minute of the time.

You must understand that it took a great deal of planning until we were able to work out an arrangement with swell people like Sonia and Ben for you fellows to spend the summer there. They are warm hearted people, good and kind and above all are doing all they can to help set us free and see that you our children are well taken care of. From your last letter I can tell you are comfortable and are able to relax and be yourselves. I know no better two people who can act as your temporary mother and father while we your parents are forced to be separated from you fighting to win our case. You went to the picnic boys and with your own eyes you could see many of the people who are behind us and you were able to hear with your own ears answers from strangers to some of the questions that are troubling you.[235]

It is true that two years have already passed since our family life was broken up and it will take more time before our fight for justice is won but you can rest assured that in the end we will be set free because as every day

---

[235]See *Sons*, pp. 201–2 for my memories of that picnic.

passes more and more people who learn the facts of our case are convinced of our innocence and are taking part in working for this just cause.

In the meantime dearests be patient and continue to play and have fun and leave it to us grownups to take care of our problems. I suppose Robbie and you Mike have found new playmates and friends and are enjoying the outdoors, swimming, games and new places. When you have an opportunity write us more about the day camp how you two are getting along and of course we want to hear more about Ben, Sonia, Leo and Maxine. Don't fail to give them our warmest greetings and love. To any friends who ask you, tell them we are confident that we will win this case.

Your sweet mother and I are very glad that you are learning new things and are receiving the best possible care, understand [*sic*] and love. There are very many wonderful people in this land who are doing their best to make this a better and happier world for all children to live in. We too are part of that and we are looking forward to the day when we will be reunited in our own home. {# 110649}

We miss you fellows very much and send you all of our hearts [*sic*] love. You are always in our hearts and in our mind. We kiss you dearly—Your Dad—Julie—Ethel gave me the pleasant job to write you this time. [A line is drawn under the last two words and "Julie" is written then erased under that line.]

Julius to Ethel

July 27, 1952

Hello Darling,

It's been a busy day for me since early this morning I've been writting [*sic*] letters. A newsy [NWI] one was sent off to our precious boys telling them that you had given me the pleasant duty to write for both of us ["to them" CO]. Then I wrote a two page letter to my sister Ethel which I will discuss with you in great detail at our next meeting.

Honey I know full well your let down feeling and I understand it. Would you believe it when I tell you that I too experienced similar reactions at this time. My opinion is that the same cause affected us both. Please sweetheart put your thoughts down in outline form because I have a great deal to talk to you about and I want us to have a very fruitful visit this next time. A great deal of strength is needed and we have to constantly call on our reserve stamina to do us stead when the going gets rough or when the blues hits us. We are under no illusions my dearest for we are aware of the forces in our land that are against us and it does not depend on miracles but on a steady tedious uphill campaign to gain the mass support we need to force a review of our case on it's [*sic*] legal merits. This can be the only guarantee the [*sic*] we will receive any decent hearing. If one does not understand that only the hysteria and the times could have produced this political frameup then he cannot see the issues in our case. Well the political circuses are over [punctuation omitted] nothing startling and new has come from the bipartisan conventions they just show a continuation of cold war politics as usual. It is therefore up to the common people in all walks of life to take effective action and give voice and reality to peace in the world now. Many important issues are being fought out to a climax and this fall will be a crucial period in the lives of all our citizens. Among all this important issues like war and peace, political democracy, civil liberties our own case as part of the whole picture will be decided too. The getting of the writ of certiorari will be an important step in our campaign for a new trial. I'm still optomistic [*sic*] because I have faith that the grass root sentiment in our country will be mobilized to our support.

Honey wife this man of yours misses you and at times finds it so difficult to be without you. When the Deputy Director of the Fed. Bureau of Prisons was down I was on the verge of asking him to grant us the right to set up housekeeping at the "C-C" but we'll be patient and suffer in silence. Anyhow Wednesday is almost here and thats [*sic*—"our" CO, N2WI] when we get together at our favorite screen. Love you with all the fibre of my being my precious woman. Life is beautiful even here, when I'm with you—Julius—Keep you [*sic*] chin up & lets [*sic*] see you smiling

Mrs. Ethel Goldberg
5347—65th Place
Maspeth, L.I. New York

July 19, 1952

Dearest Ethel,

This is a very few lines simply to reassure you that all's well. The doldrums I was in on Saturday are no more and I'm "in the groove" again. The dreary week-end is past and I am now enjoying my usual pleasant anticipation of Julie's presence on Wednesday. Your brother is the best husband a woman could have and entirely deserving of his family's love. Tell your mother for me she has a son of whom she may justly be proud!

Honey, could you possibly let me know whether or not she is definite about Monday? If you answer this letter immediately after your receipt of it, I ought to receive your reply by Saturday at the latest—you might also mention what goes with the shopping for a certain terribly important "garment"—you see, my spirits are soaring once more!

One other small matter; there is a letter I sent the children before they left the city. When I queried Mike about it, he remembered that it had been received but had not been read to them. Please find it and forward it to them; it has a little poem about the rain and a train and a song and should have a June date—I'd appreciate your attention on this score, no end—

Thanks for everything and my very best to all—

Affectionately,
Ethel—

Julius to Ethel

July 31, 1952

Precious Darling,

I received a letter from my dear sister Ethel telling me she was very pleased with what I wrote & after Lena heard it they sent it to Dave to use as he sees fit. At the same time my sister received a letter from Bach telling her that the children are having an excellent time at the day camp and at other activities and are very much at ease. He states further that he has the childrens' welfare very much at heart and love them very much. Also she mentioned that Mama got a letter last week that Sonia had asked Michael if he would like to attend school at Toms River. Monday night my mother spoke to the children and they sounded well and contented. Sweetheart I am gratified to hear that our two dears are getting along so well. I know your motherly heart glows with joy with the knowledge that our sons are receiving the care understanding and love of two swell people and are afforded the opportunity to develope [*sic*] under much less tension. We too are able to feel more relaxed because definite progress is being made in this important sphere of our family life. Perhaps now we will be able to concentrate on some other problems that confront us.

Ethel honey we had a grand visit. It is impossible to tell you in the confines of this letter all that you mean to me. Precisely at time like this when as a team we are able to have our relationship pay us its greatest dividends in [N3WI] seeing our own self respect and in the understanding of ourselves as individuals of dignity and character. Particularly is it true that you by your examplary [*sic*] actions and your high personal standards set us an example to follow and emulate and it serves us well in personal satisfaction and allows others to see us are [*sic*, probably meant "as"] we really are. I realize full well the tremendous treasure I posses [*sic*] because you are my wife. And your acceptance and love for me makes life beautiful and bolsters my morale to face this difficult situation. I've read a great deal of many loves and I simply believe that we have a fine relationship that is cemented with mutual bonds of love and even in all this misery I am able to

thrill because of it. Dearest woman of my heart for you and the children we
must win our fight to prove our innocence and then we will be able to be
reunited once again and really begin to live as one happy family. Now all I
can do is think about it and keep my spirits set on the future because [NWI]
all this [NWI] nightmare too must end and I have confidence that we will
win this case. Darling I'm awfully lonesome and I can only count the days
till I see you again at our favorite screen. Keep that pretty face smiling &
that disposition of yours in good spirits and we'll come through with flying
colors. I'll go back to dreaming about you and do a little reading in between
to pass the time. I'll write again this week end—Love you with all my heart
Julie
P.S. Dont [sic] forget. Sunday pass June 10th for Dave.—

Julius to Ethel

Aug. 3rd, 1952

Sweetheart Bunny,

Another day, another week and still another months [sic] time marches
on and we are left to suffer through monotonous, endless, loneliness productive of myriads of thought of what we face. Stripped of all we hold dear
but our own self respect how else could one maintain his strength but to
reassert the cardinal principles of his life and call on all the resources of his
past experiences to give him the necessary incentive to stand firm. Constantly striving to overcome time by reading, writting [sic] and blotting out
any thoughts of difficulties but always cognizant of the realities of the situation, steadfast in the conviction of the righteousness of our cause and the
correctness of our position. Perhaps ["it is" probably omitted here] because
we have so much to live for and we love life that we find our separation so
hard. Yet the contradiction of this is the fact that we are able to maintain our
stamina precisely because we know all this and [next word covers an erasure]
this clarity brings with it great confidence. It does not in any way lessen the
deep pain I feel for the terrible hurt that has been visited on you and the
children. However, happy am I that I walk hand in hand with you, united in
heart, mind and purpose for together we face the future with a clear perspective. For without you and our relationship life would be very bleak indeed.
Well dearest I'll give you an opportunity to thrill me with your charms next
Wednesday when we meet at our favorite screen. I am positive we will have
a great deal to share at our next tete a tete and I hope we'll both come
prepared to get the maximum out of our visit. Honey you can gather that
from Wednesday to Wednesday I feel I'm marking time and then I'm in
heaven when I'm with you.

In case you've forgotten send my brother a Sunday pass and if you can manage [one letter CO, NWI] it drop a few lines to our precious boys. Maybe it would be better to delay it untill [*sic*] after you see my mother and after our visit? Do you recall our summer vacations with the boys? Can you picture all of us together in the county [*sic*—meant "country"] or at the beach? How glorious it makes me feel just to think of it. The fact that other people are filling in for us and doing their all for our boys eases the terrible hurt and relieves some of my anxiety. But somehow I feel cheated of the opportunity to exert my fatherly prerogatives and grow up with my fellows. Two years, that were especially important for our two dears, was [*sic*] taken away from us and my only hope is that it will not take to [*sic*] much more time for us to win our freedom and be with our children again. Enoughs [*sic*] enough oh tyrants you've got more than your pound of flesh and blood from our innocent family and we hope by exposing this to be compensated for our heartaches. At least other innocent people will not be so easily hurt as we have been.

Precious woman keep giving [NWI] me strength I trive [*sic*] on the sustenance you give me. All the love of my heart —Julie

Ethel to Julius

                                                              Sunday, Aug. 3
Bunny darling, 7:30 P.M.

I'm simply carried away, enthralled, enraptured! You can't guess? Well, I've been listening to "Old Man Tosc"[236] conducting the NBC Summer Symphony. What a magnificence of sound that guy can call forth; it's positively incredible. All right, sweetheart, I'll cut it out and pay some attention to my own guy for a change, who is entirely capable of thrilling me quite as satisfactorily!

                                                         Monday 2:00 P.M.

Dearest, your letter was so moving, so wonderfully gratifying; my sweet, tender Julie who bring's [*sic*] to his love for me all the untrammelled joy and zest he brings to life itself! Always, whatever the matter under discussion, inevitably the question arises; when, oh when, is all this ardor [N2WI] to be permitted its joyous release!

To come back to more sensible subjects (sic!) according to a letter I received from Ethel, unless it rains or gets very hot, your mother ought to be seeing us to-morrow. All weather reports thus far would indicate at least

---

[236]Arturo Toscanini

no worse a day than it is at the moment. It strikes me I'm a bit behind time; certainly you'll be talking to her directly [NWI] before you [NWI] ever have the opportunity to read the foregoing lines! It strikes me further that since she'll be relaying some of our conversation to you, it would only be repetitious on my part to write at length concerning matters I intend her to bring to your attention [NWI] anyway. Still, I want to state here and now (details on Wed.) that I had such a pleasant visit with my brother[237] on Saturday that it served to counteract some of the desolate feeling that usually sets in over the week-end.

Julie dear, another of your earnest epistles just made its appearance. You're so serious-minded, so sincere; I could actually eat you in sheer extremity of feeling. I am reminded by my expression of how adoringly you look at me, sometimes, and how intensely you struggle to put your adulation into words, when I've said or done something that you find particularly appealing. You behave, then, as though you might, in fact, eat me! What did I tell you, here we go again! When, oh when, does this feast of love begin!

My darling, how did you know I was figuring to write the children after your mother's visit? I may [NWI] even work it so that I have my letter to them [NWI] only half-way through by Wednesday before I see you, so that I may add to it appropriately, afterward.

Love you, sweetest—
Ethel

P.S.—Request slip for Davy's visit has been ready and waiting since Saturday— So don't fret, honey—

Mrs. Lena Cohen
140 Baruch Place
New York New York

August 5, 1952

Dearest Lee,

Thank you so much for your letter and all your effort on my behalf. By all means have two of them sent me; that's a wiser procedure than running the risk of having me wear out one garment in short order, through constant use and frequent launderings, and then having to be bothered making another such purchase at some later date. Alternating between two insures the span of usefulness of both over a far greater period of time.

---

[237]Must be referring to Bernard.

It's good to hear that the kids are doing so well. For the first time in a long while my mind is at peace concerning them. Give our most grateful thanks and affectionate regards to Sonia and Ben; may they have returned to them in full measure all the happiness they are now showering upon two anxious little boys!

My very best to all— Please phone Ethel and tell her how much comfort her letters have been giving us—

Love,
Ethel—

Julius to Ethel

Aug. 7, 1952

My Charming Woman,

It was indeed very gratifying to me to see you in such a happy frame of mind, so vivacious beaming confidence and pride. You had just cause to feel so good and I too was quickly overtaken with a wonderful feeling. If you didn't write the boys yet would you please suggest that when they type the next letter to you to send me a carbon copy as I like to reread such gems a number of times to completely enjoy every bit that they have to offer. Just because our visit was so full and satisfying the time seemed to pass all too quickly and there was much more that we both hoped to talk about particularly to spend just a few moments to exchange some sweet words of love. We'll make up for it next time and I'm sure we'll continue the discussion until we've completed it to our satisfaction. I think we are making definite progress on a number of things and I'm glad we're taking part in some of these activities. At this time I want to caution us not to expect too much but to work in such a manner that if something good comes of it all the better but if not we're to maintain our morale because by no means can this be decisive.

Oh Ethel honey you looked so wonderful and I loved you so much and yet I could not take you in my arms and hold you close to me. But sweetheart this kind of raport [*sic*] we have established makes the time pass quickly and more pleasantly and brings us closer to the time we will be [NWI] in each others [*sic*] arms.

Darling the high regard you have for me and the way you express your love for me in your letters makes me feel so good and yet so humble because it's you who are the object of my affections. Truth is I do try very hard because I do not find the medium of words on paper adequate to express my profoundest emotions & thoughts about you and the situation we find ourselves in. Somehow when I sit across from you with my nose pressed against the screen you inspire me and words and feelings just gush forth and things are clearer and many times I forget that we are here in the death house but I actually believe us to be home and all that matters is our sharing the moments together and all else is blotted out. My wife we have arrived at a higher level of understanding each other in our relationship and that is why we can derive such great satisfaction from our visits. Constantly I hope that the week were made up of seven Wednesday's [sic] but I'll have to suffer through till I look at you again next week. In the meantime I'll prepare an agenda for my visit with my brother to make sure I pack in a maximum number of items in the alotted [sic] time. You can imagine all that I've been dreaming about being with you and the boys in the country and meeting lots of decent people— All my love—

Julie

Julius to Ethel

August 10, 1952

Hello Precious,

It is quite late now I've spent most of the afternoon sweating out a letter to my brother in between reading the Sunday paper. You don't know how much I long for us being together and working as we used on such matters. Anyhow I'll read you my letter when we meet at our favorite screen. As a team we managed very well together and with this experience behind us we'll do much better than before. I am so very happy with all the splendid news my brother brought me and I'm pleased to be able to partici- pate in the campaign but somehow at times I feel inadequate to perform my best and I am sure that were you present to inspire me I'd do much better.

Talking of my favorite subject you I can't help feeling good over our last visit and I hope we are able to continue in the same pattern to manage so beautifully. Today I had occassion [sic] to reread our letters that appeared in the National Guardian[.] Sweetheart you are a jewel a veritable literary genius, a most charming wonderful sweet woman, full of compassion and warmth, of noble character and great talent. In short your [sic] a swell person and I'm indeed luck [sic] to have you as my wife and faithful com- panion. You know honey these god-forsaken mosquitoes are annoying me to no end, dive bombing me, roaring in my ears and sinking their six inch drill bits into me and I have to continue to finish this letter to meet jewelry collection time. Then I will commit mayhem, I'll plaster them on the walls and hunt them till the're [sic] exterminated. Guess this joint is [next word illegible, it appears from context to be "making"] me bloodthirsty. Enough of this levity back to a little verbal smooching, since this is the only medium left to us to convey our feelings for each other. The genuiness [sic] [N3WI] of our feelings is definite and only the sight of you and the sound of your voice continues to revitalize my morale and soon we'll begin to hear more news of increased activities on our behalf and that will keep our spirits high.

It is my firm belief that by our present conduct we are contributing a maximum effort on our own behalf & more accomplishments in this direction will be very self satisfying. I suppose in a couple of weeks we can look forward to seeing [two letter word CO] our beloved Manny again and be brought up to date on the latest legal activity in our case. This [last word written over the word "The"] copy of "The Nation" was a tremendous advancement in the fight against the present reactionary trend and it is indicative of the maturing of a counter-force to prevent the growing fascist tendencies. This is only a beginning but it is a healthy one and let's hope it can be mobilized to help us in our fight for justice.—Goody! Goody! only a few more days— All my hearts [*sic*] love—Your Julie

Ethel to Julius

Thursday
August 7, 1952

My dear one, my darling;

I am so utterly alone today I must speak to you. Yesterday, I was quite frankly aware of myself as the dispensor [*sic*] of glad tidings, and played the role for all it was worth. Unfortunately, no amount of anticipatory feeling, prior to our actual meeting; and no degree of enjoyment experienced during it, ever compensates us for the endless hours of our separation, nor does our pitifully short "time in the sun" ever constitute the consummation we crave. Inside of me, though, (and it happens every week, even as I am disillusioned every week), there is irrational expectation of [NWI] just such [NWI] a genuine coming to-gether and the concomitant sense of anti-climax, which must inevitably flow from the very situation in which we helplessly thrash about!

Friday, August 8, 1952

Sweetheart, your letter was just what I needed to pick me up some; you see, my frustration often takes on such intensity that it helps to know you aren't completely satisfied either. I am referring specifically in this case to our last visit; I am so impatient to continue the discussion which had perforce to be brought to such an abrupt halt—Damn this confounded waiting, it drives me wild! You may gather from the foregoing the agony, the waits between visits from my dear Dr. Saul, [*sic*] represented, and how terribly I miss him, now that he isn't to put in an appearance for weeks and weeks!

Monday, August 11

Finally, this morning, I scribbled off a fairly decent letter to the children. Yes, dear, I put in your request for a carbon copy and also urged them to send us snapshots. I'll give you all the details as per usual on "Wondrous Wednesday." Ah, me, it is still only "Mis'able Monday" (just a slight edge over "Sorrowful Sunday") and Tantalizing Tuesday "is not yet in sight." (Maybe I should have stood in bed!) [A whole line of dashes divide these lines from the next line]

Actually did take time out for a restful nap; slept from 10:00–11:30 A.M. the coolness in here these mornings, of late, is most conducive to slumber, especially since it generally takes me ages to fall asleep [N2WI] at night and [NWI] I tend to be wakeful in any case. Usually, however I sleep right thru breakfast, mail collection, etc. and [NWI] am up and about before too long. Today, since I was determined to delay the kids' letter no longer, necessitated a much earlier rising with the resultant [NWI] thorough capitulation to Morpheous [*sic*; N2WI] as described. Well, the day is still young and the sun is shining brightly.

Gosh, I hope your brother made his train; through some mix-up the bus was very late. Into the bargain it [NWI] had begun to pour by 11:30—Must make my bed now and then hie me outdoors—Gee whiz, bunny, I want you— All my love, Ethel.

P.S. My sweet you sing my praise so extravagantly I'm blushing! Am referring to your letter of the 10th received this P.M.—Of course, I don't like it—not much I don't! Love you,

Ethel

Michael & Robert Rosenberg
c/o B. Bach—R.D. 2
Box 148 M
Toms River New Jersey

August 11, 1952

Dearest Children,

First, let me thank you (and Ben) for that very newsy letter. I received it just the day before Daddy was due to see me and so had the extra pleasure of looking forward to surprising him with it. You should have seen him when I waved both nicely covered pages excitedly in front of him! And how he smiled all over his dear face when I began to read; you know, that look he gets when he's very happy, as though he were [NWI] all lit up from inside! Oh, speaking of Daddy reminds me, he'd like a carbon copy of the next typewritten letter, if it's possible.

The number and variety of your activities quite takes our breath away; it sounds like just what both of you needed. (We are curious as can be about "air-Mail" in which Mike was Jugoslavia and figure to enjoy hearing it described—among many other things at the next "Rosenberg Round-Up"! Yippee!)

I've been wanting to ask and always forget—Do Sonia and Ben still have the piano Maxine used to play? Do remember us to her and wish her the best of luck with her plans. By all means, send snapshots of everybody; it would give us no end of pleasure to see our two fellers with those who are doing so much to make them happy!

Often I used to wonder what you might be doing at this moment or at that, or rather I used to worry; were you feeling good or were you perhaps feeling bad. Yesterday, as I watched the rain coming down, it made me feel wonderful to remember that you were [NWI] probably having a "hell of a time" with good friends and good material on the enclosed porch. In any case, I know that you are among people who care and who are truly concerned with your thoughts and your feelings. Yes, it is as it should be, (and as it was so well put in your letter), that it is for children to enjoy their childhood and for the grown-ups to shoulder their grown-up responsibilities. Thus, every body to-gether, each in his own way, will contribute to make the victory for us all—

Cookies, mail is being collected now. Will have to cut this short—I promise to write you once more this week, since I have lots more to say— Daddy sends his best love to all our dear friends—We are [NWI] both fine and love you with all our hearts—

xxxxx—Mommy—

Julius to Ethel

Aug 14, 1952

Honeybunch,

Whenever your letter comes and no matter how many times I reread it always exudes freshness, keeness [sic] of thought and is very emotionally stimulating. Your use of language is superb and the prose used mirrors your ideas beautifully and presents a clear picture to the reader. [last two letters written over suffix "ing"] It is one of my greatest pleasures to enjoy your creative epistles and as your foremost admirer, devoted companion and loving husband I receive a great deal of satisfaction seeing the visible expression of one of your talents. In this matter I know that I am stating a fact even though I might be considered slightly prejudiced. How could I help feeling so good about you when I consider us immeasurable [sic] enhanced in assets because of the treasure our team possesses in having one of such

noble character and analytical mind as you [N3WI] on its side. The very
nature of our case and the type of incarceration we are forced to suffer with
the ever present threat of death staring us in the face gives rise to violent and
extreme emotional feelings, plaguing us with innumerable frustrations both
physical and mental but as we have already experienced always [N3WI]
causing us to revert [suffix "ing" CO] back to a stable foundation. Because
we love life so dearly and we know how to enjoy every minute of useful
social intercourse enriching the dignity of the individual, enhancing his
potentialities for common and personal good our present physical shackles
cramps [sic] our sensitivities and doesn't allow the pain to really subside.
However we can be thankful that we have obtained the level of understanding to truthfully ascertain our position and keep uppermost in our
vision a correct perspective to guide us out of this abyss of despair and keep
our sights set on the developements [sic] in our campaign for complete
vindication from guilt and the future [NWI] which holds promise for
complete victory. The summer season is drawing to a close and with it will
come increased activities to present our side to the court of public opinion
and I am looking forward to a greatly accelerated drive to reach all the people
in our country with the facts and issues in this case. Yes to us my wife our
lives and freedom are most important to say the least but the significance
that this cause celebre holds to democratic America goes to the heart of the
political issues that are confronting our country. No doubt you've noticed
the item in todays [sic] Compass about the two day conference in Chicago
and I am sure will hear a great deal more of the same type of news in the
coming period. Take heart my love we are not alone but part of an ever
increasing army for justice and peace—your fellow— Julie

P.S.—You can guess this guy of yours is in love and you no doubt know
who is the object of his profoundest affections.

Julius to Ethel

                                                      Aug. 17, 1952
Hello Darling,
       Within a few more weeks some of our dearest friends will be back from
vacation and grace us with their presence and rekindle our waning spirits.
The emotional sustenance and mental stimulant ["of" CO, N3WI] we get
from these noble people ["give" CO, N2WI] engender in us the necessary
stamina to maintain our strength and personal dignity and reassures us that
our faith in mankind is well justified. In this respect I enjoyed my sister's
visit very much because of the swell report she gave me, particularly concerning the Chicago conference and what she told me of the committees [sic]

office. Remind me to talk to you about these items. Each and every visit from members of my family continues to be more and more fruitful and I'm sure that I do not exaggerate when I say that it does the visitor more good than we can imagine. It is true that I receive personal satisfaction from them but my family always repeat that whenever they leave us their morale is way up and they are able to transmit this good feeling to all whom they talk to about us.

By the way the P.K. happened by and we had a nice talk and all is straightened out. He really is a peach of a person. Since Wednesday is almost here I'll tell you about it then. I got a letter from my sister Ethel and the pictures you asked her to send me. I received one you didn't get. There [*sic*] all very good and I get a thrill every time I see them. In her letter Ethel said Bach called her from [NWI] the New York office this last week and said the children are very happy and he loves them dearly. Robby does not hide in corners, the shyness has left him and Michael has put on weight. I'll elaborate on all the news Lena gave me when we meet at our favorite screen. My sister is trying to make arrangements for her and my mother to get a ride to see our precious dears: I knew you'd like to hear this instead of waiting and I'm anxious to see if you ["had" CO, NWI] got the same reaction I ["had" CO, NWI] did. It is splendid to know that our sweet ones are in very good hands. Probably by the time we see each other you'll have gotten off a letter to Manny to arrange to see us at an early date for as long a time as possible to allow us to cover all the questions that we need answered. For Wednesday let's spend some time planning an agenda for our legal consultation.

Dearest let's take firm hold of our seats and be [word "prepared" CO, NWI] ready to meet the terrible storm that's brewing and resolve to keep our feet firmly planted in reality and not let ourselves be carried away with ["the" CO] extraneous matters and hysterical scares. I'm confident we'll do O.Kay but lets [*sic*] be prepared anyway. This time I'll save all the song that's in my heart for my lips and I'm sure that they'll have more meaning to your ears. All the love of my being is for you— Your—Julie

P.S. I think I'll hold up writting [*sic*] the boys till we hear from them & I see you.

Mrs. Lena Cohen
140 Baruch Place
New York New York

August 18, 1952

Dearest Lee,

Just thought I'd set your mind at rest about me. I was really not myself on Saturday and I'm afraid I was far too irritable with you. It has nothing to do with you, of course, it's just my situation. A small thing, you understand!

Look, dear, you won't knock yourself out any more about the panty, at least not for the present. I have an idea it will be a lot easier to lay your hands on something suitable after Labor Day—and thanks again for all the trouble you have already taken.

If Ethel is unable to get here this Saturday tell her not to be concerned. I would appreciate a line from her, one way or another, however, so I'll know whether or not to expect her. If not, she will be just as welcome on the following Saturday if not more so for the simple reason that the usual "cause" for my [next two words close to illegible, looks like "pain giver"] will not be present, to press attentions that are unsolicited by either myself or my visitors, and altogether unwelcome!

My very best to every one— Love, Ethel

Ethel to Julius

August 19, 1952

Julie darling,

I am interrupting my already tardy letter to the snookies, in order to send you a few words of cheer; be comforted, love, I have looked on the face of your pain and know it for my own. Indeed, I am constantly tossed upon a sea of righteous wrath for all the pettiness and iniquity that hems us in. Nevertheless, the concealed tears rose at once into my eyes as I read and I drew you close into loving arms and warmed you with my warmth. Sweetheart, I feel so hopelessly inadequate in the sight of your need and yet I long to believe I have [NWI] had some small something to do with the extraordinary stability you have by and large been exhibiting here.

Words fail me now, dearest; we'll see each other soon.

My soul loves you, my sweet—

Ever your wife—

Master Michael Rosenberg c/o B.Bach
R.D. 2 Box 148 M
Toms River N.J.

                                                    August 20, 1952
Dearest Michael & Robert,
    I had intended to write you much sooner but I deliberately waited until I
talked over a number of matters with your sweet and adorable mother Ethel.
We had a most fruitful visit which was all the more satisfactory because of
the splendid news of your well being and of the progress you are making.
We are more than pleased, indeed we are elated that it is possible to work
out a mutually satisfactory arrangement with Ben and Sonia and you boys.
Of course we accept their most kind and generous offer to care for our two
dears. We had high hopes of such a thing coming to pass in time, but we
felt it would be presumptive on our part to even ask for fear we might put
two swell people like the Bachs in a compromising position. From our
hearts thank you noble human beings.
    Your mother and I are very relieved to know you are in competent hands
and you will receive the love and security of warm hearted foster parents. As
for some technicalities we suggest immediate arrangements be made to
register Michael in school and Robert in kindergarten and if birth certificates
or records are required communicate with my sister Ethel to take care of
same.
    Mr. Bloch is due back from his vacation this week and we expect him
at an early date and we'll discuss other pertinent matters concerning these
arrangements and he'll get in touch with you directly.
    Truth is we are very happy to know you boys are surrounded by people
who accept you and are sympathetic to our cause and ["the" CO] positive
experiences are the most effective remedy for the terrible pain that has been
visited on your lives. In spite of all these good improvements nevertheless
our parental hearts ache and we are choked with emotion because we are
forcible [*sic*] kept from our beloved children. However each of us must take
himself to his job, you fellows to play, enjoy, learn and grow and we to
participate to the maximum of our efforts in fighting our case to complete
victory.
    We understand the nature and ramifications of our case. Great difficulties
face us for we are innocent victims of a political frameup in a time of growing hysteria and a hot war in Korea. Only in such an atmosphere of fear can
there be a Rosenberg case. But we have always been campaigners for better
conditions for all people and we realize only in a peaceful world can our
children grow up into healthy and happy citizens. Once the facts and issues
in our case are known to the public it will be obvious to them that our
conviction and sentence are being used as a warning against those who don't

conform. Since there is only a future in opposition to this we have faith that increasing numbers of people will come to our support and help set us free.[238]

We are confident we will be reunited with you our precious children and perhaps we'll have the opportunity to send you again to this Day Camp. You can see for yourselves we are gaining new friends daily. Keep your spirits high we're going to win—
All our love—Daddy—Mommy. —Julie—# 110649

Julius to Ethel

Aug. 21, 1952

Hello Sugar,

As we had discussed at our meeting I got off a letter to our boys yesterday. However I was not able to include enough personal news such as the childrens [*sic*] pictures, Maxine and the newsy letter they sent us so be a honey and include same in your epistle of love to our dears. If they are able to take some photos ask them to send me duplicate copies.

I intend to tell my sister of our plans for the children so that she will be able to inform the other members of my family of our views and be ready to take care of some of the details needed for the boys such as birth certificates and school records. Perhaps she may be able to tell us when our dear Manny will put in an appearance and grace us with his noble presence. I'm itching for loads of good news and I hope it wont [*sic*] be long before we begin to hear some of the latest [NWI] big doings by the committee. At least we'll know the results of the Chicago conference.

Darling I know we didn't manage to find enough time to go into the personal matters but now that we've been able to finish discussing a number of very necessary techical [*sic*] details I'm sure we'll be able to give more attention to the question you raised at our last tete a tete. No doubt you've noticed that at times I look at you in certain ways and I am at a loss for words. My tongue is tied even though a wealth of feeling ["is" CO] wells [letter "s" written over "ing" which is crossed out] up inside of me and there is a great need to express it all but it seems that circumstances prevent me from satisfying this deep need. This is symptomatic of our frustrations brought about by our separation in this tomb of despair. Only by constantly striving to overcome the ["ese" crossed out] emotional and mental

---

[238]Note how here and in the early paragraph, the letter is really addressed to the Bachs and any other adults that might read this letter, not to the nine- and five-year-old children! It is possible that my father was also thinking that we might read this later with more understanding as adults.

barriers that this situation has imposed can we succeed in overcoming these difficulties. Truth is we're not made of iron but only human and so we must suffer through as best we can considering the circumstances. Now that the matter of the childrens [*sic*] home environment looks like it will be decided as we planned we can relax on that score and turn our attentions on our own immediate problems.

Of course I found ever increasing joy in our short sharing together at our favorite screen and I can't help loving you so much till it hurts. I've noticed that when I'm with you I'm very much at ease and the rapport we have established has enhanced our relationship to ["the" CO, NWI] a high level of ["my" CO] mutual satisfaction. Comparing this with how we functioned in the past I see a marked improvement and how I hope we'll be able to have the advantage of this put to use [N4WI] in a short time in raising our beautiful family together once again. It's a long hard road but the future holds dear promise for us. Take courage my precious woman we'll see this through to complete victory. Heaven knows we deserve this justice ["and" CO, "by" CO above the previous crossed out word, N2WI] its [*sic*] our right. ["s" CO] Don't fail to write our counselor—All my love—Julie

Julius to Ethel

Aug. 24, 1952

Hello Sweetheart,

It seems so long ago that I've seen you and I guess it's due to the fact that I miss you very much and feel lonely. Our lot dearest is a very difficult one and when on top of this miserable situation there are sometimes [NWI] added unnecessary aggravations it makes one terribly sick at heart. But we must maintain our dignity of person and attach the right amount of importance to everything objectively [N3WI] as it is based on the totality of our present position. You can understand that I'm actually writting [*sic*] for my own benefit. Sort of speaking to myself. When I see you I'll tell you of a disagreeable incident that I experienced.

In examining the last set of photographs we received of our sweet children I noticed that on every one ["of them" inserted and CO] that Michael appeared in he was squinting badly even though there was no sun in his eyes. Perhaps he may need a pair of glasses and since you have already made a note of Robbie having an audiometer test add one for Mike to have his eyes examined. I explained in detail our plans for the children to my sister and also discussed the situation concerning my mother and we'll have to settle a number of questions with Manny concerning this matter. From the looks of things he may not see us until the latter part of the week. You know Honey that independently you and I made similar suggestions to my sister concerning regular visits with our boys. You can just imagine how wonderful I felt when she told me that you had just told her the same thing I had because it verifies that we think along paralell [sic] lines and react the same to situations. Ethel let's spend a little time for me to just look at you and tell you all that you mean to me. I need this kind of sustenance to keep strong and maintain my equilibrium.

My sister and I had a very good visit and I did my share to cheer her up. They certainly have their trouble and I don't like to see them hurt so I smoothed out her pained conscience. Yes my wife we, because of our understanding, have to give clarity and comfort to our loved ones and our friends and in so doing can really enjoy the personal satisfaction of knowing our own worth. Thank goodness in a few days I'll be able to see your charming and beautiful face and listen to your dear words of wisdom. Near as the time is I'm still impatient until I sit with my nose pressed against our favorite screen and devour all your loveliness with my hungry eyes. You are my right arm my dearest and I'm counting on you and I am confident that you will continue to inspire me and give me the courage I need to face the vicissitudes of the future. All my heart is for you my love—Your Julie

Julius to Ethel

Aug 28, 1952

Sweetheart,

After such a splendid satisfying session with you and Manny I'm mentally fatigued and emotionally exhausted. The consultation received my undivided attention and I keyed myself to be especially keen in analyzing our situation that after it was over I fell into a heavy sleep. At this time I'm fully recuperated [N2WI] helped along with a big bowl of macaroni and meat balls under my belt and I can [NWI] now comment on our visit. Our dear friend and esteemed counselor is a darling of a person and very precious indeed. Never does he fail to gather up the loose ends put everything in the right light and instill great strength that comes with confidence in the justice of our cause and the correctness of our campaign to win vindication. He helps reaffirm our faith in the supreme goodness and decency of man. It's wonderful to have him so completely in our corner. We covered all we had planned to take up and I believe we made a great deal of progress and I'll be glad to hear how things are developing when our boys come to visit us next time.

Concerning my mothers [sic] visit, I'm sorry we didn't make definite arrangements for regular periodic visits with the children. The important consideration being that since it is a difficult trip perhaps some special consideration should be given to my mother staying over one night in the vicinity. However, if this is not advisable at least she should get a ride back and forth. Truth is I'm concerned for her health as it will be a gruelling [*sic*] experience. Maybe you have some other suggestion and I'm sorry we did not get to explore this in greater detail. I'll talk to my mother about our plans and I hope we're both able to make her visit a pleasant one.

What pleases me most are the indications that many good things are in the works and the campaign will begin snowballing this next month. We need a real active and vigorous drive by the committee and I think our chances for certiorari are very good. Anyhow I'm optomistic [*sic*] because I believe we'll be able to obtain a growing amount of support from the public. So let's put ourselves in order in the coming weeks and we will be better able to acquit ourselves properly. If I didn't tell you by word of mouth I'm sure you sensed it in my eyes that I love you very much and adore you. We'll be able to devote part of [NWI] our next tete a tete to this lawyer visit. If you manage to write Manny or the family tell him to send us copies of the record. I'm glad you managed to send off your letter to the children because Manny will be able to read it when he sees them. I think we're doing nicely in this department and I have high hopes we'll have better success in all our undertakings particularly in the big one, our freedom. All my heart is for you—Julie

Julius to Ethel

Sept. 1st, 1952

My Adorable Woman,

The first words out of my mothers [*sic*] mouth were "your Ethel looks so pretty and sends you her love." Believe me dearest it gives me great pleasure to hear it from her lips with such sincerity and a sense of her own personal satisfaction. Indeed we had a most excellent visit and she is more than pleased that she'll be able to keep the apartment. Her seeing the children and knowing they are in competent hands and feeling secure about her own position finds her in accord with our wishes and with a family conference coming up to wrap up all the loose ends a big worry will be off our hands.

I'm sending Dave a pass for this Sunday and telling him to check with Lena and Bernie that there is no mixup for only one of them can come this week. Also to be aware that shortly our children will come to visit us and we would like them to plan it so that we don't have all the visits come at once and [NWI] then a few weeks will go by without us seeing any of the family. We can now rest assured that many of the technical details we spoke about are all being taken care of.

The next personal hurdle is how the boys take to the school and we'll know about it at their next visit. From here on in the crucial period of our case is at hand and I hope that all mankind will be graced with advances [N3WI] in the fight for peace and a better life. This will also affect the outcome of our case and I'm sure that the committee and our supporters will redouble their efforts to get the facts to larger numbers of people. We will have to patiently await news of progress in the campaign and wherever possible to do our bit. You know sweetie I read the introduction to the "Song of the Lark" (which is quite excellent) but after reading the first paragraph of the book I could not get interested enough to continue. I guess I'm just lazy but I'll get to it at my own leisure pace and then I'll be able to really enjoy it. Naturally my reading gravitates to lighter matters but I too have my deeper moments. (Don't you think so?)

Oh happy day Wednesday is almost here I am leaving it entirely up to you to plan our discussion and do it as you feel and not as you think. You get the point dearest and you'll give us sufficient time to smooch orally. Well Darling the summer is over and it's been a good one and now the time for decision is upon us. If we are able to continue in the same manner as we have in the past we'll be prepared to meet whatever [N4WI] difficulties face us in the immediate future ["face us with" CO]. Our love and our relationship will be the solid foundation to buttress our individual personal self and the knowledge and understand [sic] we possess based on them will carry us through. I'm optomistic [sic] honey—Keep smiling All my love—Julie

Julius to Ethel

Sept 4, 1952

Hello Darling,

When our visits pass so quickly and are very productive we're really hitting on all cylinders. I cannot begin to tell you how much it means to me to be able to be at one with you in this way. No doubt it has a similar effect on you and it is always stimulated by deep thinking provoked by emotional and mental satisfaction. I'm three-quarters of the way through "The Song of the Lark" and every bit of it is most enjoyable. Many of the incidents ring cordant [sic—looks like he created a word, the opposite of "discordant"] notes in me and set off a train of reactions. Both of us will have an opportunity to discuss this in greater detail and we will be able to go into the significance of certain incidents in a different manner than ["which" CO, "one in" inserted, then CO] the author went into [NWI] them. As I read this afternoon I hungered to be with you and share my thoughts. Congratulations are in order for you because you were able to be well prepared for our session and your new program of putting everything in it's [*sic*] place certainly paid off well. Of course I was so completely carried away with our talk I failed to tell you how well you looked particularly the way you had your hair set. Honey I'm so completely in love with you and I want you so strongly that at times the intensity of my feelings cause me such anguish. Believe me sweetheart with all the pain it's a very good feeling.

I was worried about my mother making it home alright because of the rain and she promised to write me. Lena sent a note said she made it home early and is fine. That Mel[239] was coming home. You know we had a long talk about visits. Well my sister Lena said she'll see us two weeks after Daves [*sic*] visit, I guess we'll have to check with her if she means the 20th or 27th. We're off again so we'll have to get it straight with my brother.

Since last Monday I've been suffering with a tough case of hay fever that has forced me to take some pills for relief. However I still find that this is one of the worse ["periods" CO, N3WI] sieges I've had in the last five years and it is verified by the newspaper reports that the pollen count is very high. You see Ethel I need you to take care of me. Maybe you can arrange it. What do you say? One thing I did was buy myself a box of Doeskin Tissues and they come in three colors, yellow blue and red. At least I can wipe my nose in real style but I'm still uncomfortable. Don't worry yourself too much as I've only you to complain to. After all what's a little suffering more on top of all our big serious troubles. I hope we'll get the trial record soon and you'll be able to review some of the testimony to be better able to refresh your memory and discuss it with precise references to incidents. Perhaps my brother will tell us when our lawyer intends to bring the children. Ethel I miss our boys very much and I'm impatient for an early visit with them and I'll be satisfied with any date you set for them to put in an appearance. Don't fail to write Manny, once you decide the date, and tell him the time he should have the children here—All my love —Julie

Emanuel H. Bloch
7 W. 16th Street
New York New York

Sept. 4, 1952

Dear Manny,

As per usual, the written reminder I always find it necessary to send you following a visit, mostly to ease my own tensions.

First, Julie wanted me to give you some idea as to when you might figure to be here with the children. Please understand, however, these dates

---

[239] Lena's son

are only tentative and subject to change, dependant [*sic*] upon further information, from David Rosenberg on Sunday, as to how his sisters plan to fit in their visits during this coming holiday month.[240] As of now, it looks like either the 13th or the 20th is the more likely; you see the 20th is Rosh Hashonah and there is [NWI] certainly less question involved about Ben[241] coming in then than either of Julie's sisters. In any case, sit tight until I write and make it absolutely definite.

I trust you have already phoned Dr. Miller to get in touch with Miss Schidell[242] so that an appointment may be arranged as soon as possible at the JBG. Since you apparently neglected to request anyone to drop me a line as to which Friday he is due to see me, I shall probably get all ready sit on pins and needles for hours (unable to concentrate on anything else, meanwhile) and then be disappointed. Oh well, it's my own fault for not having insisted you make a written note; after all, there are a hundred different matters with which you are bedevilled, and small (though important) details have a way of slipping up unless they are so noted. I hate to scold you, sweetie, but as I tried to explain to you, it does cause me extra frustration and heart-ache to sit around waiting for something that doesn't pan out, just because I don't know definitely one way or another. Certainly, you'll agree it's a good idea to try to avoid that for me, whenever it's possible, I mean.

Please if there was any doubt left in your mind concerning a tonsilectomy [*sic*] at this time, let me dispel it at once. Not only is it not to be considered, I simply want no mention of it made at the present. And no arguments.[243] Mail call—I'll give Dave a message for you on Sunday about this and other matters—

My best to all—

Ethel

Emanuel H. Bloch [ink]
7 W. 16th Street
New York New York

Sept. 7, 1952

Dear Manny,

In between sneezes brought on by my hay-fever allergy I got to think about your health. After all I find it's very difficult to function on all cylin-

---

[240]This is in reference to Rosh Hashanah, the Jewish New Year, and Yom Kippur, the Day of Atonement.
[241]Ben Bach, though Jewish, was not religious.
[242]My social worker
[243]Robby did have a tonsillectomy later, but not at this time.

ders mentally and spiritually when one is afflicted with bodily ailments. Ethel and I are concerned about you and we insist you take care of yourself. Remember sweet guy besides being our devoted friend we're counting on you to help save our lives. We hope by the time we see you ["again" CO] that you will be feeling in the pink again and are not neglecting your physical condition. The best intentions and strongest will power have been frustrated by illness. Pretty please for our sake too take care.

To save a great deal of confusion I've decided to ask you to see to it that some technical details are ["attended to" CO, N3WI] taken care of for us, then I'll be sure that they'll be attended to properly. First please send each of us a copy of the trial record. Please settle the commissary situation for us. Also I've asked for a Webster College abriged [*sic*] dictionary a number of times and as yet no dictionary. Then too the committee puts out a lot of printed matter and press releases perhaps you can send us copies of same under your stationary [*sic*] as we're interested in this phase of our case.

Ethel will be writting [*sic*] you on the childrens [*sic*] visit and I hope it wont [*sic*] be too much of a strain on them. From some of the news my brother brought me I can begin to discern a maturing of the campaign into a broad movement of all sections of the people who understand the deeper implications of our case and are working to secure justice for us as an important ["initial" CO] step in turning ["by" CO] back the attack against ["their" CO] civil liberties and the fight for peace. The political nature ["of" CO] of our trial and sentence is evident to all who are acquainted with the facts and it's imperative to reach the public with this message. You have given us the best legal defense possible but only the court of public opinioin [*sic*] can assure us the freedom that is rightfully ours. The effectiveness of the fight to save us will depend on the support we can get during this period while the high court is receiving our petition for certiorari. ["Please tell" CO] I have confidence that our friends will not let us down with "too little and too late." Clarity of purpose and perspective will help guide those who are leading the campaign to take timely action. In the meantime we need news of progress to fortify our morale and strengthen our determination to keep on a high ["er" CO] level our principled fight. You know make it a little easier for us, it's tough enough here.

Don't forget to give my best to your wife and to pop. Send my regards to all. I guess we'll be seeing you and the boys soon. (Excuse the writting [*sic*])

As ever,
Julie
#110649

P.S. I don't mean to sound discouraged only I miss my boys and Ethel very much and at times my heart aches for them because I'm lonesome and worried about their welfare.

Julius to Ethel [pencil]

Sept. 7, 1952

Ethel—My Sunshine & Light,

Now that I've begun this letter I feel much better ["now" CO] but I must say that I've had a mixture of many different emotions today. Worrying about the children missing you dreadfully, this hay-fever knocking the stuff out of me and just feeling blue once in a while. You can understand [partial word "thi" CO] because you too have run the gamut of these kind of [NWI] painful days. Even though every bit of my brother's visit was good nevertheless it was frustrating because it was so short and we didn't have time to discuss any of the things I wanted to cover with him. Well enough of despair Wednesday is almost here and I'll be seeing you soon.

I sent our beloved Manny a letter asking him to take care of a number of things for us. As for the childrens [*sic*] visit it looks like things are working out as you had planned. The P.K. was around to-day and I discussed ["this" CO] our request with him and he said he'll let me know [N2WI] the score after he talks it over with the warden. Incidentally I haven't heard from our boys and I've been awaiting their letter answering the ones we sent before I write them again. As for our lawyer, I didn't go into arrangements for the childrens [*sic*] visit. I'm leaving it up to you to go into this matter and let him know our wishes.

It looks like the campaign is begin [*sic*] to mature into a broad movement of many people who see the political nature of our case, understand it's [*sic*] deeper implications and are working to secure justice for us as an important step in defending civil liberties and fighting for peace. However I'm not going to be satisfied with half measures I believe I'm right in expecting a major effort on the part of the committee and our supporters to put over the facts of our case to mobilize the Court of Public Opinion on our behalf to help set us free. It's a tough fight but we're up to it and the need of the hour and the justness of our cause inspire us to fight for ["a" CO] complete victory.

Slowly but steadily we are coming to the date of our next major hurdle the writ of certiorari and I'm optimistic about our chances but of course I'm not positive for no one can predict the idiosyncrassies [*sic*] of the courts. I just thought of the fact that we ought to ask the Rabbi to get us New Years greeting cards to send to our family. For them it isn't going to be much of a holiday but we're closer to the time of our decision and we can hope for good results from now on. Lena will be coming up this weekend and I'm sure she'll bring us news of our two dears and of all the latest developments. Till I have the joyful pleasure of being in your presence I'll have to dream of holding you in my arms and loving you as you should be loved. It is necessary to recall how wonderful [*sic*] we used to spend our time together to gain new strength to continue the difficult fight ahead. You can tell my wife I need you more than anything else. All my being is for you—Your devoted husband—Julie

Emanuel H. Bloch
7 W. 16th Street
New York New York

Sept. 10, 1952

Dear Manny,

A very brief note simply to ask you to phone Ben about proper travel arrangements up here. Is he sure he can be here no later than 10:00 A.M. or earlier—anyway, no later. Remember he will have to meet you here when you arrive from the city by train and I want no slip-ups. Now, as soon as you are sure about same (if you aren't already, that is), please phone Ethel or Lee, so that they may set my fears at rest; I am working myself into a dither about it, probably needlessly. Nevertheless, I'd appreciate having some definite information—

At this writing, it looks like the 20th will be the day for the kids' visit, however, caution Ben to hold off telling them, as yet—First they will [NWI] all be driven half crazy a whole week in advance, and second—the date [NWI] itself is still subject to change—I am hoping to make it definite when Lena gets here on Saturday, the 13th—

In the mean time, please do take care of yourself; I hear you are not as well as you might be. Dena,[244] make him behave, won't you; he worries me!— Love, Ethel

Today—Mike is exactly $9^1/_2$!—I am fine!

Julius to Ethel

Sept. 11, 1952

My Sweet Woman,

Just after we got through talking about the fact that we haven't received any news direct from our boys a sweet newsy letter is delivered to us. Of course you can bet that I'm itching to see those photos but I'll be patient

---

[244]Manny's wife

and look forward to this extra treat at our next visit. I promptly sent our two dears an answering letter and my suggestion to you is to do the same after this weekend. Perhaps you ought to ask them if there is a day camp maybe it would be better for our Robbie to go there. Naturally we don't want to suggest anything that might not be for the best but it's a thought that should be considered. The tone of their letter pleases me very much and it is a good sign that they are getting the kind of care, security and love that will help them to withstand the difficulties of their peculiar situation brought about by our case. It will be good to see with our own eyes how they react and to see the visible improvements. I am happy but at the same time very sad that we are not with our beloved children to exercise our parental prerogatives and grow with them. However, it is fine that we have been able to make such a positive step and that will ease the burden on our boys.

Darling I'm terribly disappointed with the news the P.K. brought me as to our request. Heaven knows it is no more than right that we be allowed this little bit but I guess we will have to see what can be done to improve this situation. We will discuss this at our next tete a tete at our favorite screen. Also we'll be able to discuss the next general gathering of our sweet family at Ossining on the Hudson. I plan to send out the New Years cards this weekend after I buy some stamps in the commissary. You ought to send one to Miller.

Every time a Jewish Holiday arrives my mind flashes back to my family and all that this occassion [*sic*] signifies to them. All their prayers and wishes will be for a happy reunion of all of us in a peaceful world and they'll continue to work in every which way to contribute their share in helping us win our case. This holiday will take a lot out of them. Especially is this true of my mother. Soon all of us will be tensely awaiting the Supreme Courts [*sic*] decision on the writ of certiorari. My mind will be attuned to news of the committees [*sic*] work and each bit of progress will maintain my high spirits. It will be difficult for us these days but before the fireworks begins [*sic*] please don't expect too much of us and know we are only human and are therefore subject to all the [NWI] human frailties and I expect we'll have our difficult moments. At such times we must find in each other and in our love the strength to face with dignity and renewed determination the viscissitudes [*sic*] ahead. Long and hard [N3WI] is the fight but there is an end and it can only result [NWI] in our freedom. All my love—Julie

Julius to Ethel

Sept. 14, 1952

Sweetheart,

It's been a dull long day and I guess my mood is the same as the weather, namely I've been kind of out of sorts. Guess it's because I miss you very much and I feel lonely for the times we used to share together, discuss things and enjoy each others [*sic*] company. Our separation is the hardest sacrifice to take because we have been able to find in each other, no matter how difficult the situation may be, the necessary means to face our problems with courage, confident of our abilities to work things out satisfactorily. That is exactly why I had hoped we would be able to see each other more frequently and so put to naught painful longing and seek sustenance from emotional anguish and mental torture. But we are mature people who are thoroughly familiar with all that surrounds us and only in our [NWI] own character and person can we find the means to withstand the hardships and heartaches. Because of you my love I find new strength and vigor and I hope I can inspire in you [N2WI] added strength with my profound feelings of love for you. Perhaps I am addressing both of us when I write you and I repeat we must always keep in mind a clear prospective [*sic*] and know that we will ultimately win our fight. Since this is what really matters we can look forward to the time when we'll be together with our family building anew the [NWI] good life that we abruptly interrupted. This is the only worthwhile thing and by continuing this principled stand we are holding faith with our desires for a peaceful just and better world. I'm sure we'll come through with flying colors and I'm optimistic about our chances. Keep your pretty face smiling sweetheart so it can give me the lift I need.

Hooray for our Wednesday. This time you prepare the items for discussion making certain to allow sufficient time to talk about our boys [*sic*] visit. Above all we want this occassion [*sic*] to be a very fruitful one and if you brief us on it we might be able to get more out of it than usual. I know that you too got the idea that our little fellow should go to Day Camp if he can't go to kindergarten. Maybe you ought to write to Manny and tell him your idea so that by the time he comes he may have an answer for us. Also I'd like to suggest that he try to make arrangements for an early consultation with us. At the latest 10 days from the childrens [*sic*] visit. There is so much that I want to take up with you and I just wonder if we'll ever get to them. You understand that the kind of visit we have isn't always the most conducive to proper interchange of all ideas. Both of us will have to be patient and wait for our reunion to once again establish the kind of relationship we thrive on. I'll be thinking about you and holding you close

to my heart ["until" CO, NWI] soon I'll sit at our favorite screen and take in
all your charms. All my love—Your own Julie

Mrs. Lena Cohen
140 Baruch Place
New York New York

                                                                    Sept. 15, 1952
Dearest Lee,
    It's too bad I was not able to finish what I had begun talking about, so
perhaps I have succeeded in accomplishing nothing so much as to make you
unduly anxious. Please, I must ask you not to concern yourself until I see
you again. When I do, I'll clear it up to our mutual satisfaction. I simply
want us both to be as comfortable as possible; but, there, I'm beginning to
try to discuss it, and written words can [NWI] often be more confusing than
silence. So I just want you to promise me not to worry about it until you
visit me once more. OK?
    It's too bad I wasn't able to say it. I mean, when you tried to convince
me you weren't being conceited when you compared someone at the office
with your family. If I had said it, it would have embarrassed you into feeling you had "fished for a compliment," so I refrained. I'd like to say it now,
though, if I may. My dear girl, I have always had a soft spot for you, because you see I understand better than you imagine, that in your life you
have never [NWI] exactly had "honey to lick"—What's more, I've always
known you deserved a little of that "honey"—At the same time, when you
stick your head in the sand like an ostrich and want me to do likewise, I
can't help but holler some. Sure I wish there weren't any problems to begin
with [N4WI] the same as you, but since they [NWI] do exist, you have to
come to grips with them and solve them, not "look away" as you put it and
swallow all kinds of guff! Besides, I've seen you assert yourself very nicely
where you were convinced the need to do so existed—If you "look away"
from a situation, [NWI] however, how can you figure out whether such a
need exists or not! Savvy?
    Anyway, let's talk about something in a lighter vein. May I suggest
the following for the outfit you were wearing? Make shoulder straps out of
black velveteen material and a ruffle (same stuff) for the front of the dress in
place of the lace you have there now. With the soft black felt hat, black
shoes and bag you were wearing, and these extra rich black touches to accent
the black dots in your costume (you see, I'm very observant), and a pair of
smart white gloves for contrast, you will look like one "slick chick"! Also,
wear black, [NWI] velveteen band around throat without the cameo—To
begin with, you don't have matching ear-rings; second, it [NWI] just doesn't

"go" with your dress—And instead of the ear-rings you did wear, let me suggest medium sized button ear-rings in lustrous imitation pearl, you know, the round type that screws on and covers the entire lobe of the ear—Now you're all dressed up to go anywhere!—You don't mind all [letter continued on top of second side] this, do you—It was fun for me!—All my love—
                                                                                 Ethel—

Ethel to Julius

                                                                         Sept. 15, 1952
Sweetest Julie,
    I expect what I wish to say in reply to your letter of the 14th shall require but a very few lines and shall therefore make it less difficult for you to receive before we meet on Wednesday. My darling more and more I tend to withdraw into the [NWI] deepest recesses of myself, stimulated to emerge fully, only when you are with me; and yet I am moved by your poignantly expressed need, to [N2WI] attempt to communicate with you, even in the absence of your physical being. Day by day our separation grows the more bitterly intolerable; day by day, the assault upon mind and spirit grows the more viciously insistent. The fact that no degree of pressure will ever cause us to repudiate those principles of democracy that sit beleaguered with us behind these repugnant bars, does not in anyway mitigate the heartbreak we suffer nor render less culpable the refusal to alleviate it to some more comparable degree. Wait, wait and tremble, ye mad masters, this barbarism, this infamy you practice upon us and with which you regale yourselves presently, so gleefully, will not go unanswered, unavenged, forever! The whirlwind gathers, before which you must fly like chaff!
    Sweetheart I love you with a strength that defies my pain—Still, hold me close my heart is so heavy with wanting you—Always, your own wife—

Julius to Ethel

                                                                         Sept. 18, 1952
Sweetest Bunny,
    I must say that your last epistle was a gem and moved me very much. Fundamentally so because of its keen insight in our situation and what the future holds for our case. You have an important gift that you must bring forth for others to see because you have now become integrated in a "case." This is a duty we owe to mankind for we possess the ability to poignantly present our cause in it's [*sic*] most dramatic way especially as it effects [*sic*] the lives of our fellow Americans. This contribution to our fight we can

[NWI] make and [NWI] we ought to work hard to do our part as we see it and as we are able ["to" probably omitted here] translate for all to know the facts. Of course we must do it at our own speed and in our own way but we have the stuff and the committee can do a swell job with it.

The samples of the literature Manny sent us shows that the committee is doing a splendid job and I'm feeling a lot better, after seeing some of the results. In the last two days I've received two beautiful New Years Cards, chosen in very good taste, that ["had" CO, NWI] expressed all the typical warmth of my family [N2WI] for us on this special occassion [sic]. ["Also I" CO] There also was a letter from Lena and the wonderful letter from the boys. If we want to get these letters often we'll have to answer them as soon as possible. If you can see your way clear, after our boys visit us, drop them a line. The reason I'd like you to write them now is that you can take them to task for self deprecation. For their actions and letters show there is no lack of understanding or ability and formal education is not the key to knowing ones [sic] worth.

I'm well prepared for our visit with the boys this weekend and Ive [sic] done as you suggested to insure that things will go off smoothly. As the day approaches my anxiety increases especially since I am hoping for a very positive and constructive visit for our two precious dears. Anyway we'll be able to celebrate the New Year by being together, even though it is under this [sic] difficult circumstances. Let us look forward to a year when we will be delivered from all the misery and take up again the sweet family life we know and love so much. Our wishes and hopes are for a peaceful world because only in an atmosphere of calm can justice really triumph and can people enjoy a free democratic life. The coming year will be an important one of decision for us and many other people and we can enter it full of confidence knowing that we have progressed well in our campaign to win our freedom. Assured that there will be no letup but an intensification of the fight to win [NWI] our complete vindication.

This is the third New Year that we will spend in danger and away from our beloved children but our hopes are high and we can face the future with new courage—All the love of my heart and mind —Julie

Michael & Robert Rosenberg
c/o B. Bach—R.D. 2 Box 148 M
Tom's River New Jersey

Sept. 25, 1952

Sweetest children,

You are exactly that you know; since Saturday, I've been walking on air, remembering how you looked and what you said. How wonderfully satisfying it was to squeeze you in my arms and exchange loving kisses. As a matter of fact, I plan to have all the Rosenbergs, short and tall, [N3WI] fat and skinny, spend one solid week doing nothing else but, sometime in the near future, the nearer the better, of course! When Daddy was in to see me on Wednesday, we babbled like a couple of kids ourselves, marvelling first over one of you and then over the other, and we dearly wish for you to know how proud we are of the fine job both of you are doing, each in his own individual way, just the most worthwhile job anyone, be it adult or child, can do—that of growing and changing and developing, into healthy, happy people!

They are collecting mail now, so I'll have to write you [NWI] again over the week-end.—I simply had to drop you a few lines, [N5WI] in the mean time however just to say, "thank you," for a most enjoyable visit—and hello again!

All my love—
Mommy—

Julius to Ethel

Sept 25, 1952

Dearest Ethel,

Our visit was so wonderful and I love you so much that I find I miss you very much today. How I hunger to be with you ["and" CO, N3WI] for us to share the joys of life together. In spite of this heartfelt pain I suffer because of our separation I find the courage to keep myself on an even keel since I have you as an example and inspiration. I know that any words this letter conveys to you cannot begin to express all that you mean to me and the high regard I have for you. How much happiness you can get on this third birthday of yours, spent imprisoned in direct negation of all that is right and decent. I dont [*sic*] really know. Truth is you deserve much better and an indication of the real satisfaction is the thought people have of you. For isn't the medallion you wear the symbol of warmth love [NWI] worth and promise [three inserted words CO, first and third were "and" and "worth"]? In the past we've celebrated many of your birthdays together. We continue to do honor to this special day of yours by rededicating ourselves to fight with all our strength for what is best for our children and family and incidentally all families. For peace, justice and a better life. Working for the dignity of the human being. That means that we follow in the same principled way [N4WI] the manner in which we have lived till now ["the" CO, NWI] and campaign for complete vindication from this political frameup. Happy day my sweet wife and I have high hopes of spending your next birthday with you and our precious children. Take heart we've come a long way and there are many positive accomplishments to date and we must keep our vision fastened on a perspective of freedom.

There are a number of things we didn't cover at our visit such as Dr. Millers [*sic*] visit and the record. I finally managed to complete the entire trial record. My candid opinion is that our rights were well protected by our lawyers and we didn't get a fair and impartial trial because the D.A. and Judge's conduct was atrocious. Particularly bad from the point of view of going counter to legal precedents and the constitutional protections of [NWI] civil rights is the manifestly vicious Circuit Court opinion. For with a large record they found refuge in upholding the governments [*sic*] position and not answering the questions we raised. I still feel optimistic of our chances for certiorari and I think we have put forth a very good petition. The clincher is going to be the effectiveness of the committees [*sic*] work in rallying public support. It is my belief that a careful study of the testimony will prove helpful in suggesting matters to our distinguished counselor for investigation. Let us ["not" CO] make good use of our abilities in this direction. Please write our boys a letter and let my sister know if you do. She will be able to carry a message to me on her Sat. visit. —Many more returns of the day in happier surroundings.

All my heart—devotedly Julie

Julius to Ethel

Sept. 28, 1952

Hello Charming Wife,

In keeping with this special day of yours that I am celebrating I take myself to the pleasant chore of communicating with you, the dearest person I know. A good part of the day I spent in reminiscing [NWI] the many incidents that we have shared together. It would be a pleasure to sit and talk to you for hours on just what I recalled today. This morning I began to reread the trial record in earnest and I'm making copious notes of details we should talk over with our counselor. The progress I am making is slow but steady I expect to be able to continue at the rate I set today, one book a day. Perhaps by next weekend when Manny comes I'll have all these notes to talk over with him. Besides being usefull [*sic*] work it helps the time pass quickly.

Coming back to the thought that I'd like to spend our time discussing pleasantries I find that it is more important to cover more pressing matters. For instance the two hour visit I spent with my sister this Saturday was packed full of stuff and I'll have to condense it as much as possible and still give you all the pertinent facts. As for the news from the committee she is very sorry that she did not find the time to tell you all that is taking place but I made notes of the high lights and I'll give them to you. Also I intend to fill you in on the conversation we had about my mother and our lawyer and their actions in our case. Actually sweetheart there is so much to cover I'm beginning to worry that not only will I not be able to impart all of it to you but I won't be able to pitch any verbal woo. This next tete a tete must go off like clock work and I want you to prepare an outline to present your own views in concise form. Note that I'd like to hear about your last talk with Dr. Miller.

I hope that by the time you read this letter you will have sent our precious boys a few words. Somehow I don't find it easy to keep up my end of the correspondence on too regular a basis. One thing you can rest assured on that the committee is making very great strides in our case and their plans for Rosenberg week include many of the ["thoughts" CO, NWI] ideas you yourself suggested at our last visit.

Honey girl each passing year you are sweeter dearer and more youthful to me. With any kind of a fair shake, we will be celebrating your next birthday in the warmth of our own home with our boys close by. Autumn with its [next word or words are illegible because there is over-writing by the end of the first over the beginning of the second—best guess is what follows] quickly falling dusk, longer nights, and approaching cold is upon us. Let us keep our hopes high and we'll win our case. Ethel I miss you terribly and feel so lonely I really need you my heart —All my love—Julie

Michael & Robert Rosenberg c/o B. Bach
R.D. 2 Box 148 M
Tom's River New Jersey

                                                    Sept. 28, 1952
Dearest children,

What a glorious day it was to celebrate a birthday. I awoke to find a golden sun bright in a clear, blue sky. A mild breeze wafted in gently from the Hudson and it was heavenly good to fill the lungs with sweet, fresh air. Overhead the sea gulls floated by on indolent, gray wings, and only the sound of the starlings, noisily scolding, broke the all pervading stillness. I walked quietly about the peaceful yard, stopping every now and then to inspect the bits of green stuff struggling up through the cracks in the concrete, and trying to imagine what you two might be up to, this fine morning! My goodness, I thought, that's right; I am 37 years old to-day, old enough to have chalked up to my credit a grand family, a worthwhile life, and a host of wonderful friends; old enough also to realize why I must spend my birthday alone, but strong enough, too, to know without any doubt whatever, that those artificially induced storms about which Ben told you, will at long last no longer be permitted to rage at the expense of decent mankind! This day I spend apart from loved ones is all the proof I need that there is no loneliness too great to withstand. No task too difficult of accomplishment, for the [next three lines inserted] establishment of that kind of world that will give all peoples the opportunity to live and work and grow to-gether, in love and in dignity and in peace! Know then, my two dearest dears, that bitterly as I missed you, (and there's no two ways about it, I'll have to go on missing you until we're all to-gether again at last), know then that I was gladdened because I understood the necessity to accept my responsibility for your dear sakes, just as it warmed me to remember all the other countless parents who are standing up for their families! Our precious children deserve no less than that!

Speaking of other parents, reminds me that I have a bone to pick with a certain pair of them named "Bach." No sooner do they finish taking me to task (and rightly) for daring to feel inferior, then what do they do but up and tear themselves down! A fine thing, I must say! All kidding aside though, we must all of us feel that what [NWI] we are giving [NWI] is the most that is in us to give, else we shan't even be able to give the least—Savvy? Not that I am unable to appreciate these feelings of inadequacy, but, my dear Ben, take comfort from the fact that I must be considered an unlettered savage, if someone of your development considers himself uneducated! Nuff said! I love you all!

Robby, darling, would you please make a few pictures for me? I should like very much a drawing of the "wolfie" and the bear with the long nails, and the one of the door-knob and the two bell buttons. And you, Mike, honey, compose a poem—or if you'd rather draw something, too, I should be delighted. Such presents would bring you closer to me and make me ever so happy!

Your Daddy is fine and sends all his love—And so does your Mommy!—[the rest of the line is filled with x's]

Ethel to Julius

Sept. 29, 1952

Sweetheart, Sunday, Sept. 21

Since yesterday I have been floating in an atmosphere so rarified, that it is far more reminiscent of Mt. Olympus than Sing Sing!

Monday, Sept. 29, 1952

After you left me on Wednesday, I descended earthward with a crash; what you had told me of your problem had a necessarily depressing effect. Man's inhumanity to man has ever made men sick at heart; the hurt, fortunately, is of a temporary nature, however, and I bound back with renewed strength and determination. Especially when there is a dear husband to send me such deeply sincere and moving birthday greetings!

Darling, my sweet darling, how truly I love you! And how much I long to possess the remarkable qualities you attribute to me, and to be worthy of all that you are yourself!

I [NWI] have dropped Manny a line urging him to come as soon as possible. My mind has been in a whirl since Saturday, and I am in too agitated a state to wait too long for our next consultation—

Again, dearest—all my thanks for your beautiful card—and all my heart to you—

Your loving wife—

Mr. David Rosenberg
430 E. 63rd Street
New York N.Y.

Sept. 30, 1952

Dear Brother,

Enclosed please find a pass for this Sunday morning from 10:00–11:00 AM. I hope you will come well prepared to bring us all the latest news. Since our time is kind of short I would suggest you and Lena discuss with our sister Ethel all that we talked about at our last visit. I am positive that you my brother and sisters will exert every effort, [NWI] practical, moral and financial to help us in our time of need. Well do I know that it necessitates a sacrifice from each one of you but I'm sure you will do your part willingly and not let us down. Therefore please discuss the family problem amongst yourselves and let me know what your conclusions are on this matter. It is my hope that every one in the family had a pleasant holiday season and are in good health. This month will be of great importance to us because we expect to learn the Supreme Courts [*sic*] decision on our petition for a Writ of Certiorari. We are optimistic and we believe we'll be successful in obtaining a hearing before the highest court in our land but to ensure our success we need a great deal of public support.

The plans the committee has drawn up and already begun to put in effect for the coming period are the kind that are needed to arouse a mass movement of the people to win justice for us. They must be pushed with vigor and determination and a relentless concerted drive this month can ["and" probably omitted here] will do the trick.

Since I've received the trial record I've read it completely and now I'm rereading the testimony carefully and making copious notes to discuss with our counselor at our next legal consultation. Incidentally, we hope to see our distinguished lawyer this weekend and go over many details of our case with him. To the unbiased individual the record will prove conclusively that we are victims of a monstrous political frameup and that there is no basis in fact to warrant a conviction. The trial record speaks for itself and I believe it should receive very wide distribution. By the way I would like you to tell Manny to send a copy of our trial record to the Rabbi who is chaplain of Sing Sing. The name is Rabbi Irving Koslowe, [NWI] address Mamaroneck NY. Since we are part of his congregation here he is interested in reading the facts in the case.

Till now it's been very difficult for us but we have high hopes that our fellow Americans will recognize the true nature of our case and come to our aid. I have faith that there is enough decency and righteousness in our fellow men that they will fight for a just cause. We are confident and are awaiting the day of our freedom. We hope it will come soon.

All my love—Julie
P.S. Send my love & regards to Mama, Ethel, Lena & the whole family.—

David Rosenberg
430 E. 63rd Street
New York N.Y.

Oct. 1, 1952
Dearest Davy,
Enclosed please find usual Sunday pass. Please try, won't you, to be in a position to give us some idea as to when Manny figures to get here. I'd also like to know how soon your mother plans to come again—

All is well—On Saturday, Sept. 28, I was 37—As I told Mike at our visit with the children, his mother is getting ["to be" omitted] an old lady. He took it up promptly and said that in that case, Julie must be "an old geezer"!—A fine thing! What is this younger generation coming to! [NWI] Seriously, I am crazy about both of them—and the childish yet brave manner in which they try to keep their spirits up! Bless them!

My lord and master arrives soon, so adieu—

Until Sunday—my love to all,
Ethel—

Julius to Ethel

Oct. 2nd, 1952
Hello Honey Dearest,
It was most refreshing to the senses to see you looking so well and very pretty indeed. A buoyant and joyful feeling stirs inside of me and at

once I am captivated by your youthfulness, vitality and beautiful countenance. I mean it sincerely when I say that immediately when I see you I feel strong in our unity and confident in our victory. Therefore keep on smiling and I'm sure our spirits will remain high in spite of all the difficulties we face. This is the important month of decision darling and we must keep our feet firmly planted in reality and not allow ourselves to be stampeded into hopelessness. We've put up an excellent fight for a very good cause and we're not quitters as our experience tells us life is only worthwhile when you struggle to better yourself. I've given some thought to your idea concerning a play and I think it is a swell idea and you should do all you can to implement this and have it bear fruit. Any way you are able to contribute to this creative endeavor will be very advantageous to us and I would like to suggest that you do some preparatory work so that you'll have some of it available by the time Manny gets around to see us. Of course we never have enough time to adequately cover these pressing points. Let us not be dismayed by the proximity of the Supreme Courts [*sic*] decision but instead let us continue to do all we can to help ourselves.

As for myself I'm on schedule with the trial record. I managed to get into the sixth book before I was sidetracked by the world series game. Incidentally this promises to be a very interesting contest and I'm sure we're both rooting for the Dodgers. As a diversion it is a good one and it helps pass the time.

As yet I haven't seen any indication of the effectiveness of the campaign the committee is waging. My brother will bring us up to date on all the latest developments. Naturally I had hoped to begin to hear some favorable comments, at least in the liberal press, on our position. However we must be realists the the [*sic*] political climate has not cleared up and there is a great fear that is paralysing [*sic*] many former liberals and progressives into silence. On the other hand the progressives are putting up a very good fight and soon we'll be able to guage [*sic*] the results. Our case, the elections and above all the fight for peace these will give the answers. I'm still optimistic but I'm prepared for any eventualities.

At the moment I'm very lonely and I miss you terribly. Oh If [*sic*] I could only hold you in my arms and whisper to you all the love of my heart!! I am trying to get with the mood to send our sweet fellows a letter tonight. My sweet woman I adore you. All my devotion —Your Julie

Master Michael Rosenberg
c/o B. Bach
R.D. 2 Box 148 M
Toms River N.J.

Oct. 2, 1952

Dear Michael & Robert,

Your Mummy and I have made a sort of arrangement to try to alternate in writting [*sic*] you letters in order for you to be informed as to how we are getting along. You fellows were able to see how happy we were to visit with you and we certainly enjoyed talking to you and playing games. Mike please keep us informed of how you are doing at school with your studies and how you spend your time. Of course it was fun doing the arithmatic [*sic*] problems and discussing history and geography. I like your singing Robbie and had a good time playing mousie and pussy cat with you.

It would be wonderful if arrangements could be made for Robbie to go to Day Camp or school. I believe we are very fortunate to have children who are talented and if it is possible to give you boys the opportunity to develop these skills by piano or music lessons I would like to see such efforts made.

Please thank Sonia and Ben for the lovely New Years card. I was very pleased to receive one from them. These past two weeks I've been very busy reading the trial record. At this time I'm making thorough notes in order to discuss pertinent questions with our dear friend and distinguished counselor Manny Bloch. The committee made a very good move in printing copies of the entire trial proceeding. An impartial reading of the facts in the case will bare the monstrous miscarriage of justice that has been perpetrated as a political frameup against the freedom of the American people. This is a threat to create a paralysing [*sic*] fear throughout our land so that these evil forces, who would do away with us can have a free hand. Since we want you our sons to live in peace, to play, learn and grow in security we continue as always, even in this very difficult position, to fight for these principles. Because it is in the interests of all people mankind is rallying in it's [*sic*] multitudes to secure the peace and the democratic ways we hold dear and since our case is an integral part of this bigger fight they will also come to our aid.

The committee has outlined an ambitious program which if successful can insure a victory in this campaign. The coming months are the most crucial ones and only vigorous, relentless concerted activities [NWI] now will be timely in helping us get public support to win our freedom. It is imperative that the record be gotten into the hands of public leaders in all walks of life and that the facts & issues of this case reach millions of people. We are optimistic that with this kind of support we'll get certiorari and be able to prove our innocence and [NWI] eventually be completely vindicated. I am sure Ben and Sonia will be able to explain all this to you in a way you will be able to understand. Let us keep on hearing good reports from you our precious children. Don't worry we your parents will be together with you again when this is all over. All my love. Daddy —Julie

Regards to our friends and well wishers. Your good work will make all people proud by winning justice in this case. JR.

Ethel to Julius

Oct. 3, 1952

My darling husband,

These lines, I hope, will reassure you as to my emotional state. First, I have been getting a great deal of satisfaction in the process of composing a suitable letter to the children, commemorating my birthday; I think so well of it myself, who knows [NWI] but that it may very well be pressed into service on our behalf in some way or another.

Into the bargain, a very pleasant surprise in the form of a new dress gave my morale an unexpected boost. I shall tear myself apart until you have the chance to see it, of that you may be sure, for it really looks lovely on me!

And last but not least, our visit, though incomplete as usual, was of such a quality as to renew my spirits quite remarkably—My sweet, you are so capable and so hard-working and so sweet, I just simply adore you!—

Dearest, your lazy wife will never get her commissary slip in, in time, unless—you know—

Again, my deepest love and thanks

yours ever, Ethel

Julius to Ethel

Oct. 5, 1952

Hello Bunny,

Thanks for a lovely letter. I hope you made a copy of your literary epistle that was brought forth on the occassion [sic] of your birthday for [N3WI] the benefit of your precious children. Certainly, I will be anxiously awaiting our get together, at our favorite screen so that I can feast my eyes on your new dress especially the lovely woman in it. This Friday I sent our two dears a letter and I'm sure they'll like it. My brothers [sic] visit although short was fruitful in so far as I impressed [NWI] him with my views on the home situation. Since it isn't of real great import as far as our case is concerned and I'm positive they'll work things out I don't intend for you and I to spend too much of our short time on this matter. As yet he has not given your brother[245] a copy of the record and I don't like the slow rate some of these important matters are taken care of.

Let us try to cover a great deal of ground at our next visit. Please prepare your suggestions for Manny's visit, which I hope will come soon. Incidentally from the newspapers I gather that Oct. 13th will be the earliest date that the Supreme Court could possibly decide on our petition for certiorari. Also this Wednesday let us take up your ideas on what we can personally do. I intend to condense the more ["than" probably omitted here] 26 pages of notes I made on the record in order to pinpoint certain items for your attention. The job of carefully scrutinizing the trial record is complete and I need at least a six hour discussion period with you and our swell counselor to deal with all these points.[246] Honey the immensity of the frameup that was perpetrated against us becomes more evident with each reading of the facts. The culprit of this star chamber proceeding is Judge Kaufman[.] He is the prosecutor, Lord high executioner [last two syllables inserted] decider of the issues and he bended [*sic*] the jury to his views and in its entirety it is a grave miscarriage of justice.

Shortly, we will know the results of our fight to date. Legally we've done the best and the deciding factor will be the effectiveness of the campaign to [illegible word here] public support. I suppose at our lawyer's consultation we'll be able to glean from his report, how the court of public opinion is reacting and whether it is becoming acquainted with the issues in our case and really doing something about it. The only thing I can say to you, and of course I'm speaking collectively, is to maintain as in the past the correct perspective and we'll weather the difficult road ahead.

Since I last saw you I've missed you dreadfully and I need your comforting words, the depth of your wisdom and the warmth of your love. Darling it is true that I adore you and admire you as a wonderful person and I feel

---

[245]Almost certainly refers to Bernard, the only Greenglass who visited her in Sing Sing.

[246]Note the traditional lawyer-client relationship, even in a political case. The two defendants had had virtually no input into the original appeal and the first petition for *certiorari* because they had not even seen the full record and had no chance to give their views to their lawyers before the appeal and petition were filed. Clients, even intelligent, political clients, were deemed not to have the expertise to make any contribution to their own defense. For some very angry reactions to this approach, see Morton Sobell, *On Doing Time*, especially pp. 155–56. It is important to note that the cooperation between political defendants and lawyers in political cases changed totally in the 1960s. See, for example, *The Trial* by Tom Hayden (NY: Holt, Rinehart and Winston, 1970) and *Free Huey* by Edward Keating (NY: Dell, 1970).

such a great hunger that I can't be with you all this long time. But in my mind and in my heart I know we will be one again—Devotedly—Julie

Julius to Ethel

Oct. 9th, 1952

Dearest Ethel,

I am positive that the fresh breeze that entered your domicile [*sic*] as you read the latest letter from your boys warmed the cockles of your heart. The atmosphere was one of a warm well-knit family group with healthy energetic activities that are very wholesome and is conducive to growth and proper understanding of the dignity of social beings. Truely [*sic*] our dears are developing under the loving care of swell people who are giving them the security they need in this difficult period of their lives. The fact that they succeeded in spite of difficulties, to get Robbie to kindergarten shows how quick they are to put into effect our suggestions. Therefore, I think it is high time that you on our behalf enter into a correspondence with them on furthering plans to give Michael piano lessons and Robbie some additional release for his talents. I feel this is important and you can put our ideas in the form that they will meet the right kind of consideration from Ben and Sonia.

Before I answer this letter of theirs I intend to wait until after our decision on the writ of certiorari this coming Monday. If on the other hand you can write the boys please do the honors. Their messages mean a lot to us and our own efforts to keep in touch with them is the key to prompt and regular news from Toms River.

Perhaps, I will see you before next Monday but if Manny doesn't put in an appearance before then this letter will have to do. Incidentally Monday at 12:45 P.M[.] station WFAS carries the news which will probably have the Supreme Court decisions. Remember honey, no matter what the decision is it does not change our innocence nor our determination to fight with all our vigor in the same principled manner for complete vindication. One thing is certain that the political climate in our land is one of fear with a rising hysteria against all those who dont [*sic*] conform and this does not help us obtain a just verdict based on the merits of our case. Counterbalanced against this are the increasing activities of the committee to rally support to secure justice in our case[.] I am confident we have conducted ourselves in a manner that our conscience is clear and our self respect is preserved. Darling we can hold our head up high and justly be proud of ourselves for we are standing up to all these difficulties. I am confident we must win and I am sure the future will justify our faith in the fundamental [NWI] democratic principles of our country and its wonderful decent people. I hope I were [*sic*] able to surround you with my love and profound affection [two words erased here, look like "for you"] in this trying period but I want you to know you are uppermost in my heart and mind— Devotedly—Julie

The following letter represents the first and most detailed reaction of Julius Rosenberg to reading the trial record. It is apparent from previous letters and this one that he and Ethel never had a transcript of the record until the National Committee to Secure Justice in the Rosenberg Case duplicated the transcript which had been submitted to the Supreme Court along with the petition for a writ of certiorari on June 7, 1952. All references in the following letter are to the pagination of that reprint. The original trial transcript is on file at the Federal Records Center in Bayonne, N.J.: "U.S. vs. Rosenbergs, Sobell, Yakovlev and Greenglass" (Cr. No. 134-245). In my footnotes I will refer to this publication as "Record."

In amplifying on our father's letter, we are faced with the possibility of describing almost the entire trial in order to explain the sections of the transcript he is referring to. We choose, instead, to let the reader decide whether to go to the transcript to see what he is referring to. We will only amplify on our father's remarks if it touches on a particularly important issue about which there is further information in either the primary or the secondary sources. This letter is written in ink.

Mr. Emanuel H. Bloch
7 West 16th St.
New York N. Y.

Oct. 11, 1952

Page 1.
Dear Manny,

After reading the trial record a number of times certain questions have been troubling my lay mind and I beg your patient and understanding indulgence in considering the contents of these notes. They may be nonsense, repetitious, useless or perhaps one or two items might mean something please bear with me. Truth is I'm overwhelmingly pleased with the legal job you've done for us and I don't intend to waste too much of your time or interfere into your province. You have done magnificent [suffix "ly" CO, NWI] job ["in prote" CO] defending our rights and protecting the record.

All the pages and lines refer to the small printed trial record put out by the committee. Where something concerns Bernie I will put a B in front of the note. ["If" CO] I'll not be mad if you tear these up and throw them away without looking at them but here goes.

426 *The Rosenberg Letters*

1 [circled] The following court proceedings are missing from the record how can they be made part of it for future use?

(a) Our arrest and arraignments (The warrants too)

(b) Court hearings on bail

(c) Motion and arguments on Bill of particulars

(d) All additional pre-trial court activities such as motions and briefs in support of them.

(e) How about your brief to circuit court?

(f) Why is Dave's sentencing proceeding part of our official record for his attorney, the D.A., and Judge got in many prejudicial remarks that are put before the appeals Judges and you our attorney couldn't protect our rights. Many obvious distortions were included.

2 [circled] What effect did it have on our case when the complaint against Sobel [*sic*] listing five overt acts i. e. (a) Jan '46, (b) June '46 (c) Feb '47 (d) July '47 (e) May '48 were made part of the record after we had been on the stand and we couldn't put in our denials for it was too late?

3 [circled] On the questioning of the perspective [*sic*] jurors many derogatory questions on organizations listed as subversive by the Att. Gen. were made in spite of the Supreme Courts [*sic*] ruling on this matter.

4 [circled] In Saypols [*sic*] opening to the jury he made a number of damaging statements that the trial record did not in fact prove even from his own witnesses.

5 [circled] ["1st Book Vol. 1" written in margin above the next two words] P. 181 The courts [*sic*] initial ruling on your motion to exclude communism is that if it is for establishing a motive he will in due course rule on this matter. Doesn't this bind him to it?

6 [circled] P. 203—L. 8–12 If as Elitcher[247] says he was first approached to join the Young Communist League in 1939 while in Washington he of his own knowledge could not know of communist activities at school that Saypol used in his opening remarks and summation to the jury.

7 [circled] [A circled 7 and P 209 L. 13–18 CO, N4WI, first two on top of second two] 2nd Book. Vol. 1 P. 221–222 The prosecutor concluded [*sic*—perhaps meant "colluded"] with the court to pass over the Young Communist League so that ostensibly the record is supposed to be bear [*sic*] of this poison until 1939 but nevertheless it was allowed to reoccur numerous times after.

8 [circled] P. 236 Elitcher states the first meeting was June 1944 after D-Day how about the record of my employment at Signal Corps to disprove this?

---

[247]For a discussion of Max Elitcher as a witness, see Schneir, pp. 121–23, 323–27; Sobell, Morton, *On Doing Time*, p. 140–62; *Sons*, pp. 422f.

9 [circled] P. 236 L 9–12 from bottom. He says no other names were mentioned & then on next page Saypol gives the lead that Sobel [sic] was mentioned.

10 [circled] P. 257 L 8 from bottom—Elitcher uses "Julie" is it not [word "revealing" CO, N5WI, last two of which continue to a new line] contradictory from the witnesses testimony that I did not use "Julius" as a name that Saypol claims in his brief [N4WI] to Circuit Court which is supposed to be my "spy" name.

Page 2

Book 2 Vol.–1

P. 258 Note Elitcher statement of how I said I got into the work is the same as Greenglass's so well rehearsed before hand. Whose legal mind lays these their parralells [sic] (like asking wife to leave) this bit of poison, schools, money—Perhaps (Rat Rogge).[248]

P. 269 Many times, quite frequent [sic], he saw FBI & D.A. & lawyer thats [sic] were [sic] he learned to repeat his story so well.

Note P. 305-6 & 309 on these two occasions the end of summer social gathering & then he came to N.Y. with wife he says there was no "spy" talk how could Saypol say continuous efforts with him?

P. 341 L-3 he says he doesn't remember whether he testified to grand jury & whether the question was asked about Bently.[249] in [sic] the middle of the page the court says for him not to answer these questions because it was already answered & the Court testifies for him incorrectly that he said he wasn't asked *

DAVE Greenglass

The chronology of this testimony is important July '44 he went to Manhattan project Aug. '44 he reached Los Alamos—Middle Nov—44 Ruth said she had conversation with us at 10 Monroe—End Nov. '44 Ruth with

---

[248]O. John Rogge was the lawyer for both David and Ruth Greenglass and for Max and Helene Elitcher. He was a former left-wing liberal who in 1948 ran for a local judgeship in New York on the Progressive Party ticket headed by former Vice-President Henry Wallace. For the story of the Progressive Party and that campaign, see C. MacDougall, *Gideon's Army* (NY: Marzani and Munsell, 1965), especially Volume 2. By 1950 he had become an anti-communist Cold War liberal and was anxious to make peace with the U.S. government. For an admiring short story of Rogge's career, see Radosh and Milton, pp. 82–84. For a less admiring story, see W.E.B. DuBois, *In Battle for Peace* (NY: Masses and Mainstream, 1952), pp. 109-18. Dr. DuBois may be forgiven his less charitable attitude since Rogge became the main witness in an effort to jail the 83-year-old African-American scholar-activist for failing to register as a foreign agent after he worked to circulate the Stockholm Peace Appeal. The entire story is told in the aforementioned book. It was DuBois who coined the phrase "Rogge the Rat."

[249]See footnote 68 for information about Elizabeth Bentley.

David at Albuquerque then Jan. furlough. Note: Jan. '45 Gold saw Fuchs in Cambridge and learned about the Los Alamos project then later it is inferred he turned over information that month to Yakovlev. Now the govt. theory that they try to infer is that I had contact with Yakovlev. How can any sane man explain according to the testimony in the record. (a) That I knew Dave worked on "Atom" Bomb. Was Dave perhaps in contact with Yakovlev before Nov. 1944 [N3WI] or with Fuchs. For his wife didn't even know his exact place of work before then.[250] (b) How in heavens [sic] name could I know of the existence [last syllable illegible, "existing" is overwritten] of work on atomic bomb or of Los Alamos in Nov. 1944. 2 [circled] How could I give him Dave a description of the bomb in early part of Jan 1945 when even according to Gold's testimony Fuchs hadn't given this information as yet or at least it isn't even inferred. I hope I make myself clear. What is the possibility of obtaining depositions from people who are out of the country like Fuchs on these matters.

P. 402-3 Note Fitzpatrick, De Mars, Bob Holland his bosses. He was foreman for only two months of his stay at Los Alamos. He left in Feb '46.

P. 411—middle—He said he learned of Dr. Urey in Dec. '44 How did he tell the information to Ruth in Nov '44?

On Dave's testimony as to hero worship, discussions at home in early years & later years Bernie can know the truth about these.[251]

P. 421 bottom page—Dave said Ruth went out in Aug '44—How about the fact that Ruth might have seen Dave twice at Albuquerque? Note Dave's recital & Ruths [sic] repetition is in the same order, same highlights & even the same words—Not rehearsed? Who staged this Rogge at behest of Saypol. (Note He arrived a few day [sic] after Jan 1945 p. 427 & I gave him a description of bomb)

Vol 1—Book 3

P. 454—Delman P. 457 Bederson

P. 471 He spoke of Theta shop to get lense [sic] work done how does it check with chronology of him turning over sketches on lense [sic] mold if theta shop was his location after date he says he turned over sketch to me in Jan '45

P. 472 Marshman.

---

[250]Note here that our father is continuing to accept the defense theory of the case at that time that Greenglass and Gold were in fact spies and that our parents had been brought into the case by the Greenglasses to lighten their guilt and punishment.

[251]It is clear from this and other references that our parents hoped that Bernard Greenglass would be willing to offer testimony that would tend to impeach the credibility of David Greenglass on some issues of fact.

P. 478 12 lines from bottom Koski says to best of his knowledge no information in this field in text books or technical journals on this subject.[252] How about shaped charges used in the war before this[253] check with scientists on this important matter. Showing that the important principle of concentrating pressure waves was not new and revealing as he said so that one can get to the important slant of the work.

Page 3

Vol 1—Book 3

P. 482 Note the important answer of Koski on the relative dimensions that were missing in sketches.

P. 516 Convenient to mention Gen. Elect (Sobell) & Cleveland (Sidorovich)[254] whose mind Rogge & Saypol?

P. 517 He mentions Warner & Swasey perhaps we could check on the guest book of visitors during the period to prove I was never there.[255]

---

[252]Walter Koski was the only scientist who testified at the trial for the prosecution. His testimony (pp. 466–86) was designed to show that three sketches introduced as alleged copies (from memory) of what David Greenglass allegedly turned over to Harry Gold in June of 1945 and to our father in January of 1945 represented a "reasonably accurate" portrayal of experimental work with lens molds at Los Alamos. (See pp. 473–77 for exhibits 2 and 6, 477 for exhibit 7). The crux of the testimony is Koski's affirmative response to the prosecutor's assertion that he was "engaged in a new and original field" (p. 478).

[253]See Schneir, p. 266: ". . . the fact is that the explosive lenses made at Los Alamos were very closely related to a far earlier development—the shaped charge—which, by 1945, had been discussed in 'text books or technical journals' throughout the world for some fifty years. In the late nineteenth century, Charles E. Munroe, an American, had discovered that the effect of cutting a cavity in the side of an explosive charge is to concentrate part of the explosive force on a particular spot. This valuable technique for converging and focusing explosive waves—known as the 'Munroe effect'—soon found numerous applications. . . . A variety of shaped charges were utilized by all belligerents in World War II in many different weapons, including the bazooka. . . . In February 1945 . . . a detailed and profusely illustrated article on the shaped charge appeared in *Popular Science* magazine and was afterward reprinted in the July-August 1945 issue of the technical journal *Explosives Engineer*. The latter publication, incidentally, offered 'grateful acknowledgement' for the many 'sketches and photographs' of shaped charges supplied by the United States Army Ordnance Corps."

[254]Ann and Michael Sidorovich were considered part of the so-called "other spy ring." (See Schneir, Ch. 23) The FBI exhibited pictures of the Sidoroviches to all potential witnesses in the summer of 1950 (memo SA to file, JR NY 757; memo O'Connor to file, JR NY 770) and there was testimony about Ann Sidorovich at the trial (see Record, pp. 444–46).

[255]Greenglass testified that our father had been to Cleveland to "see one of his contacts" and had seen "the Hugh Warner-Swasey turret lathe plant" (Record, p. 517). The Sidoroviches lived in Cleveland.

P 518 L 1—(B) Sky Platform project.

(middle of page) Check this description with (B) How about previous information in publications & papers on German work on this stuff. Particularly check astounding stories popular science and mechanix.[256]

P. 519 L-9 Check on this matter with shop employees at that time & with (B)[257]

P. 514 L-12 who put in this poison Rogge-Saypol[258]

p. 527 L-3 He said he would attend to vaxcination [*sic*] crtif. cnfrs. my testimony.[259]

P. 529 on bottom He said in middle of May I told him I got a lawyer—but on June 17 I ["first" CO] saw you for the first time in my life —& I had not been in contact with a lawyer since I was fired from War Dept & only those who took care of corp. work.[260]

P. 531 L-9 He said he kept pictures in draw [*sic*] in his house & FBI searched house. He did not give them the pictures they probably found them put in by Rogge to show his willingness to cooperate—

---

[256]Note: Because of the nature of this letter, in this and in many places, words that should be capitalized often aren't and other grammatical errors are made. For easier reading, we've chosen not to "[*sic*]" all of these.

[257]Greenglass had said "He once stated to me in the presence of a worker of ours that they had solved the problem of atomic energy for airplanes . . ." (Record, p. 519).

[258]Refers to Greenglass stating that our father said "They let Barr out, Joel Barr, and he was a member of our espionage ring." (p. 524) Joel Barr had left the United States in 1948 and around the time of Greenglass' arrest he left his Paris apartment. He reappeared first in Czechoslovakia and then in the Soviet Union where he made an engineering career that was denied him in the United States. The government has always claimed Barr was a spy—Radosh and Milton certainly make a big deal about his "disappearance" (see p. 104–10) and subsequent career (see paperback edition, pp. 471–74). For a counter, see the comments of Miriam Schneir in Walter and Miriam Schneir vs. Ronald Radosh, Joyce Milton and Sol Stern, "Were the Rosenbergs Framed?" Town Hall debate, New York City, October 20, 1983 (hereinafter referred to as Debate), pp. 20–21.

[259]Refers to testimony that our father had asked the family doctor about whether you need shots for Mexico. See Record, pp. 851–57.

[260]In 1945, Julius Rosenberg was employed by the U.S. Army Signal Corps and was fired on the charge of being a Communist. He denied the charge following the usual procedure of Communists to remain "secret" except from fellow Party members, and also as a way of avoiding losing his job. At the trial, he was repeatedly badgered about his probable perjury during this period. He was fired because the FBI had engaged in what has come to be called a "black bag job" (a break-in burglary) at a local Communist Party headquarters and had forwarded a photostat of his membership card and later a photostat of a record of transfer of Julius Rosenberg to U.S. Army Intelligence. (See Radosh and Milton, p. 54–56 with extensive notes on p. 497–98.)

P. 541 (B) His wife visited him at Calif & lived there with him at a greater personal cost to them in transportation & expenses. Isn't it logical that this same pattern was followed at Albuquerque—

P. 543 (B) To show Daves [*sic*] true nature on cheating everybody including relatives.

P. 551 (B) middle of page felt it was right thing to do then he remembers Rogge's instructions & must show equivocation that he was led.

P. 553 (B) "Hero worship" how does it jibe with his philosophy & actions.

P. 555 (B) Middle He is justifying his actions (where is hero-worship or doubts)

P. 566 (B) Conveniently doesn't remember anything of F.B.I. interview just a short time before.

P. 580 (bottom) after the judge rehabilitated him got him to say that he was told of his rights to counsel only after he signed statement & that govt. was with him for almost 12 hours did they tell you "You ought to get a lawyer" Some legal rights?

P. 583(middle to end of page) He admits he was confused [next three lines inserted] during that period and yet he is able to parrot after the Court's leding [*sic*] questions. (He means confused so as not to tell the truth).

P. 586 Note after lunch recess his mind is alerted to all his statements [word "because" CO, NWI] as if he had been prompted on this.

P. 594(B) L–8 again he admits it was first time he was told he was free to get a lawyer after statement.

Check with (B) on his negotiations with a lawyer & what the family commonly knew about the purpose & subsequently how they knew of the promise to him of 5 yrs & a day & his wife to go free & the same for us if we do the prosecutions [*sic*] bidding.

P. 603(B) Tombs has daily visits & for stool pigeons [*sic*] a special room to be alone with their wife. I just found this out now from people who know the Tombs.

P. 608 B [circled] How come on so important a line of questions you ["could" CO, NWI] were not allowed by Court to pursue this line of attack?[261]

Page 4

---

[261]The line of questioning referred to was the cross-examination regarding the idea that David Greenglass's testimony would reduce his sentence and protect his wife from being charged. See "Affidavit of Henry Linschitz," 17 August 1966; "Affidavit of Philip Morrison," 2 August 1966; and "Affidavit of Harold C. Urey," 9 September 1966. Morton Sobell vs. U.S.A. 66 Civ. 1328 U.S. District Court for the SDNY. Dr. J. Robert Oppenheimer endorsed the Morrison affidavit, see "Oppenheimer to Perlin," [n.d.] submitted to the Court of Appeals, Docket #31259 U.S. Court of Appeals for the Second Circuit.

Vol 1 Book 3

P. 611 (B) Cute in answers of his failing subjects. Very revealing as to his personality; arrogance & cocksure attitude.

P. 620 Bottom William Spindel

P. 631 [Letter "B" inserted circled here] L 12 Note Dave said Julius told him he did pictures on the table (console) check with Ruth's remarks on the table.[262]

p. 634 Note he was caught in important lie that jello box was substantially the same even though he claims he didn't see it. (He meant the D.A & Rogge told him to say it was substantially the same). Then of course the Judge helped him crawl out of this one. "Some fair trial!"

P. 649 He is caught in lie on Dr. Urey the little slips that come even for a well prompted witness who was coached for 8 months.

P. 663 Check with (B) on money & quarrels.

P. 666 bottom check with (B)[263]

Vol 1 Book 4

P. 679 Again check what I said back there about chronology. For this bears out our contention that Dave probably was a spy before this Date [*sic*] and he slipped when he told Ruth right then & there only [N2WI] less than two months after being a plain machinist he knew proscribed information. (That is was not supposed to be known to him).

Note putting both Dave & Ruths [*sic*] testimony side by side besides the similarity order, use of words etc. The studied equivocations, also questions of communism, affiliation, so called "party work", daily worker, gifts from Russians & money could only be the plan of a legal mind like Rogge or Saypol's. To lay ground work for light sentence for Dave & freedom for Ruth so she put in as soon as possible her becoming agent & her doubts & that she was young & was led.

P. 682 Note she said that the scientific basis of the bomb should be made available to the Russians—Doesn't this prove it was a put up story.

P. 682–423 Dave said Ethel started the story & Ruth said I did.

P. 683 at bottom note the first name Ruth used is Dr. Urey in Nov '44.

---

[262]This is Julius' first reference to the alleged Russian gift console table. See Schneir, pp. 196–203, *Sons,* pp. 188–90, 404–7. For RM's alternative formulation, see RM, pp. 361–66.

[263]The reference is to a quarrel over how David Greenglass would separate himself from the machine shop business that they were involved in. When he left the business in 1949, he wanted a promissory note from Julius in return for his shares, but Julius wouldn't give him a note.

P. 687 L-9 from bottom Ruth said she met Ann Sidorovich prior to that evening.[264] Then why was it necessary to have her come up as they say to introduce them to an alleged courier.

P. 691 (B) Check with him on money I had & spent while we were in business together & as long as he knows us. (Clothes, furniture & pocket money)

P. 707 She puts the offer to Dave to go to school in '46 & Dave puts the time as end of his last furlough in Sept. '45

Also she said that Dave said he was no longer interested in furnishing information right after his release from army. How do they try to reconcile this lie with their other lies that I revealed to him secrets such as sky platform, atomic energy for airplanes, secrets from Schenectedy, Barr is a spy, additional monies, Mexico brokers papers—Where is the compatability [sic] of all these (Too much gilding the lily is very revealing)

P. 708 (B) On Daves [sic] going to school—check on the true facts of how I fought with him to pay attention to business give up school.

P. 709 (Note how well she remembers (coached) days—May 24, 1950 I came I told them they would have to leave country—Didn't Dave say it was sometime near Feb 1950 before birth of second child that he alleged I talked to him to leave. [parenthesis omitted]

P. 710 Ruth said Soviet Union was destination of flight & Dave said Checkoslovakia [sic].

P. 710 If the arrest was to take place in 3 weeks time why would she be told she had a month to spend the $1000?

Page 5

P. 710 She says she was asked to get a certificate & Dave said he would take care of it in his testimony. (P. 526 there was no conversation in Ruths [sic] presence according to Dave about certificate & destination).

P. 722 Reading the testimony shows how anxious Ruth was to admit she was out with Dave in Calif. as if she had been rehearsed on it.

P. 723 [next page references inserted] L 8–L 12 (B) some little weasel.

---

[264]Ann Sidorovich, according to the prosecution, was supposed to be the courier to bring information back from Albuquerque to JR. Ann Sidorovich denied this strenuously to the FBI and she and her husband were subjected to a tremendous amount of harassment. See Schneir, pp. 299–302. According to RM, she and her husband Michael were members of the "other spy ring." See RM, pp. 299, 302, 416, 417. For the Justice Department summary of what they thought they "had" on the Sidoroviches, see Thomas K. Hall, Securities Activities Section, to William F. Tompkins, assistant attorney general, Internal Security Division, Justice Department, 146-41-15-133, November 5, 1956, pp. 39–40.

P. 724 middle—Ruth says the money she got from Gold was from Julius on what basis could she say that Gold did not so testify neither did her husband.

P. 725 Interesting admission of receiving "800.00 in summer" 1948 was he doing spy work—what kind. Perhaps he was in contact with Gold even then for this time check with (B) we were being pinched [NWI] financially badly off.

P. 755 Note Ruth said that Dave told her to memorize the information this slip proves our contention that Dave was already the spy & giving her information to give to someone else.

P. 768 (B) Her position on our debt to her & the suit she brought against us.[265]

P. 769 Note how she made sure to say she did not destroy the letters even though not asked. She had been properly forewarned.

P. 770 She had been prepared after Dave's cross to beware that the style of the box (jello) had changed.

P. 773—5–6–7–8—783—5–6 for (B) on Pitt & finances.[266]

P. 790 '44 during winter. Dave Ruth Ethel & I went to movies together. How they were in the Army & we had a little baby home. (?)
ask Bernie if at 16 years of age or at any time someone could talk politics to Dottie Printz.[267]

P. 797 (B) Note he says that 1 day later after he received the package he opened it & found money. Note Dave said he wanted to flush it & his brother-in-law talked him out of it. {How does this tie in with cooperation to flush the money} very revealing. & his intention was to hid [*sic*] it where nobody would see.[268]

P. 818 Meeting [two letters CO] in Jan '45 report turned over 2nd week of month.[269]

---

[265]The Greenglasses sued Julius Rosenberg over the money still owed for the buyout of David Greenglass' shares in the business. Nothing was ever collected.

[266]The name of the business was the Pitt Machine Products Co.

[267]The witness at this time was Dorothy Abel, Ruth Greenglass' younger sister. She had introduced evidence of our parents' pro-Soviet politics. Her maiden name was Printz.

[268]The witness Louis Abel, David Greenglass' brother-in-law, had testified that he received a package with $4000 in it from David Greenglass, hid it in his house, and when David was arrested, he took the package and gave it to O. John Rogge as a retainer.

[269]This relates to one of Harry Gold's meetings with Klaus Fuchs—see above for Julius' ideas about how this shows the chronology in David Greenglass' testimony to have been untrue.

P. 820 Note Gold had meeting with Yakovlev last Sat in May. See how Ruth said we knew she was to be seen 1st week in June. How does this tie in, {Gold—Dave—Yakovlev}

P. 827 How come Ruth & Greenglass [NWI] didn't mentioned [*sic*] anything about Gold seeing his brother-in-law & a telephone number. Did they forget on so important a point of corroboration.

P. 839 How come one important thing like Greenglasses' furlough was first mentioned in Nov '45.

P. 849–50—Why was the question of wire-tapping not pushed especially of my telephone at home & the ["place" CO, NWI] business and the ["counsel" CO, NWI] consultation room at Foley Square—Note also nowhere does he say I asked him to falsify a vaccination certificate.[270]

V. 11 Book 1

P. 901—[letter CO] Look how frightened Saypol & the Judge are that the witness might answer truthfully.

P. 906–7 Note he was a liason [*sic*] man an expediter not a scientist or an expert on these matters.[271]

P. 916 Note ["objection" CO] before objection the court jumps to sustain.

P. 988 L-7 Why is Saypol allowed to say Julius an engineer she did not so testify.

---

[270]See Record, p. 856, for the doctor's denial.

[271]Julius has hit on a very important point, later developed at great length in legal proceedings and publications. See, for example, Schneir and Schneir, *Invitation to an Inquest* (New York: Penguin, 1973) (and only that edition!), pp. 432–36; Markowitz and Meeropol, "The 'Crime of the Century' Revisited: David Greenglass' Scientific Evidence in the Rosenberg Case," *Science and Society*, Vol. 44, No. 1 (Spring 1980). The point was that the government had intimidated the defense into believing that Greenglass was confessing to stealing important secrets. The witness list included Dr. Urey, Kistiakowsky, Dr. Oppenheimer and General Groves. None of these people were contacted and the government's apparent motive was to suggest to the defense that these "witnesses" supported the government's contentions. Meanwhile, having Derry, a non-scientist, "authenticate" Greenglass's sketch permitted the government to side-step the inaccuracies and crudities of the sketch—inaccuracies and crudities developed very clearly in a motion for a hearing filed on behalf of co-defendant Morton Sobell in 1967. See "Affidavit of Henry Linschitz," 17 August 1966; "Affidavit of Phillip Morrison," 2 August 1966; "Affidavit of Harold C. Urey," 9 September 1966; "Affidavit of Robert F. Christie," 28 September 1966; Morton Sobell vs. U.S.A. 66 Civ 1328 US District Court Southern District of NY. See also letter of J. Robert Oppenheimer to Marshall Perlin, submitted as part of the Record on Appeal Docket #31259 US Court of Appeals Second Circuit. Julius's point was supported by none other than Dr. Kistiakowsky himself in *New Times* ("Victims of a Desperate Age," by Daniel H. Yergin, May, 1975.)

p. 990 L-7 from bottom—Saypol said I said to Sobell I received a call from Bentley.

Page 6

(B) should read all of my & Ethels [*sic*] testimony to prove we did not lie for there are many things he can corroborate.

Vol II—Book 2

P. 1105—6–7–8 for Bernie.

P. 1164 L-5 This is a misstatement of fact I raised no Constitutional privieledge [*sic*] as yet.[272]

P. 1168 Top—If you ["look" CO] said it ["or" CO] was argumentative for Saypol legitimate cross.

P. 1196 Bottom—How different the Court rules for D.A. when defense witness is being questined [*sic*].

P. 1214 middle of page & P. 1215 middle of page Saypol deliberately makes misstatement of facts as when I was with Sobell

P. 1225 for (B)

Vol II Book 3

P. 1308 How does the Judge know they have nothing to do with case when they are used to refute Saypol questions on Photos & would prove what I say.

p. 1423 Pagano gives the lie to Ruthie on her frequent lawyer visits.[273]

P. 1428 Note he said 3 doz. pictures @ 3 for $1.00 is $12.00 not $9.00.

P. 1513 [N2WI] near Bottom He says Rosenberg to Gold—that is against the testimony of his own witness.

Vol II Book 4

P. 1515 Middle page a distortion he said Bentley said she knew him, had telephone to him as "Julie".

P 1517 Two distortions that I told Sobell who told Ellitcher [*sic*] & also I told Dave I knew Golos.

P 1518 Note Ruth did say the money was from Julius

P. 1570 middle again a distortion of fact not in record that Ann Sidorovich was the Soviet Agent.

---

[272]The most crucial tactic of the prosecution at the trial was to raise the question of our parents' belief in communism and membership in the communist party. Our parents' response was to invoke the constitutional privilege against self-incrimination. The prosecution, and the court, used that fact to damage our parents' credibility. Here, for example, there had been an objection by defense counsel on a previous page (p. 1162) to such a line of questioning but not on the grounds of potential self-incrimination.

[273]Helen Pagano was a prosecution witness. She was a secretary in the Rogge law firm and testified about receiving the paper bag from Louis Abel that turned out to have the money in it.

P. 1523 near bottom again a deliberate distortion by saying Gold saw them once it was twice in the same day according to there [sic] testimony.

P. 1530 Distortion of the fact that Elitcher admitted he was recruited into espionage ring by Sobell & me.

P. 1531 L 14—Again a distortion of the fact that Sobell & I recruited him into the Young Communist League at college—No such evidence as a matter of fact their own witness did not say this.

P. 1534 About not receiving an order from Danziger he had work to offer that our machines could not handle for it required presses not turning machinery.

P. 1545 Judge [paragraph sign] begining [sic] with Justice is in your hands—Isn't this misstating the law?

For (B) To read Saypol & Judges [sic] sentencing speech to show that sentence is political & to read all of Daves [sic] sentencing speech to see many distortions by Rogge & things he says that are not based on the record at all. (1628) shows how Rogge prepared the Greenglasses [sic] testimony with an eye to the bargain based on reservations, fuzzy thinking being led & stool pigeon work.

P. 1637 (B) The judge spelled it out but left out framed Ethel & I.

P. 1642 L 16 from bottom distortion of fact of Russian questioning about operation of atomic bomb & formula.

P.S. [N2WI] Excuse handwritting [sic] Thats [sic] all for now if I think of some other questions I'll write you again. Incidentally what should I do in regard to Ethel's letters that I'm supposed to send you? Please let me know. I feel confident. Lets [sic] keep up the good fight till we reach complete victory. Can't wait to be home with Ethel & the boys!! All my love —Julie # 110649

[The next three letters are written in pencil.]

Julius to Ethel

Oct. 12, 1952

Hello Pretty,

You were the belle of our consultation and it certainly was a good omen to see you in a new and very becoming dress. It gave me a good feeling to see you looking so well and naturally your spirits were in tune with your lovely appearance. I am elated over the splendid confab we held and I am most gratified with the results of the committee to date. Since we know exactly all the alternative legal steps that are open to us we can make our plans accordingly. I do hope Manny will be able to take his planned trip for not the least of my wishes in this matter is ["the" CO, N2WI] one of purely selfish motive. Our own participation at this meeting was very productive and I am very pleased with our creative efforts. As for you I adore you and love you with every fibre of my being. Because of you and the visit I'm in an excellent state ["of omitted] mind. Under the influence of these conditions I await with renewed confidence the Supreme Court ruling.

Lena and I had a pleasant visit and we talked the family situation through. It is most difficult to expect to change human nature and it is even harder to make people understand when these are personal blocks set up [N2WI] by them to ward off examining problems objectively because they may require additional burdens on their part. You know what I mean and I do not intend pressing this matter any further as it can only cause unnecessary aggravation on our part. I am sure they'll do what's best in this situation within the limits of their understanding. The question of my mother's visit is all up in the air, for some reason she may not come tomorrow and I suggested to Lena that if Mama can't make it you will let her know the best day for her to come.

I spent most of yesterday making a resume of my notes on the trial record and I've condensed it to 6 letters. ["At" CO, lower case "t" overwritten in next word] The next time mail goes out I hope to get these papers in Manny's hands as soon as possible in order for him to go over them and see if there is any merit to some of my thoughts. At this moment I'm sort of caught up with my reading and writting [*sic*] chores, that is those I care to indulge in at this time, and I'm awaiting the verdict of the highest court. Today I spent a good deal of time thinking about you and reliving many of our mutual experiences and I want with all my heart to go back to it all soon. Come what may this Wednesday we'll have many things to talk about and I'll not prepare an agenda until Tuesday evening.

My sister told me of the new clothes you've acquired and we were happy that you can get these things to make yourself more comfortable. I'll tell you some of the [erasure here—next word written over it] funny remarks your husband made about this matter. Darling I believe we'll be entering a new lap in our long fight to win our freedom and no matter what the difficulties we are coming closer to our final victory. All my love— Devotedly—Julie

Julius to Ethel

Oct. 13, 1952

Hello Sweetheart,

Just a word of encouragement untill [*sic*] I see you again. As for me nothing has changed. My courage, demeanor and understanding is the same but it seems to me that Supreme Court has shown callous disregard for justice in our case.[274] I got off a letter to Manny after I heard of the denial of our petition I'll tell you about it when I see you. Although I knew from hearing the news on the 12:45 [NWI] radio broadcast I didn't let on to Mama because I wanted her to be home and have people near her when she hears the bad tidings. We will have to spare her as much suffering as possible because she is just all emotions and completely heartbroken. I tried as much as possible to ease her feelings but it was too difficult a task for the kind of visit we have.

The actions of the Court in our case speaks more eloquently [N7WI] of the true nature of our government than all the propaganda that emanates from Washington. They are trying to make haste in putting us to death before the Court of public opinion gives its answer, protesting this political frameup. I believe this latest action by the highest court in our land will galvanize many people into positive actions on our behalf. The fight is not over because the people [NWI] still have to be heard from.

Of course, I realize our path becomes more difficult, ["with" CO, NWI] when each succeeding avenue of legal action ["being" CO, NWI] is denied us, but we are realists and we know other factors play a most important part in political cases such as ours. I realize I should write our children a letter but somehow at this moment I can't take myself to this usually pleasant task. Perhaps after I speak to you I'll be in the proper frame of mind to write them.

Honey we'll have to pack a great deal into our visits from now on because things are going to be popping fast and furious ["from now on" CO]. It would be a good idea if we reviewed our personal plans at our next get together at our favorite screen.

At this time I miss you and the boys most of all. If only I were able to shield you of all this pain and the horrible emotional and mental torments that you still have to face, while we fight to win the justice that we deserve. The jackals of fear are having a field day. The hirelings of the kept press are howling for our blood. The only reason they are so vocal is because they want to hide the issues from the American people.

I want to repeat to you again my sweet, wonderful wife that I face the future with courage, confidence and perspective because of what you and the children mean to me. It is our faith in the principles of democracy and the

---

[274]For a detailed investigation of the role of the Supreme Court in the case see Michael Parrish, "Cold War Justice, The Supreme Court and the Rosenbergs," *American Historical Review*, Vol. 82, No. 4 (October 1977), pp. 805–42. See also Joseph Sharlett, *Fatal Error: The Miscarriage of Justice that Sealed the Rosenbergs' Fate* (NY: Scribner's, 1989).

dignity of the human being that convinces me that we will succeed in the end.

Devotedly—Julie

Ethel to Julius

Oct 13–52

My very dear one, my darling,

The plot stands exposed at last in all its ugly nakedness, [N3WI] in all it's [*sic*] pusillanimous rottenness. Again, political necessity has over-ruled due process![275]

My sweet, understand me well; there grows within me now a deep calm, a power such as I never knew I should even be capable of possessing. Only I was in such a state of shock and daze that my brain [NWI] only began to function clearly, too late, to do full justice at this time to the barrage of ideas and words that demand expression. Suffice it then to quote [NWI] just these lines from a letter I am sending Lena:

"The blow is tempered, however, by the knowledge that there is yet time for much to be done. And so I write to earnestly beg you not to squander this time in too many useless fears, not to permit yourself to be stampeded by anything you might hear or read. The hatemongers, you know, we have always with us; please know that they leave me quite unimpressed. Mark my words; you will now begin to see an avalanche of protest! You see, Lee, strange as it may seem to you, it is "they" who are afraid, it is we who have the power to dismay them, if we will but believe in ourselves & mass our full might for decency and justice!"—

My deepest, strongest love—Your wife

always—Ethel

The next letter begins with almost a complete side labeled "October, 1952" and then concludes on January 19, 1953. We are including the first part here and will include the rest on January 19, 1953. The letter is written in ink.

---

[275]Virginia Gardner, in *The Rosenberg Story*, referred to the thoughts of Emanuel Bloch's assistant, Gloria Agrin, who remembered an exchange between Bishop Cauchon and the Earl of Warwick in Shaw's *Saint Joan*. "'I tell you now plainly that her death is a political necessity,' it was Bishop Cauchon who replied pridefully that 'The Church is not subject to political necessity, my Lord.' That was all they could ask and hope for, that the court was not subject to [political] dictates . . . " (Gardner, p. 119). The *Saint Joan* reference is to an exchange in Scene VI. See *The Complete Plays of George Bernard Shaw* (London: Constable and Co. Ltd., 1931), p. 991.

Emanuel H. Bloch
7 W. 16th Street
New York New York

October, 1952

Dearest Manny,
     Letter # 1
     Fortunately, you had prepared us so well [N3WI] at our last consultation
we took this latest hammer-blow with admirable dignity and self-control. I
think we have every right so to characterize our behavior for [NWI] while it
is no easy matter to contemplate one's own imminent demise, it is far more
horrifying to watch the cauldron boiling and the plot thickening right out in
broad day-light, while the people flee, hysterical with fear headlong down
the path to their own destruction the liberals flounder about pathetically atop
their synthetic fences!
     On Monday, Oct. 13, the Supreme Court, with the praiseworthy excep-
tion of Justice Black,[276] used its proud office to write "justice" off the
statute books. By its refusal to review a case that involved two decent young
parents, and questions of law vital to the democratic well-being of the entire
citizenry, they clearly sanctioned the scrapping of due process and the incidental scrapping of human life. They also demonstrated a reluctance to pass
upon [NWI] a record [NWI] that exposed all too effectively a creaking make-
shift of a case and a hollow mockery of a trial thereby ["also" CO] revealing
a quite astonishing lack of that independence of thought and action we had
come to associate with such a venerable body as the United States Supreme
Court!

[The next nine letters are written in pencil.]

Julius to Ethel

Oct 16th, 1952

Beautiful Woman,
     Unfortunately you do not see all the newspapers that I have access to,
for if you were able to read them you would note that just as you said, that
an avalanche of protest ["will" crossed out, N4WI] already has begun to
materialize. From a line here a bit of a statement there one can gather that
we are receiving a considerable amount of support in our efforts to get a
hearing before the Supreme Court. It is important not to lose heart for one
moment because as soon as the volume of public clamor reaches [erasure

---

[276]See Michael Parrish, "Cold War Justice: The Supreme Court and the
Rosenbergs," *American Historical Review* 82 (1977): 816–18.

here, next word written over it] sizeable proportions they will be forced to grant us our day in court. I am not dismayed by the weakness certain so-called liberals and progressives show because at every crucial point where they must take a determined stand and act on it they take a defeatist position. Again they deluded themselves with the false idea that it is possible to buy immunity by being against certain key progressive issues and claim look we're against the Communist, [*sic*] the progressives, the Rosenbergs and they even equivocate when it comes to the question of peace and war. Strange as it seems I too feel calm and more determined because I have my self-respect and I feel stronger knowing that we have consistantly [*sic*] conducted ourselves with dignity according to the principles of decency and democracy. The job of getting the facts and issues of our case before the American people is a very difficult one but the latest action of the highest Court in our country will make it easier to get the facts before the public.

I was very happy to get my sisters [*sic*] letter and it is good to know that she is working effectively to help us. Incidentally my mother rode home on the same train with someone's wife who was visiting here and ["he" crossed out N2WI] the fellow got a letter from her next day saying Mama was in good spirits, got home alright and wanted us to be reassured that she is fine and wants us not to worry. She did not find out about our adverse decision until she got home.

A couple of ideas have been percolating in my mind and I'd like to find out what you think. How about each of us sort of writting [*sic*] out a speech as if we were talking to an audience and explaining our case? How about an autobiographic account of our background, education, home life activities, the case, the trial, our situation here and the children? Let us talk about these next time for I'd like to proceed in an organized manner.

Of course, I always leave the "piece de resistance" for last. You looked so good, your beautiful smiling face, shiny rich hair, lovely dress and oh boy what a woman I was thrilled every minute I was able to feast my hungry eyes on you. To top it all, you are such a jewel of a person with nobel [*sic*] character, with courage that comes from self-worth, confidence that comes from conviction and a realistic perspective. You are a wonderful sweet mother and an excellent wife. Every word I write about you is the gospel truth and I have such a rich and beautiful life because of you. We got what it takes—Death can't change that —All my love

Julie

Michael & Robert Rosenberg
c/o B. Bach
R.D. 2—Box 148 M
Toms River New Jersey

Oct. 16, 1952

My dearest, darling children,

Forgive me for not having written you at once, but my heart simply rebelled at the thought of breaking your innocent ones. Gradually, however, I have come to the realization that since we have all been living with this situation for some time, and since the devoted people around you must certainly have assumed full responsibility for handling your disappointment with tenderness and understanding, my continued silence in the face of tidings of which you were already fully aware, would accomplish nothing so much as to heighten your anxiety. Besides, once the first shock had worn off and I was my usual calm self again, I wanted ever so much to speak with you and to reassure you about us both.

Daddy was in to see [NWI] me on Wednesday, the same cheerful, smiling Daddy as he ever was, and was delighted to find that my spirits matched his own. We did not waste any of the precious time, you may well believe, but settled right down to map out the next phase of the campaign. In a day or so, we shall have ample opportunity to exchange plans and ideas with Manny Bloch, who [NWI] and you may rely upon it, will leave no stone unturned, no legal avenue unexplored, to see that justice is truly done!

Your mother, (I hope you have gathered from the above) is in a fighting mood; and while some tears must be shed (and you should feel perfectly free to relieve yourselves in whatever way you need to), I'd like to be able to feel that I have conveyed if only in some small measure my own confidence, and have lent my children some small degree of comfort and encouragement. Nor am I faking this confidence; trust me that it is wonderfully real and strong!

Only one thing bothers me; I am never able to fully express in words, how very very much I love you. And Daddy agrees that he, too, has that difficulty! Please know that we are both fine and will continue to keep in close touch with you.

Again, let nothing dismay you; there's much to be done, and we are rolling up our sleeves to do it!—

Our best regards, and deepest love—

Always, your loving Mommy—

P.S.—Your last letter was a treasure—adored every bit of it! Let me hear from you soon—

Julius to Ethel

Oct 19, 1952

Honey Dearest,

What a pleasant surprise to see you and our beloved counselor today and of course the news was wonderful. Just as we had foreseen the avalanche of protest is already here. I really believe we've done a pretty good job in helping bring our story to the public. I am sure we'll not be found wanting in assuming our share of the burden in this fight and so each of us will participate in this important activity by putting into writing all our thoughts and ideas. Whenever we write to the family and the children I hope they will make sure that these letters are sent to Manny after they are read. Therefore at the next chance we get we must ["so" CO] direct our dear ones to get these letters to our lawyer. At our next get together I'll discuss the letter situation with you in more detail.[277]

It is only because I am attuned to searching out public reaction to our case that I can gather from the small bits of news, the howlings of the prostitutes of the press and the advertisements in the Compass that there is a great deal of activity in our behalf. Outside of this there is a press blackout on our case. Only when they can distort and hurt us do they print anything about us and the case. However the heroic job the National Guardian is doing is in the ["greatest" CO, NWI] best tradition of American journalism and will win the kind of support that counts. Just now we're beginning to get the kind of support we should have had at the time we went to trial but we understand the situation and now that the government has exposed itself completely by the latest ["action" CO, NWI] denial they have shocked the good decent people ["into a" CO] of our country & the world into action for all can now see the dagger pointing at the progressive movement.[278] This is the naked threat of fascism that all the lip service to democracy cannot adumbrate from public view. Slowly but surely each succeeding step of our federal government [N7WI] is further along this road of doom in attacking civil liberties, violating rights of political opponents, supporting more and better preparations for hotter wards and further brutalizing the people by committing legal murder against two innocent people who refuse to ["go" CO] do their bidding in this political plot against all men and women.

Our team is strong because basically we are sound for we're innocent and we are principled fighters for good and decency. Naturally this gives us

---

[277]This is the first hint that the publication of the letters in book form was being planned.

[278]This echoes our father's oral statement to his co-defendants and the lawyers in the counsel room immediately following the sentencing. See *Sons* (first edition only), p. 352.

the strength to continue our struggle to win complete freedom. The situation will probably get worse but as long as we have life we'll continue to live for this fight is the best kind of living I know. I intend to beginning [*sic*] writting [*sic*] Manny a letter tonight & then I'll communicate with our dear precious boys. Until I see you at our favorite screen your sparkling eyes and alert beautiful face will be before me. I love you with all the passion [word almost illegible, could be "power" instead of "passion"] of my heart and mind. Devotedly —Julie

Ethel to Julius

Oct. 20, 1952

Hello, (Yawn) Bunny dear,

"Oh, how I hate to get up in the morning"! It's my honest guess the song-writer had me in mind; after all, you must realize, what with the "hysteria" I am in by day the "sleeplessness" I wrestle with by night, comes 6:30 A.M. I am sim—ply ex—haus—ted, my dear sim—ply ex—haus—ted, (a la Bascom Pentland of "Of Time and the River["])! Why did I ever have to start the dratted thing; now it draws me like a magnet, and I should like nothing better than to drop everything else, (excluding meals, of course, the gutter press to the contrary notwithstanding), and indulge a craving to plow through it, uninterrupted, for as many days as necessary. What a pity the man is such an unforgiveable [*sic*] racist! But for this one fault, he should have emerged as the literary giant his ample talents indicate.

Sweetheart, I feel frustrated; there was so much left unsaid on Sunday, I am still breathless. I guess we just can't seem to grasp the simple fact that Manny, human dynamo though he be, is still only one person, not six! Look, darling, please come prepared to give me a full press report on Wednesday, among other things—I never did get to hear all the gory details concerning that first "sleepless night" we were supposed to have suffered!

My wonderful husband, I love you!—The battle rages, but I am serene! —Always, your Ethel—

Julius to Ethel

Oct 23rd, 1952

Hello Sweetheart,

You cannot be blamed because "Of Time and the River" it is so interesting and [N2WI] must be very demanding of your attention. It is a fascinating book, well written and gives the reader great satisfaction. The other day I came across an item in one of the columns of the Daily News that said that Lester Cole[279] directed a group performing a stage version of "The Web and The Rock" and a long tour is expected for the dramatic company on this production. Now that I've read the book I'd like to see the stage show. A great deal could be done with stuff like this and it would take a series of plays to do justice to the subject covered in the original text.

As for me I spent all of yesterday working my writing fingers to the bone getting out a long megillah to our dear Manny. Look darling, pretty please how about pushing out that little epistle you started to our lawyer. Also I'd like to suggest that by this <u>Monday</u> the latest you on our behalf write a statement that could be used to our benefit. Try to use the idea we discussed at our last tete a tete.

I received a letter from the kids today and as yet I didn't send them one for I agree with your criticism of the kind of thing I should communicate with them and I'll do my best to get a letter off tonight.

This Saturday my sister will bring us the latest details of the committee work and I'm impatient to hear the news. As in the past I'm sure we'll be able to encourage my sister and see to it that she brings back a good report to my family as to our morale and situation here. Before I forget Ethel, if you do manage to produce some literary chores please keep a copy of it so that I may have the pleasure of hearing your creative gems at our next visit.

Don't forget to have my sister get in touch with our counselor and tell him of our plan to see the children soon and the reason we believe it might be best to have an early visit with them. He'll probably be up to see us some time near the end of next week and we can then try to make definite plans to see the boys, if possible, before the next stage in our case.

The press campaign of the slimy weasels is in full swing against us.— To me that's a very good sign [illegible word CO, NWI] we're getting new supporters every day and they are reacting—.

In case you don't know dearest this here condemned convict is madly in love with you and it's not because I've been forced to practice celibacy— Dang it! Truely [*sic*], honey, I miss you dreadfully and feel the terrible loneliness without your charming personality, keen analytical mind, warm understanding heart and satisfying love. You understand this is not all Platonic but this too will pass with all the other horrors and we'll try to wake up for it all. Believe me, wifey, I too am calm in the face of the storm. We've got a good rudder to steer a correct course. Keep your chin up and your beautiful face smiling—Devoted & Always Yours—Julie
P.S. I sent the boys a letter.

---

[279]One of the Hollywood Ten

Master Michael Rosenberg
c/o B Bach
R.D. 2 Box 148 M
Toms River N J

Oct 23rd, 1952

Dearest Michael & Robert,

Just a quick note before mail call. I started a letter to you a couple of times, but no sooner did I get started then I had matters that had to be brought to [N3WI] the attention of our good friend and lawyer Mr. Bloch. [Next word written over an erasure] Then I got off a letter to your Sweet Mommie and this morning I finally mailed a 12 page megillah to our counselor. You no doubt understand that certain pressing things have to be taken care of. However, since you boys sent me such a lovely communication, full of warmth and affection and so very encouraging I must not put off any longer the pleasure of keeping in touch with you.

Ethel told you the news of what is happening in her last letter to you and like all things the news isn't always good. Up until this point the legal results, that is in the courts, have been against us but as you know the important part of the fight, winning the support of public opinion is beginning to reach such proportions that it will force the courts to review our case.

It is not good to burden you children with problems that are not yours and are beyond your comprehension and therefore when Manny visits you next he will read you parts of my letter that you will [N3WI] be able to understand and explain as much of the situation as possible.

One thing must be crystal clear and that is that ["the central meaning" CO] our case if allowed to stand is a very great threat [NWI] directed at the heart of the progressive movement and it is an integral part of the conspiracy to establish fear in our land. The political nature of the frameup is obvious and the facts must be presented to expose to public attention the danger [the "r" was written over the letter "s"] that this holds to those who fight for peace.

You my precious sons must continue to study, play, have fun and keep well. The news of your accomplishments and your doings warms my heart and makes me happy to know that you are in very good hands.

Even though the autumn breeze, blowing from the Hudson River keeps our exercise yard quite cool I never miss my fresh air. I still manage to play a vigorous game of handball or boxball every day. From the scores of the games I can say in all modesty I do well for myself. The signs of the changing season are all around us. The wind blows leaves and seeds over the wall and its [sic] interesting to watch the maple tree seeds spinning down slowly ["whole" CO, NWI] because the attached half wing gives it lift, making it look like a heliocopter [*sic*]. All around us are the freshness and vigor of life and we sense it here but above all we are closest to the world we know and love; when we hear from you, & see you, & read the National Guardian and visit with my family.

I see Ethel regularly and I can say we are both well & calm. You know your Mommie and Daddy and we repeat to you we will not let you down and we will continue to discharge our responsibilities to you our precious children and to our brother and sisters who are fighting for peace, decency and justice. We are confident we'll be set free and be together with you again. So be patient and let's each of us do our job and keep smiling darlings All my hearts [*sic*] love Your Daddy—Julie

Mrs. Lena Cohen
140 Baruch Place
New York New York

October 25, 1952

Dearest Lee,

I spent so much time on the soap-box to-day during Ethel's visit, I was unable to complete giving her instructions concerning next Saturday, [N2WI] Nov. 1. It occurred to me a minute after her departure that you might be due for your usual morning visit on that day, but upon checking my calendar, I find that Davy is marked [NWI] down for [NWI] Sunday, November 2, which means you must not plan to come on Saturday, November 1, but on Saturday, November 8— Since this is so, I think it would be wise for Bernie to plan to come his usual afternoon hour on the day you are expected in the morning (Sat. Nov. 8) instead of coming in the morning on Sat. Nov. 2 as Ethel and I had figured. Since he finds it so much more convenient to get here after lunch why should I place obstacles in his way by insisting on a morning visit. It's just as simple for him to postpone his usual afternoon hour until the following Saturday. I shall then be able to have my [NWI] afternoon visit with Dr. Miller, as per usual on Saturday, Nov. 1 (without interference by Bernie) and he will have to come the following Saturday, Nov. 8, the same day you will see me in the morning. I am counting on you to let him know at once, to this effect, as I don't want to run the risk of losing even a minute of my precious time with Dr. Miller.

Speaking of Dr. Miller, I am sorry to have to tell you I simply could not get around to even mentioning the problem we had discussed. I shall do so, however, the very first thing, at our next session. In the meantime, don't feel that you are imposing in any way.

I asked Ethel to let Manny know that I am [NWI] still in the process of writing to him. I neglected, however, to have her remind him not to fail to use the letters I sent you and Julie, following the action of the Supreme Court. Each of these letters, I believe, is dated Oct. 14 and between them contain enough useful material for a highly effective statement. So please phone Manny urging this course of action, in the event he does not hear from me in the next couple of days. Simply read him the foregoing paragraph. You'll be sure to phone him at once, right?

I am extremely well, Lee, and have unbounded confidence in the future!

Mail call—So all my love—

Yours, for victory,

Ethel—

Julius to Ethel

Oct. 26, 1952

Hello Bunny,

How's the book? I hope you've found sufficient time to get out some writing. My sister's visit was a very fruitful one and I'll have certain matters to discuss with you this Wednesday. We talked about Manny's next visit and the time we wish to see the kids and [N2WI] I left it is [*sic*] all up in the air for I expect you to handle this detail and let our counselor know what your plans are. Since she had to pick up some letters of ours, which were supposed to be ready for her at the gate, ["sh" CO] my sister missed the 3:00 and had to wait about $1^1/_2$ hours for the next train. She intended to deliver the letters to our lawyer on her way to 14th St. You understand she is quite a practical person and she figured on going shopping anyway. It is good to know that my family is solid and pitching in to help the committee and do whatever they can to support us.

The committee is really doing a bangup job and I'm optimistic that they'll be successful in their undertakings. I've asked my sister to have Manny send us a copy of all the latest material that is being distributed on our behalf. Whenever my people visit me they spend the first part of our talk, telling me how lovely you look and that you are cheerful and in very good spirits and it is very difficult for them to find words to praise you enough. The high regard that they hold for you and the tenor of their voices is the [NWI] real barometer of their innermost feelings. It is true I'm a little prejudiced but it is a glorious feeling to hear others talk about you in such glowing terms. Everyone who meets you and knows you sings your praise and believe me honey it is genuine. I too am terribly enamored of you, my lady fair and regardless of the present difficulties I still have great hopes of being home with you in the not to [*sic*] distant future. Before I forget send out a Sunday morning pass to my brother for Nov. 2nd.

By the way, I suggest we accumulate the next batch of letters ["fo" CO] until our ["leg" CO] next legal consultation and then our lawyer can take them when he leaves. I'm kind of restless now darling. Of course you can guess I miss you very much and I never dreamt that I could love another so dearly. Aside from my personal and parental feelings [N5WI] to you and the children, there are many times I try to analyze calmly and coldly our situation and the enormity of the horror that this portends for our fellowmen makes me want to shout from the rooftops danger! danger! but the reality of the bars makes me feel impotent and sick that I personally cannot speak of this great threat. The letters I write compensate to some degree ["and" CO] my needs but it is not enough for the situation requires more. The only thing that can fill in the gap is news of positive accomplishments by the committee in mobilizing mass action on these issues. I believe we will be hearing this kind of news soon. You can understand me, my wife and [NWI] besides I need your love and comfort, for it is part of my life blood—Devotedly—Julie

Mr. David Rosenberg
430 E. 63rd St
New York N.Y.

                                                        Oct 28, 1952
Dear Brother,

I'm enclosing the usual Sunday morning pass and I do hope you will bring us lots of news of the campaign, of our beloved mother & how everybody is feeling. You get it, I hunger to know all that is going on and so feel closer to the outside world. Most of my letter writing has been concentrated on matters pertaining to our case and therefore I've done most of it to our distinguished counselor and also to my dear wife and precious children. Since I am sure that you can get to read these letters I haven't tried to duplicate my thoughts by carrying on much of a correspondence with my wonderful family. You people understand and I am happy that you keep on sending us letters.

Today, our lawyer filed our petition for a reargument. Truth is we should receive a hearing ["of" CO, NWI] on the merits of our case before the highest court of our land. There certainly is sufficient legal grounds for an appeal but we realize, as we have from the very beginning, that political considerations will determine both the legal and practical considerations of our case. Once this fact becomes clear to the people and they understand the issues involved in this cause I am confident the public will not allow this miscarriage of justice to stand. This requires a heroic effort on the part of many decent men and women and a very vigorous and mass campaign right now in order to assure us [NWI] even the chance to prove our innocence and [NWI] ultimately win complete vindication. This is no easy task especially in the midst of a bitter election campaign, with a war hysteria that is silencing opposition by fear. Nevertheless our lives and, yes, thousands of other innocent American lives, are in grave danger unless the people expose this political frameup and act to save us and—themselves.

Many times in the past, I've told you this is a very long and difficult battle and there is lots more of a fight ["left" CO, N5WI] that has to be waged on our part. Never did we lose faith that great numbers of people will rally to our support and help us win this worthy fight.

Dave, Ethel and I are filed away in concrete death cells only 30 feet apart separated by massive steel bars locked away from each other and our family but still we are strong because we're right and our cause is a just one. But we can't touch our boys, hug or kiss them, [erasure here] scold them and accept them, comfort them when in pain and give them the security [N2WI] and love that is their birthright because evil men keep us locked away from them. Sure, my sweet wife is a wonderful woman but her heart aches [last word written over an erasure] for her children and it is hard for us because of them and we are ["torn" CO, N4WI] determined in spite of this terrible pain and anguish and also because of it to guarantee that other parents, innocent like ourselves, [next word obviously meant to be "will" but looks like "wal"] not face a similar catastrophe in an era of growing fascism and war. I would be less than candid if I did not tell you that the emotional mental and physical pressures are very great and that we are suffering but [N2WI] we are [two inserted letters CO] bearing up under this nightmare. So please keep working hard to help us with all your strength for we're depending on you. Believe me, important things, regardless of the cost must be worked for always. all my love to the family—Confident as ever—Julie

Julius to Ethel

Oct. 30, 1952

Sweetheart Darling,

The meager report that appears in the Compass of last nights [*sic*] rally is very heartening and [N3WI] already begins to indicate ["s" CO at end of last word, "already" CO] a qualitative change in the campaign. The type of fight now being waged must bring positive results. Naturally I am very impatient to hear all of the detailed accounts of these happenings for the press and radio have dropped a curtain of silence on any news that might help us and although I am positive that the truth will out I want to hear of it from Manny and my brother by the week end.

Thank goodness I received our petition for a rehearing today and I've already read it twice. In spite of the fact that our lawyer was circumscribed, to a great degree, by the Supreme Court rule, that we could not repeat our points and arguments raised in the original petition for the writ of certiorari, we have now in this brief submitted a much stronger argument on the "treason" point[280] and on the "sentence" question. The points are quite substantial, the law is well documented and I believe the cases our counselor cites prove our points and if given fair consideration will be the basis for a writ of certiorari. It is possible that at this date ["the" CO] public support may be able to turn the courts [*sic*] attention to the issues in our case and grant us ["some" CO] the relief we ask for. Of course this will depend on the effectiveness of the peoples [*sic*] clamor for justice in our case.

No doubt many of the possible forces that could ordinarily be brought to bear to aid us in this gigantic endeavor are busy in other activities [N3WI] at the moment connected with the elections, but after Nov. 4 I expect to see a very definite upsurge ["in both" CO] in the volume, vigor and effective quality of the committee's work. I hope our counselor accedes to your request for his appearance [NWI] here this Saturday and we will then be able to plan the next steps and be prepared for all contingencies.

Honey girl, I hope you've been able to hammer out ["your" CO, NWI] the creative epistle [N4WI] you've been working on and send it ['s CO] on its way, so that it can, in a very practical manner, benefit us. Know sweet wife that I have complete and unquestioning confidence in you and I am at all time [*sic*] your faithful and ardent champion. It is possible for us to tell the productiveness of our visits by how we feel at the end of the session. This last tete a tete was a most fruitful one in that respect, and it gave me

---

[280]This point is that although our parents were technically charged with "conspiracy to commit espionage," they were actually tried as if they were being charged with treason. The judge even used the word "treason" in his sentencing speech (Record, p. 1615). This charge of conspiracy coupled with the actual trial as if for treason denied our parents the stringent protections actually written into the Constitution for people accused of treason. Each overt act would have to be testified to by at least two disinterested witnesses (meaning, not accomplices), and the government must prove actual actions against the United States not merely "to the advantage of a foreign power" as in the language of the Espionage Act. Justice Hugo L. Black, who voted to review the case every time it came before him, noted in an interview many years later that he had always believed our parents were denied due process by being tried for treason without the protection of the treason statute. For more analysis, see "The Rosenberg Case: Reflections on American Criminal Law," *Columbia Law Review* (February 1954): 241n. See also Parrish.

much satisfaction to once again recapture some of our former sharing of problems together. Only the bars and this awful place marred the pleasant moments and shocked us back to the brutal reality. I'm getting along okay and I hope to see you this weekend.

I've got a confession to make Ethel and that is that you've been in my mind a great deal of late, and I believe I have designs on you, some of which are quite amorous. What do you say woman how about visiting this here lonesome fellow who is madly in love with you. Every passing day you become dearer and more precious to me my bunny and I know that we will in due time share life's joys together again. Your devoted husband Julie

[The next two letters are written in ink.]

Julius to Ethel

Nov. 2nd, 1952

Attention: Please give this letter to my wife on Monday Nov. 3rd so that she could make arrangements for our weekend visits. Thank you

Julius Rosenberg

Darling Ethel,

Your wish is my command and, of course, I'll let you make the final arrangements and be prepared to send out the passes for this Sunday unless I hear otherwise from you. However, I want you to keep the following in mind. 1 [circled] We are only allowed one more Sunday visit this month and my brother is due to come Nov. 30th.

2 [circled] Bernie will not be able to make it this coming weekend. I'll explain when I see you.

3 [circled] The children are due to be at my mother's house Friday night. See us Saturday and then take the long trip home. This will make it easier on them, the Bachs and I guess on Manny. Also they will be able to rest up on Sunday for another week of school.

4 [circled] My sister Lena can come at any time during the week and if we ask her she may be able to manage it on Friday or Monday. At any rate it is not necessary for her to come the same weekend as our boys for one visit will be satisfactory.

5 [circled] No one will interfere with Dr. Millers [*sic*] visit as they are all aware of his scheduale [*sic*].

6 [circled] Bernie will have preference next time and if he does plan to visit you on Saturday he'll be able to come in the morning if Dr. Miller comes in the afternoon.

Write Manny & family to tell them of your wishes.

As for me I'm not sending any letters to anyone ["and" CO] in order not to confuse my family as to your plans. Therefore honey write to let them know just what you prefer for them to do. To be doubly safe I'll send Lena a pass for Sunday Afternoon [*sic*] (to use it only upon your say so) and a pass for Sunday morning for the children. At least we can expect one visit this weekend. I'd prefer to see our boys as soon as possible to reassure them of our steadfastness and confidence and show them our love.

You know dearest we must have to talk to somebody to get them to let us stay together. Then there will never be any of this mixup. Perhaps you can convince them!!

How do you like the new ball point pen I bought? It's only 55¢ and very useful around here. I recommend you invest in one.

Dave and I, we had a very good visit and there will be lots of news for me to tell you at our Wednesday visit. Also we should talk about the boys coming visit here.

I'm marking time until after the elections this Tuesday because I expect a tremendous upsurge in the activities on our behalf. Do you think it would be possible for Manny to plan to come back for another hour consultation with us after Mike and Robby leave. This would kill two birds with one stone, bring us up to date on the latest, discuss our problems and save our lawyer ["from" inserted and then CO] the trouble ["to" CO, NWI] of coming again [NWI] to [*sic*] soon.

Sweetheart, I have a very empty feeling tonight, nothing seems to satisfy me. I have a great need to talk to you my wife and share my deepest emotions with you. Your sharp mind can supply the emotional uplift and mental stimulation I crave. I miss you bunny sweet—As ever your devoted husband   Julie

Mrs. Lena Cohen
140 Baruch Place
New York NY
Nov. 4, 1950 [*sic*—someone else, probably the editor of the first edition of the letters, wrote a "2" over the "0"]

Dear Lena,

I am sending you a pass that can be used by my boys for this Sunday morning or by you for the coming Sunday afternoon. Please abide by my wife's wishes as to this week end. I am only sending you this pass so that you may have it available if you plan to visit us this Sunday [N6WI] or if the boys come then. I suppose you will check with my lawyer to make certain there is no conflict with the childrens [sic] visit. You see, since we can't get together more than once a week I have to use this method to prepare for all eventualities. Note that it is not necessary for you to use this pass, if you make other arrangements. I hope I made myself clear.

This mornings [sic] New York Times carried the shocking report that the "Compass" folded up for lack of funds. Although I did not agree with it's [sic] position on our case I believe this latest happening will be a blow against the impartial presentation of ["the" CO] news as ["it" CO, NWI] this was a liberal newspaper. Now more than ever before is it necessary to [NWI] have a means to reach the public with the truth about the war danger, civil liberties and cases such as ours. One thing should be clear that at no time should principles be sacrificed, no matter what the cost. It is my sincere wish that the progressive people will find a way to get this paper publishing again.

As for [one letter CO] our campaign, I expect to hear a great deal of news of positive results on our behalf after this election is over. When my brother was here last Sunday he told me of the many different printed materials the committee is distributing and I'd like you to tell our lawyer to send us a copy of each of these items. As in the past, we haven't lost our courage, as a matter of fact we are confident that the American people will prevent this legal murder and rally to secure justice for us. Therefore, take courage and bolster up mama's [NWI] spirit and keep reassuring her of our love and devotion.

It's 6:00 P.M now and I've got a little more reading to finish in today's newspapers and then I'll begin listening to the radio election returns. Don't forget to give my best wishes to Melvin and tell him to keep trying and he'll succeed in his studies and that the important thing is that he absorb as much knowledge as possible and that marks are secondary. Give Linda a hug and a big kiss for me tell her of my affection for her. Also please give me [sic] regards and love to the entire family. You know, Lee, I've almost forgotten what my nieces and nephews look like and I'll bet they're really grown up. I'm happy to know that, in spite of the catastrophe that has befallen us, they still have a high regard for us. Thank everyone for their confidence ["in us" CO] and we'll continue to try to live up to ["your" CO, NWI] their trust in us. No doubt you can tell I've ["'ll" CO, "'ve" inserted above] just bought a new ball point pen and I'm making good use of it. Keep working hard getting the news to us and we can't fail to win our just cause.

I'm impatient to see my precious sons—Stay well and keep your chin up—As ever Your beloved brother
Julie

Mrs. Lena Cohen [pencil]
140 Baruch Place
New York New York

November 5, 1952

Dearest Lee,
You will note that the enclosed Sunday pass lists the children's names as well as your own. Let me explain. Since I have not yet heard definitely as to a Saturday or Sunday visit for the kids (perhaps Manny may not be able to get them here at all), I am sending slip [*sic*] listing both visits (in case of either materializing) just to be sure. Should it work out that the kids must be here on Sunday, (or not at all) you can come Saturday, as per usual—If they have to get here on Saturday, and you care to come Sunday, (although this throws out your visit to your mother on that day) you are properly prepared with the pass.
Now, this is important—If the kids need to come Sunday, make sure this pass is turned over to Manny, or they may be held up at this end—Also, please urge Manny to send telegram informing me one way or another about kids' visit this week-end just as soon as he knows himself. Thanks loads—
Love, Ethel—

Julius to Ethel [ink]

Nov. 6th, 1952

My Darling,
This is the first opportunity [N2WI] I have since our visit ["that I have" CO] to tell you, your [*sic*] just wonderful and I'm simply nuts about you. Really and truly your [*sic*] adorable and that is the opinion of almost all people who know you here. If you can continue to keep up your spirits on this high level we'll come through with flying colors. The more enamored of you I become the more difficult is our separation and your confidence and well being is the only mitigating factors [N2WI] on me. I guess I'll have to be patient until this weekend when we will see our precious children and visit together.
One thing this election has done, it has once and for all shown the results of the war hysteria and witch hunt in our land. Fear has conquered large sections of our population and silenced most opposition. Although the

need of the hour ["as" CO] is very great the available forces to the progressives are few and far between. However we must be realists and not be stampeded by the definite swing to the right that has taken place in our country. It is necessary to read between the lines and understand the full meaning of the election.

As to our own situation I am still optimistic as our cause is just and [NWI] that at the same time it is linked to the larger issue of the progressive fight for peace and this will allow for an all inclusive rallying point of peoples of different political inclinations and from all walks of life. Of course, we realize the task is an enormous one but we can and must win this important fight. It seems to me that our fight will be a ling [*sic*—probably a mis-written "long"] one and I am prepared to see it through. Perhaps there will be some who will get faint-hearted and avoid the struggle and if it is possible by our example to give the [there is a stain on the letter at this point and it is possible the "m" in "them" was obliterated] courage by all means we will. Therefore by our actions and in our writing we will be able to be effective in this direction.

That brings to mind the idea that you [NWI] should make some notes in concise form to aid you in discussing these matters with our dear Manny when he puts in his next appearance with our boys. We will have to stress the fact that some means be found to send us more reading material of all that is going on in our case and in the progressive movement in greater detail, than that which we can get from the National Guardian.

This time, let us try to find out more of the details of Robert's schooling, play and all he is doing and this also applies to Michael. Please take the lead in directing our attention to this as I do not seem to know enough of whats [*sic*] happening with the boys. To some degrees I am at fault because I've not been writing them on any regular basis. I am sure we'll absorb as much as possible from them and I hope we can convey, as we have in the past, our profound love and feeling ["for" CO, NWI] to them.—My precious wife I am proud and at the same time humble besides you because you accept me ["as" CO, NWI] with your love, ["and" CO, N2WI] as your husband — Always devoted to you—Julie

Ethel to Julius [pencil]

Nov. 7, 1952

Sweetheart,

Just to say good morning; all night I slept peacefully in your arms and now I feel warm and relaxed and rested. But what's the use of kidding myself; you weren't actually with me and it's better to see the light of day and find myself alone!

It is something to know at least that the children are definitely putting in an appearance to-morrow, and when the telegram arrives this afternoon, we'll also know exactly what hour to start listening for them. I can scarcely wait through the remaining hours to squeeze them in my arms! What's more, I am confident it will be the most satisfactory visit yet!

Bunny, I just can't [N2WI] seem to concentrate enough to write any more, except to repeat what I said on Wednesday: you are my man and I love you!

Always, my dear one,
Your loving Ethel—

Julius to Ethel [ink]

Nov. 9th 1952

Hello Mike & Robbie's Mommie,

I felt as you did when I saw how the boys spoke to you and how they acted and in the main it was a very good visit. True we tried to follow two diametrically opposing desires but we had to finally give in to the sweet darling bunnies. You ["have" CO, NWI] gave us a couple of wonderful human beings and I'm proud for us to see how well they are developing.

I heard a few snatches of your conversation with Manny[281] and I'm pleased to know you'll handle ["d" CO at end of last word] the details of our boys [*sic*] future plans while I take care of this other matter for us. I just managed to finish a rough draft of the letter to Manny and it's almost ten now. Don't be surprised if this letter is cut short because of the lack of time.

Lena's visit was a pleasant surprise and we had a nice time. I'm going to write a note to Mr. Wilson explaining about the difficulty concerning Dave's Nov. ["23" CO] 30th visit, I'll let you know about it. It is my opinion that Ethel should be allowed to come next [fragment "Satday" CO, NWI] Saturday and my mother can come the following week. In this way we will not put off the girls too often & thereby obtain more visits.

My brother is keeping in touch with Bernie and as soon as he has a free day he will come to see you and it will not conflict with any other visit. If you intend to write my sister telling her it is all right for her to come this Saturday explain Dr. Miller's scheduale [*sic*] so your brother will not interfere with him.

Incidentally I heartily agree with your suggestion concerning additional visitors and I've told my sister to put it to Manny and leave it to his better judgement as to whether to make the move or not.

---

[281]We have no information about what he is referring to.

Darling wife I need you so much. To [*sic*] often I have no one to talk to ["th" CO, NWI] or work things out [NWI] with and help settle problems as I think of them but I feel very confident that I'm able to contribute something to our share of this noble fight.

Naturally, after our boys left there was a decided let down and I had an empty feeling. So I take myself to concentrate all the harder on my work and keep my mind on our next meeting at our favorite screen.

We will have lots to talk about honey but I want you to know, just as your eyes filled with tears my heart cried with you, even though my outward appearance seemed calm. We've got a couple of gems for sons dearest and we must see to it that they have every chance to develop properly and are giving [*sic*] the opportunity to grow culturally, emotionally, mentally as well as physically. You know what I mean and this you must attend to for you can best accomplish the needed results. I hunger for you my precious woman[.] Accept all the love of my heart and mind— Your devoted husband Julie

Emanuel H. Bloch [pencil]
7 W. 16th Street
New York New York

Sunday,
November 9/52

Dearest Manny,

I hated to wake up this morning; I knew what it would be like after yesterday! I know I should be remembering the matchless purity of Michael's great luminous blue eyes, the velvet warmth of Robbie's sweetly serious brown ones. I knew I should be watching the two graceful, finely molded heads, the blond one bent diligently over a "problem" and the dark one eagerly raised to the father's face. I knew I should be hearing their bubbling merriment, their incredible talk. I knew in short, that my heart should be breaking! Nor was I wrong; the very air is desolate and there is no comfort anywhere. "I want them, I want them," the horribly mutilated, outraged woman feelings shriek frantically, and the longing is a wound that cannot be staunched. In the end, are there any words for the rent flesh, the escaping blood [the rest of that line and all of the next are filled with dashes]

I see by the papers that the holiday season is in full swing, and since "justice" enjoins me from "doing my shopping early", later, or other wise, it will have to be undertaken for me. In this respect, I have fairly pounced upon each copy of the more recent issues of the "Guardian," in the avid hope of finding some guide to the perplexing problem of choosing truly fine books for the children. Of course, I shall want them to have such "Guardian" recommendations as "Be My Friend", "Tony and the Wonderful Door," and "The Races of Mankind," among others but these are but a small fraction of the reading matter that is currently available, and while some of the innumerable titles listed and enthusiastically reviewed in the "Times," the "Herald Tribune" and "Parents Magazine" may very easily be mediocre, I don't want anything overlooked that might conceivably further their all around development. The same holds true of records. It might be advisable to send for the list "Bookfair" puts out, as well as the catalogue of folk music "The Record Loft" offers (addresses carried by "Guardian"); it occurs to me, however, that readers and well-wishers, generally, might welcome the opportunity to contribute in very real measure to the Rosenberg children's holiday joy by sending in suggestions for book and record purchases, based upon their own personal experience with such material, as parents, educators, etc., bearing in mind, meanwhile, that Mike is close to 10 and Robbie is just $5^1/_2$. A word of caution might be added at this point, in order to avoid duplications and consequent waste of these good people's hard-earned dough. Since all monies received and ear-marked for the children's holiday spending will be suitably disbursed, in any event, only titles of books and records are necessary.

You may be wondering why I have as yet made no mention of toys, per se, nor of clothes, for that matter; let me assure you that I have been positively wallowing in advertisements, of late, pencilling here, clipping there, now accepting, now rejecting! (You see, I am determined to go on living and planning as though aught awaited me save
c't'd—Letter # 2 Ethel

Emanuel H Bloch
7 W. 16th Street
New York New York

Dec. 9/52
[*sic*—this is a continuation of the Nov. 9 letter]

Dearest Manny, c't'd from letter # 1—Letter # 2
a husband's fond kiss, a son's noisy welcome—) You, my friend, must come prepared to give me [N2WI] at least an approximate accounting of what they already have, and what new things they want, in so far as you have been able to ascertain through visits, letters & phone calls to the Bachs, and then we'll "draw up" the "final papers," y'dig! Incidentally,

their[282] own little boy, Leo, must receive his full share of the "swag" and be an integral part of all the merry-making.

And now I want to ask you for still another favor. Ever since Michael wrote me, begging me to "allow" him to continue with his musical education, I have been most distressed to learn that no effort to find a teacher of piano in Tom's River has met with any results. Let it be understood that Michael is a highly creative child with genuine musical talent (according to both his first teacher at Knickerbocker Village, when he was only 7, and [N2WI] more recently, that very wise friend of yours who deliberately refrained from making "wild guesses" about his pupils' supposed abilities, but who was constrained to express himself [NWI] as delighted with Mike inside of a couple of months); and that, in view of same and the child's own longing ["that" CO] it would be a great pity for such a serious need to remain unsatisfied. If the Guardian were to urge all interested persons to contact the Committee, I am confident the response would be forthcoming and proper arrangement could then be worked out for transportation, fees, etc. An accredited, progressive-minded piano instructor who will conscientiously devote himself (or herself) to their child's musical growth, will constitute the most precious gift (apart from clemency!) that the Rosenbergs could possibly desire!

That is not to minimize Robbie's very real potentialities, musically and otherwise; certainly it will be stimulating to him, too, should [NWI] piano lessons in fact be made available to his brother. Nevertheless, I am anxious for you to realize that I am sorely troubled by Robbie's [NWI] very apparent (still largely unfulfilled), need for self-expression. The tone of entreaty when he asks questions, the struggle to cope with a deep-seated bewilderment and frustration and hostility, the inarticulate demand for a greater degree of [NWI] personalized attention [N2WI] the desperate need to find a self that has somehow gotten "lost",—all strongly point to skilled play therapy for him as well as for Mike. These things considered, the Bachs have been accomplishing miracles; the fact is both kids were in a badly disturbed state when they arrived in Jersey, and the remarkable improvement that is clearly evident, is a tribute to their unwavering love and devotion.[283] All honor to them and to all the People everywhere! All honor, too, to the People's Advocate!

---

[282]The Bachs'

[283]See *Sons*, pp. 138–39, 144–45, 147 for our memories of this period.

462 *The Rosenberg Letters*

All my love (that utterly repugnant liar, Oliver Pilat(e), to the contrary notwithstanding)[284] Ethel
P.S.—Would like a contribution sent to "Nat'l Guardian" in our names—

Mr. Emanuel H. Bloch [ink]
7 W. 16th Street
New York N.Y.

Page # 1 Nov. 10, 1952

Dear Manny,
   The events of the past three years will show that we have been plummeted into the public eye because we have become a very important and celebrated "case."
   In the past we have dealt with personal items and special matters but now I think it imperative to put down in concise form a recapitulation of our views on what we believe to be the important issues in our case and the meaning and effect the outcome will have on the American people.
   To reach a correct conclusion, to fully understand the case and see the facts in their right perspective we must base our analysis on the trial record and focus our attention to it, keeping in mind the political climate that existed during the period of this alleged conspiracy dating from 1944 to the present.
   What is the history of this period? What are the pertinent high lights? In 1944, ["from" CO] the government policy of being allied with the Soviet Union and the national liberation movements of the peoples of the world in a war against fascism, the Rome-Berlin-Tokyo Axis, ["in the year 1944 this official policy" CO—also CO, "if" inserted between "this" and "official"] began to change once the defeat of the common enemy was apparent. Our

---

[284]Oliver Pilat (the addition of an "e" was part of our parents' effort to dub him a modern "Pontius" Pilate) was a reporter for the *New York Post* who wrote many vicious and false articles about our parents (including perhaps a reference to a falling out between our mother and Manny?). Later when some papers stolen from David Greenglass' lawyer were sent (from France) to Manny Bloch, it was discovered, among other things, that Pilat was a secret public relations man for the prosecution. Some of these papers are reprinted in John Wexley, *The Judgment of Julius and Ethel Rosenberg* (New York: Cameron and Kahn, 1955), pp. 637–44. The information re Pilat is contained in the following quote: ". . . had lunch with Ruth [Greenglass], Pilat, and HJF [one of the law partners]. We looked at Pilat's articles. They look O.K., but HJF as a precaution, told Lane [one of the prosecutors] previously he would insist Pilat, who already had 2 Conferences with Saypol, show the draft of the articles to Saypol or Lane." From an interoffice memorandum of the Rogge law firm on August 23, 1950, quoted in Wexley, p. 642.

foreign affairs vis a vis Russia deteriorated from suspicion to containment and cold war, then to Korea, to "liberation"[285] and opposition to the Colonial people's independence fight.[286]

Today, it is obvious to all, that there exists great international tension and there is a ["dag" CO] danger of a third world war.

Domestically, in paralell [*sic*] with this foreign policy and based on it there began [at end of the word, the letter "s" is written over] an attack to break up the great coalition of labor, farmers, liberals, progressives and enlightened businessmen that rallied around the Roosevelt program. At first it was only the communist but it quickly ran the gamut of all groups until all who did not conform or support these policies ["and they were" CO] subject to smear, character assassination, loss of livelihood, contempt citations, due process persecution and jail sentences. Fear was the instrument used against those thought to harbor unorthodox views.

To be most effective and to silence all opposition to a policy that leads to war abroad and a police state at home it was necessary to establish a link, even if only for propaganda purposes that would finally connect Russia—spy—communist.

This could only take place during the cold war, in the midst of a witch hunt hysteria, ["and" CO] that would be heightened by an atom-bomb spy trial.

Against this background the facts as they appear in the trial record are these

1 [circled] The Government witnesses, who were trapped criminals, effected an arrangement with the prosecution to mitigate their punishment for testimony against us. They were well rehearsed and coached in their story and this was their reward;

Page #2

(a) David Greenglass confessed spy—15 years
    Julius Rosenberg — Death
(b) Ruth Greenglass confessed spy—never indicted permitted to go free
    Ethel Rosenberg — Death
(c) Max Elither [*sic*] — who was threatened with prosecution for espionage and faced a five year perjury charge—never indicted
    Morton Sobel [*sic*] — 30 years

---

[285]This refers to the U.S. policy to "liberate" the "captive nations" of Eastern Europe.
[286]The most obvious example of this, even in 1952, was the U.S. support for the French in their effort to prevent the Communist-Nationalist Viet Minh from taking over Vietnam.

2 [circled] No documentary evidence was introduced to connect us with the crime. The Greenglasses [*sic*] and Elitcher's oral testimony was unsupported evidence and all the overt acts were said to be conversations that could not be independently verified and were incredible to say the least.

3 [circled] The flimsy corroboration was based on inferences extended to the nth degree

4 [circled] We didn't obtain a fair and impartial trial. The prosecutor and the judge violated our rights throughout the entire trial.

5 [circled] The trial was dominated and completely permeated by the injection of alleged communist affiliations and beliefs that were constantly reiterated and used by the prosecutor and the judge to inflame and prejudice the jury against us. Thereby not giving the jury the opportunity to decide impartially the issue of guilt or innocence of the crime charged[.]

6 [circled] The evidence presented did not warrant any finding of guilt.

7 [circled] The barbaric sentence of death was to serve as a weapon against those who disagreed with our governments [*sic*] established policy. A reading of the judges [*sic*] sentencing speech and the proceedings at the Greenglass sentence will prove the political nature of this case for they make it crystal clear by stating the purpose of their actions. Special attention should be given to the Circuit Court of Appeals [*sic*] affirming opinions for if this decision is allowed to stand there is grave danger to every progressive individual and every fighter for peace because now they can face spurious "espionage" and "treason" charges and death.[287] The Supreme Court refusal to even consider our case, unmasked the plot and reveals again that due process gave way to political necessity.

This review is based solely on the trial record which should be studied by those who wish to be informed about this case. There is an abundance of material and facts that can be used to our benefit and particular attention should be paid to both of our briefs to the Supreme Court which poignantly and brilliantly presents [*sic*] our contentions.

Again I want to re-iterate with all the strength and vigor I possess that we are completely innocent of the charge. This is nothing but a political frameup whose two fold purpose is to snuff out two innocent lives to help destroy the fight for peace and democracy. Therefore we believe our fellow Americans will work to save us and themselves from this conspiracy.

The Committee to Secure Justice in the Rosenberg Case has been effectively carrying on this most difficult campaign. They have accomplished great things but as yet there hasn't been a close enough liaison established

---

[287]For analysis of this issue, see *Sons* (first edition), p. 353.

with [indent sign CO, three illegible letters inserted then CO] a [NWI] completely satisfactory rapport.[288] We wish to make clear that any constructive

Page #3

critiscism [*sic*] we make is [NWI] only in furtherance of our common interest [.] It is ["our lives that are at stake and" CO, next ten words written above the CO words] the peculiar position we find ourselves in that requires that we ["should" CO] be consulted on major policy, [a period is placed at the top of the comma, N11WI] This [the capital "T" is written over a lower case "t"] need [this word was written over an illegible word] not be construed as a dictum but merely in deference to our wishes due to our close proximity with the case [.]

First I would like them to know that all legal action pertaining to our case will ["originate with" CO, N2WI] come from us or in agreement by us and our views and decisions will have to take precedence in this sphere and you our lawyer are our official representative, no one else. Naturally we will willingly discuss in a most friendly manner these matters with the committee.[289]

Secondly, when my brother told me about Father Duffy's pamphlet that asked mercy for us, I told him we welcome all help and appreciate Father Duffy's interest but we do not ask for or want any mercy only a guilty person needs mercy. We are innocent we ask for justice. Therefore we are categorically opposed to the committee distributing in it's [*sic*] name on our behalf such a pamphlet.

Yes we go along with clemency which is a last ditch effort to save our lives in order to give us the opportunity to continue to present the truth of

---

[288]Here and in what follows, we see a glimpse of one of the most unfortunate aspects of the effort to save our parents. The Committee and Emanuel Bloch did not work well together. There were tremendous conflicts over strategy as well as outright distrust between them. Emily and David Alman have told us that one of the handicaps they operated under was the non-participation of Ethel and Julius in the struggle. They had only their letters but no interaction with them. At one point, they tried to get Julius' sister Ethel to request that they (Emily and David) be permitted to visit them in prison. Emanuel Bloch took that as an effort to undermine him. Meanwhile, we can see from the specifics of the correspondence that despite our parents' willingness to be very actively involved in their own defense, Emanuel Bloch did not credit their participation—even to the extent of not making a transcript available until the Committee had printed it. This section of the letter, then, serves as an effort to get the Committee and Emanuel Bloch to work well together, but also to reiterate Ethel and Julius' complete confidence in Emanuel Bloch.

[289]Note their willingness to speak directly with the committee, but they were never able to do this.

our innocence until we win vindication. This is the only principled way we want to carry on the fight for our lives.

It is obvious from the above that there are many excellent issues in the case some of which I have outlined including others such as scientific issues and an issue of perjured testimony that should be brought to public attention which the committee has begun to do but should be more fully gone into.

True there are Anti-Semitic overtones in this case but they are subtle and secondary issues, hard to put the finger on and by being put into the position of concentrating and stressing this as a major issue the committee has been sidetracked by the opposition which tends to weaken the main fight because the facts bearing on this issue in the trial record are not as sharply defined and clear as the others and allows for unnecessary confusion. I say it is a tactical mistake[290] when we do not concentrate on the crux of our case, the unfair and impartial [*sic*—obviously meant "un-impartial" which is not a word] trial, the political nature of the frameup and the brutal sentence and it's [*sic*] meaning.

Also this cause is broad enough to involve all sections of the country, people in all economic classes, men and women of all political opinions, labor, church and fraternal groups. This can and must develope [*sic*] into an action including millions of Americans and it should be the duty of the Committee to organize and direct this movement into one containing political significance for that is the only way to secure justice for us.

Then too we want to keep abreast of all the latest happening's [*sic*] please send us all the committee's publications as soon as they appear. We want to function actively as a part of this great undertaking.

Another thing, I want you Manny to acquaint the committee with our plans to pursue with dispatch and vigor our next legal moves to continue to press in every possible

Page #4

way to get our case back into the court. Only by coordinating the public campaign to force a court reversal can we win a just cause and destroy this plot that threatens the peoples [*sic*] interest.

Let us not be stampeded by the hysteria and the men of evil for I believe if people adopt the motto that Ethel and I have we will all stand firm. It is, courage, confidence and perspective.

With deep regard, affectionately   Julie

---

[290]There were many references to the anti-semitic overtones of the case in the committee literature. Later on, Julius was forced to attempt to defend the committee's focus on anti-semitism. See below, Julius' letter of December 3, 1952, to Emanuel Bloch, especially pp. 2 and 3.

P.S. Please help explain our position. Note I am writing for both Ethel and myself and I want the committee to know they have our whole-hearted support and I am positive we will be able to work in closer harmony. The overall policy of the campaign, by the very nature of our case, has to be based on a correct political understanding and only then can the right policy be determined and proper tactics followed to assure victory.

To my brothers and sisters on the committee I extend our warmest regards and most friendly greetings and wish them crowning success in their noble endeavor
As Ever—Julie

P.P.S. The childrens [*sic*] visit was just wonderful. I miss them terribly, I hope my thoughts are helpful. I mean well.
110649

Mrs. Lena Cohen [pencil]
140 Baruch Place
New York New York
                                          November 12, 1952
Dearest Lee,
This is simply to confirm that we expect to see Ethel on Saturday. Julie wrote me to that effect so I'm clinching it. He also suggested you let Bernie know right away not to plan on coming, since my doctor is due Saturday afternoon. You'll do it, wont [*sic*] you?—

After you had gone I realized that we had completely forgotten about a certain personal problem you had once broached. Dr. Miller suggested you phone Jewish Family Service (it's in the Manhattan book) for an appointment. Tell them a former client (and give my name), recommended the agency; they usually ask how you happened to hear of them. It might be a good idea to jot down a few notes concerning the nature of the difficulty, so that it will be easier to explain what goes and impress them with your need to see them as soon as possible.

Every thing is fine—My love to all—
Ethel—
P.S.—You won't forget to tell Bernie, huh?—Thanks loads.

Julius to Ethel [ink]

Nov. 13, 1952

My Sweetheart,

After lunch today I took a long nap in order to rest up because I'm usually emotionally drained after an intense visit with you. This in no way is to imply that ["it" CO, N2WI] the visit was any the less satisfactory as a matter of fact it [next word written over another word] was the best nourishment for my morale. I slept clean through the shift change and when I looked [the "ed" and the next word are written over something else] up I noticed a couple of letters next to the New York Times in the bars.

The first one was a note from the Warden telling me that my brother will not be able to visit us Nov. 30th as it would constitute a third Sunday visit and he will not make an exception in our case. Perhaps we'll try to impress my brother with the idea that he should come on another day just this time.

Then I noticed a letter from our esteemed friend and counselor Manny. I read it over, twice and then went back to reread it at least five times in the last 5 hours. It is impossible to put in words how moved I was to read this stirring message.

At once, the bars and the death house [N2WI] seemed to melt [suffix "ed" CO] away [N4WI] they did not count and I found myself once more involved, as ["I" CO] we ["were" CO, N2WI] have been in the past, in a great campaign for the advancement of a worthy cause. Above all I felt so proud that we from the very beginning saw that the people, men and women of principle, who love freedom and fight for decency ["will" CO, NWI] would come to realize the monstrous frame-up that has ["been" probably omitted here] perpetrated in this case and rally to our aid.

Even though we did not, ["see" CO] until now, see in [the "n" is written like an "m", three illegible words CO] writing the evidence of such support, we were positive it existed. If because of the fact that we have been singled out to die ["be the {NWI} first victims" CO, NWI] by ["of" CO] evil men who plot ["the" CO] against the peace and liberty of our people, we can help to expose and prevent ["its" CO, NWI] the fruition of this dangerous plan, then we have succeeded in ["turning" CO] destroying the purpose of the prosecution. More than ever before do we have a heavy responsibility to prove ourselves worthy of the confidence of good people all over the world. I know we will do our part well.

I've walked around my cell for hours, in my mind I wrote a long letter to men and women such as these telling them how encouraging the [last letter is extended to cover the letters "ir"] expression of their sentiments are. However I don't feel up to carrying out [the "ing" and "out" are written over something] such a task, nor do I wish to burden our lawyer by writing him about this. Maybe, I'll decide to do something about it. Better still let me know, what your thoughts are on this matter.

Please pardon the ball point pen it just doesn't always work on this glossy surface. I was very pleased to receive ["all" CO] the copies of some of the committees [*sic*] publications and I do hope they understand how we feel about their work and their efforts on our behalf.

As for you my darling. I love you with all my heart—Always devoted to you— Julie

[The rest of the letters in 1952 are written in ink by Julius.]

                                                             Nov. 16, 1952

Hello Adorable,

By the time you read this letter you will probably know the Supreme Court decision on our petition for rehearing, which will be ["carried" CO] broadcast on the 12:45 news on Monday. Since we both are of one mind on this matter our statement which we drew up a few days before the [NWI] court's last [word "court's" CO] denial still covers very adequately this present situation.

At this time again I want to assure you of my steadfastness, my complete devotion to you and of the deep regard and profound love I have for you. Even as I obtain new strength and inspiration from you my dear I am sure you too will find new courage and be heartened because of all that you mean to me and above all what you symbolize to many.

If we are able to contribute something in the great fight for peace and against fascism and I believe that we have already made an important contribution to aid in this fight, then we have turned the tables on the prosecution and have ["won" CO] advanced the cause of justice and freedom. Also I simply believe before this case is over we will win new victories for the people and we will be vindicated. It is true that when a goal is really worthwhile a great deal of energy and sacrifice must be expended before one succeeds. When the principles of democracy, decency and the dignity of the human being are involved then the effort alone is in itself a noble endeavor. We will continue to strive ahead and I believe we will succeed in our undertaking. And so my darling if I can continue to walk besides you in this way then our relationship reaches new heights and life has been good to me. There wells up in me tremendous feelings and I hope to express some of them to you when I face you this Wednesday across our favorite screen.

Ethel and I had an old fashion gab-fest this Saturday and we chewed the fat ["for" CO] the entire visit. It seems to me that we ought to take up once again our correspondence with the children. At our visit we can scheduale [*sic*] this. I'm not preparing any notes for our next visit. I want you ["the" CO] to carry the ball and plan to discuss all that your heart desires. You know, Ethel, even though I miss you very much I am very serene because I'm well satisfied with the two of us. Take a look at the childrens [*sic*] book review section of the New York Times maybe you can get some idea ["for" CO] of books for the boys.

There was a special occasion that had great meaning to us which occured [*sic*] during a [NWI] particular passover holiday. I've lived through it a number of times. Tonight again we share it's [*sic*] joy. Sweet honey wife—All my love I send you. —Julie

Mr. Emanuel H. Bloch
7 W. 16th St.
New York NY

Nov. 17, 1952
2:00 P.M.

Dear Manny,

The Supreme Court has again struck a blow against justice. By it's [*sic*] action today it is sanctioning the use of "due process" as a club against those who fight every move that leads to war and to it's [*sic*] handmaiden fascism. The rights and liberties guaranteed in our constitution, which are the foundation and strength of our country, are here again emasculated and deliberately violated for political purposes. Only the bigots, the hate-mongers, the racists, the fomentors of tensions between peoples and nations and the warmakers will be happy with this decision because it ["shows" CO, N3WI] fits in with their beastly designs.

This shameful miscarriage of justice must not be allowed to stand. We cry out!—We are completely innocent of the charge.— History will record the truth of our contentions. Before all mankind we will be vindicated.

Yes, we want to live and devote ourselves to a fruitful life of accomplishments. Therefore, while we still have ["a" CO, NWI] lifes [*sic*] breath left in our bodies we call out to our fellow Americans. "There is great danger ahead." Imprisonment and death faces those who seek to exercise their democratic prerogatives, expressions and actions, that are considered by the government in power to be opposed to their policies.

The only answer to this is an aroused and vigilant public rallied in [N2WI] in determined support of the great democratic traditions and principles of our country, that protects the rights and liberties of all.

The lessons of Hitlerism, its techniques, it's [*sic*] brutality and horror are known to all. The World has given its answer before. The only future is opposition to war and fascism.

We have faith the people will continue in increasing numbers to take this correct path again. The fight for justice in our case is one of the steps along this noble path.

We are confident we will win the support of decent men and women everywhere and that they will save us and themselves.

With courage we await the verdict of the court of public opinion that will help set us free.

As Ever

Julie

P.S I dashed this off as soon as I heard the news. This flowed from my heart and mind and I didnt [*sic*] have time to go over and polish it up. Tell our good friends to fight harder. Send [NWI] them my affection and love. ["to them." CO]

Nov. 17, 1952

Dearest Ethel,

The Supreme Court failed to redeem itself but persisted in acquiescing to this growing madness. Mass pressure is the only thing that will restore the bill of rights, maintain the Constitutional liberties and save our lives. Take hope darling the avalanche of protest we predicted will come now. We are not alone and the significance of our case is being understood by ever increasing numbers of people. Their actions in our behalf will be their answer.

After I heard the news broadcast I reread your letter of the 13th of Oct. and found your analysis very appropriate and applicable to the instant action. Then I read the letter from France again and together they gave me new strength.

I quickly dashed off a statement to our beloved friend and distinguished counselor Manny. I didn't have much time to polish it up as I wanted to get it out to him this afternoon. I'll tell you about it at our Wednesday meeting.

I am calm, confident and prepared to contribute my all to the campaign to win us justice. Keep your courage up sweetheart the toughest part of the fight is here now.

Since the pressures will become greater as time passes I propose we give all of our visit over to our personal problems. I've prepared my few remarks in concise form to give you most of the time.

I am sure that my family will devote their efforts working to save us and therefore I am not going to write them at this point. Before the week is out we should get some indication of how the wind is blowing. It would please me no end if our lawyer decides to come and see us this weekend[.] It is an ideal time because there is no ["visit" inserted here, then CO] schedualed [*sic*] ["visits" CO, NWI] visit then.

You are ever present in my mind and my heart is all for you. Every night when I go to bed I hug you close to me and feel at one with you. Although we are apart I am positive we are one in mind and spirit and that is what really counts. Remember sweetheart I am completely devoted to you and I love you more than anything else in the world because you symbolize so much that is good.

We are not deluding ourselves for we are still to go through more agony and greater kinds of hell before this nightmare is over. I have no doubts that we will come through in flying colors. The enemy does not know the source of such determination and strength. We however understand and are confident.

Keep your peace of mind my love and that pretty smile on your beautiful face and I know all will be well—Your husband and greatest admirer Julie

Nov. 20, 1952

Charming Flower of My Heart,

You looked magnificent in that elegant dress. When one puts on a new dress, especially in these surroundings, it brightens up the atmosphere and believe me darling you were actually beaming. I was so proud to see you looking so well and of course I wanted to hold you in my arms and love you with all my heart but that will have to wait. We had an excellent visit but the time just slips away [NWI] all to [*sic*] quickly and we never can cover enough ground. However, what we did manage to talk about we discussed thoroughly.

At present, I'm concentrating on the book I spoke to you about and I'm making notes which we'll discuss at our next legal consultation. I do hope Manny will get here soon. There are many things I want to talk to him about and if he agrees with my ideas, they will entail a great deal of work. Since our time is limited I want him to explore all possibilities as soon as possible. If you do happen to write to our lawyer tell him when he does plan to come we will need more time at this next meeting than we usually take at these sessions. This is most important because we will have to make complete plans for our boys, especially concerning the mattes [*sic*] you and I talked about this past Wednesday.

I intend to wait until Sunday before I write the children a letter. Maybe, we'll hear ["about" CO] from them before then. I'm sure my family [next word written over the word "are"] is busy working on our behalf and I am looking forward to hear how things are going. Within a couple of days

Judge Kaufman will probably set a date for our execution and that should signal ["the" CO] maximum effort ["of" CO, NWI] by the committee and our supporters to win us justice. The situation will be very difficult and trying and I am sure we will be able to face whatever the future brings. I am confident regardless of the dangers we face, we will conduct ourselves with dignity and courage and that eventually we'll be able to clear ourselves of the charges.

I find letter writing is to [sic] inadequate a means to share with you our mutual problems ["and" CO, N2WI] and common responsibilities and our ["common" CO] love. It is very hard for me to break loose from so much feeling and put down on paper what I wish to convey to you. I talk to you, think of you, dream of you and kiss you every night to sleep and I am strong because of you. Keep on looking pretty, my beautiful wife and you'll feel better and find yourself in the ["mind proper" CO, NWI] proper frame of mind to relax more often. Please don't get the idea that I think there is anything wrong with your appearance as a matter of fact you shine [NWI] even in this God forsaken place.

Sweetheart I'm proposing all over again for I'm madly in love with you—Wont [sic] you please accept? Always devoted to you—Your Julie

Nov. 23rd, 1952

Dearest Ethel,

You already know that the "honorable" Judge has ordered that we remain alive for only 50 odd more days. I'm sure we'll confound him again for before the ink was dry on his order our lawyer began to fight back with the various legal steps we've talked about. Naturally I'm just itching to discuss all these matters with him but we'll have to be patient as he must at this moment concentrate on these legal moves.

Now that the issue is being drawn in it's [sic] crucial stage the hirelings of the Hearst press have spewed forth some additional fabrications, products of whiskey soaked brains, to hurt our fight. It seems to me that their [sic] exists in our country a "phantom" Goebbels [NWI] type general staff with representatives on major newspapers whose purpose it is to act as the theoretical section of neo-fascism and use it's [sic] technique, anti-communism distortions, professional stool pigeons and constant repetition of big lies. Just to name a few—Rushmore on the Journal American, Riesel & Winchell on the N.Y. Mirror, Danton Walker on the News, Philbrick on the Tribune, Waltmen on the World Telegram, Lyons on the Post. They are not alone for they often receive editorial support from their pappers [sic]. I've witnessed how they distorted the anti-semitism [the "a" and "s" were originally capitalized, then over-written with lower case letters] issue in our case by raising straw men and falsifying our claim but when it suits their political purpose how quickly they raise the cry. I'm going to talk to you about this subject at our next visit, on the basis of my reading in the book I spoke to you about and also an article in the Menorah Journal on this subject. It is my belief that only a correct understanding of this issue can be had by studying the economic and political basis for it. Then one can see when it is raised as a true issue.

I still have hopes of hearing from Mr. Kelly as to our request before I see you this week. We'll need this time to help in our defense. Again I'm hesitant about writing our boys and I'll have to let it go until I think I can do justice to all that I want to tell them. I suggest you write my sister to forstall [*sic*] any possible mixup on your visits next weekend. Maybe Manny will let us know when he'll visit us. The earliest chance will probably be this coming Friday. Our's [*sic*] darling is a lot that requires endless waiting, myriads of mental torments and yet all this can be conquered because our conscience is clear. We are innocent and we have conducted ourselves in a principled way and that gives great strength. I'll have some interesting items to tell you about and I can't wait to once again look upon your beautiful radiant face and sop up all the inspiration you have to offer. Many thoughts are pounding in my head and are jammed up and can't find release. I'm sure when I see you I'll manage to unblock this dam and give free reign to my emotions and ideas. I'm constantly thinking of you— Always devoted to you my precious dear—Your Julie

P.S Don't worry the committee's really working. We'll hear of the results soon enough. All my love.

Nov. 27, 1952

Darling Bunny Wife,

It is after 8:00 P.M. now. I just awoke from a heavy sleep in time to have my coffee. At the moment I feel kind of loggy [*sic*] perhaps it's the effect of finally eating some chicken or maybe the thought I'll have to wait until Christmas to get some more. Actually, I'm keenly awaiting the outcome of our present legal moves in the district court. One thing is certain that we'll have to be very patient as this will take many twists and turns and it will be some time yet before we know the final decision on this present procedure. However one thing is very clear that we are obtaining a great deal of support from all over the world and [NWI, but below the line] from all different types of people because the pen prostitutes are setting up an organized howl. The tenor of their campaign, the nature of the lies put forth shows the strength of our position.

I have high hopes that we'll see our lawyer this weekend even though he's deeply immersed in the legal battle. Then, I intend to write the children this Sunday, expecting in the meanwhile to hear from them. I'd like to know how they spent their Thanksgiving holiday. Also I believe we should plan for them to spend the Christmas week with Mama. Hanukah week begins Dec. 14 and we ought to decide what gifts we want Manny to give them on our behalf.

Recently, there have been a number of articles in the magazines concerning the prison system, which are of current interest, because of the numerous riots that have taken place. In most of them, they tell of the progress made by the Federal Bureau of Prisons and it's [*sic*] modern outlook on Penology. They further state that even the strictest prison Alcatraz is on its' [*sic*] way out [N3WI] as an institution which is [NWI] now used for the most hardened and [partial word "hopel" CO] desperate criminals. How our government displays it's [*sic*] partiality and brutal intent by sending Sobell to that prison![291] It is only a means to pressure him but it also exposes the nature of their foul plot as a political bludgeon against the American people. For it is obvious that those who run our Government today fear the democratic [the pen skipped a bit in the next word] instincts of the people and wish to stifle freedom and true independence. Gentlemen, not even death sentences will work. I'm more confident than ever that we'll win this fight and I'm prepared for all eventualities. So keep your chin up, your spirits high and we'll come through in better shape than when we were first dragged into this nightmare.

The words come more difficult to express, especially when I try to tell you how I feel about you. Suffice it to say, now that my perception is sharpest, because of this situation, I begin to realize the tremendous worth you have to me—You brighten and enrich my life and living ["as your husband" CO with pencil] with you as my inspiration and partner [words "in life" CO with pencil] is glorious—All my love
Devoted to you—Julie

---

[291] Sobell discovered many years later that it was on the direct orders of J. Edgar Hoover, who technically had no say over where federal prisoners should be housed, that Sobell was sent to Alcatraz. See *On Doing Time*, pp. 412–13.

Mr. Emanuel H. Bloch
7 W. 16th Street
New York N.Y.

Nov. 28, 1952
Page # 1 [circled]

Dear Manny,

I know I have a heavy responsibility, a duty to the people to contribute my all to the common struggle for peace and decency. But I have been held back because I feel inadequate to the task, for I want to be worthy of the faith and support of my fellow men.

It is very difficult for me to know just where to begin. Therefore, I've decided to write a running account of my thoughts as I get them. Note, the date will be based on the remaining days that ["have been" CO, NWI] are left us as decreed by the death sentence of our government.

This will be no polished manuscript, rewritten with an eye to grammar, style or even completely coherent. Therefore, please consider my weaknesses and human frailties and I'll just put down my ideas as they occur.

I'd like this to be a conversation between me and the reader, whoever he or she may be and as I go along I'll tell you dear person why I take the liberty to communicate with you.

Our government through the instrumentality of one of it's [*sic*] Federal Judges Irving R. Kaufman has decreed that my wife and I be put to death in 45 days.

Almost daily there are individuals convicted of capital crimes and sentenced to death. But, this is the first time in the history of our country, in a civil case, that the authorities have set the death penalty [illegible letter CO] for a conviction of conspiracy to commit espionage.

The peculiar circumstances are these that two innocent people are condemned to death in a political frameup. I will discuss every element of this in detail. Particular attention will be paid to the purpose and motives of the prosecution as exemplified by their actions and statements, by the propaganda of interested parties and only incidentally ["the" CO] to the witnesses whose oral testimony against us was the only evidence. It was of poor quality, unreliable, uncorroborated, ["and" CO] full of extraneous hysteria engendered by the Cold War and anti-communist prejudice and still it was empty. It did not even warrant submission to a jury much less have [NWI] any grounds for a finding of guilt beyond a reasonable doubt.

Since this case is of great significance to you and effects [*sic*] the vital interests and very lives of all people I beg of you to hear me out and if I seem to go far afield I will tie it all up to the main theme.

Events have chosen us as the principles [*sic*] in this case. I hope you our reader are acquainted with our background, our experiences, and know a little about us from the material in the trial record and the letters we have written. Then it will be easier to understand our reactions.

— At the very outset of our trial the District Attorney Mr. Irving Saypol in his opening statement to the jury said and I quote from the record P. 183 —

(# 110649)

Nov 28
Page # 2 [circled] of 7

"We will prove that the Rosenbergs devised and put into operation, with the aid of Soviet Nationals and Soviet Agents in this country, an elaborate scheme which enabled them to steal through David Greenglass this one weapon, that might well hold the key to the survival of this nation and means <u>the peace of the world</u>, the atomic bomb"[292]

In Saypols [*sic*] summation to the jury, P. 1518-19 of the trial record and I quote, "We know of these other henchmen of Rosenberg in this plot by him, by Sobell, by the Soviet Union and it's [*sic*—no apostrophe in the source] representatives and by other traitorous Americans to deliver the safeguards of our security into the hands of a power that would wipe us off the face of the earth and <u>destroy its'</u> [*sic*] <u>peace</u>. ["]

Judge Kaufman stated and I quote from the record P. 1614-15. "I believe your conduct in putting into the hands of the Russians the A-Bomb years before our best scientists predicted Russia would perfect the bomb has already caused, in my opinion, the Communist <u>aggression in Korea</u>, with the resultant casualties exceeding 50,000, and who knows but that millions more of innocent people may pay the price of your treason.["]

I have gone to the trouble of quoting verbatim these statements even though they are complete inventions of those who made them, are false and not based on the evidence or any sane reasoning but because they touch on what I am convinced is the most significant factor of this case. It makes obvious the true purpose of the government. The issue raised is peace and should be discussed thoroughly to show how it is really threatened and what the roots of war are.

What Relation [*sic*] does our trial and death sentence have to this?

Every student of history knows that World War I, World War II and the danger of World War III stem from the same source. The existance [*sic*] of world cartels, controlled by finance capital and it's [*sic*] resultant imperialism that in the normal course of its' [*sic*] activities sets in motion economic and political forces in the state and countries it controls that inevitably lead to war.

---

[292]Here and in the next two instances, the underlining is added by Julius.

James Stewart Martin wrote a book entitled, "All Honorable Men.["] It is an account of how giant German industrial and financial combines subsidized Hitler and the Nazi military machine on the one hand and on the other hand conspired to weaken Europe and America through favorable cartel agreements in preparation for world conquest. It is fully documented [*sic*] and shows the part leaders of American business played in this scheme.

It is also an inside story of how our government's enunciated ["policy" CO, N2WI] post war program [N2WI] which was signed into the Potsdam agreement, to end the menace of the German cartels (the source of war) was frustrated and finally stopped by American and other allied powers [*sic*] industrial and financial [NWI] interests whose paramount concern was "business as usual."

(—110649)

Nov. 28
PAGE # 3 [circled] of 7

It names all the major individuals and all the major firms involved. It describes incidents of how they actually aided the enemy in wartime under the provisions of ordinary commercial agreements. And it is written from first hand experience by a man who as chief of the Decartelization Branch of our Military Government was not allowed to complete the mission set by President Roosevelt.[293]

"Defeat of the Nazi armies will have to be followed by eradication of the weapons of economic warfare" wrote President Roosevelt in 1944. It was plain that the great German cartels would have to be broken up before we could win the peace.

This clear cut objective for smashing the deadly menace in the German economy was never carried out. Obstacles blocked the path for the interests of businessmen conflicted with United States war aims. The author says there are no villains in this great economic and political drama; the generals, the administrators and businessmen who reversed the American decartelization program were all—as Anthony said of Caeser's [*sic*] murderers—"All honorable men." What he meant was that they were all fraternity brothers, representatives of finance capital, of ["and" CO] the cartels.

On page 264 of this book I quote two revealing paragraphs (The forces that stopped us had operated from the United States but had not operated in

---

[293]At the end of World War II, the initial approach to the defeated German nation was summarized as "the four D's": denazification, decartelization, demilitarization, and democratization. Very early on, the first three were stopped because of the desire to build up West Germany as an ally of the U.S. and Britain against the Soviet Union.

the open. We were not stopped by a law of Congress by an executive order of the President, or even by a change of policy approved by the President or any member of his cabinet. In short, whatever it was that had stopped us was not, "the government." But it clearly had command of channels through which the government normally operates.

The relative powerlessness of governments in the face of growing economic power is of course not new. Between the two world wars the outstanding development in world economics was the division of territories and markets, by private agreement, among the largest corporations of Britain, Germany and the United States, with minor participations by their counterparts in France, Italy and Japan. National governments stood on the sidelines while bigger operators arranged the world's affairs.]

Again I quote on P. 291 of this book (Our observations in postwar Germany did not support the theory that the Nazi regime was a runaway affair. Propaganda had been turned out in an effort to convince people that the industrialists who backed the Hitler coup did not realize they were opening a Pandora's box. We are to believe that the troubles they set loose plagued them no less than the rest of mankind. On the contrary, from all that we could gather in talking with German industrialists, the big-industry group in Germany regrets the Hitler period only because the Nazis lost the war. We found no evidence that the leading industrial groups had acquired a fundamental distaste for German nationalism as such. They are still working to-ward the organization of Europe in such a way as to support a dominant German industrial economy, and the organization of Germany's own economic life around a concentation [sic] of heavy industries.)

Documents found in files in Germany showed that the representatives of big business in Germany deposited huge sums
#110649

Nov 29
PAGE # 4 [circled] of 7

of monies in a special bank fund that Hitler and Himmler drew on to finance the Nazi movement ["at" CO, NWI] and at the crucial point in the struggle for power, all of big industry and finance threw their support openly to Hitler and he took control.

In the earlier days of the 3rd Reich Hitler never made major decisions without being sure in advance that he had the backing of the Krupps and other Ruhr and Rhineland industrialists. For their support the Krupp holdings did well under Hitler. They were greatly expanded and had the benefit of the Nazi labor policy. 50,000 foreign workers, 20,000 prisioners [sic] of war worked for them under their discipline and authority. Especially satisfactory did they find the "extermination through work" programs for certain classes of concentration camp workers.

Frederick Flick one of the steel magnates of this group showed that his $40,000 annual premiums to the Himmler fund had yielded the best from the S.S. labor procurement service. Unlimited quantities of slave labor from the concentration camps at very low rates were charged to such special "subscribes". [*sic*]

These are only a few examples [N2WI] from which you can ["only" CO, NWI] get an idea of the ["the" CO, NWI] entire picture. Of course the best way is to read the authentic documents direct from the source material.

Only a small group of men less than 100 controlled I.G. Farben, United Steel, Deutche [*sic*] Bank and Dresdner [*sic*] Bank and all the rest. So to [*sic*] in America we do have economic power concentrated in the hands of a group of not more than 100 men. Before World War II 250 of the largest American Industrial Corp. controlled $2/3$ of the industrial assets of the United States the bulk of this in the hands of the largest 100. The leading firms were arranged in eight major groups by common financial ties and interlocking directories. During the war and after these 100 corporations controlled by the same eight financial groups increased their concentration of power from $2/3$ to $3/4$ of the American Industrial economy.

Just as the six largest financial corporations in Germany inter-locked with the dominant industrial firms, so there are eight large financial units in the American economy which in recent years have assumed a comparable degree of power over here. These are: (1) the Morgan group controlling, among many others, such headliners as United States Steel, General Electric, Kennecott Copper, American Telephone and Telegraphy, International Telephone and Telegraph; (2) the Rockefeller interests, including the Standard Oil companies and the Chase National Bank; (3) the Kuhn, Loeb public utilities network (4) the Mellon holdings; including the Aluminum Company, Gulf oil, Koppers, Westinghouse Electric; (5) the Chicago group, including International Harvester and the Armour and Wilson packing houses; (6) the Dupont interests, including General Motors, E.I. duPont de Nemours, and United States Rubber; (7) the Cleveland group, with Republic Steel, Goodyear and others; and (8) the Boston group, including United Fruit, Stone and Webster utilities and First National Bank of Boston.[294]

---

[294]This analysis stems from work done by Marxist economist Paul M. Sweezy for the National Resources Committee, published originally as Appendix 13 to Part 1 of *The Structure of the American Economy*, edited by W. Leontiev (Cambridge: Harvard University Press, 1941). Based on research done in 1937,

Firms in the portfolios of these eight groups make up the Big Threes and the Big Fours of practically every basic industry in the United States.

The concluding paragraph of this book states. (The moral of this is not that Germany is an inevitable menace; but that

(110649)

Nov 29
PAGE # 5 [circled] of 7

there are forces in our own country which can make Germany a menace. And, more importantly, they could create a menace of their own here at home, not through a deliberate plot to bring about a political catastrophe but as a calm judgement of "business necessity." The men who would do this are not Nazis but businessmen; not criminals, but honorable men.)

But Mr. Martin pulled his punches I don't have to. I'll call a spade, a spade. These so called "honorable" men are very powerful. They fear the democratic instincts of the people and the wrath of the American public if they become aware of these truths that, by their very nature ["they" CO, N2WI] the cartels are the source of wars and from them alone stems the danger to the peace of the world. They control the press and radio and use it to distort, by repeating high sounding words over and over again like "free" world and peace. They control the political parties ["and use appointees" CO, N2WI] and appoint as errand boys such men as Saypol and Kaufman to create a big lie that we could possibly threaten the peace. They use us as scapegoats to confuse the people and frighten them into acceptance of governmental policies that inevitably lead to war.

But they are in power and we have only 44 days to live.

Please be patient I have a great deal more to talk to you about.

Suppose we look into this espionage business.

On P. 19 of Martin's book is found the following:

(In 1940, 1941 and 1942 ships leaving American seaports had had the same security measures to protect their departure. Yet many of their broken hulls and water-soaked cargoes had washed up onto the beaches of New Jersey, Virginia and the Carolinas, where German submarines had spotted them within sight of shore. In case after case, every man on board had been marked before the captain opened his orders. Though they may not have known it, the cargoes they carried were reinsured with Munich. The routine system of placing insurance had put precise information on their sailing date and destination in the hands of the Germans before the ship left port.)

Sweezy identified these eight major interest groups. The appendix was reprinted in Sweezy, *The Present as History* (NY: Monthly Review Press, 1953), Ch. 12.

All industrial plants were reinsured and full reports by insurance inspectors including blueprints of the installations, description of the fire hazards and risks, and inventory of the contents of the buildings, room by room. One example ["of" CO] cited of plans for a large new magnesium plant with one of the blueprints having an arrow pointing at a valve, with the legend. "Under no circumstances must this valve be closed while the plant is in operation, an explosion would result."

All these activities during ["war" CO] war and peace time come well within the scope of the Espionage Act. However these gentlemen were fraternity brothers, honorable men they were never indicted. However, on no documentary [*sic*], we [illegible cross-out here] were charged with conspiracy to commit espionage because we [NWI] always spoke ["for peace" CO] and worked for peace ["always" CO] and exposed these plutocrats.

What about the death sentence?
#110649

Nov 30
Page # 6 [circled] of 7

I think you should read Brig. General Telford Taylor's book "Doctors of Infamy". He was the chief prosecutor of the leading representatives of German medicine during a war crimes trial. I know you will find it very difficult to keep from retching when you read of these revolting, barbaric, monstrous atrocities. There were a number of very lengthy and famous trials such as the Nuremberg war crimes trials that documented the facts of their overwhelming guilt. However only a minute number ever paid fully for their crimes. The members of the fraternity did not allow justice to take it's [*sic*] course, [*sic*] Under their aegis slight legal technicalities were found to stop the trials of war criminals. Then they commuted the death sentences of these convicted criminals, released them from prison because thousands of these individuals were needed once again to take their places as errand boys doing the dirty work of the "honorable" men.

This is the kind of equal justice under the law our government metes out. And we have only 43 more days left to live.

During the course of my testimony I stated in court that I believed the Russians carried the brunt of the war and that the Allies should ["have" CO] open [suffix "ed" CO from previous word] a second front ["sooner" CO]. This didn't go well with the court but if a second front had been opened sooner the Nazis would not have had time to exterminate 6,000,000 Jewish people and millions of other victims of fascism. At Page 1079 of the trial record I gave the following testimony. (and in discussing the merits of other forms of governments, I discussed that with my friends on the basis of the per-

formance of what they accomplished, and I felt that the Soviet government has improved the lot of the underdog there, has made a lot of progress in eliminating illiteracy, has done a lot of ["progress" CO] reconstruction work and built up a lot of resources, and at the same time I felt that they contributed ["the" CO] a major share in destroying the Hitler beast who killed 6,000,000 of my co-religionists, and I feel emotional about that thing.
Q. Did you feel that way in 1945? A. Yes, I felt that way in ["194" CO, next number inserted] 1945
Q. Do you feel that way today? A. I still feel that way.)

The court didn't like this they wanted me to confess to crimes I did not do, to bear false witness against innocent people and to allow myself to be used as a tool to create anti-soviet and anti-communist propaganda to add to the hysteria and the cold war.[295] I would not allow myself to be used even for propaganda purposes to increase the tensions between the United States and Russia. Only better relations between these two countries can benefit ["both of it's" CO, "of it's" inserted after "both" then CO, NWI] the peoples [N3WI] of both lands and insure world peace.

The only documentary evidence produced by the government to tie us up with this case was a tin collection can "Save A Spanish Republican Child" and our lawyer in summation said hollow, hollow like the case against the Rosenbergs for in no way can anyone infer any connection to espionage.[296]
#110649

[The seven-page letter to Emanuel Bloch was interrupted by the following letter.]

Julius to Ethel

Nov. 30, 1952
Dearest Ethel,
    Ever since Manny's last visit I've been going through a state I am sure you are very familiar with. My conscience and my mind tells me it's my

---

[295]A year later, the CIA would come up with a detailed proposal for just such a role for our parents, should they confess. It entailed getting them to make a public declaration that the Soviet government was engaging in an anti-semitic pogrom against Jews and to warn world Jewry to get out of and become strong opponents of the world communist movement. See Memorandum, January 22, 1953, prepared by an unidentified CIA employee, enclosed in Keay to Belmont, February 2, 1953, JR HQ 1772. Also in *Hearings,* pp. 2328–32.
[296]For the way the prosecutor used the collection can, see Record, pp. 1176–78.

duty to write and very often at that [NWI] but here's the rub even though I know it, I feel inadequate to the task. I've begun and stopped at least three times daily since Friday and at the same time I've denied myself the pleasure of going into any new books. Over and over again I tell myself I'll do the best I can but it is coming harder than pulling teeth. One thing you can be sure that I will break through and get out something. The idea to [NWI] be perfect and do a real bang up job is a great detering [sic] force. However I've made some rough notes on a number of statements we ought to get in shape and I'll talk to you about them at our next visit. Also I have the general outline of my plan in mind but again the task is a gigantic and difficult one. I am positive if we were able to work together it would be a masterpiece. I'll just have to muddle through the best I can.

If we are able to spend the time I'll go into this matter more fully. Of course I must say that I'm elated that our affidavit was successful in getting Kaufman to disqualify himself from hearing the motion.[297] This is our first victory in $2^1/_2$ years of legal efforts and is only an indication of how far we've come already to have this motion granted without going to a higher court. Even more important at this point is the kind of support we're getting at home and abroad. The Committee is doing a terriffic [sic] job and so is Manny. It was just wonderful to read this weeks [sic] National Guardian a storehouse of comfort and inspiration. So principled a policy and clear in its efforts to mobilize public opinion behind the campiagns [sic] that are ["in the" CO] of cardinal importance to the peoples [sic] interest. I was particularly moved by the poem that appeared about the children. For it was exactly like it happened.

Darling wife the avalanche you predicted 19 months ago is here and they have taken us to ["y" CO] their hearts and are going all out in our behalf because they are awake to the great danger to all if this miscarriage of justice is not rectified. We ["1" CO] can take heart because this is the true barometer of the peoples [sic] feelings and this will guarantee that we live and win complete vindication. Of course, there is still a long fight ahead with the most important hurdles yet to be overcome but I have more confidence than ever that we'll succeed no matter what the obstacles are. To [sic] bad my love I have to seek inspiration by proxy from you when you in the flesh right here beside me is the best kind of stimulant. I am impatiently

---

[297]Kaufman recused himself from hearing the sec. 2255 motion after they charged he was biased against them. This motion was therefore heard by a different district court judge. However, the chief judge of the district later ruled that all subsequent motions dealing with the Rosenberg-Sobell case would start with Judge Kaufman, and so he heard the next motion in June of 1953 as well as Morton Sobell's motion of 1956.

awaiting our next tete and tete at our favorite screen—By the way write to
Lee to prevent any mixup on visits if Dave puts in an appearance this
Monday—Remember only 2 visits per week
All my love — Devoted as ever — Julie

Dec 1
PAGE # 7 [circled] of 7

This can was supposed to be used to collect funds to aid the innocent
victims of the fascist butcher Franco. We admit we are ardent anti-fascists.
Not only did we donate money to help refugees but we collected funds and
signed petitions to aid the Republican cause.

I remember when the rebellion broke into [sic, probably meant "out"]
in Spain and my wife and I decided to help them. Ethel had studied voice.
She is a coloratura soprano and she sings beautifully[.] Since I studied
Spanish in college I taught her the words to two songs. Tango de las Rosas
and Ay—Ay—Ay. Then together with a few of our friends we went to
Times Square on Saturday night. Ethel sang these two Spanish songs and
Non Pasaran and ["we" CO, N4WI] the rest of us held the corners of a
Spanish Republican flag. The people contributed generously, coins and
dollar bills. The public was overwhelmingly in favor of the Republican
Spanish cause. However, the fraternity brothers were on the side of Franco
while we fought fascism. For this we are condemned with 42 more days left
to live.

Let me digress a moment on an important item. I read in the National
Guardian that on December 12, 1952 the World Peace Congress in Vienna
will begin.

It is conceded by everyone that the American people overwhelmingly
desire peace. Since Eisenhower promised to go to Korea, end the war and
bring peace to the world he won the elections. Our government has heralded
peace as it's [sic] primary aim. The Vienna Peace Congress will not be
controlled by ["representative" CO, NWI] gentlemen of the fraternity brothers
of the [the "e" in the last word is written over "at"] international cartels and
so our government demurred to send representatives to it. They didn't even
wish to pay the usual lip service to the hopes and desires of the millions of
it's [sic] citizens for peace. In addition to opposing this congress they are
doing everything within their power to harass and prevent any Americans
from participating. However in spite of the tremendous hardships placed in
their paths the U.S. Sponsoring committee for Representation at this
Congress has been well received in every corner of the land and it's [sic] call
has even penetrated the gloom of our death house cells.

No force on earth, no matter how reprehensible can prevent the people from working for peace even death cannot silence the cry of humanity for peace.

It is particularly heart warming to us to hear of the participation of our American brothers and sisters in this noble work because, in a way, it destroys the purpose of the prosecution in our case to stifle the voice for peace. We are happy to join the millions of mankind in wishing you success in your deliberations.

For in the victory of your endeavors all the people ["s" CO at end of last word] benefit and we are vindicated.

Long live Peace—Long live Liberty.

Manny—I'll have to stop here for now & I'll send you ["these" CO] letters in two batches each week.

As Ever—Julie

P.S. I hear you'r [*sic*] doing a swell job. I know you'll keep it up. We must win this fight.

Mr. Emanuel H. Bloch
7 W. 16th Street
New York N.Y.

Dec. 2nd 1952
Page A.

Dear Manny,

I have a couple of minutes before my pencil and pen are collected for the night and I'll only have time for a few words.

I just read the Dec 1st issue of the N.Y. Post. It seems to me the truth of our case must be reaching the people and so this apologist paper must do a hatchet job to head off the growing protest movement against this infamous act of our government. The editorial gives no facts either from the record or about us but goes far afield to spew it's [*sic*] own little bit of poision [*sic*]. After all it must ingratiate itself with the F.B.I. and Winchell. Look here why bother us we are calling for the blood of ["that" CO] those "Soviet Communist Spies" the Rosenbergs.

Always they raise straw men and knock them down but their [*sic*] is no truth about our case.

By sheer coincidence the series of articles began on the same day our case goes into court again.[298]

As to the first item Pontius Pilat uses you can give the lie to him for you have the copy of my letter without the important deletions and distortions.

This series is starting out with the same pattern as our trial no facts just political propaganda, cold war hysteria and anti communist witch hunt language.

They are fuming because we refuse to be stool pigeons[.] Now as to his [NWI] socalled [*sic*] facts # 1 My views were open and known to all up to [N2WI] and after my arrest. My family knew them, my friends, my workers, my business contacts and my fellow employees wherever I worked. Where does he base his fact on?

2 We never claimed to be communist & it was never proven we were communists. Even taking the meaning of what he says gives the lie to the government. The entire trial was full of our opinions on politics. Our activity for Spain. My opinions of the 2nd front. Our union activity and our talks with friends where we expressed progressive ideas.

3 We never claimed we were "Convicted of being Jews[.]" That is his straw man but his answer has nothing to do with the question. I never had rabbinical training all I went to was Hebrew School and it was never understood that I would do anything but pursue a course of study to become a professional man.[299] Of course a cheap trick at [*sic*] distortion when the entire family knows I was the apple of my father [*sic*] eye and our relationship was extremely close. It was I who stood by him Day [*sic*] and night for 10 days taking care of him [N4WI] while in the hosp [*sic*—"until" CO, NWI below cross out] before he died from a pulmonary [word "embolism" CO, NWI] trombosis [*sic*]. But this dog will even insult the dead. Since when does a recitation of educational background in English and Hebrew constitute invoking religious respectability. Only a representative of the Judenrat could be so contemptible to justify his keep.

4 [circled] This is a complete lie—You can best document this from the record. Of course the jury took almost 6 hours to deliberate & we did categorically deny the photographer's story ["the" CO] it should be easy to expose him —Julie

[298]This refers to the first motion for a new trial under sec. 2255 of the federal criminal code. See Schneir, pp. 180–84 for a summary of the issues raised and its subsequent disposition by the district court and appeals court.
[299]Louis Nizer repeated this Pilat lie and even invented conversations about this alleged rabbinical training with my father. See Nizer, pp. 17, 22.

Mr. Emanuel H. Bloch
7 W. 16th Street
New York N.Y.

Dec. 3rd, 1952
Page # 1 of 6

Dear Manny,

I just want to continue my vebal [*sic*] stumbling. Dear friend I have permitted myself certain luxuries today for I must confess I am only mortal. It was a dull dreary morning and snow was falling so I slept late until my turn came for fifteen minutes exercise around the yard. The rest of the morning I spent doing my laundry and cleaning my cell. Today I had intended to discuss more intimate family matters but that will have to wait awhile for there are more important things to talk about.

On this 40th day left to live I want to talk about some of the servants of the abattoir such as the pen hirelings of big business. As you know it takes large sums of money to own a newspaper and it depends on advertising for the revenue needed to keep on operating. Through control of the technical means in the newspaper business such as; [*sic*] newsprint, paper, the large news services and by the very practical lever of paid advertisements, which is tantamount to a mortgage, the fraternity brothers control and in the main dominate the editorial and news slanting policies of the so called "free" press. For practical purposes it is not necessary to be too rigid nevertheless, finesse is needed to hoodwink the readers.[300]

To effectively determine just where the press stands we have to know what it's [*sic*] position is on the key issues of the day and the main orientation of it's [*sic*] program

Where do they stand on the cartels?

Are they fighting the policies of imperialism that up to date has been responsible for the shrunken bodies, the swollen bellies of children, poverty, disease and hunger, short stunted lives devoid of all but the most meager means to maintain body and soul much less the ability to raise the moral, mental and cultural standards of the colonial people? Are they supporting every move for their national liberation so that these men and women can determine for themselves their own form of government, can appropriate to themselves a larger share of their natural [partial word "resour" CO, NWI] wealth and above all walk with human dignity as free people masters of

---

[300]For some detailed analyses to support this point of view, see Noam Chomsky, *Necessary Illusions: Thought Control in Democratic Societies* (Boston: South End Press, 1989); Noam Chomsky and Edward Herman, *Manufacturing Consent: The Political Economy of the Mass Media* (NY: Pantheon Books, 1988).

their own destiny? Or do they support the robber barons in their merciless exploitation, degradation and racist policy against the interests of these people. No amount of prettied up high sounding phrases about the need for raw materials, mineral wealth and strategic positions against the bogey man communism can justify imperialism in any form.

Where do they stand on peace and coexistence?

Are they fighting militarization, alliances with every fascist and reactionary regieme [sic], superweapons that are only of an offensive nature, jingoistic programs and bellicose statements that are made in the guise of national security while preparing and concentrating massive means of aggression? Are they supporting "agreements" that only mean surrender to the program of finance capital? Are their policies only based on anti-communist belligerent propaganda?

Where do they stand on the living standards of the people?

(#110649)

Page #2 of 6

Are they fighting the policies of big business that imposes increasing burdens on the common people and in effect lowers their living standards? Or do they under the cloak of patriotism use witch hunts to harass labor unions and decrease the purchasing power of the people.

Where do they stand on Liberty and the Constitutional Rights?

Are they going along with the hew [sic] and cry that the legal rights of communists can be breached because of their politics? That those accussed [sic] as reds not be allowed to teach in the schools, speak on the radio, write in the press, earn a living, because they hold unpopular views. The law of the land is that everybody must be protected equally by the Bill of Rights and if not it is only a worthless piece of paper.[301]

The truth is that practically the entire press does the bidding of the fraternity brothers of the cartels on these key points.[302] Newspapers on the extreme right give voice to the most rabid fascist howlings. In the center we have the polished and distinguished conservative newspapers. The so called liberal New York Post occupies the left flank of this group and prints weasel philosophical excuses for the need to go along with the tide. Of course they raise pious loud noises on some revolting [NWI] reactionary measures but never on a principled or fundamentally deep basis because their

---

[301]Many times during and since the 1950s, "person on the street" polls have asked people to sign the Bill of Rights without identifying what it is. A large majority had refused to sign it, many times labelling it "communist."

[302]For an excellent summary, see James Aronson, *The Press and the Cold War.*

job is to influence the liberal, labor and progressive people to support the government policy that is leading to war.[303]

["After" CO] We'll discuss this paper's actions on our case after we talk about this topic on this 39th day we have left to live.

It has been heralded by our enemies that we claim we were convicted because we were Jews and that we are raising a false issue of anti-Semitism to win support for our cause.

Here are the plain hard facts:

1 [circled] From the very beginning starting with our arrest and going through the trial, the various appeals, [NWI] reading the trial record [the "&" symbol is written under the line and then CO, the next word is the squeezed in above the symbol] and all our letters and statements it is crystal clear that we never said nor intimated that we were selected out and convicted because we were Jews. No amount of semantic gyrations, distortions, or words out of context can change this truth.[304]

2 [circled] After our sentence the National Guardian a progressive weekly through a series of articles by William A. Reuben brought to public attention the background facts and reviewed the case. This led to the formation of the National Committee to Secure Justice in the Rosenberg Case. They were convinced we are completely innocent and then [last letter overwritten] went to work; presented the facts and held meetings.[305]

---

[303]Lest the reader believe this to be over-blown, remember that the decisions that ultimately led to the long U.S. involvement in Vietnam were already being made as our father wrote. The liberal media actually helped support the U.S. government policy of building up the Ngo Dinh Diem regime after 1954 and making it strong enough to refuse to hold the elections that would have united all of Vietnam under the communist-nationalist Ho Chi Minh. It was not until after massive U.S. troop involvement after 1965 that some elements of the media began to question the "wisdom" of such a heavy involvement, but the unanimous chorus of international anti-communism from the mainstream media helped assure that the U.S. government would have no significant challenges to its actions between the early 1950s and 1965. It took the American people an entire decade to force our government out of Vietnam, during which time hundreds of thousands of Indochinese (from Vietnam, Laos and Cambodia) were killed as well as over 50,000 Americans.

[304]It is true that some writing by committee supporters (see for instance Howard Fast's article in the French Communist newspaper *L'Humanite*, Nov. 24, 1952) had gone further than this. Also note the Nov. 10 letter from Julius which suggests this was not a good approach to take.

[305]Actually, the Committee was a coalition of people who thought they were innocent and those who believed, in the words of Emily Alman, that "grave doubt" existed as to their guilt. The Committee also argued that they did not receive a fair trial. By late 1952 and throughout 1953, the Committee supporters

3 [circled] Prior to the organization of this committee this was the chronology of the actual origin of the charge of Anti-Semitism. The first and basic charges of Anti-Semitism appeared in the anti-communist Yiddish press.

(a) Jewish Daily Forward—April 5th editorial and article by Hillel Rogoff on April 12, 1952 and Jewish Day editorials April 6 & 8[.] These papers voiced disapproval of Judge Kaufmans [*sic*] unprecedented death sentence that he handed down on April 5, 1951.

(b) M. Danzis—Day editor on [first letter of next word written over letter "A"] on April 12, 1951 said "One cannot overlook the Jewish element in this unfortunate tragic Rosenberg trial."   #110649

Page #3 of 6

H. Leivik [*sic*]—A poet in an article in the Jewish Day on April 16th said, "the Judge should have been free from the Jewish complex. In the same vein a column was written by Dr. G. George Fox Chicago Rabbi—columnist for the Sentinel.

(c) Therefore, the Rosenberg committee did not create this issue or first note anti-Semitism in the case. They only brought to public knowledge the existence of these statements and pointed out the appearance of anti-Semitic stickers and literature about the Rosenbergs as "Jew-Communist-atom-spy." For they [N5WI] as well as Jewish leaders realized that the case has potentialities not only for a dreadful anti-Semitic wave, but also for grave danger to the elementery [*sic*] liberties of the American people as a whole.

4 (circled) When it became evident that the public and especially the Jewish community were waking up to the implications of the case and were reacting to this gross miscarriage of justice, some self-appointed leaders of Jewish organizations took on the role of an American Judenrat to disrupt and abort this growing movement. To do this a great myth was created. Oliver "Pontius" Pilat. [*sic*] New York Post reporter planted the germ. He made the accusation and tried to establish his lie, prima facia [*sic*], as a fact, that we claim we were convicted because we were Jews and because of anti-Semitism. The egg was then laid in a New York Post editorial to add credence to this non-existent invention. A febrile attempt to further clothe this illegitimate offspring with some semblence [*sic*] of fact was made by S. Andhill Fineburg [*sic*—the correct spelling is "Fineberg"] paid bureaucrat of the American Jewish Committee by stating de novo this charge with some added twists. The fabricator based his "objective research job" on reports in

---

included many who supported clemency even though they were inclined to believe in the Rosenbergs' guilt.

the New York Times and on Pilat's book.[306] This was published in a 9-page single spaced memorandum $9/10$ of which was a diatribe against communists and was not based on the actual source material the trial record, our letters and statements but on ["stark" CO, N2WI] oft repeated anti-communist ["hysteria" CO, NWI] charges.

These misleaders have a large publicity apparatus available to them and also have access to a favorable press. The New York Post in it's [sic] new series of articles on our case has created an entirely new case. I charge and this can be proven.

1 [circled] That the articles are full of numerous bold lies.

2 [circled] Where the government witness made contradictory statements they rectified it in their reporting[.]

3 [circled] Where the testimony is unreliable and incredible. They add new evidence and put our testimony in the mouths of the government witnesses.

A reading of the trial record will show this to be the unvarnished truth. ["This is done" CO]

The reason this is done is to give weight to the case where there [previous word written over "their"] is none. To make important the evidence of three persons Dave & Ruth Grenlass [sic—hurriedly wrote "Greenglass"] & Elitcher, all of them unreliable as accomplices and for ["selfish" CO] reasons of self preservation. To hide that there was no corroboration of their story by any independent witness or by the F.B.I. or general public that we had ever done or said anything in in [sic] their presence or that in the search of our home any written or documentary evidence was found. ["The only" CO, N5WI] To obscure the fact there ["There" CO] was no evidence but what their three ["had" CO] said. The key to the problem is that politics, hysteria and prejudice played the strongest role in getting a conviction.
110649

Page # 4 of 6

Naturally it helps the New York Post to be on the anti-communist bandwagon and ["be aga" CO] it is now very fashionable to be against the Rosenbergs. They hope to gain immunity from the red-baiting attacks of the lunatic fringe on thought and so they outdo McCarthy in a scurrillous, [sic] vicious attack on us, replete with bold lies and will [sic—probably meant "wild"] accusations that are obvious to all who are acquainted with the record. But they are not afraid of being contradicted in the sympathetic "free"

---

[306]See Oliver Pilat, *The Atom Spies* (NY: Putnam, 1952), and S. Andhill Fineberg, *The Rosenberg Case: Fact and Fiction* (NY: Oceana, 1952).

press. They wish to discredit the efforts to secure us a new trial and hope to obfuscate the main issues by filling the air with pious incantations elaborately elucidated but based on a false nonexistent premise, the [last word written over "their," word "own" CO] strawman they raised. However, this cruel plot against the truth, against our lives, against the interest of the Jewish people and all peoples is exposed. They have to live with their own guilty consciences, they have to face the justifiable wrath of the members of their organizations and they have to answer to the entire public for this despicable performance.

It is an axiom that renascent anti-semitism is always the forerunner of fascism and the menace of war. Our position has always been and is today one that wages a most determined and relentless principled fight against the roots and [NWI] against every manifestation of this brutal infection in the world today. The only explanation I can give for this kind of blackmail is that these people in their blind anti-Soviet hatred can't see reality and are playing the role of the Judenrat in America. In their red smear campaign they are trying to use us as political pawns to prevent the effective rallying of the Jewish people together with all people against threatening fascism and war. They are frantic, they are alarmed they are unmasked and in spite of their efforts we are receiving public support in ever increasing numbers especially from the Jewish people.

We will not be provoked into extensive polemics on obvious falsehoods nor will we be sidetracked from concentrating on the major issues of our case. The fact [sic; next word written over "is"] are: We testified in our [NWI] own behalf. Our cohesive defense negated the flimsy oral evidence that was very tenuous even with the use of the conspiracy gimmick.[307]

---

[307]Under federal conspiracy law, any alleged accomplice can testify to the agreement of the defendant to engage in a criminal act. If the jury believes the "accomplice's" version of that conversation that is all the evidence needed to convict. Note the following self-serving statement by one of the prosecutors, Roy Cohn: ". . . anybody who can make a deal with the government can 'rat out' whoever the government wants ratted out—and if the jury believes his story and he's tried and convicted, the conviction will be upheld on appeal, on the accomplice's word alone. Never mind that his 'words' wouldn't be worth a six-cent verdict in a municipal court automobile accident case. Never mind that he's got a record two arms long. Never mind that he's probably going to walk free after the trial, though he admits to being part of the crime itself. His word alone can convict someone who never got a parking ticket. . . . I knew the game by heart. As a young assistant U.S. attorney I convicted my share of people on uncorroborated accomplice testimony. But it was one thing to make sure of the tools at hand—however unfair the tools may be—and another, quite another thing, to employ the extraordinary powers of the federal government in pursuit of a personal vendetta. That I never did. I never hated anybody enough to do

From the vey [*sic*—miswritten "very"] beginning we vigorously protested our innocence. We vehemently denied generally and in detail every part of the evidence introduced by the prosecution to connect us with the crime charged. ["If" CO] The evidence that was presented at the trial did not warrant any finding of guilt. [N6WI] In order to secure a conviction The [*sic*] prosecution and the judge violated our constitutional rights throughout the trial and allowed it to be dominated by inflammatory extraneous issues taking advantage of a prevalent atmosphere of war tension and anti-Soviet hysteria. The verdict could well be described as a triumph of political prejudice.

As the Chanukah holiday week approaches it recalled to mind the rich heroic traditions of my people and in the "festival of lights" it rekindles in the hearts of all Jews ["the" CO] as it has for ages the hopes and aspirations for freedom, liberty and justice. We are proud of our Jewish origin, of our Hebrew education of the culture and glorious heritage of our people. Before our arrest and even now our children are attending Jewish school so that ["they" probably omitted here] too will be inspired as their parents were by it and we are raising them in the spirit of an ["integrated" CO] progressive American and Hebrew heritage.
\# 110649

Page \# 5 of 6

It is appropriate on this 38th day we have left to life [*sic*] to present the following that appeared in the Christian Science Monitor.

Judge Learned Hand with 42 years experience on the federal bench, who was acclaimed by Supreme Court Justice Benjamin Cardozo as "the most distinguished living English speaking jurist" recently told the New York Board of Regents

"Risk for risk for myself I had rather take my chances that some traitor will escape detection than spread abroad a spirit of general suspicion and distrust, which accepts rumor and gossip in place of undismayed and unintimidated inquiry. I believe that the community is already in dissolution where every man begins to eye his neighbor as a possible enemy, where nonconformity with the accepted creed, political as well as religious is a mark of disaffection; where denunciation without specification or backing takes the place of evidence, where orthodoxy chokes freedom of dissent;

---

that." (Sidney Zion, *The Autobiography of Roy Cohn* [NY: Lyle Stuart, 1988], p. 160.) In state courts and under the federal treason statute, such testimony is not enough to convict a defendant. The *Columbia Law Review* noted that, "had the Rosenbergs been tried across the street, in a New York State Court where corroboration is required, a conviction would have been unlikely on this record." (*CLR*: 234)

where faith in the eventual supremacy of reason has become so timid that we dare not enter our convictions in the open lists to win or lose."

The danger ["to" CO] which Judge Hand eloquently presents, is daily becoming more of a reality in our land and a reading of our trial record will bear out that such an atmosphere permeated our case. Dear person no matter what is said we know we are innocent and our conscience is very clear. We are confident that in time the rest of mankind will be convinced of this truth and we will be exonerated.

The judges [sic] sentencing speech included the following paragraph— "Indeed the defendants Julius and Ethel Rosenberg placed their devotion to their cause above their own personal safety and were conscious that they were sacrificing their own children, should their misdeeds be detected all of which did not deter them from pursuing their cause[.] Love for their cause dominated their lives.—it was even greater than love for their children."

What he said is not based on the record of the trial but is purely a fabrication of his own warped imagination and is an unmitigated lie. This statement is the product of a political hack ["for" CO] who covers his appointment to a party dominated by corrupt political officials associated with gangsters who do the bidding of the "honorable" men of finance capital.[308]

But this made me think of David Greenglass the trapped self confessed spy,[309] who bore false witness against two innocent people and was responsible for his Sister, his own flesh and blood being sentenced to the electric chair. This act alone will have him go down in history as the most infamous informer. However I think the most serious crime he committed was to allow himself to be used as a tool in the interest of the fraternity brothers to serve their evil political purposes. He did [letters "nt" CO] not think of his children. he did not know where his true interest lay. he has bequeathed a great burden to them.

---

[308]Before being appointed to the federal bench, Irving Kaufman had been what is described as a "Tammany Hall Democrat," Tammany Hall being the local Democratic political machine which was periodically rocked by scandal throughout the postwar period and periodically thrown out of office by "reform" democrats beating Tammany candidates at the polls.

[309]Note the wording. It is unclear from this whether he actually believed that David Greenglass was a spy, which was the defense contention at the time of the trial and during the appeal process, or whether he thought the whole case to be a fraud, which was the position taken by pro-Rosenberg partisans from at least as early as 1955 when John Wexley's *The Judgment of Julius and Ethel Rosenberg* was published. For comparison see Malcolm Sharp, *Was Justice Done?* (NY: Monthly Review Press, 1956).

I'll tell you about our relationship with our children. Just one incident
will serve as an illustration. At night before I used to leave my machine
shop I used to call home. My three year old little Robbie would answer the
phone and I heard his happy exclamation. "Is that our Daddy"—"Yes baby" I
replied. ["]Hows [*sic*] my big fellow." and he went on,
#110649

"Bring home Cherry O'nilla ice cream and one [the next word is obviously
an attempt to capture a childish mis-pronunciation but it is hard to decipher.
It appears to be "grind-vine" but that doesn't make any sense] mulk [*sic*]"
Later as I came through the door with my arms laden down with purchases
the boys would give me a boisterous affectionate welcome and Ethel would
peek out from the kitchen smile warmly, beaming with pride on our wonderful family[.] While she prepared the supper I'd quickly change into some
work pants so we could play together on the floor.

My lovely wife and I we shared everything together and gave our all to
help our boys develop as healthy, socially conscious human beings, holding
dear the principles of democracy, liberty and brotherhood. In our behavior, in
our play with them, in the stories we told them and by our understanding
and devotion to them we gave them more than just parental love. Through
them and in them we [next word illegible, appears to be "maintained"] a
love for humanity for its basic goodness and its inherent creative glories.

You can understand how desolate and barren our existence is since we
have been forcibly torn from our boys. We can't hear the sound of our sons.
[previous punctuation mark written over a comma] The shouts, the joy, the
cry of pain when hurt, the quizzical seeking questions, the thin singing
voices, the even breathing when they slept in the stillness of the night all
gave richness and warmth to our home. Our family growing, developing
secure as a harmonious unit cemented with understanding and love. Nothing
is more precious than [words "the bond of" CO] complete acceptance and
devotion between parents and [NWI] their children.

I have to stop now for my heart aches too much for they have been
denied their birth rights. But even this we must bear to help stop similar and
greater tragedies from being visited on other children and innocent parents.
The imperialts [*sic*—probably meant "imperialists"] must be stopped in
their mad plans ["to" CO, N2WI] that will bring terror and destruction to
families.

I have great faith in the democratic instincts of the common people and
I know they will do all in their power to maintain the peace. But not always
are they aware of the facts and especially of the great danger coming from

the warmongers and the hatemongers. But you and I know the score. We must therefore not remain silent, not remain inactive but work with all our might for our children, ourselves and our world. At this point let me quote a passage from Edward Bellamy's book "Looking Backward"[.]

"It means merely that a form of society which [next word written over another] was founded on the pseudo, self-interest of selfishness, and appealed solely to the anti-social and brutal side of human nature, has been replaced by institutions based on the self-interest of a rational [first two letters of next word written over some letters] unselfishness, and appealing to the social and generous interest of men. It finds it's [sic] simple and obvious explanation in the reaction of a changed environment upon human nature."

We have always been socially conscious individuals, progressivly [sic] working in the spirit of such an enlightened philosophy and now we find ourselves in this situation with 38 days more to live.[310]
As ever Julie
I'll continue more next time I want to meet the deadline mail. add [sic] this to the other letters JR

Julius to Ethel

Dec 4, 1952
Hello Sweetheart,
    I want to repeat to you again that because of your encouragement ["and, inspiration" CO] you have [N3WI] been able to inspire me to really stick to the job and I've been working steadily. Your cooperation, corrections and suggestions go a long way is [sic—probably meant "in"] making it possible for me to do this ["job" crossed out, NWI] task. Since I've started this project I find myself busy from morning till night. The days just whiz by and I manage to get in a little reading on the side. The usual newspapers, magazines and my present heavier reading is Chaplin's "Wobbly" an excel-

---

[310]This is the first reference in any letter or any other matter of public record such as the trial transcript where Julius expresses his belief that socialism is a preferred form of social organization to the one in the United States at the time. Considering the general attempt to side-step the issue of being Communists and pro-Soviet while vaguely being "progressive" and supporting peace, this is a pretty bold assertion in a letter that he expected would be read by the general public. Edward Bellamy's socialist utopia in *Looking Backward* was a far cry from Stalin's Soviet Union, even the Soviet Union in the relatively rosy picture that most American Communists persisted in believing in in those years.

lent book.[311] I'm sure that when you feel up to it you'll take pen in hand
and get some really top notch stuff out. It is important to feel that your [*sic*]
part of something and keeping up a steady scheduale [*sic*] keeps me in very
high spirits.

Of course, as our need is increasing our visits seem all too short but
we'll just have to make it due [*sic*] the best as possible. I'm leaving it
entirely up to you to tell Manny about our suggestions for the boys to
spend Christmas week with my mother. Also I'd like you to handle the kind
of gifts we suggest for the children. However, I would like to know if it
would be possible to get some gift similar to the rings we got for our boys.
You understand they have to have more sentimental value than just the
ordinary toy or present. Perhaps a watch or pen and pencil set I don't really
know what will be best. I'm going to drop ["them" CO, N2WI] our dears a
few wods [*sic*] after I finish this letter.

The battle is raging fiercely now and the enemy has called on his
reserves the fabricators [last three letters written over some others, there is a
cross-out under the last three letters as well, NWI] the pen prostitute of the
Post and the more open reactionary writers. They are going to be nailed to
every lie they spew forth and I'm positive our committee is having excellent
results because all of the gutter press claims we've "fooled" great numbers
of people. The material the opposition puts ["it" CO] out can't hold a candle
to any of the stuff the committee prints and although they own & control
the "free" press we're reaching the public with our side. It is going to get a
great deal rougher for we've got them fuming mad because they can't use us
to do their dirty work. I will not spend any more time on these degenerate
sadists.

You know honey I didn't find the opportunity to do any verbal smooching with you and I want you to remember that no matter what I am doing or
how difficult the situation may be I think of you my darling and I get a
warm good feeling. Everything else shrinks in importance when considered
besides our relationship, the high calibre of human stature you exemplify
and your excellent understanding. It has been wonderful ["till m" CO] to
have spent these thirteen years together and the future can only bring [NWI]
greater promise ["to" CO, NWI] for us. With all the power ["that I posses

---

[311]The "Wobblies" were the Industrial Workers of the World, a radical anarcho-
syndicalist industrial union in the early twentieth century. Though Communists
felt they were politically incorrect, they admired their anti-capitalism, their
courage, and their support for industrial as opposed to craft unionism. Ralph
Chaplin was an IWW organizer who wrote the union's theme song "Paint 'Er
Red." For a history of the IWW see Melvyn Dubofsky, *We Shall Be All* (New
York: Quadrangle Books, 1969).

[*sic*] CO, N3WI] of my feelings and every fibre of my body I love you. We are approaching a crucial period and I'm sure we'll do alrigit [*sic*] —Always your devoted husband—Julie

Master Michael Rosenberg
c/o B. Bach
R.D. 2 Box 148M
Toms River N.J.

December 4, 1952

Dear Mike & Robbie,

We have been kept very busy. I am spending almost all of my time writing to our lawyer Manny. Many things are happening in court that need our cooperation but also more important than that is the growing fight by the people to [N2WI] help us win this case. Since we are a vital part of this struggle I've been concentrating on giving a running account of our views on the trial, the issues in our case and any ideas I think might be of interest to readers who want to know more about us. When our counselor is able to extricate himself from the legal jungle I'm sure he'll read some of these letters to you. Therefore don't worry because you don't hear from me directly for we are in the thick of a terrific battle. This much I can say we are very confident, we are pleased with the kind of campaign the committee is waging and [word "in" CO] the support we are getting seems like it will be successful in eventually setting us free.

As for us we're both healthy and well and just raring to get home and be with you fellows. No just because we haven't written is no excuse for not letting us know how you are doing. It is the little details that we are most interested in. The books you read Mike[.] The toys you play with Robbie. Your friends. How do you spend a typical day? What goes on at school? Tell us news about Sonia, Ben ["and" CO] Maxin [*sic*] and Leo. Anything you do or say is precious to us. We treasure every word you write. Please boys continue to keep in touch with us regularly. We'll make up for it sweethearts. Even though we haven't been writing we've been talking about you, making plans & discussing various items with our lawyer and with our family—concerning you boys. Also Mama and I now see each other twice a week on Tuesdays and Fridays and we're able to accomplish more this way and many is the time we exchange stories of our pleasant experiences with you our sons. I'd like to know if you've improved your chess game Michael because in here I'm champion. It is a little more difficult for us to play the game than usual. Each player has a complete set in front of him as a numbered board and he shouts his moves from one numbered square to another to his opponent in an another [*sic*] cell. Don't worry son you and I are going to play some good games.

It is true I've been hearing good reports about you but we like to hear directly from you. I don't know what your plans are for the Christmas week but I think it would be a splendid idea if you spent part of your vacation in Grandma Sophie's house. Then you could visit us during the holiday week and also spend time visiting places and relations in the city. What do you think about this?

You know kids when your [*sic*] in a situation [N2WI] like us and you are positive that your [*sic*] right then [word "it" CO] you are able to fight all the harder for [word "it" CO, N2WI] your cause and no matter how difficult it looks you are sure it will come out alright—All my love & kisses
Daddy Julie
P.S. Send my affectionate regards to Ben, Sonia, Maxin [*sic*] and Leo. and our fraternal greetings to our many friends. Kisses xxxxxxxxxx

Julius to Ethel

Dec. 7, 1952

My Darling Wife,

Before anything else I wish to tell you I'm terribly sorry for monopolizing our last two visits for it was very selfish of me. Therefore I resolve never to do it again. As a start I mailed out six pages more to our lawyer and I'm going to send him a few more letters tonight. Hereafter we'll only discuss mattes [*sic*] we need to and let each of us [N2WI] (meaning me) do the best ["we" CO, "his" inserted and CO, NWI] we can by ourselves except where it is really ["really" CO, NWI] very important that we confer ["about it" CO, NWI] together. Your suggestion for a lawyer consultation for this Wednesday is a good one. This time we must go over very carefully and in detail all the legal moves. Also we'll have to plan for a Christmas visit with the boys ["in" CO] two weeks ["after" CO] hence.

I am amazed at the fabulous newspaper campaign organized against us. It is obviously well planned and has the earmarks of desperation. To make this flimsy tale and brutal sentence palpable to the American people ["they" CO, N2WI] the enemy [next word written over "are"] is forced to resort to wholesale lies, (easily proven from the minutes of the trial record), fantastic incidents that never occurred, [letter CO] all of which are heavily dosed with the usual anti-communist propaganda and above all their need to have so-called liberals carry the ball and do the hatchet job on us. Truth is, the public is learning the facts and is questioning the entire case and the implications it has for all Americans. The opposition doesn't give up easily it is afraid the frameup is beginning to show and the true nature of the case is beginning to shock the sensitivities of all mankind.

The situation is fraught with great danger to all and more [N2WI] directly & immediately to us. However, I am sure we will never lend ourselves to be tools to implicate innocent people, to confess crimes we never did and to help fan the flames of hysteria and ["support" CO, NWI] help the ["gro" CO, NWI] growing witch hunt. The complete degeneracy of those who fight us is revealed by the low slimy ["misuses of our"] use they are trying to make [N2WI] of terrible [insertion continues with what appears to be three illegible words crossed out, under the last word, squeezed above the continuing text is an illegible word that could be "has," then the insertion ends with a word that appears to be "about" or "above," the word after the insertion mark (back in the main text) was probably "of" from context but it is obscured by both the insertion mark and the writing above it] our children and family.[312]

---

[312]The fifth article of the Pilat series (*New York Post,* Dec. 5, 1952), entitled "The Ones They Leave Behind," allegedly concerns the case's "impact on relatives . . ." of our parents. Most of it is full of praise for Tessie Greenglass, whose behavior is well documented in *Sons,* pp. 19–25 but ignored by Pilat. Then, he turns to Robby and me. "Letters from the parents to the boys and from the boys to their parents have been published by the Rosenberg defense committee as part of the propaganda for the convicted spies. Most of the weight of the case has fallen on Michael's frail shoulders. He has been dragged to rallies where emotionalism could be cut with a knife. He has been asked to write, or sign pathetic letters to papers. One appeal from him, entitled 'Dear God and Good People' was circularized widely in New York City. Among other things it asserted that 'Uncle David told lies to the Judge and Jury'." As Robby and I have asserted many times, this gives an entirely false impression. We were almost totally sheltered from the campaign to save our parents. We had gone to one rally (the June, 1952 rally) up to that point, and it had been I who insisted on going up on stage, against Ben and Sonia Bach's wishes. I remember writing only one letter, either to the Committee or the *National Guardian,* the only words of which I remember were "Don't let my parents die." It is possible that the letter Pilat refers to was circulated as if from me but in fact was not. The article then concludes that speakers at rallies had ridiculed "relatives on both sides of the family for refusing to help because of a supposed fear of public criticism. So far as Mrs. Sophie Rosenberg and Mrs. Tessie Greenglass are concerned, and probably other relatives, these charges are unjust and unfair. Certainly the grandmothers proved their willingness to endanger their own lives in an attempt, which could not succeed, to raise the boys." I don't know what Pilat was referring to. Certainly from the letters one can see that our father's two sisters and brother had been extremely supportive and helpful. It is true that certain members of the committee have told us that they were displeased that neither of the aunts nor our uncle offered to take Robby and me into their homes, but it is unlikely that such feelings would have been publicly expressed about the very family members whose support meant everything to our parents. Most likely, Pilat is referring to the unwillingness up to that point of Bernard Greenglass to

How wrong and hateful can they be? The antics of those who pay lip service to liberalism and democracy shows that ["they" probably omitted here] have climbed on the bandwagon, [N2WI] in order to gain immunity from attacks by [NWI] the Winchells and ["the" inserted here, then CO] McCarthys. I am sure these people will be adequately exposed.

I do not know how much longer we'll have an opportunity to continue to write but I feel it imperative that at this point we must put as much as we can on paper even though it ["we" written over "is" here, NWI] do not do a [NWI] completely polished job.

Please have an outline prepared for our next session as I want us to cover a great deal of ground. Also prepare a separate ["f" CO] one for the consultation with Manny and I'll do the same.

Sweetheart, I miss you terribly and I must keep on driving myself in order to withstand the loneliness and great hunger for you. Somewhere somehow all those who had a hand in this horrible plot will have to answer for their misdeeds. In the meantime I know that they are having a difficult time with their conscience.

I continue to hold you in my arms and share with you our consumming [*sic*] love. The feeling I have for you and the children are [*sic*] very deep and all encompassing. All my thoughts are of you and the boys. Always devoted to you my charming Ethel—Your guy—Julie

Mr. Emanuel H. Bloch
7 W. 16th Street
New York N.Y.

Dec. 7, 1952

Dear Manny,

First I want to apologize for my poor penmanship and for the haphazard writing I've been doing. Please understand my shortcomings. Also, since I feel pressed for time, I'm ["going" CO, N2WI] putting down my ideas as quickly as I get them. I agree with Ethel that Wednesday is a good day for our consultation, since we visit with each other on Tuesday and Friday. Let me add that Mr. Kelley, the acting warden, has been very nice in granting us

---

help and is attempting to obscure the fact that the Rosenberg relatives were completely supportive of their brother's claim of innocence. The attitude of the older Greenglass brother, Sam, is obvious from the letter he wrote our mother in 1950 (see above, p. 25, footnote 27). The article closes with "The convicted spies insist upon more than personal support: they want full political support. That some of the family members will not give." All the letters between our parents about their relatives as well as to their relatives prove what a bald-faced lie these sentences are.

addition [*sic*] time to confer together. Please, when you do come, I hope you are prepared to give us enough time to cover all the legal moves and other questions we might raise. Then, [NWI] too, we expect to see the children [N2WI] sometime during the week of Christmas.

I ["t" CO at end of last word] must admit that although ["I am" CO, N2WI] I am a sophisticated person I am, nevertheless, amazed at the fabulous propaganda campaign being waged against us. However, it has all the earmarks of desperation. The phenomena is even more [letter crossed out above the previous word] startling [N2WI] to them because their stock-in-trade anti-communist hysteria isn't able to make, this flimsy "spy" tale and brutal sentence, palpable to the American people. Therefore, they brazenly resort to wholesale lies, that are easily proven false to any one who reads the trial record. Fantastic incidents, that even the prosecutor never dared ["to charge" CO] raise at the trial, are dramatically portrayed to bolster this empty case. But this is not enough for these beasts, they [N2WI] have to bring the family and our little children in and pour slime and filth, to smear and tear us down in the public eye. Another very peculiar thing about this "holy crusade" to get the Rosenbergs is that the front men selected to do the hatchet job are the so called respectable liberals. They do this because they hope to gain immunity from [N3WI] the red baiting attacks ["by" CO, NWI] of the Winchells and the McCarthys.

How wrong and how low can these people be? These misleaders, under their "democratic" "liberal" mask are helping to lower the morality, brutalize the sensitivity of the public [N5WI] and are confusing the issues which [next word written over another] tends [NWI] to disarm ["ing" CO at end of last word] the fight against growing fascism [*sic*] and war. On the other hand their violent fulminations ["have been unsuccessful" CO, although the last seven letters of the last words didn't get physically crossed out] proves that they have been unsuccessful in their attempt to hide [N3WI] from the people the nature of this case and the political plot against ["the" CO] liberty and peace. The truth, the facts of the case, and it's [*sic*] implications, must be brought to world attention and these madmen must be exposed.

You know dear friend we have only 37 more days left to live and on this infamous day of Dec. 7 we call out a [NWI] warning to all our brothers and sisters that a new diabolical plan of aggression against mankind is threatening. We are just plain ordinary people like you and because the future belongs to your children and our children, we plain folks have a great job to do.

We find our senses keener and we are able to examin [*sic*—"ourselves" CO, N2WI] our values and ourselves and determine our true worth. Our conscience is clear because we have led useful lives. We have been true to our vows to each other, to our responsibility to our children and to our single-

heartedness of purpose to work to make this a better world to live in and
that can only be when there is peace. It is [a stain obscures some of the
letters in the next word but it is clear from context] important to learn as
much as possible and to know oneself well, to constantly strive to develope
[*sic*] one's potentialities and increase one's abilities by participating in life's
endeavors, socially, culturally and politically & to have the courage of
["your" CO] one's convictions. (top) [letter continued on top of second side]
Life is as fruitful as [NWI] the efforts [N2WI] we make in attaining worthwhile goals.
As ever Julie # 110649

Mr. Emanuel H. Bloch
7 W. 16th Street
New York NY

Dec. 8, 1952
PAGE # 1

Dear Manny,
    I just want to take passing notice of the latest betrayal by the right
wing Social-Democratic misleaders[313] who control the executive board of
the A.C.L.U. As has often happened in the past the so-called liberals are
trying to have ["this" CO] organizations [N4WI] such as this one] take a
middle-of-the-road position. ["by" CO, NWI] But the rapid deterioration of
civil liberties as the political climate changes, disturbs their equilibrium and
they find themselves going along with the tide all the time conceding bit by

---

[313]The term Social-Democratic is very revealing. Communists considered the
European Social-Democratic Parties as betrayers of the ideals of socialism at
least since most members of the Second International supported their national
governments in World War I. In the United States, for the most part, the
Socialist Party opposed participation in World War I, but that did not prevent a
split after the Russian Revolution from which emerged the Communist Party of
the U.S.A. (See *Encyclopedia of the American Left*, pp. 719–20, 147–48.)
Communists who lived through the internecine struggles of the left in the 1930s
adopted at times the attitudes of the German Communists who contemptuously
called their Social Democratic rivals "social fascists" and whose slogan was
"After Hitler, us!" This view that those ideologically close to one's position are
in some sense more dangerous enemies than those far away from one's position
seems to exist in many political movements, and certainly our parents had this
view. However, in fairness, we ought to note that they had good cause for feeling
this way, especially given the extreme attacks they had been subjected to by the
liberal *New York Post*.

bit until they have abandoned principles entirely.[314] Is the undemocratic, repugnant doctrine of 'guilt by association' now to be the law of the land and be allowed to be applied to cases where political topics are involved, though not part of the crime charged? Since when are permissible expressions of belief such as ["expressed" CO, NWI] statements made in private conversations showing a preference for forms of government and economic organization of society[315] admissible as material evidence in

---

[314]Refers to a decision by the American Civil Liberties Union "that the question of commutation of the death sentence of Julius and Ethel Rosenberg, convicted for atomic espionage, raised no civil liberties issue." (*New York Post*, December 8, 1952). What our father didn't know is that ACLU co-counsel Morris Ernst had expressed interest to the FBI in involving himself with the defense in order to help the government induce our parents to confess. The Morris Ernst incident is a most intriguing and revealing one. Ernst was a general counsel and Board Member of the American Civil Liberties Union which had since 1948 refused to defend Communists, even when their civil liberties were being violated. According to FBI records, Ernst had offered his services to the FBI to help them get information out of Harry Gold, when Gold was first arrested. (Nichols to Tolson, June 1, 1950 HG HQ 215. Nichols to Tolson, December 20, 1952. JR HQ 1390. Nichols to Tolson January 9, 1953. JR HQ 1438. [I am indebted to J. Kevin O'Brien, Chief of the FOIA-PA Section of the FBI for responding to queries about these documents by mail.]) Ernst told the FBI that our aunt Ethel and uncle David had come to see him in December, 1952 to try and get him involved in the clemency fight. He told the FBI he would get involved to try and secure a confession only if the FBI thought it would be a good idea. One interesting note about the last meeting was that Ernst volunteered that he had conducted a "psychological study of the Rosenbergs" (note, without having ever met them) and believed that "Julius is a slave and his wife, Ethel, the master." This ridiculous statement ended up justifying in the minds of many officials the execution of our mother. On June 16, 1953, President Eisenhower wrote to his son John, ". . . I must say that it goes against the grain to avoid interfering in the case where a woman is to receive capital punishment. . . . [H]owever . . . in this case it is the woman who is the strong and recalcitrant character, the man is the weak one. She has obviously been the leader in everything they did in the spy ring." Dwight D. Eisenhower, *The White House Years: Mandate for Change, 1953–1956* (NY: Doubleday, 1963), p. 225. Quoted in Schneir and Schneir, p. 242. For more details on the anti-communism of the ACLU see Mary Sperling McAuliffe, *Crisis on the Left: Cold War Politics and American Liberals, 1947-1954* (Amherst, MA.: University of Massachusetts Press, 1978) and Frank Donner, *The Age of Surveillance* (NY: Alfred Knopf, 1980).

[315]Refers to David Greenglass' trial testimony that our parents had preferred "Russian Socialism" to the American form of government (Record, p. 420; see also pp. 414–21 for the legal arguments as to whether such questioning was relevant or not). On cross-examination our father had circumspectly denied he made any such "direct statement" (Record, p. 1079: "The Court: Did you approve the communistic system of Russia over the capitalistic system in this country? The Witness: I am not an expert on those things, your Honor, and I did not make

criminal prosecutions for high crimes? Isn't this a violations [*sic*] of the "Bill of Rights" of freedom of expression? Since when is a sentence constitutional because it is used as a coercive force against political nonconformists? ["It" CO] Is the new criterion of Anglo-Saxon jurisprudence to be based on the reprehensible code of the stool pigeon, the debased venality of the informer where the accused must confess when ["there is" CO, N2WI] he has nothing to confess? Are the rights, liberties and lives of innocent men and women to be forfeited because the cry is communism? These hated, evil forms of abuse went out with the Stuarts and were always revived as soon as new tyrannical regimes took over the reigns [*sic*] of power. Millions of lives were sacrificed, oceans of blood were spilt in destroying the fascist beasts and eliminating these repressive practices. I am confident that humanity is opposed to these doctrines and will therefore, not allow a decision such as made in our case to stand.

It just so happens that I am in the midst of a book called Wobbly and the author, Ralph Chaplin through his story of an "American Radical" gives the reader a birds [*sic*] eye view of the growth of the labor movement [NWI] and political groups and shows the development of the struggle for economic justice, labor rights and civil liberties. Each period is high lighted [*sic*] by a "cause celebre"[.] Eugene V. Debs was one of them who died not long after release from federal penitentiary. Joe Hill is remembered for his workers songs, urging them to organize. He was framed on a trumped up murder charge and faced a Utah firing squad.[316] The great campaign waged for Sacco and Vanzetti the shoemaker and the fish peddler, innocent men put to death because they were anarchist in times of great labor unrest. The Tom Mooney Scoutsboro [*sic*—correct spelling is Scottsboro] Boys Cases went on for years until final vindication [N2WI] was won for these men.[317] The

---

any such direct statement. Q. Did you make any comparisons in the sense that the Court has asked you, about whether you preferred one system over another? A. No, I did not. I would like to state that my personal opinions are that the people of every country should decide by themselves what kind of government they want. If the English want a King, it is their business. If the Russians want communism, it is their business. If the Americans want our form of government, it is our business . . .") but in this letter he is at least tacitly admitting that the private conversations reported by the Greenglasses did include such political and economic preferences.

[316]For information on Eugene V. Debs, see *Encyclopedia of the American Left*, pp. 184–87, for Joe Hill, *ibid.*, pp. 310–12, for Ralph Chaplin, see p. 127.

[317]On Scottsboro, see *Encyclopedia*, pp. 684–86. See also Dan T. Carter, *Scottsboro: A Tragedy of the American South*. 2d ed. (Baton Rouge: Louisiana State University Press, 1984) and Haywood Patterson and Earl Conrad, *Scottsboro Boy* (NY: Doubleday,1950). On the Tom Mooney Case, see

lessons of history are very clear certain powerful entrenched intrests [*sic*] needed scapegoats to use as ["threats" CO] a weapon against those who threatened their positions of power and economic wealth in any way. These movements also started [words "from scratch" CO] from the grass roots with few supporters and all the power of the newspapers, state, business and so called respectable organizations [NWI] were against them. But the ["y" crossed out at end of last word, NWI] people [CO word inserted here] were not dismayed for their cause was just. Where they were able to rally the public and develope [*sic*] a widespread mass campaign they met with success. We have high hopes on this 35th day we have left to ["life" CO] live that in our case we will get the support of large enough numbers of people to save our lives and help us win complete vindication. #110649

Dec. 9, 1952
PAGE #2

During my high school and college days I participated with thousands of other students in these great fights for justice, liberty and equal rights. I believed in exercising my prerogatives as a conscious social being and so by participating in helping a good cause I too benefited from it. I was an active member of the Engineers unions [*sic*] for more than eight years until I became an employer and had to turn in my membership card. But I never forgot my trade union principles and I always treasured the work [N2WI] I did and [NWI] the experience I got [NWI] while [CO word squeezed between "got" and the next word] putting into practice some of my convictions ["such as" inserted, then CO, word "for" CO] helping [last three letters added to word] myself by helping to better the lot of my fellowmen [*sic*].

Getting back to the present. Every Monday night I have the pleasure of listening to $1^1/_2$ hours of pleasant music. Outside of the cells on the opposite side of the gallery are a couple of [NWI in the left margin] loud speakers wired to a central receiving set. The reception and fidelity isn't the best but what's a little inconvenience to men in the condemned block. After the officer adjusts the volume to suit the tastes of the inmates I relax on my bed and imagine myself home surrounded by my family and listening to the radio. I ["like" CO, NWI] prefer folk music, spirituals, labor songs and songs of struggle.

Each man here is given two fifteen [*sic*—word "minute" probably omitted] yard exercise periods daily. The yard is ["located" CO] bounded on one side by the gallery of cells on in [*sic*] the other side by the death

---

Encyclopedia, pp. 485–86 and Richard H. Frost, *The Mooney Case* (Stanford: Stanford University Press, 1968).

chamber and in all is [NWI] about 150 feet in circumference. When the weather was good I played handball [next word appears to be "occassional"] however now that winter is here once in a while I play bachi-ball [*sic*] but in the main I have an opportunity to walk around the yard and sing the songs I like. I am not sure but I believe that I am one of the first to fill the air in the confines of this space with favorites such as "Peat Bog Soldiers", "Joe Hill" and "Freiheit." While I sing it brings back memories, inspires me and make [*sic*] me think of all the other innocent political prisoners who experienced this type of hospitality from their Uncle Sam. In the solitude of the yard at that moment I realized humanity is imprisoned that equality before the laws of the land is an empty phrase that for political dissidents the Bill of Rights is a mere paper document. But this does not change the justness of our cause nor discourage us in anyway. To hoodwink the people it is only necessary for those who run the government to charge spy, treason[,] murder, [NWI] perjury etc. and use inflammatory issues to blind the jury and thus insure a guilty verdict. One thing is certain that our way of life, the principles we cherish and the philosophy we live by is diametrically opposite to [N7WI] that which could possibly make for the commission of any crimes especially spying. The history of the case, the trial record and the facts of life cry out against this terrible miscarriage of justice. Though the opposition is powerful, the truth will out and the overwhelming force of the people can and I am confident will save the lives of innocent Americans.

You'll have to excuse me I'm getting a little lethargic. I suppose I'll just take it easy for the [word CO, NWI] rest of the day and curl up with a book. Today I had the usual excellent visit with my adorable wife and although we have only 34 more days left to live we are planning and working right along with a tremendous will to keep right on living. The answer to this terrible problem rests with the people. We have faith in them. We know they are trying and we hope they are successful.— As ever— Julie.

Mr. Emanuel H. Bloch
7 W 16th Street
New York NY

Dec. 11th 1952
Page #1 of 4

Dear Manny,

Wednesday Dec. 10th I was just taking it easy and lolling around. Read through a Colliers and Life magazine and after lunch heard the news that Judge Ryan has denied us a hearing to present our witnesses and summarily dismissed our petition.[318] Now it is important for the reader to know that all the legal steps we have taken are those that are available to any petitioner in a court action. Nowhere along the line where it was a matter of judicial discretion did we receive a favorable ruling.

The sentence, which is in the judges [*sic*] hands, was the most extreme that could be ["had" CO, NWI] given under the statue [*sic*] and was the first such sentence in the history of American justice. The Circuit Court of Appeals refused to grant a rehearing. The Supreme Court didn't even issue a writ of certiorari to hear the many legal questions raised in our case. Now, too, we are denied a hearing. <u>Always such haste.</u> [underlining in original] The miscreants and blackguards [N5WI] who are responsible for this want to do away with the "hot potato" they have created before they have to face the full fury of the ensuing storm. Again the task falls to the "free" press to confuse the issue and distort the truth. ["But" CO] By these actions they show that the cards are stacked and they are moving heaven and earth to obscure the truth from the people. A holy crusade is on. [N3WI] The cry is get the "Rosenbergs". Anything counts, all who wish to cleanse themselves of past sins (anything remotely progressive, that is labelled pro communist) can do so by joining the pack and throwing filthy lies, [NWI] tales made of whole cloth as long as it fits in with the political propaganda of those in power.

The truth which cannot be created or destroyed is perverted by these demagogues to suit their interests. Since they control the means of communication, the press, radio, money and government they feel secure that the terrible misdeeds will not be exposed. But ["with justice on" CO] our cause is just and no matter how ["what the pro" CO] great ["is" CO] the opposition is we will nail them to their lies. All movements for decency and right start with a few, especially when it is against the tide. It requires hard work sacrifice and devotion to rigtheous [*sic*] principles to rally man-

---

[318]This was the first of two motions filed under Sec. 2255 of the Federal Criminal Code which permits a convicted defendant to have a new trial if they can introduce new evidence that indicates a substantial violation of due process at the original trial. The grounds for this motion were pretrial publicity, the timing of the unsealing of the indictment of William Perl in the middle of the trial (See Record, pp. 756–57; *New York Times,* March 15, 1951, p. 1), and perjury on the part of the photographer who testified that our parents had taken passport photos in May of 1950 at his studio contradicting their testimony on the witness stand. (See the papers filed Nov. 24, 1952 and transcripts of the oral arguments before Judge Ryan, Dec. 2 and 5, 1952, all in the Federal Records Center in Bayonne, NJ [Cr. 134–245]. See also Schneir, pp. 180–83; *Sons,* pp. 423–25.)

kind behind this noble cause. We can and we must do all in our power to ["prevent" CO] rectify this miscarriage of justice.

We received an excellent letter from the children. The joy of reading Michael's own handwriting and [two words CO, only the first one "the" is legible, N2WI] hearing about his accomplishments in his own youthful account of the activities he is participating in brought his precious presence so close to us. I am very happy they are both progressing beautifully at school, at shule,[319] at play and most of all that they are surrounded by the great love and deep affection of Ben and Sonia. It does us great honor to see such devotion and care visited upon our children. These people have indeed contributed a great share to our peace of mind and relieved us of a great deal of anxiety. To them and the rest of our dear friends we pledge to work to justify their confidence and trust in us. Such selfless dedication symbolizes in [illegible mark here] a very practical way the brotherhood of man.

The sincerity and meaningfulness of this letter washed away all the hate and falsehoods of the "free" press[.]   #110649

Page # 2 of 4   Dec. 12

It inspired me and with this stimulus I sent out a batch of Chanukah cards the Jewish Chaplain gave me. To our sweet children I composed a few verses. I must confess it is my first attempt and I hope the sentiment is properly expressed. This I want to say to the great number of people who have come to our support.

I am just a plain ordinary guy and I don't profess to be anything extraordinary or special. I feel my greatest accomplishment, is being a successful father to my two boys. I know with them I've made a success. It is because of them, and, of course, all children, that my first duty in life is to work for their future.

All my activities are concentrated on these endeavors. One thing is certain I worked very hard in this direction. Although I was none too successful as a small businessman I continued to integrate my social activities working for peace, for liberty and ["holding dear" CO] in the best tradition of American democracy. If I can help advance the fight for these noble causes I have fulfilled my mission in their behalf and my conscience is clear that I have functioned best in my own interest. Then, too, together with my wife we have built a fine relationship that has enabled us to drink deep of the

---

[319]We went to a Jewish cultural school in New Jersey, learning the Hebrew-Yiddish alphabet, songs in Yiddish and getting our first instruction in Jewish history and culture. These "shules" had a secular emphasis with no prayers involved. See *Sons,* p. 144.

fruits of life as we contribute our share ["to" CO] as progressive parents to a better world.

Therefore on the occassion [*sic*] of this Chanukah-Christmas holiday season. We join ["t" CO at end of previous word] with our fellowmen in striving for peace on earth and brotherhood among men.

We are confident this is the hope and wish of the entire world and we have faith that mankind will also be able to see the road that must be followed to make this a reality. So, too, we believe that the good people everywhere will not let two innocent people go to their death.

Let each of us implement the fine sentiments of this holiday season by practicing in our daily lives the principles ["of" CO, N5WI] of democracy & fighting for justice, liberty and ["peace working for" CO, "by" inserted above "peace" and then CO] peace. A good effort for a just cause is ["a very satisfactory" CO] spiritually and morally the greatest self achievement of the human being.

It is indeed our pleasure to extend to all peace-loving and freedom-loving decent men and women everywhere our Chanukah ["and" CO] Christmas and New Years [*sic*] best wishes.

Incidentally we hope to be around to see the future and take our rightful place ["alongside" CO, NWI] with the rest of humanity doing our part [N4WI] toward the common goal. The people will guarantee that we [ending "'re" and the word "not" CO, NWI] will live and that we will be able to prove our complete innocence.

In the normal course of events with regard to the relationship of children to their parents [N3WI] & in the many experiences over a period of time there is set up the patterns that establishs [*sic*] the diurnal rapport of family life. On this bedrock depends the stability, character and security of the future adults of our world. ["H-" CO] The point I wish to make is that children have a very keen sense and intuitively are aware of changes such as, difficulties faced by the family and   #110649

Page # 3 of 4   Dec 13

the attitudes of the grownups in the group. The remarkable fact is that they are able to know truth more accurately and quickly because they are not encumbered by extraneous emotions and prejudices. This is true in the main and in our [NWI] own case the reactions of Michael and Robbie, vis a vis we their parents, shows they ["are" CO] too are aware of the basic truths that we are completely innocent. Naturally, we don't burden them by discussing the issues of the case but they in turn freely ask very searching questions and at all times they receive direct and truthful answers. This has been the way we brought them up and ["only" CO] in this manner ["do" CO] we intend to help them develope [*sic*] and grow. The ["very good" CO] present state of their good health, physically, mentally and emotionally is a tribute [N3WI] to us, for ["to" CO] the foundation that we [three letters CO, looks like a miswritten "hav"] helped establish and is also do [*sic*] ["the" CO] to the splendid job the Bachs are doing in their own right in following in the main our ideas on how our boys should be raised. This in no way detracts from the wonderful help and care our children have gotten from strangers but it still remain [*sic*] our prerogative as parents to direct the handling of our sons. Because our dear friends have encouraged us in this way we have been able to contribute a maximum to the important fight to win our case ["in" CO, N2WI] by conducting a principled ["basis" CO] defense. It is a glorious feeling that we [NWI] get as parents because we see ["the essential" CO] brotherhood among people in action, when strangers care for our children, surround them with love and understanding and secure them with all the warmth that is good and decent. In the short time of our visits with the boys we can observe the fact that ["th" CO] our children feel their own worth as individuals that are accepted for what they are.

I don't know if I've mentioned it before ["but" CO] as to how we get books from the library. Every Monday morning the books we received the week before are collected and new ones are sent in. They come from ["the" CO] both the prison and ["cha" CO] rabbi's ["office" CO] library and if there are any books ["you" CO , NWI] one like [*sic*—"you" CO , NWI] he read them. This week I began to read, "A Reader ["of" CO] in General Anthropology" by Coon. The progress I am making is slow. This work is a sort of a textbook on this subject and besides having an academic interest in increasing my general knowledge perhaps I'll be able to find some of the answers that are still puzzling me about the vermin that bore false witness against us. So far, I find that the primates and primitive men are too humane to display ["see" CO] any traces of similar degradation. As yet I haven't made up my mind which direction to go but it seems to point to the growth of civilization for only in this misuse of the blessings of modern men can one see similar diabolical occurrences.

You know friend there is so much to learn, know and do and so very little time left. We have about 30 more days left to ["life" CO] live but we'll continue to function fully as long as there is a breath of life left in us. We also believe that the people will have the final say and we are confident they will not let this happen here.					#110649

Page # 4					Dec. 14

Manny there are a number of personal items I'd like to request from you. If there are sufficient copies available and it isn't to [*sic*] much trouble to get them to me I'd like to receive a copy of ["your" CO, NWI] our complete petition and Ryan's ["denial" CO] decision denying our motions. Also if and when available our briefs to the Circuit Court of Appeals. I'm running low on commissary and if you come this week it will be time enough then for you to leave me ["a check" CO , N2WI] some money. When you do finally [NWI] make arrangements [last syllable of previous word written under the next word, which is "time" CO] for our consultation I hope you set aside enough time so that we can adequately exhaust the question we have in mind. We have to do this, in spite of the fact that you are terribly pressed for time on the legal moves in our behalf. I know you're doing your best and I'm sure you plan to see us this week. Again, let me reassure you of our complete confidence in you and of our devotion to you[.] Our mutual understanding and close relationship has made it possible to do the good job we are doing despite the terrific odds. We need [NWI] you good friend so take care of yourself.

You know reader this is a pretty rough place to be in and you can't imagine what a wonderful feeling I get when I receive the latest issue of the National Guardian. It brings with it ["the" CO] all the news of the fight for peace and also a fresh, sincere and honest account of the happenings in our case. The sign of our times is that this is one of the few remaining voices of progressive Americans that dares to challenge the evil deeds of those in power. This paper works for the interests of the people and is keeping the torch of liberty burning brightly and it's [sic] clarion call has already resulted in the great campaign that is being waged for justice in our case. They have a proud and noteworthy record to date and have made a distinguished mark for themselves as a leading crusading journal in cold war America. The high ethical and moral standards they follow and the integrity they posses [sic], are a tribute to the heroic men and women who put this paper out. All power to them for the wonderful job they are doing.

The days are lonely and the dark long nights are empty without my wife. There is no rest and no peace of mind because I know how great her suffering is. Over and over again I drive myself to work hard to drown out the agony that grips me but there is no real relief. My Ethel is always in my mind and my heart. The only satisfaction I get is to try to emulate the example she sets. Believe me, she is a swell, sweet, person. She has an excellent character and very good qualities and her conduct under these very difficult circumstances is very admirable. I adore her because she is a noble woman, a good mother and a remarkable human being. I cannot ask for anymore than that and because of the treasure I possess in her and our children I must do my best for them. We have so much to live for and ["it"

CO, NWI] life will have greater meaning [N2WI] to us when we win this principled fight.

So long for now. I'll write again soon

As ever — Julie
#110649

Julius to Ethel

Dec. 12, 1952

Dearest Ethel,

I was deeply touched by our childrens [*sic*] letter and I am very pleased with the progress they are making. One swell and decent letter like that washes away all the mountains of filth that are being printed these days. It is indeed a tragedy how the lords of the press can mold public opinion by printing over and over again fancy stories based on blatant falsehoods. The pressure campaign is on & in very high gear and many weak people will be scared off and others will be forced to change their positions. However by these actions the oligarchs of hate show that they are very uneasy ["lest" CO, NWI] about this foul frameup backfiring on them. There is a new whipping boy in our land "the Rosenbergs" and all "respectable" people ["will" CO, N2WI] have to cleanse themselves by throwing stories at us. They are doomed to failure for the truth will out.

The situation will get rougher but I'm positive we'll be able to standup [*sic*] under it. You know we were so correct in our analysis of the governments [*sic*] purpose in our case. Even before our trial they made communism the issue and had it permeate the entire proceedings in court. But Pilat slipped, he said they only did it to dramatize the case. Now all stops are out every technique of smear is used to obscure the basic infirmities of the governments [*sic*] case ["and" CO] the unfair trial and the breaching of our constitutional rights. They have told the public the issues as they see it, Confess [*sic*] and help us fight the Communists. Of course all they do is say we are overwhelmingly guilty of espionage but they never meet our arguments & proof, all they do is yell communist. The cards are stacked but only the massed determination of the people can upset this miscarriage of justice. Because we have fought for the truth and in the interest of decency we have already won a major fight. I am still confident we'll win our freedom. But come what may I am sure that our names will eventually be cleared.

Sweetheart I'm taking it easy these last two days outside of a few Chanukah cards I haven't done any writing. As expected Judge Ryan followed true to present day American dispensation of justice, politics must reign supreme.

On the occassion [*sic*] of this Chanukah, when the festival of lights holiday is celebrated by our people as a victory of righteousness, freedom and justice, let us take new heart as did millions before us and rededicate ourselves in light of this nobel [*sic*] heritage. For what really lives and is held dearly by all mankind is contributions by men and women like the Macabees[320] ["that help liberty" CO, illegible word inserted after "help," then CO , NWI] who fight for and help establish liberty and peace. Also sweet woman and wonderful wife of mine accept all the love that I have for you. ["with" CO] With every fibre of my being I'll continue to express the beauty of our relationship and the purposefullness [*sic*] of our lives. I adore you my charming woman—
As ever— Julie

Julius to Ethel

Dec. 14, 1952

Dearest Ethel,

After I saw you this last time I went to work over the weekend and hammered out 4 more additional letters to our lawyer. It is true I'm laboring over them but at the same time there are a number of thoughts I have on the matter that are about to jell. The only thing that is holding me back is that I don't feel adequate to do a thorough enough job. I'll talk to you about it at our next visit and perhaps you'll be able to advise me on the best proceedure [*sic*] to follow.

Ethel and I had a very pleasant visit this Saturday and I'm happy to see that ["they are" CO] the family ["are" CO, NWI] is in there pitching all the time. The fact that they are confident is a very good sign and we can attribute it to the growing support that they see we are getting and [NWI] also they know they are fighting for a good cause. It is good to know that they are not letting themselves be stampeded by the pack of lies in the press.

When ["ever" CO from previous word] the National Guardian ["comes and" CO, NWI] arrives with it comes a fresh, sincere and honest account of the real occurences [*sic*] in our case. The sign of our times is that this is one of the few remaining voices of progressive Americans that dares to challenge the evil deeds of those in power. This paper is keeping the torch of liberty burning brightly and its clarion call was of sufficient magnitude to result in the great campaign that is being waged around the issues in our case. They have a noteworthy record to date and have already made a mark for themselves as ["the" CO] a leading crusading journal in cold war America.

---

[320]The heroes of Chanukah, who drove the invaders out of Israel and restored the Temple to Jewish control.

The integrity and high ethical and moral standards they follow are a tribute to the heroic men and women who put this paper out.

On this Chanukah day I don't have a card to send you but the fire that burns in my heart for you is brighter and more consuming than ever. The greatest present we can give one another is the complete acceptance and devotion to each other. Therefore now as in the past all my love is for you. Oh my darling, the Macabees and the people who ["su" and the first half of "p" CO] followed them were so few and weak against the mighty hordes of tyranny and yet their steadfastness, determination and devotion to a just cause enabled them to win out against overwhelming opposition. Our present situation is similar to theirs and I ["have" CO] am confident we too as they did, will rally to our cause the people and in the end win the fight.

The days are ["long" CO] lonely sweetheart and the dark long nights are empty without you. There is no rest or peace when I know how great is your suffering. Over and over again I work hard ["the" CO, NWI] to drown out the agony that grips me but there is no real relief. Loved one you are always in my mind and in my heart and the only satisfaction that I can get is to try to emulate the fine example you set as a great person. I admire you for all the excellent qualities ["you" CO] and [NWI] good character you have ["that" CO] especially [N3WI] are these admirable under ["these" CO, NWI] present trying circumstances. I'm so nuts about you darling that I'd even marry you again — Always devoted to you—
Julie

Julius to Ethel

Dec. 18, 1952

Dearest Wife,

I'm feeling wonderful after such an excellent consultation with you and Manny. It was particularly good because you did a fine job discussing the childrens [*sic*] problem and although I did not enter much of the verbal ["repartee" CO, NWI] views I learned quite a bit and I expect to be able to contribute some useful suggestions after this. I finished writing my Christmas cards and I went right to the task of getting out a letter to our counselor. That we had helped our own situation I am sure of ["it" CO] and I also believe we'll be able to do a great deal more in our own behalf ["in fthe" [*sic*] CO] at this time.

Remember darling all the warm expressions that many decent strangers are sending us was influenced ["I believe by" CO, "from" inserted before "by" and CO, N2WI] because of our own writings. This is the only medium ["that we" CO, N4WI] our own true selves can really be known to the public as we actually are and not as our detractors depict us to be. Michael's maturity and understanding is the most revealing [NWI] single feature of the kind of job the Bachs and Manny are doing with our boys. I am amazed at his rapid progress and at the same time I miss being with them to personally witness the wonderful growth of our children. Again I think it proper to recall to you that all the groundwork and constant vigilence [*sic*] that you maintain over our boys [*sic*] welfare is paying off in the dividends we now see. Not only did you bring me around very early on this matter but look at the very excellent change [N3WI] you brought about in our own dear Manny. We will have to set forth certain definite plans for the boys [*sic*] future and turn it over to our counselor.[321] I suggest you work on an outline. We'll discuss it and you will write it up.

Don't forget to tell my mother that we arranged with Manny to have the children stay with her during the holiday for a couple of days also I am sure you will help cheer her up. I hope our lawyer gets her a nice Chanukah present for us. She is a sweet Mommy and we both love her dearly. She has always been ["the" CO, N3WI] one of our most dependable defenders[322] ["we have" CO] and sick and troubled as she is we can count on her will and determination to lend strength to our cause.[323]

There is an interesting thing that I learned, for I found that by listening, especially when you were talking I had a splendid opportunity to keep my eyes focused on you and it did me a world of good. I just don't get a chance to sit back and take in all your charms ["with my eyes and ears" CO]. Of course, I very [*sic*] proud of you my sweet woman and I'm right to sound off about your virtues for you deserve every bit of compliment I give you. Naturally since I ["'m" CO] happen to be your husband it makes me feel kind of wonderful. You see it is both an objective and subject [*sic*— probably means "subjective"] truth and there is no denying it. This here fellow is very much enamored of you and I think something ought to be done about it. A little matter like a court reversal. [NWI] Huh! Confident & hopeful as ["ey" CO] ever[.]
Julie

---

[321]Note the willingness to contemplate their approaching death and the need to "turn over" plans for us to Manny, which they ultimately did in their last wills and testaments, see below, p. 701.

[322]See *Sons*, p. 25 for her crucial role in rallying Julius' sisters and brother to his support very early.

[323]It wasn't until later that she came to the forefront giving interviews to the press and speaking at rallies. See *Sons*, p. 204.

The following telegram was undoubtedly sent as a result of the legal consultation between Manny Bloch and our parents on December 18. The proposed demonstration did occur. It is referred to in our mother's letter of January 19, 1953. (See below, p. 559.) Meanwhile, the requested meeting with William A. Reuben, the writer of the original National Guardian *series and the first head of the National Committee to Secure Justice in the Rosenberg Case, never occurred. Emily and David Alman, who were the mainstays of the Committee and who had had conflict with Manny Bloch about strategy, wanted desperately to meet our parents and give them a direct window onto their own defense efforts but were unable get a message to our parents through family members.*

E70CC 3B 104/102 COLLECT 7 EXTRA DUPLICATE OF TELEPHONED TELEGRAM
VIA IU
OSSINING NY 5522P DEC 19 1952

EMANUEL H BLOCH
5149 [stamped]
    DLR SATURDAY AFTER TEN AM ROOM 810
401 BROADWAY NYK (EMD)

WE WELCOME ACTIVITY SAVE OUR LIVES SECURE JUSTICE STOP HYSTERICAL TIMES DEMAND DEFENSE CIVIL RIGHTS STOP OUR CONSIDERED JUDGEMENT HOWEVER DEMON-STRATION AT SING SING ILL ADVISED STOP DIRECT CONTIN-UING CAMPAIGN TO FEDERAL GOVERNMENT FOR RELIEF STOP SING SING AUTHORITIES NO LEGAL POWER TO INTERVENE IN OUR CASE STOP DESIRE LEGAL PERMISSION TO SEE WILLIAM A RUBIN [sic] IMMEDIATELY STOP URGENT YOU UNDERSTAND OUR POSITION. STOP WE SUPPORT ANY OTHER ACTION TO DRAMATIZE ROSENBERG CASE AND ITS FAR REACHING IMPLICATIONS STOP ASSURE YOU DEVOTED FRIENDS OF HEARTFELT GRATITUDE FULL CONFIDENCE IN YOUR EFFORTS STOP
    ETHEL ROSENBERG #110510 JULIUS ROSENBERG #110649
902P

Julius to Ethel

Dec 21, 1952

Dearest Ethel,

    Sweet wife of mine, so near to each other yet restrained but underneath inside of me such powerful feelings of love for you. Even on this paper it is not enough and [NWI] also when I visit with you the circumstances are not conducive to free expression. However, ["it" CO] our relationship has reached much higher heights than we've ever experienced and it is very good for our morale. This is the extra something we need to withstand the growing pressure of the coming events. Although I cannot ["still I am" CO] take you in my arms and crush you to my body and kiss you with my heat [*sic*—probably "heart" miswritten] ["I can ta" CO, NWI] nevertheless you are with me every minute of the day. I continue to be inspired by your courage and by your example and I'm proud to be your husband. Even though we disagreed with the tactic of holding a demonstration here I heard on the radio that a peaceful [NWI] clemency meeting was held to send us greetings from the people. [N6WI] All power to these wonderful people. I am very happy to receive this kind of support and coming with all these cards, letters and the report in the National Guardian we [NWI] are receiving a real Christmas present from the world we love. I am sure we'll hear the details of all that is happening sometime this coming week. Don't forget to send out a Sunday pass for my brother Dave.

    I sent a couple of letters out to Manny one of which explained in greater detail our position on the people and individuals that support us. You know honey when I read that short excerpt from Rosa Luxemburg's prison letters.[324] I thought I was reading something you wrote. It has the depth of your feeling and the fluidity of the style is very reminisent [*sic*] of your writings. I hope we have the good fortune to see the book of our letters that they intend to print.[325] Sweetheart our letters have been a very great factor in showing the kind of people we really are. Every single time you put something on paper it has such profound emotional effect on the reader because it is pure stuff straight from the heart and it hits the readers [*sic*] finer feelings right at the heart.

    Do you think we ought to try to convey any special message to our precious children at their Christmas time visit. Perhaps we should follow

---

[324]Rosa Luxemburg was a German socialist intellectual and revolutionary in the period before World War I. She was murdered during the abortive German revolution of 1919.

[325]This is the first reference in the letters to the decision to issue a book of letters. In the end, the volume *Death House Letters* was not published until June of 1953.

our usual custom—but make certain all of the time is given over to their
needs and we must pay 100% attention to them. We'll discuss it before we
see them and make our plans accordingly. This visit with our family must
be a most positive one for our boys. I am sure we'll both try very hard and I
expect us to be successful in our efforts.

From now on, after we take care of our immediate personal problems
and the pressing question of the case, we'll have to get certain plans on
paper at each visit concerning our boys and other personal matters. These
we'll take up starting with our next tete a tete.

Darling there is so much pent up feeling and I can't get it down on
paper I need you so much and oh if we could only work together again as we
did in the past in the warmth of our own home surrounded by our beloved
children. For this we give our all—Your devoted husband—Julie

Mr. Emanuel H. Bloch
401 Broadway
New York NY

                                                             Dec 22nd, 1952
Dear Manny,

Today I had served on me the enclosed papers[326] I assume similar ones
were ["filed" CO] served on my wife. It is to be noted that they are photostats, permanent records of of [*sic*] this brutal sentence. The "honorable"
gentlemen who had a hand in this foul political frameup are listed and a
record is made to go down in history.

Our government that has failed to mete out ["proper" inserted, then CO]
justice to the fascist and Nazi war criminals in it's [*sic*] custody, who
murdered tens of millions of innocent victims now ["wants" CO, N2WI] is
going to bloody it's [*sic*] hands with [N3WI] the lives of two innocent
Americans.

By their deed they shall be known. There is still time to prevent this
miscarriage of justice [N3WI] from being irrevocable and I am confident the
court of public opinion has yet to be heard from and will help save us from
this impending doom.

Keep up the fight. I believe we're going to be saved and we'll have our
day in court, yet, in spite of the wishes of these "honorable" men.

Perhaps it is in keeping with the times that these papers are delivered to
us just before Christmas. This kind of "good will to all men" makes empty
words out of their pious incantations in the spirit of the holiday season.

---

[326]Death warrants

Maybe in their ghoulish way of thinking death is the kind of peace they speak about.

However humanity whose basic instincts are good will give their [N5WI] answer in ["the true" CO] keeping with the traditional ["answer" CO] Christmas and holiday spirit. The truth has exposed the plot. I believe the decent men and women working with us will win this fight for right.

Confident As ever Julie

The following letter, though begun on December 22, was not mailed until December 25, and in fact was written over the intervening days. We have decided to include it as a whole rather than breaking it up into separate units. The letter of December 23 will follow this one.

Mr. Emanuel H. Bloch
7 W 16th Street
New York N.Y.

Dec 22nd 1952

Page #1

Dear Manny,

Today my mind went back to the year 1933 when we lived in the midst of the great depression. I was a High School senior at Seward Park H.S. and it was very difficult for me to decided [*sic*] whether to continue my schooling or take a job for the family was in very tough financial situation and the future for young people like myself didn't look so good.

Although only fifteen years old I was fully aware of conditions around me and felt deep social responsibility to do something about them. To earn a little money I used to peddle penny candies on Sundays. The ["average take" CO, NWI] profit went from [N3WI] a low of 40 [NWI] up to 80 cents for a good day.

Now one day on my way home from school I stopped to listen to a speaker at a street corner meeting on Delancey St in the lower East Side. His topic was the campaign to win freedom for Tom Mooney labor leader who was imprisoned on a frameup.[327] The same night I read a pamphlet I had bought from the speaker that presented all the facts of this case and listed how the reader could help free this innocent victim. I was determined to do my part and since I had saved up $1.10 and ["only" CO, N8WI] the cost of a box of candy was only 60¢ ["was" CO] the very next day I [N2WI] went

---

[327]For the Tom Mooney–Warren Billings frameup case, see *Encyclopedia of the American Left*, pp. 485–86.

and contributed .50¢ to this cause. Then I began to distribute literature and collect signatures on a petition from the students at school and from my neighbors[.] This is the way I implemented my convictions to fight for right.

There is an incident that occurred which is still very fresh in [NWI] my mind. It happened during my first year at City College in 1934 in the Great Hall where I had to attend freshmen [*sic*] chapel with all other freshman.[*sic*] The student council was [NWI] then responsible for the programs during this hour and usually invited guest speakers. This particular time, over their strenuous objection, the president of the school Frederick Robinson [NWI] (boo) usurped this right and on his own invited a delegation of foreign students from fascist Italy to be guests and help make good will [N3WI] for that regime among us students.

When the prexy got up to speak he was greated [*sic*—meant "greeted"] by a chorus of boos. He was forced to sit down without being able to speak but he managed to ["call" CO] state that "our conduct was befiting [*sic*] guttersnipes." After all the heinous deeds of the fascisti was not palpable to Americans with democratic instincts and everybody present booed ["some more" CO] lustily.

To ["get order" CO] reestablished [*sic*—he meant to cross off the "d," NWI] order the authorities allowed Eddie Alexander president of the student council to speak. The hall was perfectly quiet when he began, "I was given permission to speak if I don't say anything derogatory against fascism. But I want to convey a message to ["my" CO, NWI] our enslaved and tricked brothers under Italian fascism." The truth cut too deep and the ["foreign students" CO] fascisti students dragged him away from

Dec. 23rd 1952

Page # 2

the microphone and a free for all began. 3000 voices thunderd [*sic*] in the Great hall "Abasso il fascismo" ["]Demuerte de Mussilini [*sic*]"

At this point the prexy called out New York City's finest and the college student body was treated to a lesson of nightstick civics. The entire metropolitan press ["dis" CO] printed distorted accounts of what took place and heaped abuse on the students. Within a week almost the entire student body ["sported" inserted, then CO, "sported" CO, NWI] wore buttons that read "I am a guttersnipe I hate fascism." Subsequent events such as: Il Duce legions bringing "civilization" to ["the no" CO] Ethiopia via bombs, flames and death to innocent defenseless natives proved we were correct [two illegible letters CO] in our position of fighting fascism. [N6WI] But 21 students including Alexander were expelled. ["for th" CO]

I remember when the rape of Ethiopia began students from the colleges and university [sic] located in New York City [NWI] area protested this barbaric invasion and picketed the Italian Consulate but their peaceful demonstration was broken up by police clubs. Again the newspaper accounts were completely false and antagonistic. There were similar demonstrations against Nazi brutality in front of the German consulate and this time also the result was the same.

At school I took a very active part in the campaign to free the Scottsboro boys. My extracurricular time was devoted in this constant work for [NWI] the good causes. ["I studied, read, participated and learned" circled and inserted at the end of the next sentence, then CO] Together with thousands of other young people. [sic] I studied, read, participated and learned.

I took a part-time job as a clerk in a drug store on Lenox Ave near 125th Street in order [N3WI] to earn enough to make ends meet. Daily I walked through the Negro neighborhood from school to work. I saw what discrimination meant. Overcrowding in slums. 25 to 50% higher prices than those charged in other neighborhoods for the same items and [NWI] higher ["for" CO] rents. ["None" CO] The store employees in the neighborhood were all white. There were many incidents where the police were charged with brutality [circled "x" here with an arrow to the top of the page where was written "At this point include incident on page # 2A." We will produce that page in the order in which he originally wrote it. In *Death House Letters,* the insertion was made as per his request (p. 116). The same was done in *Sons,* p. 169.] Then [N6WI] there came a time when all the resentment against ["all" CO] these accumulated abuses ["build" CO] that were seething in this [NWI] boiling cauldron overflowed into the Harlem riots.[328] The public sat up and took notice and the Negro people of this area won some relief ["of" CO, NWI] for their justifiable grievances [sic]. Stores hired Negroes. The police let up on some of the rough stuff and committees of investigation went to work. Of course not enough was done to solve the problem.

What I'm getting at in reciting some of my experiences is that there are things you don't learn at school or from reading but you must see. ["This is the way" CO, N2WI] All this I integrated in my store of knowledge; the truths I saw with my own eyes together with my formal education so that I could ["better" CO] understand the world I live in and function better as a social human being.

---

[328]This occurred in 1943.

Dec 24, 1952

Page #3

There was a strike of auto workers ["in the" CO] who were locked out. ["not" CO, N3WI] This took place near our campus. A number of us helped them with their picketing and once when we went to their ["h" CO] union hall we noticed that the strikers [*sic*] families were in very bad financial straits. A student committee to help them was set up and funds were collected to buy food for these needed families. I remember well the feeling of brotherhood when we turned over crates of food to the striker's [*sic*] welfare committee.

This is part of my background and goes to make up the person that I really am a progressive individual. Is this the reason they have given us only 3 more weeks to live. They tell me in many devious ways you can save you [*sic*] wife and yourself. Make a deal. Do what the government wants.

Can I now deny all these truths [N2WI] I know?

Can I deny the principles of democracy that are [N2WI] so much part of me? This I can never do. I cannot live a lie nor can I be like the Greenglasses and the Bentleys.[329] My entire life and philosophy negates this and it is [NWI] obvious ["plain" CO, "clear" inserted then CO] that I could never commit the crime I stand convicted of[.] [a letter, either "t" or "f," is added, then CO] The plain fact is that we are completely innocent and we are confident we will prove that to the people[.]

It is Christmas eve now and 16 years ago this week the most important thing in my life happened to me. I met my wife then. Looking back now I am sure it was the best thing that occurred to me in all these years. Although I had decided to quit school and go to work because conditions were bad and the future didn't look good Ethel convinced me to finish my studies. She helped me with my work, typed all my engineering reports and lent me moral encouragement. Of course we did our share of smooching and believe me that was very inspirational[.] [N7WI] By the way I miss that now. You see I fell in love with her very soon after we met.

You must know my Ethel I cannot sing her praise to [*sic*] highly to you. She is sweet, gentle and generous. Very warm hearted, understanding ["she" inserted, then CO] and [N3WI] possess [*sic*—meant "possesses"] a ["swell" CO] keen analytical mind. Her virtue is a fine character and all who are acquainted with her know her true goodness. This situation gives me a chance to see her real worth and I am sure I have a great woman for my wife.

---

[329]Re Elizabeth Bentley, see footnote 68.

We can be so happy together. We want to be reunited with each other and our two sons. Our will to live is strong and that is the reason we fight so hard in this principled way to win our case. We have faith that the people will see to it that this will not be our last Christmas eve.

Let me tell you from the bottom of my heart we are working to make this a Merry Christmas and a Happy New Year for all the people.

Deeds of goodwill and deeds that make for Peace that is what the world wants[.]

This writing is my Christmas present to you dear friends.

Dec 23rd

Page # ["4" CO] 2 A
add to back of Page #2

One night while I was working in the store there was an accident on Lenox Ave. A speeding bus ran over a middle aged Negro man and he was brought into the store bleeding profusely from his leg that was almost completely severed off. It took the ambulance more than $3/4$ of an hour to answer this emergency call while this man bled to death. I had to mop up this mans [*sic*] life's blood and I'll never forget this crime that permits such a thing to happen to a human being.

Dec. 24th

Note: Manny the holiday cards ["I" CO] and messages of good cheer that I am receiving continue to [illegible word, looks like "mount" CO] pour in and I believe the authorities are only allowing a small portion of those that are sent to us to reach us. These expressions of support do us a great deal of good and we extend our warmest greetings to our well wishers.

Dec 25th

Manny is it possible to get our family pictures back from the F.B.I? These are the only photos that shows our children from birth on and also includes many pictures of Ethel and myself. Of course, I leave it up to you to do what you can.[330] Please continue sending us all printed matter ["s" CO at end of last word] on our case.

I'll continue to write whenever I get the urge to put a few thoughts down. Please excuse the penmanship, spelling, grammer [*sic*] and general mental wanderings[.] I'm really trying hard it is not easy to function under all this pressure. Send all my love to all of our friends.
Julie

---

[330]See footnote 14 above for information of what became of those pictures.

Dec 25, 1952
Page #4

Dear Manny,

It is Christmas Day in the death house. As usual I had a cup of coffee for breakfast. Then I stood in the center of ["this" CO] my cubicle of concrete & within arms [*sic*] length to the left, to the right, behind me, on the floor and on the ceiling stretched a solid wall of concrete except for the heavy steel ["bars" CO] that ["covered" CO, NWI] barred the entrance. Natures [*sic*] air and light was able to enter the cell through the spaces between the bars.

Across the corridor through the window on the ["far" CO] opposite side I could see it was a dark cloudy morning. The thin gray morning light did not succeed in penetrating to the inside only the cool breeze from the open window made itself felt. I stood a moment longer and reflected. It is solidly built, efficient but very cold. The only brightness was on the left wall ["where" CO, N2WI] on which ["Ethel and the boys [*sic*] pictures hung" CO] pictures of Ethel and the boys were ["ta" CO] held up by strips of [NWI] adhesive tape. A pile of ["cal" CO] Christmas cards on my desk ["lent" CO] gave additional color to the place. Even the July 4th 1952 page of the New York Times that ["was" CO] contained a copy of the Declaration of Independence and [NWI] which was also held up on the same side by strips of adhevise [*sic*] tape was brown with age and seemed to be molded into the wall a [letter "n" CO at end of last word, "empty" CO] weathered piece of paper. Yet, in this tomb there was warmth. it [*sic*] was inside of me. I reached my arm out through the bar and felt for the switch and put the light on. The rays of light projected by the reflector behind the bulb from the outside were broken into oblong rectangular patches of light by the cell bars. They made a weird pattern all over ["the" CO] my concrete cubicle.

There is no beauty, no joy and no cheer here and only within oneself is it possible to find good in this tomb.

I thought of other Christmas days and immediately my ["fa" CO] mind focused on my adorable wife and precious children. How were they spending the time? What were they doing? And I began to think of my fellowmen and of our world. It is true I miss ["ed" CO at end of last word] being with them but on the whole I don't feel so bad because I see in the confidence they honor us with. [NWI] Also that ["all that" CO, "in the main" inserted, then CO, NWI] what I believed was right and good, was ["really" CO, NWI] really so & that I always lived in truth. To struggle for good causes is the highest precepts of ["the" CO] the human being. ["Their" CO] It encompasses all spheres of life and with the attainment of a specific goal newer and greater horizons are [NWI] always ahead and in the meantime mankind benefits.

Therefore, I do not despair for I have this perspective ["also" CO] before me at all times[.]

The news on the radio today is very good. All people can take new hope and redouble their efforts for peace in the world. I believe that the people will find a way to insure peace and I also have faith in their ability to save us.

Time is getting short but I am still optimistic that we will win our freedom. A lot can be done and must be done in the 3 weeks we have left to live.

As ever Julie

Mr David Rosenberg
430 E 63rd St.
New York NY

Dec 23rd, 1952

Dearest Brother,

Enclosed please find a Sunday morning pass for Dec 28, 1952 (10–11 AM). Mama has been telling me how hard you and the girls are working on our behalf. We always knew you would support us to the limit and we hope you'll have many good things to tell us when we see you this weekend.

Since we are terribly anxious for news, don't fail to be well prepared to tell ["al" CO] us all of the latest developements [*sic*]. You know our government is telling us this will be our last Christmas but we refuse to be convinced. With each succeeding day we have more cause to renew our faith in the people. We feel confident that public opinion will make the authorities consider carefully this brutal sentence and this miscarriage of justice. The truth cannot be hidden from the people and as they learn the facts they are reacting just as ["we" CO] Ethel and ["I" probably omitted here] predicted at the start of this political frameup.

It is impossible to tell you how pleased we are with all the support we are getting from people in all walks of life from all over the country and from foreign countries. Not only are we reading about this things [*sic*] but we have received many warm hearted messages of support & of pledges to fight for our freedom. The common men and women of the world are on our side and they will help us win the justice we deserve.

Never for one moment let up in the relentless effort to make known the truths about this case. You my family know us most intimately[.] People want to find out the truth about the Rosenbergs and you can best tell them.

I'm trying to rush this letter out to catch an earlier mail because ["of" CO] the heavy Christmas mail might delay this pass.

Love Your brother
Julius # 110649

Merry Christmas

Julius to Ethel

Dec. 25, 1952

My Darling,

Christmas Day was very bleek [*sic*] and lonely without you and our children. The songs, the sentiments and the meal all mean nothing, without my being together with my family. But as I said in a letter to Manny today I don't despair because the people honor us ["with" CO] by their confidence in us. We expect to see many more Christmas days and I hope to spend them with you my beloved. You were in my mind and my heart and all day long I day-dreamed about us. It was good for a time but I couldn't touch you and I was quickly brought back to reality. However, I'm still optimistic that we'll win our freedom.

I'm beginning to think about the children's next visit and I'm already anticipating a good time for all. Every moment of it will be spent on ["their" CO] what they want to do and talk about. Naturally, I'm sure we'll get our share of hugging and kissing our sons.

The bulk of my time is still being spent writing Manny but I'm not able to get enough out. I'll just have to be satisfied with the results to date and whatever else I can do.

["Now" CO] If there are any special things that you feel we must take up now is the time to give careful consideration to them. Since we are grownups and very practical about this situation we ought to be prepared to any eventuality and act accordingly.

Incidentally, I told Manny that it was 16 years ago this week that we met and ["I talked about" CO, N5WI] in the letter to him I ["discussed about us" CO, N5WI] told him of certain incidents. Here is one of the paragraphs in that letter.

You must know my Ethel, I cannot sing her praise to [*sic*] highly to you. She is sweet, gentle and generous, very warm hearted, understanding ["she" inserted, then CO] and [N3WI] possess [*sic*—meant "possesses"] a ["swell" CO] keen analytical mind. Her virtue is a fine character and all who are acquainted with her know her true goodness. This situation gives me a chance to see her real worth and I am sure I have a great woman for my wife.

You can tell honey that I was restrained because I tried to be very objective but [NWI] but just between us [next word written over something else] you'r [*sic*] just a swell person, a charming girl and I love you with every fibre of my being. Oh If [*sic*] I could only take you ["to my heart" CO, N3WI] in my arms.

We've got to keep our courage up now dearest, the pressure is being turned on. You have already proven the indestructibility of the individual and now we must maintain our equilibrium for the difficult trials and tribulations ahead. The drama that we are the main characters in has a force of developement [*sic*] of it's [*sic*] own but I believe by our actions we have effected [*sic*] it to some extent and I believe that we can still help determine the outcome [N2WI] to be favorable to ["be" CO] us. Of course the key to the situation is the people. We'll soon know the decision. All my love—
Your devoted husband— Julie

Mr. Emanuel H. Bloch
7 W. 16th Street
New York N.Y.

Dec 27, 1952

Page # 1

Dear Manny,
It was cold in the yard this morning. Winter was asserting itself. Gusts of icy wind blew across the yard, stinging my ears and carrying to my nose the pungent fishy ["smell" CO] odor of the Hudson River. A soaring seagull was sailing upward in wide circles lifted by the strong wind and gracefully, without effort, covered the expanse of the wide open sky that my eyes could see. Yes my spirit, too, took wing with that bird. Suddenly with a roar man's invention the jet plane, intrudes ["it's [*sic*] presence with the" CO, N2WI] into nature's scene but the white puffs [N2WI] that were bunched like an endless chain ["of" CO, NWI] into clouds hid it from my sight.

Then as I took another turn around the yard my eyes ["caught" CO, N2WI] glanced at the white streak of calcium that seemed to make odd shapes as they ran in broken lines from brick to brick along the wall of the death house. I began to think of the chemistry of the building materials. Through my mind flashed a picture of coal and iron ore being dug from the bowels of the earth, trains bringing [NWI] it into to [*sic*] the mills, iron and steel pouring from the furnaces, fabricated parts making their way to Sing Sing, skilled mechanics building all these parts into a strong structure ["with" CO, NWI] using all the science of modern industry ["into" CO, NWI] to make a death house. Just as the panorama imprinted itself on my brain the exercise guard gently reminded me my fifteen minutes yard period was finished. I breathed [N2WI] once more deeply of the fresh free air and then I went to my cell. The steel door closed ["and, the sna [illegible end]" CO, NWI] a key turned [NWI] in the lock, the padlock snapped and I was once again shut in my cubicle of concrete.

Day and night, pacing back and forth, being on my bed & endless thoughts crowding through my mind. So little time left so much to say and live in a couple of weeks. What should be put down first? To whom? How?

Please listen, look, see, hear, feel. Learn the truth & get at the facts. Each for his own defense must defend right and life.

Over and over again I begin to write to my sons. I wrote a few lines and tore up the paper. Then ["and" CO] I put it off again and sent Ethel a letter and again I couldn't make it and I continue to write you dear friend. It is futile to tell a mother not to grieve for her children. Well do we realize the terror and emotional hardships our two bunnies are going through. We their parents see the terrible hurt visited on our boys and know the mark that has been made on their lives. And when I look through the screen at my wife in her cell and [N2WI] see the tears ["are" CO] streaming down her face and her body ["is" CO] straining [N4WI] with all its might to contain the sobs of pain, I try to quiet her, while inside of me I'm crying all over. It's the damnable injustice and horror of it all. We feel and live so strong. Because we are so sensitive we must do right by our children and for others like them we must do what we can to prevent a similar catastrophe, a product of hysteria and cold war, from being visited on thousands of other innocent parents.

Dec 28, 1952

Page # 2

Dear good Manny in everything I've written and all that I've said I try to explain to my sons the meaning and reason for this situation. A great part of the job and responsibility will be yours to help them understand. One thing I feel sure of that when they are older and read the trial record and all that took place they will know that all the way through we their parents were right and the knowledge of this truth will buttress their feelings and confirm their confidence in themselves and in us their parents. We are still optimistic but we are alarmed that madmen in their haste to conceal this rotten frameup will snuff out our lives. This must never be.

With each passing day more and more people are becoming aware of the facts in this case and the evil men who are responsible for this miscarriage of justice want us to save their face ["as" CO, N3WI] & hide the documented facts in the record. ["b" CO] It wont [*sic*] work and I believe the people will not let this act of desperation happen.

I just happened to think that no matter what the outcome of this case is will Judge Kaufman every [*sic*] be able to explain his action to his own children, who some day will read the facts of this case. Don't these people know they will have to account for their actions? Yes, I understand what motivates these people and the public must be told everything. I state that the type of evidence used to convict us if considered dispassionately could not be sufficient to convict a pickpocket.

Legally, judicially[,] morally and in simple truth we are completely innocent. We are hoping for the best and we have faith the people will not allow this execution to take place. If I only had the means to talk to each man and woman personally I am sure I could alert them to the danger and prove our contentions. There must be no letup in activity. Justice demands that we live to have our day in court to win complete vindication. The human conscience and our national honor demands this.

I will stop now because I want to make the mail but I'll write soon again.

As ever
Julie

P.S. Keep sending me all printed material. Address the same items to Ethel and me under separate cover. Send my deepest affection and love to all our friends and supporters. We want to live to join them in future campaigns for decency, brotherhood and peace.

Julius to Ethel

Dec. 28, 1952

Darling Wife,

Just a couple of reminders. Put the following items on your commissary list Monday evening; 1 [circled] Box of Schrafts candy, 2 ball point pens and, 1 can of chicken.

I've been thinking my dearest how terribly inadequate I feel because I can't give you much comfort in this time of our great agony. It is futile to tell a mother not to grieve for her children. Well do we realize the terror and emotional hardships our two bunnies are going through. All the reason and right in the world cannot change that. But yet you and I must together steel ourselves although our hearts are breaking and our tortured minds scream out for relief. We must do what's right for them and for other children like them, that this catastrophe, product of hysteria and cold war, [NWI] must not engulf thousands of other innocent parents.

As expected the filth hirelings of the kept press are spewing forth ["weird" CO] lies, bigger and better to hide the truth. They can never change the facts and they are frightened that they will have to account for this monstrous frameup. In this desperation to save their face they are hoping to have us do their dirty work but it won't work for the people are on to this miscarriage of justice and they are moving to stop this brutal sentence from being carried out.

I know how you feel dearest. My mind tells me write, write but I am so torn inside I can't get anything out. I must drive myself for there is so much pent up inside of me and the time to put it down on paper is getting short.

If for any reason I might have given you ["the" CO, NWI] any ideas that have prevented you from writing please consider it a mistake on my part and write ["what" CO, NWI] as your conscience directs you. This I must say again that we've done wonderfully well in this matter to date and I am confident we'll do even better in the next couple of weeks.

As we discussed at our last visit I talked to the P.K. about certain matters and I have high hopes that Warden Denno will look with favor on our requests.

Cookie girl, I miss you terribly. It is just impossible to conceive that this grotesque web of horror has been ["false" CO] spun around us by ["y" written over "ut" in previous word] such vile, evil men. Is everything decent in life to give way to a callous political bunch? I don't believe so, but I am, nevertheless, worried that madmen [NWI] might make frightful blunders and the worse [*sic*] may happen. Ethel sweetheart, my love for you is so over-whelming that it gives me great strenght [*sic*] to withstand the mounting pressure. One thing I am positive of and that is that your devotion to truth and right will conquer the terror being visited on us.

Let me send you all my love and everything I cherish and hold fine and dear. You have shown me how [N3WI] wonderful it is to be a really good humane [*sic*] being & I am happy for it. Confident as ever

Julie — Remember Courage Confident [*sic*, he meant "Confidence"] & perspective—
Julius to Ethel

1953

Julius to Ethel

Jan 1st, 1953

Hello Bunny,

Happy New Year to you Ethel darling. May this year see events [N2WI] take place that are more to our benefit than [N2WI] those that have happened in the old year. The Circuit Court of Appeals ushered out the old year with another piece of hair splitting [N3WI] in an opinion that continues to help bury us.[331] Just as we expected the cards are staked [*sic*] against us.

---

[331]The Court of Appeals, in a unanimous opinion written by chief Judge Thomas Swan, carefully scrutinized one of the arguments raised in the Sec. 2255 motion rejected by Judge Ryan in December. The issue was the alleged timing of the unsealing of the indictment of William Perl in the middle of the trial and the statement to the press by Prosecutor Saypol that Perl could corroborate some of Greenglass' testimony. The Court of Appeals wrote that such tactics "cannot be too severely condemned . . . if defendants had moved for a new trial, it should have been granted. But they did not so move. . . . They now seek to excuse the omission because when they conferred with the judge Mr. Saypol gave assurance that he had not 'timed' the Perl indictment. Such assurance they then accepted as true but they have recently concluded that it was false, because Perl has not yet been brought to trial. This is not a valid excuse. . . . Mr. Saypol's motive and 'timing' in opening the indictment are irrelevant; the wrong consisted in the statement made to the press to the effect that the government had expected to use Perl's testimony to corroborate the Greenglasses', and the intimation that because he had backed out he had been indicted for perjury. Such a statement to the press in the course of a trial we regard as wholly reprehensible. Nevertheless we are not prepared to hold that it vitiates the jury's verdict when there is no allegation or evidence that any juror read the newspaper story and the defendants deliberately elected not to ask for a mistrial." (quoted from the opinion in Schneir, pp. 183f.)

However they are forced to write opinions and from the fragments that I read in the newspapers they recognize the prejudice caused to us by the publicity as handled and have so stated.[332] Both courts are of the opinion that despite the prejudicial conditioning of complained of publicity ["prejudi" CO] the defendants [*sic*] failure to take timely corrective proceedural [*sic*] steps, ["it" CO] now forecloses the courts from giving us relief as prayed for. To all this I say bunk.

I believe that true justice is concerned with substance not forms or modes of proceedures [*sic*]. [NWI] If It [*sic*] is recognized that the publicity complained of served to deny us a fair trial and due process of law then failure to counsel to make timely objections, or passage of time, in no wise corrects the unfairness of the trial. In other words if to begin with, it was an unfair situation, the situation did not later become "cured" because of passage of time.

If the courts [*sic*] opinion is to be squared with an ordinary common-sense interpretation of whether or not their holding is good law, we come to the absurdity as follows: That because of negligence, laxity, inexperience, of ineptitude of a lawyer his clients can be deprived of life even though the courts admit that their trial was infected by prejudicial unfairness. Of course, mature reason dictates the rejection of this. Enough, it just galls me to think of this terrible injustice.

Honey I missed you terribly New Year's Eve and all day today. I spent the hours ushering in the New Year reading the material published on our behalf and rereading your letters. Naturally, I was terribly moved but I felt so close to you sweetheart.

Oh Gosh, my wife, the long many painful hours, full of longing, devoid of cheer and pregnant with [NWI] the ever present danger to our lives, becomes at times unbearable. The people responsible for this infamous deed must be made to account ["of" CO] for ["it" CO, N2WI] their actions. Before God and man we are innocent and ["human decency" CO] decency and humanity demands that we receive the justice that is rightfully ours.

I am more determined than ever to fight with every last breath to expose the monsters and this terrible miscarriage of justice. Do not think because I feel so strongly that I have lost any courage. On the contrary I am ["very" CO] confident and hopeful that our lives will be saved.

---

[332]The motion for a new trial included extremely detailed research into all the articles published in the local New York papers between the arrests and the trial and continuing during the trial to show how prejudicial they were. The newspapers basically printed press releases from the prosecution as well as hiding the role of "reporters" like Pilat (see above, pp. 487, 491, 514 and footnote 284).

Excuse the penmanship and general scribbling I'm rushing this letter through. Again my beloved I send you ["the pos" CO] my heart ["f" CO at end of last word] and my very soul—Always your own

Julie

Mr. Emanuel H. Bloch
7 W 16th Street
New York NY

January 3rd, 1953

        Page #1
Dearest Manny,
        It is now Saturday afternoon the visit is over. Our children have gone home. Through the exertion of super-human efforts I have finally succeeded in reestablishing [N2WI] my equilibrium. ["enough a [N2WI] in order suffi-cient [N3WI] amount of my faculties to" CO, N3WI] and I can continue to write [last letter written over "ing"]. The love of truth and mankind demands that I make this record.
        Because we are innocent and our cause is just I have been [N2WI] strong enough ["able" CO] to face [N2WI] all this ["anything" CO] and not once have I given free reign [*sic*] to the tormenting flood of emotions that are dammed up [three illegible letters CO] inside of me.
        Today our precious boys came and our own family lived [NWI] again for two hours. I could see the trust in little Robbies [*sic*] eyes and the sweet, warm tender feelings of love that passed between us, in all he said and in our play together. I carried ["on" CO, N3WI] the baby on my back giving him a horsey ride. We looked through the barred window at the sea gulls and the tugboat pulling ["the" CO, NWI] a string of barges on the Hudson. He zoomed through the room pretending to be an airplane as I held him [N3WI] in my arms tightly [NWI] pressed to my heart. The pictures he drew and the drawings I made for him [N2WI] were interrupted while he ["showed" inserted then CO, illegible word CO, NWI] kissed my cheeks ["with his and" CO, N2WI] as he ["and" CO] circled my neck with his [NWI] little arms. My son was happy with his daddy. Julie was a big pussy cat chasing the little mousie Robby and we had fun. Our baby got our true feelings.
        Michael was troubled, disturbed and the burdens on him were obvious to us his parents. My darling wife did so well by him. She explained patiently, carefully, firmly but all the time with a complete acceptance of him and showed such wonderful understanding. It was really a most positive visit for all of us. I promised to play him chess I hope to someday.
        Then they had to go and as I ["put" CO] helped ["him" CO, NWI] Michael with his [letter CO] coat ["and" CO] he [NWI] suddenly clutched me

with his hand ["he" CO] and stammered as he ["held his [NWI] head down" CO, N3WI] lowered his head, "You must come home, everyday ["I have a" CO, N3WI] there is a lump in my stomach ["and I" CO] even when I go to bed." I kissed him in a hurry for I was unable to say anything but, "everything will be alright."

When I was in the solitude of my cell once more and the door clanged shut behind me I must confess I broke down and cried like a baby [N6WI] because of the childrens [*sic*] deep hurt. With my back to the bars ["and facing" CO], I stood facing the concrete walls ["on all sides of me" CO, N7WI] that boxed me in on all sides. [*sic*] and I let ["my" CO] the pains that tore at my insides flood out in tears. The wretched beastliness and inhumanity of it all. Take heed tyrants you will answer for your misdeeds.

Decency and Right cries out that this danger and cruelty that faces my fellowmen [N3WI] & their children must be fought against and stopped before it is to [*sic*] late.

I am okay now and I'll copy over some of ["my" CO, NWI] the notes that I prepared for you. One thing you must do and that is that my children and all the world must know the truth. The trial records and all printed matter concerning us must be widely circulated.

The facts are with us and the foul deeds of "atomic" political monsters must be exposed.

Page # 2

It is indeed shocking that the Circuit Court of Appeals would go contrary to the Appeals Court decision as handed down in the Delancy, income tax collector, case in Boston. The distinguished gentlemen of the judiciary are going along with the hysteria of our times. They havent [*sic*] the courage to dispense justice dispassionately. They grab at any straw to hang their hat on to justify their ["hair splitting" CO] legal double talk.

From a reading of newspaper items concerning the Court of Appeals reference to defendents [*sic*] "astute" counsel's failure to object at trial or move for mistrial, I come to some conclusions that should be considered
First: Let it be assumed that we failed to
1) Move for a change of venue
2) Register objections at earliest opportunity of prejudicial news treatment
3) Move for a mistrial
Second
From a reading of Ryan's opinion on the "publicity" phase of the motion and from what I read of the fragments of the opinion of Court of Appeals as reprinted in the papers, I am left with the unmistakeable impres-

sion that both Courts have recognized the prejudice caused to us by the publicity as handled, and have so stated.

Third:

Both courts are of the opinion that despite the prejudicial conditioning of complained of publicity the defendents [*sic*] failure to take timely corrective procedural steps, it now forecloses the Courts from giving us relief as prayed for

To all the above I say bunk!

I believe as follows:

First

True justice is concerned with substance not form or modes of procedures.

If it is recognized that the publicity complained of served to deny us a fair trial and due process of law then failure of counsel to make timely objections (add one more to the hundreds we made), or passage of time, in no wise corrects the unfairness of the trial!

In other words if to begin with it was an unfair situation, the situation did not later become "cured" because of passage of time.

If the Court's opinion is to be squared with an ordinary common-sense interpretation of whether or not their holding is good law, we come to the absurdity as follows.

That because of negligence, laxity, inexperience or inaptitude [*sic*] of a lawyer his clients can be deprived of life even though the courts admit that their trial was infected by prejudicial unfairness. Of course, mature reason dictates the rejection of this.

Page # 3

(It is to be noted the same specious argument was used by the same Appellate Court in the matter of the trial Judge's prejudicial conduct. Again they seized on the straw and excused the denial of ["my" CO, NWI] our rights by taking one of counsel's statements (a [NWI] common court courtesy) thanking the court for a fair trial in the American way to be ipso facto proof that he realized there was no violation of constitutional rights [N2WI]—I say Nothing but chicanry [*sic*]

Of course I know we can try to go in on a writ of certiorari. (A discretionary power of the Supreme Court ["to" CO, N3WI] that it can withhold for any reason it sees fit. This courts [*sic*] denial of our past requests should be carefully explained and ["its" CO, N3WI] so that its significance will not be misconstrued) However, outside of that is there any possibility of ["picking" CO] using this opinion of theirs on it's face and saying alright so counsel did err in not timely raising these questions, nevertheless, a fundamental violation of due process exists here.

Or, is there another alternative that in this case where life is involved that our rights were effectively nullified because we didn't have proper objections made seasonably [*sic*] during the course of our trial.

Now I understand the cards are stacked against us in the courts but since they opened themselves up in this manner shouldn't we take advantage of this situation? Again I'm in a dilemma because in no way do I go along with the Court in their putting you on the hook with a knife in their hands all the time helping to [illegible word crossed out, NWI] bury us. (Such a legal move might put you in a funny position)

It is necessary that you clarify this matter to me, perhaps, we might find a way to turn this to our advantage.

I know that only the support of the people will help us stay alive but let us not overlook any other helpful step

[Extra line skipped here]

As it has [NWI] done so often in the past, making ex parte presentation of the case against us and only distorting our position when it did print our side, the so called "free" press gave complete coverage with the New York Times printing [N4WI] the complete text of Judge Kaufman [*sic*] sanctimonious [NWI] political propaganda tirade denying our application for clemency. This virulent anti-communist, anti-soviet blast is a warning against all political dissenters and is a coercive threat against the [NWI] free exercise of constitutional rights of our citizens. This is now being heralded ["as the "truth" CO] of course, prima facia [*sic*] as the "truth."

The plain fact is that it is not a true picture of what took place at our trial, of the facts, of the evidence, of the witnesses but is a prejudiced, inflammatory, myopic distortion of the truths. That is the reason why the newspapers refused to allow us to place paid advertisements to sell the complete transcript of the trial proceedings

Page #4

But this is the record and they can't hide it from the people. No amount of judicial semantics by the district court judge and the appellate court judges can rectify the weak case [N2WI] & record they have against us nor obscure the ["comp" CO] repeated violations of our constitutional rights and the unfair nature of our trial. But in spite of this blackout the truth will out and this is what they fear. That is the reason for their desperate efforts to make us confess to crimes we did not ["do" CO] commit. For they want us to cover up their dirty work. It will never work. Every efforts must be exerted to get our side printed in the press and to make certain that the trial record and the new evidence we presented in our petition for a new trial receive the widest possible circulation.

Kaufman is the new darling of the pro-fascist hate-mongering press. He will go down in history for his infamous deeds in our case.

[Extra line skipped here]

Although it has been almost unbearable I've [illegible two letters CO] used every ounce of my strength to be patient and waited all during the course of the legal moves[.] I had hoped some of those responsible for our situation would regain ["the some" CO] their sanity and come forth with the truth, make amends by helping us, commute our sentence to prevent an irreparable miscarriage of justice but this they did not do.

Therefore before God and man I must blazon forth these truths.

1 [circled] We are completely innocent. Nothing can change this.

2 [circled] That a monstrous frameup for political purposes has taken place in the Rosenberg case.

The ["earli" CO] genesis of this conspiracy has as its' [sic] background the worsening of relations between our government and the Soviet Union. It has it's [sic] roots in the anti-communist hysteria of the cold war and it's [sic] nefarious purpose is to justify present foreign policies and stifle opposition at home by linking atom bomb-communist-spy-Russia in a precedent setting case.

Fortuitously, at the height of this period of war scares the Greenglasses found themselves hopelessly trapped spies facing death for their heinous deeds. The scheming Ruth Greenglass hatched the idea, through her persistent efforts won over her husband to it, was aided and guided by her lawyer O. John Rogge (former [NWI] Asst Attorney-General. Government fingerman in Dubois peace case, ["repre" CO] paid agent of Tito,[333] allowed to keep $4,000 tainted spy money as his fee)[334] in consummating a deal with the District Attorney and F.B.I. participating to bargain our lives away to keep Ruth free (never even indicted ["but" CO, NWI] with a death penalty always hanging over her head if she doesn't continue to play ball) and a

---

[333]When Rogge testified for the prosecution against Dr. DuBois, he admitted to having been a registered foreign agent of Yugoslavia. Defense attorney Vito Marcantonio claimed in his summation that the government had only succeeded in identifying one foreign agent, and it was the government's own witness—a useful rhetorical flourish. See DuBois, *In Battle for Peace,* p. 141–47; Belfrage, p. 159.

[334]Refers to Greenglass' testimony that he received $4000 from our parents as expenses to help him and his wife flee but that he instead gave it to his brother-in-law Louis Abel who hid it. After David Greenglass' arrest, he had his brother-in-law bring the money to O. John Rogge as his initial fee. See Record, p. 794f.

light sentence 15 years (parole promised in 5 years) for Dave. These cannot be contradicted for they are the truth.[335]

Page # 5

Even the Circuit Court of Appeals had to admit the entire case rests on the Greenglasses and it is all made up of oral testimony of these accomplices uncorroborated, unsubstantiated by proof and incredible in spite of 9 months of coaching and rehearsing. By their own records ["He" CO, NWI] Dave perjured himself.

It was only recently that we forced another admission of ["subornation of" CO] of [*sic*] perjury on the part of the prosecution [illegible letter CO] witness Schnieder [*sic*] and the adding of deliberate fraud [N3WI] on the court by the District Attorney to his subornation of perjury. These of course are conveniently overlooked.

I charge that the judge and district attorney from the very beginning injected the false issue of communism and political beliefs to obscure the issue at bar and influence the passions of the jury against us and allowed this to dominate the trial. This was done to fit in with the grand plan to heighten the witch hunt in our land.

I charge the judge strained every effort to bind the jury to a verdict of guilt, by his constant numerous injection [*sic*, probably meant interjections] against our interest at every stage that was to our advantage. He allowed our rights to be [NWI, written over another word] repeatedly violated and prevented our lawyer from adequately defending us and did not allow the jury to judge the crime as charged in the indictment on a fair and impartial basis.

---

[335]Note the lack of logic in his reasoning. Why would guilty spies David and Ruth Greenglass be able to "fool" the government into giving them lenient treatment in return for testimony to convict two other people? Alternatively, why would the government want to let guilty people incriminate innocent people (with the prospect that the frameup might unravel)—especially innocent people who weren't prominent? The only rational reason for accepting the interpretation that Emanuel Bloch used at the trial and that our parents persisted in, up to the end—namely that the Greenglasses were in fact spies—is that the government was afraid they might not be able to convict the Greenglasses if they chose to plead not guilty and thus promised them leniency in return for testimony that could convict someone else. A much more consistent interpretation is the one that was adopted by William A. Reuben in *The Atom Spy Hoax* and John Wexley in *The Judgment of Julius and Ethel Rosenberg*, that neither the Rosenbergs nor the Greenglasses were spies. Finally, note how if our parents really were guilty, it would not have been in their interest to support an interpretation that accepted the guilt of the Greenglasses because that in fact gives them more credibility. Only a truly innocent person who doesn't quite understand how the government put together the frameup would grope to such an internally inconsistent interpretation as the one suggested in this letter.

In short he crucified us and now he is legally murdering us. A reading of the records will bear me out. I am willing to stand on the facts as they appear there and not on glib mouthings, ["unf" CO] made out of whole cloth [N2WI] in order to conform with establish [sic] policies. The judges must think the American [NWI] naive [N3WI] when he tries to invent ["ion" CO at end of last word] new scientific facts, to rewrite history and attempt to palm off such a bald fraud as the true representation of the Rosenberg case. [N19WI] The effrontery to yell communist at distinguished scientists, clergymen, men of letters & laws who petition for our lives. He only exposes himself as completely corrupt. You Irving Kaufman has [sic] damned yourself in front of all mankind and we will not save your face. The record of this case condemns you for all time and throughout your life your conscience will plague you and you will reep [sic] the future you have earned.

As for us we are confident of the righteousness of our cause and of our determination not to allow ourselves to be used as tools against the peoples [sic] interest in their fight for peace, freedom and decency.

Take heed gentlemen don't be too hasty and pull the switch. [NWI] Remember It [sic] is a two way affair. The World is watching our ["countries" CO, NWI] govt's action in this case and the consciences of men of goodwill are outraged by the brutal sentence and the miscarriage of justice in the Rosenberg Case.

Time is short there is but 10 more days left to live I will do my best to crowd in as much ["bef" CO] work as possible. I am raising a warning for I believe this is a test case of threatening fascism at home. Don't let them murder us.

As ever Julie

Mr. Emanuel H. Bloch
7 W. 16th Street
New York NY

Jan 4th, 1953

Dear Manny,

This is a continuation of the batch of letters I sent you yesterday.

It is evident that the truth is becoming known to larger numbers of individuals daily and the people are interested in learning the facts about our case. But the opposition is afraid for the record literally stinks and so to head off the rising protest in our behalf the corrupt puny man in judicial robes issues a verbose legal opinion purporting it to be the complete story of our case. The New York Times printed it in full and all the papers gave it big play. Here they say are the truths and the facts of the Rosenberg Case they failed to include [N2WI] the words de novo. Judicial pronouncements, prima facia [*sic*], even when couched in legal terms, by astute judges, cannot take the place of evidence and facts that are part of the trial record. This political propaganda document is a complete distortion of the case and is not the complete or true picture of the trial record and the facts in the case.

When the New York Times continues this ex poste presentation against us prints statements [NWI] made against us & does not permit any statements that are sent to it by prominent citizens in all walks of life that in any way help us [N4WI] or gives our side, such as, the one by 157 clergymen & educators asking for clemency, Prof. Harold Urey's letter and many more, especially not printing our concise and poignant statement which in a few lines ["demolishes" CO] exposes the long winded diatribe of Judge Kaufman against us, then [N3WI] there is no freedom of the press ["does not exist any more" CO].[336] For it is [NWI] then only freedom of those in power to crucify others [N11WI] and bloody their hands with the legal murder of innocent Americans. With each succeeding step they expose themselves more & we must bring the truth to the attention of all.

Gosh Manny I'm ["terribly" CO] concerned about Ethel, ["she" CO] it's terribly hard for her. Because I love our children so dearly I also love their mother so much. My wife is [NWI] a diamond and no amount of lies, filth or vilification can scratch her honor or mar her dignity. I believe she has risen ["above this to newer and" CO] in stature as an individual, in spite of the misery even ["in" CO, NWI] within the confines of this slaughterhouse while we face death. This to me is the singular proof of her [NWI] nobel [*sic*] character [NWI] good conscience and yes of our innocence. I hope I were [*sic*] able to give her more comfort and ease her great pain but all I can do is write.

Because I love to build, to create with my hands and mind I studied to be an engineer. My professional opinion as the crisis approaches and as the issues are sharper and clearer is that we are closest to the absolute truth and right. I am not dealing with the matter in a subjective way but refer to it objectively, the reality in nature perhaps I am confusing because this is ["a" CO, N4WI] to [*sic*] much like a physical or mathematical concept. However I believe that the idea I am trying to get across, at least the substance of it is the ultimate truth.

---

[336]The *New York Times* article printed in full Judge Kaufman's opinion denying a reduction in sentence. The *Times* finally published Dr. Urey's letter on January 8, 1953. Dr. Urey did not merely support clemency but stated he believed my parents were innocent. The *Times* actually refused to run ads put out by the National Committee to Secure Justice in the Rosenberg Case offering the sale of the trial transcript.

No matter what happens you must continue to work until you prove to all that we are innocent as indeed we are. (What happened to all the printed matter [N7WI] we want it to be sent us. It means a great deal to us)
As ever Julie

Julius to Ethel

Jan. 4th, 1953

Dearest Wife,
I hope this letter finds you in a good frame of mind because I am fully cognizant of the terrific pressures you are under at this time. After the wonderful visit we had with our children I wrote up a five page letter to our lawyer and I sent it to the Warden this morning in order for Manny to receive it sometime Monday. We'll spend our Tuesday visit discussing this get together with our family and you [*sic*] own visit.[337] Again I must repeat my amazement at the biased news reporting, particularly [illegible three or four letters CO] the New York Times. This shows how fearful they are, ["and the" CO, N2WI] ergo a concerted effort of the opposition to silence the rising protest in our behalf. Now these vicious demagogues will reep [*sic*] the storm they have ["sowed" CO, NWI] caused. As long as I work at reading and writing I'm in very high spirits and so I continue to keep at it. If only we were able to be within talking distance of each other I'm sure we would accomplish much better results. The statement we composed which was largely your formulation was concise and very poignant.[338] In a few words we demolished the verbose propaganda tirade that Kaufman ["is" CO, N2WI] tried to cloak [suffix "ing" CO] with [NWI] his judicial prestige in order to make this distortion the case against us. But this he can never do for the true picture of the case is documented in the trial record and in our petition of new evidence. Judicial pronouncements couched in legal terms cannot take the place of evidence and facts. This corrupt puny man in judicial robes has won the hearts of all reactionaries [NWI] hatemongers and pro-fascists but he will go down in history for his infamous part as [NWI] it is documented in the complete record.
You have no idea how powerful your pen is my dearest and the effect it has on the outcome of our case and on the people who read it. To me it is the essence of creative work not only for the inspiration and the talent [suffix "ed" CO, N2WI] of the person that ["puts" CO] brought it forth but what it does ["for and" CO, N3WI] to you and especially to others. If we are given the opportunity ["we must collaborate" CO] I will do all I can to help

---

[337]Perhaps referring to a prospective visit with her mother.
[338]This statement does not appear to have survived in any of the records.

you write for it is a treasure that must not be hidden from ["mankind" CO] our fellow men.

Because I love our children so dearly I can love their mother so much. You know, Ethel, a diamond is made of the hardest material [illegible letter CO] we have and therefore it cannot be scratched or marred by less coarse materials and so ["to" CO, N2WI] for us no amount of lies, filth and vilification can scratch our dignity or mar our honor. I believe we have risen above our miseries to new [N2WI] & higher stations as individuals even in the confines of this slaughterhouse while we ["await" CO] face death. This to me then is singular proof of our character, conscience, and yes innocence. Permit me my heart's desire to lend what comfort I may ["for" CO, N4WI] to you because of all that you mean to me and [NWI] for the deep feelings I have for you. As the crisis approaches the issues are sharper and clearer. The engineer is me feels that we are closest to the absolute truth and right.

All the love of my heart and soul — Always your own—Julie

Emanuel H. Bloch
7 W. 16th Street
New York, New York

January 5, 1953

My very dearest Manny,

What price perfidy! I have just read the excerpts of Judge Swan's opinion carried by the New York Times on New Year's Day. All legal considerations aside, I am sick for the unconscionably sneering attitude, the snide insinuations, you have had to suffer on our behalf. It is a shockingly deplorable level indeed to which morality has sunk when public servants of such exalted position find [NWI] entirely acceptable the questionable technique of the slur and the smear. With what extraordinary aplomb, with what high-handed unconcern for fact, with what cool disdain, your carefully organized, thoroughly documented soberly stated arguments, were dismissed! Perhaps I am naive, but it doesn't seem possible that a responsible governmental body should stoop to subject to jeers and jibes, one whose selfless devotion to justice and inspiring nobility of purpose ["should" CO] merits only the most boundless, admiration, the most [NWI] affectionate thanks. Please know that we honor and love you, as indeed do all lovers of truth and decency, beyond any measure!
Ethel—

P.S. to be continued—but I promised [N2WI] to send you some expression, no matter how incomplete, on Monday morning. More to follow re Judge Kaufman! Am well, and perfectly calm!—ER

The following is the text of a telegram sent on January 5.

EMANUEL H BLOCH
401 BROADWAY NYK
URGENT YOU GET IN TOUCH WITH MY MOTHER AT ONCE STOP
SHE WILL DO ANYTHING YOU SAY STOP DONT FAIL TO
CONTACT HER STOP LOVE
ETHEL ROSENBERG

Emanuel H. Bloch
7 W. 16th Street
New York New York

                                                    January 6, 1953

Dearest Manny,

Methinks I detect the "subtle" sounds of "delicate" machinery sliding smoothly into place as the master gun-men bring up their heavy artillary [*sic*] under cover of a suitable smoke-screen, (already [NWI] ably laid down by the kindred spirits of the "free press"), and "get set" for the surprise attack! Sound the alert; these "conditions" please me not! How many blows will the decent people have to sustain, how many losses will they bitterly lament, before the lesson is ineradicably etched into the understanding, that the enemy's "promise" is but a promise of some fresh betrayal!

One thing is certain; in that "brave, new world" that we may never see, it will be noted with shocked disbelief that in the barbaric year of 1952, ["when" CO] duplicity was the order of the day, and the august words "His Honor" came to mean, "Dishonor"!

En garde!

Ethel

P.S.—I am hoping you find time to contact my mother; she appears to be desperately anxious to do whatever she might possibly be able to do, at this late hour!

Note: The "6" in the date of the following letter is written over an erasure. It is unclear if this letter was written earlier and then delayed before being mailed, or if in fact, both this and the previous letter were written on the same day.

Emanuel H. Bloch
7 W. 16th Street
New York New York

January 6, 1953

Dear Manny,

My letter expressing wariness about Kaufman's announced intention to grant a stay on "condition" that we apply for presidential clemency by Saturday, January 10, was written without prior knowledge of the details of the stay itself. Yesterday's "Times," reporting these details, fully confirmed my previously stated suspicions that a fraud was being deliberately perpetrated. The most ignoble feature of a judicial proceeding which for sheer viciousness and double-dealing is already without parallel, is the pernicious attempt to create the impression, with the one hand that we are receiving just about all the jurisprudence that is lying around loose, while making legally available to some lucky (sic!) individual, with the other, the opportunity for a quick (and preferably adverse) disposition of that horrible headache, that ghastly political boomerang, known throughout the civilized world as the "Rosenberg Case"!

Ethel to Julius

3:00 P.M. Jan. 6

Darling, I have only just received your most heart-warmingly beautiful letter. How simply and clearly you put it! They are indeed insane who vaingloriously and contemptuously underestimate the torrential power that is the People! Shake their fists as they may, scheme and terrorize, rant and rave, the organized might and enlightened indignation of the tens of millions can no longer be ignored!

Thank you, too, for recognizing as readily as I did myself the central political fact that it was due to the relentless pounding of that tidal wave of protest against the cold-blooded contemplation of foul, deliberate murder, that this concession, wretchedly inadequate as it is, was wrung from the authorities!

Aux Armes, citoyens! For myself, I want it fully known, that it is my unaltered judgment, my most steadfast understanding, that you must fear moderation only. Do not, I entreat you, you who hold in your massive, deathless hands, all of human bondage and human liberation, do not, for [NWI] all our children's sweet sakes, allow yourselves to be cajoled by blatant blandishments nor coerced by truculent threats, into abating your righteous anger! Shun like the plague and mercilessly expose the advocates of "sha—sha" (a salty and derisive Yiddish term for the "hush-hush" policy of appeasement), for they advocate only death!

I have had the unmitigated gall to try to set words to the immortal "Peat Bog Soldiers"—as follows: (2nd verse still to be composed ahem!)

I

Far and wide as the eye can wander
Brick and steel are everywhere
Overhead the clouds are threat'ning
& Winter sky is bleak and bare!
      <u>Chorous</u> [*sic*]
We are the death-house watchers
Waiting for our doom in the chair!
Repeat chorous [*sic*]
(What do you think? Is it at all serviceable?)
      Love, Ethel—

III

Up & down we hear them pacing
Millions, millions by our side
Those who lived and those
    they buried
Shall no longer be denied!
      <u>Chorous</u>[*sic*]
Then <u>will</u> the death-house watchers
Wait no more for their doom—in the
      Repeat— chair!

Mr. Emanuel H. Bloch
7 W. 16th Street
New York NY

Jan 6, 1953

Dear Manny,

As I had ["cautioned" CO] brought to your attention last Saturday [N3WI] and as expected Judge Kaufman did pull off a ruse. This wily, corrupt, trickster in judicial robes has unabashedly exposed himself again with his latest cunning stunt. By this indecorous action he flagrantly violated his public avowal to give us adequate time, (his words "all the time we need") which is our right, to properly prepare and submit our plea for clemency to this President.

Kaufman's magic hamstrings are as follows:

First,—He effectively prevents us from even seeking a Supreme Court review of our motion for a retrial on newly discovered evidence because no other legal moves are to be in process while making this final executive appeal.

Second—Our lawyer has less than 4 days in which, to secure forms from the Presidents [*sic*] pardon attorney in Washington D.C[.], to prepare all necessary paper [*sic*] and petitions for relief, to have us at Sing Sing sign them before a notary and then file all these papers in Washington D.C[.] All by this coming Saturday.

No amount of high fluent [*sic*—perhaps meant "falutin'"] legal verbosity can hide this unseemly deed that galls the spleen of decent people.

Third—He assumes that our case will continue to be a political football, dependent, ["so they plan" CO] upon whatever strategic propaganda maneuverings are in order, at least so they plan,

Fourth—It is now obvious to all the Kaufman "opinion" which could be entitled "Alleged Communists or pro-Communists are Better off dead" was deliberately conceived ["by the government" CO] to use this distorted judicial pronouncement as the case for political propaganda; 1 [circled] By the State Dept to offset mounting foreign indignation ["with" CO, NWI] against this ["shocking" CO, NWI] monstrous frameup and brutal sentence that shocks the conscience of mankind. 2 [circled] Through the instigation of the Justice Dept [N2WI] at home a high pressure press and radio campaign [N4WI] is in full swing to oppose and stop the growing protest movement ["at home" CO] against the horrible death sentence and above all to prevent the spread among the entire people of the grave doubts that many already have about our guilt and [NWI] about the evidence ["of" CO, N4WI] that there is here a gross miscarriage of justice in the Rosenberg case. The trial record dams [*sic*] them.

How terribly afraid of the truth they are! We two little people ["are" CO], even [NWI] when facing death, are strong in our innocence and confident of the justness of our cause. Even eloquent syllogisms firmly and beautifully pyramided when based on the big lie are completely demolished by right & facts. This is the pure and simple reason we have been able to maintain our dignity as human beings and our honor which we hold sacred. We have faith that the people will not let American justice be indelibly stained with the blood of the Rosenbergs.

Since you beloved friend have the most difficult task in this fight I pray that you have the strength and good fortune to do [NWI] almost the impossible and [N3WI] are able to function at the optimum of your ["form" CO] gifted faculties, encumbered as you are ["that" CO, N2WI] by all the tremendous pressures and obstacles. Never in the hearts of men has courage been found lacking in the fight for noble principles. This situation requires heroic efforts.

Manny the three of us are giving our all for good.

As ever Julie

Julius to Ethel

January 8, 1953

Darling Wife,

I'll see you much before you get this letter but being a creature of habit I want to be certain that you receive the usual epistle of love. ["that" CO] I struggle so hard to transfer ["to the" CO, "onto" inserted then CO, NWI] on paper all the ardent desires of my heart. We my sweetheart, bound together by the strongest ties of heart and mind can find in our profound feelings for each other the strenght [*sic*] and deep satisfaction, in spite of the great danger we face and the fact that we are keep [*sic*] apart. Believe me my adorable woman many are the hours that I relive parts of our past life and there are times that I imagine [NWI] what our life ["to" CO, NWI] will be like for all my reason and senses tell me that we will live to share life's secrets together again.

Nevertheless, I continue to be amazed at the extent the newspapers are drumming up a campaign of hate and lies against us. It is not that I fail; to understand the nature of our fight to win justice but it is the plain fact that we have received such a great amount of support that even the opposition is forced to acknowledge it and say we have "duped" great numbers of non-communists. Always the charge looks good on the other side and never are they able to back up their claims with hard facts from the trial record. Now they rely on Kaufmans [*sic*] argumentative opinion as the so called "truths" in the case. Of course, they still have all the press and other means of disseminating information but we've done remarkable [*sic*] well considering all the difficulties we face. This then is the real power of truth. One thing I am sure of and that is that ["tha" CO] come what may the Rosenberg Case will ["not" CO] be read by all people [N5WI] who wish to be informed and the grave miscarriage of justice will be known to all. [N9WI] They know they've got to reckon with the people Because [*sic*] they are terribly afraid of being completely exposed they have pulled out all stops to hammer away at us. Somehow, I still feel that they will have to come to their senses and realize that they can't afford to shock the conscience of the world.

Lately, my writing has been done in spurts but I'm always thinking about our case and spend hours pacing back and forth while I mull over my thoughts. Darling I'm very pleased that you saw your mother and were able to give her the opportunity to redeem herself ["for the terrible hurt she has" CO] Always it is we who have been hurt so badly that are the first to forgive and make amends for the other persons [*sic*] wrong deeds. That my wife is because we are compassionate people and we understand and I must say it is not a sign of weakness but rather confidence in ourselves when we can be so considerate and humane to those who have repented all the ["y" at end of last word CO] harm they've done us. Naturally, just as you say we can't and wont [*sic*] allow ourselves to be used as doormats to be stepped upon. Just as we can't allow ourselves to be used as tools by anyone for political purposes that would [the next word is illegible, it appears from context to be "harm"] the people. I kiss you tenderly with all love of my heart

Always devoted to you — You [*sic*] own Julie

Emanuel H. Bloch
7 W. 16th Street
New York, New York

January 9, 1953

Dear Manny,

It strikes me that Judge Irving R. Kaufman's immortality is at last assured; future generations will ["marvel at" CO, NWI] cite his decision denying us clemency as the epitome of that artful double-talk and intellectual dishonesty so prevalent in the "Age of Hypocrisy." (More conventionally known as the 20th Century), and bestow upon him with refreshing candor, the eminently fitting title of "Master of Sophistry"! ["It strives so hard to impress and fails so dismally." CO]

Full of the most extraordinary inaccuracies and omissions, and the kind of specious reasoning that lends credibility to distortion, [illegible cross out—could be "profoundity to profoundity"] it strains so hard to be profound [NWI] and fails so dismally to be anything but puerile. Striking a pose worthy of Thomashefsky and Barrymore combined, and donning a revoltingly respectable solemnity, calculated to represent himself to the gullible as a saddened but sternly dutiful guardian of the [NWI] nation's "security," he is actually at great pains to conceal the inherent moral bankruptcy of his position. Hence the shrill and officious trumpeting of a pigmy, whose cowardly violation of the true worthiness of the human spirit, must be expiated by the "slaughter of the innocents"!

In this wise, it even becomes necessary to traduce the noble lines of a George Eliot, whose entire life, ironically enough, is a monument to those very ideals a Kaufman sees fit to slander and subvert. [NWI] Surely this is plagiarism on a signally low level; [two illegible cross outs, one above the other] for while it is true that authorship is duly acknowledged, the [NWI] cynical use to which this fine literary ["lion" CO, NWI] expression was put—a use that clearly could never have been intended by a [N2WI] great souled woman who herself rebelled at the falsity that "saves the form while damning the spirit", — such a use, [N2WI] I say constitutes a travesty and a defamation of a very repulsive [illegible word CO, NWI] sort, indeed. [Paragraph sign inserted] Enamored of quotations as the good judge seems, however, I would hazard the guess that a study of the following excerpts from Shaw's "Saint Joan" would not have inclined him to press them into service against the Rosenbergs! As you will recall, John de Stogumber, the English chaplain, who had been one of the most blood-thirsty advocates of Joan's proposed burning, comes rushing in from this "glorious" spectacle overcome with remorse and sobbing like one demented, "You don't know; you haven't seen; it is so easy to talk when you don't know. You madden yourself with words: you damn yourself because it feels grand to throw oil

on the flaming hell of your own temper. But when it is brought home to you: when you see the thing you have done; when it's blinding your eyes, stifling your nostrils, tearing your heart—then then —Oh, God, take this fire that is consuming me—She cried to thee in the midst of it:—Jesus, Jesus. Jesus! She is in thy bosom; and I am in hell for evermore!" And there shall ["shall" CO, NWI] you be, Judge Kaufman, for a crime "worse than murder"!
Ethel—

Julius to Ethel

Jan. 11, 1953

Hello Darling,

Daily I've been thinking of writing a couple of letters on things I read in the newspapers about our case, but with each succeeding day the sheer weight of newsprint used in our case [N2WI] increases & has reached unprecedented proportions [N9WI] that staggers the imagination & causes me to hesitate. This weekend alone each and every newspaper carried extensive news accounts & featured articles on our case. Since they have only presented the prosecution's side of the case in the past the only reason they have to restate and repeat themselves is because they have a difficult convincing job to do. Methinks they protest to [*sic*] much. They are using the old Goebells [*sic*] technique continuous repetition of pronouncements and they hope that this will filter into the minds of the readers but they cannot obscure the record from the public. We have to be thankful to the committee because it is bringing the truth in this case to the public attention. As soon as I finish this letter to you I'm going to write Manny a letter on the press and ask him to see if it is possible to have the metropolitan newspapers print it as an open letter. Since this is the only way we can defend ourselves I'll keep on trying.

Dearest the situation is fraught with danger not only ["to" CO] for us two insignificant individuals but for the safety and security of our countrymen. If there is no reason or sanity left in Washington then in desperation the authorities ["who" CO, NWI] may allow the switch to be pulled on us [N4WI] and who knows if ["may" CO] tomorrow [NWI] they turn around ["throw" CO, "& explode" inserted, then CO, N2WI] & drop an atomic bomb or some other means of mass destruction and set off a world war that would end civilization. It is precisely, because the people realize that [NWI] danger that our case has won such popular ["shr" CO] support in Western Europe, Asia, the Americas and even in our country in spite of the overwhelming press barrage. The cry of communism cannot always work and so the authorities continue to fumble and pile mistake on mistake.

Nonetheless, I sincerely feel our chances to win a commutation of our sentence are better now than ever before but the danger still exists for an adverse decision.

As you would expect I am very lonesome and I miss you very much. When I give myself a chance to think about it I find it hard to remember when I held you last in my arms. We are helpless here while all sort of dirt and harm is done us. I know that in time we will be vindicated but the suffering of the moment is the reality of our situation and it is very difficult to assuage pain from a deep hurt ["simply because" CO] even though we know we are right. That does not mean that we are any the less strong in our determination to win the fight for this just cause. For nothing can change the fact that in truth we are innocent.

The need to spend time with you is very great. If only they did the humane thing of letting us be within talking distance of each other for together we could do a much better job. I still have faith bunny girl and I [NWI] have hopes we [NWI] will live to celebrate our freedom. Always your devoted husband —Julie

Mr. Emanuel H. Bloch
7 W. 16th Street
New York NY

1/12/53

Dear Manny,

The stupendous propaganda campaign against us is reaching unprecedented heights. Why the sheer weight of newsprint staggers the imagination, but it sets one thinking. ["whether" CO] They are doing a selling job. ["because" CO, NWI] Are the authorities are [*sic*] adamant on going through with this madness or is it because they are having a difficult time convincing the public? This weekend alone each and every newspaper carried extensive news stories and feature articles on our case. Now they have presented the prosecutors [*sic*] side of this case only and since they have to repeat and reiterate it so often if shows that they are not meeting with to [*sic*] much success. This is the favorite Goebbels technique continuous repetition of pronouncements that they hope will become to be accepted by the people as the facts. Methinks they protest to [*sic*] much. But they cannot and the [*sic*] must not be allowed to hide the truth, the record of the trial and all the facts in the case.

The only means we have of defending ourselves is to write the facts as they are and we have authorized you to use our letters to make available this information to the public in order for them to know us are [*sic*—probably meant "as"] we really are. We must find some way to break into that impenetrable barrier [N6WI] that keeps our side out of ["the" inserted, then CO] the great newspapers of our country. Experienced and more competent writers than I could do a much better job then I ever hope to be able to do but I must make every effort. Help me all you can dear friend to get this across.

I would like you to prepare with our cooperation an open letter to the American Press answering all the lies and the common misconception ["of" CO, NWI] that the newspapers are feeding the public. We should base it on the trial record and only include such personal items that are of interest & that would present us in our true light.

Since they disseminate public information & news it is there [sic] duty and it is in the interest of fair play that they don't black out our side of the controversy and allow us the opportunity to place paid advertisement in their papers. I'm not naive but I believe it's worth a try. In a short time we'll know the decision of the President that will either doom us or spare our lives and we have a right to insist that in some small measure we be allowed to present our story. It wont [sic] be remiss to show their bias and distortion of the facts in our case.

Always it is the most rabid witch hunters that are leading the pack and driving the weak to silence. It is therefore no mere coincidence that at the hearing before Judge Kaufman and in Jan 9th Victor Riesel column in the Mirror[339] a new line of attack was opened this time against our legal defense, the selfless very competent attorney counselor Emanuel H. Bloch. He is to [sic] effective in defending our rights, exposing the frameup and performing his legal responsibilities [N3WI, illegible cross out between the second and third words] in the highest professional standards of [NWI] legal advocacy in the most ethical and moral way possible. That is the reason for these subtle and dangerous attacks. It is still another step in the tactic—fear, the method—coercion the objective—conformism and orthodoxy

Page # 2

spelling out fascism that brings with it racialism and ["war" CO] leads to war. This is a warning sign and we must be alert to combat this before it deprives people of the chance to defend themselves against charges as is their right under the constitution. The only manner we can maintain our rights is to fight for them.

Obviously the situation is fraught with grave danger. Not only are our two lives in jeprody [sic] of being snuffed out but the safety and security of our fellow countrymen is threatened. If there is no reason or sanity left in Washington then in desperation they may allow the executioner to pull the switch and murder us. Then who knows that tomorrow the authorities may

---

[339]A daily New York newspaper.

turn around drop an atom bomb or some other means of mass destruction and set off a world war that ["would well be" CO] would end civilization. It is precisely because the people are aware of this danger that we have won ["the" CO] such popular support in Western Europe, Asia, the Americas and even in our country, in spite of the overwhelming press barrage of lies and distortions. The cry of Communism is not working and all that they accomplish is to continue to fumble and pile mistake upon mistake.

The need of the hour is vigilance and action to let the government know the true feeling of the people. I sincerely believe our chances have improved to live to fight to prove our innocence but the possibility still exists for an adverse decision. But I remain confident and I continue to hope that we will succeed in our common efforts for this worthy cause.

By the way read Pilat's article on Kaufman in Sat. Post I think you'll find it revealing.

I'll have to close now. They are collecting my pen for the night. See that we receive all the literature on our case. I do hope the committee prints our plea to the president[340] and ["gives it wide circulation" CO] distributes it widely throughout our land.

All my love
Julie

Tell my friends to keep up the good work. They're doing fine. We can win this fight.

[The following letter is only available in typewritten form.]

Julius to David Rosenberg

Jan. 14, 1953

Dearest Brother,

You'll find enclosed a pass for this Sunday morning 10-11 A.M. Please come loaded down with all the latest news.

I want to take this opportunity to express to you, my sister[341] and my mother my everlasting gratitude and profoundest love for you and for your consistent relentless devotion to me and my family and for your tireless efforts in working on our behalf. It is above and beyond what one can expect and it comes of a firm realization and conviction that we are innocent and you who know us best, who've read the facts and experienced shocking

---

[340]This refers to the first petition for executive clemency which is reprinted above.

[341]This must be a typist's error, he had two sisters whose work he appreciated tremendously.

revelations in your dealings with the authorities understand the full enormity of this miscarriage of justice. The body politic in our land is sick. [There is a blank space here, the typist apparently could not read the word from the original] and our case is one of the boils that have come forth as a warning that the infection might spread and become fatal. That is why the good men and women in all walks of life and in every corner of the globe are rallying to our support. Before it is too late and leads to greater madness this political plot must be exposed, fought against and it must be stopped. The first step is to save our lives. Truth is we are winning wider and greater support daily and we are confident that the conscience of the world is with us and we have high hopes that we will live to prove our complete innocence.

But there are very dangerous signs. To one who has read the record and knows the facts the mountainous press campaign of lies and distortion in almost all the metropolitan newspapers will have no effect. However, large numbers of people are misinformed and thousands of others are frightened into inaction. The danger always exists that evil men in their desperation may pull the switch on us. Therefore, there must be no letup in putting the truth before the public. Every effort must be exerted to get the newspapers to print our side, advertisements and letters to the editor. Do not despair because the kept press does not represent American sentiment and above all it is printing a pack of lies. Given the opportunity we can easily expose and demolish them. Again I urge steady and increasing work on our behalf. This is the only way we can win this fight for life.

No matter what the situation is or what happens we must not give up because I sincerely believe we will succeed in our struggle for this worthy cause. When you pause take stock of the great deal of progress we've made in this campaign and you'll notice that it is picking up momentum. Naturally, the enemy will use every conceivable means to discredit us and all those who come to our support but hard facts and the truth can overwhelm vicious slander and distortions. It should be obvious to all now that we were correct in our estimation of the nature of this case as a political frameup and in due time the entire world will be aware of this truth.

The crisis is approaching. Right, decency and love will win out if we fight hard enough for it. We and you, my beloved family, are doing our all. We have won a partial victory. Let us go on to win the battle for truth, justice and principles. This is in the interests and welfare of all mankind and particularly is this true for our country.

As ever—Julie

[The next letters are written in ink.]

Julius to Ethel

Jan 15, 1953

My Darling,

The press is gripped with a frenzy for they are trying to offset the mountainous support we are getting by increasing the lines of newsprint used against us to greater proportions. The Journal American feature writer Bob Considine began a series of articles this last Sunday about us. Wednesday the World Telegram started a series. The [N3WI] rest of the papers chimmed [*sic*] in with Editorials and special articles. Always additional & newer stories are invented to take the place of the weak and unconvincing record that there is in this case. Ethel I read at least seven papers daily and I can truthfully say that they are showing signs of desperation. They are actually pleading with us to save them from complete exposure of this horrible miscarriage of justice. It is they who have pulled off this foul political frameup and now they will feel the full fury of the storm that they helped unleash.

It takes a great deal of strength sitting here facing our doom while such powerful forces are [NWI] in combat deciding our fate. However, our faith in the good people everywhere is more than justified because they have shown by their actions that they will not let this happen here. Every word and line I read I begin to formulate answers immediately but as yet [N2WI] this week I haven't put anything on paper. I think I'll save my say for ["wh" CO] Manny's next visit.

Another thing I've noticed is that my longing for you is increasing. I never though [*sic*] it possible to miss you so much. The pain is very severe. My love for you is overwhelmingly powerful and I continue to draw on it for new strength & [NWI] continued encouragement. Dearest wife there is no greater hurt than being falsely accused and forced to suffer separation from loved ones when all mind and body cries out against this ghastly wrong. It staggers the imagination to think that we could possibly endure such dire hardships which are greatly aggravated because we are completely innocent. Our determination to prove as you've so aptly ["put it" CO, NWI] stated before "the indestructibility of the human being" and to show the power of the dignity of the individual enables us to hold fast to our principles and withstand the mounting pressure. Bunny girl I embrace you with all the love of my heart and adore you with all the love of my mind and although we're apart the emotional and mutal [*sic*] satisfaction you've given [previous word written over "giving"] me in these difficult hours never fails to inspire me and satisfies my greatest need and assuages a great deal of my agony. No man can ask for more from another person even though she be his wife. I do hope we can once again take up our life together because there is so much [N2WI] that is beautiful in our relationship and no matter what happens to us I am happy for the sweet life we've lived together. I never asked for much but I was very lucky to have you and the children and I always got most out of life depending on how much I contributed to advancing the common good. Always devoted to you

Your own Julie.

Mr. Emanuel H. Bloch
7 W. 16th Street
New York NY

Jan. 17, 1953

Dearest Manny,

I am enclosing three of Ethel's letters that I received ["while" CO, NWI] since I've ["been" CO, NWI] come here. They were among my other personal papers. As for myself there are times that I find it difficult to write. Of course you understand it is because there is so much crowding into my mind at once and I can't get it out till I am able to unblock the log jam. Naturally, I'm pretty anxious ["le" CO] to learn the President's decision. It is because I know that it will be decided on [N3WI] the basis of higher government policy that I hope those that support us & decency and right will be successful to ["throw" CO, NWI] tip the balance to our favor. Calm reasoning dictates that it is best for our country that our lives be spared. However, I remain confident while I wait.

In the rush of events I've never been able to tell you the tremendous personal satisfaction I've derived from our relations as two human beings. Permit me to say in all humbleness that I've admired you as a kind sweet principled individual and I am honored that I have won some measure of respect from you for the person that I really am.

I'll have to stop now to make sure that this gets mailed out as soon as possible

As ever Julie

P.S. Ethel is sending you her letters also.

Affectionate regards to all ["my" CO] our friends

Julius to Ethel

Jan. 18, 1953

Hello Bunny,

Just a little reminder that you don't forget to send my brother a Sunday pass. Before I do anything else I want to apologize for being so abrupt when

you suggested arrangements be made for our boys [*sic*] next visit. I guess it
was due to the prevailing tension and the short time we had to consider your
unexpected proposal. What I am saying in no way excuses my conduct and
therefore I want you to know I'm very sorry and I feel bad that I acted in
such haste without thinking. This coming Tuesday we will discuss it
thoroughly and we will let Manny know our proposals for a visit if it is
[NWI] still possible to ["still manage to" CO] arrange one.

Because the time of decision on our executive clemency appeal is close
at hand I find it difficult to properly apply myself to the work I've planned
to do. These are the times dearest that I need you most. I need your
understanding your counsel, your warmth and your love for then I ["am able
to draw" CO, NWI] get my best inspiration that only you have been able to
supply. You know darling death doesn't hold any terror but ["but it is only
(NWI) that what" CO] it signifies a dangerous shift in basic political policy
on the part of the authorities that makes me fearful [N5WI] for the safety &
future ["for" CO] of our loved ones and ["for" CO] all the good people of our
world. It is such a terrible shame that the pen prostitutes are able to write
such outrageous lies about us that shows that nothing is sacred to them and
they can do this because we are defenseless in our present circumstances. In
their zeal to invent grounds to make this case palpable [*sic*—probably meant
to write "palatable"] to the American public they have opened themselves up
for complete exposure. I believe that in due time the complete magnitude of
the frameup and also the part the press played in it, will be brought to the
attention of the people.

It seems to me from the tone the kept press is taking they are appealing
to us to allow ourselves to be used by them as political pawns in their cold
war power struggle. [Over the last word "Don't they" is CO, N21WI] They
ought to know by now innocent people don't succumb to puely [*sic*]
blandishments and we will not let ourselves be used. The important factor
that will mean a great deal when the final determination is being made is
that those who support our plea for commutation clearly understand the
nature of the issues at stake and their sentiments on this matter relating to
the entire political picture is definitely in our favor. However, I never lose
sight of the fact that the authorities may decide to embark on a policy of
outright extermination of political opposition and so doom us. I believe we
are the test case that will either signal ["persistence" CO, N3WI, "blocking"
inserted then CO, N2WI] a stop to fascist encroachments or the open
terroristic acts of a tyrannical regime. We have resolutely stuck to our
principles of devotion to democracy freedom and justice and the peaceful
coexistence of all peoples regardless of forms of government. Since this is
also the wish and hope ["of the" CO] of mankind I have faith they will fight
hard for these goals. So too do I believe that they will succeed in helping

save our lives. Truth is ["the" CO] the sparing of our lives will be in the common good. All my love.

Your own—Julie

This next letter is added to the letter dated October 1952 (see p. 441) concerning the Supreme Court's initial denial of certiorari. It was sent by Ethel to Emanuel Bloch.

January 19, 1953

Much water has flowed under the bridge since I wrote the afore-mentioned words; a national election of unprecedented importance has taken place, the "lesser evil" theory[342] of Thackrey and Stone has been exploded by social forces which they failed utterly to comprehend, but which the Progressives evaluated with truly remarkable accuracy,[343] and the Rosenbergs' calm prediction that the people would refuse to acquiesce in legal murder has been borne out a thousand times over. Here and there a date stands out. My [NWI] personal calendar records that on Wednesday, Dec. 17, 1952, certain duly accredited gentlemen, escorted by the Warden, paid me a visit in order to inquire concerning my health and to determine what my needs might be, short of staying the hand of the executioner, [NWI] (sic!) poised to pull the Switch during the week of January 12! And on Sunday, Dec 21, 1952, I sat quietly in my cell, "listening" to the songs that close to 1000 people were singing in a heavy rain [N3WI] at Ossining Station (although I couldn't actually hear them), [NWI] and feeling a calm, and [NWI] a safety and [NWI] a spiritual bond that no deprivation, no loneliness, no danger, could shatter!

It is now [N2WI] the long-awaited January 20. "Der Tag," Jan 11th, came and went, as did those hectic ones [N4WI] just prior to it when officials of one kind or another were giving us the familiar run around and the scribes were nobly assisting with a campaign of slander that daily assumes the characteristics of the sewer, Sweet essence of putrescence!

There are, however, memories not listed in any calendar, memories of emotions that flashed by, meteor like, in bewildering succession, and that now in retrospect, are so many burned-out stars, identically pale and color-

---

[342]This refers to the practice of leftists who basically disagree with the position of both candidates put up by the two major political parties of voting for the "lesser of two evils."

[343]Progressive here refers to the Independent Progressive Party which in 1948 had run Henry Wallace as an anti-Cold War, save the New Deal candidate, and in 1952 ran Vincent W. Hallinan. See *Encyclopedia of the American Left*, pp. 600–1.

less and forgotten. Again, casting a glance backward over the shoulder of the swiftly speeding present, I remember vividly that each day then seemed to me

(c't'd—Letter # 2—) Ethel

This letter continues on p. 570, dated January 26 from Ethel to Emanuel Bloch.

David Rosenberg
430 E. 63rd Street
New York New York

January 21, 1953

Dear Davy,

Enclosed please find the usual Sunday pass. I had told Julie that he was premature last week but he wasn't taking any chances on losing a visit with you! I saw him this morning and he was in fine spirits as I am myself.

Will look for you on Sunday. In the meantime, please give our best to all—Was so sorry to hear that you had written Julie to the effect that Lena has been quite ill of late. Assure her that if she does not manage to get here on Saturday, we'll understand. Certainly she ought to be completely well before attempting the trip.

Again, all my love—
Ethel

Emanuel H. Bloch
7 W. 16th Street
New York New York

January 21, 1953

Dear Manny,

This is to let you know my mother was here on Monday; the following transpired among other things, which I think may interest you. 1 [circled] I expressed pleasure at seeing her but inquired why she had expended the time and energy [NWI] to travel to Sing Sing (and alone to boot), when she might better have saved some for a trip to see Davy.[344] She begged off, quoting her doctor for support, but when I persisted, suggesting Pullman accommodations as a solution to the problem of her health, and offering to cover all costs, she indicated she might reconsider. I am compelled to add, however, that up to the moment of her departure, there was no definite

---

[344]Ethel's brother, David Greenglass

promise forthcoming. 2 [circled] Re the crate, she insisted she knew nothing whatever about it, but when I confronted her with Bernie's admission concerning same to David Rosenberg and to you, she agreed to talk to him about it. 3 [circled] Now brace yourself for a shock; fact is, I am still in a state of stupefaction over its bold-faced immorality. At one point, while verbalizing the emotional factors she could employ in speaking with Davy, [NWI] I pointed out to her that whatever unfounded fear of reprisal he might be harboring it was my life that was in peril, not his—and further, if I while awaiting electrocution, ["had the courage to" CO] was not afraid to continue to assert my innocence and give the lie to his story, why couldn't he, in a far more advantageous position be man enough to own up at long last, to this lie, and help to save my life, instead of letting it be forfeited to save his face! Our conversation follows, and I quote almost verbatim. Said she, "So what would have been so terrible if you had backed up his story?"—I guess my mouth kind of fell open. "What," I replied, "and take the blame for a crime I never committed, and allow my name, and my husband's, and children's [N2WI] to be blackened to protect him? What, and go along with a story that I knew to be untrue, where it involved my husband and me? Wait a minute, maybe I'm not getting you straight, just what are you driving at?" Believe it or not, she answered, "Yes, you get me straight; I mean even it [*sic*, word "if" omitted here and later] was a lie, [N2WI] all right, so it was a lie, you should have said it was true, anyway! You think that way you would have been sent here? No, if you had agreed that what Davy said was so, even it wasn't, you wouldn't have got this!" I protested, shocked as I could be, "But, Ma, would you have had me willingly commit perjury?" She shrugged her shoulders indifferently and maintained doggedly, "You wouldn't be here!"

I intend speaking to David Rosenberg about all this when he gets here on Sunday; under the circumstances, I don't feel I should offer you ["a" CO, NWI] the gross insult ["by" CO, NWI] of asking you to get in touch with her, yourself!

Is it possible for you to make arrangements to bring the children up here Saturday morning, Jan. 31st? Please be very good to me, Manny, and try to let Dave know, at least tentatively, or have one of the girls write me just as soon as you know, definitely. Incidentally, it happens to be the very best day for me, because my nemesis who is with me, unfortunately, during the afternoons for the next $2^1/2$ weeks, won't be around that week-end at all. Julie and I are both agreed we must see them, even if clemency is denied us—so bend every effort you can dear, to get them here Sat. morning [NWI]

Jan. 31st ["Also, if" CO] Only caution Ben not to tell them until a day or so in advance—Mike will get all tensed up otherwise! Love—Ethel—other letters in the make! [*sic*]

Mr. David Rosenberg
430 E. 63rd Street
New York NY

January 21, 1953

Dear Dave,

I'm enclosing a pass for Sunday morning from 10-11AM. I was terribly distressed to learn that my beloved sister Lena was so ill. Please ["tell" CO, NWI] give her my best wishes for an early recovery also what does she mean taking time out to get sick when her precious help is needed at this crucial time to save our lives. Since I know she understands this I'm sure she'll be up and working hard very soon. All kidding aside it is most important to us that she be healthy and well. For our sake please take care.

Incidentally, brother please send all our letters to Manny after they've been read by the family as we want him to collect them all for safekeeping.

As we've anticipated the Truman government has passed the "hot potato" they've brought forth to the ["new" CO] President Eisenhower.[345] The situation is very delicate and since the decision as to whether we live or not will be based on higher policy of this new administration it is more imperative than ever that the sentiments of the American people be made known to the new executive of our government. Now is the time to revisit prominent people, men and women of influence and to get a maximum number of individuals and organizations to ask for clemency. The next few weeks will decide our fate.

You see that this case is finally being decided as it was at every stage of the court proceeding by political considerations and not on the merits as they are set forth in the trial record. To you, our family and those familiar with all that has taken place this has been very revealing. Only when all the details are fully known does the enormity of the miscarriage of justice become obvious. This you must promise me that you'll never stop bringing the facts to the attention of all who want to be informed and then I am confident that our name will be cleared and we will win complete vindi-cation. As time goes on we will be able to unravel more of the hidden riddles of the frameup and our innocence will then be proven. Again at this late hour I must reassert, with all the emphasis I possess, that we are completely innocent. Isn't it fantastic how spurious espionage charges,

---

[345]Truman left office without acting on the clemency petitions.

unsubstantiated by documentary evidence, uncorroborated by independent witnesses has been snowballed ["into" CO] from a weak empty case as it appears in the record into a big lie based on judicial pronouncements, surrounded by political propaganda and fed to the public in a gigantic press campaign to justify the brutal sentence and the shame on American justice known as the Rosenberg case.

Truth must win out and we are not surrendering to fear & cajoling nor do we abandon our principles of democracy, decency, right and justice. We sincerely believe that we will again be reunited with our darling boys and live [N2WI] once more as the happy family we've been before the catastrophe befell us.—We await the decision with courage, confidence & pespective [*sic*].

All my love—Julie

P.S. Tell Manny to make arrangements for an early visit by our children. Ethel will let him know when it's best for them to come.

Michael & Robert Rosenberg
c/o B. Bach
R.D. 2 Box 148M
Tom's River New Jersey

January 22, 1953

My own dear sweethearts,

All this time, I've been feeling so badly for my seeming neglect of you; actually, I've been working hard for all of us, thinking through ideas, discussing them with Daddy, with Mr. Bloch and other people, making notes for possible use in the future, and composing letters of one sort or another. As a matter of fact, so busy have I been scribbling, that I don't spend as many hours as I should like, on reading, a very important occupation, incidentally, for anyone who wishes to express himself on paper. How many valuable thoughts and feelings my reading has stimulated would be difficult to estimate; eventually my reactions to the printed word somehow find their way out [illegible two letter word CO, NWI] in my own written ones.

Do you know how I started this letter? I was completely absorbed with another one I had been composing for some days, and had promised myself time out to write my boys just as soon as I had it done. I had arrived at the following sentence, "And to my children I sent a charming, light-hearted, little poem by way of Chanukah greeting,"[346] when I suddenly decided I couldn't wait another minute! All at once the sentence had whisked you

---

[346]See below, p. 570.

straight into my presence and I was hugging you tight and not letting you go, and wetting your dear faces with my kisses and tears!

So now that you are here, let's visit a while—a little while, anyway. And if for any reason, I have to cut our visit short, at least ["you" CO, NWI] we will ["know it is only a" CO, N4WI] have had a brief one, preliminary ["one" CO] to a really nice, long one. Actually, I guess I'm writing because I got such a hankering to say "hullo," to say "I miss you," to say "I love you"! And also to assure you how keenly aware I am of all your problems and difficulties and longings, and how much I want us all to-gether again! So often have I reflected on our intolerable situation and wondered what wise thing to impart, what comforting word, to ease the hurt to lessen the anxiety, to bridge the separation. Somehow, things got kind of disorganized during our last get to-gether, and I didn't feel [NWI] quite as satisfied as usual. Already I am laying plans for another visit, [NWI] however, and am determined it shall be less hectic and more enjoyable.

I shall want to hear more about all your activities, and we'll spend more time singing and chewing the fat, and just plain relaxing. Mike dear, if I didn't get it across to you before, I'd like you to know specially that your Hebrew lettering is just about perfect. Both Daddy and I are thrilled at your progress along these lines and are ever so glad you have been able to continue studying the piano. My darling Robbie, I have followed your instructions [N3WI] to the letter, not to blow my nose into your beautiful "present" handkerchief. I use it only when I wear a pretty dress for a visit and then I fold it carefully away in your "present" envelope!

Another letter shall somehow follow this one before too long, I promise.—In the meantime, my very best to dear Sonia and Ben—My heart is full because I know you are loved in our absence. xxxxxxxxxxx—from Mommy & Daddy—

Julius to Ethel

January 22, 1953

Sweetheart,

As I sit and write this letter my mind is full of thoughts about you and I'm anxiously anticipating our big hour together tomorrow morning. Silly of me to say this for by the time you receive this epistle we'll be looking forward to our next get together. ["I never stop to marvel" CO, N4WI] How marvellous it is ["is" CO] that we are able to pack so much living in our brief tete a tete and we continue to find an endless source of strength and encouragement from each other that carries over to our next visit. This I feel is due to the fact that our love is based firmly on reality and our individual dedication both for personal and for social advancement for the common good has welded our relationship in dignity and rectitude that we are able to stand with honor and struggle in this principled way in defense of our rights and our innocence. Truth possessed by people with these simple virtues is all powerful especially is this so when there is a conviction to work for justice and a determination to guard the cherished liberties of all human beings. The sincerity of the substance of ones thoughts put in words makes beautiful harmony to my ears when it strikes [NWI] such a cordent [*sic*] note with the high ethical and moral standards of enlightened people.

This brings me to another observation perhaps because I read about eight newspapers daily it is easy for me to discern the way the propaganda is turned on and off like a faucet not only in our case but in all matters foreign and domestic reported as "facts" in the "free" press. Verily, our background, understanding and perception—has equipped us well to glean the truth from the mass of confusion and distortion put out to control the minds of men. It is unfortunate that only once a week we have access to the clear thinking and poignant facts of what is taking place in the world when we read the National Guardian. The effectiveness of this potent weapon in behalf of mankind is [N2WI] once again attested to by the great mass movement of millions that have rallied to our support which this progressive weekly initiated by bringing to public attention the Rosenberg case. The peoples of the world grasped the full significance of the issues involved in terms of their own needs and are acting to see that justice is done. The great interplay of world forces is the politics of this situation and will determine both the immediate issue of our lives and the ultimate answer to the questions raised in this case. I am confident whatever the outcome may be, for to fight for a just cause is a victory in itself.

Ethel unblievable [*sic*] as this fabulous lie is the authorities continue to press this hoax on the public and it is natural that we be concerned about our safety. However, we must [NWI] relentlessly ["press" CO, NWI] expose the frameup with truth and we will continue to gain more supporters. Of course, it is hard for us isolated from the world we know and the people whom we love to feel the temper of the times but we're managing to keep our feet planted firmly on solid ground.

Oh if the good men and women everywhere knew how terribly we are suffering because we dare to challenge evil and tyranny with decency and truth, they would ["stop this" CO] put a stop to this cruety [*sic*] and insanity— Courage my heart— Always your own—Julie

Emanuel H. Bloch
7 W. 16th Street
New York New York

January 24, 1953

Dear Manny,

The following is a poem you may recall my having mentioned in our last consultation. I am self-conscious about it, myself, but Julie was much moved and insisted I send it to you. So here goes: (Incidentally, the last stanza was written after I had already read him what I thought was the complete presentation.)

1 If We Die

You shall know, my sons, shall know
Why we leave the song unsung
The book unread the work undone
To lie beneath the sod.

Mourn no more, my sons, no more
Why the lies and smears were framed
The tears we shed, the hurt we bore
To all shall be proclaimed.

Earth shall smile, my sons, shall smile
And green above our resting place
The killing end, the world rejoice
In brotherhood and peace.

Work and build, my sons, and build
A monument to love and joy
To human worth, to faith we kept
For you, my sons, for you!

I hope it's some good. Am in the process of completing another letter to you, so keep your eyes peeled for it. It will take 2 letter-heads. Am very well and in pretty good spirits—Very much pleased that I managed to get a nice letter (Julie says so) out to the kids. Please do let me know about Saturday, Jan 31st, huh?

Love,
Ethel

P.S.—To read poem [NWI] with proper rhythm [NWI] meter is 4-4-4-3 in every verse.

Mrs. Lena Cohen
140 Baruch Place
New York N.Y.

Jan. 25, 1953

Dear Lee,

I was greatly grieved to learn from our brother Dave that you've been so ill. I should have suspected something was amiss when you did not put in your usual appearance at your visiting turn. Yes the callous actions of the authorities and their seemingly [*sic*] violation of everything moral and ethical shocks the sense of decency and outrageous [*sic*—probably meant "outrages"] all principles of justice. They have visited great hardships on our family and have hurt us deeply. It was only natural and human that my beloved family would pitch in to the limit to help their own flesh and blood particularly when right was completely on our side.

To [*sic*] often sweet sister although the mind and the heart is very willing and capable the physical body cannot stand the terrible strain. Please darling Lee for our sake take it easy and get well. Your family needs you and we need you. You've done more than enough and you can be most effective by easing our minds of an [*sic*] further anxiety. I'm going to keep in touch with our lawyer and family to asertain [*sic*] that you are recuperating satisfactorily.

Daily we are receiving growing support and we are thriving with each succeeding report of good news. Also we are well physically and mentally and are contributing our share in this noble cause.

You see as we have told you from the beginning that many people will rally to our support until ["it" CO, N4WI] as it surely will reach ["es" CO] multitude proportions. The truth must win out and large numbers of people are becoming convinced of our innocence. We had faith that once the people learn the facts they will see the nature of the political frameup perpetrated against two innocent Americans. The lieing [*sic*] campaign against us grows in volume and fury because they are being exposed and the truth is very painful for evil men bent on tyranny. We are confident and feel strong and I sincerely wish and hope from the bottom of my heart that you recover ["y" CO at end of last word] quickly and we can have the pleasure to see you soon again.

Tell Melvin that experience and knowledge will make it easier for him to take all problems in his stride. Self confidence comes from an objective understanding of ones faculties and a true perspective of each situation we meet in life. I'm rooting for my nephew and from what I know about him I am sure he'll succeed in his studies. Good luck and keep at it.[347]

---

[347]Lena's son was studying to be a pharmacist.

Don't forget to give Linda a big hug and a kiss for me and if you have pictures of them bring it up and let me take a look. It's been a long time and I want to be able to recognize them.

Send my best regards to Julius.[348]

You've made me very proud of you Lena and I've never loved you more. I'm thinking about you and I hope to hear good news about you— Always your kid brother whom you used to pinch—

Julie

Julius to Ethel

Jan. 25, 1953

Dearest Ethel,

I was terribly shocked to learn that Lena was so ill and I am glad she's getting better. I just finished a letter to her & I hope it encourages her and speeds her to an early recovery. Honey, the beasts are continuing to mark our family with very deep hurts. We'll just have to fight harder to insure an early victory.

The news my brother brought was splendid and I hope they get to send us copies of all this wonderful stuff. I can't understand what could be holding up the printed material Manny promised to send us. It is splendid to see that clear headed thinkers don't scare easily for they are fully cognizant of the lessons of history and armed with the facts cannot be stampeded by wild hysteria generated to give political advantage to [N4WI] those who wish to fan the cold war into a big hot one.

I read your letter [N7WI] that was printed in the National Guardian a number of times and I must say you did an excellent job taking the judge to task. I guess we'll never be able to measure how effective we've been in aidding [*sic*] our own cause especially since people see us in a true light. But I am sure that we've done a great deal to help ourselves and lend courage to thousands of people everywhere to have faith in themselves and stand us [*sic*—probably meant "up"] to be counted for peace, freedom and liberty. It is because their plans have backfired that the kept press is putting up such a frenzied campaign of lies against us. I am not concerned about them for I am sure they don't represent the real sentiments of the American people. Yes they can confuse and they immobilize many people who would otherwise act but I still feel we'll overcome this handicap. The job is big and must be done and the committee is doing it. Incidentally when next you write don't fail to remind them to send us the printed literature about the case. All they can possibly send us it is good for our morale.

---

[348]Lena's husband

I hope you've made all the necessary arrangements for the childrens [*sic*] visit and ["made sure" CO, N3WI] seen to it that Ethel's visit will not conflict with it. It is almost 10:00 P.M. and I'm rushing this letter to make the deadline.

Due to the short time of our visit today I didn't get to go into the things I wanted to with Dave. For some reason had to wait 25 minutes until the bus brought him down and we just touched on a few highlights. He seemed to be in very good spirits.

I'm beginning to think about our boys [*sic*] next visit and we'll talk about it when I see you. Truth is I'm very anxious to see our precious darlings and I'm sure we'll have a good visit. Sweetheart I love those boys of ours so much and I want so to be home with them. For more than 2 1/2 years of their young ["life" CO, NWI] lives ["and" CO] we've been torn away from them and nothing can completely heal this pain unless we are reunited and live together in happiness secure in our love. For them and all that is beautiful we can suffer in this way— Always devoted to you
Your Julie

Mr. Emanuel H. Bloch
7 W. 16th Street
New York NY
        Jan 26, 1953 [the second number in the date is either a "6" or a "5"]
Dear Manny,

I have a couple of minutes for a short note. Please send us as much of the printed literature the committee has put out as is possible. It is imperative that we have this encouraging stuff available to us to help our morale. Its been weeks now since we've received one piece of printed matter.

The howlings in the kept press don't affect me in the least I know them for what they are worth and I am sure they don't represent the facts as they are happening or the true sentiments of the American people.

I'm confident and feeling fine and I'm anticipating our next visit with our children. Please keep well. Find out how my sister Lena is feeling before you come up to see us next time.

It is impossible for us to acknowledge all the support we've gotten but I think it a good idea for you to contact certain people on our behalf and let them know how we feel.

Send my best wishes to all our friends.

                                                                    Julie
[Following post-script is in pencil]
P.S. That wife of mine is sure wonderful. A real treasure and can she write. We just have to win Manny I love her so much.

[Letter continues in pen] (over)
If an extra copy of our petition is available send one for the two of us. (The Appeal for executive clemency.)

Emanuel H. Bloch
7 W. 16th Street
New York New York

January 26, 1953

Dear Manny, Letter # 2 (c't'd) from #1—349
to be stretching out long and endless and golden with promise. I wrote my husband, "The battle rages, but I am serene!" And to my children, I sent a charming, light-hearted little poem [N5WI] clipped from the Sunday Times by way of Chanukah Greeting.

All, all past, and decision close at hand; for us, sitting here and fighting for breath [illegible CO here] in an ever narrowing circle of tightening time, it looms large and unknown, color-blurred and shape-less upon the gigantic canvas of a furious age. And yet, essentially, it is a simple decision, predicated as it is upon a few simple propositions.

1 [circled] Whatever the merits of the case, millions of people throughout the world today, [NWI] numbering among them some of the most outstanding figures of our times, view the refusal of the courts to grant [illegible CO, N2WI] the Rosenbergs relief as an affirmation of the [two illegible words CO, followed by "of the Rosenbergs and their outspokenly expressed" CO, followed by an illegible word CO, NWI] couple's insistence [NWI] unshaken after nearly two years in the death-house, that they are political victims of the cold-war. Accordingly, these millions have registered the most vigorous kind of opposition to the sentence.

2 [circled] The enormity of this protest, indeed the very fact of its existence, so clearly expresses the political nature of the case, that it has forced a desperate attempt in certain quarters either to minimize it by exaggerating the importance of our detractors, or to write the whole thing off as a "Communist plot"! The feverish activity of the columniators [*sic*] whether of the "Journal American" scavenger variety or the politically respectable, white-washing ACLU liberal stripe, points a) to a recognition of the validity of the campaign on our behalf and (b) to an uncertainty and an indecision on the part of the Government that [illegible word CO, NWI] poses the pivotal question, ["the heart of the matter, as it were, to be thrown into sharp relief" CO] to wit: "shall ruling authority permit itself the right to coerce citizens ["under penalty of death to plead guilty" CO, "our"

349See above, p. 560.

inserted, then CO, N8WI] to plead guilty on pain of death even when they staunchly defend their innocence and [illegible word inserted, then CO] to do ["otherwise" CO, NWI] so were to deny alike conscience and truth simply because assertion of innocence in face of such coercion, exposes ["it" CO, N2WI] said authority to the wide-spread condemnation of all decent humanity?"

3 [circled] Thus, while the entire world storms, thunders, exhorts and pleads, we are witnessing the ["most" CO] astounding spectacle of the most powerful nation on earth bound, helpless, powerless to reverse itself because it is always so much easier to commit new errors, than [NWI] to right old ["wrong" CO] ones!

4 [circled] Boiling this down to simpler even ludicrous terms, I ask in all seriousness, "Is it worth forfeiting two warm, young lives, about whose guilt [N3WI] the world says there is reasonable doubt, ["(if for no other reason than the maintenance of innocence in the shadow of the electric chair [N5WI] & threatens so many others)"CO] to save the face of the United States?"

[she filled the line with dashes]

As I have already stated, it is a remarkably simple decision, for all the hysteria that is being deliberately fomented, for to "lose face" by granting clemency to the Rosenbergs is to demonstrate in the most palpable manner

c't'd—Letter # 3 Ethel

Emanuel H. Bloch
7 W. 16th Street
New York New York

                                                        January 26, 1953
["possible" CO] Dear Manny, Letter # 3 (c't'd) from #2

possible that Justice is something more than a ruthless treadmill, which once set upon a certain course must like some horrible Frankenstein, grow stronger than the controlling hand upon its throttle and run [NWI] blindly amuck!

[another line of dashes]

We wait in the dimness of gathering doom! We wait and we hope and we do not lose faith that the sun still shines in this land of our birth—this "Sweet land of liberty"—this America!

Ethel

P.S. Re the letter I sent with the poem, you will note when you receive it that the version I read [NWI] to Davy [NWI] Rosenberg has a last line that is different. Please note this change, accordingly, on the original—Oke? [sic]

Julius to Ethel

Jan. 29, 1953

Dearest Beloved,

It is almost 8:00 PM now and since 2:30 PM when I received Manny's letter and the printed material that the "Committee to Secure Justice" has published, I've been in a dither thrilled by such spiritual and emotional encouragement as only this type of positive evidence, of increasing support in our behalf, can satisfy me, ["one who" CO] and as you know I am one who is firmly enamored of reality and objective facts. Our counselor's insight, keeness [*sic*] and clarity warms my scientific heart. ["and" CO] His warmth, sincerity and humaness [*sic*] touches me deeply. ["and" CO] His high encomiums of us is [*sic*] the greatest tribute that we've received particularly because of [illegible word CO, illegible word inserted, then CO, N2WI] of his noble dignity as a person and the high calibre of his character.

Indeed we are honored and we accept his high regard with humility. This is singular proof that humble people everywhere have the inherent means to strive for and bring into being a better rich life for all mankind. Death only becomes more horrible and [NWI] positively final when there goes hand in hand with it a destruction of the principles we hold dear for the advancement of humanity. The essence of our strenght [*sic*] is a solid premise based on truth of the laws of human ["and" CO] nature and social relations, a life devoted and dedicated to follow and enhance these always guided by the principles and a clear political perspective of where ["you" CO, NWI] we are heading.

Of course, the deep love I feel for you Ethel and the splendid relationship we have always ["had" inserted then CO, "followed" CO, NWI] shared by practicing in all our activities our precepts of this good life.

I believe we have won the understanding of the world because they are themselves in us. Yes we are plain ordinary man and wife but we are very sensitive people very compassionate to the needs of our fellow men [N6WI] and at one with them in ["to" CO] their hopes and aspirations [N4WI] and in the struggle ["for" inserted, then CO] for peace, liberty and freedom.

Already my mind is beginning to percolate again and after I visit you tomorrow I'll take pen in hand once again and put my thoughts on paper. Because we consider it a duty and a responsibility to others we want to prevent them, thousands of innocent men and women like us from facing ["such" CO, NWI] similar danger and save them [NWI] even as we are fighting to save ourselves from the terrible suffering that have been visited on us.

To you my charming woman belongs a great deal of the credit for the kind of Rosenberg family we are. One can acknowledge someone else's virtues, remain humble and still be cognizant of his own attributes and worthwhileness. It is imperative to know one's self both good and bad and to strive ["to" CO] at all time [*sic*] to improve. Then an individual can meet problems with confidence.

I'll spend the rest of the evening rereading the literature that came today. This kind of liason [*sic*] with the world we cherish is most important for our morale. Darling as your devoted husband, man of flesh and blood, I press you close and love you with all the ["fire" CO, NWI] fire and passion of my heart and soul. Always your own—

Julie

Emanuel H. Bloch
7 W. 16th Street
New York New York

January 29, 1953

Dearest Manny,

I hasten to re-assure you concerning the children's visit; what's more I feel like one awful dope not to have surmised before this that only important activity on our behalf could have decided you not to bring them on the day I had specifically mentioned. In view of your plan to see us one day next week [NWI] however (as per your letter of the 28th) ["however" CO, NWI] I hesitate to press for February 7th unless you wish to hold off our legal consultation until some time after their visit with us. If, however, you would definitely prefer to consult with us at some length prior to bringing the children at some future date, it might be wise to wait to see them, particularly since I'll need a little time to set the situation up properly, as per the explanation I set forth to you in my last communique.

Friday, Jan. 30/53

This very morning I saw Julie, just as I figured, he'd rather you came as soon as possible and make more definite plans for the kids, when you arrive. Tuesday is particularly good, since I see Julie until 10:00 A.M. and am already dressed and ready for another visit, (even if I don't know in advance that you're due), but Wednesday or Friday will do as well, if it must. In any case, Ethel will phone you and you will then be good enough to tell her when we may look for you and she will so notify us. Oke?

And now to your letters which I have read avidly perhaps half a dozen times or more. It came just in time to pick me up out of the dismal dreariness that is an inescapable by-product of solitary confinement. Not that you are mistaken about my good spirits; it so happens that I actually am maintaining a fairly consistent degree of confidence and strength. That, however, presents no ["stumbling block" CO, N2WI] serious obstacle to the poor, foolish palpitant heart that will not listen to reason and that hungers and thirsts for the [illegible word CO, N2WI] true gratification ["only worthwhile" CO, N2WI] of creative human exchange ["possible" CO]; nor does it deter the [two illegible words CO, "this" CO, three short illegible words inserted then CO, illegible word CO, "accommodations" CO, N5WI] grim fact of an endless gray monotony ["of accumulating thin [*sic*]" CO] of an existence!

May I thank you for all the affection and understanding and generosity; ["that" CO, NWI] it touched me somewhere away [NWI] down deep inside and ["made me cry" CO, NWI] brought the tears in a spontaneous rush of sheer ["happy feeling" CO, N2WI] sweet happiness. After a childhood of warping bitter cold, you see, such warm, fulsome praise ["touched off" CO, NWI] causes a rather intense emotional reaction and moves me to the most profound [N2WI] feelings of humility and gratitude. I am the more exercised, therefore, about the cowardly attacks upon your integrity and good faith. Until we see you and can properly discuss this matter among others, suffice it to say—and all the yapping cur-dogs [illegible letter CO] can make what they will of it—my husband and I shall die innocent before we lower ourselves to live guilty. And nobody, not even you, whom we continue to love and extol as our own true brother, can dictate terms to the Rosenbergs, who follow only the dictates of heart and soul, [NWI] truth and conscience, and the God-blessed love we bear our fellows!
Ethel

Mr. Emanuel H. Bloch Esq.
7 W. 16th Street
New York N.Y.

                                                    Jan. 30th, 1953
                            I
Dearest Manny,
    Yesterday a little after 2:30 P.M. your letter and a ["paquet" CO] package of printed matter put out by the Committee to Secure Justice in the Rosenberg Case arrived. It just happened to be my turn to exercise in the yard. Rain or shine snow and freezing winds have as yet never dettered [*sic*] me from seeking the freedom of the cold bleek [*sic*] yard for ["m" CO] the gloom of my solitary cell. For the fresh breath of air that expands my lungs always sets my spirits soaring and with my face pointed upward my eyes eagerly seek signs of life in the skies; birds, and airplane flying under a ["carpet" CO, NWI] layer of cirous [*sic*] clouds, that mother nature has carpeted the heavanly [*sic*] expanse, hidding [*sic*] the vastness and depths of an endless universe and as my feet measure the short perimeter of the walk and

.y shoulders brush the high walls that confine the small area as I make the 'sh" CO] right angle turns, the rhythm of of [*sic*] all this sets my mind working and my thoughts run the gamut of big and little things social and personal items for I am alive and my mind and soul are not ["shackled" CO, N3WI] and cannot be imprisoned.

You can well realize the importance I put on this exercise period. This time with the literature under my arm and your letter held in front of me I slowly circled ["the" CO] around reading while a light snow fell. I was thrilled by your spirited letter and the excitement engendered coupled with the cold air to chill the marrow of my bones and caused my hands to shake. I continued to shuffle along, gritted my teeth [N3WI] to contain myself as I avidly read through the ["multi" CO] material but the excitement was too much and for the first time I cut my stay outdoors and went to my lonely cell but now it ["was removed" CO, N2WI] had changed from it's [*sic*] former character and it was full of you ["this indicates that we are not alone" inserted, then CO] and the living reality of people participating in the turbulent problems of our day very specifically the affair [a hyphen is CO, N2WI] known as the Rosenberg case. There is cheer because [N2WI] in fact we are not alone. For a ["time" CO, NWI] while the deep suffering and pain that has been visited on us is ["obscured" CO] forgotten though it cannot be removed and always we seek complete relief as is due us in all justice.

I spent the entire evening rereading all these papers a number of times and then I sent my adorable Ethel her usual Thursday night letter. Since I've been here twice a week I've felt the need to send these communications to my wife. My love for her demands it and it [NWI] also serves to help her maintain a high degree of morale & in this ["for her to" CO, N3WI] way she can give free reign [*sic*] to her literary gifts. You understand how encompassed we are physically and mentally and the buffeting we've taken tends to fatigue [N4WI] us as it would ["was" inserted then CO, "the" CO, N2WI] any other individuals and just as your words to us are very uplifting we find that encouraging it is very ["important" CO, NWI] necessary especially is this so when praise has [illegible letter inserted, then CO] been earned. You see dear friend even in this horrible place we've established a good ["raport" CO] relationship to help one another and it is good to get comfort from a compassionate world.

You are a very fine observer but do not for one moment think that my changes in mood represents a lowering of spirits. On the contrary, it is that I feel so confident that I am a bit worried that we'll be kicked in the teeth again as we've [NWI] already experienced in all our [NWI] other court actions. Truth is, reason ["and" CO] facts, precedents

Page # 2

the good name of our country and it's [NWI] very interest will best be serve
if our lives are spared but I guess I'm ["beginning" inserted, then CO]
overcompensating for my confidence. ["I gu" CO] This may sound a bit
screwy but believe me I'm very relaxed, reading [N3WI] now it is a book of
Theatrre [*sic*] Guild plays and taking it easy. I've had many urges to write
the past two weeks but I must confess that I've been to [*sic*] indulgent with
myself and I am well aware that I ["'ve of" CO] consider ["my" CO] it my
duty and responsibility to the people to put my thoughts on paper. Your
letter has sparked me again and I'll try to do my best.

You know me well enough by ["now" CO, N2WI] this date and, ["it
seems to me that" CO] I am fully cognizant of my capabilities, both ["good"
CO, "in" inserted, then CO, N3WI] strong and weak points and I'm always
trying to improve myself and even if I say so myself I believe I'm a [NWI]
pretty level headed sort of a guy.

Again I want to thank you for your very kind expressions about Ethel
and me, I'm overwhelmed with emotion and I pledge to you and the
millions of others like you who have taken us to heart and mind that I will
["never betray me" CO] always fight for these principles that mean [N4WI]
everything to us and so much for the common weal.

It's only a short time ago that June 1950 that we met and I subsequently prevailed upon you to be our attorney and in fact you agreed and
upon my arrest ["you agreed" CO] I hired you as my counsel. Because the
plain truth is that we are completely innocent we have fought this case from
the very beginning [N3WI] in this manner. At all time the decision was ours
and you only advised us of our rights and defended us legally.[350] This is the
only way ["we" CO, N4WI] the three of us would have [At this point and at
other points in this letter, some editor was crossing out and changing the
writing. I can tell where this is happening because of the color of the ink
and the difference in the handwriting. I have not indicated those editorial
changes, but here, the crossing out and editing combined with our father's
own editing makes the intention he had a bit difficult to follow. The best
guess I can make is that he meant to write as follows:] in spite of the high
regard we have for you. ["and" CO] As a lawyer you have done honor to your
profession and as our advocate, you have acquitted yourself nobly[.] Your
conduct and demeanor in all court proceedings was exemplary in fact twice
the court passed complimentary comments on your abilities and performance
in this case. The scurrilous accusations the snide remarks now raised against

---

[350]This sentence and some indications in our mother's letter of January 29 are in
reaction to newspaper accounts that one or both of our parents were willing to
"cooperate" but that their lawyer was holding them back.

you is conduct [NWI] only befitting scoundrels [N8WI] that might be expected of the likes of ["of" CO] the lowest dregs of society. How dare they stoop to this infamy. No filth they throw can ever stain so distinguished a legal career of the highest profession [N2WI] & ethical standards [N2WI] as yours nor can they besmirch your impeccable character for they dwell in their [NWI] own slime ["they" CO] and they can't [N3WI] ever hope to reach you. Because it is you who hold us in such high ["regard we treasure" CO, NWI] esteem your warm sentiments [NWI] mean all the more to us and we treasure them. We feel very humble and consider ourselves deeply honored and we mean to give the plain decent ordinary men and women added cause to find in themselves, even as we have in ourselves, ["greater resources and new res" CO] a reservoir of great strenght [*sic*] to work for good causes and fight for right. This then builds the human being and gives him real worth.

Now his nibs Judge Kaufman among other [next word illegible, looks like "wordl" or "worel" which could be an attempt to write "world"] judicial ["precedents" CO] acts ["of his" CO] has in his unctuous sorcery, the pronouncement denying us clemency, stressed the fact we did not follow the Greenglasses [*sic*] example and this is [N8WI] the new twist in the campaign against us ["a" CO] being parrated [*sic*] by a certain circle of so called liberals, false friends of ours, ["tha" CO] who are wailing "confess" to save yourselves. Gentlemen, the last word

Page #3

in the sentence is wrong you mean to say "confess" to save ["you" CO, NWI] us. This is to there [*sic*] benefit for Saypol, Lane and Kaufman have used our bodies as stepping stones to personal glorification and power and want us to ["hide" CO, NWI] shield these perverters of justice. No we will not bail out these morally bankrupt people and ethical degenerates who are so wedded to the cold war that they are devoid of all reason and blind to the truth. You have condemned us though we are innocent. You have crucified us to serve your political interests. But you will never succeed [N3WI] even in death to torture a "confession" from us nor coerce us to admit guilt for a crime we've never committed. We will not go along with this big lie. They have created this Frankenstein miscarriage of justice and the world insists that this barbaric sentence must not be carried out and then we will have an opportunity to prove our innocence and erase the shame on the good name of our country.

At this moment there is a lull and many great political decisions are in the making. It is not easy to know that our fate will depend on higher policy [N3WI] of our government but we are hopeful that the support we have gotten will shift ["it" CO, N3WI] the decision to ["the side be" CO, N2WI] one that is [last word written over an illegible word] favorable ["one" inserted, then CO, "for" CO, NWI] to us and in so doing be [N2WI] in fact based on the [NWI] whole truth.

Understanding and deep feelings are a hard task master and because ["y" CO] we love life so much the agony [N4WI] we are going through is very difficult [N2WI] on us. It is very hard for those who don't experience it to comprehend what a sensitive person like myself goes through, who sees my wife caged like an animal, whom I can't ["care" CO, NWI] even caress to give some comfort, to assuage the terror this beloved women of ["my" CO] mine faces when the motherly instincts and longings for the babes she bore refused to be denied, ["that" CO, NWI] when the conscience and civilization is outraged by evil men who would brutally voilate [*sic*] this most sacred birthright of all mankind, when all the time I know she is only guilty of having a snake for a brother, of being married to me, of being devoted to family, children, society and beauty. For this facing death. This type of horror and torture that we are face to face with must be fought and done away with before many thousands of other innocent parents and individuals find themselves [NWI] similarly engulfed by monstrous tidal waves [NWI] coming in the wake of political expediency.

Our sons are normal children and until this catastrophe befell their parents they were just like any other boys and girls of the same age in your neighborhood. Now they come to us, they ask, they tell us and they demand that we come home. This is their right. Heaven knows we should be reunited at home with them. We are ["hopeless only" CO] incapable of acceding to them [N5WI] much as we want to and we [NWI] therefore turn to you the public who have it in your power, to give Michael and Robert back their mother and father. As we with every fibre of our bodies work to secure justice for ourselves I am confident that the people with ["you" CO, NWI] their heart and mind will support us.

There are many wonderful people who have spoken out and joined the growing numbers that are working to save our lives. I was particularly moved when I read that the Rev. H.S. Williamson delivered a prayer for our lives. As long as it is honest and sincere we welcome it and are eternally grateful for humanistic expressions in our behalf—As ever Julie

Page #4   Jan 31st, 1953

It is Saturday morning. The death house barber is giving us our shaves and I am anticipating with delight the visit today of my sweet sister. She always brings news of the family, our children and what is happening in the world. Our mutual devotion and love with my family is always a source of pleasure and adds to our strength. It has been consistent and if anything their activity on our behalf has increased. They, too, need support and help to face the fury of the storm.

I just happened to be thinking of our Saturdays of the long ago. They seem so far away I've almost forgotten them. This was my day out with Michael and Robert while Ethel took care of her personal needs, shopped etc. Usually we'd pick out a trip that required every means of ["vehicule" CO] transportation street cars, buses, trains and if possible a ferry ride. We'd leave in the morning with a bag of lunch, ["a couple of balls and a" CO] a baseball and bat. Sometimes I'd take along a couple of their friends and borrow a camera and we were off to a park, the zoo, to South Beach or some other point of interest. ["to" CO] Six to eight hours of fun and frolic with even only two kids would wear me out but oh so pleasantly. We'd always ride in the front of trains standing up and if there were a number of ways to get to our destination I chose the longest, with the most transfer points and if possible those that passed many switching tracks. Even if it rained we spent the time on trains. One of the favorites of the boys was the 3rd Ave El to South Ferry and a ride to Staten Island and the train to South Beach. The children and I were so happy together. We'd get home tired and grimy off wi [sic, probably meant "with"] our street clothes, on the floor with a game or blocks and relaxing in our play while we listened to the children's records. Then supper with Mommy a bath with boats, floating objects and water pistols. I'd be drenched [N3WI] so would Ethel in the youthful horse-play ["of" CO] that we all indulged in. Ethel took over the boys reading & singing or just being with her fellows and I'd clean up the mess in the bathroom. Then for a little while longer until bedtime we'd all share of each other and it was most satisfying for our family.

This is how it was and this it must be again.

With courage and hope. For life and love.

Julie

Mail call—See you soon—Regards to all the bestest with our mostest

Julius to Ethel

Feb 1st, 1953

My Lovely Nightingale,

Oh joy of joy I caught a couple of bars of your renditions of Gounod "Ave Maria" and the Alleluah [sic]. Imagine if only your door were open, what a lovely concert we would have. I reminisced a bit of the many time [sic] you would sing my favorite arias and folk tunes. Honey, as I thought of it I just adored you. To [sic] bad you weren't closer I'm sure I would have conveyed my deepest feelings for you in a way that is very proper indeed for two lovebirds. I send you my tender kisses as messages of my heart.

Since the usual Sunday papers didn't arrive I made use of the occassion [sic] to write a "megilah" [sic] to our lawyer on certain thoughts that have been percolating in my mind. I intend to copy these five pages of scribbled notes in a more legible hand for I've been too hard on our dear Manny's eyes. Incidentally, now that there is some respite we have an opportunity to do a little writing that will help our cause even as it gives us great satisfaction as an additional emotional reward.

My sister staid [*sic*] on until 3:30 PM because she was given a lift to New York by another visitor and we had a very fruitful visit. I'll fill in some of the news items she didn't have time to tell you about [N5WI] at our next get together. I'm very much relieved that Lena ["if" CO] is coming along nicely and I know she's just itching to get back into the swing of activity. However, my sister and brother are carrying the ball very nicely and things are being done.

As long as our counselor is so busy with work on our behalf I'm glad we're not pressing him to [*sic*] strongly on his bringing up our children. He knows how anxious we are to see the boys and I'll bet he intends to ["bring" CO, N3WI] come up with them ["out" CO] within a week after his consultation with us. Believe me sweetheart I have to fight [N2WI] not to think [suffix "ing" CO from last word] about our precious children to [*sic*] often for ["it" CO, N2WI] the longing breaks me up and hurts so badly. Oh darling, how wonderful it would be to once again [N3WI] be together & share life [NWI] with our family. ["beauty" inserted then CO, "again together" CO] I just thought about the [NWI] good times we used to have. You carrying Robbie on your back and Michael on my back and the big race was on. Do you remember the procession ["after" CO, N5WI] when it came time for the little one to be ["ing" CO from last word] put to bed. You led the way holding his feet, I held his shoulders and Michael marched in the middle with his brothers [*sic*] back resting on his head. It was loads of fun and the way we carried on, a little nutty, but happy. Such poor innocent babes suffering cruelly without any cause. This none of us will ever forget. Let us keep hoping we will someday win this case and help restore the boys [*sic*] happiness. I've got a secret to tell you my wife that I'm very deeply in love [NWI] with you (as if you didn't know it). Well what do you say? Enough of this nonsense!

Your devoted —Julie

Mr. Emanuel H. Bloch Esq.
7 W. 16th Street
New York N.Y.

Feb. 1st 1953

Page #1 of 4

Dearest Manny,

It's two days now that I haven't received the New York Times and [N2WI] I missed the Sunday edition. Will you please save clippings that might be of interest to me until the deliverers strike is over. I'm particularly interested in all news about the Emergency Civil Liberties Conference. In the situation I'm in I hunger to read each and every source of news particularly ["th" CO] since this is the only access I have to any daily paper and it's [sic] brand of information.

Happy days, yesterday I received the latest issue of the National Guardian and in there I had the extreme pleasure to read again one of my favorite writers Dr. W.E. DuBois.[351] It is wonderful to see my own true feelings [N2WI] in print expressed so beautifully and poignantly with such devastating effectiveness that [NWI] only the pen of so talented a distinguished scholar like this great man is, can so zealously proclaim for all to see. This is just what I've been yelling about, although not as well put, but you'll find references in many of my previous letters to this subject.

All of man's thinking and actions are bottomed on the facts available to him and correct conclusions can only be drawn when the entire truth is known. This is the fundamental premise of science and the basis of understanding life itself. It is a must for any progress.

Take our own case for I am most familiar with it. Now there exists a trial record that contains all the testimony of the witnesses in our case. The government obtained a verdict of guilty on this record, Although [sic] the decision was corrupt. Was the record as it stands brought to public attention by the newspapers or other media of information? No it was not. On the contrary we have had to print copies of the complete transcript of this record

---

[351]By the 1950s one of the few places in the United States that would publish the work of this outstanding African-American scholar was the *National Guardian*. For the life and radicalization of Dr. DuBois, see *The Autobiography of W.E.B. DuBois: A Soliloquy on Viewing My Life from the Last Decade of Its First Century*, ed. Herbert Aptheker (NY: International Publishers, 1968). See also Horne, Gerald, *Black and Red: W.E.B. DuBois and the Afro-American Response to the Cold War, 1944-1963* (Albany: State University of New York Press, 1986). Along with many others, Dr. DuBois had attempted to file an *amicus* brief with the Supreme Court in 1952. The day after our parents' death, Dr. DuBois spoke from their graveside, "These people died because they would not lie."

and the entire press including the New York Times refused to print our advertisements announcing that these records were available and they also refused any other paid advertisement on our behalf. They were afraid the readers would see the weak case presented against us, recognize that our rights were violated, that we didn't receive a fair trial and that this was a gross miscarriage of justice. More important not only did they omit our side of the controversy and highlight the prosecution's case but the press printed distortions and fabrications that was [*sic*] never even in the trial testimony ["It is immaterial" CO] Whether these stories were fed to them by the prosecutor or ["that" CO] they themselves invented these items of the [*sic*—probably meant "their"] own volition for the net effect was to falsely inform the people on this matter.

The future of our children, the safety of all of us and life itself makes it the most important task of everyone to break through the lie curtain of the "free" press and radio and present the

Page #2 of 4

facts as they really happen. I want to whole-heartedly join in this plea to support and build the National Guardian as a powerful weapon that brings the truth the [previous word written over "that," N3WI] life blood free men [N2WI] that is need [*sic*] in order to work for peace and make democracy survive. Just think with all the major newspapers against us we've still be [*sic*—probably meant "been"] able to reach and win to our just cause great numbers of people. Isn't it obvious that many more would have been reached with the message of the need for justice if we only had the means to accomplish this. The answer is a bigger, stronger National Guardian [NWI] which will surely be many times more effective than it is now in [N2WI] fighting for the interests of the American people.

Through their efforts they've set in motion the movement that saved the "Trenton Six" and were it not for this paper we two, who are innocent, might have been put to death by now. In many important struggles we cannot bargain & with a slim margin for victory, we must give our all. This paper means so much and these are only two instances, there are many other and their voice for peace and liberty is vital for all Americans. I would gladly like to contribute my dollar a month out of my commissary money but unfortunately the authorities wont [*sic*] let me but I'll follow with avid interest the progress of the fund campaign, [illegible CO at beginning of next word] because I am confident my fellowmen know how this insures their welfare and will come forth with the monies needed. All I can do is cheer you on from the death house.[352]

I appreciate your sending me a copy of the Le Monde letter sent by Henri Pierre to the editor of the Washington Post. It was really something to see this sample product of the foreign opinion on this case. It is a sober, intelligent and honest declaration of a sincere individual, an independent, who is raising questions to clarify the issues as he sees them from a reading of the record. More than that it was a treat to read the Washington Post's editorial especially their lame, apologetic defensive tone![353] Their main

---

[352]It is obvious from context that this letter was meant to be either published by the *National Guardian* or at least to be shared with the staff of the *National Guardian* during a fund-raising campaign.

[353]On January 4, 1953, the *Washington Post* had editorially attacked M. Pierre for supposedly equating our parents' case with the Slansky case in Czechoslovakia. The *Post* also took umbrage at the charge of antisemitism, noting that although there were no Jews on the jury, the judge, himself, was Jewish. On January 23, M. Pierre responded with a letter to the *Post* which stated in part:

> I had not the least intention of comparing the Prague trial to the one in New York . . . insofar as the judge's attitude is concerned, I . . . believe . . . that he was, whether consciously or not, inclined to be more severe toward his coreligionists. It is in this sense that anti-Semitism played an indirect part. . .

> If I am willing to modify my article in that which concerns anti-Semitism, on the other hand I feel obligated to maintain my general point of view about the affair . . .

> 1. Guilt of the Rosenbergs: I still consider it shocking that they were sentenced essentially through the testimony of Greenglass, corroborated in part through Gold's testimony, . . . from the point of view of justice it is inadmissible that Mrs. Greenglass should never have been bothered while Mrs. Rosenberg was sentenced to death for having been the moral support of her husband.

> 2. Although the judge chose to affirm his impartiality at the end of the debates, were not his references throughout the whole trial to the communistic opinions of the Rosenbergs of such a nature as to influence the jury?

> 3. As to the extreme severity of the penalty, it is sufficient to read the judge's summation before the sentence to realize that he wanted to make a terrible example of the Rosenbergs as individuals, and I repeat that it has not been irrefutably established that they were the leaders of a plot or that they transmitted vital information. . . .

rebuttal of course is false for if he read the facts the Post editor would know that Harry Gold testified orally as to the complicity of both Dave and Ruth Greenglass, also documentary evidence was adduced to connect Ruth directly with bank accounts & other items see (Govt. Exhibits 5, 9A & 9B, 16 & 17) and above all she admitted her guilt on the witness stand. Naturally the Post has no argument at all. You see the facts are on our side and we must tell all who want to know about them.

Concerning people like Walter White who might have read the record, although I have grave doubts that he did or he wouldn't make the statement he did, they seem to be interested in ["every" CO, NWI] other things ["else" CO] and not the merits of the case. What would our principles be worth if we were to join the present popular trend, the anti-communist, hate Russia, cold war bandwagon in order to enlist support for our fight for justice?[354]

Page # 3 of 4

This can never be. We are defending our innocence and only that and from the very beginning we have always proclaimed this for it is the complete truth. This is the only way we can be morally and ethically fair with ourselves and our fellowmen. To deny this is to destroy all that we want to live for and all that is honest.

I would like to request that the Committee print our petition to the President for executive clemency and distribute it widely. It's [sic] 37 pages represents a mountain of prodigious work, full of good honest fact, reasoning and a forthright statement and avowal of adherence to principle. It seems to me that here is a good concise resume of the entire case and is a very hard hitting document. I like this as an appeal it is emotional but restrained. Also in our behalf send a copy of this to Mr. Walter White perhaps he'll see the light.

At this point, although I told my sister Ethel to tell you about this incident, when [N2WI] it happened and from whom I received the information (be careful of how you use this I'm leaving it to your good judgement) I am compelled to go into details. Taking into consideration the date you submitted our petition to the President I don't think that Morris Ernst read it but I'll give him the benefit of the doubt. He said after reading it, he

---

The response from the *Post* on the same day noted that "M. Pierre's letter does not convince us, . . . that he has not fallen for the world-wide Communist-inspired propaganda campaign on Ethel and Julius Rosenberg, the atom spies . . ." (See "Le Monde Buys a Hoax," *Washington Post*, 4 January 1953, p. 4-B; Henri Pierre, "Le Monde Buys a Hoax," Letter to the Editor, *Washington Post*, 23 January 1953, p. 20; "Le Monde's Justice," *Washington Post*, 23 January 1953, p. 20. The latter two were the documents referred to in the letter.)
[354] See footnote 295.

thought it was no good and also that he was personally ["was" CO] opposed to our being granted clemency. This, his true feelings of course, he confided to this individual while at the same ["time" omitted here] he is double dealing with my family, interviewing calling and writing them, hypocritically saying he's our friend and wants to help us (murder us perhaps) while asking questions and harping on extraneous matters and acts like a provocateur or a police agent. I say beware of this man, his [NWI] hostile actions ["are hostile" CO] both publically [sic] in the American Civil Liberties Union and more so privately speak more eloquently than his beguiling words. He is our enemy and a treacherous unprincipled opportunist.[355] Since I'm without newspapers I've spent the time going through the record again and I want to apologize in advance if I'm wasting your time but please be patient with me. All pages referred to are in the eight booklets put out by the Committee.

1 [circled] P. 237 You begin to object & the judge cuts you off before you even finished the sentence he overruled you.

2 [circled] On P. 257 near the bottom Elitcher in his answer referred to me as Julie the name all my friends & relatives knew me by.

3 [circled] P. 388. beginning with the 2:20 PM recess. It was during this recess that he was told to straighten out his testimony about a "lie". See 387-388. Probably the D.A. or FBI talked to him during recess.

4 [circled] Page 411 D.A. Cohn said the name of each scientist will be directly related to ["th" CO] the two of us. I dont [sic] believe he connected it up.

Page # 4 of 4

5 (circled)

Page 415-416 don't you think it was error that all this was permitted to be argued before the jury.

6 (circled) Page 508 bottom—the court giving his personal feeling in the matter. A judicial confession of prejudice even before all the evidence is in. Also the possibility exists that he was acquainted beforehand with the important points the prosecution was going to establish. How else can you account for many times in the cross-examination of Govt. witnesses on events and dates not brought out in their direct testimony & not fitting into the prosecutions [sic] theory he brushed you off commented on them & frustrated your examination saying they probably have nothing to do with incriminating evidence. This is also true of the pattern in his hostile questioning of ["defendents" CO] defense witnesses. Only one who knows the D.A's case in advance can ever [sic] offer this.

---

[355] See footnote 314.

7 [circled] P. 535 top. Billions of brown paper wrappers. How could he positively identify that one! Perhaps it was error to receive it in evidence.

8 [circled] P. 556. Bottom page.—He can't remember such most important ["dates" CO] things in his relations with his wife but does remember minor things. This would be good to bring to Public attention on his credibility[.]

9 [circled] Beginning with P. 848 All of the Doctors testimony should be studied carefully. The direct testimony is short and not incriminating to any interest. The witness seemed ill at ease both at the trial and from analyzing his testimony. He did not give many facts the D.A. [next word written over an illegible word] got Greenglass to say about the falsified certificate. He is definitely hidding [*sic*] something & we should have pressed a line of inquiry on wire tapping. On cross examination the court was very brusque & seemed to feel we were touching a sensitive spot for he tried to prevent examination. Only when you read the Judges [*sic*] question on subsequent volunteering by the doctor about telephone call then it is obvious he must have had prior knowledge of either an FBI report, a statement of the witness or he was briefed by the D.A Note the Doctor said I did not ask him about a vaccination certificate which if anything corroborates my testimony. If there is a possibility to charge collusion on the part of the judge, I'd strongly urge it and say let's go into it.

10 (circled) Note Page 1119 my remark Dave said Julie

11 (circled) P. 1308 Refusing our pictures in evidence making the comment. Isn't that prejudging the case

That's all for now I'll discuss other matters with you when I see you. The facts are our most powerful weapon we must publicize them at all costs.

Now is the time to accelerate the activities for there are signs of a shift favorable to us and we must not falter at this crucial period. I am feeling pretty good and I want you to keep the material coming to us. We didn't get any Jewish life [*sic*] this year yet. Tell all our friends a [*sic*—probably meant "and"] well wishers we will never abandon the truth. We are fighting for justice because we are innocent.

As ever—Julie

Remember we know the score. Regards.

Emanuel H. Bloch
7 W. 16th Street
New York New York

                                                    February 4, 1953
Dearest Manny,

Shall we ever really have such an abundance of time to spend together that these after-thoughts won't be necessary! I am simply fidgeting with annoyance because of my ignorant misuse of the word "fulsome". For God's sake change it, perhaps to "gracious", or "unstinting"; my artistic integrity is at stake! Yep, you guessed right; I looked it up and was aghast at what I found!

Also, I had a point "letter-writing," about which I never said a word. So here's the word and very simply. Did you make the ["requested" CO] corrections ["in" CO] I requested ["by me" inserted then CO] re the poem (which, incidentally, I was too shy to ask you about, although I was dying to) and the letter which asked whether it was with "the savage cutting down of two warm, young lives to save the face of the U.S. Government"—All I wanted changed on the poem was the last line which originally was, "For You, My Sons, for you"—The [NWI] new version I gave David Rosenberg was "For our Sons and yours"—I trust these changes I request are [NWI] always made before the writing is ["publ" CO] printed for public consumption; it irks me no end to see mistakes of this kind or mistakes due to careless transmission into print.[356]

I [NWI] had also wanted to assure you it would be perfectly O.K. for you to edit my stuff without asking me, if [N3WI] you seriously thought a word or even a particular sentence contained error. Of course, I can trust you to use good judgment and discretion along these lines, but I ["felt" CO, NWI] feel you should know you ["had" CO, NWI] have my permission. Did Ethel ever read you a correction I gave her for the sentence we didn't like about "Shunning like the plague those who appease, etc." I trust you edited this out.

As per the Warden's request I am forwarding a couple of Julie's letters—am hard at work and want you to know that if the ["last" CO] words you offered in parting really ["are" CO, NWI] express your considered judgment, it is a great deal more the "small consolation" you imagine. I kiss your hand—dear Manny!
Ethel—
P.S.—Another poem along the way; I had the first verse by the time you came but no opportunity to read it. It happens to ["suit" CO] tie in so aptly with the task on hand, it's really odd. You'll see what I mean if it ever gets completed—Best to all—Feel wonderful
—E.R.

---

[356]In the *Death House Letters* published in June of 1953 and the more complete edition entitled *The Testament of Ethel and Julius Rosenberg* published in 1954, the original, not the corrected version of the poem was published. Apparently, Emanuel Bloch was too busy with legal activities to make this change or the person editing the book of letters made a specific editorial decision not to make the change. In *We Are Your Sons* we published the original and footnoted the change she wished to make but which was never implemented.

Julius to Ethel

Feb 5, 1953

Sweet Darling

I meant it from the bottom of my heart [N8WI] when I spoke those endearing terms to you at our legal consultation and I'm sure you understand I did not intend that [previous word written over illegible word] to be ["a" CO, NWI] mere cute expressions. We've got some wonderful lawyer dearest and I must say that he has been the single most effective person [N3WI] in all progress in our long and difficult fight. It gives me a wonderful feeling to know that he's completely devoted to our cause and is always working in our behalf. One thing is certain that he has done his best for us.

By this time I had hoped to hear from the children. I'll wait till this weekend and then I'll write them. Not that I'm worried because Manny brought us word about how they are getting along, it's just that I'd like to hear more intimate details of what they are doing. If the pressure is hard on us we can imagine how tough it is for our little boys and Ben and Sonia. Concerning our visits from the family I'm a bit confused as to when they are expected here next. After all Lena is ill and members of your family may put in an appearance and there might be as conflict so I suggest you take it upon yourself to straighten it out and write my sister Ethel a scheduale [*sic*] contain [*sic*] alternatives. Considering all [N2WI] this & the kids [*sic*] next visit ["and" CO] she will [N3WI] be able to attend to this matter and see that all are properly informed. A technicality but as always a very necessary thing to think about especially when ["it" CO, NWI] we take into account our visits.

It was a blessing to receive the daily newspapers again. I've been following the foreign news carefully and as we had anticipated the Eisenhower Government is embarking on Dulles' policy of "liberation."[357] We victims of political justice in our country know [previous word written over illegible word] to judge the authorities by their actions and not their statements. The trend is clear, a policy of spreading the Cold War in the world with a danger to peace and, of course, our lives are ["too" CO] also in greater jeopardy because of this. ["This" CO] It is the fundamentals of politics that reactionary and police state measures at home would [NWI] eventually lead to war abroad. That is why an integrated program for peace requires opposition to illiberal ["policies" CO] internal policies and a concerted effort

---

[357]The foreign policy enunciated by Secretary of State John Foster Dulles was officially aimed at "rolling back" Communism and "liberating" the "captive nations" of Europe. This was supposed to be a positive policy as opposed to the passive, reactive, policy of "containment" promulgated by George Kennan and former Secretary of State Dean Acheson.

to save our lives. We have been successful in arousing the conscience of the world by our adherence to principles and have made known the issues involved in this case ["the world public" CO, NWI] millions understand the political implications and that is the reason for their concern and their active support. You will also note that in foreign countries the character of the campaign, even more so than here at home, is based on the fact that they have grave doubts that we are guilty and moreover the sentence is barbaric and inhuman. It is my hope that more of the American people will awaken to the plain truth of our innocence before it is to [*sic*] late. The problem never was an easy one but we are holding our own in the battle. All we can do is keep up our courage and confidence.

Your devoted husband—Julie

Julius to Ethel

Feb. 8, 1953

Darling Ethel,

The weekend seemed very long since we didn't receive the usual family visit. From the time I left your presence this last Friday, I've been thinking about you and the problems you face. In a way, I want you to feel completely free to share everything with me even though you ["are" CO, N3WI] might again be forced to breakdown [*sic*] and cry. Naturally, the lack of privacy on those intimate family relations doesn't help any and aggravates the situation yet we must suffer through if we intend to release our tensions. Unfortunately, we must resort to letters as the only means of exchanging our confidences as man and wife.

Honey I understand full well the deep hurts you suffer especially the terribly [*sic*] frustrations that are magnified manyfold because we sit awaiting our doom. If the flowing tears and irrepressible sobs you uttered because you could not contain yourself anymore represented ["only" CO] the surface expression of your pain then know that the reason for my speechlessness at that time was due to ["the" CO] my agony ["watching" CO] reflecting your own. It is impossible to soothe you or protect you from the daily torture that is ["your every" CO] even present here but we've been able to stay strong in spite of it and our unity has been made unbreakable because of it and we face with confidence what awaits us. [NWI] The Greatest [*sic*] writers of all times have described love and explained the beauty and virtues of complete acceptance of each other of husband and wife but none of it can come near the painful but extreme satisfaction that our relationship has meant to me [NWI] even on the very threshold of our death. There is no greater [letter "j" in next word written over "y"] joy or happiness than to know that two separate individuals [N4WI] like you & I [*sic*] freely chose to find in each other and [first syllable of next word written over "them"] ourselves that character and humble dignity sincerely devoted to noble principles ["and life this" inserted, then CO, NWI] which is the most worthwhile endeavor of the human being. Of course this has real meaning because we are innocent. Even more than that we didn't compromise one bit with the truth and ["the knowledge of this" CO, NWI] this is the secret of our great strength.

If we were home and I held you in my arms ["with you" CO] pressed to my body then [last letter of previous word written over "re"] I could convey to you [NWI] exactly how I feel about you Ethel. The full passion of my heart and the tenderness of a sweet kiss I cannot give you with this pen and paper but ["you can" CO, NWI] please try to imagine it from what we've sensed together in the past. The close bind of mind, heart and body that ties us together has in the short span of our young lives enriched us and given us [NWI] great promise ["of" CO, NWI] for a beautiful future. I believe that because we were successful in turning this great personal force of ours into working for the best interests of our children and humanity that we have given expression to the greatest single desire of mankind [there might be an "&" sign here, it doesn't look like it but there is something and from context it fits—next word written over an illegible word] that [N3WI] is the reason we have won their favor and active support. Also I realize that around our ["issue" CO, NWI] case every trend of world opinion has crystallized into distinct positions each group for reasons of their own and whatever the outcome I feel confident we have helped the cause for good. All my best is for you—Your devoted husband— Julie

Emanuel H. Bloch
7 W. 16th Street
New York New York

February 9, 1953

Dear Manny,
    This is to inform you that I am expecting you to bring the children here for a visit on Saturday, February 14th, at 10:00 AM.—
    Don't fail to acknowledge at once.—
Thank you—

Love,
Ethel

Emanuel H. Bloch
7 W. 16th Street
New York New York

February 9, 1953

Dear Manny,

In recent weeks an ugly development has been gaining ground. It is being casually bruited about by our less than wholesome brethren that I am to be spared by commutation out of a humanitarian consideration for me as a woman and a mother, while my husband is to be electrocuted. Further, it is hopefully confided, in such an event my "spy secrets" would not die with me and the possibility would still exist for my eventual recantation. Lastly, the responsibility for the decision concerning my husband's life would be shifted squarely onto my shoulders, and his blood would be on my hands if I wilfully [sic] refused to make him "come across"!

So now my life is to be bargained off against my husband's; I need only grasp the line chivalrously held out to me by the gallant defenders of hearth and home and leave him to drown without a backward glance. How diabolical, how bestial, how utterly depraved! Only fiends and perverts could taunt a fastidious woman with so despicable, so degrading a proposition! A cold fury possesses me and I could retch with horror and revulsion, for these unctuous saviors, these odious swine, are actually proposing to erect a terrifying sepulchre in which I shall live without living and die without dying! By day there will be no hope and by night there will be no peace. Over and over again I shall see the beloved face and fancy I hear the beloved [illegible word CO, NWI] voice. Over and over again, I shall sob out the last heartbroken, wracking, good-byes and reel under the impact of irrevocable murder!

And what of our children, noble testament to our sacred union, fruit of our deep and enduring love what manner of "mercy" is it that would slay their adored father, and deliver up their devoted mother to everlasting emptiness. Know then, you warped, gross, eaters of dust, you abominations upon this beauteous earth, I should far rather embrace my husband in death than live on ingloriously upon your execrable bounty. [paragraph sign inserted here] Be under no illusions, either, magnanimous sirs, that I shall besmirch and dishonor my marital vows and the felicity and integrity of the relationship we shared, to play the role of harlot to political procurers. My husband is innocent as I am myself and no power on earth shall divide us in life or in death. Trust me, I shall remain faithful; trust me, I shall not revile him! My shattered life shall be his immortality and his memory shall ["remain green and unsullied" CO, "endure clean" inserted, then CO, NWI] be safe from your [NWI] wicked debauchery. But the savage reprisal you visited upon me shall pursue you ["up" inserted, then CO] to [N3WI] the edge of your graves [NWI] and beyond, and your names shall be anathema wherever love is the First Commandment!

Take heed, reckless [illegible word CO, NWI] speculators in human misery, lest History exhume your rotten carrion and solemnly charge you with ["rank, premeditated murder" CO, N2WI] cold-blooded killing! Take heed, despoilers of all that is ["sweet and fair" CO] good, lest you create a new and more flaming "Joan"!

Ethel

[She filled the page with lines.]

P.S—D'ye like? Please, dear, make sure Dr. Miller gets a copy of the record and the book of our letters (if ["ready" CO, NWI] available)[358] before he leaves the city ["on" CO, NWI] this Friday or Saturday for a two-week vacation. He told me yesterday he would phone you on Friday, but I'd appreciate it if you got in touch with him upon receipt of this letter and made arrangements to get the stuff to him before he departs— Thanks—

Love
Ethel

Emanuel H. Bloch
401 Broadway
New York New York

February 10, 1953

Dear Manny,

Re my letter to you of February 9th concerning the latest line of our better scribes, kindly make the following corrections:—"and his memory shall be safe from your cowardly slander". I originally wrote "wicked debauchery" which I do not like one bit. The very last sentence speaks of "cold-blooded killing".—Please make this "vengeful killing" or "wanton killing"—

Also, if you feel it needs changing, (although I don't think it's too bad as it stands)—Thusly:—

"—that I shall dishonor my marital vows and besmirch the felicitous relationship we shared"—etc.

Please ["change" CO] take care of same accordingly, huh, [illegible letter CO] before ["getting it out" CO, N4WI] letting it be seen in ["to" CO at

---

[358]Indicates that they were expecting the book *Death House Letters* to be published much earlier than in fact it was.

end of last word] print anywhere, or I shall have a conniption!
    Let me hear about Saturday, Feb. 14th—
Am fine—

                                                                    Love
                                                                    Ethel

On February 11, President Eisenhower denied clemency.

Mr. Emanuel Bloch
7 W. 16th Street
New York NY
    Page # 1

                                                            Feb 11, 1953
                                                            6:00 P.M.

Dear Manny,
    On Guard America this is tyranny.
    President Eisenhower reveals some more of his great crusade and ex-
poses his fine military hand. It reminds us of the famous Biblical story only
there is a significant shift in the roles. "The voice is the voice of Jacob but
the hands are the hands of Esau." What a mockery; benevolent words hypocritically clasping a barbaric act. This harsh and cruel decision was sired in
madness.
    Today by its action in acquiesing [*sic*] to the brutal and excessive
sentence against us the executive arm of our government has become a party
to murder. For the whole truth is we are innocent.
    We believe our legal execution has been ordained in order that we serve
as scapegoats for ulterior political purposes of higher government policy.
    We have never lost faith and we hope this atrocity against two young
Jewish parents of two small children will not be permitted to come to fruition. For it may very well set in motion a chain reaction that will threaten
the welfare and endanger the lives of the people.
    Before the irreparable is consummated it is imperative that the true facts
be known to all. Sadly, the information in the press and other mass media
of news is not the truth but instead is a distorted, truncated, myopic aber-
ration of our case. Only the complete transcript of the trial record and the
court proceedings on our motion for a new trial on the grounds that our
conviction was illegally procured can serve as the basis for a fair and impartial determination of the truth and justice in this case. As a public service
this material, the only complete story of the case has been printed and the
facts are breaking through to the people in spite of the lie curtain of the
"free" press.

The reader must come to the correct conclusion that it is for the common good and in the best interests of all concerned that we live.

It is clear that the primary purpose of our case is that it should be a means of coercion against political dissidents with government policies. Further it intends by the use of fear and hysteria to obtain conformism. Such a situation will only lead to a police state at home and war abroad.

By killing us the government hopes to obsucre [*sic*] these facts:

1 [circled] Only oral uncorroborated accomplice testimony of confessed trapped spies the Greenglasses was the basis for a guilty verdict for an alleged conspiracy to commit espionage

2 [circled] We did not receive a fair trial

3 [circled] Our constitutional rights were continuously violated

4 [circled] Extraneius [*sic*] matters concerning political ideas and alleged communism permeated the trial, prejudiced the jury and prevented an impartial, objective determination of the guilt or innocence of the crime charged.

5 [circled] The press and the authorities poisioned [*sic*] the public mind against us by an organized propaganda campaign to arouse passion and create hostility towards us.

Page # 2

Feb 11

6 [circled] Perjured testimony was knowingly used to obtain a conviction on the weak evidence presented.

7 [circled] A hoax of a secret and an atom spy plot is perpetrated contrary to science, history and the plain facts in the record.[359]

We have waited patiently hoping that somewhere along the process set down by law governing this case, sanity and sober judgement would take over and determine the ultimate outcome of our case. Instead contrary to his declared statement, by this action ["of" CO] the President has displayed an arrogant disregard of the conscience of the world, a disavowal of the fundamental elements of fair play and humane decency and a denial of justice which by all rights should be ours.

Not only is this our claim but millions throughout the world including top scientists, prominent lawyers, most distinguished representatives of the clergy, men of letters and arts, honored leaders of all shades of political opinions who are best qualified to judge the issues have grave doubts and justly so that in fact the verdict is corrupt.

---

[359]In his statement denying clemency, Eisenhower had echoed the Judge's sentencing speech that " . . . the crime for which they have been found guilty . . . could very well result in the death of many, many thousands of innocent citizens." See Schneir, p. 195.

The love we bear our two sons and each other demands that we hold fast
to these truths even in death which will destroy our little family.

We are not the first victims of tyranny. 6 million of our co-religionists
and millions of other innocent victims of fascism went to the death chambers. The war criminals who had a part in committing these crimes are daily
being freed by representatives of our government. Never in the history of
our country for the most heinous crime on our statute books treason has any
citizen been executed.[360] Here now in behalf of the sovereign people of the
United States the Administration wants to stain the good name of our country with the blood of the Rosenbergs. It is the duty of the people to give the
answer and we are confident that they will raise a mighty cry against this
new great danger that besmirches the reputation of our ["gov" CO] land, that
starts ["with" CO, N2WI] by dooming two innocent Americans and threatens
to engulf millions.

We hope that by our adherence to principle we will at least help insure
that many others after us are not visited with the kind of terror we've been
facing.

We ask only the continuance of the struggle for justice. Learn the facts
and defend the truth. [letter "s" CO at end of last word]

We continue to fight with courage and confidence for live [sic] and love.

As ever
Julie

Julius to Ethel

Feb 12, 1953

My Darling,

The Great Emancipator is whirling in his grave while the phoney [sic]
crusader is acting like a knave. Just as we had been informed by our lawyer
that it would take [previous two words written over "will be"] at least
["until next" CO, NWI] another week ["that" CO, NWI] for Eisenhower to get
the record the newspapers let the cat out of the bag and said that the
Attorney General brought over the file to the Presidents [sic] Office at 4:00
P.M. and at 5:07 PM the prepared statement was read.[361] Of course he did

---

[360]Actually, John Wilkes Booth's alleged co-conspirator was executed for
treason after the Civil War.

[361]Among the FBI documents is some evidence as to how the Eisenhower
clemency decision occurred so much faster than had been anticipated: " . . . on
January 27, . . . Assistant United States Attorney Kilsheimer called Pardon
Attorney Dan A. Lyons . . . at the request of Judge Kaufman and asked when
Lyons would get the Application for Pardon papers to the President in
connection with [the Rosenberg] case. Lyons indicated it would be at least three

not read the record nor did he see our petition. To cover up this apparent discrepancy they say on his own he's been brushing up on the case. I guess in between playing golf, playing footsie with all his big business cabinet members and playing around with the Formosa issue. Such bold hypocrisay [*sic*]. The man's just a plain liar. Why he doesn't even make sure that he's accurate in his [N2WI] haste to use ["of" CO, NWI] shopworn platitudes stating the [NWI] obvious fallacy that the Supreme Court reviewed our case. It is true that the initiative [letter "i" at beginning of last word written over "u"] and the heavy advantage is at present with the smiling General but he did not reckon with the people for [NWI] instinctively the military mind ["holds the" CO] has only contempt for them. He may be successful in that we could be put to death but ["the reaction to his disregard" CO] he has shocked the conscience of the world and revealed ["him" CO, N3WI] himself a perfidious reactionary ["self" CO] who is ready to embark on risky adventures that ["will" CO, NWI] may bring on world war 3. He will find that this move of his ["government" CO] administration is a terrible mistake. I feel certain that the people will do everything to change this decision.

I worked today Ethel but not ["as much as I hope" CO, N3WI] for any ["real" CO] length of time. It is hard to find [NWI] the proper formulation to express the way I feel. You can be certain that all my thoughts are of you. Sweetheart I never dreamt I could love anyone as much as I do you and also I have such a wonderful sense of complete satisfaction in knowing that you're all there. I am positive you understand what I mean. As I write this letter I must say that just keeping in mind all ["a" written over "w"] that my pen gives expression to makes me feel strong and I believe you'll feel better when you realize that you have been so helpful to me.

Like you, my beloved, I find it most difficult to think about what this new developement [*sic*] will do to our precious sons. The heartache is just to [*sic*] much for it is impossible to do anything to protect them from the horrible consequences of our execution nor can we assuage the deep hurt that they will have to bear. I will have to find the strength to suffer through the torment and begin to write our children a long letter. This we must do and we'll talk about whether it would be best to send it to Manny to hold ["it" CO] until ["the" CO, NWI] such time [N4WI] as he feels it is appropriate

weeks, whereupon Assistant United States Attorney Kilsheimer stated that it was desired that the matter be expedited. Lyons advised Kilsheimer that no one could get this matter expedited unless he was directed to do so by the Attorney General or the President.

Kilsheimer furnished this information to Judge Kaufman and thereafter Judge Kaufman called someone in the Department in an effort to get this matter expedited." *Hearings*, p. 2399, Cleveland to Belmont, JR HQ 1466, January 27, 1953. February 11 was two weeks after that conversation occurred.

["for him to" CO] to read ["it" CO] to our children. At this time we'll have to seriously make preparations to finish up a number of items in order that everything necessary is done ["before" CO, NWI] & is not left to the very last minute. I think we'll have to take this up with our lawyer at our next consultation. Know my darling I am happy that you have made my life is meaningful—Always devoted to you forever

Your Julie

Mr. Emanuel H. Bloch
7 W. 16th Street
New York NY
        Page # 1 of 3

Feb 12, 1953

Dear Manny,
        On Lincoln's Birthday February 12, 1953 in the the [*sic*] death house at Sing Sing prison, Ossining, New York, We Julius and Ethel Rosenberg condemned to death put our hand to this document and proclaim to the world.
        We do hereby indict for [N4WI] a conspiracy to commit murder all those who have had a hand in our case in violating the laws of Nature and the Constitution of the United States before God and Man; in that said individuals did conspire, combine, confederate and agree with intent and reason to believe, to bear false witness, directly or indirectly, to deprive of freedom, liberty and life two innocent people, to incite the public mind, by chicanery and by fraud, to misinform, mis-lead and coerce people to conform to official policies, to create fear and hysteria that inevitably leads to war abroad and a police state at home.
Overt Acts.
1—In pursuance of said conspiracy and to effect the objects thereof within the City of New York up to and including our trial publicity independently engendered and stimulated by information fed to a propaganda campaign by the F.BI, the Dept. of Justice, the office of the U.S. Attorney for the Southern District of NY and other officials of the Govt. intensely aroused the passions of the public against us and created a prejudicial atmosphere prejudging us guilty. Fact is that even the Circuit Court of Appeals in its opinion stated if we had asked for a mistrial on this basis it probably would have been granted.[362] Well?
2—And further in pursuance of said conspiracy and to effect the objects thereof, on or about June 15 thru July 16, 1950 one David Greenglass

---

[362]See footnote 331 above.

trapped spy who was already arrested and his wife Ruth about to be arrested on oral and documentary evidence in the hands of the F.B.I. given by another spy Harry Gold[363] were allowed to pay $4000 contraband spy money to an Attorney O[.] John Rogge, a former Asst. Attorney General of the U.S., the finger man for the prosecution against Dr. W.E. Dubois [sic] concerning an [NWI] alleged peace plot, acted as the Greenglasses [sic] representative and consummated a deal with the prosecution officials, U.S. Attorneys Saypol, Lane, Cohn, Kilsheimer and FBI agents Harrington & Norton, that for their testimony against us Ruth would go free and Dave would be eligible to go free after 5 years and a Day parole on a 15 year sentence.—Incontrovertible facts.[364]

3—And in further pursuance of said conspiracy and to effect the objects thereof we husband and wife were arrested and kept in custody for nine months. All this time the Greenglasses had numerous meetings with the prosecution. They were coached and rehearsed, They [sic] refined their statements and studied their testimony while hundreds of F.B.I. agents scoured the country interviewed many thousands of people all who went to school with us, all who worked with us, all our neighbors and anyone who knew us.

Page #2 of 3

Yet not one single person, nor one iota of evidence could they find to corroborate the Greenglass accomplice testimony to prove our participation in the main matter of the charge. The Court of Appeals even said "If the Greenglass testimony was disregarded, the conviction could not stand".[365] The government was forced to rely on the tenuous circumstancial [sic] inferences that could only be put forth in a conspiracy type indictment in order to put us in jepoardy [sic]. Conveniently the Greenglasses laid all the incriminating episodes to conversations between themselves and us. Also that admissions of involvement by Julius Rosenberg were alleged [sic] made to Dave Greenglass all are contained in a few words of his testimony no additional details or proof and completely uncorroborated by anyone else. Is this was the self confessed trapped spy Ruth Greenglass was never indicted

---

[363]Note, still following the defense view that David and Ruth Greenglass and Gold were spies. We doubt that they actually believed David and Ruth were spies.
[364]See Rogge's statement in *The Unquiet Death of Ethel and Julius Rosenberg,* n.p. "I felt I had an arrangement with the government whereby for providing the government with witnesses, . . . that Ruth would be left out of the indictment and she was. And that David would have a sentence of no more than three to five years. But when it came to judgment day, the judge wrapped himself in the flag, went overboard, and began with death penalties."
[365]See Record, p. 1648.

or at the very least given a suspended sentence for her crime "worse than murder"? [*sic*—This sentence is garbled, perhaps he meant to insert "the reason that" after the second word and omit the "was."] The threat of a death sentence hangs over her head and seals her lips against the truth and prevents her husband from revealing the details of the deal for he fears to jepoardize [*sic*] his wife's life never mind that he already bargained away the lives of his own sister and her husband.

4—And in further pursuance of said conspiracy and to effect the objects thereof although evidence of the substantive charge as listed in the overt acts if believed by the jury was basis enough to support a conviction, the prosecution under the aegis of the the [*sic*] judge allowed an extraneous issue to permeate the trial and inflame the jury against us and confused the issues and blunted the objective ["ity" CO at end of last word] weighing of the facts on the crime charged. The Court of Appeals said "Of course, such evidence can be highly inflammatory in a jury trial. This Court and others have recognized that the Communist label yields marked ill-will for its American wearer . . . ["] the judge cautioned the jurors "not to determine the guilt or innocence of a defendant on whether or not he is a Communist" it may be that such warnings are no more than an empty ritual without practical effect on the jurors[.][366] How come where life is at stake the danger of this possibility is permitted & for technicalities is not considered sufficient grounds for reversal?

5 [circled] And in further pursuance of said conspiracy and to effect the objects thereof the judges [*sic*] antagonistic conduct, his prejudgement of issues before all facts were in, his anticipatory examination of govt. witnesses and his protection of them when in danger because of cross examination and his ready knowledge of facts not yet adduced from the witness stand proves he had prior knowledge of either statements by witnesses, or he had read F.B.I reports or he had been briefed on the major points the U.S. Attorney planned to present. In short collusion on the part of Judge Kaufman.[367] Again a technicality was found to uphold the improper conduct of the judge.

6 [circled] And in further pursuance of said conspiracy and to effect the objects thereof and after we brought the facts to light ["the" CO, NWI] and FBI Agent Harrington was forced to admit ["ted" CO at end of last word] that at the direction of Saypol in direct violation of the Courts order excluding all witnesses

---

[366]See Record, pp. 1655–56.
[367]One of the clearest examples of this is in the cross-examination of the photographer who allegedly took passport pictures of our parents. See Record, p. 1437, see also *Sons*, pp. 423–24.

Page # 3 of 3

brought Schneider a "surprise" witness behind the rail to indentify [*sic*] us, and he was permitted the next day to testify falsely that he had not seen us from the time he took passport photos of us until the moment he took the stand. This was a deliberate fraud and knowing use of perjury which was witheld [*sic*] from the jury. The Court of Appeals again refused us relief on the technicality Schneider hat [*sic*] not meant to lie. Even in death is such a doubt ["is" CO] allowed to stand?[368]

7 [circled] And in futherance [*sic*] of such Conspiracy and in effect the objects thereof the Court of Appeals admitted that the Perl Indictment had been deliberately "timed by the prosecution to prejudice us saying "Such assumed tactics cannot be too severely condemned" and ["the statement issued by Saypol" CO] as to Saypols [*sic*] statement they said "Such a statement to the press in the course of a trial we regard as whoely [*sic*] reprehensible". They said that the damage done us was so irremediable that were it not for certain technical legal consideration [*sic*] that counsel failed to move for a mistrial, a new trial should have been granted. But we found out afterwards that Saypol induced our attorney not to move for a mistrial by falsely representing to him that the Perl indictment was procured in the regular course of the administration of criminal justice and not for ulterior purposes.[369] Judge Ryan had refused to subpoena Saypol or have him present an affidavit submitting the proof to the court. A violation of a constitutional right is not rectified by time or conduct of defendants [*sic*] attorney.

8 [circled] And in futherance [*sic*] of said conspiracy and ["in violation the" CO, N3WI] to effect the object thereof the weak testimony of the Greenglass accomplices, [next word is illegible, appears to be "alternate" or "attenuate" but neither really fit the context, we used "attenuated" in *Sons* (1st Ed.), p. 391] by their motive of self preservation was revealed from the lips of the prosecutor Saypol to be inaccurate and was contrived in the bargain for his[370] life & the freedom for his wife only "through Ruth Greenglass, his wife; came the subsequent recantation . . . their cooperation and the dis-

---

[368]For the role of Schneider from the point of view of the prosecution, see the testimony of Roy Cohn in *Hearings,* p. 2259, 2262–63, 2267. See also Radosh and Milton, pp. 164–66, 295. For the alternative point of view see Schneir, p. 164, 180–82 and *Sons,* pp. 423–25.

[369]The Court explicitly rejected this part of the defense argument. See Schneir, p. 183. Emanuel Bloch's associate Gloria Agrin told me many years later that they had "saved" the Perl indictment issue for a new trial motion as a way of delaying the execution of the death sentence in hopes that with time hysteria would fade.

[370]Referring to David Greenglass

closure of the facts by both of them"[371] and as attested by disinterested prominent scientists David could not have made replicas introduced in the trial from memory unaided.[372] The most important point is that the material he said he turned over is universally considered ["by" CO] despite propaganda to the contrary was either illegorial [*sic*—probably meant "illogical"], not workable, without quantitive [*sic*] date was no secret, that the principle of implosion was in already publically [*sic*] published before the date ["of" CO] the alleged conspiracy began.[373] And in fact there is no basic "secret" concerning atomic weapons. All the top scientists state this fact.[374]

9 [circled] And in furtherance of said conspiracy and to effect the object thereof Judge Kaufman sentenced us to death hoping to bury forever the monstrous miscarriage of justice sired for political purposes and his sentencing speech reveals the reason for his bias throughout the trial and clearly states that the ["basis of is" CO] political interest of official policies would best be served by damning us and ["would ea" CO] because we did not confess and cooperate. He did not base the sentence on the crime we were convicted of as based on the facts in the record but on extraneous matters, scientifically untrue, historically untrue and based on false reasoning. There is no better ["propo" CO] example than the fact that we are the first to be put to death for this [next word in pencil, one after it in pen] for this [letter continued in pencil] crime. While war criminals go free and convicted traitors live. & Ruth Greenglass for the crime worse than murder is free. [Letter continued on top of page in ink]

P.S. I'll continue to send you overt acts in future letters that will follow. (There are at least 5 more and a summation) JR.

---

[371] See Record, p. 1623.

[372] This point relates to the evidence sought by Emanuel Bloch in 1952 as part of an effort to discredit the scientific testimony that had not been sealed. See Radosh and Milton, pp. 438–40; see also Affidavit of J.D. Bernal. Actually, the considered scientific opinion is that Greenglass' crude drawings were in fact what "a good machinist" could have made. The most crucial point is that they did not reveal anywhere near as significant and accurate information as the prosecution claimed. On this, see Markowitz and Meeropol, "The 'Crime of the Century' Revisited: David Greenglass' Scientific Evidence in the Rosenberg Case." *Science and Society*, Vol. 44 (Spring 1980): 1–26.

[373] On this point, see Schneir, p. 264–77. On the evidence sealed at the trial and not reopened until 1966, see Markowitz and Meeropol.

[374] Unfortunately, no American top scientists would state that fact for the record at that time. See the statements of Philip Morrison in *The Unquiet Death of Ethel and Julius Rosenberg*, n.p. and Marshall Perlin in *Hearings*, p. 2305.

*The following is labeled Page #3 which suggests it is a continuation of the
February 11 letter.*

Page #3

Feb. 13, 1953

Dear Manny,

Only a cynical man whose natural instincts are affected by his military
career could show such contempt for the people and although he is the
President and has the greatest responsibility as their representative he
nevertheless boldly and publically [*sic*] displays the triumph of his perfidy.

We had been correctly informed that some time by the end of this week
Mr. Lyons the Pardon Attorney would send the only complete records of the
case to the Attorney General and the newspapers all reported that at [next
word squeezed in the left margin, with two letters blotted out by either a
water or grease spot] about 4:30 P.M "Mr Herbert Brownell Jr. brought the
records of the case to the White House." 5:07 PM a prepared statement is
given out. This proves to the world that [NWI] Pres. Eisenhower never read
the records nor did he see our clemency petition. However the solicitous
press hastens to add that he had been considering independently, "had
reasoned that the crime was enormous with frightful implications in the
atomic age and had concluded that he could not justifiably set aside the
verdict." No need for any pretense the farce is exposed. Again it completely
bears out our contention that the decision is based on a ["considered" CO]
one sided prejudicial evaluation obviously obtained from a source other than
the record and is not founded on the facts in the case nor on it's [*sic*] merits.
In short even the President joins in the political plot to murder us by
approving this excessive harsh sentence and denying us justice. The
magnitude of his crime is [N3WI] all the more staggering because we are
innocent.

Aside from the time worn platitude a reading of the text of the
Presidents [*sic*] statement will show it contains serious inaccuracies.

1 [circled] The President did not give "earnest consideration to the records in
the case" for the Attorney General brought him the records at 4:30 P.M. and
1/2 hour later a prepared statement was issued

2 [circled] Neither the indictment nor the overt acts claim we delivered
certain "highly secret atomic information" although this is tenuously
inferred. [capital "I" written over lower case "i" in next word] If the President
read the record he would find this completely upset by the most competent
top scientists who give positive proof the information claimed is not secret
and which we presented as evidence for a new trial.

3 [circled] The President too a la Judge Kaufman strains to do the impossible and make the crime fit the punishment when he says our crime far

exceeds that of taking the life of another citizen. On the one hand war criminals ["arg" CO] are daily being given freedom by our government and no other citizen was ever executed for the most serious crime treason and now the complete departure from tradition, reason and calm judgement.

4 [circled] Gen. Eisenhower charges us with betrayal. This is a complete lie for the legal term refers to treason. We were not charged with treason nor could we be. The crime we stand convicted of no-where states we gave aid or comfort to an enemy in time of war. Nor that any single overt act was corroborated by two witnesses and so judged true by a jury verdict. Once and for all let it be understood we stand convicted of a conspiracy to commit espionage and nothing more.[375]

5 [circled] The courts did not provide every opportunity for the submission of evidence. On our motion for a hearing to present evidence that our conviction was illegal Judge Ryan denied us the opportunity to subpoena documents and witnesses in order to submit proof of our contention.

6 [circled] The jury was inflamed and prejudiced by a hostile atmosphere by the press, by the reprehensible conduct of the prosecution and by the passion arousing extraneous issue of alleged communism. Its' [sic] verdict was corrupt.

7 [circled] The Supreme Court did not uphold the conviction nor did it judicially review the case. They stated so in Associate Justice Frankfurters [sic] opinion.[376]

8 [circled] Conglomerately his hypocritical statement contains distortions and is untrue and set apart from pretty words it only pays lip service to fair play. It holds fast to the mechanical form of the law and flys [sic] in the face

---

[375]The idea that my parents were convicted and sentenced for treason without the Constitutional protection of the Treason Statute in the Constitution was what led Justice Hugo Black to vote for *certiorari* every single time the case came to the Supreme Court. This confusion continues to persist. When we sued Louis Nizer, the original Judge, Harold Tyler, wrote in his first opinion that they had been convicted of treason. When informed of his error by a letter from our lawyer, he noted orally, "What's the difference?" The difference, aside from the legal facts that the evidence against them could not have supported even a treason indictment let alone a conviction, is that there was no evidence introduced at the trial that they intended to injure the United States in any way. A traitor is one who "makes war upon" his/her own country. See the U.S. Constitution, Article III, Section 3, Paragraph [1]: "Treason against the United States shall consist only in levying war against them, or in adhering to their enemies, giving them aid and comfort. No person shall be convicted of treason unless on the testimony of two witnesses to the same overt act, or on confession in open court."

[376]See memorandum of Mr. Justice Frankfurter, *Rosenberg vs. U.S.* 344 U.S. 889–890. For what Frankfurter was thinking, see Parrish.

of the spirit of the law under the "time honored traditions of justice." Therefore this makes him party to legal murder of two innocent people.

Now it's exposed for all to see. As the justice dept. witheld [sic] the Pope's appeal for clemency from the President & the Public it has witheld [sic] the true facts in the record and the real sentiments of millions of people from the President & the public. From its very inception this pattern has been followed by the justice dept in its plot against us. They hurriedly got the President to sign a statement to completely whitewash this monstrous miscarriage of Justice against two innocent Americans.

The above letter hit the nail on the head about the haste with which Eisenhower made his decision. See footnote 361 above for discussion of Judge Kaufman's role in accelerating the decision.

The following letter is the first indication that Emanuel Bloch was beginning to consider using the console table issue as the next piece of evidence used to support a motion for a new trial. We know from FBI documents about overheard conversations that at least as early as January 31 there was some conversation both between our mother and Aunt Ethel and between our parents about the table. (See teletype Boardman to Headquarters, Feb. 5, 1953)

Mr. Emanuel H. Bloch
7 W. 16th Street
New York NY

February 14, 1953

Dear Manny,

As per our discussion at today's legal consultation I am writing you this letter.

In reference to the console table my best recollection is that I bought it some time either 1944 or 1945. At first it was used mostly as a show piece and a spare family dining table. When the gate leg table broke down completely and could no longer be used to eat on it was sold and the console table took it's [sic] place and was used continuously since some time late in 1947 until the day of our arrest.

The table top was hinged in the middle and folded over on itself and a wooden plug with a flanged boss was screwed to the bottom half. The plug fits in a circular hole in a cross member attached to the frame and the table top could be rotated about this as a fixed center and then the folded leaf could be opened thus doubling the table top area. For the last three years we used it this is the way it remained and this was the only table we could eat on. The frame was rectangular but the front side ["had a" CO, NWI] was curved.

The table top was narrow and only a few of the screw threads of two screws held the plug to the top and the table on the frame. In a short time the threads were stripped & the top used to fall off and besides the table was wobbly when in use. I kept repairing it by stuffing the stripped holes with wooden matches regularly.[377]

Periodically I would get the urge and engage in a number of projects around the house such as painting a chest of draws[*sic*], building a couple of shelves or repairing a piece of furniture. I remember it was around Christmas time the end of 1949 or beginig [*sic*] of 1950 that I got the bright idea to fix the console table and steady it. I planned to fix the table top permanently and add a center leg on the long straight side to give the table greater stability. I hunted up some tools that I found a brace and a couple of [NWI] steel metal ["steel" CO] drill [*sic*] I recall I couldn't find any wood drills. Then I began to ["put" CO] drill a couple of holes but I never completed the job as a matter of fact I believe I didn't quite finish enlarging the holes as I planned. Also I didn't get to go much further I was afraid I might damage the thin table top by putting more screws in it. The possibility occurred to me it might even weaken the top sufficiently and during constant use as our dining table the top might split. This attempt at repair was done about $1/2$ year before our arrest.

You must understand it's hard to remember all the details but what I said is accurate. If you want to know something else we'll be able to talk about it at our next legal consultation.

As Ever
Julie

P.S. I've got a plan on a new investigation that I'm sure will be of substantial use to us and prove Dave lied and I told the truth. This needs immediate attention and we ought to discuss it thoroughly.

In addition to these letters, there are a number of greeting cards exchanged by my parents. One of them includes a handwritten message and so we are including it here. Though it only carries the date 2/53 it is a Valentine's Day card and therefore we are including it as if it were dated February 14.

The card shows two kittens sitting in an open, upside-down umbrella, with this printed message:

"That's my idea of HAPPINESS,
Just sharing life TOGETHER"

---

[377]See *Sons*, p. 188 for my confirming memory of this.

My mother's note (in ink) read:

Dearest, my most precious husband,
    It hurts me to see you suffer but I can't help myself. Believe me whatever I do I am doing with a full heart because it is the right thing to do. My efforts added to the many others might make the difference between life and death.
    Nevertheless I still have hopes that not all is lost & we shall know of happier days—

Always yours, Ethel

Mr. Emanuel H. Bloch
7 W. 16th Street
New York NY.

Feb. 15, 1953

Dear Manny,
    Just a few thoughts ["of of" CO, NWI] on what I can gather from the newspaper and radio reports of the rapid developements [*sic*] in our case. For only a short moment the shock let the truth through to the public. Then quickly the lie curtain took over again[.]
    This Sunday Times is the best example of the point I wish to make. This paper is clearly a master of the art of double talk. You will note that in the use of a deceptive caption they have tried to nullify in the minds of readers the "true meaning of the Pope's message." With a journalistic juggling of news items a deceptive headline and a "story" by McGranery, a back slanted quote by Haggerty [*sic*] they have attempted thru the eye, to mislead the mind.[378]
    Most readers are not "analysts" and the eye controls not only their minds but also their reason and reasoning power. The old "shell game" is a good example. Now you see it now you don't. They ["they" CO] say that a message from the Pope does not represent his sentiments. What a deliberate whitewash of the corrupt knave McGranery and a distortion of fact.

---

[378]This is in reference to the release of information by the Vatican newspaper *L'Osservatore Romano* on February 13 that the Pope had appealed to President Truman for clemency in the case. Attorney General McGranery admitted that he had received this message orally but had not transmitted it to then President Truman. The spin put on this by the press was that the Pope had not intervened but had merely called the attention of the U.S. administration to the many requests he, the Pope, had received to intervene. However, on April 16, 1953 *L'Osservatore Romano* made it clear that the Pope had requested clemency. See Schneir, pp. 193–94.

It seems to me that the magnitude of the crime, this incident is significant of, is that it strikes at the heart of our civilization. For it destroys truth. I believe that the press and radio are engaged in the most serious crime against all mankind because they are the source that prevent the correct evaluation and the right actions from being taken. Naturally it is not all black and white but the mere fact there are enough ["black" CO] deliberate lies condemns them.

Again they depend on the injection of the false issue of communism to hide the monstrous frameup. To the extent that we are successful in breaking down this lie curtain that will determine the outcome of our case and the relative position of the people in the coming struggle for peace and democracy. You and I, many of our friends and [N2WI] even our enemies know this. We must see to it that the dangers are clearly explained to the people.

It is also imperative that the quality of the work on our behalf be dignified, poignantly directed at the main issue and on the highest level of integrity. Of course it goes without says [sic] the rallying of millions is the only guarantee of victory against men of evil. They are desperate and want to bury us quickly before the entire lid is blown off and exposes the stinking messy plot to murder innocent people for political purposes. I haven't a bog [sic—probably meant "bad" or "big"] enough adjective to describe Judge Kaufman and those in the Dept. of Justice who are part of this deal against us. Let them panic in fright we must be firm and resolute in our determination to completely expose them. Go to beloved friend every fibre of our being is behind you

—As ever Julie

P.S.

Manny I got a good idea [last letter of last word written over "d"] concerning the proximity fuse and an investigation to prove Dave a liar. Please think about it.

Emanuel H. Bloch
7 W. 16th Street
New York New York

February 16, 1953

Dear Manny,

There are a number of ideas bumbling around in my head. To begin, [NWI] with there were two items in particular I wanted very badly to take up on Saturday but found no opportunity.

1 [circled] Did you manage to contact Dr. Miller before he left the city concerning a matter we had discussed once before. In any case, it would be personally gratifying to me if I could know he had read the record. He was

supposed to have left a forwarding address and phone, so if you did not manage to speak to him as [N2WI] we had ["planned" inserted then CO] planned, I would strongly urge you to do so now [N2WI] by phone and [NWI] also forward a copy of the record to him. (or write him briefly, if you prefer)

2 [circled] There was also a matter concerning a high-chair about which you wrote down some pertinent facts ["which" CO, NWI] that can very easily be corroborated by the party mentioned.[379]

It would be wonderful, incidentally, if you could get back up here soon. Both Julie & I would rather discuss certain matters with you personally, than write letters about them. And since we were unable to go into things in full detail while visiting with the kids, we shall be biting our nails off until your arrival. Could you ask Ethel to drop us a short line about your intentions as soon as you know where you stand. She's due here on Saturday, incidentally, so if you don't plan to ["come" CO, NWI] see us by this Friday, give her some idea about the week of the 23rd. Possibly Wednesday, the 25th, might suit you, unless you get such a short stay it necessitates your getting here much sooner.[380] In any case, we are anxious for an early consultation with you.

Now, concerning the "plea that wasn't a plea," ["!" CO] certainly [N5WI] one thing is very plain! Whatever message was received from the Vatican, Mr. McGranery's unwarranted assumption that it had nothing to do with the "merits of the case", and his subsequent deliberate concealment of ["its receipt" CO] the facts, would surely indicate ulterior motive. What cold ["and" CO] heartlessness is it that fails to recognize the justice and validity of recommendations for mercy during a clemency appeal, upon whatever grounds they might be forthcoming and from whatever quarter!

---

[379]In one conversation at a regular Wednesday visit between our parents, the FBI reported that they were overheard talking about telling our aunt Ethel not to mention the console table and "the high chair" during prison visits. This report (FBI teletype, February 5, 1953) mentions conversations that occurred January 31 and February 3 between our mother and aunt Ethel as well as the Wednesday visit. There is no evidence anywhere to indicate the significance of this high chair. Emanuel Bloch's files do not contain any references to the information that may have passed between client and attorney during that consultation. What is clear is that the console table was something they were thinking about at least as early as February in terms of legal strategy. Radosh and Milton attempt to paint something sinister about their telling aunt Ethel not to talk about the table in prison, but it is just as likely that they were not anxious to divulge legal strategy in advance. See RM, p. 366.

[380]The defense had appealed to the Court of Appeals for a stay of execution so that they could file a new petition for *certiorari* with the Supreme Court so the Court could review their motion for a new trial that had been denied the previous December. Without such a stay, they would have been executed in early March.

It is my spontaneous feeling that dignitaries of the Catholic Church in this country ought to be approached by proper persons and urged to seek a Papal audience for the purpose of acquainting His Holiness with the corrupt practise [*sic*] to which we have been subjected in the name of a non-existent justice, and to plead for a more directly personal expression from him. Your petition for Presidential Clemency, some of our letters, and others you have received from eminent scientists and lawyers, might serve to convince His Holiness of the righteousness of our cause.

Much more but it will have to wait until I see you. Am getting too restive to go on writing—Love,
Ethel

P.S.—My sympathy to Dena,[381] my best regards to your Pop—Tell every one I said to keep plugging—We ain't licked yet!

Mr. Emanuel H. Bloch
7 W. 16th Street
New York NY

Page # 1   Feb. 16, 1953
Dear Manny,

In the small printed booklet containing the record transcript page 510–511 Dave said "Julius told me he had stolen the proximity fuse when he was working at Emerson Radio. He told me he took it out in his briefcase. That is the same briefcase he brought his lunch in with and he gave it to Russia". This is supposed to have been done while I worked as a Signal Corps Insp. at Emerson Radio. That would fix the time somewhere during 1944.

1 [circled] We could get positive proof from Emerson Radio that no proximity fuse was missing or stolen ["&" CO] at anytime and specifically during the time I worked there. (All information pertaining to this matter, security, set up of plant can be verified by [N2WI] President Emn [*sic*] Ben Abrams)

2 [circled] Ben Yelsey man in charge of Signal Corps, Lt Col Frank Prima [last name somewhat illegible] Officer in charge of Newark Signal Corps, Lts. Samuel [next name illegible] & Bernard Olcott two area officers who were in charge of Emerson Radio could verify all pertinent information.

3 [circled] During my assignment at Emerson my briefcase was always kept in the bottom drawer right hand side of my desk in the Signal Corps office it never went anywhere else in the plant. It contained a complete Signal

---

[381]Emanuel Bloch and his wife had decided to divorce.

Corps Stampkit about 3" wide 6" X 8", extra inspection apparatus, (micrometer, paint, additional stamps cross flags etc.) Two thick files of memoranda each about 2" thick. Inspection regulations booklet and a couple of booklets on government regulations pertaining to the job. Quantities of different forms needed in my inspector's work like Vendors shipping documents, acceptance forms, time sheets, expense forms, inspection reports and quantities of franked envelopes. There were three compartments in the brief case and it was always packed full with all these items & this was the only brief case I used when I worked for the Signal Corps. I only took it from the desk when I had to go on an inspection trip to another plant where I needed all these materials to do the inspection job. Also whenever one came into the plant or left it armed security guards inspected the contents of the brief case and any packages.

When I did bring my lunch from home I always brought it in a paper bag.

4 [circled] The proximity fuse was a bulky item in size and shape and, even if my brief case were empty of the other materials and it never was, and if the fuse ["could possibly" CO] were put in one of the pockets of the brief case it would bulk it out quite a bit. It would be difficult to secure from the production line (without it being noticed or missed) a proximity fuse, pass through a number of armed security guards without being detected, conceal it properly in my brief case in the Signal Corps off. (always full of other Signal Corps employees over 20 of them & a secretary & Emerson personnell [*sic*] had access to it also.) pass at least two more security check points containing armed guards with this conspicuously bulky brief case without being detected. In short even if someone wanted to commit the crime the setup at Emerson ruled out the possibility and beside none was stolen or missing all the time I worked there.

5 [circled] Nor was I in direct contact with the inspection work of the proximity fuse but I supervised those inspectors under me who did the actual work on the production line, on the testing and in the packing.

6 [circled] The office is on the 2nd floor and in the beginning the pilot run was made on the 6th floor and when material went between floors they passed close scrutiny of armed guards & foremen the same was true when the production line on another side of the 2nd floor went into operation. Besides I never carried a proximity fuse between floors.

Page #2

7 [circled] Every unit entering the production line was accounted for even the parts. Line five kept a running account at start, during and end of the day at many points in the line and at each new process. Every subassemble & especially each complete assembly was accounted for and even the rejects

were recorded and kept. I believe the contractor was even paid for the rejects. Never while I worked there were any units missing, lost, stolen or unaccounted for.

A real thorough job can be done on this one single items [*sic*] that Greenglass slipped and said something specific. It appeared prominently in the Circuit Court of Appeals 1st opinion in our case.[382] We can discuss this in detail and really go to town here.

Perhaps we could do the same on the mere mention of mathematics for atomic energy for airplanes (what is it, where, how & maybe some scientist can give us a clue to this lie). Also on the space platforms and the public knowledge concerning Forrestals [*sic*] acknowledgement of the work being done & information in public science magazines. As much as possible should be accumulated together at one time.[383]

As ever
Julie

On February 17, the Court of Appeals stayed the execution permitting the filing of a new writ of certiorari *with the Supreme Court.*[384]

Julius to Ethel

Feb. 22nd, 1953

Hello Sugar,

You'll have to excuse the concentration on the new matters for investigations at this last legal consultation. Although I had promised faithfully that we would go into the children's situation I found I had to give this item preference. I did not wish to repeat what happened the last time when ["I" CO, NWI] our lawyer was preparing a petition for a writ of certiorari. However, this much I insist on that you write Manny as soon as you get around to it to put in motion all arrangements so that everything will be ready when Dr. Miller returns from vacation [illegible overwriting makes the next word uncertain, appears to be "then"] a lot of time ["is" CO, NWI] will not be consummed [*sic*] with new delays. This must be attended to quickly as our counselor will be wrapped in in [*sic*] his law books and [NWI] will find it difficult to allow for any interruption in the work on the Supreme Court appeal.

---

[382]See Record, p. 1659.
[383]On the proximity fuse search, see *Sons*, p. 192. See also memo to file, JR NY 596, August 17, 1950, which demonstrates that the FBI knew the facts that this letter asserts and still Greenglass was permitted to testify falsely at the trial.
[384]See Schneir, p. 194.

Imagine darling there wasn't enough time to exchange more than a couple of glances and yet I need you so very much and want to keep on repeating that I adore you and love you with all my heart. It was a swell letter we got from the kids and I like the confidence that surrounds the written sentiments. Perhaps it would be a good idea to write them and show some warm feelings for Ben and Sonia for the splendid job they are doing with our children. Yes, to [*sic*] often in the rush to concentrate on the main problems we neglect the simple expressions that do so much to encourage people who are trying very hard to do their best. I believe sincerely we owe it to them and I think you can do a much better job than I. Will you please do it for us honey?

I've finished making my notes on our statement and I intent to work it over a bit and at our next tete a tete we'll put it in final shape. I expect to send our lawyer a letter today on a couple of items I would like him to take care of and then I'll relax.

Just because I'm anxious to read the latest issue of the National Guardian, it is late in coming. My brother gave me some of the high lights and from all that he tells me my family is much encouraged by the picture as they see it and are gaining [NWI] confidence most from participating actively in our campaign.

You know, Ethel it would make a swell book to tell the full story of your family and mine and detail their actions and developement [*sic*] leading up to the arrest the trial and [appears to be "uj" CO, N2WI] to this [next word written over illegible word] very date. What do you think of the idea?

There is much to talk about darling so come prepared with an agenda and we'll squeeze 2 hours work into the small time we get. Slowly but surely little bits of truth on our case are beginning to filter into the newspapers. This Sunday Times, in spite of the usual slanting and red-baiting told the story that Europe (Western) is for clemency ["on" CO, N3WI]—using these words mercy, emotional, reason and legal grounds. That's what we've been saying all along. The same will be true of our country if the people get to know the facts. Keep you pretty face smiling and your little chin held high I expect to crush you to my chest again [NWI] smiling in the privacy of our home—All my love
Julie

Mr. Emanuel H. Bloch
7 W. 16th Street
New York NY

February 22, 1953

Dear Manny,

On this the birthday of the Father of our great country, dedicated to the heritage of democracy, freedom and individual rights the idea of truth is stressed because it is the cardinal point of all stories about this first President of the United States.

I think it is fitting to take up a distasteful matter concerning an item that appeared in the Leonard Lyons column in the New York Post Feb. 20, 1953. This vicious living viper must be stopped. There are a number of previous incidents I brought to your attention. Here now again we have this complete fabrication with intent to poison the public against us and help the murder plot against our lives to be carried through with immunity.

In the first place the U.S. Marshall William Carroll did not come to Sing Sing and if he did come he did not see us. We never made any such statement to the U.S. Marshall nor to anyone else concerning any rabbi.[385] This is on a par with the fraud on the Pope' ["s" at end of last word omitted] message and it is not amiss to note that this [last word written over "he"] pen prostitute is fast friends with Judge Kaufman, the prosecutor and members of the FBI. Even if you are to [sic] busy with other matters perhaps you can delegate this item to one of your associates and we ought to bring him to court with a criminal libel suit. One thing is certain I have nothing [suffix "ing" from last word written under next word] but contempt for this low life.

Concerning the matter of the way the newspapers are pressuring the jurors to use them as propaganda against us I believe we can also use this to good advantage. At any rate I think we should have a thorough investigation of this matter and of each and every juror. You have your hands full but I think you ought to get a staff of some of your associates to work on these matters under your able direction.

I've written [last two letters of last word written over "ing"] a number of pages on a proposed statement and I'm waiting until Ethel and I jointly

---

[385]The Lyons column echoed other propaganda that tried to paint our parents as contemptuous of religion due to their alleged Communist atheism. On this point see the comments of the Jewish Chaplain from Sing Sing rabbi Irving Koslowe: "I read some material about the fact that they had a disdain for religion. I read this in the newspapers. From my contact with them that was not apparent at all. I never found your mother or father either disrespectful in any way towards any religious practice or ritual or service. They participated in each one. They responded to each one." (*Sons*, p. 70.)

hammer out one at our Tuesday visit before I send it to you. I was glad to read this Sunday Times and find that news of how the people of Europe feel about our case is beginning to get through to the public. I feel confident that when the American people learn the facts they, too, will react as their European brothers and sisters and I hope that every opportunity will be sought to publicize the truth about our case. Please have your secretary send us printed material that the committee publishes.

By the way if other people can get court orders to visit us how about some of the people we would like to see getting court orders?[386] If there are any interruptions in my letters to you don't worry as I'm working on my notes and I'll try to send the letters in batches. Before the week is out I'll send some material to you. Incidentally send our regards to Mr. Finerty[387] and our best wishes to Pop and send Dinah [*sic*] our condolences. We're counting on you dear friend and we know you'll do a job we'll be right proud of.

As ever Julie

Mrs. Ethel Goldberg
53-47 65th Place
Maspeth, L.I.C. NY

February 23, 1953

Dearest Ethel,

I've already written to our lawyer but I'd like you and the family to consult with him on this matter and take whatever appropriate action you decide on. I am referring to the very latest turn in the campaign against us.

Some diseased mind invented out of whole cloth a complete fabrication about our alleged anti-Semitism. First Leonard Lyons in his column in the New York Post Feb. 20, 1953 reported a meeting between the U.S. Marshall Mr. Carroll and ["myself" CO] us, which never took place and ["bring" CO] gave birth to a big lie [N2WI] claiming things which ["I" CO, NWI] we never said to anyone. Walter Winchell followed this up on his Sunday night broadcast and in his Feb. 23rd column in the Daily Mirror with another similar slander on the same subject. Of course you know these are entirely false and are sired in desperation to poision [*sic*] the public against us.

---

[386]The Almans had tried to get our parents to request that they be allowed to visit, but due to conflicts with Emanuel Bloch, he opposed that.

[387]John F. Finerty, who had been associated with the cases of both Sacco and Vanzetti and Mooney and Billings, had joined the defense team for the application to the Court of Appeals for the stay on February 17.

We have an opportunity to fully expose this low type anti-Semitic trick in reverse and show it follows the same pattern of fraud that has been practiced by our enemies throughout this case. If possible legal action should be started with a criminal libel suit. We should try to obtain a complete public retraction in kind from these two lice. I believe the New York Board of Rabbis should be approached for they are directly involved in this insult as well as [next word written over "us"] we. Also Manny will tell you ["the" CO, NWI] any other people to see on this matters [sic]. It is very simple to track down these items and bring the truth to public attention. Let us continue on this offensive because we've got the opposition worried and I believe the trend is being [sic—probably meant "beginning"] to be a bit more favorable to us.

By the way don't be concerned that the papers distorted what you did on ["the" CO, NWI] your letters to the jurors.[388] You must understand they only wish to hurt us and will do everything possible to poision [sic] the people's mind in order to turn them against us & to stop them from rallying to our support. But you see they cannot succeed because they lie and are rotten to the core. Keep up the splendid work we love you very much and more so for what you are doing.

We got a very lovely letter from our children and I was especially moved to learn that one town in Italy with almost total unemployment, sent the boys a package of delicacies, and a little music box. The thought behind this gift shows you the real heart of mankind and the many encouraging letters and heart warming statements from all over the world signifies the true brotherhood of man. ["and" CO] With this force and the conscience of the world behind us we have what it takes to win this fight. You see my loved ones there is no greater worth than to be true to oneself and one's principles for high moral, ethical and social standards. The final answer is always with the people. I am confident and await good news from you. See you soon—Love to Lee, Hope she's well—Love to Mama—Dave—Your family & Regards to All

as ever your brother Julie

---

[388]We have no knowledge of letters written by our aunt or other family members to the jurors.

Mr. Emanuel H. Bloch
7 W. 16th Street
New York NY

February 23, 1953

Dear Manny,

At first I thought the Lyons item was an isolated case now I'm sure that it is the latest twist in the campaign against us. However, it still retains the singular feature of fraud that has characterized the [NWI] entire legal and public case against us.

First Lyons, then Winchell in his Sunday night broadcast and in his Monday newspaper column reported this new lie. It is obvious to me this is another deperate [*sic*] move sponsored by our enemies to stem the tide of support that is exposing this miscarriage of justice and demanding that we be saved. A psychiatrist would probably be able to analize [*sic*] these warped minds and say that the true feelings of these bigots have slipped out and by their self serving statement they vicariously indulged in this type of filthy anti-Semitism. Naturally, it fits in nicely with the present hatemonger campaign to link up "communists" & anti-Semitism and [N5WI] now too ["so" inserted then CO] they add ["now" CO] the Rosenbergs.

This big lie is made out of whole cloth for I did ["met" CO, N2WI] not see Mr. Carroll nor did I say any such thing directly or indirectly [N2WI] to anyone. Nothing ["ing" of previous word written under next word] short of a complete retraction in kind, publically [*sic*] in the press and radio would give me any degree of satisfaction in this matter. I believe both you and my family should take the matter up with the New York Board of Rabbis for this is a terrible insult to them as well as to us.

Also if possible legal proceedings should begin at once to bring these arch criminals against the truth to justice. I strongly urge you to take this up with my family and have them go to work on this matter. We can and we should use this to further expose the case and the true nature of our enemies. I realize full well that your primary responsibility at this time is to pay [NWI] your fullest attention to our petition for certiorari but you are a past master at coordinating all important features of our defense and since we have complete faith in you, I leave it to your good judgement to do the right thing.[389]

I sincerely believe we must take the initiative wherever possible particularly on key items such as this that show the public the pattern of the case against us. I must caution those who support us to go about doing the work correctly, in the most principled way. The opposition is mad ["e" written over at the end of last word], we've got to nail them to their lies for

---

[389]There is no evidence that any such action was taken.

the people to clearly see, ["that" CO, NWI] for it is we who defend the truth and fight for their interest even as we struggle to win justice that is rightfully ours.

We are hurting them Manny, that is the reason for these ["acts of madness" CO, "in" inserted between second and third words, then CO, N2WI] insane acts. It is a product of their "mental anguish." One does not have to be a genius to see the ["how the authorities have" CO] integration of the whole political picture and [N2WI] to understand just what part our case plays in it. The knowledge of the political nature of our case should give rise to the proper campaign to assure a maximum degree of success. I await to here [*sic*] news of positive accomplishments—As ever—Julie

Mr. Emanuel H. Bloch
7 W 16th Street
New York NY

February 24, 1953

Dear Manny,

At today's visit Ethel brought the following item to my attention and we decided I should write to you about it.

In the February 18, 1953 issue of the New York Times there appeared a news article reporting the proceedings before the Circuit Court of Appeals which lead [*sic*] to a stay of execution. The article states,

(Judge Frank said there was a possibility of prejudice arising from newspaper publicity about the Perl indictment but held that the Rosenberg jury could not know about the indictment itself.)

Obviously Judge Frank is mistaken for of P. 1159 in the small booklets of the record transcript when [last word written over an illegible word] ["cross" CO] cross-examination began this was the first line of questioning by Mr Saypol and the jury heard about Perl or Mutterperl, about the newspaper report, about the arrest of this man for perjury. ["and obvi" CO] Also there was a legal clash on asserting of priviledge [*sic*] against self incrimination on this point. It seems to me that the matter was prominently placed before the jury by Saypol. I know you are aware of this but we felt we ought to bring it to your attention anyway.

Last week's Guardian finally arrived today and it certainly was a swell issue. Everytime I read this paper it acts like a shot in the arm and quickly inspires me with new strength. We really need more of this kind of stimulation, for it's the only light of truth that shines in this dismal place. I hope ways will be found to expose the [N4WI] full story about the Lyons-

Brownell[390] clemency recommendation and it's [*sic*] subsequent repression. The Republicans are the other side of the [NWI] same coin [N3WI] with the Democrats when it comes to chicanery. It is a very difficult job to reach the people considering the pressure against us but we must not stop because we have an opportunity to hold back the flood gates ["of" CO] against reaction and war. It is not enough to fight for clemency we must patiently explain the meaning of this case to the people and tell them all that it signifies.

Now and then, more news is getting through that "free" press lie curtain and a conscious effort must be made to reach the reading public through the press & magazines and also through the radio. Again I'd like to ask you to have one of your secretaries send us printed material on our case. If you can send us some more good books we'd appreciate it immensely. How come since Dec. we haven't received any "Jewish Life" magazines? Perhaps we can get I F Stones [*sic*] newsletter sent to us!!

We're both feeling fine and we'd like to have more time to visit each other to work on the case and our personal problems. ["Maybe" CO] I expect my sister Ethel this weekend ["gi" CO] please give her any news you want to convey to us. I'm right proud of my sweet mother. She looks like the tower of strength [N2WI] she is ["that" CO, NWI] and only a mother's love can give ["for" CO, N2WI] this to her family.

As ever
Julie

Emanuel H. Bloch
7 W. 16th Street
New York New York

February 24, 1953

Dear Manny,

Enclosed please find a few of Julie's letters to me. I call your attention particularly to the one dated February 22nd, in regard to his feelings concerning the children. Of course, I share his sentiments entirely. You ought to get the therapist prepared to visit the kids in company with Dr. Miller, at the earliest possible date.

Also, you have to explain to them both beforehand (and of course, they need to meet once in order to become acquainted personally and ["also" CO] to compare notes), that I'd like Robbie's emotional strains carefully ["sized" CO] evaluated from the point of view of a possible tonsilectomy [*sic*] in the near future. Personally, I'd like to avoid ["a" CO] what might be a punishing

---

[390]This Lyons refers not to the columnist Leonard Lyons but to the Pardon Attorney of the Justice Department.

experience, in view of all the punishment that has already been meted out, but when a report card notes so many days out from kindergarten, his physical ["needs must" CO, N3WI] condition has to be more carefully investigated. Should the therapist find him strong enough emotionally to undergo [NWI] such medical treatment as ["will" CO, NWI] might be required, and should ["their" CO, N2WI] the Bachs' own ["opinion" probably left out here] be to find it imperative (only where both factors are present, you understand, will we give our consent), [NWI] necessary arrangements will then ["have to" CO, NWI] accordingly be made. We were distressed to note the difficulty under which the child labors when he attempts to say more than a few words at a time, and while I have no doubt he is inarticulate for other reasons, certainly a horidly [*sic*] stuffed-up nose and throat don't exactly help matters. Nevertheless, ["I" CO, NWI] we want to be very sure that the "cure" is in order, before we say "OK."

I would forget, of course, to remind you when you were here, that while he [next word written over] was on vacation, Dr. Miller could very well have done with a copy of the record. ["Of" CO, NWI] Well, I did write you to that effect [NWI] some days before you came up here, but a reminder wouldn't have been amiss. If you overlooked this item, I guess it's a little late to do anything about it now as he's due back in the city at the end of this week. Do get in touch with him as soon as ever you can, huh?

Am terribly restive—but one of these days some writing's bound to pour out of me onto paper. In the meantime, patience; [N3WI] just remember that I have to struggle bitterly to function with any degree of ease or comfort, at all. Talent, without the emotional ability to release it, humiliates and mocks one, until one is ready to shriek aloud in pain and in desperation — So please don't expect too much, too fast —

Miss everyone I love [NWI] dreadfully;—the loneliness is impossible!

My best wishes to the Guardian; why, oh why, can't I be out raising funds! Tell everyone I said the major political task is to build the Guardian! It is the one remaining shaft of light in a darkness deliberately created by the free press!—   Love, Ethel

Mr. Emanuel H. Bloch
7 W. 16th Street
New York NY

                                        February 24, 1953

Page # 1
Dearest Manny,

Due to the fact that our visits are short and because of the kind of visits they are Ethel and I weren't able to work out a joint statement. I believe you should take exerpts [*sic*] from Ethels [*sic*] previous letters particularly to [*sic*—probably means "the"] one on her mother and use the following rough draft as the basis for a polished finished document. I read the following to Ethel.

It has come to our attention that millions of people in Europe have rallied to our support and we are honored to convey ["this" CO, NWI] a fraternal [NWI] message of solidarity to you decent men and women who like ourselves are compassionate, love liberty and treasure life. ["Well do" CO]

Well do we recall the last two decades, when first as young people and then as young parents, we participated as social beings with our fellowmen always working for the good of the community and for a better world. Considering our background it was natural that we were active unionists and devoted anti-fascists. Alert to happenings, we strove to contribute our share on the side of progress. In our views and in our actions we were two among the many who practiced the principles of democracy we held dear.

After World War II with the military defeat of the Axis powers many changes took place in the world and also in our country. At first slowly, then at an increasing tempo certain forces in our land, many in high places, attacked the civil rights and liberties of our citizens, the freedoms that made our country strong and ["helped" CO] by these actions broke up the great coalition that made up the New Deal forces. In every sector of life, in the schools, the arts, the newspapers, the radio, the unions, in books and in the government service, men and women found their position in society and their very livelihood threatened. Increasing numbers of people went to jail for political unorthodoxy. Hysteria and fear swept our America. Conformism was the watchword and the Cold War became the foreign policy. However, we two continued to maintain our views and now found ourselves opposed to government policies which we felt were reactionary and would lead to war. Three years ago we Rosenbergs and our two small sons were leading ["a" CO] simple ["life" CO] lives, like most other Americans, unknown to the world except to our family and friends.

Suddenly, in July 1950, a catastrophe singled us out and visited upon us the nightmare of these criminal accusations. We cried out then, even as we do now, that we are innocent but the forces against us we [*sic*—probably meant "were"] overwhelming. The public was prejudiced by the charge of communism, the community was aroused by the accusation [last letter written over] spies for Russia and the peoples [*sic*] passions were inflamed [*sic*] by the mere mention of secret atom bomb plot. Completely alone we two found strength in ["each" CO, "one" inserted then CO, NWI] each other and in our adherence to our principles. We were determined to hold fast to the truth and maintain our faith in the people. We firmly believed in the goodness and strength of the people ["and" CO] realizing that once the facts and issues of our case became known to them, they would understand the far reaching implications and come to our aid.

Page # 2

With the hostile climate it was impossible to get a fair trial. We [next word written over] were framed on the perjured testimony of self confessed trapped spies, who by oral evidence only, tenuously inferred we two were connected in a conspiracy with them to commit espionage. Most of the evidence, both oral and documentary only connected our accusers with espionage and this uncorroborated testimony together with the issue of communism and unpopular ideas, which dominated the trial, prejudiced the jury to find us guilty.

The tensions heightened by the Korean War and ulterior political purposes were the reasons the authorities made an example of us and the judge passed the excessive barbaric sentence of death upon us. It is a coercive ["weapon" CO] force that threatens all those who dissent [sic] from established policies and demonstrate that our government will go so far as to silence opposition by death.

The pressure on us has been terriffic [sic] and our suffering is aggravated ["because" CO] by the threatening tragedy of the destruction of our small family. Because we love our children [N3WI] & our fellowmen so dearly ["and our fellowmen" CO] we shall do the right thing by them and continue to proclaim the truth about our case. It is most important to understand that our two lives are being used as pawns in the hands of evil forces in our country, who want to legally murder us, in order to help establish a police state at home and an international policy that inevitably leads to World War.

Our personal experiences have proven the efficacy of our principles and makes clear that this case of ours is a monstrous miscarriage of justice. ["Unfortunately," CO, N5WI] There [next word written over] is great danger ["whe" CO, next word written over it] because these individuals who participate in this conspiracy plot against the people's interest, are in very high places in our government and even reach to the highest policy making levels in Washington. The world is learning the truth about our case.

We are very much inspired that our faith in the people has been justified and [next word squeezed in] that they are answering to this atrocity. We embrace you our European brothers and sisters and take new strength from your support and your action for justice, decency and freedom. We want to express our heartfelt gratitude for the warm-hearted consideration and kindness you have shown to our two small children. Your encouragement ["s" CO at end of last word, "and the" CO] beautiful sentiments and the symbolic gifts for Michael and Robert are singular proof that the conscience of Europe will not rest until the executioner is stopped and we are returned to our beloved children.

As humble people we acted to protect our good name and our sacred honor. Only as democracy is defiant of tyranny so do we staunchly [*sic*] defend our integrity and the right to fight, as others do, for peace and liberty, for bread and love, for family and future.

With, confidence, courage and conviction
Julius Rosenberg # 110649[391]

The following telegram was sent on February 25, 1953.

EMANUAL [*sic*] BLOCH
401 BROADWAY NYK
=LYONS AND WINCHEL [*sic*] ITEMS FABRICATION MADE OUT OF WHOLE CLOTH STOP NEVER REFUSED SERVICES OF RABBI NOR SEE US MARSHALL CARROLL ON ARRANGEMENTS EXECUTION STOP NEVER MADE THESE TWO OR ANY STATEMENTS DIRECTLY OR INDIRECTLY ABOUT RABBIS THAT SHOWED ANTI SEMITISM STOP RABBI IRVING KOSLOWE SING SING CHAPLAIN US MARSHALL AND AUTHORITIES HERE CAN VERIFY STOP SEE MY LETTERS FEBRUARY 22 AND 23 TO YOU AND FAMILY DECRYING THESE OUTRAGEOUS FRAUDS=
    JULIUS ROSENBERG 110649

Mr. Emanuel H. Bloch
7 W. 16th Street
New York NY

February 25, 1953

Dear Manny,

A cardinal principle in my philosophy of life is the firm belief in equality and in freedom of religion. In all my actions and [next word squeezed between two words] all the things I've said throughout my adult life I have always adhered to these principles and I've respected the right of my fellowmen to think, speak and worship as they pleased. That is why I've been so terribly incensed over the monstrous lies that Lyons and Winchell made by falsely charging me with anti-Semitism. I loathe and detest any kind of ["anti" CO] racialism or anti-Semitism even the reverse kind these two pen prostitutes put forth in their columns.

---

[391]This letter was never published.

At Sing Sing Ethel and I have attended all services conducted by the Jewish Chaplain and I've had talks with the Rabbi every time he comes ["o" in previous word written over "a"] to the condemned ["all" CO, NWI] cell block. We discussed this matter he too is horrified by the viciousness of such ["u" in previous word written over "h"] irresponsible newspapermen. In the time I've been here the Rev. Thomas J. Donovan the Catholic Chaplain has come to know me well and he too has been shocked by the news reports and told me that never was their [sic] any indication of such an atitude [sic] on my part. Both of these religious leaders and the authorities here will be able to attest to the fact that my relations with all men here have been honorable and particularly have I demonstrated in that which I said and did that I am not anti-religious or bigoted in anyway against anyone for their race, color or creed.

Dear friend because I stand ["condened" CO] condemned to death although I am innocent, I am being crucified this way. In the interest of truth and fair play I demand complete satisfaction from these two lice. Do what you can to bring the culprits to justice.

In a Feb. 25th article in the New York Times it [NWI] was reported that Mr. Lane devoted most of his talk to the prosecution of the Rosenberg spy case. He spoke at a luncheon at the Lions Club of NY at the Belmont Plaza Hotel. He has added unethical professional conduct to the list of his infamous acts in our case.

The final sentence is revealing "If the Reds are out to get our lives, let's get theirs first." and also he hoped Americans would not become complacent about the threat of Communist infiltration & that the case would prevent it. Obviously that is the reason he helped frame two innocent people to use the case as a political weapon against dissenters, who are alleged by his ilk to be communists. It seems to me that the District Attorney has a little "mental anguish" of his own for he's completely corrupt.

By the way I'll be needing some commissary money I just put in a 3 months subscription for the Times. I hope you take good care of yourself for we love you very much. Also there is a great deal of responsibility [sic] riding on ["those" CO, N2WI] your very capable ["hands of yours" CO, NWI] shoulders. I sincerely believe that the best thing that has happened to us since this case is that we met you and became fast friends I can't ever praise you enough. Your [sic] a Prince of a guy Manny—fraternally—Julie

Julius to Ethel

Feb. 26, 1953

Dearest Ethel,

There are times when I'm going great guns, working hard, enthusiastic that we're fighting against tyranny and feeling good. A visit with you, Manny, the kids or the family or a letter and some good news primes my spirit and keeps my morale high. However, it is not enough because I can't go home to you and the children. Then, there is emptiness, heartaches and great suffering.

Books are wonderful things. I get so completely absorbed in them. [illegible letter at end of last word CO] They take me out of this place and are very gratifying emotionally uplifting, and are good food for the intellect. At present I'm reading "Man the Maker" by Forbes a history of technology and invention and it's [*sic*] effect on civilization. It's a very edifying work and makes interesting reading. Then when I put this book down, ["and" CO] the narrowing walls and steel bars hem me in so closely. They Point [*sic*] out the sharp contrast of the rapid advances technically but still there [N2WI] is an archaic, barbaric, spiritual and moral contrast of life all around us. He who cannot see ["or" CO] feel or understand the meaning behind words, forms and society cannot begin to get anything out of life, for the real beauty of the good life is participating in the forward movement of humanity.

We can be very thankful for one characteristic that both of us possess and that is although we are effected [*sic*] by little things we are always able to keep in mind the overall bigger picture of our situation, clearly understand our perspective and therefore maintain a firm stability at all times. Oh Sweetheart, the mind and heart will not be satisfied until it has the minimum standards [N4WI] of our relationship that we've experienced together. I hunger to share with you, my dearest, the simplest, the smallest things and of course all my love.

History ["has" CO, NWI] is recorded [NWI] by it's [*sic*] highlights with stories of a number of "Hamans" but we too, my darling are the victims of the modern "Hamans[.]" Again, in our case the motives of the present day tyrants are the same, personal agrandizement [*sic*] through a foul political plot [NWI] while spilling the blood of the innocent. The Heritage [*sic*] of our Hebrew culture has served our people throughout the ages and we have learned it's [*sic*] lessons well and it is part of us in our blood and we strive for a free, richer and better life. What we are and all that we have no one can take away from us even though they keep us apart and threaten us with death. It seems to me that perhaps it would be easier on us if we did not feel so deeply and were not so well aware of our case and its implications. Nevertheless, I am positive we would not want it any other way. We have in the past and we will in the future continue to contribute to progress in spite of the difficulties we face. That is the reason our enemies use this lowest type of tactics against us because they can't beat us down and they will ["live" CO, NWI] suffer to see us win regardless of the final outcome of this case. All the love of my heart. Your devoted husband   —Julie

Julius to Ethel

March 1st, 1953

My Precious Woman,

It's eight P.M now and I just awoke from a $1^1/2$ hour nap. After spending $5^1/2$ hours reading the Sunday newspapers I get [*sic*] very tired and welcomed the respite. I've been reading eight metropolitan newspapers regularly for the last two years and I've developed an ability to analyze news trends. Also one thing is very clear to the careful reader that this ["there" CO] is no free press but one that slants it's [*sic*] news and [N2WI] seeks to control public opinion. It is imperative for us to know that the administration is steadily moving to the right and the hysteria is reaching a new peak. Because we understand the full picture we are better able to gauge the means needed to reach the people and conduct the best possible defense. Being aware of the great difficulties we face doesn't in any way mean that we are downhearted but requires that we fight all the harder because we know the importance of this struggle and we sincerely believe, with the aid of the people, we can win a victory.

As we become more effective in our effort of rallying support and exposing the frameup and it's [*sic*] political nature the opposition will continue to react with this lowest type of campaign and vicious vituperations against us. They realize we are hurting them and they are attempting to frighten the people with their methods but they are failing because their policy, method and tactics [next word written over illegible word] are rotten and decadent and [NWI] because they hold the people in complete contempt. This affords us the opportunity to mobilize the multitudes with the clear call of the truth to save us and [N4WI] so doing also defend their own interest. ["s" CO at end of last word] If there are such low ["f" CO with a dash] lifes like the Greenglasses who barter away their own flesh and blood to save themselves, it is ["not too much" CO] easy to understand ["the" CO, NWI] what motivates the evil forces in our land who are leading our country to fascism and war. Basically, these are the big stakes in the world arena and our case has become part of this greater picture.

Of course, it was a great treat to get Manny's letter and read the inspiring words of the great French Lawyer Paul Villard. It is really good to know that the French people and the rest of the world are alert to what is taking place in our country and are doing something about it. The supreme task is to help our American people become as politically conscious of their ["last letter written over illegible letter] needs as their European brothers are. A great deal more has to be done to build up a newspaper like the National Guardian and people's organizations that stand vigilant at all times and leads [*sic*] the fight for democracy and peace.

When I see you this Tuesday we'll go into ["personally" CO] many of the things I've been thinking about. My heart and my love reaches out to embrace you my dearest to give you the deepest feelings I posses [*sic*] to comfort [NWI] you and lend you support even as I [NWI] too draw great strength from these tender feelings. Because of you and the children I am proud of our family and I can face the future steadfastly defending our principles. All my love

Your devoted husband—Julie

Julius to Ethel

March 5, 1953

Dearest Ethel,

Although it was only Tuesday morning that we had such a good visit it already appears that it's been so very long ago. I guess this is do [*sic*] to the fact that we haven't received any letters from home or from Manny this week and we're hungry for news of what's taking place. The lie curtain of the "free" press prevents any true picture from being presented on our case or on matters involving political controversies. Also I haven't done any writing this week and the time seems to drag and I'm not completely satisfied with myself even though I realize I can't mechanically force myself unless I feel the need to express my thoughts. Besides, I miss you very much for it ["s" CO at end of last word] is unhuman [*sic*] to keep us apart, away from our children and under the threat of imminent death considering the great injustice in this case. But tomorrow I see you and I'm looking forward to another wonderful visit.

I'm planning to write both boys on the occasion of Michael's 10th birthday and I'm sure our precious darlings would welcome an expression from you on this happy day for our first born. This weekend I've put my hand to writing you more details on this special day for us. To our lawyer I'll send a reminder of the kids [*sic*] birthday and suggest he get them a few presents on our behalf and remind the family to make this a pleasant remembrance for our children.

You know sweetheart when we were home together, as other people, we found many releases for our feelings ["and" CO, N3WI] and of these, the need to let off steam and gripe to someone who cares and understands is very important. This is the only way for a relationship to be fruitful and flourish to maximum advantage for all parties concerned. Painful, is the only word to express the deep hurt I feel because of our present circumstances. One compensating feature is that we are contributing our share on the side of progress in the great decisions that are [NWI] now in the making. Yet I feel the situation demands more of us and I know we could be much more effective if we were together, home with our sweet boys. You can guess dearest that I need your love and comfort, which you have always [NWI] wilingly [sic] given me, but I want you in my arms, physically close to me.

If I haven't put anything on paper you must understand I've been thinking very deeply about many ["details" CO, NWI] things and I prefer to discuss them with you and Manny personally ["instead of using" CO, N3WI] rather than use letters as the means of talking over these matters.

One thing continues to amaze me and that is the great degree of degenercy [sic] of integrity among a large section of "liberals" and intellectuals in our country. Of course, these are difficult times we live in and fear has stampeded many people to conformity and silence but they must surely know that this is suicide. Regardless of the hardships, the seriousness of the situation is known to the progressive and I'm confident the people will know how to protect their interests. This is our great hope too.

All my love—Your—Julie

Mr. Emanuel H. Bloch
7 W. 16th Street
New York NY.

March 5, 1953

Dearest Manny,

Although I haven't written you this last week, it does not signify ["that" CO] any demoralization or any lack of new ideas, for ["on" CO] the contrary is true. My mind has been very active and I've been in deep thought on many different ideas but I must wait until I consult with you and Ethel before I give expression to the many profound feelings that have occupied my time this last week.

Since I want to finish this letter and make tonight's mail I'll just make a few brief notes. March 10th is Michaels [sic] birthday. He'll be 10 years old and it's always been our practice to celebrate these occasions with gifts for both boys and all that goes with making this a happy memorable day for them. Particularly at this time we feel special effort should be made to reassure our children with love, understanding and new hope for their welfare and future. Remind my family, in case they've forgotten, about the nature of this day for I know they'll want to do something for Mike and Robbie. If it is possible, give the boys something extra on our behalf. Ethel suggests an enlarged photo of us might be a suitable present.

I was pleased to read your letter telling me about the press release concerning the Lyons and Winchell anti-Semitic frauds. Instead of reading of a retraction I find that Winchell [N2WI] in his March 5th column saw fit to repeat his bigoted falsehood. I hope you'll be able to enlist religious leaders in the fight to force a clearing of the record and get a full retraction from this filthy louse.

I know that you are very busy working on our petition to the Supreme Court and I do not wish to press you to try to see us soon but if you do mange to find the time I'm sure we'll have a very productive consultation with you.

Before I forget I want to express my appreciation and thanks for the moving fraternal message from Paul Villard, a true son of the heroic liberty loving French people. It is a source of inspiration and courage to receive the comradeship and heartfelt feelings of millions of people of France. As long as the conscience of the world is reflected by ["this type of" CO] sincerity and brotherhood in this way then peace and freedom on ["the" CO] earth are assured and the Rosenbergs will be saved.

The world is on the threshold of many important decisions and, incidently [*sic*] our two insignificant lives ["will" CO, NWI] are also linked up with these greater events. The important thing is that we fight on the side of the people, for the little and big things, that make for a better, fuller, peaceful life. If we two ordinary man and woman can suffer because we firmly adhere to these principles [next word written over illegible word] then by our example [N2WI] we can arouse our fellowmen ["to" CO, NWI] in their own ["interests and" CO, "strength" inserted then CO, NWI] interest to their own strenght [*sic*] and prove their real worth. The victory is all the sweeter.

As ever Julie

Master Michael Allen Rosenberg
c/o B. Bach
R.D. 2 Box 148 M
Toms River N. J.

March 8th, 1953

Dearest Michael,

As always in the past, as too this year, on the very special occasion of your 10th birthday on March 10th I join you in celebrating it and send you the deepest love of my heart, my most affectionate embrace and heartfelt kisses. Each time you become a birthday boy son you grow in many ways. Your knowledge increases, your understanding grows, you are able to reach out to newer and higher goals of the finest things life gives us an appreciation of the world we live and the part we play in it.

For me your father this is also an important day. I'm proud of your accomplishments and your happiness and welfare is my constant concern. ["s" CO at end of previous word] Above all Mike I always accept you for what you are, whether you eat eggs or not, with all your gripes and complaints, your joys and sorrows and hopes. As a growup [sic] the real beauty in life is ["a" CO] purposefulness in living, in working to improve the world we live in. ["and" CO] In my relationaltionship [sic] first with you and our family and then with my fellowmen both in the things ["we" CO, NWI] I do and the principles I adhere to, I find the greatest satisfaction. I believe this is the way we improve ourselves as people and find we are really worthwhile.[392]

Each one of us Mike developes [sic] at our own rate of speed [N6WI] because of the capabilities we possess from what we learn and experience. Although circumstance [sic] prevent closer contact between us I am very glad you are getting along well by doing the ordinary things boys your age do; study, play, learn music, fight around (tease) gripe etc. Sincerely son you are doing ["well" CO, NWI] fine so here is congratulations for your birthday and for your general behavior.

You know it is most important that we do not shut our eyes to reality. We are aware of the difficulties we face and of the deep meaning of events around us and particularly as it is reflected in the ["events" CO] matter that touched our lives and holds such importance for mankind. Also we must hold fast to the truth, to the fact that we are innocent and have the courage of our convictions. Daily more and more people all over the world are coming to our support and are realizing the true nature of our case and we are confident they will help set us free.

To Robbie his brother's birthday is also a happy day and soon he too will be a birthday boy. I saw your pictures in the National Guardian and I am thrilled to have such a nice picture to look at whenever I wish.

Your letter pleased me very much for it has a quality of you Michael and I want to thank Ben and Sonia for doing an extra good job. It is a

---

[392]Since he must have realized the ten-year-old he was writing to could not have understood this letter, the language indicates that he wanted to leave letters that Robby and I as adults could understand. This suggests a (perhaps subconscious) preparation for the possibility that he would not live to see us grow old enough to understand such thoughts.

wonderful feeling to know that our precious children are secure and are getting the kind of love and understanding that is helping them grow and meet the future.

Happy Birthday Michael I hope we'll spend many of them with you in the future. I send all my love to you boys. Give our best to the Bachs and all our [NWI] other dear ["freedo" CO] friends. Keep writing it does us good to hear from you.

Your Own Daddy—Julie

Julius to Ethel

March 8th, 1953

HAPPY BIRTHDAY MOTHER, My Adorable Bunny

March 10th will be 10 year [*sic*] that you gave birth to our first born. I am proud of our family, Ethel dear and in spite of all difficulties our children are growing up properly. Again my darling I want you to know that I love you with every fibre of my being. I am not happy about our dire predicament but I am pleased with the principled way we have conducted ourselves and with the steadfast fight we've waged to prove our innocence. My feeling for you is profound and overwhelming and our separation is very painful. I'll just think about our relationship, our love, our life together and our single heartedness of purpose, the great promise of the future and I can remain strong and confident.

On this occasion it's good to note that our boys are progressing nicely and that our friends are doing all they can to help them develope [*sic*] normally. Also that the people whom we believe in, are supporting us and are even taking us into their hearts. This signifies the efficacy of our principles and proves the real meaning of brotherhood among men. Life practiced in this manner is really worthwhile. After all, what is important is that we continue to strive for decency, for human dignity, for understanding for democracy and peace. Even in this horrible place we can contribute our share for progress. Regardless of the difficulties and the situation truth and morality will be effective in helping us and will work for the common good.

The critical times we're in require that we ["base" CO, NWI] maintain our faith in ourselves and the people and think clearly about the whole picture and then we will ["understand" CO, N4WI] see our way clear ["ly" CO at end of last word]. You will note how the enemy is linking our case with every major political problem he faces and we must expose this to public attention. If I were to try to keep up with every new twist in the ["h" CO] campaign against us I'd have to write reams of letters daily. I have discussed each of the developements [*sic*] with you and whenever I don't get to write Manny I make notes for our next consultation.

I sent our children a birthday letter and I hope they like it. It is hard to write them since I feel so strongly. However, I stopped a few moments to think about us in our own home. The kids are on the floor playing with their toys and we're sitting on the couch enjoying the warmth of our family circle and snatching a couple of kisses every now and then. Of course, I mean to say plenty of hugging and loving. Honey! we'll make it. Rights [*sic*] on our side and our will is very strong and besides this is the only course that will bring justice and happiness.

You know wife I'm just crazy about you and the boys. I can't wait to see you again. Every waking moment is occuppied [*sic*] with thoughts of you and the children. Good night sweet woman—As ever always devoted to you

Julie

Julius to Ethel

March 12, 1953

Dearest Ethel

From both Michael's and my sister's letters I hear a note of greater confidence and it is indeed remarkable how people working for a good cause, which is based on their convictions, can be fired with spirit, enthusiasm and courage. Actually, the most fruitful results are obtained from action ["s" CO at end of last word] motivated by a thorough understanding of the situation and a knowledge of the purpose of what ["the people" CO, NWI] one wishes to accomplish. First I must say we are honored by the solicitude shown our children and my family by the good people the world over. Most important is that great numbers of people are aware that peace and freedom are the primary ["issues" CO, NWI] goals and they are alert to all ["isses" CO, NWI] issues ["th" CO] such as our case that are an integral part of the major ["issue" CO] problem facing the world. We cannot ask any more than that we continue to work for this just cause as we fight to save ourselves.

Although I've refrained from writing these last weeks while I've been digesting all I read I can't help but comment on what I believe to be a developing dangerous situation. Practically the entire press has embarked on a jingoistic campaign. Open bellicose statements, editorials, columns [the next word is written illegibly enough so it could be either "interspersed" or "intensified"] ["between in" CO, NWI] among a welter of utterly confusing and contradictory news reports must be having a deleterious effect on the public. For it must be exceedingly difficult for ["them" CO, N2WI] the people to obtain any fair degree of facts which are essential for them ["th"

CO] to know in order to get any idea of what is taking place and what they are facing. It seems to me that the task facing the outspoken progressives, leaders and honest men and women is [N2WI] not only more difficult but also ["is" CO] most urgent.

Oh darling I feel so frustrated. I would like to stop the ordinary man on the street and talk to him for I feel sure it would be easy [N4WI] for both of us to ["show him where" CO, N2WI] agree on our joint interest. Then I begin to worry that I'm not writing ["my" CO] and putting my thoughts down and use this means to get my views across. However, somehow it just doesn't always work out as easy as it should and do not for one moment think it is because I'm worried or downhearted that I'm not very productive, on the contrary, it is precisely because I want to be crystal clear in formulating my thoughts that it requires such great efforts on my part.

One thing is certain I've been reading and listening to so many beautiful words & lively high sounding principles in lengthy disertations [*sic*]. All ["based" CO, N6WI] empty words for they are based on false premises and are leading to reaction; decay and eventual war always in the guise of peace and the "free" world. It is only necessary to keep in mind the individual actions and the apparent contradictions to see the true face of the "prophets of doom". I am very confident the people will succeed in defending peace and I sincerely believe they will help save us.

Of course you know I miss you very much and I love you with all my heart that's why ["there is enough room" CO, N4WI] I can love my fellowmen so much. Always devoted to you—your husband—Julie

Julius to Ethel

March 15, 1953

My Darling,

You can imagine how anxious I was while you went through the ordeal[393] but from all that I gathered you did very well. It is we who have a conscience and deeest [*sic*] feelings that are forced to suffer the tortures of the damned, in order, to uphold our principles. At the moment, we are in the forefront of a very important struggle and I feel confident we will continue to find the courage [N3WI] to stand firm in spite of the terriffic [*sic*—"ff" in previous word written over either an "l" or a "b"] personal pressures assailing us. It is hard for good people to believe that barbaric and bestial ["terror both" CO] mental and emotional [NWI] terror are being used against us. Why the civilized mind is revolted by such tactics. Oh how I fear for our fellow Americans that because there [NWI] are certain forces in our land are

---

[393] Another visit from Ethel's mother.

able to reverting to such evil practices.[394] The political lesson must be clear to all who are not blind that only organized opposition to the hate-mongers can save the peace and freedom. You can understand the reason for my anger ["that" CO, "because" inserted, then Co, NWI] that the Committee did not see fit to print and widely distribute our petition for Executive Clemency. Here is an opportunity to poignantly show the nature of our case and the relation it bears to the fight against the witch hunters who are paving the way, through fear, to fascism and war. I still believe they'll see the light in time to make effective use of this scholarly document. I cannot praise our lawyer Manny enough for the brilliant job he did in writing this appeal.[395]

Sweetheart, our consultation was pretty good but I would have felt much better if we had made specific plans, right then and there, for Manny to follow just as soon as he files our petition with the Supreme Court. I might suggest a detailed letter to him and Dr. Miller discussing what we'd like done, raising the problems we've talked about and ["suggesting" CO] recommending they set an early date to see our children. If you find it possible to get off a letter to our boys on the music question I think it would be very helpful. I realize there are many pressing things on your mind but I am sure you'll understand I'm only putting my thoughts down and in no way do I intend to push you to do anything you're not ready for. Oh Honey, I love you very much and I want so to be with you. Can you imagine they didn't have the nerve to face me! Your family didn't even make an attempt to see me. They are probably waiting for further instruction [*sic*] from the F.B.I. or district attorney before they venture to offer me their rotten deals. Although I don't know the details I still want to pat you on the back for the way you conducted yourself.

You know sweetheart with all the increasing tension and the confusing world situation I still feel calm because I am secure in the knowledge we are right and we are doing our part in this fight. What is really difficult for me is the constant concern over you and the children and I guess that is only

---

[394]From the corrections in this sentence it appears he originally wrote ". . . because certain forces in our land are able to revert to such evil practices." The version as it stands now (with "revert" extended to "reverting") doesn't make sense because he did not change "are able to" to fit. Perhaps the new sentence should have read ". . . because there are certain forces in our land which are reverting to such evil practices."

[395]Note because there was never any personal contact between my parents and the Committee, everything he learned about what was going on between them and Manny came from Manny alone. In reading the petition for executive clemency, the reader can decide if perhaps the committee members might have felt it too strident an insistence on innocence when the key to the campaign was clemency, on whatever grounds.

natural. We didn't make any plans for another visit with our boys but I think we ought to have them up here after Manny puts in our petitions. Think about it and make some arrangements so that we'll get in another visit before we hear from the Supreme Court. I adore you Ethel ["you are" inserted then CO] my precious wife I hold you always close to my heart— As ever devoted to you— Julie

Mr. David Rosenberg
430 E. 63d Street
New York New York

March ["17" CO, NWI] 18, 1953

Dear Davy,
    Just to send you enclosed Sunday pass—
    We are fine —
    Love, Ethel —

P.S.—No time to write— Mail collection— and I have to get ready for Julie's visit.— Ketch?
P.S.P.S.—I wrote the above the wrong day —
Julie visits me Tuesday not Wednesday which is Mar. 18—E

Julius to Ethel

March 19, 1953

Sweetheart Darling,
    Here it is still two more days before a young man's fancy turns to love and ["yet" CO, NWI] already I am "plein de amor" [*sic*] for you my sweet Ethel. [N4WI] (As always my dove) Everything seems to be in tune. The season of the year is approaching [NWI] with the bright scenery days that quickens [*sic*] the pulse, freshens [*sic*] the spirit and a glorious feeling of youthfulness encourages newer accomplishments. For in essence advancement always displays the rigor of youth. The world has come to recognize the true nature of our case and the people, the most effective force on earth, are behind us and are demonstrating a thorough awareness that they know how to fight for peace and freedom. Politically not only has this miscarriage of justice misfired but it has exposed ["those in" CO] our government by the barbaric sentence of death against two innocent people for their progressive views. Then, too, the level of the campaign at home has entered the phase where the public is beginning to understand the full meaning of our case. Therefore, my morale is at a very high point and my profound love is in harmony with it but cries out for proper expression. There is no doubt that

we've received great satisfaction from our firm maintainance of high moral and ethical standards and from working for a good cause but still the flesh and blood will not be assuaged until we are [three illegible words followed by "and" inserted, then CO] together again with our children, at home.

I've been thinking darling it ["s" CO at end of last word] is almost three years since we've lived with our children. How we treasured ever [*sic*] moment with them and how wonderful it was to share each and every accomplishment of theirs. A new painting, a nice block building, a particularly meaningful action of our boys, signs of growth, indications of abilities for music, art and the general problems of joy worry and pain that goes with the beauty of family life. And so Robbie will be six and Mike is ten and they and we have been denied our birthrights by beasts. If we write with conviction and we're strong it's because the truth is indelibly made part of us by the deep marks of pain. When I see the sign of understanding in Michael's deep blue eyes and the warm smile of feeling in Robbies [*sic*] face, then I know the reason we can stand this great suffering. Inside of me I guess I'm a softie for when I think of our sons and you I get such tender feelings and although I don't show it my heart is crying.

You know I've been reading a great deal lately, books on nature, the physical laws, economic problems, political and scientific works and because I know man can work with nature and better the world I realize how important it is to work ["for a" CO] to make this a reality. This is the only way to ["s" CO] truely [*sic*] love my children. Dearest when I sit across from you separated by the power of tyranny, my eyes, my voice and my demeanor conveys to you my wholehearted destiny and admiration for you and assures you that I will ["al" CO] forever be true. So, for the coming day, a breath of spring, the perspective that will make all ["seasons" CO, NWI] year the seasons of youth, for the full bloom of life I love you & I'm confident

Your young man—Julie

Julius to Ethel

March 22, 1953

Precious Bunny,

I'm going around with that far away look in my eyes. You guessed it. Just some more of that spring fever. Now that I've read my sister's most recent letter and the latest issue of the National Guardian I can understand the reason for the New York Times giving such prominence to something that is only a rehash, that Greenglass asserts he did not lie. You will note that now they are forced to finally fall back on the weak premise that he says so and ergo it must be so. Sweetheart, the public is questioning and very strongly so, the verdict in this case and they have reason to believe it is corrupt. Considering the period of cold war we are in I honestly feel that the results of the dinner are amazing and it should indicate to those who are working on our behalf that they should boldly go out and mobilize the people around our case.

Another very heartening thing is the new enlarged New York issue of the National Guardian.—It is such a welcome sign of the growing opposition to the press blackout and it comes at a very appropriate time when certain liberals & progressives are beginning to fight back against McCarthyism the [illegible word CO, "of" inserted, then CO] feuher [*sic*] of American fascism. It seems to me that what is needed is a bette [*sic*] clarity ["of" CO] on events that are taking place and the people will quickly recognize the demogogic acts of our governmnt [*sic*] in foreign & domestic policy. I can't help going back to our case because in it we can easily show the deeds and what they signify and that is the reason I've been stressing that [N3WI] there is a crying need for more and better literature on our case such as: our petition to the president & our letters. ["an" CO] I do hope some competent experts ["in" CO] like ["s" CO at end of last word] scientists and sociologists would analize [*sic*] the case with particular regard to their own field and I'm sure the results ["l" CO] would be most revealing and [NWI] very helpful to us. Yes darling I borrowed this suggestion from you and I think Manny ought to ask some people to go to work on this idea. By the way I haven't been writing our lawyer lately and I think you ought to send him our letters.

So let me come back to the point I raised at the beginning of the letter. The Easter season is a colorful time for the family. Some new clothes, beautiful flowers, warmer weather and a holiday spirit permeates the air. Love, closeness of family and ["dedication to" CO, N2WI] the good feeling of joy in life & to me it was always a time for rededication to the humane features of man to high moral and ethical standards and to the concentration on the deeper meaning of things. Even in here we must cultivate ["the" CO, NWI] a zest for all that is decent and I must say I've been able to drink deeply and with [NWI] great satisfaction when I read good news of happenings in the world. Naturally, I speak relietely [*sic*] because basically I'm very lonely for you the children and the life of striving to advance in the world we know. For your smile Ethel, your warm kiss, your sweet voice and your understanding mind are my greatest treasure & pleasure. Accept my heart my love—your Julie

Julius to Ethel

March 26, 1953

Beloved Ethel,

Into the narrow confines of this steel and concrete tomb, in the abattoir at Sing Sing comes a card, a message from far away France a fresh breeze of spring. I do not know who sends this particular one but our good advocate Manny informs me it is one of thousands from the French people. It comes from the mind because they think of us. It comes from the heart because they love us. It comes from feeling, emotion and reason ["because" CO, N5WI] for they are compassionate and they admire us. Above all it is life because they act.

It is simple and clear and yet all encompassing. Besides the concise language a picture, a drawing of flowers, of earths [*sic*] creation of hands reaching for beauty, for food and for life. ["for" CO] This has stirred me very deeply for here is a visual example of the true expression of the conscience of the world, of humanities [*sic*] striving for good, for plenty. ["that" CO, N3WI] They know it can only come with peace and liberty. The people of France have contributed much to civilization and know how to insure its progress. Sweetheart, we are honored, indeed I am encouraged by the wonderful sentiment and feel strong in the unity that binds us with our brothers allover [*sic*] the world against the tyrants that ["threaten us" CO] want to destroy us. Since they have no faith in the people, they fail to understand the elementary historical truth and to recognize the strength of the people. On the other hand I firmly believe in this principle and I am [NWI] therefore confident that we will win.

In every sector of American life there has lately arisen a group of self-appointed "demi-Gods" following the lead of the "God" McCarthy who have arrogated to themselves supreme powers to dictate to the rest of us what we may or may not do, read, speak, believe, etc. They hide their demogoguery [N2WI] while they ["behind" CO, N3WI] cloth [*sic*] themselves in a mask of super patriotism, & behind a cloud of wild charges and lies in an atmosphere of fear catering to the basest passions [N2WI] they hope to prevent reason and truth from exposing ["them" CO, N2WI] their game. It seems to me that because of this situation it is ever imperative to stand up to these fascists and nail them to their lies. This is the third passover holiday that we will spend in the shadow of death. Our forefathers freed themselves from bondage and we must learn the lesson that while we are able we must prevent these [N2WI] evil men from enslaving the mind as a prelude to complete subjugation. That is why they must be fought [N3WI] at every stage when they attack the free schools, the books, free speech, association and assembly. Those who struggle for freedom can rightly claim this [NWI] glorious heritage [N3WI] of our people and I am sure it will inspire them as it has always inspired me.

My mind has been working overtime and I've given you only a couple of the high lights of the thoughts that have occupied ["my mind" CO, NWI] me these last few days. Believe me it seems like ages since I've last seen you because I've been busy reading books, newspapers, Supreme Court opinions and legal briefs. I read the opinion and the briefs in the case of the four Negroes [N4WI] (The Daniels case etc.) who are due to die in North Carolina. Honey here is proof positive ["the" CO] of lynch justice. When will America wake up to the truth and stop these bestial racial murders? Look now they are adding political murders and spreading the barbarism just like the Nazis did. I am confident the people will ["not" CO] act but I hope it will be soon with sufficient force to win a victory.

All my love
As ever—Julie

Julius to Ethel

March 29, 1953

My Charming Ethel

Even though you do not have an Easter bonnet or a new spring outfit you still look very lovely and what really stands out are the important things, the sincerity of your convictions, the integrity of your character and the profound humanity of your soul. It is indeed our good fortune that our lives have been enhanced and made fuller because of the great contributions you have made to our relationship, to the essence and spirit of a happier life. Also because I've been able to observe the integration of your social actions ["with" CO] based as they are on a foundation of fine virtues that I admire you because you are such a swell woman. I see these truths and I repeat them because you more than deserve the simple acknowledgement of these objective facts and so I sing your praise and reiterate again and again my undying love for you.

I've been reading a magazine ["on" CO] Jewish Social Studies and the emotional stimulus [N3WI] derived from it made it conducive for me to wax [N2WI] a bit philosophical besides the coming Passover holidays brings back nostalgic memories of our family life together. The great heritage of our people has always been a storehouse of treasure that I've been able to draw from for inspiration, hope and understanding. I have studied, read and experienced and the lessons of the struggle for freedom of the Jewish people from bondage will continue to serve as it has in the past as an example of the endless striving for newer and broader horizons [N2WI] by mankind in every sphere of humane [*sic*] endeavor, physical, mental, social, political ["by mankind" CO]. At this time our petition for a writ of certiorari is again reaching the Supreme Court and again it ["is at the" CO] takes place when many moves are being made to bring about peace. I realize that the changing political picture, particularly foreign developments, affect our case and I am glad that we have been able to rally so much sentiment to help us obtain some equal consideration for our appeal. I am confident but I wont [*sic*] commit myself until I hear what's what for I am well aware of the political nature of our case. I guess our lawyer will be up shortly and we'll be able to read the brief and petition and hear the latest news of all that is taking place. Also we ought to make plans to see our children as soon as you think it would be best for them to come.

Incidentally, I had a very nice visit with my sister Ethel and she wants me to tell you that she is very clear now on the situation & she'll go to work on it. It is hard for [NWI] certain people to realize your reaction & her reaction to things that are obviously so indecent that it is very difficult for ["one" CO, NWI] anyone to contain themselves. ["The natural re Since" CO, NWI] Yes it is important to think of the best method to get help in our fight to expose [illegible letter CO] this frameup but we are not made of stone and we will scream when we're hurt. I understand and I want to assure you and my sister that you can not be held responsible for your natural reaction. My sister is sweet and she is very much concerned to do the right thing by us. It does her a great deal of good to contribute her share from the heart and she is doing a better job because she is convinced of our innocence. Happy holiday my love—Always devoted to you Julie

Julius to Ethel

April 2nd, 1953

Hello Bunny,

You are a very sweet one at that and all year around too and not ["only" CO, NWI] just at Easter time. I certainly enjoyed the swell Passover feed Rabbi Koslowe put on for us and I am glad that we can celebrate the holiday and enter [NWI] into the full spirit of the occasion, the birth of the struggle for freedom of our people. The road [N2WI] of progress has always been hard and bitter but the fruits have always been sweet and wonderful. I am sure we'll soon learn how our darling sons spent their holiday. Probably our lawyer will inform us of how they've been progressing lately. I know that both of us are impatiently awaiting our dear Manny's presence so that we can satisfy our deepest hunger for all the latest news.

At our last visit we both noticed the significant difference that exists at this time of our appeal to the Supreme Court. This is the first time that a court action of ours is pending while there is taking place a [*sic*] easing of world tensions in spite of the strenuous efforts of the newspaper and [N2WI] others of their ilk [N4WI] to confuse the issues and a distinct possibility of peace in Korea exists. Because of the fact that our case does have ["these" CO] political overtones these latest foreign developements will help create a favorable atmosphere. On the other hand I note there has been no letup in the hounding liberals, progressives and radicals and instead I see an increase of activities by the McCarthys and ["the" CO, NWI] other pro-fascists [N3WI] in their efforts to saddle our people with a police state. Again I rest my faith on the people because their actions will determine the ultimate outcome of our case. I know with whom we are dealing ["with" CO] and we must fight for the justice that is ours. One thing is important that those who are working on our behalf have a splendid opportunity to win an important victory for peace and for us & for people like us who work for it. The results of the last two [NWI] public meetings have been very gratifying and I'm hopefully looking forwary [*sic*] to the huge rally planned for Randalls [*sic*] Island. These ["se" written over "y" in previous word] are the surest signs that we are meeting with success in reaching the public with the truth in our case and they are acting to help us. I am confident that many people have learned a great deal about the political nature of our case and I am sure they will be better prepared to make a positive contribution to peace and a better world.

As you can well imagine I'm busy reading and thinking about the case, about you and the children. You know Honey I remember when that picture was taken. I was 16 years old then and I entered C.C.N.Y & as yet I hadn't had the good fortune to meet you but that most pleasureable [*sic*] event took place two years later. Sweetheart I am glad my sister sent you the picture of us and Mike when he was a baby and Gladys. I remember those days and even recall the outfit the little fellow had on. They were wonderful memories and I'll always treasure them. It is very helpful to me to relive some of those experiences they make these present difficulties bearable. I continue to love you with all my heart. Always.

Your devoted husband—Julie

Mrs. Ethel Goldberg [pencil]
5347—65th Place
Maspeth Long Island

April 3, 1953

Dearest Ethel,

Thanks for understanding so wonderfully; you're a peach, that's for sure! I am referring, of course, to your heart-warming letter of March 31st, detailing the Carnegie Hall rally on our behalf!

Since you say your mother is due to see us, may I suggest Monday, April 6th? First of all, there is nobody else due (if Manny gets here by Saturday, that is, and I don't see why he wouldn't). Secondly, since Julie and I see each other Tuesday, he is in a position to recapitulate all that transpired between them [N2WI] on Monday. We derive ever so much pleasure from exchanging our respective impressions of her, and what she said and how she said it. It would be particularly gratifying this time, in view of the two important events at which she was present, to have her come before rather than after our Tuesday visit. However, while I prefer to see her on Monday, she should suit her own convenience, in the final analysis.

So pleased with the snap shots you sent, although the sight of my darling Gladdy made me weep bitterly. She was such a dear person, and I loved her so much. I don't know that I shall ever really reconcile myself to the hard fact of her death. But then it wasn't too much easier, either, to behold the two parents, protectively encircling an unbelievably tiny Michael, and smiling in clearly evident self-satisfaction and pride. In fact, I stared in wonder at the entire group, finding it difficult to remember we had ever once been a part of such simple happiness, so much horror had been packed into the [N2WI] last few intervening years. Nevertheless, we do not doubt that we will be a part of it again, and gain in strength and deter-mination with each passing day. Please give my love, won't you, to Lena; she is not forgotten, by any means. I have but to recall her quiet but steadfast words before Judge Kaufman to feel a thrill of genuine admiration and respect.[396] Tell her, Ethel, that she must not fret herself about her enforced inactivity at this time, and that her complete recovery is all that concerns us.

That a traditionally joyous holiday should be marred by the calculated barbarity that has been visited upon us, is perfectly understandable. Still, I'd like to share with you a very tiny happening, but one that holds a rich meaning. Last Sunday evening, just one night before the start of the Passover festivities, I was enchanted to hear a broadcast of a Seder service, that included among other songs, the spirited "Da, da, yanu." Feeling a remarkable [N2WI] sense of inspiration and power, I chimed in so lustily [N3WI] so help me the very bars looked sheepish! You see, the love of truth and justice, symbolized by the Exodus, is so sacred a flame, it shall never be stamped out, until men learn [NWI] to revere the noblest testament to the glory of God and grow humble before their common humanity!

All my love and fond wishes— Ethel—

---

[396]Our grandmother and aunts Ethel and Lena met with Judge Kaufman to plead for a reduction of sentence. See *Sons*, pp. 204, 369.

[The following letters are written in ink.]

Julius to Ethel

April 5, 1953

Dearest Wife,

The telegram from my sister stating that Manny will be delayed until Monday or Tuesday of this week because of the district Attorneys [*sic*] reply brief means that he is putting in a rebuttal brief in our behalf. This procedure is only used when the answering brief raises questions our lawyer did not cover in his petition or where there exists flagrant distortions in the reply brief ["based" CO] as regards to facts in the record. I hope this explanation proves satisfactory to you. It is true that I'm itching to see our counselor but we'll have to be patient until he takes care of all the legal formalities that are needed to adequately defend our interests.

This weekend my thoughts have been of ["my" CO] our adorable family which are brought more sharpely [*sic*] in focus because of the holidays, ["the" CO] spring and all that goes with it. The beautiful flowers that were brought to the CC's for Easter Sunday Church services reminded me of how much you and our children like flowers. Believe me I missed you so very much and as I looked at the beautiful white lilies I had such an expansive feeling all I can say [NWI] is I felt wonderful. Also the thought that peace in the world is almost here lends real meaning and deeper significance to the promise of better days ahead. There is no question that the entire world hopes for it and is looking forward to peace in Korea and less tension in the world. It isn't hard to see how the warmongers are squirming because they haven't succeeded in stopping the drive for peace.

I am sure you realize that the improving world picture makes it more difficult for our government to carry out the miscarriage of justice in our case.[397] Since we understand the score, we know that only hard work by masses of people will ["will" CO, NWI] win us the justice we deserve and will help set us free. I eagerly listen to every news broadcast for details of the progress towards an end to the war and as soon as I get the newspapers I read them avidly from cover to cover. Darling, the news is good and I am confident the peoples [*sic*] will ["will" CO] cannot [NWI] now be denied.

Ethel I noticed that one of the Rabbis making his Sabbath sermon said exactly the same thing you did about the sacredness of peace and how evil

---

[397] Despite the complete success of the anti-communist domestic policy in marginalizing the left, there still was a great reservoir of resentment against the Korean War which by November, 1952 had been stalemated for over a year and a half. Eisenhower had campaigned on the promise that he would "go to Korea" in search of an end to the war, and it did appear by the spring of 1953 that an end to the war was likely.

people are trying to give it a bad connotation by ["saying" CO, N2WI] referring to "peace offensive" in a derogatory manner. Honey, the wisdom you posses [sic] is very profound and a person of your integrity and honesty would make an excellent preacher. ["Anyhow" CO, NWI] Besides, I have the extreme pleasure to listen to your thoughts and hear your voice and I know I'm not alone in singing your praise. Not only outside but even here everone [sic] who knows you, talks to you & sees you, speaks very highly of you and that goes for almost everyone I come in contact in ["he" CO] this miserable place. You see I have good cause to be proud of you and I have a right to boast about your virtues because ["every word I speak is" CO, "it" inserted then CO, N2WI] they are the truth. I adore you and love you my sweetest wife—Your

Julie

Julius to Ethel

April 9, 1953

Dearest Honey,

I'm still coasting along on the wonderful effects of our last legal consultation and I've spent the last few days reading our petition and appendix to the Supreme Court. If I know you I am sure you've been busy grinding out a megillah to our lawyer and I'm sure your ability to recall each and every detail and to record same with ["the" CO, N2WI] a very great degree of accuracy will be very helpful in showing the complete picture.

You will have time enough to enjoy the pleasure of reading this wonderful piece of work our beloved Manny put together in our behalf. I sent our distinguished advocate a short note of my views of his legal handywork [sic] and with my limitations I tried very hard to adequately praise him for his excellent job. Darling I believe it is a masterpiece and considering the posture of our case at this point it is by far the best possible legal appeal we can offer. The facts presented are incontrovertible and the law bears out our contestions. [sic] Of course, we'll get the relief we seek if the court sticks to law and the merits of the case but I'm afraid other extraneous circumstances will influence the decision and I'm counting on the support we're getting to help us get justice now. At any rate I'm happy about the legal papers that were filed on our behalf.

Well that's enough in the legal department now about another matter. Would you believe it Ethel ever since our visit with our counselor each night when I go to bed I see the beautiful colored picture of our precious darlings "The Rosenberg Piccilini"[398] and I feel so good. It's the warmth

---

[398]A picture from Italy used in the clemency campaign.

and comradeship of decent people, It [*sic*] is the compassionate heart of good people and the fraternal solidarity of mankind. This is what is really worthwhile and this is what is good in the world and the bonds of brotherhood will help save us as it is now saving the peace of the world. I can understand how these people feel when they see the pictures of our sons for I know my reaction when I see the children of other innocent victims whether it be Negro children in the south or Korean children in the war area. ["Bbecause" [*sic*] CO] I love children and I want them all to have the best possible opportunity while they grow ["up to" CO, NWI] & live a most fruitful life. Surely with such strong feelings I yearn to go back to our life together. However as long as we can effect [*sic*] people in such a way that they print these pictures and that the women of Lorraine France write such letters to you then we can face the trials of the days ahead with greater strength and courage. My beloved woman and faithful wife we stand together in unity of heart and mind firmly defending ["of" CO] our principles and our sacred honor. This [NWI] legacy we ["e" in previous word written over "ill"] can and will give ["our boys" CO] to Michael and Robert no matter what the outcome of this case—Always thinking of you sweetheart

Your devoted fellow—Julie

Julius to Ethel

April 12, 1953

My Charming Ethel,

Our last visit was so very satisfying that it has brightened the long lonely hours until I see you again. When I think of it, I see your beautiful beaming face and your bright sparkling eyes and the freshness and vitality of the life spirit [N2WI] you possess was conveyed to me also and I feel inspired. You can't imagine how much you impress me by your demeanor and morale and if it seems that I'm babbling nonsense by telling you I love you over and over again and repeating that in fact you are truely [*sic*] wonderful please allow me to continue to pour forth my innermost feeling, else I'll be completely frustrated. Why am I not better gifted? I would like to tell in the most descriptive language all about your virtues. Then all women can be proud that one of the average women they [NWI] might meet on the street daily has come through such difficult trials [N3WI] as you have and shown ["that" CO, N2WI] real greatness by adherence to principles and standards of decency. In maintaining human dignity in this manner you have again proved the indestructibility of the individual and one's worth as a social being. As we discussed darling the essence of bing [*sic*] "cared for" and giving to the common good for our fellowmen is in the best self interest and allows us the greatest personal gratification.

Many times when I think over our conversations I realize the profoundness of your ideas and their value and I hope that when you do get around to being in the right frame of mind and if the situation is favorable you will put your thoughts on paper and in satisfying a personal need you'll be contributing to others who will benefit from reading your ["creative" CO] experiences and [N2WI] they will understand ["ing" CO at end of last word, three illegible letters inserted, then CO] some of the creative urges that motivate you. Perhaps I haven't explained myself properly but I am positive you know exactly what I mean. Because of the great potential we must struggle all the harder to make certain that it will find expression, in spite of the great hardships and then it will be all the more fruitful when we do win our freedom. Not for one moment do I doubt that we will win our fight and be reunited with our family again. We enter into this new period with confidence and courage bolstered by the prospects of peace in the world.

Dearest with all these wonderful thoughts and good feelings I am still terribly lonely and I miss you a great deal. It's spring with bursting signs of new life all around us, new growth and the quickening harmony of beauty and love, every fibre of my being longs for you, your company, your sweetness and warmth, & the sharing and consummation of a complete relationship of heart and mind, of family—the wholesome life—We don't ask much darling for we give to receive. The hearts who wish to destroy us fail to understand that their brutality cannot make us dishonor our names or betray our love for our children and each other. It is indeed a long hard road of suffering we've been traveling and I hope will be spared to [sic] much more pain. I am heartened ["with the way" CO, NWI] because the good people everywhere are beginning to move and that is the best guarantee that we'll be saved. I believe [NWI] that the two years we've spent in this death house will save many other innocent peoples [sic] lives—I love you my precious wife—Your

Julie

Julius to Ethel

April 16th, 1953

My Darling Wife,

I've been spending a great deal of time studying the record and briefs relating to our latest legal move before the Supreme Court. Without doubt our appeal is masterfully executed and poignantly presented and we make a conclusive showing in fact and law ["that not only" CO] that our rights were violated and the conviction is therefore illegal. ["but" CO, NWI] Also that the prosecution is guilty of a deliberate miscarriage of justice to win a conviction and put [next word written over illegible word] two innocent people to death quickly before the entire rotteness [*sic*] of this frameup is exposed. I do hope that our petition and briefs are distributed widely and read by many people to acquaint them with the nature of this case.

In today's NY Times I read an item that the New York County lawyers Association is looking into the matter of the growing evil of "trial by newspapers" that effectively prevents an acussed [*sic*] from obtaining a fair & impartial trial. They could start off their work by looking into our case and studying these egregious features that point out the terrible burden placed on an accused ["in" CO, NWI] facing a passion arousing charge. Is their [*sic*] any better proof of the complete bias of the press against us ["th by" CO, N2WI] than by noting their completely [*sic*] silence on the expose of the so called Russian "gift" console table?[399] Obviously the kept press is corrupt and will not print the truth in this case. Of course whenever politics or special interest enters into the picture, honest reporting and writing true facts gives way to transent [*sic*] political needs. It is therefore of primary importance that the truth be made available to the greatest number of people that can be reached and that is the reason [N2WI] for the crucial need of the National Guardian and the Committee in this situation. We are positive that given time we will prove [NWI] that each of [*sic*] every charge of the government against us is completely false and is [NWI] only contrived [N2WI] in [from context the next word should be "order" but it is illegible] to attack the progressive movement and those people who fight for peace.

Reading the latest news of the world it is obvious to all that the warmongers and hatemongers will not bow to the will of the people unless the overwhelming majority force them and so too must we be alert in our case that a maximum of effort against these evil men is pressed in order to save us now. I always like writing this Thursday letter because I know you'll be receiving it after our visit and it will sort of extend our being together for a longer period of time. Both of us darling live from visit to visit and it is the most important source of inspiration that helps to ["continue" CO, NWI] maintain our high state of morale and enables us where possible to contribute to the struggle for all that we hold dear.

One thing I must say about the memorial services we attended and that is that I thought about your father and my father and I am sure we are honoring their memory because we are following the path ["s" CO at end of last word] and brotherhood that formed the center of their own spiritual

---

[399]The *National Guardian* had published an article about the discovery of the console table on April 1. For the importance of the console table, see *Sons*, pp. 188–90, 352–53, 404–6. Testimony in the Record is on pp. 521, 631, 707, 1136, 1211, 1296, 1357–60, 1406–12. See also Schneir, pp. 196–203 and Wexley, pp. 449–62, 644, 646–48.

beliefs. It is a satisfying feeling to have a clear conscience and with humility to have a pride in ones [*sic*] dignity.—Love you with all my heart

Your devoted husband—Julie

P.S. Don't think I forgot that your [*sic*] wonderful and swell but I'll tell you about that at our tete atete [*sic*]. Your [*sic*] always my charming adorable women [*sic*]

JR

Julius to Ethel

April 19, 1953

Hello Bunny,

As I was writing your name I recalled something my sister Ethel told me at our last visit. A weeks ago she saw the Bachs and they told her how well the children are progressing and that Robbie is doing nicely and he takes such pride in writing his name.[400] They're growing up honey our little Robbie is learning to read and write. Naturally I am pleased to hear that the boys are growing ["up" CO] normally but I want to partake of the joy of seeing them advance. There is nothing more heartless than separating parents from their [NWI] beloved children and thereby ["destroyini" [*sic*] CO] breaking up a family. It is indeed a sign of moral and ethical degenercy [*sic*] that this inhumanity should be practiced by our government in this case. This is the out and out truth as we know it and we aim to call a spade a spade. The grave danger to the rest of the American people is that the political motives that made the two of us innocent victims of a frameup might ["spread to" CO, N3WI] operate to persecute many ["of" CO] others like us. The plain fact is that there is a growing danger of fascism [N3WI] in our country and "due process" is only a legal extension of the brutality of a police state. I am sure that growing numbers of people are aware of this danger and understand the serious implications ["for the people" inserted then CO] that our case has on both the domestic and freign [*sic*] scene for all Americans.

Indeed, it was good to hear the report my sister gave me of the many positive accomplishments in the work of the committee and the mass movement on our behalf. It is at the grass root level that they will be most successful and this is the most effective way to arouse the conscience of the public and alert them to the meaning of the issues involved. Since this is definitely a political case our interests, which are at the same time the interests of the people, can best be protected by the court of public opinion and

---

[400]See *Sons*, p. 240 for Robert's own memory.

the ["y" CO at end of last word, "have" CO, NWI] people already [NWI] have
shown by their actions that they are working to save our lives. Nothing but
a strong consistent fight will insure victory because the opposition is
ruthless and vicious and will ["use" CO] exert every effort to make this
frameup stick. However, we are confident that with the help of the people
we will win. It is the pressure of the world that is forcing a peace in Korea
and I believe it will also force them to grant us the justice we deserve.

Coming back to our precious children Ethel assures me that we will not
recognize our little ones because they are making such rapid progress and
there are observable improvements in their emotional well being. Our
friends who are responsible for the boys are doing a swell job and they
deserve a great deal of credit [N2WI] for it and I know ["they have" CO, NWI]
that our heartfelt thanks goes out to them. Those who can love our children
prove the efficacy of the brotherhood of man and [N2WI] they have revealed
the tremendous amount of good will that exists among the common people
everywhere and [NWI] have shown the great strenght [*sic*] of fraternal
solidarity. It gives of [*sic*—probably meant "us"] new courage to defend our
innocence and continue our principled struggle for complete vindication.—
All my love

Your devoted husband—Julie

Julius to Ethel

April 23rd, 1953

My Dearest Wife,
    The last two days I've completely given [NWI] myself over to indulge
in a most pleasant pastime reading famous plays and I must say they are
indeed very stimulating. Each of us depending upon our individual make up
and experiences derive many different satisfactions from our reading and that
also goes for our interpretation of the creative treasures contained in plays.
    You probably recall the last scene of Maxwell Anderson [*sic*] "Mary of
Scotland" where Elizabeth tells Mary that she has seen to it that the history
of her reign will be written as she orders her writers to put down the events
although in fact they ["are" CO, "maybe" inserted, then CO, NWI] are untrue.
Also in our case and even more so, at this time, we see a similar situation
in the way the newspapers are reporting the events in Korea. Of course, if
you follow eight papers daily [N3WI] as I do you [NWI] too would be able to
immediately recognize contrived news reports to mislead the public. The
way I see it the "free" press is conditioning the people in order to blind them
to the truth and confuse them and prevent an effective rallying behind a
correct program. This is done because in spite of the efforts of the most
reactionary forces in our government the people of the world are forcing a

eace in Korea now and to continue their evil efforts they are pushing for a
ascist domestic policy under the guise of anti-communism. Since there is
an interrelation between domestic and foreign policy each of these trends
will effect the final outcome of peace in the world. It is therefore imperative
at this time that the people help us win a victory which will contribute to
advance the political trend of opposition to a police state at home and war
abroad. It seems to me that spreading the facts about our case will insure
that history will record the truth about this miscarriage of justice and give
the public a chance to right the great wrong done us. Believe me sweetheart
I'm enjoying every moment while reading the Theatre Guild Anthology.
How wonderful it would be to sit in our own living room and read theses
[*sic*] excellent plays aloud!

Talking about home I'm anxiously awaiting our precious sons [*sic*]
visit. Somehow it seems so long in coming and yet I ["ve" CO] sort of look
forward to it ["as a" CO, N4WI] for it is a high point which marks out certain periods of our trials at this godforsaken death house. Always after each
such family gathering I marvel that so much real pleasure can be crammed
into such a short space of time and that every member of our family can
share the love we do in this way. You know honey, that ["in spite of" CO]
because of the dramatic and emotionally packed nature of our family visit
the warmth and sincerity that we get across to our boys is most effective in
reassuring them of our love and [NWI] complete acceptance. It is when they
react to this positive influence that I get most from our get together.
Powerful forces such as these will never be denied. We will do all we can to
rejoin our sweet children as soon as events permit. I am confident we will
win—All my love—Julie

Julius to Ethel

April 26, 1953

My Dearest Wife,

Each succeeding time I see the children the parting becomes more difficult. It is taking a terrific [*sic*] toll and I've been terribly heartsick since
they left. The baby's crying and Michaels [*sic*] parting expressions were
very painful and if it effects [*sic*] me this way I'm much concerned for the
great hardship it visits on our beloved little ones. Truth is they are growing
nicely and getting along well but definitely they are disturbed about our
situation and their innocent young lives are being badly marked by this
brutal tragedy. I'm besides [*sic*] myself in anguish ["trying" CO] impatent
[*sic*] to help them and to assuage your own suffering ["only" CO] somewhat.
I'll try to console myself with the knowledge that I am acting in their best
interest by defending our honor and maintaining our principles for a decent

life with dignity. We really have a wonderful family and I love you all s
very much. Both of us can feel proud our our [*sic*] sons personal accomp
lishments and most important is that they recognize themselves and are
more confident in themselves as people. When will our government begin
the [*sic*] to recognize the great disgrace this case is bringing on it's [*sic*]
good name? Humanity is revolted by the cruelty involved in this case. I feel
confident that the good people will be able to save us and set us free.

I'll save most of the news about the kids for our next visit. The thing
that we need the most at this time is a through [*sic*] legal consultation to
pull together all the loose ends and plan ["n" written over "in" in last word]
the next stages of our defense. Unfortunately at this point Manny is busy
and I hope he'll not be forced to drop everything and come rushing back
because that would indicate an adverse decision by the Supreme Court. I
know we feel as one about our fight and no matter what the court's decision
will be I am sure we'll continue to fight to victory for that is the [NWI]
only true justice ["of" CO, NWI] in this case.

Darling, I looked at you and your eyes and the expression on your face
echoed my own sentiments of painful joy at sharing some moments of the
good life [NWI] together as a family. Ethel, honey we want what is rightfully ours so strongly and yet we must though heartbroken and sanity
almost gone pull ourselves together to defy all that is despicable and evil.

It is appropriate on this anniversary of the heroes of the Warsaw Ghetto
to recall the lines "May you on the outside be blessed—where are our
develiverers [*sic*]? The American people must ["destroy" CO, NWI] fight the
creeping fascism that would destroy us all and the issues involved in our
case require that we be freed to prevent the massacre of political opposition
in our country. Resistance must be mobilized before the forces of darkness
gain momentum against the peoples [*sic*] interest. To the extent that the
public is rallied to defend the causes of freedom, liberty and decency to that
extent will they defeat fascism, maintain peace and save our lives. I know
we will not be found wanting I am awaiting the positive results of the
activities on our behalf—All my love—

                                                              Your Julie

Julius to Ethel

                                                         April 30th, 1953
Dearest Ethel,

Tomorrow is May Day, traditional labor holiday. At its inception in
America it symbolized the great struggle that led to the eight hour day and
in recent time it has held great meaning to the people of the world fighting
for a better richer life in peace. We have always considered this a special day

ɔr us and so I on this occasion send my ardent greetings and deep love. "as" CO] I am sure we are not alone because all people desire peace as we do and many of them are thinking of us and working to save our lives. It is gratifying to learn that larger sections of the public are recognizing the deeds of our government when it comes to peace and anti-democratic measures at home as apart from their words that are used in propaganda. It seems to me that now the true nature of neo-fascism as represented by McCarthyism is becoming clear to the America people. Only by active opposition to reactionary measures and by positive action for peace and progress can we maintain our freedom and democracy. We have always believed this and I feel confident that our fellowmen [N4WI] also understand this & will see to it that we get the justice that is rightfully ours.

I think we are approaching a most decisive stage in our case and the events of this coming month will determine the outcome. Of course, I include [punctuation mark CO] political factors external to the case itself and other items directly bearing on the legal fight in the courts. Somehow I get the feeling that most people are pausing, marking time to see whether the Armistice is consummated in Korea and this period is most crucial for us. It is my opinion that there will be peace in Korea but there can be ups and downs [N3WI] in the meantime on ["the" CO] peripheral items such as our case. A Writ of Certiorari or a hearing of our claims which by law we are entitled to, will be a very definite victory and be the turning point in our favor. The possibility exists and I am optimistic but I will not give up hope even if we get an adverse decision.

Sweetheart, considering the added circumstances of Spring I miss you more than ever before and it's just plain agony while we're apart. There is no song or cheer, nor any beauty without you only loneliness and the depths of despair. The rotteness [sic] and oppressive nature of this place ["s" CO at end of last word] outrageous [sic] ones [sic] decency and is torturous for the mind. How much longer must we suffer the pain? True the spirit is strong but we need relief. I have great faith that we will be delivered from this hellhole and I hope it will be soon.

I want to sit besides you my love. Stroke your hair. Look into your eyes while I hold your hands in mine. Even as our minds are one our gentle caress will convey most eloquently our feelings for words are not necessary. The simple facts of our close proximity, sans [next word written over] wire [NWI] screens bars and an impending [NWI] brutal death hanging over us, will be our greatest joy. We don't ask much to be completely happy. It is evident to all with a heart that there can be no greater pleasure than to be with each other and our children—Yours to be home together next May Day—

Julie

Julius to Ethel

May 3rd, 195⁞

My Darling,

Alert as we are to events that are happening we cannot fail to recognize the political fact that the first quarterly [NWI] period of the new administration in Washington has seen a marked reactionary swing to the right. Under the aegis of the executive branch of our government a series of police-state policies have been introduced and with it's [*sic*] benign support to the pro-fascists of McCarthy's ilk it has loosed sceptre of fear throughout our land and the judiciary have fallen in line [N2WI] all of which threatens the freedom & the basic constitutional rights [N3WI] of all citizens and the democracy of our country. It is this situation which endangers the peoples [*sic*] fight for peace and concomitently [*sic*] with it our campaign for justice. The urgency of a relentless struggle against the forces of fascism and war must be clearly understood so that at every important step they can be blocked in their efforts against the best interests of our country. Therefore I am under no illusions concerning our case for I know that only the organized pressure of the people can save us and expose the heinous political frameup that would murder two innocent people. Since in truth we are guilty of no crime we will not be party to the nefarious plot to bear false witness against other innocent progressives [punctuation CO] to heighten hysteria in our land and worsen the prospects of peace in the world. Whatever the Supreme Court decision is it will not change the justness of our cause. I am confident we'll continue to maintain ["of" CO, NWI] our principles and defend the honor of our name. The accumulation of pain and torture is quite fatiguing but the spirit is strong and our faith in the people will help see us through the difficult trials ahead.

As you can see from the foregoing I spend most of my time reading the newspapers carefully and digesting the content behind the propaganda headlines and this gives me an indication of how things are going and what we might expect considering the political nature of our case. One important short coming is that I haven't been kept informed of the extent of the activities of the committee and other people in our behalf and only the history of the coming events in our fight will tell the whole story. One thing is certain our struggle is definitely helping the forces of freedom and peace and therefore it must also help us.

Of course, in my many spare moments I've ["lb" CO] been thinking of you and all that you're going through and my heart goes out to you my dearest with all my tender feelings and profound love. For what really matters is the sincerity ["of" CO, NWI] in the thoughts of our minds and in [NWI] the feelings of our hearts. Nobody welcomes suffering honey but we are not the only ones who are going through hell because of all we stand for ɪd I believe we are, in holding our own, contributing a share in doing away with the great sufferings of many others both at this time and in time to come.

This month of May has always been a special one for our wonderful family in the many happy days we celebrated together and I hope we will have the good fortune that this month will not be moved by an adverse decision. I'll be there, my heart, pressing my nose against the screen in order for my eyes to get a closer, better look of all your loveliness.

Always devoted to [NWI] you my most charming woman—Julie

Julius to Ethel

May 7, 1954 [*sic*]

My Most Precious,

I sent you a card, the only kind I could get, as a token to you on this Mother's Day May 10th. This is a most important ocassion [*sic*] because motherhood combines all the traits that are glorious, good and creative. In you the mother of our two fine sons I find the great beauty of life and the promise for a fruitful and worthwhile future. Mankinds every effort is basically directed to free himself from the physical and mental fetters that bind him and utilizing a maximum knowledge of the laws of nature and social relations to advance the general well being which, of course, includes his own family. It is true that in peace and freedom there are the optimum conditions for developing the greatest potential and gifts of the individual but in spite of all hardships and under extreme conditions motherhood has prepared women to make great contributions to society. The plain fact is that you, Ethel, my wife, are one of the best examples of a woman combing [*sic*—probably meant "combining"] all these noble traits of a mother and decent human being. I know you well and I've witnessed the proof of what kind of person you are and I say I am proud to have shared these years with so sweet and fine a wife and mother ["like" CO, NWI] as you. Painters can make you see it. Poets put it in rhyme and museums give you music to hear it. For me I feel it inside of me, in my heart and in my mind & this is the most precious thing in the world, a true person. Therefore I readily understand that your greatest suffering is due to the fact that you are denied [N4WI] the opportunity to exercise your prerogative as a mother. By now our enemies must be aware of their great mistake in fighting against such a powerful force. The more the public becomes acquainted with this situation the greater the pressure will be to struggle against the monsters who dare to perpertrate [*sic*] such bestiality. The outraged conscience of the world will not be assuaged unless this barbarous sentence is ["done away with" CO,

NWI] revoked and this miscarriage of justice is rectified. All honesty an. sane reason demands an end to this tyranny against us.

Because I am one of the people, so close to you and also another innocent victim of this frameup, I feel your pain very deeply and in anguish cry out for your suffering. Somehow, somewhere together we find in each other the strength to withstand together the rigors of our trials and the good people everywhere continue to be a source of never ending encouragement and support for our principled fight. Our faith and hopes have kept our spirits high and we are confident the ultimate victory will belong to us. Then, let me gather you in my arms, even as you are in my mind so that I may love you with all my heart.

We can face the lies, the pain and even death as long as we are united in heart and soul, in love and truth. I sincerely believe we will be returned to our children again and you will be able to discharge your duties as mother to ["you" CO, N2WI] our children Michael and Robbie as is their birthright.

Always devoted to you —Julie

The following letter is indicative of the conflicts that had developed between Emanuel Bloch and the leaders of the National Committee to Secure Justice in the Rosenberg Case. This letter was clearly designed to strengthen Bloch's hand in this conflict. What is so sad about this, with the hindsight of history, is that our parents never got to meet the members of the Committee and discuss strategy directly with them.

Mr. Emanuel H Bloch
7 W. 16th Street
New York NY
      Page #I

May 9th, 1953

Dear Manny,

On a number of occassions [*sic*] in the past I have found it necessary to write you on the delicate matter of our relations with the Committee to Secure Justice and others who are helping us and who are sincerely working very hard in our behalf. Ethel and I are mature people and we have a thorough understanding of our case. Since it is our lives that are at stake, we are naturally concerned with the legal matters in the case. We have retained you to handle all our legal actions in court and to defend our interests and any matters that relate in any way on the legal issues must be cleared with and approved by you. The fact is that we have had the best possible defense and as our lawyer you have done a most competent job and we intend to see to it that you will not be hindered in your work on our behalf.

Of late, we've been greatly perturbed by news [punctuation CO] that, although with the best of intentions, the committee against your advise [*sic*] saw fit to initiate an issue that infringes on your legal prerogatives on our behalf and we strongly insist that they desist from any such action in the future[401] ["I" CO, NWI] We are ["re" written over "m" in previous word] sure that no one on the Committee wants to do anything that would redound to our disadvantage. Precisely, because we are deeply [*sic*—he obviously left out some words here] for many other innocent progressives, who will be affected by the outcome of our case that we want our dear friends to understand they must not arrogate to themselves the right that only you can exercise in our behalf. Not only are we always willing to listen to their counsel[402] but we welcome it and we plead with them to continue to lend all possible assistance to facilitate you [*sic*] difficult task in conducting the court fight.

We ["I" CO] feel that all of us are participating, collectively, in a very important struggle for justice that vitally effects [*sic*] the interests of all Americans[.] ["Because" CO, N2WI] Truth is we in cooperation with the committee share a very grave responsibility of acting as spokesman and leader in this mass movement that must prevent this political frameup from being turned [next word written over illegible word] into a weapon of legal lynching against the peace and progressive forces.

We have read much of the material the Committee has gotten out for wide distribution and as yet they haven't printed our appeal to the President. Since it is the most comprehensive analysis and forceful presentation in our case we believe the committee has been remiss in not utilizing this petition

---

[401]This might refer to any of three separate issues. 1) The release of information about the console table had put pressure on Manny to use it in a legal motion, but as yet he had not done so. 2) The interest of some members of the Committee to help Attorney Fyke Farmer of Nashville, Tennessee, who had prepared a motion for a new trial based on the idea that the Atomic Energy Act of 1946, which explicitly stated that a jury had to recommend the death sentence, superseded the Espionage Act upon which the indictment in the case was based. For details, see J. Sharlitt, *Fatal Error*; Schneir, pp. 237–38, 242–43. Bloch had opposed Farmer's efforts and even sent a telegram to Judge Kaufman disassociating his clients from those efforts. 3) The theft of interoffice memos regarding David Greenglass from the Rogge law firm which were published by a French newspaper in April angered Emanuel Bloch, according to the members of the Rogge law firm with whom he met on May 4. Perhaps he blamed the Committee for this burglary and felt pressured to use it in some legal papers despite his personal belief that they did not amount to much. (This is certainly the position of Radosh and Milton. See RM, pp. 366–72 and the footnotes on pp. 559–60.)

[402]As noted earlier, this was not the case. There was no direct contact between our parents and any member of the committee.

for executive clemency to acquaint the public with the pertinent details of our case.

Facts and only facts are convincing. The job that has to be done is clear. All that is required is to go to the people at the grass roots level and inform them of the nature of the issues involved.—Ring doorbells—Put literature in their hands—Hold mass meetings—Demonstrations in the streets, at factories, in public halls and even at the U.N.

Page # II

We know the Committee understands all this and they have successfully rallied great numbers to our support and of course they have to decide how best to carry out the noble task they've undertaken but we're cheering them on from the death house and we feel we're with them when we are able to make a few suggestions.

Perhaps it is difficult for those on the outside to really comprehend the terrible hardships we are living through but we are certain all of us are of one heart and mind when it comes to contributing the maximum effort to save our lives and win this principled fight.

We are going to take the above matter up with my family and I don't intend to write any additional letters on this subject. Therefore please let my brother and sister read this letter and I want all of you or if not the two of them to show it to the Committee and work out a harmonious arrangement, in keeping with our suggestions, to increase the effectiveness of our campaign both legally and politically.

The stakes are high we must all rise to the occasion to defend with the best of our abilities all that we hold dear. We are confident that this urgent plea of ours will be taken in the correct light by our friends and will receive their open-hearted understanding and warmth as they have affectionately accepted us in the past. Send all our love and gratitude—Confidently

Julie

Manny—

Dear sweet person and devoted friend. I congratulate you on your birthday May 12. You are endowed with the best personal gifts, a humble honorable individual of great integrity and boundless humanity. You are the swellest guy I know. I send you my warmest heartfelt fraternal affections and brotherly love.

Julie

P.S. Please send me some commissary money. What is happening to our book of letters?[403] Don't forget to send us ["as much of" CO] the printed literature the Committee distributed which we haven't as yet received.

                                                                    JR

Julius to Ethel

                                                              May 10th, 1953
My Darling Ethel,
    Today was a really beautiful Mother's Day and I spent a great deal of time thinking about you. The usual stuff, how we spent our lives together, the sweet children we have, the kind of fight we're putting up and our future reunion when we're once again free. The will to live, enhanced but [*sic*—perhaps meant "by"] all the world beauties, by the basic worth of truth and principles continues to keep my spirits high. I'm doing a little more writing and I intend to complete a project I've talked to ["you" omitted here] about. Also by Tuesday I expect to send the children a letter for Robbie's birthday. Spring the season of new hopes keeps turning my attention to you and all my thoughts ["of" CO] are of love my lady fair. The luxury of grandiose day dreams does not assuage the deep yearnings of my demanding heart so I must find relief elsewhere in my reading and writing but all to no avail I continue to suffer. It is when I feel this way that I know how deep your pain is and all the tenderness I possess flows out to you my dearest.
    Slowly, haltingly but surely in spite of the headlines the military and politicians the logic of events, backed by the [*sic*] peoples will is forcing a truce in Korea. Unless some unforseen [*sic*] madness upsets the wishes of mankind their [*sic*] will be peace in the world this summer. Without doubt, this can only ease tensions and have a favorable effect on our case.
    You know honey I can't help but say that the last visit with our lawyer wasn't completely satisfactory. There was [NWI] not afforded to us ["the" CO] sufficient time to talk over our problems and ["comple" CO] come to some conclusions instead rush, rush, leading to misunderstanding of what I wanted Manny to get of my views. Perhaps we'll be able to straighten out the situation between the two of us and then we'll ask Manny to give us an early consultation. At any rate my sister Ethel will be here this weekend and we'll be able to discuss matters in detail with her. The visit with my brother went off nicely and he's beginning to see your family in their true light. The plain truth is almost unbelievable and indeed shocking to one who is

---

[403]Note, again, they wanted the letters to be published much earlier. Allegedly there was conflict between the individual who edited the first edition of *Death House Letters* and Attorney Bloch.

decent and sensitive. However, the importance of the task and the justness of the cause will keep him working for what is right.[404] Just as you have always pointed out, only when the people see the facts for themselves are they convinced of the difficulties we have to contend with as far as your family is concerned. In spite of the apparent overwhelming problem I still feel we are making very definite progress, although tediously slow but we must go through this stage before we are completely successful. One thing is certain and that is that I am confident that we will overcome all obstacles and eventually win this case.

In my mind I've celebrated this Mother's Day in the usual manner we used to enjoy these days together and I hope that next Mothers [*sic*] Day we will be home with our children and share our happiness the proper way. All my love—Julie

Masters Michael & Robert Rosenberg
c/o B. Bach
R.D–2 Box 148M
Toms River N.J.

                                                              May 12, 1953

Dear Children,

Today was my birthday and I started the morning off with a very wonderful visit with your charming mother Ethel. She looked very pretty and welcomed me with a Happy Birthday and a big sweet smile. I told her I sent

---

[404]This undoubtedly relates to the effort engaged in by David Rosenberg to get an affidavit from our mother's brother Bernard that David Greenglass, contrary to his sworn testimony at the trial that he had never stolen anything from Los Alamos, had indeed stolen uranium. (See Record, pp. 564–67. See also p. 626: "Q. Did you ever steal any . . . material, and take it out of the project to your home? A. I did not." Also see Affidavit of Bernard Greenglass, May 31, 1953, reprinted in Wexley, p. 645.) Of particular interest are the following words in the Affidavit: "I told this same story about the uranium to my sister Ethel during my visit to her about a month and one half ago on a Saturday at the Sing Sing death house." This would have been in mid-April. He further notes, "About a month ago, on a Friday night, David Rosenberg Julius Rosenberg's brother came to my home to discuss the case of Ethel and Julius. There were also present Ruth Greenglass, and my mother Tessie Greenglass. The subject of uranium come up. I told Dave Rosenberg the same story that I am stating here." This would have been in early May or late April. The significance of this information is not that the theft of uranium indicates criminal activity on the part of David Greenglass which would frighten him into confessing to espionage because he was really guilty of this theft. The significance is that it is an example of perjury at the trial—a trial at which credibility was the most important issue for the jury to decide: did they believe the Greenglasses or the Rosenbergs?

our good friend and lawyer Manny a letter congratulating him because he happens to have a birthday on this same day.

Of course then we talked about our precious sons and how in [NWI] this one week when we were home together we celebrated Mother's Day, My Birthday and last but by no means least our Robbie's Birthday. Brother Michael's [*sic*] was a birthday boy last [previous word written over illegible word] March, which is sort of a preview to you Robbie and now you yourself will be six years old. You must know son I am very happy on this day because we had the good fortune to have such a sweel [*sic*] boy like you as one of our children and you can rest assured that I'll find ways even here to make this day more joyful. I suppose by the time you get this letter you will already have received our presents and we hope you like them.

I remember very well and I believe Michael remembers too, the day both of us went to the hospital and took Mommy and you home. You [*sic*] brother was only 4 years then and he helped hold you while we rode in the car and I am sure that he is today proud of you Robbie as he was [N3WI] (on the whole) glad those days to have another baby home. Of course, today when one feels secure and is respected as an individual each one of us learns our own worth and even as 6 & 10 year olds we are able to be much happier[.] Therefore my greatest pleasure is to have seen with my own eyes the very marked progress both of you have made this last year and at each birthday son we are proud of our achievements and mean ["s" CO at end of last word] to better ourselves to get more out of life. It goes without saying that learning to be social beings, getting along with our neighbors and understanding the world we live in, are part of growing up and in this manner our dear friends Sonia and Ben have done a splendid job.

As for us your parents we are working to give you fellows the best present we know of and that is to win this case and come home to you. Growing up we are able to realize that at times, good things that are really important require great sacrifice but ["that" CO, NWI] difficulties must not deter us who are your mother and father from working for the best interest of you our children and all children.

I am aware that our good friends will try to make this day a joyous one for you boys and I want to send all my love, kisses & best wishes. Happy Birthday Robbie. We will look forward to spending the next one home with you. In the meantime I am glad to know that you our precious boys and busy doing your job, being boys and growing up and we your parents will work hard to do our part to win this case and come home soon—All my love—Daddy—Julie

P.S. Affectionate embrace to all our wonderful friends in Toms River

Julius to Ethel

May 14, 1953

Dearest Ethel,

Congratulations mommie our baby is 6 years old today. It seems only yesterday he was only a tiny fellow and now he's going to school, writing, doing the thinks [*sic*] little boys do and growing up. Not only have they falsely acussed [*sic*] us but they have robbed our little one of his babyhood and early boyhood and denied him the comfort and love of his parents that are his birthright. This crime against our children is the most dastardly part of the frameup against us. When decent standards no long [*sic*] exist and human considerations are destroyed then all civilized people have much to fear from those political vicious men who rule the destinies of our lives. Apparantly [*sic*] the American people are not sufficiently impressing the government with their ardent desires for peace for how else can one explain the present policies that lead only to more and larger wars. Our earliest estimates were correct that the brutal sentence against us is part of a pattern of pro fascist and bellicose actions by those who rule our land. It must be obvious to all that only positive mass action by the public will be successful in redirecting our country toward ["ward" in last word inserted] peace in the world. Also our future depends on this same fact.

I had not intended going into this type of a discussion but only to talk about our sons and the meaning of their birthday but we can't kid ourselves the most important need they have is for us to win our fight for freedom. In spite of the reactionary trend at home I still feel confident and optimistic that the thing we and our boys desire most will come to pass. You know that I'm terribly proud of our children and believe me when I say that I never loved them more dearly than I do now. The strong family bond and paternal feelings I have for Michael and Robbie give me my greatest incentive to do right by them and uphold the honor of our name. Of course you my darling are aware of the deep affection and profound love I have for each and every member of our fine family unit. To me this has always been the most vital factor in my real understanding of the life force. Understanding fundamental human relations and possessing this bulwark of strength permits me to stand fast to the principles we hold dear and to defend the truth in the interest of honesty. Surely this position is a difficult one but at the same time the most rewarding one for my self-respect and dignity. I guess after 35 years I should be more modest in what I write but in all sincerity and humbleness this is the true estimate of this way I see ["it" CO] myself and my actions.

The afternoon after I saw you I had a pleasant ride through the prison as a birthday present. The lush green lawn, rows of tulips, all the signs of spring, the wide river and open spaces were wonderful to see and then they spoiled it all by yanking out a molar. Imagine spoiling my birthday by pulling a tooth. There just ain't no justice.

The wonderful birthday cards I received were well chosen and expressed the right [NWI] kind sentiment [NWI] & they [last word written over "it"] moved me deeply. I just can't help loving my family and friends. Always your own—Julie

Julius to Ethel

May 17 ["7" written over "8"], 1953

Ethel darling,

[The first side of the letter has a wavy line down the middle. The text is written in verse down the first half and then continued from the top of the second half.]

I've reieived [*sic*] your card
it was indeed
a wonderful token
of our love
that is endless
and unbroken.

The familiar handwriting
most pleasing
to the eye
conveying sincerest sentiments
to my heart
that our love cannot die.

Take heed tyrants
before you rue
for all times
the barborous [*sic*] act
you take in desperate haste
and lay waste
to body and soul
that the whole
of mankind realize
As mortal death to love

But we my wife
fight for life
and with it goes
the bright red rose
For us
and millions more
to be free and love
to live in peace
and simple dignity.

Thanks my precious heart
for your lovely
birthday card.

Honey the card of red roses
you sent me and the beautiful
poem you composed gave such
rich expression to your feelings
that it evoked a profound
response in me. Believe me
sweetheart it was a most welcome
surprise and a very pleasant gift and
I am deeply moved. Your love, darling,
is the rock that fortifies me and gives
me great sustenance, you sweet dear.

Now as I share my thoughts with you through the inadequate medium of this paper I crave much more, and the unassuaged demands of every bit of me to be with you even though they go unanswered press to find release for the deep hunger. Truth is the only relief I find is in the knowledge of the treasure I have in you and our precious children and the understanding of the importance of our principled fight. With faith and hope I continue to maintain confidence in our ultimate victory.

My lady fair, again we have a situation that is a bit confusing, that is developing rapidly just when our case is before the court. Of course, I had hoped that a definite stage in the move for peace would be reached by the time the nine wise old men [N2WI] decide to act on our petition.[405] ["and" CO, "T" in next word written over "t"] There still is a possibility that a truce will be reached if they don't hand down a decision until June 8th in our case. Another observation I wish to make is this. That an adverse decision at this stage may well be an indication that for [NWI] every move the other side is making to ease tensions our side is [N2WI] countering by throughing [sic] more cold water on it. Naturally I want [N2WI] to see the people ["to" CO] begin to assert themselves on the side of peace before there is a possibiity [sic] that the forces that want want [sic, NWI] war may gain momentum to prevent a ["Korean" CO] peaceful [NWI] Korean solution. The political climate at home is non [sic] to [sic] promising but I must hope for the best and the issuance of a writ to us would be a very good sign. Oh my wife this very long suffering is taking a terrific [sic] toll of us. Soon there must be an end to the misery and we ought to see the bright sunshine again. You and the children, love and roses, freedom and peace that's everything.

Always your own—Julie

---

[405] Actually, according to the research of Michael Parrish in "Cold War Justice: The Supreme Court and the Rosenbergs," *American Historical Review*, vol. 82, no. 4 (Oct. 1977), pp. 823–25, the Court had decided to deny *certiorari* at their April 11 conference and were delaying the announcement while Justice Frankfurter decided whether or not to write a dissent attacking Saypol's tactics. According to his own papers, he was loath to dissent because he did not want to give aid and comfort to the Communists who supported my parents. However, he also felt that there would forever be doubts about the case if the Supreme Court did not give it a full review.

Emanuel H. Bloch
7 W. 16th Street
New York New York

May 18, 1953

Dear Manny,

Ethel tells me that Alice Citron[406] has urgently requested some word from me concerning Ethel Julia Van Haaren.[407] Will you be good enough to transmit the following message to her immediately upon your receipt of it. At the same time, you might also make it known to her that we would greatly appreciate prompt action on all the back issues of "Jewish Life" that they have been neglecting to send us. There must be at least six that are due us—So how's about it?—

For Mrs. Van Haaren

"Sing Sing to Holland! A vast aggregate of mileage, of water, of people, lies between; half a world of pitiless toil and travail of blood-shed and bondage, separates us! Yet there are no reaches of space the human heart cannot over take, no strident struggle the lusty cry of new life cannot lend new courage, new hope!

Good mother of Ethel Julia, you are very dear to us. In your face is written a tenderness and pride most beauteous to behold, and your arms encircle ["the child" CO, N2WI] your baby with a [NWI] true woman's steadfast strength. You are the universal Mother, plain, enduring, unadorned save for the grace of a benign fulfillment, patient, indomitable, fruitful, as the ["beautiful" CO, "far flung" inserted, then CO, "fertile" inserted, then CO, NWI] fecund Earth herself!

Kind and generous sister, may I share her with you, this child of my adversity though not of my body, this child ["whose" CO] named ["d" in previous word added, "is" CO, NWI] for love? Then sing out bravely, Ethel Julia, your brothers ["Michael and Robert" CO] shout in joyous welcome and crowd close to touch your flower's face! Sing out bravely, stout little

---

[406] A former New York City school teacher, fired for being a Communist, who up until late November, 1951, was working very hard in defense of Dr. DuBois and then joined the defense effort with special emphasis on the international clemency campaign. (The DuBois trial ended with a directed verdict of acquittal on November 20, 1951. See DuBois, *In Battle for Peace*, p. 141.) See *Sons*, pp. 141–43 for her very important future role.

[407] In Rotterdam, Holland, Mrs. Chr. van Haaren-Bos had named a newborn daughter Ethel Julia in honor of our parents. See *The Testament of Ethel and Julius Rosenberg*, p. 161. Emanuel Bloch had brought them a clipping from a Dutch newspaper with a picture.

Dutch girl, and rouse the sleepers across the far Atlantic! The murderous sea pounds perilously upon every shore!"[408]

P.S. Manny, please leave the words "Michael & Robert" scratched out—Everyone knows their names, anyway, and inserting them spoils the rhythm of the sentence for me—So don't change same—If there is any thing else, however, that strikes you as poor, act accordingly—I know I can trust my artistic integrity to you.[409]

Love,
Ethel—

Michael & Robert Rosenberg
c/o B Bach
R.D. 2—Box 148M
Tom's River New Jersey

May 18, 1953

My dearest, sweetest children,

So many times I have planned to write only to have something else turn up and demand first claim upon my energies. So when I received Robbie's precious expressions of love for his Mommy on her special day I was thoroughly ashamed to realize that I had not yet even wished him a happy birthday. Of course, I send messages to both of you via the crows and robins, whenever their majesties condescend to pay me one of their infrequent visits in the yard, and the other week, when a ravishingly beautiful red-winged black-bird swooped down unexpectedly to partake of the bread I had strewn for the sparrows I watched wordless, with one arm around each of my sons, filling my greedy eyes with ["the" CO, NWI] its sheer gaudy loveliness ["of it" CO], and pressing your dear warmth lovingly against me.

For a breathless moment we stood there, we three, and then he was lifting gracefully off the ground and streaking off across the sky in a [N2WI] flight of brilliant ["flash" CO, NWI] color! He was gone and you with him!

But then there have been so many enjoyments you have shared with me, without your knowledge. For days I had been checking up on a "weed" that gradually began to take on the characteristics of (was it possible?) a dandelion, when lo and behold, there sprouted from its center, as though by

---

[408] For Mrs. van Haaren's answer, which arrived too late for our parents to read, see *ibid.*, p. 162.

[409] Unfortunately, once again, the editor of *The Testament of Ethel and Julius Rosenberg* ignored her wishes and published the letter with our names inserted, in parentheses.

magic, a short, thin bit of stalk, topped by something small and brownish green and round. It had been raining dismally [*sic*] on and off all morning, when all at once a dazzling sun was splashing warmly down upon the cold, gray concrete and toasting the dull brick a golden brown. I ran eagerly down the damp stone steps towards the familiar spot along the moss-covered crack and then gasped and choked and grew very still. A silky yellow bead was blooming with a kind of regal daintiness among the green stuff! How little it was, how tender and yet how marvelously fashioned, like some tiny, softly bright, exquisite jewel!

And there was [NWI] yet another jewel, that [four words CO, N3WI] first saw the light of day in far-off Holland, ["on a da" CO, NWI] probably during March or April, as far as I have been able to figure out. Her parents have named her Ethel Julie in honor of your Daddy and me and today I addressed a message to ["her" CO, "mother" inserted, then CO, N5WI] Mrs Van Haaren, her mother, thanking [*sic*] her for having given the Rosenberg boys a sister! A very unusual birthday present, don't you think? Perhaps the family will forward some snap-shots of the baby when she's a bit larger, so you can have the pleasure of watching her grow! Already I feel she belongs to us and to all the kind people everywhere who recognize that the world must become a safe-haven for all children and who will [N2WI] care to undertake to make it that! With such a goal, ["the race" CO, "life" inserted, then CO, N2WI] the race is an exciting challenge; never mind the obstacles, run it we shall—and win!

Many hugs, many kisses—and all my love to you both—

["both" CO] xxxxxxxxx Mommy—

Julius to Ethel

May 21st, 1953

Ethel Darling,

At this moment I'm very lethargic and in a romantic mood. I guess it is the combined effect of a nice long spring day and a natural desire to be with my beloved. The constant longing is a powerful force that makes me ever conscious of my deep need for you and spurs me on to renewed endeavors to be reunited as in the past. Everything seems so unreal and out of focus. Our weeks are marked off by the two short visits we have and they ["y" in previous word written over "n", "strthen [*sic*] into" CO, NWI] the months, the years an endless period of torment and yet no sign of relief. It seems like we're suspended somewhere, far off seeing everything that's being done and not being able to do anything even though we are the center of the controversy. A realization of the situation reveals the magnitude of the horrible dilemma. The brutal attempt to stifle the life force and sterilize life of all it's [*sic*] beauty and magnificence are [N2WI] after all the issues that are involved. Only ["when" inserted then CO] understanding these things is it possible for the mind to comprehend the full meaning of our case and the fiendish death sentence against two innocent people. Perhaps what I am saying sounds a bit disjointed but you can believe me I am writing just as I feel about these things and getting them off my chest I know I'll have a sympathetic listener in you. You will note that I think the most crucial attack against the American people is the ["phychological" CO] psychological offense against a free and reasoning mind that ["at" written over two letters, N2WI] try to frighten the individual into conformism via mass hysteria. No self-respecting person with pride and dignity will be able to flourish under this situation and history has proven that the only answer to this autocratic anarchy is forthright defense of freedom, democracy and peace.

Therefore, my love it is not only a matter of life but [N2WI] also for the most worthwhile attributes of civilizations that we fight to maintain when we struggle to keep our principles of decency and the sacredness of our honor. With all this honey girl I am able to withstand the great pressures that ["that" CO, N3WI] force me to cry out for satisfaction because the mind and heart have added strength to the will. Sweetheart I hope you are able to translate these mere words into the deep honest feelings I have about this matter because then I am able to commune with you and it is my sincerest desire that we share theses [*sic*] emotions and thoughts. Of course in my mind I've [NWI] been thinking about our relationship and sometimes I am able to get across to you some of my intimate feelings in a letter even more so that [*sic*] through the screen and bars when I face you at our visits. Truth is that if we were really together there would be no obstacles to prevent our complete sharing as we have in the past. Silly me, you know there is only one answer to the problem I pose. I wanna go home with you dearest and enjoy life together. It is important that we continue to have faith and I know we'll both continue hoping. Always devoted to you—Your own—Julie.

Julius to Ethel

May 24, 1953

Ethel Darling,

You, too, no doubt have been reading the latest twist in the verbal battle against us. It is to be noted, that only recently substantive evidence has been unearthed that sharply raises the question of the corruptness of the verdict against us and yet the "free" press has raised a curtain of silence hiding this most revealing and important information from the public who have a right to know the facts in this case.[410] To obscure these truths the justice department engages in a psychological tactic to continue the process of brain washing the people in this 'trial by newspaper' technique. "Officials" of the department inspire newsreports that receive wide coverage in the mass media that is sympathetic to the prosecution. Not only is this an ex parte presentation which is indecorous and devoid of any fairness but it is outrageous because the items are made up either in part or ["th" CO] in their entirety of lies. Never do they meet our charges which are well documented but instead issue self-serving statements ["no" CO, N3WI] always without any proof. That officials of the government engage in the "most reprehensible practices" [N3WI] in this case is surely a grave threat to the foundations of American justice and the liberty of all people. However, I feel confident that they will not succeed in their plot to make this monstrous frameup stick because it is based on a foundation of a big lie for we are completely innocent. The efforts of decent men and women everywhere will insure us the time [NWI] needed to uncover all the truths in this case and prevent a gross miscarriage of justice. Moreso this case will boomerang and once the issues are understood by the people they will actively work for peace and freedom which they will see is in great danger. I firmly believe these desperate moves of the opposition are due to concern and weakness on their part. They are worried the truth will out and their wretched game will be exposed for the world to see. The pattern of events of the attacks against the democratic rights of the people followed by the attempt to deport Cedric Belfrage editor of the independ [sic] progressive National Guardian and detention of a prominent English pacifist under the McCarran Act are [NWI] indeed symptomatic of fascism![411] Once the mind is shackled there is no longer any freedom of conscience. I have faith that the American people will not let it happen here.

Perhaps some one in the justice dept has some advance information on our writ of certiorari petition[.] Anyway we might know definitely this Monday. I was pleased to read your poem in this weeks Guardian because it carrys [sic] a terriffic [sic] punch. Methinks it's about time that the book containing our letters ["got" CO] was printed. Time is of essence and I feel certain this will get us new supporters. Since I don't seem to be getting any results with my requests for the printed matter the committee has published will you please try to use your charming influence with Manny to send us

---

[410]This relates to the discussion of material in the Rogge Papers.
[411]Cedric Belfrage, a citizen of Great Britain, was ordered deported, an order he accepted in 1955. See Belfrage and Aronson, *Something to Guard—The Stormy Life of the National Guardian, 1948–1967.*

this material.[412] Hey sweetie this poor guy is nuts about you and misses you very much—All the love of my heart & mind I send you—Julie

On Monday, May 25, the Supreme Court made public its denial of certiorari.[413]

Mr. David Rosenberg
430 E 63rd Street
New York NY

                                                                    May 26, 1953
Dear Brother
This Sunday I had the misfortune to come down with a case of influenza. All night Sunday and Monday I had fever, a very sore throat and I began to take medication for relief. In the afternoon Mama came to visit and I couldn't conceal from her the fact that I was ill. Coming on top of this was the latest blow from the Supreme Court denying our petition. I am still under the weather a bit but I'm getting along considering the very trying circumstances of the latest situation.

I had intended to write to lend my voice to the truth that is being drowned but unfortunately I still don't feel completely up to it. However, you will notice again the unseemly haste to deny us a hearing to prove our claims. The only answer is that the justice department is afraid to let us prove in court that we are indeed innocent. It is obvious that this latest psychological campaign is well planned to brain wash the American people on our case and through [*sic*—meant "throw"] up a smoke screen so that they can get away from answering our new evidence by ["yelling" CO] using self serving statements and a false issue of "talk" to save our lives. Here we see the modern application of the rack and screw to coerce innocent people into false confessions and to use them ["on" CO, NWI] with the threat of death. Many people now are convinced and all the world will come to know the plain truth that we are completely innocent.

I realize the pressures on all of us are tremendous and threats and fear cower many people but we must not falter to save our ["life" CO] lives in a decent and honest way. At this time my heart goes out to Ethel, the children, Mama, the girls and you and I want our [next word written over illegible word] bond of flesh and blood to draw us closer in love, comfort

---

[412]Note the clear evidence that Manny wanted to control all their contact with the activities of the Committee.

[413]For what went on just before and at the regular Monday conference, see Parrish, pp. 823–25.

and understanding. Dave as brothers we have shared much together and what I treasure most is our close relationship as two separate [next word written over illegible word] individuals who respect each other and practice the tenets of real brotherhood. Ours is a most difficult task to prove the worth of the dignity of the individual and of human ["e" CO at end of last word] integrity in spite of a brutal sentence facing us. Take strength and help Mama and the girls stand up in the days that are ahead I can tell you that Ethel and I will remain faithful to our children and our self-respect regardless of the outcome. You must continue to help us and don't for one minute ever allow the lies and threats to frighten you. I am sure our family we'll [*sic*] do all it can to save us. Send all my love to them.

Tell our friends to work hard the crucial hour is here now. I am confident the court of the people will still have a chance to prevent this miscarriage of justice. I hope you'll have some good news to bring us this weekend.—Here's a Sunday pass—

["T" CO] My best wishes to our supporters all my love—

Your devoted brother Julie.

David Rosenberg
430 E. 63rd Street
New York New York

May 27, 1953

Dear Davy,

Enclosed please find Sunday pass—So glad you will be able to see us before leaving on your vacation—

We are O.K.—Keep your chin up—

My best to all—

Ethel—

Emanuel H. Bloch [pencil]
7 W. 16th Street
New York New York

May 27, 1953

Dear Manny,

Enclosed please find a letter sent me by Julie a day before word came of the denial of cert. I think it analyses the events that led to the Supreme Court's capitulation with exceptional clarity, so am holding in abeyance several others from him, in order to insure quick re-censorship of this lone one and immediate forwarding to you.

Heil McCarthy! Imagine! Two impudent and imprudent heretics had the audacity to challenge the line laid down by our genädige gauleiter[414] in order not to deprive two lowly citizens of due process! Seriously this is political persecution, shameless, blatant, cynical. But it must not be a cause for pessimism; the appearance of health often merely masks a rotting organism. The bravado, the display of strength must not be mistaken for victory itself; quite the contrary, it is only through a correct evaluation of the purely psychological nature of the attack that it will lose its power to cripple and immobilize the defense.

It is the relentless struggle to live life that defeats death! To put it in classic terms, "There is nothing to fear but fear itself." Tell the Bachs they must feel this great truth themselves, so that they may infect our children with their courage and ours! If we, the parents, dare not permit [NWI] ourselves the luxury of emotionalism, neither may they. More difficult yet, but unavoidable, they must be our voices, our strength and our love. On the rock of such proudly assumed burden, the hate that would cruelly damn two innocent children must surely batter itself useless! How wonderful that the sacrifice brother must make for brother and sister for sister require no apologies, no scraping, no bowing! Only an unswerving humility, an overpowering appreciation, unsolicited, but fully forthcoming, wells up out of the depths of one's being. And it is suddenly a tremendous thing to acknowledge oneself human!

Only comfort my kids; I can't help it, it hurts dreadfully for them—
All my love and all my devotion—

Ethel—

Judge Kaufman fixed the date of execution for the week of June 15. Since executions were normally carried out on Thursdays, that made the date the 18th of June, which was our parents' wedding anniversary.

Julius to Ethel [ink]

May 31st, 1953

Ethel Darling,

Taking pen in hand I question myself. What does one write to his beloved when faced with the very grim reality the [*sic*—meant "that"] in eighteen days on their 14th wedding anniversary it is ordered that they be put to death? The approaching darkest hour of our trial and the grave peril that threatens us requires every effort on our part to avoid hysteria and false heroics but only [NWI] maintain a sober and calm approach to our most

---

[414]A very literal translation from the German is "gracious commander."

crucial problems. Therefore, I wish to state that I believe that the plans you and I agreed on at our last visit are indeed the best that will help win us new support and make a very positive contribution in our own defense. Incidentally please send my letters to Manny and I do hope he will send us copies of many of the printed materials that have been put out by the committee. Of course, the job of the committee is most important now and I am confident they will do their utmost to be most effective in saving our lives. At this point a great deal of the burden will once again fall on our trusted friend and counselor Manny and we can have complete faith in him.

Dearest over and over again I have tried to analyze in the most objective manner possible the answers to the position of our government in our case. Everything indicates only one answer that the wishes of certain madmen are being followed in order to use this case as a coercive bludgeon against all dissenters. However, I still have faith that the more responsible elements in the administration will let sanity be the better part of judgement and spare our lives. It seems to me that at this moment it is still touch and go and therefore we must see to it that the maximum is done in our behalf. Surely, the American Government doesn't want such a damaging record as is documented in our case to go down in history for it will stand condemned for all time for this gross miscarriage of justice and this brutal sentence against two innocent people. For in good conscience and self-respect we could never deny the simple truth that we are innocent. By every reasoned consideration we should be allowed to live while there remains grave doubt to afford us the chance to clear our name and bring the true facts to light. At this late hour I am still confident the good people of our country will make their will felt in Washington and stop the executioner.

Sweetheart, I know that our children and our family [next word written over "is"] are suffering a great deal now and it is natural that we be concerned for their welfare. However, I think we will have to concentrate our strength on ourselves. First we want to make sure that we stand up under the terriffic [sic] pressure and then we ought to try to contibute [sic] some share to the fight. To my way of looking at the problem this is the way we can look out for our children's interest best. Honey dear, the Sunday issue of the New York Times had an excellent editorial on the essence of June with particular emphasis on the physical beauty of the [NWI] lush green around us. This month was ours because then we were united as husband and wife and found the boundless joy of a flourishing beautiful relationship. Precious noble woman [NWI] even to the end I am completely devoted to you—All the love I possess is yours—Julie

Mrs. Lena Cohen
140 Baruch Place
New York N.Y.

June 2nd, 1953

Dearest Lee,

Sweet sister you know we are most anxious to see you and we'd like nothing better than having a visit from you therefore I want you to consider what I am about to say. We are aware that you have been quite ill and unless you feel certain that the strain of the trip up here and the ensuing visit will not be detrimental to your health then [N4WI] don't come[.] Of course You [sic] yourself should decide whether to come. Of course I understand that you want to see us and you can rest assured the feeling is mutual but again I ask you to think it over carefully before you decide. At any rate what ever you decide will be alright with us. If you decide to come use the enclosed Sunday pass.

After a week of the flu I'm completely recovered [NWI] now and I'm back doing my share in our fight. Although the situation is very difficult both Ethel and I are confident that we will win this fight. Please don't worry too much everything possible is being done both in the public fight and the court battle to save our lives. Since in truth we are innocent we have high hopes that this will determine the successful outcome to our defense. Believe me darling I want nothing more than to convince you that we are well mentally & physically and that all will turn out as we work for it. It will not do us any good to know that you are not progressing nicely. The fundamental fact we must all learn is that a strong will depends on a healthy body.

You must know that your devoted support, love and warm affections have been an important source of strenght [sic] to my wife and me. Your sincere feelings for us have indeed been a great comfort in the hard trials we are going through and we love you all the more ["for" CO] because your [sic] our big sister. Keep well honey.

Please send my best to everyone and I'm happy to know the're [sic] all working hard on our behalf. Special hugs and kisses to Linda, a hearty handshake to Melvin and my personal regards to Julius. Tell Mama I hope she's keeping her spirits high.

I've got a lot of work to get off to Manny this evening and the time is short so I'll have to say good-bye for now.

I'm always thinking about my family and I hope you're all well please

don't let the opposition get you panicky. Calm and sober thinking will help
at this time.

Cheer up Sweethearts
Your kid brother
Julie
All my love.

*Although Julius did not refer to it in the previous letter, our parents had that
day had a very important visit from James V. Bennett, director of the Bureau
of Prisons. At 3:00 P.M. they sent the following telegram to Emanuel
Bloch.*

MR BENETT DIRECTOR OF FEDERAL PRISON BUREAU,
AT DIRECTION OF MR BROWNELL SAW ETHEL AND MYSELF
TODAY AND TOLD US IF WE WANT TO COOPEATE [*sic*] WITH THE
GOVERNMENT WE CAN DO SO THROUGH HIM AND HE WILL PUT
US IN TOUCH WITH THE PROPER OFFICIALS STOP WE BOTH
REASSERTED OUR INNOCENSE [*sic*] AND SAID SINCE WE ARE
NOT GUILTY WE CANNOT TELL THEM ANYTHING ABOUT
ESPINAGE [*sic*] STOP ALSO THAT HE SHOULD TELL THE
ATTORNEY GENERAL TO RECOMMEND A COMMUTATION OF
OUR SENTENCE STOP WE WOULD LIKE TO SEE YOU TO FILL IN
THE DETAILS—
    JULIE AND ETHEL—

Mrs. Lena Cohen
140 Baruch Place
New York New York

June 3, 1953

Dearest Lee,
    Davy mentioned that you were planning to see us on Sunday. I am
therefore herewith enclosing the necessary pass. However, please do not feel
you must use it, if you really don't feel up to it.
    Much as we should enjoy seeing you, we don't want you to strain
yourself in any way. So come if you are sure you can, and don't worry if
you can't—We are both very well and remarkably calm in the face of
tremendous pressure. Only innocence can so maintain itself, only complete
faith that justice will yet be won!
    My love to all our family and friends—

As ever,
Ethel

That very same day, our parents issued a press release through attorney Bloch.

"Yesterday we were offered a deal by the Attorney General of the United States. We were told that if we cooperated with the Government, our lives would be spared.

By asking us to repudiate the truth of our innocence, the Government admits its own doubts concerning our guilt. We will not help to purify the foul record of a fraudulent conviction and a barbaric sentence.

We solemnly declare, now and forever more, that we will not be coerced, even under pain of death, to bear false witness and to yield up to tyranny our rights as free Americans.

Our respect for truth, conscience and human dignity is not for sale. Justice is not some bauble to be sold to the highest bidder.

If we are executed, it will be murder of innocent people and the shame will be upon the Government of the United States.

History will record, whether we live or not, that we were victims of the most monstrous frame-up in the history of our country."[415]

Julius to Ethel

June 4th, 1953

Ethel Darling,

I think the statement we issued through our attorney is an excellent one and I am very much pleased with it. Indeed I am proud of the fact that the bulk of the words and ideas ["are" CO] put in the final draft were a product of your efforts and together this was ["our" CO, N2WI] a joint accomplishment. It is hard for people to realize the very difficult circumstances we are laboring under and the deep sense of responsibility we felt as we worked out our thoughts to make sure that everyone would know the letter and full spirit of what we tried to tell the public. After all our very lives and most cherished principles are at stake here and I am glad we met the test well. Even more important is that the American people should know the truth about our case and also about the reprehensible conduct of justice department officials in this case. I feel strongly that it is our sacred duty to expose the police state methods that are being practiced. Because we are fighting for a just cause our spirits are high but at the same time our lives are in very great jeopardy [*sic*—"ap" written over illegible letters]. Of course the strain is getting greater but I know we'll ride through this storm in good shape. Therefore my sweets I can't help admiring you and telling you over and over again

---

[415]*The Testament of Ethel and Julius Rosenberg*, pp. 168–69.

that your [*sic*] a great noble [N5WI] which in fact you are and certainly a very charming person at that. I guess it will not [next word written over "seem"] be amiss if I say I love you most dearly.

As we expected the government would be quick to deny that they indulged in this dirty business. It reminds me of the story of the ["zea" CO] overzealous district attorney who was accussed [*sic*] of offering a similar "deal" to an accussed [*sic*]. The district attorney fumed and vehemently denied this in a long loud speech to the court but he ended on this note however if the accussed [*sic*] ["does" CO, NWI] should accept, the deal still stands (sic!) One thing is certain that Mr[.] Bennett sure inflicted a great deal of mental torture on us during the course of the 1 hour he was alone with me in the counsel room (against regulations without any brass present) the $1/2$ hour he spent with you and the $1/2$ the three of us were together. Perhaps he didn't mean to say to either of us or [NWI] also in both our presences that the Attorney General sent him to see us and Mr[.] Brownell wants us to know we can cooperate ["with" CO] with the govt through Mr[.] Bennett then their [*sic*] will be a basis to recommend clemency to the President. How big can the lie get and how much deceit and fraud are they capable of before they realize the [next word is illegible but appears to be "treme," perhaps a truncated "extreme"] dishonor they are doing to our country [N8WI] with cruelty they are visiting on innocent people. It seems to me that now the good people will see to it that justice will be done in this case. I have faith we will yet win and have our day of celebration. Naturally the first step is to save our lives and I am confident that we will live to go home together to our children. Events are beginning to happen at an increasing tempo and we must continue to look to each other to find the strength and courage to stand up to the terror—United in love and spirit we will be successful—

Always devoted to you
—Your Julie

P.S. The two motions brought on our behalf are very strong point of law & the logic in the argument is unassailable. Without doubt we have more than proved our contention. But all the law goes out the window when it comes to our case. The courts must uphold the D.A. & hide the frameup but I believe it wont [*sic*] work. The truth will out JR.

Mr. Emanuel H. Bloch
401 Broadway
New York NY

June 5, 1953

Page #1

Dear Manny,

After the incident of the special visit from the emissary of the Attorney General of the U.S. I rushed off a telegram to you and I wrote up an account of what took place at the interview but when I heard you were going to see us the next day I preferred to verbally give you all the details. After reading the bald lie of the justice department that Mr. Bennett's visit was routine and that they intimated no deal was offered I feel it my duty to present the facts as they took place last Tuesday.

First let me tell you that the mental torture Ethel and I went through took a very great toll and has revealed the naked ugly brutality of police state tyranny.

On Monday June 1st Mr. Carroll and Mr. Foley U.S. Marshalls were up to serve us with papers setting down our executions for our 14th wedding anniversary June 18th 11:00 P.M. My wife and I are to be horribly united in death on the very day of our greatest happiness our wedding day. They were very pleasant but they had a job, a distateful [*sic*] one at that, to do and they pointedly asked me before they left if they could do anything for us and I said yes—bring us good news.

Their visit was routine.

Tuesday at 11:00 AM after my visit with Ethel I was ushered into the counsel room and there was Mr. Bennett Federal Director of the Prision [*sic*] Bureau. Mind you this was the first time I was alone with anyone one [*sic*] without an officer or Sing Sing official present (I believe it's against the regulations here). We were alone for about an hour while the Principle [*sic*] Keeper Mr. Kelley sat outside the room while the door was closed.

Mr. Bennett opened the conversation and said, "Mr. Brownell the Attorney General sent me to see you and he wants you to know that if you want to cooperate with the government you can do so through me and I will be able to make arrangements for you to talk with any proper officials. Furthermore if you Julius can convince these official [*sic*] that you have fully cooperated with the government they will have a basis to recommend clemency." (Routine??——No-Deal??)

You can realize how shocked I was but I didn't want to lose my temper or self-control and I said in the first place we are innocent, that is the whole truth and therefore we know nothing that would come under the meaning of the word cooperate. "By the way did you tell our lawyer that you were coming to see us about this matter". He said ["now" CO] no your lawyer will see you tomorrow. (He knew that's why he came). I told him ["it is" CO] to get in touch with you as it was the only proper thing to do and he said he would later on.

Page # 2

June 5th, 1953

You mean to tell me Mr. Bennett that a great government like our is coming to two insignificant people like us and saying "cooperate or die." It is a terrible thing to do to offer to barter life [NWI] by ["to" CO] "talking"[.] It isn't necessary to beat me with clubs but such a proposal is like [N4WI] what took place during the middle ages equialent [*sic*] to the screw and the rack. You are putting a tremendous pressure on me. He said "why do you know that I didn't sleep last night when I knew I had to see you and Ethel the next day and talk to you about this matter why I was terribly worried." How do you think we feel sitting here waiting for death for over two years when we are innocent. My family has gone through great suffering. My sister had a nervou [*sic*] breakdown. My aged ailing Mother is tormented. Our children have know [*sic*] much emotional and mental agony. Then you talk to us about this.

Remember Mr[.] Bennett we love our country it is ["the" CO, NWI] our home, the land of my children and my family and we do not want its good name to be shamed and in justice and common decency we should be allowed to live to prove our innocence. He then said no not a new trial only by cooperating will there be a basis to ask for commutation. Look here Julius he said you ["never" CO, NWI] didn't deny ["y" of last letter written over "ied"] that you do not know anything about this espionage. I certainly did and furthermore did you read the record sir. He said he did not but continued by saying you had dealing [*sic*] with Bently [*sic*]. I never did and if you read the record she ["denied on the" CO, N3WI] said on the stand she did not know me and never met me. You had dealing with Gold didn't you. Of course I didn't he said on the stand he never knew me or met me. You should have read the record to be familiar with the facts. Oh I read a newspaper account of it. (It is interesting to note how they are convinced of their own lies ["s" of last word written over two illegible letters] and of course they will not stick to the record).

Listen Julius I was just sent here but if you agree I will bring someone to see you who is thoroughly familiar with the case and you will try to convince him you have cooperated with the government. "What do you want to do have him convince me I am guilty when I am not. You want him to put ideas in my head you will only be satisfied when I say the things you want me to say but I will not lie about this matter."

Look Julius, he said, Gordon Dean the head of the Atomic Energy Commission is a very good friend of mine[416] and if he is convinced that you have cooperated fully and told all you know about espionage he will speeak [*sic*. From the different color ink, one can discern that the previous word was originally "see" and the "p" was inserted as were the "ak", NWI] to the President and recommend clemency. I don't know anything ["agan" CO] about espionage since I am innocent and I think you should tell the Attorney General to recommend clemency because it is the just, humane and proper thing to do in this case. Our country has ["s" in previously word written over illegible letter] a reputation to maintain in the world and many of it's [*sic*] friends are outraged at the barbaric sentence and the lack of justice in this case.

Page #3

June 6th, 1953

I know there has been a lot of publicity in this case but that is not germane[.] What is ["germ" CO] the point is that you have to convince the officials that you have cooperated. Well Julius why did your brother-in-law involve you. I believe he did it to save his own skin[.] Also to try to make himself out to be a minor innocent dupe dominated by someone else so that he should not be held accountable for his own actions. Besides the government had caught the Greenglasses with the goods and they had to find some way to mitigate their own punishment. With my background of being fired for alleged communism from govt. service, because I was a union organizer and since he was a relative and knew me intimately and we had violent quarrels and [N2WI] there existed personal animosity between us I was falsely involved.[417] Also the prosecution saw a chance to make great political capital out of "communist-spy-atom-bomb-plot" and my wife and I became scapegoats & were straws tossed around by the political controversies that raged in the cold war. Why not go to the Greenglasses and get them to cooperate to tell the truth about this frameup.

You yourself Mr[.] Bennett as head of the Prison Bureau know that Greenglass and Gold were together in the Tombs for 9 months, discussing the case, studying notes from a big looseleaf covered book, rehearsing testi-

---

[416]For the role of Gordon Dean, see David Gelman, "Papers Suggest U.S. Manipulated Rosenberg Case," *Newsday,* May 25, 1975, see also entry in Gordon Dean's diary, February 7, 1951 and the transcript of a meeting of the U.S. Joint Congressional Committee on Atomic Energy, February 8, 1951. See also Radosh and Milton, pp. 142–51.

[417]Note how the thesis that the Greenglasses were indeed spies continued to be believed. Note also the refusal to acknowledge, even at this late date, Communist Party membership.

mony, talking to FBI agents, the prosecution & their attorneys.[418] You
know this because the records of the Tombs will show it & yet your dept.
refused to give us an opportunity to subpoena these records to prove this.
You know that Greenglass was coached on the A bomb sketch testimony
both verbally and from notes. You know the prosecutor permitted the
Greenglasses to perjure themselves. You know the prosecution caused
Schneider to perjure himself. You know the Govt. is preventing my wife's
family from coming forth with exculpatory testimony. You know that the
prosecution has exculpatory evidence that they are withholding from the
court. In short we did not get a fair trial and we were framed. Now you want
us to admit that this big lie is the truth. That we can never do.—Sure Mr[.]
Bennett we will cooperate fully ["get" CO, NWI] give us our day in court and
under oath from the witness stand we will repeat the truth and at the same
time we will be able to subpoena witnesses to prove our claim. That is the
way to give us justice—Oh no Julius no new trial only by cooperating can
you help yourself—But you can have the district attorney to agree to one of
our motion [sic]—Then we will put up or shut up and I am sure we will be
vindicated—No that is not germaine [sic] you have to cooperate with the
government.

How about the death sentence certainly even if the verdict were a true
one, which we vehemently deny, we never should have gotten such a severe
sentence. The history of our country in freeing war criminals nazi & fascist,
in not put [sic] to death traitors and spies and yet for the first time

Page #4

June 6th, 1953

the Rosenbergs are the worse criminals in all our history you know as a
reasoning man this is not so. All the facts in the case, the trial record and
the sentence prove it was a means of coercion. The humane, proper and just
action would be for our lives to be spared. We are a leading [NWI] powerful
country with a great prestige in the world and we must consider what the
["y" crossed out at end of previous word, NWI] people will think about the
fact that our government says to two people cooperate of [sic] die. Remember it would be in the best interest of our country to commute our sentences
of death. "But Julius I am giving you the opportunity to cooperate" he said.

Sure Judge Kaufman made a terrible blunder with this outrageous sentence and he has the bull by the tail and he can't let go. That's right Julius
he needs you to help him change this sentence and you can do this by
telling all you know. I cannot bail him out for his mistake for we never

---

[418]For one extraordinary documentation of this, see HG Phila. 3-599, December
28, 1950 and the analysis surrounding it in *Sons*, pp. 362–63.

should have received this sentence and in fact we should never have been brought to trial.

Julius all the courts upheld the conviction many times and all the officials in Washington believe your [*sic*] guilty. Why most everybody believes your [*sic*] guilty. You know that only one Appeals Court upheld the verdict of the original trial & the denial of certiorari does not pass on the merits of the case. At all other court actions we didn't get a hearing but only the right to file papers. This is the form of the law not its spirit. Always such haste because they are afraid we will prove our innocence. Also people like Dr[.] Urey, Prof. Einstein, scientists, lawyers, men of letters, have grave doubts about the case after reading the record. The Pope, 3000 Christian Church leaders, prominent rabbis and millions of people have asked for clemency. No Julius the Pope did not ask for clemency—Yes he did and I have the articles from the Osservatore Romano to prove it. We had the record printed, the one that records the entire proceedings of the trial and people read it and they ["are" CO] came away with grave doubts about the justness of the verdict. This record is available and will be read and the only way to cleanse this damning record is to let us live so we can prove our innocence.

Julius the trial not being fair, the sentence being too severe and all the publicity are not germaine [*sic*] to the issue the only way is for you to cooperate and convince the officials in Washington then they will have a basis to ask for clemency.

All these three years you say ["s" CO at end of last word] I am not telling the truth then if I say what you want [N3WI] me to say that would be cooperating and then it would be the truth. In good conscience I could not lend myself to this practice and I must say ["what" CO] in effect this pressure on us is cruel and unconscionable. The only decent thing to do is tell Mr[.] Brownell to recommend clemency. It was 12:00 o'clock when he went ["into" CO, NWI] in to see Ethel for a 1/2 hour & then they brought me into the woman's wing & he continued to try to brow beat us for another 1/2 hour till 1:00 P.M. Ethel will tell you about what took place ["at" CO, NWI] during this hour.

Page #5

June 7th, 1953

At the end of our session the Warden walked into the women's wing and ask [*sic*] what is this all about and I told him Mr[.] Brownell sent Mr[.][Bennett to tell us if we cooperated with the Government he would recommend clemency to the President. You will note the Warden was not present when the offer was made.

After I was in my cell again after 1:00 P.M[.] Mr[.] Bennett came over and he tried to convince me again to let him bring people who are familiar with the case and "you would submit to answer questions of what [next word written over "I"] you know about this." Then I said why this would be like brain washing Mr[.] Bennett. He then asked if he could come to see me again & I said yes if he brings good news.

Ethel and I resolved not to see anyone except ["if" CO, NWI] when you are present also. I gave you a few of the details as best I can recollect them I also told you some more of what took place at our last consultation. excuse [*sic*] the penmanship the rambling and the discontinuity but these are the true facts. The interview & visit was not routine it was well planned cold and calculated mental torture. In an arrogant ["and" CO, N2WI] manner, in utter disregard for ethics, justice, plain common decency and humanity we were told in effect cooperate or die—A dirty deal which the Government needs to help hide a vicious frameup against two innocent people in order to make political capital with this case and our lives. Yes they run the government, the courts and the press but they are beginning to worry about the people for they are sovereign and will not let this gross miscarriage of justice stand.

This terror was visited on two defenseless people but it could not succeed because we are right and we refused to abandon our principles, our belief in democracy freedom and the integrity of the individual. The people must be told all about what took place for there is great danger in our land if this ["sort of" CO] fascist stuff is not stopped now. Anyway you look at it as it happened last Tuesday, we saw what police state methods mean and it is terrifying to behold. After all the ["p" CO] buildup ["of the public" CO] in the newspapers they weakly deny that they made a dirty deal because they were exposed. The great difficulty is that by their control of the mass media [N2WI] of information they are continuously in small doses brain-washing the readers and listens [*sic*] about our case and the public is misinformed. Every efforts [*sic*] must be made to spread the truth.

We must live to defeat the plans of the justice department to kill us because they couldn't use us. I have faith that the people will learn the facts and save our lives & force the courts to stay our execution in order to see that we get justice in the time honored tradition of our great American Heritage. What will be the answer of America to all this? We are still confident that the good name of our country will be maintaned [*sic*] & we will live—

All my love—Julie

Page # 6

June 7th, 1953

You can understand counselor that it isn't possible to remember all the words of the conversations that took place but if the brain-washing session were recorded all that I wrote would be the gist of what took place stripped of fancy words and transparent camouflage. In effect he told me you must understand we control the courts and you'll never get anywhere there. Also he displayed an utter disregard for the feelings and conscience of the people of the world as if to say we call the tune and if they don't like it they can lump it. Besides it is apparent that he has a contempt for democracy and the traditional freedoms of our country and believes in an authoritarian approach to this matter. In so many words he said, only if I become an informer do and say things that satisfys [*sic*] the officials in Washington then they will let us live. Here in practice they show the meaning of all the fine words that they give lip service to. These are acts of desperation, signs of a deep illness and I fear that in the moments of madness they will disregard better judgement and the sane counsel of calm and intelligent responsible leaders of the government and in frustration and hate commit [NWI] double murder.

I have read your papers on the writ of mandamus action and on the motion of illegal sentence and the law and logic of our argument is unassailable and without doubt ["they are" CO, N2WI] we raise substantial questions of law. Why the courts don't even bother to read and study the questions we raise. They don't even make a pretense of going through the motions of even giving us the form of the law. It seems to me that when it comes to our case there is no law any more. Then the courts have deteriorated to the point that they are meer [*sic*, last two letters written over two illegible letters] appendages of an autocratic police force and in political cases the rights of defendents [*sic*] and the protection of the constitution no longer operates. These are plain facts and I think that each and everyone of our legal papers should be printed in ["the" CO] many thousands of copies and should receive wide distribution to inform America that it is happening here.

We are supposed to be sophisticated people and we understand about the nature of our government and we've read a great deal yet would you believe it that even after the "browbeating" I am still amazed that it actually took place. Incidentally I think our concise and poignant statement was an excellent one because it told the true story, plainly for everybody to see. I must say for Ethel that she is indeed a gem, a most marvelous and heroic woman. Although the strain has been very severe I am proud that we were able to successfully resist the mental torture. It is good to know that all of us, are doing our utmost. When oh when will our agony be over and how soon will we see some daylight? We are waiting and hoping to hear the good news soon—

As ever Julie

On June 5, Attorney Bloch filed a motion for a new trial under Section 2255 of the Federal Criminal code. The grounds were the papers stolen from O. John Rogge's office detailing the early statements of David Greenglass to his lawyers which showed that in fact he had not told "the full story" right from the beginning. Also included was the affidavit of Bernard Greenglass about the theft of uranium, proving again that David Greenglass had lied at the trial when he claimed he had not stolen anything from Los Alamos. Finally, affidavits about the console table were submitted, proving that David and Ruth Greenglass lied when they claimed it was a Russian gift and further that Ruth Greenglass lied when she claimed it had a hollowed out portion for microfilming. All of this evidence was significant because it went to the issue of credibility—the most crucial issue in the case. If the jury had been informed of these Greenglass perjuries, they might not have been so willing to believe the charges against our parents.

Julius to Ethel

June 7, 1953

Ethel Darling,

I must say I had an excellent visit with my sister and it is most gratifying that my family are [NWI] all busily working on our behalf, confident of ultimate victory instead of being paralyzed with fear engendered by the latest nefarious actions of the prosecution in this case. I think that spirit that has raised their morale is indeed indicative of a trend for the better. Of course after my sister told me about the new evidence that has been uncovered I, too, was heartened. It seems to me and I believe I know a great deal about our case that the latest motion for a new trial is beyond any doubt our strongest legal action and besides it contains some devastating stuff that can break this case wide open. The only reason I have any reserve about it is that we must go before Kaufman and by past performance he will not let the law govern in our case. However if the information contained in the new evidence motion papers, [sic] is widely circulated, the courts will be forced to give them some consideration. At any rate I am still hopeful about our chances in the courts. Especially since the public campaign in our behalf is gaining strength and also because the political situation in the world is changing for the better. Considering all angles I feel that we can still be optimistic about winning this case even at this late hour.

Of course I don't want you to get me wrong I am under no illusion about the benignity of certain of the officials who run the country but I have to hope that reasonable and practical minds will [N2WI] govern and determine the final decision of our government in this case if and when it does come down to the question of life or death. At the moment nobody can tell what the exact solution will be but in a large measure our analysis of the case has always been found to be correct and I am confident that we will live to prove our innocence.

I hope that Manny sends us the latest papers on the new evidence because there are certain matters I must talk over with you and I believe we can possibly recommend new directions of investigation to uncover more of the missing parts of the puzzle. Also it will help you in talking to your brother [Bernard Greenglass]. With the latest knowledge that my sister informed me about I begin to discern ["many of" CO] the general pattern of the jig-saw [NWI] plot, that was concocted by the Greenglass [*sic*] to save themselves and frame us. Saypol and his henchmen certainly had a part in this dirty deal to make political capital out of the case and win personal glory. In justice these people should go to jail for their part in this frameup. The printed record and the new evidence brought forth by our lawyer is a major roadblock in the way of the gang in the justice dept that want to execute us to close the truth of the case from the public view. ["It looks like" CO, NWI] From their actions it looks [previous two words written over "shows"] like they are worried that the entire mess will be exposed in this sense they have already admitted defeat. I have faith that we will live to be in each others arms again—love you always—your Julie

P.S. Can't wait to see your sparkling eyes and beautiful face again. I am simply nuts about you my wonderful, charming woman. JR.

Emanuel H. Bloch
7 W. 16th Street
New York New York

June 8, 1953
Letter # 1

Dear Manny,

The lame attempts of the Justice Dept. to "brainwash" the public on an issue that had been the main burden of a sickening refrain for over two long years, brings to mind Iago's cynical assertion that "knavery's plain face is never seen till used"!

As you may recall, on Tuesday of June 2nd ([NWI] always here-after [hyphen written over "in" in previous word] to be re-["ferred to" CO, next two syllables inserted] membered as "D-eal Day"), Mr. James V. Bennett, Federal Director of Prisons, paid us a "routine" visit at Sing Sing and we wired you at once concerning same. To fully comprehend the true significance of this incident, it is necessary to examine a number of salient factors.

Even since the imposition upon us of a manifestly savage and vengeful sentence, we have been periodically advised via newspaper, ["press" CO, NWI] radio and television, that the opportunity to save ourselves rested upon our willingness to "cooperate" with the government and "confess" our "guilt". Often, these unofficial "invitations" to "talk" had risen in pitch and intensity to such an extraordinarily well-tuned and collective clamor, as would have indicated a definite purpose on the part of the government. Indeed, hot upon the heels of the Supreme Court's latest refusal to review, it was deliberately and falsely reported that an offer had ["allegedly" CO] been made us; and when you, as our counsel, roundly and publicly denounced this "news item" as an unethical fabrication, the government was forced to show its hand.

Subsequent events bear me out, to wit: After Judge Kaufman had, with his usual indelicate haste, fixed the week of June 15 for our joint execution, two U.S. Marshals in the presence of the Warden personally served me with official notification papers, setting [N3WI, middle word illegible and CO] aside Thursday, June 18 (our 14th wedding anniversary, incidentally) for the grand event. That was Monday, June 1st. The very next day, just as I was sitting down to lunch, Mr. Bennett entered the women's wing of the death house and announced himself. Contrary to all established practise [sic], he was alone with me, the Principal Keeper and the matron having discreetly stationed themselves at the outer barred gate to the corridor, and the Warden who invariably escorts official visitors through the prison, conspicuously absent.

He came right to the point, Attorney General Herbert Brownell, Jr. had directed him to inform me that he would make available to me any official to whom I might care to divulge expunge information I had hitherto withheld. If I cooperated in this fashion, the government stood ready to invalidate the death penalty. He had been visiting with Julie for an hour—since my husband's personal visit with me had ended at 11:00 A.M. as a matter of fact—and now he was anxious to get my view-point.

I made it short and sweet. I was innocent, my husband was innocent, and neither of us knew anything about espionage. And if the Attorney General were to send a highly placed authority to see me, I should simply reiterate what I had just stated and urge that clemency be recommended to remedy a shocking situation.

Gently Mr. Bennett prodded me to "cooperate". "Surely you must know something," he coaxed. I picked him up quickly, "Well, now, how could I when I did not participate in any way. In order to cooperate as you desire, I should have to deliberately concoct a pack of lies and bear false witness

Letter #2—c't'd from
<u>Letter #1</u>

Dear Manny,

against unoffending individuals. Is that what the authorities want me to do—to lie?" He was properly horrified. "Oh, dear, no, of course we don't want you to lie. But now take a family, for example. One member might not be actively engaged in certain activities, but still have knowledge concerning another member's activities."[419] I was exceedingly polite but firm. "The fact still remains that I don't know any more than I knew during the trial. I told the full and complete truth then and I don't intend to start lying now." He tried another tack. "I am a perfectly honest individual myself, yet my experience in these matters has shown me that for one reason or another, a person will sometimes plead innocent, knowing full well that he is guilty. Wouldn't you agree with that?"

"I will be just as frank," I replied evenly, "and grant you that there have been such instances. Nevertheless, I couldn't possibly concern myself as to the motives involved in such cases. I do, however, know my own mind and heart, and I tell you in all conscience that I continue to maintain my innocence for the sole reason that I am simply not guilty of the charge.["]

"Well, the government claims to have in its possession, documents and statements that would dispute that, so if only you were willing to cooperate, there might be a basis for a commutation—"

I remained entirely unimpressed. "To begin with, I ["do not at all" CO, N2WI] couldn't possibly know nor do I care what they have or don't have. Whatever it might be, it has nothing to do with me. Besides, if what they have is so damaging, why do they need me to confirm it, at this late stage. If you are persuading me to confess to activities concerning which I have solemnly sworn I have no knowledge, on the basis of evidence with which I was never confronted in court, then obviously the validity of this evidence must be strongly questioned, if ["you" CO, "they" inserted, then CO, NWI] it in fact ["have it" CO, NWI] exists at all. I will tell you this very bluntly. The most powerful government on earth has sent its representative to approach two insignificant little people with a [NWI] disgraceful propo-

---

[419]One of the more damning FBI documents shows that the government was willing to concede internally that it had no idea whether my mother was the least bit involved in any espionage activity. One of the questions on the list to be asked of my father, should he decide to "cooperate," was "Was your wife cognizant of your [espionage] activities?" See Branigan to Belmont, June 17, 1953. This internal understanding is probably the source of Bennett's question.

sition, because it is fully aware [NWI] that the convictions were illegally procured, the sentences vindictive. And rather than risk exposing their participation in a rotten frame-up, and with a double execution they are anxious not to carry out [",", CO] only days away, they have the effrontery ["do they" inserted, then CO] to try to forcibly wring from us a false confession, by dangling our lives before us like bait before hapless fish! [illegible letter CO] Pay the price we demand, or forfeit your lives, is that the idea?"

At this juncture Mr. Bennett [illegible word CO, NWI] hastened to stem the rising tide of my indignation. "Come, come, I have not said anything of the sort, you are misinterpreting me." "On the contrary", I retorted, not without asperity, "I have understood you far too well. Of course, you are not quite so cold-blooded, but I have interpreted to you, and correctly, the government's intent. So here is our answer. We will not be intimidated by the threat of electrocution into saving their horrible faces, nor will we encourage the growing use of undemocratic police state methods by accepting a shabby, contemptible little deal, in lieu of the justice that is due us as citizens. That is for

Letter #3—c't'd from
Letter #2

Dear Manny,
Hitler Germany, not for the land of liberty. A truly great, truly honorable nation has the obligation to redress greivances, [sic] not to demand tribute of those who have been wronged, for [NWI] grudgingly sparing their lives— lives that should never have been placed in ["jeoa" CO] jeopardy at all!"

"But we are trying to help you by seeking your cooperation," he pleaded, beginning to flounder in earnest now. Somehow, he was not managing things as he had doubtless intended, and the mask of nonchalant authority was beginning to slip, revealing his very real discomfiture.

"Say what you will," I declared unmoved, "Camouflage it, glamorize it, whitewash it in any way you choose, but this is coercion, this is pressure, this is torture." Here I pointed to the clock that was cheerfully ticking away my life. "Let me say to you in all sobriety. You will come to me at ten minutes of 11:00 P.M. on Thursday, June 18, and the fact of my innocence will not have changed in the slightest."

Mr. Bennett gazed at me with a look in which utter disbelief and sheepish admiration vied equally. It said so plainly. "She must be crazy to reject life when it is there for the taking—ar-r-humph—for a price of course. Nevertheless, one has to respect her stand."

I felt sorry for him; just another cog in a wheel, doing a lousy, thankless job, wanting so desperately to convince me that he was impartial and finding it increasingly difficult to maintain an untenable position against an incredibly ["devastating" CO, NWI] virile and dedicated honesty!

Throwing up his hands in despair, finally, he requested that Julie be brought in. For another half-hour he [NWI] fairly entreated us to "cooperate", even promising to enlist the aid of his good friend, Gordon Dean, chairman of the Atomic Energy commission. My husband was wonderfully poised and forthright. "How can ["this country" CO, NWI] America stoop to such tactics," he demanded, "and hope to command the [NWI] continued respect and [N2WI] affection and support of our friends. It is simply unthinkable! Frankly, as one human being to another can you offer me one reason that might possibly justify the unheard of barbarity of the sentence? And don't you feel at all called upon to recommend clemency to the Attorney General as a matter of plain, ordinary decency and common sense? How can ["our" CO] this nation afford to let such villainy ["remain" CO, NWI] go unchallenged, and be indelibly recorded to the everlasting shame of ["the" CO] incoming generations! Wouldn't it be the better part of valor to grant Mr. Bloch the opportunity to prove our contentions that the entire conduct of the case was marked by passion, prejudice and perjury? Just imagine! Even if it were true, and it is not, my wife is awaiting a horrible end for having typed a few notes! A heinous crime, "worse than murder," no doubt, and deserving of the supreme penalty, while the most atrocious and wanton killers known to civilization, the Nazi war criminals are being freed daily."

(more letters to follow—)—
Ethel

Emanuel H. Bloch
7 W. 16th Street
New York New York

June 9, 1953
Letter #4

Dear Manny,

Let me repeat the last lines of Letter # 3, so there will be some continuity. [She filled the next line with dashes]
"A heinous crime, 'worse than murder', no doubt, and deserving of the supreme penalty, while the most atrocious and wanton killers known to civilization, the Nazi War Criminals, are being freed daily!"

Mr. Bennett began to look a little distraught. "What you're saying is not germane. Please, if you would only agree to cooperate, something could be worked out. There just won't be any other way."—(*sic*!) "Of course", I interjected, "a hearing based on new evidence is not germane; after all, we might actually be able to prove our claims. But it is germane for the government of a great nation to victimize two helpless people just because a world controversy has developed as to their guilt and to tell them in effect, "to knuckle under [illegible word CO, NWI] or die!"

Oh, I neglected to mention that [illegible word CO, N3WI] a good bit after Julie's [six illegible words CO, NWI] arrival, the Warden had [NWI] finally come hurrying in. Now the visit was beginning to draw to a close. My husband was speaking. "Consider carefully, wouldn't it be more advantageous to the United States to let us live? Wouldn't it be a real proof to the peoples of the world that this country is genuinely concerned with human rights? Doesn't your coming here at the behest of the Attorney General indicate that the handling of this case has cost us a good deal of prestige on the other side? Obviously, it would be much less costly in terms of this prestige to ["let us live" CO, N2WI] give us the opportunity to prove our innocence!"

"Oh, oh, there's been so much politics made of this case—too much—and it isn't germane. You say you have never hurt your country, you say you love your country, do you?"

As we vigorously assented, he said, "Well, then, cooperate and give us the information we need to enable us to recommend a commutation!" ["Appalled" CO, N2WI] We stared at him, appalled; then Julie said slowly. "You see, Mr. Bennett, we love her so much we will not permit her [N2WI] good name to be ["degraded" CO, illegible word inserted, then CO] dishonored, by ["acquiescing to" CO, N2WI] entering into an immoral arrangement!"

He shrugged his shoulders wearily, explained to the warden that he was to expedite any messages we might care to send him, and bade us good-bye. As he turned to go, I made a final plea. ["Give" CO, NWI] "Grant us our day in court, Mr[.] Bennett. Let us live ["to" CO] that we may prove our innocence. That's the decent way, the American way!"

Afterwards, I learned that he had followed Julie back into his own corridor and had attempted yet ["again" CO, N2WI] once more to convince him ["he ought to cooperate" CO, NWI] that his only hope lay in "cooperation". "Would you like me to come ["and see you" CO, NWI] back another time," he had inquired rather timidly. "Yes", my husband had ["grinned" CO] answered ["grimly" CO, NWI] pointedly, "if you can bring me [NWI] some good news!"
[The next line is filled with dashes]

The newspapers, arriving at 3:00 P.M., helped to bring a crazily reeling world back into focus. It ["seems" CO, NWI] appeared that while we were ["being {"in" inserted, then CO} worked over for all we were worth" CO, N5WI—in pencil] "standing up and being counted" and our bargaining agent was "Whistlin' in the Dark", Britons had been "Singin' in the Rain" and pouring out their ["most" CO] tender, human feelings in fealty to youth and love and beauty. In honor, too, of human courage and human endurance, they had subdued mighty Everest

Emanuel H. Bloch
7 W. 16th Street
New York New York

June 10, 1953
Letter #5

Dear Manny,

The following is a re-write of the last paragraph of the last letter—letter # 4. Please see that the changes are made and that the original is not used. I went to so much trouble having a corrected version of "If We Die" transmitted to you, to no avail. The original last line was printed instead of the corrected version which was, "For our sons & yours," or at least, "For you, my sons, and yours."

Last paragraph of letter # 4 to read as follows:

The newspapers arriving at 3:00 P.M. helped to bring a crazily reeling world back into focus. While* we were standing up and being counted and our bargaining agent ["subjecting us" CO, NWI] making with the polite palaver at Sing Sing's death house, it appeared that Britons had been "Singin' in the Rain!" in London and pouring out their tender human feelings, in fealty to youth and love and beauty.[420] To the everlasting glory of human courage and ["human" CO] endurance, they had also conquered mighty "Everest"!

Somehow it was all of a piece. They didn't know it, these intoxicated celebrants, these intrepid challengers, but we were one with them. For had we not likewise strained the heights and laughed fearlessly at danger and

---

[420]The last paragraph was originally written like this. The asterisk is in reference to two lines written between the date and the salutation at the top of the letter: "While our bargaining agent was making with the polite palaver at Sing Sing's death house and we were standing up, etc." To show the different order she wanted, she ran an arrow from the asterisk to the word "our" nine words later and put a circled "1" above it. The line was extended from the other direction from the asterisk to encircle the entire clause "our bargaining agent . . . death house" as well as the words "we were". Just before the word "our" with the circled "1" above it, the word "and" has a circled "2" above it with a line drawn ending in a point at the "we" in "we were." It appears that what she wanted to do was change the order of the two "events" from the previous letter to this one and chose to do it by first rewriting what she had in the previous letter and then using arrows and numbers and an asterisked partial re-write to accomplish that. Neither version was published in *The Testament of Ethel and Julius Rosenberg* nor in *Sons*.

death! And had we not likewise kept faith with love, and humbly offered a gift to life!

["A free nation does not [N2WI] try to buy subservience. It was because we scorned to dignify a scandalous horse-trade and refused to barter freedom for slavery," CO]

I was perhaps therefore the more revolted at the ["outrageous characterization" CO, NWI] Justice Dept.'s unblinking disavowal of complicity and ["its" CO, NWI] the brazen characterization of ["a scandalous" CO, illegible word CO, "its offer as routine only" inserted then CO. "First a scandalous horse trade" CO, N3WI] its unscrupulous offer as "routine"! The motive for such outrageous ["lying falsification [NWI] distortions of facts" CO] misstatement is pretty transparent. ["We had s" CO] Our firm refusal to traffic in corruption had placed them in anything but a flattering position and the ["impact of the" CO, illegible word CO, NWI] scandal of two powerless individuals [NWI in pencil] boldly [illegible word inserted, then CO] defending their innocence [N2WI in pencil] in defiance ["putting" inserted then CO, "and putting to shame the" CO, illegible word CO, illegible word inserted then CO, N3WI in pencil] of their inquisitors ["needed to be softened" CO] might ["give recent" CO, N2WI in pencil] touch off such-a [*sic*] "thunderous out-cry," CO, N3WI in pencil] storm of protest that it would be difficult [NWI in pencil] indeed to persuade [she switched to pencil with the "u" in the previous word] any ethical person any where that their proposed execution was justified. On the contrary, all decent humanity must inevitably recognize that a fiendishly power-drunk, reckless authority had vented its spleen in reprisal, and silenced voices fraternally raised to champion the liberties they despise and fear.

It was Oliver Wendell Holmes with his flaming passion for truth, that forced an apathetic and conscienceless world to recognize the nobility of a Philip Semmelweis[421] who fought at the cost of [NWI] terrible self-sacrifice for the "clean hands" that alone preserved life, "The truth must not be silenced not a single mother's life taken" he thundered. "Men with un-clean hands—look to God to forgive you—man never will!"

It is "unclean hands" that have ever spread disease and contamination. It is "unclean hands" that clutch [NWI] to execute the Rosenbergs! In your immortal spirit, ["Philip" CO] Semmelweis, we will mercilessly scrub away every last vestige of filth that life may shine and sparkle & God's divine will be done.   Ethel

---

[421]A Hungarian obstetrician who discovered that puerperal fever was transmitted by the failure of obstetricians to thoroughly wash their hands between performing autopsies on mothers who had died of the disease and examining living mothers. He was the first practitioner of asepsis.

Emanuel H. Bloch [ink]
401 Broadway
New York New York

June 10, 1953

Page #1

Dear Manny

It is encouraging to hear that you are confident and most comforting to receive your sincere greetings. The latest legal papers came with your note and I read them over carefully.

Of course, people with many years of association or close interest with legal papers are more qualified than I am and can speak with greater authority than I, but in the last three years of concentrated attention to legal matters, briefs and other writings and particularly those connected with our matter I believe [N3WI] in all candor the informed reader will readily agree with me when I say never have I heretofore read anything written in language comparable to the businesslike presentation of the Supreme Court Petition and Supplementary Brief! (It is imperative that these papers receive wide circulation among members of the bar, judiciary, legislative and executive branch of the Government).

These papers should, and conceivably could shock and perhaps will shame the august court to take definitive steps in initiating a review which will allow the stinking mess to be aired, and in time correct the hypocritical parody of justice which has been palmed off on us as being a "fair trial."[422] I most heartily endorse your "J'accuse" approach at this time because the posture of the proceedings to date requires this ["aggressive" (*sic*) CO, NWI] action. Bravo!! for you and Mr. Finerty it is an excellent job and I offer my congratulations and most grateful thanks for your superb ["efforts" CO] accomplishment.[423]

---

[422]On June 8, Judge Kaufman had heard oral arguments and denied a hearing under Sec. 2255 in a charade that prompted physicist Harold Urey, who had been in the courtroom, to charge that when he saw what goes on in Kaufman's court he saw "no Kaufman but McCarthy." (See *Sons,* p. 193). The Court of Appeals insisted on hearing the appeal from Kaufman's ruling on the spot on June 9 and immediately denied the appeal and refused to stay the execution, setting the stage for one last effort at the Supreme Court. See Schneir, pp. 211–12.

[423]The Finerty affidavit was attached to an application for a writ of *habeas corpus* which was filed with the Supreme Court immediately after they denied a stay on June 15. The approach was to use the argument that had been used in the Mooney-Billings case, that knowing use of perjured testimony is grounds for reversal. (See Parrish, p. 833, RM, pp. 397–99) Finerty had himself been the lawyer who had won the landmark *Mooney vs. Halohan* Supreme Court decision in 1935.

Our moving papers show an abundance of merit. The claims are not frivolous; are documented sufficiently to even now establish our contentions; and more than enough to satisfy legal requirements for a prima facie showing of right to relief prayed for.

The Perl situation (re affidavits, etc.) and the "uranium" set-up as divulged by papers from Rogge files[424] [N5WI] & supported by Bernie's affidavit have devastatingly now established on the record as being a bit of slimy connivance and collusion which certainly (on the record) puts the government within the sphere of litigants which the courts (usually in comparable unpublicised [sic] cases) terms [sic] as "coming into court with dirty hands". I think these two items are the strongest points raised in our petition. Now in the context of the fore-going the "console" further serves to nail the Greenglasses to the big lie of our involvement into espionage. Is there then any wonder why the government and Kaufman are dreadfully afraid that we have our day in court to prove from the witness stand the truth of our contentions?

However, Manny, in an intelligent and adult appraisal of our grave situation, and of the many other worthy legal showings made to the courts, what can I tell myself as assurance that this too will not go out the window? That as applied to us,

Page # 2

the law has absconded into the never-never land of politics and maybe by vigorous tactics as these latest you our lawyers may shock or shame the judiciary to forsake the executive branch of government and act as a judiciary branch! Mind you I say this studying our legal ["position" CO, NWI] situation in the most objective manner projecting myself into the position of those responsible officials who must calmly weight ["t" CO at end of last word] what is truly in the best interest of ["justice and" CO] our country and justice.

I realize full well that the political situation is the determining factor in our case. Therefore considering the growing world opinion in our behalf and the easing of international tensions and the proximity of a truce in Korea, our execution at this time will be looked on ["by" CO] as an act of madness and a reversion to barbarism. Because of this I am able to hope that the court will decide one of our legal actions on ["their" CO, NWI] it's [sic] merits on the basis of law.

At this point we have completed a record that for all time raises grave doubts about our guilt and the government can rectify this miscarriage of

---

[424]See Schneir, p. 211 for how one Rogge memorandum confirms Bernard Greenglass' affidavit.

justice ["in many ways" CO, N2WI] very simply—if we are allowed to live. Our many legal actions give them an opportunity to give us our day in court.

I am still confident that the logic of events and the movement of the ["historical" CO] peoples [*sic*] forces, which is the modern historical truism that governs politics and is the major shaping force for changes and for important decisions of governments. That the present administration in Washington is keenly aware of this factor is attested to by it's concentration on psychological warfare and it's [*sic*] strenuous efforts to control the minds of the public in ["i" written over "o" in previous word] a way that they accept it's [*sic*] concocted false version of our case as the "truth." Even though we are completely innocent and the record, the facts, the law and the plain truth are in our favor I am still worried because the twists and turns of our governments [*sic*] policies don't always ["follow" CO, N2WI] end up in the most reasonable and correct action. Therefore with the trend in world affairs becoming more favorable it is still possible for the extreme right wing fascistic minded elements in Washington to obtain the willing consent of the administration to go along with our execution. Recent events have shown how pliable the executive branch is when it is pressured in a reactionary direction. Therefore only a most thorough and concerted campaign ["of" CO, NWI] with all the weapons we have will assure us of a victory.

The simple truths and the issues as they are drawn in and around our case demand a vigorous and determined fight for justice and life. It is now Thursday morning June 11th as I finish this letter and our date is set for next week. Will the people deliver us to celebrate our wedding anniversary or will they let us go to our doom? The answer is in their hands. (top) [Letter continued on top of last side] Again send our thanks to Mr Finerty and Mr Sharp[425] for their help. Tell our friends & everybody we are earnestly and confidently awaiting their action. All my love—as ever—Julie

---

[425]Professor Malcolm Sharp of the University of Chicago Law School joined the defense team for the filing of the motion on June 5. He later wrote a book about the case, called *Was Justice Done?* (New York: Monthly Review Press, 1956).

Emanuel H. Bloch
7 W. 16th Street
New York New York

June 11, 1953
(Why don't you try reading
some of this where it
might do some good)

Dearest Manny,

No wonder you are confident, the latest stuff is terrific. Reading it has given me a good deal of comfort!

Nevertheless, I am under no illusions and am preparing myself for the worst, while remaining just as hopeful [N3WI] and working hard for the best. Since, however, I am a grown woman, I have to figure there might be last good-byes to make. In this respect, I am fairly besides myself because of the tiny amount of time left in which legal matters must take precedence over personal ones. You know what's bothering me; how can you possibly be expected to continue making the necessary moves (and they will be [NWI] made right up to the last), and still manage to bring up the children. Tell me, magnanimous sirs, have we grown so calloused, so ["inured" CO] innured [*sic*] to [illegible word CO, NWI] kindness and simple human decency, that we unconcernedly plan to re-unite a couple in death on their 14th wedding anniversary, after having deprived them [NWI] also of a last bit of happiness with their children. After all "justice" might not triumph if too much time were frittered away on such frivolous amenities! I say mercy must also have "its day in court", ["else" CO, NWI] lest law become ["s" CO at end of last word] a jungle beast ["now stalking the" CO, N2WI] prowling for prey.

Besides, I remember very distinctly reading an article in the "Times" which quoted Justice Vinson as saying he was denying a stay because he didn't think the government would set a date before June 15—Furthermore, you yourself told us he hadn't passed on the merit of your request but that the request was made too soon [N5WI] & therefore he denied it. Doesn't it strike you as odd that ever since the date was set, everybody (press & radio alike) has been ["pha" CO] harping on the [N2WI] same old theme of June 18th as though nothing could possibly happen to upset the "proper" functioning of the well-oiled machinery! Doesn't it [N2WI] help to pressure the Supreme Court into making a hasty decision because there's a "deadline" to meet!

I should feel so relieved, if there were a stay, ["(" CO] so that come what might after it was used up, [")" CO] I should know [N2WI] at least that ["my" CO, NWI] our affairs were completely in order and that we had had ample opportunity to visit with our children—

Do something, Manny, try, won't you—It is inconceivable to me that they will permit such a piece of crudity as our execution on our wedding anniversary—But then, I am an incurably soft individual who just can't understand how men may sound and look like me and be ["nothing more nor less than" CO, NWI] only sadistic devils in disguise!

In any case, plan to see us next without the children. We deserve your exclusive legal attention emotional deprivation or not—If your back-breaking efforts yield fruit, there will be plenty of time to visit socially at our leisure—We serve the children's needs much more [N3WI] for the present by concentrating on our defense—Keep your eyes open for Letter # 5 which I sent ["today" CO] you on the 10th—Love Ethel

Emanuel H. Bloch
7 W. 16th Street
New York New York

                                                                    June 12, 1953
Dearest Manny,

It was 2:00 A.M. when I finished scribbling my letter of the 11th to you and I was too exhausted to bother very much about the grammatical niceties to say nothing of my handwriting. I was also most regretful to realize that I had altogether neglected to mention Mr. Finerty's excellent "Supplemental Brief." Will you please convey to him my heartiest congratulations on a most penetrating and hard-hitting and conscientious piece of work. I am certain that Julie will express himself in similar vein when I see him a couple of hours hence.

You know, ever since the Oatis opus, I have come to place more faith in the power of personal appeal than I ever had heretofore.[426] Legal papers have an importance, of course, that needs no mention whatever, and the kind of press statements we have been issuing are of inestimable value from a public relations point of view. Nevertheless, though I have every now and then touched on the idea of the more direct use of our letters (or appropriate excerpts thereof), to gain [NWI] the support of people in strategic positions, I have only just begun to feel strongly about it. I guess it was that feeling that prompted [N3WI] a request for a stay on personal grounds as well as legal ones, and quoting from said letter in court, if you deemed it correct, naturally! I might add at this point, the reference to Oliver Wendell Holmes and Dr. Semmelweis' fight for "clean hands" is the kind of excerpt that

---

[426]An American named William Oatis was imprisoned as a spy in Czechoslovakia but released as a result of a plea by his wife. See *Sons*, pp. 222–23.

might very well be brought to bear with telling effect upon the proper parties, or am I being youthfully starry-eyed? (over)
["The following is a" CO] Letter to the President follows—
Love, Ethel

Emanuel H. Bloch
7 W. 16th Street
New York New York

June 15, 1953

Dear Manny,
    Kindly send the following letter to:
Dwight D. Eisenhower, President of the United States
White House, Washington, D.C.
Dear Mr. President:
    At various intervals during the two long and bitter years I have spent in the Death House at Sing Sing, I have had the impulse to address myself directly to the President of the United States. Always, in the end, a certain innate shyness, an embarrassment almost, comparable to that which the ordinary person experiences in the presence of the great and the famous, prevailed upon me not to do so.
    Since then, however, the moving plea of Mrs. William Oatis on behalf of her husband has lent the inspiration. She had not been ashamed to bare her heart to the head of a foreign state; would it really be such a presumption for a citizen to ask for redress of grievance, and to expect as much consideration as Mrs. Oatis received at the hand of strangers?
    Of Czechoslovakia I know very little, of her President less than that. But my own land is a part of me, I should be horribly homesick for her anywhere else in the world. And Dwight D. Eisenhower was "liberator" to millions before he was ever "President." It does not seem reasonable to me then, that a letter concerning itself with condemned wife as well as condemned husband should not merit this particular President's sober attention.
    True, to date, you have not seen fit to spare our lives. Be that as it may, it is my humble belief that the burdens of your office and the exigencies of the times have allowed of no genuine opportunity as yet, for your more personal consideration.
    It is chiefly the death sentence I would entreat you to ponder. I would entreat you to ask yourself whether that sentence does not serve the ends of "force and violence" rather [NWI] than an enlightened justice! Even granting the assumption that the convictions had been properly procured, the steadfast denial of guilt, extending over a protracted period of solitary confinement

and enforced separation from our loved ones, makes of the death penalty an act of vengeance.

As Commander-in-Chief of the European theatre, you had ample opportunity to witness the wanton and hideous tortures that such a policy of vengeance had wreaked upon vast multitudes of guiltless victims. Today while these ghastly mass butchers, these obscene racists, are graciously receiving the benefits of mercy and in many instances being reinstated in public office, the great democratic United States is proposing the savage destruction of a small, unoffending Jewish family, whose guilt is seriously doubted throughout the length and breadth of the civilized world! As you have recently so wisely declared, ["we dare not take the risk of" CO, N4WI] no nation can chance "going it alone." That, Mr. President, is truly the voice of the sanity and of the leadership ["that is" CO] so sorely needed in these parlous times. Surely you must recognize then, that the ensuing damage ["to the" CO] to the good name of our country, in its struggle to lead the world toward a more equitable and righteous way of life, ["may" CO, NWI] should not be underestimated.

Surely, too, what single action could more effectively demonstrate this nations' fealty to religious and democratic ideals, than the granting of clemency to my husband and myself!

Such an act would [NWI] also be a fitting reply to a small boy's desperate appeal.[427] His bright young mind and homesick heart prompted him [NWI] even as his mother was ["simi" inserted then CO] prompted, to see in Mr. Oatis' release a hope for the release of his own dear parents. I approach you then as he did, solely on the basis of mercy, and earnestly beseech you to let this quality sway you, rather than any narrow judicial concern which is after-all the province of the courts. It is rather the province of the affectionate grandfather, the sensitive artist, the devoutly religious man, that I would enter. I ask this man, himself no stranger to the humanities, what man there is that History has acclaimed great, whose greatness has not been measured in terms of his goodness? Truly, the stories of Christ, of Moses, of Ghandi [*sic*] hold more sheer wonderment and spiritual treasure than all the conquests of Napoleon!

I ask this man, whose name is one with glory, what glory there is that is greater than the offering to God, of a simple act of compassion!

Take counsel with your good wife; of statesmen there are enough and to spare! Take counsel with the mother of your only son; her heart which understands my grief so well, and my longing to see my sons grow to manhood like her own, with loving husband at my ["side" CO, NWI] side

---

[427]See *Sons*, pp. 222–23 for the text of that letter and its context.

even as you are at hers,—her heart must plead my cause with grace and with felicity!

And the world must humbly honor greatness!

Respectfully yours,
(Mrs.) Ethel Rosenberg

A typed version of this letter with "parlous" rewritten as perilous, with a return address of 354 Hunter Street, Ossining, NY, dated June 16, 1953, and with her number 110-510 and "Women's Wing—C C" typed after her name was among the originals. It is the typed version that was published in The Testament of Ethel and Julius Rosenberg, *pp. 181–82 and in* Sons, *p. 224–26.*

At the end of what turned out to be their last visit with us, June 16, I left the room wailing "one more day to live, one more day to live . . ." The following letter was written in reaction to that outburst. In Sons *it is claimed to have been misdated, but in fact Wednesday was the 17th and also the day on which Julius and Ethel would have been visiting each other and from the context at the end of the letter, it appears it was written on the morning of the 17th.*

Emanuel H. Bloch
401 Broadway
New York New York

June 17, 1953

Dear Manny—Please send this letter to the kids or phone it to them [next four words placed in parenthesis under the line two words later and inserted via a connecting line] (or send by messenger) in [last word written over "as"] as short [NW] a time as possible as I don't know where they are staying now—

My dearest darlings,

This is the process known as "sweating it out", and it's tough, that's for sure.[428] At the same time, we can't let a lot of chickens that go about their business without panic, even when something's frightening them,— we can't let them put us to shame, can we! I was sorry afterward that I had not remembered the "example of the chickens" as you had put it to me in

---

[428]The applications for a stay were before Justice Douglas, the second petitions for executive clemency were in the hands of the President, and Manny had in his hands the letter of June 15 above to be delivered to the President if all else failed. For details see *Sons,* pp. 228–29, Schneir, pp. 237–42, Sharlitt, *passim.*

your last letter for it might have given you some comfort at the time of our parting.

Maybe you thought that I didn't feel like crying too when we were hugging and kissing good-bye, huh, even though I'm slightly older than 10. And maybe you thought I was just too matter of fact to stand, when your outraged feelings demanded acknowledgment in kind. Darlings, that would have been so easy, far too easy on myself; and I had to resist a very real temptation to follow your lead and break down with you. As I say it would have been only too easy, but it would not have been ["a real" CO, NWI] any kindness, at all. So I took the hard way instead of the easy, because I love you more than myself and because I knew you needed that love far more than I needed ["1" CO] the relief of crying.

Instead, I reassured you as well as I could in the minutes we had, and promised to write. There is one thing among many others I'd like you to know. The kisses are there between Daddy and myself even though we may not exchange them presently[429] —and while it would be sweet to be able to do so, it is only to the degree that parents are able to give each other and their children the strength and encouragement to cope with their problems and [quotation marks CO] to "sweat it out" if need be,—it is only to that degree, I say, that people really love.

I know, sweethearts, an explanation of this kind cannot ever substitute for what we have been missing and for what we hope to be able to return to, nor do I intend it as any such thing. Only, as I say, we need to try to remain calm and free from panic so that we can do all we can to help one another to see [NWI] this thing through!

I shall continue writing you after Daddy's visit this morning but am sending out this incomplete letter in the meantime.

All my love and all my kisses—Mommy—

Justice Douglas granted a stay based on the application of a "next friend," Irwin Edelman, whose lawyers, Fyke Farmer and Daniel Marshall, raised the idea that the Rosenbergs had been sentenced under the wrong law. Passed in 1946, the Atomic Energy Act provided that a death sentence could only be imposed by explicit jury recommendation, which had not been true under the Espionage Act of 1917. The reason Douglas granted the stay is that it was a new point that had never been addressed before. He sent it back to the District Court for determination and that meant, probably, that the case would take almost a year to get back to the Supreme Court on that issue. Unbeknownst to anyone at that time, Attorney General Brownell met with

---

[429]Once on a prison visit I had remarked, "I never saw Daddy and you kiss."

the Chief Justice, Mr. Vinson, while Douglas was considering the application and agreed that if Douglas granted it, he would "call the full Court into session Thursday morning [June 18] to vacate it."[430] *Sure enough, the day the stay was granted Brownell filed his "request" with Vinson who immediately called the Court back into session. On June 18, the arguments occurred and the Court recessed to consider their decision. In case they decided to vacate the stay before nightfall, the preparations for the execution the night of June 18 continued.*[431]

Mr. Emanuel H. Bloch
401 Broadway
New York NY

June 18, 1953

Dear Manny,

I have drawn up a last will and testament so that there can be no question about the fact that I want you to handle all our affairs and [N3WI] be responsible for the children as in fact you have been doing. Ethel completely concurs in this request and is in her own hand attesting to it.

Our children are the apple of our eye, our pride and most precious fortune[.] love [*sic*] them with all your heart and always protect them in order that they grow up to be normal healthy people. That you will do this I am sure but as their proud father I take the prerogative to ask it of you my dearest friend and devoted brother. I love my sons most profoundly.

I am not much at saying goodbyes because I believe that good accomplishments live on forever but this I can say ["tha" CO, NWI] my love of life has never been so strong because I've seen how beautiful the future ["will" CO, NWI] can be. Since I feel that we in some small measure have contributed our share in this direction, I think my sons and millions of other will ["be better off for it" Co, N4WI] have benefited by it.

Words fail me when I [next word written over illegible word] attempt to ["express" CO, N2WI] tell of ["the" inserted, then CO] the nobility and grandeur of my life's companion, my sweet and devoted wife. Ours is a great love a wonderful relationship it has made my life full and rich.

My aged and ailing mother has been a source of great comfort and we always shared a mutual love and devotion. Indeed she has been selfless in her efforts on our behalf. My sisters and my brother have supported us from the

---

[430]Belmont to Ladd, JR HQ 1823, June 17, 1953, also in Hearings, p. 2353.
[431] For details, see Parrish and Sharlitt. For other actions on the same days, see *Sons,* pp. 229–38: Arthur Kinoy, *Rights on Trial* (Cambridge: Harvard University Press, 1983), pp. 115–27.

start and were behind us 100% and worked on our behalf. We can truthfully say that my family gave us sustenance in the time of our great trials.

You Manny are not only considered as one of my family but are our extra special friend. The bound [*sic*] of brotherhood and love [N2WI] between us was forged in the struggle for life and all that it means ["and even in death" CO] and it [next word written over "was"] is a source of great strength to us. Be strong for us beloved friend and we wish you long life to continue your fruitful work in health and happiness for without doubt you are a ["great" CO, NWI] fine man, ["a humanitarian, and tops in your profession." CO, N9WI] dear friend and sincere advocate of the people. I salute you and caress you affectionately with all my heart.

Never let them change the truth of our innocence.

For peace, bread and roses in simple dignity we face the executioner with courage, confidence and perspective,—never losing faith.

As ever Julie

P.S

All my personal effects are in 3 cartons and you can get them from the Warden

All my love—Julie

June 19th Ethel wants it made known that we are the first victims of American Fascism Ethel & Julie [circled]

At noon on Friday, June 19, the Supreme Court vacated Douglas' stay.[432] *The execution was moved up from 11:00 P.M. to 8:00 P.M. so as not to desecrate the Jewish Sabbath. They were together when the following letter was written, in my mother's handwriting, sometime that afternoon.*

Mr. Emanuel H. Bloch
7 W. 16th Street
New York New York

June 19, 1953

Dear Manny,

The following letter is to be delivered to my children:

Dearest Sweethearts, my most precious children,

Only this morning it looked like we might be together again after all. Now that this cannot be I want so much for you to know all that I have come to know. Unfortunately I may write only a few simple words; the rest your own lives must teach you, even as mine taught me.

---

[432]For the Supreme Court's opinion and dissents, see Rosenberg vs. United States, 346 US 273-313. See also *New York Times* (June 20, 19530: 1, 7. For other events on that day, see *Sons,* pp. 231–38.

At first, of course, you will grieve bitterly for us, but you will not grieve alone. That is our consolation and it must eventually be yours.

Eventually, too, you must come to believe that life is worth the living. Be comforted that even now, ["we know" CO] with the end of ours slowly approaching ["that" CO, NWI] that we know this with a conviction that defeats the executioner!

Your lives ["will" CO, NWI] must teach you, too, that good cannot really flourish in the midst of evil; that freedom ["must be sometimes" CO] and all the things that [N2WI] go to make up a truly satisfying and worthwhile life, must sometimes be purchased very dearly. ["even" CO] Be comforted, then, that we were serene and understood with the deepest kind of understanding, that civilization ["had" CO, NWI] had not as yet progressed to the point where life did not have to be lost for the sake of life; and that we were comforted in the ["fact that th" CO] sure knowledge that others would carry on after ["a" CO] us.

We wish we might have had the tremendous joy and gratification of living our lives out with you. Your Daddy who is with me in these last momentous hours ["wants" CO] sends his heart and all the love that is in it for his dearest boys. Always remember that we were innocent and could not wrong our conscience.

We press you close and kiss you with all our strength.

Lovingly,
Daddy and Mommy—
Julie Ethel ["Julie" was signed in my father's handwriting]

P.S.—to Manny:—The Ten Commandments religious medal and chain—and my wedding ring—I wish you to present to our children as a token of our undying love—

P.S.—to Manny: Please be certain to give my ["deepest love, affection and regard" CO, NWI] best wishes to ["my" CO] Saul Miller. Tell him I love ["him so dearly and regarded h" CO, "honor" inserted, then CO] and honor him with all my heart—["He" CO] Tell him I want him to know that [N2WI] I feel he shares my triumph—For I have no fear and no regrets—Only that the release from the trap was not ["permitted to continue and" CO, illegible word inserted, then CO, N2WI] completely effectuated [NWI under the line] and the qualities I possessed could not expand to their fullest capacities—I want him to have the pleasure of knowing how much he meant to me, how much he did to help me grow up—All my love to all our dear ones

Love you so much—Ethel

At 7:20 my parents were separated for the last time. The following letter was written in pencil.

Emanuel H. Bloch
7 W. 16th Street
New York New York

June 19, 1953

Dear Manny,

These are some notes I want you to give to Saul—they are atttached to this letterhead—There are also a few last notes—[N10WI] for you—the one beginning with quote from Geo Eliot—Dearest person, you and Saul must see to my children—Tell him it was my last request of him—They must have professional help [N2WI] if needed & he must see that they are tested to find if it is needed.

All my heart I send to all who held me dear—I am not alone—and I die "with honor and with dignity"—knowing my husband & I must be vindicated by history. You will see to it [NWI] that our names are kept bright and unsullied by lies—as you did while we lived so whole-heartedly, so unstintingly—you did everything that could be done—

We are the first victims of American Fascism.

Love you, Ethel—

On a scrap of paper attached to the letterhead were these last pencilled notes in my mother's handwriting:

Geo Eliot said, "This is a world worth abiding in while one man can thus venerate & love another—"

Honor means you are too proud to do wrong—but Pride means: [NWI] that you will not own that you have done wrong at all—

["I cry" CO] I cry for my self as I lie dead—how shall they know all that burned my brain & breast—

the fat's in the fire to say nothing of the books—(My best to Pop Bloch)

Second Petition
for Executive Clemency

Death House
Sing Sing Prison
Ossining, New York

June 16, 1953

THE PRESIDENT OF THE UNITED STATES

We, JULIUS ROSENBERG and ETHEL ROSENBERG, husband and wife, are now confined in the Death House in Sing Sing Prison, awaiting electrocution on June 18, our fourteenth wedding anniversary. We address this petition to you for the exercise of your supreme power to prevent—"a crime worse than murder"—our unjust deaths.

We appealed to you once before. Our sentences, we declared there, violated truth and the instincts of civilized mankind.

We told you the truth: we are innocent.

The truth does not change.

We now again solemnly declare our innocence.

The guilt in this case, if we die, will be America's. The shame, if we die, will dishonor this generation, and pervade history until future Americans recapture the heritage of truth, justice and equality before the law. Our case has made new precedents in the law of this land—evil precedents, unjust, inhuman and with not even that concern for human life shown the protection of the rights of property.

The highest court of the United States—its Supreme Court enshrined in pure white marble halls—has just denied us a stay of our executions, although with death so close, it closed its doors to us to seek its review of weighty questions going to the heart of the justice of our convictions and sentences. And yet, unheard of in the annals of our law, four judges—four of the most distinguished members of that bench—had voted to let us live, at least long enough to vindicate our rights before them. Thus, the opportunity we struggled to achieve is now denied.

Instead our accusers torture us, in the face of death, with the guarantee of life for the price of a confession of guilt. Close upon the execution date—as though to draw upon the last full measure of dread of death and love of life—their high negotiator came bearing this tainted proffer of life. We refuse this iniquitous bargain, even as perhaps the last few days of our young lives are slipping away. We cannot besmirch our names by bearing false witness to save ourselves. Do not dishonor America, Mr. President, by considering as a condition of our right to survive, the delivery of a confession of guilt of a crime we did not commit.

You may not believe us, but the shamefulness of our convictions has already bitten deeply into the consciences of reasoning men. Justices Black and Douglas (and perhaps Frankfurter, as well) of the United States Supreme Court, have noted their unwillingness to leave history to ponder the justice of death sentences responsive to a verdict, procured by prosecution conduct which a reviewing court held could not be "too severely condemned," so "wholly reprehensible" and productive of prejudice to us so beyond recall that "a new trial . . . should have been granted."

You may not believe us, because there is in the court record an undisturbed verdict of guilt. But we defended our innocence on that very record. Printed unabridged in the tens of thousands, the record itself, according to the Government the strength of its case, has convinced untold numbers of our innocence and instilled, in more, grave doubts of the correctness of the verdict.

The world-wide sense of disbelief in our guilt is epitomized by the considered conclusion, from the record, of Dr. Harold C. Urey, our foremost nuclear physicist whose scientific labors represent a major contribution to the defense of our country.

"The case against the ROSENBERGS," he declared, "outrages logic and justice . . . it depends on patently perjured testimony."

You may not believe us, but the passage of even the few short months, since last we appealed to you, is confirming our prediction that, in the inexorable operation of time and conscience, the truth of our innocence would emerge.

Evidence recently discovered, reveals proof positive, short of recantations by the Greenglasses, the prosecution witnesses-in-chief—the one, imprisoned, under the aegis of the Government; the other, free, under the constant threat of indictment for her admitted capital crime—that a case was constructed against us on a pyramid of lies. The new evidence should, at the very least, persuade you that doubt of our guilt is not so aggravated that good conscience demands that we live.

We submitted proof to the courts that Greenglass was said by his own wife, to have a "tendency to hysteria" and, from her knowledge of him since he was ten years old, to "say things were so even if they were not."

We submitted documentary evidence to show that David Greenglass, trapped by his own misdeeds, hysterical with fear for his own life and that of Ruth, his wife, fell back on his life-long habit of lying, exploited by his shrewd-minded and equally guilty wife, to fabricate, bit by bit, a monstrous tale that has sent us, his own flesh and blood, down and long and terrible path toward death.

We submitted proof to show that David Greenglass stole uranium from Los Alamos, in a venture concededly unconnected with us. This fact both he and Ruth concealed at the trial, to avoid destruction of their claim that they were pawns in our hands and to cloak their independent motivation to bargain with the Government for the "cooperation" which inculpated us and saved them.

In fact, who knows the real crime of the Greenglasses that moved David to the dreadful penance of sending his own sister to her death. For on his apprehension, we showed, he admitted he lied to the authorities about the "espionage" material he gave to Gold.

But that his trial testimony against us resulted from the later fabrications of his animal desire to preserve himself and his wife, the mother of his children, is evident from our new proof that at first, he incriminated neither of us, or mentioned that the crime committed was "the crime worse than murder": the theft of the "secret" of the atom bomb.

We submitted actual physical evidence (the missing console table), never produced in court against us, to show the Greenglasses and the Government collaborated to bring into the trial false testimony that we had in our home an expensive console table, given to us by the "Russians" and equipped for micro filming purposes. The table itself belies the Greenglass testimony. It is not a specially constructed table, but one bought by us at R.M. Macy's for about $21.00, as we testified at our trial.

We submitted documentary evidence to show the unconscionable *quid pro quo,* for the Greenglass' testimony implicating us. Here, where we face death, the Government offered first that neither of the Greenglasses should even be charged with crime. The brazenness of the "deal" was transparent.

The proposal changed in form but not in substance. Ruth, the wife, would go free and David, although to be named as a defendant, would receive no penalty. Finally, only after the suspicions of our attorney that this filthy bargain was in the making were revealed in open court, did the Government, to save face, first propose that David Greenglass might be required to serve some prison term. The sordid "deal," all know, has been fulfilled: Ruth is free; David may soon be; we are in the Death House.

We asked the courts to overturn the scandalous convictions, conceived in fraud and consummated in perjury. But the disposition we received was summary. Our right to an open trial of our proof was frustrated. We were foreclosed from the opportunity to expose the fraud and perjury. We were prevented from exhausting our appellate remedies. We were accorded only the trappings, but not the substance of justice.

Can our deaths, hastened by the assumed blindness of those who refuse to see the travesty, exonerate American justice where history will resurrect the unburied doubts?

The present mirrors the future. Never before have more people in all lands and in all walks of life been so shaken as by our imminent fate. Our inhuman sentences of death have already produced a traumatic shock to the moral sense of the world.

If you will not hear our voices, hear the voices of the world.

Hear the Pope: who spoke three times in the name of Christian compassion. Hear his Cardinal in France who "is passionately hoping" that our lives be spared in the name of "charity and peace." Listen to the pleas of 5,000 of our Protestant ministers beseeching in the name of God; the Rabbis of France, "in the very name of our common ideal of justice and generosity."

Hear the great and the humble: from Einstein, whose name is legend, to the tyros in the laboratories of Manchester; from struggling students at Grenoble to Oxford professors; from the world-famous movie directors of Rome to the bit players of London; from the dock workers at Liege to cotton spinners of India; from the peasants of Italy to the philosophers of Israel; from Mauriac, the Nobel literatteur, to reports in Mexico City; from the stenographers of Rotterdam to the transport workers of England; from the auto workers of Detroit to the auto workers of Paris; from Nexo of Denmark to Sequeiros [*sic*] of Mexico to Seghers of Germany to Duhamel of France; from Australia to Argentina; from Uruguay to Sweden; from Cuba to Canada to New Zealand.

Read the tons of petitions, letters, post-cards, stacked high in your filing rooms, from the plain and gentle-folk of our land. They marched before your door in such numbers as never before, as have their brothers and sisters in London, Paris, Melbourne, Buenos Aires, Ottawa, Rome. They ask you not to orphan our two young boys. They ask you in the name of the conscience of the world, in the name of humanity, brotherhood and peace to spare our lives.

Hear the great and the humble for the sake of America.

Do not hear only our accusers in the Department of Justice whom the law makes advisers to you on our right to clemency. Does not their self-interest to secure the challenged verdict, by our deaths, tarnish their advice? Does not their conceded concealment from you of most persuasive pleas on our behalf, impair the integrity of their counsel?

Let us recall John de Stogumbur, the English chaplain of Shaw's "St. Joan," who had been one of the most bloodthirsty advocates of Joan's proposed burning, as he came rushing in from this "glorious" spectacle, overcome with remorse and sobbing like one demented:

> "You don't know; you haven't seen; it is so easy to talk when you don't know. You madden yourself with words; you damn yourself because it feels grand to throw oil on the flaming hell of your own temper. But when it is brought home to you; when you see the thing you have done; when it's blinding your eyes, stifling your nostrils, tearing your heart—then, then—Oh, God, take away this sight from me—Oh, Christ! deliver me from this fire that is consuming me—she cried to thee in the midst of it: Jesus! Jesus! she is in thy bosom; and I am in hell for ever more."

We ask you, Mr. President, the civilized head of a civilized nation to judge our plea with reason and humanity. And remember, we are a father and a mother.

Ethel Rosenberg
Julius Rosenberg

Index